THE LEGAL ENVIRONMENT OF BUSINESS

PRINCIPLES AND CASES

THE LEGAL ENVIRONMENT OF BUSINESS

PRINCIPLES AND CASES

GEORGE W. SPIRO

University of Massachusetts, Amherst

 PRENTICE HALL, Englewood Cliffs, N.J. 07632

Spiro, George W.
    The legal environment of business : cases and principles / George
W. Spiro.
        p.   cm.
    Includes bibliographical references and indexes.
    ISBN 0-13-529884-9
    1. Industrial laws and legislation—United States.
2. Business enterprises—United States.   I. Title.
KF1600.S66   1993
346.73'07—dc20   92-28825
[347.3067]   CIP

Editor in chief: Joseph Heider
Acquisitions editor: Donald Hull
Development editor: Ronald Librach
Production editor: Joanne Palmer
Interior design: Rosemarie Paccione
Cover design: Rosemarie Paccione
Prepress buyer: Trudy Pisciotti
Manufacturing buyer: Patrice Fraccio
Supplements editor: Lisamarie Brassini
Editorial assistant: Wendy Goldner

The book's epigraph from Proverbs is reproduced
in the translation contained in *Gates of Prayer:
The New Union Prayerbook* (New York: Central
Conference of American Rabbis, 1975).

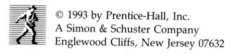 © 1993 by Prentice-Hall, Inc.
A Simon & Schuster Company
Englewood Cliffs, New Jersey 07632

Printed in the United States of America
10 9 8 7 6 5 4 3 2 1

ISBN 0-13-529884-9

Prentice-Hall International (UK) Limited, *London*
Prentice-Hall of Australia Pty. Limited, *Sydney*
Prentice-Hall Canada Inc., *Toronto*
Prentice-Hall Hispanoamericana, S.A., *Mexico*
Prentice-Hall of India Private Limited, *New Delhi*
Prentice-Hall of Japan, Inc., *Tokyo*
Prentice-Hall of Southeast Asia Pte. Ltd., *Singapore*
Editora Prentice-Hall do Brasil, Ltda., *Rio de Janeiro*

Happy is the one who finds wisdom,
the one who gains understanding;
For its fruits are better than silver,
its yield better than fine gold.
It is more precious than rubies;
No treasure can match it.

-PROVERBS 3: 13-15

This book is dedicated with affection
to my mother, father, wife, and son.

CONTENTS IN BRIEF

vii

CONTENTS

PREFACE

The primary goal of this text is to introduce students to the rapidly changing legal environment of business. We will work hard to provide students with a thorough introduction to the nature and functions of our legal system and its importance to citizen managers. *Legal Environment* accomplishes this goal using three main components: (1) a careful explanation of appropriate legal concepts, (2) an integrated approach to ethics and global legal issues in accordance with the most recent AACSB guidelines, and (3) a practical group of cases and materials designed to assure that students understand legal issues in a way that will be useful to their lives.

LEGAL CONCEPTS. I have made a great effort to present legal concepts as clearly as possible. To this end, major concepts are supplemented with numerous examples. Each chapter contains at least four major case excerpts that provide opportunities for students to develop their critical thinking and reasoning skills. Because it is most important that students know more than just what the law is today, major concepts are placed in context. Students must be able to think about what the law ought to be, how it might change in the years ahead, and how these changes will affect their lives. Finally, they should recognize that as intelligent, informed manager-citizens, they can have a voice in molding both law and public policy.

Several learning aids have been incorporated into this text in an effort to enhance student learning. Each chapter includes several *Concept Checks*—objective questions disbursed throughout the chapter to test and reinforce student learning. A *Marginal Glossary* has been designed so that students can quickly identify key terms and their definitions. Chapters have boxes that integrate coverage of international issues and provide students with biographical sketches and organizational profiles that reflect law in action. Photographs, charts, and figures further illustrate chapter materials.

ETHICAL/GLOBAL ISSUES. The American Assembly of Collegiate Schools of Business (AACSB) is the accrediting agency for schools of business and management in the United States. Accreditation standards set by the AACSB "have evolved to meet the contemporary needs for business, professions, government, and graduate and professional schools so that students who study management have the educational background to effectively serve society."

The AACSB guidelines were *completely redesigned in 1991,* and *Legal Environment* reflects and incorporates these new guidelines. One set of standards addresses the curriculum. For those who teach law courses, a curriculum guideline of particular importance requires that all programs should provide an understanding of perspectives that form the context for business. Coverage "should include: (1) ethical and global issues, (2) the influence of political, social, legal and regulatory environmental and technological issues, and (3) the impact of demographic diversity on organizations." This book includes ethical and social considerations along with legal concepts, not only to meet the AACSB standards but to help promote a better understanding of the importance of ethics and social responsibility in the world in which we live. *Legal Environment* is not just about law; it is also about justice, morality, and individual rights. Chapter 2 introduces social and ethical concepts, which are then integrated throughout the text. In a similar fashion, we recognize that all of us are part of a global network of business and law, and international law is thus an integral part of this comprehensive text.

PRACTICAL BASE. One goal of the legal-environmental course is to ensure that students understand legal issues in a way that will be useful to their lives as managers. An understanding of the legal environment of business is a necessary component of successful management practice.

What legal issues will managers confront in their lifetimes? Financiers need to know about securities law. Accountants will face issues involving contracts. Human-resources managers will face issues of labor standards and labor relations. Marketing professionals will face questions of copyrights, product liability, and the like.

As students climb the managerial ranks, each of these subjects will become more important. Indeed, an understanding of how specific subject areas integrate with one another is essential even at the highest levels of management. The sole proprietor of a manufacturing firm, for example, might need to know what effect changing the business to a partnership or corporation will have on his or her life and on the health of the organization. A grounding in the legal environment of business will help.

■ STRUCTURE OF THE TEXT

Legal Environment is written for readers who have had little or no prior exposure to legal studies. That assumption has influenced organization and content throughout.

Part 1: The Nature of Law and the U.S. Legal System

Chapters 1 and 2 explain the concept of law, its functions and sources, and its relationship to ethics. Chapters 3, 4, 5, and 6 provide the context for the legal issues that managers face. They introduce the content of our Constitution and explain how it provides a framework for our government. They look at the structure of the federal and state court systems and examine how disputes are resolved there. They next turn to other systems for dispute resolution, including arbitration and mediation. Finally, they examine the workings of the "fourth branch of government," our administrative agencies, in some detail.

Part 1 thus provides a systematic overview of the basic parts of the U.S. legal system. A special effort has been made to illustrate these basics with examples drawn from the world of management. With this basic foundation in place, the student is in an excellent position to concentrate on the public and private laws that affect business. These laws are the subject of the balance of the text.

Part 2: Organizing to Do Business

Almost every student will work for an organization, and each organization has a legal and managerial form. Chapter 7 begins with a brief introduction to agency law as it applies to the three basic organizational forms designed to provide a structure for doing business. The sole proprietorship, the partnership, and the corporation are then the subject of the bulk of the chapter. The whole of Chapter 8 is devoted to securities regulation, a subject of importance not just to future financiers and accountants but to entrepreneurs. A basic explanation of the 1933 and 1934 acts is followed by a discussion of the ramifications of insider trading.

Part 3: Regulating Private Business Conduct and Crime

Contracts and torts share the bond of being largely private law and being rooted in the common-law tradition. Product liability has its origins in contract and tort law. Separate chapters on these three related subjects begin Part 3 and define the businessperson's private relations with other members of the legal environment. Chapter 12, on business crime, defines the responsibilities of the individual in society as a whole. Unfortunately, criminal law is an ever-increasing part of the world of management. The chapter attempts to develop a realistic picture of the world of criminal law and, in particular, the world of corporate crime.

Part 4: Employment and the Law

Many students are interested in a career in human-resources management. Three chapters cover critical areas of the employment relationship. First, we look at the union movement in the United States as an introduction to a discussion of the legal framework for collective bargaining. A labor-relations executive cannot practice his or her craft without understanding this material. The next chapter deals with the ever-growing number of laws regulating labor standards. Workers' compensation, minimum wage laws, and the problems of occupational disease are among the subjects treated. A separate chapter on equal employment opportunity and affirmative action completes this part.

Part 5: The Legal Environment of the Marketplace

Antitrust has been an area of most rapid change in the late 1970s and 1980s. The very goals of antitrust legislation are being questioned, and enforcement reflects changing values, attitudes, and beliefs. Chapters 16 through 18 present the student with both the historical and current picture of antitrust legislation.

Antitrust enforcement involves the Federal Trade Commission, which is also charged with regulating trade practices. Chapter 18 thus deals with this aspect of the FTC's work. Some monopolies are deliberately granted by the government in the form of patents, copyrights, and trademarks, and the regulation of this intellectual property is the subject of the final part of Chapter 18.

The work of the FTC in debtor-creditor relations provides a bridge into the world of credit management, credit abuse, and bankruptcy. Chapter 19 discusses both personal and business bankruptcy.

Environmental protection issues are everyone's concern. Business leaders and civic leaders alike struggle to find ways to help our economy grow without sacrificing our treasured natural resources. Chapter 20 describes the current state of legislation. However, we first build a careful base of understanding through an overview of basic property law—groundwork that students need in order to understand the issues of environmental protection.

The book concludes with a look at international business law. Students can no longer assume that a knowledge of U.S. business law and management practice is sufficient. They will be part of a world of multinational exchange. Chapter 21 looks at how other countries' businesses become involved in our market and how differences in law are resolved. Specifically covered are the Foreign Corrupt Practices Act, the act of state doctrine, licensing, and joint venturing.

■ SPECIAL FEATURES

ORDER OF THE CHAPTERS. I have attempted to group the chapters in a way that coincides with certain logical pedagogical concerns. However, each instructor may wish to regroup them to fit the particular needs of his or her own educational philosophy. Certain chapters obviously need to be handled together; as far as possible, however, chapters have been written to be independent of each other. Numerous cross references facilitate the use of chapters in differing orders, and an extensive glossary assures that any unfamiliar terms encountered in a chapter read out of its original sequence will be easily accessible to students.

CASES. One hundred classic and contemporary cases have been carefully selected for their pertinence to a major point in a chapter, for their intrinsic interest, and for their usefulness in exemplifying the process of legal reasoning. Each case has been carefully edited and includes a brief headnote to assist student learning. Discussion questions are included for each case. In keeping with my goal of showing the background of current law, classic cases complement the most recent excerpts.

CHAPTER SUMMARIES. Each chapter has a carefully written summary that reviews the most important ideas and concepts contained in the chapter.

BIBLIOGRAPHY. The sources on which I drew in the writing of this book are listed by chapter at the end of the book. Students may find this list useful in the preparation of research papers or as a guide to further information.

CASE PROBLEMS. At the end of each chapter, ten case problems give students an opportunity to apply the information contained within the chapter. Many of these cases are hypothetical; most of the actual cases have been disguised. (Citations for the actual cases are given at the end of each problem.)

MARGINAL GLOSSARY. A Marginal Glossary has been designed so that students can quickly identify key terms and their definitions. Each new term is highlighted and clearly defined in the margin of the text as it appears.

THE INTERNATIONAL AND ETHICAL ENVIRONMENT. Boxes incorporating ethics and global issues are dispersed throughout the text in order to incorporate and highlight these important elements of law. These boxes enrich the entire book and complement separate chapters on ethics and international business law.

PERSONAL AND ORGANIZATIONAL PROFILES. Chapters are also enhanced by boxed inserts that give students an insight into law in action. Biographies of noteworthy lawyers, judges, or managers and profiles of organizations that are dealing with legal issues are included. Profiles of Thurgood Marshall, Sandra Day O'Connor, Dow, Inc., Union Carbide, and others make the book stimulating reading.

PHOTOGRAPHS, CHARTS, AND FIGURES. Each of these items is used to illustrate chapter material. These items can capture students' interest and enable them to learn the concepts embodied in the chapter.

CHAPTER SUMMARIES. Chapter summaries have been designed to focus studeent attention on the most important themes developed in the chapter. These summaries are followed by carefully constructed chapter case questions.

CONCEPT CHECKS. Objective questions have been dispersed throughout each chapter. These questions help students review critical chapter topics.

SUPPLEMENTS. Supplements for *Legal Environment* include a *Study Guide* prepared by Bradley J. McDonald, Greg C. Anderson, and Timothy P. Atchison of Northern Illinois University.

Developed by Teresa Brady of Holy Family College, the *Instructor's Manual* also includes a completely redesigned *Test Item File*. In order to ensure that questions are of the highest quality, the test bank that accompanies *Legal Environment* has been reviewed by a group of instructors within the legal environment of business.

A joint venture between ABC News and Prentice Hall, the *ABC News/PH Video Library* is a comprehensive library of videos, including features and documentary excerpts from a variety of such ABC News programs as *World News Tonight*, *Nightline*, *Business World*, and *This Week with David Brinkley*. Videos have been selected on topics which pertain to the important concepts and current debates in the discipline and which work well in the legal-environment curriculum.

A carefully prepared "mini-newspaper," *The New York Times/PH Contemporary View* supplement, provides instructors and students with recent articles selected from the pages of *The New York Times*. Linking both the text and the classroom with today's real-world business and legal environment, *The Contemporary View* is designed to enhance the student's reading appreciation of both textbooks and newspapers.

Acknowledgments

I would like to thank the following teachers and writers for their contributions to this book: Susan Rothstein, Paula Berg, and Marcia Leest. Professor Linda K. Enghagen was primarily responsible for an early draft of Chapter 7 on forms of business organization. Professor Paul Lansing provided the benefit of his experience as an expert in international law; Attorney Patricia Rogers wrote the original text of Chapter 21.

The following people contributed seemingly endless time and patience in researching cases and law-review articles: Attorney Catherine Z. Rossi, David Block, and Lisa Leggiardro. In addition to helping prepare end-of-chapter material, Anne Stephenson provided research assistance on numerous matters. John Wall and Maureen Walsh provided much-needed library assistance.

I am especially indebted to the following reviewers who provided invaluable comments, suggestions, and guidance at several critical stages of this project:

Richard Asebrook, University of Massachusetts at Amherst
Robert B. Bennett, Jr., Butler University
Harvey Boller, Loyola University, Maryland
Donald W. Cantwell, University of Texas at Arlington
Patrick J. Cihon, Syracuse University
Richard L. Coffinberger, George Mason University
Michael J. Costello, Thompson & Mitchell, Attorneys at Law, St. Louis, Missouri
Steven B. Dow, Michigan State University
Nancy S. Erickson, Ohio State Law School
James Frierson, East Tennessee State University
Pamela Giltman, Salisbury State University
Martin Grace, Georgia State University
Gerard Halpern, University of Arkansas
Marsha Hass, College of Charleston
James P. Hill, Central Michigan University
Jack M. Hires, Valparaiso University
James Holloway, East Carolina University
Carolyn Hotchkiss, Babson College
Sandra N. Hurd, Syracuse University
James E. Inman, University of Akron
Robert Randolph Jesperson, University of Arkansas at Little Rock
Mary Kate Kearney, Loyola University of Chicago
Kurt Klumb, University of Wisconsin at Milwaukee
Ruth B. Kraft, Hofstra University
Paul Lansing, University of Iowa
Seth E. Lipner, Baruch College
Michael P. Litka, University of Akron
Diane Macdonald, Pacific Lutheran University
Nancy R. Mansfield, George State University
Donald O. Mayer, Oakland University

Sharlene A. McEvoy, Fairfield University
Gregory G. Naples, Marquette University
Julianna Nelson, New York University
James M. Owens, California State University, Chico
James L. Porter, University of New Mexico
Daniel L. Reynolds, Middle Tennessee State University
Allan Roth, Rutgers University
Mark A. Schlesinger, University of Massachusetts at Boston
S. Jay Sklar, Temple University
Clyde D. Stoltenberg, University of Kansas
Larry Strate, University of Nevada at Las Vegas
Gary L. Tidwell, College of Charleston
Wayne R. Wells, St. Cloud St. University

I also owe a great debt to the professionals at Prentice Hall who provided insight, advice, suggestions, and the editorial skills that contribute throughout to the readability and clarity of this book. I would like to acknowledge the following people: Garret White, Publisher, Business and Economics; Ray Mullaney, Editor in Chief, College Book Development; Senior Managing Editor Joyce Turner and Managing Editor Fran Russello, B&E Production; Designer Rosemarie Paccione; Supplements Editor Lisamarie Brassini; and Editorial Assistant Wendy Goldner. The production of the book was supervised by Joanne Palmer and Colette Conboy. Don Hull, Senior Editor, Accounting and Information Systems, managed every detail of the project from inception to publication.

A special statement of appreciation goes to Cecil Yarbrough, whose commitment to this project went well beyond any of my expectations. As Development Editor on the first edition, he offered expert advice on the entire manuscript based on years of professional experience. His professional judgment, thoughtfulness, and attention to detail were greatly appreciated; he made writing this book a real joy. I am most of all grateful for something I will always treasure—his friendship.

Editorial assistance can be invaluable. Ron Librach, Senior Development Editor on this new edition, provided such service to this book. He was a constant source of ideas. Further, he is a colleague who generously and constructively critiqued the manuscript and produced a much improved final product. He helped in virtually every phase of this project and made superb suggestions at each point along the way. I thank him for his time and dedication to this project.

At the University of Massachusetts at Amherst, I am thankful for all of the suggestions provided by my colleagues in the law group. All of my friends in the dean's office deserve credit for putting up with my idiosyncrasies as this book was produced, but a special word of thanks goes to Mrs. Janice Degilus. Her great patience, her capacity for hard work, and her constant good humor made this book possible.

Finally, as I spent the hours working and reworking this manuscript I often thought of Lucia and Jeff and how much they mean to me. I appreciate their loving kindness.

GEORGE W. SPIRO

WHAT IS LAW?

Most of us are aware of the effect of law in our daily lives: We charge dinner on credit cards; we pay parking fines; we get notices of rent increases from our landlords. We realize, however, that each of these events has a legal component. But this very pervasiveness of law makes it hard to define. Most of the time, when we try to define *law* we are really identifying its applications in concrete laws and rules. "Law" clearly has more than one meaning.

Law is not unusual in that respect. For example, think of the word "aircraft." *Webster's New World Dictionary* defines it as "any machine designed to travel through the air, whether heavier or lighter than air; airplane, dirigible, balloon, helicopter, etc.; sometimes, in a restricted sense, an airplane."

The word *aircraft* sometimes means any machine capable of flying and sometimes just one of those machines—the *airplane*. For certain purposes, the broadest definition would be the most useful one; in other cases, a more limited definition is required. For example, if an airport's regulations say that any aircraft is permitted to use its facilities, people who wanted to use it would have to know whether "aircraft" included or excluded balloons, dirigibles, and the like.

So, too, does the word "law" have broader and narrower meanings. Lon Fuller, whose theories of law will be considered later in this chapter, has defined law as "the enterprise of subjecting human conduct to the governance of rules." That, of course, is a very broad definition. Some people, for example, identify with the law in the Ten Commandments and would define it as being based on higher principles. Others might define it as the United States Constitution and all of the laws passed under its authority by Congress and the legislatures of our fifty states, as well as case law developed by judges. Some people think of law as a synonym for the police. All of these senses of the word "law" are now in use.

It is important therefore to understand where law comes from and how it functions. This chapter explores the objectives that our law aims to serve and the philosophic traditions that form its foundation. It examines the various branches of American law and its sources, such as the Constitution, legislation, and judicial cases. This chapter also examines the basic ways of finding a particular law and how to read and analyze a case.

■ THE FUNCTIONS OF LAW

MAINTAINING SOCIAL CONTROL WHILE FACILITATING SOCIAL LIFE.   Perhaps the most important function of law is maintaining social control by enforcing a set of accepted behavioral norms. By spelling out in advance a set of rules and the penalties (or sanctions) that will be imposed for breaking those rules, the law allows for a needed level of predictability among individuals. In turn, this set of rules makes social life easier by providing people with expectations about how others will behave in a given situation. For example, when you take your car onto the road, you need to know that, like you, every other driver will be driving on the right side of the road. The law grants you this necessary expectation by establishing both this rule and the threat that those who disobey it will be punished. Such legal guidelines foster the kind of cooperation that is necessary to build and run a society.

Law, of course, is not the only force maintaining social control: Morals, ethics, culture, tradition, habit, manners, and even fashion determine how individuals behave in particular situations. To a large extent, these nonlegal determinants of social behavior contribute to making society work. Nonetheless, helping to maintain social control is perhaps the primary function of law.

PROTECTING THE PUBLIC ORDER.   On the most apparent level, the law maintains public order by punishing those who deviate from accepted norms. The criminal justice system, which includes the police, judges, and jails, exists to enforce a system of order upon all of society's members. Criminal laws operate to punish those who actually commit crimes and to discourage others from committing illegal acts by promising criminal penalties. (*See* Chapter 12 *for the application of criminal law to the business sector.*)

One way to look at our legal system is to divide it into *criminal* law and *noncriminal,* or *civil,* law. Civil law, like criminal law, can protect the public order. As we shall see, the law of torts (*see* Chapter 10) permits individuals who have been harmed by others to sue in court to collect money damages as compensation for injuries. In this way, the civil law defends the public order: If those whose unreasonable behavior causes injury to others know that they may be sued in court, they may be less likely to cause the injury.

RESOLVING DISPUTES.   Our behavior is often governed by customs, ethics, and traditions. However, one group's idea of acceptable behavior may give rise to conflict with another group that adheres to a different set of ethical or cultural norms. For example, members of a community located near a river may find it acceptable to dispose of garbage by tossing it into the water. Environmentalists, on the other hand, would find this behavior objectionable. The law functions to resolve this dispute both by enacting statutes to establish environmental regulations and by permitting environmentalists to sue the community in court.

The law similarly permits individuals who are unable to iron out their differences to bring disputes to courts where judges or juries can resolve them.

Obviously, not all disputes arise between bad people or between a good person and a bad person: Conflicts are an inevitable, though unpleasant, effect of social interaction.

PROTECTING THE STATUS QUO. Another important function of the law is to protect the *status quo*—that is, the existing state of affairs at a given time. The structure of our legal system—that is, its rules and procedures—will outlive all of the lawyers, judges, and litigants who currently operate within it. The durability of the law thus fosters a sense of order by permitting people to predict how certain things will run both during their lifetimes and beyond.

FACILITATING ORDERLY CHANGE. As in nature, change is an inevitable and wonderful aspect of social life. People are born and die, businesses are created and go out of business, and human relationships begin and end. The law permits change to occur while ensuring that it is a rational and minimally disruptive process.[1]

■ THE NATURE OF LAW

Since the ancient Greeks, philosophers and other thinkers have attempted to define *law*. They have tried to (1) elucidate the nature and functions of law, including the values that a legal order is supposed to promote; (2) investigate the historical, psychological, and sociological roots of law; and (3) analyze the institutions and methodological means that are necessary to carry the purpose of the law into effect.

All of these subjects belong to a branch of legal studies called *jurisprudence*—Latin for "the knowledge of what is just and unjust." Jurisprudence looks at "the institution of the law as a whole, at the forest of the law, so to speak, rather than the individual trees in the forest."[2] **Jurisprudence,** then, is the study or science of law, including the study of how to *interpret* the law.

jurisprudence The science or philosophy of law, including its interpretation (*see* Chapter 5)

Concepts of Jurisprudence: The Case of the Speluncean Explorers

In 1949, Harvard Law School professor Lon Fuller devised a hypothetical case that he called *The Case of the Speluncean Explorers*. The jurisdiction is that of the supreme court of the imaginary country of Newgarth, and the projected year is A.D. 4300.

Fuller's intention was to show how people supporting different theories of jurisprudence could respond quite differently to a very basic set of common facts. The first part of the case—Chief Justice Truepenny's official account of the facts—appears here. The remainder of the case excerpt—the opinions of Chief Justice Truepenny and four of his associate justices—appears at the end

---

[1] This section draws on Lawrence M. Friedman, *American Law* (New York: Norton, 1984), pp. 8-13; Hazel B. Kerper and Jerold H. Israel, *Introduction to the Criminal Justice System*, 2nd ed. (St. Paul, MN: West, 1979), pp. 3-11; and State Education Department, *Teaching about Basic Legal Concepts* (Binghampton: University of the State of New York, 1973), pp. 1-4.

[2] Edgar Bodenheimer, "Jurisprudence," in *Guide to American Law* (St. Paul, MN: West, 1984), p. 416.

of the section. In between the segments is a description of three different perspectives on the law—that is, three different schools of jurisprudence: the *natural-law, positivist,* and *social-science perspectives.* After examination of the justices' opinions, some conclusions are drawn about each justice's preferred school of legal thought.

THE CASE OF THE SPELUNCEAN EXPLORERS
In the Supreme Court of Newgarth, 4300

The defendants, having been indicted for the crime of murder, were convicted and sentenced to be hanged by the Court of General instances of the County of Stowfield. They bring a petition of error before this court. The facts sufficiently appear in the opinion of the Chief Justice.

Truepenny, C. J.:
The four defendants are members of the Speluncean Society, an organization of amateurs interested in the exploration of caves. Early in May of 4299 they, in the company of Roger Whetmore, then also a member of the society, penetrated into the interior of a limestone cavern of the type found in the central plateau of this Commonwealth. While they were in a position remote from the entrance to the cave, a landslide occurred. Heavy boulders fell in such a manner as to block completely the only known opening to the cave. When the men discovered their predicament they settled themselves near the obstructed entrance to wait until a rescue party should remove the detritus that prevented them from leaving their underground prison. On the failure of Whetmore and the defendants to return to their homes, the Secretary of the Society was notified by their families. It appears that the explorers had left indications at the headquarters of she Society concerning the location of the cave they proposed to visit. A rescue party was promptly dispatched to the spot.

The task of rescue proved one of overwhelming difficulty. . . . The work of removing the obstruction was several times frustrated by fresh landslides. In one of these, ten of the workmen engaged in clearing the entrance were killed. . . . Success was finally achieved on the thirty-second day after the men entered the cave.

Since it was known that the explorers had carried with them only scant provisions, and since it was also known that there was no animal or vegetable matter within the cave on which they might subsist, anxiety was early felt that they might meet death by starvation before access to them could be obtained. On the twentieth day of their imprisonment it was learned for the first time that they had taken with them into the cave a portable wireless machine capable of both sending and receiving messages. . . . The imprisoned men described their condition and the rations they had taken with them, and asked for a medical opinion whether they would be likely to live without food for ten days longer. The chairman of the committee of physicians told them that there was little possibility of this. The wireless machine within the cave then remained silent for eight hours. When communication was reestablished the men asked to speak again with the physicians. The chairman of the physicians' committee was placed before the apparatus, and Whetmore, speaking on behalf of himself and the defendants, asked whether they would be able to survive for ten days longer if they consumed the flesh of one of their number. The physicians' chairman reluctantly answered this question in the affirmative. Whetmore asked whether it would be advisable for them to cast lots to determine which of them should be eaten. None of the physicians present was willing to answer the question. Whetmore then asked if there were among the party a judge or other official of the government who would answer this question. None of those attached to the rescue camp was willing to assume the role of advisor in this matter. He then asked if any minister or priest would answer their question, and none was found who would do so. Thereafter no further messages were received from within the cave, and it was assumed (erroneously, it later appeared) that the electric batteries of the explorers' wireless machine had become exhausted. When the imprisoned men were finally released it was learned that on the twenty-third day after their entrance into the cave Whetmore had been killed and eaten by his companions.

From the testimony of the defendants, which was accepted by the jury, it appears that it was Whetmore who first proposed that they might find the nutriment without which survival was impossible in the flesh of one of their own number. . . . After much discussion of the mathematical problems involved, agreement was finally reached on a method of determining the issue by the use of the dice.

Before the dice were cast, however, Whetmore declared that he withdrew from the arrangement, as he had decided on reflection to wait for another week before embracing an expedient so frightful and odious. The others charged him with a breach of faith and proceeded to cast the dice. When it came Whetmore's turn, the dice were cast for him by one of the defendants, and he was asked to declare any objections he might have to the fairness of the throw. He stated that he had no such objections. The throw went against him, and he was then put to death and eaten by his companions.

After the rescue of the defendants, and after they had completed a stay in a hospital where they underwent a course of treatment for malnutrition and shock, they were indicted for the murder of Roger Whetmore. . . . In a lengthy special verdict the jury found the facts as I have related them above, and found further that if on these facts the defendants were guilty of the crime charged against them, then they found the defendants guilty. On the basis of this verdict, the trial judge ruled that the defendants were guilty of murdering Roger Whetmore. The judge then sentenced them to be hanged, the law of our Commonwealth permitting him no discretion with respect to the penalty to be imposed.

After the release of the jury, its members joined in a communication to the chief executive asking that the sentence be commuted to an imprisonment of six months. The trial judge addressed a similar communication to the chief executive. As yet no action with respect to these pleas has been taken, as the chief executive is apparently awaiting our disposition of this petition of error.*

How would you decide this case? Look first at three major perspectives of jurisprudence.

The Natural Law Perspective

The earliest theory of jurisprudence is **natural law.** According to its adherents, government, including the legal system, should reflect fundamental or absolute principles of justice that are inherent in human life. Proponents of natural law do not believe that legal principles should be the product of reasoning alone. Rather, they hold that law should reflect some moral and ethical scheme. They view law as "neutral" in that it is not formulated to advance any particular perspective or system. Instead, it reflects innate human qualities and the natural laws of human society.

> **natural law** Law based on fundamental or absolute moral principles inherent in human life rather than written codes

Aristotle (384–322 B.C.), one of the most famous philosophers of ancient Greece, devoted much of his work to understanding and explaining the difference between *natural* and *conventional* law. According to Aristotle, natural law "everywhere has the same force and does not exist by peoples' thinking this or that." Thus, *natural laws* are moral principles that are universal in human societies. For example, murder is inherently wrong—and thus a violation of natural law—according to Aristotle, because it is universally regarded as a bad act.

Conventional laws, on the other hand, reflect the values and morals that are accepted by a particular society at a particular time. In our own time, for example, laws establishing minimum-age requirements for voting or drinking are not products of some divine scheme, but rather reflect the prevailing views of a particular society and a particular time.

St. Thomas Aquinas (A.D. 1225–1274), a medieval theologian, tried to reconcile Aristotle's philosophy of natural law with Christianity. According to Aquinas, there are four types of law. *Eternal law* is God's plan for the universe. *Natural law* is made up of those aspects of eternal law that are accessible to humans through reason. *Divine law* is God's direct revelation to humankind through the Scriptures. Finally, *human laws* are specific rules created by men and women to address particular problems or circumstances.

Aquinas believed that particular laws created by humans were often influenced by such human vices as selfishness and ignorance. Human laws, therefore, must never conflict with natural laws. In fact, Aquinas believed that human laws that conflict with natural laws ought to be disobeyed. Such acts of disobedience vindicated the superiority of natural law.

In our own time Lon Fuller has attempted to apply natural-law principles to an analysis of the legal system. In *The Morality of Law* (1964), Fuller examined our legal system to understand its "internal morality." In so doing, he laid out certain requirements for an internally moral legal system:

- The legal system should comprise reasonably clear general rules that are known to all citizens in advance.
- These rules should not be retroactive—that is, they should not be applied to situations that occurred before those rules were established.
- Laws should not be contradictory or require the impossible.
- Laws should remain constant over time and should be administered in a consistent manner.

Although Fuller's formulation of natural law certainly differs from that of Aristotle, it shares with it an attempt to identify certain unchangeable moral principles that should form the foundation of every legal system.

The Positivist Perspective

The natural-law approach suggests that a law is truly a law only if its content reflects certain higher principles. In effect, then, natural-law theorists believe that a law whose *substance* is illegitimate is no law at all. Another approach to the law is called **positivism** or **(formalistic** or **analytical jurisprudence).** Its supporters argue that a law is truly a law if it has the *form* of a law—that is, if it can be *enforced*. This approach eliminates the distinction between *general* legal principles (natural law) and their expression in *positive* (that is, specific) laws. Any positive (specific) law that can be enforced *is* a law. There are no higher laws.

positivism Legal theory holding that a law is dependent not on content or morality but on form and is truly a law if it can be enforced

JOHN AUSTIN: COMMAND AND SOVEREIGNTY. John Austin (1790–1859), one of the most important thinkers in the tradition of legal positivism, did agree that morality should play some role in shaping the law. But Austin, like other positivists, believed that moral theory has no role in defining what law actually *is*. A bad law is as much a law as a good one: "The existence of law is one thing," he wrote; "its merit or demerit is another."[3]

To Austin, the difference between a law and an opinion lies in the fact that a law must be obeyed on pain of punishment: A law is thus a "command" issued by a "sovereign." A *command*, according to Austin, has two components. The first is the expression of a desire that someone do or not do something; the other is a threat or implied threat against anyone who does not comply with that desire.

The *sovereign*, meanwhile, must be "an uncommanded commander—that is, a person or institution "not in the habit of rendering habitual obedience" to anyone else and "habitually obeyed by the bulk of the people in that society."[4] In addition, the sovereign must always be "determinate": that is, it must consist of specific individuals or institutions.

---

[3] John Austin, *The Province of Jurisprudence Determined* (1832) (New York: Noonday Press, 1954), p. 184.

[4] Quoted by George C. Christie in "Positive Law," *Guide to American Law* (St. Paul, MN: West, 1984), p. 237.

HVGO, GROTIVS, IVRISCONSVLTVS,
De. Larmeßin fcul.

War and Peace, Humanist Style The origins of European international law can be found in the Italian city-states of the fourteenth century. During the fifteenth and sixteenth centuries, it developed primarily in Spain, then the leading world power, until rivaled in the seventeenth century by the Dutch school. Although no one figure can be regarded as the "father" of international law, the Dutch jurist, theologian, and humanist Hugo Grotius (1567–1641) produced what is undoubtedly the most important single body of juridicial work in the era. Although it is now recognized that Grotius's greatest contribution lies in his successful synthesis of work that had come before him, his masterwork, *On the Law of War and Peace* (1625), attained unparalleled fame and influence. In particular, Grotius emphasized the self-destructive nature of war and the sovereign state as the basic unit of international law. While maintaining the right of states to institute policy according to their own discretion, Grotius also insisted that states were bound by a *natural law* that he defined as independent of God and a reflection of human nature. Subsequent schools of thought included the *naturalist* school, which equated natural and international law, and the *positivist* school, which distinguished sharply between natural and international law in actual state practice. Grotius found followers in a so-called *eclectic* school that tried to adapt both naturalist and positivist principles.

H. L. A. HART: OBLIGATIONS AND RULES. Another legal positivist, the Englishman H. L. A. Hart (*b.* 1907), emphasized the difference between being *obligated* to do something and being *obliged* to do it. Suppose, suggests Hart, that a gunman holds you up and says, "Hand over your wallet!" The gunman is probably not in the habit of taking orders from anyone—and no doubt gives a lot of orders himself. He is therefore an "uncommanded commander:" Because he has the gun and you don't, you are *obliged* to follow his order much as you would be if a legitimate government authority gave you an order—indeed, more so. Yet, as Hart points out, "We should misdescribe the situation if we said, on these facts, that [the victim] 'had an obligation' or a 'duty' to hand over the money."[5]

If, however, we received a command from a duly constituted official, it would have legal force even if it was not backed up by an immediate threat of violence. An order has legal force, says Hart, only if we feel obligated as well as obliged to follow it: In other words, compulsion is a necessary condition of law but not a sufficient condition. In order to have law, therefore, we need something else: namely, the sense that we have an obligation, a duty, to follow the order in question. This understanding of obligation, according to Hart, is the central characteristic of law.

According to Hart, a mature legal system also comprises two kinds of rules. *Primary* rules are the actual directives requiring us either to do or not do things or to do them in certain ways if we want to do them at all. *Secondary* rules tell us both who has the right to issue primary rules and under what circumstances they may be issued.

Hart suggests in addition that there are three kinds of secondary rules. Rules of *adjudication* tell us how to settle disputes. Rules of *change* explain how the system can be modified. Rules of *recognition* are standards that tell us whether or not a particular law is valid. By "valid," however, Hart does not mean *morally* valid. Like Austin, Hart was a positivist: He held that although morality can and should influence law, it does not help us decide what is a valid law.

What sort of "practical" conclusions can be drawn from this debate between natural-law and positivist theories? THE ETHICAL ENVIRONMENT box in this chapter is concerned with one extreme instance in which legal theory played an important role in government legal practice.

Social-Science Perspectives

Natural law theorists focus on the content of law as the driving force of its creation and legitimacy. Positivists focus on the way in which a law was made as the determinant of its validity. Some theorists, however, believe that neither of these theories sufficiently takes into account the circumstances—especially the *social* circumstances—in which laws are made and obeyed. These theorists argue "that law cannot be understood without regard for the realities of social life."[6]

We can divide this perspective into two schools of thought: *sociological jurisprudence*, which argues for the application of sociological principles in legal decision making, and *legal realism*, which focuses on the factors that affect the actual working of the courts as a social institution.

---

[5] H. L. A. Hart, "A New Conception of Law," from *The Concept of Law* (London: Oxford, 1961), in Joel Feinberg and Hyman Gross, *The Philosophy of the Law*, 3rd ed. (Belmont, CA: Wadsworth, 1986), p. 55.

[6] Steven Vago, *Law and Society* (Englewood Cliffs, NJ: Prentice Hall, 1981), p. 41.

The conflict between the theories of natural law and positivism is perhaps nowhere more clearly illustrated than by the events that occurred before, during, and after the Holocaust. Under a system of natural law, the Holocaust could never have happened because the systematic "execution" of millions of "enemies of the state" violates the underlying moral and ethical foundations of that legal theory. Positivists, however, view a law as a rule that can be enforced: "Good" ("moral" and "ethical") and "bad" ("unethical") do not have a role in whether the law should or should not exist. Accordingly, even a moral horror like genocide can be made legal—as in fact it was in Nazi Germany.

The Nazi attempt to exterminate an entire population was not implemented in a single day. It took about twelve years from the time of the first major anti-Semitic riots until the enactment of the Nuremberg Laws in September 1935. The Nuremberg Laws were in fact constitutional amendments. The first of these laws, the Reich citizenship law, separated the population into two categories: Aryans and non-Aryans (Jews, of course, were considered non-Aryans). The law was expanded through thirteen implementing ordi-nances, issued between November 1935 and July 1943, that systematically excluded the Jews from the fundamental rights under law that made everyday social functioning possible. The second Nuremberg law—the law for the protection of German blood and honor—prohibited marriages and extramarital intercourse between Jews and Germans, forbade Jews from employing German maids younger than forty-five, and banned Jews from raising the German flag.

These laws lifted the burden of deciding whether anti-semitic activities were "right" or "wrong." In the simplest terms, such laws made it legal to rob, beat, and murder Jews. The fact that German Jews had been an integral part of German culture, education, and social life since the twelfth century was irrelevant. Under positivism, the morality of the crimes committed against the Jewish population was, theoretically, not at issue. The laws were legal and enforceable. In fact, after World War II, when the existence of the persecution campaign was graphically illustrated by photographs of the concentration camps and their survivors, many German citizens and soldiers claimed that they were simply obeying the law.

As enforcers of new laws enacted earlier that year, members of the Nazi *Sturmabteilung* (storm troopers) demonstrate against the "enemies" of the German state in 1935. The banner reads, "We admit no sabotage of the constructive work of the Fuhrer," and Nazi "enemies" are pictured above (in the center, a lascivious old Jew fondles a young Aryan woman).

SOCIOLOGICAL JURISPRUDENCE. Sociological jurisprudence suggests that both the law and judicial interpretations of it should take into account the findings of sociology. Consider, for example, the case of *Brown v. Board of Education* (1954)—the famous case in which the Supreme Court declared racial segregation of the public schools to be illegal. In explaining its decision, the Court introduced information, stemming from the work of sociologists, which suggested that black children learn more readily in integrated than in segregated schools. When the Court put these findings forward as a reason for banning segregation in public schools, its reasoning was an example of sociological jurisprudence.

Perhaps the leading exponent of sociological jurisprudence was Roscoe Pound (1870–1964). Pound eagerly incorporated the findings of social-science research into his own legal writings and even looked forward to the creation of "laboratories dedicated to legal science." Pound argued that legal systems in civilized countries are based upon certain shared assumptions or expectations.[7] In such countries, he believed, we must be able to assume that:

- no one will deliberately harm anyone else;
- property rights, not only in fixed and movable property but also in such intellectual property as patents and copyrights, will be respected;
- anyone who enters into a contract will observe it;
- people will try to prevent needless injury to others;
- people who use dangerous materials and processes will do so only in ways that do not threaten the public.

We do not expect that these assumptions will hold true in every case. We do, however, expect that when they do not, those responsible will be punished.

LEGAL REALISM. Similar to sociological jurisprudence in that it, too, recognizes the role of the social sciences in the making of laws is the school of **legal realism,** which focuses on how judicial systems actually work.

Before the emergence of legal realism, most legal theorists tended to argue that the function of courts and judges was logically to apply principles of law to each case that came before them: because these principles were universally valid and accepted, all judges and juries would reach the same conclusions when presented with the same given sets of facts.

In the real world, of course, such consistency does not exist: Courts decide similar cases differently even though the same legal principles are applied. Focusing upon this phenomenon, legal realists contend that law is distinct from universal notions of morality. Unlike legal positivists, however, they believe that judges, lawyers, and juries are influenced by *their own* values, beliefs, attitudes, and the dominant belief system of the times. In other words, judges and juries draw upon legal principles reflected in statutes and cases, they also bring to them their own perspectives and ethics.

One influential legal realist, Karl Llewellyn (1893-1962), viewed judges' decision-making as an interplay between their own value judgments and their interpretation and application of judicial precedents, which are previous rulings by judges in similar cases. (*See* Chapter 4.) For Llewellyn, the law is a product of these two forces.

---

[7] Pound called these shared assumptions *jural postulates*. See his *Jurisprudence*, Vol. 1 (St. Paul, MN: West, 1959).

The school of legal realism remains influential among jurists today—although in a more complex form than has been presented here. Many different disciplines—economics, sociology, political science, anthropology, and history—explicitly influence law-making, whether through judges, juries, or legislatures. U.S. Supreme Court Justice Oliver Wendell Holmes, who advocated the application of a judge's experience and reason to legal principles, was also an early proponent of legal realism. His views are discussed in the PERSONAL PROFILE box in this chapter.

Concepts of Jurisprudence: Back to the Case

But what happened to the defendants in *The Case of the Speluncean Explorers*? How did Lon Fuller's judges decide that case? Although abridged here, each judge's opinion reflects a different legal philosophy. Can you identify which of the theories that we have just discussed each judge adheres to? Before reading the opinions, however, consider Fuller's postscript to his invented case:

> There is probably no need to observe that the *Speluncean Case* itself is intended neither as a work of satire nor as a prediction in any ordinary sense of the term. As for the judges who make up Chief Justice Truepenny's court, they are, of course, as mythical as the facts and precedents with which they deal. . . . The case was constructed for the sole purpose of bringing into a common focus certain divergent philosophies of law and government. These philosophies presented men with live questions of choice in the days of Plato and Aristotle. Perhaps they will continue to do so when our era has had its say about them. If there is any element of prediction in the case, it does not go beyond a suggestion that the questions involved are among the permanent problems of the human race.

THE CASE OF THE SPELUNCEAN EXPLORERS (cont.)

Trupenny, C.J.:

It seems to me that in dealing with this extraordinary case the jury and the trial judge followed a course that was not only fair and wise, but the only course that was open to them under the law. The language of our statute is well known: "Whoever shall willfully take the life of another shall be punished by death." N. C. S. A. (N.S.) § 12-A. This statute permits of no exception applicable to this case, however our sympathies may incline us to make allowance for the tragic situation in which these men found themselves.

In a case like this the principle of executive clemency seems admirably suited to mitigate the rigors of the law, and I propose to my colleagues that we follow the example of the jury and the trial judge by joining in the communications they have addressed to the chief executive. . . . I think we may therefore assume that some form of clemency will be extended to these defendants. If this is done, then justice will be accomplished without impairing either the letter or spirit of our statutes and without offering any encouragement for the disregard of law.

Foster, J.:

I am shocked that the chief justice, in an effort to escape the embarrassments of this tragic case, should have adopted, and should have proposed to his colleagues, an expedient at once so sordid and so obvious. I believe something more is on trial in this case than the fate of these unfortunate explorers; that is the law of our commonwealth. If this court declares that under our law these men have committed a crime, then our law is itself convicted in the tribunal of common sense, no matter what happens to the individuals involved in this petition of error. . . .

For myself, I do not believe that our law compels the monstrous conclusion that these men are murderers. I believe, on the contrary, that it declares them to be innocent of any crime. I rest this conclusion on two independent grounds, either of which is of itself sufficient to justify the acquittal of these defendants.

The first of these grounds rests on a premise that may arouse opposition until it has been examined candidly. I take the view that the enacted or positive law of this commonwealth, including all of its statutes and precedents, is inapplicable to this case, and that the case is governed instead by what ancient writers in Europe and America called "the law of nature."

This conclusion rests on the proposition that our positive law is predicated on the possibility of men's coexis-

---

tence in society. When a situation arises in which the coexistence of men becomes impossible, then a condition that underlies all of our precedents and statutes has ceased to exist. When that condition disappears, then it is my opinion that the force of our positive law disappears with it. . . .

. . . .

Had the tragic events of this case taken place a mile beyond the territorial limits of our commonwealth, no one would pretend that our law was applicable to them. . . .

I conclude, therefore, that at the time Roger Whetmore's life was ended by these defendants, they were, to use the quaint language of nineteenth-century writers, not in a "state of civil society" but in a "state of nature." This has the consequence that the law applicable to them is not the enacted and established law of this Commonwealth, but the law derived from those principles that were appropriate to their condition. I have no hesitancy in saying that under those principles they were guiltless of any crime.

What these men did was done in pursuance of an agreement accepted by all of them and first proposed by Whetmore himself. Since it was apparent that their extraordinary predicament made inapplicable the usual principles that regulate men's relations with one another, it was necessary for them to draw, as it were, a new charter of government appropriate to the situation in which they found themselves

. . . .

. . . My second ground proceeds by rejecting hypothetically all the premises on which I have so far proceeded. I concede for purposes of argument that I am wrong in saying that the situation of these men removed them from the effect of our positive law, and I assume that the consolidated statutes have the power to penetrate five hundred feet of rock and to impose themselves upon these starving men huddled in their underground prison.

Now it is, of course, perfectly clear that these men did an act that violates the literal wording of the statute which declares that he who "shall willfully take the life of another" is a murderer. But one of the most ancient bits of legal wisdom is the saying that a man may break the letter of the law without breaking the law itself. Every proposition of positive law, whether contained in a statute or a judicial precedent, is to be interpreted reasonably, in the light of its evident purpose. . . .

The statute before us for interpretation has never been applied literally. Centuries ago it was established that a killing in self-defense is excused. There is nothing in the wording of the statute that suggests this exception. Various attempts have been made to reconcile the legal treatment of self-defense with the words of the statute, but in my opinion these are all merely ingenious sophistries. The truth is that the exception in favor of self-defense cannot be reconciled with the *words* of the statute, but only with its *purpose*.

The true reconciliation of the excuse of self-defense with the statute making it a crime to kill another is to be found in the following line of reasoning. One of the principal objects underlying any criminal legislation is that of deterring men from crime. Now it is apparent that if it were declared to be the law that a killing in self-defense is murder, such a rule could not operate in a deterrent manner. A man whose life is threatened will repel his aggressor, whatever the law may say. Looking therefore to the broad purposes of criminal legislation, we may safely declare that this statute was not intended to apply to cases of self-defense.

When the rationale of the excuse of self-defense is thus explained, it becomes apparent that precisely the same reasoning is applicable to the case at bar. If in the future any group of men ever find themselves in the tragic predicament of these defendants, we may be sure that their decision whether to live or die will not be controlled by the contents of our criminal code. Accordingly, if we read this statute intelligently it is apparent that it does not apply to this case. The withdrawal of this situation from the effect of the statute is justified by precisely the same considerations that were applied by our predecessors in office centuries ago to the case of self-defense.

. . . .

I therefore conclude that on any aspect under which this case may be viewed these defendants are innocent of the crime of murdering Roger Whetmore, and that the conviction should be set aside.

Tatting, J.:

In the discharge of my duties as a justice of this Court, I am usually able to dissociate the emotional and intellectual sides of my reactions, and to decide the case before me entirely on the basis of the latter. In passing on this tragic case I find that my usual resources fail me. . . .

As I analyze the opinion just rendered by my brother Foster, I find that it is shot through with contradictions and fallacies. Let us begin with his first proposition: these men were not subject to our law because they were not in a "state of civil society" but in a "state of nature." . . .

. . . .

Let us look at the contents of this code of nature that my brother proposes we adopt as our own and apply to this case. What a topsy-turvy and odious code it is! It is a code in which the law of contracts is more fundamental than the law of murder. It is a code under which a man may make a valid agreement empowering his fellows to eat his own body. Under the provisions of this code, furthermore, such an agreement once made is irrevocable, and if one of the parties attempts to withdraw, the others may take the law into their own hands and enforce the contract by violence—for though my brother passes over in convenient silence the effect of Whetmore's withdrawal, this is the necessary implication of his argument.

. . . .

All of these considerations make it impossible for me to accept the first part of my brother's argument. I can neither accept his notion that these men were under a code of nature which this court was bound to apply to them, nor can I accept the odious and perverted rules that he would read into that code. I come now to the second part of my brother's opinion, in which he seeks to show that the defendants did not violate the provisions of N. C. S. A. (N.S.) § 12-A. Here the way, instead of being clear, becomes for me misty and ambiguous, though my brother seems unaware of the difficulties that inhere in his demonstrations.

. . . .

Now let me outline briefly, however, the perplexities that assail me when I examine my brother's demonstration more closely. It is true that a statute should be applied in the light of its purpose, and that *one* of the purposes of criminal legislation is recognized to be deterrence. The difficulty is that other purposes are also ascribed to the law of crimes. It has been said that one of its objects is to provide an orderly outlet for the instinctive human demand for retribution. *Commonwealth v. Scape.* It has also been said that its object is the rehabilitation of the wrongdoer. *Commonwealth v. Make-over.* Other theories have been propounded. Assuming that we must interpret a statute in the light of its purpose, what are we to do when it has many purposes or when its purposes are disputed?

. . . .

Now the familiar explanation for the excuse of self-defense just expounded obviously cannot be applied by analogy to the facts of this case. These men acted not only "willfully" but with great deliberation and after hours of discussing what they should do. Again, we encounter a forked path, with one line of reasoning leading us in one direction and another in a direction that is exactly the opposite. . . .

. . . .

There is still a further difficulty in my brother Foster's proposal to read an exception into the statute to favor this case, though again a difficulty not even intimated in his opinion. What shall be the scope of this exception? Here the men cast lots and the victim was himself originally a party to the agreement. What would we have to decide if Whetmore had refused from the beginning to participate in the plan? Would a majority be permitted to overrule him? Or, suppose that no plan were adopted at all and the others simply conspired to bring about Whetmore's death, justifying their act by saying that he was in the weakest condition. . . .

. . . .

I have given this case the best thought of which I am capable. I have scarcely slept since it was argued before us. When I feel myself inclined to accept the view of my brother Foster, I am repelled by a feeling that his arguments are intellectually unsound and approach mere rationalization. On the other hand, when I incline toward upholding the conviction, I am struck by the absurdity of directing that these men be put to death when their lives have been saved at the cost of the lives of ten heroic workmen. It is to me a matter of regret that the Prosecutor saw fit to ask for an indictment for murder. If we had a provision in our statutes making it a crime to eat human flesh, that would have been a more appropriate charge. If no other charge suited to the facts of this case could be brought against the defendants, it would have been wiser, I think, not to have indicted them at all. Unfortunately, however, the men have been indicted and tried, and we have therefore been drawn into this unfortunate affair.

Since I have been wholly unable to resolve the doubts that beset me about the law of this case, I am with regret announcing a step that is, I believe, unprecedented in the history of this tribunal. I declare my withdrawal from the decision of this case.

Keen. J.:

I should like to begin by setting to one side two questions which are not before this court.

The first of these is whether executive clemency should be extended to these defendants if the conviction is affirmed. Under our system of government, that is a question for the Chief Executive, not for us. I therefore disapprove of that passage in the opinion of the chief justice in which he in effect gives instructions to the chief executive as to what he should do in this case and suggests that some impropriety will attach if these instructions are not heeded. . . .

The second question that I wish to put to one side is that of deciding whether what these men did was "right" or "wrong," "wicked" or "good." That is also a question that is irrelevant to the discharge of my office as a judge sworn to apply, not my conceptions of morality, but the law of the land. . . .

The sole question before us for decision is whether these defendants did, within the meaning of N. C. S. A. (N.S.) § 12-A, willfully take the life of Roger Whetmore. The exact language of the statute is as follows: "Whoever shall willfully take the life of another shall be punished by death." Now I should suppose that any candid observer, content to extract from these words their natural meaning, would concede at once that these defendants did "willfully take the life" of Roger Whetmore.

Whence arise all the difficulties of the case, then, and the necessity for so many pages of discussion about what ought to be so obvious? The difficulties, in whatever tortured form they may present themselves, all trace back to a single source, and that is a failure to distinguish the legal from the moral aspects of this case. To put it bluntly, my brothers do not like the fact that the written law requires the conviction of these defendants. Neither do I, but unlike my brothers I respect the obligations of an office that requires me to put my personal predilections out of my mind when I come to interpret and apply the law of this commonwealth. . . .

. . . .

There was a time in this commonwealth when judges did in fact legislate very freely, and all of us know that during that period some of our statutes were rather thoroughly made over by the judiciary. . . . It is enough to observe that those days are behind us, and that in place of the uncertainty that then reigned we now have a clear-cut principle, which is the supremacy of the legislative branch of our government. From that principle flows the obligation of the judiciary to enforce faithfully the written law, and to interpret that law in accordance with its plain meaning without reference to our personal desires or our individual conceptions of justice. I am not concerned with the question whether the principle that forbids the judicial revision of statutes is right or wrong, desirable or undesirable; I observe merely that this principle has become a tacit premise underlying the whole of the legal and governmental order I am sworn to administer.

Yet though the principle of the supremacy of the legislature has been accepted in theory for centuries, such is the tenacity of professional tradition and the force of fixed habits of thought that many of the judiciary have still not accommodated themselves to the restricted role which the new order imposes on them. My brother Foster is one of that group; his way of dealing with statutes is exactly that of a judge living in the 3900s.

. . . .

The process of judicial reform requires three steps. The first of these is to divine some single "purpose" which the statute serves. This is done although not one statute in a hundred has any such single purpose, and although the objectives of nearly every statute are differently interpreted by the different classes of its sponsors. The second step is to discover that a mythical being called "the legislator," in the pursuit of this imagined "purpose," overlooked something or left some gap or imperfection in his work. Then comes the final and most refreshing part of the task, which is, of course, to fill in the blank thus created. *Quod erat faciendum.*

My brother Foster's penchant for finding holes in statutes reminds one of the story told by an ancient author about the man who ate a pair of shoes. Asked how he liked them, he replied that the part he liked best was the holes. That is the way my brother feels about statutes: the more holes they have in them the better he likes them. In short, he doesn't like statutes.

One could not wish for a better case to illustrate the specious nature of this gap-filling process than the one before us. My brother thinks he knows exactly what was sought when men made murder a crime, and that was something he calls "deterrence." My brother Tatting has already shown how much is passed over in that interpretation. But I think the trouble goes deeper. I doubt very much whether our statute making murder a crime really has a "purpose" in any ordinary sense of the term. . . .

. . . .

. . . . As in dealing with the statute, so in dealing with the exception, the question is not the conjectural *purpose* of the rule, but its *scope*. Now the scope of the exception in favor of self-defense as it has been applied by this court is plain; it applies to cases of resisting an aggressive threat to the party's own life. It is therefore too clear for argument that this case does not fall within the scope of the exception, since it is plain that Whetmore made no threat against the lives of these defendants.

The essential shabbiness of my brother Foster's attempt to cloak his remaking of the written law with an air of legitimacy comes tragically to the surface in my brother Tatting's opinion. In that opinion Justice Tatting struggles manfully to combine his colleague's loose moralisms with his own sense of fidelity to the written law. The issue of this struggle could only be that which occurred, a complete default in the discharge of the judicial function. You simply cannot apply a statute as it is written and remake it to meet your own wishes at the same time.

. . . .

I conclude that the conviction should be affirmed.
Handy, J.:
. . . . The problem before us is what we, as officers of the government, ought to do with these defendants. That is a question of practical wisdom, to be exercised in a context, not of abstract theory, but of human realities. When the case is approached in this light, it becomes, I think, one of the easiest to decide that has ever been argued before this Court.

. . . .

I have never been able to make my brothers see that government is a human affair, and that men are ruled, not by words on paper or by abstract theories, but by other men. They are ruled well when their rulers understand the feelings and conceptions of the masses. They are ruled badly when that understanding is lacking.

. . . .

. . . . I believe that all government officials, including judges, will do their jobs best if they treat forms and abstract concepts as instruments. We should take as our model, I think, the good administrator, who accommodates procedures and principles to the case at hand, selecting from among the available forms those most suited to reach the proper result.

The most obvious advantage of this method of government is that it permits us to go about our daily tasks with efficiency and common sense. My adherence to this philosophy has, however, deeper roots. I believe that it is only with the insight this philosophy gives that we can preserve the flexibility essential if we are to keep our actions in reasonable accord with the sentiments of those subject to our rule. . . .

Now when these conceptions are applied to the case before us, its decision becomes, as I have said, perfectly easy. In order to demonstrate this I shall have to introduce certain realities that my brothers in their coy decorum have seen fit to pass over in silence, although they are just as acutely aware of them as I am.

The first of these is that this case has aroused an enormous public interest, both here and abroad. Almost every newspaper and magazine has carried articles about it; columnists have shared with their readers confidential information as to the next governmental move; hundreds of letters-to-the-editor have been printed. One of the great newspaper chains made a poll of public opinion on the question. "What do you think the supreme court should do with the Speluncean explorers?" About ninety percent expressed a belief that the defendants should be pardoned or let off with a kind of token punishment. It is perfectly clear, then, how the public feels about the case. We could have known this without the poll, of course, on the basis of common sense, or even by observing that on this court there are apparently four-and-a-half men, or ninety percent, who share the common opinion.

. . . .

Now I know that my brothers will be horrified by my suggestion that this court should take account of public opinion. They will tell you that public opinion is emotional and capricious, that it is based on half-truths and listens to witnesses who are not subject to cross-examination. . . .

But let us look candidly at some of the realities of the administration of our criminal law. When a man is accused of crime, there are, speaking generally, four ways in which he may escape punishment. One of these is a determination by a judge that under the applicable law he has committed no crime. This is, of course, a determination that takes place in a rather formal and abstract atmosphere. But look at the other three ways in which he may escape punishment. These are: (1) a decision by the prosecutor not to ask for an indictment; (2) an acquittal by the jury; (3) a pardon or commutation of sentence by the executive. Can anyone pretend that these decisions are held within a rigid and formal framework of rules that prevents factual error, excludes emotional and personal factors, and guarantees that all the forms of the law will be observed?

. . . .

My brother Tatting expresses annoyance that the prosecutor did not, in effect, decide the case for him by not asking for an indictment. Strict as he is himself in complying with the demands of legal theory, he is quite content to have the fate of these men decided out of court by the prosecutor on the basis of common sense. The chief justice, on the other hand, wants the application of common sense postponed to the very end, though like Tatting he wants no personal part in it.

. . . .

I come now to the most crucial fact in this case, a fact known to all of us on this court, though one that my brothers have seen fit to keep under the cover of their judicial robes. This is the frightening likelihood that if the issue is left to him, the chief executive will refuse to pardon these men or commute their sentence. As we all know, our chief executive is a man now well advanced in years, of very stiff notions. Public clamor usually operates on him with the reverse of the effect intended. As I have told my brothers, it happens that my wife's niece is an intimate friend of his secretary. I have learned in this indirect, but, I think, wholly reliable way, that he is firmly determined not to commute the sentence if these men are found to have violated the law.

No one regrets more than I the necessity for relying in so important a matter on information that could be characterized as gossip. If I had my way this would not happen, for I would adopt the sensible course of sitting down with the Executive, going over the case with him, finding out what his views are, and perhaps working out with him a common program for handling the situation. But of course my brothers would never hear of such a thing.

. . . .

I must confess that as I grow older I become more and more perplexed at men's refusal to apply their common sense to problems of law and government, and this truly tragic case has deepened my sense of discouragement and dismay. I only wish that I could convince my brothers of the wisdom of the principles I have applied to the judicial office since I first assumed it. . . .

. . . .

. . . . I conclude that the defendants are innocent of the crime charged, and that the conviction and sentence should be set aside.)

. . . .

The supreme court being evenly divided, the conviction and sentence of the Court of General Instances is *affirmed*. It is ordered that the execution of the sentence shall occur at 6:00 A.M., Friday, April 2, 4300, at which time the public executioner is directed to proceed with all convenient dispatch to hang each of the defendants by the neck until he is dead.

In addition to reflecting different schools of jurisprudence, the *Speluncean Case* illustrates both how judges' perceptions of the purpose of law affect their decisions and how judges' interpretations of facts are affected by what they conceive to be a fair outcome:

- Obviously, Chief Justice Truepenny is a *positivist*. For him, the task of a judge is to ensure that applicable statutes—in this case the law defining murder—are accurately applied. The final result does not matter: If the men's actions constituted murder as defined by a duly enacted law, then they must pay the consequences—no ifs, ands, or buts.

- Justice Foster would toss out the murder statute and rely instead upon *natural law* in analyzing the facts of the case: Because they found themselves in a state of nature in which they all could not survive, it would be unfair to hold these men accountable to a statute that was enacted to apply to civil society.

- Justice Handy reaches his decision in keeping with the traditions of *legal realism:* In reversing the lower court, he considers such pragmatic factors as public opinion and the likely effects of punishing the defendants.

Serving for 30 years, Oliver Wendell Holmes, Jr. (1841-1935) was one of the most famous and most respected justices to ever sit on the Supreme Court. Holmes—son of an aristocratic Boston family, graduate of Harvard Law School, and proud Civil War veteran—brought a wealth of life experience to the bench. This background might help to explain his commitment to legal realism—the belief that the law is always human and can never be absolute. Holmes contended that all people—whether "good" or "bad"—wish to avoid breaking the law. The difference, however, is that a good man will uphold the law because it is the right thing to do; the bad man is likely to break a law if he feels that he will not get caught. Laws, therefore, should be formed from the perspective of the bad man. Holmes explained his views in two of his most famous writings.

The first of these works, The Common Law, was published in 1881. It is here that Holmes stated his two-part legal theory: (1) "The life of the law has not been logic, it has been experience"; (2) "The substance of the law, at any given time, pretty neatly corresponds, so far as it goes, with what is understood to be convenient. . . ."

The second (and possibly more famous) work is "The Path of the Law," which was published in the Harvard Law Review in 1897. Holmes's definition of a legal duty appears in this article. It states that a legal duty is "nothing but a prediction that if a man does or omits certain things he will be made to suffer in this or that way by a judgment of the court." Holmes, in other words, viewed laws as predictions of what the courts actually would do in a given set of circumstances.

These concepts informed some of the most important opinions rendered by Holmes during his tenure on the Supreme Court. For example, Lochner v. New York, 198 U.S. 45, 25 S. Ct. 539, 49 L. Ed. 937 (1905), involved a

Oliver Wendell Holmes, Jr., associate justice of the Supreme Court, 1902–1932. Renowned as much for his rhetorical skills as for his juridicial reasoning, Holmes was once called the only "authentic sage" in U.S. legal history.

New York law limiting the hours that bakers could be required to work. At issue was whether or not the statute violated Section 1 of the Fourteenth Amendment, which provides that no state can "deprive any person of life, liberty, or property, without due process of law." The Supreme Court struck down the state law by a 5-4 margin. Not surprisingly, Holmes dissented, saying that the majority ruling was grounded in a personal ideology favoring freedom of contract rather than a strict interpretation of the Constitution.

In a later case, Abrams v. United States (250 U.S. 616[1919])—Holmes wrote a passionate defense of free speech. His opinion argued that "we should be eternally vigilant against attempts to check the expression of opinions that we loathe and believe to be frought with death, unless they so immediately threaten interference with the lawful and pressing purposes of the law that an immediate check is required to save the country." Perhaps it can be said that this language—and this way of thinking—has colored such recent Supreme Court opinions as the one rendered in the flag-desecration case of Texas v. Johnson (which is the subject of the YOU DECIDE feature in Chapter 3, p. 85).

Each of the other justices presents a decision based on his own philosophical perspective—after all, judicial decision making is a complex task. The case thus highlights how the same set of facts can be viewed so differently by different people. In the chapters that follow, you will be reading many opinions written by many judges. When you examine these cases, read between the lines and think about what factors—factors of experience and philosophy—may have influenced the judge.[8]

■ Concept Check 1-1   The Functions and Nature of Law

- Identify and explain the most important *function* of law.
- Define *jurisprudence*.
- Describe the *natural-law, positivist,* and *social-science* perspectives on jurisprudence.
- Define *legal realism* and explain how it is similar to but different from *sociological jurisprudence*.

■ LEGAL TRADITIONS

So far, we have examined various conceptions of what law is. Now we will take a very brief look at the two great historical traditions of Western law: *civil law* and *common law*. Most Western countries, as well as a great many Third World countries, follow one of these traditions. In many of these countries, because the traditions of religious law also influence secular (that is, nonreligious) law, we will touch upon three religious traditions that have had an important influence on the development of both common- and civil-law systems in the West: *talmudic, canon,* and *Islamic law.*

Civil Law

We have already seen that our system of law can be divided into two branches: criminal law and noncriminal, or civil, law. However, although "noncriminal" is indeed one meaning of the term "civil law," it is not the one with which we are concerned here. **Civil law** is the name of a particular system of jurisprudence that is followed in a great many countries of the world. Put in its sim-

civil law Roman-based legal system still operative in Europe and based on legal *codes* or *statutes*

---

[8] Gerald L. Gall discusses the case in *The Canadian Legal System,* 2nd ed. (Agincourt, Ont.: Carswell, 1983), pp. 6-8.

legal codes *Statutes* enacted by lawmaking bodies and defining a society's basic laws on various subjects

plest form, we can say that civil-law systems are those based on **legal codes,** (or *statutes*) that spell out a society's basic laws on a variety of subjects, such as acts that constitute crimes, tax obligations, and rules about owning and transferring property.

The term "civil law" and the basis of the law itself are derived originally from the law of ancient Rome, the *jus civile.* As time passed, ancient Roman law was reworked into comprehensive legal codes. The code of the emperor Justinian (A.D. 483-565) was revived after the Dark Ages, and it became the basis of modern law in Italy, the German Empire, the Netherlands, France, and Spain, as well as in their colonial offshoots. Our own state of Louisiana historically also shares the civil-law tradition. Each country that has turned to civil law, however, has adapted it to local needs and traditions. Moreover, the *customary laws* of these countries—as well as those of their separate regions—has survived alongside official civil law.

Today, most Western European countries have civil-law systems, as do the countries of Latin America, most African countries, Japan, Thailand, and Turkey. Some roots of Western civil law are discussed in the INTERNATIONAL ENVIRONMENT box in this chapter.

Common Law

Besides the United States and England, a system known as *common law* prevails in Australia, Burma, Canada, India, Iraq, Liberia, Malaya, New Zealand, Singapore, and in Britain's former colonies in Africa, such as Ghana and Nigeria.

THE INTERNATIONAL ENVIRONMENT
The Rise of Civil Law in the West

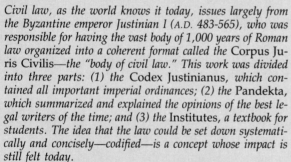

Civil law, as the world knows it today, issues largely from the Byzantine emperor Justinian I (A.D. 483-565), who was responsible for having the vast body of 1,000 years of Roman law organized into a coherent format called the Corpus Juris Civilis—*the "body of civil law." This work was divided into three parts: (1) the* Codex Justinianus, *which contained all important imperial ordinances; (2) the* Pandekta, *which summarized and explained the opinions of the best legal writers of the time; and (3) the* Institutes, *a textbook for students. The idea that the law could be set down systematically and concisely—codified—is a concept whose impact is still felt today.*

The monumental Corpus *commissioned by Justinian still influences the evolution of law in virtually every civil-law country. (The roots of civil law are so deeply imbedded in French jurisprudence that French universities did not even teach common law until 1689). It affects legal rules, legal thought, legal classifications, the treatment of legal precedents and techniques, and the organization of court systems. The emphasis remains on rules, principles, and authoritative explanations of the law. Legal precedents thus carry relatively little weight, only contract law remains the area that is most heavily influenced by the* Corpus.

One interesting aspect of civil law is that it transfers from place to place more easily than common law. For instance, largely because of the influence and conquests of Na-

poleon, books on the French civil code have been translated for use in numerous other civil-law countries throughout the world. It is sometimes said that there are two branches of civil law: French and German. The civil codes of both countries have proven particularly adaptable.

For example, the French Code Civil (or Napoleonic Code), *first promulgated by Napoleon I in 1804, is the basis of the laws of Belgium, the Netherlands, Luxembourg, and parts of Germany, Switzerland, and Italy. Spain, Romania, and parts of Africa and South America also borrowed the* Code Civil *as a guide for local civil codes. In North America, for example, the civil laws of both the state of Louisiana (1808) and the Canadian province of Quebec (1884) are rooted in the* Code Civil. *Inherited from the Holy Roman Empire, Germany's Civil Code, which was enacted in 1900, also reveals the strong influence of Roman civil law. Although its reach has been much narrower than that of the French* Code Civil, *it has been important in such far-reaching sites as Thailand, China, Japan, Eastern Europe, and Greece.*

Two other countries enacted civil codes that have been adopted elsewhere. The Swiss Civil Code, which took effect in 1811, became the Turkish Civil Code in 1926 when it was adopted by Turkey; the Chilean Civil Code (1855) is the model for other South American countries.

The basis of **common law** is not a comprehensive code: Rather, the basic building block of common-law systems is *case law*, which is composed of decisions handed down by judges who rule on individual cases. Because each judicial opinion serves as a precedent for later decisions, judges trying cases are somewhat bound by prior rulings in similar cases (albeit with numerous exceptions—*see* Chapter 4). As a result, common law is sometimes called *judge-made law*. Common-law judges have very wide powers of interpretation to apply previous judicial rulings and to interpret statutes. The basis of the common law in the United States is the subject of chapters in this book on the Constitution, the courts, civil litigation, and criminal procedures. For now, however, we will distinguish common law from civil law.

common law Legal tradition based on *case law*, or the rulings of individual cases that serve as *precedents* for later decisions

The Influence of Religion

Although secular in nature, both civil law and common law, especially in the West, were influenced by Christianity. When both of these systems were taken to other parts of the world, they were influenced by other religious traditions, especially those of Islam.

TALMUDIC LAW. The Jewish code of law is the Talmud (Hebrew for "learning"), which is a "summary of oral law that evolved after centuries of scholarly efforts by sages who lived in Palestine and Babylonia until the beginning of the Middle Ages."[9] The Talmud seeks to interpret the Hebrew Bible. It has two major parts. The first part is called the Mishnah (a book of law). The second part, known as Gemarah, is an elaboration and discussion of the Mishnah. Although the Talmud is constructed as a legal tract, it also includes discussions of ethics and custom.

CANON LAW. Around A.D. 500, local meetings of Catholic bishops adopted certain *canons*—rules or norms—applicable to Christian communities in their regions. For the next 700 years, these canons were developed and applied to larger and larger regions. In the twelfth century, these rules were systematized by Gratian, an Italian legal scholar. In the thirteenth century, they were replaced by the Decretals of Pope Gregory IX, a summary of important judicial decisions made by the papacy. Until the twentieth century, these two works remained the foundation of Roman Catholic canon law.

A new code was established in 1917, and yet another, the current code, in 1983. Although this code sets forth the rights and obligations of all church members, for the ordinary Roman Catholic today, most of the domain of canon law has been taken over by secular law.

ISLAMIC LAW. In countries where most of the population is Muslim, Islamic law has a powerful impact on the legal system. In some countries—for example, Pakistan, and Saudi Arabia—Islamic law is enforced by the courts.

Unlike Christian canon law, Islamic law can serve this function because it is much broader. It covers not only constitutional, criminal, and commercial law but also such matters as morality and the correct performance of religious rituals. Most religious Muslims regard the law as divine in origin, and for them, it is unchangeable.

---

[9] Adin Steinsaltz, *The Essential Talmud* (New York: Basic Books, 1976), pp. 3-4.

Classic and Modern Shari'ah There are actually two separate sites of worship in this islamic mosque: one for men and one for women. Considered an expression of Allah's command for Islamic society, Islamic law is highly *canonical*. Known as the Shari'ah, classical Islamic jurisprudence differs from Western legal systems in two significant ways. First, the Shari'ah regulates not only the individual's relationships with other individuals and the state but also relationships with God and the personal conscience; it is thus much broader in scope than Western legal conceptions. The Shari'ah is concerned as much with ethical as with legal standards, and it prescribes such ritual practices as prayer and pilgrimage. Second, Islamic law, considered an expression of divine will, presupposes that law precedes and molds society rather than the reverse. Such a philosophy poses basic problems in the application of law to circumstances of social change such as the Islamic world is now experiencing, and these problems constitute a central issue in current Islamic legal thought. Because traditional Islamic law is patriarchal in outlook, this issue has been central to the question of reform in family-relations law. For example, two seminal developments in legal reform, the Syrian Law of Personal Status (1953) and the Tunisian Law of Personal Status (1957), both enacted measures regarding the two subjects of polygamy and divorce. Islamic jurisprudence has since struggled to find its place in a transitional phase of social evolution, defining its task as the solution to problems facing contemporary Islamic society.

- Define *civil law* and explain the role played in civil-law systems by legal *codes*.
- Define *common law* and explain how *case law* is the "building block" of common-law systems.

■ BRANCHES OF LAW: THE ADVERSARY SYSTEM

As we have seen, law can be studied in many different ways and from many different perspectives. One of the most important practical perspectives is legal categories—different subject areas of the law.

Our system of law is based on an *adversary* notion of justice: A main goal of our legal system is to uncover truth, and we use the courts, lawyers, court employees, and judges to help reveal the truth in particular situations. However, as any person who has observed our court system in action can tell, the search can be arduous. In an **adversary system,** dispute resolution requires that the parties involved are responsible for initiating lawsuits, defining the issues, and providing evidence to support claims. The word "adversary," however, also means opponent, and in such an adversary system, while lawyers on both sides present their particular points of view accurately, they also do so in the best possible light for their clients' interests. It is the job of the judge and jury to determine which perspective to accept. It is therefore quite important that the mechanism in place for determining the truth should be carefully constructed.

adversary system *Dispute-resolution system* requiring involved parties to initiate lawsuits, define issues, and provide supporting evidence for their claims (*see* Chapter 5)

Procedural versus Substantive Law

The branches of our legal system can be divided into *procedural* and *substantive law*.

PROCEDURAL LAW. **Procedural law** establishes the rules or the guidelines—that is, the procedures—under which our legal system operates. It creates the mechanism for resolving disputes and explains *how* substantive laws are to be enforced. In our legal system, for example, procedural law specifies the length of a statute of limitations for instituting a lawsuit or for arresting a wrongdoer; it also specifies the steps involved in instituting a lawsuit or making an arrest.

Procedural law can be divided into **criminal procedures,** such as the list of rights that must be read to a suspect before being questioned by the police (*see* Chapter 12), and **civil procedures** such as *pleadings,* the written statements of the positions to be advanced at trial by the parties in a lawsuit (*see* Chapter 5). Some *procedures* are common to both civil and criminal law.

procedural law Branch of the legal system that establishes rules and guidelines under which legal systems operate, including mechanisms for resolving disputes and enforcing *substantive law*

criminal procedure Division of *procedural law* dealing with offenses deemed to be against society as a whole (*see* Chapter 12)

civil procedure Division of *procedural law* dealing with disputes between individual parties (*see* Chapter 10)

SUBSTANTIVE LAW. **Substantive law** embraces rights, obligations, or limitations applicable to people and businesses in a variety of situations. Substantive law may be based in the Constitution of the United States, in legislative enactments such as statutes, or in case law developed by judges. In criminal law, for example, the actual definitions of the acts that constitute crimes are substantive law.

substantive law Laws concerned with public or private rights, duties, and obligations

In the law of contracts (*see* Chapter 9), substantive law includes the rights and remedies that are available when one party to a contract violates the terms of the agreement.

Public versus Private Law

Substantive law can in turn be divided into laws that affect *the public generally* and those that affect only *private individuals*. Consider the following incident:

Smith drives Jones to a baseball game. On the way into the parking lot, Smith's car is hit from behind by the car of White. Smith gets so angry with White that he screams at him. White punches Smith in the nose. Everybody, however, eventually calms down. Smith and White exchange insurance information, and everyone goes to the game.

On the way back to the parking lot after the game, Jones carelessly drops an empty soft-drink cup onto the ground. A policeman on duty at the game sees Jones do this and gives him a ticket for littering.

Public law is the body of law affecting the public generally; **private law** extends to actions affecting private individuals. Both are involved here. In fact, from a legal standpoint, the situation can be surprisingly complex:

- The automobile accident involves *tort law*, which provides redress for a person who has been injured by the act of another. Tort law (*see* Chapter 10) is a branch of private law covering one person's concerns with another. Specifically, tort law will be used to determine who was at fault for the accident and how to allocate responsibility.

- Similarly, if the fight that Smith got into resulted in a broken nose, he would have had medical bills. These bills would be of concern to Smith but of little concern to the rest of the world. Private law deals with these private concerns. The branch of private law that would apply here is the tort of *battery*—an individual cause of action for compensation for the unwarranted offensive touching of Smith by White, the driver of the other car.

- On the other hand, all of us in society are offended by certain actions of individuals. Collectively, we may choose to categorize some of those offensive actions as criminal offenses. When people commit crimes, it is the state (representing all of us collectively), not the "offended individual," that prosecutes them. If Smith was punched in the nose by White, the state might prosecute White for *criminal battery*, a public offense. Criminal law is a branch of public law.

- Moreover, private disputes may affect the public interest because they affect a larger social realm or involve costs to society. In the case of the car accident, many states have passed laws that require all motorists to obtain automobile insurance to ensure that the costs of accidents are borne by the people involved, not by society as a whole. In this example, such a law would be a public law.

- Furthermore, a state's traffic laws may require that "points" be added to drivers' records if they are at fault in automobile accidents. Once a driver accumulates a certain number of points, his or her license is suspended. The purpose of this public law is to deter people from behavior that causes accidents and to remove hazardous drivers from the road.

- Finally, when Jones drops a soft-drink cup onto the ground, he may be offending a collective sense of appropriate behavior—an offense that we have in this instance defined as the criminal act of *littering*. If society as a whole is offended, littering is a crime against all of us collectively and therefore an example of public law.

A much more significant element of public law is the structure of government established by our Constitution—a social structure that quite clearly affects all of us. Another important branch of public law is *administrative law*, which defines the structure and operation of government agencies such as the Federal Trade Commission and the National Labor Relations board.

A contract, on the other hand, defines private relations—one-to-one or group-to-group. A contract between you and me or between one company and another does not affect the public generally. It is a part of private law.

Figure 1-1 charts some branches of law but does not represent all of them. It gives examples of those that will concern us in this book. In some cases, we include a single chapter for a branch of law, such as contracts. In others, we devote more than one chapter for a major category, such as labor relations (Chapters 13, 14, and 15). There is a single chapter on the role of administrative agencies in our government (Chapter 6), but it is hard to think of another chapter that does not have to do with administrative agencies of one kind or another.

FIGURE 1-1 Some Branches of Law

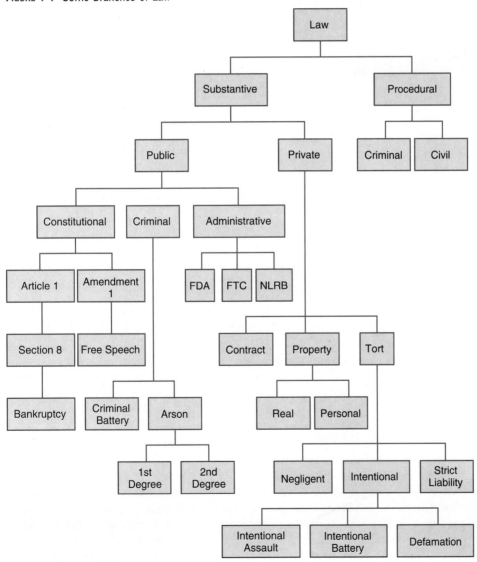

- Define the *adversary concept of justice* and explain the ways in which ours is an *adversary legal system.*
- Describe the key differences between *procedural* and *substantive law,* including the difference between *criminal* and *civil procedure.*
- Describe the difference between *public* and *private law.*

■ THE SOURCES OF LAW

How can we discover the *content* of different substantive and procedural laws? How can we find out, for instance, the rules for forming a corporation in Colorado or the definition of arson in Alabama? The American legal system is a network of legislation, executive actions, and court decisions ruled by our 200-year-old Constitution—the supreme law of the land. Thus, we have three basic *forms* of law: constitutional, statutory, and judicial. We also have three *levels* of government promulgating laws: federal, state, and local; and three *branches* of government at each level: executive, legislative, and judicial.

The Constitution

The federal Constitution outlines the basic structure of the federal government and sets forth principles governing the relationships between citizens and their government which apply at the federal, state, and local levels. (*See* Chapter 3 *for discussion of the Constitution, the constitutional powers of government, and the rights of citizens.*) State constitutions function similarly, setting forth basic principles of governance for their respective states. A state constitution reigns supreme over all other laws promulgated by the state or any of its local governments but not over federal laws. The highest courts at the federal and state levels are the ultimate arbiters of their respective constitutions.

Legislation

statutes Laws established by lawmaking bodies like Congress or state legislatures

ordinances Laws enacted by lawmaking bodies at the local level

Laws promulgated by Congress or the state legislatures are generally called **statutes;** laws promulgated at the local level (by a city council, for example) are called **ordinances.** A broad range of federal and state statutes and local ordinances governs nearly every aspect of American life—from the amount of money we pay in taxes to the punishments we prescribe for jaywalking.

Some of these laws establish *administrative agencies* within the executive branch that are empowered to issue regulations that have the force of law in specified areas. (*See* Chapter 6.) For example, the Securities and Exchange Commission is an agency established by the Securities Exchange Act of 1934 and empowered to regulate the securities industry. By establishing administrative agencies like the SEC, both Congress and state legislatures effectively delegate some of their lawmaking powers.

Case Law

case law Law developed through individual court case rulings and decisions

Courts make law on an *ad hoc* basis when they decide cases that are brought before them. Court decisions, at the federal and state levels, make our **case law**—that is, law which, unlike statutes, is developed through decisions made in court cases. Courts make case law by interpreting constitutions, statutes, and ordinances as well as principles of common law that the courts themselves have developed over the years. (*See* Chapter 4 *for a discussion of the court system.*)

Executive Order

A fourth, less common form of law is the **executive order**: an order issued by the president pursuant to a specific statute or his inherent constitutional powers. The president may also enter into *treaties* with foreign nations, but only with the consent of the Senate. The treaty-making power is, therefore, split between the executive and legislative branches. Executive orders may also be issued by the executive of a city or state, that is, the mayor or governor.

executive order Order issued by the president in accordance with a specific *statute* or the executive's constitutional powers

■ FINDING THE LAW

Statutes

Laws enacted by Congress and each of the state legislatures are compiled into federal and state **codes.** Codes are then organized by subject—for instance, public health, domestic relations, taxation, labor law, and criminal law. Each subject then becomes a numbered **title.** Thus, federal and state codes consist of series of books including laws on the many subjects addressed by legislation.

codes Sets of *statutes* enacted by federal or state legislatures and assembled and organized by subject

title Major category of a code or statute

Subject groupings vary in specificity. The United States Code, for example, is broken down into fifty subjects and titles. The Maryland State code includes over 100 subjects, the California code only twenty-eight.[10] Indexes to the codes (which usually make up several books by themselves) will tell you under which subject and title you may find laws governing specific topics. For example, laws governing mortgage transactions would be included under the title *Real Property.* Because new laws are enacted every year and existing ones amended or repealed, code books are updated annually, with **pocket parts** (pamphlets slipped into pockets in the back of each volume) or separately bound supplements. Once you locate a statute, you should check the pocket part or supplement to find out whether it has been amended or repealed.

pocket parts Pamphlets inserted into the backs of law books updating them on developments in the law

Titles within each code are also subdivided by section and subsection. To cite a particular statute, you state the title, the name of the code, and then the section: For example, the citation *18 U.S.C. 320* refers to *Title 18 of the United States Code, section 320.* Codes are usually published in annotated versions that include brief legislative histories and summaries of specific cases interpreting each statute.

Finally, when they are enacted, statutes are published in pamphlet form as *slip laws.* These are the first official statutory publications. Slip laws of Congress and each of the state legislatures are collected in volumes of *session laws;* federal session laws are called *Statutes at Large.* In the states, session laws are named variously: In New York, for example, they are called the Laws of New York; in Massachusetts, the Acts and Resolves of Massachusetts.

Administrative Regulations and Executive Orders

Regulations issued by the federal administrative agencies are collected in the **Code of Federal Regulations (CFR).** Like the statutory-code collections, the CFR is arranged by subject and numbered title, with titles broken down into sections and subsections. The CFR includes fifty titles, which are updated an-

Code of Federal Regulations (CFR) Collection of regulations issued by the federal administrative agencies, organized by subject and title, and updated annually

---

[10] Morris L. Cohen and Robert C. Berring, *How to Find the Law,* 8th ed. (St. Paul, MN: West, 1983), p. 171.

REFUSING TO GIVE THE LADY A SEAT.

Executive Action and Reaction When President Woodrow Wilson returned from Europe from the peace conference that ended World War I in 1919, he brought with him a treaty that included a "covenant" calling for the establishment of a League of Nations. However, although the U.S. president himself had labored hard to hammer out the treaty, he returned home to renewed isolationist sentiment, and as this contemporary cartoon suggests, public opinion was sharply divided in what was to become the most notable instance of an American president's efforts to initiate law through *executive action*. Opposition in the Senate—which had to ratify the treaty—included William E. Borah of Idaho, Hiram W. Johnson of California, and, especially, Henry Cabot Lodge of Massachusetts, here depicted by a treaty proponent as refusing to give "Lady Peace" a seat on the railroad car of state. Opponents' strategy included modifying the treaty so heavily that even Wilson objected to the watered-down version, and despite public pressure on the Senate to reconsider its opposition, the treaty was finally defeated in 1920—ironically, by a combination of "irreconcilable" Republicans and Democrats loyal to the president. Wilson's successor, Warren G. Harding, eventually signed a separate treaty with Germany, and although the League of Nations subsisted from 1919 until (officially) 1946, the United States never joined.

nually. Agency names and subjects are indexed in a separate CFR volume, *Index and Finding Aids*. You cite a federal regulation in the same way that you cite a statute: title, source, and section: *2 C.F.R. 9* refers to *Title 2 of the Code of Federal Regulations, section 9.*

Administrative regulations, proposed regulations, and executive orders are announced daily, Monday through Friday, in the ***Federal Register,*** an official publication chronicling the activities of the federal government. Both the *Federal Register* and the CFR date back to the 1930s and were mandated, respectively, by the Federal Register Act (FRA) of 1935 and amended in 1937. Until passage of the FRA, the growing number of federal regulations and executive orders were not effectively organized or readily accessible.

Federal Register Official, daily publication of the federal government announcing federal *regulations* and *executive orders*

State administrative regulations are organized in varying degrees from state to state. In about a third of the states, publication of regulations is discretionary and often determined by the agencies themselves. The remaining states, however, publish updated volumes of regulations, and about twenty states publish monthly or weekly newspapers chronicling administrative actions.

Case Law

Court decisions (both case law or common law) are compiled in books known as **reporters.** There are federal and state reporters for the federal and state courts and separate reporters for each federal and state court system. For example, decisions of the United States Supreme Court are published in three different reporters: the United States Reports, the Supreme Court Reporter, and the Lawyer's Edition. United States appeals-courts decisions are published in the Federal Reporter, district court decisions in the Federal Supplement. At the state level, decisions of supreme, intermediate-appellate, and some trial courts are also published in separate reporters. In addition, regional reporters collect the state court decisions for various regions, like the Northeast, South, and Northwest. Like code systems, each reporter system contains many separate, numbered volumes. Cases are cited by case name, volume number, source (name of reporter), and page number: The citation *335 F. Supp. 421* refers to *volume 335 of the Federal Supplement, page 421.*

reporters Books compiled from *case law* or *common-law court decisions*

Reporters publish the complete majority opinion in each case, as well as any concurrences and dissents (see the next section). In many reporters, the text of the opinion is preceded by headnotes—brief paragraphs organized by subject that highlight key points of the case. In the *West reporting system,* which is comprehensive and commonly used, each subject has a key number, with key numbers and subjects used to index the massive number of cases.

Other essential research tools are the *Shepard citator tables,* which list (by volume, reporter system, and page number) all the cases in which another given case has been cited. These citations can give you the precedential value of a case, telling you how many times it has been followed and whether it has been overruled. Tracing the history of a case in this way is called "shepardizing."

■ *Concept Check 1-4   The Sources of Law & Finding the Law*

- What are the three basic *forms* of American law? Given an example of each.
- Describe the subject organization of U.S. *codes.* What is a *title?*
- Describe the *Code of Federal Regulations* and the *Federal Register.*

■ READING AND BRIEFING A CASE

To learn how the law evolves and how, in a practical way, legal principles are applied to various sets of facts, you need to learn how to read cases. A non-lawyer encountering a case for the first time may find it rather daunting, but judicial decisions are not nearly as difficult as they look.

Consider the case of *Rosenblum v. Adler,* which involves the issue of liability when an accounting firm performs an audit negligently (*see* Chapter 10, pp. 367–368, *for major portions of the opinion*). *Rosenblum v. Adler* is used here to demonstrate case format and to explain how to read and *brief* a case.

Figure 1-2 is a brief excerpt from *Rosenblum* as it would appear in a reporter. The case as shown is a second appeal, heard by the New Jersey Supreme Court, the highest court in the state. There is a lower appeals court in New Jersey, the Superior Court, and below that are the trial courts, the county

FIGURE 1-2 Sample Excerpt: The Parts of a Case

Case Name	ROSENBLUM v. ADLER
Court rendering the opinion	New Jersey Supreme Court
Citation ("cite") to volume 93 of the New Jersey Reports and to volume 461 of the Atlantic (regional) reporter, second series, the case was decided in 1983. J[ustice] Schreiber wrote the opinion.	93 N.J. 324, 461 A.2d 138 (1983)

Schreiber, J.

This case focuses upon the issue of whether accountants should be responsible for their negligence in auditing financial statements. If so, we must decide whether a duty is owed to those with whom the auditor is in privity, to third persons known and intended by the auditor to be the recipients of the audit, and to those who foreseeably might rely on the audit. Subsumed within these questions is a more fundamental one: to what extent does public policy justify imposition of a duty to any of these classes?

Opinion: stating the issue raised, describing the parties and facts, discussing the relevant law, and rendering judgment.

. . . The plaintiffs Harry and Barry Rosenblum brought this action against Touche Ross & Co. (Touche), a partnership, and the individual partners. Touche, a prominent accounting firm, had audited the financial statements of Giant Stores Corporation (Giant). . . .

. . . .

The judgment granting defendants' motion for partial summary judgment with respect to the 1971 financial statements is reversed and that denying defendants' motion for partial summary judgment with respect to the 1972 financial statements is affirmed. The cause [sic] is remanded to the trial court for further proceedings consistent with this opinion.

For reversal and remandment—Chief Justice Wilentz and Justices Clifford, Schreiber, Handler, Pollock, O'Hern and Garibaldi—7.

For affirmance—None.

Votes of the court. This case was heard by all 7 justices of the court, and all joined in the decision to reverse the lower courts' decision and remand the case, or send it back to the lower court with instructions on what to do.

courts. This appeal was heard by all seven justices of the New Jersey Supreme Court, and Justice Schreiber, whose name appears at the beginning of the opinion, wrote the decision. All six other justices joined in the opinion, which was to reverse the findings of the two lower courts and send the case back—that is, *remand* it—to the trial court for rehearing. If any justice had disagreed with the reasoning of the opinion—that is, its *reasoning*, not its *conclusions*—he or she could have written a **concurring opinion;** any justice who disagreed with the result could have written a **dissenting opinion.**

Once the citations and abbreviations have been deciphered, the text of the opinion is readily accessible. A good opinion is written in clear, jargon-free prose and is organized quite logically. It states the issue or issues raised by the case, identifies the parties, and recites the facts, describing both the incident or transactions that precipitated the dispute and the record of its progress through the lower courts. It then discusses the law of the case, which may involve constitutional principles, statutes, ordinances, and/or case law (the relevant legal principles established in earlier cases). The law is interpreted, or reinterpreted, in light of the facts in the case, and the opinion concludes with the judgment of the court.

In this course or in other courses in which you read cases, you may be asked to prepare an abstract or **case brief.** Whether or not you are given such assignments, the preparation of a case brief is the best way to understand a case. To *brief* a case, you employ a logic similar to that of the writer of the case. The purpose of a brief is to highlight important facts and cull out the principles of law at the heart of the case. Give the title and citation ("cite") for the case and then summarize the facts and lower-court proceedings; state the issue or issues involved and the judgment of the court, including its rationale. Figure 1-3 is a sample abstract of *Rosenblum v. Adler*.

concurring opinion *Opinion* written by a judge agreeing with the majority's conclusion but not its reasoning (see Chapter 5)

dissent (or **dissenting opinion**) *Opinion* offered by a judge disagreeing with the majority panel of judges' conclusion (see Chapter 5)

case brief Written abstract of a case highlighting important facts and pivotal legal principles of the case

FIGURE 1-3 Sample Case Brief

ROSENBLUM v. ADLER
New Jersey Supreme Court
93 N. J. 324, 461 A.2d 138 (1983)

Facts: The plaintiffs agreed to sell their businesses to Giant Stores Corp. in June 1972 in exchange for shares of Giant stock. Before the merger, Touche Ross & Co. had audited Giant and had issued opinions in 1971 and 1972 certifying that the company's financial statements fairly represented its financial position. In fact, however, Giant had manipulated its books by falsely recording assets and omitting accounts payable. Giant's fraud was discovered in 1973 and the company soon filed for bankruptcy, making the plaintiffs' stock worthless. The plaintiffs contended they had relied on Touche's opinions that Giant was financially sound, and sued Touche and its individual partners for fraudulent misrepresentation, gross negligence, negligence, and breach of warranty.

In courts below: the trial court dismissed the claims that were based on the 1971 audit. The court ruled there could be no liability because in 1971 Touche was not aware of the plaintiffs or the proposed merger. The court upheld the claims based on the 1972 audit. The appellate division affirmed the trial court's rulings.

Issue: Can an accountant be liable to a third party for negligence in auditing financial statements when the accountant has no direct relationship with the third party?

Resolution: Yes. The state supreme court held that an accountant's duty to provide accurate representations extends to all parties who can reasonably be foreseen to rely on the representations for business purposes. Previously, most courts had held that accountants could be liable only to parties with whom they were in privity, i.e., in a direct relationship. The court rejected this reasoning, observing that under tort law a claim involving a defective product does not require privity between the manufacturer and the customer; the duty to provide a suitable product extends to all foreseeable users. Here, it was foreseeable that Touche's opinions would be used for many business purposes and relied on by anyone with whom Giant did business. The fact that Touche was not specifically aware of the plaintiffs when it conducted the 1971 audit did not relieve it of liability. Therefore, the plaintiffs had a valid cause of action based on both the 1971 and 1972 audits.

FIGURE 1-3 (continued)

■ **Concept Check 1-5   Reading and Briefing a Case**

- What is the primary purpose of *briefing* a case?
- Define a *concurring opinion* and a *dissent.*

SUMMARY

- The law serves a variety of functions. It maintains a system of social control while facilitating social life. It protects the public order by punishing those who deviate from accepted norms. It also exists as a way to resolve disputes that arise between individual members of society. On a societal level, the law protects the status quo while allowing for change to take place in an orderly manner. *Jurisprudence* is the study of the nature, purpose, and functioning of law and its institutions.

- There are three major philosophical perspectives on what constitutes law. The *natural-law* school, which originated in ancient Greece, stresses the moral and absolute basis of law: Only those laws that conform to natural law—that is, to absolute moral values—are viewed as valid. Laws that conflict with higher ethics are not laws at all. As opposed to natural laws, *conventional laws* reflect the values a particular society has accepted at a particular time.

- *Positivists* believe that a law is valid if it was properly issued: A law is a command issued by a person who has the power to enforce it. Positivism, therefore, is not concerned with the content of a law but rather with its form—that is, a law is true and legitimate if it can be enforced. Unlike adherents to natural laws, positivists are unconcerned with the moral or ethical validity or acceptability of a law.

- *Sociological jurisprudence,* dissatisfied with the natural-law and positivist schools' lack of attention to social circumstances that help create and affect laws, argues that the law and its interpretations must take into account the findings of sociology. The school of *legal realism,* much like sociological jurisprudence, asks that law recognize the impact of social realities on the formation of laws. Legal realism looks to the participants in the legal system—judges, lawyers, and juries—as determinants of the law. Its proponents believe that law is the product of human beings who are themselves the products of and influenced by social and economic circumstances. Law, this school argues, is separate from absolute moral principles. Although courts and judges apply the same universally accepted values to cases, the conclusions of judges and juries vary. They are influenced by their own values and beliefs.

- Most of the world's legal systems are based on one of the two great historical traditions of Western law. The first is the *civil-law* tradition, which is based on legal *codes* or *statutes* that define a society's basic laws on various subjects. The second tradition is *common law,* whose cornerstone is *case law* or the accumulation of judicial decisions, as opposed to a comprehensive code. Common law is also known as *judge-made law*. Civil law is more adaptable—that is, easier to transfer from place to place—than common law. In addition, *religion* includes various laws which have had and continue to have varying degrees of influence upon the legal systems of certain countries.

- Our legal system, which is based on common law and employs an *adversary system* of dispute resolution, can be divided into two branches: *procedural* and *substantive law*. Procedural law creates the guidelines by which our legal system operates and spells out the mechanisms for resolving disputes, as well as the steps that must be followed to enforce a certain law or bring a lawsuit. Procedural law can be divided into *criminal procedures* and *civil procedures*. Substantive law embodies the actual rights, obligations, and limitations upon human action that a society has embraced. Substantive law is found in the Constitution, statutes, and cases; procedural law is generally found in statutes, regulations, and court rules.

- Law can also be broken down into *public* and *private law*. Public law addresses issues and incidents that are of interest to society as a whole. One important branch of public is *administrative law*, which defines the structure and functioning of government agencies such as the National Labor Relations Board. Private law is concerned only with disputes that arise between private parties.

- In the U.S., there are three basic forms of law: constitutional, statutory, and judicial. Moreover, there are three levels of government with three branches each, and all the levels promulgate laws. Thus, our society has many sources of laws: the federal and state constitutions, legislative enactments, judicial decisions, and executive orders. *Statutes* are laws promulgated by Congress or state legislatures. *Ordinances* are laws promulgated at the local level. *Case law,* unlike statutes, is comprised of court decisions, both at the federal and state levels. A less common form of law is the *executive order,* an order pursuant to a President's constitutional powers or to a particular statute.

- Laws are grouped systematically. Statutes are organized by subject and title into *codes*. The *Code of Federal Regulations* is a collection of regulations issued by federal administrative agencies. The *Federal Register* is a daily, federal publication that announces the proposed and adopted regulations and orders of the federal government. Books termed *reporters* are compilations of court decisions.

QUESTIONS AND PROBLEMS

1. Three seamen and a young boy drifted for twenty days in a small boat in the ocean 1,000 miles from the African coast when the yacht they were in was wrecked in a storm. There was no fresh water, there had been no food for the past eight days, and there was no sign of rescue. One of the men, with another's consent, told the boy that he was going to be killed and eaten. The man then cut the boy's throat; the three men ate the boy and survived four more days until they were rescued. The two men who agreed to sacrifice the boy were later tried for murder and raised the defense of necessity. Note the similarity of this actual case to Lon Fuller's *Case of the Speluncean Explorers* in this chapter. Should the deliberate killing of a person be murder if the killing is necessary in order for others to survive? If so, should the sentence be the same, lighter, or heavier than for other murders? Why? [*Regina v. Dudley*

& Stephens, Queens Bench L.R., Q.B. 61 (1884)].

2. The state of Pennsylvania passed a law prohibiting the unauthorized tampering of computer software and hardware. The law includes unauthorized retrievals of information, using information for one's own, unauthorized use or changing data. Such tampering is classified as a third degree felony. Describe this law in regards to the following: civil/criminal law; public/private law; legislative/case law.

3. A laundromat hired an employee who had a past history of mental illness. One evening, the employee and a customer got into an argument over money. The employee subsequently stabbed the customer to death. At trial, the laundromat claimed it was not responsible for the customer's death because it had no way of knowing of its

employee's mental illness. Should businesses be sued for an employee's unauthorized actions, like in this instance, stabbing a customer to death? In this case, an actuary estimated that the customer, a laborer, would have earned over his lifetime, $800,000. Is it ethical to put a "price tag" on how much a person would have earned if he had lived and use this for a calculation of damages?

4. Is a law valid simply because it is a law?

5. A thief attempts to enter a home at 3:00 A.M. and the window he raises falls out and injures him. Should the thief be able to sue the homeowner for the injuries received? Explain.

6. In April of 1989, on the way to file a case at a crowded courthouse in Pasadena, a lawyer was humiliated when his shoes set off a metal detector. The attorney was forced to pull off his favorite pair of steel-shanked penny loafers and walk over a filthy floor. The 9th Circuit Court of Appeals has a budget of $37.9 million for the 6,725 appeals filed for this year. That means each filing, including this one, costs $5638. Should backlogged and budget-tight court systems allow such appeals to be heard?

7. What if baseball fans want to attend night games but the ball park owner refuses to install stadium lights? Should the law be used to address such issues? Why or why not?

8. Many states have laws governing what types of sexual acts can and cannot be performed in private between consenting adults. Should such laws exist? What purpose do they serve? Where does morality end and law begin in such situations? Does it make a difference if people are rarely prosecuted for breaking the law, or that the law is virtually impossible to enforce? Why or why not?

9. In the 1960s the speed limit on most highways was 70 miles per hour. During the oil crisis of the 1970s the speed limit was lowered to 55. In 1987 the speed limit on some stretches of highway was moved up to 65 again. What purpose do speed limits serve? Do they serve the same purpose on a seldom traveled stretch of highway as they do on a busy interstate? What does it do for citizens to be told that it saves lives and energy to have a speed limit of 55 rather than 65, and then have the speed limit raised to 65 again? Should the law be enforced if it is 3:00 A.M. and there is no other traffic?

10. If you are a police officer and your partner routinely has sex with females who wish to avoid traffic charges on their driving records, would you report your partner's actions? If you fail to report these actions, should you be held in violation of law? Explain your answer.

ETHICS AND SOCIAL RESPONSIBILITY

Why do we accept the rule of law? Could it be that legal rules are also *ethical* rules? **Ethics** is the study of good and bad conduct—that is, of morality. Many laws—such as those that forbid murder, rape, and theft—suggest that rules of law have moral content. Yet not all legal rules have this character. Some laws were passed to forbid acts that we regard as bad in themselves, such as murder. Other laws were passed mainly to provide *rules,* whatever they might be. For example, it is legal to cross a street when the light is green and illegal to cross when the light is red. But would it be immoral if we decided to make it legal to cross on the red and illegal to cross on the green? Of course not. It makes no difference whether we cross on the green or the red, so long as we all understand the rule and obey it. In contrast, legalizing murder would surely be seen as immoral. Thus, the concepts of law and morality, though distinct, are somehow related.

Figure 2-1 shows two overlapping circles. The circle on the right symbolizes all actions required by morality. The circle on the left symbolizes all actions

ethics The study of standards of conduct and morality

FIGURE 2-1 The Intersection of Law and Morality

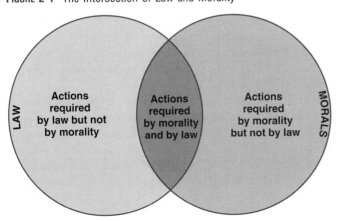

required by law. The overlapping parts of the two circles symbolize actions required *both* by morality and by law; the remaining parts of the circles symbolize actions that are required *either* by morality or by law, but not by both.

■ THE CONCEPT OF VALUES

We can all say more or less what we mean by *values;* in fact, most of us can say what we mean by values in several different ways. For example, we could say something about values by filling in the blanks in any or all of the sentences in the following list:

1. I *value* _____ .
2. I *value* _____ over _____ .
3. _____ is a traditional *value.*
4. The *value* of _____ cannot be measured in dollars and cents.
5. We ought to *value* _____ .
6. Because Mr. Smith did _____ , he apparently *values* _____ .

The idea of *value,* of course, is central to all six sentences. However, as the blanks indicate, the idea of *value* is not by itself completely meaningful in any of them. Sentence 2, for example, suggests *relative values.* Sentence 5 could be interpreted as a statement of *moral values.* Sentence 6 is the most complicated of all: It suggests that *value* can be inferred from someone's real-life *behavior.*

In order to show how such issues can arise when we apply questions of value and ethics to business principles and practices, we will look first at the relationship between the idea of *value* on the one hand and the ideas of *morality* and *norms* on the other.

Values and Morality

Very often, the connection is made between morality and law by our word choice. Consider the famous Preamble to the Constitution of the United States:

> We the people of the United States, in Order to form a more perfect Union, establish *Justice,* insure domestic Tranquility, provide for the common defence, promote the *general Welfare,* and secure the Blessings of *Liberty* to ourselves and our Posterity, do ordain and establish this Constitution for the United States of America [emphasis added].

The italicized words have a *moral* content: It would not be moral to undermine justice, liberty, or the general welfare. But why? The answer is that justice, the general welfare, and liberty are things that we desire *in themselves.* We do not want them only for the sake of having rules or as means to other things. In other words, we *value* justice, the general welfare, and liberty.

"Justice" has other meanings as well. One such meaning lies within our system of criminal justice. One of the most important living moral philosophers, John Rawls, has compared this moral sense of justice to "fairness." Rawls asks us to imagine that we had the power to organize society without knowing anything about its social class, intelligence, or strength. Rawls calls this scenario the "original position." In this frame of mind, we would probably organize society in ways that benefited everyone, not just a lucky few. In so doing, we would adopt two basic principles:

John Rawls

First: Each person is to have an equal right to the most extensive basic liberty compatible with a similar liberty for others. Second: Social and economic inequalities are to be arranged so that they are both (a) reasonably expected to be to everyone's advantage, and (b) attached to positions and offices open to all.[1]

Rawls assumes that we would want *liberty* to mean an ethical notion of *freedom of choice* that implies an *obligation* to respect the *rights* of others. Although each of us would want to be as wealthy as possible, we would not know how much we had of those qualities that help human beings become rich. Therefore, only those inequalities that made *everyone* wealthier by increasing the overall wealth of society would be accepted. For instance, a rule that permitted people of great ability to earn more might encourage people to work harder and produce more. If production was higher, there would be more wealth to distribute. Consequently, we might all be better off.

We would also want positions of power and wealth to be open to anyone with the necessary talent; otherwise, many talented people would have no reason to use their talents fully, and society would not reap the full benefit of their abilities. To put the argument in another way, it would be unfair to grant individuals any advantage that did not benefit *society as a whole*.

We can easily imagine a society that failed to provide for justice, the general welfare, and liberty. But we cannot imagine wanting to live in such a society. Who would choose to live in a country where the government enforces racial segregation, or in one that practices religious terrorism against its own citizens? In contrast, we can easily imagine living in a society with a different speed limit on the roads.

As we have discussed them above—that is, on a basically *conceptual* level—the ideas of *value* and *morality* are quite closely related: Because of certain shared *values*, a certain society's set of *legal principles* can provide a fairly good window onto its sense of *morality*. On this level, we can define **values** as relatively stable personal or social principles, standards, or goals that are desirable in themselves.

values Comparatively stable, intrinsically worthwhile personal or social beliefs and standards

Before we go on to a discussion of business and social responsibility, we should also point out that problems like those suggested above are further

---

[1] John Rawls, "Justice as Fairness," reprinted in W. M. Hoffman and J. Mills Moore, *Business Ethics* (New York: McGraw-Hill, 1984), p. 25.

CHAPTER 2 • ETHICS AND SOCIAL RESPONSIBILITY

35

complicated by at least two other factors. First, the so-called *Protestant Work Ethic* that has traditionally influenced both business-related and social values in the United States has been changing over the past two decades. Think, for example, of a television advertisement that promotes personal self-fulfillment over the traditional workday grind: Which of these two values is likely to be emphasized in the factory that makes the product being advertised?

Second, ethics reflect values and cannot be legislated. Our *adversarial* legal system (*see* Chapter 4) is comprised of ever-changing legislation and regulations and develops on an *ad hoc* basis through *case law* (*see* Chapter 1). It thus responds to changes in our social values and norms, and one of the reasons why it is so hard to reach consensus on public policy in the United States is that we have traditionally preferred flexible—and even relative—values to fixed, "universal" values. That preference is reflected in the development of our legal system itself.

■ Concept Check 2-1   The Concept of Values

- Describe the interrelationship between *law* and *morality*, giving an example of an action required by morality but not by law.
- Discuss the relationship between *accountability* and *social responsibility*.

■ THE SOCIAL RESPONSIBILITY OF BUSINESS

People in business cannot ignore their own personal interests. Does it follow that they have no moral responsibility? If they do have such a responsibility, what is it?

In traditional societies, before 1750 or so, the answers appeared to be self-evident. A business was thought to have duties to itself, to all other businesses in its own line of trade, and to society at large. Every aspect of business—prices, methods, materials, workers, and workmanship—was regulated in great detail. These attitudes and practices, according to one social historian, "reflected the values of the medieval village or town community, which saw wealth as more or less fixed and assumed that the only way one got rich was at the expense of one's neighbor."[2]

Customers, however, were not free to buy what they wanted to buy, and producers were not free to make what they wanted to make. Trade guilds, governments, and religious authorities assumed that they knew what was good for everyone else, and everyone else, by and large, accepted this assumption.

Let's look, however, at a contemporary example. What if the owner of a successful chain of locally owned restaurants gave money to an area college? We could assume that although the gesture might well be in the best interest of the individual's business, it would also be in his or her own best interest—the interests of the business and its sole proprietor are essentially indistinguishable. But what if the managers of a national corporation headquartered in the community donated money to the same college? In whose best interest was this money invested—that of the company's stockholders or that of the managers themselves? Was the donation part of a community-relations program in

---

[2] David Landes, *The Unbound Prometheus* (London: Cambridge University Press, 1969), p. 19.

the long-term best interests of the company or did the managers want to upgrade their favorite on-campus tennis courts?

Questions like these arise with the emergence of the modern corporation, in which a company's ownership is distinct from its **management**—that is, from the individuals responsible for planning, organizing, and controlling its activities. (THE ETHICAL ENVIRONMENT box in this chapter takes up some issues in managerial behavior in the corporate context.) This section will discuss several models of *corporate social responsibility*. The corporation itself will be discussed in Chapter 7, but this section will locate the corporation within its *stake-*

management Body of individuals that plans, organizes, and controls a company's activities

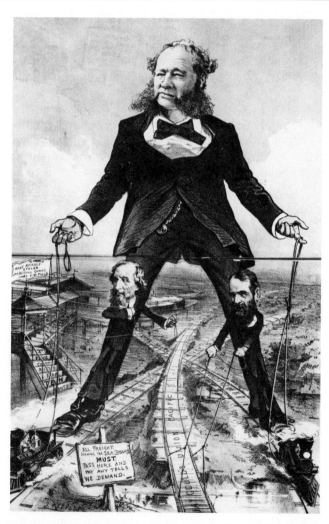

Workin' the Railroad A contemporary cartoon depicts financial speculator Jay Gould (1836–92) at the autocratic reins of the Union Pacific Railroad—one of four Western railroads over which Gould manipulated control (as well as stock values and commercial access) in the 1870s. As director (along with fellow speculators James Fisk and Daniel Drew) of the Erie Railroad in 1867, Gould "watered" the company's stock by issuing huge amounts of new securities unjustified by any increase in the company's profitability. Unsuspecting buyers—including railroad tycoon Cornelius Vanderbilt—tried in vain to buy into the company by picking up the overvalued stock until Vanderbilt (supposedly an "ally" of Gould) put two and two together and went to court. The bitter legal wrangling finally ended when Gould bribed the New York state legislature into legalizing his scheme.

holder environment and will describe three levels of *corporate social responsibility* that can affect that environment.

The Corporate Stakeholder Environment

stakeholder environment The greater community of individuals influencing or influenced by a company's activities

The **stakeholder environment** is the larger community of individuals affecting or affected by a company's activities. As Figure 2-2 shows that environment is both *external* and *internal*. Externally, for example, customers exchange money for a company's products or services; suppliers exchange labor, raw materials, and equipment for the company's financial resources; governments, both domestic and foreign, regulate a company's activities within various jurisdictions. Internally, its stockholders and employees are part of the company's stakeholder environment in the sense that management is responsible to them.

Not surprisingly, a company's stakeholder environment can be extremely complex. For one thing, the external environment can be thought of as both *direct-action* and *indirect-action*.[3] Whereas stockholders, for example, can directly influence company activities, those elements that influence the *climate in which those activities take place* are part of the company's indirect environment. Government, for example, is part of the indirect-action external environment, and, as Figure 2-3 illustrates, this environment can be a vast web of jurisdictions (local, state, federal, foreign, international) and legal actions (legislation, regulation, and, even more indirectly, special-interest pressure).

---

[3] *See* Alvar O. Elbing, "On the Applicability of Environmental Models," in Joseph W. McGuire, ed., *Contemporary Management: Issues and Viewpoints* (Englewood Cliffs, NJ: Prentice Hall, 1974), pp. 283–89.

THE ETHICAL ENVIRONMENT
The Accountable Manager

There was a time, not too long ago, when white-collar crime was more or less winked at. Perhaps many people agreed with Milton Friedman's contention that the only social responsibility of business was the maximization of profits. That is no longer the case. After federal regulation eased in the mid-1980s, many states assumed the responsibility of the duty of overseeing business activities within their own jurisdictions. And these states are tough. The price of plea bargaining, for example, has soared, and such deals are more difficult to negotiate.

The B.C.C.I./First American scandal, the Salomon Brothers/Treasury scandal, and the Drexel Burnham Lambert fiasco all have one thing in common: Corporate management has had to shoulder some of the responsibility both for errors of judgment and ethical missteps made by their firms. On some occasions, management has been able to show that it simply did not know what was going on. At other times, however, managers who committed crimes went to prison.

Managers who want to survive in this kind of environment must assess their own situations. They must be able to defend the decisions that they make on behalf of their companies from both legal and ethical standpoints. Some analysts of contemporary management practices have suggested that it might be appropriate for managers to take an "ethical litmus test" before deciding whether to proceed with a particular deal or project. The key points of such a test might be whether a reasonable employee, shareholder, or competitor—someone in the company's stakeholder environment—would (1) view the activity as moral and ethical and (2) believe the defense of a managerial decision in a court of law.

Many big corporations have already taken the initiative by issuing policy statements or codes of ethics in order to minimize liability and control the effects of various managerial decisions on stakeholder relations (see Figure 2-6, p. 49.). However, few corporations have an ongoing program of ethical oversight. This situation, however, may very well change in the future. It has been suggested, for example, that Congress take over the task of overseeing business ethics through legislation. Some suggestions include an executive-responsibility statute and a federal reporting law concerning health and safety in the workplace. The latter might include a provision to protect whistleblowers—that is, individuals who bring unethical or unlawful acts to the attention of lawmakers, the media, or the public. Other recommendations involve mandatory publication of corporate litigation records. Still other proposals call for stiffer penalties for white-collar criminals.

Although it is still being drawn, the bottom line appears to be this: Corporations must weigh profit margins against the possibility of a criminal prosecution. Each individual manager must make the same assessment.

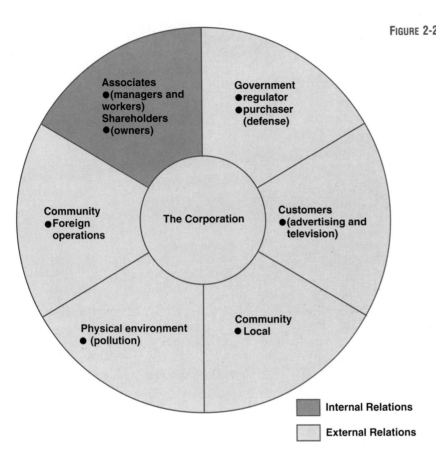

FIGURE 2-2 The Corporate Stakeholder Environment

Source: Adapted from Gerald F. Cavanaugh and Arthur F. McGovern, Ethical Dilemmas in the Modern Corporation (Englewood Cliffs, NJ: Prentice Hall, 1988).

Associates
● (managers and workers)
Shareholders
● (owners)

Government
● regulator
● purchaser (defense)

Community
● Foreign operations

The Corporation

Customers
● (advertising and television)

Physical environment
● (pollution)

Community
● Local

Internal Relations

External Relations

Models of Corporate Social Responsibility

We will describe three models of corporate social responsibility before concluding with a brief discussion of specifically *legal perspectives* on the issues raised by these theories. However, we should note first that some students of management and ethical theory would make a distinction between theories of corporate *social responsibility* (general doctrines describing the broad relationships of business to society) and theories of corporate *social responsiveness*—that is, less "philosophical," more pragmatic approaches to the requirements of corporate activity. In this sense, the approaches of Milton Friedman and E. M. Dodd might be considered theories of social responsibility, that of Archie Carroll a theory of corporate social responsiveness.[4]

MILTON FRIEDMAN AND "ETHICAL CUSTOM." Milton Friedman, an influential economist, assumes that a company's stockholders want "to make as much money as possible while conforming to the basic rules of society, both those embodied in law and those embodied in ethical custom."[5] Although Friedman

---

[4] *See* R. Edward Freeman and Daniel R. Gilbert, Jr., *Corporate Strategy and the Search for Ethics* (Englewood Cliffs, NJ: Prentice Hall, 1988), pp. 88-91.

[5] "The Social Responsibility of Business Is to Increase Its Profits," in W. Michael Hoffman and Jennifer Mills Moore, eds., *Business Ethics: Readings and Cases in Corporate Morality* (New York: McGraw-Hill, 1984), p. 128.

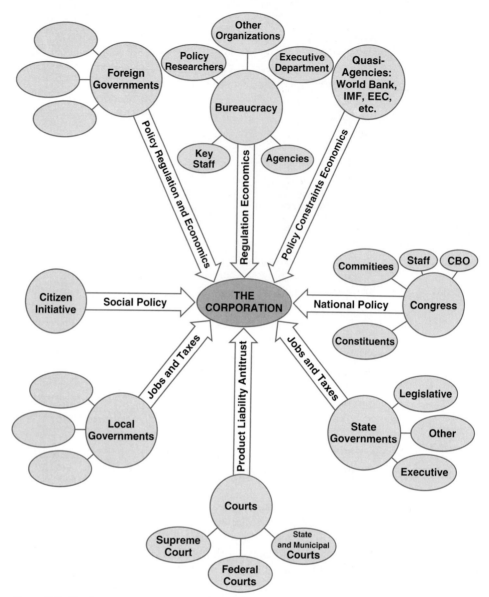

FIGURE 2-3 The Business-Government Environment in the U.S. *Source: R. Edward Freeman,* Strategic Management: A Stakeholder Approach *(Boston: Pitman, 1984). © 1984 by R. Edward Freeman.*

never actually defines "ethical custom," he does give examples of what it does *not* mean: attempts to help the poor by hiring the hard-core unemployed or to improve the environment by spending more money on pollution control than either the law or the corporation's interests require. Managers who use corporate funds for either purpose are spending "someone else's money." In the first case, they are spending the money of more qualified workers, whose scarce skills are made less valuable when unqualified workers are hired. In the second, they are spending the money of the stockholders, whose dividends may be reduced, and the money of customers, who may have to pay more for the company's goods.

Perhaps this country should do more about poverty and pollution, but Friedman contends that it is the government's job to promote these goals—not the managers': As voters, we can force politicians to enact stricter pollution controls. We may have not done so, but we must ultimately be considered the best judges of our own interests. Managers who spend more money on pollution control than they must are "in effect imposing taxes . . . and deciding how the proceeds shall be spent. . . ."

Charitable contributions, however, may be in a company's best interests. For example, a firm having trouble finding certain kinds of workers may have an interest in contributing money to schools that train them. Such expenditures are justified by Friedman's standards.

THE TRUSTEESHIP MODEL. Not all legal and economic thinkers or all people in business accept the free-market model in its pure form. Even Friedman concedes that (1) business does have certain undefined ethical responsibilities and (2) it may be in the narrow self-interest of a company to help others. In fact, it may be that a general sense of social responsibility is in the best interest of business.

Shortly after law professor A. A. Berle argued in the 1930s that managers should run their corporations in trust solely for stockholders, E. Merrick Dodd proposed a quite different model of trusteeship.[6] Dodd put forward his views in 1932, during the Great Depression. In that year, a Republican president, Herbert Hoover, was defeated for reelection by a Democrat, Franklin D. Roosevelt.

The public, it seemed, no longer bought the pure free-market model, and the spirit of the times suggested to Dodd that there had been a "substantial change" in public opinion about the social responsibilities of business that would affect the attitudes of managers.

Dodd proposed a four-fold model of trusteeship. A person to whom another's property has been entrusted for safekeeping is a *trustee*. According to Dodd, the corporation has a responsibility not only to its stockholders, its employees, and its customers, but to the general public. In turn, the stockholders have a right to expect that managers will use the corporation's assets safely, honestly, and wisely, so that stockholders will receive a fair rate of return. The employees, "who put their labor and lives into this concern," also have a right to fair wages and continuity of employment. The customers have a right to good value for their money, and the general public has the right to expect that the company will perform its duties "as a great and good citizen should."

However, "fair" profits, wages, and prices are not self-evident. Friedman, for instance, clearly thinks that the "fair" price is merely the highest price that customers are willing to pay. Although Dodd's argument seems to imply that a "fair" price might be lower, he does not explain how to determine what it is.

THE SOCIAL PERFORMANCE MODEL. Writing in the depths of the Great Depression, Dodd was impressed by a change in public attitudes toward business. Yet another change took place in the 1960s and 1970s, when the Vietnam War led many Americans to question national social values, including the value of private enterprise. Issues like employment discrimination, pollution, and occupational safety suddenly clamored for attention. A new definition of the social responsibilities of business was needed.

Archie B. Carroll has provided an ambitious definition.[7] His three-dimen-

---

[6] E. M. Dodd, "For Whom Are Managers Corporate Trustees?" 45 *Harvard Law Review* 1145 (1932).

[7] Archie B. Carroll, "A Three-Dimensional Conceptual Model of Corporate Performance," 4 *Academy of Management Review* 497 (Oct. 1979).

sional model, shown in Figure 2-4, not only identifies the social responsibilities of private enterprise but also describes the issues that generate them and the possible responses of business.

Friedman distinguishes between all-important economic responsibilities of business and its social responsibilities. Carroll rejected this distinction. He instead argued that the social responsibilities of business include four categories of business performance: (1) *economic*, (2) *legal*, (3) *ethical*, and (4) *discretionary*.

According to Carroll, the economic responsibility of business is "to produce goods and services that society wants and to sell them at a profit." The legal responsibility of business is "to fulfill its economic mission within the framework of legal requirements." It is profitable to sell heroin, for example, but not legal. Ethical responsibilities are "ill defined," Carroll admits, but real: "Society has expectations of business over and above legal requirements." Carroll adds a fourth category, discretionary responsibilities, that Friedman rejects. Society has "no clear-cut message for business" about them, says Carroll, so they are quite voluntary: Although we would not, for example, condemn a business that failed to help the hard-core unemployed, Carroll insists that we do expect business to assume responsibilities over and above those in the first three categories.

Friedman argues that because the social responsibilities reduce profits, the social responsibilities of business are not only distinct but adverse to its economic responsibilities. Carroll, however, suggests that his four categories are neither *mutually exclusive* (that is, wholly separate, like apples and oranges) nor *continuous* (that is, like the range from small apples to large apples).

Figure 2-4 Caroll's Model of Corporate Social Performance   *Source: Adapted from Archie B. Carroll, "A Three-Dimensional Conceptual Model of Social Performance,"* Academy of Management Review 4 *(1979).*

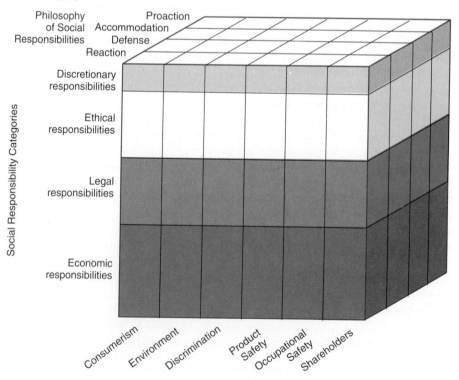

Global Relativism In what was planned as the country's last all-white national referendum, South African voters in March 1992 endorsed by a two-to-one margin the continuation of talks designed to create a new political system guaranteeing full participation by the nation's black majority. By the mid-1980s, such American companies as General Motors, IBM, Exxon, Honeywell, and Mobil had already responded to public pressure to divest their South African operations (Mobil, as it turns out, was disenchanted with the host country's tax codes), and although the South African chapter in the story of international business ethics may finally be drawing to a close, the authors of one book on corporate ethics (R. Edward Freeman and Daniel R. Gilbert, Jr., *Corporate Strategy and the Search for Ethics*) remind us that the case of South Africa still offers a fairly clear study guide to such concepts as *cultural relativism:* "CR," they observe, "tells us to understand 'South African morality' and 'U.S. morality' and 'Japanese morality,' but not to judge among them. . . . The implications of Cultural Relativism for business are vast. . . . Must American managers in Saudi Arabia treat women as the Saudis treat them?"

Carroll's argument is unusual because he believes that each of his four categories is linked to the others. Economic duties are social duties because society depends upon business to satisfy material needs, and it cannot do so unless it is making money; legal, ethical, and discretionary duties are even more obviously social in nature. Moreover, an ethical responsibility (for example, the obligation to make safe goods) can become a legal responsibility if public opinion is aroused. In this case, because many people refuse to buy unsafe goods, it may also even become an economic responsibility. The same action "may simultaneously involve several of these kinds of social responsibilities." As another management theorist has put it, "Social responsibility is a moving target."[8]

The definition of social responsibilities is only the first dimension of Carroll's model. The second dimension involves the issues that give rise to those responsibilities. Those issues vary both from industry to industry and from time to time. For example, there was much less concern about the environment thirty years ago than there is today. The third dimension of Carroll's model thus involves a company's "philosophy of responsiveness." Responsiveness is a *continuum of action:* It ranges from absolute resistance to proposals that a company accept some sort of social responsibility, through attempts to deal with it through public relations, legal maneuvers, or bargaining, through acceptance, and finally to enthusiasm.

Legal Perspectives on Corporate Responsibility

The idea that businesses have obligations beyond mere profits is not mere philosophical speculation: It is in fact reflected in the law. In 1919, the Supreme Court of Michigan considered the question of whether corporations, which exist largely for the benefit of their stockholders, might also act directly to benefit other stakeholders (in this instance, the company's customers). In 1915, Henry Ford, who had founded the Ford Motor Co. in 1903, announced plans to build new facilities that would double the company's output. The plan was in keeping with Ford's primary competitive strategy—namely, to take advantage of "economy of scale" to build as many cars as possible and to sell each unit at the lowest possible price. That strategy may not have been exactly "humanitarian" in nature, but it was, Ford argued, consumer-oriented and in the company's long-term best interests. Because Ford's plan was quite costly, the company decided that extra dividends to stockholders would have to cease in order to pay for it. Two stockholders—John F. and Horace Dodge—sued to demand dividends. The court's decision is given in the following case.

---

[8] Neil Churchill, "Toward a Theory of Social Accounting," 15 *Sloan Management Review* 266 (1974).

DODGE v. FORD MOTOR CO.
Michigan Supreme Court, 170 N.W. 668 (1919)

John and Horace Dodge commenced this action against the Ford Motor Company. The Dodge brothers were shareholders of Ford Motor Company. From the time of its inception in 1903 the business of the company continued to expand. The cars it manufactured met a public demand, and were profitably marketed, so that in addition to regular quarterly dividends equal to 5% monthly on its capital stock, from 1911 to 1915 its board of directors paid special dividends.

Beginning as a mere assembly plant, the Ford Motor

Company's factory came to be a manufacturing plant, where it made many of the car parts that, in the beginning, it had purchased from others. At no time has it been able to meet the demand for its cars.

No special dividends were declared after 1915 and Plaintiffs ask for a decree requiring the distribution to stockholders of at least 75% of the accumulated cash surplus, and that for the future directors be required to distribute all of the earnings of the company except such as may be reasonably required for emergency purposes in the conduct of business.

Appeal from Circuit Court, Wayne County, in Chancery; George S. Hosmer, Judge.

When plaintiffs made their complaint and demand for further dividends, the Ford Motor Company had concluded its most prosperous year of business. The demand for its cars at the price of the preceding year continued. It could make and could market in the year beginning August 1, 1916, more than 500,000 cars. Sales of parts and repairs would necessarily increase. The cost of materials was likely to advance, and perhaps the price of labor; but it reasonably might have expected a profit for the year of upwards of $60,000,000. It had assets of more than $132,000,000, a surplus of almost $112,000,000, and its cash on hand and municipal bonds were nearly $54,000,000. Its total liabilities, including capital stock, was a little over $20,000,000.

As early as in June, 1915, a general plan for the expansion of the productive capacity of the concern by a practical duplication of its plant had been talked over by the executive officers and directors and agreed upon. It was determined not to reduce the selling price of cars for the year beginning August 1, 1915, but to maintain the price and to accumulate a large surplus to pay for the proposed expansion of plant and equipment.

It is the contention of plaintiffs that the apparent effect of the plan is intended to be the continued and continuing effect of it, and that it is deliberately proposed, not of record and not by official corporate declaration, but nevertheless proposed, to continue the corporation henceforth as a semi-eleemosynary institution and not as a business institution. In support of this contention, they point to the attitude and to the expressions of Mr. Henry Ford.

Mr. Henry Ford is the dominant force in the business of the Ford Motor Company. No plan of operations could be adopted unless he consented, and no board of directors can be elected whom he does not favor. One of the directors of the company has no stock. One share was assigned to him to qualify him for the position, but it is not claimed that he owns it. A business, one of the largest in the world, and one of the most profitable, has been built up. It employs many men, at good pay.

"My ambition," said Mr. Ford, "is to employ still more men, to spread the benefits of this industrial system to the greatest possible number to help them build up their lives and their homes. To do this we are putting the greatest share of our profits back in the business."

"With regard to dividends, the company paid sixty per cent, on its capitalization of two million dollars, or $1,200,000, leaving $58,000,000 to reinvest for the growth of the company. This is Mr. Ford's policy at present, and it is understood that the other stockholders cheerfully accede to this plan."

He had made up his mind in the summer of 1916 that no dividends other than the regular dividends should be paid, "for the present."

The record, and especially the testimony of Mr. Ford, convinces that he has to some extent the attitude towards shareholders of one who has dispensed and distributed to them, large gains and that they should be content to take what he chooses to give.

We have no doubt that certain sentiments, philanthropic and altruistic, creditable to Mr. Ford, had large influence in determining the policy to be pursued by the Ford Motor Company—the policy which has been herein referred to.

It is said by his counsel that—

"Although a manufacturing corporation cannot engage in humanitarian works as its principal business, the fact that it is organized for profit does not prevent the existence of implied powers to carry on with humanitarian motives such charitable works as are incidental to the main business of the corporation."

And again:

"As the expenditures complained of are being made in an expansion of the business which the company is organized to carry on, and for purposes within the powers of the corporation as hereinbefore shown, the question is as to whether such expenditures are rendered illegal because influenced to some extent by humanitarian motives and purposes on the part of the members of the board of directors."

In discussing this proposition, counsel have referred to decisions such as Hawes V. Oakland, 104 U.S 450, 26 L. Ext. 827; Taunton v. Royal Ins. Co., 2 Hem. & Miller, 135;

These cases, after all, like all others in which the subject is treated, turn finally upon the point, the question, whether it appears that the directors were not acting for the best interests of the corporation.

A business corporation is organized and carried on primarily for the profit of the stockholders. The powers of the directors are to be employed for that end. The discretion of directors is to be exercised in the choice of means to attain that end, and does not extend to a change in the end itself, to the reduction of profits, or to the non-distribution of profits among stockholders in order to devote them to other purposes.

There is committed to the discretion of directors, a discretion to be exercised in good faith, the infinite details of business, including the wages which shall be paid to employees, the number of hours they shall work, the conditions under which labor shall be carried on, and the price for which products shall be offered to the public.

It is said by appellants that the motives of the board members are not material and will not be inquired into by the court so long as their acts are within their lawful powers. As we have pointed out, and the proposition does not require argument to sustain it, it is not within the lawful powers of a board of directors to shape and conduct the affairs of a corporation for the merely incidental benefit of shareholders and for the primary purpose of benefitting others, and no one will contend that, if the avowed purpose of the defendant directors was to sacrifice the interests of shareholders, it would not be the duty of the courts to interfere.

We are not, however, persuaded that we should interfere with the proposed expansion of the business of the Ford Motor Company. In view of the fact that the selling price of products may be increased at any time, the ultimate results of the larger business cannot be certainly estimated. The judges are not business experts. It is recognized that plans must often be made for a long future, for expected competition, for a continuing as well as an immediately profitable venture. The experience of the Ford Motor Company is evidence of capable management of its affairs.

We are not satisfied that the alleged motives of the directors, in so far as they are reflected in the conduct of the business, menace the interests of shareholders. It is enough to say, perhaps, that the court of equity is at all times open to complaining shareholders having a just grievance.

The Ford Motor Company was able to estimate with nicety its income and profit. It could sell more cars than it could make.

If the total cost of proposed expenditures had been immediately withdrawn in cash from the cash surplus (money and bonds) on hand August 1, 1916, there would have remained nearly $30,000,000.

So that, without going further, it would appear that, accepting and approving the plan of the directors, it was their duty to distribute on or near the 1st of August, 1916, a very large sum of money to stockholders.

Case Questions

1. Did the court accept Ford's argument that it was permissible to run a company with "incidental" charitable motives?

2. What standard did the court use to evaluate the directors' decision?

■ Concept Check 2-2　The Social Responsibility of Business

- Define the *stakeholder environment* and discuss its role in the ethics of *management* decision making.
- Describe the following *models of corporate social responsibility:* (1) *ethical custom* (2) the *trusteeship model* (3) the *social performance model.*

■ APPROACHES TO ETHICAL BEHAVIOR

As individuals and societies progress, abstract principles begin to replace personal interests as the chief influence upon behavior, especially moral behavior, and ethical theories soon emerge. These theories suggest approaches to every kind of human activity, including business.

In this section, we will consider two basic schools of philosophical thought on the question of ethical behavior. As a representative *teleological theory,* we will discuss *utilitarianism* and, in order to suggest the kinds of complexities that can arise in the realm of ethical theory, offer a brief critique. We will then survey some classic *deontological theories* and show briefly how these theories apply to a modern approach—that of John Rawls—which we have already encountered. Finally, we will look at the *business-judgment rule* as a specific issue in legal perspectives on ethical theory.

Teleological Theories: Utilitarianism

teleological theories Theories of ethical behavior holding that an act's outcome determines its morality—that good consequences signify good actions and vice versa

The Greek word *telos* means "end," or "result." Some moral philosophers argue that we must judge the morality of an act chiefly by its *consequences.* These theories suggest that a good action is one that has a good *outcome,* and vice versa, and are thus called **teleological theories.** The most important of them is

utilitarianism, which seeks to promote the greatest happiness for the greatest number of people. To implement the principle, according to utilitarian theorists, we must answer two questions:

utilitarianism Teleological theory of ethical behavior promoting the greatest good for the greatest number of people

1. How do we decide what "happiness" really means?
2. How do we resolve conflicts between the happiness of one person and that of another?

Jeremy Bentham. The English philosopher Jeremy Bentham (1748–1832) had a fairly clear answer to the first of the two problems presented above. As he put it somewhat brutally, "Pleasure for pleasure, pushpin is as good as Plato." Pushpin was a simple child's game; Plato is often regarded as the greatest of all philosophers. Bentham meant that many people get as much pleasure from playing pushpin as from reading Plato, and we must accept their value judgment as valid for them. In other words, we know only that something is desirable if it is actually desired.

Bentham formulated what has come to be known as the *principle of utility:* Actions are to be evaluated according to the balance of happiness or unhappiness that they produce when one considers alternatives. In other words, an action is good or right if it produces the greatest balance of happiness over unhappiness or pleasure over pain. A key feature of utilitarianism is the maximization of good or pleasure.

John Stuart Mill. Many utilitarians were dissatisfied with Bentham's definition of happiness. The problem, as they saw it, was the difficulty of maintaining Bentham's view consistently unless one is prepared to say that anything which the majority desires strongly must be right, no matter what it is. Bentham's most important disciple, John Stuart Mill (1806–1873), broke with him completely on this issue.

Mill distinguished between what he called the "higher" pleasures (those of the mind) and the "lower" pleasures (those of the body). He insisted that "It is quite compatible with the principle of utility to recognize the fact that some *kinds* of pleasure are more desirable and more valuable than others." How do we know this? Because, he claims, "It is an unquestionable fact that those who are equally acquainted with" the two "give a most marked preference to the manner of existence which employs the higher faculties."

PROBLEMS WITH UTILITARIANISM. Utilitarianism suggests in any form that we should judge the morality of an act or an institution by considering its results—that is, its impact on the happiness of the greatest number of people.

One problem often expressed with respect to utilitarianism has to do with the difficulty of quantification. Can all happiness or unhappiness be exactly quantified? Business must make trade-offs that are difficult to measure. For example, how does one compare the value of adding a child-care facility at a company to the value of having an on-site medical facility to care for injured workers?

Another critical approach points out that utilitarian theory focuses exclusively on *aggregate* social welfare, ignoring how welfare should be *distributed* among individuals.[9] From this perspective, there are at least three considerations that apply to questions of ethical or moral standards: *utilitarian, moral*

---

[9] *See* Manuel G. Velasquez, *Business Ethics: Concepts and Cases* (Englewood Cliffs, NJ: Prentice Hall, 1982), pp. 90-93.

rights, and *justice.* As they might apply to a specific moral or ethical judgment, questions reflecting these considerations are summarized in Figure 2-5.

When all three issues are considered, the following, more general criticism comes into focus:

1. *Utilitarian standards* ignore the distribution of aggregate welfare among individuals.
2. *Moral-rights standards* ignore both aggregate rights and the question of their distribution in favor of individual considerations.
3. *Standards of justice* focus on the question of distributing rights but slight the questions of both aggregate and individual rights.

Proponents of these perspectives point out that the application of any of these three standards could be relevant—and even decisive—in a given case. They argue that all three should therefore be considered quite systematically whenever an issue of moral or ethical reasoning is being considered. Try to apply this three-fold model of ethical reasoning as you complete this chapter, applying questions like those posed in Figure 2-5 both to the following theories of ethical behavior and to the perspectives on ethical business behavior discussed in the next section.

Deontological Theories

deontological theories
Theories of ethical behavior focused on the means used to achieve an end and arguing that an act's rightness is dependent on its intent rather than its consequence

Deontological theories focus on the *means* used to achieve an end. Proponents claim that the rightness and goodness of an act are determined by the *intentions* of the actor, not by the consequences of the act. Just as teleological theory derives from the Greek word meaning "outcome," deontological theory derives from the Greek word meaning "duty." In the next section, we will describe the deontological theory of Immanuel Kant. Notice, as you read, that deontologists argue that we have certain duties to behave in ways that assure good results: Behaving in accordance with these duties or obligations, regardless of outcome, is critical to deontological theorists.

Immanuel Kant and the Categorical Imperative. Immanuel Kant (1724–1804), perhaps the greatest deontological philosopher, proposed the **categorical imperative.** For Kant's purposes, "categorical" means absolute and "imperative" means *requirement.* According to Kant, there is one absolute requirement: "Act only according to that maxim by which you can, at the same time, will that it should become a universal law." This principle, of course, is an extension of the Golden Rule: Do unto others as you would have them do unto you.

categorical imperative
Doctrine of ethical behavior holding we are under absolute obligation to treat people as ends in themselves instead of as means to our ends

Kant gives us an example of what he means. A man, he proposes, must borrow money. He fears that he will not be able to repay it but knows that he

FIGURE 2-5 Three Moral Considerations   *Source: Manuel G. Velasquez,* Business Ethics: Concepts and Cases *(Englewood Cliffs, NJ: Prentice Hall, 1982).*

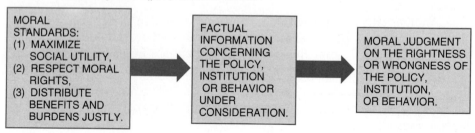

- We believe our first responsibility is to the doctors, nurses and patients, to mothers and fathers and all others who use our products and services.
- In meeting their needs everything we do must be of high quality.
- We must constantly strive to reduce our costs in order to maintain reasonable prices.
- Customers' orders must be serviced promptly and accurately.
- Our suppliers and distributors must have an opportunity to make a fair profit.
- We are responsible to our employees, the men and women who work with us throughout the world.
- Everyone must be considered as an individual.
- We must respect their dignity and recognize their merit.
- They must have a sense of security in their jobs.
- Compensation must be fair and adequate, and working conditions clean, orderly and safe.
- We must be mindful of ways to help our employees fulfill their family responsibilities.
- Employees must feel free to make suggestions and complaints.
- There must be equal opportunity for employment, development and advancement for those qualified.
- We must provide competent management, and their actions must be just and ethical.
- We are responsible to the communities in which we live and work and to the world community as well.
- We must be good citizens—support good works and charities and bear our fair share of taxes.
- We must encourage civic improvements and better health and education.
- We must maintain in good order the property we are privileged to use, protecting the environment and natural resources.
- Our final responsibility is to our stockholders.
- Business must make a sound profit.
- We must experiment with new ideas.
- Research must be carried on, innovative programs developed and mistakes paid for.
- New equipment must be purchased, new facilities provided and new products launched.
- Reserves must be created to provide for adverse times.
- When we operate according to these principles the stockholders should realize a fair return.

FIGURE 2-6 The "Credo" at Johnson & Johnson   *Source: Johnson & Johnson.*

will not get the loan unless he promises to do so. Would it be right to lie? The man thus applies the categorical imperative: "How would it be if my maxim [to lie for a loan] became a universal law? He immediately sees that it would never hold as a universal law of nature and be consistent with itself; rather, it must necessarily contradict itself." Obviously, if such promises were *always* broken, *no one* would lend money to anyone else.

Indeed, few people if any would enter into *contracts*—perhaps the most basic device of business—if people who signed them generally failed to deliver. A contract is a promise to do or not do something. Lenders, for example, promise to give borrowers money which they, in turn, promise to repay. In recent years, however, borrowers have become more and more prone to default on that promise. As a result, more and more businesses refuse to extend credit to their customers and insist on immediate payment—exactly what Kant would have expected.

Kant also has a second formulation of the categorical imperative. It, too, has a direct application to business: Kant insists that we have an absolute obligation to treat other people as *ends in themselves*, not as mere means to *our ends*. You may remember that the free-market model of the social responsibilities of business suggests that its only responsibility is to maximize profits legally. Suppose, however, that you were a manager and found that the most effective way of getting your employees to work hard was to abuse and insult them. In general, although this is not the best way to get results, it may work in particular situations. Kant's perspective suggests that even if it did, it would be morally wrong to treat your subordinates in ways that suited your interests but denied their right to self-respect and human dignity.

contract theories Theories of ethical behavior dedicated to formulating rules for organizing society at large

CONTRACT THEORY. Another deontological tradition—**contract theories** like John Rawls's theory of justice—was mentioned earlier in this chapter. Unlike Kant, who tried to devise a rule to guide the acts of *individual* men and women, contract theorists devoted their attention to rules for organizing *society at large*. Unlike utilitarians, they regard those rules as absolute.

Not every contract theory, however, is deontological in character; in fact, one of the first contract theorists, Thomas Hobbes (1588-1679), was also a founder of utilitarianism. As we noted previously, Rawls's views are deduced from an imaginary state in which we choose the principles that govern society. Hobbes, starting from an imaginary "state of nature," holds that human nature is selfish and aggressive. For him, the state of nature is a "war of all against all" in which each human being seeks to promote his own interests at the expense of others. In addition, we fear the selfishness and aggression of other human beings. According to Hobbes, this fear makes it rational for us to submit to an all-powerful government capable of controlling the aggressions of others. He suggests that we make a "contract" delegating our political liberty to the government and confining our aggressiveness to the sphere of private life, including business competition.

Another great contract theorist, John Locke (1632-1704), also derives his principles from the so-called "state of nature," which he believed was governed by the "law of nature." Locke's conception differed from Hobbes's because he had a different conception of human nature: According to Locke, "Reason, which is that law [of nature], teaches all mankind who will consult it [that] no one ought to harm another in his life, health, liberty, or possessions. In other words, while Hobbes thought that society originates in a contract to surrender our "natural liberty," Locke saw the contract as a means of protecting that liberty.

When Rawls argues that, in the original position, we would agree to certain principles, he is also making a contract argument. Rawls analyzes contracts in ways that recall Kant. Private individuals (including business executives) seek to "establish and stabilize their private ventures by giving one another their word."[10] This practice is often hard, he notes, because contracts typically require one party to act before the other parties do so. If the first party does not believe that the others will follow the contract, he has no reason to follow it himself—or to sign contracts at all.

Rawls's principles are not derived from human nature or natural rights. Nevertheless, his two principles of justice, like natural rights, receive "absolute precedence" over individual interests.

---

[10] Rawls, *A Theory of Justice* (Cambridge, MA: Harvard University Press, 1971), p. 346.

The Private Sector and the Public Interest Made from a videotape played at his trial in October 1980, this photo shows Representative Michael Myers (second from left) holding an envelope containing $50,000, which was received from undercover FBI agent Anthony Amoroso (left). With the assistance of players like convicted con man Mel Weinberg (right), the Justice Department launched a widespread investigation into corruption among interest groups and lobbyists working the Congressional beat. Posing as Arab potentates seeking immigration and investment assistance, agents created criminal opportunities for suspected corruptible officials and prosecuted those who seized their opportunities. Called *Abscam,* the operation concluded in 1981 with the conviction of six members of Congress and ten other defendants. Because the Federal Regulation of Lobbying Act (1946) requires registration only of interest-group representatives whose "principal purpose" is lobbying, many people whose jobs include the indirect influence of public officials need not register.

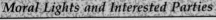

YOU DECIDE

Moral Lights and Interested Parties

The Chicago Cubs of the National Baseball League have not won the National League pennant since 1945, and they have not participated in a World Series since 1918. Until recently, the Cubs were also the only major league baseball team that did not have lights for night games in their home park, venerable Wrigley Field on the north side of Chicago. In 1966, a minority owner named Shlensky sued the team, arguing that its policy of exclusive day baseball caused financial hardship to investors. The plaintiff asserted that management and the team's principal owner, chewing-gum mogul Philip K. Wrigley, were acting in the interests of the neighborhood in which the stadium was located instead of the interests of the team's stockholders.

The issue, then, involves both social and legal responsibility: How should the interests of the various parties to this dispute be weighed? (For further discussion, see p. 58.)

- Define *teleological* and *deontological* as theoretical approaches to ethical behavior. Explain how *utilitarianism* is a teleological theory of ethical behavior.
- Explain the difference between the principle of the *categorical imperative* and *contract theory*.

■ ETHICAL STANDARDS FOR CORPORATE DECISIONS

Moral philosophy often deals with abstractions—for example, "the greatest benefit for the greatest number." Such abstractions would clearly be more useful if they were applicable to personal situations, professions, and employers' demands, among other things. Therefore, moral philosophy must be supplemented by *personal standards, corporate codes of conduct,* and *standards for professional associations.*

Personal Standards

In 1958, Harvard's Theodore Levitt argued that "the cultural, spiritual, social, and moral consequences [of a businessperson's acts] are none of his occupational concerns.[11] A few years later, the *Harvard Business Review* asked a group of businesspersons whether they accepted or rejected this claim. No less than ninety-four percent of the respondents rejected it outright.[12]

At the same time, however, men and women responding to polls often say what they think other people want to hear rather than what they really think. The same group of respondents, for example, was presented with a number of ethical problems and asked:

- What would you do in these situations?
- What would the "average executive" do?

The designers of the poll assumed that in talking about the probable behavior of average executives, the respondents would in fact be saying something about themselves. For example, the executives were asked to judge the conduct of a manager who padded his expense account by five percent of his annual income. These were the results:

- Six percent of them found such conduct acceptable if the man's colleagues had been doing the same, and twenty-seven percent thought that the average executive would accept such conduct in these circumstances.
- Eleven percent thought it was acceptable if the executive's supervisor knew about it, and twenty-eight percent thought the average executive would accept such an arrangement.

---

[11] Levitt, "Are Advertising and Marketing Corrupting Society? It's Not Your Worry, Levitt Tells Business," *Advertising Age,* Oct. 6, 1958, p. 89. Levitt's words leave open the possibility that these issues may be of interest to businessmen in their other capacities, for example, as citizens.

[12] R. C. Baumhart, "How Ethical Are Businessmen?" 39 *Harvard Business Review* (July-Aug. 1961), pp. 36-50.

- Eighty-six percent regarded manipulating expense accounts as unacceptable "regardless of the circumstances," but only sixty percent believed that the average executive would think so.

The authors of the study concluded that "actual business practice is probably closer to what respondents say 'the average executive' would do," if only because so many of us seem to think that other people are not ethical. The problem has evidently gotten worse. For example, a 1987 survey of 671 executives found that twenty-five percent thought high ethical standards were likely to hinder their career prospects, and fifty percent admitted that they would bend the rules to get ahead.[13]

Why do we sometimes behave ethically and sometimes unethically? The 1961 respondents said that when they behaved ethically, they were following their own ethical outlook. They blamed unethical behavior mostly on pressure from supervisors, the ethical climate of their industries, and the failure of many companies to develop codes of ethics.

Codes of Conduct

The 1961 respondents were also asked if their industries tolerated "practices which you regard as unethical." Fully fifty-nine percent answered affirmatively: Most executives wanted their industries to develop codes of ethical behavior. They felt that such codes would serve a dual purpose: (1) to clarify what is ethical and (2) to provide an impersonal reason for refusing to engage in questionable practices.

CORPORATE CODES. Not all codes work effectively. For example, a large, well-known company once issued a code of conduct that all decision-making executives had to read and sign once a year. The code consisted mostly of general statements requiring them to obey the federal antitrust laws. Except for provisions explicitly forbidding the executives to talk to their counterparts in rival companies about industry prices, the code was vague and contradictory. The executives could interpret the code as a directive to compete vigorously, to compete not at all, or to compete only enough to avoid prosecution. In fact, a number of the executives were prosecuted under the antitrust laws.

Corporate codes of conduct, the interviewers concluded, should:

- be consistent in both their actual provisions and their overtones;
- provide both positive and negative guidance, telling the executive what to do as well as what to avoid; and
- create a sense of responsibility, not just of caution.

Sometimes, they added, it is wise to have different codes of conduct for different employees: A single code is sometimes so general that people conclude that it does not apply to them.

Johnson & Johnson, the giant consumer-goods company, is highly decentralized, with managers at all levels making decisions with varying degrees of autonomy. In 1945, the company thus issued its corporate code to insure not only its ongoing commitment to product quality but commitment among all

---

[13] "A Question of Ethics," *The Wall Street Journal*, Sept. 8, 1987, p. A1.

employees to corporate goals of ethical behavior. The Johnson & Johnson "Credo" in Figure 2-6 on page 49 specifies the company's policy on stakeholder relationships.

PROFESSIONAL CODES. Certain codes apply to entire professions. In a real sense, a profession is a trust from society: On the one hand, society grants the profession a monopoly over a certain kind of activity; on the other, society requires that this monopoly be exercised for the common good.

Professional codes must ensure that everyone in the profession meets a certain standard of competence. They must be imposed and enforced by the profession itself, not by outsiders like the government. They must also require that the interests of society, and of the profession itself, come before the private interests of the men and women who practice it.

Certain lines of work, notably law and medicine, are universally recognized as professions. Business management is not. However, certain groups of managers, such as certified public accountants, are so recognized.

■ *Concept Check 2-4   Ethical Standards for Corporate Decisions*

- Describe the primary goals of a *corporate code of conduct.*
- What are the primary purposes of *professional codes of conduct?*

■ THE LIMITS OF LAW

Recall from Chapter 1 our discussion of *natural law*—in particular, the ideas of St. Thomas Aquinas. St. Thomas believed that an unjust law should not be obeyed. Consider what might happen in our society if we put such a belief into practice. Two famous Americans also believed that an unjust law should not be obeyed and were moved to civil disobedience to protest that injustice.

HENRY DAVID THOREAU. In 1845, after a successful war of secession from Mexico, the independent nation of Texas was admitted to the United States as a slaveholding state. Then in 1846, the United States went to war with Mexico in a one-sided conflict in which the United States secured vast amounts of former Mexican territory in what is now the American Southwest. The Texan cause, then, was tainted by its association with slavery. Moreover, the United States had provoked the war even though many Americans opposed it. One of them was a young writer named Henry David Thoreau (1817-1862), who was then living in a shack that he had built along the shore of Walden Pond, near Concord, Massachusetts.

Most opponents of the war merely argued against it. Thoreau, however, went further: He refused to pay a tax that had been levied to support it. Thoreau's friend Sam Staples, the town constable, offered to pay the tax for him. When Thoreau declined the offer, he was arrested.

There is an unconfirmed story that Thoreau's friend and fellow writer Ralph Waldo Emerson came to the jail to see him and asked, "Why are you here?" Thoreau is said to have replied, "Why are you not here?" In any event, someone (perhaps Thoreau's aunt) paid his tax, and he went free in the morning. Thoreau, however, was angry because he regarded his refusal to pay the tax as a deliberate action intended to make a point. He ultimately made his position clear in his famous essay on "Civil Disobedience."

Thoreau's premise was that the moral power of a democratic government is that it is a government by the *majority*. Suppose, however, that such a government—with the support of the people—follows policies that are immoral. What are moral men and women to do?

Thoreau begins by denying, in effect, that any kind of government, democratic or otherwise, has any *moral* foundation. "That government is best," he tells us, "that governs not at all; and when men are prepared for it, that will be the kind of government which they will have." In the meantime, although we must have government, the kind we have is a matter of practicality rather than morality.

According to Thoreau, rule by a majority makes sense "not because they are most likely to be in the right, nor because this seems fairest to the minority, but because they are physically the strongest." We thus have no absolute obligation to obey the laws of such a government: "The only obligation which I have . . . is to do at any time what I think right." Respect for law, he adds, is wrong in principle, for through it even good people "are daily made the agents of injustice."

Slavery is unjust, and the war had been fought partly for its sake. How then should a moral man "behave toward this American government today?" asks Thoreau. "I answer, that he cannot without disgrace be associated with it. I cannot for an instant recognize that political organization as *my* government." Those who are in the minority have a duty to deny it practical support: "It is enough that they have God on their side;" besides, "any man more right than his neighbors constitutes a majority of one already." And if a moral man goes to jail, so much the better, for in an unjust society, "the true place for a just man is also a prison."

Thoreau's argument assumes that individuals have the right not only to decide that the government's conduct is immoral but also to act on that belief.

MARTIN LUTHER KING, JR. Thoreau's ideas and example influenced the Reverend Dr. Martin Luther King, Jr., when he challenged the historical aftermath of slavery: racial discrimination. King had been active in the civil rights movement for about a decade when, in 1963, he went to Birmingham, Alabama. Local black leaders had been negotiating with the city fathers for some time. Promises had been made and broken. King and his colleagues replied with a campaign of nonviolent civil disobedience. The campaign included sit-ins at which protesters blocked the entrances to local businesses, boycotts against those businesses, and marches held without permits.

Early in April 1963, city officials went to court seeking a temporary injunction that would halt the protest. Their complaint charged that the protesters had violated many state and local statutes and ordinances. This contention was not in doubt. When the injunction against holding street parades without a permit was granted, the protesters deliberately violated it. King and others went to jail for criminal contempt. While in jail, King wrote a famous letter explaining his actions. A brief portion of his letter follows:

> One may well ask: "How can you advocate breaking some laws and obeying others?" The answer lies in the fact that there are two types of laws: just and unjust. I would be the first to advocate obeying just laws. One has not only a legal but a moral responsibility to obey [them]. Conversely, one has a moral responsibility to disobey unjust laws. . . .
>
> Now, what is the difference between the two? How does one determine whether a law is just or unjust? A just law is a man-made code that squares with the moral

Martin Luther King, Jr., Birmingham, Alabama, 1963. Although the Supreme Court upheld an Alabama state court's injunction barring King's march in the city, it left room for doubt about the constitutionality of both the injunction and the municipal ordinance that it enforced. Writing for the majority, Justice Potter Stewart rejected the idea that individuals are "constitutionally free to ignore all the procedures of law and carry their battles to the streets." Four dissenting justices, however, suggested that there is a right to defy—peacefully—patently unconstitutional laws and court orders.

law or the law of God. An unjust law is out of harmony with the moral law. . . . An unjust law is a human law that is not rooted in eternal law and natural law. Any law that uplifts human personality is just. Any law that degrades human personality is unjust.[14]

THEORY AND PRACTICE. Laws must be enforceable. Can the rule of law survive if citizens decide which laws they wish to obey, just or not? Dr. King's approach to civil disobedience suggests answers that other writers have developed into a theory. One of these writers is John Rawls, whose theory of justice has already been discussed. **Civil disobedience,** he says, is "a public, nonviolent, conscientious yet political act contrary to law." Its aim is to change particular laws, not to subvert all law. In other words, civil disobedience "expresses disobedience to law within the limits of fidelity to law. The law is broken, but fidelity to law is expressed by the public and nonviolent nature of the act, by the willingness

civil disobedience Conscientious and nonviolent criticism policy demonstrated by refusal to comply with the rule of law

---

[14] Martin Luther King, Jr., "Letter From Birmingham Jail," *Why We Can't Wait* (New York: Harper & Row, 1964), pp. 84-85.

Satyagraha *Satyagraha,* according to Mohandas K. Gandhi, "is the Force which is born of Truth, Love or Nonviolence." In practice, the hallmark of *Satyagraha* was for Gandhi (1869–1948) nonviolent civil disobedience to British rule in his homeland of India—a spiritually nourished political conviction that he organized into nationwide campaigns of resistance to colonial oppression. India gained its independence in 1949—a year after Gandhi was assassinated by a disaffected Hindu fanatic. He is pictured here in 1932, celebrating the 75th anniversary of the Indian mutiny of 1857—what Indians call their "first war of Independence." Revered by his followers as *Mahatma* ("the Great Soul"), Gandhi is regarded as the catalyst for no less than three of this century's major revolutions: the revolutions against colonialism, racism, and violence.

to accept the legal consequences of one's conduct." Those who engage in civil disobedience base their criticisms of individual laws upon "the commonly shared conception of justice that underlies the political order,"[15] not upon purely personal moral insights.

Civil disobedience of this sort can only exist in a democratic society—that is, a society that respects both individual rights and majority rule. As a citizen of a democratic state, you too may someday have to ask yourself which laws you will and will not obey, much as Martin Luther King did.

---

[15] J. Rawls, *A Theory of Justice* (Harvard Belknap, 1971), pp. 363-370.

The specific issue to be decided in the case of Shlensky v. Wrigley (237 N.E.2nd [1968]) was whether lights should be installed at Wrigley Field so that the Chicago Cubs could play night games at home. The plaintiff argued that if there were night games, attendance would rise and the financial problems currently faced by the ball club would be alleviated. Although the defendant acknowledged that it had a duty to its stockholders, team management also contended that it had a duty to the neighborhood in which its stadium was located. In its most basic terms, then, the conflict was between financial and social responsibility. Because baseball is not simply business—it is a national institution—the dilemma was even more pronounced.

The Illinois Appellate Court cited Dodge v. Ford Motor Co.:

Plaintiff argues that the allegations of his amended complaint are sufficient to set forth a cause of action under the principles set out in Dodge v. Ford Motor Co. (1919). . . .

From the authority relied upon in that case it is clear that the court felt that there must be fraud or a breach of that good faith which directors are bound to exercise toward the stockholders in order to justify the courts entering into the internal affairs of corporations. This is made clear when the court refused to interfere with the directors' decision to expand the business. . . .

Plaintiff in the instant case argues that the directors are acting for reasons unrelated to the financial interest and welfare of the Cubs. However, we are not satisfied that the motives assigned to Philip K. Wrigley, and through him to the other directors, are contrary to the best interests of the corporation and the stockholders. For example, it appears to us that the effect on the surrounding neighborhood might well be considered by a director who was considering the patrons who would or would not attend the games if the park were in a poor neighborhood. . . .

In strictly practical terms, this was the tradeoff: If lights were installed, leisurely nights previously enjoyed by the neighborhood surrounding the park would be sacrificed because crowds would be going to and from the facility at all hours. The safety of neighborhood children might be jeopardized. The streets might be littered. Overnight parking might become a problem for area residents. On the other hand, the corporate stockholders were entitled to the best possible return on their investment. Under the business-judgment rule, the appellate court upheld the decision of the lower court in Wrigley's favor: As in Dodge, the court refused to interfere because there was evidence of illegality in team management's decision.

Shlensky lost his case, but lights were eventually installed at Wrigley Field in 1988.

■ Concept Check 2-5   The Limits of the Law

- Discuss Thoreau's concept of the *moral foundations* of government.
- Describe Martin Luther King, Jr.'s distinction between *just* and *unjust laws.*
- Define the concept of *civil disobedience* and give at least one specific example of an act of civil disobedience that has resulted in a change in the legal system.

SUMMARY

- Many laws seem to suggest that rules of law are moral—that is, they are involved with *ethics,* or the study of good and bad conduct. Yet not all legal rules have this chapter. Some laws forbid acts, such as murder, rape, and theft, that we regard as bad in themselves. These rules are *moral.*

- It is important in reconciling morality and law—and morality and business—to distinguish between *values,* which are personal or social standards desirable in themselves, and *norms,* or standards by which values are translated into judgment, and behavioral principles. It is also necessary to remember that ethics reflect values and so can never be legislated in our everchanging adversarial system, which is based in turn on shifting case law.

- The social responsibilities and moral concerns of business have been complicated by the inherent structure of the rising modern corporation, whose ownership is distinct from its *management,* or those individuals responsible for planning and handling a business' activities.

- In general, businesses have been under more pressure to maintain ethical standards since the mid-1980s, at which point federal regulations eased but states began to wield more rigorous jurisdiction. Increasingly, the different facets of the *stakeholder environment*—the internal and external community of individuals influencing or influenced by a company's activities—is carefully considered to determine and monitor the various responsibilities of a company.

- One model of corporate responsibility is the model of *ethical custom,* which denies that business has any responsibility other than earning the highest possible profit consistent with the law. Another is the *trusteeship model,* which E. Merrick Dodd proposed following Adolph A. Berle's argument in the early 1930s that a corporation's managers hold their power in trust only for its owners—that is, its stockholders. The *social-performance model,* prompted by the upheaval of national social values during the 1960s and 1970s, has been defined by Archie B. Carroll in an attempt to define the budding social responsibilities and underlying issues of private business. Carroll erases the distinction between the economic responsibilities and social responsibilities of business, and insists that business has four kinds of responsibilities—economic, legal, ethical, and discretionary.

- *Teleological theories* of ethical behavior suggest that we must judge the morality of an action chiefly by its consequences. *Utilitarianism,* the most important of these theories, seeks to promote "the greatest happiness for the greatest number" of people. *Pluralistic utilitarianism* is the doctrine that we must take the wants of humanity as we find them, whether or not we approve. Two general problems of utilitarianism are, first, that happiness or unhappiness can hardly be quantified or exactly measured; second, utilitarian theory focuses on *aggregate* social welfare but ignores how welfare is to be *distributed* among individuals.

- *Deontological ethical theories* focus on the means used to achieve an end. Proponents claim that the rightness of an action should be determined by certain rules or duties, not by its consequences. One such theorist, Immanuel Kant, believed that good conduct was conduct that could be followed by all people. In contrast, *contract theorists* such as John Locke and John Rawls devote their attention to rules for organizing society at large. Unlike utilitarians, these theorists regarded those rules as absolute. Locke, whose views deeply influenced our Declaration of Independence and Constitution, saw life, liberty, and property as natural rights that are part of human nature.

- Laws may be objectionable on moral grounds. In this case, we must decide which laws we will and will not obey. This problem is addressed by theories of *civil disobedience,* which aims to change particular laws; it does not intend to subvert all law.

QUESTIONS AND PROBLEMS

CASE PROBLEMS

1. Executive Order 11246 prohibits those with contracts with the federal government of $10,000 or more from discriminating in employment on the basis of race, color, religion, sex, or national origin. Those with contracts of $50,000 or more must develop written affirmative-action plans that set forth goals and timetables for remedying any underrepresentation found in the employer's workforce in the groups targeted in the executive order. Suppose you are an employer subject to the executive order. You know that the regional office of the federal agency responsible for enforcing the order must monitor businesses in a 50-county area and that funding cutbacks have re-

sulted in a shortage of agency personnel. Although you have always considered equal-employment efforts an administrative burden, you have nothing personal against the requirements. Would you slacken your efforts to comply with the order, knowing that the chances of your being discovered are virtually nonexistent? Why or why not?

2. On November 1, 1991, the new Federal Guidelines for Sentencing were passed that provide for tougher fines and sanctions against corporate lawbreakers. Under the new system, a company can be sued for millions of dollars for wrongdoing, but if the company has instituted preventive measures like an

in-house ethics program, the fines can be reduced to hundreds of thousands of dollars. Is it ethical for our government and our courts to follow such a system? Should all companies and executives who commit business crimes suffer the same penalties? How can a law with such varied penalties act as a deterrent for companies and their executives from committing crimes?

3. A group of dentists in Florida advertised on television that they are HIV negative. The ads had the purpose of easing patients' concerns that they could contract AIDS from their dentists, following reports about Kimberly Bergalis, the Florida woman who apparently contracted AIDS from her dentist. Is it ethical for professionals to use the public's fear of a terminal disease to advertise their business? Should the District Attorney step in to stop these ads?

4. You are a candidate for your party's nomination for high political office. You are married and have two teen-aged children. While your spouse and children are away, you plan to invite a young, attractive friend who lives in another city to visit you for the weekend. It is not planned as a romantic weekend and there is no romantic relationship between you and the friend. Should you go through with your plan? Explain your answer.

5. Assume you married young, attended medical school while your spouse supported you, then divorced shortly after finishing school and before realizing any significant earnings. Your spouse gets only a small divorce settlement and feels used. Would you put the assets you earn in the future in your parents' name to avoid having assets that your ex-spouse would be able to use as a basis for modifying the settlement decree to receive more money? Explain.

6. Assume you are a parent who needs someone to care for your small children in your home. You cannot afford the rates charged for in-home care. If someone approached you and offered to care for the children in your home for a price you could afford in exchange for your not reporting the payments because the sitter would lose Social Security benefits, would you do it? Why or why not? Explain. Would your answer change if the sitter told you that the benefits barely support her and that they would be cut back if any supplemental income was reported?

7. Suppose you are an assistant district attorney (DA) and your best friend is picked up on drug charges. Your friend tells you she did not commit the crime. The DA handling the case is a good friend of yours. You know that if you ask about the case and the DA finds out it is your friend, the DA will recommend a favorable disposition even if you did not ask for one. Would you tell the DA? Why or why not?

8. A famous, well-respected female sports star is sued by her female ex-lover for breach of contract for failing to carry out promises made when the two were lovers. Your company has endorsement contracts with the sports star. It is general knowledge that she is lesbian. Would you ask her to withdraw from the endorsement contracts?

9. It has been found that tissue from aborted fetuses has medical value and can contribute to advances in tissue transplants and treating Parkinson's disease and other nerve disorders. What ethical questions are involved in the use of fetal tissue for medical purposes?

10. Teleological (utilitarian) theories argue that we judge the morality of an act chiefly by its consequences—that is, a good action is one that has a good outcome and vice versa. Deontological theories focus on the means used to achieve an end—that is, the rightness and goodness of an act should be determined by certain rules or duties, not by its consequences. Using the fact pattern in Question 9 above, give an analysis of the facts and your decision under each theory.

3

THE CONSTITUTION AND BUSINESS

The United States has been guided by the same basic Constitution since June 21, 1788, when the state of New Hampshire voted to ratify the document drawn up a few months earlier in Philadelphia. Since then, although we have amended the Constitution, we have never deviated from the basic political philosophy of a representative, democratic government.

Our system of government was partly based on the British system because it provided for representative institutions and limited government power. However, that system merged the executive and legislative functions: Under a parliamentary system, the leader of the majority party becomes the head of the cabinet (that is, the prime minister). The framers of our Constitution believed firmly that executive, legislative, and judicial functions ought to be separated. They also had to contend with the fact that the founding states were older and more powerful than the central government that they had created. Consequently, the U.S. government is among the few governments that have never been sovereign over their constituent parts. Although the government is supreme in relation to the states, it cannot abolish them.

Our constitutional system also differs from the British system in another way: Instead of securing individual rights with ordinary laws (that is, statutes that can readily be repealed), the Constitution authored by the framers is a higher form of law that cannot simply be changed or disregarded by either Congress or the president.

Constitutional questions about government power are, and always will be, central to American politics, because the Constitution is a statement of general principles that are often subject to conflicting interpretations. We started arguing about constitutional issues—albeit those involving the British constitution—well before the American Revolution, and we have been debating about our Constitution ever since it was written. Few constitutional questions can be resolved simply by a literal reading of appropriate phrases. The framers intentionally chose language that was clear enough to signify their general inten-

U.S. v. Nixon (418 U.S. 683, 94 S.Ct. 3090 [1974]) On April 29, 1974, President Richard M. Nixon, acknowledging that his refusal to submit tapes and records of White House conversations to the Special Senate Watergate Committee "had heightened the mystery about Watergate"—and called into question his own role in the episode—agreed to send (edited) transcripts to the House Impeachment Committee, which was then conducting an independent investigation into the president's actions. Citing *executive privilege* (the asserted prerogative of the president to deny testimony that he believes will compromise the independence of the executive branch), Nixon had denied the tapes to the Senate committee in the summer of 1973 despite the committee's issuance of a *subpoena* (a court order that can carry punishment for refusal to comply). He then refused the request of special Watergate prosecutor Archibald Cox, whom he had himself appointed and then removed in November 1973. Cox's successor, Leon Jaworski, subsequently presented evidence to a *grand jury,* which, on March 1, 1974, indicted seven high-level presidential aides for "obstruction of justice" (and secretly named Nixon himself an "unindicted coconspirator"). When Jaworski petitioned a federal district court for a subpoena for additional tapes, Nixon released the edited transcripts shown here but also sought to have the new district-court subpoena nullified. On July 8, the Supreme Court, recognizing its extraordinary constitutional significance, agreed to hear the case. After 15 days of intense negotiation, the Court ruled that the Chief Executive had to comply with the district-court subpoena. Perhaps more importantly, the justices had labored intently—conferring, redrafting portions of the opinion, and maneuvering in the interest of compromise—to achieve a *unanimous* decision so tightly presented that it provided no room for the president to acknowledge but ignore it: The president, in other words, could conceivably have accepted the Court's opinion as a ruling on a point of law and simply refused to act on it. The potential constitutional crisis was resolved when Nixon resigned 16 days later.

tions and guiding principles but broad enough to accommodate any changes that the future might hold.

The final interpreter of the Constitution is the Supreme Court. In the past 200 years, the Court has tackled almost every issue considered by the framers themselves—and some they could have barely imagined, like the rights and responsibilities of the business community in a postindustrial age. Thus, both the Court and the Constitution itself help shape the legal environment of business.

■ CREATING A SYSTEM OF GOVERNMENT

The starting point for thinking about the U.S. system of government is understanding that ours is simply one model of governance among many others. For example, one commonly accepted definition of government is a "social organization that has the authority to rule the state." A government, then, provides a very important function that makes it different from any other group to which individuals might belong: Governments make laws that members of societies are bound to follow.

The Purposes of Government

All of us belong to different groups during our lives. These groups vary in their importance to us and in their power over how we act. For example, most of us are members of work groups, religious institutions, and social circles, and each of these groups provides us with some amount of direction. A religious institution, for example, might suggest rules for marriage or divorce. Work groups might have rules for how we do a particular job. This approach to understanding governments might suggest that all disputes could easily be settled by merely referring to a particular group's values. Unfortunately, the needs of different groups often come into conflict. You might, for example, know of instances in which people could not agree about whether to spend tax dollars on new schools or public hospitals. Such a dispute reflects different *group values* and different *group needs:* While young families with children feel a greater need for schools, older couples might sense a need for greater public medical care. As these values and needs clash, people turn to governments for resolutions because government has both the *power* and the *authority* to weigh different needs and to help different groups live together.[1]

POWER AND AUTHORITY.   In the sense that we will use it here, **power** is a government's capacity to make people act in accordance with collective needs even when they might prefer to act otherwise. As a child, for example, although you may not want to wash the dishes after dinner, your parents have the power to force you to do the task. They also have the *authority* to exercise that coercive force if necessary—that is, **authority** is *recognized power* or the *legitimized use* of power. Society has thus legitimized parental use of power to make children dry dinner dishes. On a broader scale, governments use power and authority to make individuals and groups behave in ways that seem appropriate to both those who govern and those who are governed. Competing values and needs are ordered and collective decisions are enforced. These decisions—however rightly or wrongly arrived at—become the substance of our laws and public policies.

power In a political sense, a government's ability to make individuals act in accord with collective needs even when they might prefer to act otherwise

authority In a political sense, the recognized or legitimized use of *power*

SECURITY.   One extremely important function of governments—and thus of laws and public policies—is providing for *security* within the bounds granted them by collective decisions. Sometimes, for example, differences between

---

[1]For an excellent treatment of the origins and purposes of government, see Leslie Lipson, *The Great Issues of Politics: An Introduction to Political Science* (Englewood Cliffs, NJ: Prentice Hall, 1989).

Crisis and Security The wave of reforms that allowed Boris Yeltsin to sweep to the presidency of the Russian republic with sixty percent of a historic vote in 1990 may have made the failed coup of August 19–21, 1991, inevitable, but in the immediate two-month aftermath of the coup, the republics of what is now commonly called the "former Union" had not yet formulated a coherent governmental structure to fulfill one of the primary needs that governments should, ideally, meet: *security*. In the case of Russia and the eleven other republics of the "former Union," that need was and is for economic security. Thus, in October 1991, Yeltsin, accused by both Soviet and foreign economists of failing to seize the opportunity presented by the coup's failure, announced drastic plans for coming to grips with potential economic disaster in the republic—plans that entailed some adjustments, both legislative and political, in the operations of the republic's untried governmental structure. Yeltsin proposed combining his own chief-executive functions as president with the administrative functions of the vacant prime minister's office. Promising that he proposed a "path to democracy, not to empire," Yeltsin offered to assume personal leadership of the republic at a time when extremely painful reform might generate a backlash that only personal leadership and popularity could forestall. He also argued the need to postpone promised regional elections which he claimed would be an unwarranted "luxury" during a period of traumatic economic change, and again, constitutional adjustment reflected uncertainties in security: Yeltsin aides worried that opponents of change might use elections to empower regional officials willing to obstruct reform.

groups in a particular nation come into conflict and violence may even erupt. The government has the job of resolving these differences, thus, the police step in to quell an urban riot. At other times, however, groups may feel that the government no longer adequately reflects their values or satisfies their needs. In June 1991, for example, the Croatians declared their independence from Yugoslavia and sparked a civil war largely because of a clash of cultures and religion. Similarly, even governments clash with one another (as in World War II) as each government—at least according to its own interpretation of the needs and values of its members—attempts to provide security for those members.

COMMON NEEDS. At the same time, governments also find ways of cooperating with each other when they share common needs. Often, for example, countries find it advantageous to establish trade agreements. Such agreements outline a series of rules for expediting business transactions. The European Community (EC), for instance, is composed of twelve member countries. Its members have been working, since the community came into existence in 1958, to simplify and eliminate trade barriers among themselves and, ultimately, to organize themselves as a unified common market by the year 1992. The result, it is hoped, will be quite beneficial for the economy of each nation and for the economic security of their citizens.

■ THE PURPOSE OF FORMING THE U.S. SYSTEM OF GOVERNMENT

The goals of governments differ according to their societies' different values and needs. The U.S. Constitution, for example, was written by men seeking to correct abuses to certain political and economic rights under the governance of the English monarchy and parliament when the British government exercised sovereignty over Colonial America. They gathered in Philadelphia to create a stronger government than had existed under our first interstate compact, the Articles of Confederation, but they still feared a strong central authority. They also knew, however, that the various states which they represented feared such authority even more. James Madison acknowledged these fears when he wrote: "In framing a government which is to be administered by men over men, the great difficulty lies in this: you must first enable the government to control the governed; and in the next place oblige it to control itself."

In a representative system like ours, the first defense against abuse of power is the electoral process: Voters can throw those who betray their trust out of office. In the United States, another safeguard is the *federal system*, which divides power between national and state governments. But the framers of our Constitution, firmly convinced that free elections and federalism were not enough to prevent tyranny, devised yet another protection: The **separation of powers** within the federal government itself, including a system of *checks and balances*, allocates powers among the branches of government at a specified level—and prohibits the intrusion of one branch upon the domains of the others.

separation of powers The division of a government body, including a system of *checks and balances*, which allocates powers among its branches at a specific level and prohibits the intrusion of one branch on the domains of the others; the division of the U.S. government into executive, legislative, and judicial branches

The framers divided the powers of the federal government among three distinct and equal branches:

- a *legislature* to make laws,
- an *executive branch* to carry them out, and
- a *judicial system* to interpret them.

To ensure that the new president, for example, could not control the new legislature—Congress—the framers also provided for separate congressional and presidential elections and forbade members of the executive branch from holding seats in the legislature. Moreover, after dividing the government into three branches, the founders gave each branch certain authority over the other two, thereby creating a system known as **checks and balances** in which government institutions or branches exercise *checks* on, and *balance* the activities of, other institutions and branches. Congress thus passes our laws, but the president can veto any of them, subject to a congressional override. The judiciary can invalidate laws that violate the Constitution (*see* the discussion of *Marbury v. Madison*

checks and balances A system in which government institutions or branches exercise *checks* on, and *balance* the activities of, other branches and institutions

later in this chapter). Although the president appoints both the executive officials of government, and all federal judges, the Senate approves these appointments and also ratifies any treaty that the president negotiates. And because the president, members of Congress, and federal judges all get their authority in different ways, in different years, and for different lengths of time, they are unlikely to represent exactly the same interests.

In this way, the framers believed, the federal government would control itself. It was, wrote James Madison, the "accumulation of all powers, legislature, executive, and judiciary, in the same hands" that "may justly be pronounced the very definition of tyranny." By ensuring that the powers of the federal government were not only *separate* but could actually *confront* one another, the framers sought to forestall impulses toward "tyranny" over the political and economic lives of new country's citizens. Some of the major points of separation and confrontation in federal power are summarized in Figure 3.1.

Separation of Powers

Neither the separation of powers alone nor the democratic process itself is always the most efficient system of governance. The framers therefore sacrificed the efficiency of consolidated power for the political and economic freedoms insured by a system in which conflicts would naturally arise because of the lim-

FIGURE 3-1 Separation and Confrontation of Powers in the Three Branches of the Federal Government

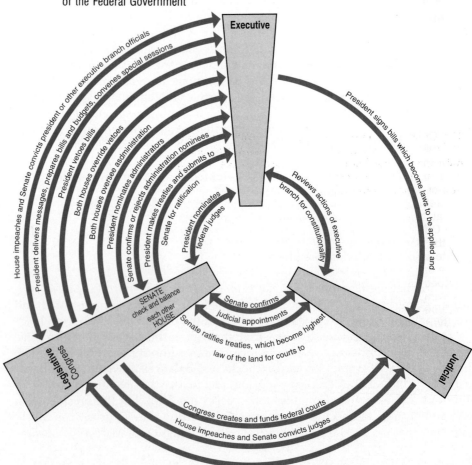

ited authority of any one branch to overrule another. Confusion, however, sometimes arises from the fact that separation of powers is not and cannot be complete. As Supreme Court Justice Louis Brandeis remarked sixty years ago, each branch has "functions in their nature executive, legislative, and judicial."

For example, when Congress considers legislation, it takes testimony from expert witnesses—as does the *judiciary* in deciding cases; in ruling on constitutional questions, the judiciary sometimes makes decisions that function as *legislative* acts. For example, the Supreme Court has made racial integration the law of the land. As we saw in Chapter 1, judicial decisions pronounced or developed in cases comprise *case law*. Certain presidential orders also have the force of law (presidents could not manage foreign relations or command the armed forces if their orders were not binding), and administrative agencies are generally empowered by Congress to enforce binding regulations. Thus, federal law has three sources: the legislative, executive, and judicial branches of government.

Bowsher v. Synar. Executive authority itself may also be divided. Congress, for example, has given itself certain quasi-executive powers. In the case of *Bowsher v. Synar*, for instance, the court ruled that "the Capitol police can arrest and press charges against law breakers, the Sergeant at Arms manages the Congressional payroll, the Capitol Architect maintains the buildings and grounds" (*Bowsher v. Synar* [1986])—all of which are routine administrative matters. Sometimes, however, congressional assumption of what appears to be executive power is highly controversial. The Gramm-Rudman Act of 1985, for example, gave the comptroller general—who reports to Congress rather than the president—the power to suggest cuts in the federal budget. In 1986, the Supreme Court considered this provision.

BOWSHER v. SYNAR
United States Supreme Court, 478 U.S. 714 (1986)

The Gramm-Rudman Act became law on December 12, 1985. This act was Congress' attempt to eliminate the federal budget deficit through the setting of a "maximum deficit amount." A progressive series of annual automatic reductions was to be used whereby this number would be reduced to zero by fiscal 1991. The Act provided that the directors of the Offices of Management and Budget (OMB) and of the Congressional Budget (CBO) were to estimate what reductions would be necessary to ensure that the maximum deficit amount would not be exceeded. Then the Comptroller General, after reviewing these figures, was to decide the actual reductions to be made.

Synar, the plaintiff, brought this action claiming that the Gramm-Rudman Act was unconstitutional. The trial court ruled in Synar's favor on the basis that Congress, through the Act, was giving the Comptroller executive power and the Constitution forbids it from doing this. Bowsher appealed.

Chief Justice Burger delivered the opinion of the Court.

. . . .

The Constitution does not contemplate an active role for Congress in the supervision of officers charged with the execution of the laws it enacts. The President appoints "Officers of the United States" with the "Advice and Consent of the Senate. . . ." Article II, Section 2. Once the appointment has been made and confirmed, however, the Constitution explicitly provides for removal of Officers of the United States by Congress only upon impeachment by the House of Representatives and conviction by the Senate. An impeachment by the House and trial by the Senate can rest only on "Treason, Bribery, or other high Crimes and Misdemeanors." Article II, Section 4. A direct congressional role in the removal of officers charged with the execution of the laws beyond this limited one is inconsistent with separation of powers.

. . . .

. . . Congress cannot reserve for itself the power of removal of an officer charged with the execution of the laws except by impeachment. To permit the execution of the laws to be vested in an officer answerable only to Congress would, in practical terms, reserve in Congress control over the execution of the laws. . . . The structure of the Constitution does not permit Congress to execute the laws; it follows that Congress can grant to an officer under its control what it does not possess.

. . . .

To permit an officer controlled by Congress to execute the laws would be, in essence, to permit a congressional veto. Congress could simply remove, or threaten to remove, for executing the laws in any fashion found to be unsatisfactory to Congress. This kind of congressional control over the execution of the laws. . . .is constitutionally impermissible.

. . . .

We conclude the District Court correctly held that the powers vested in the Comptroller General under Sec-

tion 251 violate the command of the Constitution that the Congress play no role in the execution of the laws. Accordingly, the judgment and order of the District Court are affirmed. . . .

Case Questions:

1. What fundamental principle of the Constitution is violated by the Gramm-Rudman Act?

2. What in the Court's decision suggests that the Comptroller General is not an agent of the executive branch?

3. How might the analysis differ if the Comptroller General exercised purely legislative functions?

■ *Concept Check 3-1   Creating a System of Government and Forming the U.S. Government*

- Explain what is meant by *separation of powers* within our federal government, and explain how it provides us with a defense against abuse of power.
- Why do people form systems of government?
- Give an instance in which the principle of *checks and balances* played an important role in federal-government activity.
- Explain the principle of *separation of powers* and give an example of how its incompleteness can affect governmental activity.

■ FEDERALISM

There was virtually no central government in 1787. The states each claimed to be sovereign; Massachusetts and Vermont even fought a war. Under the Articles of Confederation drawn up in 1781 to create a loose affiliation of sovereign states governed by a weak unicameral legislature, the central government could not compel the states or their citizens to act according to legislative or regulatory statutes. Although it could make treaties, it was powerless to enforce them and could not resolve conflicts between the states. For instance, when New York restricted use of the New York harbor, the Confederation could not intervene in the interests of neighboring states and the national economy. By contrast, the Constitution ensured that the new government had the power to enforce such actions.

Three Government Systems

At the same time, however, the Constitution reserved certain powers to the states, and in order to understand some of the key principles of central-government power under the U.S. Constitution, we should first look more closely at federalism as one of three types of government systems: the *federal, confederal,* and *unitary* systems.

federalism A government system in which a central government shares *power* or *authority* with constituent state or local governments

Federalism. The sharing of power by a central or national government with its state or regional governments is a system known as **federalism.** Each layer of government has sovereignty over particular spheres of activity usually defined by a written constitution. Our federalist system thus allows for two sources of sovereign law; because companies frequently operate in more than one state, the result is often a complex regulatory environment for business.

Confederation. In their debates about which system of government to establish in America, some of the Founding Fathers argued for a **confederation:** a league of sovereign states that delegate authority over areas of common concern (typically, defense and economic and foreign policy) to a central government. The only powers of the central government are those expressly assigned to it by the states. Unlike the reciprocal flow of power in a federal system, power in a confederation flows from the local to the national level. With its weak central government, however, confederation is relatively rare, although it is interesting to note that the republics of the former Soviet Union are currently considering just such a system.

Unitary System. At the other end of the spectrum from confederation is a **unitary system** of government, in which a strong, centralized national government holds supreme authority; state or local governments have no authority other than that delegated by the central government. The great majority of countries (Japan, Singapore, and Iran, for example) have unitary governments.

Figure 3-2 summarizes the flow of authority in these three different systems.

confederation A league of sovereign states that delegate *power* or *authority* over areas of common concern to a central government

unitary system A government system in which a centralized government holds supreme *authority*, with state or local governments having only the authority delegated by the central government

The Flow of Authority in a Federal System

With its shared powers, federalism is thus a compromise between unitary and confederated systems. Federalism accords to the states control over purely local issues and the general, inherent power to protect the public health, safety, and welfare. The Constitution delegates to the states authority to establish local governments, conduct elections, and regulate intrastate commerce and further reserves to the states all those powers not expressly delegated to the national government. In turn, the Constitution specifically delegates **enumerated (or express) powers** to the national government, granting it authority over national economic development and stability, national security, and foreign policy: The national government is constitutionally authorized to make treaties and declare war, regulate interstate and foreign commerce, coin money, and maintain an army and navy. In addition, the national government has certain inherent or **implied powers**—powers not mentioned in the Constitution but necessary to

enumerated (or express) powers Powers specifically granted to a branch of the central government by the Constitution

implied powers Powers of a branch of the central government that are not mentioned in but are consistent with the Constitution; such powers are deemed "necessary" to the functioning of the central government

FIGURE 3-2 The Flow of Authority in Three Government Systems

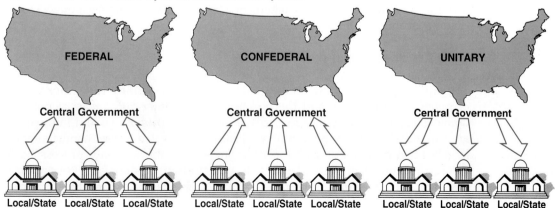

FEDERAL

Central Government

Local/State   Local/State   Local/State

CONFEDERAL

Central Government

Local/State   Local/State   Local/State

UNITARY

Central Government

Local/State   Local/State   Local/State

its functioning (for example, the authority to regulate arms sales). Thus, ours is a government of both express and implied powers.

In addition, state and federal governments share certain **concurrent powers**—powers that are exercised at both levels as long as they do not conflict. Both levels of government, for example, have authority to levy taxes, regulate business, and prohibit housing or employment discrimination. The jurisdictions of state and national governments further overlap because the power of the national government has been broadly interpreted to include the power to regulate local activities that affect national interests. Congress cannot, however, regulate domestic affairs simply in the name of the public interest, as the states may. Its *domestic* acts must be authorized by the Constitution.

concurrent powers Shared powers exercised at more than one level of government that do not conflict

THE LAYER-CAKE AND MARBLE-CAKE THEORIES. Scholars sometimes compare the federal system to a layer cake. In this metaphor, the top layer represents the national government and the middle layer state government. City, county, and other local governments form the bottom layer. In areas of concurrent power, however, the limits on the sovereignty of these layers of government are not always clear. Local, state, and national governments, for example, all regulate and fund education and health care. In addition, citizens must obey the laws of each government that has jurisdiction over them; national, state, and local governments have simultaneous authority over citizens. It has thus been suggested, however, that a marble cake would be a more accurate analogy for federalism: The responsibilities of various levels of government intermingle in almost every area of our lives.

Arguments for Federalism

Despite inevitable confusion and conflict over jurisdiction, the federal form of government has the advantage of keeping substantial political power close to its citizens, allowing regional differences to flourish while enabling a strong central government to provide both national defense and regulation in areas of common concern. Moreover, sheer size may make highly centralized government unworkable: In the American colonies, for example, decisions made in Washington might take weeks to reach the furthermost states. In large countries, federalism also allows diverse regions (for example, French-speaking Quebec in Canada and the Muslim states of India, which is primarily Hindu) to develop politically according to their own values and customs. The citizens of these regions exercise greater local political control than they could if Canada and India had unitary governments. Finally, in a federalist system the states serve as political laboratories where new politicians can gain experience and new government initiatives can be tried.

Some Key Principles of U.S. Federalism

The rapid expansion of the union soon brought to the surface numerous points of political controversy, and the pressures of resolving differences of political opinion resulted in pressure to clarify the powers, enumerated and implied, of an expanding federal government. Efforts to resolve these conflicts have largely been played out in the courts, and out of this ongoing process have emerged several key principles of U.S. constitutional federalism. We will discuss in some detail four of the most important of these principles: the *necessary-*

and-proper clause, the *preemption doctrine,* the *police power,* and the principle of *judicial review.*

THE NECESSARY-AND-PROPER CLAUSE. As we saw earlier, the framers of the Constitution wisely did not attempt to anticipate every national issue that the federal government might be empowered to address. Congress was given the open-ended power to "make all Laws, which shall be Necessary and Proper for carrying into execution" all congressional powers specified in the Constitution—for example, the power to tax, coin money, regulate interstate commerce, and establish a postal system. These and other specified powers are set forth in Article 1, Section 8 of the Constitution. Thus, the **Necessary-and-Proper Clause** (also called the **Elastic Clause**) gives Congress implied powers in addition to the express powers enumerated in Section 8.

M'Culloch v. Maryland. This extraordinary grant of implied power was opposed by early advocates of **states' rights**—a movement advocating more power for state and local governments and opposing the expansion of congressional powers not expressly mentioned in the Constitution. However, the broad interpretation of the Necessary-and-Proper Clause was upheld and consolidated by the Supreme Court in 1819, in the landmark case of *M'Culloch v. Maryland,* 4 Wheat. 316 (1819), which involved a challenge by the state of Maryland to the federal government's establishment of a national bank. Maryland imposed a tax on the bank that federal authorities refused to pay, arguing that the state lacked power to tax the federal government. Maryland argued, in turn, that the federal government lacked power to establish the bank because that power was not specifically listed in the Constitution.

Daniel Webster, counsel for the Bank of the United States, asserted that Congress could incorporate a national bank under the Necessary-and-Proper Clause because "necessary and proper" should be interpreted broadly to mean *reasonable* and *appropriate,* not just *essential:* The incorporation of a national bank, Webster contended, was a reasonable way for Congress to exercise its enumerated power to regulate the nation's finances. Furthermore, he argued, because federal law was supreme pursuant to the Supremacy Clause, states should not be permitted to use their taxing powers to frustrate legitimate actions of Congress or the executive branch.

The Supreme Court unanimously adopted Webster's *broad construction* of the Necessary-and-Proper Clause and affirmed the supremacy of federal law. Chief Justice John Marshall's opinion established a tradition of broadly interpreting the Constitution as a statement of *general* principles and a *general* scheme of governance, not a simple list of rules and regulations: "We must never forget," he declared, "that it is a Constitution we are expounding, intended to endure for ages to come and therefore to be adapted to the various crises of human affairs."

Although the federal government's complete immunity from state taxation as suggested by *M'Culloch* was later qualified, Marshall's assertion that the state cannot tax the federal government so as to subvert its functions still has full force. Today, the doctrine of **intergovernmental immunities,** which is rooted in *M'Culloch,* exempts various levels of government from certain legal obligations to the others and provides that neither the states nor the federal government can tax each other's "instrumentalities." For example, corporate bonds pay higher interest rates than municipal or state bonds because interest on corporate bonds is subject to federal income taxes from which publicly is-

Necessary-and-Proper Clause (Elastic Clause) Article I, Section 8 of the Constitution, granting Congress the open-ended power to "make all laws which shall be necessary and proper" to execute its *enumerated powers*

states' rights Principle or movement advocating more power for state and local governments and opposing the expansion of central-government powers not expressly mentioned in the Constitution

intergovernmental immunities Doctrine exempting each level of government from certain legal obligations to the others and providing that neither state nor federal governments can tax each other's "instrumentalities"

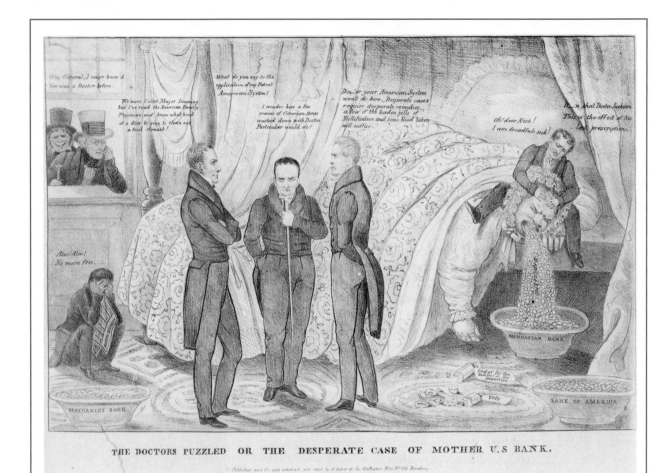

THE DOCTORS PUZZLED OR THE DESPERATE CASE OF MOTHER U.S. BANK.

Principles, Policy, and Partisanship John Marshall's opinion in *M'Culloch v. Maryland* (p. 71) reflected federalist sympathies that saw strong national power as conducive to economic growth, and his "loose construction" interpretation of the federal Constitution supported this view. By 1832, the Second Bank of the United States, with $35 million in capital, was by far the country's largest corporation and, with its assumptive role of overseeing the national economy, its politically most influential. In this 1830s cartoon, Nicholas Biddle, the bank's president (upper-right), comforts a bloated bank suffering from attacks by supporters of President Andrew Jackson (upper-left), while bank supporter (and one of its founders) Henry Clay (center-left) proposes the cure of his "American system"—a program that projected a federal government that was paternalistic in establishing tariffs, nurturing business, and fostering internal improvements. In 1832, Jackson, appealing to Jeffersonian values and denouncing the bank as a privileged monopoly, vetoed renewal of its charter. At center-right is John C. Calhoun, whose proposal of "nullification" refers, ironically, to the so-called "nullification crisis," also of 1832. When Jackson disappointed southern interests by declining to press for substantial reductions in import duties, Calhoun's home state declared federal tariff regulations "null" within the borders of South Carolina. In this instance, Jackson, avowing, "Our federal union, it must be preserved," secured the Force Bill, which empowered the president to use the military to enforce federal law within the states. Subsequent compromise resolved the crisis.

sued bonds are exempt. Marshall's broad construction of the federal government's implied powers is also followed today. We have, in general, one test to determine whether a congressional act infringes upon a fundamental right: Does it bear a *reasonable relation* to an enumerated power? (The REASONABLE RELATION TEST is discussed on page 94.)

THE PREEMPTION DOCTRINE. The Supremacy Clause does not preclude the states from exercising powers similar to federal powers or from regulating areas also regulated by federal law. It does, however, prevent the states from passing laws that interfere or conflict with federal legislation. The **preemption doctrine** holds that because certain matters are of national, as opposed to local, concern, federal law prevails when federal and state laws regulating the same activity are inconsistent. The principle of preemption has developed because, as we have seen, federal and state governments have some concurrent powers and share concurrent areas of jurisdiction. For example, there are both state and federal laws regarding the power to tax and prohibiting housing or employment discrimination.

> **preemption doctrine** Doctrine, issuing from the *Supremacy Clause*, holding that because certain matters are of inherent national concern, federal law prevails when federal and state laws are inconsistent

Sometimes, Congress expressly declares its intent to preempt—or not preempt—parallel state laws. The Wholesome Meat Act, for example, prohibits the states from imposing on meat "marking, labeling, packaging, or ingredient requirements" that differ from federal requirements. More often, however, Congress will insert a "savings clause" in federal legislation that validates parallel, nonconflicting state laws. When Congress does not declare its intent to preempt and a controversy arises over the interplay of state and federal laws, the courts are sometimes called upon. However, because preemption is in general a matter of congressional discretion and not a constitutional requirement, the courts are usually reluctant to invalidate state legislation when congressional intent is unclear.

THE POLICE POWER. The **police power** is the general, inherent power to protect the public health, safety, and welfare. Because the federal government does not have such power, it cannot act without a constitutional grant of authority simply to protect the public interest. The states, however, can.

> **police power** The general, inherent power, expressly granted only to the states, to protect the public health, safety, and welfare

Many of the laws regulating daily life—traffic laws, zoning laws, building and fire codes, consumer-protection laws, public-health laws—are enacted by state and local governments pursuant to their police powers. Unless those laws infringe upon either fundamental constitutional rights (such as the First Amendment right to free speech) or exclusive federal powers (such as the power to regulate interstate commerce), such laws are considered valid so long as they are reasonable means of protecting the public health, safety, and welfare. Judges are not supposed to "second-guess" legislators in formulating public policy. The public may effectively veto unwise laws by voting the legislators who passed them out of office.

Compelling State Interest. Judges are charged, however, with enforcing the Constitution. An exercise of police power that interferes with either a fundamental constitutional right (that is, one explicitly guaranteed by the Constitution) or a federal power must be more than a reasonable way of protecting the public: It must be an essential way of protecting a "compelling" state interest. In these cases, courts directly scrutinize the law at issue and balance the competing interests. If the state's purpose in passing the law is not as compelling as the fundamental constitutional right that is impaired, the courts can invalidate the law. For example, the Supreme Court has invalidated antilittering ordinances that broadly proscribe the distribution of circulars and pamphlets because fundamental First Amendment rights of freedom of speech outweigh the noncompelling public interest in trash-free streets (*Lovell v. Griffin,* 303 U.S. 444 [1938]).

In cases involving state laws affecting interstate commerce, the courts use a similar balancing test to weigh the state's interest in protecting the public with the federal interest in commerce. A "reasonable" state law that only incidentally affects commerce generally will be upheld while one that unduly burdens or discriminates against commerce usually will be struck down. Thus, the court employs similar standards of review in cases involving violations of individual constitutional rights and burdens of interstate commerce.

JUDICIAL REVIEW.   The courts have the power to assess not only the actions of individuals and agencies but laws enacted by Congress, states, and localities in order to determine whether they are in accord with the Constitution. This power of **judicial review** is now widely considered an essential check on both Congress and the president. The Constitution itself, however, gives only the slightest hint of that power, in Article III: "The judicial Power of the United States, shall be vested in one Supreme Court, and in such inferior Courts as the Congress may . . . ordain and establish. . . . The judicial Power shall extend to all Cases, in Law and Equity, arising under this Constitution."

judicial review   Principle whereby the courts have the power to assess laws enacted by Congress, states, and localities to determine their constitutionality

It is clear that many delegates to the Constitutional Convention wanted the Supreme Court to review the constitutionality of state legislation. It is much less clear, however, whether they wanted the Court, not the president or even Congress itself, to have the power to review acts of Congress. The problem arises because the Supremacy Clause defines the relationship of federal and state law, not the relationship between the three coequal branches of the federal government.

The framers considered two forms of judicial review but were unable to agree on either. One group, led by James Madison and James Wilson, proposed giving a veto power over federal law to a council composed of the president and a "convenient number" of judges. The delegates defeated this plan three times on the grounds that it violated the division of powers. Madison and Wilson then proposed that all bills go to the president and the Supreme Court: If *either* objected to a bill, it could be enacted into law only if two-thirds of Congress voted for enactment. If *both* objected, a three-fourths vote would be necessary to override the veto. This plan also was rejected. Instead, the president was given a *qualified* power to veto legislation and Congress the power to override the president's veto with a two-thirds vote. The Supreme Court was given no *express* power to review federal legislation. Under the leadership of Chief Justice Marshall, however, the Court found an *implied* power of review in its responsibility to uphold the Constitution.

Marbury v. Madison.   The future of the Supreme Court did not seem promising when Marshall took over as chief justice in 1801. Although the Court was still dominated by Federalists—the party that had grown out of support for the new constitution and its establishment of federal power—both Congress and the presidency had been captured in the 1800 elections by Thomas Jefferson and his party. The Jeffersonians (formerly the "Anti-Federalist Party") were not supportive of a national court system.

The conflict between the Federalists and the Jeffersonians over the federal judiciary began even before Jefferson took office. At the very last minute, the lame-duck Federalist Congress created numerous judgeships. Outgoing Federalist President John Adams ordered Marshall, then his secretary of state, to complete these formal appointments before the end of his term. Marshall failed to do so. When Jefferson assumed office, he ordered Marshall's successor, James Madison, to ignore the undelivered commissions.

The case of *Marbury v. Madison*, 1 Cranch 137 (1802), grew out of this dispute. It was brought by William Marbury, one of the noncommissioned appointees, against Secretary of State Madison. Marbury, a Federalist, led a group of four appointees in petitioning the Supreme Court for a *writ of mandamus*. "Mandamus" is Latin for "we command," and such writs are issued by courts to compel executive officers to perform duties required of them by law. Marbury, then, was asking the Supreme Court to force Madison to deliver the remaining judicial commissions.

Marshall was faced with a formidable challenge to the prestige and power of his court. One the one hand, ordering Madison to deliver the commissions would merely show the nation that the Court could not enforce its own decree—Jefferson would surely ignore it with impunity. On the other hand, refusing to issue the writ because of presidential opposition would establish the supremacy of the executive. Marshall found an ingenious way to do neither: He avoided both confrontation and retreat by striking down the mandamus statute that gave the Court authority to issue the writ that Marbury sought.

Speaking for a unanimous court, Marshall scolded Jefferson and Madison for withholding Marbury's commission. He noted, however, that Marbury's case did not fall within the Court's jurisdiction as defined by the Constitution. Therefore, the Court was simply not empowered to grant Marbury the relief he sought.

In effect, Marshall declared that the Constitution was a higher form of law than statutes passed by Congress—it is, after all, the Constitution that enables Congress to enact legislation. Moreover, by stressing the obligation of judges to uphold the Constitution, he reasoned that the Court was not only obliged to refrain from enforcing invalid laws but was empowered—even compelled—to strike them down. It was, in other words, the Court's job to choose between the laws and the Constitution, and for Marshall, the choice was clear: "If a law," he declared,

> be in opposition to the constitution; if both the law and the constitution apply to a particular case, so that the court must either decide that case conformable to the law, disregarding the constitution, or conformable to the constitution disregarding the law; the court must determine which of these conflicting rules governs the case; this is of the very essence of judicial duty.

As we will see in Chapter 5, although the courts are supposed to exercise restraint in deciding constitutional cases, self-restraint is not one of their primary responsibilities. Standing at the top of an increasingly overburdened legal system, the Supreme Court must still struggle to meet the needs of a complex and changing society. Few statutes or constitutional provisions are so clear as to need no judicial interpretation, especially in the context of changing social and political values. In 1857, for example, the Court declared that the Constitution conferred no rights of citizenship upon black slaves or their descendants (*Dred Scott v. Sandford*, 60 U.S. [19 How.] 393 [1857]); in 1954, however, it invalidated segregated schools (*Brown v. Board of Education*, 347 U.S. 483 [1954]. One job of the judiciary, then, is to respond—within the terms of the Constitution—to social and political change.

Perhaps no part of American life has changed faster or more fundamentally than the economy. In the next section, we will consider the Court's changing views, over the past 150 years, of the scope of congressional power to regulate commerce.

MAD TOM in A RAGE

Principles, Policy, and Partisanship (II) When Thomas Jefferson agreed to join George Washington's cabinet as secretary of state in 1789, he did so reluctantly: Wary of the new Constitution's lack of a bill of rights, Jefferson feared a compromise to republican principles and individual liberties under Federalist policies, especially those of Treasury Secretary Alexander Hamilton, who sought to use financial policy to strengthen the new central government. As Hamilton emerged as symbol of the new Federalist party and Jefferson of the Democratic-Republican party, partisan politics began to play a significant role in the interpretation of constitutional principle and governmental power. Divisive politics were often conducted with passion and anger, and as this 1801 cartoon suggests, Jefferson's open letters on diverse matters sometimes launched angry ideological and personal attacks on political foes who countered in kind: Jefferson was elected president in 1800, and "Mad Tom in a Rage," as this Federalist cartoon was titled, attacked Jefferson as a brandy-soaked anarchist assaulting the pillars of a stable federal government fostered by Washington and John Adams. As the case of *Marbury v. Madison* indicates, Jefferson was particularly rankled by Federalist control of the judiciary: "The Federalist's," he charged, "have retreated into the judiciary as a stronghold . . . and from that battery all the works of republicanism are to be beaten down and erased." The Judiciary Act of 1801, which had occasioned the *Marbury* dispute, was repealed by the Jefferson administration in 1802. Congressional Federalists assailed the repeal as unconstitutional, and Chief Justice Marshall would probably have nullified the repeal had not the act also altered Supreme Court sessions so that it did not reconvene for fourteen months, by which time the acquiescence of affected judges had made judicial review impractical.

■ Concept Check 3-2 *Federalism*

- What is the function of the *Necessary-and-Proper Clause* in our Constitution?
- States are not precluded from exercising powers similar to federal powers. How does the Constitution deal with situations in which federal and state laws regulating the same activity clash?
- Define *police power* and give some examples of its use by state and local government.
- How does the power of *judicial review* provide a check on Congress and the president?

■ THE COMMERCE CLAUSE

The **Commerce Clause,** Article 1, Section 8, gives Congress the power to "regulate Commerce with foreign Nations, and among the several states, and with the Indian Tribes." These few words are the source of considerable federal power: The federal government can regulate any aspect of the delivery of any product or service (including tangible goods, the transmission of gas, electricity or radio waves, and the sale of insurance policies) across state lines. Broadly construed, the Commerce Clause also gives the federal government the power to regulate purely local commercial and noncommercial activities that *affect* interstate commerce. For example, the 1964 Civil Rights Act, which includes prohibitions against employment discrimination and segregation in hotels and restaurants, was based on the Commerce Clause: The adverse economic effects of discrimination were used to justify federal regulation of social practices that had traditionally been considered the business of the states.

But the Commerce Clause has not always been construed so broadly. During the past 150 years, both commerce and federal-state interactions have changed, and the need for broad-reaching federal regulations has increased. The development of federal commerce power provides a valuable lesson in how the Constitution may be made to accommodate fundamental economic and social changes.

A threshold question about the Commerce Clause is whether its reach should extend to activities contained wholly within the borders of one state. Over the years, the Supreme Court has taken different analytical approaches to this issue, confronting in Commerce Clause cases important questions about the components of a national economy, federal jurisdiction, and states' rights.

Gibbons v. Ogden. Today, an expansive view of the commerce power prevails which dates back to the Depression and the New Deal of the 1930s. It was, however, anticipated over 160 years ago by Chief Justice Marshall in the landmark case of *Gibbons v. Ogden.* Gibbons ran a steamboat between New York and New Jersey that had been federally licensed to engage in trade along the Atlantic Coast. The state of New York, however, had granted a competitor, Ogden, the exclusive right to operate steamboats in New York waters. Ogden sued Gibbons for venturing into his territory, and Gibbons responded that Ogden's state-granted monopoly violated the Commerce Clause. Marshall focused on the constitutionality of federal power to license coastal trade: He held that

Commerce Clause Article I, Section 8 of the Constitution, granting Congress the power to "regulate commerce with foreign nations" and "among the several states"; basis of the federal government's authority to regulate both the delivery of goods and products across state lines and local commercial activities that affect interstate commerce

the federal licensing statute at issue was a valid exercise of commerce power and invalidated the New York State-granted monopoly under the Supremacy Clause, ruling that it conflicted with a legitimate federal law. Marshall declared that the commerce power extended to "that commerce which concerns more states than one" and that it "may be exercised within a state." *Gibbons* thus provides a basis for preemptive federal regulation of commercial activities within the concurrent jurisdiction of the states.

Dual Federalism

Forty years after *Gibbons*, federal commerce powers once again became an issue when the Supreme Court began to accord the states greater powers to control economic activity under the doctrine of **dual federalism.** Dual federalism actually refers to a political pattern whereby influence shifted away from economic interests that desired greater nationalization of business regulation to interests (for example, farmers and working persons) less dependent on economic nationalization. In response to these developments, the court expanded its definition of purely "local" activities to include activities that had only *indirect* effects on interstate commerce. In general, goods or services that did not cross state lines were considered within the exclusive jurisdiction of the states. This definition placed much economic activity beyond the reach of federal regulation.

Manufacturing, for example, was for a long time generally immune from federal antitrust regulations. In the Sugar Trust case of 1895, the Court held that a sugar company, which refined more than ninety percent of the sugar produced in the entire country, could not be prosecuted under the Sherman Antitrust Act.[2] Sugar refining was considered a manufacturing process, and manufacturing, the Court held, was not commerce but a "mere local" matter. The Court later included mining and factory production in this category. Such a *narrow construction* of the Commerce Clause created formidable barriers to later federal efforts to curb the abuses of industrialization.

Similarly, in *Hammer v. Dagenhart,* 247 U.S. 251 (1918), the Court struck down a federal child-labor law that forbade interstate transportation of items made at factories with child workers. The Court held that manufacturing was not commerce and that the "power to regulate commerce [was not the power] to equalize the economic conditions in the States." The Court invoked states' rights under the Tenth Amendment to regulate local manufacturing and trade.

Expanding the Commerce Power

The Great Depression and the New Deal dramatically changed popular notions of federalism. As a result, Congress and President Franklin D. Roosevelt enjoyed a broad new mandate to regulate the economy. However, it took Roosevelt several years to influence the Supreme Court. During his first term, the Court continued to limit federal regulation of intrastate activities under such laws as the National Industrial Recovery Act of 1933 (designed to increase prices and improve labor conditions) and the Agricultural Adjustment Act of 1933 (which paid farmers to decrease production). Some justices actively op-

---

[2]*United States v. E.C. Knight & Co.,* U.S. 1 (1895).

posed the expansion of federal power, and the Court persisted in finding no "direct" connection between interstate commerce and the management practices and agricultural production levels that the federal government was trying to control. The tide turned with both Roosevelt's landslide reelection in 1936 and the changing composition of the Court. By 1941, Roosevelt had appointed seven new justices. The stage was set for dramatic expansion of the federal commerce power.

NLRB v. Jones & Laughlin Steel Corp. The modern view of the Commerce Clause as a broad, preemptive mandate for federal regulation of local activities with *direct or indirect* effects on commerce is rooted in the case of *NLRB v. Jones & Laughlin Steel Corp.*, 301 U.S. 1 (1937). In this case, the Court upheld by a five-to-four majority the National Labor Relations Act, which regulated employer/worker relationships that "affected commerce." The act, bitterly opposed by the business community, gave workers the right to unionize and required collective bargaining in all industries that affected interstate commerce. Refusing to distinguish between commerce and manufacturing, the Court thus enunciated the **affectation doctrine,** ruling that labor practices at the manufacturing facility of a national corporation were subject to federal regulation because a strike could have an appreciable effect on interstate commerce. Local activities were within federal jurisdiction if they had "a close and substantial relation to interstate commerce." (*See* excerpts from NATIONAL LABOR RELATIONS Act in *Appendix C*.)

affectation doctrine Doctrine granting federal *jurisdiction* over local commercial activities if those activities have "a close and substantial relation to interstate commerce"

The Commerce Clause Today

In cases following *NLRB v. Jones & Laughlin,* the Court expanded on the affectation doctrine and gave Congress the far-reaching commerce powers that it enjoys today. Congress may regulate a local activity with merely a *possible* effect on interstate commerce, such as the marketing within one state of a local product that may compete with a product in interstate commerce. For example, in *United States v. Wrightwood Dairy Co.*, 315 U.S. 110 (1942), the Court held that federal milk regulations could be applied to milk produced and sold within a single state because the marketing of intrastate milk could adversely affect the marketing of milk on an interstate basis.

In such cases, the Court has essentially deferred to congressional evaluation of the relationship between an intrastate activity and interstate commerce. Thus, in ruling on the applicability of a federal law to a local activity, the Court tends to look to the *intent of Congress.* Commerce Clause cases now tend to be cases of statutory construction, not constitutional law.

Bacchus Imports, Ltd. v. Dias. The Court will also act to protect federal interests in regulating commerce in the absence of a specific federal statute. As we have seen, in the absence of an overriding, compelling state interest, the Court will strike down a state law that burdens or discriminates against interstate commerce. It is important to remember, however, that federal and state laws regulating commerce often coexist and that the Court avoids invalidating legislation whenever possible. For example, it recently upheld a state law protecting local corporations from hostile takeovers, finding that the state was preempted by neither a federal statute (the Williams Act) nor the federal commerce power (*CTS Corp. v. Dynamic Corp. of America*, No. 86-71 and 86-97).

In the case that follows, the Court balances the state's interest in achieving legitimate objectives against the burdens imposed on interstate commerce.

BACCHUS IMPORTS, LTD. v. DIAS
United States Supreme Court, 468 U.S. 263 (1984)

In 1939, the Hawaii Legislature enacted a 20-percent excise tax on wholesale liquor sales. This tax was to help defray the increased cost of governmental services necessitated by liquor consumption. However, in order to foster the growth of its liquor industry, the legislature created certain local exemptions from the tax on the production of fruit wine and okolehao, a type of Hawaiian brandy.

The plaintiff, Bacchus Imports, as a wholesaler is subject to this tax. Bacchus brought this action protesting the tax as a violation of the Commerce Clause, claiming that the exemption unfairly benefited local producers by not providing a corresponding benefit to out-of-state wholesalers. After losing in the initial proceeding, the plaintiff lost on two successive appeals to the Tax Appeals Court and the Hawaii Supreme Court. Plaintiff has finally appealed to the Supreme Court of the United States.

Justice White delivered the opinion of the Court.

. . . .

A cardinal rule of Commerce Clause jurisprudence is that (n)o State, consistent with the Commerce Clause, may "impose a tax which discriminates against interstate commerce. . . by providing a direct commercial advantage to local business." Despite the fact that the tax exemption here at issue seems clearly to discriminate on its face against interstate commerce by bestowing a commercial advantage on okolehao and pineapple wine, the State argues—and the Hawaii Supreme Court held—that there is no improper discrimination.

Much of the State's argument centers on its contention that okolehao and pineapple wine do not compete with the other products sold by the wholesalers. The State relies in part on statistics showing that for the years in question sales of okolehao and pineapple wine constituted well under one percent of the total liquor sales in Hawaii. It also relies on the statement by the Hawaii Supreme Court that "(w)e believe we can safely assume these products pose no competitive threat to other liquors produced elsewhere and consumed in Hawaii." . . . as well as the court's comment that it had "good reason to believe neither okolehao nor pineapple wine is produced elsewhere." However, neither the small volume of sales of exempted liquor nor the fact that the exempted liquors do not constitute a present "competitive threat" to other liquors is dispositive of the question whether competition exists between the locally produced beverages and foreign beverages; instead, they go only to the extent of such competition. It is well settled that "(w)e need not know unequal the tax is before concluding that it unconstitutionally discriminates."

The State's position that there is no competition is belied by its purported justification of the exemption in the first place. The legislature originally exempted the locally produced beverages in order to foster the local industries buy encouraging increased consumption of their product. Surely one way that the tax exemption might produce that result is that drinkers of other alcoholic beverages might give up or consume less of their customary drinks in favor of the exempted products because of the price differential that the exemption will permit. Similarly, young drinkers, such as the maturing young, might be attracted by the low prices of okolehao and pineapple wine. . . . (w)e are unwilling to conclude that no competition exists between the exempted and the non-exempted liquors.

The State contends that a more flexible approach, taking into account the practical effect and relative burden on commerce, must be employed in this case because (1) legitimate state objectives are credibly advanced, (2) there is no patent discrimination against interstate trade, (3) the effect on interstate commerce is incidental. . . . On the other hand, it acknowledges that where simple economic protectionism is effected by state legislation, a stricter rule of invalidity has been erected. . . .

A finding that state legislation constitutes "economic protectionism" may be made on the basis of either discriminatory purpose, . . . or discriminatory effect. . . . (In this case) we need not guess at the legislature's motivation, for it is undisputed that the purpose of the exemption was to aid Hawaiian industry. Likewise the effect of the exemption is clearly discriminatory, in that it applies only to locally produced beverages, even though it does not apply to all such products. Consequently, as long as there is some competition between the locally produced exempt products and non-exempt products from outside the State, there is a discriminatory effect.

No one disputes that a state may enact laws pursuant to its police powers that have the purpose and effect of encouraging domestic industry. However, the Commerce Clause stands as a limitation on the means by which a state can constitutionally seek to achieve that goal. One of the fundamental purposes of the clause "was to insure. . .against discriminating State legislation."

. . . .

. . .We observed that competition among the States for a share of interstate commerce is a central element of our free-trade policy but held that a State may not tax interstate transactions in order to favor local businesses over out-of-state businesses. Thus, the Commerce Clause limits the manner in which States may legitimately compete for interstate trade, for "in the process of competition no State may discriminatorily tax the products manufactured or the business operations performed in any other State." It is therefore apparent that the Hawaii Supreme Court erred in concluding that there was no improper discrimination against interstate commerce merely because the burden was borne by consumers in Hawaii.

The State attempts to put aside this Court's cases that have invalidated discriminatory state statutes enacted for protectionist purposes. . . . The State would distinguish these cases because they all involved attempts "to enhance thriving and substantial business enterprises at the expense of any foreign competitors." Hawaii's attempt, on the other hand, was "to subsidize nonexistent (pineapple wine) and financially troubled (okolehao) liquor industries peculiar to Hawaii." However, we perceive no principle of Commerce Clause jurisprudence supporting a distinction between thriving and struggling enterprises under these circumstances. . . In either event, the legislation constitutes "economic protectionism" in every sense of the phrase. It has long been the law that States may not "build up (their) domestic commerce by means of unequal and oppressive burdens upon the industry and business of other States." Were it otherwise, "the trade and business of the country (would be) at the mercy of local regulations, having for their object to secure exclusive benefits to the citizens and products of particular States." It was to prohibit such a "multiplication of preferential trade areas" that the Commerce Clause was adopted. Consequently, the propriety of economic protectionism may not be allowed to hinge upon the State's—or this Court's—characterization of the industry as either "thriving" or "struggling."

We also find unpersuasive the State's contention that there was no discriminatory intent on the part of the legislature because "the exemptions in question were not enacted to discriminate against foreign products, but rather, to promote a local industry. . . ." The determination of constitutionality does not depend on whether one focuses upon the benefited or the burdened party. A discrimination claim, by its nature, requires a comparison of the two classifications, and it could always be said that there was no intent to impose a burden on one party, but rather the intent was to confer a benefit on the other. Consequently, it is irrelevant to the Commerce Clause inquiry that the motivation of the legislature was the desire to aid the makers of the locally produced beverage rather than to harm out-of-state producers.

We therefore conclude that the Hawaii liquor tax exemption for okolehao and pineapple wine violated the Commerce Clause because it had both the purpose and effect of discriminating in favor of local products.

Case Questions:

1. What was the motive behind the exemption granted by the Hawaii legislature? What factor did this play in the Court's decision?

2. Would there be any effect on the Court's decision if the local producers within the exemption did not compete with any out-of-state concerns for its business?

3. Is there anything in the U.S. Constitution that prohibits economic protectionism?

■ *Concept Check 3-3   The Commerce Clause*

- Define the concept of *dual federalism*.
- How did the court's interpretation of the Commerce Clause change as a result of the Great Depression and the New Deal?
- Review the contemporary view of the Commerce Clause. Is there any local activity that Congress may not regulate?

■ CONSTITUTIONAL AMENDMENTS AND BUSINESS

There are two ways to propose constitutional amendments and two ways to ratify them. Amendments can be *proposed* by (1) a two-thirds majority in both the House and Senate, or (2) a national convention called by Congress at the request of two-thirds of the state legislatures. An amendment can be *ratified* (following proposal) by (1) three-fourths of the state legislatures or (2) state conventions in three-fourths of the states. The process, then, is complex; Figure 3-3 summarizes the four possible ways of amending the federal Constitution.

Four Routes to Constitutional Amendment

Proposal

Either:

Congress proposes an amendment by passing it by two-thirds vote in each house. It also states a time limit for completion of ratification (if it chooses to) and which of two possible ways of ratification will be used.

Or:

The legislatures of two-thirds of the states request a convention for proposing amendments, at which point Congress is obliged to call such a convention. The national convention then proposes an amendment for ratification by whichever of two routes Congress specified.

Ratification

Route One
Three-quarters of the state legislatures must vote favorably on it, but each can decide whether to require a simple majority vote or an unusual majority such as two-thirds in favor.

Route Two
Special conventions are called in each state, and three-quarters of them vote favorably on it.

Route Three
Three-quarters of the state legislature must vote favorably on it but each can decide on whether to require a simple majority vote or an unusual majority such as two-thirds in favor.

Route Four
Special conventions are called in each state and three-quarters of them vote favorably on it.

In practice, routes three and four have never been used; route two was used only for the Twentyfirst Amendment; thus the normal route has turned out to be route one. Note also that a state cannot legally rescind (or "take back") its ratification, but it can change its mind by voting to ratify after first rejecting an amendment. After ratification by whichever route, the amendment is automatically in force—"valid to all intents and purposes, as part of this Constitution," in the language of Article V.

FIGURE 3-3 Four Routes to Constitutional Amendment

Congress has recently required that ratification must occur within seven years. For example, the first time-limit for the Equal Rights Amendment prohibiting sexual discrimination fell on March 22, 1979. However, because the seven-year period had been written into a companion law and not into the amendment itself, Congress extended the ratification deadline, requiring a mere majority vote in both houses, to June 2, 1982. If the seven-year period is actually part of a specific amendment, a two-thirds majority of both houses of Congress would have had to approve it.

With the exception of the Twenty-first Amendment, passed in 1933, all amendments have been ratified by state legislatures rather than by state conventions. The provision allowing two-thirds of the state legislatures to ask Congress to call a second Constitutional Convention has never been exercised. However, a group called the National Taxpayers Union has had some success in pressuring state legislatures to request such a convention. Their goal is an amendment requiring the federal government to balance its budget. It is not clear whether a convention called to consider a balanced-budget amendment could consider other amendments as well. Some opponents of a constitutional convention fear that balanced-budget proposals could become an occasion for broad constitutional revisions.

In addition, it is not clear who would attend such a convention. Congress has considered various proposals, both to limit discussion at any convention to a specified subject and to limit a state's delegation to the number of its senators and representatives. Congress' authority to regulate a convention is as questionable as the scope and makeup of the Convention itself.

Including the first ten amendments, known as the Bill of Rights, the U.S. Constitution has been amended twenty-six times—the last amendment, passed in 1971, specifying the voting age as eighteen years. Some amendments, such as the Sixteenth Amendment (Income Tax, 1913) and the Eighteenth Amendment (Prohibition, 1933), have reflected changes in the role and powers of the federal government. However, the expansion of citizenship rights and of democratic values seems to be the major thread running through the history of the amendment process. In this section, we will discuss the Bill of Rights and four amendments that bear on the protection and expansion of citizenship rights: the First Amendment (which protects such rights as freedom of speech and assembly), the Fourth Amendment (which protects privacy and security against potential abuse of police power), the Fifth Amendment (which insures due process of law), and the Fourteenth Amendment (which not only extended citizenship rights, but also extended to the states the limitations placed on the federal government by the Bill of Rights).

The Bill of Rights

The first efforts to amend the Constitution began before it was even ratified. Anti-Federalists feared that the central government established by the Constitution would become tyrannical even without a general grant of police power. They successfully demanded the addition of provisions protecting individual rights, and the Bill of Rights, the first ten amendments to the Constitution, was adopted in 1791, shortly after its ratification.

The first eight amendments set forth specific limits on the power of the federal government to interfere with freedom of speech or religion, to arrest people or invade their homes without good cause, and to deprive them of due process of law or speedy public jury trials for criminal offenses. The Ninth Amendment simply declares that the rights enumerated in the Bill of Rights are not exclusive—that is, that people's rights are not limited to those specified in the first eight amendments. The Tenth Amendment states that all powers not constitutionally delegated to the federal government or expressly denied to the states "are reserved for the states respectively, or to the people."

Remember that the Bill of Rights was originally enacted as a limitation of *federal* power: It did not, and does not, apply to purely private actions by purely private citizens. Constitutional rights exist not between citizens, but between citizens and their government. For example, if private citizens break into your home, they have committed a burglary, and although they may be prosecuted, they have not violated your constitutional rights.

THE BILL OF RIGHTS AND THE STATES. The Bill of Rights did not apply to state governments until after passage of the Fourteenth Amendment, which prohibits the states from denying any person due process. In a series of cases, the Supreme Court has since held that the *Due Process Clause* (discussed below under the Fifth and Fourteenth Amendments) makes certain provisions of the Bill of Rights binding on the states. Thus, First Amendment rights of free speech, Fourth Amendment rights against unreasonable searches and seizures, and the Sixth Amendment right to jury trials in criminal cases also apply to the states. The Court has explicitly held only three provisions to be *inapplicable* to the states: the Second Amendment right to bear arms, the Fifth Amendment guarantee of a grand-jury indictment to initiate criminal proceedings, and the Seventh Amendment right to jury trials in civil cases.

The First Amendment

The First Amendment states that "Congress shall make no law respecting an establishment of religion, or prohibit the free exercise thereof; or abridging the freedom of speech, or of the press; or the right of people peaceably to assemble, and to petition the government for a redress of grievances." It protects our right to believe what we choose and to express our beliefs in churches and synagogues, at public meetings, in books and newspapers, on television and radio,[3] on the streets, and in other public places. However, First Amendment freedoms against government oppression in practice are not absolute: Speech can be prohibited if it consists merely of epithets aimed at provoking a fight (the "fighting-words" doctrine), if it offends community moral standards and lacks "redeeming social value" (obscenity is not considered protected speech), or if it poses an immediate "clear and present" danger to the national security. As a general rule, however, speech is *presumed* protected.

THE "FIRST FREEDOMS." The First Amendment freedoms are considered the "first freedoms" because they are vital to the political process: An open marketplace of ideas in which dissenting views are freely circulated is essential to an informed public, and an informed public is essential to a democracy. Thus, the Supreme Court has always accorded the most protection to speech that concerns social, economic, or political issues and opinions. Even the most unpopular political advocacy of illegal conduct would probably not be prohibited unless it was intended to, and likely would, incite an immediate criminal act.[4] *Commercial speech*, discussed more fully below under "UNPROTECTED SPEECH," is lower on the hierarchy of protected speech. Therefore, legislatures may curtail or ban deceptive advertising or the advertising of illegal activities.

prior restraint Principle, issuing from the First Amendment, whereby the courts encourage legislative and regulatory bodies to permit the expression of speech rather than to *restrain* it *prior* to expression

At the heart of the First Amendment are its procedural safeguards against the imposition on speech of **prior restraint**: That is, the courts encourage legislative and regulatory bodies to permit the expression of speech rather than to restrain it prior to expression or publication. The First Amendment, then, protects the *act* of speaking, not simply the *substance* of what is said. Thus, the government may not suppress an instance of allegedly unprotected speech, like obscenity, or speech that allegedly endangers the national security without first proving that the speech is either unprotected or clearly and presently dangerous. This principle, for example, prevented the federal government from enjoining publication of the Pentagon Papers in 1971 (*New York Times Co. v. U.S.*, 403 U.S. 713 [1971]).

UNPROTECTED SPEECH. The First Amendment also requires that laws against unprotected speech be narrowly drawn so as not to interfere with protected speech. The Court will thus invalidate laws using vague, value-laden terms to

---

[3]Because access to the airwaves is limited, Congress has some special power to regulate the electronic media. Stations are licensed, and the Fairness Doctrine—the familiar principle whereby a group with an opposing view may be entitled to reply to advocacy advertising in the broadcast media—regulates the airing of political opinions. There remains some disagreement, however, over whether the Fairness Doctrine violates the First Amendment.

[4]*Brandenburg v. Ohio*, 395 U.S. (1969). The clear-and-present-danger standard invoked by the Court to review allegedly subversive speech has evolved over the past sixty years. During the 1950s, the Court adopted a more expansive view of government power to suppress speech considered to undermine the national security. In some now discredited cases during the McCarthy era, the Court upheld the convictions of Communist Party organizers charged with advocating the overthrow of the U.S. government. These cases are beyond the scope of this text.

define the type of speech restricted. In 1974, for example, it struck down a statute prohibiting "contemptuous" treatment of the flag on these grounds (*Smith v. Gogeun*, 415 U.S. 566). (The question of flag-desecration statutes is the subject of the YOU DECIDE feature in this chapter.)

YOU DECIDE
Free Speech and Flag Burning

Attempts to restrict speech by law often provoke controversy. In 1989, the Supreme Court considered a First Amendment case that sparked a national debate about the appropriate limits of free speech as expressed in a political act: burning the American flag.

During the Republican National Convention in Dallas in 1984, Gregory Johnson participated in a political demonstration against Reagan-administration policies. As he chanted protests in front of Dallas City Hall, he soaked an American flag in kerosene and set it afire. Johnson was the only one of the approximately 100 demonstrators to be charged with a crime: He was subsequently convicted in a Texas court of desecrating a venerated object in violation of a state law. The Texas Court of Criminal Appeals, however, reversed the lower court's ruling, holding that the conviction was inconsistent with Johnson's First Amendment right to free speech. The state of Texas appealed to the Supreme Court, which ruled on the case in Texas v. Johnson, *1095 S. Ct. 2533 (1989).*

Although the First Amendment explicitly protects only "speech," the courts have long extended constitutional guar-

antees of free speech to certain kinds of "expressive conduct": They have held that acts intended to convey a particular message which will be readily understood by onlookers may be covered by the First Amendment. Burning the American flag may therefore be construed as a political message consistent with the meaning of "expressive conduct" and therefore subject to First Amendment protection.

In Texas v. Johnson, *the Supreme Court had to resolve a conflict between the individual's right to free speech and the state's obligation to preserve public order. Johnson maintained that his burning of the flag was a political protest protected by the First Amendment. The state of Texas claimed that his act was so offensive that it went beyond the protection of the First Amendment because it was likely to cause a breach of the peace; the state also argued that Johnson had violated a state law intended to preserve the flag's unique status as the symbol of our nationhood.*

Some states are considering the passage of flag-desecration statutes. Do you favor or oppose such laws? (For further discussion, see p. 98.)

The fact that speech may not, in general, be prohibited, does not mean that it may not be *regulated*. This is an important principle to remember in cases involving *commercial speech* (speech made for such purposes as commercial advertising). A legislature may regulate the time, place, and manner of speech as long as the regulations are *content-neutral*—that is, they cannot prohibit any *specific* message content. A particular kind of unpopular speech may not be singled out for special restrictions. For example, billboards may be regulated in the interests of highway safety and aesthetics, but the restrictions may not distinguish between commercial and noncommercial speech. It is the medium, not the message, that may be restricted.

FREEDOM OF THE PRESS.   One of the most cherished aspects of the First Amendment is freedom of the press. We learn of world events through newspapers, magazines, and books. What would happen if these major industries were censored? Should any restraints be placed on what appears in print? For many years, the Supreme Court would not offer protection to obscene or libelous statements. Today, however, even potentially libelous speech receives some protection. For example, in *New York Times Co. v. Sullivan*, 376 U.S. 254 (1964), the Supreme Court ruled that the defamation of public officials and public figures is protected unless it is done with "actual malice," which the Court defined as knowledge of the falsity of the remarks made or reckless disregard for whether they were true or false. The case of *New York Times Co. v. Sullivan* is the subject of the ORGANIZATIONAL PROFILE in this chapter.

In the *Masson v. New Yorker* case that follows, the Court ruled that if a reporter deliberately alters quotations attributed to a named individual in print, and if the misquoted individual is injured by the false report, then the alterations can constitute "actual malice" and fall outside the protection of the First Amendment.

MASSON v. NEW YORKER
111 S. Ct. 2419 (1991)

Janet Malcolm, a journalist with *The New Yorker*, conducted a series of in-person and telephone interviews with Jeffrey Masson, Projects Director of the Sigmund Freud Archives. Despite the fact that the sessions yielded more than 40 hours of taped interviews, certain statements that appeared in Malcolm's article as direct quotations cannot be found on the tapes. Among the statements included in the article are those quoting Masson as having said that both Kurt Eissler and Anna Freud, the two people responsible for Masson's hiring, considered him to be an "intellectual gigolo." The article has since been made into a book, *In the Freud Archives*, which paints a very unfavorable picture of Masson.

Masson, the plaintiff, brought this suit against the defendants, *The New Yorker* and Janet Malcolm, for libel on the basis that statements appearing in the article because direct quotations were published with knowledge that they differed from those actually uttered by Masson. Both the trial court and the Court of Appeals ruled in favor of the defendants. Masson now appeals to the Supreme Court of the United States.

Justice Kennedy delivered the opinion of the Court.

. . . .

The First Amendment limits California's libel law in various respects. When, as here, the plaintiff is a public figure, he cannot recover unless he proves by clear and convincing evidence that the defendant published the defamatory statement with actual malice, i.e., with "knowledge that it was false or with reckless disregard of whether it was false or not." *New York Times Co. v. Sullivan*. Mere negligence does not suffice. Rather, the plaintiff must show that the author "in fact entertained serious doubts as to the truth of his publication. . . ."

We have used the term actual malice as a shorthand to describe the First Amendment protections for speech injurious to reputation and we continue to do so here. . . .

The constitutional question we must consider here is whether, . . . the evidence suffices to show that the respondents acted with the requisite knowledge of falsity or reckless disregard as to truth or falsity. This inquiry requires us in turn to consider the concept of falsity; for we cannot discuss the standards for knowledge or reckless disregard without some understanding of the acts required for liability. . . .

In some sense, any alteration of a verbatim quotation is false. But writers and reporters by necessity alter what people say, at the very least to eliminate grammatical and syntactical infelicities. If every alteration constituted the falsity required to prove actual malice, the practice of journalism, which the First Amendment standard is designed to protect, would require a radical change, one inconsistent with our precedents and First Amendment principles. Petitioner concedes this absolute definition in the quotation context is too stringent, and acknowledges that "minor changes to correct for grammar or syntax" do not amount to falsity for purposes of proving actual malice. . . .

Petitioner argues that, excepting correction of grammar or syntax, publication of a quotation with knowledge that it does not contain the words the public figure used demonstrates actual malice. . . .

. . . .

We reject the idea that any alteration beyond correction of grammar or syntax by itself proves falsity in the sense relevant to determining actual malice under the First Amendment. . . .

. . . .

In all events, technical distinctions between correcting grammar and syntax and some greater level of alteration do not appear workable, for we can think of no method by which courts or juries would draw the line between cleaning up and other changes, except by reference to the meaning a statement conveys to a reasonable reader. To attempt narrow distinctions of this type would be an unnecessary departure from First Amendment principles of general applicability, and, just as important, a departure from the underlying purposes of the tort of libel as understood since the latter half of the 16th century. From then until now, the tort action for defamation has existed to redress injury to the plaintiff's reputation by a statement that is defamatory and false. . . .

. . . .

The common law of libel overlooks minor inaccuracies and concentrates on substantial truth. . . .

We conclude that a deliberate alteration of words uttered by a plaintiff does not equate with knowledge of falsity for purposes of New York Times Co. v. Sullivan. . .unless the alteration results in a material change in the meaning conveyed by the statement. The use of quotations to attribute words not in fact spoken bears in a most important way on that inquiry, but is not dispositive in every case.

Deliberate or reckless falsification that comprises actual malice turns upon words and punctuation only because words and punctuation express meaning. Meaning is the life of language. And, for the reasons we have given, quotations may be a devastating instrument for conveying false meaning. In the case under consideration, readers of In the Freud Archives may have found Malcolm's portrait of petitioner especially damning because so much of it appeared to be a self portrait, told by petitioner in his own words. And if the alterations of petitioner's words gave a different meaning to the statements, bearing upon their defamatory character, then the device of quotations might well be critical in finding the words actionable.

The Court of Appeals. . . .concluded that an altered quotation is protected so long as it is a "rational interpretation" of an actual statement. . . . Application of our protection for rational interpretation in this context finds no support in general principles of defamation law or in our First Amendment jurisprudence. . . .

. . .The record contains substantial additional evidence. . . .that Malcolm deliberately or recklessly altered the quotations.

. . .Malcolm contests petitioner's allegations, and only a trial on the merits will resolve the factual dispute. But at this stage, the evidence creates a jury question whether Malcolm published the statements with knowledge or reckless disregard of the alterations.

The Court of Appeals majority found it difficult to perceive how the "intellectual gigolo" quotation was defamatory, a determination not supported by any citation to California law, but only by the argument that the passage appears to be a report of Eissler's and Anna Freud's opinions of petitioner. We agree with the Court of Appeals that the most natural interpretation of this quotation is not an admission that petitioner considers himself an intellectual gigolo" but a statement that Eissler and Anna Freud considered him so. It does not follow, though, that the statement is harmless. Petitioner is entitled to argue that the passage should be analyzed as if Malcolm had reported falsely that Eissler had given this assessment (with the added level of complexity that the quotation purports to represent petitioner's understanding of Eissler's view). An admission that two well-respected senior colleagues considered one an "intellectual gigolo" could be as or more damaging than a similar self-appraisal. . . . To the extent that the Court of Appeals based its conclusion in the First Amendment, it was mistaken. . . .

. . . .

The judgment of the Court of Appeals is reversed, and the case is remanded for further proceedings consistent with this opinion.

Case Questions

1. What test does the Supreme Court use with regard to finding actual malice in the context of statements published as direct quotations but differing from the statements as originally uttered?

2. Is the decision consistent with the definition of actual malice given in the case?

3. Does the decision in *Masson v. New Yorker* now mean that every time a statement published as a direct quotation differs from what was actually stated it will constitute actual malice?

COMMERCIAL SPEECH. Commercial speech—that is, messages designed specifically to promote commerce—has only recently been brought under the aegis of the First Amendment. In 1942, in *Valentine v. Christensen*, 316 U.S. 52, the Supreme Court upheld a New York Sanitary Code provision prohibiting the distribution of "commercial and business advertising" on the city's streets because purely commercial advertising was not protected by the First Amendment. In 1951, in *Breard v. Alexander*, 341 U.S. 622, the Court upheld a prohibition on unsolicited door-to-door magazine sales: A sales pitch, the Court suggested, was not protected speech because it was aimed at generating profits, not ideas.

Bigelow v. Virginia. In *Bigelow v. Virginia*, 421 U.S. 809 (1975), the Court invalidated a state prohibition on advertising for abortion services, declaring that advertising a legal activity conveyed what might be valuable information to the public and could not summarily be prohibited. In 1976, in *Virginia State Board of Pharmacy v. Virginia Citizens Consumer Council*, 425 U.S. 748, the Court struck down a state law prohibiting pharmacists from advertising prices for prescription drugs: The court stressed that consumers had an interest in receiving information about drug prices (note that the First Amendment protects the listener as well as the speaker). In further observing that the message in this case was *truthful*, the Court also reaffirmed the state's power to prohibit *false* or *deceptive* advertising.

commercial speech *Protected speech consisting of messages made for economic or business purposes*

On March 29, 1960, The New York Times *ran a full-page advertisement soliciting money for civil-rights activists seeking to end racial segregation in the South. Entitled "Heed Their Rising Voices," it described incidents in which nonviolent student protesters in South Carolina and Montgomery, Alabama, had been "met by an unprecedented wave of terror." The ad also referred to an official campaign of "intimidation and violence" against the Reverend Dr. Martin Luther King, Jr., the leader of the civil-rights movement. Among the dozens of church and labor leaders and entertainers who endorsed the ad were Eleanor Roosevelt, Jackie Robinson, and twenty southern ministers.*

Referring to "southern violators"—implicitly meaning state and local governments—the ad mentioned no officials by name. Nevertheless, L. B. Sullivan, city commissioner of Montgomery, Alabama, sued the Times *for libel, as did the governor of Alabama and three other Montgomery city officials. Citing several factual errors in the ad and claiming that their professional reputations had been harmed, they*

asked for $3 million in damages. An Alabama court ruled in Sullivan's favor. Its decision was upheld by the state supreme court.

In 1964, in New York Times Co. v. Sullivan, 376 U.S. 254, the U.S. Supreme Court ruled that defamatory statements about public officials and public figures are constitutionally protected free speech unless they are made with "actual malice"—that is, either with prior knowledge that the remarks are false or with reckless disregard for whether or not they are false. Although it was a clear vindication of the Times, *the ruling was more important as a landmark decision broadening the constitutional protection of speech.*

In New York Times Co. v. Sullivan, the court upheld a newspaper's right to report freely on public figures involved in important national events. In the process of pursuing a recognized business interest, the Times *secured a major reinterpretation of the First Amendment guarantee of the public's right to a free and informed debate of political and social issues.*

The *Bigelow* case underscores the fact that restrictions on commercial speech need not be content-neutral: False advertising or advertising of an illegal activity may be prohibited. Protected commercial speech is not as protected as political speech, but the Court has set forth a fairly stringent standard for determining when it may be prohibited: The prohibition must be directly related to a substantial state interest, and it must be narrowly drawn so as to apply only to speech that it is necessary to prohibit. In the case that follows, the Court outlined a *four-part test* for protection of commercial speech. The case involved a state regulation banning advertising by a public utility promoting electrical use. In other words, why does a monopoly enterprise need to advertise?

CENTRAL HUDSON GAS & ELECTRIC CORPORATION v. PUBLIC SERVICE COMMISSION OF NEW YORK
United States Supreme Court, 447 U.S. 557 (1980)

In an administrative order, the New York State Public Service Commission prohibited all electrical utilities from engaging in promotional advertising. The Commission stated that promotional advertising could not be allowed during an energy shortage because such advertising is designed to encourage the purchase of utilities. The order, however, permitted all advertising not clearly intended to promote sales.

At trial, the plaintiff, Central Hudson, attacked the Commission's order as restrictive of its right to commercial speech as protected by the First and Fourteenth Amendments. Both the trial court and the New York Court of Appeals upheld the Commission's order. Central Hudson now appeals to the United States Supreme Court.

Mr. Justice Powell delivered the opinion of the Court.

. . . .

The Commission's order restricts only commercial speech, that is, expression related solely to the economic interests of the speaker and its audience. . . . The First Amendment as applied to the states through the Fourteenth Amendment, protects commercial speech from unwarranted governmental regulation. Commercial expression not only serves the economic interest of the speaker, but also assists consumers and furthers the societal interest in the fullest possible dissemination of the information. In applying the first Amendment to this area, we have rejected the "highly paternalistic" view that government has complete power to suppress or regulate commercial speech.

Nevertheless, our decisions have recognized "the

commonsense distinction between speech proposing a commercial transaction, which occurs in an area traditionally subject to government regulation and other varieties of speech."

The Constitution therefore accords a lesser protection to commercial speech than to other constitutionally guaranteed expression. The protection available for particular commercial expression turns on the nature both of the expression and of the governmental interests served by its regulation.

The First Amendment's concern for commercial speech is based on the informational function of advertising. Consequently, there can be no constitutional objection to the suppression of commercial messages that do not accurately inform the public about lawful activity. The government may ban forms of communication more likely to deceive the public than to inform it, . . . or commercial speech related to illegal activity.

If the communication is neither misleading nor related to unlawful activity, the government's activity is more circumscribed. The State must assert a substantial interest to be achieved by restrictions on commercial speech. Moreover, the regulatory technique must be in proportion to that interest. The limitation on expression must be designed carefully to achieve the State's goal.

. . . .

In commercial speech cases, a four part analysis has developed. At the outset, we must determine whether the expression is protected by the First Amendment. For commercial speech to come within that provision, it at least must concern lawful activity and not be misleading. Next, we ask whether the asserted governmental interest is substantial. If both inquiries yield positive answers, we must determine whether the regulation directly advances the governmental interest asserted, and whether it is not more extensive than necessary to serve that interest.

We now apply this four-step analysis for commercial speech to the Commission's arguments in support of its ban on promotional advertising.

. . .The New York Court of Appeals questioned whether Central Hudson's advertising is protected commercial speech. Because appellant holds a monopoly over the sale of electricity in its service area, the state court suggested that the Commission's order restricts no commercial speech of any worth. The court stated that advertising in a "noncompetitive market" could not improve the decisionmaking of consumers. . . .

This reasoning falls short of establishing that appellant's advertising is not commercial speech protected by the First Amendment. Monopoly over the supply of a product provides no protection from competition with substitutes for that product. Electric utilities compete with suppliers of fuel oil and natural gas in several markets, such as those for home heating and industrial power. . . . Each energy source continues to offer peculiar advantages and disadvantages that may influence consumer choice. For consumers in those competitive markets, advertising by utilities is just as valuable as advertising by unregulated firms.

. . . .

The Commission offers two justifications for the ban on promotional advertising. The first concerns energy conservation. . . . In view of our country's dependence on energy sources beyond our control, no one can doubt the importance of energy conservation. Plainly, therefore, the state interest asserted is substantial.

The critical factor lies in the provisions of the statute defining the Comptroller General's office relating to removability. Although the Comptroller General is nominated by the President. . . . and confirmed by the Senate, he is removable only at the initiative of Congress.

. . . .

. . .The statute permits (Congressional) removal for "inefficiency," "neglect of duty," or "malfeasance." These terms are very broad and, as interpreted by Congress, could sustain removal of a Comptroller General for any number of actual or perceived transgressions of the legislative will. . . .

. . . .

. . .In constitutional terms, the removal powers over the Comptroller General's office dictate that he will be subservient to Congress.

. . . .

Against this background, we see no escape from the conclusion that, because Congress had retained removal authority over the Comptroller General, he may not be entrusted with executive powers. The remaining question is whether the Comptroller General has been assigned such powers in the (Gramm-Rudman) Act of 1985.

Appellants suggest that the duties assigned to the Comptroller General in the Act are. . . . not. . . . "execution of the law" in a meaningful sense. On the contrary, we view these functions as plainly entailing execution of the law in constitutional terms. Interpreting a law enacted by Congress to implement the legislative mandate is the very essence of "execution" of the law. Under Section 251, the Comptroller General must exercise judgment concerning facts that affect the application of the Act. He must also interpret the provisions of the Act to determine precisely what budgetary calculations are required. Decisions of that kind are typically made by officers charged with executing a statute.

The executive nature of the Comptroller General's functions is revealed in Section 252(a) (3) which gives the Comptroller General the ultimate authority to determine the budget cuts to be made. . . .

Congress of course initially determined the content of the (Gramm-Rudman) Act; and undoubtedly the content of the Act determines the nature of the executive duty. However, . . . once Congress makes its choice in enacting legislation, its participation ends. Congress can thereafter control the execution of its enactment only indirectly—by passing new legislation. . . . By placing the responsibility for execution of the (Gramm-Rudman) Act in the hands of an officer who is subject to removal only by itself, Congress in effect has retained control over the execution of the Act and has intruded into the executive function. The Constitution does not permit such intrusion. . . .

No one can doubt that Congress and the President are confronted with fiscal and economic problems of unprecedented magnitude, but "the fact that a given law or procedure is efficient, convenient, and useful in facilitating functions of government, standing alone, will not save it if it is contrary to the Constitution. . . .

The Commission also argues that promotional advertising will aggravate inequities caused by the failure to base the utilities' rates on marginal cost. The State's concern that rates be fair and efficient represents a clear and substantial governmental interest.

Next, we focus on the relationship between the State's interests and the advertising ban. Under this criterion, the Commission's laudable concern over the equity and efficiency of appellant's rates does not provide an adequate reason for restricting protected speech. . . . The impact of promotional advertising on the equity of appellant's rates is highly speculative. Advertising to increase offpeak usage would have to increase peak usage, while other factors that directly affect the fairness and efficiency of appellant's rates remained constant. Such conditional and remote eventualities simply cannot justify silencing appellant's promotional advertising.

In contrast, the State's interest in energy conservation is directly advanced by the Commission order at issue here. There is an immediate connection between advertising and demand for electricity. . . .

We come finally to the critical inquiry in this case: whether the Commission's complete suppression of speech ordinarily protected by the First Amendment is no more extensive than necessary to further the State's interest in energy conservation. The Commission's order reaches all promotional advertising, regardless of the impact of the touted service on overall energy use. But the energy conservation rationale, as important as it is, cannot justify suppressing information about electric devices or services that would cause no net increase in total energy use. In addition, no showing has been made that a more limited restriction on the content of promotional advertising would not serve adequately the State's interests. . . .

The Commission's order prevents appellant from promoting electric services that would reduce energy use by diverting demand from less efficient sources, or that would consume roughly the same amount of energy as do alternative sources. In neither situation would the utility's advertising endanger conservation or mislead the public. To the extent that the Commission's order suppresses speech that in no way impairs the State's interest in energy conservation, the Commission's order violates the First and Fourteenth Amendments and must be invalidated. . . .

The Commission also has not demonstrated that its interest in conservation cannot be protected more adequately by more limited regulation of appellant's commercial expression. . . .

Accordingly, the judgment of the New York Court of Appeals is Reversed.

Case Questions:

1. What was the test used by the Supreme Court in determining whether the First Amendment had been violated in the commercial speech context?

2. What other methods could the Commission have used to achieve its avowed objective of conserving energy?

3. How was the Court able to conclude that Central Hudson's promotional advertising was protected by the First Amendment?

The Fourth Amendment

The Fourth Amendment guarantees the "right of the people to be secure in their persons, houses, papers, and effects, against unreasonable searches and seizures. . . ." It also provides that search warrants must be based on "probable cause, Supported by Oath or affirmation, and particularly describing the place to be searched, and the persons or things to be seized." In brief, the Fourth Amendment protects people (not places) from unreasonable intrusions by the government.

SEARCHES AND SEIZURES. These provisions insure individual privacy and the sanctity of the home, the workplace, and, to a lesser extent, the automobile and serve as important checks on exercises of government power. The government cannot arrest people or search their homes or possessions without some *objective reason* to believe that a crime has been or is about to be committed. This caveat is enforced by the **exclusionary rule,** a judicially created remedy for violating the Fourth Amendment that prohibits the use of—*excludes*—evidence obtained illegally through an unreasonable search. Searches and seizures are broadly construed to include (1) arresting people, (2) taking samples of their blood, (3) exploring their premises or automobiles, (4) inspecting their possessions, and (5) wiretapping their telephones.

exclusionary rule Judicial principle, issuing from the Fourth Amendment, prohibiting the use of evidence obtained through a legally unreasonable search

Generally, a *reasonable search* is one conducted pursuant to a warrant issued by a judge or magistrate and based on a showing of **probable cause**—that is, reasonable grounds for believing that evidence exists. Police officers, for example, must demonstrate that they have objective reasons for suspecting someone of engaging in criminal activity; they must describe the area to be searched and the objects that they are searching for. Warrantless searches are reasonable only under the following, limited circumstances:

probable cause Judicial principle, issuing from the Fourth Amendment, defining a *reasonable search* as one conducted on the belief that evidence exists

- Police may seize evidence in "plain view" (for which they need not search at all) without a warrant.
- Police may frisk a suspect under arrest and search his or her immediate surroundings without a warrant.
- People may consent to being searched without a warrant.
- "Exigent circumstances" requiring immediate action may justify a warrantless search and seizure. For example, police in "hot pursuit" of a subject may make an arrest and search of the surrounding area without a warrant.

It is impossible to list every "exigent circumstance" or every exceptional case in which a warrantless search may be considered reasonable. The courts thus determine *reasonableness* on a case-by-case basis. In making this determination, they must balance the individual's right to privacy with the government's need to prevent or prosecute an alleged crime.

THE FOURTH AMENDMENT AND BUSINESS. Like individuals, corporations are considered "persons" protected by the Fourth Amendment. Therefore, warrantless seizures of corporate records are prohibited, as are warrantless health, safety, or fire-code inspections. Remember, however, that the exceptions for warrantless searches outlined above also apply to cases involving corporations. Moreover, commercial property is not considered quite as sanctified, or protected against searches, as is a home. Thus, the courts are likely to apply a looser standard of reasonableness in reviewing searches of commercial property.

An important Fourth Amendment issue for business today is the legality of mandatory, random drug testing. A drug test may be considered a search and an unreasonable invasion of privacy. Mandatory, random testing of government workers at federal, state, and local levels is currently being challenged in the courts. Private employers, however, have broader power to conduct drug tests. Remember that the Bill of Rights, in general, is a limitation of state action. Although a handful of states have passed laws restricting drug testing, it is not yet clear whether the Fourth Amendment will eventually be construed to limit random, mandatory drug testing by private companies. (The issue of drug testing in the workplace is the subject of the YOU DECIDE feature in Chapter 13.)

The Fifth and Fourteenth Amendments: Due Process

The Fifth Amendment prohibits the federal government from denying any person "life, liberty, or property, without due process of law." The Fourteenth Amendment applies the same prohibition to the states and also prohibits them from denying any person "equal protection of the laws." Together, these two amendments assure all "persons" (including corporations) of due process and equal protection pursuant to both state and federal law. The concepts of *due* process and *equal protection* are the Constitution's most important safeguards against unfair or discriminatory laws and procedures. Basically, they provide all of us with an assurance that the government will not act in a manner that is unfair.

The Fifth and Fourteenth Amendments are designed to prevent the government from depriving people of certain basic rights—namely, life, liberty, or property—without **due process.** The intent is to guarantee fundamental fairness in the way laws are applied and in what they proscribe. Thus, the Supreme Court has enunciated principles of *procedural* and *substantive* due process. The Due Process Clause applies to all civil and criminal cases, and procedural due process is essential in insuring the integrity and fairness of criminal prosecutions. We will, however, consider only the meaning of due process in civil transactions. In addition to the Due Process Clauses of the Fifth and Fourteenth Amendments, we will discuss the Equal Protection Clause expressed in the Fourteenth Amendment and extended to the Fifth Amendment. Finally, we will examine Sunday-closing or so-called "blue" laws, which have withstood both due-process and equal-protection challenges.

due process Principle, issuing from the *Due Process Clauses* of the Fifth and Fourteenth Amendments, that refers to fundamental fairness in the ways laws are applied and in what they proscribe

PROCEDURAL DUE PROCESS. **Procedural due process** ensures that laws will be fairly enforced. In civil cases, this principle generally means that no one may be deprived of liberty or property without notice and a meaningful opportunity to be heard. The Court, therefore, must find that a property interest or an aspect of personal liberty is in jeopardy in order to apply procedural due process requirements to any given case. The definitions of "liberty" and "property" determine the scope of due-process guarantees.

procedural due process Principle under the *Due Process Clause* that laws will be fairly enforced

Liberty. *Liberty* has been defined to include not just freedom from physical constraints but some freedom of choice in life-style and personal beliefs. As the Court ruled in 1923:

> [Liberty] denotes not merely freedom from bodily restraint but also the right of the individual to contract, to engage in any of the common occupations of life, to acquire useful knowledge, to marry, establish a home and bring up children, to worship God according to the dictates of his own conscience and generally to enjoy those privileges long recognized . . . as essential to the orderly pursuit of happiness . . . (*Meyer v. Nebraska*, 262 U.S. 390 [1923]).

Property. The Court has had greater difficulty defining the *property* protected by due process. Pervasive government regulation of professions, public education, highway safety, and social-service programs has created government benefits and licenses that do not fit readily into a traditional definition of property. For example, while real estate and personal effects are obvious property, welfare benefits, drivers' licenses, or the services of a public utility are not so easily definable forms of property. The courts decide these questions on a case by case basis often deciding whether the particular claim is a mere expectation of a property claim or an **entitlement.** For example, public employees who hold their jobs at the will of the public employer have no legal entitlement to continued employment and may be dismissed without due process. The courts will thus look to the federal, state, or local law governing terms of employment to decide whether the employee has an entitlement and so a legal claim to continued employment or merely an expectation of employment.

entitlement *Property*, such as welfare benefits, resting on a continuing legal claim to interest in a benefit established by legal right

Finally, it is important to remember that due-process cases may involve public benefits: The Due Process Clause, like other provisions in the Bill of Rights and the Fourteenth Amendment, applies only to actions by the government, not private individuals or businesses.[5] Therefore, the jobs of public employees are sometimes protected by certain constitutional provisions.

The Due Process Clause also applies to a private taking of property through a public process. For example, a creditor who goes to court to recover a debt invokes the power of the state, and the right to a prejudgment seizure of property is strictly limited. A debtor's wages, for example, may not be garnished without the notice and a hearing required by due process.

SUBSTANTIVE DUE PROCESS. Substantive due process—a principle for evaluating *substantive laws* to determine whether they violate fundamental rights granted by the Due Process Clause—is a controversial concept that involves the judiciary in quasi-legislative policy decisions about the soundness, fairness, and necessity of a given law. In the early 1900s, the Court relied on the Due Process Clause to strike down progressive economic regulations. In *Lochner v. New York*, 198 U.S. 45 (1905), for example, the Court invalidated a New York State maximum-hours law applying to bakeries by declaring that it interfered unreasonably with the workers' "liberty" to contract and establish their own maximum-hour rules. The principles handed down in *Lochner* have been criticized for ignoring the unequal bargaining positions of employers and employees and, more importantly, for substituting its judgment for the judgment of a legislature in evaluating the public need for a regulated workplace. (The *Lochner* decision has in fact been discredited as both a matter of law and public policy.)

Today, maximum-hour laws are considered legitimate exercises of both the state's police power and the federal commerce power. Economic regulations that do not infringe upon fundamental rights need only be reasonably related to a legitimate government purpose. This position reflects a permissive standard of review that requires the Court to defer to legislatures in formulating social and economic policies. The Supreme Court enunciated this "rational-relation" test in *Williamson v. Lee Optical of Oklahoma, Inc.* 348 U.S. 483 (1955):

> The day is gone when this Court uses the Due Process Clause of the Fourteenth Amendment to strike down state laws, regulatory of business and industrial conditions, because they may be unwise, improvident, or out of harmony with a particular school of thought. It is enough that there is an evil at hand for correction and that it *might be thought* that the particular legislative measure was a rational way to correct it.

Substantive due process, however, is invoked often today in cases involving laws that allegedly violate fundamental rights. In order to protect freedom of speech, freedom of religion, and other individual constitutional rights, and to prevent racial discrimination, courts will scrutinize the content of a law and balance the individual right with the state interest at issue: When a fundamental right is involved, the state must demonstrate that the law is necessary to serve a compelling state interest.

EQUAL PROTECTION. The Fourteenth Amendment's Equal Protection Clause says that no state shall "deny to any person within its jurisdiction the equal protection of the laws." **Equal protection** has thus developed into the principle that under like circumstances, individuals will receive the same benefits—and bear the same responsibilities—of the law. Originally applied to the states, "equal

substantive due process Principle for evaluating the soundness, fairness, or necessity of a law and whether it violates a fundamental right granted by the *Due Process Clause*

equal protection Principle, issuing from the Fourteenth Amendment's *Equal Protection Clause*, holding that under like circumstances, individuals will receive the same benefits and bear the same responsibilities under the law

---

[5]The Constitution may apply to private entities that fulfill public functions or to private transactions involving a governmental body.

protection" has since been extended to the federal government by means of the Fifth Amendment's Due Process Clause. Because both amendments guarantee "due process of law" and because the Fourteenth Amendment also mentions equal protection, the argument has successfully been made that Fifth Amendment due process includes equal protection. The courts may apply one of two tests to determine if either the Due Process or Equal Protection Clause has been violated: the *reasonable or rational relation test* and *the strict scrutiny test.*

The Reasonable or Rational Relation Test. Equal protection does not mean that everyone is entitled to precisely the same treatment. It does mean, however, that under the **reasonable** or **rational relation test,** everyone in the same *class* or *category* must be treated equally and that legislative classifications must be reasonably related to a legitimate government interest. As we have seen, a law that interferes with a fundamental right of all citizens will be tested by courts under the Due Process Clause. If a law interferes with the fundamental right of even one group of citizens, it will be tested under the Equal Protection Clause to determine whether the grouping or classification under scrutiny is legitimate. However, the burden of proof falls on those attacking the law in question. In addition, only those laws that are *designed* to discriminate are struck down.

For instance, an Alaska statute that discriminated against newcomers to the state when it distributed its oil fund-surplus revenues was overturned. However, veterans can be singled out for preference by government personnel offices at the expense of women applying for public jobs. The burden on women is considered incidental to a reasonable law that provides benefits for veterans. A zoning law that effectively prevents poor people from moving into certain neighborhoods is legal until its stated purpose is proved to camouflage discriminatory intent. Such laws, for example, require houses to be built on large plots of land, thus raising their cost (*see* Chapter 20). The intention to discriminate cannot be proved unless a state or community has a history of discrimination.

The Strict Scrutiny Test. The **strict scrutiny test** is invoked when fundamental rights or "suspect" classifications are involved. Because the state must assume the burden of proof, this test is much more difficult to satisfy: The state must prove that its interest in the law is compelling and that no other action will serve that interest.

But what are "suspect" classifications? In *San Antonio School District v. Rodriquez*, 411 U.S. 1 (1973), the Court declared that groups that have historically suffered discrimination, political powerlessness, or other handicaps deserve special judicial protection. Suspect classes are those based on race, national origin, or ethnic origin. Religion is probably another suspect basis for discrimination, but this argument has yet to be tested in the Supreme Court. Poverty is not a suspect classification. Laws classifying citizens by sex have been subject to something less than strict scrutiny. The Court has staked out a middle ground in cases involving sex discrimination. Essentially, this means that sex-based classifications are not quite as suspect as racial ones. (Employment discrimination by sex is discussed in Chapter 15.)

With one notable exception, legal classifications have not been upheld under the strict scrutiny test: In *Korematsu v. United States*, 323 U.S. 214 (1944), the Court used the language of strict scrutiny to sanction the government's forced evacuation of Japanese-American citizens from parts of the West Coast during World War II. Ten years later, strict scrutiny was used in the case of *Brown v. Board of Education*, 347 U.S. 483 (1954) to order the desegregation of the public

reasonable or **rational relation test** Judicial test to insure *equal protection* by requiring that legislative classifications of individuals be *reasonably related* to a legitimate government interest

strict scrutiny test Judicial test to insure *equal protection* by requiring that states justify legislative classifications by demonstrating that no other action will serve the state's compelling interest

Strict Scrutiny and Segregation Thurgood Marshall (*see* the PER-
SONAL PROFILE on p. 96), who was later to become the first black
Supreme Court justice, was the chief attorney for the NAACP-
sponsored battle to overturn the legal bases of racial segregation
in public education. Here, Marshall is flanked by fellow lawyers
George E. C. Hayes (left) and James M. Nabrit upon hearing
news of the Court's decision in *Brown v. Board of Education,* in
which the principle of "strict scrutiny" was applied to rule on legislation affecting fundamental rights like the provisions of the Bill
of Rights and suspect classifications like race and national origin.
The Court subsequently used strict scrutiny to invalidate segregated public beaches, parks, buses, and courtroom seating, but by
the early 1970s, Marshall, then himself on the Court, had begun
to question what he believed to be too rigid an approach to equal-
protection review. Marshall objected to the premise that because
the broad variety of equal-protection cases was presumed to fall
into one of two categories, such cases called for review based on
either rational relation or strict scrutiny tests. Instead, he argued
for what has since been labeled *mid-level scrutiny*: In *San Antonio
Independent School District v. Rodriguez,* he proposed variable degrees of scrutiny based on such factors as the constitutional and
societal importance of "the interests adversely affected" and the
"invidiousness" of a particular classification.

schools. This landmark holding was later applied to a broad range of public facilities, overturning Jim Crow laws—antiblack discrimination measures—
throughout the country. The *Brown* case and the career of Supreme Court Associate Justice Thurgood Marshall are surveyed in the PERSONAL PROFILE box in
this chapter.

BLUE LAWS. The rational relation test has been used to judge state statutes
which require businesses to close or which prohibit certain business activities

Thurgood Marshall, the great-grandson of slaves, was born in 1908 in Baltimore, then a strictly segregated city. After graduating from Lincoln College in Pennsylvania, he was prevented from enrolling in the University of Maryland Law School, which excluded blacks. Marshall went on to graduate first in his class at the all-black Howard University Law School.

Marshall's personal experience of poverty and discrimination decisively shaped his ideas about the law and his own career: For more than fifty years, he championed civil rights and individual liberties in cases that profoundly changed American society. As a young lawyer for the Baltimore branch of the National Association for the Advancement of Colored People (NAACP), Marshall helped force the integration of the same University of Maryland law school that had refused to admit him. In 1940, he became director of the Legal Defense Fund at the NAACP. During the next twenty years, he initiated civil-rights cases throughout the South and won twenty-nine of the thirty-two cases that he argued before the Supreme Court.

Among his victories was Brown v. Board of Education, *the landmark decision that integrated public schools and paved the way for other minorities and women to claim their civil rights in the courts. In 1951, Linda Brown, the daughter of a black minister in Kansas, tried to enroll in an all-white school in Topeka. Like many other states, Kansas maintained school systems segregated by race, the legality of which had been upheld by the Supreme Court in* Plessy v. Ferguson (1896). *The Brown family, supported by the NAACP and joining with students from other segregated states, appealed the school board's refusal to admit Linda.*

The Court specifically put aside the question of educa-

tional resources and assumed (although the assumption had no basis in fact) that black school systems had the same financial and educational resources as white school systems. Noting the different facts and local conditions concerning the various plaintiffs, the Supreme Court addressed one central issue: the constitutionality of the "separate-but-equal" doctrine. Marshall, arguing the case for the NAACP, maintained that racial separation was by its very nature unequal and discriminatory. Noting that sound education is essential both to a healthy democracy and to individual economic success, the Court judged that segregated schools stigmatized blacks and made them feel inferior to the rest of society. The Court unanimously held that race-based school systems violated the Equal Protection Clause of the Fourteenth Amendment, ruling that "separate educational facilities are inherently unequal."

In 1961, President John F. Kennedy appointed Marshall to the Federal Appeals Court. He became President Lyndon Johnson's solicitor general four years later. In 1967, Marshall became the first black ever to be named to the Supreme Court. Joining a predominantly liberal court, Marshall influenced decisions on cases involving civil rights, free speech, and the rights of the accused; he was instrumental in the decision legalizing abortion in Roe v. Wade (1973). *As a succession of conservative Republican appointees left him in a shrinking liberal minority, he continued to argue powerfully for the court's role as a "protector of the powerless" until his retirement in July of 1991. Harvard Law School Professor Laurence Tribe has said of Marshall, "It is hard to think of another lawyer in the twentieth century who has played a more important role."*

---

blue laws (or Sunday-closing laws) Statutes requiring businesses to close or prohibiting certain business activities on Sundays

on Sundays. These so-called **blue laws** have sustained three different constitutional challenges based on due process, freedom of religion, and equal protection, respectively. The *substantive-due-process challenge* argues that the Constitution denies state governments the power to regulate business hours. The *freedom-of-religion challenge* charges that blue laws establish a government-enforced holy day. The *equal-protection challenge* contends that many exemptions in state laws allow some businesses to remain open while forcing others to close.

All three challenges were turned back in *McGowan v. Maryland*, 366 U.S. 420 (1961), in which the Court held that state police powers include the authority to create a common day of rest by dictating business hours. Although Sunday-closing laws have a long history of promoting religion, the Court asserted that modern statutes do not have a primarily religious purpose. Rather, it claimed, they provide for a common day of rest, recreation, and family togetherness—which just happens to be Sunday, the Christian day of rest. This change of rationales is apparent in the fact that Sunday-closing laws now usually exempt businesses offering recreation (movie houses, restaurants, and the like). As it happens, the Maryland statute that the Court upheld contained many exemptions that the Court allowed to stand.

States work hard to adapt blue laws to our needs—although not always as hard as the Massachusetts legislators who came up with fifty exemptions, including permission to open stores on Sundays between Thanksgiving and Christmas. According to the Massachusetts statute, one common purpose of blue laws is to "preserve a diverse mix of small and large businesses." Thus, the rationale behind requiring most businesses to close Sundays is to counteract the competitive disadvantages of family-run stores. For example, many of these laws require big stores to close but allow small stores to remain open to enjoy some of the big stores' business.

A number of state courts have overturned various blue-law exemptions as unconstitutional. The Supreme Court of Louisiana considered the issue in 1982.

HARRY'S HARDWARE, INC. v. PARSONS

Louisiana Supreme Court, 410 So. 2d 735 (1982)

The Louisiana State Legislature enacted a four-section Sunday Closing Law intended to regulate the conduct of business on Sundays. While Section 191 of the Closing Law mandated a general prohibition on Sunday business, Section 192 made several exceptions, allowing certain types of businesses, such as drug stores, grocery stores, and hotels, to remain open on Sunday.

The plaintiff, Harry's Hardware, brought suit in the trial court seeking a permanent injunction against Parsons, the Superintendent of the New Orleans Police Department, to prevent enforcement of the Closing Law. The trial court denied the permanent injunction. The plaintiff then appealed to the Louisiana Appeals Court. The Appeals court found for the plaintiff and ordered the trial court to grant the permanent injunction. The issue is now in the Louisiana Supreme Court.

Blanche, Justice.

. . . .

It is undisputed that Sunday Closing Laws are not per se unconstitutional. State legislatures within their general police powers may enact legislation setting aside a uniform day of rest and regulating or restricting sales on that day. The ultimate constitutionality of such a statute can only be determined by an examination of its particular provisions. A closing law may not create arbitrary and unreasonable business classifications which have no bearing on the public health and welfare considerations that prompted its enactment.

In both lower courts the plaintiff contended that (Section 192 of the Closing Law) creates an arbitrary and unreasonable classification. There is no doubt that drug and grocery stores are treated differently from hardware stores under the law. Drug stores and grocery stores (as public and private markets) may remain open on Sunday, while hardware stores must be closed. Moreover, those drug and grocery stores may sell any item of their inventory not expressly prohibited from sale on Sunday by (Section 194 of the Closing Law).

According to the plaintiff, there is no rational reason for the differing treatment. A majority of the non-food and non-drug items sold on Sundays by the drug and gorcery stores are available for sale in plaintiff's hardware stores. The court of appeal found merit in this argument, and declared the Sunday Closing Law unconstitutional. . . .

We cannot agree that any discrimination inherent in the Closing Law is of such an unreasonable nature as to render the statute constitutionally infirm. Not every discrimination promulgated by statute is unconstitutional. The constitutional safeguard is offended only if the discriminatory classification rests on grounds wholly irrelevant to the achievement of the State's objective.

. . . .

The statement of legislative purpose in (Section 194 of the Closing Law) expresses a twofold objective: promotion of the health, recreation, and welfare of the citizens of this state, and prevention of unfair competition among persons, firms, or businesses. To this end, the law provides for a forced day of rest. . . .

The exemptions created by the statute are those that the legislature deemed necessary to safely provide for the welfare of the public while mandating a forced closing of most businesses. Drug stores and public markets are exempted to allow the sale of food and medicine on Sunday. . . . The exemptions for theatres, book stores, and art galleries are consistent with the intent to provide a day of rest and recreation. Hotels are exempted to provide a place of residence for out-of-town visitors.

Each of the exemptions provided by the Sunday Closing Law is rationally related to the state's objective in enacting such a statute. The discrimination suffered by the plaintiff's hardware stores is a by-product of a rational legislative scheme whereby the leisure and recreation of the populace without concomitant deprivation of access to essentials such as food and medicine. This discrimination does not become invidious merely because those drug and grocery stores which are allowed to remain open may also sell non-food and non-drug items.

. . . .

. . . It is a legislative prerogative to ascertain which stores should and should not be open. That prerogative has not been exercised arbitrarily or unreasonably in this case.

For the foregoing reasons, the decision of the court of appeal is reversed and the injunction prohibiting the enforcement of (the Sunday Closing Law) is hereby vacated.

Case Questions

1. If it is clear that the Sunday Closing Law discriminated against hardware stores, why wasn't it found unconstitutional?

2. What reasons might there be for exempting only certain types of businesses?

3. Is there a greater public interest in allowing a drugstore to operate on Sunday, while denying the same privilege to a hardware store?

■ Concept Check 3-4   Constitutional Amendments and Business

- Explain the ways that one can amend the U.S. Constitution.
- Explore the arguments for and against regulating *commercial speech*.
- Contrast *procedural due process* and *substantive due process*.

YOU DECIDE: ANSWER/DISCUSSION
Free Speech and Flag Burning

The Supreme Court ruled in Texas v. Johnson *that Johnson's act was political protest protected by the First Amendment. Justice William Brennan noted in the majority opinion that no breach of the peace occurred or threatened to occur in Dallas. The Court held that the state could not distinguish between verbal and nonverbal conduct toward the flag: Just as it could not prohibit spoken or written words critical of the flag, it could not prohibit "expressive conduct," no matter how offensive that conduct might be. The Court's historical record of First Amendment decisions, Brennan wrote, having established that "the Government may not prohibit expression simply because it disagrees with its message, is not dependent on the particular mode in which one chooses to express an idea."*

The Court's ruling, however, was not the last word on flag burning. The deep disagreements among Americans on this issue were reflected on the Supreme Court itself: Three justices vigorously dissented from the majority opinion. Chief Justice William Rehnquist, writing for the minority, stated that the flag's uniqueness as a national symbol "justifies a governmental prohibition against flag burning." He denied that Johnson's act was the expression of a political

idea, calling flag burning "the equivalent of an inarticulate grunt or roar" which was gravely offensive to many people and which might well cause a breach of the peace. Citizens denied the right to burn the flag could express their disagreement with national policy in a variety of other ways. President Bush agreed and proposed a constitutional amendment allowing the states to prohibit desecration of the American flag.

Democracy relies on an electorate informed by the free exchange of political, religious, and other ideas and capable of holding the government to account. The Supreme Court has acknowledged the primary importance of a free flow of political ideas and, where rights are in conflict, has traditionally given preference to First Amendment rights, even where the protected speech is offensive. Justice Oliver Wendell Holmes, for example, defended the principle of "freedom for the thought we hate," and those who wish to prohibit the expression of ideas that they find offensive or dangerous are opening a complex debate. Among the questions they must answer are: What does "offensive" mean? Dangerous to whom? And who should decide where the law draws the line?

SUMMARY

- The U.S. Supreme Court is the final interpreter of the U.S. Constitution, which provides for a *legislature* to make laws, an *executive* to carry them out, and a *judiciary* to interpret them. This division of powers, with built-in *checks and balances*, was intended to prevent the new central government from consolidating dictatorial powers.

- Under the *Supremacy Clause,* federal law is supreme over state law in all areas of federal jurisdiction. Federal jurisdiction has steadily expanded since 1789. The Tenth Amendment reserves for the states and people any power not given to the federal government, but the Constitution stretches the government's reach with a flexible grant of *implied powers.* Although Congress lacks the general *police power* granted to the states, it has often substituted its power to regulate commerce.

- *Judicial review*—that is, the Supreme Court's power to declare any law unconstitutional—is a creation of *case law,* with a sound basis in the logic of the Constitution. Judicial restraint counsels judges to avoid "unnecessary lawmaking" while meeting the nation's changing needs. The historical development of the *commerce power* is a good example of how judicial interpretations change over time.

- The *Bill of Rights* (the first ten amendments to the Constitution) and the Fourteenth Amendment limit federal and state power to restrict individual rights. The First Amendment guarantees *freedom of speech and expression.* Although *political speech* is the most valued form of expression, *commercial speech* that is truthful and describes a legal activity is also protected. The Fourth Amendment protects individuals and businesses against *unreasonable searches and seizures.*

- The Fifth and Fourteenth Amendments guarantee *due process* and *equal protection* of law in both state and federal jurisdictions. Due process means fundamental fairness in the way laws are applied and in what they proscribe. *Procedural due process* insures that no one will be deprived of liberty or property without notice and a hearing. *Substantive due process* refers to the fairness and wisdom of a law. It ensures that laws do not interfere with certain basic rights unless justified by a significant government interest.

- The *Equal Protection Clause* insures against discriminatory laws that single out special groups of individuals for special burdens or benefits. Certain legislative classifications—such as those based upon race, ethnicity, or religious affiliation—are considered "suspect" by the Court and trigger a strict standard of judicial review similar to the standard used in substantive due process cases involving fundamental rights.

QUESTIONS AND PROBLEMS

CASE PROBLEMS

1. Becoming increasingly concerned about the political and religious violence in the Middle East, the owner of a hotel near an airport decides not to permit Moslems to stay at the hotel. Abdul Ramallah is turned away from the hotel after the owner learns of his religion by reading the religious preference stated on the hotel registration card. Abdul frequently travels and needs to stay close by the airport. He brings an action to enjoin the hotel owner from barring him from the hotel based on his religion. Will Abdul be successful? [*Heart of Atlanta Motel v. United States,* 379 U.S. 241 (1964)]

2. In order to prevent fraud, the state of Scarborough passes a law requiring that anyone wishing to solicit donations at the Scarborough Fair do so from a booth. Members of a local religious sect are arrested after approaching fairgoers and soliciting donations on the fairgrounds. They argue that it is a requirement of their religion to approach those who do not belong to the religion, tell them about the religion, and seek donations. Therefore, they argue, their arrest for practicing their religion was unconstitutional because the First Amendment gives them the right to freedom of religion. Are they correct? Explain. [*International Society for Krishna Consciousness, Inc., v. Barber,* 650 F. 2d 430 (1981)]

3. A law was passed in Illinois whereby the statutory period for a child to bring suit to determine parentage was longer than the time for a putative or alleged father to claim his paternity. Which test will the court use in determining if the adult's right to equal protection is violated by the law? Explain. [*Majidi v. Palmer,* 530 NE 2d (1988)]

4. Jennifer Greene applies for a job with the state government. The state has an absolute lifetime preference for veterans. Therefore, the state law mandates that all veterans who qualify for state civil service positions must be considered for appointment ahead of any qualifying nonveterans. The preference operates overwhelmingly to the advantage of males. Since Ms. Greene is not a veteran, she brings an action alleging that the state's preference operates to exclude women from consideration for the state's best civil service jobs and, therefore, unconstitutionally denies women the equal protection of the laws. Is she correct? [*Personnel Administrator of Massachusetts v. Feeney*, 442 U.S. 256 (1979)]

5. A small city refused to allow low-income multifamily dwellings to be constructed within its borders. John Robbins, a member of a minority, brings suit. He alleges that the city's regulation discriminates against minorities, thereby denying them equal protection, because most of those who are low-income and will live in the disputed units are minorities who will have to move out of the city because of the regulation. Is this sufficient for the court to analyze the claim using the strict scrutiny test? [*Village of Arlington Heights v. Metropolitan Development Corp.*, 429 U.S. 252 (1977)]

6. Pat Scanlon, a maker of handwoven baskets, becomes well known around the state for his baskets, and soon receives requests from out of state. State law prohibits any product made of once-live vegetation from being sent out of state without meeting expensive registration and inspection requirements. Since the baskets are made out of sweetgrass, palm, grape vine, hemp, and pine straw, Pat Scanlon is subject to the state law. He challenges the law as unconstitutional primarily through his assertion that the state did not have the power to pass the legislation because the area is preempted by the federal government. In support of this position, he points to the "Once-Live Vegetation Shipment Act" passed by the federal legislature under the Commerce Clause. That act merely requires that the shipping package clearly states that the goods contain once-live vegetation. In the statute, Congress did not state whether it was preempting the area of once-live vegetation. Assess the validity of Mr. Scanlon's position. [*New York State Dept. of Social Services v. Dublino*, 413 U.S. 405 (1973)]

7. If Patricia Haney's parents take her motorcycle and sell it, has she been deprived of her constitutional rights?

8. The Employee Polygraph Protection Act is a federal law passed in 1988. The Act prohibits employers from conducting polygraph examinations on all applicants, and most employees, with just a few exceptions:
—local, state, and federal employees
—industries with national defense or security contracts
—business with nuclear power-related contracts with the Department of Energy.
Private businesses may use polygraphs under certain conditions: for private security personnel, when hiring persons with access to drugs, and during investigations of economic injury or loss by the employer.
State X would like to pass a law to allow for polygraphs to be administered to anyone applying for a teaching position. State Y would like to ban all polygraphs in all situations even where permitted by the Federal Act. Does the Preemption Doctrine apply in either scenario? Discuss.

9. During the Republican National Convention in Dallas in 1984, Gregory Johnson participated in a political demonstration in which he took an American flag, doused it with kerosene, and set it on fire. Johnson was arrested and charged with the desecration of a venerated object in violation of the Texas Penal Code and sentenced to one year in prison and fined $2,000. In 1988 the Supreme Court overturned his conviction. What was the Constitutional basis? [*Texas v. Johnson*, 109 S. Ct. 2533 (1989)]

10. Jane Price, who is unmarried, discovers that she is two months pregnant. She calls WeCare Municipal Hospital to make an appointment to have an abortion, but is told that WeCare, a publicly operated municipal hospital, does not perform elective abortions. The order not to perform elective abortions came from the hospital's director and board of trustees. She sues WeCare, alleging violation of her constitutional rights. Will the court agree? [*Doe v Hale Hospital*, 369 F. Supp. 970 (D.C. Mass. 1974)]

4

THE COURT SYSTEM

The United States is a litigious country, with some 140 lawyers for every 100,000 people. Even in our society, however, although litigation is often a first resort, few people would claim that the courts are capable of mediating every conflict, and most differ about which conflicts they should address. Should judges decide profound personal questions about procreation or sexual preferences? Should they decide social policies about integration in schools and the workplace? When prompted by such issues as these, discussions about the nature and function of law can trigger heated debates.

In this chapter, we will discuss the structure of the federal and state judicial systems and the kinds of cases that they can and should decide. We also will review the kinds of remedies available in civil cases As we will see, the judicial process is an *adversarial process* that operates on a case-by-case basis: In other words, our system allocates rights and responsibilities in specific instances according to federal and state *constitutions, statutes,* and *case law* (*see* Chapter 1). In doing so, that system regulates social and economic behavior, helps to order our personal and business relationships, and shapes the way our country does business.

■ WHICH CASES SHOULD THE COURTS ADDRESS?

Courts *react* to resolve the specific disputes brought before them: Unlike legislatures, they neither take the initiative in addressing general issues confronting society nor formulate general public policies. In the United States, the concept of **adjudication**—the process of determining the nature of a controversy and making a judgment about it—as an ad-hoc, adversarial process is rooted in the Constitution: Article III limits the federal judicial power to deciding cases and controversies. Thus, only *cases* and *controversies* are "justiciable." Because "justiciability" is largely a matter of case law (*see* Chapter 1), it is a somewhat

adjudication The process of determining the nature of a *case* or *controversy* and making a judgment about it

fluid concept that changes, sometimes subtly, over time. The Supreme Court itself has described justiciability as a "concept of uncertain meaning and scope."[1]

The basic question of adjudication—the question of which cases courts should address—thus involves two closely related but distinct principles: *jurisdiction*, which refers to the power or authority of a particular court to hear a particular case, and *justiciability*, which refers to the criteria by which a court may determine the applicability of its jurisdiction to a dispute. We will first define *jurisdiction* and some of the principles that the courts have applied in both exercising and restraining it; we will then discuss in some detail the basic standards that the courts have used to determine justiciability.

Jurisdiction and the Doctrine of Judicial Restraint

jurisdiction The authority of a court, with discretionary exercises of *judicial restraint*, to hear and decide a case; court authority over both the *subject matter* and *parties* involved in a case

In order to hear a case, a court must satisfy two jurisdictional requirements: It must have jurisdiction over the *subject matter* of the case and over the *parties*—individuals or organizations—against whom a suit is brought. **Jurisdiction**, then, refers to the complex relationship between the courts and the parties involved in the cases that courts decide. In order to understand that relationship more fully, we need to introduce three important legal concepts: the development and scope of *long-arm statutes*, the principle of *diversity of citizenship*, and the concept of *venue*.

long-arm statute The legislated authority of a state court to exercise *jurisdiction* over defendants who are cited in one state but who are citizens or residents of another (*see also* Chapter 5)

LONG-ARM STATUTES. **Long-arm statutes** permit a state court to exercise jurisdiction over defendants who are citizens or residents of another state. For example, if you are a Texas resident injured by a car driven by a New Jersey driver who then returns to New Jersey, you need not go to New Jersey to file suit: An out-of-state defendant can be subjected to the jurisdiction of a court in the state where the civil wrong is alleged to have occurred. The plaintiff, however, must show that the action in question is specified by a given state's long-arm statute, and defendants' constitutional rights to due process cannot be violated by the requirement that they defend themselves in plaintiffs' jurisdictions.

diversity of citizenship Principle whereby *federal* district courts may exercise *jurisdiction* over *state* law when (1) the parties to the controversy are citizens of different states and (2) the contested amount exceeds $50,000

DIVERSITY OF CITIZENSHIP. **Diversity of citizenship** refers to the jurisdiction of *federal* district courts over *state* courts when two criteria are met: (1) the parties involved are citizens of different states and (2) the contested amount exceeds $50,000. If there is more than one plaintiff, *each* must claim $50,000 in damages, and *all* plaintiffs must be citizens of different states—that is, if a defendant in California is being sued by three plaintiffs, two of whom are citizens of Ohio and one a citizen of California, the diversity-of-citizenship principle does not obtain; the California plaintiff would have to withdraw from the suit.

In some instances—for example, claims involving real estate—the court need have jurisdiction only over *property* in question; ownership of or interest in the property may be sufficient for a court to establish jurisdiction over a defendant. Corporations are usually considered citizens of both the states in which they are incorporated and those in which they conduct their principal business.

---

[1] *Flast v. Cohen*, 392 U.S. 83 (1942).

VENUE. Venue is specified by statute and designates jurisdiction over *geographic* sites. A particular county, for example, may be the specified venue according to the residence of a person or the location of property. Thus, while jurisdiction determines whether a court *can* hear a case, venue determines whether a particular court *should* hear a case—and, when more than one court may have jurisdiction, *which* court should hear the case. One factor in deter-

venue Statutory designation of *jurisdiction* according to geographic site (*see also* Chapter 5)

The International Forum An account of the disaster at a Union Carbide plant in Bhopal, India, in December 1984 can be found in the INTERNATIONAL ENVIRONMENT box in Chapter 10. In 1986, a U.S. court of appeals applied the principle of *forum non conveniens* in transferring litigation from a New York federal district court (where Union Carbide expected speedier resolution) to the Indian court system. The U.S. defendant agreed to Indian jurisdiction, and after a trial judge had ordered interim payments of $270 million, the case eventually made its way to the Indian High Court in Jabalpur, where Carbide appealed. Factual disputes in Indian courts are usually heard by a trial judge who listens to testimony. High Court Judge S. K. Seth, however, applied the principle of Indian law whereby decisions concerning rules governing cases can be heard by a judge who has listened to no testimony about the facts. Citing Indian law that holds companies engaged in hazardous operations liable even if they have not been negligent, Judge Seth ordered Carbide to pay $190 million in damages *before* any liability had been determined.

mining venue is *convenience:* Venues can be changed for such reasons as witness costs, access to evidence, congested court dockets, and the possibility of local controversy or bias. The doctrine of **forum non conveniens** provides that a defendant may petition to transfer a case to a more convenient site.

Justiciable Controversy

forum non conveniens Doctrine providing that a defendant may petition to transfer a case from one *venue* to a more convenient site

justiciability Principle according to which a court determines its *jurisdiction* to decide a *case* or *controversy*

justiciable controversy *Case or controversy* that is "real and substantial" and capable of being decided in a court

Justiciability refers to the principle whereby a court determines its jurisdiction to decide a dispute. A classic definition of a **justiciable controversy** was given by Chief Justice Charles Hughes in *Aetna Life Insurance Co. v. Haworth* (300 U.S. 227 [1936]). Justice Hughes stated that a justiciable controversy may not be *hypothetical, abstract,* or *moot.* Instead, it must be "definite and concrete, touching the legal relations of parties having adverse legal interests . . . , a real and substantial controversy admitting of specific relief through a decree of a conclusive character." How do the courts determine which cases fit this definition? In deciding the question of justiciability, the courts examine both the nature of the case and the litigants' interest in it. The following discussion summarizes the basic standards of justiciability that can be gleaned from the case law: *standing, ripeness, mootness, advisory opinions, finality,* and *political questions.* Bear in mind that these standards have resulted from attempts to identify the *active, actual disputes* that courts were created to resolve.

standing Standard of *justiciability* holding that the parties to a case must have actual, personal interests in the issue under consideration

STANDING. The parties to a case must have the **standing** to litigate it: They must have actual, personal interests in the issues under consideration. A law, for example, cannot be challenged unless you are actually injured by it or actual injury is threatened. Your belief that a law is unwise or unfair or a belief that others will be injured does not establish the legal *standing* necessary to challenge a law.

class-action suit Suit filed by a plaintiff on his or her own behalf and on behalf of a specified party or parties with similar claims

The question of standing often arises in **class-action suits**—that is, suits on behalf of a specified plaintiff or plaintiffs and "all others similarly situated." Although class-action suits do not eliminate the requirement that a plaintiff demonstrate actual injury, they do broaden the concept of *injury.* For example, in *Sierra Club v. Morton* (405 U.S. 727 [1971]), the Supreme Court refused to hear a challenge to federal parkland development brought by the Sierra Club because the environmental organization failed to allege any injury to its members; it alleged only that the environment was injured. Two years later, however, in *U.S. v. SCRAP* (412 U.S. 669 [1973]), the Court granted standing to an environmental organization which alleged that its members would be endangered by pollution caused by federal regulations regarding the recycling of waste products. Unlike the first suit, the second alleged actual, personal injury to parties with an interest in the litigation.

Standing requirements are also important in identifying the range of economic interests recognized by the Court. For example, in actions brought by private utility companies against the Tennessee Valley Authority in the late 1930s, the court held that businesses do not have standing to challenge government action that undercuts their business by creating or supporting competing activities (*Tennessee Electric Power Co. v. TVA,* 306 U.S. 118 [1939]). The court found that because there was no common-law right of freedom from competition, the utilities did not have a "legally protected interest." In *Data Processing v. Camp* (397 U.S. 150 [1970]), the Court granted standing to sellers of data-processing services who challenged the entry of national banks into the data-processing business. The Court held that the plaintiff's assertion of actual economic injury changed the status of whether the plaintiff's interest was legally protected from a threshold question of standing to an issue to be decided on the merits of the case: Standing requirements were satisfied as long as the interests alleged by plaintiffs were within the "zone of interests" protected by a relevant statute. In recent years, courts have tried to limit the number of class actions by requiring plaintiffs to pay all court costs and requiring that actual notice be given to all members of the class no matter how large.

RIPENESS. To satisfy the justiciable requirement of **ripeness,** a case must be "ripe" or ready for adjudication—that is, it must be based on an *active conflict.* It is sometimes difficult to distinguish between ripeness and standing. For example, the decision that a case is not ripe may reflect the failure of a litigant to allege (or the court to recognize) an actual personal injury. Thus, the question of whether a case is considered ripe may depend on such issues as the court's evaluation of the actual hardships posed by the threatened application of a statute rather than on constitutional questions.

> **ripeness** Standard of *justiciability* holding that a case is ready for *adjudication* only if based on an active conflict

In *United States Workers v. Mitchell* (330 U.S. 75 [1947]), for example, the Supreme Court refused to allow federal employees to challenge Hatch Act provisions prohibiting them from engaging in political activities before they had in fact engaged in them. The Court suggested that the act had to be violated before it could be challenged. The *hypothetical* threat posed by the act was not considered sufficient injury to create a justiciable controversy, and the Court ruled that until the act had been violated, no active conflict existed.

MOOTNESS. A case is moot when the issue it raises no longer has practical consequences for the parties. Although **mootness** may seem a simple question of fact, it is often difficult to predict whether a case is legally moot. For example, in *Doremus v. Board of Education* (342 U.S. 429 [1952]), the court refused to review a state court dismissal of an action challenging Bible reading in public schools, partly because the child involved had already graduated. In the landmark abortion case *Roe v. Wade* (410 U.S. 113 [1973]), however, the Court heard a challenge to a Texas antiabortion law by a woman who was no longer pregnant. Refusing to hear the case on grounds of mootness can mean that the Court will never review abortion statute.

> **mootness** Standard of *justiciability* holding that the issue raised by a case must still have practical consequences for the parties involved

The Supreme Court also has made exceptions for arguably moot cases that are "capable of repetition, yet evading review." This principle has been invoked in election-law cases involving *continuing* election practices that come before the court after a *particular* election has been held (*Moore v. Olgivie*, 394 U.S. 814 [1969]).

ADVISORY OPINIONS. The federal judiciary branch will not advise members of the executive or legislative branches on abstract questions of law. This caveat against **advisory opinions** dates back to 1793, when the Supreme Court declined to answer President George Washington's questions about America's rights and responsibilities as a neutral nation in a war between England and France. The Court stated that rendering "extrajudicial" opinions for the president would violate the separation of powers by effectively making the Court a presidential law firm (and thus involved in the formulation of executive policies). On the other hand, courts can make **declaratory judgments**—judgments which state the rights of parties on a point of law but which do not order any specific action.

> **advisory opinion** Formal judicial advice to the legislative or executive branches as to how a court would rule on a case that is not actually before it; federal courts will not issue such opinions

> **declaratory judgment** Judicial determination on a point of law which states the rights of the parties involved but which orders no specific action

FINALITY. Just as the Court will not give advisory opinions, it will not issue opinions that may be reviewed by the executive or legislative branches. This is the principle of **finality,** the simplest and perhaps least important principle of justiciability. In *Hayburn's Case* (2 Dall. 409 [1792]), for example, the Court declined to decide a veteran's pension rights because its decision would have been subject to review by the Secretary of War. Thus, such an opinion would violate the integrity of the judiciary and the separation of powers.

POLITICAL QUESTIONS. The notion that the courts should not decide political questions was until recently a generally accepted principle based both on the separation of powers and practical constraints of the adjudicative process. The **political-question doctrine** was enunciated in 1849, in *Luther v. Borden* (7 How. 1). The Court has held that matters like the conduct of foreign relations and military actions and the status of Indian tribes are political questions that the courts are neither empowered nor equipped to address.

However, the Court's obligation to uphold the Constitution requires it to decide some questions that might readily be called political. This obligation was made clear in the landmark case of *Baker v. Carr* (396 U.S. 196 [1962]), in which the Court held that a Fourteenth Amendment challenge to a state plan for apportioning seats in its legislature was a justiciable controversy. The fact that the case involved political rights was not deemed controlling. Instead, Justice William Brennan wrote that the Court must ask three relevant questions:

1. Is a *federal* court being asked to interfere with *federal* (not state) political issues?
2. Does the Court have the resources to decide the issue or are *legislative findings of fact* required?
3. Have *judicial criteria* for deciding the issue been presented? In a later case challenging the legality of the Vietnam War, the Second Circuit Court of Appeals declined to rule on the constitutional propriety of congressional involvement in the war because there were no "manageable standards" that the Court could apply (*Orlando v. Laird,* 443 F.2d 1039 [1971]).

The political-question doctrine is quite elusive. It is a *jurisdictional* constraint that federal courts may invoke when they feel compelled to defer to Congress as a matter of either necessity or principle. Therefore, it is a good example of how the standards of justiciability generally reflect both practical and legal considerations. In determining whether a given dispute presents a "case or controversy," the courts must decide both their competence to resolve the dispute and the constitutionality of their attempt.

■ *Concept Check 4-1   Which Cases Should Courts Address?*

- Describe an instance in which someone might lack *standing* to sue.
- Under what circumstances is a case considered *moot?*
- Define *jurisdiction* and *judiciability* and explain the differences between them.
- What doctrine prevents judges from making the broadest possible decisions?

■ How Courts Decide Cases

It is said that ours is a government of law, not of people: In other words, our rights and responsibilities are supposed to be determined by an objective, reliable set of democratically determined principles. Legal principles, however, are interpreted and applied by individual judges who bring to their jobs human ideals, preferences, and prejudices. Good judges struggle to find the proper balance between their personal beliefs and the rules of law that they are obliged to uphold. Legal decision making is, after all, largely a matter of interpreting rules. Judges must make decisions that interpret statutes and constitutional provisions that mean different things to different people.

In addition to interpreting federal and state statutes and constitutions, judges interpret previous cases. In making decisions, the courts are guided by the principles enunciated in previous decisions in similar cases. The obligation of courts to follow their own precedents is known as the doctrine of *stare decisis* ("let the decision stand"). This doctrine is an important check on unduly subjective decision making.

The Doctrine of Stare Decisis

The doctrine of **stare decisis** is the doctrine that requires courts to consider established *precedents* when deciding cases based on similar facts. Developed in England in the thirteenth century, stare decisis is at the heart of the common-law system. Under King Edward I, common-law courts began keeping records of previous cases to guide judges in deciding current ones. This practice helped make the *common law* (*see* Chapter 1) more objective and predictable. Like statutes, previous cases became forms of notice of illegal or tortious behavior. If you can count on the courts to follow past rulings or precedents, you know that your actions will be treated as similar actions were treated in similar cases. Similarly, if you want to bring a lawsuit against someone, you can assess your chances for success by reviewing previous, similar lawsuits. In the same way, you can determine which defense will serve you best if you have a suit brought against you.

stare decisis Doctrine requiring courts to consider established *precedents* when deciding cases based on similar facts

PRECEDENT AND DISCRETION. Stare decisis, however, does not eliminate the use of judicial discretion: No two cases are exactly alike, and lawyers for opposing sides can usually find grounds for arguing which precedents ought to be followed. Which aspects of the case are the most significant legally? Or, as lawyers ask, which facts are *controlling?* How a case is described determines which precedents ought to apply: Any one case may be—and usually is—described in opposing ways by opposing lawyers.

Although the judge determines how best to decide a present case, he or she must also decide how to describe the available precedents: A decision in an earlier case is meaningless without an evaluation of the precedents on which it was based. Through description and evaluation, precedents may be *distinguished, extended,* or *overruled.* We will briefly explain each of these principles for evaluating precedents and then note some differences in the applicability of stare decisis to *constitutional law* and *legislative policy.*

Distinguished Precedent. A judge may decide that a decision in an *apparently* similar prior case should not be followed because it was based on an important factual difference between it and the present case. In this way, precedents are *distinguished* from cases to which they arguably *might* apply. The precedential value of a case may also be limited by subsequent determinations that it was based on a unique set of controlling facts.

Extended Precedent. A precedent may be *extended* if a judge decides that it enunciates broad and basic principles of law intended to apply to a general practice rather than a specific set of facts. For example, the landmark case of

Brown v. Board of Education (347 U.S. 483 [1954]), which outlawed segregation in public schools, was later relied upon to outlaw segregation in other public facilities, such as parks, pools, and golf courses. Thus, this case was interpreted primarily as a case about segregation, not education.

Overruled Precedent. A precedent that announces equally broad but outmoded principles may be *overruled*. Although judges prefer to *limit* precedents in deference to stare decisis, some cases establish rules of law that stand in the way of generally desired change. We saw examples of this practice in Chapter 3, where we discussed changing interpretations of the commerce clause and in *Brown v. Board of Education's* overruling of *Plessy v. Ferguson*.

Stare decisis, then, does not bind judges to the status quo: Case law evolves as judges respond, in general, to the changing society and to the facts of the individual case. Every judicial decision is grounded as much, if not more, in the facts of the present case as it is in the law of a previous one. In addition, judges sometimes fashion new rules in the process of applying old ones. It has been said that although legal reasoning is reasoning by example, choosing and applying appropriate examples is a discretionary and creative endeavor. Justice Benjamin Cardozo once said that "the serious business of the judge begins [when there is no decisive precedent]. He must then fashion law for the litigants before him. In fashioning it for them, he will be fashioning it for others."[2] As the ETHICAL ENVIRONMENT box below suggests, this fairly unique relationship of the judiciary to ourselves and our posterity raises the question of judicial discretionary power and the potential demands brought to bear on the judgments of individuals whose positions are, theoretically, shielded from both political and popular attitudes toward the changing course of social events.

---

[2] Justice Cardozo was Chief Judge of the New York State Court of Appeals from 1927 to 1932. This quote is from "Determining the Ratio Decidendi of a Case," 40 *Yale Law Journal* 161 (1930).

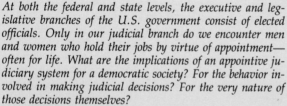

THE ETHICAL ENVIRONMENT
Discretion and Judicial Job Security

At both the federal and state levels, the executive and legislative branches of the U.S. government consist of elected officials. Only in our judicial branch do we encounter men and women who hold their jobs by virtue of appointment—often for life. What are the implications of an appointive judiciary system for a democratic society? For the behavior involved in making judicial decisions? For the very nature of those decisions themselves?

In practice, of course, we have a dual system of populating the bench—in most states, and at most levels within state courts, judges are indeed elected officials. The federal judiciary, on the other hand, is entirely appointed. With both processes at work, we are thus left with the following issue: At least theoretically, who hands down the fairest, least biased, most responsive decisions, an elected or an appointed judge?

When individuals—usually attorneys—are entered on ballots for election to the judiciary, they have usually paid

their political dues: They have probably worked on prior political campaigns, been visible supporters of local and state candidates, and demonstrated clear allegiance to their political parties. After all, even if the judiciary is not supposed to be a partisan function, the electoral process certainly is. Would-be judges, then, are like other individuals who hope to be elected to office—namely, they are to some extent political animals.

Once in office, however, judges, unlike mayors and senators—unlike executives and legislators at all governmental levels—are supposed to make rulings without regard to political agendas. Moreover, in their general judicial behavior and particular decisions, judges are not expected to carry out promises made to certain segments of the electorate in the course of political campaigns. However, even assuming that judges are ethical, maintaining an independent judiciary requires a watchful citizenry—one that makes sure that its judges don't "owe" anyone anything.

In addition, judges may be "political" in the sense that they respond to particular social issues and have certain goals for society that they feel should be accomplished. It would be naive to think otherwise. Of course, both as an electorate and as a society, we enjoy constitutional and statutory means of keeping our judges accountable. If, after all, judges must stand regularly for reelection, then they must—again, theoretically—answer for their behavior while on the bench. We the people have the opportunity to examine and question them in public forums and to express our opinions about the ramifications of judicial decisions.

In reality, however, incumbent judges are seldom held up to the same kind of scrutiny as incumbents in other government branches. For one thing, people are frequently apathetic about judges, their performances, and the elections that put and keep them in office. For another, judges standing for reelection can cite "the law" as the basis for their actions, short-circuiting debate by arguing that they are interpreters of a body of accepted "rules" and not makers of policy. Thus, although voters can theoretically "fire" their judges, in actuality, an elected judge probably has almost as much "job security" as an appointed one.

All judges on the federal bench, whether on the district or circuit court, or the Supreme Court, are appointed for life—or at least "during good behavior"—by the president with the advice and consent of the Senate (see Chapter 3). On the surface, this constitutional provision (Article II, Section 2) should mean that they are free of such partisan attachments as elected judges have. A deeper look, however, suggests that federal judicial appointments are in fact often "political" appointments themselves. A conservative or a liberal administration, for example, will probably appoint likeminded individuals—jurists who, they hope, will hand down decisions that will reflect certain social sentiments and, by extension, a certain political philosophy. (See the section below on politics and the makeup of the federal courts). Is a judiciary thus constituted more or less "independent" than an elected one? Are its decisions fairer?

As a judge in the U.S. Circuit Court of Appeals, for example, you know that you have lifetime tenure. Assuming that you are a fair and ethical person, this security means that you can formulate your decisions with an eye focused on judicial principles, free of worry about reelection. Still, you were appointed with the knowledge that if you would not adhere exactly to certain policies, at least you would not impede their implementation. Thus, your dilemma will be about the same as that of the elected judge—can you remain nonpartisan in this environment?

Whether appointed or elected, a judge must determine how to work reasonably free both of partisan pressure and personal prejudice. This is not to say, of course, that judges come to their tasks without philosophies, social views, and the like—obviously, they will carry such "baggage" with them in whatever system they work. Ultimately, it might be best to look at the bigger picture of that system, and some judicial analysts point out that one can, in general, say at least two important things about that system.

First, because the United States is not a civil-law country, we do not have a "professional" judiciary. In many countries, for example, the judiciary is a career in which individuals who wish to become judges pursue a professional path quite different from that pursued by individuals who wish to practice bar. In such a system, "entry-level" judges pursue their careers through "promotions" as civil servants who thus face bureaucratic pressures in addition to political and social pressures. (See the INTERNATIONAL ENVIRONMENT box in Chapter 5.) In the United States, judges are lawyers. Admittedly, although at least one survey has found that about four out of five U.S. judges acknowledged having been "political activists" at some point in their careers, these same people have been trained as lawyers: They are subject to peer scrutiny, both professional and academic, and again theoretically, the process of becoming a good lawyer is the same process as preparing to become a good judge.

Second, although doing so may require impeachment for "treason, bribery, or other high crimes and misdemeanors" (Article II, Section 4), the voters—and nobody but the voters, either directly or through their elected representative—can remove a judge from the bench. Or, to put it conversely, because neither executives nor legislators can do so, partisan powers cannot dominate the judiciary. The effects of what can happen when a regime dominates the judiciary can be extreme. (See the ETHICAL ENVIRONMENT box in Chapter 1.) Some of the cases presented in this book reflect an equally interesting phenomenon: In the United States, although the "regime" recommends employment and promotion and signs judicial paychecks, it loses several important cases every year.

STARE DECISIS AND THE CONSTITUTION. The doctrine of stare decisis is most limited in constitutional cases. The Constitution reigns supreme over case law as well as statutes. Sometimes, a constitutional amendment changes the precepts on which prior cases were based. (The Civil War Amendments, for example, effectively overruled the Dred Scott decision denying black slaves the rights of citizenship [see Chapter 15].) Sometimes, different judges interpret the Constitution differently and write *dissents*. In any event, judges are bound by the Constitution, not by previous cases construing it.

STARE DECISIS AND LEGISLATION. On the other hand, stare decisis can have considerable effect in cases involving legislative policy decisions and not constitutional law. It is sometimes argued that legislators should decide whether to

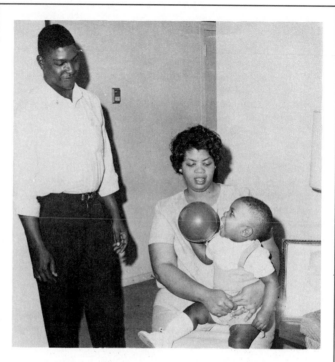

Interpretation and Stare Decisis Mrs. Charles K. Smith and family, Topeka, Kansas, 1964. Ten years earlier, when she was Linda Brown, Mrs. Smith's name appeared on the Supreme Court's ruling in the case of *Brown v. Board of Education of Topeka*. That decision had overturned the Court's own ruling in the 1896 case of *Plessy v. Ferguson*, in which the principle of "separate-but-equal" educational facilities for blacks had been upheld (both cases are discussed in Chapter 3). Justice John Harlan, who dissented in *Plessy*, had argued then that "Our Constitution is color-blind and neither knows nor tolerates class among citizens." It was also Justice Harlan who once reminded a class of law students that "if we [the Supreme Court] don't like an act of Congress, we don't have too much trouble to find grounds for declaring it unconstitutional" and the Court announced in *Brown* that, in effect, Justice Harlan's opinions were accurate on both counts: the doctrine of *stare decesis* is not engraved in stone when the Court seeks to interpret the Constitution. In other words, it is the Constitution itself that is binding—not any interpretation of it—and the Court may reverse its decisions as its current members deem necessary.

overrule long-standing precedents that are not constitutionally mandated. If legislators disagree with the court's construction of a statute, they can amend it or write a new statute in order to make their original intention clear. By not acting, they are effectively agreeing with the way a law has been construed.

This principle was invoked by the Supreme Court in the case of *Flood v. Kuhn*, which considered the exemption of professional baseball from federal antitrust regulation. Baseball was originally declared exempt from the antitrust laws in 1922 because it was not then considered part of interstate commerce. Today, although congressional power to regulate baseball is clear, Congress has not attempted to exercise that power since 1922.

FLOOD v. KUHN
United States Supreme Court, 407 U.S. 258 (1972)

In 1969, the baseball All-Star center fielder Curt Flood was traded by the St. Louis Cardinals to the Philadelphia Phillies. Because he was not given notice of the trade before it occurred, Flood asked the Commissioner of Baseball to allow him to become a free agent. Free agency would have meant that Flood could have bargained with any major league team to seek the best possible contract.

After being refused his request for free agency, Flood, the plaintiff, sued the defendant, baseball commissioner Bowie Kuhn, on the theory that denial of his request for free agency violated federal antitrust laws. Both the trial court and the Court of Appeals ruled in Kuhn's favor. Flood now appeals to the U.S. Supreme Court.

The Legal Background

A. *Federal Baseball Club v. National League* (1922) was a suit for treble damages instituted by a member of the Federal League (Baltimore) against the National and American Leagues and others. . . . The main brief filed by the plaintiff with this court discloses that it was strenuously argued, among other things, that the business in which the defendants were engaged was interstate commerce; that the interstate relationship among the several clubs, located as they were in different States, was predominant. . . .

Mr. Justice Holmes, in speaking succinctly for a unanimous Court, said:

"The business is giving exhibitions of baseball, which are purely state affairs. . . . But the fact that in order to give the exhibitions the leagues must induce free persons to cross state lines and must arrange and pay for their doing so is not enough to change the character of the business. . . . [T]he transport is a mere incident, not the essential thing. That to which it is incident, the exhibition, although made for money would not be called trade or commerce in the commonly accepted use of those words. . . .

"If we are right . . . the restrictions by contract that prevented the plaintiff from getting players to break their bargains and the other conduct charged against the defendants were not an interference with commerce among the states."

B. . . . In the years that followed, baseball continued to be subject to intermittent antitrust attack. The courts, however, rejected these challenges on the authority of *Federal Baseball.* . . .

C. . . . [I]n *Toolson* [(1953)], . . . *Federal Baseball* was cited as holding "that the business of providing public baseball games for profit between clubs of professional baseball players was not within the scope of the federal antitrust laws," and:

"Congress has had the ruling under consideration but has not seen fit to bring such business under these laws by legislation having prospective effect. The business has thus been left for thirty years to develop, on the understanding that it was not subject to existing antitrust legislation. The present cases ask us to overrule the prior decision and, with retrospective effect, hold the legislation applicable. We think that if there are evils in this field which now warrant application to it of the antitrust laws it should be by legislation. . . ."

D. *United States* v. *Shubert* (1955) was a civil antitrust action against defendants engaged in the production of legitimate theatrical attractions throughout the United States and in operating theaters for the presentation of such attractions. The district court has dismissed the complaint on the authority of *Federal Baseball* and *Toolson.* This Court reversed. Mr. Chief Justice Warren noted the Court's broad conception of "trade or commerce" in the antitrust statutes and the types of enterprises already held to be within the reach of that phrase. He stated that *Federal Baseball* and *Toolson* afforded no basis for a conclusion that businesses built around the performance of local exhibitions are exempt from the antitrust laws . . . :

"In *Federal Baseball,* the Court, speaking through Mr. Justice Holmes, was dealing with the business of baseball and nothing else. . . . "In *Toolson,* where the issue was the same as in *Federal Baseball,* the Court was confronted with a unique combination of circumstances. . . . In short, *Toolson* was a narrow application of the rule of *stare decisis.*"

. . . .

E. *United States* v. *International Boxing Club* (1955) was a companion to *Shubert* and was decided the same day. This was a civil antitrust action against defendants engaged in the business of promoting professional championship boxing contests. . . . [The Supreme Court] stated:

". . . *Federal Baseball* did not hold that all businesses based on professional sports were outside the scope of the antitrust laws. The issue confronting us is, therefore, not whether a previously granted exemption should continue, but whether an exemption should be granted in the first instance. And that issue is for Congress to resolve, not this Court."

. . . .

F. The parade marched on. *Radovich* v. *National Football League* (1957) was a civil Clayton Act case testing the application of the antitrust laws to professional football. The district court dismissed. The Ninth Circuit Court affirmed in part on the basis of *Federal Baseball* and *Toolson.*

This Court reversed . . . :

"[S]ince *Toolson* and *Federal Baseball* are still cited as controlling authority in antitrust actions involving other fields of business, we now specifically limit the rule there established to the facts there involved, *i.e.,* the business of organized professional baseball. As long as the Congress continues to acquiesce we should adhere to—but not extend—the interpretation of the Act made in those cases. . . ."

G. Finally, in *Haywood* v. *National Basketball Assn.* (1971), Mr. Justice Douglas, in his capacity as Circuit Justice, reinstated a district court's injunction *pendente lite* in favor of a professional basketball player and said, "Basketball . . . does not enjoy exemption from the antitrust laws."

. . . .

In view of all this, it seems appropriate now to say that:

1. Professional baseball is a business and it is engaged in interstate commerce.

2. With its reserve system enjoying exemption from the federal antitrust laws, baseball is, in a very distinct sense, an exception and an anomaly. *Federal Baseball* and *Toolson* have become an aberration confined to baseball.

3. Even though others might regard this as "unrealistic, inconsistent, or illogical," the aberration is an established one, and one that . . . has been with us now for half a century, one heretofore deemed fully entitled to the benefit of *stare decisis,* and one that has survived the Court's expanding concept of interstate commerce. It rests on a recognition and an acceptance of baseball's unique characteristics and needs.

4. Other professional sports operating interstate—football, boxing, basketball, and presumably, hockey and golf—are not so exempt. . . .

6. The Court . . . has concluded that Congress as yet has had no intention to subject baseball's reserve system to the reach of the antitrust statutes. This, obviously, has been deemed to be something other than mere congressional silence and passivity.

7. The Court has expressed concern about the confusion and the retroactivity problems that inevitably would result with a judicial overturning of *Federal Baseball.* It has voiced a preference that if any change is to be made, it come by legislative action that, by its nature, is only prospective in operation.

8. . . . Accordingly, we adhere once again to *Federal Baseball* and *Toolson* and to their application to professional baseball. We adhere also to *International Boxing* and *Radovich* and to their respective applications to professional boxing and professional football. If there is any inconsistency or illogic in all this, it is an inconsistency and illogic of long standing that is to be remedied by the Congress and not by this Court. If we were to act otherwise, we would be withdrawing from the conclusion as to congressional intent made in *Toolson* and from the concerns as to retrospectivity therein expressed. Under these circumstances, there is merit in consistency even though some might claim that beneath that consistency is a layer of inconsistency.

. . . .

We repeat for this case what was said in *Toolson:* "Without reexamination of the underlying issues, the [judgment] below [is] affirmed on the authority of *Federal Baseball Club of Baltimore* v. *National League of Professional Baseball Clubs, supra,* so far as that decision determines that Congress had no intention of including the business of baseball within the scope of the federal antitrust laws." And what the Court said in *Federal Baseball* in 1922 and what it said in *Toolson* in 1953, we say again here in 1972: the remedy, if any is indicated, is for congressional, and not judicial, action.

The judgment of the Court of Appeals is Affirmed.

Case Questions

1. What must occur before the courts can no longer apply baseball's somewhat curious exemption from the antitrust laws?

2. What phenomenon has allowed only baseball to enjoy an exemption from antitrust laws?

3. How does *Flood v. Kuhn* illustrate the concept of stare decisis?

■ *Concept Check 4-2   How Courts Decide Cases*

- Describe the concept of *stare decisis* and explain how it works.
- Explain the differences among *distinguished, extended,* and *overruled precedents.*
- In what ways does stare decisis have more effect on *legislative policy* than on *constitutional cases?*

■ HOW COURTS REMEDY DISPUTES

In medieval England, routine civil cases involving private disputes were generally heard by the Court of Common Pleas—the court established to hear cases not involving the king. To obtain *relief* for an alleged wrong, a plaintiff obtained from the king's chancellor a *writ* describing his case and demanding that the defendant either provide the requested relief or appear in court.[3] Although writs were originally tailored to specific cases, they were eventually standardized: Instead of fashioning his writ to satisfy the particulars of his case, the plaintiff had to characterize his case so that it satisfied more or less technical requirements of legal form and procedure. Courts hearing cases according to this procedure were known as **courts of law.**

Although this system of seeking relief contributed to a more systematic application of judicial rules and procedures, it gradually bogged down in its own complexity, and plaintiffs who could receive no satisfaction in courts of law began petitioning the king directly. In turn, the king referred petitions to his chancellor, and the practice of petitioning the chancellor directly soon became quite common, primarily because the chancellor was not bound by the increasingly rigid rules of the courts of law. Rather, the chancellor administered *discretionary* justice: Referring to generally accepted principles of right and wrong, he redressed injuries and granted relief as he saw fit.

From this practice developed the system of **equity**—that is, a body of law based on "fairness" or "conscience" rather than rules; courts administering this body of law were known as *chancery courts* (from the office of the *chancellor*) or **courts of equity.** Although this system was generally more flexible and responsive to the nuances of individual cases, it could also be subjective and imprecise—a court of equity was only as just as the chancellor who presided over it and certainly less predictable than a court of law. Out of this situation emerged an interesting paradox in the system of judicial decision making from which our own system developed: If law courts reflected an unwieldy system of rules untempered by human sensitivity (and perhaps common sense), courts of equity encouraged the often arbitrary judgment of individuals under no practical constraint to apply rules of law.

Consequently, the nature of the *remedies* provided by each of these two systems became one of the most important practical differences between the principles of law and equity. For example, while law courts could award money damages and secure the return of wrongfully appropriated property, they could not order a defendant to fulfill a *duty* to the plaintiff—nor could they order the defendant to refrain from avenging himself by harming the plaintiff. Courts of equity, meanwhile, could issue *decrees of specific performance* ordering defendants to fulfill contracts and *injunctions* ordering defendants to refrain from specified activities.

Our justice system no longer maintains a codified distinction between judicial decisions of law and equity (except in the state of Delaware, which preserves courts of chancery to decide cases of equity). Instead, federal and state courts are **courts of general jurisdiction**—that is, courts of both legal and equitable jurisdiction. In our system, judicial decision making in civil cases is also *remedial*, and in courts of general jurisdiction, a **remedy** can be either the means of enforcing a right or the means of preventing a wrong; a defendant can be ordered by the court either to *do* something that the plaintiff requests (for example, pay monetary damages) or to *refrain* from doing something (for example, interfering with the use of property).

At the same time, however, it is important to remember that the basic dis-

courts of law Historically, courts hearing only cases satisfying certain technical requirements of legal form and procedure and awarding only monetary damages or the return of wrongfully appropriated property; courts administering *remedies at law*, especially *monetary damages*

equity Body of law based on general concepts of "fairness" rather than on strict legal precepts

courts of equity Historically, courts that applied principles of common-law "fairness" to cases in which a *remedy at law* was unobtainable; courts administering a relatively discretionary system of justice based on concepts of right and wrong, justice and injustice

courts of general jurisdiction Federal and state courts in which are combined the jurisdictions of both *courts of law* and *courts of equity*

remedy Judicial means, either *at law* or *at equity*, of either enforcing a right or preventing a wrong

---

[3] In contemporary legal usage, a *writ* is a formal court order directing an individual or an organization to do something. *Writs of certiorari* are discussed later in this chapter; the *writ of mandamus* was defined in Chapter 3, and the *writ of garnishment* is explained in Chapter 19.

tinction between legal and equitable remedy does in fact persist in our system. Monetary damages, for example, constitute a legal remedy, an injunction an equitable remedy. In other words, the *kind* of relief sought by the plaintiff and/or awarded by the court largely determines whether a case is regarded as legal or equitable. We will therefore examine the kinds of *remedies at law* and *remedies at equity* available to the courts.

Remedies at Law: Monetary Damages

Because financial remedy is sought and/or awarded in virtually every case of a breached contract, we will here on **monetary damages** (or **damages at law**)—financial remedy for monetary loss resulting from a wrongful action. The three main categories of monetary damages are *compensatory, punitive,* and *nominal.*

monetary damages (or damages at law) Financial *remedy* for monetary loss resulting from a wrongful action

COMPENSATORY DAMAGES. **Compensatory damages** are intended to redress, in dollars, an actual injury sustained. In a contract action (*see* Chapter 9), the compensation is intended to put the plaintiff in the same position that he would have enjoyed had the contract not been violated. In a tort action (*see* Chapter 10), the purpose of the compensation is to put the plaintiff in the position he would have been in if the injury had not occurred. For example, if someone violates a contract from which you would have realized $10,000, an award of $10,000 would be compensatory damages. If your neighbor puts a dent in your car that costs $800 to fix, an award of $800 is compensatory damages.

compensatory damages *Remedy*, usually monetary, intended to redress an actual injury sustained; in breaches of contract, compensatory damages are intended to restore the plaintiff to a position occupied before the breach

Plaintiffs may also be compensated for injuries caused indirectly by defendants. *Indirect compensatory damages*, sometimes called **consequential damages,** are limited to injuries that were natural and probable consequences of the defendant's act: In other words, the act must have been the proximate (legal) cause of the injuries. **Speculative** or **avoidable damages**—losses that *may* have resulted or may be incorrect from a wrongful action—are not recoverable. Consider these examples:

consequential damages *Remedy* limited to injuries which, although indirect, were natural and probable consequences of a defendant's action

speculative (or avoidable) damages *Remedy* intended to provide for losses that *may* have resulted from a wrongful action

- You are injured in an auto accident caused by the defendant's negligence, and you lose three weeks of work; while recovering, you may be compensated for lost earnings in addition to medical expenses; you may not, however, recover speculative profits like the bonus that you might have received for work performed during those three weeks.
- Your car is wrecked in an accident, but you are not injured; if you can commute to work by train, you cannot recover for lost earnings while you search for a new car.

In tort actions, you may be compensated for several types of injuries, including physical and mental impairment, physical and mental pain and suffering, lost earnings or impairment of earning capacity, injury to your reputation and business standing, and reasonable and necessary expenses. (Expenses do not include legal fees, which are generally not compensable in tort cases unless compensation is authorized by statute.)

Consequential damages are more difficult to specify in a contract action. Some contracts thus stipulate the amount of damages, called **liquidated damages,** recoverable in case of breach. As a general rule, you may recover for consequential business costs and loss of profits occasioned by a breach. For example, damages for a defective product delivered under a contract may include both the cost of correcting the defect and the profits that the plaintiff lost while

liquidated damages Contractually stipulated *remedy* recoverable in case of breach

waiting for the defendant to correct it. To be compensable, the business loss must have been a *foreseeable* consequence of the contract breach. Anticipated and contingent profits or profits that cannot reasonably be determined are not recoverable.

Obviously, determining the amount necessary to compensate the plaintiff for an injury or breach of contract is not an exact science. Therefore, the parties rarely agree on how to arrive at this figure. In the following case, the court took issue with the plaintiff's method of calculating compensatory damages.

RODGERS v. FISHER BODY DIVISION GENERAL MOTORS CORPORATION
U.S. Court of Appeals, 6th Circuit, 739 F.2d 1102 (1984)

Sammie Rodgers was hired for the position of temporary guard at General Motors' Fisher Body Plant in Lansing, Michigan. Upon his hiring, it was represented to Rodgers that if he passed a six-month probationary period, he would be eligible for a permanent position. Five months into his employment, Rodgers, who was black, was called into a meeting where he was told that he was being laid off and that a white temporary guard had been given the position for which he was vying.

Rodgers brought this employment-discrimination suit against the defendant, Fisher Body Division, for intentional racial discrimination. The jury returned a verdict for Rodgers in the amount of $300,000 compensatory and $500,000 punitive damages. The defendant appeals based on the excessiveness of the verdict.

. . . .

The Court now considers the troubling issue of the excessiveness of the verdict. All the federal circuits today agree that there should be appellate supervision of the size of jury verdicts. In determining whether a verdict is so excessive that appellete review is proper, the Court must find the verdict to be "shocking" or to manifest "plain injustice." Before an appellate court reverses on the basis of excessive damages, it must make a detailed appraisal of the evidence bearing on damages.

The Court has made this appraisal, as stated above, and finds both the compensatory and punitive damages awarded in this case to be so excessive as to shock the conscience of the Court. These awards resulted from several errors which prevented the jury from receiving adequate guidance on the damages issues.

Errors which affected the compensatory damages award include: (1) the failure of either party to request a charge and the failure of the District Court to charge the jury on reduction of future damages to present value; (2) plaintiff's closing argument in which plaintiff's counsel calculated on a blackboard plaintiff's damages for lost wages; (3) the limited evidence of mental distress.

The Court *sua sponte* [on its own] raises the first two of these three issues.

It is settled law in this Circuit that an award of future damages must be reduced to present value in order to take into account the earning power of the money.

. . . The error in question here was obvious and it affected the fairness and integrity of the judicial process in that it was undoubtedly to some degree responsible for a shockingly large verdict. When an appellate court determines that the jury did not have before it a correct statement of the law regarding damages, it can remand solely for a redetermination of damages.

Not only did defendant not request a charge that future damages must be reduced to present value, but General Motors also failed to object to plaintiff's extremely speculative estimate of his damages for lost wages. In her closing argument, plaintiff's counsel, using a chalkboard, calculated these damages to be $220,770. . . . The $220,770 figure thus includes future damages which were not reduced to present value. . . . It was plain error for the court not to instruct on reducing future damages (loss of income) to present value.

Furthermore, in the case of an injury of an economic nature, the injured party is to be placed, as nearly as possible, in the position he would have been in had the wrong not occurred. . . . Although juries are thus accorded great discretion in determining the amount of damage awards, damages must be proved; they must not be speculative.

. . . .

With so little actual evidence of lost wages before it, the jury was no doubt unduly influenced by the extremely hypothetical figures presented by plaintiff's counsel in closing argument.

General Motors' counsel made no objection to the use of these highly speculative figures. Nor did he attempt, in any detail, to rebut them. . . . The jury was, in short, given little guidance which would be of aid in reaching a reasonable damage figure for lost wages.

Plaintiff also claimed compensatory damages based on the mental distress which he suffered as a result of being discriminatorily laid off by defendant. In her closing argument plaintiff's council stated that plaintiff was seeking $500,000 for mental stress.

Virtually the only evidence of the mental stress which plaintiff suffered as a result of his layoff was plaintiff's brief testimony in this regard. Because of an error for which defendant was not responsible, the Michigan Employment Security Commission denied plaintiff's eligibility to receive unemployment benefits; this error resulted in his not receiving benefits for 13 weeks. Plaintiff, his wife and child went on welfare for approximately seven months.

. . . .

Plaintiff's evidence of mental distress is too slight to support a sizeable damages award for the intangible injury of mental harm. While jurors might easily infer that going on welfare and losing one's car would cause emotional distress, plaintiff has not demonstrated his mental distress with the specificity required. . . . The jury did not have sufficient evidence to place a high dollar value on plaintiff's emotional harm.

It is impossible for the Court to determine what part of the $300,000 award the jury apportioned to each of the two aspects of plaintiff's injuries, lost wages and emotional distress. It is clear, however, that plaintiff's evidence was insufficient to support such a large award in regard to either aspect of his claim for compensatory damages.

. . . .

Accordingly, we affirm the District Court's judgment on the issue of liability and reverse on the issue of damages. The cause is remanded for trial solely on the issues of compensatory and punitive damages.

Case Questions

1. What error does the decision suggest that the trial judge had made?

2. What reasons does the court give for concluding that the jury verdict was excessive?

3. Would it have made any difference if the jury had evidence before it that the plaintiff experienced fits of dizziness and nausea after being laid off?

---

punitive (or **exemplary**) **damages** *Remedy*, generally awarded for acts considered reckless or malicious; imposed in order to punish or deter

PUNITIVE DAMAGES. **Punitive damages,** sometimes called **exemplary damages,** are awarded to *punish* and *deter*. Unless authorized by statute or awarded by a judge, they are not generally recoverable in contract actions. Generally associated with tort actions, they reflect the *harm posed to society* by defendant's actions rather than the actual injury suffered by plaintiff.

In some jurisdictions, punitive damages are awarded instead of compensatory damages. They are usually awarded for acts that are reckless, malicious, fraudulent, or generally abhorrent and that pose considerable social costs. Remember, punitive damages are supposed to serve the *public*, not the *individual plaintiff*. In the following case, Browning Ferris Industries "willfully and deliberately attempted to drive Kelco Disposal out of the market." The lower court awarded compensatory and punitive damages. The Supreme Court is called upon to decide if the punitive damages in this case are constitutionally excessive under the Eighth amendment.

TOOLE v. RICHARDSON-MERRELL, INC.

California Court of Appeals, 60 Cal. Rptr. 398 (1967)

Under his doctor's direction, Toole, a 43-year-old man, took triparinol to combat arteriosclerosis. However, because of its side effects, Toole had to stop using this drug, which was manufactured by Richardson-Merrell under the trade name MER/29. The side effects that occurred while he had used the drug disappeared. But now Toole, already suffering from cataracts and reduced vision by reason of his use of MER/29, faces a future of potential health disorders and possible blindness. The history of MER/29 from its development is replete with numerous instances of wrongful activity by Richardson-Merrell. After tests done on laboratory animals clearly demonstrated the harmful effects it could have on human beings, Richardson-Merrell nevertheless sought FDA permission to market the drug. After approval by the FDA, due to a series of false statements made by the company, MER/29 was placed on the market. Despite receiving letters from established members of the medical profession advising them of its harmful effects, Richardson-Merrell refused to take MER/29 off the market.

Toole, the plaintiff, sued the defendant, Richardson-Merrell, for the injuries he sustained by reason of his use of MER/29. The jury awarded him $175,000 general damages and $500,000 punitive damages. The defendant appeals on the theory that the plaintiff did not show that he was entitled to recover punitive damages.

Appellant contends that a verdict should have been directed for it on the issue of punitive damages. It argues that if wrongful acts were done by its agents it must be shown that such acts were authorized or ratified by responsible management in order to hold the corporation liable.

A corporation may be held liable for punitive damages for the acts of its agents and employees when the act is done in ill will, or is motivated by actual malice, or done under circumstances amounting to fraud or oppression, providing that the act is done with the knowledge or under the direction of corporate officials having power to bind the corporation.

Appellant argues that none of the wrongdoing upon which respondent relies to show fraud was known to any officer or principal having power to bind the corporation; that all of the alleged wrongful acts were done by agents and employees below the level of responsible management. . . . This argument cannot succeed here. . . . There was ample evidence from which the jury could infer that high level management had knowledge of wrongdoing on the part of department heads and other employees and agents. As we have related in a statement of the evidence, Dr. Van Maanen was appellant's associate director of research, in charge of the Biological Science Division. . . . Dr. Van Maanen directed falsification of the test results. . . . Falsification of these results permitted appellant to conceal the toxicity of MER/29 and tended to deceive the FDA into allowing appellant to market a potentially injurious drug. Dr. Van Maanen was high enough on the executive scale of responsibility to hold appellant liable in punitive damages for his wrongful acts. . . .

. . . Moreover, there is evidence that Vice President Woodward, who was just one step below President Getman, admitted in an inter-company memorandum that ". . . the full body of company knowledge . . ." had not accompanied appellant's supplemental application to the FDA—an admission made at a time when appellant was accused by the FDA of withholding test data.

From all of this evidence the jury could reasonably infer that corporate management, at least from the level of Vice President Woodward on down, had knowledge of the true test results of MER/29 when used in animals, and that some or all had joined in a policy of nondisclosure of vital information. Thus corporate responsibility for the wrongdoing of its officers and agents is fully established.

Appellant next argues that the punitive damage award cannot be sustained because malice in fact was not proven.

Civil Code section 3294 allows punitive damages where the defendant has been guilty of ". . . oppression, fraud, or malice. . . ." . . . At appellant's request, the court instructed the jury that "Malice . . . implies an act conceived in a spirit of mischief or with criminal indifference toward the obligations owed to others. There must be an intent to vex, annoy and injure. Defendant's conduct must have been so recklessly disregardful of the rights of others, so as to be characterized as wanton or willful conduct. Mere negligence, even gross negligence, is not sufficient to justify such an award."

. . . .

. . . Appellant says there is no showing of any deliberate intent to do harm to respondent, and that in the absence of a showing of deliberate intention on the part of appellant to injure respondent the award of punitive damages must fall. But malice in fact, sufficient to support an award of punitive damages on the basis of malice as that term is used in Civil Code section 3294, may be established by a showing that the defendant's wrongful conduct was willful, intentional, and done in reckless disregard of its possible results. . . .

In our case there is evidence from which the jury could conclude that appellant brought its drug to market, and maintained it on the market, in reckless disregard of the possibility that it would visit serious injury upon persons using it. . . . Even after a number of cases of cataracts in humans from use of MER/29 had been reported to appellant, and when its own tests had established blindness in its test animals, appellant continued to defend sale of its drug. . . .

From all of the evidence the jury could find that appellant acted recklessly and in wanton disregard of possible harm to others in marketing, promoting, selling and maintaining MER/29 on the market in view of its knowledge of the toxic effect of the drug. Such a finding would necessarily be a finding of malice in fact, and since the jury was instructed only on malice as a foundation for an award of punitive damages and made such an award of punitive damages and made such an award in respondent's favor, we must presume they found malice in fact.

. . . .

The judgment is affirmed.

Case Questions

1. What statement is made by a court when it awards punitive damages?

2. What elements are necessary before a plaintiff may recover punitive damages? Were such elements met in the case?

3. Might the court have ruled differently if Richardson-Merrell had conducted no tests prior to marketing MER/29 and had no knowledge of its ill effects?

"Americans are the most litigious people on earth, and they pay dearly for it." Such were the sentiments expressed by one business analyst in the late 1980s—and he acknowledges having echoed the sentiments of the French commentator Alexis de Tocqueville, who toured America over 150 years ago. Today, some of the dearest of court-ordered payments are made by corporations when plaintiffs are awarded astronomical punitive damages in tort cases. As this chapter's YOU DECIDE feature illustrates, such awards may forge a double-edged sword in so-called "mass-disaster" cases.

nominal damages *Remedy awarded when plaintiff proves an unlawful act but not compensable damages*

NOMINAL DAMAGES. **Nominal damages** are insignificant amounts, often $1 awards given in cases in which a plaintiff proves that a defendant has committed an unlawful act but fails to demonstrate a compensable loss. In effect, nominal damages are a statement by the court that the plaintiff's rights have been violated. They offer psychological satisfaction and, with certain restrictions, make the defendant liable for court costs.

Remedies at Equity

equitable remedies *Generally, court orders for a party to refrain from doing something; usually issued only when monetary damages cannot resolve a dispute*

Equitable remedies generally involve court orders to do or *refrain* from doing specified activities: They are considered "extraordinary" remedies, and are awarded only in cases that cannot be resolved by monetary damages. The inadequacy of remedies at law is a general precondition to the exercise of equity jurisdiction. Equity is still a relatively discretionary system of justice that is governed by standards that have developed over the years. Usually, these standards are expressed in maxims and doctrines.

The most common—and perhaps most important—of these standards is

118

the **doctrine of unclean hands:** Equity is available only to those who come to court with "clean hands"—that is, those who have acted in good faith. For example, the courts may refuse equitable relief to those who have not vigilantly protected their rights. In other words, the courts will not take extraordinary measures to protect plaintiffs who have been negligent in protecting themselves.

doctrine of unclean hands Standard whereby *equitable remedy* is available only to plaintiffs who have acted in *good* faith

Equitable relief is not limited to any particular type of case. For example, it is available in cases involving contracts, torts, property rights, or trusts and estates. We will briefly review three types of equitable relief: As we have seen, *injunctions* and *decrees of specific performance* originate in medieval English equity law, while actions for an *accounting* are frequently made as a result of such fiduciary cases as business-partnership disputes (*see* Chapter 7).

INJUNCTIONS. **Injunctions** are court orders to perform or not to perform a specified act. Injunctions are generally issued *preventatively*. For example, a builder who has violated zoning laws may be required to dismantle that part of the building in violation; one neighbor may be required to tear down a fence that encroaches on another's property. When we refer to injunctions, we are usually referring to court orders *enjoining* the commission of harmful acts.

injunction Court order to perform or not to perform a specific act

As previously noted, injunctions may be temporary or permanent. *Temporary injunctions* (also known as **preliminary injunctions**) are issued during the pendancy of a lawsuit to preserve the status quo and to prevent irreparable harm. For example, a court may issue a temporary injunction against a real-estate developer to prevent the destruction of a landmark building pending determination of the developer's right to destroy the building. A case like this might start with the issuance of a *temporary restraining order*—a very brief injunction (usually for a period of days), issued *ex parte* (that is, without notice to the other side), pending a hearing on a motion for a preliminary injunction. A preliminary injunction is issued only after notice and a hearing. Plaintiffs must demonstrate that they have a good chance of succeeding on the merits and that they will suffer irreparable harm if an injunction is not issued. *Permanent injunctions,* issued after trial, reflect the court's determination on the merits of plaintiff's claim.

preliminary injunction Injunction issued during a lawsuit to preserve the status quo and prevent irreparable harm

Injunctions are extraordinary, discretionary remedies that require courts to balance the interests of the parties involved. As the following case demonstrates, although injunctions are not issued lightly, they can be awarded in a broad range of circumstances as a means to remedy *breaches of duty*—that is, a defendant's failure to exercise the same care as would be exercised by a "reasonable person under similar circumstances" (*see* Chapter 10). Such injunctions are often ordered when there is otherwise no adequate remedy at law.

SMITH v. WESTERN ELECTRIC
Missouri Court of Appeals, 643 S.W. 2d. 10 (1982)

The plaintiff, Paul Smith, an employee at the defendant Western Electric's Missouri plant, filed a complaint seeking an injunction to prevent his exposure to cigarette smoke at the plant. With the aid of medical records, Smith claimed that since he suffered adverse physical symptoms whenever exposed to such smoke, it was necessary for him to work in a smoke-free environment. He further alleged that because efforts to relocate him to less smoky areas had proven unsatisfactory and because the management failed to make a reasonable effort in implementing its policy of segregating smokers and nonsmokers in working areas, it was impossible for him to work under the prevailing conditions.

The lower court dismissed Smith's complaint on the basis that a trial was not necessary because even if all of the facts alleged therein were true, they were not sufficient to support an injunction. Smith now appeals to the Missouri Court of Appeals.

The petition seeks an injunction to prevent plaintiff's employer from exposing him to tobacco smoke in the workplace and from affecting his pay or employment conditions because of his medical reaction to tobacco smoke. The petition alleges that by allowing smoking in the work area, defendant permits its employees to be exposed to a health hazard and thereby breaches its duty to provide a safe place in which to work.

Plaintiff contends the trial court erred in dismissing his petition in that it invokes legal principles entitling him to relief and shows that injunctive relief is appropriate. . . .

The petition includes the following allegations. Plaintiff has been employed by defendant since 1950 and has worked in defendant's Missouri branch since 1967. He is a nonsmoker sharing an open office area with other employees, many of whom smoke tobacco products as they work. In 1975 plaintiff began to experience serious respiratory tract discomfort as a result of inhaling tobacco smoke in the workplace. A subsequent medical evaluation determined that plaintiff suffers a severe adverse reaction to tobacco smoke. His symptoms include sore throat, nausea, dizziness, headache, blackouts, loss of memory, difficulty in concentration, aches and pains in joints, sensitivity to noise and light, cold sweat, gagging, choking sensations, and light-headedness. The symptoms have become increasingly severe over the years, however. Doctors evaluating and treating plaintiff have advised him to avoid contact with tobacco smoke whenever possible.

The petition further alleges that plaintiff first complained to defendant about the tobacco smoke in the workplace in 1975. Defendant thereafter moved plaintiff to different locations within the plant, but no improvement resulted because each location contained significant amounts of tobacco smoke. In 1978 plaintiff was informed that he should no longer submit complaints about the smoke through defendant's anonymous complaint procedure since defendant would not process them. In response to recommendations of the National Institute for Occupational Safety and Health, defendant adopted a smoking policy in April 1980. The declared policy was to protect the rights of both smokers and nonsmokers by providing accommodations for both groups and by making a reasonable effort to separate the groups in work areas. Because defendant has failed to implement its policy by making such a reasonable effort, improvement of the air in the workplace has not resulted.

According to the petition, in August 1980 plaintiff filed with defendant a Handicapped Declaration Statement that he was handicapped by his susceptibility to tobacco smoke. Refusing to segregate smokers or to limit smoking to non-work areas, defendant informed plaintiff he could either continue to work in the same location and wear a respirator or apply for a job in the computer room (where smoking is prohibited). The latter option would entail a pay decrease of about $500 per month. Defendant thereafter provided plaintiff with a respirator that has proven ineffective in protecting plaintiff from tobacco smoke.

The petition states that plaintiff has exhausted all avenues of relief through defendant; he has no adequate remedy at law; he is suffering and will continue to suffer irreparable physical injuries and financial losses unless defendant improves working conditions. The petition alleges that defendant is breaching its common law duty as an employer to provide plaintiff a safe place to work, and that defendant has available reasonable alternatives to avoid the continuing breach of duty, as demonstrated by defendant's ability to protect its computer equipment from tobacco smoke. The petition further states that, although "second-hand smoke" is harmful to the health of all employees, defendant is permitting them to be exposed in the workplace to this health hazard which is neither related to nor a necessary by-product of defendant's business. Construing these allegations favorably to plaintiff, we must determine whether they invoke principles of law entitling him to relief.

[1] It is well-settled in Missouri that an employer owes a duty to the employee to use all reasonable care to provide a reasonably safe workplace, . . . and to protect the employee from avoidable perils. . . . Whether the employer has fulfilled its duty depends upon the facts of each case. *Lathrop v. Rippee*, 432 S.W.2d 227. . . .

[2] The allegations of the instant case, taken as true, show that the tobacco smoke of co-workers smoking in the work area is hazardous to the health of employees in general and plaintiff in particular. The allegations also show that defendant knows the tobacco smoke is harmful to plaintiff's health and that defendant has the authority, ability, and reasonable means to control smoking in areas requiring a smoke-free environment. Therefore, by failing to exercise its control and assume its responsibility to eliminate the hazardous condition caused by tobacco smoke, defendant has breached and is breaching its duty to provide a reasonably safe workplace. . . .

[3] If plaintiff's petition establishes defendant's failure to provide a safe place for plaintiff to work, we must next consider whether injunctive relief would be an appropriate remedy. An injunction may issue "to prevent the doing of any legal wrong whatever, whenever in the opinion of the court an adequate remedy cannot be afforded by an action for damages." § 526.030 RSMo 1978. Injunctive relief is unavailable unless irreparable harm is otherwise likely to result, and plaintiff has no adequate remedy at law.

[4] The petition alleges that plaintiff's continuing ex-

posure to smoke in the workplace is increasingly dele-terious to his health and is causing irreparable harm. Assuming the allegations and reasonable inferences therefrom to be true, we think it is fair to characterize deterioration of plaintiff's health as "irreparable" and as a harm for which money damages cannot adequately compensate. This is particularly true where the harm has not yet resulted in full-blown disease or injury. Money damages, even though inadequate, are the best possible remedy once physical damage is done, but they are certainly inadequate to compensate perma-nent injury which could have been prevented. Plaintiff should not be required to await the harm's fruition be-fore he is entitled to seek an inadequate remedy. . . . Finally, the petition states that plaintiff has no adequate remedy at law and alleges facts indicating that prior to this action plaintiff unsuccessfully pursued relief, both through his employer's in-house channels and through administrative agencies. Viewing the petition favorably, as we must to determine its sufficiency, we find that in-junction would be an appropriate remedy.

[5] Defendant contends the trial court lacks jurisdic-tion to provide relief, and therefore the petition fails to state a claim upon which relief can be granted, because the subject matter of this case is preempted by the Oc-cupational Safety and Health Act (OSHA), 29 U.S.C. §§ 651-678 (1970). The Act specifically states, however, that it does not affect the common law regarding "injuries, diseases, or death of employees arising out of

. . . employment." The Act also declares that it does not prevent a state court from asserting jurisdiction over an occupational safety or health issue for which no OSHA standard is in effect. We are unpersuaded by de-fendant's argument that refers only to the common law pertaining to workers' compensation laws. In addition, defendant has not directed our attention to any OSHA standard which would appear to cover tobacco smoke. No such standard figured in the opinions of other courts considering OSHA and tobacco smoke. Furthermore, defendant conceded in oral argument that a court may retain jurisdiction in the absence of an OSHA standard.

We conclude that plaintiff has stated a claim upon which relief can be granted and that the trial court therefore erred in dismissing the petition. Plaintiff should be allowed the opportunity to prove his allega-tions.

The judgment is reversed and the cause remanded.
Gunn and Crandall, JJ., concur.

Case Questions

1. What must a plaintiff show in order to be eligible for an injunction?
2. How is an injunction similar to specific performance?
3. Why did the Court of Appeals in *Smith v. Western Electric* believe that an injunction was the only remedy?

DECREES OF SPECIFIC PERFORMANCE. As mentioned earlier, **decrees of specific performance** are awards to compel parties to fulfill contractual obligations. Such decrees are the exception, not the rule: Partly because they are difficult to en-force, the courts often are reluctant to issue decrees of specific performance.

Specific performance is often awarded in divorce cases and, most fre-quently, in real-property cases. An owner, for example, may be compelled to proceed with the sale of real property: Monetary damages are considered inad-equate compensation for a disappointed buyer in real estate cases because land is considered *unique*. (*See* Chapter 20 *for a full discussion of property law.*) As a general rule, specific performance will be awarded only in those purchase and sale transactions involving unique goods. Again, monetary damages are in these cases considered inadequate. Specific performance is not available in per-sonal-service contracts, in which it would be a form of involuntary servitude. Some commentators have argued that specific performance should be more readily, even routinely, available in contract cases because often only perfor-mance of the contract will redress the breach. The following case involves an effort to obtain specific performance for a breach of contract to sell an automo-bile.

decree of specific performance *Equitable remedy* compelling a party to fulfill a contractual obli-gation

---

SEDMAK v. CHARLIE'S CHEVROLET, INC.
Missouri Court of Appeals, 622 S.W.2d 694 (1981)

The Sedmaks, a couple greatly interested in cars, had plans to purchase one of the limited edition of only 6,000 Chevrolet Corvettes manufactured to **commemorate that car's selection as the official Pace Car of the Indianapolis 500. Charlie's Chevro-let informed the Sedmaks that the price of the spe-**

cial-edition Corvette was to be about $15,000, of which $500 was to be required as down payment. Charlie's represented to the couple that payment of the deposit would ensure their ownership. In addition, the Sedmaks were told that they would be receiving a written contract to sign. When the car arrived at Charlie's, the Sedmaks were informed that despite their payment of the $500 deposit, they could not purchase the automobile for the price previously mentioned. They could only submit a bid on it, because a great demand for the car increased its present value far above the $15,000 suggested sales price.

The Sedmaks sued the defendant, Charlie's Chevrolet, in the trial court for specific performance, arguing, as was necessary to become eligible for such a remedy, that an oral contract was made. The court granted the Sedmaks specific performance. Charlie's Chevrolet appeals.

Charlie's first contends the Sedmaks' evidence is "so wrought with inconsistencies and contradictions that a finding of an oral contract for the sale of a pace car at the manufacturer's suggested retail price is clearly against the weight of the evidence." We disagree. The trial court chose to believe the Sedmaks' testimony over that of Mr. Kells and the reasonableness of this belief was not vitiated by any real contradictions in the Sedmaks' testimony. Charlie's examples of conflict are either facially not contradictory or easily reconcilable.
. . . .

Finally, Charlie's contends the Sedmaks failed to show they were entitled to specific performance of the contract. We disagree. Although it has been stated that the determination whether to order specific performance lies within the discretion of the trial court, this discretion is, in fact, quite narrow. When the relevant equitable principles have been met and the contract is fair and plain, "'specific performance goes as a matter of right.'" Here, the trial court ordered specific performance because it concluded the Sedmaks "have no adequate remedy at law for the reason that they cannot go upon the open market and purchase an automobile of this kind with the same mileage, condition, ownership

and appearance as the automobile involved in this case, except, if at all, with considerable expense, trouble, loss, great delay and inconvenience." Contrary to defendant's complaint, this is a correct expression of the relevant law and it is supported by the evidence.

Under the [Uniform Commercial] Code, the court may decree specific performance as a buyer's remedy for breach of contract to sell goods "where the goods are unique or in other proper circumstances."

. . . The pace car . . . was not unique in the traditional legal sense. It was not an heirloom or, arguably, not one of a kind. However, its "mileage, condition, ownership and appearance" did make it difficult, if not impossible, to obtain its replication without considerable expense, delay and inconvenience. Admittedly, 6,000 pace cars were produced by Chevrolet. However, as the record reflects, this is limited production. In addition, only one of these cars was available to each dealer, and only a limited number of these were equipped with the specific options ordered by plaintiffs. Charlie's had not received a car like the pace car in the previous two years. The sticker price for the car was $14,284.21. Yet Charlie's received offers from individuals in Hawaii and Florida to buy the pace car for $24,000.00 and $28,000.00 respectively. As sensibly inferred by the trial court, the location and size of these offers demonstrated this limited edition was in short supply and great demand. We agree with the trial court. This case was a "proper circumstance" for ordering specific performance.

Judgment affirmed.

Case Questions

1. Should there be any significance to Charlie's Chevrolet that the Sedmaks already owned six Corvettes?

2. What was the primary reason given by the court supporting its decision that specific performance was an appropriate remedy?

3. How might the result have changed if Chevrolet had manufactured 100,000 of the limited-edition Corvettes?

accounting Statement of money owed, spent, or held in trust ordered as *equitable remedy* in cases involving allegations of breaches of *fiduciary duties*

ACCOUNTING. An **accounting**—a statement of money owed, spent, or held in trust—may be ordered in cases involving alleged breaches of fiduciary duties, for example, those of estate administrators, trustees, or guardians. (*See* Chapter 7.) The guardian of a minor child, for instance, may be ordered to account for the use and administration of funds held in trust for the ward. An accounting may include a detailed listing of all transactions involving such funds. The court will rely on it in determining whether the guardian has misappropriated or squandered money.

■ *Concept Check 4-3   How Courts Remedy Disputes*

• Describe the development of *courts of law* and *courts of equity* in the English justice system.

- Explain the key differences between *remedies at law* and *remedies at equity* available to U.S. courts today.
- Under what circumstances will courts award *punitive* as opposed to *compensatory damages?*
- Describe a hypothetical case that might include the issuance of both *temporary* and *permanent injunctions.*

■ THE STRUCTURE OF THE COURT SYSTEM

In our country, the federal and state court systems are separate. The federal system was established by Congress, under Articles I and III of the Constitution; state constitutions provide for the establishment of state courts. Both federal and state courts are empowered to adjudicate questions of federal and state law. As a general rule, however, federal courts are considered the ultimate arbiters of federal law and state courts of state law: In other words, a federal court will defer to a state-court construction of a state law, and a state court will defer to a federal-court construction of a federal law.

The Three-Tier Judicial System

The federal government and most states have three-tier judicial systems consisting of *trial courts, appellate courts,* and a *supreme court.* Although the specific functions of each tier of courts differ on the federal and state levels, it will be helpful to provide general definitions and descriptions of the courts on each tier.

TRIAL COURTS. Trial courts (or **general trial courts**) are the first point at which disputes enter the judicial system. Although evidence may be heard by a jury, most trial-court cases are in fact **bench trials**—that is, they are heard only by a judge. Generally a verdict or judgment is rendered without a summary of the facts. Most trial-court disputes go no further than the trial-court stage—in fact, because of expense and other factors, only a small number of cases filed in trial court actually reach trial.

trial court (or general court) First point at which disputes enter the *judicial system*

bench trial *Trial-court case* heard only by a judge and not by a jury

APPELLATE COURTS. Appellate courts (or **reviewing courts**) neither conduct trials nor hear evidence. Instead, they review case records—pleadings, evidentiary exhibits, testimony transcripts—for errors that may have been made during the original trial. Both the party requesting the review (the **appellant**) and the opposing party (the **appellee**) file **briefs**—written arguments outlining the points that they want considered—with the appellant charging error and requesting that the verdict or judgment be overturned, the appellee asking that it be affirmed. Although it is sometimes difficult to determine precisely when an issue is *factual* or *legal* in nature, appellate courts are generally supposed to correct errors of law, not make judgments concerning the facts of the case.

appellate court (or reviewing court) Court that reviews case records for errors made during an original trial whose findings have been appealed

appellant Losing party to a dispute requesting review of a lower-court decision by an *appellate court* (see also Chapter 5)

appellee Winning party to a dispute opposing the *brief* for review by an *appellate court* (see also Chapter 5)

briefs Written arguments, filed by both *appellant* and *appellee,* outlining points that each wants reviewed by an *appellate court* (see also Chapter 5)

SUPREME COURTS. State **supreme courts** are actually appellate courts—in states with no tier of appellate courts between trial courts and the supreme court, they are the only courts of appeal. As such, supreme courts decide questions of law not questions of fact. Litigants are entitled to only one appellate review, and because a successful petition for a case to be heard by the supreme court

supreme courts *Appellate courts* that act as the final courts of review in a judicial system

may actually grant a second appeal, the supreme court itself decides whether it will hear a case. (The special constitutional functions of the United States Supreme Court are discussed below.)

The Federal System

The federal court system is not constitutionally mandated in its current form: Although Article III established the Supreme Court, Congress was empowered—not *required*—to establish lower federal courts. Its decision to do so, which dates back to the Judiciary Act of 1789, had a dramatic effect on the development of American federalism (*see* Chapter 3). That decision has meant that federal courts, not state courts, are available to decide both questions of federal law and many disputes between citizens of different states. Figure 4-1 illustrates the structure of the federal court system.

The permissible judicial power of the United States is defined by the Constitution. Article III limits the jurisdiction of the Supreme Court and all lower federal courts created by Congress according to subject matter and identity of the parties. Pursuant to Article III, *subject-matter limitations* extend to cases and controversies arising under the Constitution, laws, or treaties of the United States and to maritime and admiralty cases. Federal *party jurisdiction* extends to those cases (1) in which the United States is a party; (2) involving foreign diplomats; (3) between two or more states; (4) between a state and citizens of another state; (5) between citizens of different states; (6) between citizens of the same state claiming land under grants from different states; and (7) between a state or its citizens and foreign states, citizens, or subjects. (The Eleventh Amendment qualified these provisions by eliminating from federal jurisdiction lawsuits against states brought by individual United States or by foreign citizens or subjects.)

Thus, the Constitution describes the limits of federal judicial power. Because Congress is not required to establish lower federal courts, it is not required to give those courts that it does establish the full range of federal party and subject-matter jurisdiction allowed by the Constitution. The Judiciary Act of 1789, for example, did not give lower federal courts original (trial) jurisdic-

FIGURE 4-1 The U.S. Federal Court System   *Source: Adapted from Administrative Office of the United States Courts, The United States Courts: Their Jurisdiction and Work (1989).*

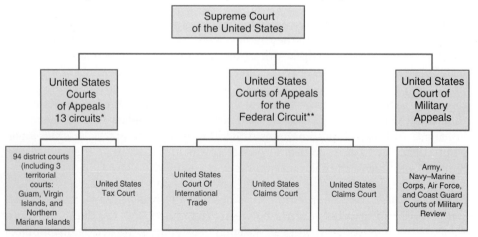

* The 13 regional courts of appeals also receive cases from a number of federal agencies.
**The Court of Appeals for the Federal Circuit also receives cases from the International Trade Commission, the Merit Systems Protection Board, the Patent and Trademark Office, and the Board of Contract Appeals.

PART ONE   THE NATURE OF LAW AND THE U.S. LEGAL SYSTEM

tion of "federal-question" cases. Cases arising under the Constitution, federal laws, or treaties were tried in state courts. **Federal-question jurisdiction** was not given to the federal trial courts for nearly 100 years. The Judiciary Act of 1875 gave them Article III federal-question and diversity-of-citizenship jurisdiction. However, Congress does not have the same power to limit the jurisdiction of the Supreme Court, which was created by the Constitution as a coequal branch of government.

federal-question jurisdiction *Jurisdiction* granted lower federal courts by the Judiciary Act of 1875 to hear cases arising under the Constitution, federal laws, or treaties

The federal judicial system consists largely of courts created under Article III, sometimes called *constitutional courts.* These include: the *federal district courts* (with general criminal and civil trial jurisdiction), the *Court of International Trade* (a special court with jurisdiction over tariff-law cases), and the *U.S. Court of Appeals* (with general intermediate appellate jurisdiction). In order to insure the integrity of the judicial process, the judges of these courts are appointed for life (although they may be removed for acts of misconduct), and their salaries are guaranteed. (*See* the ETHICAL ENVIRONMENT box earlier in this chapter.)

Congress may also establish courts under Article I. Such courts, sometimes called "legislative courts," are special courts that essentially serve Congress. They are neither constitutionally limited in jurisdiction nor vested with the "judicial power" of the United States as outlined in Article III. Today, Article I courts include the court of claims, the court of military appeals, and the tax court. The judges in these courts serve for definite terms of years.

THE DISTRICT COURTS.   Nearly all criminal and civil cases entering the federal system begin in the district courts, which are the federal trial courts. They have exclusive original jurisdiction in federal criminal cases and in bankruptcy cases. (Bankruptcy courts are considered part of the district court systems.) The broad range of federal-question and diversity cases within district court jurisdiction are within **state concurrent jurisdiction**—that is, state jurisdiction in cases which involve more than $50,000 and which may also be heard in a federal court.

state concurrent jurisdiction State *jurisdiction* in *federal-question* and *diversity-of-citizenship cases* within federal district court jurisdiction

There is at least one district court in every state and ninety-one throughout the United States. Every state as well as Puerto Rico, Guam, the Canal Zone, the Virgin Islands, and the Northern Mariana Islands have at least one court. The larger states contain several judicial districts; Texas, California, and New York each have four. Usually, one-to-three judges preside over a court. Congress may add district court judges when they are needed. The judges themselves may appoint magistrates who serve for eight-year terms and handle pretrial proceedings such as bail hearings and pretrial conferences.

U.S. COURT OF APPEALS.   District court decisions are reviewed by the U.S. Court of Appeals. As an appellate court, the court of appeals reviews questions of law, not facts; appellate courts rely on trial-court findings of facts, although a case may be sent back to a trial court for further factual determinations. The court of appeals is divided geographically by circuit (appeals courts were known previously as *circuit courts*). There are now thirteen circuits throughout the United States and its territories, including a circuit for the District of Columbia and the Federal Circuit, established by the Federal Courts Improvement Act of 1982 (*see* Figure 4-2). The Federal Circuit reviews: (1) cases from specialized federal trial courts; (2) district court patent, trademark, and copyright cases; and (3) cases in which the United States is a defendant. There are usually three-to-fifteen judges in each circuit. Each case is generally heard by a three-judge panel although cases considered especially significant may be

FIGURE 4-2 Circuits of the U.S. Courts of Appeal   *Source: Administrative Office of the United States Courts, The United States Courts: Their Jurisdiction and Work (1989).*

heard *en banc*—that is, by all members of the circuit. In addition to reviewing district court decisions, the court of appeals also reviews decisions of some administrative agencies and commissions.

THE FEDERAL JUDICIAL WORKLOAD.   Despite an increase in appointments to the federal bench, the federal docket has been so overwhelmed by a flood of litigation over the past several decades that some scholars have proposed such solutions as rescinding the diversity jurisdiction granted by the Judiciary Act of 1875. Because the problem of heavy judicial workloads has a significant impact on both the principles of jurisdiction and the practical application of the law, we might glance, if only briefly, at some recent developments concerning the workload in U.S. federal courts.[4]

Table 4-1, for example, presents civil and criminal findings in district courts for 1980 and for 1986 through 1990. On the one hand, filings per authorized judgeship dropped from 473 in 1989 to 399 in 1990. On the other hand, these figures reflect an addition of seventy-four judgeships authorized by Congress in December of 1989, and although the total number of 1990 filings is nine percent below the 1988 figure, the total of 258,961 filings in 1990 represents an increase of 55,000 over the 1980 total. Moreover, much of the decrease in civil filings has occurred in relatively less complex areas like Social Security filings. Finally, while *civil* filings decreased, *criminal* filings increased in 1990, with filings outnumbering terminations and the pending caseload rising by eleven percent—an increase of forty-six percent since 1986.

As Figure 4-3 shows, drug-related cases, although down in 1990, made up twenty-six percent of the total criminal workload; because the Anti-Drug Abuse Act of 1988 designated drug offenses as "crimes of violence" and so added immigration and weapons laws to the war against drugs, immigration and weapons filings rose fifteen and twenty percent, respectively, in 1990. Fraud cases also set a new record with a five-percent increase—including a

---

[4] Data in this section comes from the *Federal Judicial Workload Statistics Report* issued in December 1990.

| TABLE 4-1 | Civil and Criminal Cases Filed, U.S. District Courts, 1980 and 1986–1990 | | | | | | |

TYPE OF CASE	1980	1986	1987	1988	1989	1990	PERCENT CHANGE 1990/1989
Total	203,265	285,366	278,028	284,038	272,124	258,961	−4.8
Civil	174,369	243,946	234,748	240,370	225,329	211,626	−6.1
Recovery of Debt[1]	15,652	28,831	20,832	18,344	13,488	8,127	−39.7
Asbestos	*	7,934	6,570	11,846	11,691	9,994	−14.5
Food and Drug Forfeiture[2]	647	606	707	1,051	1,886	2,803	48.6
Social Security	9,338	11,523	15,002	12,633	8,846	6,797	−23.1
Criminal[3]	28,896	41,420	43,280	43,668	46,795	47,335	1.2
Drugs	3,536	8,370	9,663	10,904	12,810	12,221	−4.6
Weapons	1,112	2,013	1,938	2,085	2,388	2,870	20.2
Immigration	1,870	1,843	1,833	1,792	2,115	2,434	15.1

[1] Includes overpayments of veteran's benefits and defaulted student loans.

[2] Cases filed by the U.S. to seize profits and/or assets obtained through the sale of illegal or unapproved drugs.

[3] Excludes transfers.

* Data not available separately.

Source: Administrative Office of the United States Courts, Federal Judicial Workload Statistics (December 1990).

twenty-percent increase in cases involving lending institutions, primarily because of the savings-and-loan scandal.

Table 4-2 shows figures for the U.S. Courts of Appeals. Appeals filed in the twelve regional Courts of Appeals rose a modest two percent in 1990 (to almost 41,000 cases), and although the number of dispositions increased six per-

FIGURE 4-3 Criminal Filings, U.S. District Courts, Year Ended 31 December 1990   Source: Administrative Office of the United States Courts, Federal Judicial Workload Statistics (December 1990).

Total = 47,335

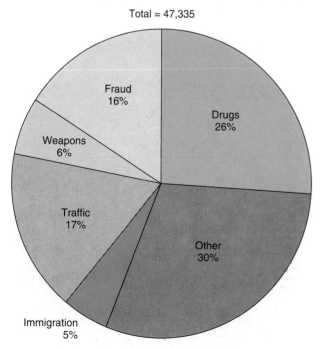

High Court Overload Warren Burger (right) succeeded Earl Warren as Chief Justice of the United States Supreme Court and served in that capacity from 1969 until 1986. Having announced his retirement in 1985, Burger warned that "Unless some relief is given . . . there may be some judges . . . who will exploit the reality that, since the chance of being reviewed by the Supreme Court is swiftly diminishing, they need not pay very much attention to what the Supreme Court decides." Citing the Court's burgeoning workload, Burger and five other justices proposed an experiment: the creation of a new federal court of appeals composed of nine federal judges who would review the conflicting rulings of U.S. Court of Appeal judges. Critics of the plan—including some Supreme Court justices—have replied that the Court tends to overburden itself by taking on issues of relatively minor significance. Although current Chief Justice William Rehnquist has endorsed the Burger proposal, there has yet to be any substantial Congressional action.

| TABLE 4-2 | *Appeals Commenced, Terminated, and Pending, U.S. Courts of Appeal, 1980 and 1986–1990* |

YEAR	AUTHORIZED JUDGESHIPS	COMMENCED		TERMI-NATED	PENDING
		NUMBER	CASES PER PANEL		
1980	132	24,122	548	28,886	21,429
1986	156	34,753	668	33,936	26,470
1987	156	35,698	687	35,272	26,896
1988	156	38,962	749	36,684	29,174
1989*	156	40,245	774	37,591	31,579
1990	167**	40,982	732	39,825	32,736
Percent Change					
1990 over 1989		1.8	−5.4	5.9	3.7

*Revised

**Public Law 101-650, signed on December 1, 1990, authorized 11 additional positions.

Source: Administrative Office of the United States Courts, Federal Judicial Workload Statistics *(December 1990).*

cent over 1989, because filings outpaced terminations, the pending caseload went up four percent. Criminal appeals rose eleven percent (to almost 10,000 cases), with drug offenses leading the way with a fourteen-percent increase (compared to a six-percent increase in 1980). Despite increased terminations, the number of appeals pending increased four percent, led by a sixteen-percent increase in criminal appeals. With a twenty-two-percent increase, drug-related appeals now account for about sixty percent of all pending criminal appeals.

THE U.S. SUPREME COURT. The U.S. Supreme Court is, at least in theory, the court of last resort for some ten million cases heard every year. About 300,000 of these cases are appealed through higher state courts and the federal system. The Supreme Court is petitioned to hear about 5,000 cases each year. It can actually hear only 150 to 175 of these.

Only a very small number of cases are *guaranteed* Supreme Court review—that is, those that fall within either the Court's exclusive original jurisdiction or its obligatory appellate jurisdiction. Although the Supreme Court is primarily an appellate court, it does have original, trial jurisdiction of all cases in which any states or foreign diplomats are parties. Congress has codified these constitutional grants of jurisdiction in 28 U.S.C. § 1251.

The vast majority (ninety-eight percent) of all cases heard by the Supreme Court are appeals. Congress defines the Court's appellate jurisdiction, pursuant to Article III. (The extent to which it can limit that jurisdiction, depriving the Court of the power to decide constitutional questions, is a highly debatable point of constitutional law.) The U.S. Code (*see* Chapter 1), 28 U.S.C. §§ 1252, 1254, and 1257, defines the Court's discretionary and obligatory appellate jurisdiction. Cases within its discretionary jurisdiction are reviewed on **writs of certiorari**—requests by one of the parties that the Court hear the case. Cases within its obligatory jurisdiction (which the Court must accept) are reviewed by appeal and must satisfy one of two circumstances: (1) civil, federal district court cases in which the United States is a party and an act of Congress has been declared unconstitutional; and (2) cases in which a state court has either struck down a federal law or treaty or upheld a state law against a constitutional or federal statutory challenge.

writ of certiorari Request that the U.S. Supreme Court hear a case within its *discretionary jurisdiction*

The majority of cases heard by the Court are those that fall within its discretionary jurisdiction and in which a *writ of certiorari* is granted. Only five percent of all writs that come before the Court are granted; the lower-court decision becomes final in the remaining ninety-five percent of cases. That decision, however, does not have the same force of law as a lower-court decision summarily affirmed by the court in an appeal. According to current Chief Justice William Rehnquist, the Court should agree to hear a case within its discretionary appellate jurisdiction when: (1) the federal circuit court decision conflicts with an earlier decision of another circuit; and (2) the case raises issues that "seem both important to a much larger segment of society than the litigants themselves, and of debatable correctness."[5]

THE FEDERAL COURTS: SELECTION AND MAKEUP. As we have seen, Article II, Section 2 of the Constitution empowers the president to appoint members of the Supreme Court and other federal judges "with the advice and consent of the Senate." In reality, of course, the process is much more complex. We will look

---

[5] Address delivered by Chief Justice Rehnquist, delivered at St. Louis University on 7 April 1983, quoted in 28 *St. Louis University Law Journal* 3 (1984).

briefly at the following factors in the nomination and confirmation of Supreme Court justices: the roles of *politics, ideology,* and *race* and *sex.*

Politics. Although it no longer applies to Supreme Court appointments and now applies less often to courts of appeals judges, the practice of *senatorial courtesy* offers veto power over nominations to a senator if (1) a federal judge is to sit in that senator's state and (2) that senator is of the president's party. As a rule, in addition to the president, the Senate as a whole, political-party leaders, and the Department of Justice are involved in the judicial bargaining process. In addition, the Standing Committee on the Federal Judiciary of the American Bar Association evaluates nominees' competence and integrity and issues critical ratings; while these ratings are not binding, most presidents have hesitated to forward the names of nominees considered "unqualified" by the Committee.

Until fairly recently, most presidents made no secret of the fact that judgeships were used as partisan political rewards. In general, presidents have only seldomly nominated judges from opposing parties, and recently, Presidents Ronald Reagan and George Bush have been quite open about the importance of partisan affiliation and ideological leaning. Table 4-3 shows the party affiliation of judges appointed by U.S. presidents since Franklin D. Roosevelt.

TABLE 4-3	*Party Affiliation, Federal Judges Appointed by Presidents from Roosevelt to Bush*

PRESIDENT	PARTY	APPOINTEES FROM SAME PARTY
Roosevelt	Democrat	97%
Truman	Democrat	92%
Eisenhower	Republican	95%
Kennedy	Democrat	92%
Johnson	Democrat	94%
Nixon	Republican	93%
Ford	Republican	81%
Carter	Democrat	90%
Reagan	Republican	97%

Source: David M. O'Brien, Judicial Roulette: Report of the Twentieth Century Fund Task Force on Judicial Selection *(Dallas, TX: Priority Press, 1988).*

Ideology. Even President Jimmy Carter, who openly disavowed partisan considerations in his selection of judicial nominees, appointed only a few individuals outside his own party. However, because he assigned initial screening to bipartisan panels and then deferred to the recommendations of minority and women's organizations, President Carter—who appointed almost forty percent of the federal judiciary during his one-term tenure—bequeathed a lower federal bench that was generally more "liberal" than the Supreme Court. Virtually every president has acted upon some concern for ideology—or "policy consideration"—in selecting nominees for the federal bench, and although more than one president has failed in his prediction of a key nominee's subsequent judicial comportment, analysis has shown that at least Supreme Court appointments have satisfied expectations about seventy-five percent of the time.[6]

---

[6] See especially Laurence H. Tribe, *God Save This Honorable Court: How the Choice of Supreme Court Justices Shapes Our History* (New York: Random House, 1985).

NEWARK (NJ) EVENING NEWS

Of Course He Can't Want This!

"The Switch in Time That Saved Nine" With the New Deal running out of steam after his reelection in 1936, President Franklin D. Roosevelt opened his second term with an attack on the Supreme Court. The Court had declared unconstitutional several New Deal measures enacted during Roosevelt's first term, and the president, who regarded the justices as guardians of conservative policy, asked Congress for the power to nominate six additional members. As this 1937 cartoon shows, many people, conservatives and liberals alike, feared that Roosevelt's "Court-packing" scheme was a prelude to autocratic rule, and not surprisingly, the proposal ignited a firestorm of controversy. Ultimately, however, the Court, possibly responding to the aggressiveness of the president's stance, began ruling in his favor, sustaining numerous pieces of New Deal legislation. Although the controversy subsided, some observers recognized the real possibility of Roosevelt's eventual success, and one commentator thus referred to the Court's reversal as "the switch in time that saved nine."

Although it is often difficult to assign the labels *liberal, conservative,* and *moderate* to the "philosophical" leanings of federal-court appointees and nominees, widely held assessments of opinions and other sources do tend toward some general consensus, and Figure 4-4 reflects the changes in the basic makeup of the Supreme Court at ten-year intervals between 1962 and 1992.

Race and Sex. As we have seen (Chapter 3), President Lyndon Johnson appointed Thurgood Marshall as the first black to the Supreme Court in 1967, and George Bush appointed the second, Clarence Thomas, as Marshall's successor in 1991. In selecting 40 women, 38 blacks, and 16 Hispanics to the federal bench, Carter appointed more minorities and women than all other presidents combined. Although Reagan appointed the only woman, Sandra Day O'Connor, to the Court in 1981 (*see* the PERSONAL PROFILE box in this chapter), his administration's stringent screening of candidates for ideological compatibility resulted in the selection of far fewer women and minorities.

Year									
'62	Earl Warren	Hugo Black	Arthur Goldberg	William Douglas	William Brennan	Charles Wittaker	Potter Stewart	John Harlen	Tom Calrk
'72	Warren Burger	Lewis Powell	Harry Blackman	William Douglas	William Brennan	Byron White	Potter Stewart	William Rehnquist	Thurgood Marshall
'82	Warren Burger	Lewis Powell	Harry Blackman	John Paul Stevens	William Brennan	Byron White	Sandra Day O'Connor	William Rehnquist	Thurgood Marshall
'92	Anthony Scalia	Anthony Kennedy	Harry Blackman	John Paul Stevens	David Souter	Byron White	Sandra Day O'Connor	William Rehnquist	Clarance Thomas

☐ Liberal   ☐ Moderate   ☐ Conservative

FIGURE 4-4 The Changing Ideology of the U.S. Supreme Court, 1962-1992 *Source: Henry J. Abraham,* Justices and Presidents: A Political History of Appointments to the Supreme Court, *3rd ed. (New York: Oxford Univ. Press, 1992).*

PERSONAL PROFILE
Sandra Day O'Connor

In September 1981, Sandra Day O'Connor was unanimously confirmed by the Senate to sit on the U.S. Supreme Court. O'Connor broke historical precedent by being the first woman elected to sit on the highest court in the land. Moreover, her nomination and acceptance constituted a radical restructuring of what was previously and commonly considered sacred male terrain.

O'Connor brought with her to the Supreme Court a stockpile of knowledge and experience. She had worked in all three branches of state government—as an attorney, an Arizona appeals court judge, and an Arizona state legislator. Still, from the moment O'Connor stepped across the threshold into the male sanctum of the Supreme Court, an added psychological burden was placed on her: She was immediately prey to—and, to a debatable degree, answerable to —the pressing and varied demands and desires of American women. This extension of concern and duty is one that the other Supreme Court judges, by virtue of their being male, simply do not experience. In strictly mathematical terms, it was predictable from the start that O'Connor would likely bear the world of particularly female concerns on her shoulders because the other judges had generally deadlocked four to four on the abortion issue.

Due in part to her background, it seems that O'Connor is well prepared to handle the stress of being a pivotal judical figure. She was born in 1930 and grew up on an isolated cattle ranch in southeastern Arizona and southwestern New Mexico. Raised out of step with accelerated, crowded urban society, she was forced to establish her own mental stride and practical self-sufficiency at an early age. By the age of eight, O'Connor knew how to shoot, mend fences, and drive a truck.

Fueled by a strong work ethic, O'Connor excelled when sent off to school, first in Texas and later at Stanford University. After graduating, O'Connor tried unsuccessfully in the early 1950s to penetrate the blue-chip male bastion of California corporate law. Forced to fall back on her own resources, O'Connor settled instead into a small private practice begun with one other partner.

Simultaneously, O'Connor began a family, having married fellow Stanford graduate John Jay O'Connor, a corporate lawyer. O'Connor abandoned private practice after the birth of their second son and began a five-year interim away from paid employment. Although she devoted most of her attention to her family, O'Connor stayed heavily involved in legal practice through community volunteer work, anticipating—and facilitating—her future re-entry into the mainstream of law and politics.

In 1965, O'Connor recommended work as an assistant attorney general in Arizona. Four years later, she was chosen to finish out the remaining term of a state senator who resigned. She won the senate seat herself in 1970 and 1972 and the following year was elected majority leader, establishing a landmark as the first woman in a state legislature to secure the position.

Upon examination of O'Connor's career as an Arizona state senator, it is clear that she is an issues-oriented person and thus tends to be a "swing" voter. As a state senator, O'Connor voted to repeal Arizona's strong anti-abortion statutes, and she cosigned a bill to make contraception information more readily available. However, since then, her suspicions of the inherent value and legitimacy of Roe v. Wade have been aired. Also as state senator, O'Connor exercised conservatism—for example, her advocacy of fiscally-conservative federal government—that ran counter to her liberal tendencies.

The next step in O'Connor's career was service in the Arizona judiciary, first as an elected judge to the superior court and subsequently as an appointee to the state Court of Appeals. In the former position, O'Connor was considered tough on law and order.

Considering O'Connor's current residence on the

Supreme Court bench, we recall that Ronald Reagan was adamantly opposed to the ERA and was fulfilling a campaign promise by nominating a woman to the highest court. It follows that O'Connor has for the most part met Reagan's expectation that she would prove a conservative justice. In a large percentage of cases, she has voted with conservative Chief Justice Rehnquist. Basically, O'Connor navigates a course of judicial restraint, the compass points for which were (publicly) set in her nomination hearings when she stated: "Judges are not only not authorized to engage in executive and legislative functions, they are ill-equipped to do so."

Known for her meticulous attention to constitutional precedent, O'Connor has in her role as Supreme Court justice pleased liberals by siding with them on a sex-discrimination case in which she grounded her decision in the equal-protection guarantee of the Constitution. In another decision perceived as liberal, O'Connor maintained in an affirmative-action case that, in certain situations, an employer may hire and/or promote minorities and women over slightly better qualified men in order to balance the workplace.

O'Connor's preference for restrained judgment on the abortion issue manifested itself in 1989 in the Webster v. Reproductive Health case. The outcome of the case was the Court's qualification, by a five to four vote, of the 1973 Roe v. Wade ruling that a woman has a constitutional right to an abortion. O'Connor voted with the majority in Webster forcing the adoption of her own vague standard: namely, that states may impose abortion restrictions at any stage of pregnancy so long as they do not place an 'unnecessary burden' on the woman's abortion decision. In her individual concurring opinion, O'Connor wrote, "There will be time enough to re-examine Roe. And to do so carefully."

In June 1992, O'Connor signed the five-to-four majority opinion in the case of Planned Parenthood v. Casey, which reaffirmed the Roe v. Wade ruling that legalized abortions. "The Constitution," wrote O'Connor, "serves human values, and while the effect of reliance on Roe cannot be exactly measured, neither can the certain cost of overruling Roe for people who have ordered their thinking and living around that case be dismissed."

July 7, 1981: Arizona appeals-court judge Sandra Day O'Connor meets the press after having been selected by President Ronald Reagan as the only woman ever nominated for the U.S. Supreme Court. Justice O'Connor's stature remains unique—and so does the issue of the standards to which she will be held. In 1989, for example, with her colleagues apparently deadlocked at four-four on the question of abortion, a member of the faculty at one of the nation's preeminent law schools voiced the opinion of many Court observers: "If Justice O'Connor wants to continue protecting abortion rights, they will be protected. If she does not, they will not. It is her decision."

State Court Systems

Because court systems and procedures vary from state to state, we can only give a general overview of them here. As noted earlier, most include three levels of courts: trial courts, intermediate courts of appeals, and a supreme court. In this, of course, they mirror the federal court system. A typical state-court system appears in Figure 4-5.

Trial courts at the state level may be divided into *civil* and *criminal divisions*. They function as trial courts generally do, hearing evidence and testimony and delivering verdicts. Intermediate appellate courts review the legality of trial-court proceedings. Like the Supreme Court, the state high courts hear appeals from the intermediate appellate courts on *writs of certiorari* and select most of their own cases.

FIGURE 4-5 Typical State Court System   *Source: John H. Jackson and Vernon A. Musselman,* Business: Contemporary Concepts and Practices *(Englewood Cliffs, NJ: Prentice Hall, 1987).*

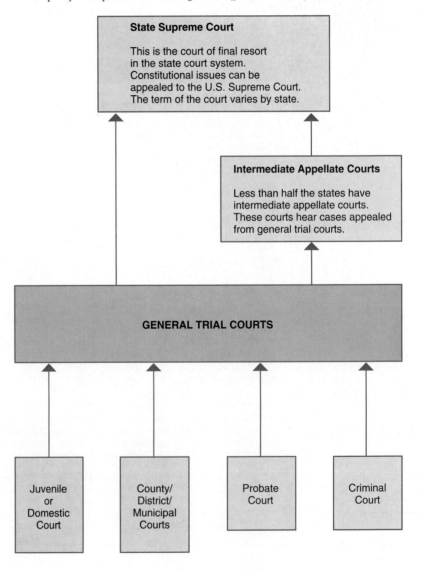

In the case of Roginsky v. Richardson-Merrell, *the district court judgment regarding compensatory damages was affirmed and the judgment regarding punitive damages reversed. The appellate found that "evidence was insufficient to warrant a finding of recklessness required . . . for an award of punitive damages," although there was "evidence of carelessness, failure to exercise proper supervision, and possible bad judgment in regard to failure to issue timely or appropriate warnings or to withdraw drug from the market based on evidence" that it could cause cataracts (378 F.2d 832).*

The judge recognized that punitive damages were a significant monetary issue to Richardson-Merrell in terms of the hundreds of pending claims over the drug MER/29. He also acknowledged the implications for the "entire pharmaceutical industry and to all present and potential users of drugs" (378 F.2d 838). In addition, because the claims for hundred of plaintiffs would be enormous, he acknowledged that punitive awards could far outweigh criminal fines for such an act and thus constitute a denial of due process to the defendant.

However, even in this case of "mass-disaster" litigation, where there was no finding of recklessness on the defendant's part and thus no punitive award, the policy issue of punitive damages still remains open: If such an award might indeed deter future similar actions by this firm and others like it, then it might be warranted.

On the other hand, even if a drug company is held to be reckless—for example, in not testing its products long enough or on enough subjects or under the right circumstances—do compensatory damages not provide individual plaintiffs with a sufficient amount? Would not a corporation whose funds are diverted to the payment of high punitive-damage awards be less able to respond fairly to everyone seeking to recover compensatory damages? Moreover, are very high punitive-damage awards in civil suits out of proportion to the actual damages found—and far in excess of fines imposed in analogous criminal proceedings?

Clearly, even with the many cases of compensatory and punitive damages being decided each day in federal and state courts, there are still questions to be settled. In particular, both students of these questions and the courts themselves are still grappling with two major issues.

1. Generally speaking, punitive damages constitute a "windfall" for the plaintiff: They are not a matter of right and are to be awarded at the discretion of a judge or jury. Most courts thus rule that when there is no finding for compensatory damages, there is no cause for action to support the award of punitive damages. Moreover, some courts decline to find such cause of action when only nominal compensatory damages are awarded. And herein lies an important problem: The prospect of punitive-damage awards derives from a policy of providing an incentive for plaintiffs to file claims for "petty outrages" for which only nominal damages can be expected.

2. It is frequently assumed or argued that punitive damages should bear some "reasonable proportion" to the amount of compensatory damages awarded. This proportion, however, remains undefined, and in practice, although very few courts have rejected outright the idea of some proportion, there is often a great deal of inconsistency in punitive-damage awards: In some cases, courts are hesitant to support large penalty verdicts with small compensatory awards, while in others punitive awards quite out of keeping with compensatory awards have been affirmed.

Such problems, of course, are highlighted in "mass-disaster" cases, and to date, a few states have acted to resolve issues like these. Some, for example, have established limitations on punitive damages. Others have decided that when extremely large punitive awards—like those in "mass-disaster" cases—are analogous to criminal fines, they are to be payable in part to the state, which would ordinarily be the recipient and custodian of fine payments.

State court systems often have an additional, lower level of specialized trial courts with limited jurisdictions. Juvenile courts, probate courts (dealing with trusts and estates), and family courts fall into this category (Municipalities often have their own municipal courts, which are generally limited to hearing minor civil or criminal matters. In rural areas of a few states, **justices of the peace**—usually elected officials who are not required to have any formal legal training—conduct very simple legal proceedings like performing marriages and disposing of traffic tickets. In addition, the states have **small-claims courts**—informal forums for the resolution of cases involving small dollar amounts. Such courts are intended to allow people to settle claims themselves, without hiring lawyers, by presenting claims or defenses to hearing officers who decide cases and fix damages.

justice of the peace Generally, an elected official without formal legal training who conducts such simple proceedings as marriages and traffic-ticket disposition

small-claims court In most state judicial systems, an informal forum for resolving disputes over small monetary amounts

- Describe the *three tiers* of the U.S. judicial system and explain the key differences between *trial* and *appellate courts.*
- Define *federal-question* and *concurrent jurisdiction.*
- Explain the differences between the U.S. Supreme Court's *discretionary* and *obligatory appellate jurisdiction.*

SUMMARY

- The general purpose of *adjudication* is the resolution of disputes and the definition of rights and responsibilities. As a practical matter, *jurisdiction*—a court's authority to hear and decide a case—is limited by the exercise of judicial restraint. In order to hear a case, a court must have jurisdiction over the subject matter and over the parties against whom a suit is brought. *Long-arm statutes* extend the judicial reach of U.S. courts over parties. *Diversity of citizenship* extends the jurisdiction of federal district courts over state law when certain criteria are met. *Venue*, defined by statute, designates jurisdiction over geographic areas.

- *Justiciability* is defined broadly by the Constitution; pursuant to Article III, the judicial power of the United States extends only to *cases and controversies.* Construing this provision, the Supreme Court has set forth the following standards of justiciability: (1) plaintiffs must have *standing* to sue; and (2) the case must be an active controversy, not a *moot* or hypothetical situation, which is *ripe* for judicial review. The courts will not issue *advisory opinions* or nonfinal orders subject to executive review.

- *Case law* is based on the principle of *stare decisis*, which gives each case decided by a court precedential value to guide courts in deciding future cases. Based on this doctrine, judges may *distinguish, extend,* or *overrule* precedents only through careful description and evaluation. Thus, the stare decisis principle helps insure the predictability and fairness of the legal system.

- In civil cases, the role of courts is essentially *remedial*. Remedies may be either *legal* or *equitable* in nature. *Monetary damages* are legal remedies. *Injunctions* and *decrees of specific performance* are equitable remedies. Although our society distinguishes between legal and equitable remedies, under our legal system, both federal and state courts are *courts of general jurisdiction*—that is, they are courts of both legal and equitable jurisdiction.

- The U.S. court system includes both federal and state courts. The federal system and most state systems have three-tier judicial systems consisting of *trial courts, intermediate appellate courts,* and a *supreme court.* Both federal and state courts may decide matters of federal or state law. State courts have *concurrent jurisdiction* with federal district courts in many civil cases involving *federal questions* and disputes between citizens of different states.

- The Constitution established the Supreme Court and defined the limits of federal jurisdiction. Congress has established a lower federal court system at its discretion, under Articles I and III of the Constitution. Article I courts function essentially as administrative arms of Congress. Article III courts are vested with the judicial power of the United States and constitute the independent federal judiciary.

- *State courts*, which are established by state constitutions, function in the same general way as the federal courts in deciding state and sometimes federal disputes. State courts often have an additional lower level of specialized trial courts (for example, juvenile, probate, and family courts). In addition, state *small-claims courts* provide informal forums for the resolution of simple disputes, usually involving less than $1,500.

CASE PROBLEMS

1. Justine Smith, a claims intake worker for the Veterans Administration (VA), receives several claims from returning veterans who have a range of medical complaints including headaches, nausea, anxiety, and inability to sleep, concentrate, or hold coherent conversations. Most of these applicants have been on duty where a certain chemical was used in the war effort. Ms. Smith forwards the applicants' claim requests, which are rejected by agency officials who are unwilling to find a connection between the chemical and the veterans' nonspecific illnesses. She then brings a class action suit on behalf of the applicants to have their illness recognized as one for which the VA will approve benefits. What will be the outcome and why?

2. Over thirty years ago, many pregnant women were given the antimiscarriage drug DES which subsequently caused cancer in the women's daughters years later. The courts allowed for the women's daughters to sue all DES manufacturers even when they could not determine which company made the drug their mother ingested. Now, a granddaughter is trying to sue the manufacturers of DES by asserting that her premature birth, cerebral palsy and grand mal seizures were caused by the DES effects on her mother's reproductive organs when her mother was exposed to DES in the womb! Does this granddaughter have standing to sue? Discuss.

3. Valerie Johnston owns a business adjacent to a busy street. The city council votes to widen the street to accommodate the growing traffic burden. Ms. Johnston challenges the city council's action by suing. She alleges that it is an unconstitutional taking of her property without due process of law for the council to vote to widen the street and deprive her of customers while the construction is in progress. By the time the case reaches the appellate court, however, the business is sold. Will this case be heard by the court? Why or why not?

4. In reviewing a lower court decision, the Supreme Court is called upon to determine a court's authority to grant certain types of relief in cases involving consent decrees. The Court's decision discusses the issue in question and then goes on to give its views as to relief that can be granted in other types of cases. Can the Court legitimately do this? [*Firefighters Local 1784 v. Stotts*, 467 U.S. 561 (1984)]

5. John Abrams contracted to perform at the Epic Theater on April 30, but does not appear as scheduled. Epic sues him for $20,000 in compensatory damages, which it can prove, and $50,000 in punitive damages. How much can Epic recover and why?

6. Jean Cragmere, from Ohio, has an accident with Roland Quincy, from California, on Interstate 25 in Iowa. She sustained serious injuries totaling over $25,000, and sued Roland Quincy in federal court. However, he claims that since there is no federal law involved, he must be sued in state court if at all. Is this correct?

7. Darby Sullivan, who is employed as a waiter at the Coral Gables Country Club, buys new tires for his car from Tire Company and pays for them on credit. He is current in his payments, but the tire company's computer shows that he is delinquent. Therefore, Tire Company removes the tires from his car while it is parked at work, and leaves the car standing on the rims of the wheels. Mr. Sullivan suffered embarrassment, humiliation, and wounded feelings. He lost two nights of sleep and took medication. He also became the butt of jokes and was asked to remove his car from the lot since it was an embarrassment to the club. As a result, he sues for compensatory and punitive damages. What will the court decide? [*Santiesteban v. Goodyear Tire Co.*, 306 F.2d 9 (5th Cir. 1962)]

8. Jacques walks across Rusty's land without Rusty's permission. Jacques does not interfere with Rusty's use of

his property but Rusty repeatedly tells him to get off. What types of damages could Rusty get for Jacques' interference with Rusty's possessory interest?

9. Jewel was employed for four years as a hair stylist at Connie's Hair Salon. When Jewel first began her employment she was asked to sign a one year contract that said if she left her employment at Connie's Hair Salon for any reason, she was prohibited from working in a competing hair salon within a one mile radius of Connie's Salon for two years. Jewel leaves her employment and works at George's Hair Salon three blocks away. Connie's Hair Salon files suit asking for specific performance and $10,000 in punitive damages. Who do you think will win and why?

10. After Adam Boyle purchased four lots for future homes in the residential section of town, Brian Green constructs a fuel gas reservoir for storing gas to be distributed to customers directly across the street. No applicable laws or zoning ordinances have been violated, but Mr. Boyle asserts that the reservoir (1) pollutes the air so as to injure the health of those living there, (2) has depreciated his lots, (3) prevents the sale of his lots for any reasonable price, and (4) ruins the area for residential purposes. Mr. Green counters that the lots are vacant, so Mr. Boyle's comfortable enjoyment of them is not invaded. What, if any, recourse is available? [*Romano v. Birmingham Ry., Light and Power Co.*, 182 Ala. 335, 62 So. 677 (1913)]

5

LITIGATION AND DISPUTE RESOLUTION

Governments are established, in part, because the body politic has a general interest in preserving peace among its members. The family, tribe, township, or nation establishes rules and procedures to maintain order and settle disagreements. A government's chosen form of dispute resolution may derive from tradition, philosophy, economic necessity, or a combination of the three, and may be modeled on various sources. However it develops, an effective system of dispute resolution must be consistent, in conformance with prevailing concepts of justice, and must have the consent and support of its participants.

In the United States, the settlement of controversies between parties is carried out in an **adversarial system**: Although the courts provide a forum, the participants involved in a civil disagreement bear the major responsibility of initiating the suit, defining the issues, and providing evidence in support of their claims. However, all prospective plaintiffs should first weigh the costs and benefits of going to court. They should understand both the substantive law governing the case and the procedural steps whereby a suit moves through the courts. Procedural rules and strategies often determine the outcome of a case.

This chapter follows the progress of a lawsuit from inception to appeal, paying particular attention to how a suit begins, what is required of each of the parties, how the jury and the judge assess the evidence and the applicable law, and what recourse there may be for the losing party. Because litigation is costly, exhausting, and slow, alternative forms of dispute resolution are gaining in popularity and credibility, and this chapter concludes with a look at some of these alternatives.

adversarial system
Dispute-resolution system in which the involved parties must initiate the lawsuit, define the issues, and provide supporting evidence for their claims (*see also* Chapter 1)

■ JURISDICTION: BEYOND SUBJECT MATTER

jurisdiction A court's legal authority to hear and decide a case (see also Chapter 1)

The subject matter of a case can determine whether a state or federal court has **jurisdiction**—that is, the legal authority to hear and decide it (*see* Chapter 4). However, subject matter is not the sole determinant of jurisdiction. Once a specific court system has been identified according to the principles discussed in Chapter 4, the question of jurisdiction becomes a matter of which court has the *territorial* right to summon and hear the people involved in the case. Questions raised by this issue include the following:

- Does it matter whether the parties to the case are "natural persons" (human beings) or corporations (state-created beings)?
- How do we decide the extent of a court's personal jurisdiction—its power over individuals and business entities?

As we previously saw, two jurisdictional requirements must be met in order for a court to hear a case: jurisdiction over *subject matter* and jurisdiction over the *party* against whom a suit is brought. We saw that *parties* may be either individuals or organizations, and we will now clarify that distinction by discussing jurisdiction over *natural persons* and, for purposes of focusing on litigation in the context of business, jurisdiction over *corporations*. We will also expand on the discussion of *venue*, which was introduced in Chapter 4. Clearly, the development of court systems and principles of jurisdiction are closely related. As the INTERNATIONAL ENVIRONMENT box below shows this fact also holds true for the legal system in Japan, which, although modeled on the U.S. system, offers some interesting contrasts.

THE INTERNATIONAL ENVIRONMENT
Jurisdiction in the Japanese Legal System

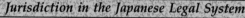

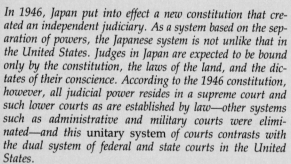

In 1946, Japan put into effect a new constitution that created an independent judiciary. As a system based on the separation of powers, the Japanese system is not unlike that in the United States. Judges in Japan are expected to be bound only by the constitution, the laws of the land, and the dictates of their conscience. According to the 1946 constitution, however, all judicial power resides in a supreme court and such lower courts as are established by law—other systems such as administrative and military courts were eliminated—and this unitary system of courts contrasts with the dual system of federal and state courts in the United States.

Japanese courts are empowered to adjudicate all legal disputes; to determine the constitutionality of laws; to make rules regarding procedures, practice, and the administration of judicial affairs; and to exercise such powers as the law provides. Under this last category, courts decide a wide range of cases—for example, trust and estate matters, corporate reorganizations or liquidations, and domestic property disputes.

Structurally, the Japanese judicial system resembles the U.S. system: Cases flow from a lower to higher court for ap-

peals, and higher courts have original jurisdiction over certain kinds of cases. The diagram below shows the five types of courts and their interrelationships.

At the head of the Japanese system is the supreme court, which hears only appeals except in the following instances: (1) cases regarding the impeachment of the commissioner of the National Personnel Authority, and (2) cases in lower courts with pending petitions for habeas corpus—that is, writs ordering a person to be brought before a court. In order for an appeal to be heard in the supreme court, it must meet some very strict criteria: (1) in a criminal case, a constitutional issue or a conflict with a prior decision of the supreme court or a high court, (2) in a civil case, a constitutional issue or a question of law regarding the judgment being appealed. The supreme court also conducts administrative affairs for the whole system.

Below the supreme court are the High Courts, which also hear appeals from lower courts but which have original jurisdiction in a few areas. Of the eight high courts, the one in Tokyo is similar to the U.S. Court of Appeals for the federal circuit in that it hears cases from certain governmental agencies. The fifty district courts, which have territorial jurisdiction, are where all cases originate, except those specifically coming under higher courts. District courts also hear appeals from summary courts.

Located within the district courts are family courts, which decide family disputes and all related legal matters. To obtain a divorce in Japan, for example, one must first apply to the family court, where an attempt is made to reconcile differences or terminate the marriage in an equitable manner. If agreement proves impossible, only then may one of the parties sue for divorce in district court. The family courts are also the original jurisdiction for criminal cases in which the offender is a minor. Finally, there are 575 summary courts. They try civil cases in which the monetary value does not exceed $7,000 and certain minor criminal cases.

In Japan, all practicing lawyers and public prosecutors, as well as individuals aspiring to judgeships, must receive two years of training at the Legal Training and Research Institute after having passed the national bar exam. Although it might seem impossible to train so many professionals at a single institution, the task looks less daunting when we realize that Japan has only about 14,000 lawyers. Japan is clearly not as litigious a society as the United States, where we require 140 lawyers for each 100,000 people—and a consequent number of law schools to train them all.

All judges in Japan are appointed by the Cabinet. Judgeships involve a two-tier system in the high, district, and family courts. Aspirants to assistant judgeships, in addition to meeting the two requirements cited above, must also pass a final qualifying exam. After ten years of service, these judges—as well as public prosecutors, practicing attorneys, and a few other legal positions requiring ten years' experience—may become full-fledged judges.

Interestingly, not all judges in the supreme and summary courts of Japan must fulfill the same requirements. Of the fifteen judgeships in the supreme court, for example, five need not be filled by qualified jurists as long as the proposed judges know the law. In summary court, a person may simply demonstrate knowledge of the law to qualify for a judgeship.

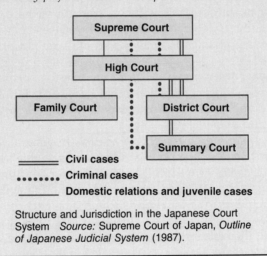

Structure and Jurisdiction in the Japanese Court System   *Source:* Supreme Court of Japan, *Outline of Japanese Judicial System* (1987).

Jurisdiction over Natural Persons

Courts may determine their jurisdiction over *natural persons* according to two criteria: *territorial* and *personal*. As we shall see, although *territory* is a factor in both criteria, distinctions between the two types of jurisdiction have developed in the modern legal system, and we will discuss each by focusing on those distinctions.

TERRITORIAL JURISDICTION.   Fundamental notions of fair play and substantial justice are involved in determining whether a particular state court has sufficient contact with the parties to decide the case. For example, suppose you are on vacation from New Jersey. You travel to Casco Bay in Maine, and, while you are there, your car is damaged in an auto accident involving a driver from Massachusetts. You want to recover the cost of repairs from the other driver, but you do not know which state's courts should resolve the dispute. How do you decide? In other words, which state has **territorial jurisdiction?**

In early common law, accused persons had to be physically present for

territorial jurisdiction A court's authority to resolve a legal conflict on the grounds that the accused person or property at issue falls within the physical jursidiction of the court

court to pass judgment. Defendants had a right to confront accusers and to be judged by peers or neighbors. Furthermore, unless the court had physical control, the accused could not always be compelled to honor the terms of any judgment against him. Thus the early court's *territorial* limits defined its power over people and property. Today's notions of *territorial jurisdiction* reflect similar practical limitations. There are three types of actions over which courts have territorial jurisdiction:

action *in personam* Action involving human or corporate entities

action *in rem* Action in which the court holds authority over a piece of property but not its owner

action *quasi in rem* Action in which a piece of property serves as the court's basis for exercising limited control over the property's owner

- **actions *in personam,*** which are those involving human or corporate entities
- **actions *in rem,*** where the court has power over a piece of property, but not its owner
- **actions *quasi in rem,*** in which a particular piece of property is used as a basis for exerting limited control over the owner—for example, the property may be attached by the court to satisfy an unrelated claim against the owner when that owner is beyond the court's reach and cannot be compelled to physically come to court and submit to judgment

In all three situations, either the accused person or the property at issue must be within the *physical* jurisdiction of the court. In recent years, scholarly and judicial debate has most often focused on when to expand the limits of *in personam* jurisdiction over parties who are not physically present.

PERSONAL JURISDICTION.   Historically, the person who initiates the lawsuit—the plaintiff—must seek a court that has jurisdiction over the defendant. There are three traditional tests for personal jurisdiction over a defendant: *presence, domicile,* and *consent.*

Determining Physical Presence. In general, a person who lives in or conducts business in a state is subject to that state's jurisdiction and can be served with a *summons* within the state. A defendant must be within the court's jurisdiction voluntarily. In other words, although even a brief visit to the state is an adequate jurisdictional basis, the defendant's presence cannot be the result of fraud or compulsion; the defendant cannot have been forced or tricked into entering the state in order for a suit to be instituted there.

domicile   The single place that an individual considers, or intends as, his or her permanent home

Defining Domicile. A person's **domicile** is determined by two factors: (1) the individual's intent to make a particular location his permanent home and (2) facts indicating that the party has physically located there.[1] A person may have residences located in one or more states but can have only one domicile. The notion of a *unique domicile* is a guarantee that there is always *some* place where a defendant may be sued.

Principles of Consent. A party may always agree to be bound by the jurisdiction of a state's courts even if he is not present or domiciled there. Explicit *consent* occurs in two situations (1) when a defendant files an answer to a suit and thereby waives any jurisdictional defects without contesting jurisdiction in that court; (2) when a party to a contract agrees to be sued in a particular jurisdiction in any contractual disputes that later arise and result in litigation.

A defendant's consent may also be implied. As communication and transportation among the states has accelerated, the courts have found *implied consent* with increasing frequency. The courts have held, for example, that doing business within a state implies consent to that state's jurisdiction, even in matters not directly connected to the business activity itself.

---

[1] Friedenthal, Kane, and Miller, *Civil Procedure* (Minneapolis, MN: West Publishing Co., 1985), p. 109.

Jurisdiction over Corporations

Eighteenth-century American jurisprudence viewed corporations as strictly state-created beings. Thus, corporations could be sued only "domestically"—that is, within the boundaries of the state in which they "existed." The tests applied to the question of corporate jurisdiction were the same as those for persons—that is, presence, domicile, and consent. In cases involving domestic corporations, jurisdiction was easily found. However, because corporations had no existence outside the borders of the state that had *chartered*, or created, them, they could not be sued in any other state.

In order to address the problems of jurisdiction created by the rapid expansion of business activities, American courts have developed several criteria for extending jurisdiction over commercial organizations that are not strictly subject to "domestic" litigation. Three such criteria are the *"doing business" standard*, the clarification of this standard in the case of *International Shoe Co. v. the State of Washington*, and the principle of the *long-arm statute.*

THE "DOING BUSINESS" STANDARD. As the legal system struggled to find a theory supporting such jurisdiction, some courts used the rationale that doing business in a state carried implied consent to be sued there. Other courts used the test of *presence*—that is, the location of in-state offices, facilities, and activities. The law reports, however, became cluttered with inconsistent decisions as to what constituted "doing business" in a state.

THE TEST OF *INTERNATIONAL SHOE*. In *International Shoe Company v. State of Washington* (326 U.S. 310 [1945]), the Supreme Court finally relieved much of the uncertainty and confusion surrounding the concept of doing business. International Shoe was a Delaware corporation whose main office was in St. Louis. The corporation hired approximately a dozen salesmen who lived in the state of Washington to sell shoes in their home state. These salesmen, who were paid on commission, carried and displayed samples, sometimes rented showroom space, and took orders. Washington demanded that International Shoe pay unemployment compensation tax on the salesmen's commissions. When the company refused, the state served an order of assessment on one of the salesmen, as the company's representative, and mailed a copy of the order to the company's home office.

International Shoe claimed that the state's action was a denial of due process: Because it kept neither inventory nor contracts within the state, its activities were insufficient to demonstrate presence. It further asserted that the salesman was not a suitable agent on whom process could be served. The Court rejected both contentions and declared that a defendant not present in the territory of the forum need have only "certain minimum contacts with it such that the maintenance of the suit does not offend 'traditional notions of fair play and substantial justice' " for *in-personam jurisdiction* to be established. Subsequent rulings have refined and elaborated the minimum contacts and traditional notions of "fair-play" and "substantial-justice" standards.

LONG-ARM STATUTES. Since *International Shoe*, most states have enacted jurisdictional laws known as **long-arm statutes.** As we saw in Chapter 4, these laws give the state jurisdiction over nonresident persons and foreign corporations with certain in-state ties. Typically, long-arm statutes confer jurisdiction over nonresidents who:

long-arm statutes State legislative act giving courts of the state *jurisdiction* over certain defendants who are nonresidents of the state and who generally have some limited contact with the state (*see also* Chapter 4)

- do business in the state
- commit a tort in the state
- own real estate in the state

Some liberal long-arm statutes even confer jurisdiction over nonresidents who commit an out-of-state tort, such as the manufacture of a defective product that causes injury inside the state.

The fundamental aim of long-arm statutes is to provide a local forum in which a state's citizens may sue nonresidents. Thus, broadly written long-arm statutes may undermine the defendant's traditional right to be heard in a convenient forum. For this reason, courts generally examine long-arm statutes closely for violations of due process. Not only must the letter of the law be satisfied but both federal and state constitutional standards of fairness must also be met.

Accordingly, if a defendant's activities are sporadic and "not purposeful," contact is generally considered insufficient to establish jurisdiction (*Helicopteros nacionales de Colombia, SA v. Hall*, 104 S. Ct. 1868 [1984]). However, national marketing programs increasingly provide injured plaintiffs with jurisdictional

The International Court of Justice A principal organ of the United Nations (see Chapter 21), the International Court of Justice (ICJ) is mandated by the UN charter. It is composed of 15 judges elected concurrently by the General Assembly and Security Council; all judges must be of different nationalities, and if a state involved in a specific case is not represented on the Court, such state may appoint a national judge to participate with full voting rights. The major deficiency of the IJC is the lack of any compulsory jurisdiction: states may choose whether or not to surrender their sovereign freedom to international authority. Nor is there any satisfactory means for the IJC to enforce its determinations: although states agreeing to submit cases to the Court are bound by international law, refusal to comply has occurred on several occasions. States may, however, declare that, *in relation to another state accepting the same obligation,* they recognize the Court's jurisdiction in the following disputes: (1) treaty interpretation; (2) questions of international law; (3) the existence of a fact that constitutes violation of an international agreement; (4) reparations to be remitted for violation of an international obligation.

bases. In *World-Wide Volkswagen Corp. v. Woodson* (444 U.S. 286 [1980]), for example, the Supreme Court held "if the defendant purposefully caters to a national market, distributing its product across the country through its own efforts or the efforts of middlemen, a plaintiff can still constitutionally assert jurisdiction over that defendant in virtually any state where the product malfunctions."

Can a franchisee who enters into a substantial, long-term contract with an out-of-state corporation be sued in the foreign state? The Supreme Court considered this question in 1985.

BURGER KING CORPORATION v. RUDZEWICZ
United States Supreme Court, 471 U.S. 462 (1985)

A contract was entered into between Burger King Corp., a Florida concern with headquarters in Miami, and Rudzewicz and MacShara. Through the terms of this contract, the latter two individuals agreed to pay Burger King $1 million over 20 years to operate a franchise in Birmingham, Michigan. After Rudzewicz and MacShara became unable to keep their payments current, Burger King brought suit against them as defendants for breach of contract in the Florida District Court. The court rendered judgment against the defendants, rejecting their argument that the franchise contract was not sufficient contact with Florida to justify the court's exercise of personal jurisdiction. The Court of Appeals reversed, finding the district court's judgment invalid due to a lack of personal jurisdiction. The plaintiff, Burger King, appeals to the U.S. Supreme Court.

Justice Brennan delivered the opinion of the Court.

Burger King Corporation is a Florida corporation whose principal offices are in Miami. . . . Burger King conducts approximately 80% of its business through a franchise operation that the company styles the "Burger King System"—"a comprehensive restaurant format and operating system for the sale of uniform and quality food products." . . .

. . . .

Burger King oversees its franchise system through a two-tiered administrative structure. The governing contracts provide that the franchise relationship is established in Miami and governed by Florida law, and call for payment of all required fees and forwarding of all relevant notices to the Miami headquarters. The Miami headquarters sets policy and works directly with its franchisees in attempting to resolve major problems. Day-to-day monitoring of franchisees, however, is conducted through a network of 10 district offices which in turn report to the Miami headquarters.

The instant litigation grows out of Burger King's termination of one of its franchisees, and is aptly described by the franchisee as "a divorce proceeding among commercial partners." . . .

Rudzewicz and MacShara jointly applied for a fran-

chise to Burger King's Birmingham, Michigan district office in the autumn of 1978. . . . By signing the final agreements, Rudzewicz obligated himself personally to payments exceeding $1 million over the 20-year franchise relationship.

The [franchised] facility apparently enjoyed steady business during the summer of 1979, but patronage declined after a recession began later that year. Rudzewicz and MacShara soon fell far behind in their monthly payments to Miami. . . . Burger King [brought suit in Florida and] alleged that Rudzewicz and MacShara had breached their franchise obligations "within [the jurisdiction of] this district court" by failing to make the required payments "at plaintiff's place of business in Miami, Dade County, Florida." . . . Rudzewicz and MacShara entered special appearances and argued, inter alia, that because they were Michigan residents and because Burger King's claim did not "arise" within the Southern District of Florida, the District Court lacked personal jurisdiction over them. . . .

. . . Finding that Rudzewicz and MacShara had breached their franchise agreements with Burger King and had infringed Burger King's trademarks and service marks, the court entered judgment against them. . . .

Rudzewicz appealed to the Court of Appeals for the Eleventh Circuit. A divided panel of that Circuit reversed the judgment, concluding that the District Court could not properly exercise personal jurisdiction over Rudzewicz. . . . [T]he panel majority concluded the "[j]urisdiction under these circumstances would offend the fundamental fairness which is the touchstone of due process."

. . . .

We have noted several reasons why a forum legitimately may exercise personal jurisdiction over a non-resident who "purposefully directs" his activities toward forum residents. A State generally has a "manifest interest" in providing its residents with a convenient forum for redressing injuries inflicted by out-of-state actors. Moreover, where individuals "purposefully derive benefit" from their interstate activities, it may well be unfair to allow them to escape having to account in other States for consequences that arise proximately from such activities; the Due Process Clause may not readily be wielded as a territorial shield to avoid interstate obligations that have been voluntarily assumed. . . .

. . . [T]he constitutional touchstone remains whether the defendant purposefully established "minimum contacts" in the forum State. International Shoe Co. v. Washington.

. . . Jurisdiction is proper . . . where the contacts proximately result from actions by the defendant *himself* that create a "substantial connection" with the forum State.

. . . So long as a commercial actor's efforts are "purposefully directed" toward residents of another State, we have consistently rejected the notion that an absence of physical contacts can defeat personal jurisdiction there.

Once it has been decided that a defendant purposefully established minimum contacts within the forum State, these contacts may be considered in light of other factors to determine whether the assertion of personal jurisdiction would comport with "fair play and substantial justice." International Shoe Co. v. Washington. Thus courts in "appropriate case[s]" may evaluate "the burden on the defendant," "the forum State's interest in adjudicating the dispute," "the plaintiff's interest in obtaining convenient and effective relief," "the interstate judicial system's interest in obtaining the most efficient resolution of controversies," and the "shared interest of the several States in furthering fundamental substantive social policies." . . . As we previously have noted, jurisdictional rules may not be employed in such a way as to make litigation "so gravely difficult and inconvenient" that a party unfairly is at a "severe disadvantage" in comparison to his opponent. . . .

In this case, no physical ties to Florida can be attributed to Rudzewicz other than MacShara's brief training course in Miami. Rudzewicz did not maintain offices in Florida and, for all that appears from the record, has never even visited there. Yet this franchise dispute grew directly out of "a contact which had a *substantial* connection with that State." . . . In light of Rudzewicz's voluntary acceptance of the long-term and exacting regulation of his business from Burger King's Miami headquarters, the "quality and nature" of his relationship to the company in Florida can in no sense be viewed as "random," "fortuitous," or "attenuated." Rudzewicz's refusal to make the contractually required payments in Miami, and his continued use of Burger King's trademarks and confidential business information after his termination, caused foreseeable injuries to the corporation in Florida. For these reasons it was, at the very least, presumptively reasonable for Rudzewicz to be called to account there for such injuries.

. . . [W]e believe the Court of Appeals gave insufficient weight to provisions in the various franchise documents providing that all disputes would be governed by Florida law. . . . The Court of Appeals reasoned that choice-of-law provisions are irrelevant to the question of personal jurisdiction. . . . Nothing in our cases, however, suggests that a choice-of-law *provision* should be ignored in considering whether a defendant has "purposefully invoked the benefits and protections of a State's laws" for jurisdictional purposes. Although such a provision standing alone would be insufficient to confer jurisdiction, we believe that, when combined with the 20-year interdependent relationship Rudzewicz established with Burger King's Miami headquarters, it reinforced his deliberate affiliation with the forum State and the reasonable foreseeability of possible litigation there. As Judge Johnson argued in his dissent below, Rudzewicz "purposefully availed himself of the benefits and protections of Florida's laws" by entering into contracts expressly providing that those laws would govern franchise disputes.

. . . .

. . . Because Rudzewicz established a substantial and continuing relationship with Burger King's Miami headquarters, received fair notice from the contract documents and the course of dealing that he might be subject to suit in Florida, and has failed to demonstrate how jurisdiction in that forum would otherwise be fundamentally unfair, we conclude that the District Court's exercise of jurisdiction pursuant to Florida Stat §48.193(I)(g) (Supp 1984) [Florida's long-arm statute] did not offend due process. The judgment of the Court of Appeals is accordingly reversed, and the case is remanded for further proceedings consistent with this opinion.

Case Questions

1. Is there anything about a 20-year contract that might be more persuasive in getting a court to find valid personal jurisdiction when that is the defendant's only contact with a forum state?

2. To what inquiry is it relevant that the defendants in the Burger King case had voluntarily connected themselves with Florida?

3. Doesn't it seem unfair to make the defendants travel all the way to Florida to appear in court? Are there considerations that weigh against this?

The Question of Venue

After the questions of subject matter and territorial jurisdiction are answered, the issue of which of the courts that can hear the case should in fact hear it is next to be decided. If the case does not involve a question of federal law, parties from different states, or a suit to which the federal government is a party, then the case will be heard in a state court. Rules determining **venue** vary from state to state.

venue The locality in which a court holding *jurisdiction* may hear a case (*see also* Chapter 4)

COMMON RULES OF VENUE IN STATE COURTS. Proper venue for an action exists in either

- the county where the defendant is domiciled
- the county where the cause of action (such as an automobile accident) arose
- the county where the subject matter (such as a piece of land of disputed ownership) is located
- the county of plaintiff's residence in the case of a nonresident defendant
- the seat of a local government in a suit involving some branch of that local government

VENUE IN THE FEDERAL COURTS. As we saw earlier in this chapter, the kinds of actions that may be brought in federal court are limited. Federal venue requirements are relatively simple: Suit may be brought in the district where the claim arose or where all defendants reside. When federal jurisdiction is based on the fact that the litigants live in different states, venue is properly the state in which all plaintiffs reside.

When the suit involves individuals, place of residence tends to determine venue. Generally, residence is the same as domicile. In a suit involving a corporation, either the corporation's home office, the state of incorporation, or any place where it does business may be considered a corporate residence. Labor unions and similar associations also fall under this rule.

Where venue properly lies in more than one district, the courts have generally applied a formula involving the "weight of contacts" to determine venue.

SEEKING A CHANGE OF VENUE. Defendants have the right to seek "removal"—that is, transfer to another court where venue is also proper. This right must be exercised promptly or it is forfeited. In granting or denying removal, the court looks to the convenience of the litigants and witnesses as well as to the practicalities of the particular suit—for example, considering whether a trip to the scene of the accident is necessary. Because plaintiff made the initial choice of forum, removal is a defendant's remedy.

■ *Concept Check 5-1   Jurisdiction: Beyond Subject Matter*

- What tests are used to determine whether a court has *jurisdiction* over people or organizations?
- What is the purpose of *long-arm statutes*?
- Explain the concept of *venue*.

■ BEFORE THE TRIAL

Let's consider initiating a dispute between a tenant and a landlord. Suppose that you enter into a contract (or lease) to rent an apartment. Further, suppose that the landlord failed to replace the wall-to-wall carpeting in the apartment before you moved in even though he had agreed in writing to do so. You decide to take the matter to court.

Your first act will probably be to select and visit a lawyer. Next, you and your lawyer will gather information about the case, such as a copy of the lease and any related correspondence. After this is done, *pleadings* are drafted and served on the landlord. You have initiated your suit, and in drafting your pleadings, you have taken the first step, known as *summons and complaint*. You and your lawyer may then conduct the process known as *discovery*, and you may participate in a *pretrial conference*.

Summons and Complaint

pleadings The series of written statements defining each party's claims and defenses

plaintiff The person who initiates a lawsuit

defendant The person sued or accused by the plaintiff

complaint Written statement of the *plaintiff's* complaint, served to the *defendant* as the first step in a lawsuit

summons Court document, delivered by a sheriff or professional process server, directing the defendant to appear in a certain court at a certain date and time because a *cause of action* is being initiated

PLEADINGS. **Pleadings** are a series of formal statements between the parties to a suit that define their respective positions, or their claims and defenses. The person who initiated the claim—in this case, the tenant—becomes the **plaintiff.** The person whom the plaintiff wishes to call to court for trial and judgment is the **defendant.** In contemporary civil procedure, the first step in this process is to draft a **complaint,** which, in most jurisdictions, is served on the defendant at the same time as the **summons**—a court document that directs the defendant to appear in a particular court at a particular date and time because a suit has been initiated.

The summons is delivered either by a sheriff or by a professional process server. Because the summons is a critical notification device, failure to serve it properly can create fatal problems for plaintiff's suit. The rules governing *service of process* differ from state to state. Constitutional guarantee of due process requires the best effort at locating the defendant that can reasonably be made.

A defendant may try to avoid being served with process by leaving the jurisdiction of the court in which the complaint was made. This problem has been addressed by statutes that permit "substituted service": If the defendant cannot be located after diligent effort, the summons and complaint can be left at a defendant's home or published in a local newspaper.

In *Milliken v. Meyer*, the Supreme Court addressed the issue of serving process outside the state in which suit was brought.

MILLIKEN v. MEYER
United States Supreme Court, 311 U.S. 454 (1940)

Milliken sued Meyer in Wyoming court. Despite the fact that Meyer never appeared to present his case, the court ruled in Milliken's favor.

Meyer then brought suit against Milliken in Colorado court, alleging that due to his absence from Wyoming at the time of service, the judgment entered against him was invalid because the Wyoming court failed to obtain jurisdiction. The Colorado trial court ruled in Milliken's favor. Meyer then appealed to the Colorado Supreme Court which reversed. Milliken now appeals to the Supreme Court of the United States.

Mr. Justice Douglas delivered the opinion of the Court.
. . . .

The controversy is over a 1/64th interest in profits from operation of certain Colorado oil properties.

Transcontinental on August 31, 1922, contracted to pay Meyer 4/64ths of those profits. Milliken asserted a claim to a two-thirds interest in that 4/64ths share. . . .

Later Milliken instituted suit in the Wyoming court alleging a joint adventure with Transcontinental and Meyer and charging a conspiracy on their part to defraud him of his rights. . . . Meyer, who was asserted to be a resident of Wyoming, was personally served with process in Colorado pursuant to the Wyoming statutes; but he made no appearance in the Wyoming cause. . . . The court found . . . that there was a joint venture between Milliken and Meyer. . . . Thereafter the 1/64th share was withheld from Meyer and paid over to Milliken. In 1935 respondent instituted this suit in the Colorado court praying, *inter alia*, . . . for an injunction against Milliken attempting to enforce the Wyoming judgment, and for a decree that the Wyoming judgment was a nullity for want of jurisdiction over Meyer or his property. The bill alleged, *inter alia*, that Meyer at the time of service in the Wyoming court had long ceased to be a resident of Wyoming and was a resident of Colorado; that the service obtained on him did not give the Wyoming court jurisdiction of his person or property; and that such judgment was violative of the due process clause of the Fourteenth Amendment. . . . The Colorado court, on issues joined, found that Meyer was domiciled in Wyoming when the Wyoming suit was commenced, that the Wyoming statutes for substituted service were constitutional, that the affidavit for constructive service on Meyer was filed in good faith, substantially conformed to the Wyoming statute and stated the truth, that Wyoming had jurisdiction over the person of Meyer, that the Wyoming decree was not void, and that the bill should be dismissed.

That judgment was reversed by the Supreme Court of Colorado. . . .

Where a judgment rendered in one state is challenged in another, a want of jurisdiction over either the person or the subject matter is of course open to inquiry. But if the judgment on its face appears to be a "record of a court of general jurisdiction, such jurisdiction over the cause and the parties is to be presumed unless disproved by extrinsic evidence, or by the record itself." In such case the full faith and credit clause of the Constitution precludes any inquiry into the merits of the cause of action, the logic or consistency of the decision, or the validity of the legal principles on which the judgment is based. . . .

On the findings of the Colorado trial court, not impaired by the Colorado Supreme Court, it is clear that Wyoming had jurisdiction over Meyer in the 1931 suit. Domicile in the state is alone sufficient to bring an absent defendant within the reach of the state's jurisdiction for purposes of a personal judgment by means of appropriate substituted service. Substituted service in such cases has been quite uniformly upheld where the absent defendant was served at his usual place of abode in the state as well as where he was personally served without the state. . . . Its adequacy so far as due process is concerned is dependent on whether or not the form of substituted service provided for such cases and employed is reasonably calculated to give him actual notice of the proceedings and an opportunity to be heard. If it is, the traditional notions of fair play and substantial justice implicit in due process are satisfied. Here there can be no question on that score. Meyer did not merely receive actual notice of the Wyoming proceedings. While outside the state, he was personally served in accordance with a statutory scheme which Wyoming had provided for such occasions. And in our view the machinery employed met all the requirements of due process. Certainly then Meyer's domicile in Wyoming was a sufficient basis for that extraterritorial service. . . . One such incident of domicile is amenability to suit within the state even during sojourns without the state, where the state has provided and employed a reasonable method for apprising such an absent party of the proceedings against him. Here such a reasonable method was so provided and so employed.

Reversed.

Case Questions:

1. What is the test used to determine whether service of process has violated due process?

2. How does the Court go about enforcing the Wyoming judgment against Meyer in Colorado?

3. Does the Milliken case tell us that a defendant can go on a two-week vacation to avoid being served with process?

Figure 5-1 is a sample complaint, which must accompany the summons and contain the following elements:

- a statement establishing the jurisdiction of the court in which the complaint was filed
- a description of the relationship between the plaintiff and the defendant
- a brief statement showing why the plaintiff is entitled to relief—for example, monetary damages, enforcement of the contract, an injunction, collection of a debt, or other remedies
- a demand for that relief

Under current rules of civil procedure in most jurisdictions, complaints and other pleadings have been greatly simplified from earlier forms. At common law, for example, a plaintiff was required to select the correct form of a complaint in order to ensure that the proper theory of substantive law would be applied to the facts (*see* Chapter 4, *p.113*); until recently, the courts relied on pleadings to sharpen the controversy and identify uncontested points. Today, however, discovery and pretrial conferences have assumed many of the func-

```
             UNITED STATES DISTRICT COURT
             EASTERN DISTRICT OF NEW JERSEY

    Kelley's Electronics World, Inc.,
                          Plaintiff

             v.

    John Doe,

                          Defendant

       1. Jurisdiction is based upon diversity of citizenship and
    monetary amount in controversy.
       2. Defendant is a citizen of the State of New Jersey.
       3. Plaintiff is a corporation duly incorporated under the
    laws of the Commonwealth of Massachusetts.
       4. The amount in controversy exceeds, exclusive of in-
    terests and costs, the sum of $10,000.
       5. On December 24, 1992, plaintiff entered into a con-
    tract wherein plaintiff agreed to deliver 125 personal com-
    puters to defendant on or before January 16, 1993, and de-
    fendant agreed to pay $193,823.86.
       6. On or about January 12, 1993, plaintiff shipped the
    contracted for goods to defendant.
       7. On January 14, 1993, defendant received the con-
    tracted for goods.
       8. Demand has been made for the amount due under the
    contract.
       9. Demand has been made for payment for goods sold
    and delivered.
       10. Defendant has refused to pay the sum due and owing.
       WHEREFORE, plaintiff demands judgment against de-
    fendant John Doe in the amount of $193,823.86, exclusive
    of interests, costs, and disbursements.

                          /s/ _____
                          Amy Amherst, Esq.
                          Attorney for Plaintiff

    Dated: June 3, 1993
    TO: John Doe, Defendant
```

FIGURE 5-1 Sample Plaintiff's Complaint

tions originally filled by the pleadings. In addition to the complaint, pleadings include the answer by defendant, and, when required, plaintiff's reply.

Consider the case of the home-drawn complaint drafted by John Dioguardi in his attempt to sue the Collector of Customs. As the case of *Dioguardi v. Durning* shows, pleadings retain a certain degree of formality even under contemporary rules.

DIOGUARDI v. DURNING

U.S. Court of Appeals, Second Circuit, 139 F2d. 774 (1944)

The plaintiff, Dioguardi, brought suit against the defendant, Durning, the Collector of Customs at the Port of New York, in U.S. District Court for conver-sion and violation of federal customs law. Although Dioguardi's complaint clearly stated that Durning had done away with several cases of his "bottles of tonics" that were supposed to be sold at public auction, it was not so clear about how the cases came into Durning's possession.

The district court dismissed Dioguardi's complaint on the basis that it failed to state facts sufficient to constitute a cause of action. The case is now in the U.S. Court of Appeals for resolution of the standard to be used in determining the sufficiency of a complaint.

Clark, Circuit Judge.

In his complaint, obviously home drawn, plaintiff attempts to assert a series of grievances against the Collector of Customs at the Port of New York growing out of his endeavors to import merchandise from Italy "of great value," consisting of bottles of "tonics." We may pass certain of his claims as either inadequate or inadequately stated and consider only these two: (1) that on the auction day, October 9, 1940, when defendant sold the merchandise at "public custom," "he sold my merchandise to another bidder with my price of $110, and not of his price of $120," and (2) "that three weeks before the sale, two cases, of 19 bottles each case, disappeared." Plaintiff does not make wholly clear how these goods came into the collector's hands, since he alleges compliance with the revenue laws; but he does say he made a claim for "refund of merchandise which was two-thirds paid in Milan, Italy," and that the collector denied the claim. These and other circumstances alleged indicate (what, indeed, plaintiff's brief asserts) that his original dispute was with his consignor as to whether anything more was due upon the merchandise, and that the collector, having held it for a year (presumably as unclaimed merchandise under 19 U.S.C.A. §1491), then sold it, or such part of it as was left, at public auction. For his asserted injuries plaintiff claimed $5,000 damages, together with interest and costs, against the defendant individually and as collector. This complaint was dismissed by the District Court, with leave, however, to plaintiff to amend, on motion of the United States Attorney, appearing for the defendant, on the ground that it "fails to state facts sufficient to constitute a cause of action."

Therefore plaintiff filed an amended complaint. . . .

It would seem . . . that he has stated enough to withstand a mere formal motion, directed only to the face of the complaint, and that here is another instance of judicial haste which in the long run makes waste. Under the new rules of civil procedure, there is no pleading requirement of stating "facts sufficient to constitute a cause of action," but only that there be "a short and plain statement of the claim showing that the pleader is entitled to relief," Federal Rules of Civil Procedure, rule 8(a); and the motion for dismissal under Rule 12(b) is for failure to state "a claim upon which relief can be granted.". . .

We think that, however inartistically they may be stated, the plaintiff has disclosed his claims that the collector has converted or otherwise done away with two of his cases of medicinal tonics and has sold the rest in a manner incompatible with the public auction he had announced—and, indeed, required by 19 U.S.C.A. §1491, and the Treasury Regulations promulgated under it. As to this latter claim, it may be that the collector's only error is a failure to collect an additional ten dollars from the Springdale Distilling Company; but giving the plaintiff the benefit of reasonable intendments in his allegations (as we must on this motion), the claim appears to be in effect that he was actually the first bidder at the price for which they were sold, and hence was entitled to the merchandise. . . . [A]s it stands, we do not see how the plaintiff may properly be deprived of his day in court to show what he obviously so firmly believes and what for present purposes defendant must be taken as admitting. . . .

. . . .

Judgment is reversed and the action is remanded for further proceedings not inconsistent with this opinion.

Case Questions

1. What must a plaintiff include in his complaint in order to avoid a dismissal under the Federal Rules of Civil Procedure?

2. Is the standard espoused by the court in *Dioguardi v. Durning* a looser or a more rigid standard than that used under the common law?

3. What reasons support the use of a more relaxed standard?

ANSWER, COUNTERCLAIM, AND REPLY. When the defendant receives the summons and complaint, he then has a fixed period of time to file an answer. If he fails to answer, a **default judgment** may be entered.

The defendant's **answer** either admits or denies each of the individual allegations made in the complaint. (*See* Figure 5-2 *for a sample answer.*) The process of admission and denial narrows and defines the controversy, eliminating the need to argue before a judge about certain agreed-upon facts. Some states allow defendants to answer with a general denial. When the complaint is totally defective as a matter of law, the defendant may file a **motion to dismiss** instead of an answer: A motion to dismiss essentially declares that even if everything written in the plaintiff's complaint is true, the plaintiff is still not entitled to relief. Grounds for dismissal may be either *procedural* or *substantive*—for

default judgment Judgment rendered by the court on default in the event of a defendant's failure to answer a *summons* within an allotted time

answer A defendant's submitted *pleading* to the plaintiff's *complaint*

motion to dismiss Motion filed by the defendant requesting that the court dismiss a case because of the inherent legal defectiveness of the plaintiff's *complaint*

```
            UNITED STATES DISTRICT COURT
            EASTERN DISTRICT OF NEW JERSEY

Kelley's Electronics World, Inc.,
                        Plaintiff


                        v.


John Doe

                    Defendant


     1. Defendant admits the allegations contained in para-
graphs 1, 2, 3, and 4 of the complaint.
     2. Defendant denies that a contract was entered into on
December 24, 1992.
     3. Defendant denies the allegations contained in para-
graphs 6, 7, 8, 9 and 10 of the complaint.
Wherefore, defendant demands dismissal of the within ac-
tion.


                            /s/ _____
                            Jim Jersey
                            Attorney for Defendant Doe


Dated: June 23, 1993

TO: Amy Amherst, Esq.
    Attorney for Plaintiff
```

FIGURE 5-2 Sample Defendant's Answer

example, the summons may have been served on the wrong person (a procedural defect), or there may be no basis on which to grant plaintiff the relief
sought (a substantive flaw).

In addition to denying or admitting specific facts stated in the complaint,
the defendant may also raise **affirmative defenses.** Generally, affirmative defenses involve issues which are not raised in the complaint and which justify or
mitigate the defendant's actions. So that plaintiff will not be caught by surprise, the defendant is required to raise these defenses specifically (or forfeit
the opportunity to do so later). Examples of affirmative defenses include plaintiff's contributory negligence, fraud, a lapsed statute of limitations, and so
forth.

The defendant can also make a **counterclaim,** in which damages or other
relief are sought from plaintiff. The final stage in the pleadings is plaintiff's **reply** to counterclaims and affirmative defenses.

At this point, if either party decides that there is no factual disagreement
between them that party can move for **summary judgment.** In such cases,
where only questions of law exist, the judge can decide the case on motion papers, without a jury trial or additional court procedure. If summary judgment
is neither sought nor granted, the parties commence discovery.

Discovery

Discovery is the pretrial process by which both parties to a suit gather evidence
about the case. Following the adoption of the Federal Rules of Civil Procedure
26-37, in 1938, "[t]hese discovery rules virtually revolutionized the practice of

affirmative defenses
Assertions raised by the
defendant which involve
information not otherwise
detailed in the *complaint* and
which could relieve or mitigate
the defendant's liability

counterclaim Claim, distinct
from the plaintiff's cause of
action, raised by a defendant
against the plaintiff

reply Final stage of the
pleading, consisting of the
plaintiff's response to
counterclaims and *affirmative
defenses*

summary judgment Court
decision that the party in a
lawsuit who made a *motion for
judgment* is entitled to that
judgment as a matter of law
because no real issue of fact
exists

discovery Pretrial process by
which parties to a lawsuit collect
and assemble *evidence* about a
case

law in the United States. Of all the Federal Rules, they have been the most widely copied; nearly every state has adopted a similar set of provisions permitting broad, intensive discovery."[2]

Prior to the expansion of discovery, for example, litigants could learn about their opponents' evidence and witnesses only from the pleadings or from private investigations. In order to "ambush" the opposition, each party sought to keep secret any strategy to be used at the trial. The rules on discovery fundamentally altered this state of affairs: Discovery provides a useful way for each party to evaluate its case relative to that of its opponent. The purpose of discovery includes the preservation of testimony, the identification of contested facts, and the acquisition of as much admissible evidence as can be had on the disputed issues.

There are, however, limitations to both the content of discovery information and the procedures for taking discovery. We will examine some distinctions among types of *accessible* information, describe some types of information that are *exempt* from discovery, and then summarize four different procedures or *forms* of discovery: *depositions*, *interrogatories*, the *physical examination* of evidence, and the collection of *tangible information*.

INFORMATION ACCESSIBLE TO DISCOVERY. A clear distinction is drawn between the kind of evidence that may be taken during discovery and the kind of evidence that may be used in the trial. Under the rules on discovery, very few categories of information are protected. For example, a plaintiff can discover the names of witnesses in a proposed litigation, even when those witnesses have been located by the defendant. Similarly, a plaintiff may be required to disclose, through discovery, names of witnesses that he has located who can impeach or refute the testimony of the defense's witnesses.

The location of all documents that may prove relevant to the case can also be learned through discovery. However, a party may not see these materials automatically. For example, if the opponent claims that opening certain records would violate a third party's privacy or endanger a corporation's competitive position through the revelation of trade secrets, the documents may remain unavailable. However, the existence and location of documents must be revealed.

EXEMPTIONS FROM DISCOVERY. One important category that is exempt from discovery is the *lawyer's work product*. A second limitation is that discovered material, although not necessarily admissible at the trial, must be relevant to the subject matter of the case. In addition, the material must not be *privileged*, as in communications between husband and wife, doctor and patient, or priest and penitent. Privileged communications generally enjoy complete statutory immunity: The social fabric is presumed strengthened by maintaining the integrity of these intimate relationships.

The treatment of expert witnesses is also governed by special rules. If experts are to testify at the trial, the opposite side may learn, by interrogatories, both the subject matter and the substance of facts and opinions to which they will testify. Experts who will not testify need not offer subject matter or substance during discovery; indeed, they may not even be identified.

---

[2] Friedenthal *et al.*, note 1 *supra* at 380.

FORMS OF DISCOVERY. Each of the four principal types of discovery procedures has its own special advantages and limitations.

Depositions. Prior to trial, it is often useful to question, under oath, both witnesses to the incident in question and the opposing parties. This process of gathering oral testimony is known as obtaining a **deposition.** Both sides have an opportunity to depose. However, reasonable notice of the deposition must be given to the opposing side. Subpoenas may be used to make sure that witnesses—*deponents*—will appear at depositions. The testimony gathered during this process is recorded by an independent court reporter. In addition to a stenographer's recording, some courts permit videotaping of depositions.

deposition Form of pretrial *discovery* in which the oral or written testimony of a witness or opposing party is obtained

Oral depositions are expensive. They involve court costs, fees for court stenographers, and hourly rates for lawyers. Therefore, they are not always taken. Some reasons for taking depositions include (1) the possibility of gaining information and locating additional sources of evidence, (2) obtaining testimony for possible use at the trial, (3) discerning the extent of a witness's knowledge, and (4) committing the deponent to a specific version of the facts.

Remember that several years may elapse between the time that an incident occurs and the time it reaches trial. Discovery provides a way of preserving testimony. Over time, memories fade or are distorted. Furthermore, people may say one thing during discovery and another thing at trial. The conflicting testimony can be used to impeach a person's credibility.

Interrogatories. Sometimes, a party is not able to appear for oral questioning; perhaps the lawyer may want the opposing side to respond in writing to written questions. These written questions, which are known as **interrogatories,** can be used if the defendant is too ill to appear for questioning or if the responses to the questions require some research. However, interrogatories may be sent only to parties in the dispute, not to witnesses.

interrogatories Pretrial written questions served by one party on the opposing party, who must then respond in writing

The advantages of interrogatories are: (1) they are relatively inexpensive, (2) they reveal to each side what the other side knows, and (3) the respondents may consult with others in preparing their responses. However, because the answers are written, the responding party may answer vaguely or evasively.

Physical Examination. In many cases, the defendant may dispute the actual extent of injury or contend that some physical or mental impairment was the cause of the incident in question. In such cases the attorney can ask that a physical or mental examination of the plaintiff be conducted as part of the discovery process. The rules are the same for both sides. The person examined receives a copy of the examiner's report. He must also supply his own prior medical records of the same condition to the opposing party's attorney.

Documents or Other Tangible Items. In many cases, a lawyer will wish to examine a particular document or object in preparation for the trial. In a product-liability case, for example, the lawyer might want to examine the defective item or the records of the company that designed the failed part.

Pretrial Conference

pretrial conference Pretrial meeting between the judge and opposing attorneys, designed to define the issues of the case and to encourage an out-of-court settlement

A **pretrial conference** may address matters of *law* (such as defining the issues and ruling on admissibility of evidence) or matters of *procedure* (such as the scope of discovery and amendments to the pleadings). Such conferences have two purposes: (1) to encourage the parties to reach an out-of-court settlement and (2) to aid in the management of the case as it proceeds toward trial. Although these functions may appear incompatible, they actually serve the same end. A well-managed case ensures adequate discovery and a preview of the witnesses' statements, which, in turn, ensures an efficient, well-ordered trial. The same organizational clarity may show the parties that an out-of-court settlement would be to their advantage.

A pretrial conference may be requested by either party or by the court itself. The judge has the latitude to decide how many conferences a given case requires and what the procedure will be for each one. Lawyers for both sides are required to attend, and sometimes they must submit special memoranda.

In cases involving great amounts of data, there may be as many as four pretrial conferences, the first of which generally sets a timetable for discovery procedures. However, most pretrial conferences take place after discovery and before trial. At this point in the process, the judge may seek voluntary agreements from both sides. After the conference, the judge issues a pretrial order that controls the subsequent action of the case.

■ Concept Check 5-2   Before the Trial

- Describe the difference between a *summons* and a *complaint*.
- What is the purpose of a *pleading*?
- What is the name of the pretrial process by which parties to a suit gather evidence about the case?
- Explain the value of a *pretrial conference*.

■ TAKING THE CASE TO TRIAL

Most of the civil litigation begun in the United States never goes to trial. In other words, it is not heard by a judge and jury. Most cases are either dismissed on legal or procedural grounds or are settled out of court. To avoid the time and expense of a jury trial, the courts encourage such settlements. For this reason, any rejected offers to compromise or statements associated with them are not admissible as evidence during the subsequent trial.

The Right to Trial by Jury

There is an important distinction between types of juries. Trial juries are known as **petit juries. Grand juries** are part of the *pretrial*, criminal process. A grand jury decides whether the evidence in a case is sufficient to indict—for example, whether there is probable cause that a crime has been committed by the person accused. If their answer is yes, grand jurors will hand down an indictment, pursuant to which the defendant will be tried.

petit jury For civil or criminal cases, a trial jury

grand jury Jury summoned to decide whether the evidence in a case warrants indictment

Criminal procedure is examined in detail in Chapter 12. In this section, we will focus on the right to trial by jury in *civil* cases—both the guarantees of that right and the circumstances under which it can be waived. We will then examine the process of *jury selection*, including the extremely important process known as *voir dire*—that is, the process whereby adversaries for each party evaluate prospective jurors.

THE JURY: CIVIL CASES. The right of parties to a jury trial in a federal civil case is guaranteed by the Seventh Amendment to the Constitution, which states that "In suits at common law, where the amount in controversy shall exceed $20, the right of trial by jury shall be preserved. . . . " In state courts, the right to

Lights, Camera, Adjudication In the state of New Jersey, television cameras first appeared in the courtroom on May 1, 1979. In this trial (a murder trial in Atlantic City), members of the pool of admitted camera crews can be seen frame-right; the defendant and his attorney are forgeground/frame-left, and the prosecutor (standing) is frame-center. In the case of *Chandler v. Florida* (1981), the Supreme Court ruled that while no state is required to admit TV cameras into its courtrooms, their presence does not, per se, violate defendants' rights. Today, we even have *Court TV*, a cable channel dedicated to the 24-hour presentation of trials whose first "scoop" was the trial of William Kennedy Smith in 1991. Public debate continues, but most observers agree that the following questions are *not* at issue: (1) *freedom to report*—although heavy media attention on highly dramatic trials may warp further public perception of the judicial process, journalists are free to cover trials: (2) *obtrusive presence*—not only is modern equipment increasingly unobtrusive, such facilities as external monitors actually reduce the activity of reporters during proceedings; (3) *video recording*—as long as tapes are shown after the trial and the exhaustion of appeals, they may be used for educational purposes (a practice already allowed by the Code of Judicial Conduct). The issue, say many critics, is the historical relationship between the *mass media,* which represents—and is subject to—pervasive cultural and popular pressures, and the *judicial process,* which in effect, tries to conduct proceedings—the application of law to individual cases—in a context removed from those extrajudicial pressures.

jury trials in civil cases is determined by state constitutions and statutes. However, state courts typically require that the amount in controversy must be more than $20. The right to a jury must be asserted by any party within ten days of defendant's answer pursuant to most state codes and in "timely fashion" under the Federal Rules of Civil Procedure. The right to a jury trial may also be waived.

Be aware that the Seventh Amendment right to trial by jury depends, in part, on whether such a right existed at common law when the Constitution was adopted and is therefore "preserved." For example, if the case involves a matter of *equity jurisdiction* (*see* Chapter 4, *p. 113*), the right is not automatic because such cases were heard without juries at the time the Constitution was adopted. Thus, cases such as divorces or disputes of wills, for example, do not ordinarily have juries.

During the 200 years since the Seventh Amendment was written, however, questions of law and equity have become intertwined. New questions arose as to which facts, relating to which issues, could properly be considered by a jury. In decision after decision, the federal courts have expanded citizens' right to jury trial in civil cases. As the right to jury trial has expanded, however, court dockets have sometimes stretched to four or five years even though only a small number of cases actually go to trial. Instead, many cases now go to *arbitration*, which is discussed more fully below. It is important to remember, however, that although arbitration has been shown to be a highly effective method of alternative dispute resolution, an individual who gives up the constitutional right to a trial by jury and agrees to arbitration must do so voluntarily. In the case below, the court determined that even when a legal contract provides for arbitration, it may be possible for a party to that contract to resist arbitration.

RAMIREZ v. SUPERIOR COURT, SANTA CLARA COUNTY
103 Cal. App. 3d. 746 (1980)

Ms. Ramirez had arranged to have her pediatrician examine her infant daughter at the defendant hospital to determine the cause of certain heart, pulse, and breathing irregularities. The examination was instead performed by an emergency room doctor who sent the baby home without performing a diagnosis. The baby was later determined to have had meningitis, from which she is now blind and paralyzed. Prior to the emergency room examination, Ms. Ramirez signed an admission agreement, written in Spanish, requiring arbitration of all medical malpractice claims. Although Ms. Ramirez looked at the agreement before signing, it was not clear whether she was aware of the arbitration provision.

Ms. Ramirez sued the defendant hospital on behalf of the plaintiff, her daughter Corina, to recover damages caused by the alleged malpractice of the emergency room doctor. The Superior Court ordered arbitration. Ms. Ramirez now argues in the appeals court that the arbitration clause was not enforceable due to a lack of consent.

. . . The question raised by this petition is whether a patient who has signed an admission agreement which complies with Code of Civil Procedure section 1295 (hereinafter section 1295) and which requires arbitration of all medical malpractice claims may resist arbitration on the ground that the agreement was not entered into knowingly and voluntarily. We conclude that the statute must be read to permit such a challenge in order to avoid constitutional defects. . . .

On October 19, 1977, Ms. Ramirez arranged to have her pediatrician examine Corina at defendant hospital. Corina, then nine months old, had had an eight-day history of elevated temperature, pulse, and respiration rate. At the emergency room, before her daughter was examined, Ms. Ramirez was handed a Spanish version of the arbitration agreement specified in section 1295.

. . . Ms. Barbara Meninger, the nurse who handled the admission of Corina Ramirez, stated in her declaration that she can speak Spanish although she understands it better than she can speak it. She did not say,

however, whether she spoke Spanish to Ms. Ramirez. There were other people in the hospital available who did speak Spanish.

Nurse Meninger asked Ms. Ramirez to read the agreement. Although she did not know whether Ms. Ramirez read the agreement, Ms. Ramirez looked at it before signing it. Nurse Meninger made no attempt to explain the agreement. Nurse Meninger did state, however, that she did not tell Ms. Ramirez that the agreement had to be signed before her baby would be treated. Nurse Meninger stated that a copy of the agreement was given to Ms. Ramirez.

In her declaration, Ms. Ramirez stated that a hospital employee who spoke very little Spanish handed her a piece of paper and told her to sign it, where the "X" was located. No attempt was made to explain the paper or its meaning. Ms. Ramirez, worried about her daughter and believing she had to sign all the papers handed to her before her child would be examined, signed the arbitration agreement without reading it. She cannot remember whether she was given a copy of the agreement, but she has never read it.

. . . The plaintiff-wife stated that her husband had signed the admission form without reading it, no one at the hospital called their attention to the arbitration provision, and the plaintiffs were never provided with a copy of the agreement. The trial court ordered arbitration when Mr. Wheeler and his wife brought a medical malpractice suit. After arbitration on the merits resulted in an award for the defendants, the plaintiffs sought to vacate the award inter alia on the trial court's alleged abuse of discretion in ordering arbitration.

[3] On appeal, the court recognized that while arbitration is favored as a method for settling disputes, it is consensual in nature. When there is no agreement to arbitrate, an essential jurisdictional fact is missing and a court abuses its discretion if it compels arbitration. To compel arbitration there must be a voluntary agreement to arbitrate which is openly and fairly entered into. (*Id.*, at p. 356, 133 Cal.Rptr. 777.)

. . . Section 1295 [of the code of Civil Procedure] prescribes the exact language to be used for an arbitration provision in a medical services contract, prescribes the form and placement of a warning notice to the person signing the contract, and provides for rescission of the contract by written notice within 30 days of signature. In subdivision (e) it states: "Such a contract is not a contract of adhesion, nor unconscionable nor otherwise improper, where it complies" with the requirements as to form, language and rescission.

. . . [However] We conclude that in order to avoid constitutional infirmity section 1295 must be read as permitting a very limited species of attack by one who has signed an agreement in proper form. Our conclusion is drawn from our reading of the constitutional right to trial by jury in civil cases.

Under the federal Constitution, "In Suits at common law, where the value in controversy shall exceed twenty dollars, the right of trial by jury shall be preserved . . . " (U.S.Const., 7th Amend.) Under the California Constitution, "Trial by jury is an inviolate right and shall be secured to all, but in a civil cause three-fourths of the jury may render a verdict. . . . In a civil cause a jury may be waived by the consent of the parties expressed as prescribed by statute." (Cal.Const., art. 1, 16.) The importance of the right to jury trial has been expressed in the following terms: "The right to jury trial is immemorial; it was brought from England to this country by the colonists, and it has become a part of the birthright of every free man. The right to have a trial by a jury is a fundamental right in our democratic judicial system, including our federal jurisprudence. It is a right which is justly dear to the American people, and, whether guaranteed by the Constitution or provided by statute, should be jealously guarded by the courts. Any seeming curtailment of this right should be scrutinized with the utmost care."

. . . In light of the constitutional protection for the right to jury trial in civil cases, we conclude that the Legislature may not establish a conclusive presumption that one signing an agreement meeting the requirements of section 1295 has in fact consented to arbitration. We therefore read section 1295 as permitting a party to seek to show that he or she was coerced into signing or did not read the many waiver notices provided and did not realize that the agreement was an agreement to arbitrate. Because of the nature of the warnings on the form, a party attacking the arbitration agreement will doubtless have a difficult time: she will have to explain how her eyes avoided the 10-point red type above the signature line; she will have to explain why she did not ask questions about what she was signing; she will have to show that no one explained the document to her or asked her to read it before signing it; and she will have to explain why she did not rescind the agreement within 30 days after it was signed. The trial court will then make a factual ruling on the questions of coercion and of whether the person signing the document actually knew or reasonably should have known that he or she was waiving jury trial rights and agreeing to arbitrate any medical malpractice controversy. We do not believe the trial courts will be unduly burdened by the requirement that they make such a factual determination when ruling on a petition to compel arbitration. To the extent a burden is imposed, the Constitution requires it.

. . . We must annul the prior ruling and return the matter for redetermination.

Let peremptory writ of mandate issue, directing the Santa Clara County Superior Court to vacate its order of February 22, 1979 compelling arbitration, and to reconsider the motion in light of the views expressed herein.

Case Questions

1. What does one give up by signing a valid agreement to arbitrate?

2. What relation does the Constitution have to the enforceability of arbitration provisions?

3. How heavily does the Seventh Amendment weigh into the court's analysis?

JURY SELECTION. A jury may be selected by the court or by the opposing lawyers from a pool of eligible citizens. Under early common law, jurors were selected because they knew the parties involved or were familiar with the dispute. Later, jurors were appointed according to recommendations made by leading citizens. Modern jury-selection procedure aims to produce an impartial, disinterested jury from a pool that fairly represents the local community. In some federal district courts, the "local community" may include millions of people from different towns, cities, and villages.

In the past, the pool of veniremen was artificially restricted to exclude women, minorities, the indigent, and the handicapped. Many of these barriers have been removed or minimized in the past 20 years. The eligibility requirements for federal jury service are: (1) valid registration to vote (2) age 18 or over (3) U.S. citizenship (4) ability to read and write English (5) physical ability to serve (6) no criminal convictions or pending indictments.

Race and the "Cross-Section" Principle A drawing from an edition of *Leslies'* magazine, 30 November 1867, depicts both blacks and whites sitting on a trial jury. The Sixth Amendment to the Constitution requires the "impartial" composition of a jury, and in 1880 a West Virginia law limiting juries to white males was declared unconstitutional (*Strauder v. West Virginia*). Nevertheless, for another half century, the absence of black members on juries was not grounds for constitutional objections to their makeup: it was sufficient that state statutes made no specific discrimination against black jurors. In *Norris v. Alabama* (1935), however, the Court reversed a conviction on the ground that blacks had been systematically excluded both from the grand jury that had returned the original indictment and from the jury in a second trial (the first had been reversed because the defendant had been denied counsel). No black had ever been called for jury duty in the living memory of either Alabama county involved, and the *Norris* decision thus made it possible to *infer* discriminatory practice from a record of the actual facts. (As late as 1961, the courts upheld exemptions for women as "the center of home and family life," and it was not until 1975 (in *Taylor v. Louisiana*) that the Supreme Court, acknowledging "the current judgment of the country," invalidated a state statute exempting women from jury service.)

The categories of people able to escape jury duty by claiming exemption has also been reduced. For example, Massachusetts used to exempt ministers, teachers, lawyers, doctors, and most politicians. That state's revised rules now forbid exemption on the basis of occupation.

Some states and judicial districts are also changing the old two-week or one-month term of service to a one-day/one-trial jury system. Under such a system, citizens can be called just once a year, for one day only. If they are not selected for a case on that day, their obligation is fulfilled. If they are chosen to hear a case, their obligation is discharged when the case is concluded. Under older systems, potential jurors might sit on three or four cases during their terms of service.

VOIR DIRE. Jury selection is a crucial stage of a trial. Lawyers for both sides want a jury that will be sympathetic—or at least not hostile—to their respective cases. How do lawyers evaluate prospective jurors? What criteria do they use in jury selection?

voir dire Questioning of
prospective *jurors* in order to
determine eligibility to serve and
to discover any pre-existing bias
or prejudice that they may hold

When a case is ready to be tried, a group of potential jurors goes through an interview known as **voir dire.** The term "voir dire" comes from the Old French meaning "truly to speak" or "to speak the truth." The object of the questions is to determine jurors' eligibility to serve and to ascertain whether a potential juror has any preexisting bias, interest, or prejudice. For example, is the juror related to the plaintiff or the defendant? Might the juror have had significant, perhaps unpleasant, contact with a corporation or industry involved in the trial? These questions and many others may be posed either by the court or by attorneys for either side.

Juror Challenges. Any potential juror can be *challenged for cause* and excused if bias or prejudice is uncovered. In addition, each lawyer has a fixed number of *peremptory challenges* that can be used to remove a potential juror without explanation or reason. However, a prosecutor in a criminal case cannot systematically remove minority-group jurors out of a general fear that such jurors will not convict "one of their own." The Supreme Court so ruled in *Batson v. Kentucky* (476 U.S. 79 [1986], and many commentators feel that *Batson* signifies the beginning of the end of the peremptory challenge.

Lawyers commonly look to race, sex, age, religion, educational background, and marital and professional status to predict how a juror will feel about a case. Remember that neither lawyer wants an unbiased jury; each wants a jury biased in favor of his case. So, in an employment discrimination case brought by a minority or woman plaintiff, the plaintiff's attorney may prefer minority or women jurors. The defendant's attorney may prefer white males.

Lawyers also assess a juror's apparent assertiveness or passivity, favoring jurors who are both strong-minded and sympathetic, in the hope that they will sway their fellow jurors. Conversely, a lawyer might decline to challenge an unsympathetic but weak juror who may be easily swayed.

There is no sociological evidence proving or disproving these or similar theories about jury selection. However, it seems self-evident that a juror's personality and background will affect his verdict. Therefore, it is impossible to predict anyone's verdict with certainty.[3]

The Ethics of Voir Dire. Sometimes, lawyers are criticized because they seek a panel of sympathetic rather than objective jurors. Some critics charge that by seeking such a selection, lawyers undermine the trial process. To this lawyers respond that because a trial is an adversarial process, the efforts of opposing lawyers will balance out. Of course, if one lawyer is more adept at jury selection, then the outcome of the trial may be affected by such a skill. In addition, many lawyers point out that selecting a sympathetic jury is part of their primary obligation—namely, to represent their clients as effectively as possible. To do anything less, they argue, would be an abdication of professional responsibility.

An instructive example of the voir dire process is provided by *Edmonson v. Leesville Concrete Co.*, 111 S.ct 2077 (1991) decided by the Supreme Court in 1991. In the voir dire of the original jury trial, Leesville had used peremptory challenges to exclude blacks from the prospective jury in order to get a more sympathetic panel (Edmonson is black). The *Edmonson* case is the subject of this chapter's YOU DECIDE feature.

---

[3] Wrightsman, *Psychology and Legal Systems* (Brooks/Cole, 1987), p.234.

Voir dire is a courtroom procedure with constitutional implications. This process reminds us that the broad principle of equal protection under the law enters into both criminal trials and civil litigation—especially when issues regarding race are concerned. Attorneys selecting juries in civil proceedings are well aware of the fact that using peremptory challenges to exclude racial minorities in order to get a sympathetic panel is not a simple matter.

As we follow it through the courts, the case of Edmonson v. Leesville Concrete Co. raises several questions about this issue. Consider: Is the process of jury selection in private, civil litigation suit also a "state action"—that is, is it subject to the guarantee of equal protection under the law? If the guarantee of equal protection holds, must both sides prove that their choice was devoid of any "racial" selection? As a litigant, what are your rights and protections? As a prospective juror, what can you expect to happen in a court considering you for a jury?

In Edmonson, a black construction worker, Donald Edmonson, was injured in an on-the-job accident at a federal site in Louisiana. Edmonson sued Leesville in federal district court for negligence, seeking a jury trial under his Seventh Amendment right. During voir dire, Leesville's attorneys used two of their three peremptory challenges to remove blacks from the prospective jury. They were not required to state their reasons for doing so.

Edmonson's attorneys then requested that Leesville give

a "race-neutral" explanation for removing the prospective black jurors with peremptory challenges. They cited the criminal case of Batson v. Kentucky (476 U.S. 79 [1986]), in which the Supreme Court held that prosecutors who use peremptory challenges to exclude potential jurors in any way suggesting racial discrimination must provide a "race-neutral" explanation for the action. However, the district court maintained that because Edmonson was a civil case Batson did not apply. The jury (1 black person and 11 white people) found that Edmonson had contributed to the negligence and awarded him only 20 percent of the requested damages.

Edmonson appealed this decision, but the circuit court did not reverse, arguing that because the parties to the civil litigation were private, using a peremptory challenge was not a "state action" with its implied constitutional guarantees.

The decision was appealed once more, and the Supreme Court agreed to hear it. If you were a Justice, what would you hold? Is a civil process indeed private? Does a decision made regarding criminal cases hold in civil cases? Should prospective jurors be given equal protection under the law in the selection process? What will provide the litigants with a fair hearing—allowing race to be a determinant without explanation in jury selection or requiring attorneys to provide an explanation if they use race in peremptory challenges? (For further discussion, see p. 172.)

Conduct of the Trial

When the jury has been empaneled, its responsibility is to decide whether the plaintiff has met the **burden of proof**—that is, the requirement that the government proves a defendant's guilt "beyond a reasonable doubt." In a civil case, the burden of proof is much less stringent and, hence, easier to meet. The plaintiff must prove the case only by a "preponderance of evidence."

burden of proof Duty or burden of proving the disputed issues at trial

In reaching a verdict, the judge and jury perform complementary functions: The jury concerns itself with the facts of the case, the judge with the applicable law. However, the judge, as the arbiter of the law, interprets the *rules of evidence* and decides what facts are relevant or can be heard by the jury. The rules also govern *hearsay evidence.*

RULES OF EVIDENCE. The plaintiff must present enough evidence for each of the allegations made in the pleadings to convince the jury to find in his favor. The evidence presented must conform to the firmly established standards laid down in state and federal codes of evidence. The evidence may be either direct or circumstantial. **Direct evidence** directly establishes a fact at issue; **circumstantial evidence** implies it. For example, the statement by a witness "I saw David hit Peter" is *direct* evidence of an assault. The statement "I saw Peter walk out of David's office with a black eye" is *circumstantial* evidence. Both

direct evidence Evidence that directly proves the existence of a fact

circumstantial evidence Indirect evidence from which a fact is inferred, often used if no direct evidence exists

statements are **testimonial evidence.** Documents and other physical objects shown to the jury are **real evidence.**

An important rule in business litigation concerns real evidence: The **best-evidence rule** refers to the standard whereby the best evidence of the contents of a *written document* is the *original* document itself. Developed out of application to *promissory notes*—the first form of all contracts—this rule holds that contracts should be properly signed by the parties involved and filed for potential use as evidence. *Authenticated* copies are acceptable as exceptions to the best-evidence rule when originals cannot be produced.

HEARSAY EVIDENCE. **Hearsay evidence** consists of statements made by a witness *as reported by someone who is not a witness.* Such evidence is generally offered to prove the truth of a statement. Hearsay evidence, however, is not always admissible. It may be admissible if it is (1) relevant and not obtainable in any other way, (2) clearly attributable to a source whose access to the information is appropriate, and (3) more helpful in proving the case than it is prejudicial to either party.

Many appeals are based on the judge's ruling as to the admissibility of hearsay evidence, as was the case in *Cook v. Hoppin* (783 F.2d 684 [1986]). In that case, Cook was permanently injured when he fell while visiting friends in an apartment complex owned by Hoppin. Cook sued Hoppin for the injuries that he sustained.

Part of the evidence admitted into the trial was Cook's medical records. He had stated to an unknown person—perhaps a nurse or unknown hospital admitting clerk who recorded his words—that he had been involved in a "shoving or wrestling match" just before his fall. Cook initially lost the case. The U.S. Court of Appeals, however, awarded Cook a retrial because the statements recorded in his medical records were not relevant to his medical condition. An unknown person's report of Cook's statement was not admissible as medical information and was unfairly prejudicial to his case. The court of appeals ruled that the jury might consider whether or not the "shoving or wrestling match" could have made it appear that Cook's negligence, rather than the apartment owner's, was the cause of his accident.

The Order of the Trial

As we have seen, the right to trial by jury can be waived, and, especially in civil cases, that right is increasingly being waived by the agreement of both parties. However, our discussion of open-court procedures will proceed on the assumption that the trial is being heard by a jury. For the sake of clarity, we will divide open-court procedures into three stages. Stage 1 consists of opposing attorneys' *opening statements,* which are summary arguments designed to familiarize the jury with the case and not presentations of evidence. Stage 2 concerns the presentation of evidence in open court, including *direct* and *cross-examination, motions for a verdict, rebuttal evidence,* and *closing arguments.* Stage 3 describes the actions of the court taken after the close of arguments: the judge's *instructions to the jury,* the jury's *verdict,* and the motion for *judgment non obstante veredicto.*

OPENING STATEMENTS. A jury trial begins with the **opening statements** made by lawyers for each side. In most trials, the plaintiff's lawyer speaks first because the plaintiff generally has the burden of proof. The defendant's lawyer opens

testimonial evidence Statements issued by a witness in court

real evidence Documents or physical objects displayed to the jury

best-evidence rule Rule whereby the original document in a case involving written documents provides the most reliable evidence or highest degree of proof

hearsay evidence Testimony offered by a witness based on what someone else has told him

opening statements Statements made by the lawyers of each side at the beginning of a jury trial, defining the facts to be established or proved

first only if all the plaintiff's assertions in the pleadings have been agreed to by the defendant and the case rests on affirmative defenses pleaded by the defendant.

For example, if the plaintiff has accused the defendant of breach of contract and the defendant asserts that he fulfilled the contract, the plaintiff's lawyer will open. If, however, the defendant states that he broke the contract because the plaintiff failed to pay agreed-upon installments, the defendant's lawyer makes the opening statement.

In the opening statement, the plaintiff's lawyer describes for the jury what facts will be demonstrated or proved. In most courts, the opposition's opening statement immediately follows. Occasionally, however, the plaintiff will present both the opening statement and all of his evidence before the defendant's opening statement. Most trial specialists believe that it is important to the defendant's case to present an opening statement at the earliest possible moment in the case—that is, before jurors have begun to be convinced of the plaintiff's version and while their minds are still open to other interpretations of the evidence.

DIRECT EXAMINATION AND CROSS-EXAMINATION. Following opening statements, the plaintiff's lawyer begins the **direct examination.** During this phase of the trial, witnesses are called and asked to respond to direct questions about the case. The lawyer may not ask *leading questions,* such as, "Didn't defendant shout threats at you?" Rather, questions must be open-ended and neutral. Examples of such questions include "Did the defendant address you directly, and, if so, what was said?" and "What tone of voice was used?"

> **direct examination** Initial questioning of a witness by the lawyer who called him

As each witness's direct examination is completed by the plaintiff's lawyer, the lawyer for the defendant has the opportunity for **cross-examination.** The witness may be cross-examined only on topics raised in the direct examination. The style of the defendant's counsel, however, is less restrained, and leading questions are allowed in cross-examination.

> **cross-examination** The questioning of a witness by the lawyer opposing the party who called the witness for *direct examination*

In the course of direct examination, the plaintiff's attorney is permitted to introduce real evidence that is shown to be pertinent and authentic. If, at any point in the examination or cross-examination of any witness, the opposing lawyer believes that evidence of any kind is being introduced in a way that violates evidentiary rules, that lawyer may object. The judge will immediately rule on the objection, and, in most situations, either order the examination to continue or the jury to disregard the objectionable material. If counsel for either side believes that a point of law has been violated and does not object promptly, the right to appeal the case on that particular point is waived.

At the close of cross-examination, the plaintiff's attorney is entitled to **re-direct examination** of the same witness. If the plaintiff's attorney conducts a *redirect,* as it is often called, then the defendant's attorney is permitted to *re-cross.*

> **re-direct examination** The plaintiff lawyer's questioning of a witness at the end of *cross-examination*

MOTION FOR A DIRECTED VERDICT. When all of the plaintiff's witnesses have been thoroughly examined by both sides, the lawyer for either party may call for a **directed verdict.** In a directed verdict, the judge—not the jury—essentially decides the case: The judge will direct a verdict if he finds that there is insufficient evidence to go to a jury or that the evidence compels only one verdict. What is sufficient evidence to go to a jury? Standards range from a "scintilla of evidence" to "substantial evidence" favoring the nonmoving party.

> **directed verdict** Order by the trial judge that the judge rather than the jury decide the case because there is insufficient evidence to proceed to the jury or because the evidence compels only one verdict

If the motion for a directed verdict is overruled, the spotlight turns to the defense attorney. The defense now calls its witnesses. The same procedure is followed: direct examination by the defense, followed by cross-examination by the plaintiff's lawyer, followed by redirect and recross. When the defense has presented all direct evidence, either side is permitted once again to ask for a directed verdict.

REBUTTAL EVIDENCE. If the directed verdict is not granted, the plaintiff has an opportunity to present **rebuttal evidence** in response to any new issues raised in the defense's presentation. Rebuttal evidence is evidence offered to disprove or contradict evidence presented by the opposing side.

CLOSING ARGUMENTS. When all evidence has been presented by both sides, the lawyers deliver their final arguments. These statements sum up the presentation of the case in the way most favorable to each party. In most cases, the plaintiff presents the initial **closing argument.** Counsel for the defense then makes defendant's closing argument. Lastly, plaintiff offers *final* closing argument.

JUDGE'S INSTRUCTIONS TO THE JURY. At this point, the judge instructs the jury: That is, he explains the principles of law that the jury must follow in reaching a verdict. In a negligence case, for example, the judge may explain the legal definition of *due care* that the jurors must apply to the defendant's behavior. In a criminal case, the judge will instruct the jury on the elements of the crime involved and tell them what the defendant must have done or apparently intended to do in order to be held guilty. The judge will also instruct the jury on the burden of proof by explaining, in lay terms, what "beyond a reasonable doubt" or a "preponderance of the evidence" means.

Questions of law and fact sometimes merge when the case goes to the jury. For example, negligence is generally determined by a *reasonableness standard*. If the facts of the case are clear and undisputed, however, the reasonableness of the defendant's behavior may be considered a matter of law. Nonetheless, juries and not judges decide the question of negligence. In commercial cases involving a reasonableness standard, appeals courts are divided as to whether the judge or jury should apply the standard to an undisputed set of facts.

It is the jury's job to take the judge's instructions and reach a **verdict**: That is, it must find for one side or the other.

THE JURY VERDICT. Some critics of the jury system believe that today's complex society makes it very difficult for a jury to reach a correct verdict. They feel that the rights of civil litigants may be better protected by "special juries" with knowledge of the industry in question and that juries should be trained in the law prior to service. Although most legal professionals believe that our present jury system fulfills its mandate, the late Judge Jerome Frank was harshly critical of it:

> Often [jurors] cannot understand what the judge tells them about the legal rules. To comprehend the meaning of many a legal rule requires special training. It is inconceivable that a body of twelve ordinary men and women casually gathered together for a few days, could, merely from listening to the instructions of the judge, gain the knowledge necessary to grasp the true import of the judge's words. For these words have often acquired their meaning as the result of hun-

dreds of years of professional disputation in the courts. The jurors usually are as unlikely to get the meaning of those words as if they were spoken in Chinese, Sanskrit, or Choctaw.[4]

Judgment non obstante veredicto (notwithstanding the verdict), also called **judgment n.o.v.,** asks the judge to reverse the jury's decision. Like a motion for a directed verdict made earlier during the course of a trial, it rests on the claim that the evidence does not prove the findings. The trial judge can grant the motion of judgment n.o.v. only if he believes that the jury's verdict is contrary to the weight of the evidence. Lawyers frequently accompany a motion for judgment n.o.v. with a motion for a new trial. Both are postverdict motions that are considered part of the original trial.

> **judgment *non obstante veredicto*** (or ***n.o.v.***) Decision by a trial judge that reverses the jury's verdict, based on the perception that the clear weight of evidence contradicts that verdict

Procedures and Grounds for Appeal

When all motions in the original trial have been concluded, the losing party may decide to appeal the verdict. Not everything that happens in a trial, however, can be the subject of an appeal: Appeals can only relate to *issues or questions of law.* Furthermore, any alleged error of law must have been objected to *at the time it was made during the trial:* The objection and the disputed ruling must appear in the record of the trial. Questions of fact decided by the jury may not be appealed.

It is not mandatory that the appeals courts accept every appeal. In fact, they lack the resources to do so. The role of appellate courts is not that of "policeman" to the trial courts. As seen in Chapter 4, an appeal may be heard to clarify an important question of law.

If an appeal is taken, the party filing the appeal is designated the **appellant,** and the party against whom the appeal is filed is called the **appellee** or **respondent.** These terms apply regardless of which party was the original plaintiff. If, for example, the plaintiff was successful in providing the burden of proof at the trial, then the losing defendant would become the appellant.

> **appellant** The party who files an appeal (*see also* Chapter 4)
>
> **appellee** (or **respondent**) The party against whom an appeal is filed (*see also* Chapter 4)

Intermediate appellate courts are often composed of three-judge panels (*see* Chapter 4, *p. 125*). The appellant's lawyer appeals on a question of law, and both sides submit **briefs**—legal arguments consisting of statements of the issues presented for review, statements of the case, arguments on the points of law or issues being appealed, and conclusions stating the precise relief sought.

> **brief** A court document submitted by both sides in an appeal and stating each party's view of his case (*see also* Chapter 4)

On the day the case is heard, the lawyers are questioned by the judicial panel. The appellate court then reviews the relevant portion of the trial court record, along with the lawyers' briefs. Sometimes, the appellate court must review the entire trial record.

Generally, following a period of deliberation, the judges issue written decisions known as **opinions.** An opinion sets forth the questions of law applied to the appeal and delineates the reasons on which the decision was based, which becomes part of the permanent record (*see* Chapter 1, *p. 29*).

The decision is based on a majority vote of the judges hearing the case. Thus, the **majority opinion,** which is usually written by one of the judges who joins in it, is binding. However, the minority may write a **dissenting opinion.** The dissenting opinion disagrees with the reasoning by which the majority reached its conclusion, and with the ruling itself. Such opinions often provide

> **opinion** Statement of court's decisions, describing its conclusions and the reasoning of trial judges' decisions
>
> **majority opinion** Opinion of an appellate court stating the conclusion and reasoning of its majority members
>
> **dissenting opinion** (or **dissent**) Opinion written by the minority panel of judges, disagreeing with the majority's conclusion (*see also* Chapter 1)

---

[4] *Courts on Trial,* p. 116 (1949), quoted in Julius Paul, "Jerome Frank's Views on Trial by Jury," 22 *Missouri Law Review* 28 (1957).

The En Banc Panel When an issue of particular national importance reaches a federal appeals court from a district court within its circuit, the appeals-court judges, at the call of the chief judge of the circuit, may sit as an *en banc* panel to decide the case in a "collegial" manner—that is, with authority shared equally among colleagues. Such was the case in the summer of 1958, when seven federal judges sitting in the Eighth Circuit convened in St. Louis, Missouri, to hear arguments in a school-desegregation case originating in Little Rock, Arkansas, in the aftermath of the Supreme Court's historic ruling in the case of *Brown v. Board of Education* (see Chapter 3). While the Supreme Court often reverses the rulings of three-judge appeals-court panels, those of such en banc panels are rarely overturned.

useful insights. In many instances, dissenting opinions become majority opinions when similar cases are subsequently overruled.

The appellate court may either *affirm* a lower court decision or *reverse* it. A reversal makes the loser of the trial battle the winner of the war. Sometimes, a decision will be affirmed despite legal errors made during the trial. Some errors are considered *harmless*—that is, deemed not to have affected the jury's verdict. Verdicts are reversed only for *prejudicial errors*—that is, errors that are deemed to have affected the outcome. For example, the admission of an illegally obtained confession in a criminal trial would clearly be prejudicial error. An appellate court may also remand a case—that is, send it back to the trial court. Cases are remanded when further factual findings are required that the appellate courts are neither empowered nor equipped to make.

■ *Concept Check 5-3   Taking the Case to Trial*

- Compare your *right to trial by jury* in *civil cases* to your right in *criminal cases*.
- Not everything that happens during the course of a trial can be subject to *appeal*. Explain this statement.

■ ALTERNATIVES TO LITIGATION

Should every dispute between parties be solved through a lawsuit? Is a judgment resulting from the litigation process worth the time and money expended on acquiring it? Critics have long questioned the suitability and efficiency of our system for settling disagreements. In litigation, the differences between parties are exaggerated, and one party must always lose. Both may suffer economically as both lawyers' fees and the length of time for pretrial activity increase. As expenses rise and court calendars clog, more lawyers and legislators are thus turning to alternative modes of dispute resolution. Table 5-1 compares several methods of settling a dispute with the process of adjudication. We will consider in some detail two methods of alternative dispute resolution: *arbitration* and *mediation*.

TABLE 5-1   *Methods of Settling Disputes*

CHARACTERISTICS	ADJUDICATION	ARBITRATION	MEDIATION	PRIVATE JUDGING	MINI-TRIAL
Voluntary/ Involuntary	Involuntary	Voluntary	Voluntary	Voluntary	Voluntary
Binding/ Nonbinding	Binding, subject to appeal	Binding, subject to review on limited grounds	If agreement generally enforceable as contract	Binding, subject to appeal	If agreement enforceable as contract
Third Party	Imposed neutral decision maker, generally without specialized subject expertise	Party-selected decision maker, usually with specialized subject expertise	Party-selected outside facilitator	Party-selected decision maker	Party-selected adviser, sometimes with specialized subject expertise
Degree of Formality	Formalized and highly structured by predetermined, rigid rules	Procedurally less formal; procedural and evidentiary rules may be set by parties	Usually informal, unstructured	Statutory or contractually developed procedure, but highly flexible as to timing and place	Less formal than adjudication; procedural and evidentiary rules may be set by parties
Nature of Proceeding	Opportunity for each party to present proofs and arguments	Opportunity for each party to present proofs and arguments	Wide latitude in presentation of evidence, arguments, and concerns	Opportunity for each party to present proofs and arguments	Opportunity for each party to present summary proofs and arguments
Outcome	Principled decision, supported by reasoned opinion	Sometimes principled decision supported by reasoned opinion, sometimes compromise without opinion	Mutually acceptable agreement or no agreement	Principled decision, sometimes supported by finding of fact and conclusions of law	Mutually acceptable agreement or no agreement
Private/Public	Public	Private, unless judicial review sought	Private	Private, unless judicial enforcement or review sought	Private

Source: Adapted with permission from Goldberg, Green, and Sander, Dispute Resolution *(Boston: Little, Brown, 1985). © Ohio State Bar Foundation.*

Arbitration: A Third-Party Decision

arbitration Form of dispute resolution in which a neutral third party is chosen to resolve a dispute and deliver a decision that both parties agree beforehand to accept

submission Document signed by both parties in a dispute that initiates arbitration by specifying the arbitrator, his duties, and his intended procedure

The procedure followed in arbitration is summarized in Table 5–2. When **arbitration** occurs, the parties contesting the question refer the matter to a neutral third party who is chosen and accepted by both sides. Both sides agree in advance to accept the decision of the arbitrator as final and subject to limited review. Many arbitrations are voluntary. However, some labor contracts, especially those involving public employees, have provisions for compulsory arbitration. When there is no advance agreement to arbitrate, the arbitration process can be initiated by a **submission.** A submission is a document signed by both parties, specifying the arbitrator's selection and duties, the procedure to be followed, and the facts at issue. In other circumstances, initiation may be by notice or court order. The American Arbitration Association is an organization parties frequently turn for help with dispute resolution. Their submission form is illustrated in Figure 5-3.

TABLE 5-2   *The Steps to Arbitration*

STEP 1: AGREEMENT TO ARBITRATE

The agreement to arbitrate is achieved by a demand for arbitration, which cites a future-dispute arbitration clause in a contract, or by a submission of a dispute to arbitration. Proper notification of the claim to the defending party, in the former case, and to the American Arbitration Association (AAA), in both cases, is sufficient to start the process. Location of the arbitration hearing is determined at this point.

STEP 2: SELECTION OF ARBITRATOR

The parties receive a list of arbitrators from the AAA panel of qualified professionals in a field pertaining to their dispute. Each party eliminates those not acceptable and lists the order of preference of the remaining ones. Taking into account the mutual choices, the AAA case administrator selects an arbitrator. In some cases, each party selects an arbitrator and the AAA a third, neutral one; all three hear the dispute.

STEP 3: PREPARATION FOR THE HEARING

The case administrator, not the arbitrator, may hold conferences to arrange details and expedite the proceedings. In a complex case, the administrator may hold a preliminary hearing to specify issues, stipulate uncontested facts, and consider other matters. The involved parties should prepare very carefully the facts and exhibits for their presentation, paying particular attention to assembling all needed documents, interviewing witnesses, summarizing each witness's testimony, and studying the opposition's case in order to be prepared to reply to evidence.

STEP 4: PRESENTATION OF THE CASE

There is no "burden of proof" as in a jury trial, and each party must try to convince the arbitrator that the position he is arguing is correct. Although arbitrators must hear all evidence (unlike the rules of evidence operative in a courtroom), they can then decide what is relevant and important.

As with their preparation, the parties should prepare carefully as well. They should provide a brief opening statement of the controversy and point to be proved, discussing the remedy sought, introducing witnesses to clarify the dispute, and summarizing evidence.

STEP 5: THE AWARD

The award must be rendered within thirty days of the hearing. The award rules on each part of the claim, finally and conclusively. It is briefly stated—a decision, not an explanation—on one sheet of paper and cannot be changed unless both parties agree to restore the arbitrator's power or the law provides for a change.

Source: American Arbitration Association, A Commercial Arbitration Guide for Business People *(New York: AAA, 1991).*

American Arbitration Association
SUBMISSION TO DISPUTE RESOLUTION

Date: _____

The named parties hereby submit the following dispute for resolution under the _____
_____ Rules* of the American Arbitration Association:

Procedure Selected: ☐ Binding arbitration   ☐ Mediation settlement
                      ☐ Other _____
                                        (Describe)

FOR INSURANCE CASES ONLY:

_____   _____ to _____   _____
Policy Number   Effective Dates   Applicable Policy Limits

Date of Incident _____   Location _____

Insured: _____   Claim Number: _____

Name(s) of Claimant(s)	**Check if a Minor**	**Amount Claimed**
_____	☐	_____
_____	☐	_____

Nature of Dispute and/or Injuries Alleged (attach additional sheets if necessary):

Place of Hearing: _____

We agree that, if binding arbitration is selected, we will abide by and perform any award rendered hereunder and that a judgment may be entered on the award.

To Be Completed by the Parties

Name of Party _____	Name of Party _____
Address _____	Address _____
City, State, and ZIP Code _____	City, State, and ZIP Code _____
( ) _____ Telephone ___ Fax	( ) _____ Telephone ___ Fax
Signature† _____	Signature† _____
Name of Party's Attorney or Representative	Name of Party's Attorney or Representative
Address _____	Address _____
City, State, and ZIP Code _____	City, State, and ZIP Code _____
( ) _____ Telephone ___ Fax	( ) _____ Telephone ___ Fax
Signature† _____	Signature† _____

Please file three copies with the AAA.

* *If you have a question as to which rules apply, please contact the AAA.*
† Signatures of all parties are required for arbitration.   Form G1–6/91

FIGURE 5-3 AAA Arbitration Submission Form   *Source: American Arbitration Association, A Commercial Arbitration Guide for Business People (New York: AAA, 1991).*

Arbitration procedures somewhat resemble those in a trial. There may be prehearing conferences and discovery. Although there is generally a face-to-face hearing, arbitrations may be conducted entirely through written submissions. At no time does the arbitrator consult with just one party: All communications take place in the presence of both sides. Although the hearing is not open to the public, interested parties may attend. The proceedings are generally not recorded.

At the hearing, each party makes an opening statement and each presents evidence. The arbitrator may rule on the admissibility of evidence, call witnesses, and inspect property. The parties generally make closing arguments. In most cases, the arbitrator's decision, called the *award*, is made within thirty days.

ARBITRATION AND BUSINESS.   More than 50,000 disputes are administered by the American Arbitration Association (AAA) each year. Businesses submit their controversies in such large numbers because arbitration is faster and less expensive than litigation. Moreover, the arbitration process, which is conducted privately and more informally than a trial, fosters ongoing commercial relationships.

When drafting a commercial contract today, many parties include a *future-dispute arbitration clause*: By so doing, they acknowledge the inevitability of controversies in normal business dealings and provide for their speedy resolution. Disputes handled by arbitration fall into such general categories as *licensing agreements, franchises, joint venture, purchase and sale agreements, loans, leases and other property matters,* and *management contracts.* The construction industry is a major user of arbitration, especially for building contracts and claims involving cost overruns and delays.

Other areas of business have also incorporated arbitration into their dispute-resolution procedures. For example, in labor contracts, arbitration is specified to resolve grievances that cannot otherwise be settled. Even without union membership, an employee may request arbitration from an agreeable employer. Claims cover such areas as pensions, discharge, promotion, and safety.

Recently, disputes in the securities industry, especially between brokers and their clients, have been settled through arbitration. In the computer industry, with its emerging technology, arbitration has also become quite common. Claims involving hardware and, more frequently, software are growing. On the international business scene, companies often include future-dispute arbitration clauses in contracts in order to avoid going to court in a foreign country.

In the case of *Sablosky v. Gordon Company, Inc.,* an arbitration clause was part of an employment agreement. Although the plaintiff, a salesman, maintained that this contract was unreasonable, the court upheld arbitration as a method to resolve the dispute between the parties in this commercial agreement.

SABLOSKY v. EDWARD S. GORDON CO., INC.
535 N.E.2d 643 (N.Y. 1989)

The plaintiff, Thomas Sablosky, instituted an action in the trial court to recover a $3.6 million commission that he claimed was due to him under his employment agreement with the defendant, Edward S. Gordon Co. The plaintiff argued that even though his contract with the defendant contains an arbitration clause, such a contract could not be enforced because the contract itself was unreasonable.

The trial court compelled the parties to arbitrate the dispute. The plaintiff then appealed to the Appellate Division, which reversed. The defendant now appeals to the Court of Appeals, New York's highest court, seeking an arbitration order.

Plaintiff, Thomas Sablosky, was formerly employed as a commission salesman for defendant, Edward S. Gordon Company, Inc., a New York City real estate brokerage firm. In this action, he alleges that he helped defendant sell the Exxon Building in Midtown Manhattan at a price of $610 million, and claims that he is entitled under his employment agreement to a commission of $3.6 million. Defendant has moved to stay the action

and to compel arbitration, and plaintiff has made a cross motion to stay arbitration permanently. Plaintiff contends that the arbitration clause should not be given effect as a matter of public policy because the employment agreement constitutes a contract of adhesion and is unconscionable. Supreme Court granted defendant's motion and directed the parties to proceed to arbitration. The Appellate Division, 139 A.D.2d 416, 526 N.Y.S.2d 820, reversed and granted plaintiff's cross motion. . . . We granted defendant leave to appeal and now reverse and reinstate the judgment of Supreme Court.

. . . It is noteworthy that an increasing number of jurisdictions enforce commercial arbitration clauses notwithstanding the lack of mutuality of remedies . . . Nor should the court refuse to enforce the clause on policy grounds. Over the last 20 years arbitration has emerged as a preferred method for the settlement of many controversies. . . . Arbitrators customarily have an expertise over a particular subject matter and are able to offer parties a relatively expeditious and inexpensive forum to resolve their disputes. Although a party gives up an important right when it agrees to submit a dispute to arbitration, such proceedings are not less effective in discovering the truth than are judicial proceedings and it is not, as a matter of public policy, per se unfair to give one party the right to select them.

Plaintiff also relates his argument on mutuality to underlying principles of unconscionability and fairness. Indeed, some courts have invalidated unilateral arbitration clauses for want of mutuality although their decisions might as well rest on the doctrine of unconscionability or public policy.

The doctrine of unconscionability contains both substantive and procedural aspects, and whether a contract or clause is unconscionable is to be decided by the court against the background of the contract's commercial setting, purpose and effect. . . . Substantively, courts consider whether one or more key terms are unreasonably favorable to one party. . . . There is no general test for measuring the reasonableness of a transaction but we have recently provided this guidance: "[a]n unconscionable contract [is] one which 'is so grossly unreasonable or unconscionable in the light of the mores and business practices of the time and place as to be unenforcible according to its literal terms.' " . . . Measured against this standard, the arbitration clause in plaintiff's contract is not unreasonable as a matter of law. The real-estate brokerage business, by nature, is bound to generate a substantial number of disputes. An employer, who may hire hundreds of employees, should be able to protect itself from the delays and costs of extensive litigation by including as a condition of employment an agreement by the employee to arbitrate claims rather than litigate them.

Nor do we accept plaintiff's claim that the contract is one of adhesion or that it results from procedural unconscionability in the contract formation process. Such claims are judged by whether the party seeking to enforce the contract has used high pressure tactics or deceptive language in the contract and whether there is inequality of bargaining power between the parties. . . . Plaintiff's claim here relates almost exclusively to the fact that the employment agreement was prepared by the employer or the employer's attorney. As noted by Supreme Court, however, almost all employment contracts are prepared by the employer; that circumstance cannot render the arbitration clause contained in the contract unconscionable.

Plaintiff's remaining claim, alleging that the arbitration panel may be biased, is premature (see, CPLR 7511, 7506).

Accordingly, the order of the Appellate Division should be reversed, with costs, and the judgment of Supreme Court, New York County, reinstated.

Case Questions

1. What is it about arbitration that might make it a more favorable method of dispute resolution than court proceedings in the commercial setting?

2. Why does the decision reject the plaintiff's claim that the contract was unreasonable?

3. What is the difference between substantive and procedural unconscionability? If the court had found the contract to be unconscionable, do you think it would have ordered arbitration?

Mediation: Seeking a Voluntary Solution

Arbitration is a relatively formal process, with a neutral, impartial third person who binds the parties to a particular decision. In contrast, **mediation** is an informal procedure conducted by a third party who is often an active intervener and initiator. Mediators are persuaders with no power to bind the parties to a ruling. The disputants themselves control the mediation process by setting forth its rules and accepting or rejecting its result.[5]

Most experts agree that mediation must be a voluntary process and that the concept of compulsory or mandated mediation is a contradiction. Nevertheless, both Maine and California have enacted statutes that mandate mediation in divorce cases. Maine's experience has been instructive: Of the nearly 5,000 cases of required mediation handled in the state each year (approximately eighty percent of which are contested divorce cases), less than twenty percent were unable to resolve their disputes and subsequently went to trial.

This represents a significant savings both to the parties and the courts. Mediation is inexpensive because it is relatively fast. It may be completed within days or even hours. Although mediators may charge as much as lawyers, they accumulate fewer billable hours.

mediation Form of dispute resolution in which a third party actively intervenes in a dispute but whose decision holds no binding power

---

[5] Phillips and Piazza, "Using Mediation to Resolve Dispute," 3 *California Lawyer* 11 (Oct. 1983).

However, the skills that make a successful mediator are often quite different from those of an adversarial lawyer. Even though some mediators are lawyers, many mediators are drawn from the ranks of psychologists and the clergy. As states consider the possibility of enacting statutes requiring mediation, they are faced with the difficult task of specifying qualification for mediators. In the state of Maine, for example, no correlation has been found between the mediator's professional background and his performance. Thus, it is difficult to develop objective criteria for determining who will be a good mediator.[6]

BUSINESS AND MEDIATION. Through mediation as through arbitration, commercial enterprises can settle their disputes quickly with a minimum disruption of ongoing business relationships. The American Arbitration Association, for example, reports a settlement rate in excess of eighty percent in cases submitted to it under the Commercial and Construction Industry Mediation Rules. Mediation has also worked well for the insurance industry, with thousands of claims settled under its Dispute Resolution Procedures for Insurance Claims.

The basic steps to mediation are presented in Table 5-3.

■ Concept Check 5-4   Alternatives to Litigation

- Describe the differences between *arbitration* and *mediation* as two alternatives to litigation.
- Why are alternatives to litigation so important in cases of international dispute?

YOU DECIDE: ANSWER/DISCUSSION
Race-Neutral Jury Selection

In a six-to-three ruling in June 1991, the Supreme Court reversed the appeals-court decision and held that a juror may not be excluded by either side in a civil case on account of race. The majority held that a jury is a "quintessential governmental body" and that the process of selecting one is a state matter subject to equal protection of the law. This ruling extended the Batson decision, and the court further stated that although private lawyers on both sides argue the case and select a jury, this procedure occurs with the court's "overt, significant assistance." By exercising a challenge, an attorney is "invoking the formal authority of the court." Moreover, because the government confers on these private attorneys "the power to choose the government's employees or officials"—that is, the jury—then this "private body" becomes a "government actor" and is thus bound by the "constitutional mandate of racial neutrality."

The majority holding in Edmonson must be put within the context of judicial attempts to eliminate racial bias in society as a whole. The finding that race-based exclusion in the courtroom violates the equal protection rights of challenged jurors is part of that larger picture. The Court's dissenting justices agreed that "the specter of racial discrimination" must be eliminated from the courtroom but felt that the "Constitution does not sweep that broadly." They maintained that a civil trial is essentially a private matter; "although the government erects the platform"—that is, the courtroom—it is not necessarily responsible for everything that occurs there.

The majority opinion in Edmonson removes racial bias from civil proceedings. Two important issues remain, however. First, does logic suggest that in a criminal proceeding, defense as well as prosecuting attorneys will be barred from exercising peremptory challenges on the basis of race? (Batson covered prosecutors—government employees—only.) Second, having limited this selection of jurors by race, will the Court's ruling be extended to sex? Given the number of sex-discrimination cases expected to be heard in the next few years, this question could be especially important.

---

[6] Clark and Orbeton, "Mandatory Mediation of Divorce: Maine's Experience," 69 *Judicature* 311 (Feb.-Mar. 1986).

TABLE 5-3	*How the Mediation Process Works*

STEP 1: THE AGREEMENT TO MEDIATE

Mediation, a voluntary process, is initiated by (1) a request for mediation by the parties to the American Arbitration Association (AAA), accompanied by the mediation clause from their contract; (2) a submission to mediation by the parties to the AAA if no prior clause had been established; or (3) a request for the AAA to invite the other parties to join in either of the first two initiation procedures.

STEP 2: THE SELECTION OF A MEDIATOR

The case administrator assigned by the AAA will select a qualified mediator from its panel but will replace any mediator with another if the parties are not satisfied.

STEP 3: PREPARATION FOR THE MEDIATION CONFERENCE

Careful preparation by both parties should include the following: defining and analyzing the issues, making reasonable proposals, recognizing what can be accomplished within the present situation, determining strategy, gathering evidence and documents, and understanding the other side's position.

STEP 4: THE MEDIATION CONFERENCE

Each party describes its view of the dispute and responds to the other party's presentation, as the mediator gathers information and tries to clarify discrepancies. The mediator may then meet privately with each side in an attempt to bring the parties closer together and narrow the range for a settlement. Acting as a facilitator, the mediator tries to get the parties to agree on issues and then negotiate a final settlement in a joint session.

STEP 5: THE SETTLEMENT

Upon agreement, the parties put the terms in writing and exchange documents. They may also request that the AAA put the agreement in the form of a consent award. If no settlement is reached, the parties may agree to binding arbitration.

Source: American Arbitration Association, A Guide to Mediation for Business People *(New York: AAA, 1991).*

SUMMARY

- The prevailing method of dispute resolution in the U.S. is the *adversarial system,* in which the courts provide a forum for settling disputes but the involved parties are responsible for initiating the lawsuit, defining its issues, and providing supporting evidence for their claims.
- Not all courts have the power to hear all cases. The court must have *jurisdiction* over the person, corporate entity, or property involved. Courts determine their jurisdiction over *natural persons* according to two criteria: territorial and personal. The three types of actions over which courts have territorial jurisdiction are: *actions in personam, actions in rem,* and *actions quasi in rem.* The three traditional tests for personal jurisdiction over a defendant are *presence, domicile,* and *consent.*
- The *"doing business" standard* and the *long-arm statute* extend jurisdiction over commercial organizations that are not subject to "domestic" litigation. As a general rule, a defendant must have minimum contacts with a state in order to be subject to its jurisdiction, and those contacts must satisfy due-process standards of fairness to be used as a basis for jurisdiction.
- Often, more than one court has jurisdiction over a case. In such cases, determining the proper *venue* in which the case will be heard is the next step. Federal venue requirements are straightforward: Suit may be brought in the district where the claim arose or where all defendants reside.

- Civil actions are begun by the service of a *complaint* by the plaintiff upon the defendant; generally, the court *summons* is served on the defendant simultaneously. If the defendant fails to answer, a *default judgment* may be proposed. If the complaint is legally defective, the defendant may file a *motion to dismiss*. The defendant may also cite *affirmative defenses* justifying or mitigating his behavior and may impose a *counterclaim* against the plaintiff. The plaintiff may then reply to any affirmative defenses or counterclaims. The complaint, answer, and reply are called the *pleadings*. If at this point either party decides that no factual disagreement exists, a *summary judgment* may be called for.

- *Discovery* procedures facilitate the exchange of information between parties before the trial. In the belief that neither side should be surprised by the evidence against it, federal discovery rules encourage liberal exchanges. The four principal types of discovery procedures are: *deposition, interrogatories,* physical examination, and documents and other tangible objects. Recently, *pretrial conferences* have also become a common part of pretrial procedure.

- Complicated *rules of evidence* determine what *real* and *testimonial evidence* will be admissible (that is, heard by the jury). The *burden of proof* in a civil case is a "preponderance of the evidence." In criminal cases, the burden of proof rises to "beyond a reasonable doubt," a much stricter standard. In federal civil cases, *jury trials* are guaranteed by the Seventh Amendment, state constitutions, and statutes. The right to a jury trial in a criminal case is guaranteed by the Sixth Amendment. The defendant may waive this right.

- The process of jury selection, or *voir dire,* is an important stage of the trial. The pool of eligible citizens from which potential jurors are selected is known as *veniremen.* The two types of juries are *petit juries* (or trial juries), and *grand juries*—the panel of citizens that decides before a trial whether there is sufficient evidence for indictment.

- The order of the trial itself is as follows: *opening statements, direct examination* and *cross-examination,* motion for a *directed verdict, rebuttal evidence, closing arguments,* the judge's instructions to the jury (concerning how the verdict is to be reached) and the delivery of the jury's *verdict.* After a verdict is rendered by the jury, either side may ask the judge for a *judgement non obstante veredicto;* which sets the verdict aside.

- Although litigation provides extensive protections and remedies, it is exhausting, expensive, and slow. Dissatisfaction with this method of dispute resolution has prompted the search for alternatives. These alternatives include *arbitration* and *mediation* in which neutral third parties are involved in the resolution of a dispute.

QUESTIONS AND PROBLEMS

1. On July 5, Pete was injured in an automobile accident when Lorraine, the driver in the next lane, swerved to avoid hitting a deer that ran onto the highway and slammed into Pete's car. Pete, the plaintiff, sustained injuries to his neck, back and shoulders. He is asking for $50,000 compensatory damages. Lorraine, the defendant, believes the amount is excessive due to the fact that Pete has not missed a day of work and has been seen playing tennis and lifting weights at the gym. The following is taken from the court transcript. Discuss whether it is cross examination, direct examination or hearsay:

   —"Please tell the jury what happened on July 5"

   —"Isn't it true Pete, that you have not missed one day of work is three years?"

   —"What did the witness to the accident say regarding the speed of Lorraine's vehicle?"

   —"Isn't it true, Pete, that you recently renewed your membership at Wonder Man Gym?"

   —"Did you suffer any injuries as a result of the accident?"

2. Jeremy borrowed $500 from Bob while they were both in college. After graduation Bob left the state and returned home. Bob needed his money and decided to sue Jeremy. In order to serve process on Jeremy, Bob wired Jeremy that a fraternity brother had died. In fact, their fraternity brother had not died. When Jeremy got off the plane, he was served with a summons and complaint. Does the court have legitimate jurisdiction over Jeremy?

3. When Kenyon's new, locally purchased haybaling machine injures a worker while in use, Kenyon sues the California-based manufacturer in her home state of Nebraska, using the Nebraska long-arm statute. The manufacturer responds by asserting that the Nebraska court has no jurisdiction over it because it does not conduct business in Nebraska. Is the manufacturer's argument valid?

4. Weiss's attorney sends Schwartz a document by a process server, informing Schwartz he is being sued for breach of contract and setting forth the specifics. Schwartz's attorney responds in writing. In the responsive document, Schwartz's attorney sets forth Schwartz's side of the controversy, sets forth a claim by Schwartz against Weiss, and also gives a reason why Schwartz's breach does not lead to liability. Analyze these facts and give the correct legal terms for what has taken place.

5. Lowell sued Marcott for injuries sustained when Marcott negligently caused him to fall from his porch. At the trial, Lowell's attorney raises no objections and makes no motions. The jury finds for Marcott and judgement is entered in her favor. Outside the courthouse, Lowell vows to the press that he has not received justice and will appeal the judgement and be vindicated. Can Lowell's attorney make good on Lowell's statements?

6. During voir dire questioning. Husted, a potential juror, is asked if she would tend to give greater weight or belief to testimony of a witness simply because the witness is a police officer. The judge disallows the question. Is the judge's decision to prohibit the question during voir dire erroneous? [*Commonwealth v. Walker*, 350 N.E.2d 678]

7. The plaintiff, in a federal suit against tug boat owners to recover for the death of a seaman in the sinking of a tug boat, filed numerous interrogatories to the defendant, including one that inquired whether any statements of witnesses were taken in connection with the accident and requesting that exact copies of all such statements be attached and that the defendant "set forth in detail the exact provisions of any such oral statements or reports." The defendants answered by giving the names and addresses of the witnesses but did not include the witnesses' statements because the defendants believed they were not discoverable. Plaintiff disagreed and had a hearing before the court. What was the result? [*Hickman v. Taylor*, 329 US 495 (1947)].

8. Plaintiff is injured in an auto accident and defendant has no insurance. Plaintiff sues the defendant, driver. Plaintiff also sues her insurance company to recover damages for uninsured motorist coverage. The trial court grants plaintiff 6 peremptory challenges, and each of the defendants 6 challenges also. Plaintiff alleges that it is error for the court to grant both defendants 6 peremptory challenges. Is she correct? [*Larusso v. Members Mutual Insurance Co., Inc..* 603 S.W.2d 818 (1980)]

9. When Brady, who is white, does not rent an apartment to Caitland, who is black, because of her race, Caitland brings an action against Brady for damages, alleging violations of Title VIII of the Civil Rights Act of 1968. Title VIII authorizes private plaintiffs to bring civil actions for violations of the Fair Housing provisions of the Act and states that the court "may grant relief, as it deems appropriate, . . . and may award to plaintiff actual damages and not more than $1,000 punitive damages." Caitland requests a jury trial. Brady asserts that Caitland is not entitled to a jury trial under the statute, nor under the Seventh Amendment to the Constitution which entitles a party to demand a jury trial in suits at common law which exceed $20, because this is a statutory right, not a common law right. Is Caitland entitled to a jury trial? [*Curtis v. Loether*, 415 U.S. 189 (1974)]

10. Ward, of Virginia, operates a public warehouse there. Ward alleges that Moore, who owns a company organized to do business in Pennsylvania, violated the laws of Virginia when delivering a shipment of oil to him and caused an explosion which destroyed over $400,000 in property. Ward sues Moore in federal district court in New York. Moore tries to have the place of the trial (venue) changed because he says though he is qualified to do business in New York and Virginia, New York is not a convenient forum in which to litigate the case. Moore feels the appropriate court is Virginia, where the event took place, the plaintiff lives, defendant does business, and most of the witnesses reside. Ward wishes to have the case brought in New York because he is afraid that Virginians sitting on a jury would think that the $400,000 damages he is asking would be too much, and people in New York might be less provincial about the issue. Will the case be moved? [*Gulf Oil Corp. v. Gilbert*, 330 U.S. 501 (1947)]

6

REGULATION
AND
ADMINISTRATIVE
AGENCIES

The U.S. Constitution divides the powers of the federal government into the legislative, executive, and judicial branches. Some students of the U.S. government would argue that administrative agencies form a fourth branch of government. Although it is clear that our government could not survive without them, the Constitution does not mention them.

Three facts about agencies are in good part responsible for their being considered a fourth branch of government: (1) their power is pervasive, (2) the agencies labeled "independent" by Congress work side by side with the three branches defined by the Constitution, and (3) a single agency may have the power to make rules with the force of law, to enforce these rules, and to decide specific cases hinging upon them.

This chapter discusses basic questions about how agency tasks ought to be carried out, and how Congress, the courts, and the president all oversee and influence federal agencies. These questions are important because the actions of the independent agencies shape American life in countless ways. In fact, the scope of agency action is so great that many Americans take it for granted.

■ THE SCOPE OF AGENCY ACTION

The scope of administrative agency action shows just how big "big government" is. The first thing to know is that there are actually two kinds of administrative agencies. The largest group, the *executive agencies*, includes the departments of the President's Cabinet, their subgroups, and other organizations subject to executive control. The second group is composed of *independent agencies* and *government corporations* that are separate from the executive branch. In outlining the basic configuration of the federal bureaucracy, Figure 6-1 shows the relationship of both types of agency to the federal executive branch.

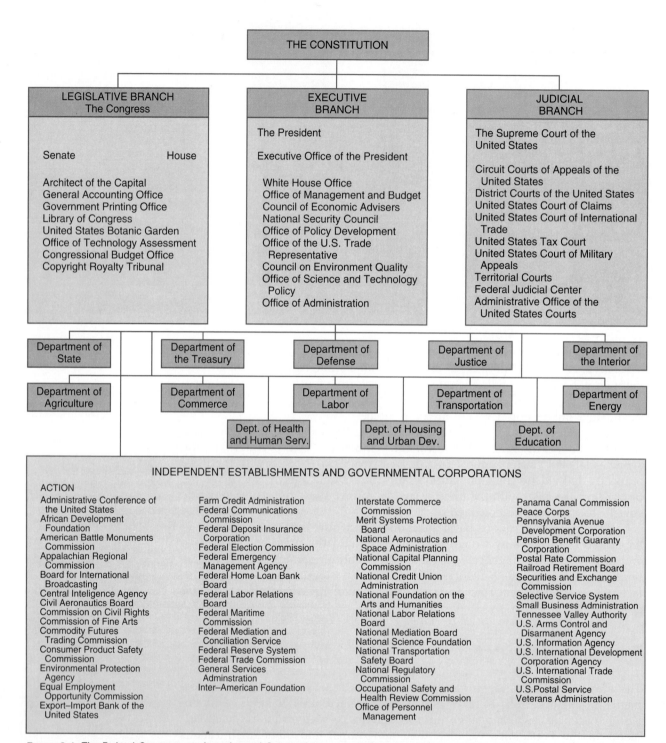

THE CONSTITUTION

LEGISLATIVE BRANCH
The Congress

Senate   House

Architect of the Capital
General Accounting Office
Government Printing Office
Library of Congress
United States Botanic Garden
Office of Technology Assessment
Congressional Budget Office
Copyright Royalty Tribunal

EXECUTIVE BRANCH

The President

Executive Office of the President

White House Office
Office of Management and Budget
Council of Economic Advisers
National Security Council
Office of Policy Development
Office of the U.S. Trade
  Representative
Council on Environment Quality
Office of Science and Technology
  Policy
Office of Administration

JUDICIAL BRANCH

The Supreme Court of the
United States

Circuit Courts of Appeals of the
  United States
District Courts of the United States
United States Court of Claims
United States Court of International
  Trade
United States Tax Court
United States Court of Military
  Appeals
Territorial Courts
Federal Judicial Center
Administrative Office of the
  United States Courts

Department of State | Department of the Treasury | Department of Defense | Department of Justice | Department of the Interior

Department of Agriculture | Department of Commerce | Department of Labor | Department of Transportation | Department of Energy

Dept. of Health and Human Serv. | Dept. of Housing and Urban Dev. | Dept. of Education

INDEPENDENT ESTABLISHMENTS AND GOVERNMENTAL CORPORATIONS

ACTION
Administrative Conference of
  the United States
African Development
  Foundation
American Battle Monuments
  Commission
Appalachian Regional
  Commission
Board for International
  Broadcasting
Central Inteligence Agency
Civil Aeronautics Board
Commission on Civil Rights
Commission of Fine Arts
Commodity Futures
  Trading Commission
Consumer Product Safety
  Commission
Environmental Protection
  Agency
Equal Employment
  Opportunity Commission
Export–Import Bank of the
  United States

Farm Credit Administration
Federal Communications
  Commission
Federal Deposit Insurance
  Corporation
Federal Election Commission
Federal Emergency
  Management Agency
Federal Home Loan Bank
  Board
Federal Labor Relations
  Board
Federal Maritime
  Commission
Federal Mediation and
  Conciliation Service
Federal Reserve System
Federal Trade Commission
General Services
  Adminstration
Inter–American Foundation

Interstate Commerce
  Commission
Merit Systems Protection
  Board
National Aeronautics and
  Space Administration
National Capital Planning
  Commission
National Credit Union
  Administration
National Foundation on the
  Arts and Humanities
National Labor Relations
  Board
National Mediation Board
National Science Foundation
National Transportation
  Safety Board
National Regulatory
  Commission
Occupational Safety and
  Health Review Commission
Office of Personnel
  Management

Panama Canal Commission
Peace Corps
Pennsylvania Avenue
  Development Corporation
Pension Benefit Guaranty
  Corporation
Postal Rate Commission
Railroad Retirement Board
Securities and Exchange
  Commission
Selective Service System
Small Business Administration
Tennessee Valley Authority
U.S. Arms Control and
  Disarmanent Agency
U.S. Information Agency
U.S. International Development
  Corporation Agency
U.S. International Trade
  Commission
U.S.Postal Service
Veterans Administration

FIGURE 6-1 The Federal Government: Agencies and Corporations   *Source: Adapted from David V. Edwards,* The American Political Experience: An Introduction to Government, *4th ed. (Englewood Cliffs, NJ: Prentice Hall, 1988). Data from* United States Government Manual, 1987/ 1988 *(Washington, DC: Government Printing Office).*

178

The Growth of Regulation

At the start of our national history, there was hardly any government regulation at all. Industry was restrained only by various attitudes toward social responsibility (*see* Chapter 2). Today, much of the work of administrative agencies involves regulating business. The Federal Trade Commission (FTC), for example, administers antitrust laws (Chapter 18); the National Labor Relations Board (Chapter 13) regulates labor-management relations, and the Food and Drug Administration regulates (among others) the pharmaceutical industry. In fact, government agencies regulate almost every corporate function, from personnel to finance.

In 1887, the Interstate Commerce Commission (ICC) was set up to regulate the railroads, chiefly by outlawing price discrimination against small businesses and Midwestern farmers. The ICC was the first modern regulatory agency and the first independent agency. It was also the first indication that the rule of laissez-faire—of a governmental policy of "hands-off" business activities—was not ironclad.

In 1903, the Antitrust Division of the Department of Justice was established to prosecute agreements "in restraint of trade" that violated the Sherman Antitrust Act. A decade later, the Federal Reserve System began to regulate commercial banking. In 1914, the FTC was created to enforce the Clayton Act, which was another attempt to promote economic competition.

During the next spate of regulation in the 1930s, President Franklin D. Roosevelt's New Deal created a great many new administrative agencies to regulate specific industries or sectors of our economy:

- The Federal Home Loan Bank Board (FHLBB), the Federal Deposit Insurance Corporation (FDIC), and the Farm Credit Administration (FCA) stabilized banking and credit.
- The Securities and Exchange Commission (SEC) supervised the issue and trading of securities (*see* Chapter 8).
- The National Labor Relations Board (NLRB) guaranteed the right of workers to join unions.

There were also many other new agencies: The New Deal reflected the now common belief that government intervention was needed to revive and strengthen our economy.

THE EXPANSION OF FEDERAL REGULATORY AGENCIES. The scope of federal regulatory activity has grown noticeably since the early 1960s. Agencies established prior to that time have generally focused on *economic* regulation of specific portions of the private sector—for example, the securities business or the railroads. By contrast, the agencies created in the last thirty years or so are empowered to provide broad regulation across the whole economy to achieve certain *social* objectives. They are organized by function or issue rather than by specific industries. Their enforcement practices focus on such goals as clean air, safe working conditions, adequate product testing, the elimination of job discrimination, and business practices free of corruption. The public interest—not the needs of a particular industry—is primary. Figure 6-2 presents an overview of the growth in numbers of federal regulatory agencies.

Interestingly, although the overall scope of federal regulation has expanded, compared with older agencies each of the individual new agencies has

The Rational Bureaucrat According to the German sociologist Max Weber (1864–1920), the ideal organization took the form of a *bureaucracy:* Its management was a well-defined hierarchy whose objectives and activities were the product of *rational* decision making and rule setting. Weber's view has long been regarded as the classical model for bureaucratic administration and is still sometimes called the "rational-person" model. Although Weber favored routine activities and an impersonal climate in which to perform them as factors contributing to efficiency, he also emphasized the importance of technical competence and the need to evaluate performance on the basis of merit. Today, of course—especially when we think of the gargantuan apparatus of the federal government—we tend to think of "bureaucracies" as immense, inflexible, and often inefficient organizations, but Weber sought primarily to make organizational activity, both economic and social, more productive by making it more predictable. Perhaps President Woodrow Wilson is the best-known American disciple of Weber's principles to reach high office, and numerous limitations on contemporary government-agency activity reflect the "rational" model of organizational functioning—for example, the management procedures required of the administrators of the Office of Management and Budget and the General Accounting Office.

a somewhat narrow sphere of responsibility. For instance, whereas the SEC supervises the whole securities business, the Equal Employment Opportunity Commission (EEOC) looks only at job discrimination cases within that industry. By the same token, no one industry can unduly influence the EEOC. In addition, whereas the SEC and other regulators are interested in the economic issues relevant to specific industries, the EEOC and similar agencies are not, and some of their activities may even entail additional costs to business. Figure 6-3 illustrates the nature of certain changes in federal regulation. The vertical lines show the traditional agency-industry relationship. The horizontal lines show the areas regulated by newer agencies, which overlap large economic sectors.

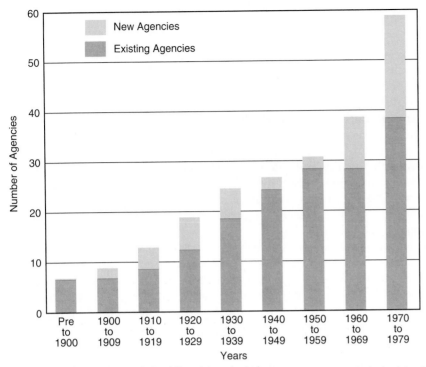

FIGURE 6-2 The Growth of Federal Regulatory Agencies *Source: Center for the Study of American Business, Washington University*

Nevertheless, in response to the activities of agencies designed to enforce *social regulation*, businesses have begun to consider the public interest as well as their own bottom-line concerns. Many now realize that the programs were established by Congress in response to rising public expectations about corporate performance. Indeed, many executives now operate their businesses as if public service were a fundamental goal. However, critics maintain that attitudes such as this are not widespread and that firms would not act for the public good unless compelled to by federal regulation.

FIGURE 6-3 Variations in the Federal Regulation of Business

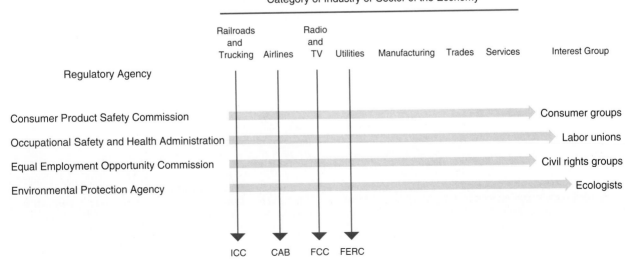

Executive Agencies

The term **executive agency** encompasses three different types of agencies. The first type includes each of the departments represented in the president's Cabinet. These departments are the U.S. Departments of State, Treasury, Justice, Interior, Agriculture, Commerce, Labor, Defense, Housing and Urban Development, Transportation, Energy, Health and Human Services, and Education.

The term "executive agency" also refers to the organizations *within* each Cabinet department. For example, the Food and Drug Administration (FDA), which insures the quality and safety of foods and drugs, is part of the Department of Health and Human Services; the Occupational Safety and Health Administration (OSHA), which inspects work sites to see that they meet the safety standards set by the secretary of labor, falls within the purview of the Department of Labor.

Finally, the seven agencies which are organizationally separate from the Cabinet departments but which have not been designated "independent" by Congress are called executive agencies. The Office of Management and Budget, which reviews the budgets of all the other parts of the federal government, is in this category. It is easy to see why this type of agency should be organizationally distinct from Cabinet departments.

Independent Agencies and Government Corporations

Congress created the first independent agency in 1889, when it moved the two-year-old Interstate Commerce Commission out of the Department of the Interior. Congress seems to have decided that the new agency needed protection from the influence of an incoming Republican administration. However, Congress may have had another reason for making subsequent agencies independent: They would be easier for Congress to control.

Independent agencies are made up of five- or seven-member commissions that work together like judges in an appellate court. The commissioners are appointed by the president and confirmed by the Senate. Their terms are set at various lengths, depending upon the agency. The president can name only a bare majority of an independent agency's members from his own political party. By contrast, Cabinet officers can be dismissed at will by a president and are nearly always members of the president's party.

The Peace Corps, an independent agency now in operation for thirty years, is the subject of this chapter's INTERNATIONAL ENVIRONMENT box.

THE INTERNATIONAL ENVIRONMENT
The Peace Corps

When the Peace Corps was established by Congress in 1961, its birth was attended by the lofty idealism of President Kennedy's "New Frontier." In fact, Sargent Shriver, its chief organizer and first director, financed the launch of the *new agency with a presidential emergency fund even before Congress had passed the enabling legislation or appropriated money. Such was the mood of the times, when idealistic Americans volunteered to go abroad to serve in Third World* countries to foster world peace. Indeed, the response was so positive that within two years, 6,000 volunteers had been sent to forty-seven countries. Ghana was the first and still remains in the program.

The Peace Corps, however, has never been free of controversy and criticism. Opposing its creation were critics like Richard Nixon, who called it a "haven for draft dodgers," and President Dwight Eisenhower, who denounced it as a "juvenile experiment." Even as it was getting started, news commentator Eric Sevareid argued that the Peace Corps merely provided "spot benefits" and would have little effect on the real need for "long-term economic development" in Third World countries.

The greatest criticism of the Peace Corps came during the Vietnam War, at which time the number of volunteers fell to a low of 5,500 from a high of 13,600 in 1965. In a statement of antiwar sentiment, the Committee of Returned Volunteers called in May, 1970 for access to the communications system of the Department of State to recall all volunteers until the war ended. In fact, the widespread social criticism of this period extended to some of the general problems besetting the Peace Corps. For instance, out of a feeling of nationalist pride, some countries in the program were becoming increasingly uncomfortable with foreigners teaching in the schools where their very history and culture were being transmitted. "Parachuting" volunteers into countries without enough training or local support came to be seen as a failure of the program.

Throughout the 1970s it became increasingly clear that, whatever its noble mission, the Peace Corps was still a federal agency subject to reorganization and decreased funding at executive and legislative discretion. In 1971, the Peace Corps was made part of ACTION, a "super agency" that included all volunteer programs, domestic and international. The effect was a loss of identity for the Peace Corps. Nicholas Craw, director from 1973 to 1974, says, "I remain convinced that the [Nixon] administration wished—by design or accident—to downgrade the status of the Peace Corps by submerging it under ACTION." In 1979, however, the Peace Corps was made organizationally viable again when an executive order signed by President Jimmy Carter made it an autonomous agency within ACTION.

In the thirty-plus years since its creation, over 100 nations have received 125,000 Peace Corps volunteers. This independent agency of the federal government has sought to fulfill its original goals while evolving in the face of world events, the changing needs of foreign cultures, and the always-shifting political arena in the United States. Although the Peace Corps has expanded and contracted during its history, its fundamental goals still remain to help promote world peace, to help fill the needs of developing nations for skilled people, and to help foster mutual understanding between peoples of developing countries and the people of the United States. In fact, this third goal has been updated for the 1990s with the World Wise Schools program. As described by current Peace Corps director Paul Coverdell in 1991, this program "links volunteers serving overseas with elementary and secondary schools in this country . . . promoting geographical and international knowledge, as well as a spirit of volunteerism."

Although quantifying Peace Corps achievements has never been easy, the successes do fall into three general categories: teaching English, the necessary language of commerce and international communication; improvement of agricultural productivity and techniques; and nutrition and health programs.

The most recent developments in the Peace Corps argue for its continued viability as it adapts to the needs of a changing world. For one thing, with the growth of market economies, business and technical skills are now in great demand by host countries. Thus, Peace Corps recruitment is now going on in such places as graduate schools of business, where such skills as marketing, budgeting, and human-resources management may be found.

The greatest call for these business specialties, as well as other needs like English-language instruction, comes from the nations of Eastern Europe, the Baltic republics, and other former Soviet republics. As they make the transition from centralized to market-based economies, they recognize that they must learn many things and learn them quickly. The Peace Corps has begun to supply volunteers and expects to send more than 600 people to the former Soviet republic by the end of 1993. The agency is not, as The New York Times reported in early 1992, "having trouble luring business executives from comfortable jobs to endure two years in an area of political unrest, economic uncertainty, scant food and hyperinflation."

Thus, the Peace Corps, without lessening its commitment to Third World countries, is evolving to meet changing world needs. Many analysts today feel that it will undoubtedly remain a unique voice within the federal bureaucracy.

There are 57 independent agencies and government corporations. **Government corporations** are nonprofit and owned entirely by the government. They are distinct from public-private partnerships, such as the Federal National Mortgage Association, which operate at a profit while meeting a specific need of the government. The United States Postal Service is a government corporation overseen by the Postal Rate Commission, which is an independent agency. *See* the ORGANIZATIONAL PROFILE box for a description of Amtrak, which was established as a private corporation by an act of Congress in 1970.

government corporation
Nonprofit government-owned corporations that are distinct from public-private partnerships

Although "Amtrak" is the common name by which we know the intercity passenger railroad system created by act of Congress in 1970, its official title—the National Railroad Passenger Corporation—really tells the story of its history, operations, and future.

By 1970, United States railroad-passenger service had seriously deteriorated in quality, usage, and profitability, far from its heyday at the turn of the century. The individual railroads had not met the challenge of a changing American lifestyle in which long-distance travel by private car had become commonplace and airplane transportation had developed a competitive advantage. Congress, however, ultimately felt it to be against the national interest to let the railroad-passenger-service portion of the transportation system die. Through the Rail Passenger Service Act, it created Amtrak, a private corporation, and gave it the mandate to manage—and, ideally, breathe life back into—this nationwide passenger rail system. Amtrak's marching orders from Congress included operating railroad passenger service as a profit-making business, meeting the needs of intercity transportation through innovative operating and marketing methods, and making its overall service run efficiently.

In many ways, then, Amtrak's relationship with the federal government is unique. Although Congress created it, Amtrak is not a federal agency, nor do its employees belong to the federal civil-service system. It has a board of directors and an executive staff. However, although it was the congressional intent that Amtrak be a for-profit firm, the federal government provides the corporation with the financial support that it needs to operate. In 20 years, operating subsidies have decreased to $520 million for fiscal year 1990, down from a high of $873 million in fiscal year 1981. The Omnibus Budget Reconciliation Act of 1981 required Amtrak to have a revenue-to-expense ratio of at least 50 percent, and it has in fact met this goal, achieving 72 percent for fiscal year 1990. (See Figure 6-A for the increase in Amtrak's revenue-to-expense ratio between 1987 and 1990.)

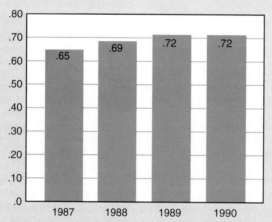

FIGURE 6-A Amtrak, Revenue-to-Expense Ratio, 1987–1990

Source: National Railroad Passenger Corporation,
1990 Annual Report *(1991)*

Nevertheless, continued federal subsidies for Amtrak are controversial, especially when federal budget balancing is mandated by law, and when some critics do not think Amtrak's performance justifies continued subsidies. Each year, when the Department of Transportation submits its budget to Congress, with Amtrak's request for operating and capital funding included, the debate flares up. However, when the final appropriations bill is signed each year, it is clear, according to the Congressional Digest, that the federal government has still decided that "public policy requires continuation of rail passenger service at public expense." Figures 6-B and 6-C show (1) Amtrak's operating subsidy and (2) its increase in passenger miles per dollar of federal support between 1987 and 1990.

In 1991, Amtrak celebrated its twentieth anniversary—a good point at which to examine not only past achievements but current problems and proposed solutions. For example, although Amtrak has had several notable marketing successes—including the Metroliner in the Northeast Corridor and the Auto Train to Florida—it faces the 1990s with a fleet which needs upgrading and faces shortages. Amtrak equipment requires a very large capital investment to replace and modernize engines and cars and so to prevent collapse of its infrastructure.

Moreover, the intercity rail network needs this maintenance program in order to provide the high-level service necessary to continue increasing ridership and remain competitive with airlines. Operating as a business with a mar-

FIGURE 6-B Amtrak, Operating Subsidy, 1987–1990 (in constant FY 1990 dollars) (in millions)
Source: National Railroad Passenger Corporation, 1990
Annual Report *(1991)*

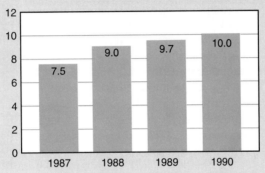

FIGURE 6-C Amtrak, Passenger Miles per Dollar of Federal Support, 1987–1990 (in constant FY 1990 dollars) *Source: National Railroad Passenger Corporation, 1990 Annual Report (1991)*

keting, or customer focus, Amtrak thus took innovative steps to build its Metroliner service between New York City and Washington, D.C. Facing heavy competition from air shuttles, Amtrak executed its marketing strategy of learning its customers' needs through market research and then shaping its service to meet them. It successfully drew its primary market of business travelers from the airlines by selling "civilized" service that was almost as fast as the shuttle.

In addition to increasing ridership, Amtrak must take other steps to increase revenues so that, by the year 2000, it will meet its goal of self-sufficiency—that is, breaking even with no federal subsidy. In fact, in 1981 Amtrak was empowered by Congress "to maximize the use of all resources—employees, facilities, and real estate—and to enter into agreements with the private sector and undergo initiatives designed to minimize federal financial support." Although intercity passenger service will always remain Amtrak's main line of business, the corporation has thus pursued other ventures in order to diversify its revenue.

At present, Amtrak runs several rail commuter services for various local authorities—for instance, in Massachusetts leading out from Boston—and tries to bid on new opportunities when possible. At 18 million passengers, the 1991 ridership for these "contract commuters" was close to the figure of 22 million for the entire national system ridership in fiscal year 1990. Other sources of revenue include real estate and maintenance services.

The greatest potential for new revenue seems to be in the mail and express business. Using both baggage-express cars and RoadRailers (which detach from a passenger train's rear end and then go over highways to serve off-line points), Amtrak hopes to continue carrying shipments for the U.S. Postal Service and, especially, to attract corporate shippers. According to Railway Age, Amtrak's competitive advantage appears to be "speeds that are truck competitive to certain locations, and reliability at lower cost."

How does the future look to Amtrak? Is it realistic to think that the experiment that Congress launched two decades ago will be a viable enterprise when the twenty-first century arrives? The best measure will be Amtrak's independence from federal financial support. Past performance indicates some optimism, and although it will be difficult, there is definitely an entrepreneurial spirit at work.

- Briefly trace the evolution of government regulation in the United States. What are the major differences between agencies established in the last thirty years and those established earlier?
- Explain the key differences between an *executive agency* and an *independent agency*.
- Characterize the activities of agencies concerned with *social regulation*.

■ DELEGATING LEGISLATIVE POWER

delegating statute Law by which Congress delegates some of its power to an *administrative agency* by allowing the agency to impose its own rules

The power of an administrative agency to impose its rules comes from Congress, which *delegates*, or transfers, that power to the agencies in **delegating statutes.** These laws broadly state each agency's purpose but leave the details to the agency's expert staff. Time, continuity, and technical knowledge are crucial to regulation, especially the regulation of complicated industries like communication.

Such delegation of power attempts to resolve conflicts between the need to delegate legislative power and the need to preserve the Constitution's formal arrangement of powers. Article I, Section 8 of the Constitution grants Congress the power to make all laws "necessary and proper" for carrying out the powers granted to it. The United States Supreme Court has held that this clause justifies only the delegation of legislative power if a clear congressional purpose is served. Thus, the courts may review the delegating statutes to ensure that they contain clear directions and standards. This process is called **Article I review.**

Article I review Court review of an administrative agency's *delegating statutes* to ensure that it is not regulating too much Congressional power and thus violating the Constitution's *Necessary and Proper Clause*

The Supreme Court has denied a congressional delegation of power as unconstitutional only twice. The first case, *Panama Refining Co. v. Ryan* (293 U.S. 388 [1935]), hinged on the section of the National Industrial Recovery Act of 1933 which empowered the president to forbid commercial interstate transportation of "hot oil." At the time, state laws decreed the amount of petroleum that could be produced or taken out of storage. "Hot oil" was petroleum obtained in violation of those laws. The ruling was made because Congress had not spelled out the conditions under which the delegated power should be exercised.

Four months later, a different part of the act came under judicial review in *Schechter Poultry Corporation v. United States*. Here, the delegated power was arguably equal in scope to Congress's own power to regulate interstate commerce.

A.L.A. SCHECTER POULTRY CORPORATION v. UNITED STATES
United States Supreme Court, 295 U.S. 495 (1935)

Under Section 3 of the National Industrial Recovery Act of 1933, the President of the United States was authorized to adopt codes of fair competition in cooperation with particular industries. The defendant, Schecter Poultry, was convicted for violation of the "Live Poultry Code," enacted pursuant to the President's authority in Section 3. On appeal by the defendant to the Supreme Court of the United States, the issue is whether Congressional delegation to the President through Section 3 of the N.I.R.A. is constitutional.

Mr. Chief Justice Hughes delivered the opinion of the Court.

The "Live Poultry Code" was promulgated under § 3 of the National Industrial Recovery Act. That section . . . authorizes the President to approve "codes of fair competition." Such a code may be approved for a trade or industry, upon application by one or more trade or industrial associations or groups, if the President finds (1) that such associations or groups "impose no inequitable restrictions on admission to membership therein and are truly representative," and (2) that such codes are not designed "to promote monopolies or to eliminate or oppress small enterprises and will not operate to discriminate against them, and will tend to effectuate the policy" of Title I of the Act. . . .

. . . .

The question of the delegation of legislative power. We recently had occasion to review the pertinent decisions and the general principles which govern the determination of this question. *Panama Refining Co. v. Ryan* (1935). The Constitution provides that "All legislative powers herein granted shall be vested in a Congress of the United States, which shall consist of a Senate and House of Representatives." Art. I, § 1. And the Congress is authorized "To make all laws which shall be necessary and proper for carrying into execution" its general powers. Art. I, § 8, par. 18. The Congress is not permitted to abdicate or to transfer to others the essential legislative functions with which it is thus vested. We have repeatedly recognized the necessity of adapting legislation to complex conditions involving a host of details with which the national legislature cannot deal directly. We pointed out in the *Panama Company* case that the Constitution has never been regarded as denying to Congress the necessary resources of flexibility and practicality, which will enable it to perform its function in laying down policies and establishing standards, while leaving to selected instrumentalities the making of subordinate rules within prescribed limits and the determination of facts to which the policy as declared by the legislature is to apply. But we said that the constant recognition of the necessity and validity of such provisions, and the wide range of administrative authority which has been developed by means of them, cannot be allowed to obscure the limitations of the authority to delegate, if our constitutional system is to be maintained.

Accordingly, we look to the statute to see whether Congress has overstepped these limitations,—whether Congress in authorizing "codes of fair competition" has itself established the standards of legal obligation, thus performing its essential legislative function, or, by the failure to enact such standards, has attempted to transfer that function to others.

. . . .

. . . Section 3 of the Recovery Act is without precedent. It supplies no standards for any trade, industry or activity. It does not undertake to prescribe rules of conduct to be applied to particular states of fact determined by appropriate administrative procedure. Instead of prescribing rules of conduct, it authorizes the making of codes to prescribe them. For that legislative undertaking, § 3 sets up no standards, aside from the statement of the general aims of rehabilitation, correction and expansion described in section one. In view of the scope of that broad declaration, and of the nature of the few restrictions that are imposed, the discretion of the President in approving or prescribing codes, and thus enacting laws for the government of trade and industry throughout the country, is virtually unfettered. We think that the code-making authority thus conferred is an unconstitutional delegation of legislative power.

. . . .

. . . [W]e hold the code provisions here in question to be invalid and that the judgment of conviction must be reversed.

Case Questions

1. What was the Supreme Court's foremost concern with Section 3 of the N.I.R.A.?

2. Did the Court believe that the delegation was inconsistent with Congressional power under the "necessary and proper" clause? If so, how?

■ *Concept Check 6-2 Delegating Legislative Power*

- Describe the nature and intent of *delegating statutes*.
- Describe the process of *Article 1 review*.

■ WHAT AGENCIES DO

As far as business is concerned, agency actions fall into one of two groups: either friendly support or efforts at control or restraint. Business and government can be adversaries in a court of law, but they need each other in a capitalistic democracy such as the United States.

The U.S. government—indeed, all of us—needs business for the goods and services that it supplies. What business needs from government are secure property rights, rules for the marketplace, reliable currency, infrastructure such as roads and sewers, and a stable social environment for employees and managers. In short, business needs government to provide a stable economic environment.

Supporting Business

Calvin Coolidge, the thirtieth president of the United States (1923-1929), once said that "the business of America is business." Several decades later, Charles E. Wilson, President Eisenhower's first secretary of defense (1953-1957) and a former president of General Motors, suggested that "what's good for General Motors is good for the country." For better or worse, the U.S. government supports business in a great variety of ways.

FOREIGN ACTIVITIES. In foreign affairs, for example, it seeks to establish good trade relations with other countries and to protect American business from foreign competition. This protection may consist of tariffs (that is, taxes on imported goods) or agreements with foreign countries (notably Japan) to limit how much of certain products can be exported to the United States. Supporters of free trade protest that protectionism actually harms American consumers and businesses that rely on imported products. Moreover, by leading other countries to protect their own manufacturers, it may also hurt the many U.S. industries that now enjoy substantial exports.

DOMESTIC ACTIVITIES. At home, the U.S. government offers direct cash grants to farmers who raise feed corn, wheat, and several other crops. It also imposes production restrictions that raise the market prices of other crops, such as tobacco and peanuts, and thus protects the incomes of those who grow them. It also gives low-interest loans to farmers and owners of small businesses, as well as tax breaks to many industries.

In recent years, the government has also bailed out several troubled companies—for example, Lockheed (1981), Chrysler (1980), and the Continental Illinois Bank (1984)—by offering them guaranteed loans when they could not raise money in private credit markets. The Small Business Administration (SBA) routinely guarantees up to ninety percent of an eligible company's bank loans. The SBA also has programs to support certain kinds of investment and to help businesses owned by veterans or members of minority groups.

Half of the money spent in the United States for research and development comes from the federal government. Both the government's own research and the private research that it subsidizes encourage new technologies that can inspire new products and increase the productivity of existing industries.

Finally, the government is an important customer for everything from automobiles to zippers. During the Great Depression of the 1930s and at various times thereafter, government spending has been used to stimulate our economy as well as to provide the government with needed supplies.

Controlling Business

"Business and industry are no longer simple," according to one legal scholar, "and the rules required for their control are exceedingly complicated; they are no longer rules, indeed, but codes of regulation, as ramified [wide-ranging] as the business they regulate."[1] This comment was made in 1938, but it is even more true today.

Failure of the marketplace to provide what is needed is the usual explanation of why the government should intervene in the economy. For example, competition may be absent from or destructive to an industry, the market may allocate resources inefficiently, or it may produce socially undesirable effects such as pollution. Therefore, much regulatory work consists of setting **standards** for safety or quality and monitoring business activity to ensure compliance. Legal requirements for disclosing information create a good deal of the paperwork that many business executives object to. Agencies created to protect consumers have the power to issue recalls removing dangerous products from the market. The government also regulates industries by attaching conditions when it gives them subsidies or when it buys products and services.

standards Marketplace levels of safety or quality set and monitored by *regulatory agencies*

Numerous federal agencies are responsible for setting marketplace standards—one of the most well-known is the Food and Drug Administration.

CASE: THE FDA: A STANDARD-SETTING FEDERAL AGENCY. The federal **Food and Drug Administration (FDA)** is charged with ensuring that the medicines we use, the foods we eat, the blood supplies we need, and indeed the cosmetics we enjoy are safe, pure, and effective. Its mission includes setting standards and then enforcing them. For example, under the 1990 Nutrition Education and Labeling Act, new rules were promulgated to ensure that food labels are less confusing and more useful to consumers. Such label terms as "serving size" and "lite" were regulated, as were such health claims of "no cholesterol" and "fat-free." In 1991, for example, the FDA seized a shipment of orange juice because the manufacturer had labeled it as "fresh" but the cartons of juice had been made from concentrate.

Food and Drug Administration (FDA) Federal agency that regulates, by setting and enforcing certain *standards*, the safety and quality of marketed foods and drugs

As the agency responsible in many ways for the nation's health, the FDA is watched very carefully by both consumer and business groups (especially food producers and the pharmaceutical industry). The FDA has been criticized by both sides for such problems as ineffective enforcement, slowness in and methods of new-drug approvals, and even misconduct. Some of this criticism has arisen from the sort of bureaucratic sluggishness that occurs in many federal agencies. Another possible explanation, however, has been an increasing deemphasis on regulation—for example, through budget cuts—in the 1980s and early 1990s by successive administrations whose policies called for less control of business. Nevertheless, as its responsibilities have grown over the past few years—for instance, in the field of AIDS research—the funds and staff allocated to the FDA have not caught up with expanding responsibilities, making it more difficult for the agency to get its job done.

Remedies, of course, have been proposed and action taken on several points by Dr. David A. Kessler, the commissioner who took over the FDA in

---

[1] Walter F. Dodd, "Administrative Agencies as Legislators and Judges," 25 *American Bar Association Journal* 924 (1939).

late 1990. In 1992, for example, in a dramatic case affecting millions of women, the FDA under Kessler called for a moratorium on the use of silicone breast implants, stating that the scientific evidence provided by the manufacturer was insufficient to prove the safety of the implants.

Another controversial issue facing the agency involves so-called "orphan drugs." The Orphan Drug Act of 1983 was designed to stimulate pharmaceutical manufacturers to develop drugs for rare diseases. The YOU DECIDE feature in this chapter examines some of the implications of the Act as well as proposed changes for public policy and business.

YOU DECIDE
The Orphan Drug Act

The interests of the general public, citizens with health problems, and the pharmaceutical industry meet, and sometimes conflict, over the Orphan Drug Act of 1983. When Congress enacted this law, its intent was to give pharmaceutical companies an incentive to develop drugs to treat people with rare diseases—rare meaning under 200,000 accounts of the disease. Firms were reluctant to develop new drugs for rare diseases because the potential for profit was seen as relatively small—that is, so few people needed the product. In many ways, the act has succeeded. Under its provisions, firms made the substantial Research and Development investment needed because they were given generous tax credits and seven years to market drugs exclusively. In fact, from 1983 to 1990, the industry marketed thirty-nine orphan drugs—compared to thirty-four in the preceding seventeen-year period.

Despite these favorable numbers, however, each of the concerned parties has raised questions about the costs and benefits of the act. Does the lack of competition give an unfair profit advantage to certain firms? Are those who need the drugs being denied speedy access to them? Is the tax-paying public shouldering an uneven part of the cost burden?

The thinking behind the law is quite clear: It seeks, according to the Journal of the American Medical Association, to eliminate the "major disincentives [that] limited commercial interest in orphan products: small market size relative to development expenses, lack of product patents . . . , and product liability." By allowing the FDA to award exclusive approval for seven years for a "specific orphan indication of a drug," the act encouraged the development of drugs such as PEG-ADA. A small biotech firm invested $2.5 million and five years developing PEG-ADA, which is used to treat children throughout the world who have SCID, an autoimmune disease.

Criticism of the law, reports the Journal, rests heavily on the argument that "exclusivity confers monopoly benefits on potentially profitable products." Although most orphan drugs have sales of less than $1 million, three have sales revenue of over $100 million each. Does such a large market, with real and potential profits, eliminate the need for the protection given by market exclusivity?

In 1990, changes were proposed in the law to foster competition. They included: removal of orphan status for a drug if, within three years of approval, its projected population exceeds 200,000; revocation of exclusivity for an approved drug when the cases exceed 200,000 and shared-market access if two firms simultaneously develop a drug. Would you support these amendments? Do they resolve the issues raised here? Are they fair to all sides? For further discussion, see p. 218.

Regulation against Market Failure

destructive competition Form of *market failure* based on destructive business competition that results in the bankruptcy of involved businesses and less consumer choice in the affected industry

economic regulation Federal regulatory intervention, in the form of *antitrust laws*, that prevents the growth of monopolies, unfair business practices, and destructive marketplace competition

Economists have identified four kinds of market failure: *destructive competition*, *inadequate information*, *externalities*, and *natural monopoly*.

PREVENTING DESTRUCTIVE COMPETITION. The first kind of market failure to be recognized was **destructive competition**: Competition is destructive when the companies involved lose money for a long time or go bankrupt, leaving customers at the mercy of the few that survive. The government intervenes against unfair business practices, promotes constructive competition, and breaks up monopolies (or trusts) through federal antitrust laws—that is, the Sherman Act of 1890, the Clayton Act of 1914, and the Federal Trade Commission Act of 1914. This type of regulation is called **economic regulation**.

COMPENSATING FOR INADEQUATE INFORMATION.   Another kind of market failure is **inadequate information** for consumers or workers. Laissez-faire theories argue that consumers will themselves reward the producers of the best products by purchasing them. In order to do this, however, consumers must have "perfect" information. Regulators assume that government experts are better able to determine the safety of some products than consumers. To make our task as consumers easier, we Americans have chosen to let the government prevent the sale of certain products such as dangerous toys or rotten meat. As employees, we also rely on the government to identify and outlaw hazardous working conditions.

inadequate information Form of *market failure* based on the communication of imperfect or *inadequate product information* to consumers

CONTROLLING EXTERNALITIES.   A third kind of market failure is called an **externality** and refers to a cost or benefit that is external to an economic transaction: It falls on a party other than the seller or the customer and is therefore not accounted for in either party's decisions.

externality Form of *market failure* that results when costs or benefits are external to economic transactions

Suppose, for example, that a factory's operations create pollutants as a by-product. The factory is on a river. In the past, if the pollutants were released into the water, the cost of cleaning up the river would have fallen on the people who lived downstream. Neither the factory nor its customers was responsible for the cost of the clean-up. In other words, the cost would be an *externality* from the factory's point of view.

The risk to a region posed by a nuclear power plant is also an externality. Today the government, representing the interests of those affected by externalities, forces producers to take them into account when making decisions about what to produce or how. Without government intervention, the market would very often fail to prevent pollution. The case that follows considers the role of the courts in reviewing agency action in controlling externalities.

BALTIMORE GAS AND ELECTRIC CO. v. NATURAL RESOURCES DEFENSE COUNCIL, INC.
United States Supreme Court, 462 U.S. 87 (1983)

In 1979, the Nuclear Regulatory Commission enacted the "Table S-3" rule, which instructed boards considering the licensing of nuclear plants not to consider the environmental impact of waste storage. The essential reason for the rule was the assumption that storage of nuclear waste was not a concern because technology would develop a way to deal with it.

The plaintiff, National Resources Defense Council, sought review of this agency rule in the Court of Appeals for the District of Columbia for a redetermination of the decision to grant a license to Baltimore Gas and Electric. The Court of Appeals ruled in favor of the plaintiff, finding the rule to be unreasonable. Baltimore Gas and Electric appeals to the U.S. Supreme Court.

Justice O'Connor delivered the opinion of the Court.

Section 102(2)(C) of the National Environmental Policy Act of 1969 . . . (NEPA), requires federal agencies to consider the environmental impact of any major federal action. As part of its generic rulemaking proceedings to evaluate the environmental effects of the nuclear fuel cycle for nuclear powerplants, the Nuclear Regulatory Commission (Commission) decided that licensing boards should assume, for purposes of NEPA, that the permanent storage of certain nuclear wastes would have no significant environmental impact and thus should not affect the decision whether to license a particular nuclear powerplant. . . .

The environmental impact of operating a light-water nuclear powerplant includes the effects of offsite activities necessary to provide fuel for the plant ("front end" activities), and of offsite activities necessary to dispose of the highly toxic and long-lived nuclear wastes generated by the plant ("back end" activities). The dispute in these cases concerns the Commission's adoption of a series of generic rules to evaluate the environmental effects of a nuclear power plant's fuel cycle. At the heart of each rule is Table S-3, a numerical compilation of the estimated resources used and effluents released by fuel cycle activities supporting a year's operation of a typical light-water reactor. . . .

. . . The original Table S-3 contained no numerical entry for the long-term environmental effects of storing solidified transuranic and high-level wastes, because the Commission staff believed that technology would be developed to isolate the wastes from the environment. The Commission and the parties have later termed this assumption . . . as the "zero-release" assumption: the reasonableness of this assumption is at the core of the present controversy.

. . . .

In 1979, following further hearings, the Commission adopted the "final" Table S-3 rule. . . . The Commission . . . continued to adhere to the zero-release assumption that the solidified waste would not escape and harm the environment once the repository was sealed. It acknowledged that this assumption was uncertain because of the remote possibility that water might enter the repository, dissolve the radioactive materials, and transport them to the biosphere. Nevertheless, the Commission predicted that a bedded-salt repository would maintain its integrity, and found the evidence "tentative but favorable" that an appropriate site would be found. . . .

The NRDC [Natural Resources Defense Council] and respondent State of New York petitioned for review of the final rule. The Court of Appeals . . . concluded that the Table S-3 rules were arbitrary and capricious and inconsistent with NEPA because the Commission had not factored the consideration of uncertainties surrounding the zero-release assumption into the licensing process in such a manner that the uncertainties could potentially affect the outcome of any decision to license a particular plant. . . .

We are acutely aware that the extent to which this Nation should rely on nuclear power as a source of energy is an important and sensitive issue. Much of the debate focuses on whether development of nuclear generation facilities should proceed in the face of uncertainties about their long-term effects on the environment. Resolution of these fundamental policy questions lies, however, with Congress and the agencies to which Congress has delegated authority, as well as with state legislatures and, ultimately, the populace as a whole. Congress has assigned the courts only the limited, albeit important, task of reviewing agency action to determine whether the agency conformed with controlling statutes. . . .

. . . The controlling statute at issue here is NEPA. NEPA has twin aims. First, it "places upon an agency the obligation to consider every significant aspect of the environmental impact of a proposed action." Second, it ensures that the agency will inform the public that it has indeed considered environmental concerns in its decisionmaking process. Congress in enacting NEPA, however, did not require agencies to elevate environmental concerns over other appropriate considerations. Rather, it required only that the agency take a "hard look" at the environmental consequences before taking a major ac-

tion. The role of the courts is simply to ensure that the agency has adequately considered and disclosed the environmental impact of its actions and that its decision is not arbitrary or capricious.

In its Table S-3 rule here, the Commission has determined that the probabilities favor the zero-release assumption, because the Nation is likely to develop methods to store the wastes with no leakage to the environment. The NRDC did not challenge and the Court of Appeals did not decide the reasonableness of this determination, and no party seriously challenges it here. The Commission recognized, however, that the geological, chemical, physical, and other data it relied on in making this prediction were based, in part, on assumptions which involve substantial uncertainties. . . . After confronting the issue, though, the Commission has determined that the uncertainties concerning the development of nuclear waste storage facilities are not sufficient to affect the outcome of any individual licensing decision.

It is clear that the Commission, in making this determination, has made the careful consideration and disclosure required by NEPA. The sheer volume of proceedings before the Commission is impressive. Of far greater importance, the Commission's State of Consideration announcing the final Table S-3 rule shows that it has digested this mass of material and disclosed all substantial risks. . . . Given this record and the Commission's statement, it simply cannot be said that the Commission ignored or failed to disclose the uncertainties surrounding its zero-release assumption.

. . . .

. . . [A] reviewing court must remember that the Commission is making predictions, within its area of special expertise, at the frontiers of science.

. . . .

In sum, we think that the zero-release assumption . . . is within the bounds of reasoned decisionmaking. . . . Our only task is to determine whether the Commission has considered the relevant factors and articulated a rational connection between the facts found and the choice made. Under this standard, we think the Commission's zero-release assumption, within the context of Table S-3 as a whole, was not arbitrary and capricious.

. . . .

For the foregoing reasons, the judgment of the Court of Appeals for the District of Columbia Circuit is

Reversed.

Case Questions

1. Does the decision in Baltimore Gas and Electric represent a failure to account for a significant externality?

2. Should the standard to be used by a reviewing court be heightened when there is a potential for great public harm?

3. What factors justify the prevailing standard of review with regard to agency action to control externalities?

REGULATING NATURAL MONOPOLIES. **Natural monopolies** are industries, such as suppliers of electric power, in which it is most efficient for one producer to serve a large area. Because there is little or no competition in these industries, the government intervenes to protect the consumer by regulating prices. (*See* Chapter 16.)

> **natural monopoly** Industry in which it proves natural for one producer to service a large area or share of the market (*see also* Chapter 16)

■ *Concept Check 6-3   What Agencies Do*

- In what ways can government agencies *support* business?
- Describe the main forms of *market failure* against which government agencies may take regulatory action.

■ CREATING POLICY

As we noted previously, federal agencies have only the powers expressly given to them in delegating statutes: In short, an agency may do what Congress created it to do, and nothing else. Nonetheless, agencies have broad discretion within these limits. Few statutes, for example, actually compel agencies to take an action. Instead, they authorize agency officials to do so when and if those officials see fit.

The **Administrative Procedure Act of 1946** supplements the laws creating individual agencies by outlining three basic procedures for regulating agency action: *rule-making, adjudication,* and *nonjudicial informal action.* Delegating statutes generally refer to this act, sometimes modifying it or adding to it in order to suit a particular agency's functions. However, if an agency's delegating statute does *not* instruct it to follow any of the act's procedures, the agency is free to ignore them.

> **Administrative Procedure Act of 1946** Statute establishing the basic procedures followed by most *administrative agencies*

Rule Making

The Administrative Procedure Act outlines two ways that an agency can make rules: *informal rule making* and *formal rule making,* the latter being the more complicated and less common approach.

INFORMAL RULE MAKING. When an agency issues rules through the **informal rule-making** procedure—also known as **notice-and-comment**—it acts very much like a legislature: The public receives notice of a proposed rule and has an opportunity to respond before the rule becomes binding.

> **informal rule-making (or notice-and-comment)** Process in administrative law by which an agency sets new rules and in which the public is informed of proposed rules and allowed to respond before rules become binding

This procedure is illustrated in Figure 6-4. It applies only to substantive rules, not to general statements of policy, rules about agency practices, or interpretative rules (ones that clarify the terms of existing rules). The act also specifies exceptions by subject matter. For example, rule-making procedures do not apply to "a military or foreign affairs function of the United States; or a matter relating to agency management or personnel or to public property, loans, grants, benefits, or contracts."[2] In addition, agencies can choose not to follow the informal rule-making procedure "for good cause," if their delegating statutes let them avoid it.

---

[2] 5 U.S.C. 553 (a)(1)-(2).

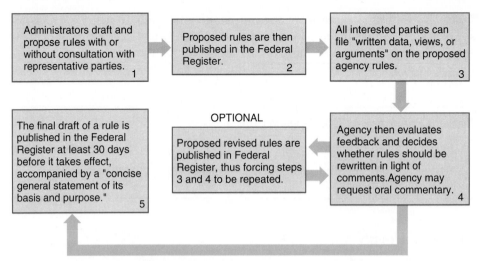

FIGURE 6-4 Informal Rule-Making Procedure *Source: Kenneth F. Warren,* Administrative Law in the American Political System *(Minneapolis, MN: West, 1982). Reprinted by permission. All rights reserved.*

The Administrative Procedure Act specifies that general notice of proposed rule making shall be published in the Federal Register and shall include:

1. a statement of the time, place, and nature of public rule-making proceedings
2. reference to the legal authority under which the rule is proposed
3. either the terms or substance of the proposed rule or a description of the subjects and issues involved.

The specific rule for obtaining public comment states that "the agency shall give interested persons an opportunity to participate in the rule making through submission of written data, views, or arguments with or without opportunity for oral presentation." Note that there is considerable leeway in the definition of an "opportunity to participate."

On the one hand, an agency may conduct informal hearings, much as Congress does. On the other, it may do no more than announce the proposal, along with a deadline for responses, in the *Federal Register,* a daily publication that prints the rules and regulations which the U.S. government (including the president, the rest of the executive branch, and Congress) has adopted or wishes to adopt. Any federal rule or regulation that imposes a penalty for noncompliance must appear in its pages.

Federal Register Daily publication of the federal government announcing proposed and adopted *federal regulations* and *executive orders*

As the agency reviews responses from the public, it also conducts its own investigation. It then reviews the record of the hearing (if one was held) and written comments, as well as its own files, to determine whether any changes in the proposed rule are needed. Any changes that are made at this point are final; no public airing is required.

At the end of the process, the agency publishes the final version of the rule in the *Federal Register.* This statement of the rule must include a general explanation of its purpose and the agency's reason for adopting it. Barring emergencies, the rule must be announced at least thirty days before it takes effect. If any interested parties believe that the record does not make a reasonable case for the final rule, they may petition a federal appeals court to consider their arguments. The court then has three choices: (1) to uphold the rule (2) to alter it or (3) to request that the agency evaluate it further.

FORMAL RULE MAKING. The informal rule-making procedure is intended to be an efficient process suited to the everyday workings of government. By contrast, formal rule making offers the public a more extensive opportunity to influence policy.

Like the informal procedure, **formal rule making** begins with a public notice proposing a rule. Next, the agency holds a hearing, presided over by the agency head or an administrative law judge to determine the relevant facts. This proceeding is more like a trial than a legislative hearing. Interested parties have the right to present evidence, cross-examine witnesses, and answer charges. An agency can also decide to receive evidence in written form.

Note that the goal of both formal and informal rule making is to shape

formal rule making In administrative law, a procedure that offers the public an opportunity, in the form of a public hearing, to influence *administrative agency policy*

Administration and the New Deal In the opinion of many historians, Franklin D. Roosevelt forged the first "modern" presidency by solidifying the roles defined by his predecessors and defining the additional presidential role of *economic manager*. Among the most visible apects of FDR's strategy for countering the effects of the Great Depression was a veritable "alphabet soup" of federal programs and agencies conceived both to stimulate a speedy recovery and to initiate long-term reform. During the so-called First Hundred Days of Roosevelt's first administratioin, for example, the Federal Emergency Relief Administration (FERA) allocated $500 million for distribution to the unemployed by state relief agencies; the Civilian Conservation Corps (CCC) paid 2.5 million unemployed men $30 per week to work on public lands at such jobs as planting trees and building ranger stations; by 1934, the Civilian Works Administration (CWA) had put 4 million men and women directly on the federal payroll at $15 per week. The Works Progress Administration (WPA), the major distributor of federal funds to the unemployed, included artists, writers, and musicians in its support for such community-enrichment jobs painting courthouse murals and writing travel pamphlets. New Deal legislation also established the Securities and Exchange Commission (SEC), Federal Deposit Insurance Corporation (FDIC), and Tennessee Valley Authority (TVA), but as this cartoon illustrates, disenchantment with Roosevelt's policies included charges of sweeping socialism, unwarranted extension of federal executive power, and general bureaucratic overkill.

rules that can be *generally* applied. In addition, both procedures recognize that behind every prospective rule there is a *controversy*. Nevertheless, whereas the informal procedure calls vaguely for public participation, the formal process grants the parties affected nearly all the rights of a plaintiff and a defendant in an actual court case.

Most often, agencies make rules that settle controversies involving many issues. Therefore, legal, factual, moral, economic, and social questions will be raised. The problem with formal rule making is that all of the parties may present witnesses, who will be subject to cross-examination by lawyers representing each of those parties.

Not surprisingly, formal rule-making hearings can take a decade or more to complete. Lawmakers, lobbyists, and agency staffs know that agencies cannot regulate efficiently and effectively through rules when they are forced to follow the formal rule-making policy. The Interstate Commerce Commission, for example, was threatened with this fate twice when the Supreme Court considered challenges to ICC rules developed by notice-and-comment procedure from plaintiffs who demanded trial-like hearings as a matter of due process. Fortunately for the ICC, the Supreme Court affirmed its legal authority to follow informal rule-making procedures.[3]

Adjudication

Like rule making, agency *adjudication* may be either *formal* or *informal*. Unlike rule making, however, it is intended only to settle factual disputes among a relatively small group of parties, not to settle controversies involving the public at large. Yet adjudication also produces general policy, if only because each case sets a *precedent*.

AGENCY HEARINGS. Agencies hold formal trial-like hearings to charge individuals or companies with violating regulations, to set utility rates, and to grant licenses. Different agencies have different ways of deciding which cases to pursue. Most have the power to launch enforcement action when evidence of wrongdoing emerges from their own monitoring or investigations. The agencies thus act as prosecutors. The Consumer Product Safety Commission (CPSC) is an example of an agency that searches out targets for regulation. By contrast, the FTC is more likely to respond to allegations of unfair or illegal business practices by a competitor of the firm that engages in them.[4]

Unless they are successfully appealed, decisions reached by adjudication are binding on the parties to the dispute. Unlike the rules developed by rule-making procedures, adjudication can remedy past wrongdoing. As a policy-making tool, this trial-like procedure is properly used only for problems the agency could not have foreseen, problems in which the agency lacks experience, or problems demanding special solutions.

Case-by-Case Consideration. In some instances, case-by-case consideration is clearly most appropriate. This is true, for example, when the Federal Power Commission sets utility rates, when the Department of Justice decides whether a corporate merger threatens competition, or when the Nuclear Regu-

---

[3] *United States v. Allegheny-Ludlum Steel Corp.*, 406 U.S. 742 (1972) and *United States v. Florida East Coast Ry. Co.*, 410 U.S. 224 (1973).

[4] *Congressional Quarterly, Federal Regulatory Directory*, 5th ed. (Washington, D.C.: Congressional Quarterly, Inc., 1986), p. 40.

latory Commission licenses nuclear power plants. In addition, a hearing is generally required before an agency takes any action that will seriously harm an individual, such as cutting off welfare benefits. These hearings are held not to establish policy but to determine the facts of a particular case and to protect individuals from arbitrary harm.

General Rulings. Finally, some agencies prefer to establish a general rule through individual cases, sometimes for political reasons. The NLRB, for example, is widely criticized for relying too much on adjudication. However, the agency may, in certain instances, regard a decision in an individual case less obvious a matter of general policy—and less vulnerable to political attacks—than a rule emerging from a rule-making procedure.

FORMAL ADJUDICATION HEARINGS. Formal adjudication begins with procedures much like those of court trials. Complaints and summonses are filed and copies sent to the defendants, who are legally required to respond. As in a civil case, the response may either dispute jurisdiction or raise defenses. The agency staff then begins to gather evidence, if it hasn't already done so.

The next step is to hold a hearing before staff members of the agency or an **administrative law judge (ALJ).** The defendants do not have the right to a jury at an agency hearing. However, everyone involved is entitled to a timely announcement of the time, place, and form of (1) the upcoming hearing (2) the source of its legal and jurisdictional authority and (3) the controversy to be considered. The Administrative Procedure Act also gives disputants or their attorneys the right to present oral and documentary evidence at the hearing, to present evidence in rebuttal, and to cross-examine witnesses.

> **administrative law judge (ALJ)** Federal public official who presides over hearings at which *administrative agency policy* is litigated

One major difference between administrative hearings and trials held in other courts is that, for two reasons, administrative hearings follow much less restrictive rules of evidence. This practice does not mean, however, that ALJs can make decisions on a hunch: The **legal-residuum rule** requires that the finding of fact rely on at least *some* evidence that would be admissible in a jury trial. The degree of necessary proof depends on the consequences of the agency's decision. For example, more evidence is required to revoke a license than to decree a nonpenal remedy against a license holder.[5]

> **legal-residuum rule** Rule requiring that *administrative law judges* base their fact finding on at least some evidence that would prove acceptable in a jury trial

Once the hearing is over, the ALJ must produce a written decision stating the facts determined and the conclusions based on those facts. The parties may choose to appeal to the head of the agency on the sole basis of the hearing's record of facts. Thus the agency as a whole functions as a two-tier court system, including both a trial court and a forum for appeals. The agency's final decision upholds or rejects the complaint, and this decision can be appealed only to the federal courts.

Administrative Law Judges—The Hidden Judiciary. The so-called "hidden judiciary" includes more than 1,000 judges with the power to enforce agency rules and to grant or withhold federal benefits for individuals, for example, welfare.

By law, ALJs must have at least ten years of experience as lawyers or judges. Although they do not enjoy the same protections from public pressure as other federal judges, they do have a great deal of independence from the agencies that they represent. Their salaries are set by the Office of Personnel Management, which also evaluates their work. Cases are assigned on a rotation basis. In order to take action against an ALJ, an agency must (1) hold a for-

---

[5] Stephen A. Ecenia, 56 *Florida Bar Journal* 571 (June 1982).

mal hearing to establish its reasons and (2) convince another agency of the need for such action.

INFORMAL ADJUDICATION. You may be surprised to learn that the procedures described in the Administrative Procedure Act account for only about ten percent of all agency actions. The other ninety percent consists of informal actions governed by methods that individual agencies devise to meet their own needs. Because most agencies handle huge caseloads, efficiency may be crucial. Perhaps the best examples of informal agency action are the thousands of rulings made yearly by the Internal Revenue Service (IRS).

Agencies also have a great deal of discretion when acting informally. The main guideline for agency-made procedures is the Constitution's due-process requirement, which applies whenever an agency action might threaten an individual's life, liberty, or property (*see* Chapter 3). In devising procedures to settle individual cases, agencies must weigh the government's interest against that of individuals affected. In doing so, they apply a court-decreed *balancing test*.

NONJUDICIAL INFORMAL AGENCY ACTION. There are a variety of agency activities that seem more *managerial* than judicial. Like private corporations, agencies can express their will merely by lifting an eyebrow, so to speak, or by *threatening* to take action.[6] They also give advice and attempt to negotiate disputes. On a daily basis, they answer letters and telephone calls requesting advice or information, grade food, and conduct inspections (including licensing inspections).

In addition, agencies can also use publicity as a tool. For example, they may hold news conferences or issue reports to publicize facts that promote agency policy. They may even wage telephone campaigns. (The 1962 campaign to prevent smaller steel companies from raising prices after U.S. Steel did so is an example of such an appeal.)

RULE MAKING OR ADJUDICATION? As you can see, although agencies have a great deal of flexibility in choosing procedures, that same flexibility often leaves them open to criticism. Perhaps the most controversial issue is whether agencies should rely more on rule making and less on adjudication. Because they are more likely than social regulatory agencies to set policy through individual decisions, the question applies mainly to the relatively old agencies engaged in economic regulation.

The FTC, for instance, relied on adjudication for most of its first fifty years. In 1964, however, the agency followed notice-and-comment procedure to create its famous rule concerning cigarette advertising and the labeling of cigarette containers. From then on, it announced, any manufacturer whose packaging failed to display a warning that cigarette smoking may be hazardous to one's health was guilty of an unfair or deceptive practice.

An alternative approach would have been to hold adjudicatory hearings, considering charges of unfair business practices against one or more cigarette manufacturers. Meanwhile, the cigarette industry argued that the FTC did not even have the power to make rules. In its defense, the agency responded that the adjudicatory approach would have put targeted companies at a competitive disadvantage.

---

[6] David L. Shapiro, "The Choice of Rulemaking or Adjudication in the Development of Administrative Policy," 78 *Harvard Law Review* 923 (Mar. 1965).

Interestingly, as the following case shows, the FTC has also come under fire for choosing an adjudication procedure.

FORD MOTOR COMPANY v. FEDERAL TRADE COMMISSION
U.S. Court of Appeals, Ninth Circuit, 673 F2d. 1008 (1981)

Consistent with what seemed to be a common practice in repossession in the car dealership industry, Francis Ford Co., an automotive dealership in Oregon, credited defaulting buyers for the retail value of repossessed automobiles with a deduction for repossession costs and lost profits. In response, the Federal Trade Commission held an adjudicatory proceeding to stop Francis Ford Co. from engaging in such practices.

The F.T.C., through an interpretation of Oregon state law on debtor-creditor relations, found the repossession method to be a violation of F.T.C. law and ordered Francis Ford to cease the practice. Francis Ford now appeals the decision to the appeals court, arguing that the dispute should have been resolved through rule making.

Goodwin, Circuit Judge.

Francis Ford, Inc. petitions this court to review an F.T.C. order finding it in violation of § 5 of the F.T.C. Act, 15 U.S.C. § 45 (unfair trade practices). We have reviewed the petition, and set aside the order.

Francis Ford, Inc. is an Oregon automobile dealership. Its practice in repossessing cars has been to credit the debtor for wholesale value of the car, charge him for indirect expenses (i.e., overhead and lost profits) as well as direct expenses (i.e., refurbishing) associated with repossession and resale, and sell the repossessed vehicle at retail keeping the "surplus." In doing so, Francis Ford claims it is doing what is commonly done throughout its industry.

The F.T.C. does not approve of the described practice. Nor does it approve of a number of other credit practices now commonly in use in a wide variety of industries.

. . . .

In order to attack Francis Ford's practice, the F.T.C. began in 1976 an adjudicatory action against Ford Motor Co., Ford Credit Co., and Francis Ford, Inc. The commission alleged that the respondents had violated § 5 of the F.T.C. Act by failing to give defaulting customers more than wholesale value for their repossessed cars, and by improperly charging them with indirect expenses such as overhead and lost profits. Parallel proceedings were commenced against Chrysler Corp. and General Motors, their finance subsidiaries, and two dealers. . . . Eventually, all the respondents except Francis Ford settled with the F.T.C.

Shortly after the consent decrees were entered, the administrative law judge held that Francis Ford's credit practices had violated § 5 of the F.T.C. Act, but that the the commission had failed to establish that Francis Ford's acts were substantially injurious to its customers. Both Francis Ford and complaint counsel for the F.T.C. appealed to the full commission. The commission deleted the portion of the order favorable to Francis Ford, and affirmed the administrative law judge's decision. The order directed Francis Ford to cease its present credit practices, and to adopt the F.T.C.'s view of proper credit practices under ORS 79.5040 (U.C.C. § 9-504).

The narrow issue presented here is whether the F.T.C. should have proceeded by rule-making in this case rather than by adjudication. The Supreme Court has said that an administrative agency, such as the F.T.C., "is not precluded from announcing new principles in the adjudicative proceeding and that the choice between rulemaking and adjudication lies in the first instance within the [agency's] discretion." But like all grants of discretion, "there may be situations where the [agency's] reliance on adjudication would amount to an abuse of discretion. . . ." The problem is one of drawing the line. On that score the Supreme Court has avoided black-letter rules. Lower courts have been left, therefore, with the task of dealing with the problem on a case-by-case basis.

The Ninth Circuit recently made such an attempt in *Patel v. Immigration & Naturalization Serv.* (1980). . . . The thrust of the *Patel* holding . . . is that agencies can proceed by adjudication to enforce discrete violations of *existing* laws where the effective scope of the rule's impact will be relatively small; but an agency must proceed by rulemaking if it seeks to change the law and establish rules of widespread application.

In the present case, the F.T.C., by its order has established a rule that would require a secured creditor to credit the debtor with the "best possible" value of the repossessed vehicle, and forbid the creditor from charging the debtor with overhead and lost profits. The administrative decision below so holds. Framed according to *Patel*, the precise issue therefore is whether this adjudication changes existing law, and has widespread application. It does, and the matter should be addressed by rulemaking.

The F.T.C. admits that industry practice has been to do what Francis Ford does—credit the debtor with the wholesale value and charge the debtor for indirect expenses. But the F.T.C. contends that Francis Ford's particular practice violates state law (ORS 79.5040); that the violation will not be reached by the proposed trade rule on credit practices; and that this adjudication will have only local application. The arguments are not persuasive.

By all accounts this adjudication is the first agency action against a dealer for violating ORS 79.5040 by doing what Francis Ford does. Although the U.C.C. counterpart of ORS 79.5040 is enacted in 49 states, nearly word for word, we have been cited to no case which has interpreted the provision to require a secured creditor to credit the debtor for the "best possible price" and not charge him for overhead and lost profits. It may well be that Oregon courts will interpret U.C.C. § 9-504 in the manner advocated by the F.T.C. if the question is put to them. But it is speculation to contend, as does the F.T.C. here, that Francis Ford is in violation of *existing* Oregon law. One of the basic characteristics of law is that potential violators have, or can obtain notice of it. No notice of the F.T.C.'s view of the law has been pointed out to us.

. . . .

Ultimately, however, we are persuaded to set aside this order because the rule of the case made below will have general application. It will not apply just to Francis Ford. Credit practices similar to those of Francis Ford are widespread in the car dealership industry; and the U.C.C. section the F.T.C. wishes us to interpret exists in 49 states. The F.T.C. is aware of this. It has already appended a "Synopsis of Determination" to the order, apparently for the purpose of advising other automobile dealerships of the results of this adjudication. To allow the order to stand as presently written would do far more than remedy a discrete violation of a singular Oregon law as the F.T.C. contends; it would create a national interpretation of U.C.C. § 9-504 and in effect enact the precise rule the F.T.C. has proposed, but not yet promulgated.

Under these circumstances, the F.T.C. has exceeded its authority by proceeding to create new law by adjudication rather than by rule-making.

The order is vacated.

Case Questions

1. What reasons does the court give for its conclusion that the FTC should have proceeded by rule making rather than by adjudication?

2. Is there any particular fact that the court of appeals finds very persuasive in determining how to characterize the proceeding?

3. Would the result have been different if the FTC had been able to cite an Oregon case establishing that the repossession practice was a violation of state law?

■ *Concept Check 6-4   Creating Policy*

- Describe the chief differences between *informal* and *formal rule making*.
- Describe the process of agency *adjudication* and explain how it differs from rule making.
- Define the *legal-residuum rule* and explain the role of an *administrative law judge*.
- It has been argued that administrative agencies should rely more on rule making and less on adjudication. Why?

■ CONTROLLING AGENCY ACTION

How do the three formal branches of American government cooperate and conflict in controlling the fourth, unofficial branch? As you will see, the president continually exerts control over executive agencies, in part by appointing sympathetic officials to head them. Only Congress can repeal an agency's delegating statute or approve changes in agency budgets. However, agency action can only be overridden by the passage of new legislation or through judicial review. Finally, agencies are accountable to the public they serve. When Americans are dissatisfied with an agency's actions, they can demand changes from Congress and the president, they can appeal cases to the federal courts, and they can simply decline to cooperate. Few agencies can enforce rules without the cooperation of most of the people whom they affect.

Executive Control

Executive oversight of our huge federal bureaucracy is concentrated in the president's office. There, the president, his personal advisers, and such organizations as the National Security Council (NSC), the Council of Economic Advisers, and the Office of Management and Budget (OMB) coordinate policy and help to ensure that executive agencies pursue the president's agenda. The five main presidential controls over executive agencies are:

1. the appointment and removal of officials
2. the power to reorganize the executive branch
3. the issuing of executive orders
4. the power to influence fiscal decisions
5. the power to deny an agency legal representation

The president appoints the heads of executive agencies, either with the advice and consent of the Senate or—if Congress agrees—at his own discretion. The president can also dismiss the heads of executive agencies at will. Many observers complain that these appointments are often of poor quality because presidents typically choose on partisan grounds regardless of whether appointees are good administrators or sympathetic to the purposes of the agencies they head.

Under President Jimmy Carter, the 1978 Civil Service Reform Act provided for many changes in the appointment and management of officials in federal agencies. The goal was to increase the overall competency level with such modifications as merit raises for midlevel managers and bonuses for top officials. (One provision was to protect whistle blowers at federal agencies; see the ETHICAL ENVIRONMENT box for a fuller discussion of this subject.) However, control over the bureaucracy remains difficult to maintain, even from the Executive Office, and politics sometimes interferes with putting and keeping the best people in the right jobs.

ORGANIZATIONAL CONTROL. Presidents have used their power to reorganize the executive branch more often than they have removed their own appointees. Even then, however, they cannot reorganize without congressional approval. Reorganization can promote such goals as effective management, lower spending, and the coordination of policies and the elimination of overlap among different agencies. Unfortunately, however, it is usually easier to create new offices or layers of bureaucracy than to remove old ones.

Reorganization may be proposed in response to shifts in social and environmental concerns. In creating cabinet-level departments of education and energy, for example, President Carter, with the approval of Congress, recognized the growing need to centralize agency decisions on these two important matters. Although reorganization also means the termination of some agencies, many agency-level departments have remained intact despite President George Bush's attempts to abolish or severely weaken many of the agencies slated for reduced responsibility.

Executive Orders. Executive orders can also be used to extend the president's control over executive agencies. In 1981, for example, President Reagan issued Executive Order #12,291, requiring agencies to prepare a regulatory impact analysis comparing the costs and benefits of any "major" proposed rule. In 1985, Executive Order #12,498 required executive agencies to prepare a yearly plan for important regulatory actions. Although the OMB reviews both kinds of documents for consistency with the president's aims,[7] the Administrative Procedure Act makes Congress and the agencies themselves the only sources of changes in their own procedures.

BUDGETARY CONTROL.   As we noted earlier, Congress makes the final decisions on agency spending. However, nearly all agencies must submit their budgets for approval to the OMB, which tries to impose the President's priorities on their spending plans. The OMB also separately reviews the budgetary impact of proposed rules and laws. (Although some independent agencies do not have to submit their proposals to OMB for clearance, most do so to avoid trouble when they submit their budgets.)

LEGAL CONTROL.   Finally, the fact that most executive agencies do not have sufficiently large budgets to defend themselves against many lawsuits gives the president a certain amount of power over their actions. Executive agencies depend for legal defense on the U.S. Department of Justice, which can deny them representation. For example, in 1977, President Carter's Attorney General, Griffin Bell, advised all agencies that he would protect them from suits brought under the Freedom of Information Act only if they could prove that the release of documents might cause harm.

Within the overall executive power of overseeing of federal agencies, presidential administrations, beginning with that of Jimmy Carter, have attempted to reform agency action, particularly regarding regulation.

Congressional Control

Congress controls the agencies in four basic ways: (1) by the Senate's power to *veto* presidential appointments, (2) by the power to withdraw or *restructure* the operating authority of executive agencies, (3) by *fiscal control* over their budgets, and (4) by *direct oversight* of their actions.

VETO POWER.   Although Congress cannot appoint agency heads, the Senate must approve the president's nominations of top executive officers. One aspect of this power is the practice of "senatorial courtesy" within the president's party: If the president, for example, is a Republican, the senior Republican senator of any state has an informal veto over the president's nominees within its borders.

POWER TO RESTRUCTURE.   Congress may act either on its own or jointly with the president to restructure the whole federal bureaucracy or to redefine the scope of any particular agency's authority. For example, Congress abolished the Atomic Energy Commission, which had been attacked for overpromoting nuclear power, and created in its place the Nuclear Regulatory Commission, which has only regulatory authority.

---

[7] Peter L. Strauss and Cass R. Sunstein, "The Role of the President and OMB in Informal Rulemaking," 38 *Administrative Law Review* 186 (Spring 1986).

The Ethical Environment
Whistleblowing

Two decades ago Ralph Nader, the pioneering consumer activist, argued that if, as a part of U.S. public policy, whistleblowing were legally protected and encouraged, then the public would receive some protection from illegal and arbitrary actions by administrative agencies, most of whose activities occur behind closed doors where the public cannot scrutinize them. However, engaging in whistleblowing is risky and makes the individual vulnerable on a number of fronts. What motivates whistleblowers, in government or in business, despite the possible consequences? What laws and public policies address the issues of making disclosures easier and protecting whistleblowers from reprisals?

Motivating most whistleblowers seems to be a belief that an individual is responsible for his or her actions—that if one does not disclose corruption, one is as much at fault as the wrongdoer being exposed. As Myron and Penina Migdal Glazer, psychologists who have researched the subject, point out, this "strong belief in individual responsibility that drives ethical resisters is often supported by feelings of professional ethics, religious behavior or allegiance to the community."

In examples ranging from the Department of the Interior and the Nuclear Regulatory Commission to the pharmaceutical industry and social-service organizations, those who have shown personal courage to come forward and report wrongdoing have often been "punished" for their stands. Reprisals—which the Glazers describe as including "transfer, demotion, firing, blackballing, personal harassment and intimidation"—have been used to get back at them. Still, people continue to speak out in order to have their charges investigated by outside authorities despite threats of ostracism, humiliation, and more.

An 1863 federal law known as the "Abraham Lincoln law" and officially called the False Claims Act is the basis for many whistleblowing suits against government contractors. (The nickname carries over from the Civil War, when the law was enacted to get citizens to expose military contract fraud against the Union.) In 1989, for example, there was a settlement of four civil suits brought against General Electric under a provision of this law, which allows private citizens to sue suspected cheaters on behalf of the federal government. These suits alleged that GE, as a defense contractor, had cheated the government of millions through such illegal activities as falsifying test certificates for military engines and a time-card altering scheme.

Blowing the whistle on Medicare fraud is another area in which concerned employees can step in to call attention to illegal corporate activities. Suits brought by individuals against Medicare and other government-contract frauds such as insurance and environmental permits would also be pursued under the False Claims Act, which once focused almost exclusively on defense-contract fraud. In fact, new suits might be encouraged by the fact that the 1986 changes to the False Claims Act provide winning plaintiffs with up to thirty percent of the awards assessed against guilty defendants.

Due in part to such suits, businesses are beginning to recognize certain forms of management failure, realizing that attention should have been paid earlier to employee notifications of errors, fraud, and so on, within the firm. On the other hand, one defense-industry coalition is currently challenging the constitutionality of the whistleblower provisions and arguing that only the federal government itself can initiate action.

At the same time, however, not all businesses seek to discourage whistleblowing. In 1990, for example, the association for the accounting profession, the American Institute of Certified Public Accountants, supported proposed federal legislation (changes to the 1934 Securities Exchange Act) that would require auditors to notify regulators of possible illegal acts they uncover in the course of regular audits. Previously, accountants had maintained that making such disclosures would injure client relationships. The intent of Congress in such legislation is to hold business responsible for reporting the illegal activities of officers.

In 1978, under the Civil Service Reform Act, Congress established the Office of Special Counsel, whose mandate was to protect federal employees coming forward with charges of fraud and waste in administrative agencies. However, because the special counsel's office had been found to be passive in its role, Congress has yet to enact further legislation. Among the provisions of a proposed reform act to make whistleblowing safer for employees is easing the burden of proof for federal employees claiming that they were fired or disciplined because they had exposed fraud; the imposition of greater burden on federal agencies to prove that personnel decisions regarding whistleblowing employees were legitimate; and the requirement that the special counsel serve as the whistleblowers' advocate.

Thus, it would seem that, as a matter of public policy, the whistleblower has been receiving encouragement. Still, as one "ethical resister" still employed by a federal agency has put it: "If you have God, the law, the press and the facts on your side, you have a 50–50 chance of winning."

BUDGETARY POWER. Congress approves the funding of agencies in two stages. First, lawmakers set the terms for the basic grant, or **authorization,** of money for an agency. The amount is usually stipulated in the statute that creates it. Second, each year Congress appropriates funds. After approval by the OMB, each agency's proposed budget goes to the appropriations committees of the

authorization the first stage, consisting of a basic grant of money, in Congressional approval of agency funding

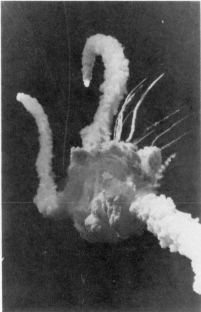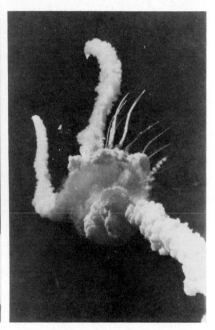

Personal Policy, Private and Public Allan McDonald and Roger Boisjoly were both engineers at the defense-contracting company Morton Thiokol, which manufactured the now-notorious O-rings (rubber gaskets between large stages of the booster rocket) that contributed to the explosion that destroyed the space shuttle *Challenger* in full view of a worldwide audience on January 28, 1986. Both men also testified before a presidential commission investigating procedures at Morton Thiokol, and both reported having had reservations about the potential performance of the rings. Both men said that they wrote memos, filed official warnings, and "blew whistles," but that the company declined to respond. Even though the episode and its aftermath were highly publicized, both McDonald and Boisjoly report having been reassigned to jobs far inferior to those for which they were qualified and hired, working at obscure punitive tasks until ultimately reinstated. To be fair, Thiokol engineers had warned NASA officials the night before the launch that impending cold weather might affect the performance of the O-rings, and much of the story of the *Challenger* disaster is the story of bureaucratic breakdown in the agency responsible for the country's space program. A meeting, for example, between Thiokol engineers and NASA officials who were concerned about the rings almost two years before the disaster had been postponed by the agency and ultimately never took place. In fact, when a senior Thiokol engineer at the launch site refused to approve the launch (which had already been postponed twice), officials at the Marshall Space Flight Center in Alabama (which oversees the shuttle rockets) went over his head to company management; no agency officials, either in Washington, at the Kennedy Space Center in Florida (the launch site), or at the Johnson Space Center in Houston (from which the shuttle program is directed), were informed of this unusual step.

House and the Senate. Both houses must approve the final appropriations bill for that year.

DIRECT OVERSIGHT. The authorizing committees for each house, and perhaps the committees dealing with the related areas, directly oversee each agency. For example, these committees hold public investigations into suspected misconduct. In addition, the government-operations committees of both houses have the job of exposing poor or corrupt management. Congress has also created its own agencies to help it oversee the executive: the Congressional Research Service, the Office of Technology Assessment (OTA), and the General Accounting office (GAO), which audits agency budgets and evaluates programs. Congress can also ask the agencies themselves to report on their progress.

Judicial Review

Nearly all federal agency actions may be appealed to federal courts. However, the *scope* and *availability* of judicial review varies from agency to agency and from case to case.

SCOPE. Some agency decisions are not legally subject to any review, others are subject to partial review, and still others may be reviewed in every aspect if a concerned party brings suit. Partial review is by far the most common: If the courts had to reconsider in full the facts of every administrative case under appeal, they would be overwhelmed.

When hearing a case on appeal, a judge must distinguish between questions of *fact*—that is, who did what and when—and questions of *law*. The distinction has sometimes been lost in gray areas defined as "mixed questions of law and fact." Generally, however, the scope of review over questions of fact is limited on appeal. Special circumstances must hold for the facts to be determined *de novo*—that is, anew or from the beginning. However, judges are entirely free to override an agency's interpretation of legal questions. These are precisely the sort of questions that judges may be better equipped to answer than an agency staff.

Section 706 of the Administrative Procedure Act outlines several grounds on which a judge may overrule or compel an agency action. Two of these grounds—*arbitrary actions* and *insubstantial evidence* concern questions of fact. Three other grounds—*unconstitutional actions, unauthorized actions,* and *improper procedures*—concern questions of law.

Arbitrary Actions. Was the agency's action "arbitrary" or "capricious"? This question applies to discretionary action, informal rule making, and informal adjudication. It must be asked in order to protect citizens from potentially monstrous abuses and to preserve the public's trust in rational government. Some judges will strike down informal agency decisions that rely on guesswork as arbitrary; others will accept a degree of uncertainty as inevitable.

Insubstantial Evidence. Was the decision or rule "unsupported by substantial evidence"? This more demanding question comes into play if the action was based on a formal hearing. "Substantial evidence" was defined in *Consolidated Edison v. National Labor Relations Board* (305 U.S. 197, 229 [1983]) to be "such relevant evidence as a reasonable mind might accept as adequate to support a conclusion." Some circumstances permit the judge to hear the case *de novo*, if necessary.

Unconstitutional Actions. The Administrative Procedure Act provides for redress against any agency violation of "constitutional right, power, privilege, or immunity."

Unauthorized Actions. Was the agency's action authorized by its delegating statute? This is a straightforward question: If the Food and Drug Administration tried to regulate airlines, it clearly would be acting above and beyond the limits of its authority. However, the limits of delegating statutes have been subjected to far more subtle tests. In *Whirlpool Corporation v. Marshall,* for example, the company challenged a Department of Labor regulation based on

OSHA's statutory authority. The regulation sought to prevent employers from treating workers unfairly because they had walked off the job to avoid unsafe conditions.

WHIRLPOOL CORPORATION v. MARSHALL
United States Supreme Court, 445 U.S. 1 (1980)

The Secretary of Labor, acting under Congressional authority granted by the Occupational Safety and Health Act, enacted a regulation giving workers the right to refuse to perform jobs involving reasonable risk of serious injury or death.

One of the tasks of maintenance workers at Whirlpool's Marion, Ohio, manufacturing plant is to remove appliance components from an elevated steel mesh screen. The screen is in place to protect plant employees from the danger that these components may slip off the plant's overhead conveyor. Due to concerns about the safety of the screen, Whirlpool began efforts to make it stronger. Despite these efforts, a maintenance employee died from injuries resulting from a fall through a yet-to-be-repaired portion of the screen. Shortly thereafter, two of his co-workers were sent home without pay and placed on written reprimand for their refusal to work on the unrepaired portion.

Marshall, the Secretary of Labor, brought this action in Ohio District Court, citing the plant's disciplinary action against the two maintenance workers as a violation of OSHA. The District Court ruled in Whirlpool's favor, concluding that Marshall had exceeded his authority under the Act. The Court of Appeals reversed the District Court's determination, prompting this subsequent appeal by Whirlpool to U.S. Supreme Court.

Mr. Justice Stewart delivered the opinion of the Court. . . .

The Court of Appeals for the Sixth Circuit reversed the District Court's judgment. Finding ample support in the record for the District Court's factual determination that the actions of Deemer and Cornwell had been justified under the Secretary's regulation, the appellate court disagreed with the District Court's conclusion that the regulation is invalid. . . .

The Act itself creates an express mechanism for protecting workers from employment conditions believed to pose an emergent threat of death or serious injury. Upon receipt of an employee inspection request stating reasonable grounds to believe that an imminent danger is present in a workplace, OSHA must conduct an inspection. In the event this inspection reveals workplace conditions or practices that "could reasonably be expected to cause death or serious physical harm immediately or before the imminence of such danger can be eliminated through the enforcement procedures otherwise provided by" the Act, the OSHA inspector must inform the affected employees and the employer of the danger and notify them that he is recommending to the Secretary that injunctive relief be sought. At this juncture, the Secretary can petition a federal court to restrain the conditions or practices giving rise to the imminent danger. By means of a temporary restraining order or preliminary injunction, the court may then require the employer to avoid, correct, or remove the danger or to prohibit employees from working in the area.

. . . .

. . . [T]he Secretary is obviously correct when he acknowledges in his regulation that, "as a general matter, there is no right afforded by the Act which would entitle employees to walk off the job because of potential unsafe conditions at the workplace." By providing for prompt notice to the employer of an inspector's intention to seek an injunction against an imminently dangerous condition, the legislation obviously contemplates that the employer will normally respond by voluntarily and speedily eliminating the danger. And in the few instances where this does not occur, the legislative provisions authorizing prompt judicial action are designed to give employees full protection in most situations from the risk of injury or death resulting from an imminently dangerous condition at the worksite.

As this case illustrates, however, circumstances may sometimes exist in which the employee justifiably believes that the express statutory arrangement does not sufficiently protect him from death or serious injury. Such circumstances will probably not often occur, but such a situation may arise when (1) the employee is ordered by his employer to work under conditions that the employee reasonably believes pose an imminent risk of death or serious bodily injury, and (2) the employee has reason to believe that there is not sufficient time or opportunity either to seek effective redress from his employer or to apprise OSHA of the danger.

Nothing in the Act suggests that those few employees who have to face this dilemma must rely exclusively on the remedies expressly set forth in the Act at the risk of their own safety. But nothing in the Act explicitly provides otherwise. Against this background of legislative silence, the Secretary has exercised his rule-making power under 29 U.S. § 657 (g)(2) and has determined that, when an employee in good faith finds himself in such a predicament, he may refuse to expose himself to the dangerous condition, without being subjected to "subsequent discrimination" by the employer.

. . . .

The regulation clearly conforms to the fundamental objective of the Act—to prevent occupational deaths and serious injuries. . . .

To accomplish this basic purpose, the legislation's remedial orientation is prophylactic in nature. The act does not wait for an employee to die or become injured. It authorizes the promulgation of health and safety standards and the issuance of citations in the hope that these will act to prevent deaths or injuries from ever occurring. It would seem anomalous to construe an Act so directed and constructed as prohibiting an employee, with no other reasonable alternative, the freedom to withdraw from a workplace environment that he reasonably believes is highly dangerous.

. . . .

In urging reversal of the judgment before us, the petitioner relies primarily on two aspects of the Act's legislative history.

Representative Daniels of New Jersey sponsored one of several House bills that led ultimately to the passage of the Act. As reported to the House by the Committee on Education and Labor, the Daniels bill contained a section that was soon dubbed the "strike with pay" provision. This section provided that employees could request an examination by the Department of Health, Education, and Welfare (HEW) of the toxicity of any materials in their workplace. If that examination revealed a workplace substance that had "potentially toxic or harmful effects in such concentration as used or found," the employer was given 60 days to correct the potentially dangerous condition. . . . If these conditions were not [corrected], an employee could "absent himself from such risk of harm for the period necessary to avoid such danger without loss of regular compensation for such period."

This provision encountered stiff opposition in the House. Representative Steiger of Wisconsin introduced a substitute bill containing no "strike with pay" provision. . . . The House ultimately adopted the Steiger bill.

The bill that was reported to and, with a few amendments, passed by the Senate never contained a "strike with pay" provision. . . .

. . . .

. . . The petitioner argues that Congress' overriding concern in rejecting the "strike with pay" provision was to avoid giving employees a unilateral authority to walk off the job which they might abuse in order to intimidate or harass their employer. Congress deliberately chose instead, the petitioner maintains, to grant employees the power to request immediate administrative inspections of the workplace which could in appropriate cases lead to coercive judicial remedies. As the petitioner views the regulation, therefore, it gives to workers precisely what Congress determined to withhold from them.

We read the legislative history differently. Congress rejected a provision that did not concern itself at all with conditions posing real and immediate threats of death or severe injury. . . . [I]n rejecting the Daniels bill's "strike with pay" provision, Congress was not rejecting a legislative provision dealing with the highly perilous and fast-moving situations covered by the regulation now before us.

. . . .

For these reasons we conclude that 29 CFR § 1977.12 (b)(2)(1979) was promulgated by the Secretary in the valid exercise of his authority under the Act. Accordingly, the judgment of the Court of Appeals is affirmed.

Case Questions

1. How does the Supreme Court in the Whirlpool case determine that the Secretary did not exceed his statutory authority?

2. Can the Secretary ever exercise greater power than OSHA gives him?

3. What considerations justify Congress in giving broad authority to agencies in their delegating statutes?

Improper Procedures. Whenever agencies conduct proceedings that may result in depriving an individual of liberty or property, the proceeding must grant that individual due process of law. At the same time, however, agencies must be able to act with reasonable speed and economy. To decide what due-process safeguards are necessary, agencies conduct the balancing test set forth in the following case.

MATHEWS v. ELDRIDGE

United States Supreme Court, 424 U.S. 319 (1976)

Beginning in June 1968, Eldridge, a disabled worker, received Social Security benefits. After evaluating his medical condition and determining **that his disability ended in May 1972, the State Social Security Agency made a tentative decision that Eldridge was no longer entitled to these payments.**

In addition to including a statement of reasons for the termination, the agency informed Eldridge that he would be allowed to petition for reconsideration if final termination were decided upon.

Eldridge, deciding to forgo the reconsideration process, brought this suit against Mathews, the Secretary of Health, Education, and Welfare, claiming that he was entitled to an evidentiary hearing prior to the termination of his benefits. The District Court, finding for Eldridge, issued an injunction preventing termination of the disability payments before such hearing. The Court of Appeals affirmed. The case is now in U.S. Supreme Court for determination of whether, in terms of due process, an evidentiary hearing is a necessary precondition to the termination of disability benefits.

Mr. Justice Powell delivered the opinion of the Court.

The issue in this case is whether the Due Process Clause of the Fifth Amendment requires that prior to the termination of Social Security disability benefit payments the recipient be afforded an opportunity for an evidentiary hearing.

. . . Respondent Eldridge was first awarded benefits in June 1968. . . . [T]he agency informed Eldridge by letter that it had made a tentative determination that his disability had ceased in May 1972. The letter included a statement of reasons for the proposed termination of benefits, and advised Eldridge that he might request reasonable time in which to obtain and submit additional information pertaining to his condition.

In his written response, Eldridge disputed one characterization of his medical condition and indicated that the agency already had enough evidence to establish his disability. The state agency then made its final determination that he had ceased to be disabled in May 1972. This determination was accepted by the Social Security Administration (SSA), which notified Eldridge in July that his benefits would terminate after that month. . . .

Instead of requesting reconsideration Eldridge commenced this action challenging the constitutional validity of the administrative procedures established by the Secretary of Health, Education, and Welfare for assessing whether there exists a continuing disability. He sought an immediate reinstatement of benefits pending a hearing on the issue of his disability. . . . In support of his contention that due process requires a pretermination hearing, Eldridge relied exclusively upon this Court's decision in *Goldberg v. Kelly* (1970), which established a right to an "evidentiary hearing" prior to termination of welfare benefits. . . .

The District Court concluded that the administrative procedures pursuant to which the Secretary had terminated Eldridge's benefits abridged his right to procedural due process. . . . [The] Court held that prior to termination of benefits Eldridge had to be afforded an evidentiary hearing of the type required for welfare beneficiaries under Title IV of the Social Security Act. Relying entirely upon the District Court's opinion, the Court of Appeals for the Fourth Circuit affirmed the in-

junction barring termination of Eldridge's benefits prior to an evidentiary hearing. We reverse.

. . . .

Procedural due process imposes constraints on governmental decisions which deprive individuals of "liberty" or "property" interests within the meaning of the Due Process Clause of the Fifth or Fourteenth Amendment. The Secretary does not contend that procedural due process is inapplicable to terminations of Social Security disability benefits. . . . Rather, the Secretary contends that the existing administrative procedures, detailed below, provide all the process that is constitutionally due before a recipient can be deprived of that interest.

. . . .

[O]ur prior decisions indicate that identification of the specific dictates of due process generally requires consideration of three distinct factors: First, the private interest that will be affected by the official action; second, the risk of an erroneous deprivation of such interest through the procedures used, and the probable value, if any, of additional or substitute procedural safeguards; and finally, the Government's interest, including the function involved and the fiscal and administrative burdens that the additional or substitute procedural requirement would entail.

We turn first to a description of the procedures for the termination of Social Security disability benefits and thereafter consider the factors bearing upon the constitutional adequacy of these procedures.

. . . .

The continuing-eligibility investigation is made by a state agency acting through a "team" consisting of a physician and a nonmedical person trained in disability evaluation. . . .

Whenever the agency's tentative assessment of the beneficiary's condition differs from his own assessment, the beneficiary is informed that benefits may be terminated, provided a summary of the evidence upon which the proposed determination to terminate is based, and afforded an opportunity to review the medical reports and other evidence in his case file. He also may respond in writing and submit additional evidence.

The state agency then makes its final determination, which is reviewed by an examiner in the SSA Bureau of Disability Insurance. If, as is usually the case, the SSA accepts the agency determination it notifies the recipient in writing, informing him of the reasons for the decision, and of his right to seek *de novo* reconsideration by the state agency. . . .

If the recipient seeks reconsideration by the state agency and the determination is adverse, the SSA reviews the reconsideration determination and notifies the recipient of the decision. He then has a right to an evidentiary hearing before an SSA administrative law judge. . . . If this hearing results in an adverse decision, the claimant is entitled to request discretionary review by the SSA Appeals Council, and finally may obtain judicial review.

. . . .

Despite the elaborate character of the administrative

procedures provided by the Secretary, the courts below held them to be constitutionally inadequate, concluding that due process requires an evidentiary hearing prior to termination. . . . [W]e think this was error.

. . . .

Only in *Goldberg* has the Court held that due process requires an evidentiary hearing prior to a temporary deprivation. It was emphasized there that welfare assistance is given to persons on the very margin of subsistence. . . .

. . . .

. . . [T]he disabled worker's need is likely to be less than that of a welfare recipient. In addition to the possibility of access to private resources, other forms of government assistance will become available where the termination of disability benefits places a worker or his family below the subsistence level. In view of these potential sources of temporary income, there is less reason here than in *Goldberg* to depart from the ordinary principle, established by our decisions, that something less than an evidentiary hearing is sufficient prior to adverse administrative action.

An additional factor to be considered here is the fairness and reliability of the existing pretermination procedures, and the probable value, if any, of additional procedural safeguards. . . . In order to remain eligible for benefits . . . a medical assessment of the worker's physical or mental condition is required. This is a more sharply focused and easily documented decision than the typical determination of welfare entitlement. . . .

. . . [T]he decision whether to discontinue disability benefits will turn, in most cases, upon "routine, standard, and unbiased medical reports to physician specialists," concerning a subject whom they have personally examined. . . . The potential value of an evidentiary hearing, or even oral presentation to the decision maker, is substantially less in this context than in *Goldberg.*

. . . .

In striking the appropriate due process balance the final factor to be assessed is the public interest. This includes the administrative burden and other societal costs that would be associated with requiring, as a matter of constitutional right, an evidentiary hearing upon demand in all cases prior to the termination of disability benefits. The most visible burden would be the incremental cost resulting from the increased number of hearings and the expense of providing benefits to ineligible recipients pending decision. . . .

. . . [T]he Government's interest and hence that of the public, in conserving scarce fiscal and administrative resources is a factor that must be weighed. At some point the benefit of an additional safeguard to the individual affected by the administrative action and to society in terms of increased assurance that the action is just, may be outweighed by the cost. Significantly, the cost of protecting those whom the preliminary administrative process has identified as likely to be found undeserving may in the end come out of the pockets of the deserving since resources available for any particular program of social welfare are not unlimited.

. . . The ultimate balance involves a determination as to when, under our constitutional system, judicial-type procedures must be imposed upon administrative action to assure fairness. . . . [H]ere, the prescribed procedures not only provide the claimant with an effective process for asserting his claim prior to any administrative action, but also assure a right to an evidentiary hearing, as well as to subsequent judicial review, before the denial of his claim becomes final.

We conclude that an evidentiary hearing is not required prior to the termination of disability benefits and that the present administrative procedures fully comport with due process.

The judgment of the court of Appeals is Reversed.

Case Questions

1. Under what circumstances will a worker be entitled to a hearing before the termination of disability benefits?

2. Does the Eldridge court adequately distinguish welfare entitlement from disability entitlement for purposes of procedural due process?

3. Once a particular interest is determined to be protected by due process, what else needs to be determined and how?

AVAILABILITY. The statutes that delegate power to the agencies generally provide a procedure for appealing their decisions or rules to the court system. Therefore, judicial review is only available if the statute permits it *and* the following tests are met: (1) the plaintiff has the *standing* to sue, (2) the case is *ripe*, and (3) agency remedies have been *exhausted.*

Standing. You will recall from Chapter 4 that the Constitution permits federal courts to hear only cases brought by parties with a personal interest in the outcome. To sue under the Administrative Procedure Act, then, you must also be within the "zone of interests" or class targeted by the statute authorizing the rule or decision that has harmed you. Finally, your injury must be traceable to the agency action, and you must show that a court has the *power* to remedy any harm done. The merits of the case should not influence the judge's decision as to whether you have standing.

Since the late 1960s, standing requirements have been remarkably relaxed, especially in state courts. The result has been a flood of cases concerning consumer, environmental, and housing law. Often, the petitioner for standing in these cases is an organization that claims to act on behalf of a group or the general public. Such claims raise the question of whether the petitioner has a personal or unique interest in the outcome.

In 1975, the Supreme Court denied standing to a group challenging zoning laws that excluded low- and moderate-income persons from a white suburb near Rochester, New York. The justices reasoned that the petitioners, who were not themselves of low or moderate income, did not have a direct, personal stake in the issue. Two years later, however, the Court granted standing to a nonprofit group challenging a zoning law that prevented it from building a low-income housing project. This time, the justices stressed that the group stood to gain from a favorable ruling.

Ripeness. Even after standing has been proven, judicial review may be denied if the court considers the case "unripe." The ripeness requirement is intended to prevent courts from becoming entangled in situations that are still developing.

To determine ripeness, the court must decide whether the issues are fit for review and whether the potential harm from *delaying* a decision is great enough to warrant immediate action. Suppose, for example, you feel so threatened by a new policy that you challenge it in court even though it has not yet been applied to you. In *Abbott Laboratories v. Gardner* (387 U.S. 136 [1967]), the Supreme Court ruled that a drug manufacturer could bring suit to overturn an FDA regulation that had not yet been enforced. According to the Court, the case was ripe because drug manufacturers were already injured: Either they bore the cost of compliance or had already risked prosecution and costly penalties for noncompliance. The risk alone was a hardship.

Exhaustion of Remedies. Judicial review is a last resort. Therefore, unless circumstances make it difficult or harmful to do so, it is only available when the plaintiff has exhausted all avenues for relief within the agency itself. This requirement is implied by the ripeness rule. It recognizes that because Congress expects agencies to exercise their discretion and expertise, they ought to have every chance to do so. An agency decision ought to be the agency's final word as determined by top-level staff before it is scrutinized by a judge. Otherwise, judicial review might be rendered unnecessary by further agency action.

Furthermore, the efficiency, autonomy, and authority of agencies may be undermined by frequent interruptions of their decision-making processes. In fact, one purpose of the exhaustion principle is to prevent plaintiffs from undermining an agency's right to decide certain kinds of cases.

■ Concept Check 6-5   Controlling Agency Action

- In what ways can the executive branch of government oversee federal agencies?
- In what ways can Congress control federal agencies?
- What are the scope and limitations of *judicial review* of agency action?
- Describe the criteria whereby judicial review of agency action is *available.*

210

■ STATE AND LOCAL AGENCIES

Like Congress, state legislatures are under great pressure to give administrators the power to regulate, especially when federal laws are seen as incomplete or inadequate. For instance, environmentalists may demand that state rules be more protective of the environment than federal rules, perhaps by imposing additional penalties for violations.

It should also be noted that one of the ways in which the federal government has been able to camouflage the growth in its own regulatory activities is the shifting of responsibility and workload to state and local governments. For example, about one-fourth of all money spent by state and local governments comes from the federal government. As Figure 6-5 shows, the result has been a dramatic increase in the number of civilian employees on the state and local levels, even when compared to the increase on the federal level. Estimates of the number of jobs all created in state and local government have run as high as 12 million. In addition, the efforts at deregulation by the federal government, especially during the Reagan administration, have put added pressure on state and local governments to carry a heavier burden. As a result, many industries face a greater regulatory threat on the state and local level than on the federal level.

Some of the major areas of state and local agency action are (1) *utilities* or basic services, (2) *education,* (3) *public health, safety,* and *welfare,* (4) *licensing,* and (5) *subsidizing business.*

UTILITIES.   Every state has a utility commission responsible for supervising public utilities such as water plants, electric power companies, railroads, buses, and regional providers of local telephone service. Most utilities are privately owned. However, more than two-thirds of American cities own and operate their own waterworks. There are about one hundred city-owned gas utilities, and an increasing number of cities also run transit systems.

EDUCATION.   Although parents may send their children to approved private schools, every child is entitled to education at the public expense and no child may legally avoid schooling altogether. Education is the single largest cost of

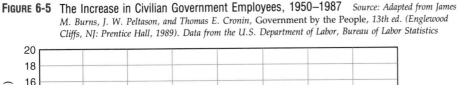
FIGURE 6-5 The Increase in Civilian Government Employees, 1950–1987   *Source: Adapted from James M. Burns, J. W. Peltason, and Thomas E. Cronin, Government by the People, 13th ed. (Englewood Cliffs, NJ: Prentice Hall, 1989). Data from the U.S. Department of Labor, Bureau of Labor Statistics*

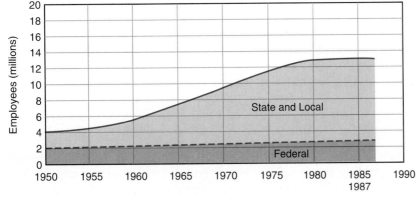

state and local governments, accounting for about thirty-six percent of their spending.

Vast efforts have been made to protect schools from politics by keeping education agencies independent from other parts of government. Every city, county, township, or school district is responsible for providing public education from kindergarten or first grade through twelfth grade. The typical unit is a school district headed by a board of education. The members of the board are elected by the voters at large.

State commissioners of education and boards of education distribute state funds for public schools. Many state education officials certify teachers and set minimum salaries. In some states, districts must conform to courses of study and minimum standards established by state agencies. In some areas of the country, textbooks used in the public schools are often chosen by state officials.

HEALTH, SAFETY, AND WELFARE. State and local governments are primarily responsible for ensuring the public health, safety, and welfare.

Safety. Traffic laws, minimum drinking ages, and penalties for drunken driving are all examples of ways that states protect the public safety. Other law enforcement agencies include state, county, and city police, state liquor-law enforcement officers, state fish and game wardens, and state fire wardens. Some cities and some townships have their own police forces, and some counties have sheriffs and deputies.

Health. Every state has an agency responsible for running a public-health program that supervises programs run by counties, cities, townships, and special health districts. Their purpose is to prevent epidemics and generally maintain a healthy environment.

Welfare. State departments of welfare or human services either directly administer social services programs or supervise the local officials who do. County departments deal with people needing or desiring aid. In fact, welfare programs are the second-largest expenditure for most states, which usually pay for about twenty-five percent of all state social-service costs.

The federal government pays for (1) aid to the aged, blind, and disabled; (2) the Medicare program, which provides health care for the elderly; and (3) the Food Stamp program for the poor. State governments fund and run unemployment-compensation programs, specialized hospitals for the insane or handicapped and caretaking institutions for the poor, and any other assistance needed to supplement federal aid. In addition, the states contribute about twenty percent of the cost of Medicaid (a federal program that delivers free medical care to the poor) and help to pay for Aid to Families with Dependent Children (AFDC).

Working Conditions. State and local regulators also have a large role in regulating labor conditions. Health, building, and labor inspectors visit work sites to see that they fulfill state requirements for lighting, heating, ventilation, fire escapes, and bathrooms. Every state has a program that compensates employees for work-related injuries and illnesses. State law sets the minimum age at which children may begin working (usually at fourteen years). Higher age minimums apply to dangerous jobs. In addition, states supplement federal law with their own rules regarding unions and labor-management relations.

LICENSING. State officials issue charters to corporations and tests to potential drivers before granting licenses. They also license banks, insurance companies, doctors, lawyers, teachers, barbers, and other professionals.

As we saw in *Mathews v. Eldridge,* the Supreme Court recognized that while different situations call for different safeguards, three factors must always be considered: (1) the importance of the individual's interest; (2) the risk of mistake involved in any procedure and the extra security that other procedures would provide; and (3) the impact of the procedure on the government's interest, including the "fiscal and administrative burdens" the procedure would entail.

The case that follows involves an order by a state licensing board revoking a physician's license, the court's reversal of this decision, and the board's subsequent appeal, in which the order was reinstated. The issues here include whether the state board was capricious in its order and whether the original court hearing the case had exceeded its authority in modifying that order.

SLAWEK v. COMMONWEALTH OF PENNSYLVANIA
State Board of Medical Education and Licensure
586 A.2d 362 (Pa. 1991)

An administrative complaint was registered in the State Board of Medical Education and Licensure against Slawek, a physician, in response to his practicing for nine months without medical malpractice insurance in violation of the Pennsylvania Malpractice Act. Following a hearing, the board ordered a three-month revocation of Slawek's license to be followed by probation.

Slawek appealed to the Commonwealth Court, Pennsylvania's appeals court, for review of the board's order. The Commonwealth Court reversed. Following a subsequent appeal by the Board to the ruling of the Commonwealth Court, the case is in the Pennsylvania Supreme Court on the question of the power possessed by an appeals court on review of agency action.

. . . OPINION OF THE COURT
FLAHERTY, Justice

Because of Slawek's failure to secure medical malpractice insurance in a timely fashion, an administrative complaint was filed before the State Board of Medical Education and Licensure for violation of Section 701 of the Health Care Services Malpractice Act. . . .

On remand, Commonwealth Court modified the board's order and removed the suspension. 124 Pa.Cmwlth. 481, 556 A.2d 525. This court then granted the board's petition for allowance of appeal. . . .

[The issue that] Slawek raises on appeal to this court is whether the board abused its discretion in revoking his medical license. As Commonwealth Court correctly stated, the revocation of the license was not an abuse of discretion because the statute requires it. If that is what the case is about, all discussion should end here, for Commonwealth Court properly resolved this question against Slawek below. We believe, however, that a more accurate statement of the question in the case is

that presented by the board: whether Commonwealth Court exceeded its scope of review when it reversed the order of the board revoking Slawek's license for a three-month period.

Section 704 of the Administrative Agency Law, 2 Pa.C.S. 704, sets forth a court's authority on review of an agency decision:

> The court shall hear the appeal without a jury on the record certified by the Commonwealth agency. After hearing, the court shall affirm the adjudication unless it shall find that the adjudication is in violation of the constitutional rights of the appellant, or is not in accordance with law, or that the provisions of subchapter A of Chapter 5 (relating to practice and procedure of Commonwealth agencies) have been violated in the proceedings before the agency, or that any finding of fact made by the agency and necessary to support its adjudication is not supported by substantial evidence.

Act of April 28, 1978, P.L. 202, No. 53, 5.

This standard of review of agency action, which provides that agency action shall be affirmed unless it violates any of the enumerated requirements, is self-explanatory, except, perhaps for the provision that agency action may be reversed in the event that it is "not in accordance with law." This phrase might refer to other applicable statutes or to the common law as it has been established in this court's or the intermediate appellate courts' case law. At a bare minimum, it refers to this court's statement of the broad guidelines governing review of agency decisions. In what is perhaps this court's seminal case on appellate review of administrative decisions, *Blumenschein v. Pittsburgh Housing Authority,* 379 Pa. 566, 572-73, 109 A.2d 331, 334-35 (1954), some rather fundamental principles were established:

By a host of authorities in our own and other jurisdictions it has been established as an elementary principle of law that courts will not review the actions of governmental bodies or administrative tribunals involving acts of discretion, *in the absence of bad faith, fraud, capricious action or abuse of power;* they will not inquire into the wisdom of such actions or into the details of the manner adopted to carry them into execution. It is true that the mere possession of discretionary power by an administrative body does not make it wholly immune from judicial review, but the scope of that review is limited to the determination of whether there has been a manifest and flagrant abuse of discretion or a purely arbitrary execution of the agency's duties or functions. That the court might have a different opinion or judgment in regard to the action of the agency is not a sufficient ground for interference; *judicial* discretion may not be substituted for *administrative* discretion. What this court stated in *Blumenschein* is as valid in 1990 as it was in 1954. In the absence of bad faith, fraud, capricious action or abuse of power, reviewing courts will not inquire into the wisdom of the agency's action or into the details or manner of executing agency action. It is conceivable, of course, that our requirement that the agency not act capriciously might, in a given case, be coterminous with Commonwealth Court's requirement in its *Hendrickson* case that the penalty be reasonable in light of the violation. As a general rule, however, Commonwealth Court's statement of its rule is overbroad in that it invites the court to substitute its view of what is reasonable for that of the agency. For that reason, we believe that the proper review of the agency's action, assuming that it is not defective under the self-explanatory requirements of the Administrative Agency Law, is not whether its order was reasonable, but whether it was made in "accordance with law" (i.e., whether it was made in bad faith, and whether it was fraudulent or capricious). As the *Blumenschein* court put it, a reviewing court may interfere in an agency decision only when "there has been a manifest and flagrant abuse of discretion or a purely arbitrary execution of the agency's duties or functions." Since there is no allegation of fraud or bad faith—also mentioned *supra* by *Blumenschein*—our inquiry in this case resolves itself into whether the agency's action was capricious or a flagrant abuse of discretion.

[4] The board justified its decision as follows:

The Board's burden is to craft a disciplinary order that takes into account mitigating factors, yet, deter others from engaging in similar conduct, and maintains public confidence in the integrity of the medical profession. If there was a market for professional liability insurance which covers a past uninsured period, the Board would order that the Respondent's license be revoked and that after a designated active period of revocation, the revocation be stayed if and when the Board would receive evidence that such insurance was secured. However, the Board recognizes that it is extremely difficult, and perhaps impossible, to find an insurance carrier that will write insurance to cover a past uninsured period. Alternatively, the Respondent could self-insure his liability for the presently uninsured nine-month period of his practice, but the Board recognizes that this is a prohibitively costly alternative. Consequently, the Board has decided to issue an order which will preclude the Respondent from practicing medicine for a brief time, but which does not require him to cure his past insurance violation as a pre-condition to returning to practice.

Adjudication and Order, The State Board of Medicine, 10.

Slawek practiced medicine for a nine-month period without securing professional malpractice insurance in blatant violation of law. The board considered mitigating factors, viz., that Slawek was "thrust into a situation where he unexpectedly had to supply medical services," Board's Adjudication at 9, and was mindful of its duty to deter others who might wish to engage in similar irresponsible conduct. It is self-evident that the board's decision was not capricious or a flagrant abuse of discretion, and it is not for this court or any reviewing court to substitute its judgment of what is reasonable for that of the agency whose decision is being reviewed.

Commonwealth Court's approach, left unchecked, would swallow up the whole system of administrative adjudications, in which administrative bodies having expertise in specific areas of law are entrusted to fashion administrative remedies that are fair and appropriate. Absent abuses of the sort specified in the Administrative Agency Law or *Blumenschein,* appellate courts should exercise judicial restraint in reviewing administrative orders.

The Order of Commonwealth Court is reversed and the order of the State Board of Medicine is reinstated.

Case Questions

1. What well-established principle does the Slawek court apply with regard to the authority possessed by an appeals court on review of agency action? Did the Pennsylvania Supreme Court find that the Commonwealth Court had exceeded its authority?

2. Do you think that the standard of review articulated in Slawek gives agencies too much power?

3. If the agency order in Slawek was permanent revocation, how might the Commonwealth Court have held?

SUBSIDIZING BUSINESS. More and more state and local governments across the nation are exempting businesses from taxes. They may also provide low-cost loans, donate land for buildings, or float industrial bonds to help finance new operations. For instance, when the U.S. Department of the Navy was seeking a home port for its battleship *Wisconsin* and other ships, it chose Corpus Christi after the state of Texas pledged $25 million and the people of Corpus Christi pledged to raise another $25 million through a bond issue.

The purpose of such incentives is attract, keep, and develop local businesses that will provide jobs and enhance an area's tax base. State commerce or development departments also frequently provide management assistance to local firms, job training, and help in obtaining private financing or federal contracts. Half of the states provide direct financing for new firms through state employee pension funds or public nonprofit companies.

■ Concept Check 6-6   State and Local Agencies

- What are the major areas of state and local regulatory action? Discuss reasons why state and local regulatory agencies are so active in these areas.
- Give some examples of administrative agencies in your own state. Describe the regulatory areas in which they are active.

■ REFORMING AGENCY ACTION

The reform of federal agency action is always a topic of concern among the interested parties—the bureaucrats themselves, the executive branch, Congress, and the various constituencies affected by agency rules. The impetus for reform has included such motives as increasing or decreasing the regulation of business, increasing government efficiency, righting wrongs when the marketplace has been unable to do so itself, and the conservative political principle of a hands-off government when it comes to the economy.

Regulation versus Deregulation

Regulatory policies of the federal government can often be explained by one or more of the following six reasons: *politics, morality, efficiency, convenience, risk reduction,* and *equity.* For example, the goal of market efficiency accounts in part for the breakup of AT&T in 1983—a case of *deregulation.* The many regulations of the Equal Employment Opportunity Commission were promulgated with the aim of social equity.[8]

In the 1960s and 1970s, the movement for social regulation changed the rules of the game for almost all businesses. First, the number of rules increased. The *Federal Register,* never a thin book, grew immensely fatter. Its pages doubled to 20,000 between 1955 and 1970; by 1980, it filled 87,012 pages. Some 41,000 federal and state rules deal with hamburgers alone. When Congress considered changing the legally defined term "mobile home" to "manufactured housing," the lawmakers were told that four federal laws, 36 regulations, 15 interpretative bulletins, 36 state pacts, 27 monitoring contracts, and the laws and rules of 35 states would need revision.[9]

---

[8] Theodore J. Lowi and Benjamin Ginsburg, *American Government* (New York: W.W. Norton, 1990), pp. 677, 679.

[9] John Hyson and William Bolce, *Business and Its Environment* (Minneapolis, MN: West, 1983), pp. 314, 319.

Too often, many observers felt, the real impact of social regulation was higher costs for everyone. Murray Weidenbaum, President Reagan's first chairman of the Council of Economic Advisors, puts the private cost at $20 for each dollar appropriated for regulation—or twenty times $7 to $8 billion.[10]

ECONOMIC DEREGULATION.   Purely economic regulation has also come under criticism—primarily for discouraging competition. That is why Presidents Ford, Carter, and Reagan all took important steps to promote **deregulation** and regulatory reform. The basic argument for deregulation is that when businesses must adapt themselves to politically imposed requirements, they become less able to serve their basic economic function: supplying goods and services at the lowest price. Many chief executive officers claim, for example, that they spend one-third of their time dealing with government regulation. If that is so, they had one-third less time to make their businesses more profitable and productive. Other reasons in favor of deregulation include the following arguments:

deregulation The removal of economic and federal regulations governing business in order to promote expansion and control consumer prices

- The more independence a business has, the more creative it is.
- Regulations lead business to be more conservative about expansion.
- Regulations raise consumer prices by making new competition difficult and by protecting weak competitors already in the industry.

The actual legislation enacted in the Ford and Carter administrations to deregulate business included the following: the Securities Act Amendments of 1975, the Airline Deregulation Act of 1978, and the Motor Carrier Act of 1980. In fact, President Ford took one of the first steps toward deregulation in 1974 by ordering agencies to consider the inflationary aspects of new rules. Then, in 1980, President Carter created a Regulatory Analysis Review Group to study the impact that new rules would have on the economy.

Under President Reagan, who took office opposed to economic intervention both through efforts to promote commerce and through efforts to regulate business, a practice called "regulation management," rather than elimination of agencies, became the preferred tool of deregulation.[11] Reagan's approach was to weaken federal regulatory agencies both by cutting budgets and staff and by appointing commissioners unsympathetic or even hostile to agency mandates. He also instituted a new review process for agencies under the Office of Management and Budget—an action that had the effect of shrinking the number of new regulations proposed.[12] In addition, Reagan sought to shift the burden of regulation to the states.

Table 6-1 is a selected listing of some of the efforts of the Reagan administration to eliminate federal programs and activities, partially by selling some public services to private industry. Not all of these proposals, of course, were enacted by Congress. It is interesting to note that despite an announced intention to deregulate numerous business activities, the administration largely drew up short of attempting to terminate regulatory programs. In practice, "regulation management" was more a matter of reducing the number of regulations and tempering the vigor of regulatory rule making and enforcement.

During President Bush's administration, proposals have been made to de-

[10] Murray L. Weidenbaum, "The Changing Nature of Government Regulation of Business," *Journal of Post Keynesian Economics* (Spring, 1980) in Thomas R. Swartz and Frank J. Bonello, eds., *Taking Sides: Clashing Views on Controversial Economic Issues* (Dushkin, 1983), p. 80.

[11] *See* Lowi and Ginsburg, p. 671.

[12] *Ibid.* at p. 672, 673, 674.

TABLE 6-1	*Selected Proposals for Eliminating or Privatizing Federal Programs during the Reagan Administration*
PROPOSALS	**PROGRAMS**
Termination proposals	*Regulatory Programs:* Interstate Commerce Commission.
	Service and Patronage Programs: Agency for International Development housing guarantees; commercial fishing industry assistance; Community Services and Urban Redevelopment block grants; energy conservation grants; EPA loans for asbestos removal; Farmers Home Administration housing and rural-aid programs; GI enhanced recruitment; postal service subsidy; railroad rehabilitation loans; rail service assistance to states; revenue sharing; Rural Electrification Administration; Small Business Administration credit assistance programs; State Student Incentive Grants.
	Welfare and Education Programs: scholarships to encourage teaching; categorical aid to migrant health centers, black-lung clinics, and family-planning clinics; college housing loans; graduate education programs; HUD grants for rental housing; Legal Services Corporation; library aid; Work Incentive Program (WIN) for AFDC recipients.
Privatization proposals	*Service and Patronage Programs:* Power Marketing Administrations (sell the power-generating and transmission facilities, but not the dams); naval petroleum reserves (sell the oil fields at Elk Hills, Calif., and Teapot Dome, Wyo.); compensatory education (provide vouchers for disadvantaged children, to be spent on private schooling); housing vouchers (provide housing vouchers in place of federally supported housing assitance); Amtrak (sell passenger rail service to private business, or to states or localities).

Source: Congressional Quarterly Almanac, *1986.*

crease federal regulation further as a means of reviving a national economy in the midst of a recession. Reasoning that some regulations and rules were burdensome to business, Bush maintained that without the imposition of new regulations in the short term, the economy would have the opportunity to flourish.

Reform and Regulation: The Future

Proposals to reform agencies continue to abound. Managerial reforms might include attracting better employees, cutting paperwork and delays, and improving coordination among agencies. Congress might also exercise tighter oversight by providing for **zero-based budgeting,** which would force the agencies to justify their entire budgets, rather than only proposed increases each and every year.

Another proposal for reforming the agencies would be to establish **sunset laws** that would require each agency to undergo periodic reviews to assess its effectiveness; if an agency should fail the review, it could be abolished. This method would address the problem of bureaucratic growth and stagnation, although not necessarily the issue of agency responsiveness. One device suggested to remedy this problem is the **ombudsman**—a citizen advocate whose role is to intervene for citizens with the bureaucracy in order to get grievances heard and to seek redress for them.

Recent reforms have increased executive control of agencies while limiting the scope of regulation. For example, the securities, banking, airline, trucking, railroad, and telephone industries were largely deregulated during the

zero-based budgeting Congressional requirement that administrative agencies justify their entire budgets annually

sunset laws Form of proposed agency reform in which laws would require every agency to undergo public assessment reviews

ombudsman Advocate who intervenes for citizens with the beauracracy in order to get grievances heard and to seek redress

1970s and early 1980s. Has deregulation succeeded? The answer depends upon who the beneficiaries are. In industries in which prices have been slashed, workers have been forced to accept pay cuts. In other industries, deregulation has created opportunities for enterprising newcomers (for instance, long-distance telephone companies like US Sprint and MCI).

Consumers have lost or gained from deregulation depending upon what they buy. Banks and thrift institutions, for instance, now compete hotly to offer the most attractive high-interest checking accounts. Customers with small deposits, however, have suffered because of higher fees for routine services, like processing bounced checks.

■ Concept Check 6-7   Reforming Agency Action

- Why has it been so difficult to make major changes in federal administrative agencies?
- Describe the role of the Carter, Reagan, and Bush administrations in the move toward *deregulation*.

YOU DECIDE: ANSWER/DISCUSSION
The Orphan Drug Act

In 1990, Congress passed revisions to the Orphan Drug Act of 1983. President Bush, however, vetoed them, maintaining that drug companies would not be inclined to develop orphan drugs if they lost the privilege of exclusivity. Nevertheless, the issues remain with us and require discussion on an ongoing basis.

AIDS activist groups, for example, are among the strongest proponents of changes in the law. They argue that without a monopoly, the high prices of drugs that fight AIDS could be lowered. They also contend that since AIDS cases passed the 200,000 threshold in 1992, it is no longer a "rare" disease and that the drugs that fight it should no longer be given market protection. For example, one drug that fights an AIDS-related pneumonia costs about $2400 a year; its manufacturer, Lymphomed, won the exclusivity race and got orphan-drug status first. However, another company, Fisons, produces a similar drug; activists would like to see that drug marketed as well in the hope that competition would bring prices down. Obviously, Fisons and biotechnology firms developing drugs for other rare diseases favor shared-market access so that they can profit as well.

The key issues, then, revolve around matters of protection, profits, and price. To benefit the public interest at large, we must determine, according to the AMA, "how to

maintain the balance of protecting R&D investments while fostering development competition." Such a balance, suggests one of the Congressional sponsors of the revisions to the 1983 Act, should involve retaining "incentives for most orphan drugs [while providing] more competition in the case of 'extremely profitable' drugs"—that is, those in which the pharmaceutical industry would invest R&D money even without the Orphan Drug Act.

In the past, the issue of orphan-drug prices has mostly involved one's ability to pay, an ethical issue in itself. However, third parties, such as insurance companies and the government, have now assumed more of the payments for prescription drugs. The public, therefore, is now "paying" more—even beyond the tax-credit advantage given to manufacturers. The prices of orphan drugs have thus become a more general matter of public concern. Is the cost becoming too high for the public to bear?

Finally, the social benefits of protecting the development of orphan drugs are a factor in any evaluation. Allowing people with rare diseases to participate fully in society and the possibility of lowering society's health-care costs are two such benefits. Whether they outweigh the costs must be considered as the Orphan Drug Act of 1983 is continuously reassessed.

SUMMARY

- *Administrative agencies,* often described as an informal "fourth branch" of government combine legislative, executive, and judicial powers. The two categories of administrative agencies are *executive agencies* and *independent agencies* and *govern-*

ment corporations. Congress delegates its power to agencies when it lacks the time or expertise to delve into details.

- Laws dealing with *delegating statutes* attempt to resolve conflicts between the need to delegate on the one hand and the need to preserve the Constitution's formal arrangement of powers on the other.

- The history of federal agencies is largely a history of increasing government regulation of the marketplace. Agencies created before and during the New Deal tend to regulate specific industries. In the 1960s and 1970s, Congress set up agencies that attempted to achieve social goals by cutting across industry lines, unlike earlier agencies, whose actions focused on the *economic regulation* of the private sector. The recognition of *market failure*—manifest in the marketplace by *destructive competition, inadequate information,* and *externalities*—is one source of the government's efforts at regulation. Business and government can be adversaries, but the U.S. government also supports business in many ways.

- Congress transfers power of self-rule to federal administrative agencies in the form of *delegating statutes.* As this power is expressed in action relating to business, agencies either support business or work to restrain and control it. The Food and Drug Administration is an example of the latter efforts.

- The *Administrative Procedures Act of 1946* outlines the process for *informal rule making* (or *notice-and-comment rule making*), *formal rule making,* and *formal adjudication,* all of which cover only a small fraction of agency actions. Formal adjudication remedies past wrongdoing by settling factual disputes between individuals. Rule making applies to the future and to the public at large, but adjudication also produces general policy because each case sets a precedent. Many scholars think that it would promote fairness and efficiency if the older agencies relied more on rule making and less on adjudication. Agency-made procedures that provide for due process constitute the remaining ninety percent of agency actions.

- All three formal branches of government control the "fourth branch." The president runs executive agencies by appointing and removing executive officials, reorganizing the structure of the executive branch with the consent of Congress, issuing executive orders, wielding substantial fiscal power, and controlling litigation on behalf of agencies. The fifty-seven independent agencies and government corporations are protected from executive control. However, all agencies receive both their political authority and their budgets from Congress, which controls them in four basic ways: control over budgets, the power to withdraw or modify operating authority, and direct oversight of agency action.

- Nearly all the decisions and rules that federal agencies make can be appealed to the federal courts. Federal courts, however, usually judge questions only of law, not questions of fact, and they consider only cases that meet the tests of *standing, ripeness,* and *exhaustion.* When the federal courts do try cases arising from agency action or failure to act, they can compel action or set aside agency action that has been ruled *arbitrary, unconstitutional,* or *unwarranted.*

- Major areas covered by state and local agency action include utilities and such basic services as education, public health, welfare, and business subsidy. State legislatures are often under citizen pressure to grant these agencies more regulatory power. It has been widely charged that the federal government can and does conceal its regulatory activity behind the transfer of power and responsibility to state and local agencies.

- Federal agency reform, an ongoing issue and concern encompasses the ongoing debate between the virtues of *regulation* versus *deregulation* and has produced such proposals for reform as *zero-based budgeting, sunset laws,* and *ombudsmen.*

QUESTIONS AND PROBLEMS

1. Sheila Jones is notified that she is about to have her Social Security benefits terminated. The notification further informs her that she has the right to a hearing regarding the termination. She responds to the notice by requesting a hearing and jury trial. What response will be forthcoming?

2. The Food and Drug Administration (FDA) is an executive branch agency that is part of the U.S. Department of Health and Human Services. Assume that it has issued decisions and rulings over the past 18 months which are at odds with the President's position on such matters. What controls can the President exercise regarding the agency?

3. OSHA is under pressure from anti-smoking groups to take positive steps to ban or limit smoking in the nation's workplaces. The EPA is completing a revised study on passive tobacco smoke that shows, that about 3700 deaths annually are the result of cancer caused by workplace smoke. The EPA will suggest some voluntary guideliness to OSHA for handling workplace smoking. If OSHA bans smoking in the workplace across the US, and a group of disgruntled employees files suit in Federal Court, discuss the scope and availability of judicial review.

4. One of the hottest business issues today is the outrageousness of CEO pay in regards to corporate profits. In 1990, United Airlines' CEO got $18.3 million—1200 times what a new flight attendant makes, even though United profits had fallen by 71%! The Interstate Commerce Commission would like to regulate CEO pay. Discuss.

5. The Federal Trade Commission (FTC) institutes proceedings against The Soft Drink Bottling Co. (Soft Drink Bottling) alleging violations of laws prohibiting unfair methods of competition. The complaint against Soft Drink Bottling challenges the validity of exclusive bottling agreements between Soft Drink Bottling and franchised bottlers who have agreed not to sell the company's products outside a designated territory. Soft Drink Bottling asks the FTC to include the 513 bottlers in the case. When FTC refuses to do so on the ground that the case would be unmanageable, although any bottlers who wish to may intervene in the case, Soft Drink Bottling appeals the decision to the federal court. Will the court entertain the action? [*Pepsico, Inc. v. Federal Trade Commission*, 343 F. Supp. 396 (1972)]

6. The Department of Health and Rehabilitative Services (HRS) files a complaint against Nursing Home, Inc., and its director, Noel Brown, for failure to comply with certain nursing home rules and regulations. In the administrative documents filed by their representative, it becomes apparent that the representative is not admitted to the practice of law in the state. HRS objects to this in proceedings before the administrative law judge and alleges that since a corporation cannot represent itself, it must have a licensed attorney to do so. How will the judge rule? [*Magnolia Nursing and Convalescent Center v. Department of Rehabilitative Services, Office of Licensure and Certification*, 428 So. 2d 256 (Fla. 1982)]

7. During a Department of Health adjudicatory hearing regarding whether a local restaurant's license should be suspended for failure to meet health code standards, Anne Lyons, an employee, testifies that she was told by one of the night workers that the owner of the restaurant had given the order not to throw away uneaten bread and rolls from customers' plates. The owner's legal counsel objects to this evidence on the grounds that it is hearsay and therefore inadmissible at the hearing. Is she correct?

8. The Soybean Development Agency (SDA) does not provide its grant applicants with the amount of research and development money Congress thinks it should for several years in a row. It also refuses to take an aggressive stand regarding the development of new uses for soybeans. Congress then notifies SDA that in 60 days it will withdraw SDA's power to grant funding. The SDA protests this move and says that it is an unwarranted strongarm tactic by Congress to get it to bend to Congress's will. If SDA sues for injunctive relief to prevent the removal of its grant-funding power, will its position be sustained in court?

9. Jack Castro is an Alaskan king crab and deep sea scallop catcher. He is caught without the proper protective equipment on his boat and is given a citation for violation of the appropriate rule. The rule was duly enacted after an appropriate notice and comment period in the *Federal Register* and publication of the final version of the

rule in the *Federal Register*. Mr. Castro opposes the citation on the basis that he never knew of the rule and it is a denial of his Constitutional right to due process for the agency to pass a rule without his knowing about it personally, since it affects him so closely. Is there any legal validity to his argument?

10. The Secretary of Commerce under the Flammable Fabrics Act issued a flammability standard which required mattresses, including crib mattresses, to pass a cigarette test, that consisted of bringing a mattress in contact with a burning cigarette. The petitioner, Bunny Bear, Inc. challenges the ruling as arbitrary and capricious because children do not smoke. Will this rule be overturned on appeal? [*Bunny Bear, Inc., v. Peterson*, 473 F.2d 1002 (1973)]

7

FORMS OF BUSINESS ORGANIZATION

Businesses are created because someone thinks he or she can offer needed goods or services at a profit. The success of a business depends upon the entrepreneur's savvy in correctly perceiving the existence of such a need and his ability to fill it.

An enterprise's success is also dependent on the *form* in which it does business. Contrary to popular belief, a firm's *size* does not dictate its form: A multimillion-dollar hardware store may be run as a sole proprietorship while a "mom-and-pop" grocery may be incorporated. The extent of the owner's personal liability, control over day-to-day operations, and share of the profits are some of the issues that affect the organizational form that is best for a given business.

Sole proprietorships, general and limited partnerships, and *corporations* are the most common forms of business enterprises. Surprisingly, sole proprietorships and partnerships outnumber corporations in the United States. Corporations, however, earn the most income.

The choice of a legal business form should not be approached lightly. The owner should carefully weigh the advantages and disadvantages associated with each option with the help of an attorney and an accountant. For example, although sole proprietorships are easy to form and dissolve, a sole proprietor also faces unlimited liability for all business debts—that is, the proprietor faces losing personal assets to pay off the enterprise's debts. On the other hand, with few exceptions, corporate stockholders are not personally responsible for corporate debts.

■ AGENCY LAW

It is a rare business in which the owner does everything. Even in small businesses, people other than the owner carry out critical functions. For example, the office manager of a small firm may be responsible for ordering supplies. In even a small retail firm, sales clerks assist customers and make sales. In each of these examples, the firm's owner (the **principal**) has authorized another person (the **agent**) to conduct business on his behalf. Agents must take direction on all matters from the principal. (Thus, they are different from *independent contractors*, who are vested with significant control over the manner in which they produce desired results.)

The delegation of authority from the principal to the agent is both the cornerstone of conducting business and the source of many problems. For example, what recourse do principals have if agents cast aside their interests in pursuit of their own ends? Are principals responsible for their agents' careless or illegal acts? Are agents authorized to sign contracts on behalf of the principal bound by the contract if the owner defaults? The law of agency addresses these issues for all business forms in which principals and agents operate.

The Nature of the Agency Relationship

An **agency relationship** is defined in the American Law Institute's *Restatement of Agency* as "the fiduciary relation which results from the manifestation of consent by one person to another that the other shall act on his behalf and subject to his control, and consent by the other so to act." In other words, an agency relationship is created whenever two parties agree that one (the agent) will be trusted to act as a representative of the other (the principal). In the examples noted earlier, the office manager is an agent authorized to represent the owner for purposes of procuring office supplies; as agents, sales clerks have the power to act on behalf of store owners in dealing with customers and consummating sales.

AGENCY AGREEMENTS. Agency relationships are formed by the mutual agreement of the principal and agent. With limited exceptions, the creation of an agency relationship need not be in writing. Assume, for example, that Alan, the owner of a taxi fleet, hires Bob as a driver. Alan and Bob will probably not enter into a formal agreement that spells out each party's duties to the other. Nevertheless, by voluntarily entering into the relationship, Alan and Bob are subject to common-law agency doctrines that govern both parties' rights and obligations. In addition, because Alan and Bob are employer and employee, certain terms of their relationship may be covered by legislation, such as minimum-wage laws (*see* Chapter 14).

Because a written instrument is not required, how do we know when an agency has been created? Generally, any words or actions by the principal and agent that indicate that the agent agrees to act on the principal's behalf are sufficient to create an agency.

Because agency relationships are consensual, they may be terminated at any time by either party. However, there may be undesirable consequences for the terminating party. For example, an employer who fires an employee in violation of an antidiscrimination law will be held legally liable. In addition, the law stipulates that agency relationships end automatically upon the occurrence of certain events. For example, the relationship automatically terminates if the principal or agent dies or becomes insane.

Agency Obligations

PRINCIPALS' OBLIGATIONS TO AGENTS. Unless the agency is gratuitous, the principal must compensate the agent for his performance. The amount of compensation is usually established when the relationship is created. The principal also must

principal Person who authorizes another person (an *agent*) to conduct business on his or her behalf

agent Person authorized by another person (a *principal*) to conduct business on his or her behalf

agency relationship Fiduciary relationship resulting from a mutual agreement between *principal* and *agent* to act in the conduct of business

reimburse the agency for any reasonable expenses or losses incurred during the course of conducting the principal's business. For example, assume that Taxidriver B paid $25 to repair a flat tire that occurred while he was cruising for fares: Because the cost was incurred within the scope of the agency activities, Fleetowner A must reimburse the driver. If the flat had occurred while Taxidriver B was using the taxi to take his wife to the doctor, however, the cost of the repair would not be reimbursed.

AGENTS' OBLIGATIONS TO PRINCIPALS. A fiduciary relationship is based upon trust and confidence. As **fiduciaries** of their principals, agents owe a wide range of duties:

- *Loyalty*: Even though each party has a different stake in the principal's business, the agent is expected to act in the principal's best interest.
- *Exercise of skill and care*: The agent is required to perform his responsibilities while using the same degree of caution and skill used by others in the community who are performing the same type of work; this duty extends to the principal's property and to third parties.
- *Obedience*: The agent is required to follow the principal's instructions concerning the performance of the services that he or she was retained to deliver.
- *Accountability*: The agent is responsible for all money and other property belonging to the principal that is in the agent's possession or control; the agent must keep records of these items and all transactions entered into on the principal's behalf; there must be no comingling of funds.
- *Conveyance of information that impacts on the principal's business*: This duty is particularly important because the law imputes the agent's knowledge to the principal.

Agents are generally liable for any losses incurred by their failure to perform their duties adequately. The following case illustrates the fiduciary duties of an agent.

FAULTERSACK v. CLINTONVILLE SALES CORPORATION
Wisconsin Supreme Court, 253 Wis. 432, 34 N.W.2d 682
(1948)

The defendant, Clintonville Sales Corporation, is a Wisconsin corporation. The plaintiffs are Walter Faultersack and his wife, Leona Faultersack. On March 18, 1946, the plaintiffs entered into a written contract with the defendant to conduct an auction sale to sell plaintiffs' farm and personal property. The farm was encumbered by a mortgage and other liens totaling approximately $6250.

Pursuant to the contract, the defendant was to advertise, hold an auction sale, pay the auctioneer and real estate broker, and account to the plaintiffs for the balance of the proceeds of the sale. The plaintiffs were to pay for the advertising and to pay the defendant a commission of ten percent of the proceeds. Prior to the auction, Arthur Umland, president of Clintonville Sales Corporation, arranged to make a loan to Frank Challoner, if needed, to enable Challoner to bid on the plaintiffs'

farm at the sale. The arrangement consisted of a loan, secured by a mortgage on Challoner's personal property, and an additional loan secured by the plaintiffs' farm. Umland did not disclose this fact to the plaintiffs at any time before or during the sale.

At the auction Walter Faultersack informed Umland, as auctioneer, that he would not sell the farm for a price less than the amount of the mortgage. The farm was finally sold to Frank Challoner for $6250. After deducting the commission and the cost of the advertising, the defendant gave Faultersack the net proceeds from the sale of the farm and the personal property. Faultersack rejected the sale of the real estate and demanded the refund of the commission retained by defendant for the sale of the real estate. Defendant refused to comply with the demands.

The plaintiffs brought this action to recover $625, which the plaintiffs claim the defendant wrongfully retains as commission. The trial court found that a valid and binding sale had been made; that Frank Challoner was the highest bidder and his bid had been accepted by the plaintiffs; that, since the defendant had fulfilled the terms of its contract in obtaining a buyer who was and is ready and willing to buy the property, it was entitled to the commission provided for in the contract. The plaintiff appeals.

Fairchild, Justice.

The difficulty with the judgment entered at the circuit is that it overlooks the rule that the auctioneer loses his right to compensation by assuming a position inconsistent with his fiduciary relation as agent of the seller.

The auctioneer is deemed to be the agent of the seller. He can be the agent of both parties only for certain limited purposes such as the signing of the contract of sale. . . . Until the hammer goes down, the auctioneer is exclusively the agent of the vendor is the way the authorities have generally stated the rule.

. . . .

An agent's duties require a full disclosure of all facts that have a material bearing on the subject of the agency. Especially is he bound to disclose acts that have a tendency to favor the other party as against the principal. Acts which may directly limit or chill a bid at an auction are within that category. Here the arrangement between Umland, the defendant's president, and one Challoner, the proposed bidder, certainly had a relation to the subject of the agency. It contained elements directly affecting the agent's attitude toward and his activities in respect to the sale of the plaintiffs' farm.

Challoner did not have the means to meet the obligations of a good faith bidder, ready, able, and willing to buy. He sought defendant's help. . . . There was to be a loan secured by a chattel mortgage on Challoner's personal property and an additional loan to be secured by a mortgage on the plaintiff's farm. This was not disclosed to plaintiffs at any time prior to or during the auction. However, it affected the sale of the farm. . . .

. . . Umland did not tell plaintiffs that one of the bidders was able to bid only because defendant would assist with a loan toward the purchase price and that the amount of his bid would depend on what defendant would loan him. Instead Umland went back to the auction block and sold the farm to Challoner at a price below that which plaintiffs had specified. It may be that plaintiffs agreed to let the farm go at that price. But had they known all the circumstances connected with the bid there is good reason to conclude that they would have rejected it.

. . . .

This failure to disclose facts on the part of the defendant's officers amounted to a breach of the fiduciary relationship existing between the defendant and the plaintiffs. In the absence of full disclosure of the facts to the principal he can refuse to pay the commission or recover a commission already paid. Plaintiffs are entitled to judgment in their favor as prayed for in their complaint.

Case Questions

1. Explain the fiduciary relationship between the plaintiff and the defendant. How did the defendant breach his fiduciary duty to the plaintiffs?

2. Specifically, what facts should defendant have disclosed to the plaintiffs in connection with the sale of the farm?

3. Why does it matter that an agent owe some fiduciary or "special" duty to a principal?

PRINCIPALS' OBLIGATIONS TO THIRD PARTIES

Contracts. Under agency law, principals are bound by contracts (*see* Chapter 9) entered into on their behalf by their agents. When an agent who has the *express, implied,* or *apparent authority* to make contracts reaches an agreement with a third party, an enforceable contract exists between the principal and the third party: It is as if the principal and the third party had themselves negotiated and agreed to the contract.

- **Express authority** consists of oral or written instructions from the principal giving the agent the right to sign contracts on his behalf.
- **Implied authority** is the automatic authority granted to agents to perform functions that are customarily an incident of their job. For example, if the owner of a department store expressly authorizes an employee to sign contracts to purchase furniture for sale in the store, then that employee has the implied authority to enter into a contract with a trucking company to deliver furniture to the store. Such contracts would be viewed as a *necessary incident* of his job as a furniture buyer. Taken together, express authority and implied authority are known as *actual authority*.

express authority Oral or written instructions authorizing an *agent* to sign contracts on the behalf of a *principal*

implied authority Automatic authority granted to an *agent* when performing customary aspects of a job for a *principal*

apparent authority Authority binding a *principal* to an *agent's* contract if a third party has cause to believe that an *agency relationship* existed

• **Apparent authority** is the authority that binds principals to agents' contracts if the principal's own words or conduct caused a third party to believe that the agent had the authority to contract on his behalf. For example, suppose that the owner of a trucking firm fired a driver on Friday but permitted that driver to use a truck emblazoned with the company's name during the following weekend. Say that the truck breaks down on Saturday and the driver takes it to the service station where the owner maintains an account. The driver then signs the owner's name to the repair bill. The service station can collect from the owner under the doctrine of apparent authority because the termination of *actual* authority did not terminate *apparent* authority. (However, because the agency relationship had terminated by the time the truck was repaired, the owner can then sue the driver to recover any monies paid to the service station.)

In the following case, a retailer brought a breach-of-contract action against a seller to recover damages that resulted when the seller failed to ship orders. This issue was whether the seller's salesman had actual and apparent authority to bind the principal to an enforceable contract.

MIGEROBE, INC. v. CERTINA USA, INC.
United States Court of Appeals, Fifth Circuit 924 F.2d 1330 (1991)

Plaintiff-Appellee, Migerobe, Inc., owns and operates jewelry counters in McRae's department stores. Defendant-Appellant Certina USA is a watch manufacturer in Lancaster, Pennsylvania. Migerobe brought action against Certina to recover for breach of contract for refusal to ship an order of watches. The jury verdict below held that Certina had breached an oral contract to deliver watches to Migerobe. Certina appeals.

Thornberry, Circuit Judge:

. . .

Certina sells its watches through the efforts of traveling salesmen, who are either salaried employees of Certina or independent representatives paid on a commission basis. Gerald Murff was one such representative. . . . Migerobe contacted Murff to notify him that Migerobe would be interested in buying Certina watches if the company decided to sell a large portion of its inventory at reduced prices. . . .

In a letter dated September 14, 1987, Murff responded to Migerobe's request, saying that he was "pursuing a special price on the Certina inventories on [Migerobe's] behalf" and that he would keep the company informed of his progress. . . . At the time, Murff was attempting to negotiate a special discounted price with Certina's vice president of retail sales, William Wolfe. On October 21, 1987, Wolfe provided Murff with a list of watches from Certina's inventory that Murff could offer to Migerobe at a price of forty-five dollars each. Murff scheduled an October 29 meeting with Migerobe to present the offer. Prior to this meeting, Murff requested and received an additional list of watches from Wolfe, which were to be included in the offer to Migerobe.

Murff kept his October 29 appointment with Miger-

obe. During the course of the day, Murff made several phone calls to Certina's home office in Lancaster, Pennsylvania, to verify the number of watches in Certina's inventory, and to secure specific payment terms. After a full day of negotiating for particular quantities and styles as well as payment terms and a shipping date, Migerobe agreed to purchase over 2000 Certina watches at a price of forty-five dollars each. Murff phoned Certina's Lancaster office one final time to report the sale, and Wolfe's administrative assistant recorded it onto a Certina order form.

On November 4, 1987, Certina's national accounts manager, Don Olivett, called Migerobe to say that Certina would not ship the watches that had been ordered on October 29. The president of Certina, John Gelson, later explained that the order was being rejected because the offered price was lower than that offered to other customers, and he feared that the offer might constitute a violation of the Robinson-Patman Act. Migerobe brought suit in district court for repudiation of the contract and, after a five-day trial, a jury awarded it $157,133. . . .

Certina filed a timely appeal. Certina urges us to reverse the district court based on several alleged errors. . . . [Among these] it argues that Migerobe presented insufficient evidence to establish that Certina's salesman acted with actual, implied, or apparent authority in contracting for the sale of watches. Finally, Certina argues that Migerobe presented insufficient evidence to establish that Certina's failure to deliver the requested watches caused Migerobe to suffer a loss in corollary sales. . . .

We use a deferential standard to determine whether the jury could have found that Murff had authority to contract with Migerobe for the sale of Certina watches. We will not overrule the findings of the jury unless the facts and inferences point so strongly in favor of Certina that a reasonable jury could not have arrived at a verdict to the contrary.

Actual authority may be express or implied. "It is deemed express if granted in either written or oral specific terms." It is deemed implied if the authority is a necessary or incidental part of the express authority.

The sale of Certina watches to Migerobe developed over a time frame of at least six weeks. During that time, Murff discussed the Migerobe sale with William Wolfe, Certina's vice president of retail sales, and Wolfe, ultimately, provided him with a list of Certina watches to offer Migerobe. Wolfe's follow-up memo to R. B. Oliver, Certina's chief financial officer, confirmed that "Jerry Murff ha[d] been authorized to sell" the watches. Based on these facts, a reasonable jury could easily conclude that Murff had been given express authority to conduct this particular transaction.

Murff's express authority was supplemented by the implied authority to do that which would be proper, usual and necessary for an agent in the exercise of his express authority. In negotiating the sale with Migerobe, Murff possessed the implied authority to settle on the specific terms of the contract such as price (anything above $45), the specific quantity (within the limits set by Wolfe), and the specific styles.

Citing section 50 of the *Restatement (Second) of Agency,* Certina argues that the authority to solicit business for the principal does not translate into authority to contract for the principal. Although this proposition may be correct, Certina ignores the evidence which tends to show that, in this instance, Murff had received express authority not only to solicit business but to contractually secure that business as well.

Apparent authority exists when the principal clothes his agent with the semblance of authority such that a reasonably prudent person having knowledge of the business involved would be justified in believing, that the agent has the power the person assumes that he has. . . . In order to recover under a theory of apparent authority, a plaintiff must demonstrate the existence of the following three elements: (1) acts or conduct of the principal indicating authority, (2) reasonable reliance on those acts, and (3) a change of position by the third person to his detriment. "Whether the evidence sufficiently meets the three-prong test of apparent authority is an issue for the fact-finder."

Therefore, we will not reverse the jury's finding unless the evidence is such that no reasonable jury could have found apparent authority to exist.

It is uncontested that Migerobe contacted Murff sometime during the summer of 1987 to express its interest in obtaining Certina watches at a discounted price. Murff responded with a September 14, 1987, letter stating that he was "pursuing a special price" for Migerobe. Murff was, in fact, negotiating for a special price with William Wolfe, Certina's vice president of retail sales. Wolfe eventually provided Murff with a list of watches that were to be offered to Migerobe for forty-five dollars each. By the time Murff arrived at Migerobe for his October 29 meeting, it was obvious to all involved that this was not a "routine" sales call. Migerobe reasonably expected Murff to present it with an offer in response to the company's request for special pricing, and Murff, with the blessing of Wolfe, fully expected to make such an offer. Wolfe was aware that Murff was to present this offer to Migerobe, and he provided Murff with all the materials necessary to make that offer. He provided Murff with an inventory list containing specific quantities and styles of watches that could be offered to Migerobe, and he authorized the selling price. While at Migerobe's offices, Murff referred to this inventory list and made phone calls to Lancaster, while negotiating with Migerobe, to double-check on the accuracy of the list. Murff concluded his day, as he had done many times before, by phoning the order into the home office at Lancaster where Wolfe's administrative assistant accepted the order and completed a Certina order form.

Under the circumstances, a reasonable jury could have found that Wolfe's actions, together with Certina's operating procedures, clothe Murff with the apparent authority to act on its behalf in concluding this particular transaction. Also, we believe that a reasonable jury could have found that Migerobe was acting reasonably when it relied on the transaction. Finally, Migerobe presented sufficient evidence of a detrimental change in position as a result of its reliance; Migerobe had planned an entire Thanksgiving advertising campaign around the Certina watches, and the scope and thrust of that campaign had to later be changed as a result of Certina's breach. . . .

For the foregoing reasons, we AFFIRM the jury's finding of a contractual breach by Certina as well as the jury's award of damages to Migerobe in the amount of $157,133.00.

Case Questions

1. What is actual authority? What must a plaintiff prove in order to recover under the theory of an agent's apparent authority? Which authority, or both, was demonstrated in this case? Explain.

2. How did the nature of the evidence in the case contribute to the court's interpretation of express and implied authority as a contract of actual authority?

TORTS AND VICARIOUS LIABILITY. In certain situations, the law also holds principals liable for torts (*see* Chapter 10) that are committed by agents who are acting within the scope of the agency. Under the doctrine of **respondeat superior**—which literally means "let the master answer"—the principal is deemed vicariously liable to third parties who are injured by an agent's wrongful acts.

respondeat superior Doctrine imposing liability on a *principal* for injuries resulting from an *agent*'s wrongful acts committed within the scope of the agent's employment

vicarious liability Doctrine holding an employer liable for the negligent acts of an employee even though the employer performed no wrongful act

The doctrine of **vicarious liability,** for example, usually operates to hold an employer liable for the negligent acts of the employee even though the employer himself performed no wrongful act. The doctrine is intended to permit third parties who have been injured by employees to bring an action against someone who is likely to have the financial resources to compensate them for their injuries.

This doctrine applies only when an employee is acting "within the scope of his employment." Holding liable the *master*—the term used for an employer in an employer/employee relationship—is based on common-law notions that a master has more or less "control" over behavior of his *servant* (employee): Either he has set the action in motion and is therefore responsible for what happened or he has selected and trusted the servant and so should suffer his wrongs rather than an innocent stranger who has had no opportunity to protect himself.

There have been thousands of cases about the meaning of "within the scope of employment." Courts agree that the master cannot insulate himself from liability by imposing safety rules or by instructing employees to proceed carefully no matter how specific and detailed those orders may be. Consider, for example, a truck driver who, during his afternoon, runs down a pedestrian who is taken to the local hospital. Will the employer be held liable? Would the results be different if the trucker did so while running a personal errand?

How far can the concept of "within the scope of employment" be stretched? What happens in instances when an employee somehow deviates from his task and causes injury? In a much cited 1834 case, Baron Parke offered the classic opinion that a master is not liable for the torts of his servant who is not at all on his master's business but is "going on a frolic of his own."

Difficult questions of fact arise, however, in determining whether a servant's conduct is an entire departure from the master's business or only a roundabout way of doing it. A "detour" exists when the employee deviates from his route on a personal errand and later returns to it. In such cases, the courts have looked at the *forseeability* of the deviation, thereby holding the employer liable for torts occurring in a "zone of interest" within which the employee might reasonably be expected to deviate, even for purposes entirely his own. Time and distance of the detour tend to be relevant factors: The master will be liable at least for those slight departures from the performance of work that might be reasonably expected on the part of the servant. The issue of vicarious liability is examined in this chapter's ETHICAL ENVIRONMENT box.

■ *Concept Check 7-1   Agency Law*

- What are the *duties* owed by an *agent* to a *principal*? By a principal to an agent?
- Explain the legal definition of an *agency relationship*.
- Describe the doctrine of *vicarious liability* and give an example of a tort as defined by this doctrine.

■ SOLE PROPRIETORSHIPS

A *sole proprietorship* (also known as an *individual proprietorship*) is the oldest, simplest, and most common form of doing business in the United States. As this chapter's ORGANIZATIONAL PROFILE box on Sears shows, even some of the

Imputing the liability of one party to another raises many ethical issues. To what extent, for example, should an employer be held liable for the actions of an employee? Consider the following facts from a real case.

William Roberson drove to a loading dock at Bethlehem Steel's plant to pick up a shipment of steel. He pulled his truck into an empty loading bay, observed the conspicuously noted sign "First come, first served," and waited while three other trucks pulled in behind him. While Roberson waited, the other trucks were loaded and the workers then took a break. This delay was apparently due to the fact that the truck number on Roberson's gate pass did not match the number on his truck. When his truck was finally loaded, the load was so off-center that it rendered his truck unsafe to drive. Incensed by a worker's offer to remove but not recenter the load, Roberson asked to speak to the foreman. Thereafter, witnesses disagree as to the violence of the exchange and as to whether verbal threats were actually exchanged. When all was said and done, however, the foreman struck Roberson, breaking his jaw and causing him to miss two months of work while his jaw healed. This case arose in Indiana, where an employer is not liable under the theory of respondeat superior for an act committed by an employee unless the employee acted within the scope of his employment. The jury was presented with the issues both of whether the foreman was acting within the scope of his employment and in furtherance of Bethlehem Steel's business when he struck Roberson, and whether the foreman acted in self-defense.

The court dismissed the significance of whether Roberson was justifiably angered over the time it took to load his truck and the way it was loaded as irrelevant to the scope-of-employment issue. It also rejected the self-defense argument.

In reaching its decision, the court did not believe Bethlehem Steel's argument that if the facts were read in the light most favorable to plaintiff Roberson, the court would find the foreman acted out of his own personal motives and totally beyond the scope of his employment. More importantly, however, the court noted that even if the foreman acted without a feeling of ill will, Bethlehem Steel could still be liable because "even though the employee's predominant motive is to benefit himself," if his action can nonetheless further his master's business to some appreciable extent (such as keeping the loading dock running smoothly), the master will be liable.

---

country's largest concerns started out as modest sole proprietorships. A **sole proprietorship** is a business enterprise with one owner who personally holds title to the business and its assets. Sole proprietorships and their owners are considered one and the same. Therefore, they terminate automatically when the owner either closes the business or dies. The simplicity of a sole proprietorship is its most attractive option, especially for a fledgling enterprise.

sole proprietorship Form of business organization with one owner who holds personal title to its assets and who is liable for its obligations

LEGAL FORMALITIES. Essentially, this type of business entity is created when an individual begins to engage in a business. There are only two legal formalities relating to doing business as a sole proprietorship:

1. If the sole proprietorship is engaging in a business that requires a *state license* (for example, a hairdresser or a chiropractor), such a license must be obtained.
2. If a sole proprietor is doing business under a *trade name*, most states require the business name to be registered with a "doing-business-as" certificate. For example, if Sally Jones owns a business under the name of "Management Consultants," she must register it as Sally Jones d/b/a Management Consultants. Registration requirement protects the public by providing access to the owner's identity.

Advantages. The operation of a sole proprietorship is quite straightforward. The sole proprietor owns the business individually. The advantage of this procedure is that the owner is in complete control. The owner makes all of the decisions concerning the business: day-to-day operations, acquiring equipment, incurring debt, hiring, and firing. The owner also reaps the benefit of all after-tax profits. Even the taxes are not complicated—a sole proprietor reports the business profit or loss on his individual income tax return. Unlike a partnership or corporation, there is no separate tax return for the business.

Disadvantages. However, the disadvantage of operating as a sole proprietorship is a major one. As we have seen, the sole proprietor is *personally liable* for all of the business' debts and other legal liabilities. This provision means that the sole proprietor is putting his personal assets (for instance, bank accounts, home, automobile, and investments) at risk for the debts and liabilities of the business. This aspect of a sole proprietorship also makes it more difficult for the owner to raise capital by acquiring loans: From the standpoint of potential creditors, it is risky to lend money to a sole proprietorship because in the event of a default, recovery can only be sought against one person's assets. Table 7-1 summarizes some advantages and disadvantages of sole proprietorships.

TABLE 7-1	*Sole Proprietorships*

ADVANTAGES	DISADVANTAGES
Easy to start up and terminate	Limited in duration by proprietor's interest or his death
Owner has complete control over business decisions	Unlimited personal liability for business debts
Subject to less government regulation than other business forms	May have difficulty in raising capital

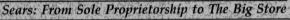

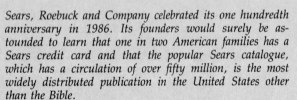

ORGANIZATIONAL PROFILE

Sears: From Sole Proprietorship to The Big Store

Sears, Roebuck and Company celebrated its one hundredth anniversary in 1986. Its founders would surely be astounded to learn that one in two American families has a Sears credit card and that the popular Sears catalogue, which has a circulation of over fifty million, is the most widely distributed publication in the United States other than the Bible.

This dramatic success story is actually the story of a sole proprietorship that became the legendary "Big Store." The story began in 1886, when an unwanted shipment of watches was sent to an unsuspecting jeweler in Minnesota. This became teenage Richard Sears' first purchase of goods. Sears was able to resell the watches, and he discovered not only a need for more orders but a healthy market for watches and jewelry. Within a couple of years, his expanding business, which operated out of Chicago, needed an assistant. Alvah Roebuck was hired in 1893, and the legendary partnership was formed.

Sears, Roebuck and Company was the answer to farmers' prayers. It offered an alternative to high-priced rural stores, and the outgoing and intense Richard Sears proved to be something of an advertising genius who understood the needs of the mostly rural clientele.

In 1895, the company was reorganized and Roebuck replaced as Sears' associate by Julius Rosenwald, who had remarkable business skills and unparalleled idealism. He and Sears worked jointly for the first several years of his tenure. During this period, gross sales exceeded $10 million and for

the first time topped those of archrival Montgomery Ward. In 1905, Sears and Rosenwald for the first time sold common and preferred stock on the open market to raise additional capital. The company has been publicly owned ever since.

For the next dozen years, catalogue sales continued to soar when Sears created an ingenious way to boost catalogue distribution: Sears wrote to the company's best customers, asking each of them to distribute twenty-four catalogues among friends and neighbors. The customers sent Sears the names of the people who received the catalogues. When, in turn, these people sent orders, the original customers received premiums for their work—for example, a stove, a bicycle, or a sewing machine. Today, more than 350 million Sears catalogues roll off the presses every year.

Sears's popularity eventually made its way into urban areas, where an untapped urban market welcomed the establishment of retail stores that offered quality merchandise at affordable prices. By the early 1920s, under the leadership of Rosenwald's hand-picked successor, Robert E. Wood, Sears was able to capitalize on a growing urban population that, for the first time, outnumbered the rural population. These urban stores were a booming success. During one twelve-month period in the late 1920s, for example, a Sears store opened every other business day.

Much of Sears' success was due to the fact that when the first retail stores were opened, Sears was highly centralized and efficient. Besides the merchandising and operating vice-

presidents, there was a third vice-president who served as the controller—or chief financial officer—of the company. Wood, however, opposed the centralized organization he inherited in 1928, and by the late 1930s with sales and profits improving, decentralization began. During the Depression era, Allstate insurance was added to Sears' operation to respond to the nation's growing reliance on automobiles. The nation's increasingly mobile population also needed more stores in suburban areas. Stores with huge parking areas soon accommodated the thousands who shopped at Sears. During the 1940s, formal decentralization at Sears occurred when the Pacific Coast territory was created. There were soon five headquarters, representing a model of progressive corporate management.

Sears also managed to inspire great loyalty among its staff. The company actually made a "psychological contract" with its employees, assuring employees that they would be fired only for stealing from the company. In exchange, employees promised lifelong services for which they were handsomely rewarded.

By the mid-1960s, Sears, Roebuck was nothing less than a retailing superstar—the "Big Store." Articles about Sears often referred to the company as the "colossus of American retailing," with sales bigger than that of the entire tobacco or furniture industries.

The era of invincibility came to a sharp halt, however, just before the world's oil prices quadrupled during the winter of 1973. U.S. retail sales declined both because of oil shortages and because many Americans had made their first purchases of such longlasting appliances as washing machines, freezers, and color televisions in prior decades. Sears had become the place to shop for many first-time purchases of durable goods and by the 1970s, there simply were not that many consumers left in the country who did not already own these items.

Sears sustained another blow in the early 1970s. In 1973, the Federal Equal Employment Opportunity Commission (see Chapter 15) charged the firm with discrimination on the basis of race, color, sex, and national origin in its hiring, pay-promotion, and other practices. When negotiations with the EEOC broke down amidst rumors that the government was about to file a massive discrimination suit against the company, Sears filed a class-action suit against ten federal agencies on behalf of all retailers employing more than fifteen people, charging that the laws under which the government was trying to stop discrimination were unfair, confused, and contradictory. A federal judge dismissed the suit, and Sears was forced to reassess its hiring policies and commitment to affirmative action.

When chairman Arthur Wood (no relation to Robert) chose his successor in the mid 1970s, it was under the pall of an impending crisis in management. His successor, Ed Telling, was a self-described maverick who openly disliked the company's regionalism. In 1985, Telling tapped Edward Brennan as his successor. Brennan, described by associates as a no-nonsense executive with an endless ability to absorb detail, introduced the ambitious, unprecedented "Store of the Future" program, which spruced up stores with new fixtures and lighting and an emphasis upon big-brand names. His goal was to regain customer trust and loyalty. Low pricing on national brand names as well as familiar Sears brands was introduced to enable retailers to avoid the steepest ups and downs of promotional cycles. Unfortunately, this plan did not succeed, and in 1990, costs exceeded profits.

Although the current times are tough for Sears, the pride and loyalty of its employees, as well as generations of satisfied customers that it has served, make it likely that the "Big Store" will have staying power.

■ Concept Check 7-2 Sole Proprietorships

- Explain how an individual starts and terminates a *sole propietorship.*
- Describe the *legal formalities* relating to sole proprietorships.
- Explain the key advantages and disadvantages of sole proprietorships.

■ PARTNERSHIPS

As we have seen, a sole proprietorship's efforts to raise capital may be hampered by the fact that there is only one owner. By organizing a business as a *partnership,* two or more owners can improve their ability to raise capital without becoming involved in the complicated process of incorporation.

Partnerships are often created when an individual decides that it is preferable to acquire needed capital and resources by jointly owning the enterprise with others rather than by borrowing money. Generally, partnerships dissolve automatically either upon the death or retirement of a partner or the admission of a new partner.

Each partner contributes capital and/or services to the firm in exchange

Whatever Happened To . . . Alvah Curtis Roebuck The birthplace of Sears, Roebuck and Co.—a railroad station in North Redwood, Minnesota, ca. 1887. In 1890, Alvah Roebuck, who had answered a Sears Watch Company ad for a watchmaker in 1887, bought Richard Sears' interest in a Minneapolis-based firm, the Warren Company, for $14,000. In 1893, Sears, who had been on the verge of retirement, bought back a two-thirds interest in what had then become the A. C. Roebuck Company, and the two entrepreneurs joined forces to create Sears, Roebuck & Company on September 16 of the same year. In 1895, Roebuck announced his desire to sell his share of the business. Agreeing to his partner's wishes, Sears held Roebuck's shares in trust for two years, until he found a buyer named Julius Rosenwald. Roebuck received $25,000 for his one-third interest in Sears, Roebuck. Gross sales under Sears and Rosenwald topped $10 million in 1900 and $50 million by 1907.

for the right to participate in controlling the enterprise. Like sole proprietors, partners are personally liable for the partnership's debts and liabilities. However, partnerships are a less risky prospect for a lender because the enterprise is backed up by more than one person's assets.

Partnerships are often the business form of choice for small firms that provide a single professional service, such as law, accounting, or medical care. There are two types of partnerships—*general* and *limited*. In almost all states, the law governing partnerships is the **Uniform Partnership Act (UPA)**.

The Nature of a Partnership

Uniform Partnership Act (UPA) Uniform source of law, adopted in most states, governing the formation, dissolution, rights, and liabilities of *partnerships*

partnership Form of business organization in which two or more persons hold joint ownership in the interest of profit and are liable for debts and other obligations

A **partnership** is defined in Section 6 of the UPA as "an association of two or more persons to carry on as co-owners a business for profit." Two aspects of this definition merit elaboration: First, the word "persons" is not limited to human beings: Corporations—and even other partnerships—may own a partnership. Second, the partners must specifically intend to profit from the undertaking *personally*. The latter requirement excludes charities and other nonprofit organizations from being organized as partnerships. Similarly, labor unions are not partnerships under this definition.

LEGAL IDENTITY. At common law, partnerships did not have a legal identity separate from their individual members—that is, a partnership represented a business arrangement but had no other significance. For instance, even today partnerships are not separate taxpaying entities. They are required only to file "information returns" that reflect their financial life in a given year; profits and losses are reported on each partner's individual income tax return.

The UPA has modified this common-law rule so that (1) a partnership can own property in its name, (2) property owned in an individual partner's name can be partnership property, and (3) a partnership can in some states be sued in its own name instead of or in addition to in the names of the partners.

PARTNERSHIP AGREEMENTS.   Neither the UPA nor common law requires a written agreement or contract as a prerequisite to the formation of a partnership. Thus, such an agreement can be merely oral. Indeed, a partnership may be implied from the *conduct* and *activities* of the parties. Consequently, it is possible for a partnership to be created even though the parties did not intend or even know of its creation. The UPA addresses this problem at Section 7(4), where it outlines what constitutes *prima facie* evidence—that is, evidence adequate to establish a fact or the presumption of a fact—that an individual is a partner in a business association.

The receipt by a person of a share of the profits of a business is *prima facie* evidence that he is a partner in the business, but no such inference shall be drawn if such profits were received in payment: (1) as a debt by installments or otherwise; (2) as wages of an employee or rent to a landlord; (3) as an annuity to a widow or representative of a deceased partner; (4) as interest on a loan, though the amount of payment varies with the profits of the business; (5) as the consideration for the sale of a good-will of the business or other property by installments or otherwise.

As a general rule, a written partnership agreement is certainly a good idea. Such a document can guide the partners through such difficult issues as control, the division of profits, and dissolution. There are several other reasons to have a written partnership agreement. First, if a dispute between the partners cannot be resolved and winds up in court, a written partnership agreement will greatly assist the judge in determining the partners' original intent. Second, the agreement will specify each partner's tax burdens. Third, such an agreement can specify that the partnership should continue despite the death or retirement of one member. Finally, partners who lend money, services, or property to the partnership are protected if the terms of the loan are included in a written agreement.

In the absence of a written agreement, the courts examine such factors as how a business is managed and how profits and losses are distributed in determining whether a partnership was formed. The courts analyze these factors objectively—they do not consider the subjective *intent* of the parties. The following case illustrates the kinds of evidence examined by a court in determining whether a partnership exists.

JOHNSON v. UNITED STATES
United States District Court, 632 F. Supp. 172 (1986)

Plaintiff, Vera H. Johnson, and her brother, Everette M. Huffman, became "loosely associated" in a sawmilling operation known as H&J Lumber Company, according to the complaint. The business did **not do well financially and eventually ceased operations altogether. The United States Government contends that certain federal employee withholding taxes, social security taxes, and unemployment**

---

taxes were never paid to the Internal Revenue Service by plaintiff, Huffman, or the entity known as H&J Lumber Company. The Internal Revenue Service has made assessments against plaintiff as a partner of H&J Lumber Company for the amount of the alleged deficiency. Plaintiff paid $2000 in federal employment taxes, but she alleges that she was not legally obligated to pay the taxes. Plaintiff institutes this action seeking refund of the amount paid. The United States counterclaims, seeking collection of the unpaid balance of a tax assessment which it contends is still due and owing from the plaintiff.

Woodrow Wilson Joes, District Judge.
. . . .

The primary issue before the Court at this stage of the proceedings is whether there is a genuine issue of material fact concerning Plaintiff's status as a partner in the H & J Lumber Company. Plaintiff is in apparent agreement with the government's contention that if she were a partner in H & J Lumber Company then she is liable, jointly and severally, for any taxes due the government by H & J Lumber Company. Plaintiff strenuously denies the government's allegations that she was a partner in the H & J Lumber Company.

[1-4] The question of whether an entity is a partnership for tax purposes is generally a question of fact and hinges primarily upon the presence or absence of an intention of the parties to join together to carry on a business and to share in the profits or losses of such business. The parties' intention is not to be determined from their protestations that a partnership was not intended. True intent must be determined by examination of the relevant facts and circumstances governing the parties' relationship. The relevant facts and circumstances to be considered are: (1) whether a partnership agreement exists; (2) whether the parties have represented to others that they were partners; (3) whether the parties have a proprietary interest in the partnership profits and an obligation to share the losses; (4) whether the parties have a right to control the partnership income and capital; and (5) whether the parties have contributed capital or services.

The "H & J" in H & J Lumber Company stood for Huffman and Johnson, the last names of Plaintiff's brother and Plaintiff. Plaintiff contributed approximately $20,000.00 to the capital of the company. It was Plaintiff's understanding that she and her brother were forming a partnership and were to "share and share alike," and that she and her brother were to have a one-half interest in the business. . . .

In their dealings with the Internal Revenue Service Plaintiff and her brother always represented themselves to be partners. . . . Plaintiff and her brother filed partnership tax returns as well as other tax documents indicating their status as partners. Plaintiff took half of the yearly losses of the business as a deduction on her individual income tax returns for the years in question.

[5] It appears clear from the deposition testimony of both Plaintiff and her brother that a partnership agreement between the two did exist, albeit that the agreement was verbal rather than written. Whether the Plain-

tiff and her brother represented to their customers, suppliers, employees or others that they were partners is unclear, but it is certain that they represented to the Internal Revenue Service that they were partners. Plaintiff and her brother agreed to share the profits of the business fifty-fifty. As it turned out there was no profits to be shared but they did equally claim the tax benefits to be gained by the business losses. Plaintiff had the right to control the partnership income and capital even though she might have lacked sufficient knowledge of the nature of the business to exercise that right responsibly or her brother might have by his own action prevented her from exercising her right to control of the business. Finally Plaintiff contributed both capital and services to the business. If Plaintiff were an employee of the business rather than a partner it seems odd that she would contribute substantial services for which she was not paid. Thus in examining all of the factors set forth in *Levasseur* it appears that each factor points to the conclusion that Plaintiff and her brother formed a partnership rather than to the conclusion assessed by the Plaintiff, that is, that she was merely an employee in her brother's business.

It should further be kept in mind that the purpose in examining the *Levasseur* factors is to determine whether two or more persons intended to form a partnership. Huffman readily admits that it was his intention to form a partnership with his sister. Plaintiff goes to great lengths to avoid the use of the word "partnership" to describe her agreement with her brother, but does state that at the inception of the business Huffman "got me to think it was partners. . . ." Even assuming that Huffman later took it upon himself to conduct the day-to-day operation of the business and the finances, and that he excluded Plaintiff from active participation in the affairs of the business, those facts would not support the Plaintiff's denial that a partnership existed. Since it appears that the only legitimate basis upon which the Plaintiff could deny her partnership status is her lack of actual control in conducting the affairs of business, and that such lack of control is an insufficient basis upon which to determine that Plaintiff was not a partner, the Court concludes that Plaintiff was a partner with her brother in the H & J Lumber Company, that there is no genuine issue of material fact as to her status as a partner and that the government is therefore entitled to partial summary judgment as to such issue. . . .

IT IS THEREFORE ORDERED that the Defendant's motion for partial summary judgment is granted as to the issue of whether Plaintiff was a partner in the H & J Lumber Company.

Case Questions

1. What standard did the court use in determining whether an entity is a partnership for tax purposes?

2. Applying that standard to the facts of this case, is it possible that the determination may be made that H&J was indeed a partnership? Explain.

3. Why did the court refuse to grant the Government's motion for summary judgment?

Partnership Liability

Even though both the UPA and state procedural laws recognize partnerships as separate entities for some purposes, the liability for all partnership debts, liabilities, and obligations rests with the partners. Although creditors are usually required to pursue partnership assets before those of the individual partners, the personal assets of the individual partners are ultimately at risk because agency law holds that partners are each other's agents. Thus, the conduct of one partner binds the others and carries all proportionate liability to them.

Partnership Management

Unless the partnership agreement provides otherwise, each partner has an equal voice in management and control. If there are more than two partners, the usual rule is that a majority prevails. However, the partnership agreement cannot be changed without unanimous consent. Partners usually authorize each other to manage a particular aspect of the business. For example, one partner may deal with all personnel matters while another handles all sales questions.

Dissolution and Termination of the Partnership

Section 29 of the UPA defines the dissolution of a partnership as a change in the relationship of the partners caused by any partner ceasing to be associated in the operation of partnership business. Thus, a partnership may be dissolved by (1) the death, retirement, or incapacity of a partner; (2) the bankruptcy of the partnership or of any of the partners; or (3) the courts, under the circumstances outlined in UPA Section 32, such as a court determination that one of the partners has become physically or mentally incapacitated.

UPA Section 30 specifically states that a partnership is not *terminated* upon dissolution: It continues until all unfinished partnership business is completed, all partnership accounts are inspected, the partnership property is sold, all monies due are collected, and such agreements as the circumstances demand in order to liquidate and distribute the partnership assets are entered into. As a general rule, rights to cease operation are vested in all of the partners when the partnership is dissolved by agreement or by the expiration of an agreed term. Remember that the partnership can continue despite these UPA stipulations if the written partnership agreement provides for such a contingency.

Table 7-2 summarizes some advantages and disadvantages of a partnership.

TABLE 7-2   *Partnerships*

ADVANTAGES	DISADVANTAGES
Partners contribute additional capital.	Partners are personally liable for all debts.
Partners contribute expertise.	Potential for conflict among partners.
Partners share work and accountability.	Life of partnership limited by life of partner.
Taxed like sole proprietorships.	More difficult to dissolve than sole proprietorship.

Types of Partnerships

limited partnership Partnership including a *general partner* responsible for management and *limited partners* who have invested in the business but do not share in its management

Uniform Limited Partnership Act (ULPA) Source of law, enacted by most states, establishing uniform provisions for the formation, operation, and dissolution of *limited partnerships*

Revised Uniform Limited Partnership Act (RULPA) Revised uniform law updating provisions concerning *limited partnerships*

limited partner Investor in a *limited partnership* who does not share in the management of the business and whose liability for its obligations cannot exceed the value of his or her investment

LIMITED PARTNERSHIPS. **Limited partnerships** are creations of statute—that is, they did not exist at common law. Over 40 states have adopted the **Uniform Limited Partnership Act (ULPA)** (1916), which sets forth prerequisites for the formation of a limited partnership. Generally, a written agreement must be filed with the appropriate state office (such as the secretary of state). A more modern comprehensive law governing limited partnerships was established by the **Revised Uniform Limited Partnership Act (RULPA)** of 1976, which replaces the ULPA in those states that have adopted it.

The designation "limited partnership" means that **limited partners** have no right to manage or control the business even though they have invested in it. The benefit that they receive in exchange for their investment is limited personal liability: A limited partner's personal liability is limited to the value of his investment.

Each limited partnership must have at least one **general partner** who is responsible for managing and controlling the business. The general partner has unlimited liability for partnership obligations. General partners sell limited partnerships to generate capital. The following case illustrates how the courts view partnership liability.

COURTS OF THE PHOENIX v. CHARTER OAK FIRE INSURANCE COMPANY
U.S. District Court, Northern District of Illinois, 560 F. Supp. 858 (1983)

Plaintiffs, the Courts of the Phoenix ("the Partnership"), a partnership, and Lakeview Trust & Savings Bank ("Lakeview Bank"), the legal owner of the building operated by the partnership, brought this action on an insurance policy issued by defendant, Charter Oak Fire Insurance Company ("Charter Oak").

In May 1980, a fire occurred in the partnership's building, which housed several racquetball and handball courts. The Chicago Fire Department later determined that the fire had been intentionally set. Charter Oak denied the partnership's claim on the insurance policy on the basis that William Reich ("Reich"), the partnership's general partner, had set the fire or had arranged for it to be set in order to liquidate what Charter Oak claims was a filing investment.

Prentice H. Marshall, District Judge.
. . . Reich was the general partner of the partnership, and the other named plaintiffs, with the exception of Lakeview Bank, were limited partners. Reich had the majority interest (over 50%). Defendant has alleged that as general partner, Reich had sole control over the operation and management of the racquetball-handball club. For the purpose of the present inquiry, because we are only determining the sufficiency of the arson defense, we will assume the validity of defendant's assertion.

. . . .
There are no Illinois cases that address the specific question at issue here, that is, whether a "limited partnership" can be denied recovery on a fire insurance policy where the partnership's sole general partner has procured the setting of the fire that gave rise to the claim on the policy. . . .

. . . .
. . . However, on the more general issue—whether the wrongful conduct of one partner may be imputed to another partner—both common law and statutory law exists. As a matter of Illinois law, the tortious or fraudulent wrongdoing of one partner, not within the scope of his authority or in furtherance of the partnership business, does not subject the other partners (or the partnership) to liability. *Saikin v. New York Life Insurance* (1977). This doctrine is also embodied in an Illinois statute. Section 13 of the Uniform Partnership Act, upon which the court relied in *Saikin*, provides that

[w]here, by any wrongful act or omission of any partner acting in the ordinary course of business of the partnership, or with the authority of his co-partners, loss or injury is caused to any person, not being a partner in the partnership, or any penalty is incurred, the partnership is liable therefore to the same extent as the partner so acting or omitting to act.

. . . .

While §13, taken literally, addressed only the *liability*

---

of partnerships, we think that it provides persuasive authority for the proposition that the legislature intended that responsibility for the wrongful acts of one partner, even the general partner, is not to be attributed to other partners unless those acts are in the ordinary course of the partnership business or are undertaken with the express or implied authority of the other partners. . . .

Our determination that *Saikin* and § 13 of the Uniform Partnership Act state the applicable rule raises two important questions. First, we must decide whether Reich's alleged acts were either within the course of business of the partnership or were done with the authority of the other partners. Second, if we determine that Reich's acts were outside of his authority and thus are not attributable to the limited partners, we must address the question whether the insurance contract here modified the common law and statutory rule.

We do not have before us the partnership agreement entered into among the limited partners and Reich. However, this does not prevent us from determining whether burning down the partnership's sole property was something that could be considered to have been done in the ordinary course of the partnership's business. Section 52 of the Uniform Limited Partnership Act provides that absent the written consent or subsequent ratification of all the limited partners, a general partner does not have the authority to "[d]o any act which would make it impossible to carry on the ordinary business of the partnership." It is not alleged that there was any such consent here. Moreover, we would find it somewhat incongruous were the law to provide that an act taken to destroy a business' sole asset is an act "in the ordinary course of business."

. . . .

The question becomes, therefore, whether the insurance contract here modified in any way the statutory and common law doctrine that the wrongdoing of one partner not within the scope of his authority or in furtherance of the partnership's business is not attributable to the other partners. . . . The most general exclusion of potential relevance here provides that

[t]he Company shall not be liable for loss occurring while the hazard is increased by any means within the control or knowledge of the Insured unless the Company has received prior written notice. However, except as otherwise provided, permission is granted to make alterations and repairs.

Other than this, we can find no provision specifically excluding coverage as to damage to the building due to the fraud or criminal acts of an insured. The same is true concerning the "business interruption" coverage. . . . Therefore, the limited partners cannot be barred from recovery as to the "business interruption" and "building" claims, which amount to all but $50,000 of plaintiffs' $1.7 million-plus claim. If Charter Oak can demonstrate that any of the limited partners expressly or impliedly authorized Reich's conduct, however, any such partner may be barred from recovery as well. Reich will, of course, be barred from any recovery if Charter Oak can demonstrate by a preponderance of the evidence, that he set the fire or procured its setting.

The result we reach is that the total amount that would be due on the policy absent Reich's alleged arson is to be reduced by a percentage that equals the percentage of the partnership owned by the wrongdoers, if any. The innocent partners may recover the balance in proportion with their interest in the partnership. . . . It is also the result that we believe the Illinois Supreme Court would reach if faced with the issue.

Case Questions

1. On what grounds did the court hold that the limited partnership, excluding the wrongdoers, could recover on the fire insurance policy?

2. Explain the distinction between a limited partner and a general partner.

3. Under what circumstances would the wrongful acts of one partner be attributed to other partners?

MASTER LIMITED PARTNERSHIPS. The **master limited partnership (MLP)** is a hybrid form of business organization that falls between a limited partnership and a corporation. Like corporations, master limited partnerships raise capital by selling shares of stock on the open market. Prior to the 1987 tax-reform package, however, income from such partnerships was taxed as income to the individual partners.

Currently, however, master limited partnerships are subject to the corporate tax. There is a ten-year grace period for existing master limited partnerships, and gas and oil deals remain exempt. This provision makes master limited partnerships a far less attractive investment because (1) the new corporate tax reduces net worth and (2) income from these partnerships can no longer be used to offset tax-shelter losses.

Master limited partnerships originated in 1981 in the oil and gas industry. Since then, increasing numbers of master limited partnerships have been formed in a wide variety of industries. In 1986, for example, the Boston Celtics

general partner Member of a *limited partnership* who is responsible for the management of the business and who has unlimited liability for its obligations

master limited partnership (MLP) Form of business organization combining the features of the *limited partnership* (e.g., taxation based on individual partner income) and the *corporation* (e.g., the capacity to raise capital by selling stock shares)

organization offered for public sale 2.6 million limited partnership units of the master limited partnership that owns the basketball team. This offering produced a handsome profit for the team's three principal owners: It yielded $119 million on an initial investment of $19 million.

Case: Burger King as MLP. Following the footsteps of the Boston Celtics, Burger King created an MLP that was intended to turn long-term assets into quick cash. Its organizers relished the idea of reorganizing to avoid corporate tax and having more cash to pass along to stockholders.

In 1986, the Minneapolis-based Pillsbury Company, the parent of Burger King, created Burger King Investor's Master Limited Partnership. It sold 98 percent of its equity to the public at $20 million a unit, for a total of $92.7 million. Once the terrain of institutional buyers lured by oil and gas MLPs, eager retail investors seized the opportunity to invest in Burger King, the nation's number-two hamburger chain, and the new MLP sold out in three days. In return, Pillsbury transferred to the partnership the deeds and leases to 128 restaurants scattered from Maine to Seattle. Investors were lured by a return on the rental income paid by the independent franchises that operated restaurants on the partnership's properties.

As an added incentive, franchise rent was tied to restaurant revenues: Any surge in sales could prove a bonus to the partnership because rent payments increased. In addition, there was the chance that the properties would appreciate in value and result in sizable capital gains for investors. Figure 7-1 explains how investors reaped profits from the deal.

MLPs can, of course, satisfy corporate financing objectives. For example, companies can realize instant returns on untapped asset values without relinquishing control over properties, operation, and residual appreciation. When a highly leveraged company is involved, an MLP can also be the catalyst for operators to strip some assets and liabilities from balance sheets.

As with any speculative investment, however, the Burger King MLP was replete with pitfalls. First, the 128 properties sold to the partnership were not

FIGURE 7-1 Pillsbury's Burger King MLP   *Source: Adapted from Robert Sonenclar, "To Catch a Rising Star,"* Financial World, *June 24, 1986, p. 48.*

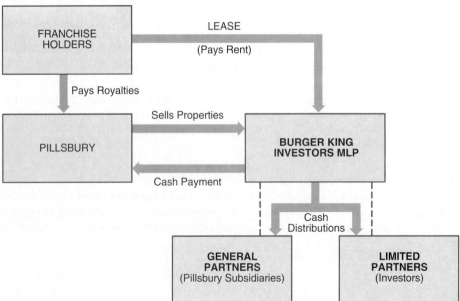

PART TWO   ORGANIZING TO DO BUSINESS

necessarily the most profitable franchises. Second, when closely scrutinized, the partnership agreement reveals some forbearing qualifiers to the would-be investor. Income and cash available for distribution, for example, would be divvied up just like the partnership equity—98 percent to public partners and two percent to Pillsbury, until the public received a 12 percent return in any given year. At that point, income and cash would be split 75 to 25 percent until public partners saw a 17.5 percent return. Beyond that, the deal would be 60 percent to partners and 40 percent to Pillsbury.

Other pitfalls included the possibility that investors would lose out if rental income from the preassigned franchises failed to meet projections. In addition, the agreement provided that Burger King was free to demand that any of the partnership's restaurants undergo remodeling or expansion—with the partnership paying 70 percent of the price tag.

Although 1987 tax legislation eliminated many of the tax benefits of MLPs, the Burger King MLP continues to survive. Economists hope, however, that future investors will have more realistic expectations about the hidden dangers of this and other MLPs. The lesson imparted from a short-lived history much like that of the notorious "junk bond" seems to be simple: Don't shop for yield. If the enticing high yield is being paid out of the capital account and not earnings, the yield is illusory and investment may be tantamount to treading water.

■ Concept Check 7-3   Partnerships

- What are the most important ways in which a *partnership* differs from a sole proprietorship?
- Identify and explain the key legal features of a *partnership agreement.*
- Define *limited* and *master limited partnerships* and explain the chief differences.

■ CORPORATIONS

Many people who emigrated from England to America carried with them a heavy dose of suspicion of political monarchies and state-run monopolies. To colonial Americans, the individual, and not the state, was king. Thus, the very idea of incorporating a business under state law was reminiscent of the monarch's favoritism in meting out monopolies to members of the nobility.

By the late 1700s, however, Americans began to understand that the formation and incorporation of a business was not necessarily the first step to the creation of a monopoly, and states began to pass laws allowing businesses to incorporate. The formation of freely competing business organizations became a natural outgrowth of a government whose purpose was restricted to protecting the property of individuals. The individual's right to form business organizations in pursuit of private interests was viewed as part of the inherent rights of citizenship.

However, even the most farsighted colonial American could not have foreseen the enormity of the modern corporation's size and influence. The yearly revenues of the largest corporations in the United States exceed those of all but a handful of countries. Figure 7-2 shows the revenues of the 20 largest international corporations. The rankings, however, include *nations* as well: When corporations are ranked according to revenue and nations according to gross national product, General Motors is the 25th largest financial entity in the

Dodge v. Ford Motor Co. **[Supplement]** The case of *Dodge v. Ford Motor Co.* (1919) is excerpted in Chapter 2. The subsequent activities of Henry Ford, pictured here enjoying a spin in his first car, are of some interest in themselves. Recall that the case originated when Ford announced plans to further the Ford Motor Co.'s best interests by building expensive new production facilities, intending to withhold stockholder dividends to finance the project. As stockholders, the Brothers Dodge sued for their dividends. It should be noted that the Dodge brothers were not only cofounders of the Ford Motor Co. but, in 1914, founders of the Dodge Motor Co.—a struggling enterprise that no doubt benefitted significantly from the approximately $1 million per year in dividends that the brothers received from Ford. Although the fact did not enter into the court's decision, Ford's proposal to benefit consumers by cutting the dividends of stockholders like the Dodges certainly threatened the ability of the younger company to compete. Ford, meanwhile, had already adopted a somewhat broader policy of stockholder relations. In 1917, he had founded another company, Henry Ford & Son, and in 1918 had resigned as president of Ford Motor Co., citing obligations to "other organizations." Probably interpreting the move as an implied threat, Ford stockholders began selling their shares. The most avid buyers—those seemingly undaunted by the threat of Ford's departure—turned out to be agents working for Ford himself, who was then able to assume autonomous control over *both* companies, which he promptly combined.

world. In perspective, consider that the United States ranks No. 1, Saudi Arabia No. 32, and the Philippines No. 47.

Taken in the aggregate, corporations are the backbone of our economy. Although corporations comprise only 20 percent of the total number of firms, they are responsible for 90 percent of the sales and take in 90 percent of the annual receipts; the net earnings of corporations exceed those of sole proprietorships and partnerships by 3.5 to 1 (*see* Figure 7-3).

Corporate Formation and Powers

Like a limited partnership, a corporation is a creation of statute: A corporation cannot come into existence until the requirements of the state incorporation statutes have been met. More than two-thirds of the states have adopted the

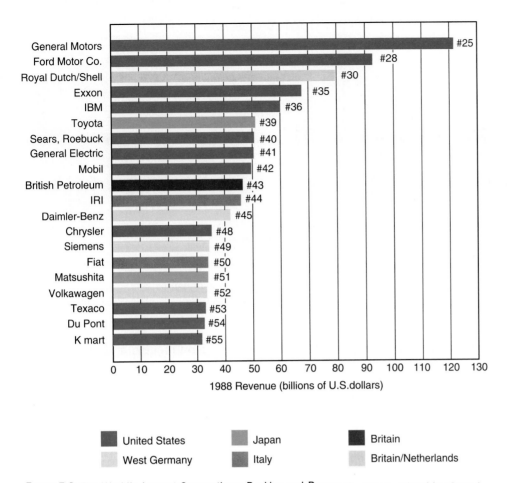

FIGURE 7-2 The World's Largest Corporations: Ranking and Revenues *Sources: Adapted from James A. F. Stoner and R. Edward Freeman,* Management, *5th ed. (Englewood Cliffs, NJ: Prentice Hall, 1992). Data from* Handbook of Economic Statistics *(Central Intelligence Agency, 1989) and "The 100 Largest U.S. Multinationals,"* Forbes, *July 24, 1989.*

Model Business Corporation Act (MBCA) as their state incorporation law. The MBCA was drafted by the Committee·on Corporate Laws of the Section of Corporation, Banking, and Business Law of the American Bar Association, and it has been revised.

Generally, the main prerequisite for incorporation is the filing of **articles of incorporation** with the proper state agency, usually the secretary of state. When articles of incorporation have been approved, the state has granted the corporation permission to operate. Articles of incorporation spell out the corporate name, the powers and purposes of the corporation, the number and types of shares of stock to be issued, the members of the first board of directors, and the initial officers of the board.

CORPORATE POWER AND AUTHORITY. Once incorporated, a corporation has the power and authority to act. Corporate power derives from two sources: the articles of incorporation and the state's incorporation law. Under the MBCA, these powers include but are not limited to the ability to maintain perpetual succession, sue and be sued in its own name, maintain a corporate seal, ac-

Model Business Corporation Act (MBCA) Statute, drafted by the American Bar Association and adopted as incorporation law by most states, establishing rules for corporate formation, operation, and governance

articles of incorporation Document, detailing such items as *corporate governance* and types and number of shares to be sold, filed with an appropriate state agency as a prerequisite for incorporation

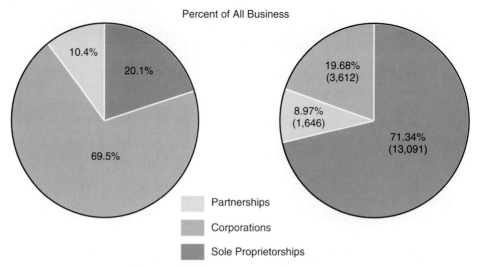

Percent of All Business

Partnerships
Corporations
Sole Proprietorships

Figure 7-3 Corporations: Percentages of Businesses and Sales Revenues *Source: Data from U.S. Department of Commerce, Bureau of the Census, Statistical Abstract of the United States (Washington, DC: Government Printing Office, 1986).*

quire and sell both real and personal property, lend money, and make and alter its bylaws.

Ultra Vires. Any act beyond the scope of the powers of a corporation, as specified under state law and in the corporation's charter, is unlawful and has no effect. Such an act is *ultra vires*—"beyond the powers [of the corporation]." At common law, the doctrine of **ultra vires** was critical to the power of a corporation. It was frequently invoked by corporations in an attempt to avoid contracts that became undesirable.

Because the result was usually unfair to the other party, ensuing law has severely limited its impact. First, the breadth of powers enumerated by state law has reduced the types of activities that are not lawfully authorized. Second, it is a relatively simple procedure to amend the articles of incorporation to broaden the purposes and powers of a corporation. Finally, many lawyers include a broad statement in the articles of incorporation empowering the corporation to "engage in any other lawful activity." This provision is codified in the MBCA, which gives a corporation the implied power "to have and exercise all powers necessary or convenient to effect its purposes."

Table 7-3 lists some of the advantages and disadvantages of the corporate form of organization. Table 7-4 summarizes and compares some important dif-

> **ultra vires** Doctrine holding that acts specified under state law and/or in its *articles of corporation* are beyond a corporation's scope of powers, unlawful, and without effect

TABLE 7-3	*Corporations*
ADVANTAGES	**DISADVANTAGES**
Limited liability[1]	Separation of ownership and control
Easy transfer of ownership	High taxes
Unlimited life	Work involved in formation and dissolution

[1] Although small corporations, with just a few shareholders, are usually not able to borrow money unless the corporate debt is personally guaranteed by the shareholders.

242

TABLE 7-4 **Summary and Comparison: Four Basic Forms of Business**

BUSINESS FORM	LIABILITY	CONTINUITY	FEATURE TRANSFERABILITY	MANAGEMENT	EQUITY INVESTMENT
Proprietorship	Personal, unlimited	Ends with death or decision of owner	Free to sell at any time	Personal, unrestricted	Personal
Partnership— General	Personal and unlimited, joint and several	Ends with death or decision of any partner	Individual interest can be sold with consent of all partners	Unrestricted or depends upon partnership agreement	Personal by partner(s)
Partnership— Limited	For limited partners, only invested capital; as above for general partners	Limited partners do not affect; as above for general partners	Limited partners free to sell: as above for general partners	Limited partners may not participate, dependent upon agreement	Personal by partner(s)
Corporation	Capital invested	As stated in charter, perpetual or specified period of years	Stock may be sold or trader without affecting other stock	Under control of board of directors, which is selected by stockholders	Purchase of stock

Source: Melvin J. Stanford, New Enterprise Management *(Englewood Cliffs, NJ: Prentice Hall, 1982). Reprinted by permission of Prentice Hall, Inc.*

ferences among four major types of business forms—proprietorship, general and limited partnership, and corporation.

Corporate Entities

The generic term "corporation" has been described by the U.S. Supreme Court as an "artificial being, invisible, intangible and existing only in contemplation of law" (*Dartmouth College v. Woodward*, 17 U.S. 518, 4 L.Ed. 629 [1819]). Despite this seemingly slippery definition, there are tangible corporate characteristics that can be identified and examined.

The fundamental characteristic of a **corporation** is that it is a separate entity: It has an existence separate from its shareholders. Even if a particular corporation has only one shareholder, it is an entity apart from that shareholder—a principle that courts have been reluctant to disregard. This characteristic most clearly distinguishes a corporation from a partnership, which is not a separate entity for most legal purposes.

The following section is designed to familiarize the reader with the characteristics of corporations and is presented in a way that will allow for identifying and understanding the different types of corporate entities. The key role of the international corporation in both the domestic and global economy should also add another perspective to this understanding.

corporation Form of business organization recognized as distinct from its owners and officers and solely liable for its obligations

CORPORATIONS: CHARACTERISTICS. Corporations are made up of:

- shareholders, who contribute capital in exchange for an opportunity to share in the profits
- directors, who manage the corporate board
- officers, through whom the corporation acts

Compared to a sole proprietorship or partnership, the chief advantage of the corporate form is that corporations can raise an almost limitless amount of capital by selling shares of stock. In fact, shareholders may sell their stock or die without affecting the corporate entity.

Corporations are, however, solely liable for the debts of the business: In other words, the owners of a corporation generally have no *personal* responsibility for corporate obligations. Unless a creditor requires stockholders to guarantee loans to the corporation personally, a shareholder's risk in purchasing corporate stock is limited to the amount of the investment.

CORPORATE RESPONSIBILITIES. Along with the benefits of the corporate organization come certain responsibilities and disadvantages. First, the formation of a corporation is considerably more complicated and costly than that of a partnership or sole proprietorship. It requires the preparation and filing of several documents and the payment of fees to the state of incorporation. Second, because corporations are separate legal entities, they are required to pay income taxes on their profits. Third, for years in which dividends are declared, shareholders pay income taxes on individual income-tax returns for dividends received. This system of paying income taxes twice on the same profit (first as a profit of the corporation and second as profit distributed to shareholders in the form of a dividend) is characterized as **double taxation.**

"Piercing the Corporate Veil." As we have seen, the fundamental characteristic of a corporation is that it exists as an entity apart from its shareholders. The law permits the incorporation of a business for the very purpose of enabling its proprietors to escape personal liability. The doctrine known as *piercing the corporate veil* is the major exception to this general rule. This doctrine permits a court to ignore the corporate entity and impose personal liability on shareholders for the purpose of promoting certain public policies, such as protecting the public from fraud. The following case illustrates how courts use this doctrine.

double taxation System whereby taxes are paid both by a *corporation* on its profits and by *shareholders* on income from dividends

---

LABADIE COAL COMPANY v. BLOCK
U.S. Court of Appeals, D.C. Circuit, 672 F.2d 92 (1982)

Plaintiff-appellant is Labadie Coal Company (Labadie), a Kentucky corporation engaged in processing and selling coal in Kentucky. Defendant-appellee is Black, the director, president, and sole employee of FAI, a "closely held family corporation." Through FAI, Black served as the "broker" between buyers and sellers of coal. Black and Labadie entered into agreements that called for purchases from Labadie and the use of Labadie's facilities for shipping coal, which FAI was to purchase from other sources. Labadie delivered coal under the contracts, but then terminated its relationships with Black (or FAI) because FAI was behind in its payments. Subsequently, Labadie sued both Black and FAI in United States District Court for the District of Columbia, seeking the payments allegedly owed for shipments made.

Prior to trial, defendant Black moved to dismiss the action on the ground that he had no business **relationship with Labadie in his individual capacity, and that he could not be held personally liable for FAI's corporate obligations, if any. The district court dismissed the action on the issue of Black's individual liability. The court refued to "pierce the corporate veil" and hold Black personally liable for money allegedly owed for coal sold to or through the entity FAI. Labadie appeals.**

Wilkey, Circuit Judge.

. . . .

1. The Purpose of the Veil

The common purpose of statutes providing limited shareholder liability is to offer a valuable incentive to business investment. Although the greatest judicial deference normally is accorded to the separate corporate entity, this entity is still a fiction. Thus, when particular circumstances merit—e.g., when the incentive value of limited liability is outweighed by the competing value of basic fairness to parties dealing with the corporation—courts may look past a corporation's formal existence to hold shareholders or other controlling individuals liable for "corporate" obligations. . . . On our examination of the record as it stands, we emphasize the following considerations which the district court should include in its examination on remand.

In evaluating the factors outlined below, it is helpful to group them under a two-prong test: (1) is there such unity of interest and ownership that the separate personalities of the corporation and the individual no longer exist?; and (2) if the acts are treated as those of the corporation alone, will an inequitable result follow? Relevant to the first question is the issue of the degree to which formalities have been followed to maintain a separate corporate identity. The second question looks to the basic issue of fairness under the facts.

2. Formalities

. . . .

(a) The nature of the corporate ownership and control.

This court has previously suggested that a corporate form may be ignored whenever an individual so dominates his organization "as in reality to negate its separate personality." . . .

The question before the court in a case like this is whether the corporation, rather than being a distinct, responsible entity, is in fact the alter ego or business conduit *of the person in control.* In many instances, the person "controlling" a close corporation is also the sole, or at least a dominant, shareholder. In other cases the controlling person may seek to avoid personal liability by not formally becoming a shareholder in the corporation. The question is one of control, not merely paper ownership.

It is apparent from the existing record that Mr. Black is in fact the dominant figure in FAI enterprises even though he *formally* controls no shares. The fact that the stock may be in his wife's name rather than in his may be of little consequence in the court's consideration of the entire picture. . . . Mr. Black alone holds the reins of FAI's activities. It was certainly by his actions alone that a relationship with plaintiff was established and business transacted.

. . . .

(b) Failure to maintain corporate minutes or adequate corporate records.

The failure of defendant to produce any corporate records, such as minutes, bylaws, articles of incorporation, lists of directors, and so on, creates a strong inference that these records do not exist. . . . If FAI has been viewed as a separate and distinct entity, one would expect appropriate records to be kept. If it is merely a separately-named business conduit for defendant's own activities, a "d/b/a" in all practicality, such records would not be as important and therefore might not be carefully maintained.

. . . [T]here is no evidence that FAI's directors, whoever they are, have ever played a meaningful role in FAI's activities, or have even formally held a meeting. It appears from the record—especially from Black's own testimony—that he alone controlled FAI and made all decisions.

(c) Failure to maintain the corporate formalities necessary for issuance or subscription to stock, such as formal approval of the stock issue by an independent board of directors.

The only evidence in the record relating to the stock of this corporation is a somewhat informal "stock book" of blank certificates and indications on stubs from which the certificates have been removed that 130 shares have been issued to defendant's wife and three children. There is no indication that any stock issue was authorized, or even of how issues were to be authorized. . . .

. . . .

(d) Commingling of funds and other assets of the corporation.

Although no evidence of such a commingling was presented by the plaintiff in this case, a key source of any such evidence would have been the checks and financial records, both of Black and of the corporation. These were all denied plaintiff by defendant's failure to produce them. . . .

(e) Diversion of the corporation's funds or assets to non-corporate uses such as the personal uses of the corporation's shareholders.

. . . .

The court may also take a close look at the salaries paid to defendant Black, his wife or other members of his family, if raised in evidence, and should be sensitive to possible asset diversion through these salaries. Asset diversion may be inferred from disproportion between the salaries paid and the services actually rendered to the corporation. . . .

(f) Use of the same office or business location by the corporation and its individual shareholders.

Black testified that although there is a corporate office in Washington, D.C., bearing the name of FAI Trading, Ltd., much of his business necessarily occurs after business hours in telephone conversations with mining operators or owners to and from his own home phone. . . . .

3. The Element of Unfairness

The [district] court correctly observed . . . that a case must only "present an element of injustice or fundamental unfairness" to justify the court's piercing the veil. The court simply found that this factor was absent in the *Labadie Coal* case. We disagree.

Ultimate resolution of at least one issue raised at trial may provide the required "injustice" to the court's evaluation. That issue is whether there was a failure adequately to capitalize the corporation for the reasonable risks of the corporate undertaking. . . .

. . . Although Black described FAI's business as that of a brokerage of sorts, the trial court would be justified in looking closely at the nature of the business actually conducted, including the types of liabilities that FAI might be expected to incur in the normal course of its dealings with suppliers and purchasers, before concluding that existing capital, whatever it is, is adequate under the circumstances.

. . . .

. . . [F]or reasons outlined above, the order of the district court dismissing the case against defendant Black is vacated, and the case is remanded to the trial court with instructions that the record be reopened and further discovery be permitted, if requested. The plaintiff should be allowed the fullest discovery into defendant Black's private financial records, as well as FAI's corporate records (such as they are), to determine facts bearing on whether FAI's corporate existence should be ignored in this case. The district court may make such determinations upon the expanded record as are appropriate on the facts and under the guidelines provided herein.

Case Questions

1. On what grounds did the court find that there was no separation between the personalities of Black and the corporation?

2. What are the factors that the appeals court analyzed in determining whether to ignore FAI's corporate form? Explain how each factor fits with the specific facts of this case.

3. What does the court suggest could be the element of injustice or "fundamental unfairness" that justifies its piercing the corporate veil? Explain.

CORPORATIONS: CATEGORIES. Corporations can be divided into four basic categories. The first of these consists of *domestic* and *foreign* corporations. A corporation is organized under the laws of a particular state and is a **domestic corporation** in the state where it receives its corporate charter. It is a foreign corporation to every other state. Thus, a **foreign corporation** is chartered in a different state from the one in which it is operating.

The second classification is the *publicly held* and *closely held corporation*. In a general way, this distinction refers to the *number* of shareholders. Usually, a **publicly held corporation** is one that has outstanding shares owned by a large number of people. By contrast, a **closely held corporation** generally has relatively few shareholders. However, there is no specific number of shareholders that definitively creates the distinction. Another factor is that the stock of a publicly held corporation is usually sold in the stock exchange, whereas the stock of closely held corporations is normally privately traded. The nature of corporate management is another distinguishing characteristic: Directors—not shareholders—are generally responsible for managing publicly held corporations, while most closely held corporations are run by shareholders. A number of states have enacted **close corporation statutes** that allow corporations to pass bylaws providing for management by shareholders rather than directors.

The third form of corporation, which is favored by small businesses, is the **S corporation** (formerly referred to as a *"subchapter S"* corporation). S corporations are afforded favorable tax treatment by the Internal Revenue Service (IRS). (The "S" refers to the section of the Internal Revenue Code that permits such corporations to be taxed as partnerships.) Essentially, this means that the corporation's income is taxed to the corporation's individual shareholders rather than to the corporation itself.

There are, however, very strict requirements to qualify as an S corporation:

1. The business may have no more than 35 shareholders.
2. The corporation may not issue more than one class of stock.
3. The corporation's shareholders must unanimously consent to being designated as an S corporation.

The fourth classification includes business and nonprofit (or not-for-profit) corporations. This is perhaps the most complex category.

Nonprofit Corporations. Business corporations are organized for the pur-

---

domestic corporation
Corporation recognized as being organized under the laws of a specific state in which it does business

foreign corporation
Corporation recognized as being organized under the laws of a state other than those in which it also does business

publicly held corporation
Corporation which has outstanding stock shares (usually offered on a stock exchange) and for which its directors, not its shareholders, are responsible for management

closely held corporation
Corporation whose stock is privately traded and which has relatively few shareholders, who generally share in its management

close corporation statutes
Laws, enacted by a number of states, providing for corporate *bylaws* that permit management by shareholders rather than directors

S corporation Small business in which income is taxed to the corporation's *shareholders* rather than to the corporation itself

pose of generating profits for the private benefit of stockholders.[1] By contrast, **nonprofit corporations** are organized for charitable, religious, or educational purposes. Nonprofit corporations are permitted to generate a profit, in the sense of making more money than they spend. However, such profits may not be distributed the way a business corporation distributes profits when it declares a dividend: Nonprofit corporations must *reinvest* any surplus in further charitable, religious, or educational undertakings.

Nonprofits constitute an important and growing sector of our economy. They provide the major forum for activity in education, scientific research, medical care, the performing arts, and charity.

Nonprofits can be organized in a variety of ways. The main distinctions are the ways in which the organization acquires its income and the kind of control group that manages it.

Financing may take the form of grants and donations ("donative" income) or may result from fees charged for services rendered ("commercial" income). The Salvation Army and the American Red Cross are examples of donative nonprofits; nursing homes and hospitals are commercial nonprofits. (Some organizations like universities are hybrids because they depend both on donations and received fees.)

There are two basic types of control groups. Those that draw their management directly from those who give or pay money to the organization—for example, country clubs and citizens' lobbies like Common Cause—are categorized as "mutual" nonprofits. Nonprofits run by self-perpetuating boards of directors who are not directly accountable to those who provide the organization's income are termed "entrepreneurial." Hospitals and nursing homes, for example, fall into this category because they are run by hospital administrators rather than patients and other service recipients. The two basic financing forms and the two control groups combine to form the four basic categories of nonprofit organizations shown in Figure 7-4.

Nonprofits enjoy special treatment in the form of exemptions from a host of regulatory laws and provisions, including antitrust, minimum-wage, and income-tax laws. These exemptions give nonprofits a certain competitive advantage over business corporations. However, nonprofits face numerous problems

nonprofit corporation
Corporation organized for charitable, religious, or educational purposes, with profits reinvested rather than paid to shareholders as dividends

FIGURE 7-4 Forms of Nonprofit Organization   *Source: Henry B. Hansmann, "The Role of Nonprofit Enterprise," 89 Yale Law Review 842 (1980). Adapted by permission.*

	FORM OF CONTROL	
	Mutual	Entrepreneurial
FORM OF FINANCE Donative	Political clubs National Audubon Society	Art museums March of Dimes
Commercial	Country clubs American Automobile Association	Nursing homes Educational Testing Service

[1] *See* Henry B. Hansmann, "The Role of Nonprofit Enterprise," 89 *Yale Law Journal* 838 (1980).

that business corporations do not encounter. For instance, nonprofits cannot raise capital by selling stock. In addition, some nonprofits have difficulty obtaining debt financing because their assets frequently lack liquidity or ascertainable market value. Moreover, lenders are sometimes reluctant to extend loans in case they are later forced to foreclose and face a public-relations embarrassment.

The International Corporation

Fifty years ago, it was relatively easy to distinguish an international company from one that was national or regional in scope. Since World War II, however, it has become increasingly more difficult to make these distinctions. As business has become more and more international in nature, the study and practice of business management has become the study and practice of international business management. Understanding the growth of international business thus requires an understanding of the problems of international management. Such an understanding also offers a better appreciation of the barriers to international trade and the resources available to increase such trade.

THE GLOBAL ECONOMY. International business plays an increasingly large role in modern society. The volume of international trade, for example, rose almost 2000 percent between 1960 and 1985. Foreign investments in the United States have also risen—from $27 billion in 1975 to $209 billion in 1986 to $329 billion in 1988. As more and more firms engage in international business, the economy of the world is rapidly becoming a single interdependent system. In his best selling book, *Megatrends,* for instance, author John Naisbett cited globalization as one of the ten most important trends affecting the world's future.

The basis for the increasing globalization of the economy is simple: Regardless of its resources, no country can produce all of the goods and services demanded by its citizens. Thus, countries naturally *export* those things that they can produce better or less expensively than other countries. Then they use the proceeds to *import* those things they cannot produce effectively. For example, according to one study, in 1989 U.S. manufacturers' top export was aircraft, followed by auto parts and computer equipment.

However, although the advantages of international trade are obvious, trading with other nations can also pose problems if a country's imports and exports do not balance out. A nation's *balance of trade* is the total economic value of all products imported into a country compared to the total economic value of all other products exported out of a country. In deciding whether a balance does or does not exist, economists use two measures: balance of trade and balance of payment. *Balance of payments* refers to the flow of money into or out of a country. Figure 7-5A illustrates the fate of the U.S. balance of trade when compared with that of three partners between 1976 and 1990. Figure 7-5B shows the steep decline in U.S. balance of payments between 1960 and 1987.

THE DECISION TO GO GLOBAL. Entering the international market also poses potential problems for management. Success in one country does not necessarily guarantee success in another country, and difficulties can be compounded by language barriers, lack of familiarity with custom, and the demands of managing and controlling a foreign work force. Moreover, management techniques that may increase worker productivity in the United States may offend workers in Japan or the United Kingdom.

The threshold question, however, is whether the firm should go international in the first place. Although the world economy is becoming more and

248

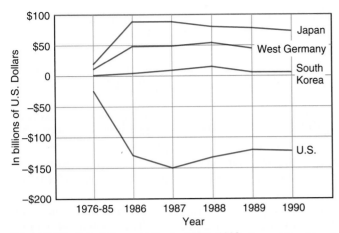

FIGURE 7-5A U.S. Balance of Trade, 1976–1990 *Source: Adapted from* Fortune, *July 31, 1989.*

more globalized, and although more and more firms are dealing internationally, this route is not appropriate for every company. Factors to be considered include the business climate of other nations, which encompasses the cultural, legal, and economic structures of the other country. There also must be a clear demand for the goods or services that the company is seeking to sell in the international market. Products that are vital in one country may be irrelevant in another.

Another consideration is whether a product can be modified to fit a foreign market, and a firm must also determine if it has or can acquire the necessary skills and knowledge to do business abroad. If there is a demand for its product, the firm must then consider how to adapt its current product to meet the special demands of foreign customers.

Level of Global Involvement. If a firm does go international, it must decide its level of involvement in the international market and, in so doing, may act as an exporter, organize as an international business, or operate as a multinational firm. An *exporting firm* that merely exports products to one or more countries may enter at the lowest level of involvement. *International firms* do a

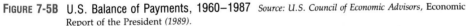

FIGURE 7-5B U.S. Balance of Payments, 1960–1987 *Source: U.S. Council of Economic Advisors,* Economic Report of the President *(1989).*

significant portion of their business in several foreign countries and sometimes have manufacturing plants overseas. Although an international firm may have an appreciable impact on the global economy, it is still rooted domestically in its international activity. Examples of international firms include McDonalds, BMW, and Procter & Gamble (which is discussed in this chapter's INTERNATIONAL ENVIRONMENT box).

The highest level of involvement in international business is the *multinational firm*. In multinational corporations, planning and decision making are geared toward international markets, and the firm does not think of itself as having a "domestic" part of its business and an "international" part. World corporations, or "stateless" corporations, represent a dramatic evolution for the U.S. multinational.

For many companies, going global is a matter of survival, and the decision means radically changing the way they work. The global or "transnational" corporation looks at the whole world as one market. It manufactures, conducts research, raises capital, and buys supplies wherever it can do the job best. It keeps in touch with technology and market trends all around the world. It tries to orchestrate the efforts of all its subsidiaries on a regional or global level. Its corporate headquarters could be anywhere. The global corporation tends to help the economy of its host country, creates new sales, sustains jobs at home, and helps to retain control of technologies.

OBSTACLES TO GOING GLOBAL.   As U.S. companies like IBM, Gillette, and Xerox begin to reap half or more of their sales and earnings from abroad, they are blending into the foreign landscape to win acceptance and avoid political complications. Similarly, foreign-based world corporations are setting up plants in the United States, employing Americans, lending technology, and bolstering the U.S. trade balance and economy.

Some of the difficulties faced by these world companies include trade problems posed by import bans, political problems, and regulatory and licensing problems. One example of a trade problem is as follows: Taiwan, South Korea, and Israel have traditionally been off-limits to Japanese auto companies. Taiwan and Korea ban the import of Japanese cars, and Japan observes the Arab embargo of Israel. Thanks to its U.S. output, however, Honda Motor Co. has found a way to circumvent these problems: It ships four-door Accords to Taiwan and Korea and Civic sedans to Israel, all from Ohio.

It is likely that the end of the Cold War will further increase opportunities for corporate globalization, as new conditions will expand existing markets and introduce countries and corporations long unrepresented in the global economy.

THE INTERNATIONAL ENVIRONMENT
Procter & Gamble Markets to Latin America

Although many multinational companies gave up on Peru's economy, Procter & Gamble, the Cincinnati-based corporation founded in 1837 by a soapmaker and a candlemaker, remained. Today, the consumer-products company, whose products include Mr. Clean, Clearasil, and Pampers, is expanding in South America. The Latin American division *that began as a fledgling detergent company is now a $1-billion business that contributes 15 percent of P&G's international sales. The company expects the division, which has subsidiaries in nine countries and sells in ten others through distributors, to double its revenue again in five years. P&G also says the division's profit margins exceed its interna-*

tional average—and for a multinational competing in over 140 countries and reaping 46 percent of its total sales outside the United States, that is no small feat.

Currently, P&G has operations in fifty-one countries outside the United States. Latin America is viewed as central to its global strategy. The region is rich in raw materials as well as consumers eager to purchase the many and varied personal-care products and laundry and cleaning products seen as essential to modern life.

The international side of P&G's business is relatively young, most of it created after World War II. It is, however, the fastest-growing part of the corporation's business, with over $5.5 billion in sales attributed to the international division. Procter & Gamble Mexico was one of the firm's first foreign ventures.

However, more than 25 percent of top management was born outside the United States, and P&G learned an important lesson in Mexico: U.S. management and marketing plans often do not work outside the United States. For example, Ace laundry detergent, introduced in Mexico in the early 1950s, was decidedly trounced by local competitors. Developed for U.S. washing machines, the product had a low-suds formula. Many Mexicans, however, still washed clothing in the river or a basin of water. For them, the efficiency of a cleaner was measured by the amount of suds sent wafting down the river while laundering. P&G eventually changed the formula and switched to smaller quantities for people who shopped almost daily and could not afford larger amounts.

Although P&G was able to forge new ground in Mexico, until 1987 doing business in Latin America was not considered viable and appealing to managers who felt that the area lacked the glamor and appeal of the Far East and Europe.

Originally, P&G encountered political and economic chaos when it set up shop in Peru and Venezuela. And although opportunities began to increase in Peru since the collapse of a military regime that had forced foreign businesses to yield control to local workers, so did the inflation rate in the late 1980s. The company's response to staggering inflation in Peru was to try to preserve its disappearing market while maintaining quality products. In addition to maintaining product quality, P&G has been forced to pursue the wholesale and retail trade. At one point, that meant that

it was raising prices 20 to 30 percent every two weeks and thus causing some small shops to reduce their orders. For these outlets, P&G hired a local fleet of delivery people to deliver orders, sometimes in exchange for such necessities as toothpaste.

Despite the turmoil in Peru, P&G has actually widened its product line, hoping that such initiatives will ultimately make business grow. It now sells 15 brands of toothpaste, detergent, soap, and health-care products in Peru. It also has tried to retain employees who might be tempted to flee Peru by adjusting salaries on a monthly basis to keep up with inflation.

Similarly, P&G has weathered hard times in Venezuela. In the early 1980s, that country was rocked by economic shocks set off by rising debt and falling oil prices. Coupled with Venezuela's strict pricing controls, these events complicate life for P&G, and to compound matters, there were times the Venezuelan government competed with P&G. In the late 1970s, for example, the government itself imported Pampers disposable diapers—one of P&G's main products—and locked up half of the disposable-diaper market. Meanwhile, the P&G subsidiary also imported Pampers, selling them to retailers and wholesalers not supplied by the government. When the local market was devalued, the subsidiary suffered because the government got a preferential exchange rate and cheaper transportation. Domestic Pampers thus lost market share to imported Pampers, and for a while, all imports of P&G diapers were halted.

One thing about the Venezuelan economy, however, is certain and predictable: Venezuelan consumers price value above all else. Thus, P&G not only keeps producing a line of products consistent with these values, it continues to strive to introduce products that best fit the needs of this Latin American country.

Indeed, founders William Procter and James Gamble could never have imagined how their soap-and-candle company would blossom. It seems clear that after more than 150 years, P&G continues to maintain the same standards of quality that its founders introduced by investing heavily in research and development and remaining committed to marketing products that are often superior to those of competitors.

■ Concept Check 7-4   Corporations

- Explain the primary differences between a partnership and a *corporation*.
- Discuss the chief articles of a corporation's power and authority to act. Define the *doctrine of ultra vires*.
- Describe the four major categories of corporations and explain the requirements for qualifying as an *S corporation*.
- Explain the doctrine known as *piercing the corporate veil*.
- Describe the major differences between *nonprofit corporations* and those falling into one of the other three categories.
- Discuss the basic decisions faced by a corporation in deciding to expand globally.

■ CORPORATE GOVERNANCE

corporate governance The corporate decision-making process, involving shareholders, directors, and other members of management

Corporate governance refers to the way in which a corporation's shareholders, directors, and officers make decisions. The corporate hierarchy is fairly easy to understand. *Shareholders* own the corporation and elect the *board of directors*. The board manages the corporation and appoints or elects its *officers*. Officers run the corporation's day-to-day operations and hire employees.

The Statutory Model

shareholder Person who owns shares of stock in a corporation

CORPORATE SHAREHOLDERS. **Shareholders** are the owners of the corporation. The precise nature of the relationship between a shareholder and a particular corporation depends upon the particular corporation. In a large, publicly owned corporation, the average shareholder neither has control over the operations of the corporation nor bears any fiduciary relationship to the corporation or to the other shareholders. As seen earlier in this chapter, a *fiduciary relationship* is based on confidence or trust and good faith. The shareholder's primary responsibility and power in corporate governance is electing the board of directors. In turn, the board of directors sets corporate policy and ensures that it is properly executed. Executing corporate policy and making routine management decisions is the responsibility of officers who derive their authority from the directors.

Shareholders also derive power from their ability to amend the corporate charter and its bylaws. The corporate charter is recognized as having the characteristics of a contract between the state and the individual corporation, which

bylaws Contractual agreement, enacted to supplement the *articles of incorporation*, between a corporation and its shareholders

has only the powers granted it by the legislature. **Bylaws,** which are enacted to supplement the corporate charter, are like a contract between the corporation and its shareholders.

Voting on shareholder issues usually occurs at annual meetings, although special meetings can be called at other times as long as proper notice is given to shareholders; unless there is a contrary provision in the corporate charter, each shareholder is entitled to one vote per share of stock owned.

Voting rights. The two most common types of voting rights are *straight* and *cumulative voting.* Straight voting means that each shareholder is entitled to one vote per share owned for each issue being voted on and for each seat on the board of directors. Straight voting often prevents minority shareholders from having their say on issues and electing directors to the board. An example of straight voting is as follows: Assume Shareholder A has 50 shares and Shareholder B 100 shares. If there are six seats to be filled on the board, A will cast 50 votes for each of the six candidates and B will cast 100 votes for each of the six candidates. It is easy to see why shareholder B will always win through straight voting.

Cumulative voting, on the other hand, gives minority shareholders more voting power. Cumulative voting works this way: Shareholder A, with 50 shares, has a total of 300 votes for the six director's seats to be filled (50×6). Because there are six seats in contention, the shareholder's amount of votes is multiplied by six. These votes may either be *cumulated* and used for one candidate or spread out over several candidates. This method of voting is designed to protect small shareholders from being outvoted at least for one seat on the board.

Voting by proxy allows a shareholder to vote even though he or she will not be present at the meeting. A *proxy* authorizes one shareholder to cast the vote of another. It must be in writing and signed to be valid.

Although majority shareholders often have the voting power to defeat minority shareholders, such power must be properly exercised. Majority shareholders have a fiduciary relationship with minority shareholders and must abide by principles of fairness and good faith in corporate matters.

Shareholder's Derivative Action. A minority shareholder who feels that the majority is either acting illegally or failing to act in the best interests of the corporation may bring a suit against the majority on behalf of the corporation. This type of suit, called a **derivative action,** is brought by an injured party for the protection of the corporation. The action may seek an award of damages from the majority or offending corporate player. It is important to note that a wrong to a shareholder in his *individual capacity*—that is, in some capacity other than shareholder—cannot be the basis of a derivative action by the shareholder. Moreover, the action cannot be brought by a shareholder who agreed to the acts complained of or for wrongs done in his or her individual capacity. Derivative actions may also be brought by officers in their capacity as officers.

derivative action Suit to enforce a corporate cause of action brought by a shareholder against other shareholders on the behalf of the corporation

Those sued must prove that they have not abused their duty to act fairly and honestly. Any money that is recovered goes to the corporation after expenses are paid. Other types of claims that may be asserted in a shareholder's derivative action include improper use of corporate materials, inside information by officers and directors to secure profits from trading in the corporation's shares, breach of the fiduciary obligation of an officer or director to the corporation, and an action to compel a wrongfully withheld dividend. Recall the case of *Shlensky v. Wrigley* (1968) in Chapter 2 (*see* p. 58), in which a minority shareholder in the Chicago Cubs organization sued to have lights installed at Wrigley Field so that the corporation could increase its profits by offering night games to loyal Chicago fans.

CORPORATE BOARD OF DIRECTORS. As we have seen, the basic responsibility of the board is to manage the corporation's affairs. The board establishes corporate goals and strategies, elects and removes officers, declares dividends, and proposes fundamental changes for shareholders' consideration. A fundamental change could concern voting rights, the acquisition of or merger with another corporation, or dissolution.

Directors are fiduciaries of the corporation's shareholders: Each director is an agent of the shareholders and owes each shareholder the duties of care, diligence, and loyalty. The director's duty of loyalty is especially important because many directors of large corporations sit on several boards—an arrangement that often leads to potential conflicts of interest.

CORPORATE OFFICERS. In most corporations, officers include the president, vice-president, secretary, and treasurer. The chief executive officer (CEO) of a corporation may serve either as its board chairman or president. As we have also noted, corporate officers are chosen by the board of directors and are its agents. The corporation's bylaws, custom, or employment contracts may delineate their specific duties. The job of corporate officers is to manage the company's day-to-day operations according to the board's policies and directives. They are fiduciaries of the board of directors and, as such, owe the duties of care, loyalty, and diligence. When corporate officers exercise the opportunities offered by their positions, the question arises as to how much freedom they should have in pursuing legitimate personal interests.

Corporate Responsibility and the Charity Principle Scottish-born Andrew Carnegie (1835–1919) was the prime mover behind the consolidation, in 1901, of several of the country's largest steel producers into U.S. Steel, whose gross income 15 years later was greater than that of the Treasury. The debate about bigness in U.S. business was not new at the turn of the century: Jeffersonians had railed against monetary policies favoring monied interests at the dawn of the 19th century, and in the 1840s, Jacksonian democrats had assailed the same interests through attacks on the Second Bank of the U.S. (see Chapter 3). By the 1870s, however, concern over the size and power of American business interests had begun to focus on the large corporation, whose social and political accountability is of a quite different order than that of smaller businesses. Carnegie himself made a classic statement of *corporate social responsibility* (see Chapter 2) and the "charity principle" in his *The Gospel of Wealth* (1889), arguing that personal and corporate wealth is held "in trust" for society as a whole. Turning capitalism to philanthropy, Carnegie spent the rest of his life giving away much of his vast fortune, but even though U.S. Steel may have been an exception, historians generally agree that much corporate philanthropy between the Civil War and the Depression was activated either by law or labor-union pressure. A related idea, the *stewardship principle*, which argued that those with personal and corporate wealth held property as "caretakers" for society, was a favorite of Sears CEO Robert Wood.

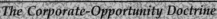

YOU DECIDE
The Corporate-Opportunity Doctrine

As fiduciaries of their corporations, officers are subject to the rule of undivided loyalty, which restricts them from competing with the corporation. Although directors and officers are not necessarily precluded from engaging in other businesses, they may not use their corporate positions to prevent the corporation from competing with them, use corporate personnel, facilities, or funds for their own businesses, disclose corporate trade secrets to others, or violate reasonable agreements not to compete.

Another aspect of the rule of undivided loyalty is the corporate-opportunity doctrine. It states that neither directors, officers, nor controlling shareholders may acquire or divert to themselves property or opportunities which the corporation needs or is seeking, of which the corporation has a reasonable "expectancy" of taking, or which those officers were otherwise under a duty to acquire for the corporation. Such directors, officers, or controlling shareholders may be held liable for the diversion of business opportunities and property from the corporation, such as assets, contracts, and the like.

The corporate opportunity doctrine does not usually affect acquisitions which the corporation has refused or opportunities that it would not have been able to take advantage of or that are not feasible, appropriate, or logically related to the corporation's business.

There remains, however, a certain amount of tension between directors or officers who, in addition to their corporate responsibilities, have personal interests to advance. In these cases, too strict an application of the rule of undivided loyalty would not only restrict free enterprise but would discourage competent people from serving in corporate directorships, which are generally part time and/or for nominal compensation.

The logical question for a corporation trying to form and maintain a productive board is how restrictive should its corporate-opportunity doctrine be? Stringent application might discourage otherwise competent potential directors from serving if their personal interests, participation on other boards, or business ventures do not fit with those of the corporation. On the other hand, reasonably strict application of the rule may encourage undivided loyalty and foster a sense of equality among board members.

Corporations have grappled with this question of balancing its interests with those of free enterprise and autonomy among its board members. Perhaps the classic case dealing with the corporate-opportunity doctrine is Guth v. Loft, 23

Del.Ch. 255, 5A.2d 503 (Sup. Ct. 1939). Guth was president of Loft, a Delaware corporation that manufactured candies, syrups, and beverages that it sold at wholesale prices in the Middle Atlantic states. It seems that Guth became angered at Coca-Cola's refusal to give Loft what he thought was a suitable discount. At the same time, he heard about a company called Pepsi-Cola, which also had a formula and trademark and which was facing a waning market in the South. When National Pepsi-Cola went bankrupt, Guth and a friend formed a new Pepsi-Cola, acquiring both formula and trademark. For the next four years, Guth poured Loft's resources into Pepsi, using its plant, its working capital, and its work force.

Loft made the Pepsi concentrate and sold it to Grace, a Guth-owned firm, at a nominal mark-up. In turn, Grace resold the syrup, with sugar and water, to Pepsi's customers—chiefly Loft—at an appreciable profit. In a short time, Pepsi-Cola became a financial success and Guth denied that Loft had any interest in it. When all was said and done, replacing Coca-Cola with Pepsi cost Loft losses of profits estimated at $300,000 (a grand sum in 1935) plus advertising expenses. To add insult to injury, Guth owed Loft over $100,000. Consequently, Guth was fired and Loft slapped him with a lawsuit.

Did Guth go too far with his venture? Would this instance suggest a stringent application of the corporate-opportunity doctrine or should Guth be lauded for his burgeoning enterprise? For further discussion, see p. 259.

THE BUSINESS-JUDGMENT RULE. The *duty of care* has a distinct role in corporate law. It requires directors—and all agents—to exercise sound business judgment. The **business-judgment rule** was created to protect directors from shareholders' unreasonable expectations and prevents the courts from second-guessing corporate directors. The rule shelters a director from liability in instances in which his mistaken belief or action was reasonably and honestly undertaken. When a director's bad faith, fraud, or dishonest purpose can be proven by a shareholder, the business-judgment rule will not protect the director. The following case illustrates how this rule works.

business-judgment rule
Doctrine holding that corporate management cannot be held liable to shareholders for management decisions unless fraud, bad faith, or dishonest purpose can be proved

SMITH v. VAN GORKOM
Delaware Supreme Court, 488 A.2d 858 (1985)

In order to realize a favorable tax situation, defendant Van Gorkom, chief executive of Trans Union Corporation ("Trans Union" or "the Company"), solicited a merger offer from Pritzer, an outside investor. Van Gorkom acted on his own and arbitrarily arrived at a buyout price of $55 per share. Without any investigation, the full Trans Union board accepted the offer. The offer was proposed two subsequent times before its formal acceptance by the board. Plaintiff Smith and other shareholders brought this derivative suit on the basis that the board had not given due consideration to the offer. The trial court held that the shareholder vote approving the merger should not be set aside because the stockholders had been "fairly informed" by the board of directors before voting on it; and that because it considered the offer three times before formally accepting it, the board had acted in an informed manner so as to be entitled to protection of the business-judgment rule. The plaintiffs appeal.

Horsey, Justice (for the majority).

. . . .

On Friday, September 19, Van Gorkom called a special meeting of the Trans Union Board for noon the following day. . . .

. . . .

Van Gorkom began the Special Meeting of the Board with a twenty-minute oral presentation. Copies of the proposed Merger Agreement were delivered too late for study before or during the meeting. He reviewed the Company's ITC and depreciation problems and the efforts theretofore made to solve them. He discussed his initial meeting with Pritzker and his motivation in arranging that meeting. Van Gorkom did not disclose to the Board, however, the methodology by which he alone had arrived at the $55 figure, or the fact that he first proposed the $55 price in his negotiations with Pritzker.

Van Gorkom outlined the terms of the Pritzker offer as follows: Pritzker would pay $55 in cash for all outstanding shares of Trans Union stock upon completion of which Trans Union would be merged into New T Company, a subsidiary wholly-owned by Pritzker and formed to implement the merger; for a period of 90 days, Trans Union could receive, but could not actively solicit, competing offers; the offer had to be acted on by the next evening, Sunday, September 21; Trans Union could only furnish to competing bidders published information, and not proprietary information; the offer was subject to Pritzker obtaining the necessary financing by October 10, 1980; if the financing contingency were met or waived by Pritzker, Trans Union was required to sell to Pritzker one million newly-issued shares of Trans Union at $38 per share.

. . . .

The Board meeting of September 20 lasted about two hours. . . . [T]he directors approved the proposed Merger Agreement. . . .

. . . .

On February 10, the stockholders of Trans Union approved the Pritzker merger proposal. Of the outstanding shares, 69.9% were voted in favor of the merger; 7.25% were voted against the merger; and 22.85% were not voted.

The determination of whether a business judgment is an informed one turns on whether the directors have informed themselves "prior to making a business decision, of all material information reasonably available to them."

Under the business judgment rule there is no protection for directors who have made "an unintelligent or unadvised judgment." *Mitchell v. Highland-Western Glass* (1933). A director's duty to inform himself in preparation for a decision derives from the fiduciary capacity in which he serves the corporation and its stockholders. . . .

In the specific context of a proposed merger of domestic corporations, a director has a duty under 8 *Del.C.* 251(b), along with his fellow directors, to act in an informed and deliberate manner in determining whether to approve an agreement of merger before submitting the proposal to the stockholders. Certainly in the merger context, a director may not abdicate that duty by leaving to the shareholders alone the decision to approve or disapprove the agreement. . . .

. . . .

On the record before us, we must conclude that the Board of Directors did not reach an informed business judgment on September 20, 1980 in voting to "sell" the Company for $55 per share pursuant to the Pritzker cash-out merger proposal. Our reasons, in summary, are as follows:

The directors (1) did not adequately inform themselves as to Van Gorkom's role in forcing the "sale" of the Company and in establishing the per share purchase price; (2) were uninformed as to the intrinsic value of the Company; and (3) given these circumstances, at a minimum, were grossly negligent in approving the "sale" of the Company upon two hours' consideration, without prior notice, and without the exigency of a crisis or emergency.

. . . .

Without any documents before them concerning the proposed transaction, the members of the Board were required to rely entirely upon Van Gorkom's 20-minute oral presentation of the proposal. No written summary of the terms of the merger was presented; the directors were given no documentation to support the adequacy of $55 price per share for sale of the Company; and the Board had before it nothing more than Van Gorkom's statement of his understanding of the substance of an agreement which he admittedly had never read, nor which any member of the Board had ever seen.

. . . .

. . . [T]here was no call by the Board, either on September 20 or thereafter, for any valuation study or documentation of the $55 price per share as a measure of the fair value of the Company in a cash-out context. It is undisputed that the major asset of Trans Union was its cash flow. Yet, at no time did the Board call for a valuation study taking into account that highly significant element of the Company's assets.

. . . .

The record also establishes that the Board accepted without scrutiny Van Gorkom's representation as to the fairness of the $55 price per share for sale of the Company—a subject that the Board had never previously considered. The Board thereby failed to discover that Van Gorkom had suggested the $55 price to Pritzker and, most crucially, that Van Gorkom had arrived at the $55 figure based on calculations designed solely to determine the feasibility of a leveraged buy-out. No questions were raised either as to the tax implications of a cash-out merger or how the price for the one million share option granted Pritzker was calculated.

We do not say that the Board of Directors was not entitled to give some credence to Van Gorkom's representation that $55 was an adequate or fair price. . . . [T]he issue is whether the directors informed themselves as to all information that was reasonably available to them. Had they done so, they would have learned of the source and derivation of the $55 price and could not reasonably have relied thereupon in good faith.

. . . .

The defendants ultimately rely on the stockholder vote of February 10 for exoneration. The defendants contend that the stockholders' "overwhelming" vote approving the Pritzker Merger Agreement had the legal effect of curing any failure of the Board to reach an informed business judgment in its approval of the merger.

. . . .

We find the Board's recital in the Supplemental Proxy of certain events preceding the September 20 meeting to be incomplete and misleading. . . . Although by January 26, the directors knew the basis of the $55 figure, they did not disclose that Van Gorkom chose the $55 price because that figure would enable Pritzker to both finance the purchase of Trans Union through a leveraged buy-out and, within five years, substantially repay the loan out of the cash flow generated by the Company's operations.

. . . .

The burden must fall on defendants who claim ratification based on shareholder vote to establish that the shareholder approval resulted from a fully informed electorate. On the record before us, it is clear that the Board failed to meet that burden.

. . . .

To summarize: we hold that the directors of Trans Union breached their fiduciary duty to their stockholders (1) by their failure to inform themselves of all information reasonably available to them and relevant to their decision to recommend the Pritzker merger; and (2) by their failure to disclose all material information such as a reasonable stockholder would consider important in deciding whether to approve the Pritzker offer.

We hold, therefore, that the Trial Court committed reversible error in applying the business judgment rule in favor of the director defendants in this case.

Case Questions

1. Why did the court find that the business-judgment rule was not applicable to "shield" the decision by the directors of Trans Union to approve the merger?

2. On what basis did the court hold that the decision by the directors was not an "informed" one?

3. Under what different circumstances could the business-judgment rule have shielded the directors' decision?

The business-judgment rule, however, does not protect directors completely. Consider the plight of the directors of Trans Union Corporation, who were held liable for negligence: Only $10 million of the plaintiffs' $23.5 million award was covered by a special insurance policy (purchased to protect directors against such suits).

About half of the states have laws that restrict directors' liability in some way. These statutes help to fill seats on the board because they remove potential exposure to lawsuits. In states lacking such statutes, it may be more difficult to find people to serve as directors.

Fourth, although two major players (the corporate creditor and the federal government) and one minor player (public-interest groups) do not formally appear on the theoretical organization of a corporation, their importance cannot be underestimated. Most corporate ventures cannot be accomplished without financing from commercial banks, and as a result, many boards welcome the addition of bankers. The federal government's interest is clear when one looks at the many laws enacted concerning the issuance of stocks and bonds, corporate taxes, labor laws, protection of the environment, and even laws that expose corporations to criminal liability for wrongful acts. Public-interest groups can and often do gain influence in corporate decision making by lobbying the federal government for the enactment of certain laws. Environmental public-interest groups have been especially effective (*see* Chapter 20).

The Reality: Separation of Ownership and Control

In many corporations, corporate reality bears only a vague resemblance to the model envisioned by statutes. First, the shareholders' role in choosing corporate directors rarely conforms to the scheme outlined above. For example, in a closely held or closed corporation, there are relatively few shareholders, and their form of governance is often informal and more like a partnership. However, in publicly held corporations, which may have thousands of shareholders, this situation is less often the case.

Second, because it is unlikely that a single shareholder owns either a controlling number of shares or enough shares to organize a voting block, shareholders may actually have only minimal incentive to participate in the governance of large corporations. Accordingly, a shareholder's opinion may be heard only on questions dealing with fundamental corporate changes—mergers, consolidation, dissolution, and the like. Quite simply, it is much easier for a disgruntled shareholder to sell his shares than to seek a real say in corporate decisions.

Third, because logistics make it impossible to convene every time a serious issue arises, modern boards are often quite remote from corporate affairs. Consequently, much of the overall management and supervision of corporate affairs is the responsibility of the CEO and other corporate executives.

An *interested director* is one who has a conflict of interest because he or she has the opportunity to compete directly or indirectly with the corporation for a purchase or for an asset to the firm or may expose it to losses or liability. When there is the possibility of such conflict, a director must reveal his interest to the board and offer the opportunity to the corporation.

Figure 7-6 presents a simplified look at corporate governance.

Proposals for Corporate Reform

Today's modern corporation is faced with two major issues that must be examined to assure its future. First is the question of who really governs modern giant corporations—shareholders, management, directors, or the government.

FIGURE 7-6 Model of Corporate Governance   *Source: Keith Davis, William C. Frederick, and Robert L Blomstrom,* Business and Society: Concepts and Policy Issues *(New York: McGraw-Hill, 1980).*

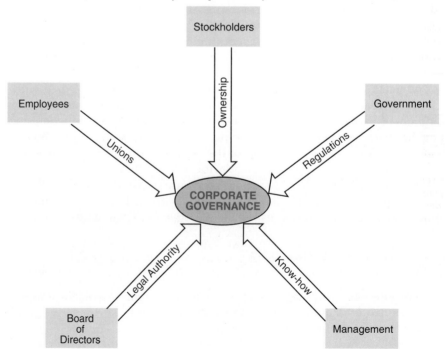

Once that is determined, it is logical to consider who is really in the best position to govern. Because each corporation has its unique needs based on its purpose, size, and shareholders, this question must be considered on a corporation-by-corporation basis. Second is the question of whose interests should be supreme in determining a corporation's direction. Determining whether it should be those of the shareholders, employees, or the public may also be a decision unique to a particular corporation.

Two proposals for corporate reform have garnered the most attention. The most radical is the federal chartering of corporations. Corporations are presently chartered by the states of their incorporation. This allows corporations to shop for states, such as Delaware, which offer the most favorable regulations, tax, and incorporation laws. Critics of this proposal fear placing more power over corporate affairs in the hands of the federal government and contend that corporations would not be adequately monitored and regulated. Proponents assert that federal chartering will allow more uniform imposition of requirements which, they argue, will benefit the public interest.

The second proposal is to reform the role of the board of directors in order to make them less subject to management domination and more sensitive to shareholder interests. Proponents suggest that the company's profit level should not be the only measure of its success and should more accurately include management's use of capital and the achievement of long-term planning goals. This trend started to gain notoriety in the late 1970s. An example of reformation includes increasing the number of outside directors who have no interest in the company and who are less likely to have conflicts of interest. This trend has also led to the SEC's requirement that all corporations listed on the New York Stock Exchange have audit committees comprised of outsiders.

■ Concept Check 7-5   Corporate Governance

- Identify and explain the major roles in the *statutory model* of corporate governance.
- Discuss the ways in which corporate reality differs from the statutory model of corporate governance.
- Discuss some of the proposals for reform of modern corporate governance.

YOU DECIDE: ANSWER/DISCUSSION
The Corporate-Opportunity Doctrine

The court found that Guth had wrongfully appropriated a corporate opportunity and ordered him to turn over to Loft all the shares of Pepsi stock (by then worth millions of dollars), all dividends thereon, plus all salary received from Pepsi.

At issue for the court were the following questions: Was the opportunity to secure a substantial stock interest in a corporation formed for the purpose of exploiting a cola beverage on a wholesale scale too closely related to the existing business opportunities of Loft? Would the acquisition of the property throw the corporate officer into competition with his company?

The court determined that the facts and circumstances demonstrated that Guth's appropriation of the Pepsi-Cola opportunity to himself placed him in a competitive position with Loft with respect to a commodity essential to it, thereby rendering his personal interests incompatible with the superior interests of his corporation. It also found that this undertaking was accomplished not openly and with his own resources, but secretly and with the money and facilities of the corporation that was committed to his protection.

SUMMARY

- Certain rules about the formation, internal operation, taxation, and legal liability apply to each form of business organization. An understanding of *agency law* is critical to understanding business relationships. An agency relationship exists whenever the owner (or *principal*) delegates authority to another person—that is, an *agent*—to act on his behalf for the good of the company. Agents may have either *express authority* or *implied* or *apparent authority*. Agents—who may be employees, corporate directors, or officers or partners—owe principals certain duties, including loyalty and obedience, to exercise skill and care, to inform, and to account. Deviation from the expected standard of care owed to third parties may expose the principal to liability. Under the concept of *respondeat superior*, principals are responsible for all torts committed by their agents when they act within the scope of their agency. Under the concept of *vicarious liability*, an employer may be held responsible for the negligent acts of its employees.

- The most common forms of doing business are sole proprietorships, partnerships and corporations. The biggest advantage of *sole proprietorships*, which are the most common forms of doing business in the U.S., is that they are easy to start up and easy to dissolve. Unless a license is required by the particular state, sole proprietorships are created by simply beginning to do business. As the sole owner of all the firm's assets, the proprietor has a unilateral right to make all significant business decisions; the sole proprietor is also personally liable for all business debts and other legal obligations. Moreover, a sole proprietorship's ability to raise capital depends upon the sole proprietor's personal credit rating.

- A *partnership* is an association of two or more people who join together for the purpose of making a profit. Partnerships allow several owners to pool resources and expertise to create and manage a new enterprise or may be formed by professionals such as doctors and lawyers. Although a partnership agreement need not be in writing, written agreements can spell out partners' respective rights and make provisions for management, profits and losses. Unless the partnership agreement has contrary provisions, partnerships dissolve automatically with the death, insanity, bankruptcy, withdrawal, or expulsion of a partner. The chief disadvantage of partnerships is that *general partners* are personally liable for all business debts and obligations; *limited partners*, however, are personally liable only to the extent of their investment. A hybrid form of business organization that falls between a limited partnership and a corporation is the *master limited partnership*.

- *Corporations* are the most complex form of business organization. They can be (1) *foreign* or *domestic*, (2) *closely* or *publicly held*, (3) *S corporations*, or (4) for-profit or nonprofit. *Nonprofit corporations* can be classified by looking at their sources of funding and types of management. The hallmark of a nonprofit corporation is that it does not distribute profits to its owners.

- Corporations have a distinct form of internal organization. *Shareholders*, who own the corporation, contribute capital, receive a share of profits, and vote and elect the board of directors. Shareholders are not usually personally liable for corporate debts. Corporations are required to pay taxes and are subject to numerous government regulations. Because the shareholders, who own the company, are not usually involved in corporate decision making, there is a separation of ownership and control in most large modern corporations. This situation is problematic because the interests of the corporate officers may not be in accord with the interests of the corporation as a whole. If this conflict becomes acute, shareholders may bring a shareholder's *derivative action* against directors or officers. This kind of lawsuit is brought on behalf of the corporation when an officer or director has violated a *fiduciary duty* or there has been some form of impropriety or mismanagement that may expose the corporation to liability or losses.

- As more and more firms engage in international business, the world's economy is becoming a single interdependent system. If a firm does go international, it must decide its level of involvement in the international market and, in so doing, may act as *exporter*, organize as an *international business*, or operate as a *multinational*. Global or *transnational corporations* look at the whole world as one market. Global corporations face political, social, and regulatory hurdles that pose numerous problems for corporate managers.

QUESTIONS AND PROBLEMS

1. The owner of the P.W. Company hired Jake to drive his truck and deliver goods for his business. Between two deliveries, Jake stopped at his home to briefly attend his son's birthday party. While Jake was in the house eating cake and ice cream, two of the children left the party, got into the truck, and released the brake. They were injured when the truck rolled down the hill and hit a tree. The children's parents sued Jake and the owner of the P.W. Company. Discuss the outcome if the parents sued under agent/principal liability.

2. Terry Segal is Todd Martin's property manager. He agrees to collect rents, disburse money from the proceeds for repairs and mortgage payments, and deposit the remainder to Todd's bank account. In April, Mr. Martin writes a check on his bank account and the check bounces. Upon investigation, he discovers that his manager has collected rents for the past four months, but has not paid the mortgage or paid for repairs. When approached about what is owed, Mr. Martin insists that the creditors contact Terry Segal because he is the one who has not paid the bills as agreed. What should the creditors do?

3. An employee on a ferry boat is responsible for making sure that the doors to the automobile hold are closed after all passengers have boarded the ferry. One day, the employee forgets to close the door. No one notice until a car rolls back and off the boat. Is the employee liable to the principal?

4. Four persons agreed to incorporate themselves for the purpose of constructing a cotton gin under the name "The Coweta Gin Company" and to buy, sell, and gin cotton for profit under the name "The Corveta Cotton & Milling Company." Before the articles of incorporation were filed, the four ordered goods from the plaintiffs and began business as a corporation. Later the articles were filed. A dispute arose over the price. Was a corporation formed before the goods were purchased? Who do you believe is liable for the purchase of the goods?

5. A customer slips on water by the vegetable bin in Jimmy Kane's sole proprietorship grocery store. His injuries are $25,000, but the business is worth only $20,000. Can the customer recover the remaining $5,000? Would the answer be different if the grocery store were a general partnership?

6. Casey Miller owns several shares of stock in XYZ Corp. He inherited them from his grandfather. When he reads in the newspaper that XYZ Corp. is being sued for $65 million, he immediately makes arrangements to sell the shares. He feared that he would be liable if a judgment was entered against XYZ. Should he have worried?

7. The president and vice-president of Adams Corp. decide to start a business of their own. While still employed at Adams, and using Adams' budget, they order paper products with their new logo. They also solicited clients through Adams' billing process. Eventually, they recruited 30 of Adams' employees to resign and work for them. When Adams Corp. learns about their scheme, it sues them. What will the outcome be? [*ABC Trans National Inc. v. Aeronautics Forwarders, Inc.* 413 N.E.2d 1299 (Ill., 1980)]

8. The stockholders of AT&T bring a shareholder's derivative action against AT&T and its directors because of the failure to collect a $1.5 million debt owed by the Democratic National Party for services rendered during the 1968 convention four years before. Is the directors' decision not to seek payment in full from the Democratic National Committee protected by the business-judgment rule? [*Miller v. AT&T* 507F.2d 759 (3d Cir. 1974)]

9. (A). T.J., Jacques, and Chiro are interested in opening a deli together and need your advice on which type of business entity would be best for them. T.J. is not interested in manag-

ing the business. He has $50,000 to invest and would just like to collect a salary. Jacques likes to run everything! He is interested in quitting his job and working full time at the deli. Chiro has $20,000 to invest but does not care if he manages the business or not. Based on these facts, what type of business entity is best for T.J, Jacques, and Chiro?

(B). Suppose T.J. and Chiro want to manage and contribute money to the business and Jacques can only contribute his services, what type of business would you suggest?

(C). Suppose Jacques decides not to get involved in a business with his friends and opens a deli on his own as a sole proprietor. Discuss with him the advantages and disadvantages of such an arrangement.

8
SECURITIES REGULATION

Selling securities—that is, stocks and bonds—is one of the primary ways in which corporations raise the capital they need to operate. A *bond* is a certificate of indebtedness; the corporation is borrowing money that must be repaid at a specified date. A *stock* represents a share in ownership of the corporation. A corporation is not required to buy back its stocks. However, at the discretion of its board of directors, it may distribute shares of its profits to stockholders in the form of *dividend payments*. Stocks are riskier investments than bonds because there are no legal guarantees that stockholders will recoup their initial investments or receive periodic shares in the corporation's profits.

Corporations generally sell stocks to finance business expansion. Individuals buy them seeking a range of financial benefits from short-term profits to long-term security. Some stocks are relatively safe investments that offer moderate yields. Higher-risk stocks offer the possibility of higher yields. The purchase and sale of securities can generate substantial profits and equally substantial losses. The temptation to speculate is strong, and the risks can be high.

The issuance and sale of securities are governed by two laws that we will discuss in this chapter: the *Securities Act of 1933*, which governs the issuance of new stock; and the *Securities Exchange Act of 1934*, which governs the trading of existing stocks. The purpose of both acts is to ensure that investors get the information they need in order to make rational decisions.

■ DEFINITION OF A "SECURITY"

Figure 8.1 shows a sample common-stock certificate; various items identified on the certificate are discussed in this section and the next. In the broadest and least technical sense, a **stock** (or an **equity security**) is a symbolic representation of an interest in a business entity. This is a rather simple definition. The Securities Act of 1933 defines equity securities as follows:

stock (or equity security) A symbolic representation of an interest in a business entity

263

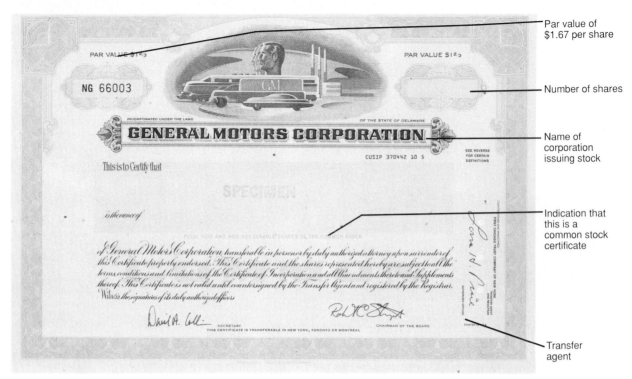

FIGURE 8-1 Sample Common-Stock Certificate

The term "security" means any note, stock, treasury stock, bond, debenture, evidence of indebtedness, certificate of interest or participation in any profit-sharing agreement, collateral-trust certificate, preorganization certificate or subscription, transferable share investment contract, voting-trust certificate, certificate of deposit for a security, fractional undivided interest in oil, gas, or other mineral rights, any put, call, straddle, option, or privilege on any security, certificate of deposit, or group or index of securities (including any interest therein or based on the value thereof), or any put, call, straddle, option, or privilege entered into on a national securities exchange relating to foreign currency, or, in general, any interest or instrument commonly known as a "security," or any certificate of interest or participation in, temporary or interim certificate for, receipt for, guarantee of, or warrant or right to subscribe to or purchase, any of the foregoing.[1]

This is a broad definition, covering many different kinds of financial instruments and investment contracts. Its very broadness has generated an enormous amount of legal controversy. As a result, the SEC and the courts must decide which securities meet the definition on a case-by-case basis. In 1985, the Supreme Court suggested just how broad and flexible an interpretation it uses:

> Where an instrument bears the label stock, and possesses all of the characteristics typically associated with stock, a court will not be required to look beyond the character of the instrument to the economic substance of the transaction to determine whether the stock is a security within the meaning of the [Securities] Acts.[2]

---

[1] 15 U.S.C. 77b(1).

[2] *Gould v. Ruefenacht,* 105 S.Ct. 2308 (1985).

The following case illustrates the difficulties that the courts encounter in making such a determination.

REVES v. ERNST & YOUNG
United States Supreme Court 108 L.Ed.2d 47 (1990)

To raise money, an Arkansas agricultural cooperative comprised of 23,000 members sold promissory notes that paid the holder on demand a higher rate of interest than local financial institutions. The co-op, which offered the notes to both members and nonmembers, told potential investors that the notes were not federally insured but stated that their money would be safe, secure, and available when they needed it. In 1984, the co-op filed for bankruptcy. At the time, more than 1,600 people held notes worth $10 million. A class made up of holders of these notes sued Arthur Young & Co., the accounting firm that had audited the co-op's financial statements. The plaintiffs claimed that Arthur Young violated standard accounting procedures in an effort to inflate the co-op's net worth and assets in violation of both the federal Securities Exchange Act of 1934 and state law. The trial court awarded the plaintiffs $6.1 million, but the Eighth Circuit Court of Appeals reversed the judgment, holding that the promissory notes were not "securities" within the meaning of the federal law. Plaintiffs appealed to the U.S. Supreme Court.

Justice Marshall delivered the opinion of the Court.
. . .

This case requires us to decide whether the note issued by the Co-op is a "security" within the meaning of the 1934 Act. Section 3(a)(10) of that Act is our starting point:

"The term 'security' means any note, stock, treasury stock, bond, debenture, certificate of interest or participation in any profit-sharing agreement or in any oil, gas, or other mineral royalty or lease, any collateral-trust certificate, preorganization certificate or subscription, transferable share, investment contract, voting-trust certificate, certificate of deposit, for a security, any put, call, straddle, option, or privilege on any security, certificate of deposit, or group or index of securities (including any interest therein or based on the value thereof), or any put, call, straddle, option, or privilege entered into on a national securities exchange relating to foreign currency, or in general, any instrument commonly known as a 'security'; or any certificate of interest or participation in, tempo-

rary or interim certificate for, receipt for, or warrant or right to subscribe to or purchase, any of the foregoing; but shall not include currency or any note, draft, bill of exchange, or banker's acceptance which has a maturity at the time of issuance of not exceeding nine months, exclusive of days of grace, or any renewal thereof the maturity of which is likewise limited."

. . . The fundamental purpose undergirding the Securities Acts is "to eliminate serious abuses in a largely unregulated securities market." . . . In defining the scope of the market that it wished to regulate, Congress painted with a broad brush. It recognized the virtually limitless scope of human ingenuity, especially in the creation of "countless and variable schemes devised by those who seek the use of the money of others on the promise of profits," . . . and determined that the best way to achieve its goal of protecting investors was to "define 'the term "security" in sufficiently broad and general terms so as to include within that definition the many types of instruments that in our commercial world fall within the ordinary concept of a security.' " . . . Congress therefore did not attempt precisely to cabin the scope of the Securities Acts. Rather, it enacted a definition of "security" sufficiently broad to encompass virtually any instrument that might be sold as an investment.

Congress did not, however, "intend to provide a broad federal remedy for all fraud." . . . Accordingly, "[t]he task has fallen to the Securities and Exchange Commission (SEC), the body charged with administering the Securities Acts, and ultimately to the federal courts to decide which of the myriad financial transactions in our society come within the coverage of these statutes." . . . In discharging our duty, we are not bound by legal formalisms, but instead take account of the economics of the transaction under investigation. . . . Congress' purpose in enacting the securities laws was to regulate *investments,* in whatever name they are called.

. . .

The Second Circuit's "family resemblance" approach begins with a presumption that *any* note with a term of more than nine months is a "security." . . . Recognizing that not all notes are securities, however, the Second Circuit has also devised a list of notes that it has decided are obviously not securities. Accordingly, the "family resemblance" test permits an issuer to rebut the presumption that a note is a security if it can show that the note in question "bear[s] a strong family resemblance" to an item on the judicially crafted list of exceptions . . . or convinces the court to add a new instrument to the list.

. . .

Because we think the "family resemblance" test provides a more promising framework for analysis, however, we adopt it. The test begins with the language of the statute; because the Securities Acts define "security" to include "any note," we begin with a presumption that every note is a security. We nonetheless recognize that this presumption cannot be irrebutable. As we have said . . . Congress was concerned with regulating the investment market, not with creating a general federal cause of action for fraud. In an attempt to give more content to that dividing line, the Second Circuit has identified a list of instruments commonly denominated "notes" that nonetheless fall without the "security" category.

. . .

We agree that the items identified by the Second Circuit are not properly viewed as "securities." More guidance, though, is needed. It is impossible to make any meaningful inquiry into whether an instrument bears a "resemblance" to one of the instruments identified by the Second Circuit without specifying what it is about *those* instruments that makes *them* non-"securities." Moreover, as the Second Circuit itself has noted, its list is "not graven in stone," ibid., and is therefore capable of expansion. Thus, some standards must be developed for determining when an item should be added to the list.

An examination of the list itself makes clear what those standards should be. In creating its list, the Second Circuit was applying the same factors that this Court has held apply in deciding whether a transaction involves a "security." First, we examine the transaction to assess the motivations that would prompt a reasonable seller and buyer to enter into it. If the seller's purpose is to raise money for the general use of a business enterprise or to finance substantial investments and the buyer is interested primarily in the profit the note is expected to generate, the instrument is likely to be a "security." If the note is exchanged to facilitate the purchase and sale of a minor asset or consumer good, to correct for the seller's cash-flow difficulties, or to advance some other commercial or consumer purpose, on the other hand, the note is less sensibly described as a "security." . . . Second, we examine the "plan of distribution" of the instrument . . . to determine whether it is an instrument in which there is "common trading for speculation or investment," . . . Third, we examine the reasonable expectations of the investing public: The Court will consider instruments to be "securities" on the basis of such public expectations, even where an economic analysis of the circumstances of the particular transaction might suggest that the instruments are not "securities" as used in that transaction. . . . Finally, we

examine whether some factor such as the existence of another regulatory scheme significantly reduces the risk of the instrument, thereby rendering application of the Securities Acts unnecessary.

. . .

We conclude, then, that in determining whether an instrument denominated a "note" is a "security," courts are to apply the version of the "family resemblance" test that we have articulated here: a note is presumed to be a "security," and that presumption may be rebutted only by a showing that the note bears a strong resemblance (in terms of the four factors we have identified) to one of the enumerated categories of instrument. If an instrument is not sufficiently similar to an item on the list, the decision whether another category should be added is to be made by examining the same factors.

. . .

Applying the family resemblance approach to this case, we have little difficulty in concluding that the notes at issue here are "securities." . . . The Co-Op sold the notes in an effort to raise capital for its general business operations, and purchasers bought them in order to earn a profit in the form of interest. Indeed, one of the primary inducements offered purchasers was an interest rate constantly revised to keep it slightly above the rate paid by local banks and savings and loans. From both sides, then, the transaction is most naturally conceived as an investment in a business enterprise rather than as a purely commercial or consumer transaction.

[1c] As to the plan of distribution, the Co-Op offered the notes over an extended period to its 23,000 members, as well as to nonmembers, and more than 1,600 people held notes when the Co-Op filed for bankruptcy. To be sure, the notes were not traded on an exchange. They were, however, offered and sold to a broad segment of the public, and that is all we have held to be necessary to establish the requisite "common trading" in an instrument.

. . .

The third factor—the public's reasonable perceptions—also supports a finding that the notes in this case are "securities." We have consistently identified the fundamental essence of a "security" to be its character an an "investment." . . . The advertisements for the notes here characterized them as "investments," . . . and there were no countervailing factors that would have led a reasonable person to question this characterization. In these circumstances, it would be reasonable for a prospective purchaser to take the Co-Op at its word.

Finally, we find no risk-reducing factor to suggest that these instruments are not in fact securities.

. . .

The court below found that the "[t]he demand nature of the notes is very uncharacteristic of a security," on the theory that the virtually instant liquidity associated with demand notes is inconsistent with the risk ordinarily associated with "securities." This argument is unpersuasive. Common stock traded on a national exchange is the paradigm of a security, and it is as readily convertible into cash as is a demand note. The same is true of publicly traded corporate bonds, debentures, and any number of other instruments that are plainly within the purview of the Acts. The demand feature of a note does permit a holder to eliminate risk quickly by making a demand, but just as with publicly traded stock, the liquidity of the instrument does not eliminate risk altogether. Indeed, publicly traded stock is even more readily liquid than are demand notes, in that a demand only eliminates risk when and if payment is made, whereas the sale of a share of stock through a national exchange and the receipt of the proceeds usually occur simultaneously.

We therefore hold that the notes at issue here are within the term "note" in § 3(a)(10).

. . .

Relying on the exception in the statute for "any note . . . which has a maturity at the time of issuance of not exceeding nine months," . . . respondent contends that the notes here are not "securities," even if they would otherwise qualify. Respondent cites Arkansas cases standing for the proposition that, in the context of the state statute of limitations, "[a] note payable on demand is due immediately." . . . Respondent concludes from this rule that the "maturity" of a demand note within the meaning of § 3(a)(10) is immediate, which is, of course, less than nine months. Respondent therefore contends that the notes fall within the plain words of the exclusion and are thus not "securities."

. . .

Respondent's contention that the demand notes fall within the "plain words" of the statute rests entirely upon the premise that Arkansas' statute of limitations for suits to collect demand notes is determinative of the "maturity" of the notes, as that term is used in the *federal* Securities Acts. The "maturity" of the notes, however, is a question of federal law. To regard States' statutes of limitations law as controlling the scope of the

Securities Acts would be to hold that a particular instrument is a "security" under the 1934 Act in some States, but that the same instrument is not a "security" in others. . . . We are unpersuaded that Congress intended the Securities Acts to apply differently to the same transactions depending on the accident of which State's law happens to apply.

. . .

For the foregoing reasons, we conclude that the demand notes at issue here fall under the "note" category of instruments that are "securities" under the 1933 and 1934 Acts. We also conclude that, even under a respondent's preferred approach to § 3(a)(10)'s exclusion for short-term notes, these demand notes do not fall within the exclusion. Accordingly, we reverse the judgment of the Court of Appeals and remand the case for further proceedings consistent with this opinion.

So ordered.

Case Questions

1. What are the advantages and disadvantages of including a broad definition of "securities" in the Securities Act of 1934, which does not include a straightforward list of the types of financial instruments that are covered by it?

2. Is the statute's definition of "securities" consistent with the underlying public-policy objectives of the Securities Act of 1934? Is the test that the court articulates for applying this definition consistent with the underlying public-policy objectives of the Act?

3. Did the court reach the right decision? Is it fair to subject a small agricultural co-op to the rigorous record-keeping and bureaucratic requirements of the Securities Act of 1934?

■ SECURITIES MARKETS

Most securities are bought and sold in organized securities markets. In terms of volume or the number and value of shares traded daily, the New York Stock Exchange (NYSE), known as the "big board," is the largest exchange in the United States. Only relatively large companies that meet the rigorous requirements set by the NYSE may use it to list or trade stocks. Collectively, these companies produce about 50 percent of the country's gross national product.

The American Stock Exchange (AMEX) is the nation's second-largest exchange. AMEX lists smaller but still substantial companies and also has strict listing requirements. For example, to be listed on the AMEX, a company must have at least $4 million of tangible assets. Like the NYSE, the AMEX is located in New York. However, stocks listed there also may be traded in smaller regional stock exchanges—for example, Chicago, Philadelphia, and other cities.

Shares in companies which are too small or which do not choose to be listed on any stock exchange are traded in the over-the-counter (OTC) market.

Market makers for each of these stocks offer to buy and sell shares, sending in their prices daily to a computerized network called the National Association of Securities Dealers Automatic Quotation System (NASDAQ).

Figure 8-2 illustrates the relative volume of shares traded on selected organized exchanges; the rapid growth of OTC trading through NASDAQ is due in large part to advances in communications technology. The pie-charts in Figure 8-3 show the change in stock values on international exchange between 1980 and 1988. In terms of overall market value, for example, U.S. exchange transactions are now behind those on the Tokyo exchange, and overall, international exchanges have become increasingly important to U.S. investment professionals.

Securities markets perform several crucial functions in today's economy:

- They are arenas for providing and trading information about prices and sales.
- They provide a continuous securities market, made possible by large volumes of sales, large number of buyers, sellers, and brokers, and the rapid execution of orders.
- They help establish fair stock prices that reflect supply and demand; through a bidding process that includes traders on a computerized network of exchanges, prices are set at auctions.
- They facilitate corporate financing by establishing recognized standards of value for corporate offerings (which makes them more attractive to investors) and by providing for continuous trading.[3]

FIGURE 8-2   Shares Traded on Organized U.S. Stock Exchanges (in million of dollars)   *Source: Ricky W. Griffin and Ronald J. Ebert, Business, 2nd ed. (Englewood Ciliffs, NJ: Prentice Hall, 1991). Data from Securities Industries Yearbook, Rosalie Pepe, ed. (New York: Securities Industries Association, 1987); The Dow Jones Investor's Handbook, Phyllis S. Oierce, ed. (Homewood, IL: Dow-Jones Irwin, 1989); and NASDAQ Fact Book 1989 (Washington, DC: National Association of Securities Dealers, 1989).*

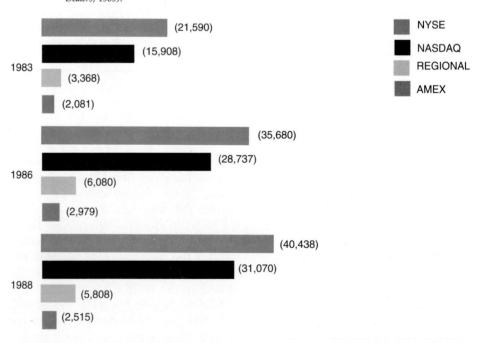

---

[3] F. Amling, *Investments: An Introduction to Analysis and Management*, 5th ed. (Englewood Cliffs, NJ: Prentice Hall, 1984), pp. 241–247.

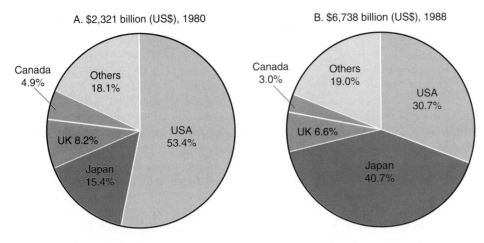

A. $2,321 billion (US$), 1980

Canada 4.9%
Others 18.1%
UK 8.2%
USA 53.4%
Japan 15.4%

B. $6,738 billion (US$), 1988

Canada 3.0%
Others 19.0%
USA 30.7%
UK 6.6%
Japan 40.7%

FIGURE 8-3 Stock Values, Selected International Exchanges *Source: Data from* The Handbook of International Investing, *Carl Beidelman, ed. (Chicago: Probus, 1987).*

The Mechanics of Investing

Through the process of investment banking (*see* Figure 8-4), a corporation that has issued a new security sells it to an investment bank, which then resells it to a retail brokerage firm, which sells it to the individual investor.

In order to invest in a corporation listed on a public exchange, you must enlist the services of a brokerage firm. Whether your investment is in common or preferred stock, bonds, or options—and whether these are new issues or se-

FIGURE 8-4 Purchasing Stock: Five Steps *Source: Adapted from Samuel C. Certo, Stewart W. Husted, and Max E. Douglas,* Business, *3rd ed. (Boston: Allyn and Bacon, 1990).*

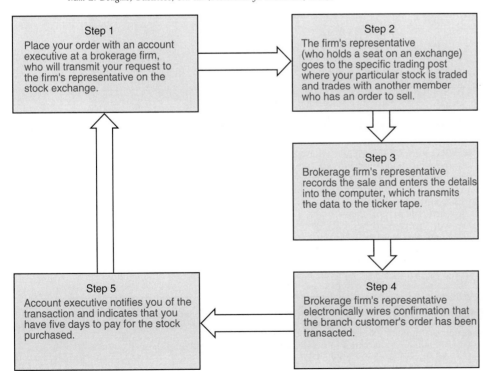

Step 1
Place your order with an account executive at a brokerage firm, who will transmit your request to the firm's representative on the stock exchange.

Step 2
The firm's representative (who holds a seat on an exchange) goes to the specific trading post where your particular stock is traded and trades with another member who has an order to sell.

Step 3
Brokerage firm's representative records the sale and enters the details into the computer, which transmits the data to the ticker tape.

Step 4
Brokerage firm's representative electronically wires confirmation that the branch customer's order has been transacted.

Step 5
Account executive notifies you of the transaction and indicates that you have five days to pay for the stock purchased.

curities that are being resold—brokerage firms buy and sell securities on the orders of their customers. Both individuals and such institutions as pension funds and mutual funds trade securities. Because they trade such large amounts, institutional investors have in recent years come to wield enormous influence on securities prices.

A typical stock transaction begins when you contact your *stockbroker* (also called an *account executive* or *registered representative*) to execute your trade. As employees of a brokerage house, brokers earn their income from commissions on each buy or sell order that they execute. Thus, the more their customers trade, the more the stockbrokers earn. Their income is not affected if a customer loses money—that is, if the price of a security falls after it is purchased.

In addition to taking an order, many brokers have the experience to offer investment advice, and the larger brokerage firms provide advice with a great deal of information gathered by in-house research departments or outside sources. As always, however, the process operates according to the classic

Securities in the '80s (I) October 27, 1988: Investment banker Michael Milken leaves the Grand Hyatt Hotel in New York after addressing the Annual Fixed Income Investors Group luncheon.

In 1978, Milken joined the New York investment-banking firm of Drexel Burnham Lambert, eventually becoming head of the company's high-yield department. He moved the department to the West Coast in 1978, and throughout the 1980s, Milken's unit revolutionized the sale of securities through the aggressive sale of *junk bonds*—high-yield low-rated bonds generally issued to raise money by companies with low credit ratings. Carrying interest rates 3 to 6 points higher than other types of bonds, junk bonds—at least until Milken—were generally perceived as particularly risky investments. Milken, however, began issuing bonds for small- and medium-sized companies which, while strapped for credit, were not especially subject to default. A number of these companies—including promising high-tech newcomers like MCI—proved successful, and before the decade was over, the junk-bond market skyrocketed, ultimately peaking at about $200 billion. By 1988, Drexel enjoyed 50 percent of the market for underwriting junk bonds; of every dollar earned by Milken's department, two-thirds went to Drexel, one-third to Milken's group. Meanwhile, Milken, as head of Drexel's West Coast golden goose, was thriving himself. When he was indicted in 1989, it was revealed that he had earned $1.2 billion between 1984 and 1987. In 1987, his salary and bonuses totaled $550 million (as a matter of perspective, it costs $350 million to launch a space shuttle); Drexel itself had earned a total of only $522.5 million in 1986.

principle of *caveat emptor*—let the buyer beware. For one thing, remember that brokers earn on the "churn"—that is, according to how much is traded. For another, if brokers were clever enough to pick stocks whose prices always went straight up, they would invest their own money and retire, and not take orders from others.

Interpreting the stock tables in your daily newspaper in order to keep tabs on your investment requires knowing a few points to get through the "sea" of numbers. For example, stocks are quoted in fractions of dollars; a quote of $12\frac{1}{2}$ means that the stock price is $12.50, and $12\frac{5}{8}$ means $12.625. The increments, in other words, are $12\frac{1}{2}$ cents each. The highest and lowest prices in the last year are also given so that you can see if the stock is volatile—that is, relatively active. In addition, although names seem mysterious at first glance, they are really just abbreviations; for instance, *GM* is *General Motors*. High, low, and closing prices for the day are also given; the *close* is what the value of the stock will be when the exchange opens the next morning. The other columns in the tables give you such information as the dividend, the yield, and the number of shares traded that day. See Figure 8-5 for a sample daily stock-market quotation.

Investor Protection

In the long-run, insuring a fair playing field is in the interests of the securities industry—rampant dishonesty could drive away customers and disable the market. The SEC is the primary industry watchdog. However, abuses occur despite its best efforts. The insider-trading scandals of recent years are the most obvious case in point. However, such abuses are not nearly as common as they were before the establishment of the SEC, when the market was essentially unregulated.

The Security Investors Protection Corporation. In addition, while the federal government protects investors against loss from fraud or the financial insolvency of investment firms, the securities industry itself offers a certain de-

FIGURE 8-5 Sample Daily Stock-Market Quotation

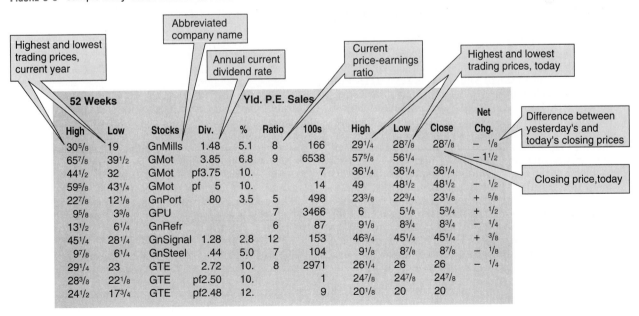

gree of protection. The NYSE, for example, used to compensate customers of member firms that went bankrupt by levying assessments on solvent member firms. When this compensation fund itself went bankrupt, Congress established the Security Investors Protection Corporation (SIPC) in 1970. It provides investors with up to $500,000 of bankruptcy insurance. However, only $100,000 of that amount can be paid by the SIPC. The rest must be paid out of the assets of the bankrupt firm.

The securities industry also includes a standard agreement to arbitrate disputes in contracts between brokers and clients: Arbitration is less costly and faster than litigation; results, however, cannot be appealed (*see* Chapter 5).

In the case that follows, Eugene and Julia McMahon went to federal court, alleging that they had lost more than $300,000 of their $500,000 portfolio (their life savings) when their broker put their money into options contracts. They charged that $200,000 of that amount went to the broker in commissions through fraudulent and excessive trading. Shearson, the brokerage firm, argued that the McMahons had waived access to the courts when they signed an agreement to arbitrate any disputes they had with Shearson. The question before the Supreme Court was whether such arbitration agreements are binding on the parties or clients like the McMahons can receive the protection of the courts under the Securities Exchange Act.

SHEARSON/AMERICAN EXPRESS, INC. v. McMAHON
United States Supreme Court, 107 S.Ct. 2332 (1987)

Between 1980 and 1982, respondents Eugene and Julia McMahon, individually and as trustees for various pension and profit-sharing plans, were customers of petitioner Shearson/American Express Inc. Two customer agreements signed by Julia McMahon provided for arbitration of any controversy relating to the accounts the McMahons maintained with Shearson.

The McMahons filed a complaint against Shearson and Mary Ann McNulty, the broker who handled their accounts, in the United States District Court for the Southern District of New York. The complaint alleged that the McMahons had lost more than $300,000 of their $500,000 portfolio when their broker put their money into options contracts. Further, they alleged that McNulty, with Shearson's knowledge, had violated the Securities Act by engaging in fraudulent, excessive trading on their accounts and making false statements and omitting material facts from the advice given to them. Shearson argued that the McMahons had waived access to the federal courts when they signed the agreement to arbitrate any disputes they had with Shearson. Relying on the customer agreements, Shearson moved to compel arbitration of the McMahons' claims. The District Court found that the McMahons' claims were arbitrable under the terms of the agreement, concluding that such a result followed from the "strong national policy favoring the en-

forcement of arbitration agreement." The Court of Appeals reversed on the Exchange Act claims. Shearson appeals.

Justice O'Connor delivered the opinion of the Court.

. . . .

The Federal Arbitration Act provides the starting point for answering the questions raised in this case. The Act was intended to "revers[e] centuries of judicial hostility to arbitration agreements," *Scherk v. Alberto-Culver Co.* [(1974)], by "plac[ing] arbitration agreements 'upon the same footing as other contracts.'" The Arbitration Act accomplishes this purpose by providing that arbitration agreements "shall be valid, irrevocable, and enforceable, save upon such grounds as exist at law or in equity for the revocation of any contract." The Act also provides that a court must stay its proceedings if it is satisfied that an issue before it is arbitrable under the agreement, and it authorizes a federal district court to issue an order compelling arbitration if there has been a "failure, neglect, or refusal" to comply with the arbitration agreement.

. . . .

The Arbitration Act, standing alone, therefore mandates enforcement of agreements to arbitrate statutory claims. . . .

. . . .

When Congress enacted the Exchange Act in 1934, it did not specifically address the question of the arbitrability of § 10(b) claims. The McMahons contend, however, that congressional intent to require a judicial forum for the resolution § 10(b) claims can be deduced from § 29(a) of the Exchange Act, which declares void "[a]ny condition, stipulation, or provision binding any person to waive compliance with any provision of [the Act]."

First, we reject the McMahons' argument that § 29(a) forbids waiver of § 27 of the Exchange Act. Section 27 provides in relevant part:

> The district courts of the United States . . . shall have exclusive jurisdiction of violations of this title or the rules and regulations thereunder, and of all suits in equity and actions at law brought to enforce any liability or duty created by this title or the rules and regulations thereunder.

The McMahons contend that an agreement to waive this jurisdictional provision is unenforceable because § 29(a) voids the waiver of "any provision" of the Exchange Act. The language of § 29(a), however, does not reach so far. . . . By its terms, § 29(a) only prohibits waiver of the substantive obligations imposed by the Exchange Act. Because § 27 does not impose any statutory duties, its waiver does not constitute a waiver of "compliance with any provision" of the Exchange Act under § 29(a).

We do not read *Wilko v. Swan* (1953), as compelling a different result. In *Wilko,* the Court held that a predispute agreement could not be enforced to compel arbitration of a claim arising under § 12(2) of the Securities Act. The basis for the ruling was § 14 of the Securities Act, which, like § 29(a) of the Exchange Act, declares void any stipulation "to waive compliance with any provision" of the statute. . . . *Wilko* must be understood . . . as holding that the plaintiff's waiver of the "right to select the judicial forum" was unenforceable only because arbitration was judged inadequate to enforce the statutory rights created by § 12(2).

. . . .

The second argument offered by the McMahons is that the arbitration agreement effects an impermissible waiver of the substantive protections of the Exchange Act. . . . They reason, as do some commentators, that *Wilko* is premised on the belief "that arbitration clauses in securities sales agreements generally are not freely negotiated." According to this view, *Wilko* barred enforcement of predispute agreements because of this frequent inequality of bargaining power, reasoning that Congress intended for § 14 generally to ensure that sellers did not "maneuver buyers into a position that might weaken their ability to recover under the Securities Act." The McMahons urge that we should interpret § 29(a) in the same fashion.

We decline to give *Wilko* a reading so far at odds with the plain language of § 14, or to adopt such an unlikely interpretation of § 29(a). . . . Section 29(a) is concerned, not with whether brokers "maneuver[ed cus-

tomers] into" an agreement, but with whether the agreement "weaken[s] their ability to recover under the [Exchange] Act." The former is grounds for revoking the contract under ordinary principles of contract law; the latter is grounds for voiding the agreement under § 29(a).

The other reason advanced by the McMahons for finding a waiver of their § 10(b) rights is that arbitration does "weaken their ability to recover under the [Exchange] Act." That is the heart of the Court's decision in *Wilko,* and respondents urge that we should follow its reasoning. *Wilko* listed several grounds why, in the Court's view, the "effectiveness [of the Act's provisions] in application is lessened in arbitration." First, the *Wilko* Court believed that arbitration proceedings were not suited to cases requiring "subjective findings on the purpose and knowledge of an alleged violator." *Wilko* also was concerned that arbitrators must make legal determinations "without judicial instruction on the law," and that an arbitration award "may be made without explanation of [the arbitrator's] reasons and without a complete record of their proceedings." . . . *Wilko* concluded that in view of these drawbacks to arbitration, § 12(2) claims "require[d] the exercise of judicial direction to fairly assure their effectiveness."

. . . .

. . . [T]he mistrust of arbitration that formed the basis for the *Wilko* opinion in 1963 is difficult to square with the assessment of arbitration that has prevailed since that time. This is especially so in light of the intervening changes in the regulatory structure of the securities laws. Even if *Wilko*'s assumptions regarding arbitration were valid at the time *Wilko* was decided, most certainly they do not hold true today for arbitration procedures subject to the SEC's oversight authority.

. . . .

We conclude, therefore, that Congress did not intend for § 29(a) to bar enforcement of all predispute arbitration agreements. In this case, where the SEC has sufficient statutory authority to ensure that arbitration is adequate to vindicate Exchange Act rights, enforcement does not effect a waiver of "compliance with any provision" of the Exchange Act under § 29(a). Accordingly, we hold the McMahons' agreements to arbitrate Exchange Act claims "enforce[able]. . . in accord with the explicit provisions of the Arbitration Act."

Case Questions

1. Did the arbitration agreement signed by the McMahons effect a waiver of either the procedural (jurisdictional) protection or the substantive protection of the Exchange Act? Explain.

2. How is Justice O'Connor justified, today, in finding that an arbitration agreement does not weaken one's ability to recover under the SEC Act?

- Explain the term *equity security.*
- Describe the process required to purchase 100 shares in a stock listed on the NYSE.
- Describe the functions performed by *securities markets.*
- Describe the ways in which the securities industry works to protect consumers against loss from fraud or the financial insolvency of investment firms.

■ LEGAL PERSPECTIVES ON SECURITIES TRANSACTIONS

The laws that have been established in the United States to regulate securities transactions provide a framework within which the federal government can control, through disclosure, those who manage our capital markets. The intent of these laws is to protect investors.

Historically, the 1929 Stock Market Crash and the Great Depression were the parents, so to speak, of the Securities Act of 1933 and the Securities Exchange Act of 1934: Both mandate that investors have access to information and both provide punishment for wrongdoers. The latest generation of securities laws, enacted in 1990, expands on the government's enforcement powers, especially in light of the turbulence in the stock market in the late 1980s. Table 8-1 describes important securities-market legislation from 1933 to 1990.

The Securities Act of 1933

The 1933 Securities Act protects investors against fraudulent acts on the part of companies that issue new securities. In attempts to ensure full disclosure of facts about all equity securities sold in interstate commerce and sent through the mails as material regarding offerings. The law cannot and does not ensure that an investor who buys a newly issued stock will make a profit: It guarantees only that all investors have the information necessary to make rational choices about which stocks to purchase. In addition, the SEC, which enforces the act, does not guarantee that this information is either accurate or sufficient.

The work of James M. Landis, who helped to draft early securities-regulation legislation and who served as chairman of the SEC from 1935 to 1937, is the subject of this chapter's PERSONAL PROFILE.

THE REGISTRATION PROCEDURE. Section 5 of the 1933 Securities Act created a registration procedure that makes information available to investors and to anyone else who is interested. This fairly complex registration procedure requires that a registration statement be filed with the SEC for the benefit of potential investors. All nonexempt securities that meet the definition of the 1933 Securities Act must be registered. The registration process involves three different time periods, with restrictions imposed by the SEC. These periods, which are discussed below, are the *prefiling period*, the *waiting period* for SEC approval, and the *post-effective period*.

The Prefiling Period: The Registration Statement. A company planning to issue a new security must prepare a **registration statement** for the SEC during

registration statement
Document, generally filed with the SEC before securities can be issued, disclosing financial data about the issuing company

TABLE 8-1 — *Landmark Securities-Market Legislation*

LEGISLATION	REGULATED ACTIVITY
Glass-Steagall Act (The Banking Act of 1933) →	Separates commerical banking from investment banking. Prohibits commercial banks from underwriting initial security offerings.
The Securities Act of 1933 →	Requires "truth in securities" be published. Companies must provide full and accurate information when selling new securities to the public.
Securities Exchange Act of 1934 →	Extends the Securities Act of 1933 to cover existing as well as new securities. Created the Securities and Exchange Commission (SEC) to oversee stock exchanges and limit their operations.
Maloney Act of 1938 →	Extends the terms of the Securities Exchange Act of 1934 to cover the over-the-counter (OTC) market. Creates the NASD to oversee the OTC market.
Investment Company Act of 1940 →	Extends the Securities Exchange Act of 1934 to cover mutual funds. Authorizes the SEC to oversee and control those funds.
Investment Advisors Act of 1940 →	Prohibits fraud and deception by paid investment advisors. Requires advisers to register with the SEC.
Securities Investor Protection Act of 1970 →	Creates the Securities Investor Protection Corporation (SIPC), a government corporation that acts as an insurance company to protect investors in cases of broker fraud or failure. Covers investors up to $100,000 per account.
Securities Enforcement Remedies and Penny Stock Reform Act of 1990 →	Strengthens enforcement powers of the SEC and adds new remedies such as civil money penalties and disgagement, temporary and permanent cease-and-desist orders against securities violations, and petitioning civil courts for penalties. Also expands disclosures of penny stocks and gives the SEC authority to bar those acting improperly from the penny stock market.
Market Reform Act of 1990 →	Amend the 1934 act by giving the SEC increased authority, broader emergency powers, and more flexible tools to prevent market crashes.
Securities Acts Amendments of 1990 →	Extends the SEC's ability to cooperate with foreign governments to combat international securities fraud.

this time. No offers to buy or sell the security may be made. The statement must contain the following kinds of information about the company:

- past earnings of the company
- certain financial statements (balance-sheet and profit and-loss-statements) that must be certified by independent accountants
- capital structure (shares outstanding, debt, etc.)
- the company's business, history, and size
- the names of anyone who plays an important role in managing or controlling the company's business
- the shareholdings, pay, stock options, bonuses, or profit-sharing plans that these people enjoy
- the company's property in areas other than its usual lines of business, plus what-

ever financial interest its officers, directors, and important shareholders may have in that property

- all legal proceedings in which the company may be involved
- the commission fee that will be paid to the underwriters of the issue
- the uses to which the money obtained through the new issue will be put.

The Prospectus. The statement must bear the signatures of a majority of the directors and executive officers of the company. Besides the registration state-

PERSONAL PROFILE
James M. Landis

Regulation of the securities industry by the federal government became an important goal of the New Deal administration of Franklin D. Roosevelt in the wake of the 1929 crash, the moribund state of the national economy, and the inadequacy of existing laws to protect investors. Among those who designed the new legislation and then stayed on to administer the regulatory process was James M. Landis, who emphasized that the most effective way to regulate the stock markets was to foster voluntary participation rather than to rely on government policing by the Securities and Exchange Commission. In fact, the SEC, created in 1934, has been hailed as the most successful of federal regulatory agencies in large part because of the principle of "participatory regulation" championed by Landis.

After growing up in Japan as the son of missionaries, Landis (1899–1964) completed a brilliant academic career at Princeton and Harvard Law School, where he was a protégé of Supreme Court Justice Felix Frankfurter. Landis idolized Frankfurter, with whom he collaborated on The Business of the Supreme Court *(1927) and who became the mentor he sought. After a stint as law clerk to Justice Louis Brandeis in 1925 (see Chapter 14, p. 502) and a return to Harvard Law where he was made the first professor of legislation, Frankfurter called Landis to Washington in 1933, where, along with Thomas Corcoran and Benjamin Cohen, he was given the task of drafting federal securities regulations.*

The three "Happy Hot Dogs," as Frankfurter's protégés were known, faced a complex situation. There was a need to regulate the issuance of new securities, mainly by requiring greater disclosure, and to control the securities exchanges, which were beset by power struggles, oligarchic management, and a tradition of disclosure. Interestingly, however, Landis saw the project as an opportunity for government, believing the industry would be receptive to changes that would buoy investor confidence and encourage growth.

Five pieces of landmark legislation emerged in a short time from the work of Landis and his colleagues: the Securities Act (1933), the Securities Exchange Act (1934), the Public Utility Holding Act (1935), the Maloney Act (1938), and the Glass-Steagall Banking Act (1933). As the team drafted the legislation, Landis contributed to the administrative aspects—namely, how to get such loftily intended laws effectively enforced—for instance, the Securities Exchange Act has as its purpose the "public interest" and "protection

of investors." His solution was to use private incentives inherent in the industry to achieve the SEC's goals.

Under the umbrella of the enabling legislation, the SEC in its early rules pursued a strategy of encouraging self-regulation. Thus, the accounting industry was wooed because of its great importance in certifying audit information for full disclosures. As SEC commissioner, Landis promoted cooperation with accountants and was successful in getting industry groups to standardize practices.

Landis followed a similar strategy with the New York Stock Exchange and regional exchanges. Asking for "institutional support," for example, served to make the specter of government regulation far less threatening to the exchanges; although the SEC originated the rules then, the exchanges were able to promulgate them as their own. Using this methodology in 1937, the SEC was successful under Chairman William O. Douglas (Landis's successor) in "cleaning house" at the New York exchange, whose entrenched and aristocratic leadership had long resisted change. The corruption of the exchange president, Richard Whitney, was exposed and an internal reform group took over to put through tough new rules, including those requiring exchange members to make additional disclosures.

As viewed after the passage of sixty years, Landis's contribution to securities regulation holds up well. For one thing, the system of participation has made the industry itself a catalyst for change and reform that does not always wait for the federal government to call for needed measures. Moreover, the industry has adopted the practice of imposing its own sanctions, often very quickly. By getting industry participants like accountants and exchange officials involved in creating regulations, Landis was able to establish administrative methods that the industry itself could exercise. In Landis's own words, his role and that of the SEC had been to "discover how to make the chosen policies effective. . . . The administrative phase . . . is enduring in character."

After leaving Washington and his accomplishments as drafter of legislation and SEC commissioner, Landis returned to Harvard Law School, and his final contribution to federal regulatory policy was a report produced for President-elect John F. Kennedy in 1960 on the status of the federal regulatory agencies. His analysis found them lacking in all promise of the achievement he had envisioned in the 1930s, and he made strong arguments for reform on which the Kennedy administration began action in 1961.

ment, it must also give the SEC copies of its charter and by-laws, important contracts, and pension plans, as well as its agreement with the firm that will underwrite the new issue. The **prospectus** is a brochure that describes the company offering the new securities and its history. It also provides financial data. A prospectus must be sent out to every person who has been offered newly registered securities.

Essentially, the discussion above reviews the *minimum* registration requirements. The initial registration statement does not yet include the public offering price. It is also subject to review by the SEC, which may require additional information that it deems relevant to the offer so that investors may make informed decisions. The registration statement is not effective until it is amended (if necessary) and approved.

Shelf Registration. Under the regular registration procedure, companies must make a separate filing for each new offering of securities. They must then sell those securities immediately even if market conditions are not promising. This provision places a significant burden on big companies offering large amounts of securities to the public. In 1982, therefore, the SEC made it easier for large companies to bring new issues to market. Although these companies must still make regular, detailed SEC filings, they no longer have to file detailed reports every time they bring out new issues. Instead, they can file a much shorter and simpler amendment to that report. Thanks to this procedure, called **shelf registration,** big companies can bring new issues to market in days rather than weeks or even months. As a result, it is much easier for these companies to gear their new issues to actual market conditions.

The Waiting Period: SEC Review. Although offers may be solicited between the time the statement is filed and its effective date—the waiting period—only *oral* sales may be transacted during this period. Because oral contracts involving more than $500 are unenforceable under the Statute of Frauds (*see* Chapter 9), offerers are effectively barred from making sales before the registration statement becomes effective. Thus, the company planning the new issue may send prospective buyers a document known as a **red-herring** (or **red-line**) **prospectus,** which is identical to the prospectus filed with the SEC except for a warning printed in red on the first page:

> A registration statement relating to these securities has been filed with the Securities and Exchange Commission, but has not yet become effective. Information contained herein is subject to completion or amendment. These securities may not be sold nor may offers to buy be accepted prior to the time the registration statement becomes effective. . . .

The information in the red-herring prospectus and the rest of the registration statement usually changes in two ways. First, when the issuing company wishes to respond to last-minute changes in the market price of its stock, it often leaves the new offering price out of the first version of the statement filed with the SEC. Second, the commission attempts to examine filings in detail and almost always requests changes in a statement's wording. In turn, because the SEC has the power to take them to court and thereby delay new issues long enough to kill them, issuing companies almost always agree to make changes of some kind. Any company that does not register a security falling within the scope of the 1933 Securities Act may be fined or punished criminally.

During the period between the filing of the registration statement and its approval by the SEC, the issuing company may also publish or send out a

tombstone advertisement
Black-bordered advertisement,
published between SEC filing and
approval, with information about
a new security issue,

tombstone advertisement (so called from the black borders in which it is enclosed). These ads are usually printed in financial periodicals and in the financial pages of daily newspapers. They inform the public that a new issue is to be launched, give its price (if known), and name its underwriters.

The Posteffective Period. In theory, the registration statement becomes effective twenty days after both the SEC and the issuing company agree on its wording. In practice, the SEC can accelerate the effective date—and almost always does. In any event, the new security cannot be sold to the public until the statement becomes effective. This interim is called the **posteffective period.**

posteffective period   Interim
period between SEC and
company agreement on the
registration of a new security,
during which period the issue
can actually be sold to the public

EXEMPTIONS FROM REGISTRATION.   Two classes of securities are exempt from the registration requirements. First, certain *kinds* of securities are exempt from registration. Second, certain securities are exempt because of the nature of the *transaction* in which they are offered to investors.

Type-of-Security Exemption. Certain kinds of securities are exempt from registration no matter how they may be offered or to whom. Most of these securities have been issued either by the government itself or by companies that are subject to regulation by some government agency other than the SEC. Securities that are subject to this type of exemption include the following:

- government securities
- securities issued by nonprofit organizations
- credit or banking instruments that mature in less than nine months
- securities issued by a Federal Reserve Bank, national or state bank, or savings-and-loan association
- securities issued by common and contract carriers
- insurance policies and annuities
- securities issued by trustees in connection with bankruptcy proceedings.

Nature-of-Transaction Exemption. Certain securities are exempt from regulation under the Securities Act of 1933 because of the transaction in which they are issued or sold. The most important of these exemptions concern Regulations A and D, which establish special rules for small businesses. There are also private offerings and transactions that involve *intrastate* offerings.

Regulations A and D. Over the years, the SEC has adopted a number of regulations meant to help small businesses raise money by issuing securities. **Regulation A** provides a simplified form of registration for offerings of less than $1.5 million. Under this procedure, there is much less paperwork, and the company offering the securities can use the preliminary circular to sell them without having to wait for SEC clearance.

Regulation A   SEC exemption
providing simplified registration
of securities offerings under $1.5
million

Regulation D exempts small companies from registration completely if the offering is small enough or if those to whom the securities will be offered or sold are sufficiently knowledgeable.

Regulation D   SEC regulation
exempting small companies from
registration of securities
offerings which are small or
which will be sold to
knowledgeable buyers

Three rules—Rules 504, 505, and 506—form the heart of Regulation D. *Rule 504* exempts offerings that will be sold for a total sum of $500,000 or less during any twelve-month period. Neither investment companies nor companies that report under the 1934 Securities Act can take advantage of this provision.

Rule 505 exempts offerings and sales for an annual amount of $5 million or less as long as the securities are offered or sold to no more than thirty-five nonaccredited investors and any number of accredited investors. There are eight categories of accredited investors, including institutional investors, corporate insiders, and people with net worth of at least $1 million or annual incomes of at least $200,000. *Rule 506* grants exemption without regard to the dollar amount of the offering (or sales). All of the investors involved must be accredited, "sophisticated," or represented by a sophisticated person—that is, by someone with knowledge and experience in financial matters.

Private Offerings. The 1933 Securities Act does not define nor even mention private offerings. It does exempt "transactions by an issuer not involving a public offering." Whether an offering is private, and therefore exempt, is a question of fact which must be determined on a case-by-case basis. Two practical considerations are important: how many people are offered the securities and how many securities they are offered.

According to SEC rule of thumb, for the transaction to be treated as public, more than thirty-five people must be offered a security. This is not, however, a hard-and-fast rule. The position of these people can also be important: Investors who know a good deal about financial affairs can often unearth, on their own, the sort of information that the prospectus contains. If a security is offered only to such people, the SEC would be likely to regard the offering as private no matter how many people were involved. After all, one of the main purposes of the law is to protect inexperienced investors against fraud; experienced investors are better able to protect themselves.

The means used to offer securities must also be taken into account. Sometimes, the company that issues them makes direct contact with potential investors and negotiates with them individually. In this case, the SEC might be willing to consider the offering a private one. By contrast, if the securities were offered through companies that specialize in selling them—that is, through securities dealers—it would be public in nature: The activities of such dealers are not intended to be exempt from the 1933 Securities Act.

The number of shares that may be sold through a private offering is even less clear than the number of people who may be involved. In general, because large numbers of shares are likely to be bought only by people who intend to resell them quickly, such as securities dealers, the more shares offered, the less likely the transaction will be regarded as private. The following case raises the issues discussed here.

SECURITIES & EXCHANGE COMMISSION v. RALSTON PURINA CO.
United States Supreme Court, 346 U.S. 119 (1953)

Defendant Ralston Purina manufactures and distributes feed and cereal products and is staffed by some 7,000 employees. In light of a company policy of encouraging stock ownership among its employees, Ralston Purina has made authorized but unissued common shares of stock available to some employees. Between 1947 and 1951, Ralston Purina sold nearly $2,000,000 of stock to employees without registration and in so doing made use of the mails. A corporate resolution authorized the sale of common stock to "key employees," those employees who have taken the initiative and are interested in buying stock at present market prices.

Plaintiff Securities and Exchange Commission brought a complaint seeking to enjoin Ralston Purina in unregistered offerings. Ralston Purina claims its offerings of stock to its "key employees" fall under the private offering exemption of the Act.

Mr. Justice Clark delivered the opinion of the Court.

Section 4 (1) of the Securities Act of 1933 exempts "transactions by an issuer not involving any public offer-

---

ing" from the registration requirements of §5. We must decide whether Ralston Purina's offerings of treasury stock to its "key employees" are within this exemption. . . . The question has arisen many times since the Act was passed; an apparent need to define the scope of the private offering exemption prompted certiorari.

. . . .

Exemption from the registration requirements of the Securities Act is the question. The design of the statute is to protect investors by promoting full disclosure of information thought necessary to informed investment decisions. The natural way to interpret the private offering exemption is in light of the statutory purpose. Since exempt transactions are those as to which "there is no practical need for [the bill's] application," the applicability of § 4 (1) should turn on whether the particular class of persons affected needs the protection of the Act. An offering to those who are shown to be able to fend for themselves is a transaction "not involving any public offering."

. . . .

The exemption, as we construe it, does not deprive corporate employees, as a class, of the safeguards of the Act. We agree that some employee offerings may come within § 4 (1), e.g., one made to executive personnel who because of their position have access to the same kind of information that the Act would make available in the form of a registration statement. Absent such a showing of special circumstances, employees are just as much members of the investing "public" as any of their neighbors in the community. . . .

Keeping in mind the broadly remedial purposes of federal securities legislation, imposition of the burden of proof on an issuer who would plead the exemption seems to us fair and reasonable. . . . The focus of inquiry should be on the need of the offerees for the protections afforded by registration. The employees here were not shown to have access to the kind of information which registration would disclose. The obvious opportunities for pressure and imposition make it advisable that they be entitled to compliance with § 5. Reversed.

Case Questions

1. Explain the purpose of the registration requirements under the Securities Act.

2. Why are some transactions exempt from the act, such as those transactions under §4(1)?

3. Why did the court find that the employees at Ralston Purina needed the protection afforded by registration, just as any other member of the investing "public"?

Intrastate Offerings. Under the Commerce Clause of the U.S. Constitution the federal government has authority over *interstate* commerce (commerce among persons in different states), but not over *intrastate* commerce (commerce among persons in the same state). This distinction is less important than it might seem, however, because most forms of commerce have been ruled to involve more than one state.

Nonetheless, if an offering can be shown to take place entirely within one state, it is subject to state rather than federal regulation and need not, therefore, be registered under the 1933 Securities Act. The company offering the securities must be incorporated and do business in the same state as the people who buy them. There are strict tests (under Rule 147) for both requirements.

ENFORCEMENT. Besides the SEC, private individuals can enforce the 1933 Securities Act. Anyone who has bought securities promoted by a registration statement that contains *material false statements* may sue for damages. Liability under the act extends to all those who signed the statement, including a majority of the board of directors and the independent accountants who prepared and certified the financial data that it contains.

due diligence Defense against fraud used by signatories to an SEC registration found to have material false statements, arguing that a reasonable inquiry into a firm's finances led to the conclusion that the statement was accurate at the time

Accountants and other signators can defend themselves against a suit of this kind by claiming to have exercised **due diligence:** Even if certain facts turn out to be wrong, accountants can argue that they made a reasonable inquiry into the financial affairs of the company filing the statement and believed that their contributions to it were accurate at the time. The following case illustrates how the courts treat this matter.

ESCOTT v. BARCHRIS CONSTRUCTION CORPORATION

U.S. District Court, Southern District of New York,
283 F. Supp. 643 (1968)

Plaintiffs, purchasers of convertible subordinated fifteen-year debentures of Defendant BarChris Construction Corporation (BarChris), brought this action under Section 11 of the Securities Act of 1933. Plaintiffs allege that the registration statement with respect to these debentures filed with the Securities and Exchange Commission contained material false statements and material omissions.

McLean, District Judge.

Defendants fall into three categories: (1) the persons who signed the registration statement; (2) the underwriters, consisting of eight investment banking firms, led by Drexel & Co. (Drexel); and (3) BarChris's auditors, Peat, Marwick, Mitchell & Co. (Peat, Marwick).

. . . On the main issue of liability, the questions to be decided are (1) did the registration statement contain false statements of fact, or did it omit to state facts which should have been stated in order to prevent it from being misleading; (2) if so, were the facts which were falsely stated or omitted "material" within the meaning of the Act; (3) if so, have defendants established their affirmative defenses?

Before discussing these questions, some background facts should be mentioned. At the time relevant here, BarChris was engaged primarily in the construction of bowling alleys. . . .

. . . .

In general, BarChris's method of operation was to enter into a contract with a customer, receive from him at that time a comparatively small down payment on the purchase price, and proceed to construct and equip the bowling alley. When the work was finished and the building delivered, the customer paid the balance of the contract price in notes, payable in installments over a period of years. BarChris discounted these notes with a factor and received part of their face amount in cash. The factor held back part as a reserve.

. . . .

By early 1961, BarChris needed additional working capital. The proceeds of the sale of the debentures involved in this action were to be devoted, in part at least, to fill that need.

. . . .

By that time BarChris was experiencing difficulties in collecting amounts due from some of its customers. Some of them were in arrears in payments due to factors on their discounted notes. As time went on those difficulties increased. . . .

. . . In October 1962 BarChris came to the end of the road. On October 29, 1962, it filed in this court a petition for an arrangement under Chapter XI of the Bankruptcy Act. BarChris defaulted in the payment of the interest due on November 1, 1962 on the debentures.

. . . .

Peat, Marwick, BarChris's auditors, who had previously audited BarChris's annual balance sheet and earnings figures for 1958 and 1959, did the same for 1960. These figures were set forth in the registration statement. In addition, Peat, Marwick undertook a so-called "S–1 review," the proper scope of which is one of the matters debated here.

The registration statement in its final form contained a prospectus as well as other information. Plaintiff's claims of falsities and omissions pertain solely to the prospectus, not to the additional data.

The prospectus contained, among other things, a description of BarChris's business, a description of its real property, some material pertaining to certain of its subsidiaries, and remarks about various other aspects of its affairs. It also contained financial information. It included a consolidated balance sheet as of December 31, 1960, with elaborate explanatory notes. These figures had been audited by Peat, Marwick. . . .

Plaintiffs challenge the accuracy of a number of these figures. They also charge that the text of the prospectus, apart from the figures, was false in a number of respects, and that material information was omitted. . . .

1960 Net Sales, Net Operating Income and Earnings per Share

The earnings figure set forth at page 4 of the prospectus shows net sales for the calendar year 1960 of $9,165,320. Plaintiffs claim that this figure was overstated by $2,525,350. . . .

. . . .

. . . I find that the 1960 sales figure of $9,165,320, as stated in page 4 of the prospectus, was inaccurate. . . . The total figure, instead of $9,165,320, should have been $8,511,420.

It necessarily follows that the figure for net operating income for 1960 appearing on page 4 of the prospectus was also incorrect. . . .

. . . .

Contingent Liabilities as of December 31, 1960

. . . .

. . . [I]nstead of $750,000, the contingent liability figure under the alternative method of financing should have been $1,125,795. Capitol [an alley owned and operated by BarChris] should have been shown as a direct liability in the amount of $325,000.

. . . .

Net Sales, Gross Profit and Net Earnings Plaintiffs correctly contend that the net sales of $2,138,455 for the three months ended March 31, 1961 were overstated.

. . . .

Materiality

It is a prerequisite to liability under Section 11 of the Act that the fact which is falsely stated in a registration statement, or the fact that is omitted when it should have been stated to avoid misleading, be "material." The regulations of the Securities and Exchange Commission pertaining to the registration of securities define the word as follows.

The term 'material,' when used to qualify a requirement for the furnishing of information as to any subject, limits the information required to those matters as to which an average prudent investor ought reasonably to be informed before purchasing the security registered.

What are "matters as to which an average prudent investor ought reasonably to be informed"? It seems obvious that they are matters which such an investor needs to know before he can make an intelligent, informed decision whether or not to buy the security.

. . . .

Judged by this test, there is no doubt that many of the misstatements and omissions in this prospectus were material. . . .

. . . .

Peat, Marwick
Section 11(b) provides:

Notwithstanding the provisions of subsection (a) no person . . . shall be liable as provided therein who shall sustain the burden of proof—

. . . .

(3) that . . . (B) as regards any part of the registration statement purporting to be made upon his authority as an expert . . . (i) he had, after reasonable investigation, reasonable ground to believe and did believe, at the time such part of the registration statement became effective, that the statements therein were true and that there was no omission to state a material fact required to be stated therein or necessary to make the statements therein not misleading . . .

This defines the due diligence defense for an expert. Peat, Marwick has pleaded it.

. . . .

The 1960 Audit
Peat, Marwick's work was in general charge of a member of the firm, Cummings, and more immediately in charge of Peat, Marwick's manager, Logan. Most of the actual work was performed by a senior accountant, Berardi, who had junior assistants, one of whom was Kennedy.

Berardi was then about thirty years old. He was not yet a C.P.A. He had had no previous experience with the bowling industry. This was his first job as a senior accountant. He could hardly have been given a more difficult assignment.

. . . .

Capitol Lanes
First and foremost is Berardi's failure to discover that Capitol Lanes had not been sold. This error affected both the sales figure and the liability side of the balance sheet. Fundamentally, the error stemmed from the fact

that Berardi never realized that Heavenly Lanes and Capitol were two different names for the same alley.

. . . .

. . . The vital question is whether he failed to make a reasonable investigation which, if he had made it, would have revealed the truth.

. . . .

The burden of proof on the issue is on Peat, Marwick. Although the question is a rather close one, I find that Peat, Marwick has not sustained that burden. Peat, Marwick has not proved that Berardi made a reasonable investigation as far as Capitol Lanes was concerned and that his ignorance of the true facts was justified.

. . . .

Contingent Liabilities
Berardi erred in computing the contingent liability on Type B leaseback transactions at 25 percent. He testified that he was shown an agreement with Talcott which fixed the contingent liability at that amount. In this testimony he was mistaken. No such document is contained in Peat, Marwick's work papers. The evidence indicates that it never existed. Berardi did not examine the documents which are in evidence which establish that BarChris's contingent liability on this type of transaction was in fact 100 per cent. Berardi did not make a reasonable investigation in this instance. . . .

The S-1 Review
The purpose of reviewing events subsequent to the date of a certified balance sheet (referred to as an S-1 review when made with reference to a registration statement) is to ascertain whether any material change has occurred in the company's financial position which should be disclosed in order to prevent the balance sheet figures from being misleading. The scope of such a review, under generally accepted auditing standards, is limited. It does not amount to a complete audit.

Peat, Marwick prepared a written program for such a review. I find that this program conformed to generally accepted auditing standards. . . .

Berardi made the S-1 review in May 1961. He devoted a little over two days to it, a total of $20\frac{1}{2}$ hours. He did not discover any of the errors or omissions pertaining to the state of affairs in 1961 which I have previously discussed at length, all of which were material. The question is whether, despite his failure to find out anything, his investigation was reasonable within the meaning of the statute.

What Berardi did was to look at a consolidating trial balance as of March 31, 1961 which had been prepared by BarChris, compare it with the audited December 31, 1960 figures, discuss . . . certain unfavorable developments which the comparison disclosed, and read certain minutes. He did not examine any "important financial records" other than the trial balance. . . .

. . . He asked questions, he got answers which he considered satisfactory, and he did nothing to verify them. . . .

. . . .

Berardi had no conception of how tight the cash position was. He did not discover that BarChris was holding up checks in substantial amounts because there was no money in the bank to cover them.

. . . .

There had been a material change for the worse in BarChris's financial position. That change was sufficiently serious so that the failure to disclose it made the 1960 figures misleading. Berardi did not discover it. As far as the results were concerned, his S-1 review was useless.

Accountants should not be held to a standard higher than that recognized in their profession. I do not do so here. Berardi's review did not come up to that standard. He did not take some of the steps which Peat, Marwick's written program prescribed. He did not spend an adequate amount of time on a task of this magnitude. Most important of all, he was too easily satisfied with glib answers to his inquiries.

This is not to say that he should have made a complete audit. But there were enough danger signals in the materials which he did examine to require some fur-

ther investigation on his part. Generally accepted accounting standards required such further investigation under these circumstances. It is not always sufficient merely to ask questions.

Here again, the burden of proof is on Peat, Marwick. I find that the burden has not been satisfied. I conclude that Peat, Marwick has not established its due diligence defense.

Case Questions

1. Upon what basis did the court find the registration statement misleading?

2. What standard was used by the court in defining "materiality" within the meaning of the act? Were the facts that were misstated or omitted in the prospectus "material"?

3. Did the defendants establish an affirmative defense in order to avoid liability?

The Securities Exchange Act of 1934

As we have seen, the 1933 Securities Act was designed mainly to regulate *new* issues of securities—that is **primary distribution.** The Securities Exchange Act of 1934 was intended mainly to regulate **secondary distribution**—the trading of securities on the floors of the exchanges and in OTC markets. To that end, the 1934 Securities Act created the Securities and Exchange Commission, which also enforces the Securities Act of 1933.

primary distribution The sale of new issues of securities

secondary distribution The trading of securities in stock exchanges and OTC markets

REGISTRATION. Like its forerunner, the 1934 Securities Exchange Act provides for the registration of three categories of people and institutions: (1) securities exchanges, such as NYSE and AMEX; (2) stockbrokers and dealers involved in interstate commerce; (3) companies involved in interstate commerce, holding assets worth more than $3 million, and having issued equity securities owned by 500 or more people or traded on national securities exchanges. Although registration under the Securities of 1934 Act is quite distinct from registration under the Securities Act of 1933, the information that a company must provide is the same in most respects. The 1933 act requires companies to register nonexempt securities with the SEC whenever they are issued. By contrast, a company must register securities under the 1934 act only when it issues a new *class* of securities. If it floats additional new issues in an existing class, it need not register them separately under the 1934 act. The only exemptions to the 1934 act are for mutual funds (which register under a different act), savings-and-loan associations, and certain not-for-profit organizations.

REPORTING. The 1934 Securities Act also requires companies that fall within its scope to file certain *reports* with the SEC. These reports are completely separate from registration under both the 1933 and the 1934 acts.

10K Report. Every year, each of these companies must file an annual report, called the *10K report,* no more than 120 days from the end of its fiscal year. This report must include the following:

Securities in the '80s (II) *February 20, 1987: Investment Banker Dennis Levine leaves U.S. District Court in White Plains, New York, after being sentenced for securities fraud, perjury, and tax evasion.*

April 23, 1987: Wall Street trader Ivan Boesky is led into Federal District Court in New York to enter pleas on criminal charges of insider trading.

Boesky had originally been indicted in 1986 for securities violations in dealings with Levine, like Milken an investment banker at Drexel Burnham Lambert. When Levine, for example, had shared with Boesky his inside knowledge about a stock buyout of Carnation by Swiss-based Nestlé, Boesky had bought and sold at a profit of $28 million. In the hands of an *arbitrager* like Boesky, high-yield securities like those in which Michael Milken specialized had already developed even more innovative and highly profitable uses. According to the indictment against Milken, raiders like Carl Icahn and T. Boone Pickens would inform Milken of their intention to take over a given company. Milken would then issue junk bonds in the raider's company—bonds to be purchased and held by other raiders who planned to avail themselves of Milken's services in the future. In this way, buyout specialists were able to raise the immense sums of capital necessary to finance such takeovers as Pickens' $8.1 billion Drexel-financed raid on Unocal Corp., the 12th-largest U.S. oil producer, in 1985. Meanwhile, Milken passed along his intimate knowledge about such arrangements to arbitragers like Boesky, who was first connected with Drexel through Levine. Levine, who was sentenced to two years in prison and fined $362,900, pleaded guilty in June 1986, agreeing to help investigators snag Boesky.

- the number of outstanding securities
- the number of people who hold them
- the names of all people who hold more than 10 percent of them
- the names, salaries, stock holdings, and stock options of the directors
- any important changes in the company's business

10Q Report. The company must also supply a quarterly document called the *10Q report*. This report includes the most recent figures for net income and gross sales.

8K Report. Each company also must file an *8K report* after any major change in its affairs. Important new acquisitions or a change in the control of the company must be reported this way. The report must be submitted no more than ten days after the end of the month when the event occurred.

Major Securities Statutes of the 1990s

In 1990, Congress enacted three major pieces of securities legislation. These statutes extend the powers of the SEC and give the agency more flexible tools to respond to new kinds of illegal behavior. The legislation was necessitated by the severe stock-market shift in October 1987, as well as by a variety of new financial products, markets, and practitioners—and attendant abuses—that have developed in the past decades.

THE SECURITIES ENFORCEMENT REMEDIES AND PENNY-STOCK REFORM ACT. This law encompasses two different areas—SEC remedies for securities-laws violations and penny-stock reform. The former enhances the SEC's previously limited enforcement and remedial powers, allowing the agency to act more quickly and with greater vigor to remedy violations of securities laws. The so-called "remedies" act provides the SEC with a comprehensive program, both administrative and judicial, to maximize compensation to those injured when securities laws are violated. The SEC also has increased powers to impose and extract penalties from offenders to deter repeat violations and to ensure that those found guilty enjoy no profits from their activities.

There are several significant provisions in this law. First, the SEC can issue both temporary and permanent cease-and-desist orders against securities violations. These orders are functionally equivalent to preliminary injunctions under federal civil procedure. The SEC can also require respondents to take "steps to ensure future compliance."

Second, the law authorizes the SEC to impose monetary penalties on offenders. This provision extends the 1934 Securities Exchange Act, the 1940 Investment Company Act, and the 1941 Investment Advisors Act. In addition, the SEC can now issue administrative orders for offenders to give an accounting and penalty payment of profits made or losses avoided by illegal activities.

Third, the SEC can now request the federal courts to order offenders to pay civil monetary penalties over and above penalty payment. Before the enactment of the "remedies" act, this penalty was limited to violations by inside traders. There are three tiers of penalties, with the seriousness of the illegal activity determining the amount.

Fourth, the law now expressly authorizes federal courts to issue injunctions forbidding individuals guilty of fraud from serving as officers or directors of any company subject to federal securities conditions. Previously, this authorization was ambiguous, and courts had to rely on the authority implicit in SEC-imposed injunctions.

Reform of the lower-priced, penny-stock business is the subject of the second part of the act. The intent of this law is to repair abuses in the issuance and trading of these stocks on the OTC market—stocks which are issued by new firms that may not have a real product or service to offer or even a plan to use funds from stock issuance. Such securities often sell for under $1 a share and are not listed on any exchange. By the late 1980s, fraud in the penny-stock business was rampant, with potential investors subject to high-pressure tactics and unethical recommendations to buy highly speculative stocks.

The law specifically seeks reform without retarding investment in small, developing companies by first providing a new statutory definition of "penny stock": A *penny stock* is any equity security *other than* one traded on national exchanges, authorized for trading on NASDAQ, or issued by a registered investment company. The SEC is also empowered to exclude certain stocks using other criteria.

Second, the law expands disclosure of penny stocks. It requires brokers and dealers to give customers a "risk-disclosure" statement prior to any penny-stock transactions. Other information that must be provided includes pricing, commission, and the trading volume of the stock.

Third, the SEC is now empowered to bar individuals from the market if their conduct is deemed improper. This sanction applies to any person participating in a penny-stock offering, with "person" defined as "any promoter, finder, consultant, agent" engaged in issuing and trading activities.

Finally, the law directs the SEC to facilitate creation of an automated quote system for penny stocks and to study self-regulatory bodies overseeing penny stocks.

THE MARKET REFORM ACT. The intent of this act is to broaden the authority of the SEC to take action under conditions of unusual activity in the stock markets. It is hoped that with these expanded emergency powers, the SEC will now have the ability to ensure fair and orderly markets and thus to combat market volatility and prevent market crashes. The Market Reform Act puts specific limits on *program trading*—that is, trading that uses a computer system with automatic triggers to execute buy and sell orders—and the law also authorizes the SEC to require increased reporting from brokers and dealers, thus allowing the agency to identify risks to the integrity of these practitioners.

THE SECURITIES ACTS AMENDMENTS. This law (P.L. 101-550) extends the power of the SEC to combat securities fraud of an international scope and to cooperate with foreign governments to achieve this goal.

■ *Concept Check 8-2   Legal Perspectives on Securities Transactions*

- In what way does the *Securities Act of 1933* ensure full disclosure of facts about equity securities?
- Describe a *registration statement* and a *prospectus*.
- Explain the major policies providing for *exemptions* from securities regulations.
- Explain the difference between the *primary* and *secondary distribution* of securities.
- List the key provisions of the *Securities Enforcement Remedies and Penny-Stock Reform Act*, including measures to protect investment in small, developing companies.

During the past decade, there has been dramatic growth in international securities trading. This expansion includes both U.S. citizens buying shares of foreign corporations on foreign exchanges and foreign investors buying shares in U.S. companies on U.S. exchanges.

Several factors have contributed to this globalization. First, non-U.S. markets provide opportunities for U.S. investors to diversify portfolios in order to protect themselves against domestic market risks. Second, the mechanics of trading across borders has been simplified: Through increasingly sophisticated automated systems, execution and settlement of trades are handled smoothly, and securities are now traded twenty-four hours a day on international exchanges. Third, funds now move more easily because of less stringent foreign-exchange controls as well as tax reforms.

As always, the mission of the SEC is to maintain the integrity of U.S. capital markets and, above all, to protect investors. Conducting investigations into international trades and enforcing sanctions against violators of securities laws provide unique challenges not met in domestic regulatory situations.

Until the enactment of the 1990 Securities Acts Amendments, the SEC was limited in its ability to investigate and sanction when it suspected that U.S. securities laws had been broken abroad. For one thing, disclosure was often prohibited by foreign secrecy and blocking laws. The SEC's primary tool in aiding the discovery process, the investigative subpoena, was generally limited to uncovering evidence from sources in the United States. Although this power could be extended abroad in some cases, the process was time-consuming and expensive. In addition, the "letter-of-request" power could be used only in connection with judicial proceedings, not for purposes of investigation.

The SEC's position was that because of such limitations, its hands were tied in its ability to protect U.S. investors. Its goal was the enactment of new regulations that would permit it to fulfill its mandate through uniform standards across international boundaries. In the past, individual countries have maintained standards of regulation and enforcement that are generally less stringent and less vigorously enforced than in the United States. The SEC's proposed solution is that its leadership position should be used to minimize these differences and achieve a global system based on the U.S. model. However, not all foreign market regulators have been disposed to implement U.S.-proposed requirements—for example, mandatory disclosure.

Japan offers an instructive case on the difficulties that the SEC has faced in protecting U.S. investors internationally. In Japan, insider trading is not viewed as the serious problem it is here. In fact, many Japanese politicians participate in it. Because the Japanese stock market is the world's second-largest, the issue is magnified. Although a stricter law was passed under U.S. pressure in 1988, the Japanese attitude may continue to encourage lax enforcement. Moreover, because of U.S.-Japanese tensions on the trade front in general, it may be hard to convince the Japanese to cooperate and enact further "model" laws based on our own.

"Cooperation," however, remains the operative word on the international front. It was within this framework that the International Securities Enforcement Cooperation Act was passed in 1990. The act reflects the basic need for the bilateral exchange of information between the SEC and foreign securities regulators so that investigations of violations can occur. It does not, however, impose the U.S. system globally. There are four major components.

First, the act clarifies SEC authority to provide foreign regulators with documents and other information. At the request of a foreign official, the SEC can require a person or institution in the United States to produce evidence of potential violations of foreign securities laws when foreign officials have agreed to provide the SEC with the same help for possible violations of U.S. securities laws in their countries. Voluntary reciprocity is crucial.

Second, the act exempts confidential documents that foreign regulators provide to the SEC from disclosure requirements under the Freedom of Information Act: If those documents are confidential under foreign law, they will remain so in the United States if under a good-faith representation it is shown that their disclosure would contradict foreign law.

Third, the SEC is authorized to impose administrative sanctions on securities-market professionals found to have engaged in illegal activities in foreign countries. If an individual has been convicted in a foreign court of violations similar to those specified by U.S. federal law, the SEC can impose sanctions.

Finally, the act authorizes the SEC to investigate violations of U.S. securities laws that occur in foreign countries. This is particularly important regarding enforcement of regulations limiting insider trading.

The SEC now has the tools to conduct investigations and impose sanctions globally. Integral to the operation of such mechanisms, however, are bilateral evidence-gathering agreements—memoranda of understanding—between countries. Although they existed prior to the 1990 law, such mutual agreements are still needed if the SEC is to pursue its mission on a global scale.

■ INSIDER TRANSACTIONS

Both the 1933 and 1934 Securities Acts are based on the assumption that investors must have information to make rational choices and that rational choices make securities markets function efficiently. Sometimes, however, cer-

Securities in the '80s (III) *December 12, 1989: Ivan Boesky prepares to leave custody after serving less than two years on a conviction for securities-law violations.*

Boesky had plead guilty to one felony and had been fined $100 million. His sentence was relatively light because he had assisted the government in bringing indictments against Drexel Burnham Lambert and Michael Milken. At Drexel, November 14, 1986, came to be known as "Boesky Day": on that day, Boesky pleaded guilty to SEC charges—supported by allegations made by Drexel's Dennis Levine—of insider-trading violations. In the process, he had opened the government's eyes to investment-banking practices that went far deeper than the insider trading that they had originally suspected. The SEC filed suit against Drexel and Milken in September 1988, and in March 1989 Milken was indicted on 98 felony counts not only of insider trading and fraud but of racketeering—of masterminding an elaborate network of client and investor relations that included the use of inside information to enforce so-called *greenmail:* threats of raider takeover made possible, like takeovers themselves, by the kind of capital that Milken could generate. Testimony in 1987 by a former Boesky bookkeeper had already provided solid evidence to link Boesky and Milken in a *stock-parking* scheme—the holding of one trader's stocks by another to conceal ownership from the SEC or the stock exchanges. Profit and losses on such arrangements are usually shared through mutual payments on phony deals, and records of $56.3 million payable from Boesky to Drexel for "consulting fees" reevealed the "smoking gun" that allowed investigators to unravel the illegal entanglements by which Boesky and Milken had been conducting business in securities.

tain investors have information that other investors do not have. Often, this information is the result of shrewdness or hard work. For example, if exploration for rare minerals were being conducted in a remote country whose language was known to very few people and you learned that language, you would have information that most people in this country lacked. Anyone else, however, could have done exactly the same thing.

Now suppose that you worked for a company that wanted to make a bid to buy another company. You learn about the bid before it is made. Realizing that the stock of the second company is likely to rise after the deal is announced, you buy a large number of shares. The information on which you acted was not available to the general public.

From both a legal and ethical point of view, the latter kind of information—**insider information**—is different than information available to anyone

insider information Knowledge about companies and transactions not available to the general public, the use of which may enable a securities trader to profit and perhaps injure others

prepared to put in the effort needed to uncover it. First, because buying the shares of the other company would help raise its price, you would injure your employer and this would force your own company to put in a higher bid than it would otherwise have made. Second, you would injure the exchange or market in which you bought the shares because ordinary investors would be much less likely to invest and trade in securities if they saw them as biased toward the interests of people who can acquire insider information. Finally, you would injure society as a whole: If people can profit from information they had no right to get or use, others will doubt the fairness of the social institutions that made such activity possible.

Section 10b/Rule 10b-5 of the 1934 Act

Section 10b of the 1934 Securities Act deals with this issue by prohibiting "any manipulative or deceptive device or contrivance, including frauds and deceits, in connection with the purchase or sale of any security. . . . " In 1942, the SEC adopted Rule 10b-5, which implements Section 10b. Rule 10b makes it illegal "to employ any device, scheme, or artifice to defraud . . . in connection with the purchase or sale of any security."

Neither the 1934 Securities Act nor Rule 10b-5 defines the term "insider" or "insider information." For years, the SEC employed what was called the "possession theory." As stated in *SEC v. Texas Gulf Sulphur* (401 F.2d 833 [1968]), this interpretation of the rule required that

> anyone in the possession of material inside information must either disclose it to the investing public, or, if he is disabled from disclosing it in order to protect a corporate confidence . . . must abstain from trading in or recommending the securities concerned while such inside information remains undisclosed.

The key word in this passage is "anyone." Thus, someone who accidentally discovered insider information could not use it for his personal benefit unless he also publicly disclosed it. This provision became known as the "abstain or disclose doctrine."

Alleged insider transactions have occasioned a number of shareholder lawsuits in the past few years, especially as related to the junk bond schemes of the 1980s—for example, against Drexel Burnham Lambert. However, a Supreme Court ruling in 1991 (*Lampf et al. v. Gilbertson* 11 S.Ct. 2773) decreased the statute of limitations that private investors have to file securities-fraud suits under Section 10b of the 1934 Securities Act and SEC Rule 10b-5. In its attempt to impose uniformity, the Court gave shareholders a year from discovery and three years from the fraud to file suit. Potentially, this could deprive shareholders of their rights because such cases are extremely complex and require several years for discovery and then development of the suit. Ultimately, federal legislation will be required to set a period that both protects investors and discourages frivolous suits.

THE *CHIARELLA* AND *DIRKS* RULINGS. The possession theory was overthrown in the early 1980s by two related rulings: *United States v. Chiarella* and *Dirks v. SEC*. In *Chiarella* (445 U.S. 222 [1980]), the Supreme Court held that the mere possession of insider information does not require anyone who has it to "abstain or disclose." The Court decided instead that these obligations exist only for persons who have some fiduciary relationship with the party that might be injured.

As we saw in Chapter 7, a means a relationship of trust that obliges someone to act in the interests of someone else. Thus, a buyer need not tell a seller that he believes the value of his purchase will rise—buyers and sellers do not have a fiduciary relationship. However, if you ask a stockbroker for investment advice, he must tell you everything important about anything he recommends that you buy because the broker-client relationship is a fiduciary one.

As a result of the *Chiarella* ruling, someone who accidentally discovered insider information about a company that was issuing new securities could use that information however he liked as long as no fiduciary relationships existed. Among those who would have a fiduciary relationship to a company that issues securities are its executives, directors, and employees, as well as the executives, directors, and employees of the firms that help it issue new securities— for example, the underwriters.

The Court fleshed out the *Chiarella* ruling three years later in the *Dirks* decision, which concerned "tippees"—people who receive tips from others. Under the possession doctrine, it would not have mattered whether or not the "tipster" (the person who supplied the tip) had a fiduciary relationship to anyone who might suffer as a result of a failure to abstain or disclose. In *Dirks*, however, the Court ruled otherwise.[4]

---

[4] R. B. Titus and P. G. Carroll, "Netting the Outsider: The Need for a Broader Restatement of Insider Trading Doctrine," 8 *Western New England Law Review* 127 (1986).

DIRKS v. SECURITIES & EXCHANGE COMMISSION
United States Supreme Court, 463 U.S. 646 (1983)

Defendant Dirks, a tippee and an officer of a brokerage firm, was told by Secrist, the insider, that Equity Funding of America (EFA) was engaging in corporate fraud. Based on this nonpublic information, Dirks investigated EFA to verify Secrist's information. During Dirks' investigation, he openly revealed the information to investors and caused many of them to sell their EFA stock. However, by his investigation, Dirks aided the SEC, plaintiff, in convicting EFA for corporate fraud, and was then sued by the SEC for violating §10(b) because he openly disclosed the nonpublic information to investors. Dirks appealed the original trial-court finding to the U.S. Court of Appeals, which affirmed the findings. He now appeals to the Supreme Court.

Justice Powell deliverd the opinion of the Court.
. . . .

In the seminal case of *In re Cady, Roberts & Co.* (1961), the SEC recognized that the common law in some jurisdictions imposes on "corporate 'insiders,' particularly officers, directors, or controlling stockholders" an "affirmative duty of disclosure. . . when dealing in securities." . . . In *Chiarella* [v. *United States* (1980)], we accepted the two elements set out in *Cady, Roberts*

for establishing a Rule 10b–5 violation: "(i) the existence of a relationship affording access to inside information intended to be available only for a corporate purpose, and (ii) the unfairness of allowing a corporate insider to take advantage of that information by trading without disclosure." In examining whether Chiarella had an obligation to disclose or abstain, the Court found that there is no general duty to disclose before trading on material nonpublic information, and held that "a duty to disclose under § 10(b) does not arise from the mere possession of nonpublic market information." Such a duty arises rather from the existence of a fiduciary relationship.
. . . .

We were explicit in *Chiarella* in saying that there can be no duty to disclose where the person who has traded on inside information "was not [the corporation's] agent, . . . was not a fiduciary, [or] was not a person in whom the sellers [of the securities] had placed their trust and confidence." . . . Unlike insiders who have independent fiduciary duties to both the corporation and its shareholders, the typical tippee has no such relationships. . . .

The SEC's position, as stated in its opinion in this case, is that a tippee "inherits" the *Cady, Roberts* obligation to shareholders whenever he receives inside information from an insider:

"In tipping potential traders, Dirks breached a duty which he had assumed as a result of knowingly receiving confidential information from [Equity Funding] insiders. Tippees such as Dirks who receive nonpublic, material information from insiders become 'subject to the same duty as [the] insiders.' . . ."

This view differs little from the view that we rejected as inconsistent with congressional intent in *Chiarella*. . . .

. . . .

. . . The need for a ban on some tippee trading is clear. Not only are insiders forbidden by their fiduciary relationship from personally using undisclosed corporate information to their advantage, but they also may not give such information to an outsider for the same improper purpose of exploiting the information for their personal gain. Similarly, the transactions of those who knowingly participate with the fiduciary in such a breach are "as forbidden" as transactions "on behalf of the trustee himself." *Mosser v. Darrow* (1951). . . .

Thus some tippees must assume an insider's duty to the shareholders not because they receive inside information, but rather because it has been made available to them *improperly*. . . .

In determining whether a tippee is under an obligation to disclose or abstain, it thus is necessary to determine whether the insider's "tip" constituted a breach of the insider's fiduciary duty. . . . Whether disclosure is a breach of duty therefore depends in large part on the purpose of the disclosure. This standard was identified by the SEC itself in *Cady, Roberts*: a purpose of the securities laws was to eliminate "use of inside information for personal advantage." Thus, the test is whether the insider personally will benefit, directly or indirectly, from his disclosure. Absent some personal gain, there has been no breach of duty to stockholders. And absent a breach by the insider, there is no derivative breach. . . .

. . . .

Under the inside-trading and tipping rules set forth above, we find that there was no actionable violation by Dirks. It is undisputed that Dirks himself was a stranger to Equity Funding, with no pre-existing fiduciary duty to its shareholders. He took no action, directly or indirectly, that induced the shareholders or officers of Equity Funding to repose trust or confidence in him. There was no expectation by Dirks' sources that he would keep their information in confidence. Nor did Dirks misappropriate or illegally obtain the information about Equity Funding. Unless the insiders breached their *Cady, Roberts* duty to shareholders in disclosing the nonpublic information to Dirks, he breached no duty when he passed it on to investors as well as to *The Wall Street Journal*.

It is clear that neither Secrist nor the other Equity Funding employees violated their *Cady, Roberts* duty to the corporation's shareholders by providing information to Dirks. The tippers received no monetary or personal benefit for revealing Equity Funding's secrets, nor was their purpose to make a gift of valuable information to Dirks. As the facts of this case clearly indicate, the tippers were motivated by a desire to expose the fraud. In the absence of a breach of duty to shareholders by the insiders, there was no derivative breach by Dirks. Dirks therefore could not have been "a participant after the fact in [an] insider's breach of a fiduciary duty."

We conclude that Dirks, in the circumstances of this case, had no duty to abstain from use of the inside information that he obtained. The judgment of the Court of Appeals therefore is reversed.

Justice Blackmun, with whom Justice Brennan and Justice Marshall join, dissenting.

The Court today takes still another step to limit the protections provided investors by § 10(b) of the Securities Exchange Act of 1934. This innovation excuses a knowing and intentional violation of an insider's duty to shareholders if the insider does not act from a motive of personal gain. Even on the extraordinary facts of this case, such an innovation is not justified.

. . . .

The fact that the insider himself does not benefit from the breach does not eradicate the shareholder's injury. It makes no difference to the shareholder whether the corporate insider gained or intended to gain personally from the transaction; the shareholder still has lost because of the insider's misuse of nonpublic information. The duty is addressed not to the insider's motives, but to his actions and their consequences on the shareholder. Personal gain is not an element of the breach of this duty.

. . . .

. . . The Court justifies Secrist's and Dirks' action because the general benefit derived from the violation of Secrist's duty to shareholders outweighed the harm caused to those shareholders—in other words, because the end justified the means. . . .

Although Secrist's general motive to expose the Equity Funding fraud was laudable, the means he chose were not. Moreover, even assuming that Dirks played a substantial role in exposing the fraud, he and his clients should not profit from the information they obtained from Secrist. As a citizen, Dirks had at least an ethical obligation to report the information to the proper authorities. The Court's holding is deficient in policy terms not because it fails to create a legal norm out of that ethical norm, but because it actually rewards Dirks for his aiding and abetting.

Case Questions

1. What was the purpose of Secrist's tip to Dirks?

2. How is the purpose of disseminating the information to a "tippee" relevant for finding liability under Rule 10b-5?

3. Under what circumstances would Dirks have derivately assumed liability from Secrist?

The Law and Insider Trading

THE INSIDER TRADING SANCTIONS ACT. In 1984, Congress passed the Insider Trading Sanctions Act, under which the SEC can ask the courts to impose a fine of up to three times the sum that an inside trader might have made through illegal activities. However, the SEC can charge someone with insider trading only if it can show that the person had a "close" relationship with the injured party. The concept of an insider with fiduciary responsibilities was later broadened to include "temporary" insiders such as lawyers, accountants, underwriters, and other professionals.

THE INSIDER TRADING AND SECURITIES ENFORCEMENT ACT. In 1988, in response to continuing insider-trading scandals, Congress passed the Insider Trading and Securities Enforcement Act to enhance enforcement and thus help restore public confidence in the integrity of the securities market. The act codifies previous case law on insider trading, in particular the **misappropriation theory,** as a way to establish liability. The misappropriation theory states that anyone who acquires nonpublic material information by violating a fiduciary or other duty of trust or confidence, and who then trades on that information, is liable: You commit *fraud* when you breach your trust. The misappropriation theory is the subject of the YOU DECIDE feature in this chapter, which involves the case of a *Wall Street Journal* writer who traded on information that he obtained during the normal course of his activities as a journalist. The question is: Did he violate his fiduciary responsibility to the paper?

misappropriation theory
Theory establishing the liability of anyone who acquires nonpublic material information by violating a fiduciary or other duty of trust or confidence and who then trades on that information

YOU DECIDE
The Information Insider

The Wall Street Journal *is a daily financial newspaper with influence far beyond the street named in its title. It disseminates information worldwide, and its reputation rests on its readers' confidence in both the accuracy of its information and the unbiased nature of its analysis. In the mid-1980s, Wall Street and the financial community was shocked to learn that prior to the publication of the news in the paper, a financial writer for the* Journal, *R. Foster Winans, had taken knowledge that he obtained about certain stocks and given it to a broker, whereupon trades were executed and all the parties involved made a lot of money.*

The issue of misappropriation is crucial here: Did Winans violate a fiduciary responsibility to the Journal? *Certainly, he had used the information for his own advantage, but was he legally liable for crossing the border into fraud because he breached a trust? As the case unfolds, it is interesting to observe the relationship between individual and institution and to ask yourself whom did he harm?*

Winans wrote the column "Heard on the Street," which provided information about companies and stocks in a popular format that was widely read. It was the policy of Dow Jones, the Journal's *parent, to inform employees that all*

news material which they gathered in doing their job was the property of the company and that such nonpublic information was confidential. Winans was well aware of the policy but nonetheless gave the knowledge collected for his columns to some brokers at Kidder, Peabody the day before the series began. Based on Winans's information, trades were executed that netted almost $700,000 in profits. The scheme was uncovered by the brokerage house, and prosecutions for insider trading followed.

The court had to decide if Winans, acting in concert with a Journal *clerk and a stockbroker, had violated federal securities laws by "misappropriating material, nonpublic information in the form of the timing and content of* The Wall Street Journal's *confidential schedule of columns of acknowledged influence in the securities market" (791 F.2d 1024 2nd Cir. [1986]). Did Winans violate a position of trust at the paper? Did he "steal" the* Journal's *property? What would have been the difference, if any, had he used the information the day* after *the articles appeared? How crucial are the words "timing," "content," and "confidential schedule"? For further discussion, see p. 304.*

Securities in the '80s (IV) In December 1988, Drexel Burnham Lambert agreed to plead guilty to six felony counts, pay $650 million in fines, and cooperate with continuing investigations into the actions of clients and employees, including Milken. On April 24, 1990, Milken pleaded guilty to six felony charges, including conspiracy, aiding and abetting the filing of false statements with the SEC, and securities fraud; Milken also agreed to pay $200 million in fines and penalties and another $400 million to settle a civil suit filed by the SEC. At his criminal sentencing in October 1990, Milken received ten years from a judge who estimated that the actions to which he had pleaded guilty had cost victims a fairly modest $318,082. Some of those victims, however, proposed some far different numbers in a raft of potential civil suits. In March 1990, for example, shareholders in Unocal Corp. accused Milken and Drexel of systematically conspiring with takeover specialists during T. Boone Pickens' 1985 raid on the company to manipulate its stock prices; the civil suit, filed under the Racketeer Influenced and Corrupt Organizations statute (RICO), seeks $2.3 billion in treble damages. The FDIC has also cited Milken and Drexel for $12 billion in damages for "deliberately and systematically" plundering the U.S. savings-and-loan industry.

Short-Swing Profits

Section 10b is not the only provision of the 1934 Securities Act that attempts to control insider trading. The other provision that does so is Section 16b, which deals with any corporate officer, director, or shareholder with a ten percent interest in the corporation. Moreover, this section deals with a very specific kind of abuse—"short-swing" profits made by officers, directors, and ten percent shareholders who have insider information by virtue of their positions. The section prohibits them either from (1) buying shares in the company and then selling them within six months of the original purchase or from (2) selling shares and then buying them again within six months. Either the corporation or anyone who holds its securities can sue offenders and force them to give illegal profits to the company whose stock was bought or sold.

Today, Section 16b is widely regarded as old-fashioned because it tends to prevent activities it was not intended to prevent. Suppose, for example, that a ten percent shareholder decides to make a bid to take over the company, offering to buy stock from other shareholders at a certain price. The company then finds a so-called "white knight"—someone who agrees to offer even more per share to keep current management in control. After a struggle of less than six months, the shareholder gives up and sells his newly acquired shares to the white knight, making a profit because the white knight has paid a higher price for his shares. Under Section 16b, the company can sue the shareholder to recover that profit even though it was earned in the course of surrendering to the company that is now suing him for having done so.

The Supreme Court faced this problem in *Kern County Land Co. v. Occidental Petroleum Corp.* (411 U.S. 582 [1973]). The defendant, which had owned more than ten percent of the plaintiff's stock, attempted to acquire the plaintiff company. That company, Kern County Land, then recruited a white knight and the defendant's effort failed. As part of the settlement, Occidental proceeded to exchange its shares in the plaintiff's stock for preferred stock in the white-knight company. Because the exchange was in effect a sale, the plaintiff then turned around and attempted to force the defendant to give up the profits. In finding for the defendant, the Court pointed out that insider information was never abused during the course of these events.

Solicitation of Proxies

Other sections of the 1934 Securities Act deal with certain aspects of the shareholders meetings held by all corporations. In the sense that it elects the directors who control the corporation's affairs, the shareholders meeting is a form of final authority. All shareholders have the right either to attend the meeting and vote in person or to assign their voting rights to some other person by signing a formal authorization. This assignment is known as a **proxy.**

proxy A shareholder's formal assignment of voting rights to another person at a shareholders' meeting

Anyone who can control the shareholders meeting controls the company. Those who do not own enough stock to control the meeting themselves can attempt to solicit enough proxies to control it. If more than one side seeks control, a full-fledged proxy contest can result. Such contests can (1) resolve disputes between the management of a corporation and a group of stockholders by giving the victory to one side or the other, (2) help outsiders take control of companies that cannot be taken over through offers to buy outstanding shares, and (3) permit various groups to raise questions of corporate or social policy—for example, whether to do business in countries on whom certain sanctions have been imposed. (As the ETHICAL ENVIRONMENT box in this chapter shows, a proxy battle can be a forum for other aspects of stockholder-management disagreement—such as executive pay.)

SECTION 14(A) AND REGULATION 14A. Changes of this sort can have a profound effect on the companies in which they take place. Therefore, the SEC tries to ensure a reasonable standard of corporate behavior by regulating the process of soliciting proxies through Section 14(a) of the 1934 Securities Act and Regulation 14A, its implementing regulation.

(In early 1992, the American public learned that selected U.S. managers, many of whose companies were doing poorly (especially in the automobile industry), were earning large multiples of what their Japanese counterparts earned. The outrage further fueled the fires in a period in which our economy was stagnant, layoffs were massive, and stockholders were wondering why these individuals were being so handsomely rewarded for such poor performance. In turn, such questions have provoked questions about fairness (the difference between CEO and employee compensation is enormous); about disclosure (shareholders very often cannot decipher the plans under which executives are rewarded); and about accountability (who should decide executive pay, stockholders or the executive-compensation committee of the board of directors, and what the criteria should be for the payments.

Often cited as one of the worst offenders in the corporate pay bonanza is Steve Ross, CEO of Time Warner, the media conglomerate formed when Time Inc. purchased Warner Communications. In 1990, Ross received compensation of $78.2 million, of which $74.9 million was a one-time payment for his stock options in Warner. Coinciding as it did with the layoffs of over 600 people at the new company, Ross's compensation caused considerable fireworks. A Newspaper Guild spokesperson put it bluntly in human terms: "Ross's 1990 pay was two and a half times the combined salaries of the people laid off. That's absurd." Although Ross is credited with providing a windfall for Warner stockholders, observers note that his payment was for options—not actual stock that he owned—and that he incurred no risk if Warner's stock had fallen. This is a critical issue, and as one analyst puts it, "huge rewards without corresponding performance or risk appear to be feeding the current outcry against the excesses of executive compensation."

The New York City Retirement System, which owns almost 260,000 shares of Reebok stock, has tackled executive salaries at that company. In 1990, Reebok chairman Paul Fireman received $33.3 million in cash and stock options al-

though the firm's earnings had not risen for four years. As shareholder fiduciaries, the system's board wants executive compensation to be tied more directly to performance. They would like to put a shareholder proposal in the annual proxy statement requiring that a committee of independent directors without business ties to Reebok establish the compensation for corporate officers.

The idea of a shareholder vote on this topic has been reviewed by the SEC for Reebok and other corporations. In general, votes can be omitted from proxy statements if the subject is the "ordinary business" of the company—for instance, whether to buy new production equipment. In the case of Reebok, however, the SEC determined that the issue was one of significant policy. The proposal was therefore to go before the shareholders.

The SEC has also been pressured to bring about more general reform. Moreover, if the commission is not more active in doing so, Congress has threatened legislation on the subject. The SEC is thus expected to conduct trial proxy votes like that conducted at Reebok in several corporations. Pay issues that the SEC will allow shareholders to vote on in 1992 include ending management's bonus plan at Bell Atlantic, disclosing severance packages at Eastman Kodak, and ending cash bonuses at Grumman unless the company's stock price approaches the 1986 high. Under the SEC plan, any shareholder with one percent of a company's stock of $1000 can place into the proxy statement a proposal for a vote on an executive compensation package.

In its attempts at reform, the SEC will also rule that noncash payments—stock options in their various forms—be disclosed clearly to shareholders; that the present value of such payouts be given; and that a standard measure be used so people can make comparisons between firms. At present, making one's way through the jargon used to describe a stock-option plan is like being tangled in a bowl of spaghetti. Although executive pay may not decline as a result of these initiatives, at least shareholders will be better informed and in a better position to rally for their rights.

Rules 14a-3 to 14a-10 of Regulation 14A require that any person whose proxy is solicited must receive a *proxy statement*. This requirement is imposed on anyone who attempts to solicit more than ten proxies for a company that must file under the 1934 Securities Act.

Solicitation is broadly defined to include (1) direct requests for proxies and (2) any kind of communication with shareholders that might influence them to grant, not to grant, or to revoke a proxy. Private meetings at which people seeking proxies attempt to influence shareholders are solicitations under Rule 14a-1 of Regulation 14A, even if no actual request for proxies is made at a particular meeting.

Proxy Statements. An attempt to solicit a proxy must be preceded or accompanied by a **proxy statement,** which includes:

proxy statement SEC-required information that must be supplied to shareholders about those soliciting proxies and about all management and shareholder proposals

- Information about those who are soliciting the proxy. (If a company's directors, hoping to be reelected, send out a proxy statement, it must include details about their occupations, salaries, and shareholdings.)
- All proposals made by management or by shareholders who have owned one percent of the voting stock or voting securities worth at least $1000 at current market value for at least a year. The proposals, which must be listed separately, have to be phrased so as to evoke a "yes" or "no" response.

Securities in the '80s (V) *February 13, 1990: Charles H. Keating, Jr., arrives at a U.S. District Court hearing of his suit to block government seizure of his Lincoln Savings & Loan.*

When the debacle in the U.S. savings-and-loan industry erupted in 1988–89, investigators for the SEC and FDIC were less than surprised to find that the paper trail often led back to Drexel Burnham Lambert and Michael Milken. Many of the thrift institutions that went boom and bust in the 1980s, including Keating's Lincoln Savings & Loan in Irvine, California, were big Milken customers—avid buyers of the high-yield bonds which were Milken's stock-in-trade and which helped to inflate their own profit statements with resale values quoted by Drexel. In December 1986, for example, Lincoln paid $1 each for 79,000 shares in the computer-peripherals company Memorex; the stocks were being sold by Drexel as part of a leveraged buyout of the company. When Lincoln's parent company, Keating-owned American Continental Corp. (ACC), wanted to buy the stock from its own subsidiary at $35.32 per share in the spring of 1987, the SEC blocked the sale. Lincoln then sold the shares to a "straw buyer" at a mere $12.61 per share for a modest $920,000 profit. ACC then repurchased the stock from Lincoln's obliging trader at $25.32 per share and subsequently bought more Memorex stock from another Drexel customer at seven times that price: Drexel had revalued the stock at $170 per share—an increase in value of 16,900 percent. When computer-terminal manufacturer Texlex announced plans to merge with Memorex, ACC sold its Memorex holdings at a profit of $11.3 million. Such transactions, according to regulators, were merely *exchanges* of paper resulting in phantom "profits." In Lincoln's case, the thrift's on-paper holdings delayed its government seizure at a cost to taxpayers of $25 million. Total cost for the S&L bailout is expected to reach $300 billion. The FDIC sued Drexel for $6.8 billion for its part in S&L dealings, but on February 12, 1990, the firm filed for bankruptcy.

PART TWO   ORGANIZING TO DO BUSINESS

At least ten days before the final statement is sent to the shareholders, a preliminary version must be filed with the SEC. The SEC staff reviews and "clears" the statement. In some cases, it may do so in less than ten days. This practice is important toward the end of a proxy contest, when arguments on both sides come thick and fast.

In keeping with the SEC's goal of full disclosure and the prevention of fraud, the staff attempts to ensure that statements observe common standards of fair play. Rule 14a-9(a) of Regulation 14A forbids false or misleading statements, including omissions of important facts.

Federal Litigation. Most federal suits dealing with the solicitation of proxies have been brought under Rule 14a-9(a). Because failure to include important information can be misleading, Rule 14a-9(a) covers errors both of omission and of commission. The omitted information does not have to be so important that by itself, it would make a reasonable investor vote one way or the other. The following case illustrates this issue.

TSC INDUSTRIES, INC. v. NORTHWAY, INC.
United States Supreme Court, 426 U.S. 438 (1976)

Petitioner TSC Industries, Inc. and petitioner National Industries, Inc. issued a joint proxy statement to their shareholders, recommending approval of a proposal to liquidate and sell all of TSC's assets to National. The proxy solicitation was successful, TSC was placed in liquidation and dissolution, and the acquisition of TSC by National was effected. This action is brought by respondent Northway, a TSC shareholder, against TSC and National, claiming that their joint proxy statement was incomplete and materially misleading in violation of the Securities Exchange Act of 1934, and Rules 14a-3 and 14a-9 claiming that material facts relating to the degree of National's control over TSC and the favorability of the terms of the proposal to TSC shareholders were omitted from the proxy statement. Northway moved for summary judgment on the issue of TSC's and National's liability. The District Court denied the motion. On appeal, the Court of Appeals reversed the District Court's denial of summary judgment to Northway on its Rule 14a-b claims, holding that certain omissions of fact were material as a matter of law. TSC and National appeal.

Mr. Justice Marshall delivered the opinion of the Court.
. . . .

The question of materiality, it is universally agreed, is an objective one, involving the significance of an omitted or misrepresented fact to a reasonable investor. Variations in the formulation of a general test of materiality occur in the articulation of just how significant a fact must be or, put another way, how certain it must be that the fact would affect a reasonable investor's judgment.

The Court of Appeals in this case concluded that material facts include "all facts which a reasonable shareholder *might* consider important." [emphasis added.]

This formulation of the test of materiality has been explicitly rejected by at least two courts as setting too low a threshold for the imposition of liability under Rule 14a-9. . . .
. . . .

The general standard of materiality that we think best comports with the policies of Rule 14a-9 is as follows: An omitted fact is material if there is a substantial likelihood that a reasonable shareholder would consider it important in deciding how to vote. . . . It does not require proof of a substantial likelihood that disclosure of the omitted fact would have caused the reasonable investor to change his vote. . . . [It does require] that the disclosure of the omitted fact would have been viewed by the reasonable investor as having significantly altered the "total mix" of information made available.

. . . The determination requires delicate assessments of the inferences a "reasonable shareholder" would draw from a given set of facts and the significance of those inferences to him, and these assessments are peculiarly ones for the trier of fact. Only if the established omissions are "so obviously important to an investor, that reasonable minds cannot differ on the question of materiality" is the ultimate issue of materiality appropriately resolved "as a matter of law" by summary judgment.

The Court of Appeals concluded that two omitted facts relating to National's potential influence, or control, over the management of TSC were material as a matter of law. First, the proxy statement failed to state that at the time the statement was issued, the chairman of the TSC board of directors was Stanley Yarmuth, National's president and chief executive officer, and the chairman of the TSC executive committee was Charles Simonelli, National's executive vice president. Second, the statement did not disclose that in filing reports required by the SEC, both TSC and National had indicated that National "may be deemed to be a 'parent' of

TSC as that term is defined in the Rules and Regulations under the Securities Act of 1933." The Court of Appeals noted that TSC shareholders were relying on the TSC board of directors to negotiate on their behalf for the best possible rate of exchange with National. It then concluded that the omitted facts were material because they were "persuasive indicators that the TSC board was in fact under the control of National, and that National thus 'sat on both sides of the table' in setting the terms of the exchange."

We do not agree that the omission of these facts, when viewed against the disclosures contained in the proxy statement, warrants the entry of summary judgment against TSC and National on this record. . . .

The proxy statement prominently displayed the facts that National owned 34% of the outstanding shares in TSC, and that no other person owned more than 10%. It also prominently revealed that 5 out of 10 TSC directors were National nominees. . . . These disclosures clearly revealed the nature of National's relationship with TSC and alerted the reasonable shareholder to the fact that National exercised a degree of influence over TSC. In view of these disclosures, we certainly cannot say that the additional facts that Yarmuth was chairman of the TSC board of directors and Simonelli chairman of its executive committee were, on this record, so obviously important that reasonable minds could not differ on their materiality.

Nor can we say that it was materially misleading as a matter of law for TSC and National to have omitted reference to SEC filings indicating that National "may be deemed to be a parent of TSC." . . .

. . . .

The final omission that concerns us relates to purchases of National common stock by National and by Madison Fund, Inc., a mutual fund. Northway notes that National's board chairman was a director of Madison, and that Madison's president and chief executive, Edward Merkle, was employed by National pursuant to an agreement obligating him to provide at least one day per month for such duties as National might request. Northway contends that the proxy statement, having called the TSC shareholders' attention to the market prices of the securities involved in the proposed transaction, should have revealed substantial purchases of National common stock made by National and Madison during the two years prior to the issuance of the proxy statement. . . . The theory behind Northway's contention is that disclosure of these purchases would have pointed to the existence, or at least the possible existence, of conspiratorial manipulation of the price of National common stock, which would have had an effect on the market price of the National preferred stock and warrants involved in the proposed transaction.

. . . .

The Court of Appeals agreed with the District Court that "collusion is not conclusively established." But observing that "it is certainly suggested," the court concluded that the failure to disclose the purchases was materially misleading as a matter of law. . . .

The Court of Appeals' approach would sanction the imposition of civil liability on a theory that undisclosed information may *suggest* the existence of market manipulation, even if the responsible corporate officials knew that there was in fact no market manipulation. We do not agree that Rule 14a-9 requires such a result. Rule 14a-9 is concerned only with whether a proxy statement is misleading with respect to its presentation of material facts. If, as we must assume on a motion for summary judgment, there was no collusion or manipulation whatsoever in the National and Madison purchases—that is, if the purchases were made wholly independently for proper corporate and investment purposes, then by Northway's implicit acknowledgment they had no bearing on the soundness and reliability of the market prices listed in the proxy statement, and it cannot have been materially misleading to fail to disclose them.

. . . .

In summary, none of the omissions claimed to have been in violation of Rule 14a-9 were, so far as the record reveals, materially misleading as a matter of law, and Northway was not entitled to partial summary judgment.

Case Questions

1. What is the general standard of materiality used in this case?

2. Upon what basis did the Court find that the omissions claimed to have been in violation of Rule 14a-9 were not materially misleading as a matter of law?

3. In what ways could the omissions be held to violate Rule 14a-9?

■ *Concept Check 8-3   Insider Transactions*

- Discuss the importance of the rulings in the *Chiarella* and *Dirks* cases.
- What is the purpose of the *Insider Trading Sanctions Act*? Of the *Insider Trading and Securities Enforcement Act*?
- Explain the concept of *misappropriation theory*.
- What is a *short-swing profit*?
- Define a *proxy* and explain the regulatory requirements of *Section 14(a)* and *Regulation 14A*.

■ TAKEOVERS AND TENDER OFFERS

Corporations can join together in several quite distinct ways. Sometimes, one company is simply folded into another and loses its separate identity. This arrangement, called a **statutory merger,** is especially common when the purchasing company is much bigger than the company that it acquires. When the two companies are roughly equal in size, they usually form a new corporation wholly distinct from the companies that combined to form it. This kind of arrangement is called a **statutory consolidation.**

There are various forms of *statutory consolidation* with laws that apply to them, including takeovers by boards of directors and *leveraged buyouts*. We will begin by discussing the Williams Act, which covers the disclosure of consolidation deals, and we will conclude with an overview of *state takeover statutes*.

statutory merger Merger in which one company is acquired by and then folded into another, thereby losing its identity

statutory consolidation Arrangement in which companies combine to form a wholly distinct new firm

Statutory Consolidation

Companies get together for as many reasons as people do. Some want to achieve economies of scale or to offer customers a broader product line. Others decide that they can expand their operations more cheaply by purchasing existing facilities than by creating their own from scratch. Still others hope to diversify their activities in order to become less dependent on any particular line of business.

Companies often attempt to take control of other companies with the consent of their boards and officers. Frequently, however, hostile takeover attempts occur: The company mounting the **takeover** must try to seize control of a company against the opposition of its board and officers. The usual method of doing so is to make a **tender offer**—that is, an offer in which one company offers to buy shares in another company for the purpose of taking it over. Such offers are made directly to the shareholders of the target companies, not to management. Shareholders stand to benefit because the company mounting the takeover bid generally offers a premium above the current market price of their stock—usually at least twenty percent. Shareholders are generally made aware of the offer through ads placed in newspapers, but if the purchasing company can acquire a list of shareholders, it may attempt to reach them directly.

takeover Attempt by one company to seize control of another, frequently over the opposition of the latter's management

tender offer Direct bid by one company to shareholders of a target firm to purchase their shares in order to take over the firm

THE WILLIAMS ACT. Until the 1960s, tender offers were rare, and acquiring companies had to register offerings only when they were stock-for-stock, not cash offers. In order to make takeover bids public so that ordinary investors would receive information affecting the value of publicly traded securities involved in cash-tender offers, Congress passed the Williams Act in 1968. The Williams Act amended the 1934 Securities Exchange Act. Prior to 1968, target-company shareholders were given only the prices and expiration dates of tender offers. Under the Williams Act, bidders must disclose to both shareholders and the SEC all material information relevant to the transfer of ownership for the shareholders to evaluate in deciding whether to accept a bidder's offer; this information includes the terms of the offer and the identity of the bidder. Specifically, any person or company acquiring more than five percent of another company's stock must file Form 13-D, which names the purchasers and lists their other holdings.

The Williams Act has not, however, discouraged takeover bids, which became virtually epidemic in the 1980s. In fact, investment banks have become heavily involved in financing such bids further and questions, as yet unresolved, have arisen about the need for forcing these institutions to disclose additional information.

TAKEOVERS AND THE BOARD OF DIRECTORS. It is the responsibility of a corporation's board of directors to take appropriate defensive measures to fend off takeover bids. Their fiduciary duty to stockholders requires them to become well informed about bids and bidders and to respond when a threat is perceived. They may even accept a lower bid if, in their judgment, such action will maximize the stock value in the long term.

Boards have developed elaborate strategies—so-called *shark-repellent devices*—for the purpose of resisting tender offers. Some companies use the *crown-jewel option:* They sell off the assets (for example, subsidiaries or patents) that might tempt another company to take them over. Other companies use the so-called *poison-pill strategy*—amending their charters of incorporation by adding provisions that penalize potential purchasers who acquire more than a certain percentage of the company's stock. Still other companies defend themselves by dispensing *greenmail*—payments meant to buy off would-be purchasers. In general, such companies buy back the other company's shares at an attractive price; in return, the would-be purchaser may consent to a *standstill agreement* in which it promises not to seek control of the target company for a set number of years. Table 8-2 is a brief glossary of takeover terms that became popular in the 1980s, a decade particularly active in mergers and acquisitions.

LEVERAGED BUYOUTS. Another device often used to thwart takeover attempts is paying off shareholders. For example, suppose one company offers $60 a share for another company. The target company might then mount a **leveraged buyout (LBO),** in which it *borrows* nearly all the funds needed to purchase the target itself (generally using the target's assets as security). In this example, the target would borrow $60 a share against its own assets and then give the money to its shareholders, who thus eat their cake and have it too: They receive the money that the would-be purchaser offered them but can still keep the stock and sell it at a later date.

In the 1980s, over 2800 companies were involved in LBOs in the United States (there are just over 1700 firms listed on the NYSE); some $235 billion—most of it borrowed—went into financing these deals. Figure 8-6 illustrates the explosion of LBOs in the decade in both numbers of deals and billions of dollars. Table 8-3 lists the ten largest LBOs of the 1980s—a decade that *Fortune* magazine has already characterized as "an age of excess."

Understandably, LBOs are very popular with shareholders. Nonetheless, there are opposing views on the overall contribution that they make to the economy. For one thing, a firm's existing bondholders are hurt by the large amounts of new debt, usually in the form of junk bonds. In addition, employees are frequently laid off. Furthermore, the firm's annual expenses rise steeply simply to pay off the loan—a fact which, in turn, makes the company less willing to invest in risky or long-term projects that might lose income. Loan repayment then becomes even harder. The biggest potential problem is that a firm with so much debt has limited flexibility in a recession and may end up bankrupt or in default. In this view, a leveraged buyout ultimately throttles economic growth.

Some businesspeople, however, see positive aspects to LBOs. For instance, because managers have a greater equity stake in the firm, they work harder to improve earnings. Moreover, because interest on the debt is tax-

leveraged buyout (LBO)
Strategy used by a firm resisting a takeover attempt in which the target company borrows funds against its assets in order to purchase the company itself and then returns the funds to the shareholders

TABLE 8-2   *A Brief Glossary of Takeover Terms*

Crown-Jewel Strategy
Making the company undesirable to a takeover effort by selling its most attractive units. Dayton Hudson sold its profitable B. Dalton bookstore chain to ward off an unwanted suitor.

Greenmail
The repurchase by a company of a raider's stock at above-market prices, usually as part of an agreement to stop a takeover effort. Phillips Petroleum and Goodyear Tire both maintained their independence in this manner.

Junk Bonds
High-risk, high-yield bonds, often issued to finance a change of control. The takeover of giant Beatrice Foods by a far smaller group of investors/speculators was engineered in this manner.

Pacman Defense
Turning the tables on the attacker. Martin-Marietta used this approach to stave off a takeover effort by Bendix. Simultaneously, Allied Chemical, serving as a white knight, wound up taking over Bendix.

Poison Pills
Technically called "shareholders rights plans," this is a method for deterring a hostile takeover by making the cost prohibitively expensive. By late 1986, 121 of the *Fortune* 500 (ranging from Alcoa to Upjohn) had adopted poison pills.

Raider
A minority shareholder who attempts to dislodge the existing management of a corporation. The term, of course, is pejorative. The contrary view holds that a "takeover specialist" competes against "entrenched management" in the market for corporate control.

Shark Repellent
An action to deter a takeover. Includes issuing a "poison pill," using a "crown-jewel" or "pacman" strategy, or voting for a staggered board. The latter means that it will take several years to gain majority control of a board of directors.

White Knight
A third party who comes to the aid of an embattled management. Most knights turn out to be "tattletale grey," in that they wind up taking over the company they are supposed to be rescuing.

Wolf Packs
Friendly groups of investors who support each other's efforts to take over the control of a corporation—and enjoy the enhancement of their stock portfolios in the process.

Source: Murray L. Widenbaum, Business, Government, and the Public, *4th ed. (Englewood Cliffs, NJ: Prentice Hall, 1990).*

deductible, tax savings give the firm more money to reinvest in itself. In addition, bankrupt firms often continue to function productively after restructuring. In this view, the economy does not suffer because of LBOs. In this chapter's ORGANIZATIONAL PROFILE box, the LBO organized by the management of the famous department store Macy's is discussed in depth; both the positive and negative aspects of this undertaking in the retail industry are examined.

State Takeover Statutes

Some states have passed laws intended to make takeover bids harder to mount. In 1986, for example, Indiana passed a law that made it more difficult for would-be purchasers to exercise the voting rights ordinarily attached to stock ownership: No matter how much stock purchasing companies buy in any Indiana company, they must ask (and pay) for a meeting at which "disinterested" shareholders—that is, everyone but themselves, the target company's executives, and inside directors—decide whether or not to give them voting rights. The meeting must be held no more than fifty days after the request has been made. This law was challenged immediately. In 1987, *CTS*

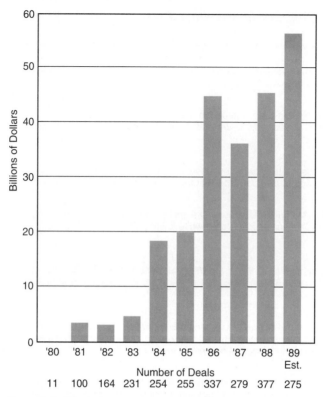

FIGURE 8-6 The Growth of LBOs in the 1980s   *Source:* Business Week, *January 15, 1990.*

Corp. v. Dynamics Corp. of America (481 U.S. 69 [1987]) wound up in the Supreme Court. Speaking for a 6-3 majority, Justice Powell upheld the Indiana law. The Court stated that the state law neither interfered unduly with interstate commerce nor conflicted with federal securities laws or SEC rules regarding tender offers. Passing similar laws, about half of the states have followed in Indiana's footsteps.

TABLE 8-3	*The Ten Biggest LBOs of the 1980s*	
BIGGEST DEALS OF THE DECADE	**YEAR**	**BILLIONS OF DOLLARS**
RJR NABISCO	1989	$24.7
BEATRICE	1986	6.3
BORG-WARNER	1987	4.4
SAFEWAY	1986	4.2
SOUTHLAND	1987	3.9
MONTGOMERY WARD	1988	3.8
OWENS-ILLINOIS	1987	3.7
FORT HOWARD	1988	3.6
MACY'S	1986	3.5
BURLINGTON INDUSTRIES	1987	2.9

Source: Business Week, *January 15, 1990.*

With great fanfare and enormous optimism, R. H. Macy's, the legendary retailer, launched the ship U.S. Leveraged Buyout in 1986, hoping to sail across the buoyant waters of the 1980s flourishing economy and into the realm of unprecedented profits. Instead, it hit the shoals of enormous debt and a flagging retail market to land on the shores of bankruptcy. Herein lies a story of ambition, probably greed, and certainly a lack of planning. The voyage is a cautionary tale.

Chairman Edward Finkelstein and his upper-level managers considered Macy's outlook in 1985 and saw much room for improvement. The 134-year-old retailer had performed well for a decade under Finkelstein (who ultimately resigned in 1992) with good profits and innovative lifestyle merchandising. Since the late nineteenth century, Macy's had grown from a single store—the landmark Herald Square location in New York City—to a system of branches and six regional store groupings. Management decided, however, that an entrepreneurial approach—giving employees a real stake in the business—was just what the department-store chain needed to grow as well as to motivate and keep on board its Macy's-trained, Macy's-nurtured staff.

In July 1986, almost 350 managers took Macy's private through the largest internal LBO in the history of retailing. Admittedly, debt financing was relatively easy to get in the mid-1980s. Using Macy's assets and cash flow as collateral, they borrowed about $3.7 billion to purchase a twenty percent stake in the company. Some stockholders, however, opposed the LBO, charging that given the value of the company's stores, the $70 per share they were offered in the buyout was much too low. Moreover, they felt that they were being kept from sharing in growth and turnaround opportunities. Veteran New York Times retailing reporter Isidore Barmash asked whether management's personal greed, rather than the desire to run the company at its optimum, might not have been the motivation: According to Barmash, the usual reasons for an LBO—financial problems, need for new capital, and a threatened hostile takeover—were absent here.

Undaunted by the huge debt that they had taken on, the managers' initial attitude was almost joyful. Finkelstein projected that the entrepreneurial spirit would cause managers to cut waste and sloppiness and devise innovative marketing schemes that would both pay off the debt quickly and begin to realize significant profits. One goal, for example, was to diversify the chain; others included developing private labels and using commission sales to boost produc-

tivity. Finkelstein also felt that management could now concentrate on neglected long-range strategies.

In this climate of good ideas but apparently overconfident aspirations, the billions of dollars of debt with which Macy's was saddled proved the firm's undoing. In early 1988, consumer spending began to slow, and with the downturn in retail sales, Macy's was hard-pressed both to run the business and pay interest on its debt. As if these circumstances were not grim enough, Macy's made a bad error in judgment. Also in 1988, it borrowed another $1.1 billion to purchase the I. Magnin and Bullock's chains, adding further to its debt in order to finance expansion in uncertain economic times. Magnin and Bullock stores in the West were being hurt as badly by the recession as Macy's other properties, mostly in the Northeast. Macy's fiscal picture was consistently poor, with a $188-million loss for fiscal 1988, $53.6 million for fiscal 1989, $215.3 million in fiscal 1990, and $150.2 million in fiscal 1991.

In order to keep afloat, Macy's undertook a variety of financial dealings. In 1990, it sold its credit operation to GE Capital Corporation, erasing $1.5 billion of its debt. In the same year, it bought back more than $550 million in bonds on the open market, again reducing its debt. In 1990 and again in 1991, Hong Kong financier Run Run Shaw bought Macy's stock for a total of $50 million.

Despite these efforts at debt reduction, however, the earnings picture was bleak due to the recession, and by the beginning of 1992, Macy's cash flow was insufficient to both cover interest payments and pay suppliers. The department store kept delaying supplier payments so that it could comply with the terms of its agreements with lenders. It enlisted Loews Corporation, under Chairman Lawrence Tisch, to save the company with an investment of $1 billion. To complete the deal, however, Loews required Macy's creditors to accept lower interest rates; when one major creditor, Prudential, refused, Tisch canceled the offer. When Macy's could no longer pay its bills after the poor 1991 Christmas selling season, Chairman Finkelstein at last recognized that Macy's no longer had a choice, and the company filed for Chapter 11 restructuring and bankruptcy protection (see Chapter 19).

Ego-bruising though this choice was—coupled with the certainty of equity loss for managerial owners—Macy's continues to do business under bankruptcy protection. Although the bright promise of the 1986 LBO has not been fulfilled, the realistic continuation of a venerable and successful retailer seems assured.

■ Concept Check 8-4 Takeovers and Tender Offers

- How does *statutory consolidation* differ from a *statutory merger*?
- What is the purpose of the *Williams Act*?
- Define *leveraged buyout*.

The U.S. Court of Appeals, Second Circuit, decided U.S. v. Carpenter in 1986, affirming the lower-court finding that Winans had unlawfully misappropriated information from his employer under Section 10(b) and Rule 10b-5. The court held that he had defrauded the Journal, to which he had a fiduciary responsibility. Subsequently, the Supreme Court upheld this ruling (108 S.Ct. 316 [1987]). Because it also affects numerous other business and personal relationships, it is useful to examine the appeals-court reasoning.

Winans stole the information when he had a duty of confidentiality. He defrauded the Journal, and although the publication suffered no monetary loss, the "exclusivity" of the information was what earned the paper its reputation and the confidence of its readers.

The timing of the theft was also deemed important. The publication of this information the next day frequently affected the price of the stock in question. Had the information not been published in such a timely way, it would not have had the same value to fraudulent traders. Therefore, the Journal's "schedule" was as much stolen property as the news itself.

It was Winans's exploitation of the information, however, that seemed to the court his greatest violation. Although he protested that he was protecting this confidential information, according to the court, he was using it for his own benefit and then concealing the scheme. He thus perpetrated fraud, not merely broke Dow Jones's own company rules.

When one expands on these issues, taking them beyond the context of securities-law violations, they reappear in a variety of circumstances. For example, does receiving—and using—information always mean misappropriation? If a college professor tells his graduate assistants in confidence that a cover-up is being investigated regarding the use of federal government research funds at the university and one of them sells the story to the largest newspaper in the state, is this merely use or is it misappropriation? In other words, is profiting from a relationship of trust unethical?

Although Winans actually profited illegally from the special knowledge that he had received because of his fiduciary relationship with the paper, other cases may not present themselves so forcefully. Thus, keeping in minding the criteria of misappropriation will always be important.

SUMMARY

- *Securities markets* are among the most important means of allocating resources among competing companies. The Great Depression marked the beginning of federal regulation. The first federal law in this area was the *Securities Act of 1933*, which regulates the way new securities are offered to the public. The 1933 Securities Act attempted to ensure that any investor would have access to full and accurate information about all securities sold in interstate commerce. It was meant to help individual investors make rational choices and thus to make financial markets more efficient.

- The *Securities Exchange Act of 1934* was intended mainly to regulate secondary distribution. To that end, the 1934 Securities Act created the *SEC*, which also enforces other securities laws. The Act provides for registration of the *securities exchanges*, stockbrokers, and dealers involved in interstate commerce and of fairly large companies involved in interstate commerce; it requires companies that fall under its authority to file regular reports with the SEC.

- In addition, the 1934 Securities Act prohibits the use of *insider information*. Since the early 1980s, however, mere possession of insider information has not required those who possess it to disclose the information or to refrain from trading securities whose value might be affected by it. These obligations exist only for persons who have a *fiduciary relationship* with parties that might be injured by a failure to "abstain or disclose."

- *Section 16b* deals with corporate officers, directors, and ten percent shareholders who have insider information by virtue of their positions. This section, which prohibits such people from making "short-swing" profits, is today regarded as old-fashioned.

- The regulation of securities markets attracted little interest in the 1940s and 1950s. But during the 1960s, American industry's need for new capital boomed and, along with it, the volume of the securities business. In 1963, the SEC asked Congress for a number of new powers, especially over OTC trading. Congress agreed in 1964. Five years later, Congress amended the 1934 Securities Act so that anyone who now attempts to take over a company must make his intentions public.

- The 1980s were marked by highly publicized securities scandals and by federal legislation designed to impose sanctions and restore public confidence in securities markets. In 1990, Congress enacted new securities laws to expand government power to enforce existing statutes.

QUESTIONS AND PROBLEMS

1. Silas Greening arrives early at the brokerage firm where his friend works and must wait a few minutes before they can leave for lunch. While in the men's room, he overhears a conversation in which one senior broker tells another of a company's decision to divest itself of a major part of its operations. He does not mention the conversation to anyone, but he invests heavily in the companies which stand to benefit by the removal of one of their toughest competitors from the market. He makes a bundle of money from his investments. Have the insider trading rules been violated?

2. R. Foster Winans, a *Wall Street Journal* reporter and one of the writers of that paper's widely read and influential column "Heard on the Street" in the *Wall Street Journal*, participated in a scheme with two stockbrokers, Peter Brant and Kenneth Felis, to provide the two with security-related information. Based on this information the two would buy or sell the subject securities. In total, the scheme netted profits of $690,000. Approximately two years later, when the compliance department of the stock brokerage house of Kidder,Peabody noticed a correlation between "Heard" articles and trading in certain accounts, the SEC filed charges. What were those charges? [*U.S. v. Carpenter*, 791 F.2d 1024 (1986)]

3. ABC Co. issues new stock in an existing class. It does not prepare a 1934 Act registration for the new securities. Has the 1934 Act been violated?

4. The Board of Directors of XYZ Corp., a publicly held corporation whose stock is traded on AMEX, is involved in an important battle over new directions for the corporation. In an effort to win support, the directors solicit proxies from shareholders by sending a letter telling their side of the story and requesting the shareholders to permit them to vote their shares. Proxies are returned by several hundred thousand shareholders, but they are challenged by the corporate opponents. Why?

5. A Tennessee corporation, which only does business within the state, makes a public offering of its securities to Tennessee inhabitants only. Must the corporation comply with the registration requirements of the 1933 act?

6. Vito Leone recently won the lottery and would like to invest in the securities of a local college. He asks for a registration statement. Vito is surprised when he is told that the securities are not registered with the SEC but he decides to invest anyway, based on information the college sends him regarding its financial situation. In an effort to raise more money, the college's financial officer adds two zeros to the end of all the asset amounts. Vito invests based on this information. Does the SEC have any authority in this matter?

7. Sara White and her broker Chas D'Orio discuss securities for two companies. The first company's registration statement is already final. The second company's is not, but the broker assured the client that shares would be reserved for her at the public offering price if and when the statement became final. It eventually did become final, and Mr. D'Orio purchased the shares as promised. However, upon receipt of the final prospectus, Ms. White demands recision. The broker refuses. Ms. White brings an action claiming that the 1933 Act was violated. Who wins and why? [*Diskin v. Lomasney & Co.*, 452 F.2d 871 (2d Cir. 1971)]

8. David G. Hill was an officer and Director of PPG Industries between February 17, 1954, and September 28, 1971, when he resigned. On Septem-

ber 29 and 30, 1971, Mr. Hill exercised options granted to him in the course of his employment with PPG, acquiring 7,282 shares of PPG common stock. During the same two-day period in September, Mr. Hill sold 6,800 shares of PPG common stock. Is a retired officer and director an "insider" for purposes of 16 (b)? Were Mr. Hill's September transactions "short swings"? [*Lewis v. Mellon Bank, N.A.*, 513 F.2d 821 (1971)]

9. The brokers of an experienced brokerage firm supplied an apartment complex's owners with a list of potential clients carefully screened for suitability as investors in the complex. The group of potential investors was given a "fact sheet" containing information. They had an opportunity to ask questions regarding the offer and were required to complete a questionnaire claiming net worth and financial sophistication. Mary Jones purchased an interest in the offering as an investment. She expected to have a positive cash flow from the investment approximately two years after the purchase. When no income was realized, she initiated an action alleging violations of the 1933 act and Section 10b of the 1934 act. The owners of the apartment complex contend that the sale was a private offering that is exempt from registration requirements. Who is right? [*Mary S. Krech Trust v. Lake Apartments*, 642 F.2d 98 (5th Cir. 1981)]

10. Black Inc. is a consumer finance company. Smith Co. is the exclusive underwriter of promissory notes issued by Black Inc. Smith Co. prepared and circulated to prospective customers reports on the notes Black Inc. held for sale. Forty-two people purchased the notes. Seven months later, the company defaulted on the notes. The default was the result of fraud perpetrated by Black Inc. and the certified public accountants who audited its financial statements and rendered opinions on them. Smith Co. was not aware of the fraud and thought that the financial statements were accurate. The investors sue Smith Co., alleging that it failed to make a reasonable investigation as underwriter, and lied when it issued the prospectus on Black Inc. Is Smith Co. liable? [*Sanders v. John Nuveen & Co.*, 619 F.2d 1222 (7th Cir. 1980)]

CONTRACTS

Contracts permeate our society. We tend to think of them as formal, written documents drafted by lawyers, signed by all parties, and sealed with a notary stamp. Contracts, however, can be very simple. Many are not even in writing. Oral contracts can be just as legal as written ones.

Contracts are important not only for business, but for individuals going about everyday life. When you buy an airplane ticket, arrange to have a picture framed, or take out an insurance policy, you have entered into a contract. The next time you park in a downtown garage, check the ticket stub. You will probably find that it contains contractual language that purports to limit the liability of the garage for your car and its contents.

Essentially, a *contract* is nothing more than a legally enforceable agreement. You enter into agreements with other people all the time. For example, you agree to go to the movies together. You agree to meet at the library to study. You promise to pick up a quart of milk before coming home in the evening. The key distinction between a contract and these other agreements is that a court of law can intervene to enforce a contract.

■ CONTRACT LAW

Some branches of the law—for example, criminal law—attempt to control human conduct by imposing obligations on people. By contrast, the role of **contract law** is simply to facilitate voluntary agreements: It allows people to enter into agreements with others and to accept obligations willingly in return for some **quid pro quo**—that is, one thing for another. Specifically, contract law has three functions:

1. to specify which agreements are *legally binding*

contract law The branch of law that facilitates voluntary agreements

quid pro quo Literally, one thing for another; in *contract law*, the gain for which people enter into agreements and accept obligations

307

2. to define the *rights* and *duties* created by enforceable but ambiguous agreements

3. to determine the *consequences* of breaking an agreement.[1]

The study of contract law, therefore, is the study of (1) the circumstances under which a court will enforce an agreement and (2) how it will do so.

Why Is Contract Law Necessary?

INDIVIDUAL TRANSACTIONS. Contract law plays a critical role in promoting efficiency and fairness in relationships between individuals. Individuals come together to exchange goods and services because it is mutually beneficial to them to do so, and many exchanges are successful even though the parties never created an explicit agreement. Indeed, in certain situations, a contract would not help—and could even hurt—the parties' chances of attaining their desired objectives.

The following example illustrates what contracts can and cannot do in the context of individual transactions: Howard and Rogers share a duplex and the winding driveway that leads up to it. The top of the driveway is wide enough to accommodate both Howard's and Rogers's cars. The bottom of the driveway, however, is only wide enough for passage of one car at a time. During a heavy thunderstorm, a bolt of lightning causes a tree to fall across the narrow portion of the driveway. The tree is too heavy for Howard or Rogers to move alone, but together they can lift it. Howard and Rogers discuss their plan of attack, Howard yells, "Heave ho!" and in unison they remove the obstacle. Howard and Rogers exchanged services for their mutual benefit. Would this transaction have been made easier by an agreement that expressly stated their obligation to use all their strength to lift the tree? No, on three counts. First, the shared necessity of removing the tree from the driveway was a sufficient inducement for them to fulfill their obligations to each other. Second, it is likely that the result of one party's insistence upon a contract would be suspicious and suggestive of a lack of willingness to participate. Finally, the primary obligation of Howard and Rogers to use all their strength is intangible: Even if this duty could be described in a contract, how could a court determine if one of them breached it?[2]

To bargain successfully, parties must recognize that both sides stand to benefit from reaching an agreement, and each party must accept the other's right to make demands that are in his own interest. Thus, individuals can collaborate in increasing their mutual satisfaction through a process of give and take. In both commercial and noncommercial settings, contracts are needed only if interdependence, shared customs, or necessity are insufficient to make both parties feel that their expectations of the other will be fulfilled.

SOCIAL AND ECONOMIC ORDER. On a socioeconomic level, contract law reflects and advances certain long-held philosophical values. For example, the notion of the sanctity of the *promise* is embodied in the law of contracts. According to this concept, which has its roots in the late Middle ages and the Renaissance, one

---

[1] *See* Anthony T. Kronman, "Contract Law and Distributive Justice," 89 *Yale Law Review* 472 (1980).

[2] Based on an example in Lon L. Fuller and Melvin A. Eisenberg, *Basic Contract Law* (Minneapolis, MN: West, 1972), p. 97.

who reneges on a promise commits a moral offense. Thus, the idea of "reliance" on another's promise is a cornerstone of contract law. This idea reflects the belief that people who legitimately rely upon the promises of others should have a right of recovery against promisors who fail to perform their obligations.

Individual Freedom. The law of contracts also promotes individual freedom by allowing people to regulate their own lives and bind themselves to others as they see fit. By establishing rules for those who wish to form contracts and by enforcing agreements against parties who breach them, the law of contracts ensures that both commercial and noncommercial relationships operate in accordance with longstanding principles of fair play and justice.

Marketplace Efficiency. The legal system's recognition and enforcement of private contracts also maximizes the efficiency of the marketplace. Many economists believe that private contracts and the law that enforces them help to maximize a society's wealth. Underlying this view is the idea that an open market allows resources to move toward their most valuable uses. In other words, the same item may be worth more in one setting than another. For example, an airplane may be worth less to an airline company that is in financial trouble than it is to an airline that is expanding and picking up new routes.

Because relative values are determined and exchanges are carried out through the *bargaining* process, contract law is an essential part of this process in market economies. People enter into contracts because variations in value and the division of labor allow all parties to benefit. For example, the airplane described above may be worth only $1 million to the troubled company but $1.5 million to the expanding company. If they negotiate a contract to sell it for $1.25 million, each party profits—as do consumers who purchase airline tickets.

■ DEFINING A CONTRACT

Like so many basic legal terms, the term "contract" is difficult to define. According to Section 1 of the *Restatement (Second) of Contracts,*[3] a **contract** is "a promise or a set of promises for the breach of which the law gives a remedy, or the performance of which the law in some way recognizes as a duty." This formulation means that all contracts are promises even though not all promises are contracts. A promise is defined in Section 2 of the restatement as "a manifestation of intention to act or refrain from acting in a specified way, so made as to justify a promisee in understanding that a commitment has been made." Only those promises that are made in a way prescribed by our legal system rise to the level of contract. This requirement explains why "social promises" often fail to become binding legal contracts.

contract *Promise* or set of promises the performance of which is legally recognized as a duty and the breach of which the law gives *remedy*

Rights and Duties. This definition is also concerned with the *binding* nature of the promise: Contracts establish *rights* and impose legal *duties* on the parties involved, and those duties may be enforced in a court. Thus parties may turn to the courts with an action for breach of contract and a request for a

---

[3] In 1932, the American Law Institute compiled contract-law principles as the *Restatement of the Law of Contracts;* the second edition of this compilation is known as the *Restatement (Second) of Contracts.* Although merely an agreement among its drafters with no official legal status, its stature makes it an important reference tool for lawyers and judges.

remedy, such as specific performance or a money judgment (*see* Chapter 4).

Exchanges. Another important characteristic of contracts, which is not explicitly mentioned in the definition given above, is that contracts are concerned with *exchanges* between at least two parties: A mere promise to do something is not an enforceable contract unless some *promise, performance,* or *forbearance* (the temporary foregoing of a right) is given in return. Thus, although the promise of a Christmas gift is a legally recognized agreement, it is not a contract—it is a one-way flow of benefits.

Note that for legal purposes the term "contract" refers to the *agreement itself*. Do not be misled by the casual use of the word by laymen and lawyers alike to refer to written documents setting forth the *terms* of an agreement. The contract is the agreement itself, *not the record of it.*

■ *Concept Check 9-1   Contract Law & Defining a Contract*

- Why is *contract law* necessary?
- How does the *Restatement (Second)* define a *contract*? A *promise*?
- What three criteria distinguish an exchange as an *enforceable contract*?

■ TYPES OF CONTRACTS

There are many different ways in which contracts can be classified, each serving a different purpose. Two of the most important classification schemes are *bilateral* or *unilateral,* and *express* or *implied.*

Bilateral or Unilateral Contracts

bilateral contract Agreement between parties that involves a promise in exchange for another promise

reciprocal promises Promises made by both parties to a bilateral *contract*, each being obligated to perform as promised and having a right to expect the other party to perform as promised

BILATERAL CONTRACTS.   The vast majority of contracts are **bilateral contracts**—that is, they consist of **reciprocal promises.** Each party to a bilateral contract makes a promise, is obligated to perform as promised, and has a right to expect the other party to perform. For example, suppose that a contract to paint a house stipulates that the painter promises to paint the house in exchange for the homeowner's promise to pay him $1500. The contract is made in the spring even though the promises will not be acted on until midsummer. Both the painter and the homeowner are bound by the bilateral contract.

unilateral contract Agreement in which only one party promises to perform in return for an act

UNILATERAL CONTRACTS.   In **unilateral contracts,** only one party makes a promise, and only that party has any obligations under the terms of the contract. The promise is exchanged not for another promise, as in bilateral contracts, but for the *actual performance* of an act. The classic example of a unilateral contract concerns the offer of a reward. A distraught pet owner promises to pay $100 to anyone who finds and returns a lost dog. No one is obligated by this contract to search for the dog, nor is the pet owner legally bound by the contract until someone returns the dog. When, however, someone does perform the act stipulated by the contract—that is, when someone finds and returns the lost dog—

the pet owner is obligated to carry out his half of the bargain and pay the finder $100.

Unilateral Contracts: Business Applications. Although unilateral contracts make up a small minority of all contracts, they do have some business applications. For example, the concept of a unilateral contract is routinely used by the courts in deciding cases involving employer-employee relationships. Disputes often arise over employees' rights to such benefits as pensions, bonuses, and profit-sharing plans. The courts have generally interpreted the very existence of a benefits plan—even when the employer has not specifically pledged to continue such benefits indefinitely—as a promise inviting a unilateral contract. Employees fulfill the conditions of that contract and make it binding simply by working for the employer.

The following case concerns just such an employee-employer relationship. Its central concern, however, is the freedom of the party making a unilateral offer to *revoke* it: What happens when somebody has begun to perform as requested in the offer but has not yet had time to complete the performance? Does this in some way bind the offeror and prevent him from revoking the offer?

SYLVESTRE v. STATE OF MINNESOTA
Minnesota Supreme Court, 214 N.W. 2d 658 (1973)

Here for review are consolidated cases brought by six district judges involving retirement compensation. Retirement laws for district court judges have been comprehensively revised and recoded and have undergone several changes. Only those pertaining to the amount of a judge's retirement compensation are of significance here.

Each judge argues that he is entitled to receive the retirement compensation that was promised to him by the state when he took office.

Knutson, Chief Justice.

Prior to the 1967 and 1969 amendments Minn. St. 1965, § 490.102, subd. 2(a), provided:

If, at the time of retirement, he [a district judge] has attained the age of at least 70 years and he has served for 15 years as such judge, or as such judge of a court of record, he shall receive for the remainder of his life, one-half the compensation *allotted to the office.* (Italics supplied.)

Ex. Sess. L. 1967, c. 38, § 5, amended this provision to read in pertinent part:

. . . [H]e shall receive for the remainder of his life, one-half the compensation allotted for the office *at the time of his retirement.*

This provision was again amended by L. 1969, c. 987, to read:

. . . [H]e shall receive for the remainder of his life, one-half the compensation allotted to the office *at the time of his retirement or on July 1, 1967, whichever is greater.* (Italics supplied in part.)

In 1971, each of the judges was receiving retirement compensation in the amount of $11,000 per annum. The legislature in that year increased the compensation allotted to the office of district judge from $22,000 to $29,000 per annum. Under the pre-1967 formula, the retirement compensation of these judges would have increased to $14,500. Under the 1967 and 1969 formulae they continued to receive $11,000 per annum. Each made a written demand for an increase in compensation based on the fact that they were entitled to one-half the compensation allotted to the office, not one-half the compensation allotted to the office at the time of retirement. In other words, they claim they are entitled to the benefit of the increase in salary. Their demands were refused, and they commenced these actions. . . .

The trial court held that Judges Forbes, Sylvestre, Jaroscak, and Hall had contractual rights to retirement benefits based on the statutes as they existed at the time of their retirement and that the amendments of the statute so as to diminish the amount of such compensation were unconstitutional as to them. The court found that Judge Flynn had no such rights since he retired after the enactment of the amendments and therefore there was no impairment of his contractual rights. With respect to Judge Underhill, the court held that he was entitled to the retirement benefits existing at the time he submitted his request for retirement, even though the retirement became effective after the 1967 amendment of the statute was enacted.

Article I, § 10, of the Federal Constitution, and article 1, § 11, of the Minnesota Constitution prohibit the state from passing any law impairing the obligation of contracts.

. . . .

While cases involving private employment are not controlling, we think the rationale of the case of Hartung v. Billmeier (1954) is persuasive. That case involved a promise by an employer to give his employees a stated bonus if they stayed with him 5 years. The employee stayed with the employer for 6 years and 9 months. When the employer thereafter sued him for the price of goods sold to him, the employee counterclaimed to collect the bonus which had been promised to him. In upholding his right to recover, we said:

> . . . Inasmuch as plaintiff's offer or promise to pay a bonus was not accepted by a promise of the defendant to work continuously for him for five years, no bilateral contract resulted when the offer was made.
>
> '. . . A bilateral contract is one in which there are mutual promises between two parties to the contract; each party being both a promisor and a promisee.' Restatement, Contracts, § 12.
> A promisee may, however, accept an offer or promise to pay a bonus by performing the act or forbearance specified in the offer, but such act or forbearance must differ from what the promisee is already obligated to do either by law or by existing contract. When a promise is thus accepted by performance of the designated act or forbearance, the promisor's offer is converted into a unilateral contract which comes into being the moment the act or forbearance has been fully performed.
> Here the defendant accepted plaintiff's offer by forbearing to leave plaintiff's employment for five years. The moment plaintiff's offer was thus converted into a contract, the bonus became due and payable.

The same is true of the case now before us. When these judges entered upon their judicial position, the state in effect said to them, "If you will stay on the job for at least 15 years and then retire after having reached the specified retirement age, we will pay you a part of your salary for the remainder of your life." . . .

. . . .

Here, a judge gives up the right to continue in the only field of endeavor in which he has been educated and is experienced in order to accept a position, often for a much smaller financial reward, anticipating that upon retirement the state will continue to pay him part of his salary. . . .

. . . .

As to Judge Flynn, the trial court held that he could receive only the retirement compensation provided at the time of his retirement.

. . . The better rule is that retirement compensation constitutes deferred payment of part of the judge's salary, if he is willing to retire, which cannot be diminished during his continuance in office; and upon his re-

tirement the contract is fully performed. He is then entitled to be paid what the state promised him when he took office, which is one-half the compensation allotted to the office then and at any time thereafter. . . . It is only on that theory that assurance can be given a judge that, if he stays in the office for the required length of time, attains the required age, and then retires, he will receive retirement compensation as promised him when he took office. On this theory, Judge Flynn is entitled to the same protection as the other judges involved; that is, he is entitled to receive one-half of the pay allotted to the office, which was the promise made by the state when he took office and remained so throughout his continuance in office.

We think the same reasoning applies to Judge Underhill. . . .

. . . .

Judges Flynn and Underhill are essentially in the position of offerees who, after partial performance, found that the offer made to them was revoked and a new offer attempted to be substituted. While the problem of the revocability of offers for unilateral contracts after part performance has not been decisively treated by this court before and is not without theoretical difficulties, see 1 Williston, Contracts (3 ed.) §§ 60 and 60A, we believe the better view is that adopted by the Restatement. Under the Restatement view, part performance by the offeree prevents the revocation of the offer (Restatement, Contracts, § 45).

. . . A change in the terms of the offer which reduces the terms of the original offer is, of course, tantamount to a revocation of the offer and the substitution of a new offer.

Thus, following the analogy to private employment cases, once Judges Flynn and Underhill began their service as judges, the state was bound by a contract to pay "one-half the compensation allotted to the office" in retirement benefits, although of course the state's duty of immediate performance did not arise until the judge's completion of the requisite years of service. Since under the principle advanced by the Restatement the state was irrevocably bound by this contract from the time Judges Flynn and Underhill took office, there is no reason for treating their situation differently from that of the other judges.

Affirmed as to plaintiffs Sylvestre, Jaroscak, Underhill, Hall, and Forbes; modified as to plaintiff Flynn.

Case Questions:

1. Explain the difference between a bilateral contract and a unilateral contract. What was the unilateral contract in this case?

2. What was the partial performance rendered by the judges? What was the state then bound by contract to do?

3. Explain the significance of partial performance in terms of revocability of offers.

Express or Implied Contracts

An **express contract** is an explicit agreement in which the parties spell out the terms and manifest their assent either in writing or orally. By contrast, an **implied contract** is one that is inferred to exist by the law: Although there is no explicit agreement between the parties, behavior and the circumstances demonstrate a tacit understanding that a contract exists. Some business transactions are routinely carried out by implied contracts. Consider, for example, what happens when a car owner leaves the family sedan at a garage to have it fixed. The implication is that the car owner is willing to pay a reasonable fee for the mechanic's services and that the mechanic is willing to fix the car. Although the contract is inferred and not written, there is no doubt that the car owners and the mechanic have made a contract.

CONTRACTS IMPLIED IN FACT. The law treats this kind of implied contract, more technically known as a contract "implied in fact," just as it treats an express contract. It is a true contract because both parties have assented to it; their agreement, although implied, is nonetheless real. The only difference is that the implied contract results from *conduct*, not *words*.

CONTRACTS IMPLIED IN LAW. Implied contracts can also refer to another category of contracts *"implied in law."* Unlike the contracts just described, contracts implied in law are not based on any promises actually made or intended by the parties: Rather, the court imposes these contractual obligations on the parties after the event in order to do justice. For example, a physician who treats an unconscious stranger lying in the street has a valid legal claim to a fee for the medical services rendered. The court assumes, for policy reasons, that the patient would have contracted for the physician's services if circumstances had allowed.

QUASI-CONTRACT. Contracts implied in law are just one facet of the larger phenomenon known as quasi-contract. Black's Law Dictionary defines **quasi-contract** as a "legal fiction invented by common law courts to permit recovery by contractual remedy in cases where, in fact, there is no contract, but where circumstances are such that justice warrants a recovery. . . ." Quasi-contract also becomes important when a negotiated agreement is judged by the courts to be unenforceable even though justice requires the courts to allocate gains and losses between the parties. Quasi-contract takes contract law into the realm of ethics (*see* Chapter 2).

The ETHICAL ENVIRONMENT box in this chapter explores the nature of both express and implied contracts in an increasingly common, but legally muddy, relationship—the unmarried couple who live together.

> **express contract** Explicit agreement in which the parties spell out terms and manifest assent either orally or in written form
>
> **implied contract** Legal agreement implied by a tacit understanding demonstrated by behavior and circumstance

> **quasi-contract** *Common-law* legal fiction invented to provide contractual *remedy* when no contrast exists

---

■ *Concept Check 9-2   Types of Contracts*

- Describe the key differences between *bilateral* and *unilateral contracts*.
- Explain the differences between *express* and *implied contracts* and give an example of each.
- Explain the difference between *contracts "implied in fact"* and *contracts "implied in law"* and give an example of each.
- Define *quasi-contract*.

Because a quasi-contract is one that is implied in law, a court deciding a case between such an unmarried couple must determine first if indeed such an implied contract (the "legal fiction") exists and then if recovery is warranted under any contractual obligations that may be found. In addition, the matter may become more complex if there are any express contracts between the partners.

The ethical considerations in such cases involve certain assumptions that the parties may have: Namely, if I act as a husband or a wife even though there is no legal obligation that I do so, am I not then in fairness—and by implied contract—entitled to the same benefits and protections of the law afforded to married partners who have an express contract?

The case of Morone v. Morone (New York Court of Appeals, 407 N.E.2d 443 [1980]) explores the nature of both express and implied contracts in a living-together arrangement. Was there a contract implied in law? Was there an express contract between the parties? What is recoverable in each case?

The plaintiff in Morone, the woman, maintained that she and the defendant had lived together since 1952 as husband and wife and that he acknowledged her two children as his. She sought the sum of $250,000, alleging that in this long-term relationship, she had "performed domestic duties and business services" requested by the defendant with the expectation she would be compensated for such work. Moreover, she alleged that he always accepted her services "knowing she expected compensation for them." The idea here is that the contract was implied in law by her rendering and his accepting of services and that she was thus entitled to remedy.

The court, however, rejected the argument that there is a "contract which is implied from the rendition and acceptance of services," stating that "it is not reasonable to infer an agreement to pay for the services rendered when the relationship of the parties makes it natural that the services were rendered gratuitously." The court maintained that, in "hindsight," it could not sort out the intentions of parties in what is a private and noncontractual relationship: In other words, in living together a man and a woman behave in personal ways that, general fairness aside, hold no weight as obligations as viewed in a court of law. As the judge interpreted New York law, in order to receive remedy, the plaintiff would have had to show that there was an "explicit and structured understanding of an express contract."

The plaintiff's second allegation was that the partners had entered into an oral agreement whereby she would provide domestic services and he would be responsible for business transactions, including taking care of her. Furthermore, she contended, all "net profits were . . . for . . . the equal benefit of plaintiff and defendant." In fact, he had demanded that she not work or he would leave her. In addition, during the course of the time that they were together, he had received a considerable amount of money from his business dealings. Finally, she stated that from 1975 on, he had provided no support, and her request for an accounting of his funds indicates that there was indeed an express contract between them and that she was due remedy based on this.

In this second allegation, the New York court did find that the plaintiff had a basis for remedy because the interpretation of the idea of a contract differed from that in the first allegation. Here, it was found, there was an express agreement between unmarried people that was enforceable by law. One must judge for oneself the fairness of this interpretation as opposed to the first. Nonetheless, the theory is that although people who cohabitate do not have the property or financial rights of married partners, they "are not disabled from making an agreement within the normal rules of contract law." Even though the plaintiff was providing what are called "housewifely" services, the court did not view them as "personal"; a contract was in operation. The oral agreement in Morone was interpreted as an express contract, and the plaintiff was entitled to the support that was due her under it.

Thus, living together is not, in and of itself, automatically regarded as a quasi-contract. However, if there is some kind of oral agreement, then the contract may be enforceable by law. One ethical issue may go deeper, and perhaps future cases will rule that implied in every arrangement of living together is a quasi-contract.

■ ELEMENTS OF A CONTRACT

In order for a contract to be *legally binding*:

- It must involve two or more parties having the *capacity to contract*.
- It must show *agreement*, including *offer*, *acceptance*, and *mutuality*.
- It must be made for *consideration*.
- It must be for a *legal purpose*.
- It must be in the *correct form*—for example, certain contracts must be in writing.

valid contract Properly executed contract enforceable by the courts as a legal obligation

Contracts may be fully or partially enforceable. **Valid contracts** are properly ex-

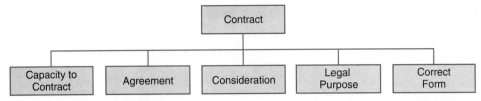

FIGURE 9-1 Elements of a Contract

ecuted contracts that cannot rightfully be overthrown or set aside. **Void contracts** have no legal force whatsoever. **Voidable contracts** have some defect but may still be enforceable if one party decides not to have them set aside. The elements of a contract are summarized in Figure 9-1.

void contract Contract without legal force

voidable contract Defective contract that may nevertheless be enforceable

Capacity to Contract

Agreements are not binding if one of the parties lacks **capacity to contract.** At issue is the idea that a fair contract demands that the parties have the ability to participate in a meaningful way in the bargaining process. Those who lack this capacity must be protected from their own unwise acts and from others who may take advantage of them.

capacity to contract Ability of the parties to a contract to bargain meaningfully

YOUTH. Individuals are not legally competent to enter into a contract until they reach the age of legal majority. Under common law, the age is 21, but most states have lowered the age of majority to 18. Under the age of eighteen a person is considered by the law to be an "infant" or "minor."

Admittedly, the law's designation of an age of majority is somewhat arbitrary—there is little difference in the experience and understanding of a seventeen-year-old and an eighteen-year-old. Nevertheless, the decision by most states to lower the age of majority from twenty-one to eighteen reflects the reality that many people in this age group do in fact engage in adult activity, such as marrying, having children, and entering into the work force. By lowering the age of majority to eighteen, these statutes have both eliminated the legal impediments to such activities among this age group and diminished the likelihood of litigation involving minors.

The assumption behind the view that infants or minors are not competent to make contracts is that adults and children have unequal bargaining power. Children lack discretion and experience and must be protected by the courts. Therefore, when a minor enters into a contract, it is generally voidable at the minor's request—but not that of the adult. The following case covers these issues in an instance when a minor entered into an otherwise legal contract—a release from liability for accidents that might be incurred as a result of the minor's participation in gymnastic activities.

SIMMONS v. PARKETTE NATIONAL GYMNASTIC TRAINING CENTER
670 F. Supp. 140 (E.D. Pa. 1987)

Tara A. Simmons, a minor, and her mother sued a gymnastic training center after Tara was injured while receiving gymnastic instruction. The complaint charged that Tara's injuries were caused by the negligence of the gym's employees. In its defense, the gym asserted that it was not responsible for Tara's injuries because both she and her mother had signed a release absolving the gym from any li-

ability for personal injuries. To resolve this dispute, the court addressed the issue of whether the release was valid and binding.

TROUTMAN, Senior District Judge.

The plaintiffs instituted this action claiming that the minor plaintiff, Tara A. Simmons, suffered personal injuries as a result of the negligent acts and/or omissions of one or more of the defendants' employees. The minor plaintiff's mother asserts causes of action against the defendants in her own right and on behalf of her minor daughter as the child's parent and natural guardian.

The defendants assert as an affirmative defense a "release" alleged to have been executed by the plaintiffs on February 12, 1984. The defendants seek judgment against the plaintiffs on the ground that the release absolves them from all liability for the damages allegedly suffered by the plaintiffs. . . .

> The "release" asserted by the defendants provides as follows:
> In consideration of my participation in Parkettes, I, intending to be legally bound, do hereby, for myself, my heirs, executors, and administrators, waive and release any and all right and claims for damages which I may hereafter accrue to me against the United States Gymnastic Federation, the Parkette National Gymnastic Team, their officers, representatives, successors, and/or assigns for any and all damages which may be sustained and suffered by me in connection with my association with the above gymnastic program, or which may arise out of my traveling to or participating in and returning from any activity associated with the program.
>
> Gymnast's Signature _____
>   /s/ Tara Simmons
>
> Signature of Parent _____
> or Guardian   (Father)
>
> _____
>   /s/ Sharon Grenell   (Mother)

(Defendants' Motion for Judgment on the Pleading, Doc. #5, Ex. "A").

As can be seen, the release is prospective in nature, i.e., it purports to exculpate the defendants from future liability, as opposed to a release compromising and settling an already existing claim for damages. . . .

It is axiomatic under Pennsylvania law that,

> A valid release is an absolute bar to recovery for everything included in the release, and it can only be set aside *as any contract* . . . in the presence of clear, precise and indubitable evidence of fraud, accidental means or *incompetence of the party who is alleged to have signed it.*
> . . .

A. The Adult Plaintiff.

[1] As to the minor plaintiff's mother's claim, i.e., Count II of the complaint, we conclude that her cause of action is indeed barred by the exculpatory agreement she signed. . . .

B. The Minor Plaintiff.

[2] The effect of the exculpatory agreement upon the minor plaintiff's claim for damages, i.e., Count I of the complaint, presents a somewhat more difficult question. It is hornbook contract law that a minor, with certain exceptions, is not competent to enter into a "valid" contract. . . . Where a minor executes a contract, however, the agreement is not "void," but rather, "voidable." . . . After reaching the age of majority, the minor may disaffirm the contract, thereby rendering it a nullity. . . . An exculpatory agreement such as that involved herein is simply a specific type of contract. Syllogistically, therefore, one would assume that the minor plaintiff may nullify the release by disaffirming it and, apparently in response to the defendants' motion, this is what she has purported to do. . . .

[3] In *Apicella v. Valley Forge Military Academy, supra,* the Court was faced with an issue similar to that presented here. The parents of a minor, in order to induce the defendant military school to allow their son to enter the academy, executed an agreement releasing Valley Forge "from all claims and damages arising from or related to or in any way connected with their son Jerry's hemophiliac condition." As a defense to the plaintiffs' suit for personal injuries allegedly suffered by the minor plaintiff, the defendant asserted that the release executed by the minor's parents insulated the defendant from any liability. The court rejected the defendant's argument, and found that under Pennsylvania law, the parents did not "possess the authority to release the claims or potential claims of a minor child merely because of the parental relationship," but, rather, could only release the defendants from any potential claims that the parents might assert. We concur in Judge Shapiro's interpretation of Pennsylvania law. Thus, we find that the mother of the minor plaintiff, by executing the release involved, did not exculpate the defendants from the potential claims that eventually accrued to her daughter and which she now seeks to assert before this Court. . . .

The common law rule that minors, with certain exceptions, may disaffirm their contracts has as its basis the public policy concern that minor should not be bound by mistakes resulting from their immaturity or the overbearance of unscrupulous adults. As stated by the Pennsylvania Supreme Court some years ago:

> All lawyers know that the protection of infants is one of the chief concerns of the law. The rule is that no one may deal with a minor, except for necessaries. Lord Coke said that an infant may bind himself for his meat, drink, apparel, necessary physic and other such necessaries, and likewise for his good teaching or instruction, hereby he may profit himself afterward: 27 Am.Jur. 759. This, generally speaking, has been accepted as the true doctrine. An infant is not com-

petent to contract. This positive inhibition is the way of the law to protect infants against their own lack of discretion and against the snares of designing persons.

We do not believe that the Pennsylvania courts would bind the minor plaintiff to the agreement which she signed. Thus, we will deny the defendants' summary judgment motion as to those claims asserted by the minor plaintiff.

It is this Court's experience that agreements such as that involved herein have become commonplace in our society with regard to organizations such as little league, scouting, midget football and so on. Thus, we believe our decision represents an important one because of the impact it may have upon such organizations.

An appropriate order follows.

Case Questions

1. In light of the court's ruling, can you conceive of any types of release that an athletic program for minors could develop to protect itself from liability in the event that one of its students is injured?

2. What is the likely impact of the court's ruling upon businesses engaged in providing athletic training to minors?

3. The court applied an across-the-board approach to the issue of whether minors should be held to contracts that they sign. Do you agree with this approach, or should the courts inquire into whether the particular minor, irrespective of age, was sufficiently mature to understand the ramifications of signing the contract?

Such guidelines generally mean that although the minor can get out of the agreement by pleading age, the adult party may still be bound by it. If the minor has received something of value by virtue of the contract, it must be returned upon the contract's disaffirmance. For example, suppose a seventeen-year-old signs a contract to buy a car and a week later decides to back out of the contract. His action is legal even though the car dealer cannot exercise that same right. At first glance, incompetence may appear to be a privilege—after all, it allows a minor to make a contract that binds only the other party. It is a real disadvantage, however, because adults are likely to refuse to enter into contracts with minors. Recall, however, that *the goal of the legal system is to provide protection to those who lack capacity.*

Necessities. One exception to the general rule limiting the liability of minors is when adults provide items that are necessary for the child's existence. Children are obligated to pay the reasonable value for such necessities. However, because their liability is a matter of quasi-contract, it does not contradict the fundamental idea that minors lack the capacity to contract. In addition, what constitutes "necessities" is a matter of some debate. Although it depends on circumstances, food, shelter, clothing, medical care, and education are often considered necessities by the courts. The legal reasoning is that because children contract to purchase these items in order to stay alive, they cannot avoid contracts for them.

Ratification. Once minors legally come of age, they can surrender their power of avoidance by ratifying contracts made when they were minors—that is, they can decide to be bound by the contract that was previously voidable. **Ratification** does not need to be in the form of a written or oral agreement; any behavior indicting an intention to remain bound by the agreement is sufficient. Let us return to the example of the seventeen-year-old car buyer. If that person makes a single car payment after his eighteenth birthday, that payment ratifies the contract. The teenager is now legally bound by the contract.

ratification Approval by an adult to be bound by a *contract* made when that individual was a minor

MENTAL INFIRMITY. This category covers a wide range of problems including mental illness or retardation, brain deterioration in old age, drunkenness, and drug use. According to Section 15 of the *Restatement (Second) of Contracts*, mental incompetency is either the inability "to understand in a reasonable manner the nature and consequences of the transaction" or the inability "to act in a reasonable manner in relation to the transaction and the other party has reason to know of this condition." Contracts entered into by the mentally infirm, like those entered into by minors, are voidable rather than void.

Inability to Understand. The first restatement test—inability to understand—is almost universally accepted by the courts. It does not depend upon whether the other party was *aware* of the mental disability: At issue is simply the contracting party's capacity at the time the agreement was made. Nor is a person's overall mental state important. Thus, it is sufficient for a senile person to have a lucid interval in order to conclude a valid contract.

Inability to Act in a Reasonable Manner. The second test—inability to act in a reasonable manner—concerns cases in which people understand the nature and consequences of their actions but are nevertheless unable to *control* them. A New York case, *Faber v. Sweet Style Manufacturing Corporation* (242 N.Y.S.2d 763 [1963]), illustrates this situation. The case was brought by a manic-depressive businessman. While manic and before being hospitalized, the plaintiff had begun several large construction projects against the advice of his lawyers. Later, he sued to rescind a contract for land purchase. There was no question that he had understood the transaction in question. The court concluded, however, that his illness compelled him to take actions that he would not otherwise have taken. However, in an effort to balance the protection of the impaired party against the rights of people bargaining in good faith, the mentally infirm party must make restitution for any benefit received as a result of a contract.

Note that people who drink or ingest drugs to the point of incapacity may fall into this category. Such a person may avoid a contract, however, only if the other party knew or had reason to know of the impairment. A person who willfully becomes intoxicated but appears relatively normal will be bound by the contract. However, involuntary intoxication or drug impairment is grounds to avoid a contract if the individual's mental state renders that person unable to understand or behave reasonably with respect to the transaction.

Agreement to the Contract

The next prerequisite for a legally binding contract is the agreement of all parties to the same terms at the same time: In other words, there must be a **manifestation of assent.** This mutual assent usually grows out of a process of bargaining. The process begins when one party makes an **offer**—that is, a tentative promise that is conditional on some action or promise by the other party. The offer creates a *power of acceptance* in the other party. A *binding* contract comes about with the other party's **acceptance** of the offer—that is, when the other party agrees to its terms. Together, offer and acceptance constitute **mutual assent.** The person making the offer is the **offeror;** the person receiving the offer is the **offeree.** The elements of the agreement process are summarized in Figure 9-2.

OFFER. An *offer* is a promise to do or refrain from doing something in the future. There are three prerequisites for a legally binding offer: *intention, specificity,* and *communication* (see Fig. 9-3).

Intention. The first concerns the *intentions* of the offeror: Offerors must behave or speak in such a way that it is reasonable to believe that they intend to make a contract and will consider themselves bound by their promises if their offers are accepted. Thus, promises made as jokes, promises made in

manifestation of assent In *contract bargaining,* the mutual agreement by all parties to the same terms at the same time

offer In *contracting bargaining,* the tentative *promise* by one party that is conditional on an action or promise by the other party

acceptance The agreement by one party to a *contract* to the terms of the *offer* of the other party

mutual assent In *contract law,* the *offer* and *acceptance* together

offeror Person making the *offer* that is the basis of a *contract*

offeree Person receiving the *offer* that is the basis of a *contract*

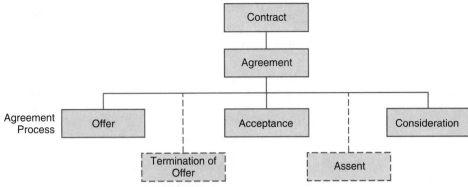

FIGURE 9-2 Elements of the Agreement Process

anger, and promises having to do with social engagements are not really offers in the legal sense. In each instance, the person making the promise does not intend to be bound legally. However, a person who does not intend to make an offer may nevertheless be deemed to have made one if he or she behaved or made statements that reasonably gave the other party the impression that a serious offer was made. Courts apply an objective standard when asked to determine whether an offer was, in fact, made.

Specificity. The second prerequisite is that the offer must be *detailed and specific.* If there is any uncertainty about the terms of the offeror's promise or about the act or promise requested in exchange, the contract fails for indefiniteness and cannot be enforced. Price, the time of performance, and the work to be done are examples of the kinds of terms that must be specified. Some details may be inferred rather than stated, like delivery in a reasonable time.

Communication. Finally, an offer cannot be accepted unless it has first been *communicated* to the offeree. For example, suppose two letters cross in the mail. One is an offer to sell goods at a certain price. The other is an offer to buy the same goods at the same price. These two letters do not add up to an offer and acceptance, because the offer was not communicated to the offeree before acceptance and the offer to sell did not induce the offer to buy.

Counteroffer. In practice, the bargaining process is often extended by a series of **counteroffers.** Instead of agreeing to the terms of an offer, the offeree rejects it and proposes different terms. For example, consider the negotiations

counteroffer Proposal by an offeree of different contract terms from those submitted by the offerer

FIGURE 9-3 Elements of a Legally Binding Offer

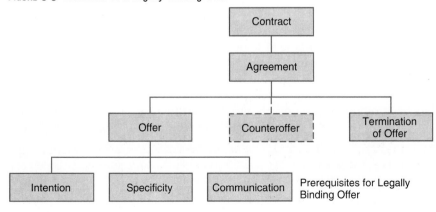

involved in buying a car. The salesperson begins by quoting a price for the car. The customer usually rejects this offer and makes a counteroffer of a lower price. This process of offer and counteroffer continues until either an agreement or an impasse is reached.

TERMINATION OF OFFER.   Offers do not stay open forever. If they are not accepted, offers can and do terminate in a variety of ways:

1. The offeror can withdraw an offer at any time before acceptance, either by notifying the offeree or by giving the same publicity to the revocation as to the offer.
2. The offeree can either reject the offer outright or make a counteroffer. The counteroffer terminates the offer just as the rejection does.
3. The offer itself may specify that it will lapse after a set length of time.
4. The offeror may die or lose the legal capacity to contract—for example, become mentally ill.

Some offers are accepted by virtue of *performance.* For example, if one party agrees to perform a service for another for a set consideration (say, $100), the acceptance of the offer is signified by performance of the act. Under common law, the offer can be revoked until the performance is completed. Today, however, most courts hold that once performance has begun, the offeree must be given a reasonable time to complete the job during which the offer cannot be revoked.

Because they are not easily distinguished from *counterinquiries* or requests for the *modification* of an offer, counteroffers can pose difficult problems. For example, here are three possible responses to an offer to sell a car for $5000: "I'll pay $4800"; "Will you take $4800?"; and "Send lowest cash price." Under common law, only the first is a true counteroffer that terminates the offer.[4]

A dispute over counteroffers was at the heart of *Thurmond v. Wieser* 699 S.W.2d 680 (1985), which involved a real-estate sale. The court found that the plaintiff's counteroffer of $250,000 for the property was a rejection of the original offer of $260,000 because the plaintiff did not expressly state that the original offer was being kept under advisement. Thus, when the plaintiff decided to meet the asking price of $260,000, the plaintiff no longer had the power of acceptance. The defendant's offer had been revoked by the counteroffer. Therefore, no contract was formed.

ACCEPTANCE.   Acceptance is an overt act by the offeree that demonstrates assent to the offer. Three requirements must be met for the offeree's acceptance to create a contract. First, the offeree must *make the promise* or *perform the act* requested by the offer. Second, the offeree must *express assent* to the bargain. (Of course, fulfilling the terms of the offer itself implies assent.)

These two requirements lead logically to the third: the offeree must *have knowledge of the offer* in order to accept it. This requirement often results in problems for unilateral contracts that offer rewards. For example, consider an honest citizen who returns some stolen property without being aware that a reward has been offered. Many courts would hold that the citizen is not entitled to the reward because he or she acted without either knowledge of the offer or

---

[4] Example from Calamari and Perillo, note 3 *supra*, p. 80. Section 2-207 of the Uniform Commercial Code changes this common-law rule. Under this provision, an expression of acceptance is binding even if it states terms different than those of the offer, unless the acceptance is expressly made conditional on acceptance of the new terms.

intent to accept it. There is, however, contrary judicial authority that would require payment of the reward on essentially public policy grounds.[5] The process of acceptance and assent is outlined in Figure 9-4.

ASSENT. How can you determine whether a party has *assented* to an agreement? This question is the subject of a great deal of debate. There are two schools of thought on the matter. According to the **subjective theory of assent**, assent can only be measured by a person's *actual or subjective intentions*. Legally binding assent would thus require that a person intends—in his own mind—to enter into the contract.

In contrast, the **objective theory of assent** argues that the state of someone's mind is not important. This theory measures assent by *outward appearances*—that is, whether a person's words and actions appear, by the standards of normal and ordinary behavior, to indicate an intention to assent. Thus, mental assent is not necessary for a legally binding agreement. What matters is whether one party had good reason to believe that the other party intended to assent.

By the end of the nineteenth century, the objective theory dominated the law and it is still accepted by courts today. Thus, according to the *Restatement (Second) of Contracts*, "The mental assent of the parties is not requisite for the formation of a contract. If the words or other acts of one of the parties have but one reasonable meaning, his undisclosed intention is immaterial except when an unreasonable meaning which he attaches to his manifestations is known to the other party."

Interpretation of Assent. There is no standard phrase or action used to signify legally binding assent to a contract. The courts simply interpret the contracting party's language and actions in the same way that any reasonable person would under the circumstances. The problem results when the same words and the same behavior can mean different things in different contexts.

Lucy v. Zehmer (84 S.E.2d 516 [1954]), a Virginia case involving a contract to sell a farm for $50,000, is a good illustration of how the objective theory of assent is applied by the courts. The seller contended that he had never intended to sell. He further argued that the offer to buy was a joke made while

subjective theory of assent
Theory stating that a person is legally bound to a *contract* by actual or subjective intentions to assent

objective theory of assent
Theory stating that a person is legally bound to a *contract* only by words and actions that indicate intention to assent

FIGURE 9-4 Acceptance and Assent

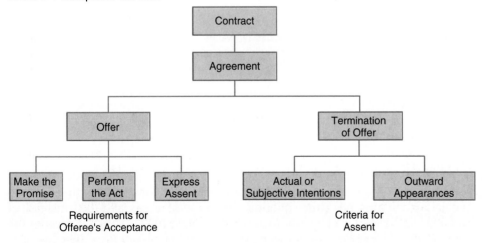

[5] *See* John D. Calamari and Joseph M. Perillo, *Handbook of the Law of Contracts* (Minneapolis, MN: West, 1977), p. 59.

drunk. He had, he claimed, written and signed the agreement on the assumption the offer was a joke. The court, however, found that the circumstances surrounding the transaction—the writing of two drafts, the signing by two people, the length and detail of the discussion, the completeness of the instrument—all pointed to its being "a serious business transaction rather than a casual, jesting matter." Following the objective theory, the court ruled:

> Whether the writing signed by the defendants and now sought to be enforced by the complainants was the result of a serious offer by Lucy and a serious acceptance by the defendants, or was a serious offer by Lucy and an acceptance in secret jest by the defendants, in either event it constituted a binding contract of sale between the parties.

The decision by an Illinois court in a case brought by an applicant rejected by the Chicago Medical School shows how assent fits into the larger process of offer and acceptance. The case of *Steinberg v. Chicago Medical School* (1976) is the subject of the YOU DECIDE feature below.

YOU DECIDE
Truth in Recruiting

Questions about matters of assent *arise in situations other than what one would think of in a strictly "business" environment. In fact, instances like that which led to the case of* Steinberg v. Chicago Medical School *(354 N.E.2d 586 [1976]) provide some of the most thought-provoking examples of contract law.*

In 1973, Robert Steinberg applied for admission as a first-year student to the Chicago Medical School, a private, nonprofit institution. When he was rejected, he filed a class-action suit against the school, maintaining that it had "failed to evaluate his application and those of other applicants according to the academic entrance criteria printed in the school's bulletin." His complaint was not that he had not been accepted but that the measures used to evaluate him were "unpublished criteria"—that is, they were not the criteria published in the bulletin. Steinberg maintained that the criteria applied by the school were nonacademic criteria, such as the applicant's familial relationship to the school's faculty and board, and the ability of the applicant and his family to make a donation to the school.

The case enters the area of contract law in the following way. Steinberg held that the Chicago Medical School had breached its contract with him. How was the contract created? Steinberg maintained that the informational brochure of the school constituted an invitation to make an offer; that

his application and payment of $15 (a legal consideration) was the offer; and that the school's retention of the fee was an acceptance. Under the terms of this contract, the school, Steinberg maintained, was bound to evaluate his application by the criteria stated in its bulletin and had failed to do so.

The school argued that there was no contract because the bulletin was not an offer (although Steinberg had only said it was an "invitation"), but rather a "general proposal to consider, examine and negotiate." In addition, the school argued that the fee was not a legal consideration but a "pre-contracting expense."

In addition to examining the issues of offer and acceptance to determine if there was a valid contract in Steinberg, one must consider the principle of assent. In order to form a contract, both parties must assent to the same thing in the same sense and their minds meet on essential terms and conditions. According to Steinberg, such mutual consent existed on the formation of the contract, and he contended that by making his application, he had acted in good faith based on the school's overt intention.

Was there a valid and enforceable contract? Did assent, offer, and acceptance exist? Or, had Steinberg interpreted the informational bulletin incorrectly? Did the school have the right to use unpublished criteria as admissions standards? (For further discussion, see p. 343.)

Advertisements. How should advertisements be treated under contract law? Are they offers that can be accepted? Suppose, for instance, that a newspaper ad contains an error, quoting the price of a car at $1000 instead of $10,000? Is the dealer obligated to sell the car for $1000 if a reader accepts the offer? The answer is no. Advertisements are not generally offers; they are simply *invitations* to the public to make an offer or to enter into a negotiation. Likewise, displaying a tennis racket in a store window or listing it in a mail-order catalog does not constitute an offer. For one thing, there is no guarantee that anyone who wants to buy the racket will be able to do so. After all, it would be impossible for the average store to judge ahead of time how much stock it would need to satisfy the public's demand for an item. Thus, it is assumed that advertisements do not manifest the *intent* to make a contract. The public-policy rationale for this rule is simple: If the law required advertisers to abide by inadvertent mistakes in their ads, it would be a great deterrent to advertising, which is needed to promote the flow of commerce.

There are, however, some exceptions to this general rule. Advertisements may in fact be worded so definitely as to be offers. The following ad, for example, would be so considered: "Baseball Memorabilia, Inc., will pay $150 for every baseball signed personally by Mickey Mantle and delivered to our office by August 30, 1989." In addition, federal and state consumer-protection laws may require advertisers to abide by offers if the content of ads is intended to deceive the public.

THE PROCESS OF AGREEMENT. The following case illustrates how offer, acceptance, and termination of an offer add up to a process that may or may not create a legally binding agreement. The dispute revolves around a reward offered on television.

NEWMAN v. SCHIFF
U.S. Court of Appeals, Eight Circuit, 778 F.2d 460 (1985)

Plaintiff, John A. Newman, is a practicing attorney in St. Louis, Missouri. Defendant is Irwin Schiff of Hamden, Connecticut. Newman brings this action against Schiff alleging breach of contract. Newman claimed that Schiff had made a public offer of reward to anyone who could cite any section of the Internal Revenue Code that says an individual is required to file an income tax return. Newman asserted that he accepted Schiff's offer, and that Schiff breached the contract by failing to pay him the reward. The district court ruled in favor of Schiff by finding that Newman's acceptance was not timely. Newman appeals.

Bright, Senior Circuit Judge.

Irwin Schiff is a self-styled "tax rebel," who has made a career and substantial profits out of his tax protest activities. Schiff's basic contention is that the federal income tax is a voluntary tax which no one is required to pay. . . . .

On February 7, 1983, Irwin Schiff appeared live on CBS News Nightwatch (Nightwatch), a nighttime television program with a viewer participation format. Schiff was interviewed by host Karen Stone from approximately 3:00 a.m. to 4:00 a.m. Eastern Time. The words "Nightwatch Phone-In" and the telephone number (212) 955-9555 were flashed on the screen periodically during Schiff's appearance. In addition, Ms. Stone repeated the telephone number and encouraged viewers to call and speak directly with Schiff on the air.

During the course of the Nightwatch program, Schiff repeated his long-standing position that, "there is nothing in the Internal Revenue Code which I have here, which says anybody is legally required to pay the tax." Following a discussion of his rationale for that conclusion, Schiff stated: "If anybody calls this show—I have the Code—and cites any section of this Code that says an individual is required to file a tax return, I will pay them $100,000."

Newman did not see Schiff's live appearance on Nightwatch. He did, however, see a two-minute taped segment of the original Nightwatch interview that was rebroadcast several hours later on the CBS Morning News. The CBS Morning News rebroadcast included Schiff's reward proposal.

Newman felt certain that Schiff's statements regarding the Internal Revenue Code were incorrect. Upon arriving at work that day, he researched the issue and located several sections of the Code that to his satisfaction demonstrated the mandatory nature of the federal income tax system. The next day Newman telephoned CBS Morning News and cited the following provisions of the Internal Revenue Code as authority for his position that individuals are required to pay federal income tax: 26 U.S.C § 1, 6012, 6151, 6153, 7201, 7202 and 7203. . . . He then reduced this conversation to writing and sent it to the CBS Morning News. Newman's letter stated that it represented "performance of the consideration requested by Mr. Schiff in exchange for his promise to pay $100,000."

CBS responded to Newman's letter on March 3, 1983, informing him that a copy of it had been forwarded to Schiff at Freedom Press. On April 13, 1983, after not hearing from Schiff for over a month, Newman wrote to him at Freedom Press. Newman repeated the portion of his previous letter which discussed Internal Revenue Code provisions that stand for the mandatory nature of the federal tax system. He then reiterated his claim for the $100,000 reward.

On April 20, 1983, Schiff wrote to Newman and stated that: "[y]our letter to Mr. O'Regan at CBS Morning News was forwarded to me. I did make an offer on the February 7, 1983 news (which was actually part of an interview conducted earlier in the week)." Schiff said, however, that Newman had not properly accepted his offer for both substantive and procedural reasons.

Newman then sued Schiff in federal district court for breach of contract. The district court decided that: (1) Schiff intended for his offer to remain open only until the conclusion of the live Nightwatch broadcast; (2) the rebroadcast on CBS Morning News did not renew or extend Schiff's offer; and therefore (3) Newman's acceptance of the offer was untimely. . . .

 . . . .

[W]e affirm the judgment of the district court on grounds that Newman did not accept Schiff's initial and only offer that had been made on the Nightwatch program.

 . . . .

Courts determine whether the parties expressed their assent to a contract by analyzing their agreement process in terms of offer and acceptance. An offer is the "manifestation of willingness to enter into a bargain, so made as to justify another person in understanding that his assent to that bargain is invited and will conclude it." *Restatement (Second) of Contracts* § 24.

 . . . .

In the present case, Schiff's statement on Nightwatch that he would pay $100,000 to anyone who called the show and cited any section of the Internal Revenue Code "that says an individual is required to file a tax return" constituted a valid offer for a reward. In our view, if anyone had called the show and cited the code sections that Newman produced, a contract would have been formed and Schiff would have been obligated to pay the $100,000 reward, for his bluff would have been properly called.

Newman, however, never saw the live CBS Nightwatch program upon which Schiff appeared and this lawsuit is not predicated on Schiff's Nightwatch offer. Newman saw the CBS Morning News rebroadcast of Schiff's Nightwatch appearance. This rebroadcast served not to renew or extend Schiff's offer, but rather only to inform viewers that Schiff had made an offer on Nightwatch. The rebroadcast constituted a newsreport and not a renewal of the original offer. An offeror is the master of his offer and it is clear that Schiff by his words, "If anybody calls this show. . . ", limited his offer in time to remain open only until the conclusion of the live Nightwatch broadcast. A reasonable person listening to the news rebroadcast could not conclude that the above language—"calls this show"—constituted a new offer; rather than what it actually was, a newsreport of the offer previously made, which had already expired.

 . . . .

We affirm the judgment of the district court for the reasons discussed above.

Case Questions

1. Analyze the situation in this case. What was the offer? What was the acceptance?

2. Upon what grounds did the court hold that no valid contract between the parties had been formed?

3. As master of his offer, what was Schiff bargaining for by his broadcast on the *Nightwatch* program?

Consideration

The concept of *consideration* was developed in the sixteenth century in order to set limits on the kinds of promises that would be enforced by the courts. As a matter of social policy, the law does not enforce *gratuitous* or *free promises*. Suppose, for example, that a millionaire tells a homeless man, "You can have my mansion and all of my money." The homeless man cannot enforce the promise in court if the millionaire changes his mind: The homeless man is not giving anything in exchange for the mansion and millions of dollars.

> **consideration** In *contract law*, a reciprocal arrangement in which something of value is exchanged

Traditionally **consideration** has been defined as either some *benefit* enjoyed by the promisor or some *detriment* suffered by the promisee. In other words, the promisee either gives something up or offers something in return for the promise. More recent legal theory emphasizes the *reciprocal* nature of bargains. From this perspective, consideration is something *valuable* that changes hands between the parties to a contract (see Fig. 9-5). According to the *Restatement (Second) of Contracts*:

1. To constitute consideration, a performance or a return promise must be bargained for.
2. A performance or return promise is bargained for if it is sought by the promisor in exchange for his promise and is given by the promisee in exchange for that promise.
3. The performance may consist of:
   a. an act other than a promise
   b. a forbearance
   c. the creation, modification, or destruction of a legal relation.

Promissory Estoppel. Occasionally, however, an offeror will make an offer in such a way that one would not reasonably expect that it will be revoked. If the offeree suffers a detriment because he actually relies on the offer, a court may stop the offer from being revoked. The court is applying the doctrine of **promissory estoppel**—that is, a device for stopping a promisor from revoking a promise when the promisee suffers *detriment*.

promissory estoppel Doctrine invoked by the courts to stop a promisor from revoking a promise when the promisee suffers detriment

ADEQUACY OF CONSIDERATION. Strictly speaking, the law is not concerned with the "fairness" of a bargain or the "value" of the consideration: As long as the consideration has *some value*, it is legally sufficient to support a contract.

However, there are circumstances in which courts will refuse to uphold a contract because the consideration is deemed legally inadequate. For example, strictly nominal consideration, which is intended to cover up the existence of an essentially gratuitous agreement, is not adequate. The sale of a house by a parent to a child for consideration of $1, for instance, is a gift masqueraded as a contract rather than a true bargain. Nor is agreeing to perform a preexisting duty in exchange for consideration considered adequate. For example, a witness cannot agree to tell the truth in exchange for cash because he is legally obligated to be honest anyway.

Promises to do or not do something illegal also are insufficient consideration to support a contract. **Illusory promises**—that is, promises which are so vague or full of loopholes that they really do not obligate the promisor to do anything—are not sufficient consideration to support a contract. For example, a contract to be performed in the future that gives one party the unilateral right to cancel at any time without penalty is illusory.

illusory promise Promise that is so vague that it does not obligate the promisor to act and is thus insufficient consideration to support a *contract*

FIGURE 9-5 Elements of Consideration

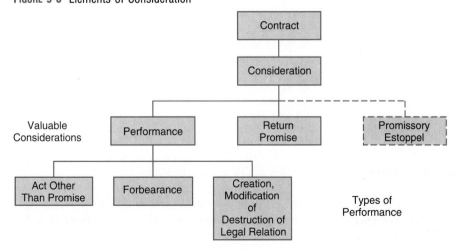

The following nineteenth-century case is a classic illustration of what constitutes adequate consideration.

HAMER v. SIDWAY
New York Court of Appeals, 27 N.E. 256 (1891)

William Story promised to pay $5,000 to his nephew, William Story 2d, if he would refrain from drinking, using tobacco, swearing, and playing cards or billiards for money until he became twenty-one years of age. The nephew fully performed the conditions. Upon becoming twenty-one years of age, the nephew informed his uncle that he had performed his part of the agreement, and he consented that the money be kept with his uncle at interest for him. The uncle died without having paid his nephew the $5,000 or the interest.

This action was brought by Hamer, the assignee of William Story 2d, plaintiff, against Sidway, the executor, defendant, of the estate of William Story. Judgment was entered in favor of William Story 2d at the trial at Special Term and was reversed at General Term of the Supreme Court. The assignee of William Story 2d, plaintiff, appeals.

Parker, J.,

. . . The defendant contends that the contract was without consideration to support it, and therefore invalid. He asserts that the promisee, by refraining from the use of liquor and tobacco, was not harmed, but benefitted; that that which he did was best for him to do, independently of his uncle's promise—and insists that it follow that, unless the promisor was benefitted, the contract was without consideration—a contention which, if well founded, would seem to leave open for controversy in many cases whether that which the promisee did or omitted to do was in fact of much benefit to him as to leave no consideration to support the enforcement of the promisor's agreement. Such a rule could not be tolerated, and is without foundation in the law. . . . Courts "will not ask whether the thing which forms the considerations does in fact benefit the promisee or a third party, or is of any substantial value to any one. It is enough that something is promised, done, forborne, or suffered by the party to whom the promise is made as consideration for the promise made to him."

Pollock in his work on Contracts, after citing the definition given by the exchequer chamber, already quoted, says: "The second branch of this judicial description is really the most important one. 'Consideration' means not so much that one party is profiting as that the other abandons some legal right in the present, or limits his legal freedom of action in the future, as an inducement for the promise of the first." Now, applying this rule to the facts before us, the promisee used tobacco, occasionally drank liquor, and he had a legal right to do so. That right he abandoned for a period of years upon the strength of the promise of the testator that for such forbearance he would give him $5,000. . . . It is sufficient that he restricted his lawful freedom of action within certain prescribed limits upon the faith of his uncle's agreement, and now, having fully performed the conditions imposed, it is of no moment whether such performance actually proved a benefit to the promisor, and the court will not inquire into it; but, were it a proper subject of inquiry, we see nothing in this record that would permit a determination that the uncle was not benefitted in a legal sense. . . .

[I]t must be deemed established for the purposes of this appeal that on the benefitted day of January, 1875, defendant's testator was indebted to William E. Story, 2d, in the sum of $5,000. . . . The order appealed from should be reversed, and the judgment of the special term affirmed, with costs payable out of the estate. All concur.

Case Questions

1. What consideration did the nephew advance to induce his uncle's promise?

2. Must the promisee suffer or be harmed in some way in order for there to be "legal detriment" borne by the promisee?

3. What was the uncle bargaining for in making his promise to the nephew? What value did the consideration advanced by the nephew have to his uncle?

4. Would the result of the case be different if it was unlawful for the nephew to perform the acts contained in his promise?

Contractual Legality

illegal agreement *Contract that is illegal because it is expressly prohibited by statute, violates public policy, or offends public morals*

Obviously, it would violate public policy to have the courts endorse **illegal agreements.** For example, a businessman's contract with an assassin to kill a detective investigating his shady dealings is illegal. Agreements can be illegal for many different reasons. Some contracts, such as gambling contracts or contracts in restraint of trade, are expressly prohibited by statute. Others, such as contracts to defraud or to injure third parties, violate public policy. Still others, such as contracts that impair family relations or interfere with the administration of justice, offend public morals.

The requirement of *legality* affects business transactions by precluding certain kinds of contracts. Contracts that modify legal relationships in ways that are objectionable to the courts are illegal. Thus, businesspersons cannot agree to disregard certain laws—for example, laws on usury or consumer protection. They cannot agree to exculpate (hold harmless) a contracting party from liability for harm caused by intentional, reckless, or negligent conduct.

EXCULPATORY CLAUSES. Although businesses offering public services generally cannot use them to avoid liability to their public-service functions, **exculpatory clauses** are a particularly complicated area of the law. Thus, a railroad cannot avoid liability for the negligent operation of its trains and a hospital cannot avoid liability to its patients.

> **exculpatory clause** Contract clause allowing a business that does not provide required services to the public to avoid liability for its functions

Exculpatory clauses are, however, permissible for businesses that do not provide *required* services to the public. For example, a health-and-racket club may legitimately include a clause in its membership contract that exculpates it from liability for personal injuries associated with playing racket sports. Indeed, many recreational businesses will pay high-liability insurance premiums unless they include such clauses in their contracts with patrons.

LICENSING. Legality also comes into play when *licensing* is an issue. When the government has established a licensing system to protect the public from unqualified persons, contracts with unlicensed practitioners are usually illegal. Thus, an unlicensed doctor, lawyer, or accountant could not collect on a contract for professional services. However, licenses created to raise revenues are treated differently. For example, a limousine company that failed to obtain a city business license would not be prevented from enforcing its agreements.

In general, an illegal contract is void. The courts will not intervene on behalf of either party. Sometimes, however, a contract can be divided into legal and illegal portions, whereby the courts may enforce the legal portion. At other times, the courts may use the principles of quasi-contract to intercede. When deciding whether to enforce all or part of an illegal contract, the courts consider the seriousness of the illegality and the relative guilt or innocence of the parties involved.

A Case Study In Contract Law: The Franchise Agreement

The entity known in federal and state law as a **franchise** is actually a right or privilege, not the business itself, such as a fast-food outlet: When you purchase a franchise, you are buying the right to operate the business. Legally, a franchise is defined by the Federal Trade Commission as "an arrangement in which the owner of a trademark, a trade name, or a copyright licenses others, under specified conditions or limitations, to use the trademark, trade name, or copyright in purveying goods and services."

> **franchise** The right to operate a business selling goods and services that are licensed by a trademark, trade name, or copyright owner

In addition, the FTC specifies that the franchisor (the seller of the franchise) exerts "significant control" over the "method of operation" of the franchisee (the buyer of the franchise) and gives "significant assistance" to this operation. Finally, the FTC definition includes the franchise's financial arrangement: In order to obtain or begin to operate a franchise, the franchisee must pay a franchise fee.

FTC GUIDELINES. To protect prospective purchasers of franchises from deception and to facilitate more informed decisions regarding purchases, the FTC mandates certain disclosure requirements in the franchise offering. The prospectus must follow the FTC format in Rule 436.1 or the Uniform Franchise Offering Circular (UFOC). It must, for example, contain information regarding the franchisor's business experience, litigation and bankruptcy history, obligations to purchase and other facts about the franchise, and the conditions of termination, cancellation, and renewal. All franchisors must comply with FTC rules. In addition to the federal government, 15 states also regulate franchises.

franchise agreement Contract spelling out the mutual responsibilities of *franchisor* and *franchisee*

FRANCHISE AGREEMENTS. The **franchise agreement** is the contract spelling out in detail the mutual responsibilities of the two parties. The franchisor sees the agreement as a tool to create uniform quality among franchised outlets and to obligate the franchisee to meet these standards. For the franchisee, the agreement is a means to get the franchisor to provide promised assistance.

Some of the important topics generally covered in a franchise agreement include the following: exclusive territory, training programs, royalty payments, quality control, enforcing and terminating the agreement, and agreement of noncompetition with the franchisee. Frequently, these agreements are made for a term of one year, subject to renewal; this term is set by franchisors in order to ensure that the conditions of the franchise are being met. It is important to note that this complex relationship is *not* a partnership: The franchisee *owns* the business and the franchise under which it operates.

Under the terms of a typical franchise agreement, there are several areas in which franchisors may exert control over franchisees: accounting practices, site approval, inventory controls, personnel practices, and production techniques. On the other hand, franchisors may assist franchisees with sales training, detailed operating manuals, establishing an accounting system, management training, and selecting a site.

TYPES OF FRANCHISES. Franchises fall into four categories:

1. *Distributorship* (or *manufacturer-retailer*): a manufacturer licenses a dealer to sell its product; exclusive territory is usually part of the arrangement, which is common in the auto and gasoline industries.
2. *Chain:* the franchise operates under the trade name of the franchisor, follows the franchisor's standardized operating methods, and is considered a member of a select group; this type of arrangement occurs in fast foods, car rental locations, and some hotel chains. (McDonald's, of course, is the most well-known chain franchise in the world; see the ORGANIZATIONAL PROFILE box in this chapter.)
3. *Wholesaler-retailer:* the franchisor is a wholesaler who recruits independent retail outlets to become franchisees; this practice is common among drugstore and automotive-aftermarket chains.
4. *Manufacturer-wholesaler:* the franchisor provides the franchisee with essential ingredients or a formula (as in the soft-drink industry) or a finished product (as in the beer industry); the franchisee then markets the product to retailers.

PROS AND CONS. From the point of view of a prospective purchaser, the franchise arrangement has the advantage of being less risky than other new-business ventures. Under the best circumstances, owning such a "prepackaged enterprise" means that you are selling a product that has been tested in the market, that the franchisor will advertise and promote the product or service for you, that you will receive a manual of tried-and-true methods for managing your business, and that the franchisor may help you secure financial aid. On the downside can be a loss of management freedom, the requirement to make purchases from the franchisor even if the prices are higher than a competitor's, the high initial cost of purchasing the business, and the possible difficulty in selling the franchise.

A number of interesting problems have arisen in franchising. For example, franchisors have been known to make inflated revenue and profit projections that proved unfounded after the purchase was made. Franchisees may also be hurt by promotional price-cut offerings run by the franchisor—that is, promotions in which they must bear the expense of the lower price out of their profit margins. In addition, franchisors have been known to overpopulate markets with too many outlets in order to sell more franchises and, in the process, hurting both themselves and existing outlets in a territory.

For the franchisor, the franchise arrangement is a way to expand a successful business. This strategy, for example, is increasingly proving to be the case as franchisors with saturated domestic markets seek international markets. Overseas, some of the same opportunities that gave rise to the domestic explosion in franchises (which now account for one-third of U.S. retail sales) can generally be found—a mobile population looking for uniform products, an increase in disposable income, and the need for time-saving products. Currently, although fast-food businesses dominate foreign franchises, especially in Japan, the growth market today seems to be in service-oriented franchises.

■ Concept Check 9-3 Elements of a Contract

- Explain the differences among *valid, void,* and *voidable contracts.*
- Explain the policy rationale whereby contracts made by minors are *voidable.*
- What are the three prerequisites of a *legally binding offer*?
- Describe a situation in which *performance* may constitute *acceptance* of an offer.
- Explain the key differences between *subjective* and *objective theories of assent.*
- Define *consideration.*

■ CONTRACTUAL DEFENSES

There are many reasons why contracts may prove to be partially or totally unenforceable. Two have already been discussed: capacity and legality. Lack of capacity by one of the parties makes a contract voidable; illegality of contractual terms may make the contract void. Contracts may also fail on account of *mistake, misrepresentation, duress, undue influence,* or *lack of written evidence.*

Mistake

One of the goals of contract law is to allow parties to *rely* on contracts that they have made. Therefore, there is considerable pressure on the courts not to overturn contracts simply because one party made a mistake when it agreed to the contract. However, it is not proper for one party *knowingly* to take advantage of

In the fast-food industry, the undisputed leader is the Mc-Donald's Corporation. With almost 12,000 restaurants worldwide and the second best-known brand name in the world (Coke is first) McDonald's serves many millions of customers a year. Of every $100 spent on eating outside the home in the United States, $7 goes to McDonald's. The company has combined successful marketing with a flexible response to consumer demand (witness the recent development of no-fat or low-fat foods). In large part, however, its great success is due to the establishment, careful management, and well-planned growth strategy of its franchise system, both domestically and internationally.

Although McDonald's has very strict requirements for potential franchisees, and although a McDonald's franchise is expensive to obtain (no financing is provided), the company definitely enjoys a sellers' market in recruiting franchisees because of the potential profit of a well-chosen location. In its own words, McDonald's says that it seeks people with "motivation, entrepreneurial talent, and a business background." From 1955, when Ray Kroc opened his first business in Illinois, until today, the brand name, strong advertising support, marketing, ongoing training for managers and staff, and constant new-product development make a Mcdonald's restaurant franchise extremely valuable. An owner gives up some control over his or her own business for the opportunity for high earnings.

Over seventy-five percent of McDonald's restaurants are owned by independent businesspeople (a number kept relatively constant for several years), and three purchase options are available: buying a new business, an existing outlet from McDonald's, or an existing outlet from a current franchisee. Initially, a franchise can cost an average of $450,000 for expenses ranging from kitchen equipment to the installation of signs. This cost is entailed by the conventional arrangement. There is also the business-facilities lease program, in which potential franchisees with good qualifications but limited funds can get a franchise; under this program, initial costs are closer to $65,000, and the option to buy comes in the second or third year.

Franchisees' profits come from sales; McDonald's derives its earnings through franchise fees paid as a percentage of sales. In the conventional arrangement, McDonald's receives three percent of a restaurant's monthly sales performance plus 8.5 percent of monthly sales or a minimum monthly fee, whichever is greater.

There are several steps to becoming a McDonald's franchisee. First, a candidate must be an on-premise, hands-on owner; no investors or investor groups are accepted. The candidate must then serve as an intern in a company-owned restaurant for about 50 hours so that the firm can evaluate if he or she has the proper entrepreneurial skills. If accepted, the candidate next attends Hamburger University and works part time at a McDonald's restaurant; this training can take 18 to 24 months, and expenses, except for the training itself, are the responsibility of the candidate.

During this initial training period, the company is selecting the site for the franchise (relocation is almost always required). McDonald's has traditionally taken the real-estate burden from the franchisee's hands and, using research to determine population patterns and volume potential, buys property that the company then leases to the franchisee under a long-term arrangement.

The franchise agreement has a term of 20 years. The franchisee must adhere to strict standards of quality, service, cleanliness, and value. Equipment and decoration in the restaurant must match company specifications. Although McDonald's is not a supplier to its franchises, it does help to negotiate high-volume discounts with independent suppliers while enforcing stringent quality standards with those suppliers. One McDonald's requirement is that the franchisee be actively involved in the community, supporting local charities and civic events.

Advertising, of course, is a crucial component of the support that McDonald's gives its franchisees. Its national campaigns over the years have provided a consistent message and a memorable brand image. Franchisees make contributions to the cost of advertising through a voluntary program based on a percentage of sales. In addition, franchisees contribute to regional advertising campaigns run by regional marketing managers.

As with other business enterprises, new McDonald's franchises are growing at the fastest rate in international locations. Of its almost 12,000 restaurants, McDonald's has more than 3200 in 53 non-U.S. markets, with nearly 80 percent in Canada, Germany, England, Australia, France, and Japan. Moreover, McDonald's intends to add about 600 outlets per year internationally over the next few years.

---

another party's mistake in order to enhance an agreement. There are five different kinds of mistakes that may render a contract voidable:

1. *Mutual mistake.* When both parties share a mistaken *factual* assumption about external conditions, the contract usually is voidable by the adversely affected party. For example, suppose the parties entered into a contract for the sale of a painting. Unknown to both of them, the painting was destroyed by fire at the time of the contract. This contract would be voidable by the adversely affected party—in this case, the buyer.

2. *Unilateral mistake.* This type of error is made by *one* of the parties. The contract is binding only if the other party is unaware of the mistake. The classic example of a unilateral mistake involves a group of bids submitted for a project. If one bid is much lower than all the others for no apparent reason, it should be obvious that it is based on mistaken calculations. If the low bid is accepted, the contract is not binding.

3. *Mistranscription.* Mistranscription occurs when an oral agreement is not correctly transcribed when it is written down. In such instances, the injured party can reform the written agreement to conform to the oral agreement.

4. *Misunderstanding.* A misunderstanding is a difference of *interpretation* of contractual terms. If one interpretation is more reasonable than the other, then it prevails. If the two interpretations are equally reasonable, there is *no contract*.

   In a landmark nineteenth-century British case, the differing interpretations concerned a ship that was to deliver a load of cotton. The contract specified the ship *Peerless* from Bombay. There were, however, two merchant ships of that name in Bombay. Each was a reasonable carrier, and the parties to the contract were thinking of different ships (operating on different schedules). There was no enforceable contract (*Raffles v. Wichelhaus*, 159 Eng. Rep. 375 [1864]).

5. *Mistakes in Transmission by an Intermediary.* This situation occurs when an intermediary (for example, an attorney drawing up a contract) makes a mistake in transmitting an offer between parties. For practical purposes, the liability of the intermediary is the more important legal issue.

Misrepresentation

Misrepresentation is the making of a statement that is not in accordance with the facts. In general, *nondisclosure* is not considered misrepresentation—for example, not mentioning the results of a mineral survey during negotiations for a land sale is not a misrepresentation. There are, however, some instances in which there is a specific duty to disclose information. For example, silence is misrepresentation when one party knows that the other party is operating under a mistaken assumption.

In order to void a contract, misrepresentation must (1) be material or fraudulent and (2) have significantly contributed to the party's decision to enter into the contract. Regardless of whether it is intentional, innocent, or negligent, misrepresentation is considered *material* if it is likely to induce a reasonable person to assent to a bargain. By contrast, *fraudulent* misrepresentation is by definition an act of intentional dishonesty designed to persuade the other party to agree to a contract.

misrepresentation Statement that is not in accordance with the facts and may therefore make a *contract* unenforceable

Duress

When a party is coerced into assenting to a contract by threats of physical or economic harm, that action is **duress.** According to the *Restatement (Second) of Contracts)*, "If a party's manifestation of assent is induced by an improper threat by the other party that leaves the victim no reasonable alternative, the contract is voidable by the victim."

Not every threat, however, is considered duress: The threat must be so intimidating that the victim is justified in agreeing to a contract that is otherwise distasteful. To determine if duress motivated a contractual agreement, the court will assess whether the threat was of *sufficient gravity* to induce the other party's capitulation. The nature of the threat and the particular facts of the case are critical. For example, in most circumstances it is unlikely that a threat to never speak to a person again would constitute duress. However, such a threat

duress The threat of physical or economic harm that coerces a party into assenting to a contract

might be viewed as duress if the parties had a history of successful business dealings.

Threats of physical violence against the victim or members of the victim's family, threats of blackmail, threats to fire a victim-employee, threats to begin criminal or civil actions against the victim, or threats not to engage in business dealings with the victim also may constitute duress.

Undue Influence

undue influence   The use of excessive pressure to get an especially vulnerable individual to agree to a contract

Undue influence occurs when people take advantage of *special relationships* with others in order to persuade them to agree to a contract. Although the victims of undue influence do not lack capacity, their judgment and the independence of their decisions are weakened by their trust in the other party. Bereaved widows, for example, may rely excessively on the advice of a trusted financial adviser. Doctors and patients, lawyers and clients, and parents and children all have relationships that create this kind of dependence and confidence. Thus, there are two criteria for a finding of undue influence: (1) The victim must have been *especially vulnerable* to the influence of the other party, and (2) the other party must have used *excessive pressure* in persuading the victim to assent to the contract. For example, it would be undue influence for a lawyer to pressure an elderly, ailing client into signing a contract to sell his house for less than market value instead of leaving it to his children. When a contract results from undue influence, the victim has the option of voiding it.

Statute of Frauds

Statute of Frauds   Doctrine that the terms of certain business-related *contracts* require written evidence, the lack of which may make the contract unenforceable

It is a statutory requirement, dating back to the English **Statute of Frauds** of 1677, that there must be *written evidence* of the terms of the following business-related contracts:

1. *Contracts for the sale of land.* This category includes changes in ownership, the sale of any kind of interest in land, including leases (generally over a year in length), easements, and licenses.
2. *Contracts for sale of goods.* This category includes the sale of all tangible, movable property, sold for $500 or more. (Note that this requirement has been extensively modified by the Uniform Commercial Code.)
3. *Contracts that cannot be performed within one year of making.* This category includes contracts whose terms make it impossible that they can be fully performed within one year after the contract is signed.

surety contract   *Promise* to be responsible for or to guarantee another person's debt

4. *Surety contracts.* **Surety contracts** are promises to be responsible for or to guarantee another person's debt.

parol evidence rule   Principle that a written *contract* takes precedence over all oral agreements as long as there is no evidence of fraud, mistake, or accident

THE PAROL EVIDENCE RULE.   According to the **parol evidence rule,** a written contract takes precedence over all oral agreements as long as there is no evidence of fraud, mistake, or accident. When there is a dispute over a contract, the courts will not generally accept any evidence of oral discussions or agreements that modify the terms of the contract as they are set down in writing. However, many courts apply the parol evidence rule only to *fully integrated contracts.* The courts will, however, consider oral evidence about the nature of any missing terms.

■ Concept Check 9-4 Contractual Defenses

- Can a person avoid contractual responsibility if there is a *unilateral mistake*? Explain.
- What is the difference between a contract made under *duress* and a contract made under *undue influence*?
- Describe the purpose of the *Statute of Frauds*.

■ REMEDIES FOR BREACH OF CONTRACT

There are a range of remedies available to a party who prevails in a lawsuit for breach of contract. They depend upon the nature of the agreement and the facts of the case. (*See* Chapter 4 for remedies, both *at law* and *at remedy*.)

Monetary Damages

Nonbreaching parties are entitled to vindication even if they have suffered no significant losses as a result of a broken contract. In such cases, courts will award **nominal damages,** usually of under $1, to signify that one party has not fulfilled his obligations.

nominal damages Remedy for breach of contract that awards under $1 to signify the failure of one party to fulfill its obligations (*see also* Chapter 4)

COMPENSATORY DAMAGES. More frequently, however, a nonbreaching party is entitled to recover **compensatory damages.** The objective of compensatory damages is to put the nonbreaching party in the position in which he would have been had the contract been performed. Computing compensatory damages usually involves calculating what the nonbreaching party lost and gained by virtue of the nonperformance. For example, suppose you hire someone to build a fence around your house for $500. When that person reneges, you hire someone else to do the job for $600. You are entitled to collect compensatory damages of $100 from the first fence builder. The $100 in damages puts you in the same position you would have been had the original contract been performed. Note that no compensatory damages would be allowed if the second fence builder charged $400.

compensatory damages Remedy for breach of contract that awards damages to the nonbreaching party in order to put that party in the position he or she would have occupied had the contract been performed (*see also* Chapter 4)

CONSEQUENTIAL DAMAGES. **Consequential damages** are reasonably foreseeable losses that arise from a contractual breach. For example, if your lawn was damaged directly because a contractor did not install a fence on the day stipulated in the contract, a court might require the contractor to reimburse you for the cost of repairing the lawn as consequential damages. However, if the damage was caused by a mudslide, the fencing contractor would not be liable for any losses (a mudslide cannot be foreseen).

consequential damages Damages awarded for reasonably foreseeable losses arising from a contractual breach (*see also* Chapter 4)

PUNITIVE AND LIQUIDATED DAMAGES. **Punitive damages** are intended to punish the breaching party and to deter him from committing the same offense again. Although they are rarely awarded in contract actions, they may be awarded in cases involving fraud, malice, or violence.

Liquidated damages are damages that the parties have agreed to pay in the event that the contract is breached. A liquidated-damages clause in a con-

punitive damages Damages awarded to punish a party breaching a contract because of fraud, malice, or violence and to deter future such offenses (*see also* Chapter 4)

liquidated damages Damages that the parties have agreed to pay in the event a contract is breached (*see also* Chapter 4)

tract might say: "If either party fails to perform his obligations as specified in this agreement, he shall pay the other party the sum of $1000 as liquidated damages." The courts generally do not uphold liquidated-damages clauses that are intended to punish the breaching party.

Equitable Remedies

specific performance Court order that the party breaching a contract involving unique goods or real property perform in accordance with the contract (*see also* Chapter 4)

The courts have long recognized that a contractual breach cannot always be remedied by the payment of money. An order of **specific performance** thus requires the breaching party to perform in accordance with the contract.

Specific performance is an extraordinary remedy that is available only if a contract involves *unique goods* or *real property*. The courts rarely order specific performance in cases involving personal services, even though there is often no substitute for the loss of a certain person's services. Orders of specific performance in such cases are scorned as a form of court-ordered involuntary servitude.

restitution An equitable remedy for breach of contract that seeks to restore the nonbreaching party to his or her pre-contract position

RESTITUTION. **Restitution** is another form of equitable remedy that is available when a contract has been breached. When one party totally breaches an agreement, the other party may cancel the contract and seek restitution: Whereas damages seek to place the nonbreaching party in a postperformance posture, restitution aims to restore the nonbreaching party to the position that he or she was in *before* the contract was formed. For example, assume that Ethel Merson hired Acme Construction Co. to build her a garage for $5000. However, in the middle of the project, Ms. Merson decides that she does not like the way the garage looks and tells the workers to stop. Because the contract was totally breached, Acme Construction would be entitled to restitution equal to the value of its workers' labor and the cost of construction materials. This remedy would restore the company to the position it was in before the contract was made.

rescission Mutually agreed-upon cancellation of a *contract* before performance has begun

RESCISSION. **Rescission** refers to the cancellation of a contract. Generally, parties are free to agree mutually to rescind an agreement before performance has begun. A party may not unilaterally rescind an agreement unless a statute or a provision of the contract provides otherwise. Consumers have a right of unilateral rescission in certain transactions, usually for some specified short period of time. Banks, for example, usually give prospective homebuyers a day or two to decide if they wish to rescind a mortgage-loan agreement after their application has been accepted.

■ *Concept Check 9-5 Remedies for Breach of Contract*

- Define *equitable remedy*.
- Describe situations in which each of the following remedies would be appropriate: *consequential damages*, *specific performance*, and *rescission*.

■ THE UNIFORM COMMERCIAL CODE

In 1944, the National Conference of Commissioners on Uniform State Law and the American Law Institute joined together to prepare a single, comprehensive commercial code to modernize and replace a multitude of conflicting laws. Before it was all over, this ambitious project would draw upon the talents of more than 1500 lawyers over a fifteen-year period. (The career of one lawyer who played a particularly important role in this drive, Karl Llewellyn, is discussed in this chapter's PERSONAL PROFILE box.)

A first draft was finished by 1950, and the first official text was published in 1952. In 1953, Pennsylvania became the first state to enact the **Uniform Commercial Code (UCC).** Continuing comments from a variety of sources, including the New York State Law Revision Commission, led to modified official texts in 1957, 1958, 1962, and 1972. Today, all fifty states (with the partial exception of Louisiana), the District of Columbia, and the Virgin Islands have adopted the code. The UCC comprises ten articles dealing with a large but select area of law.[6] Note that the UCC is not a comprehensive codification of all commercial law. It does not cover, for instance, real estate, insurance, or bankruptcy.

Purpose of the UCC

Section 1-102(2) of the UCC explicitly spells out its purposes and policies and the means by which it should be interpreted. In essence, the UCC is to be "liberally construed and applied" in order to promote its three purposes and policies:

- to simplify, clarify, and modernize the law governing commercial transactions
- to permit the continued expansion of commercial practices through custom, usage, and agreement of the parties
- to make uniform the law among the various jurisdictions

The courts have generally followed the code's call for liberal, as opposed to narrow and technical, interpretation.

In general, the UCC tries to liberalize commercial law by reducing the importance of technical requirements and emphasizing instead general obligations such as good faith and commercial reasonableness. The drafters wanted to incorporate a sense of *social responsibility* and *ethics* into commercial dealings. Thus, the UCC's provisions are not mandatory and can be modified or displaced by the parties to a contract—contracting parties cannot disclaim "the obligations of good faith, diligence, reasonableness, and care."

The UCC and the Common Law of Contracts

The portion of the UCC that is relevant to contract law is Article 2, which deals with the sale of goods. Thus, the UCC is strictly limited in scope; it covers contracts for goods but not labor contracts or contracts for land. (For a discussion of developments in international law governing contracts for the sale of goods, see the INTERNATIONAL ENVIRONMENT box on p. 338.)

In addition, the UCC does not attempt to replace entirely the common law of contract for the sale of goods. Nor does it deal with every aspect of a transaction, and it assumes that common-law rules will fill in the gaps. For ex-

---

[6] The articles are: (1) general provisions, (2) sales, (3) commercial paper, (4) bank deposits and collections, (5) letters of credit, (6) bulk transfers, (7) documents of title, (8) investment securities, (9) secured transactions, and (10) effective date and repealer (a list of acts that the UCC replaces).

ample, the UCC uses the common-law concept of "offer" but never defines it. Other portions of the UCC simply codify the *preexisting* common law. Thus, the common-law contract rules already discussed are still a vital part of commercial law.

The effects of the common law and the UCC on each other have been reciprocal. The *Restatement (Second) of Contracts* has incorporated some of the UCC's formulations and has thus expanded their influence to the whole realm of contract law. For example, the courts and the restatement have both applied the UCC's doctrine of unconscionability to noncommercial contracts. We will examine five areas of contract law in which the UCC diverges from the com-

PERSONAL PROFILE
Karl Llewellyn

Part of the movement for American legal reform in this century was the impetus for the unification, simplification, and modernization of the law. The creation of the Uniform Commercial Code represents the large-scale efforts, over many years, by literally thousands of practicing attorneys and legal scholars to make the laws dealing with commercial transactions consistent among the states. At the forefront of the work was Karl Llewellyn (1893-1962), a law professor whose philosophy of legal realism (see Chapter 1) reformed changes in U.S. law in general and the development of the UCC in particular.

Llewellyn's criticism of U.S. law centered on the idea that law is not one objective, coherent system of preexisting rules and that "especially in the business field, what courts have done and will do is, in the main, understandable only in terms of what men do." Llewellyn felt, in other words, that legal decisions are the product of numerous outside influences as well as judicial precedents.

Llewellyn sought to expand the field of jurisprudence "out beyond the rules, the imperatives and the norms" and into a "wider view of rules-in-their-setting." For Llewellyn, jurisprudence must place itself in the world: "Sound sociology," he argued, "is the precondition for sound legal technique." It is within Llewellyn's context of law as "a going institution" that his great contribution to the UCC should be viewed.

Llewellyn was concerned with commercial and banking law as well as jurisprudence, and from 1937 to 1952, much of his energy went into the UCC project. In fact, the UCC has been referred to as "Llewellyn's Code" and "Karl's Kode," among other things, although Llewellyn emphasized—and we should remember—that the project was a massive undertaking involving teamwork among over 1000 lawyers and businesspeople, not the least of whom was Llewellyn's wife, Soia Mentschikoff, also a noted legal scholar.

Within the overall movement to remedy the twin problems of "uncertainty" and "complexity" in U.S. law, the initial impetus for the UCC was a movement to enact a federal sales bill that would apply both to foreign and interstate transactions. Llewellyn saw this act as a way to promote general reform of the law of sales. As events evolved, how-

ever, Llewellyn and others came to see that the best way to achieve this goal—as well as commercial law uniformity in general—was to establish a Revised Uniform Sales Act with which the federal law would conform.

The first public airing of the idea of a comprehensive code came in 1940 from William Schnader, who stated the need to rid commercial law of "piecemeal" acts, but it was Llewellyn who then took over the development of strategy for the scope, objectives, method, and style of the commercial code. Although the UCC drafting committee was established with final responsibility resting in its editorial board, the chief reporter was the lynchpin of the project. In this role, Llewellyn, with Mentschikoff as assistant chief reporter, wrote over half the articles in the UCC and revised or redrafted the rest. Although he occupied a very strong strategic position, he did not operate unilaterally and welcomed and included the expressions of a great many individuals.

When the first draft was completed in 1949, it was opened for comments. Among the more conservative observations was the view that the code would reduce rather than promote uniformity. In general, however, there was little organized opposition to the UCC. Then, in the 1950s, as the code went before various state legislatures for approval, revisions were made. Although the earliest version probably best represented Llewellyn's influence, he ultimately agreed that the 1957 version was an improvement.

A comment by American law historian Grant Gilmore on Llewellyn's contribution sums it up well and indicates the influence of Llewellyn's view on the law's place in society: Llewellyn's "preferred solutions turned on questions of fact (reasonableness, good faith, usage of trade) rather than on rules of law. He had clearly in mind the idea of a case-law Code: one that would furnish guidelines for a fresh start, would accommodate itself to changing circumstances, would not so much contain the law as free it for new growth."

In Llewellyn's own words, the uniform laws of the UCC have these advantages: "gain in clarity . . . accessibility . . . cheapness of use . . . provision of an easy and effective filing system for the ensuing cases. . . . Finally to the degree that the law has become not only more certain in fact but easier to find and also to see (or feel) in advance as certain, that result makes for easy and for fair settlement."

mon law: the *creation of contracts, firm offer, acceptance, modification,* and *unconscionability*. First, however, we must understand two definitions used in Article 2: those of *goods* and *merchant*. The UCC governs the sale of goods by merchants.

> According to Section 2-105, *goods* are defined as:
> all things (including specially manufactured goods) which are movable at the time of identification to the contract for sale other than the money in which the price is to be paid, investment securities . . . and things in action. "Goods" also includes the unborn young of animals and growing crops and other identified things attached to realty. . . .
> Section 2-104 defines a *merchant* as:
> a person who deals in goods of the kind or otherwise by his occupation holds himself out as having knowledge or skill peculiar to the practices or goods involved in the transaction or to whom such knowledge or skill may be attributed by his employment of an agent or broker or other intermediary who by his occupation holds himself out as having such knowledge or skill.

THE CREATION OF CONTRACTS. The UCC generally endorses the common-law principles of offer, acceptance, and assent. However, it rejects the common-law prerequisite of *definiteness:* Under the common law, contracts are unenforceable even if they do not include all essential terms. This principle poses a problem in business transactions. For example, while some contracts—generally, those drawn up after protracted negotiation—may inadvertently omit terms, other contracts deliberately leave some things, like price, for future determination. In many industries, it is also common practice to set some terms during the actual performance of the contract.

Section 2-204(3) of the UCC recognizes these business realities. It states that "even though one or more terms are left open a contract for sale does not fail for indefiniteness if the parties have intended to make a contract and there is a reasonably certain basis for giving an appropriate remedy." Thus, the courts must consider the nature and commercial needs of the industry involved when deciding whether the parties intended to be bound. An agreement that is adequate in one industry may thus be found void for indefiniteness in another: Determination depends on the industry's customary usage in preparing future sales contracts.

Sections 2-304 through 2-311 of the UCC contain "gap-filler" provisions that the courts may use to interpret contracts that lack certain definite terms. For example, if a contract for the sale of goods fails to specify the time of delivery, UCC Section 2-305 provides that delivery shall be made within a reasonable period of time.

FIRM OFFER. Another frequent business practice is to promise to keep an offer "open." In common law, because a promise cannot be enforced without consideration, an offer can be withdrawn by the offeror any time prior to acceptance. UCC Section 2-205 recognizes that this practice can cause hardship to the offeree and thus permits merchants to make a binding assurance to keep an offer open.

Such an offer must be made by a merchant, must be in writing and signed, and must contain an assurance that it will be held open. The option lasts for the time stated in the offer. If no time is stated, it remains open for a reasonable length of time. It never lasts longer than three months, although renewal is possible.

The UCC supplements, but does not preempt, the traditional common-law approach to the problem of making a firm offer. When options longer than three months are desired or when nonmerchants wish to keep an offer open, the only recourse is the common-law principle of the firm offer supported by consideration.

ACCEPTANCE. On the principle of acceptance, the UCC differs from the common law on two important matters: the *manner* of acceptance and the interpretation of offer *forms*. In addition, the UCC perspective on forms addresses the issue known as *material alteration*.

THE INTERNATIONAL ENVIRONMENT
The United Nations Convention on Contracts for the International Sale of Goods

International trade is a major focus of many business enterprises in the United States and abroad, especially with the realization of the European community and the emergence of market economies in the former Soviet Union and Soviet bloc. In an attempt to reduce the uncertainty inherent in international sales and purchases, the United Nations Commission on International Trade Law drafted the Convention on Contracts for the International Sale of Goods (CISG) in order to create uniform laws that would govern such transactions. On January 1, 1988, CISG became part of U.S. federal law, and as a treaty, it overrides conflicting state laws on such contracts (see Chapter 3). By early 1992, CISG was in effect in thirty countries; it is currently the law in nations ranging from Argentina to Hungary to Zambia.

As multinational markets grow, both U.S. businesses and their attorneys will need to take CISG into account as they revise their sales documentation. For one thing, CISG provisions, although similar to those of the UCC (due in part to the influence of the U.S. legal community) are not always the same. In addition, documentation used for international trade prior to the adoption of CISG may no longer be adequate.

The applicability of CISG is quite specific: It automatically covers all contracts for the sale of goods between commercial buyers and sellers in different countries that have ratified CISG. Parties can, however, reject all or part of CISG or include choice-of-law clauses in contracts, thereby selecting laws other than CISG to govern transactions (in practice, lawyers recommend doing both in writing). In any event, the uniformity desired by the drafters of CISG would be achieved. For example, CISG would apply if a seller—for example, a U.S. manufacturer of picture frames—wanted to make a sale to an art gallery in Germany: Even if the U.S. firm has an office in Germany, CISG applies if the transaction is conducted with the U.S. office.

Because misinterpreting them could mean loss of business and even unintended liability, it is very important for firms to know the provisions of the CISG. Two crucial areas are offer and acceptance and material terms. In the former, explains an attorney for the U.S. Chief Council for International Trade, the Convention "requires that an acceptance of an offer 'mirror' the terms of the offer for a contract to be formed. Non-mirroring acceptances will operate as counteroffers only." If the acceptance is viewed as a coun-

teroffer, then it is viewed as a rejection and the contract is not concluded. Clearly, if businesses do not take this principle into account, they might be left holding the goods that they want to sell. In the case of the picture-frame maker, although the company may have already shipped to Germany, the art gallery would not have to accept the frames. This precept reflects the drafters' goal of achieving certainty as to a contract's exact contents.

The case of material terms is similar. Under the CISG, says one U.S. attorney specializing in international commercial law, "all terms relating to the price, payment, quality and quantity of goods, place and time of delivery, liability and dispute resolution are deemed to be material." If the acceptance contains additional or different terms that are material—that is, that deal with these areas—the acceptance also constitutes a counteroffer, whereby the contract is nonbinding. In the picture-frame example, if the art gallery's acceptance states that the frames must be delivered to Berlin rather than Frankfurt, then this stipulation would be a counteroffer.

Because U.S. firms operate so generally under the UCC provisions, it is critical that they recognize that in the two cases given above, as in other areas, as well, the UCC and the CISG differ: In other words, must learn the rules of a new game. Under CISG, for instance, a contract is formed when the seller receives the acceptance, whereas under the UCC it is formed when the acceptance is mailed or otherwise transmitted. In addition, although any sales contract under the CISG can be oral, the UCC requires a written contract for sale of goods over $500. Under the CISG, no contract is formed unless a price is specified—a stipulation not found in the UCC. Finally, under the CISG, irrevocable (or "firm") offers are held open even if they are not in writing, whereas under the UCC, willingness to hold open an offer must be stated affirmatively.

If a business pays attention to the details of the CISG and modifies its documentation accordingly, benefits can accrue as it operates in a truly global economy. The CISG, notes one observer, "provides internationally the same kind of level playing field established here by the UCC." According to the American Bar Association, benefits of CISG include decreased time and legal costs for researching unfamiliar foreign laws and fewer difficulties over choice-of-law issues when the CISG can be used for compromise.

The Manner of Acceptance. According to common law, the offeror is master of the offer and can prescribe how the power of acceptance is to be exercised. The offeror determines whether acceptance must be in the form of a return promise, performance, or forbearance. The acceptance is ineffective if it is made in any other way. When there is any doubt, the contract is assumed to be bilateral so that acceptance requires a return promise.

Although the UCC has retained the rule that acceptance must objectively manifest an intent to contract, it has loosened rules regarding the *manner* of acceptance. According to Section 2-206, "unless otherwise unambiguously indicated by the language or circumstances . . . an offer to make a contract shall be construed as inviting acceptance in any manner and by any medium reasonable in the circumstances." The offeree can choose the manner of acceptance if it is not prescribed. This principle is consistent with business goals: Business offerors simply want to complete a sale; they do not care whether acceptance occurs by promise or performance.

The "Battle of The Forms." Under the *mirror-image rule,* a response to an offer that does not exactly "mirror" the terms of an offer is a counteroffer, not an acceptance. Unfortunately, companies routinely exchange offers and acceptances for the sale of goods on standard form documents that can be purchased at stationery stores. The forms include a lot of fine print about warranties, credit terms, complaints, transportation and packing, and the like. General business practice, however, is to ignore the "boilerplate"—that is, the standardized language on the forms. Clerks in charge of transactions often check only the important terms, such as price, goods, and delivery date.

Common-Law View. When there is a dispute, the common law may find that there is no enforceable contract because the fine print on the two documents exchanged was not identical. Alternatively, each succeeding form may be interpreted as a counteroffer superseding the last form. The buyer's acceptance of the goods is interpreted as acceptance of the counteroffer, and the offeree's form establishes the terms of the contract.

Economic considerations outweigh the legal risks involved in doing business this way. The use of form documents for routine transactions is efficient because it reduces costs and allows lower-level personnel to process routine sales and purchases.

UCC View. Section 2-207 of the UCC was designed expressly to remedy this situation. The first question is whether a contract exists. According to the UCC, a contract exists as long as the acceptance is definite, reasonable, and not conditional on assent to new terms. Thus, the UCC recognizes that the routine exchange of form documents creates a contract as long as there is agreement on the negotiated terms.

The second question concerns which terms are in effect when the offer and acceptance disagree. UCC Section 2-207(2) interprets any differences in the acceptance as proposals for additions to the contract. Thus, in transactions between two merchants, such proposals become part of the contract unless (a) the offer expressly limits acceptance to the terms of the offer, (b) those terms materially alter the offer, or (c) notification of objection to the terms has already been given or is given within a reasonable time after notice of them is received. If the transaction involves any nonmerchants—for example, consumers—the additional terms do not become part of the contract unless the parties explicitly agree.

Material Alterations. **Material alterations** are generally considered to be

material alterations Changes in a *contract* that contradict customary usage

changes in a contract that contradict customary usage. Under the UCC, clauses negating a standard warranty or requiring that complaints be made in a shorter time than usual or reasonable are material alterations. By contrast, a change that follows customary usage—such as clauses that fix a reasonable time for complaints or that provide for interest on overdue invoices—are not considered material.

The Court's Interpretation. An example of the UCC approach to the "Battle of the Forms" can be seen in *Boese-Hilburn Co. v. Dean Machinery Co.* (616 S.W.2d 520 [1981]). The *Boese-Hilburn* dispute concerned the sale of four diesel engines that did not meet the buyer's (Boese-Hilburn) specified power requirements. In addition to a description of the equipment and the price, the seller's (Dean) quotation stated that "[t]he equipment we have proposed above may or may not meet the specifications as written and is subject to engineers approval." The seller, however, provided oral assurances that the engines would indeed meet the buyer's requirements. In response, the buyer prepared a purchase order that included the following statement in longhand on the front page: "Supplier warrants that he will provide equipment to meet specifications for the sum of $287,590.00." Also written in longhand (on the last page) and signed by the seller's manager was the phrase "Accepted subject to above."

In accordance with the guidelines set down by the UCC, the court considered the quotation to be a valid offer and the purchase order to be an acceptance. Although the warranty clause did materially alter the agreement, the manager's signature was an express assent to that change. Therefore, the court ruled that the warranty clause became part of the basis of the contract.

Offer and Acceptance at Auctions. At first blush, concepts of offer and acceptance are difficult to apply to auctions. Who is the offeror—the auctioneer who asks for bids or the bidder? Is "acceptance" marked by the fall of the auctioneer's hammer or by the bidder's act of making the highest bid?

The common law and the UCC answer these questions in essentially the same way—with one notable exception. Under both sources of law, if the auctioneer merely asks for bids (called an auction "with reserve"), he is inviting offers to purchase that can be accepted or rejected. If, on the other hand, the auctioneer offers to sell to the highest bidder (called an auction "without reserve"), the power of acceptance rests with the bidder. The auctioneer cannot withdraw the goods from sale even if the top bid is far below the goods' value. Under the common law, bidders, like the auctioneer, cannot withdraw their offers during auctions without reserve. Section 2-328 of the UCC, however, permits bidders during auctions without reserve to withdraw their bids until they are accepted by the auctioneer.

CONTRACT MODIFICATION. Under the common law, modification of an existing contract requires additional consideration—that is, consideration in addition to or promised under the original contract. This requirement can easily be an annoyance in business, where contracts are frequently altered to deal with a change in circumstances or a change of heart.

The UCC has made it easier to modify contracts: Its only requirement is that revisions be made in good faith; additional consideration is not necessary. (However, because the Statute of Frauds still applies, some contract changes must be in writing.)

This difference in approach is illustrated by the following example:

Assume that ABC Construction Corp. contracts with Acme Lumber Co. to purchase lumber. Under the terms of the agreement, a certain amount of lumber is to be delivered by Acme on the first day of each month for a year. ABC's payment of $500 for each shipment is due by the fifteenth of each month. Assume that after six months, Acme demands $600 for each shipment as a precondition to performing the remainder of the contract. ABC agrees because it needs the lumber to fulfill its construction contracts. Under the common law, the modification of the agreement regarding payment of $600 per shipment would not be enforceable because it is not supported by any additional consideration. Under the original contract, Acme was under a preexisting duty to make six more shipments at $500 each. Under the UCC, however, the modified agreement would be valid and enforceable—assuming that it had been made in good faith.

The case of *Skinner v. Tober Foreign Motors Inc.* (187 N.E.2d 669 [1963]) provides an example of how the UCC's good-faith doctrine is applied to contract modifications. The disputed contract was for the purchase of an airplane. When the plane's engine broke down, the buyer could not afford to repair it while continuing to make regular monthly payments on the plane. When the buyer offered to return the plane, the seller proposed instead to reduce the size of the payments and extend the payment period. The buyer agreed. Later, however, when the seller wanted to disaffirm the change in the contract, the court refused. Although there was no new consideration, both parties acted in good faith and benefited from the change.

UNCONSCIONABILITY. The UCC doctrine of **unconscionability** holds that a contract may be deemed unconscionable if (1) its terms are unreasonably favorable to one of the parties and (2) that same party enjoys significant bargaining power. The assumption of common law is that everyone who signs a contract has read and understood the terms. The UCC recognizes that this is not always true in real life, especially when one of the parties is a consumer rather than a businessman.

> **unconscionability** *UCC doctrine by which the terms of a* contract *include absence of meaningful choice for one party with terms that are unreasonably favorable to the other party*

The UCC addition of the doctrine of unconscionability has added an entirely new approach to the problems of fairness and unequal bargaining strength between the parties to a contract. As part of the recent trend toward more government intervention and regulation of business, it provides a defense against harsh contracts and gives the courts a more flexible tool with which to police the contract-making process and protect against abuses. Thus UCC Section 2-302(1):

> If the court as a matter of law finds the contract or any clause of the contract to have been unconscionable at the time it was made the court may refuse to enforce the contract, or it may enforce the remainder of the contract without the unconscionable clause, or it may so limit the application of any unconscionable clause as to avoid any unconscionable result.

Strictly speaking, although this rule applies only to contracts for the sale of goods, the courts and the *Restatement (Second) of Contracts* has extended it to other kinds of contracts.

The principle of unconscionability is illustrated in the following case. Note that the majority and dissenting opinions provide two interpretations of the same series of events.

LANGEMEIER v. NATIONAL OATS COMPANY, INC.
U.S. Court of Appeals, Eight Circuit, 775 F.2d 975 (1985)

Plaintiff Leon Langemeier and defendant National Oats Company ("National Oats") entered into a written agreement to grow popcorn. The agreement provided that Langemeier would grow 260 acres of popcorn at $.14 a pound for sale to National Oats, and that National Oats would furnish the seed. National Oats informed Langemeier that the popcorn would take 99 days to mature but did not disclose that the corn required an additional 20 days in the field to dry down to prevent freeze damage. With National Oats' approval, Langemeier planted the seed on May 26 and 27. Due to freezing weather in September and October, the crop was badly damaged. Pursuant to paragraph 7 of the agreement, National Oats rejected the crop. Langemeier harvested the crop and sold it to Cornhusker Foods, a company that sells lower grade popcorn, for $.12 a pound for the pounds that were usable, for a total of $31,916.

Langemeier commenced this action claiming that National Oats breached the contract by rejecting an acceptable popcorn crop. National Oats contended that it was not in breach because the popcorn was damaged and the terms of the contract enabled it to reject damaged corn. The district court awarded $5,321 in damages to Langemeier, the difference between the contract price and the amount received. National Oats appeals.

Heaney, Circuit Judge.

. . . .

. . . Paragraph 7 [of the agreement], in pertinent part, provides:

7. DELIVERY: GROWER SHALL CONSULT WITH CONTRACTOR OR ITS REPRESENTATIVE PRIOR TO DELIVERY OF THE POPCORN. Contractor, at its discretion, may (1) reject popcorn containing excessive portions of one or more foreign materials or defects [which includes damage due to freezing weather.]. . .

. . . .

The district court determined that the popcorn crop was indeed damaged by freezing weather, and that paragraph 7 of the contract authorized National Oats to reject it. The court further determined, however, that "under the circumstances of this case, paragraph 7 is an unconscionable provision and its application must be restricted in the interest of justice." The court reasoned that National Oats' "defective disclosure (as to the time needed for growing) unfairly distorted the bargaining process." . . .

National Oats contends that the district court erred in holding paragraph 7 unconscionable. In assessing whether a particular contract provision is unconscionable, courts generally look for gross inequality in bargaining power, and a misunderstanding or unawareness of the provision in question. Those factors are then examined in light of the totality of the circumstances.

Applying this test to the facts of this case, we conclude that the district court did not err in determining that paragraph 7 was unconscionable. The contract required National Oats to select and supply the popcorn seed. The company represented to Langemeier that the seed it would supply would reach maturity 99 days after planting. The company did not disclose, however, that an additional 20 days was required beyond maturity to field-dry the popcorn. . . . .

Although National Oats argues that Langemeier, an agronomist and agricultural financier, knew or should have known of the drydown period, the district court determined that he did not know and this finding of fact is not clearly erroneous.

. . . .

We affirm the judgment of the district court.

Fagg, Circuit Judge, dissenting

I respectfully dissent.

The contract at issue in this action is a simple, relatively standardized contract used by National with many commercial popcorn growers. Paragraph 6 of this contract expressly provides that "defects" in the popcorn will include "damage due to . . . weather." Paragraph 7 of the contract provides further that National, "at its discretion, may . . . reject popcorn containing excessive portions of one or more . . . defects referred to in paragraph 6." These provisions clearly place the risk of adverse weather on the grower of the popcorn, here Langemeier.

Whether the provision in paragraph 7 allowing National to reject popcorn with excessive weather damage is unconscionable under the circumstances of this case is a "[question] of law," focusing on the "circumstances existing at the time of the making of the contract."

. . . .

Unanticipated events occurring after the creation of the contract are, as a result, irrelevant and cannot be considered. Further, in determining unconscionability, the court must bear in mind that the principle of unconscionability is intended to prevent "oppression and unfair surprise"; it is not intended to disturb the "allocation of risks" resulting from "superior bargaining power."

Applying these principles to the facts of this case, I conclude the provisions in question are not unconscionable. First while inexperienced as a popcorn grower, Langemeier is by no means a newcomer to the business of agriculture. He has significant expertise in agricultural finance. . . . Further, prior to agreeing to the contract with National, Langemeier had a full opportunity to review the contract, including paragraphs 6 and 7, and understood that these paragraphs placed the risk of adverse weather on him. Finally, unlike Langemeier, the individual retained by him to farm the popcorn was quite experienced in the growing of popcorn.

. . . .
Given this factual background, I believe the contract provisions at issue are enforceable. Langemeier has significant agricultural experience. There is no evidence of oppression or gross inequality of bargaining power between the parties to this commercial contract. Also, the provision struck by the court is commercially reasonable and in fact commercially necessary if National is to exercise effective quality control over the popcorn it purchases. Finally, it is clear that absent unanticipated adverse weather, the contract provided ample time in which to grow and field dry the popcorn prior to harvest.

I conclude the district court misapplied the applicable law to the facts of this case. I would reverse the district court's decision and enforce the contract as written.

Case Questions

1. Upon what basis did the court hold that paragraph 7 was unconscionable?

2. Upon what basis would the dissent find that the provisions in question were not unconscionable?

3. Describe the "gross inequality in bargaining power" between the parties referred to by the majority.

■ *Concept Check 9-6   The Uniform Commercial Code*

- In common law, an offer can be withdrawn by the offeror at any time prior to acceptance. How does the UCC change this view?
- How has the UCC eased the rules regarding the manner of *acceptance?*
- What is meant by the *"Battle of the Forms"?*
- Describe the UCC doctrine of *unconscionability.*

YOU DECIDE: ANSWER DISCUSSION
Truth in Recruiting

In the Steinberg case, the judge agreed with Steinberg's position. He found that Steinberg and the school had entered into an enforceable contract under which the school was obliged to follow its application criteria as stated "in a definitive manner" in its bulletin. Moreover, by accepting Steinberg's application fee, which the court viewed as a valuable consideration, the school was bound to fulfill the promise extended in the bulletin. Steinberg, having accepted this promise in good faith, was entitled to have his application judged by the stated criteria, whatever additional agenda the medical school might have.

Although the basic issues of the case would seem to be resolved by this decision, we might still ask what its important implications might be. Will an institution issuing an infor-mational bulletin feel compelled to write into it a caveat that this is not an invitation to apply, but rather merely a "proposal to consider"? Although this practice would surely constitute "truth in recruiting," it might seriously hamper recruiting efforts and cause applicants to wonder about the institution's true agenda. Barring such warnings, any party responding with an offer to what he views as an invitation will have consideration if application is really the first step in the creation of contract mutually agreed upon.

In general, the issue will not always be clear cut as to whether there is a legally enforceable contract, and "language employed by the parties or manifested by their word or acts" will still be used to interpret whether there is legally binding assent to a contract.

SUMMARY

- The law recognizes the freedom of individuals to enter into agreements with one another and enforces certain types of agreements as a matter of social policy. *Contract law* is of vital importance to business. By providing sanctions against violators and rules to cover all possible contingencies, the law protects individuals, discourages careless bargain-making, and reduces the cost of transactions.

- *Contracts* involve binding *promises:* Either or both of the parties concerned may promise to perform at some future date rather than immediately. Contracts are also bargains: They govern exchanges between two or more parties who have (1) negotiated to set the terms of the deal and (2) freely assented to the agreement.

- Most contracts are *bilateral*—that is, they involve promises by both parties. In *unilateral contracts*, a promise is exchanged for some *actual performance*. Contracts of either type may be *express agreements* set out in words or *implied agreements* established by behavior alone (unless the *Statute of Frauds* requires the contract to be in writing). When justice demands, the courts may even use the concept of *quasi-contract* to impose contracts on people who have not agreed to them.

- Four prerequisites must be met to create an *enforceable contract:*

  1. All parties to the contract must be competent (over age 18 and not mentally impaired). The law protects incompetents and infants by allowing them to back out of contracts at will.

  2. All parties must agree to the same terms at the same time through the process of *offer and acceptance*. Assent is determined objectively—that is, by interpreting the parties' deeds.

  3. Legally binding promises require that something of value—that is, some *consideration*—be given in return for a promise. Consideration may consist of a return promise, an action, some forbearance from action, or a change in a legal relationship.

  4. The contract's substance must be legal. The courts will not enforce agreements that violate legal statutes, public policy, or public morals.

- Contracts that meet these four prerequisites may still be flawed. *Mistakes, misrepresentation, duress, undue influence,* and *lack of written evidence* of the terms of the contract may all make contracts fully or partially unenforceable.

- Over the past 30 years, the *Uniform Commercial Code* has made the laws governing the sale of goods consistent among the states and has had a major impact on contract law. Although the UCC did not repudiate the common law of contracts, it did make changes in order to better deal with business realities and minimize technicalities. Thus, the UCC relaxed the rules regarding offer and acceptance; dealt with problems arising from the use of form documents for offer and acceptance; simplified contract modification; and, with the doctrine of *unconscionability*, created a new flexible tool for policing the contract process.

QUESTIONS AND PROBLEMS

1. A teacher decides to sail his boat to Maine for the summer. He hires a student to drive his car there for a $500 fee. When the student arrives to pick up the keys, however, she is told that someone else will be driving the car. Does the student have a cause of action?

2. Machine Shop, Inc., sends the following offer to Industrial Machine Company on June 1: "Offer to perform overhaul, repair and regular periodic maintainance on all used machines you receive as trade-ins. If over 50 machines per month, unit price of $65 per machine. Will pick up and deliver. Reply by return mail." Industrial replies by return mail as follows: "Accept offer of June 1. Due to demands of different machinery, Industrial will pick up and deliver." When Industrial delivers the first load of machines for overhaul and repairs, Machine Shop refuses delivery. Is there a breach of contract? Explain.

3. On July 1, Chloe Typewriter Ribbon Co. sends a letter to its customer, which says in pertinent part: "We have a surplus of the type of printer ribbons you use because we get so little demand for them. We offer to sell them to you for half the list price. This offer is good until the end of the month." On July 14, a major printer manufacturer comes out with a popular new printer that uses the ribbons, and the demand for the ribbons is great. The customer goes to Chloe Typewriter Ribbon Co. on July 30 and requests 100 ribbons at half the list price. Chole refuses to sell them for under list price. Is the customer entitled to the ribbons at half the price? Explain.

4. A 17-year-old and a 22-year-old are

going to a formal dance. They each hire tuxedos at Drake's Dress-Up Shop. The outfits get ruined on the night of the party. Who is responsible for paying for the damaged clothing? Explain.

5. Plaintiff, a wholesale dealer engaged in the buying, selling, and shipping of fruits, received a dispatch from Cornforth & Co. fruit merchants in Colorado asking for prices of oranges. In response, a message was sent offering Santa Ana, San Gabriela, and Los Angeles oranges for $1.50 and Riversides for $2.60 per box, which was considerably low for these oranges. Cornforth & Co. ordered two carloads of Riverside oranges, which were immediately shipped. Cornforth refused to pay $2.60 for the boxes and insisted on $1.60. Who wins? Under that theory? [*Germaine Fruit Co. v. Western Union Tel Co*, 70 p. 658 (1902)]

6. In setting up her new business Donna Miller entered into the following contracts through phone calls to local business people on July 7: (1) a five-year lease on the commercial property housing her business entered into with Commercial Properties, Inc.; (2) the purchase of $7,000 worth of office furniture from Office Mart Furniture Co; and (3) the hiring of three employees for one-year periods, starting July 15. On July 9, she decides not to go into business after all. What is her liability on the contracts she entered into?

7. While Judy was walking to school a vicious Doberman cornered her and was ready to bite her but a passerby saw what was about to happen, and saved Judy. Judy sustained no injuries, not even a scratch, but the passerby was brutally attacked and will require plastic surgery and a lengthy stay in the hospital. Judy's mother decides to pay the passerby his weekly salary while he is in the hospital, but she stops after two weeks. The passerby files suit for the payments. Will he be successful? Explain.

8. Mr. White enters into an oral agreement with Stopleak Plumbing Co. to have Stopleak provide drainage from his basement. Mr. White dies before the bill is paid and Stopleak sues Mrs. White for the amount due. Mrs. White claims that the contract was only between Mr. White and Stopleak and she therefore owes Stopleak nothing. Stopleak says that Mrs. White was present along with Mr. White at all negotiations with Stopleak, discussed what Stopleak was to do, called Stopleak to come to the house, paid part of the account with her personal check, tried to get a loan for the work to be performed, and, when that failed, told Stopleak she would try elsewhere. Who wins and why? [*Shepard d/b/a/Raytown Plumbing & Sewer Service v. Glick (McGinty)*, 404 S.W.2d 441 (Mo. App. 1966)]

9. Bette is at an antique auction and sees a vase that will look perfect in her bedroom. Although she only has $500 in savings, Bette bids $450. After making the bid, Bette is very upset and wonders how she will ever pay for the vase and where she will get the rent money for next month. No one knows what she is thinking. Did a valid offer take place?

10. Upon being admitted to General Hospital, Tim O'Shea signed a document stating that he released the hospital from any and all liability for the negligent or wrongful acts or omissions of its employees. When he dies, his wife sues the hospital. She claims that the alleged negligence of two of its doctors caused her husband personal injury. Is O'Shea's waiver of his rights against the hospital effective? Explain. [*Tunkl v. Regents of University of California*, 60 Cal. 2d 92, 32 Cal. Rptr. 33, 282 P.2d 441 (1963)]

10

TORTS

Torts constitute a kind of legal grab bag that includes many of the most familiar kinds of liability cases. Auto accidents, fist fights, libel, trespass, and the infliction of mental suffering are all examples of conduct that may be *tortious*. Some torts pose recurrent problems for businesses. A retail store that holds suspected shoplifters, for example, risks being found liable for false imprisonment. On other occasions, businesses are plaintiffs in tort cases. For example, a business may recover for defamation when its credit rating is wrongfully injured.

Tortious behavior can be divided into three categories: (1) *intentional* interference with another's interests, (2) *negligent* interference with another's interests, and (3) interference with another's interests *without reference to fault*. These categories make up the three different bases on which tort liability may rest. Tort suits allow those injured to seek compensation for their losses from wrongdoers.

Tort law determines how losses will be distributed or harm redressed. Although tort law is predominantly of common-law origin, there are also statutes defining tortious behavior and liability. In general, tort law weighs each plaintiff's claim to compensation for injuries sustained against each defendant's claim to freedom of action. It answers important questions about individual and corporate responsibility for harmful behavior. The courts' mandate is extraordinarily broad: Tortious behavior includes intentional and accidental conduct (acts of *commission*) as well as acts of *omission*. Tort law defines wrong conduct and sets standards for acceptable, responsible behavior.

Thus, the law of torts changes as society changes. For example, the right of privacy emerged in this century as industrialization, urbanization, and the development of modern communications systems made it difficult for people to be left alone. New technologies speed the development of new torts. Thus, the invention of the automobile gave rise to automobile accidents—and new, still evolving torts to govern them. Toxic wastes, asbestos-related disease, and wiretapping are also examples of "modern" phenomena that have created "modern" torts. Courts must continually recognize new torts: If progress has its costs, tort law distributes them.

■ DEFINING A TORT

It is difficult to define a *tort* precisely because of the wide variety of injuries considered tortious. The late William Prosser, a leading authority in the field, characterized a tort as "a civil wrong, other than breach of contract, for which the court will provide a remedy in the form of an action for damages."[1] Prosser was well aware that even this broad definition is not entirely accurate.

Know 2)

In general, we can say that every **tort** shares these three elements: (1) a legal *duty* owed by the defendant to the plaintiff, (2) a *breach* of that duty, and (3) *damage* caused to the plaintiff as a result. A major purpose of tort law is to prevent injuries and to compensate the victims of injuries caused by another's unreasonable conduct. **Injury** is a broad term that includes any wrong or damage to a person's body, property, reputation, or rights.

tort Civil wrong or injury other than breach of contract for which there is a legal remedy

injury Any wrong or damage to a person's body, property, reputation, or rights

DISTINGUISHING TORTS FROM CRIMES.   A *crime* is an offense against society as a whole (*see* Chapter 12). The state acts as society's representative in criminal proceedings and prosecutes criminal cases. The purpose of criminal proceedings is to protect the public and satisfy its sense of justice by punishing wrongdoers and removing dangerous people from society. The twin goals of the system are to *reform* the wrongdoer and to *deter* others from committing the same offense.

No need on exam.

By contrast, a tort is a *civil* action brought by an injured party. Its primary purpose is to protect the interests of individuals by *compensating* them at the expense of wrongdoers. Deterrence is a secondary goal. Thus, plaintiffs in a tort suit generally seek money damages, and money damages do, of course, serve a deterrent effect: People are less likely to engage in harmful behavior when they are made to pay for its consequences.

The same act may both be a tort and a crime. The victim of an assault and battery, for example, may bring a civil tort action against the perpetrator in order to get compensation for any mental distress and physical injuries suffered. The state may also prosecute and imprison the offender on criminal charges. Such civil and criminal cases are not dependent on each other. In fact, with few exceptions, the result of the criminal case may not be used as evidence in the tort action.

DISTINGUISHING TORTS FROM BREACH OF CONTRACT.   People who voluntarily enter into contracts with each other create mutual obligations (*see* Chapter 9). Breach of contract cases involve these essentially *self-imposed* duties.

By contrast, torts involve obligations that are *involuntarily* imposed by the law itself. Explicit consent is not required. One example of such an obligation is the duty to drive a car with reasonable care for the safety of others. Although this duty stems from the freely made decision to drive the car, it is automatically incurred once you sit behind the wheel.

---

[1]*See Prosser and Keeton on the Law of Torts*, 5th ed. (Minneapolis, MN: West, 1984), p. 2.

The History of Torts

The kinds of liability problems raised in tort suits have existed for centuries. The first tort laws were simply lists of miscellaneous rules that were adopted in response to some particular problem. For example, under early English law, a person could only bring an action in the King's common law courts with one of a few, strictly prescribed *writs of summons*—that is, a written order by the court ordering or prohibiting an action (*see* Chapter 4).

The Advent of Intent and Negligence. By focusing on *intent*, the Industrial Revolution immunized factory owners from actions for injuries as long as they exercised "due care." As industrial accidents became more common, however, the concept of *fault* was gradually expanded to include unintentional injuries.

No

Legislative reforms in the nineteenth century reclassified torts into *intentional* and *negligent* actions and eliminated the older procedural categories of trespass and action on the case. It was at this time that the term "tort" came into use to designate actionable civil wrongs. (The word is derived from Latin *tortus,* which means twisted.)

Today, tort law varies from state to state. Much of this chapter, including the definitions of key terms, is based on the American Law Institute's *Restatement (Second) of the Law of Torts.* The restatement, which was promulgated in 1965, is a model for uniform state laws. (Other branches of law have similar models—for example, the widely adopted Uniform Commercial Code in contract law. Although not every state law matches the model, most state legislatures have passed tort laws based on portions of the ALI's restatement. In addition, judicial opinions frequently cite the Restatement as an authority.

Corporate Responsibility, Ethics, and Torts

Torts are closely related to the ideas about the social responsibility of business discussed in Chapter 2. What constitutes a tort is not determined by legislative fiat: In every tort case, the courts must decide whether the defendant crossed the bounds of socially acceptable behavior. At the heart of tort law are *value judgments* that reflect prevailing *social standards* of abnormal and unacceptable behavior. More than any other branch of law, tort law incorporates a common *moral code* of behavior. Issues in tort law, then, reflect the overlap of legal and ethical concerns of a society, and the ETHICAL ENVIRONMENT box below illustrates the complexity of such issues.

THE ETHICAL ENVIRONMENT
Social Host Liability

In the United States today, many people tend to think of parties as occasions to drink alcoholic beverages. Many of these same people drive automobiles to and from these events. Statistically, the combination of drinking and driving leads to approximately two million automobile accidents per year. The fact, of course, is disturbing enough in itself, and it is also a fact that about 725,000 Americans are either killed or injured in those accidents. It is reasonable to assume that if the drunk drivers who caused these accidents did not drink, those accidents, injuries, and deaths would not have occurred.

Given these numbers, it is surprising that the numbers continue to go up rather than down: One of the common effects of alcohol consumption is impaired judgment. Should someone else—perhaps the host of the party or the owner of the establishment—bear legal responsibility for ensuring that his or her guests/customers do not drive if they drink? Should that party be legally responsible to the third party who is unwittingly at risk? Should it matter whether the driver is a minor? Each of these questions has both a legal and a moral component.

In fact, some states do hold hosts and/or proprietors legally responsible for the acts of the people whom they are entertaining. These states have enacted statutes that argue against the traditional common-law view that the act of consuming the liquor—not the act of supplying the liquor—is the proximate cause of the harm: Lawmakers in these states contend that the server incurs civil liability for injuries caused by drunk drivers.

Some of these laws are based on the same theory as the dramshop laws that were on the books between the end of the Civil War and at the end of Prohibition. These laws generally are associated with tavern and restaurant owners, managers, and servers but have not yet been applied to social hosts. Instead, the common-law theory of negligence has been applied to such cases. The courts have reasoned that the server is liable because accidents are a foreseeable consequence of driving while intoxicated and have in some cases argued that social hosts, too, have a legal duty not to serve minors or intoxicated persons. Social hosts, they argue, should also be liable to third parties injured in such accidents.

One important case in this area is McGuiggan v. New England Telephone and Telegraph Co. (368 Mass. 152, 496 N.E.2d 141 [1986]). The court held that the host of a party at which alcohol was served might be liable for the actions of a guest who was intoxicated when he left the party. This case involved the driver of the vehicle and a passenger. The passenger (who was the host's son) was killed when he put his head outside the car window and struck a cement post maintained by the telephone company. The telephone company filed a complaint against the host parents, among others. The court dismissed the complaint on the ground that there was insufficient evidence that they knew that the driver was drunk. The court indicated, however, that its finding might have been different had there been evidence that the hosts knew or should have known that liquor was served to an intoxicated person.

Courts and state legislatures are beginning to respond to the public outcry against drunk driving, maintaining that if a server is to avoid liability, he or she must be aware of the consequences. In the case of a social host, the choices are either not serving liquor or attempting to monitor guests' behavior. In some cases, it might be prudent for the host to collect car keys at the beginning of the event. The answer is a bit more complicated for commercial establishments. Here, the best answer might be creating a policy limiting promotions (Figure 10-A), offers of free or low-cost food or transportation alternatives, and a written agenda specifying services policies.

> If a guest is refused service, but is determined to drive, we will offer the guest the following transportation alternatives:
>
> - Call a cab for the guest.
> - Provide information about bus routes.
> - Provide a list of public-service driver programs offered by community groups.
> - Offer to check the guest into a hotel room.
> - Offer to pay for taxi or bus fare home or to a hotel.
>
> We will offer free parking if the guest accepts an alternative to driving home.

FIGURE 10-A Sample Transportation Policy for an Intoxicated Patron   *Source: Denney G. Rutherford, "Managing Guest Intoxication: A Policy to Limit Third-Party Liability,"* Cornell HRA Quarterly, *Nov. 1985.*

Archie Carroll's model of social responsibility (*see* Chapter 2) suggests that business has economic, legal, ethical, and discretionary responsibilities. Tort law elevates ethical responsibilities into legal responsibilities. For example, drug manufacturers have always been ethically responsible for the safety of their products. But how far does their legal responsibility extend?

Are there areas of conduct that are offensive to our moral sensibilities and our corporate responsibilities but that are properly beyond the reach of law? For example, it has long been recognized that a person passing by a lake has no *legal* duty to rescue a stranger who is observed to be drowning. The moral issue might be decided differently. Consider the following case.

MILLER v. ARNAL CORPORATION
Arizona Court of Appeals, 632 P.2d 987 (1981)

On December 31, 1972, a group consisting of the appellant, Clint Miller, and five friends left the Snowball Ski Lodge and embarked upon a hiking expedition to climb Humphrey's Peak in the mountains of Arizona. After reaching an elevation of over 11,000 feet, the hikers met with a blizzard whose severe conditions caused Miller to suffer from frostbite. When on the next day the remaining members of the group, with the exception of one Alison Clay, climbed back down the mountain to get help for Miller, the lodge's mountain manager, Kuntzleman, refused the group's request to rescue Miller via a ski lift that had already been shut off because of the storm. A rescue party under the authority of the County Sheriff, which left four hours later, finally found Clay, who had frozen to death, and Miller, whose severe frostbite led to the loss of all his toes and four fingers.

The appellant, Clint Miller, sued the appellee, Arnal Corporation, owner and operator of the Snowball Lodge, claiming that Kuntzleman's decision not to pursue the rescue attempt with full knowledge of the potential harm that could result to Miller and Clay amounted to the negligent performance of an undertaking to render services. The trial court ruled in Arnal's favor. Miller appeals.

O'Connor, Presiding Judge.

Appellant's first contention is that the trial court erred in failing to submit his requested instruction 14 to the jury. It reads as follows:

> One who undertakes, gratuitously or for consideration, to render services to another which he should recognize as necessary for the protection of the other's person or things, is subject to liability to the other for physical harm resulting from his failure to exercise reasonable care to perform his undertaking, if the harm is suffered because of the other's reliance upon the undertaking.

The requested instruction is taken directly from *Restatement (Second) of Torts* § 323 dealing with negligent performance of an undertaking to render services. Appellant contends that he was put in a worse position by appellee's termination of a rescue attempt by its own ski patrol and the jury should have been allowed to compensate him for his loss of the chance of being rescued by the ski patrol.

Appellant concedes that the law presently imposes no liability upon those who stand idly by and fail to rescue a stranger who is in danger.

. . . .

... The Arizona Legislature has also limited the liability of persons who render "emergency care" gratuitously and in good faith to circumstances of *gross* rather than ordinary negligence, whether liability is alleged to exist as a result of an act or a failure to act.

. . . .

In determining whether an instruction is justified, we must consider the evidence in the strongest possible manner in support of the theory of the party asking for the instruction. Even viewed in this light, there is no evidence that appellant relied on any rescue undertaking by appellee in the sense that he chose rescue by the ski patrol over any other available alternative. Appellant's companions did not rely on appellee by choosing not to pursue other possible avenues of rescue on his behalf. Appellee's employee Rich telephoned the county search and rescue unit almost immediately after appellant's companions arrived at the lodge. The county unit then began organizing equipment and personnel for its rescue attempt. The evidence shows that the county's rescue efforts were not delayed, discouraged, or prevented by any act of appellee's. It is error to instruct in relation to a matter not supported by the evidence. Thus, the trial court properly refused to give appellant's requested instruction 14.

. . . .

Next appellant argues that the trial court erred in refusing to give his requested instructions 5 and 8.

. . .

His requested instruction 8 read: "If defendant intentionally or negligently interfered with the Ski Patrol's efforts to rescue plaintiff, it is liable for any harm suffered by plaintiff as a result of such interference."

Appellant's instructions 5 and 8 were based on §§ 326 and 327, *Restatement (Second) of Torts,* which state that one is liable for physical harm resulting from the intentional or negligent prevention of the giving of aid to another by a third person.

. . . .

Appellant's instruction 8 refers to an intentional or negligent interference with a rescue effort. He contends that, as far as this issue is concerned, appellee is in fact two parties although it "prefers to see itself as one entity." In the *Restatement* terms, Kuntzleman is seen as the one who wrongfully prevented the "third person," the ski patrol, from continuing the rescue attempt. Appellant would hold appellee liable for Kuntzleman's act by *respondeat superior.* While appellant concedes that Kuntzleman and the ski patrol members were all employees of Arnal Corporation and that Kuntzleman had the authority to direct the ski patrol's activities, he contends that Kuntzleman nevertheless had no right to interfere with or prevent the proposed rescue operation by the ski patrol.

On the other hand, appellee argues that because Kuntzleman and the ski patrol members were all employees of the corporation, there were only two parties involved, the corporation and the appellant. The corporation could not be said to have "interfered with itself." *The corporation did not interfere with an attempt; rather, it chose not to make an attempt.* We agree. The Restatement sections upon which appellant relies require three parties: an imperilled plaintiff, a rescuer, and one who prevents or interferes with the rescuer. A corporation is an impersonal entity which can act only through its officers and agents. The acts of a corporation's agents are the acts of the corporation. The concept of a corporation as a separate entity is a legal fact, not a fiction. In this case one group of corporate employees, the ski patrol, decided to attempt a rescue. A higher-ranking corporate employee, Kuntzleman, told the patrol members that they could not undertake the rescue as they had planned. The effect was that the corporation as an entity decided, through the interactions of its employees, not to begin a rescue. The corporation cannot be held liable for interfering with a rescue attempt, because it chose not to make any attempt.

As discussed above, there is no duty to rescue an endangered stranger. Thus there is no basis upon which to hold appellee liable for interfering with or preventing a rescue attempt.

The orders of the trial court are affirmed.

Case Questions

1. Why did the court in Miller refuse to find any liability on the part of the defendant corporation?

2. What did Miller need to show in order to win?

3. In terms of Carroll's model, what type of business duty did the defendant have?

■ Concept Check 10-1   Defining a Tort

- Explain the key elements that define a *tort* and describe the differences between a tort and *breach of contract*.

- Discuss the roles of *intent* and *negligence* in the development of the modern tort concept.

Generally, tort law defines *reasonable behavior* and then holds persons culpable for overstepping its bounds. In some cases involving inherently dangerous activities, it may even hold people or businesses liable for "reasonable" conduct. There are three types of torts: *intentional* torts, *negligent* torts, and torts that have their base in *strict liability*. Each type deals with a different kind of behavior.

■ INTENTIONAL TORTS *EXAM*

Intentional harmful acts are, of course, considered the most serious, precisely because they are deliberate actions intended to cause harm. Such torts, however, can also be deterred most effectively: People can avoid committing conscious wrongs more readily than accidental ones. An **intentional tort** occurs when the actor either desired to bring about the harm caused or understood that the harm was a substantially certain result from the action. Liability for intentional torts *does not* require hostility or malice toward the injured party.

intentional tort Civil wrong in which the actor desires to bring about the harm caused or understands it to be the likely result of the action

Therefore, people can actually be held liable for practical jokes. In the case of *Garratt v. Dailey* (304 P.2d 681 [1956]), the Supreme Court of Washington ruled that a five-year-old boy who had pulled a chair out from under a woman as she sat down was guilty of the intentional tort of battery—that is, intentional harmful or offensive contact. The boy did not want to injure the woman physically. He was probably too young to realize that any harm was likely to result from his joke. However, he did know with substantial certainty that he was causing the woman to come into bodily contact with the ground. Thus, he had committed a battery.

Although the legal definition of *intent* is not concerned with the wrongdoer's motivation, the courts do not entirely ignore the maliciousness of the act. In cases involving conduct that is deemed immoral or malicious, the court is likely to hold the defendant liable for a broader range of consequences and damages. Remember that the courts weigh a plaintiff's claim to protection against a defendant's claim to freedom of action: The freedom to act immorally is likely to be legally restrained.

The law recognizes dozens of intentional torts. Several of those relating to business are discussed below.

Battery

battery *Intentional tort involving harmful or offensive contact with another person*

Battery involves harmful or offensive unpermitted contact with another person. People may be held liable for battery if either they intend to bring about such a contact or if such a contact results, directly or indirectly, from their actions. In a Texas case, a woman was injured when she pushed her hand through a glass door while being chased by employees of the local Chamber of Commerce. They were trying to lasso her because she was not wearing western clothing during the rodeo season. Although the injury was indirect and unintended, it was the result of attempted, intended contact (lassoing) that was not privileged or based on consent (*Moore v. El Paso Chamber of Commerce*, 220 S.W.2d 327 [1949]).

Battery has repercussions for business because it can be interpreted very broadly. Battery need not involve touching a person's body: It may result from an unlawful contact with anything attached to the body, including clothing, a briefcase or package held in the hand, the chair in which someone is sitting, or even the car in which someone is driving. In the following case, a restaurant manager pulled a dinner plate out of a customer's hand.

FISHER v. CARROUSEL MOTOR HOTEL
Texas Supreme Court, 424 S.W. 2d 627 (1967)

A group of approximately 30 people was gathered for buffet lunch in the Brass Ring Club, a restaurant within the Carrousel Hotel, as guests for a one-day convention about telemetry equipment. Fisher, a mathematician for the Manned Spacecraft agency of N.A.S.A., was waiting in line as one of the guests. As Fisher was waiting to be served, the manager of the Brass Ring accosted him, grabbed the plate he was holding from his hand, and yelled that blacks could not be served in the club.

Fisher, the plaintiff, brought suit in the trial court against Carrousel, the Brass Ring, and Flynn, the manager, for battery. The court ruled in the defendant's favor and the Court of Civil Appeals affirmed. The issue on this subsequent appeal by Fisher to the Texas Supreme Court is whether the legal elements of battery had been met.

Greenhill, Justice.

The Court of Civil Appeals held that there was no assault because there was no physical contact and no evidence of fear or apprehension of physical contact. However, it has long been settled that there can be a battery without an assault, and that actual physical contact is not necessary to constitute a battery, so long as

there is contact with clothing or an object closely identified with the body. . . .

Under the facts of this case, we have no difficulty in holding that the intentional grabbing of plaintiff's plate constituted a battery. The intentional snatching of an object from one's hand is as clearly an offensive invasion of his person as would be an actual contact with the body.

. . . .

. . . Damages for mental suffering are recoverable without the necessity for showing actual physical injury in a case of willful battery because the basis of that action is the unpermitted and intentional invasion of the plaintiff's person and not the actual harm done to the plaintiff's body. Personal indignity is the essence of an action for battery; and consequently the defendant is liable not only for contacts which do actual physical harm, but also for those which are offensive and insulting. We hold, therefore, that plaintiff was entitled to actual damages for mental suffering due to the willful battery, even in the absence of any physical injury.

The judgments of the courts below are reversed, and judgment is here rendered for the plaintiff for $900 with interest from the date of the trial court's judgment, and for costs of this suit.

---

1. Does the court define battery too broadly?
2. Remembering that a battery does not have to in-

volve physical injury, how did intent factor into the court's decision?

3. Would the court have found a battery had the defendant used a gun to shoot the tray out of Fisher's hand, causing him no physical injury?

Assault

Although *assault* and *battery* are often classed together in a single phrase, they are legally distinct torts. According to Section 21 of the *Restatement (Second) of Torts*, a person is liable for **assault** if "(a) [the person] acts intending to cause a harmful or offensive contact with the [other] person . . . or an imminent apprehension of such a contact, and (b) the other [person] is thereby put in such imminent apprehension." Assault does not necessarily involve physical contact with the injured party; rather, it creates the *fear* that a physical contact is imminent. Note that liability for assault also requires that the defendant *intended* to do harm, either by causing a battery or by causing the imminent *apprehension* of a battery.

assault *Intentional tort* in which the defendant intends harmful contact with another person or creates the fear of such harm

CRITERIA FOR ASSAULT.   All the following acts may be instances of assault: shaking a fist under somebody's nose, aiming or striking at a person with a weapon, holding a weapon in a threatening position, and chasing somebody in a hostile manner. Although mere words are not enough, words may make otherwise inoffensive movements appear hostile.

Reasonable Apprehension. The general test is whether a reasonable person in like circumstances would normally feel apprehensive. Therefore, assault can occur even when the plaintiff is too "courageous" to be frightened or intimidated. Conversely, the exaggerated fears of an exceptionally timid person are not grounds for assault. *Reasonable apprehension* also requires showing the offender has the ability and opportunity to carry out any threats immediately. Finally, to arouse apprehension, a display of force must be directed specifically towards the plaintiff.

Battery does not necessarily involve assault. If the injured party is unaware of the unlawful contact when it takes place—for example, when asleep or unconscious—then he or she obviously cannot be afraid of it. Likewise, assault can take place without battery. For instance, a wrongdoer may deliberately fire a gun to frighten somebody without either aiming at or intending to shoot that person.

Although assault and battery can occur independently, they generally go hand in hand: After all, assault depends on the apprehension of battery. For example, assault occurs when a victim sees a fist coming toward him; battery occurs when the fist actually hits him.

False Imprisonment

False imprisonment is not necessarily a matter of locking someone in jail unjustly. It is a much broader tort that involves the involuntary restriction of another person's movements, either intentionally, directly, or indirectly.

false imprisonment *Intentional tort* in which a person's movements are involuntarily restricted, either intentionally, directly, or indirectly

CRITERIA FOR FALSE IMPRISONMENT.   The restriction must be enforced by either physical barriers, fear of force, or the false assertion of legal authority. Confining a person to a certain city, dictating the movement of passengers in an automobile, and compelling a person to accompany someone else are all examples of false imprisonment. The restrictions on the injured party's movements need only last a matter of minutes.

This tort also requires that the injured party be either conscious of his confinement or harmed by it. _Harm, however, m_ay consist simply of the restraint of_ a person's freedo_m. Victims of false imprisonment may seek compensation for a wide variety of damages, including loss of time, physical discomfort or inconvenience, physical illness or injury, mental suffering, humiliation, harm to reputation, or the loss of the company of their family.

Although most false imprisonment suits are brought against security guards or police officers, other citizens are also at risk. In _Sindle v. New York City Transit Authority_ (307 N.E.2d 245 [1973]), for example, a school-bus driver in New York announced to his passengers that he was taking them to the police station because of the damage they were doing to his bus. He then passed several regular stops and left his normal route to drive toward the police station. The driver was held liable for false imprisonment in a suit brought by a fourteen-year-old who jumped out of the bus window and was seriously injured.

CASE: SHOPLIFTING. Retailers run the risk of being sued for false imprisonment whenever they detain suspected shoplifters. The most difficult kind of arrest to justify is arrest without a warrant for a misdemeanor that does not involve a breach of the peace. Standards of liability in these cases vary from state to state. In some states, the arrest is valid only if the theft occurs in the presence of a store employee and the suspect is subsequently proven guilty. In other states, court decisions and statutes confer a limited privilege upon storekeepers to detain people reasonably suspected of shoplifting.

Without this privilege, it would be relatively easy for a suspected shoplifter to prove false imprisonment because a wide variety of actions by store employees may be considered restraint. Grabbing the suspect's arm, confiscating the suspect's property, or threatening to make a public scene if the suspect resists are all forms of restraint. Even asking a suspect to cooperate and prove his innocence is restraint if the suspect feels compelled to comply so as not to appear guilty. The following case illustrates the problems facing retailers when their employees apprehend shoplifting suspects.

ROBINSON v. WIEBOLDT STORES INC.

Appellate Court of Illinois, 433 N.E. 2d 1005 (1982)

After purchasing a scarf on the first floor of Wieboldt's Department Store, 66-year-old Sarah Robinson decided to wear the scarf as she continued to shop. Robinson was met on the third floor by a 290-pound security guard who suspected her of shoplifting. Upon seeing what he believed to be a price tag but which really was a care tag, the guard immediately gripped Robinson's upper arm tightly, even after she had told him that she purchased the item on the first floor and after he saw the sales receipt. Only after the guard had escorted Robinson back to the scarf department, where the cashier told him that Robinson had indeed purchased the

article earlier, did the guard release her.

Sarah Robinson brought an action for false imprisonment in the Illinois trial court against the defendant, Weiboldt Stores. Robinson appeals following a decision in the defendant's favor.

Stamos, Presiding Justice:

Defendant's first contention on appeal is that. . . . there is no evidence that a false imprisonment occurred. False imprisonment consists of the unlawful restraint, against a person's will, of that individual's personal liberty or freedom of locomotion. . . .

. . . A review of the record reveals that plaintiff's assertions do, in fact, present a case of false imprisonment. She testified that the security guard grabbed her tightly on her upper arm while they were on the third floor of defendant's store, restricting her freedom of locomotion. Even after presenting the guard with a sales receipt, she was forced to travel to the first floor of the store, further restricting her liberty and freedom of locomotion. To claim that plaintiff could have refused to go to the first floor and unilaterally ended the confrontation ignores the realities of the situation.

Defendant also contends that punitive damages are inappropriate. . . .

. . . [W]e believe there was a factual basis for the punitive damages instruction. Such damages are permitted where an arrest is effected recklessly, oppressively, insultingly or wilfully [sic], with a design to oppress and injure. The security guard's actions in grabbing plaintiff tightly by the upper arm and continuing to hold her tightly after he had been shown a sales receipt provide a sufficient basis for an instruction on punitive damages.

. . . .

Defendant's next contention is that it was reversible error for the trial court to permit plaintiff to testify about pre-existing conditions such as high blood pressure and that the incident caused her to have angina and an "attack." Defendant argues that plaintiff was not competent to testify to these conditions and that since her testimony was the only evidence that such conditions

existed, it was reversible error to admit the testimony. . . .

. . . Plaintiff was not qualified as an expert and was therefore incompetent to testify regarding specific medical diagnoses.

Since plaintiff's testimony was the only evidence concerning the extent of her injuries, the error in admitting her incompetent medical testimony, which was a substantial portion of the testimony, was prejudicial and mandates reversal of the award of damages.

. . . .

We affirm the judgment in favor of plaintiff on the issue of liability. We reverse the award of both compensatory and punitive damages and remand the case to the trial court on the issue of those damages alone.

Case Questions

1. When in the *Robinson* case did the actual false imprisonment occur?

2. Might the case have been decided differently had the plaintiff been a 25-year-old 350-pound professional wrestler rather than an older, smaller person?

3. What can shopowners do to protect themselves against theft while also trying to guard against being sued? Should the legislature make an exception for retailers?

Defamation

Defamation consists of the two related intentional torts of *libel* and *slander*. **Libel** and **slander** are *false* communications made with the intention of harming an individual or corporate reputation. Historically, libel is *written* and slander is *oral*. However, modern forms of communication have blurred this traditional distinction.

CRITERIA FOR DEFAMATION.   The defamation laws are intended to protect the right to a reputation unblemished by the publication of false claims or statements. This practice reflects the basic concept of libel and slander as injuries to reputation, not personal feelings. Libel and slander may cause injury to a reputation by a variety of means, including lowering the person or business in the estimation of the community, deterring others from associating or doing business with them, stirring up derogatory emotions and opinions against them, or lessening the existing esteem, respect, good will, and confidence in which they are held.

Publication is defined as the written or oral communication of defamatory material to at least one person other than the person defamed. It may be conveyed by gestures or by works of art. All that is required is that a third person receive the defamatory communication. Examples of publication include a defamatory statement overheard by a third person, a libelous message sent on a postcard that is read by a third person, a libelous message dictated to a secretary, a libelous memo sent via intracompany communications, and even a defamatory remark made to members of one's own family.

defamation   *Intentional tort* in which a person's reputation is harmed by false statements or claims

libel   *Defamation* in the form of a false written communication intended to harm an individual or corporate reputation

slander   *Defamation* in the form of a false oral communication intended to harm an individual or corporate reputation

Defamation and the Media Defendant On September 14, 1982, after Israeli army troops under the command of Defense Minister Ariel Sharon entered West Beirut, Lebanon, massacres occurred in Palestinian refugee camps that had been entered by elements of the pro-Israeli Christian Lebanese Front. When *Time* magazine published reports in 1984 that linked him to the massacres, Sharon charged libel and sued the news organization for $50 million. Sharon is shown here leaving a New York federal court, where a jury had decided that although certain *Time* employees had been "careless" in assembling details of the magazine's stories, it had not libeled Sharon. The verdict, at least in one sense, was fairly unusual: Recent studies have shown that in defamation cases brought against media defendants, juries have returned verdicts favorable to plaintiffs about 90 percent of the time. The same studies, however, reveal that approximately 75 percent of those verdicts are overturned on appeal; so-called "megaverdicts" are frequently reduced or eliminated, either by trial judges or appeals courts. Nevertheless, *Time*'s defense in the Sharon case cost the company $4 million. It has also been pointed out that the costs of the defamation insurance carried by journalistic organizations have threatened to become prohibitive and that the willingness of juries to return verdicts with astronomical awards stems in part from the inherent complexity of defamation laws. Finally, many observers worry that in response to the number and size of defamation suits being brought against media defendants, journalism may become too timid to perform its function; advocates of the media's First Amendment rights hope that decisions like that in *New York Times Co. v. Sullivan* (see the ORGANIZATIONAL PROFILE in Chapter 3) will ease the burden placed on media defendants in defamation cases.

DEFENSE AND PRIVILEGE. Because libel and slander are by definition false statements, *truth* is an absolute defense in a defamation case. Some arguably defamatory statements enjoy immunity from liability as a matter of public policy. For example, relevant statements by judges, lawyers, jurors, and witnesses in judicial proceedings are absolutely *privileged* (that is, exempt from liability), as are statements by legislators and witnesses in judicial proceedings.

Constitutional Privilege: The Press. The most important and controversial privileges in defamation cases are the constitutional privileges enjoyed by the press. The interplay between libel law and First Amendment freedoms is beyond the scope of this book. However, it is important to recognize that the courts must balance the private rights of citizens and business entities to protect their reputations with the constitutional rights of the press and public to the free flow of information.

The fact that newspapers, magazines, and radio and TV stations are profit-making businesses does not undermine their claim to First Amendment protections. It is therefore especially difficult for public officials or public figures who enjoy the dubious honor of being newsworthy to recover damages from the press for defamation: They must prove that a false statement was made *with malice*—that is, knowledge of its falsity or reckless disregard for the truth. This principle was enunciated more than twenty years ago in the landmark case of *New York Times v. Sullivan* (376 U.S. 254 [1964]) (see the ORGANIZATIONAL PROFILE box in Chapter 3), in which an Alabama official sued *The New York Times* for an allegedly libelous advertisement placed in the paper by a civil-rights group.

Actual malice, however, is difficult but not impossible for a public figure to prove. In the case of *Burnett v. National Enquirer* (144 Cal. App. 3d 991 [1983]), for example, actress Carol Burnett sued the newspaper over a short item it printed stating that she had had a loud argument in a restaurant with Henry Kissinger (presidential advisor to Richard Nixon) and strongly implying that she had been drunk at the time. Burnett was not satisfied with the paper's retraction and sued for libel. The court determined that the newspaper had been "clearly determined" to print defamatory statements that would expose Burnett to contempt and ridicule—in other words, had published with malice. She was awarded both compensatory and punitive damages.

Invasion of Privacy

Invasion of privacy is a relatively recent tort that protects the right of the individual to be left alone and unnoticed. It was first proposed in 1890 in a famous law review article coauthored by Louis Brandeis, who would later become a Supreme Court justice (*see* Chapter 14). Since then, it has slowly been recognized by all the states. It is actually a combination of four different torts:

1. *Appropriation* of a plaintiff's name or likeness for a commercial purpose such as advertising.
2. Unreasonable *intrusion* into another's home, such as by wiretapping or persistently making unwanted telephone calls.
3. Public *disclosure* of private facts about a person of an offensive nature that are not reasonable concerns of the public.
4. Publicity placing the plaintiff in a *false light*. (If, for example, a television news report on toxic wastes shows pictures of a company that does not produce such wastes, the studio would likely be liable even though it did not claim that the company pictured was creating toxic wastes.)

invasion of privacy *Intentional tort* with four grounds— appropriation of a person's name for commercial purposes, unreasonable intrusion into a person's home, disclosure of personal facts, or placing a person in a false light

Intentional Infliction of Emotional Distress

The tort of **intentional infliction of emotional distress** recognizes the right to be free from serious, intentional, and unprivileged invasions of mental and emotional tranquility. It covers severe emotional distress of any kind, including fright, grief, shame, humiliation, embarrassment, and anger. The key is that the emotional distress is so substantial or persistent that no reasonable person in a civilized society should be expected to endure it. For many years, the courts required that physical injury (illness, miscarriage, etc.) accompany emo-

"Vehement, Caustic, and Sometimes Unpleasantly Sharp Attacks" In its November 1983 issue, *Hustler* magazine published an "ad parody" that included a purported interview with the Reverend Jerry Falwell, founder of Moral Majority in America. Specifically labeled a *parody*, the "interview" contained the "revelation" that Falwell's "first-time" experience with a certain liqueur included a drunken (and incestuous) episode in the family's outdoor facilities. Falwell sued the magazine for defamation, invasion of privacy, and intentional infliction of emotional distress. Ruling in the magazine's favor on the invasion-of-privacy claim, the trial judge sent the other two charges to the jury. The jury found for *Hustler* on the defamation claim: No reasonable person, according to the jurors, could misinterpret the details of the "ad" as facts of Falwell's life. As for the claim of emotional distress, however, the jury awarded Falwell $200,000. A federal appeals court upheld the verdict, but in *Hustler Magazine v. Falwell* (1988), the Supreme Court reversed the decision. Citing *New York Times Co. v. Sullivan* (see Chapter 3), Chief Justice William Rehnquist stated that "in the world of debate about public affairs," caustic assaults, tasteless commentary, and even certain "falsehoods" are "inevitable"; although the requirement that plaintiffs demonstrate "reckless disregard" in addition to falsity may be stringent, constitutionally protected speech—however questionable its "value"—enjoys "adequate 'breathing' space" in a political forum.

tional distress in order for it to be compensable. Increasingly, however, the courts find extreme distress by itself to be grounds for awarding damages.

This tort can become an issue in employee relations. In the following case, a former employee sued for infliction of emotional distress as well as invasion of privacy, assault, and battery.

ROGERS v. LOEWS L'ENFANT PLAZA HOTEL
U.S. District Court, District of Columbia, 526 F. Supp. 523
(1981)

The plaintiff, Norma Rogers, was hired as assistant manager of the Greenhouse Restaurant located within the defendant hotel in September of 1979. Soon after her hiring, James Deavers, the restaurant manager, engaged her in a continuous course of sexually suggestive verbal and written conduct. Although Rogers met each of his advances with refusal, Deavers persisted for a two month period both at work and when she was off duty. When it was absolutely clear that Rogers was not going to yield to him, Deavers retaliated by employing various tactics, including exclusion of Rogers from staff meetings, abusive language, and refusal to cooperate with her on important business matters.

Due to Deaver's conduct and as the result of the lax attitude taken by the Hotel's Management in resolving the problem, Norma Rogers now seeks recovery against the defendants, Loews L'Enfant Plaza Hotel and Deavers, for the torts of intentional infliction of emotional distress, invasion of privacy, and assault and battery.

Joyce Hens Green, District Judge.
  Right to Privacy: . . .
  Plaintiff has alleged in this case that defendant Deavers called her at home, as well as at work when he was off duty, and that he made leering comments about plaintiff's personal and sexual life to her. . . .
  Cases involving persistent and unwanted telephone calls, as alleged here, where invasion of privacy has been found, have generally concerned calls by debt collectors. This situation is analogous, and since tort law exists "to protect citizens from other citizens" where "intrusion is not reasonably expected," it is sufficient for the purposes of this motion to dismiss to find that invasion of plaintiff's privacy as alleged in the pleadings could be such a violation of her right of privacy, constituting a tort for which she may recover damages to the extent that it can be proved. Although in most circumstances it is obviously not an intrusion to call someone at home, or even at his/her place of business, in this particular situation, with allegations of sexual harassment in personal, as well as professional life, under the standards to be followed in determining whether to dismiss a claim, the pleadings are sufficient to indicate an intrusion into a sphere from which plaintiff Rogers could reasonably expect that defendant Deavers should be ex-

cluded. Defendant's motion to dismiss plaintiff's claim of invasion of privacy must, therefore, be denied.
  Assault & Battery:. . . .
  To constitute the tort of assault, the apprehension must be one which would normally be aroused in the mind of a reasonable person and apparent ability and opportunity to carry out the threat immediately must be present. The mental injury which results could include, for example, fright or humiliation. Here, plaintiff Rogers has asserted that she was frightened and embarrassed by defendant Deavers' actions, and was put in imminent apprehension of an offensive contact even though, or especially because, they were in a public restaurant, and she was attempting to perform her duties of employment.
  . . . Plaintiff alleges that although she expressed to defendant Deavers that his suggestions and advances were distressful and unwanted, he continued to engage in that conduct. In construing plaintiff's pleadings as required in a motion to dismiss, plaintiff has made adequate claims to defeat a motion to dismiss her assault cause of action.
  To constitute the tort of battery, a defendant can be found liable for any physical contact with the plaintiff which is offensive or insulting, as well as physically harmful. Of primary importance in such a cause of action is the absence of consent to the contact on the part of the plaintiff, rather than the hostile intent of the defendant, although intent is required. The intent, however, is only the intent "to bring about such a contact."
  Here, clearly, an absence of consent has been asserted, since plaintiff specifically told Deavers that his advances were unwanted. Plaintiff also recites a touching, which included pulling her hair, and that Deavers intended to bring about this conduct. These allegations are sufficient to survive the motion to dismiss as to the battery claim.
  Infliction of Emotional Distress:
  Plaintiff's third and final tort claim, infliction of emotional distress, can result from either intentional or negligent conduct. Negligent infliction of emotional distress, recognized in the District of Columbia, requires a physical injury, whereas intentional infliction of emotional distress, also recognized in the District of Columbia, allows recovery in the absence of physical impact. Since plaintiff has alleged only intentional tortious acts in her complaint, only intentional infliction of emotional distress will be considered.

Clark v. Associated Retail Credit Men (1939), the "landmark case in this jurisdiction" states that:

> The law does not, and doubtless should not, impose a general duty of care to avoid causing mental distress. [However] one who, without just cause or excuse, and beyond all the bounds of decency, purposely causes a disturbance of another's mental and emotional tranquility of so acute a nature that harmful physical consequences might be not unlikely to result, is subject to liability in damages for such mental and emotional disturbance even though no demonstrable physical consequences actually ensue.

For a prima facie case to be made out, the tortfeasor's conduct must be "wanton, outrageous in the extreme, or especially calculated to cause serious mental distress." *Shewmaker v. Minchew* [(1980)] . . . Severe emotional distress must have occurred and the conduct must have been intentional.

> Of course, subjective intent can rarely by proven directly; therefore, the requisite intent must be inferred, either from the very outrageousness of the defendant's acts or, for example, when the circumstances are such that "any reasonable person would have known that [emotional distress and physical harm] would result. . . . " *Id.*

In her complaint, the plaintiff has clearly alleged conditions and circumstances which are beyond mere insults, indignities and petty oppressions and which, if proved, could be construed as outrageous. Emotional distress and physical harm could reasonably result from the conduct of Deavers, as stated, as well as from the conduct of the Hotel management in response to plaintiff's plight. A cause of action for intentional infliction of emotional distress does, therefore, lie.

. . . .

. . . Should plaintiff prove her allegations, her right to damages, including punitive damages, from all defendants will exist.

In the District of Columbia, punitive damages, which are awarded to punish and deter outrageous conduct, can be recovered for willful tort actions which are founded on the defendant's "outrageous conduct such as maliciousness, wantonness, gross fraud, recklessness and willful disregard of another's rights." As to an employer, "although most jurisdictions hold to the contrary, in the District of Columbia plaintiff is entitled to punitive damages only if he is able to show that the corporation, through its officers and directors, either participated in the wrongful act or ratified the conduct." Plaintiff has alleged reckless, willful and malicious disregard of her rights by all defendants. She has further alleged that the Hotel management knew of Deavers' conduct and harassment of other women and that by its lack of action, in esence, silent acquiescence, condoned the behavior. Such allegations, if proven by plaintiff, could entitle her to punitive damages. Of course, here as in all other such cases, whether plaintiff received punitive damages would be determined solely by the jury, which may decide to reject such award. Defendants' motion to dismiss will be denied.

Case Questions

1. Did the court decide that the plaintiff was entitled to judgment in her favor for infliction of emotional distress?

2. What is the primary distinction between negligent infliction of emotional distress, recognized only in certain jurisdictions, and intentional infliction of emotional distress?

3. If there is no real way to show one's actual subjective intent to cause emotional distress, how can intent be shown?

Other Intentional Torts

There are dozens of other intentional torts recognized by the law. Here are brief descriptions of three torts related to business management.

intentional interference with contractual arrangements Tort in which an individual seeking to advance his own interests causes a plaintiff or third party to breach a contract

INTERFERENCE WITH CONTRACTUAL RELATIONS. **Intentional interference with contractual relations** is an important intentional tort. A defendant may be held liable for the consequences under the following circumstances: He knows of a contract between the plaintiff and a third party; he interferes with it intentionally, seeking to advance his own interests; and he therefore causes the plaintiff or the third party to breach the contract or to lose the rights or profits under it. The defendant's act need not be malicious but it must be intentional; *negligently* interfering with another's contract is not tortious.

Defendants bear the burden of justifying their acts, and justifications may be moral or economic. Interference is not justified, however, by a mere desire to steal another's customers or obtain a competitive advantage.

Interference with contractual relations is a potentially costly tort: A multibillion dollar damage award levied against Texaco in 1987 arose out of Texaco's interference with an agreement between Pennzoil and Getty Oil.

WRONGFUL USE OF TRADE SECRETS.   Wrongful use of a competitor's trade secret is also an intentional tort. A **trade secret** is, above all, *secret*: It is separated from information available to the general public. Although a trade secret need not be patented, it must be relatively novel and must give its holder a competitive advantage. Trade secrets include computer programs, formulas, and patterns. Liability arises when a trade secret is wrongfully obtained, usually through a breach of contract or confidence or spying.

Many trade-secret cases involve claims by employers against former employees. Employees cannot be held liable for making use of the skills or general knowledge that they acquired at a previous job. However, they may not make use of confidential information or other forms of property that qualify as trade secrets.

ECONOMIC RETALIATION.   Although people have the right to exercise their economic power to further their own interests, they may not use it to compel someone to commit an illegal act or to forfeit a right. The tort of **economic retaliation** permits a plaintiff to recover economic losses that result when a defendant retaliates against him for exercising a legal right. This tort generally reflects public-policy interests, such as the interest in a safe, honest workplace or in decent housing. For example, an employer may not threaten to fire an employee for filing a workers' compensation claim or for refusing to violate a law. (See *Flesner v. Technical Communications Corp.*, Chapter 13, pp. 455–458.) Landlords may also be held liable for threatening to evict tenants who assert their legal rights or report housing, fire, or health-code violations.

Defenses to Intentional Torts

The law provides specific lines of defense for each kind of intentional tort. Two of the more widely used defenses are privilege and consent.

PRIVILEGE.   Privilege is a special exemption from liability for allegedly tortious behavior. Privileges, which may be either *absolute* or *conditional*, are granted to individuals or corporations fulfilling important public functions in order to protect them from liability for acts related to those functions. For example, police officers are privileged to make arrests without warrants if they have reasonable grounds for believing that a felony has been committed and that the person arrested committed it. This privilege protects them from the tort of false arrest even when the suspect turns out to be innocent and no felony has been committed. It allows the police to protect the public more effectively.

Absolute Privileges. If **absolute privilege** is granted, defendants are immune from all liability regardless of motive or purpose. Consider the tort of defamation. Justice demands that all participants in a trial be able to speak and make judgments freely and without fear of consequences. Therefore, everyone involved in a trial (judges, jurors, witnesses, lawyers, plaintiffs, defendants) has an absolute privilege against liability for defamation as long as allegedly defamatory statements are relevant to the case. Of course, anyone who provides false testimony can be prosecuted for perjury. Society's interest in justice outweighs the individual interest in preserving a reputation.

Absolute privilege also extends to people entering another person's land for the purpose of averting public disaster. For example, people fighting a large fire threatening many homes may destroy one person's house in the interest of

trade secret   Confidential information that gives a firm a competitive advantage

economic retaliation   *Intentional tort* in which a defendant acts with economic consequences against a plaintiff who has exercised a legal right

privilege   Exemption from liability for an intentional tort granted to individuals and corporations fulfilling important public functions

absolute privilege   Immunity from all liability for an intentional tort granted regardless of motive or purpose

saving many houses. The same principle allows a person to kill another's rabid dog in the interest of protecting the public.

Conditional Privileges. Most privileges are only *conditional privileges:* Immunity is granted only when a defendant has acted in good faith. Self-defense is an example of a conditional privilege. This privilege applies to situations in which people reasonably believe that they are under attack and use reasonable force to protect themselves. It does not shield defendants from liability if they use excessive force. A force calculated to kill or severely wound an attacker is deemed excessive unless it is based on a reasonable fear of severe injury or death and no safe retreat is available. Force exerted after the danger has passed is also deemed excessive. Thus, it is unlawful to inflict a beating on an attacker who has already been repulsed.

consent Voluntary agreement, implied or expressed, by one party to an activity that exempts another party from liability for any damage or injury caused

CONSENT. The defense of **consent** operates on the theory that a person who has agreed to some activity cannot receive damages for an injury thereby incurred. For example, suppose two men engage in a wrestling match and one man's arm is unintentionally broken by his opponent: The opponent is protected from a charge of battery because the injured man voluntarily agreed to wrestle.

Criteria for Consent. Consent may be implied as well as expressed. For instance, surgery performed without the patient's consent is generally considered to be a battery. In an emergency, however, when the patient is unconscious or irrational and any delay would endanger his life, consent to the surgery is implied and the physician can proceed without liability.

informed consent Defense of intentional tort based on a voluntary agreement made after receiving full disclosure of potential risk

INFORMED CONSENT. Consent is not a defense when a wrongdoer deliberately takes advantage of another person's ignorance. For example, suppose a man gives a box of poisoned candy to a woman. The woman voluntarily eats a piece and is made ill. The woman's consent does not shield the man if he knows that the candy was poisoned. This principle of **informed consent** is especially important in medical malpractice cases: In order to obtain a patient's valid informed consent, a doctor must fully explain a proposed treatment, disclosing its risks. Consent must also be voluntary; it is not valid if given under *duress*.

■ *Concept Check 10-2 Intentional Torts*

- Distinguish between *battery* and *assualt* and describe a case in which one may occur without the other.
- Describe a criminal action that may also involve the tort of *false imprisonment.*
- Define *defamation, slander,* and *libel* and describe the distinctions among them.
- Discuss a well-known case in which the defense of *constitutional privilege* for the press was applied.
- Describe a case in which *interference with contractual relations* occurs.
- Distinguish between *absolute* and *conditional privileges.*

■ NEGLIGENT TORTS

Intentional torts reflect the principle that people should not deliberately injure each other. The law also recognizes, however, that people should not injure others through *carelessness.* The tort that addresses this issue is the tort of negligence. Negligence has developed into the dominant cause of action for accidental injury. (The well-known negligent-tort lawyer Melvin Belli is the subject of this chapter's PERSONAL PROFILE box.)

According to Section 282 of the *Restatement (Second) of Torts*, **negligence** includes any "conduct which falls below the standard established by law for the protection of others against unreasonable risk of harm." The standard of conduct for adults is that of a reasonable person under like circumstances.

Negligent behavior creates a situation in which people are subjected to the risk of injury. In order to prove negligence, a plaintiff must demonstrate the existence of these four elements: (1) the existence of a legal *duty of care* owed by the defendant to the plaintiff, (2) the *breach* of that duty, (3) *actual injuries*, and (4) a *close causal connection* between the defendant's conduct and the plaintiff's injuries. To establish causal connection, two determinations must be made: "actual" or "cause in fact," and "proximate" or "legal cause."

negligence Any conduct that falls below the standard in law to protect others against unreasonable risk of harm

Duty of Care

Negligence is not simply a matter of careless behavior. People can behave as carelessly as they like without being held liable unless they owe another person some *duty*. Before there can be an act of negligence, the defendant must have some legally recognized obligation to behave responsibly toward the plaintiff—that is, some **duty of care.** This does not mean that the defendant must be acquainted with the plaintiff. For example, driving a car involves a duty to drive carefully in order to protect the general public. You may be liable for injuring a total stranger if you drive carelessly. The law limits the scope of the duty of care by applying the *reasonable-person standard.*

duty of care The legally recognized obligation of one person to another to behave responsibly

THE REASONABLE PERSON STANDARD. The **reasonable person standard** is an objective one: A reasonable person is expected to consider the foreseeable harm caused by an act and either attempt to minimize it or refrain from acting. A reasonable person thus weighs the risks of his behavior with the need or desire to engage in it.

It is important to keep in mind that the reasonable person is a *model* of a person who is always prudent, always careful, and never has unexplained behavioral lapses. Although the reasonable person may have human shortcomings and weaknesses, they are limited to those that the community is willing to tolerate on some specific occasion. For example, a reasonable person may have his attention drawn away from the road while driving, but only for a specific reason, such as the glare of the sun. The reasonable person in the standard is never distracted because he is having a bad day. In fact, jurors are instructed *not* to make decisions based on what *they* would have done in the defendant's place.

Note that this standard takes into account the defendant's physical disabilities—for example, blindness or deafness. A reasonable blind person will act differently from a reasonable sighted one. Thus, the standard is sufficiently flexible to deal with the vagaries of human behavior.

reasonable-person standard Measure of conduct for *negligence* whereby a reasonable person is expected to consider an act's foreseeable harm and try to minimize it or not act at all

Breach of Duty

A **breach of duty** is a failure to act (1) in the manner that a reasonable person would act under the same or similar circumstances or (2) a failure to act when it is necessary to protect or help another person. Determining what constitutes breaches of legal duty in negligence cases is a subject of great controversy.

breach of duty In *negligence* claims, the failure to exercise a reasonable person's duty of care either through acts of omission or violation of professional standards of care

California native Melvin M. Belli was born in 1907. While in high school, he discovered he had a natural gift for speaking. Contrary to what one might think from the long career and prestigious client list of the so-called "King of Torts," he did not grow up intending to be a lawyer. He graduated from the University of California at Berkeley in 1925 but did not get his law degree until 1933.

At that time—in the midst of the Great Depression—it was difficult to get a job at a law firm. Consequently, the enterprising Belli got a job as an undercover agent for the National Recovery Administration. His work involved posing as a hobo and riding the railroad, and it was during this time that he developed the strong feeling for the underdog that has been the focus of his career. Belli went on to become one of the most famous litigators of this century. During the 1940s and 1950s, many of his cases involved the application of warranty law. This work evolved into the consumer and class-action suits that are so common today.

His courtroom style revolutionized the presentation of courtroom evidence in both civil and criminal cases. In addition to his personal flamboyant style—suits lined with red silk and hand-fitted cowboy boots—Belli's technique in-

Melvin Belli. On November 4, 1979, a group of Iranian students, acting in support of the new fundamentalist government of the Ayatollah Ruholla Khomeini, seized over 60 American hostages at the U.S. Embassy in Teheran. The hostages were ultimately released in 1981. In January of that year, Belli announced that despite a guarantee made by the U.S. government, he had been retained by families of some of the hostages to sue the Iranian government for damages. "I would like to sue Khomeini himself," said Belli, "but I think you're limited to suing the government."

volves using demonstrative evidence which, according to Belli, allows jurors to learn through all of their senses rather than just their sense of hearing. Belli accidentally learned the value of dramatic presentations early in his career. While defending a San Quentin inmate who had murdered a fellow inmate, Belli tripped and dropped a drawer full of knives and other weapons that had been confiscated from other convicts who had lived in the same area of the prison. The jury was quite startled: The verdict upheld Belli's contention that the defendant had acted in self-defense.

Perhaps his most notable criminal case was his defense of Jack Ruby, the man who shot President John F. Kennedy's alleged assassin, Lee Harvey Oswald. The murder took place on live television two days after Kennedy's death. The crux of Belli's defense was that Ruby was temporarily insane as the result of "some kind of blackout" caused by psychomotor epilepsy. Although he lost the case, Belli's name became a household word.

Belli's civil cases also run the gamut—from the 1950s case filed on behalf of seventy-nine persons who contracted polio from a defective batch of polio vaccine produced by Cutter Laboratories, to the 1980s cases involving the tobacco industry and the poison gas leak caused by a defect at a Union Carbide insecticide plant in Bophal, India (see the INTERNATIONAL ENVIRONMENT box in this chapter), to the 1991 toxic pesticide spill in the Sacramento River caused by a train derailment near Dunsmuir, California. His contention that plaintiffs need not prove negligence because of the res ipsa loquitor doctrine—a presumption of negligence that requires defendants to prove that they were not negligent—helped change the face of civil litigation.

Breach of duty pertains to professionals and nonprofessionals. Under what constitutes breach of duty, *acts of omission* apply to both of these groups. An act of omission concerns the consequences that follow an action undertaken *gratuitously*—that is, without a legal duty to perform such action. Professional standards and liability only apply to professionals. There is a legal duty that professionals, such as accountants, owe to their clients and to third parties who could reasonably be expected to rely on their work. For example, accountants are liable for the actions of third parties who invest in a company on the basis of the audited figures published in that company's annual report.

ACTS OF OMISSION. There is no legal duty to come to the aid of a stranger. There must be some preexisting relationship between the plaintiff and the defendant in order for there to be a positive legal obligation to act. Thus, landlords have a legal duty to supply heat to the tenants in their buildings, physicians have a legal duty to continue to treat their patients, and people operating a train have a legal duty to blow a whistle or apply the brakes when it is appropriate. If these people fail to carry out these actions, they may be liable for negligence.

When there is no preexisting relationship between the plaintiff and the defendant, the defendant does not have any legal obligation to act. For instance, although physicians must continue to treat people who are already under their care, they are under no obligation to treat anyone else, including strangers dying on the street.

Case: Good Samaritans. There is a sharp distinction between the *legal* and *moral* obligations to act. It is most clearly seen in "Good-Samaritan" situations: When someone is injured, an observer may have a moral obligation to help but not necessarily a legal one. The law has persistently refused to impose on a stranger the moral obligation to go to the aid of another human being who is in danger. For example, an expert swimmer has no *legal* obligation to rescue a drowning child.

The *voluntary* offer of aid, however, *creates* the kind of relationship that entails legal duties. Thus, well-meaning people who try to help strangers, even when there is no legal obligation to do so, open themselves to torts for negligence: If one helps, one owes a duty of reasonable care in so doing. Good Samaritans can be held liable if they inadvertently make a situation worse and increase the danger, if they mislead a person into believing that the danger is gone, or if they deprive someone of help from other sources.

Efforts to Change the Law. The current legal situation actually discourages people from helping one another. Some state legislatures, however, have made an effort to change the law. Some states have imposed a positive duty to render aid; others have exempted certain classes of people, such as doctors, from liability for negligence when they volunteer to help strangers.

There has also been a trend in the courts to expand the number and kinds of preexisting relationships that impose positive duties. For example, judicial decisions have held that hotel operators and guests, ship captains and seamen, and employers and employees have relationships that carry this type of legal obligation.

PROFESSIONAL STANDARDS AND LIABILITY. The doctrine of the reasonable person takes into account the knowledge, training, and skills possessed by defendants. The reasonable-person concept assumes a special status in cases involving defendants who are professional persons. In such cases, a defendant is held to possess at least the minimum knowledge and skills required to be a member of his profession.

Case: Accountant Liability. Accountants are professionals, held to professional standards of care in performing their services. This does not mean that they are expected to be infallible, and it is commonly said that accountants are not *insurers*. It does mean, however, that they must serve their clients prudently, in good faith, and in accordance with at least minimum codes of professional conduct. In recent years, civil and criminal actions against accountants and accounting firms for breaching their professional duties, willfully or carelessly, have increased dramatically. (For the response of major U.S. accounting firms to this changing environment, *see* the ORGANIZATIONAL PROFILE box in this chapter.)

Accountants who violate standards of care or morality may be criminally liable for their actions under the Securities Acts of 1933 and 1934, which prohibit knowingly making false statements, or conspiring with or inducing others to make false statements, in connection with the issuance or sale of securities. Although these provisions have been in effect for fifty years, they have only recently been used against accountants in criminal cases. In 1969, for example, a case brought by the government against a major accounting firm held that conscious nondisclosure by a firm of relevant information could constitute criminal fraud (*United States v. Simon*, 425 F.2d 796). Figure 10-1 summarizes the legal exposure of accountants under the Securities Act of 1933 and the Securities Exchange Act of 1934.

Breach of Contract and Negligence. Accountants may also be held liable in civil actions for breach of contract or negligence. Most civil actions brought against accountants are negligence actions alleging a violation of professional codes of conduct. Accountants (and/or their firms) may be held liable for such lapses as disclosing confidential information, overlooking evidence of fraud, giving incorrect tax advice, or incompetent financial management.

Liability extends to clients as well as to any third parties whom the accountants knew or should have known would rely on his work. General principles of negligence apply in these cases: Damages are limited to injuries that are the proximate results of the breach and also by plaintiff's contributory negligence.

This duty was explained and adopted by the New Jersey Supreme Court in the following case.

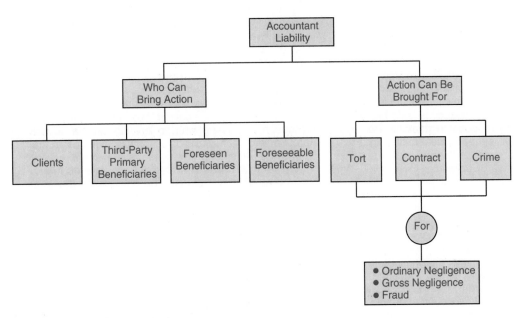

FIGURE 10-1 Legal Exposure of Accountants

ROSENBLUM v. ADLER
New Jersey Supreme Court, 461 A.2d 138 (1983)

Giant Corporation undertook negotiations with Harry and Barry Rosenblum beginning November 9, 1971, for the acquisition of their two New Jersey businesses. Pursuant to a formal merger drawn up on March 9, 1972, the Rosenblums, largely on the strength of a pair of audits performed by the reputable accounting firm of Touche, Ross, and Co., agreed to take a percentage of Giant stock in consideration for the merger. Each of these audits, the first of which was issued in connection with a large public offering of Giant stock on December 14, 1971, and the second of which was issued on April 18, 1971, portrayed Giant as a stable corporation and bore attached statements by Touche attesting to their reliability. However, in early 1973 it was discovered that Giant had fraudulently represented its financial status, thus making the 1971 and 1972 Touche audits inaccurate. As a result, all of the Giant stock held by the Rosenblums had become worthless.

The Rosenblums brought suit against Touche for negligence due to the misrepresentation of Giant's financial position as stated in the 1971 and 1972 audits. Both the trial court and the intermediate appellate court dismissed the defendant from liability with regard to the 1971 audit but found it liable as to the 1972 audit. The case is now on appeal to the New Jersey Supreme Court.

Schreiber, J.

This case focuses upon the issue of whether accountants should be responsible for their negligence in auditing financial statements. If so, we must decide whether a duty is owed to those with whom the auditor is in privity [i.e., had a contractual relationship with], to third persons known and intended by the auditor to be the recipients of the audit, and to those who foreseeably might rely on the audit. Subsumed within these questions is a more fundamental one: to what extent does public policy justify imposition of a duty to any of these classes?

. . . .

A claim against the auditor is realistically one predicated upon his representations. Though the theory advanced here by the plaintiffs is directed to the service performed by accountants and thus is in the nature of malpractice, their claim can be viewed as grounded in negligent misrepresentation. In the complaint the plaintiffs seek recompense for economic loss from a negligent supplier of a service with whom the claimants are not in privity. It has generally been held with respect to accountants that imposition of liability requires a privity or privity-like relationship between the claimant and the negligent actor. . . .

. . .

It is clear that an action for negligence with respect to an injury arising out of a defective product may be maintained without privity. The negligence involved may be that ascribable to negligent misrepresentation.

. . .

Why should a claim of negligent misrepresentation

be barred in the absence of privity when no such limit is imposed where the plaintiff's claim also sounds in tort . . . ? The maker of the product and the person making a written representation with intent that it be relied upon are, respectively, impliedly holding out that the product is reasonably fit, suitable and safe and that the representation is reasonably sufficient, suitable and accurate. The fundamental issue is whether there should be any duty to respond in damages for economic loss owed to a foreseeable user neither in privity with the declarant nor intended by the declarant to be the user of the statement or opinion.

. . . .

. . . It is now well recognized that the audited statements are made for the use of third parties who have no contractual relationship with the auditor. Moreover, it is common knowledge that companies use audits for many proper business purposes, such as submission to banks and other lending institutions that might advance funds and to suppliers of services and goods that might advance credit. The SEC twenty-five years ago stated: "The responsibility of a public accountant is not only to the client who pays his fee, but also to investors, creditors and others who may rely on the financial statements which he certifies." . . .

. . .

When the independent auditor furnishes an opinion with no limitation in the certificate as to whom the company may disseminate the financial statements, he has a duty to all those whom that auditor should reasonably foresee as recipients from the company of the statements for its proper business purposes, provided that the recipients rely on the statements pursuant to those business purposes. . . .

. . .

A. The 1971 Audit

Both the trial court and the Appellate Division ruled that the plaintiffs claim based on negligent preparation of the 1971 audit could not be sustained because the accountants were not aware at the time the audit was prepared of the existence of the plaintiffs or of a limited class of which the plaintiffs were members. The defendant's audit had been completed on April 16, 1971 and Giant's merger discussions with the plaintiff did not begin until the following September. Therefore the defendants had no knowledge of the Rosenblums or the prospective merger at the time of the preparation of the audit and there could be no liability. . . .

. . .

When the defendants prepared the Giant audit, they knew or should have known that Giant would probably use the audited figures for many proper business purposes. They knew that it was to be incorporated in Giant's annual report, a report that would be transmitted to each Giant stockholder, and would be filed with the SEC in conjunction with Giant's proxy solicitation material for its annual stockholder meeting. The defendants also knew or should have known that the audited financial statements would be available and useful for other proper business purposes, such as public offerings of securities, credit, and corporate acquisitions.

These were clearly foreseeable potential uses of the audited financials at the time of their preparation. Giant and the defendant auditors knew that these financial statements would be used at least until the next financial statements had been audited and released.

. . . .

Defendant's ignorance of the precise use to which the statements would be put does not eliminate their obligation. . . . There was no limitation in the accountants' opinion. They could reasonably expect that their client would distribute the statements in furtherance of matters relating to its business. Having inserted the audit in that economic stream, the defendants should be responsible for their careless misrepresentations to parties who justifiably relied upon their expert opinions.

. . . Under these circumstances, the courts below erred in striking the cause of action predicated on the negligent auditing of the financial data for the year ending January 30, 1971.

B. The 1972 Audit

. . . The defendants contend that the plaintiffs had already signed and were bound by the merger contract executed on March 9, 1972 at the time the audit was issued in April 1972. Therefore, the defendants argue that there could be no causal relationship between defendants' alleged fraud and negligence and the plaintiffs' damage. . . .

Irrespective of whether the defendants had actual knowledge of Giant's proposed use of the 1972 audit in connection with the merger, it was reasonably foreseeable that Giant would use the audited statement in connection with the merger and its consummation. This is particularly so since the defendants were familiar with the merger agreement and had been engaged by Giant to audit the books and records of the plaintiffs' enterprises for the purpose of the merger. The trial court properly denied defendants' motion.

The judgment granting defendants' motion for partial summary judgment with respect to the 1971 financial statements is reversed and that denying defendants' motion for partial summary judgment with respect to the 1972 financial statements is affirmed. The case is remanded to the trial court for further proceedings consistent with this opinion.

Case Questions

1. What reality of modern business is behind the court's decision? Is the decision simply a response to common practice?

2. What is "privity" and how important is this concept for accountant liability after Rosenblum?

3. What principle are accountants governed by after Rosenblum?

Table 10-1 briefly explains the key cases in the expansion of accountant liability, and Figure 10-2 illustrates the resultant expansion in potential plaintiffs who may bring suit against accountants on the grounds of negligence.

TABLE 10-1	*Key Cases in the Expansion of Accountant Liability*

CASE AND DATE	HOLDING
Landell v. Lybrand (1919)	Parties not in privity cannot hold an accountant liable for negligence; fraud must be proved.
Ultramares v. Touche (1931)	Although liability for fraud can be inferred from gross negligence (i.e., negligence so gross that it amounts to fraud), third parties can claim negligence only if identified as primary beneficiaries when the audit is performed.
Rusch Factors v. Levin (1968)	Lessened the importance of *Ultramares:* Auditors are responsible to "foreseen and limited classes" when ordinary negligence is proved; third parties need not be identified as primary beneficiaries.
RI Hospital Trust National Bank v. Swartz (1972)	An accountant can be held liable for ordinary negligence by foreseeable parties even if a disclaimer has been issued.
Bonhiver v. Graff (1976)	Weakened *Ultramares:* A state commissioner of insurance, acting as general agent for an insurance company, could act as a third party in holding the company's accountants liable.
White v. Guarante (1977)	Weakened *Ultramares:* One partner in a limited tax shelter can hold accountants auditing a company liable for negligence.
Rosenblum v. Adler (1983)	Weakened *Ultramares:* Applied the standard of foreseeability to accountants for the first time.
Citizens State Bank v. Timm, Schmidt (1983)	Weakened *Ultramares:* A negligent accountant may be fully liable for all foreseeable consequences not limited by "policy factors."
Credit Alliance v. Andersen (1985)	Confirmed *Ultramares:* An auditor could not be held liable by a third party because no contractual relationship of privity could be found.

Source: Information adapted from Wanda A. Wallace, *Auditing*, 2nd ed. (Boston: PWS-Kent, 1991).

Actual Injury

Negligent conduct alone is not tortious: In order to incur liability, the negligence must cause some actual loss or damage. Nominal damages that vindicate technical rights are not available in negligence actions in the same way that they are in cases involving intentional torts. The purpose of awarding damages in negligence cases is to compensate the plaintiff for injuries suffered, not to punish the defendant. Courts may, however, act preventively in negligence cases: If an irreparable injury is threatened, a court of equity can issue an injunction to prevent the harm before it occurs.

Causal Connection

The final element in an action for negligence is a close causal connection between the defendant's conduct and the injury that occurred. Although *causation* seems to be a fairly simple concept, it raises considerable practical difficulties because there is no precise legal definition of causation. In fact, the chain of causation may be endless.

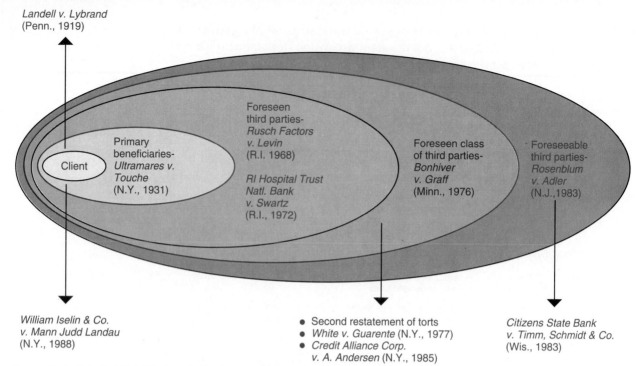

Landell v. Lybrand
(Penn., 1919)

Client

Primary
beneficiaries-
*Ultramares v.
Touche*
(N.Y., 1931)

Foreseen
third parties-
*Rusch Factors
v. Levin*
(R.I. 1968)

*RI Hospital Trust
Natl. Bank
v. Swartz*
(R.I., 1972)

Foreseen class
of third parties-
*Bonhiver
v. Graff*
(Minn., 1976)

Foreseeable
third parties-
*Rosenblum
v. Adler*
(N.J.,1983)

*William Iselin & Co.
v. Mann Judd Landau*
(N.Y., 1988)

● Second restatement of torts
● *White v. Guarente* (N.Y., 1977)
● *Credit Alliance Corp.
v. A. Andersen* (N.Y., 1985)

*Citizens State Bank
v. Timm, Schmidt & Co.*
(Wis., 1983)

FIGURE 10-2 Potential Plaintiffs in Suits for Accountant Negligence   *Source: Wanda A. Wallace,* Auditing, *2nd ed. (Boston: PWS-Kent, 1991). Prepared by Jagdish Gangolly, California State Univ. at Fuller-
ton and State Univ. of New York at Albany. Used by permission.*

Consider, for example, the case of a woman involved in a traffic accident.
Did her husband cause the accident by breaking the coffee machine, depriving
her of her morning coffee so that her concentration was reduced, and making
her late for work so that she had to speed? What about the truck involved? Is
the real cause of the accident the worker who failed to close the truck's tailgate
properly so that it popped open in traffic, spilling the truck's contents onto the
road? Where should the law draw a line? Who should be held responsible for
causing the accident?

The determination depends on the following questions: Would the injury
not have occurred but for the defendant's action? Is it fair to hold the defendant
legally responsible for all of the harmful effects of his actions? If not, how far
does the defendant's responsibility extend?

CAUSE IN FACT.   **Cause in fact** asks whether the injury would have occurred even
without the defendant's negligent conduct. The question can be stated: "*But for*
the defendant's conduct, would the injury have occurred?" The defendant is
not held liable for negligence that did not actually contribute to an injury. For
example, suppose a sailor falls overboard in a heavy storm and drowns. There
were no lifeboats on board. The company owning the boat was negligent because it failed to provide lifeboats. It was not liable in the sailor's death, however, because no lifeboat could have been launched in such a heavy storm. The
sailor would have drowned even if a lifeboat had been available.

The exception to this rule is the case in which there are *two* forces acting
independently, *each* of which would have been sufficient to bring about the
harm. The classic example of this involves two unrelated fires that merge before burning down some property. Either fire alone would have done the damage. In a strict sense, the injury would have happened even had one of the two

cause in fact   Test for
determining liability by asking
whether an injury would have
occurred without the defendant's
negligence

370

PART THREE   REGULATING PRIVATE BUSINESS CONDUCT AND CRIME

In recent years, the entire accounting profession has paid a great deal of attention to professional responsibility. Professional responsibility is a function of the corporate culture. It permeates the firm's standards, ethics, and educational development.

The accounting profession has attempted to regulate itself through professional licensing and standards developed by the American Institute of Certified Public Accountants (AICPA). The "Big Six" accounting firms—that is, the six U.S. firms with the most billable hours—have been particularly active in this area. The six firms in this category are Price Waterhouse, Deloitte & Touche, Coopers & Lybrand, KPMG Peat Marwick, Ernst & Young, and Arthur Anderson. Each of them represents a large list of clients and maintains offices all over the world.

In 1978, AICPA instituted a peer-review program under which each participating firm's system of quality control for its accounting and auditing practice is scrutinized by another firm. In 1990, Price Waterhouse became the first accounting firm to receive a perfect score on a peer review of compliance with AICPA standards.

Price Waterhouse recognizes employee initiative by choosing three quarterly winners in its Client Service Awards program. The prize winners are chosen on the basis of how well they know their clients' accounting policies and procedures and how effectively they apply that knowledge to help clients achieve their goals. Designed to foster professional responsibility, the program also makes it obvious that professionalism and integrity are increasingly important elements of Price Waterhouse corporate climate.

Coopers & Lybrand emphasizes similar goals. That firm asks its auditors to be attuned to the company, industry, and economy in which each client functions. It also stresses the importance of meeting generally accepted professional and ethical standards. Arthur Anderson is another firm that recognizes that meeting changes in the business environment is an essential part of its corporate mandate.

In short, each of the Big Six firms recognizes that it has increased responsibility for meeting the professional and ethical standards set for its industry. Additionally, of course, higher standards must also be met in an evolving global marketplace.

fires not been set negligently. In this case, a broader test of causation is applied: There is liability if the act of negligence is a *substantial* factor in bringing about the injury.

PROXIMATE CAUSE. **Proximate cause** puts negligent conduct into a broader context by considering *all* the causes contributing to an injury. The goal of the proximate-cause test is to limit legal responsibility to those actions which were likely to cause injury and which were, in fact, *significant* causes of it. The theory of proximate cause recognizes that a whole series of events—including multiple acts of negligence—may have contributed to the ultimate injury. It is not necessary for a defendant's negligent action to be the sole cause of an injury—or even the predominant cause—in order for the defendant to be held liable.

One important element of proximate cause is *foreseeability*: Could the defendant reasonably foresee the injurious results of his or her actions? One landmark New York case (*Palsgraf v. Long Island Railroad Co.*, 162 N.E. 99 [1928]) raised precisely this question. The case concerned a passenger who was carrying a package while running to catch a train. Some railroad workers tried to help the passenger aboard but in the process negligently knocked the package onto the rails. The package contained fireworks that exploded and knocked over a set of scales on the platform thirty feet away. The passenger sued the railroad company for negligence. The New York Court of Appeals ruled that the railroad company was not liable. There could be no duty—and therefore no negligence—for an unforeseeable injury.

The concept of proximate cause continues to provoke debate, and there is no single test for it. *Black's Law Dictionary* sums it up as "the primary or moving cause, or that which, in a natural or continuous sequence, unbroken by an efficient intervening cause, produces the injury and without which the accident could not have happened, if the injury be one which might be reasonably an-

proximate cause In determining liability, the narrowing of *negligent actions* to those likely to have caused injury and to those who were significant causes of it

ticipated or foreseen as a natural consequence of the wrongful act." This definition includes the test for cause in fact and stresses both the importance of the negligent conduct and the foreseeability of the injury.

The INTERNATIONAL ENVIRONMENT box below focuses on a case involving a proximate-cause dispute on a multinational scale.

Defenses to Negligent Torts

Defendants in negligent tort suits have multiple lines of defense open to them. Three of the most common defenses are *contributory negligence, comparative negligence,* and *assumption of the risk.*

contributory negligence
Defense in *negligence torts* that the plaintiff's own negligence was partly responsible for the injury involved

CONTRIBUTORY NEGLIGENCE. In this standard defense, the defendant contends that the plaintiff's own negligence was partly responsible for the injury. **Contributory negligence** is conduct that falls below the standard required for a person's own protection and is thus a contributing cause of an injury.

THE INTERNATIONAL ENVIRONMENT
Union Carbide and the Bhopal Disaster

The tragic consequences of the December 2, 1984, disaster in Bhopal, India, may have changed the face of international tort law forever. It can be argued that this incident was the worst single-incident industrial accident ever reported.

The leak of insecticide from a chemical plant operated by Union Carbide, Inc., killed approximately 2500 people immediately and injured another 30,000 to 40,000 people— some irreparably. The plant was operated by an Indian affiliate of Union Carbide, Union Carbide India, Ltd. (UCIL). However, the plant was designed in the United States, and Union Carbide owned 50.9 percent of it.

At first, Union Carbide tried to avoid blame by saying that the toxic leak was probably caused by political extremists or an unhappy employee. No proof was ever offered to support these theories, and it is more likely that the leak was caused by a combination of factors, including human error, inadequate risk assessment, poor maintenance, technical failure, and the lack of community planning for the possibility of an accident at the plant.

The combination of possible causes for the disaster is a problem in and of itself because the tort system requires plaintiffs to trace causes back to the acts or omissions of responsible parties. This is nearly impossible in a case such as this one, involving thousands of victims, the laws of two sovereign states, and millions (if not billions) of dollars in damages. As a result, individual victims took a back seat to the economics and politics of the situation. They became parties to massive lawsuits. Venue and blame became the key issues of the case.

Should the case be tried in the United States because the parent company is an American company or should it be tried in India, the scene of the tragedy? Indian activists wanted the case tried in the United States in order to afford the victims the advantages of American tort law and damage awards. Remember, most of the victims were quite poor and had no other means of gaining compensation. Union Car-

bide, seeking to avoid a large dollar penalty, argued that the case should be tried in India. The American judge who heard the arguments, Judge John Keene of the District Court of New York, sent the case back to India: In essence, he found that because the plant was operated according to Indian law, and because the victims, witnesses, and documentary evidence were located there, the case should not be brought in the United States.

Although this ruling seems to make sense, it ignores one major fact: It was Union Carbide—not UCIL—that was being sued. Should not parent companies be responsible for the actions of foreign affiliates? Eventually, although India's courts determined that Union Carbide was liable for the disaster, no monetary damages were awarded to the victims until April 1988—more than four years after the leak occurred. At that time, an interlocutory decree was upheld. During that period, Union Carbide argued that it was being denied due process in the Indian court system. Finally, in February 1989, Union Carbide was ordered to pay $470 million in damages. In exchange, the company would be discharged from all future civil and criminal liability. Although the case had not made it all the way through the Indian court system, the judges felt something had to be done.

The public, however, did not agree with the ruling. Victims groups sought to have the ruling overturned on the ground that the victims were deprived of their right to the access of justice. They also argued that it was illegal to use a civil case to dismiss criminal charges.

The result of all of the controversy now finds funds from the settlement still in the bank. The victims have not seen any of it. The Supreme Court of India is deciding whether to set aside the award and to press criminal charges against the former chairman of Union Carbide and the plant managers at UCIL. Under Indian law, top management can be held personally liable for corporate negligence. However, there is no provision for punitive monetary damages.

Let us once more consider the most common problem in negligence—the traffic accident. Assume that the defendant was driving a car at sixty miles an hour in an ice storm when he smashed into the plaintiff's car as it pulled out of a driveway. Although the plaintiff demonstrates each of the required elements of actionable negligence, the defendant argues that the plaintiff was also at fault in not looking for traffic before pulling into the street: The defendant argues that the plaintiff failed to act as a reasonable person would have acted in the same or similar circumstances. In a state where contributory negligence prevails, the plaintiff's negligence would bar any recovery of damages.

Business Applications. Contributory negligence, of course, is not limited to traffic accidents. Many business-related cases revolve around it. One example is the case of a restaurant that sued a company which installed and serviced fire-extinguishing equipment that failed to operate during a fire (*Cartel Capital Corp. v. Fireco*, 410 A.2d 674 [1980]). The defense claimed contributory negligence, arguing that the restaurant negligently stored paper plates near a hot grill and allowed grease to accumulate on the walls and grill. The court decided that the restaurant's negligence might have helped cause the fire, but not the failure of the equipment to operate.

Accountants have also frequently turned to this defense when sued by clients for negligence.[2] Many of these cases concern routine company audits that fail to uncover employee embezzlement. Accountants generally assert that clients made the frauds possible by giving employees too much discretion and by improperly supervising them. Specific acts of client negligence cited have included failure to recognize discrepancies in certain records, preparing memos in pencil so that they are easy to alter, signing checks without questioning their purpose, and ignoring accountants' advice about handling petty cash.

Although these cases have had mixed results, the general trend has been to limit the use of the contributory negligence defense. As a rule, the courts have accepted this defense only when client firms actually *interfered* with accountants' ability to perform their duties or when clients acted unreasonably in not taking the accountants' advice.

COMPARATIVE NEGLIGENCE. If both plaintiff and defendant were negligent, should the defendant be freed from all liability? This question is especially disturbing when the plaintiff's negligence has been relatively minor—for example, a simple error in judgment or a brief loss of concentration. More than 40 states have turned to the defense of comparative negligence, which reduces but does not eliminate the defendant's damages when the plaintiff has also been negligent. **Comparative negligence** measures the *relative* negligence of both parties and apportions the damages accordingly. Thus, if the defendant is 60 percent responsible for an accident and the plaintiff 40 percent responsible, the defendant pays only 60 percent of the damages due.

Many states have adopted two different forms of comparative negligence: pure and partial. **Pure comparative negligence** allows a plaintiff to recover a portion of damages regardless of the level of negligence. For example, a plaintiff found to be 75 percent at fault may still collect 25 percent of his damages. **Partial comparative negligence** generally requires that the defendant be found to be at fault at least as much as or more than the plaintiff.

comparative negligence Rule of *negligence torts* that plaintiff will receive damages reduced by the amount that he or she was at fault for the injury

pure comparative negligence In *negligence torts*, principle allowing the plaintiff to recover a portion of damages regardless of the defendant's level of negligence

partial comparative negligence In *negligence torts*, principle requiring the defendant to be found at fault at least as much as or more than the plaintiff in order for damages to be recovered

---

[2]David L. Menzel, "The Defense of Contributory Negligence in Accountant's Malpractice Actions," 13 *Seton Hall Law Review* 292 (1982).

assumption of the risk Defense in *negligence torts* that the plaintiff volunteered for a risky activity and should thus be barred from recovering damages for injuries suffered

ASSUMPTION OF THE RISK. According to the doctrine of **assumption of the risk,** volunteering for a risky activity may later bar a person from recovering damages for any injuries suffered. A person can "assume" a risk and, in so doing, relieve another party of liability in one of four ways:

1. A person can expressly consent to relieve the other party of all obligation to exercise care for his protection—for example, by signing a waiver. Because a waiver is a form of consent, it must be *informed,* and as a matter of public policy, certain rights—like the right to a safe workplace—may not be considered waivable.

2. A person can voluntarily enter into a relationship that carries known risks—for example, by attending a baseball game and taking the chance of being hit by a ball.

3. A person can voluntarily continue to expose him or herself to a known risk created by another person's negligence—for example, continuing to work with equipment known to be defective.

4. A person can act so unreasonably in accepting a risk that it is tantamount to negligence—for example, accepting a ride with a drunk driver, late at night, in a car without headlights.

In the first three instances, the assumption of the risk is really a matter of *suspending* the duty owed by the defendant to the plaintiff. The last situation is essentially contributory negligence. Because of this overlay, there is a continuing controversy about whether this defense deserves an independent existence. Nevertheless, assumption of the risk is an important issue for any business involved with sports activities in which injuries are frequent and often unavoidable and pose a major liability risk.

YOU DECIDE
Assumption of the Risk

The controversy over who assumes the risk when there is an accident gains a lot of attention when the injury is incurred during a sporting event. Among other factors, the issues of contributory negligence and comparative negligence are constantly in question.

Consider this dilemma in the context of an accident that occurs during a school-sponsored sporting event. Should the school district be held responsible? Should the student be expected to know all of the risks of participating? For instance, should a student who is blinded during a game of touch football during which he wore no protective equipment assume at least partial responsibility for his injuries? Can even an experienced amateur athlete be expected to know that the risk of injury is heightened by the lack of safety equipment? Would your answer change if the student was required to take part in the game in order to get a place on the high school football team? (Rutter v. Northeastern Beaver County School District (437 A.2d 1198 [1981]).

The above situation clearly involves a voluntary relationship with known risks: Anyone who plays football is aware that he can be injured. The next scenario, however, is quite different. It involves an experienced skier who consciously chose to ski on a trail marked "most difficult." The skier noticed that other skiers were having trouble negotiating the trail, which was on an icy hill with a series of unprotected poles down the center. Nevertheless, he continued down the slope until he slid into a pole and was seriously injured. Does this injured party have grounds for initiating a negligence suit against the owner and operator of the ski slope, or did he assume the risk on his own? Did the slope operator have responsibility for warning skiers of the specific conditions on the trail, or was the posted sign enough warning? (Smith v. Seven Springs Farm, Inc. 716 F.2d 1002 [1986]).

The issue of who assumes the risk of injury takes on yet another dimension at sporting events. In Neinstein v. Los Angeles Dodgers, Inc. (185 Cal. App.3d 176, 229 Cal. Rptr. 612 [1986]), an injured spectator sued the Los Angeles Dodgers when she was struck by a foul ball. Neinstein was seated in an unscreened area of the stadium. Her argument was that team management was responsible for protecting spectators from injury from any source. Do you think that people who attend such sporting events are given such blanket protection, or do they voluntarily assume some of the risk in exchange for being at the event? Exactly what duty do sports-team owners have to patrons of their events and facilities? For further discussion, see p. 376.

- Discuss the crucial elements in a *negligent tort*.
- Explain *duty of care* by describing a case to which the *reasonable person standard* is applied.
- Describe the basic differences between *acts of omission* and torts resulting in *professional-standard* liability.
- Describe the evolution of third-party liability in cases concerning accountant duty.
- Define and distinguish between *cause in fact* and *proximate cause*.
- Define and distinguish between *contributory* and *comparative negligence*.
- Explain the doctrine of *assumption of the risk*.

■ STRICT LIABILITY IN TORT *Know*

The third type of tort assigns liability without reference to fault as a matter of social policy: Defendants are held liable even when they have not departed from a reasonable standard of care. Because strict product liability is a relatively new development and is so important to business that it merits a separate chapter (*see* Chapter 11), this section discusses only the earlier cases of strict liability. In addition, Chapter 14 will examine workers' compensation statutes, which are designed to provide compensation to employees for work-related injuries without reference to fault.

ABNORMAL DANGER. The earliest cases of strict liability held people accountable for any damages connected with abnormally dangerous activities, such as blasting at a construction site, even when they were not at fault. It is the extreme danger of the activities that justifies the courts in imposing liability. Even when conducted with the greatest prudence and care, such activities will almost inevitably lead to injuries. The defendant is held responsible simply because his activities created the abnormal danger. Social policy dictates that people who carry out dangerous activities must be prepared to compensate anyone who suffers from them—in most cases by carrying the necessary insurance. This is the only way in which society can tolerate such activities.

Activities are considered abnormally dangerous if they can potentially cause serious harm to persons or property, if reasonable care cannot completely prevent that risk, and if the activities are not commonly performed in the area. Some examples of abnormally dangerous activities are pile driving, the storage of toxic gas, crop dusting from airplanes, and blasting with explosives. *Spano v. Perini Corporation* (302 N.Y.S.2d 527 [1969]) is a typical case. It concerns a company engaged by the government to excavate a tunnel. The concussion from the dynamite blasts at the construction site damaged a garage 125 feet away and the car inside the garage. The construction company was held liable although there was no evidence of negligence.

Livestock and Liability. There is also a long legal tradition concerning the dangers of keeping animals—a tradition that reflects the agrarian origins of our society. Traditionally, the owners of domestic livestock, including cattle, horses, sheep, and hogs, have been held strictly liable for any damage caused by their animals when they trespass on land belonging to others. Wild animals are treated differently because the law never regards them as safe. Their keepers are subject to strict liability at all times and for all types of harm.

In *Eyrich v. Earl* (495 A.2d 1375 [1985]), a recent New Jersey case concerning the mauling of a five-year-old child by a leopard, the courts expanded the application of strict liability: They held not just the owner of the animal, but everybody involved in organizing and running a circus on school property, including the board of education, strictly liable. The suit was brought by the neighbors of the child, who had taken him to the circus, watched the mauling, and consequently suffered emotional damages.

■ *Concept Check 10-4   Strict Liability in Tort*

- Discuss the important differences between *intentional* and *negligent torts* on the one hand and *strict liability in tort* on the other.
- Define the principle of *abnormal danger*.

YOU DECIDE: ANSWER DISCUSSION
Assumption of the Risk

In Neinstein, *the trial court granted the defendant's motion for summary judgment. In the court's view, management's duty is limited to that of ordinary care: In effect, the court held that the fact that the defendant sat in an unprotected area meant that she willingly assumed the risk of injury. In addition, the court found that Neinstein's knowledge of the nature of the sport, coupled with the warning printed on the back of her ticket, were sufficient to relieve the team's owners of any further duty of care.*

As in Neinstein, most cases involving assumption of the risk turn on an implied assumption, and most courts recognize that this defense is consensual in nature: That is, it is not the result of a contract between the parties. The logic behind this reasoning can be quite confusing. A plaintiff such as Neinstein who voluntarily participates in a "dangerous" activity does not necessarily agree to assume the risk of any future negligence on the part of the defendant. The fact that the risk may be assumed does not mean that it was assumed. In most circumstances, three factors must be present before the plaintiff will be found to have assumed the risk: (1) knowledge of the specific risk that caused the harm; (2) understanding of the risk; and (3) voluntary assumption of

the risk. This combination of elements is essentially the same as the reasonable person standard.
Consider these scenarios:

- *Neinstein attended another ball game and was hit by another ball. Her implied assumption of the risk protects team management from being sued again.*
- *Neinstein attended another ball game and the bleacher she was seated on collapsed. Neinstein did not necessarily assume the risk of a defective bleacher when she attended the game because (1) the injury was unrelated to the sporting event and (2) team management is expected to keep the premises in good repair.*

If the three-pronged standard outlined above was applied to the second scenario, Neinstein would have a good chance of winning her suit.
In the words of Justice Benjamin Cardozo (Murphy v. Steeplechase [1929]), "The timorous may stay at home."

SUMMARY

- Generally, *torts* are civil wrongs other than breach of contract for which the court will provide a remedy in the form of an action for damages. The primary purpose of a tort action is to exact compensation from wrongdoers. Injuries may range from some physical harm to a person's body or property to some intangible harm done to a person's reputation or peace of mind. The unreasonable behavior may be *intentional*, *negligent*, or *abnormally dangerous*. It may be an *act of commission* or an *act of omission*. Thus, torts encompass a wide variety of injuries.
- Tort law judges the conduct of each defendant by the standard of the behavior of a reasonable person. The *reasonable person* is a model of good judgment who is nonetheless susceptible to normal human weaknesses. This standard embodies the community consensus about socially acceptable behavior, which changes with society and the demands of new technologies. This flexibility allows the courts to

recognize new causes of action. For business, this means that the courts can, at any time, elevate what was previously an ethical responsibility to the status of a legal responsibility. For example, tort law governs *product liability*—an area of law that has transformed business.

- There are three types of torts: intentional torts, torts involving negligence, and strict liability torts. *Intentional torts* involve the deliberate conduct of one person that results in an injury to another. *Assault, battery, libel, slander,* and *invasion of privacy* are all intentional torts. *Negligent torts* focus on acts of carelessness. Typical negligence cases involve automobile accidents and malpractice claims against doctors. *Strict tort liability*—the newest area of tort law—assigns liability, regardless of fault, as a matter of social policy. Thus, companies carrying out abnormally dangerous activities, such as blasting with explosives, are responsible for any injuries that result, no matter how careful they have been. Drug manufacturers may also be strictly liable for harmful side effects of their products.

- There are standard *defenses* to each of these torts which bar recovery. Thus, defendants to intentional torts may (1) claim immunity from liability based on a *conditional* or *absolute privilege* granted by the law or (2) argue that the plaintiff consented to the activity. Defendants in negligence cases may argue that the plaintiff's own negligence contributed to the injury or that the defendant knowingly assumed the risks involved.

- Many torts are of special interest to business. In an increasingly litigious society, customers, colleagues, and other businesses are more likely to sue when they feel that they have been injured. The possibility of financial compensation is a potent lure. Companies, which are perceived as both impersonal and wealthy, are often the object of tort suits. Businesses are at risk for insulting customers, defaming employees in internal memos, or restricting the movements of suspected shoplifters. Tort law, however, can also provide a remedy for businesses that are injured—for example, by negligent accountants or slanderous competitors.

QUESTIONS AND PROBLEMS

1. During a Saturday night campus dance, two fraternity brothers "spike" the punch with grain alcohol in order to "liven up the party." A fraternity brother who does not drink alcoholic beverages drinks the punch without being aware of the alcohol until he begins to feel its effects. He then discovers how the alcohol got into the punch. Does he have any legal recourse against the two fraternity brothers, and, if so, for what?

2. Jean Craig, the complaints clerk at a local department store, is approached by an irate customer who wants to return merchandise. When she refuses because the customer has no sales receipt for the merchandise, the customer becomes verbally offensive. She finally makes an obscene gesture to the customer. Later, Craig, as well as the department store, receive a complaint and summons indicating that the customer is suing for assault and battery. Who wins and why?

3. On the evening of October 1, 1990, a police officer was on the premises of the Admiralty Condominium Complex to investigate a rash of burglaries. While engaged in a stake out, he received a report of a suspicious vehicle on the condominium grounds. After investigating this report and finding nothing, he proceeded to his stake out position. Rather than passing through the condominium complex gate or security gate, he scaled a five foot high wall separating the condominium complex from Montauk Highway and was injured when he landed on a pile of hardened concrete which had been discarded at the base of the wall by defendant landowner. Plaintiff alleged the landowner was negligent for failing to maintain the premises in a safe condition. Decide.
[*Rubsam v. Alexander*, 575 NY 2d 698 (1991)]

4. Anne wakes up one morning to find her picture on the front page of Sunday morning's magazine section of the newspaper. Under the picture is the caption "Teen Alienation: Is Suicide the Answer?" Anne realized that the picture had been taken without her knowledge when she attended an ex-

change program at a local high school. Anne was on one side of the picture walking along a high school corridor alone, and a group of students were on the other side of the picture talking together. In reality, Anne had simply been going to the bathroom and passed by the students, who attended the school and happened to know each other. Does Anne have a cause of action in tort?

5. A letter was sent by defendant to the New York Department of Health and to the medical administrators of two hospitals in which Plaintiff had privileges. The body of the letter contained nothing defamatory but the caption in each of the letters read: "Complaint of Professional Misconduct." Based on this caption, the defendant sues for libel. Can he recover damages? [*Herman v. Cullen*, 567 NYS 2d 846 (1991)]

6. Gene Haxon, a famous rock star, indulges his passion for animals by keeping on his property several snakes, a giraffe, a llama, a chimpanzee, and a tiger. All of the animals have caretakers and appropriate cages. One day, the giraffe leans over the fence to nibble the leaves on a passing pedestrian's hat. The pedestrian is startled and suffers injuries upon falling down. The pedestrian sues Gene Haxon on the theory of strict liability. Mr. Haxon defends by asserting that the animal was not harmful and was quite properly maintained. Is this is a good defense?

7. Plaintiff, Mary Vassilades, contacted Dr. Magassy for plastic surgery she wanted to have performed. The Doctor took "before" and "after" pictures as part of his regular routine and as a protective measure in the event a patient later claimed there had been no improvement in appearance. Several months later, the Doctor participated in a program with Garfinckel's entitled "Creams versus Plastic Surgery." The program entailed a television presentation and a department store presentation by Dr. Magassy using slide photographs of several of his patients including two "before" and "after" of Mrs. Vassilades. Mrs. Vassilades' picture appeared less than one minute on the screen and no mention was made of her name, nonetheless, people who knew Mrs. Vassilades recognized her. Which torts may Mrs. Vassilades allege and will she be successful? [*Vassiliades v. Garfinckel's, Brooks Bros.*, 492 A 2d 580 D.C. App. (1985)]

8. Zina Corbett was exiting a department store after purchasing some items, when the store's electronic merchandise detection device was triggered. The store detective requested that she accompany him back into the store and to the security office. She did so. While in the office, the contents of her package were emptied onto the counter and it was discovered that the store check-out clerk had neglected to remove a tag on merchandise she purchased. The clerk apologized. Ms. Corbett was detained a total of 5–10 minutes. She sues the store for false imprisonment. The store defends by asserting that it had a qualified privilege to detain her. Is the defense good here?

9. Bill Ferris is taking karate lessons. During practice with Kim Valentine, a friend who also takes karate, he is injured while trying to execute a "leg sweep" maneuver. He sues his friend for negligence. The friend defends by saying that he voluntarily assumed the risk in practicing with him. Who wins and why?

10. Archie Spencer, an accountant, prepared a regular financial statement for a client company. Based on the statement, a bank loaned the company $70,000. The bank later learns that the financial statements were incorrect and that the accountant had not used standard accounting procedures. The bank files suit against the accountant for negligence. Archie Spencer's defense is that the bank was a third party to the action and therefore could not sue him for negligence. Who wins and why?

11

PRODUCT LIABILITY

There are as many legal approaches to product liability as there are product flaws and imperfections; in addition, several areas of the law merge in product liability, including tort, contract, and administrative law. According to Section 102(2) of the Uniform Product Liability Act, **product liability** includes "all claims or actions brought for personal injury, death, or property damage caused by the manufacture, construction, design, formula, preparation, assembly, installation, testing, warnings, instructions, marketing, packaging, or labeling of any product." This definition raises several complex legal issues:

product liability Claims brought for death, personal injury, or property damage caused by the defective manufacture, design, instructions, packaging, or labeling of any product

- How much *risk* is acceptable before marketing a new product?
- Should the manufacturer be *responsible* for warning consumers of every possible danger of a product?
- How far does the *chain of liability* extend? In other words, who is responsible if a consumer is injured by a defective product—the manufacturer, the wholesaler, or the retailer?
- Should the manufacturer *compensate* just for the buyer's injuries? What is compensation if a member of the buyer's family or a neighbor is injured?
- Should the victim's misuse of a product relieve the corporation of responsibility?

Broader social and ethical issues are also at stake. For example, every product liability case raises clear questions about the extent of corporate social responsibility (*see* Chapter 2). Less obvious are questions about the costs of product liability to society: Manufacturers pass the costs of product liability on to their customers by raising prices. How much extra are we willing to pay in order to compensate individuals who are injured? What happens when product liability costs are so high that they drive products off the market?

Even assuming that society is willing to bear these costs, there is serious doubt that the current system of product-liability litigation is the best way to compensate victims.

■ POLICY BASES OF PRODUCT LIABILITY

Product liability is, of course, a *business* matter, especially as a result of managerial decision making in foreseeing and taking risks. This chapter discusses how public policy on product liability is formulated on the basis of risk from two perspectives: *risk management* on the part of business itself and *consumer protection* as a legal response to the developing nature of the producer-consumer relationship.

Business Policy: Risk Management

Business managers frequently approach product liability from the perspective of *quality control* and *risk management*. Quality control is usually a matter of testing samples from each batch of goods. Depending on the results of the tests, managers decide to scrap or accept each batch. There are four possible outcomes for each batch, and they fall into the matrix diagrammed in Figure 11-1. In the best of outcomes, good batches are accepted, bad batches are rejected, and there are no risks either for the manufacturer or for the consumer. However, misleading test results may cause an inspector to reject a good batch and so increase costs unnecessarily; this is the risk to the manufacturer. Alternatively, an inspector may accept a bad batch and send it on to the market; customers then run the risk of buying defective goods.

Within limits established by law, a manufacturer can set higher or lower test standards. Unfortunately for the consumer, the manufacturer and consumer risks are direct trade-offs: Setting the test standards higher—that is, accepting fewer batches—increases the manufacturer's risk and reduces the consumer's; lowering the test standards reduces the manufacturer's risk at the consumer's expense. The manufacturer is restrained not only by the law but by the market itself—that is, a reputation for poor quality may drive customers away. (For a discussion of one company's attention to product quality as a risk-management strategy, see the ORGANIZATIONAL PROFILE box in this chapter.)

In this way, manufacturers deliberately allocate the risks of injury from defective products among themselves and their customers. Most often, consumers do not participate in the process; risks are simply imposed on them by the producer. Litigation such as that detailed in the following case underscores the conflicting interests of manufacturers and consumers when it comes to making a product safer.

FIGURE 11-1 Risk Matrix for Product Testing   *Source: Thomas A. Cowan, "Some Policy Bases of Products Liability," 17 Stanford Law Review 1091 (1965).*

True State of Sample or Batch

	Good	Bad
Accept	No Risk	*Consumer's Risk*
Reject	Manufacturer's Risk	No Risk

GREENMAN v. YUBA POWER PRODUCTS INC.

California Supreme Court, 377 P.2d 897 (1962)

How

Greenman was seriously injured when a piece of wood flew from the Shopsmith power tool on which he was working and hit him in the forehead. After giving written notice of his injuries approximately 10.5 months later to Yuba Power Products, the manufacturer of the Shopsmith, and to the retailer, Greenman, the plaintiff, sued both of them in California trial court on charges of negligence and breach of express and implied warranty. The jury returned a verdict for Greenman against Yuba upon which the court entered judgment, although it was not clear whether the verdict was based on the negligence or the warranty claim. Yuba appealed to the California Supreme Court, arguing that because of the possibility that the jury may indeed have based its decision on breach of warranty and that a breach of warranty action was barred by the law of sales since Greenman failed to give timely notice, the chance that they could have decided in such a way was unfairly prejudicial. The California Supreme Court, however, takes a different approach.

Section 1769 of the Civil Code provides: In the absence of express or implied agreement of the parties, acceptance of the goods by the buyer shall not discharge the seller from liability in damages or other legal remedy for breach of any promise or warranty in the contract to sell or the sale. But, if, after acceptance of the goods, the buyer fails to give notice to the seller of the breach of any promise or warranty within a reasonable time after the buyer knows, or ought to know of such breach, the seller shall not be liable therefor."

Like other provisions of the uniform sales act, section 1769 deals with the rights of the parties to a contract of sale or a sale. It does not provide that notice must be given of the breach of a warranty that arises independently of a contract of sale between the parties. Such warranties are not imposed by the sales act, but are the product of common-law decisions that have recognized them in a variety of situations. . . .

The notice requirement of section 1769, however, is not an appropriate one for the court to adopt in actions by injured consumers against manufacturers with whom they have not dealt. "As between the immediate parties to the sale [the notice requirement] is a sound commercial rule, designed to protect the seller against unduly delayed claims for damages. As applied to personal injuries, and notice to a remote seller, it becomes a booby-trap for the unwary. The injured consumer is seldom 'steeped in the business practice which justifies the rule,' and at least until he has had legal advice it will not occur to him to give notice to one with whom he has had no dealings." . . . We conclude, therefore, that even if plaintiff did not give timely notice of breach of warranty to the manufacturer, his cause of action based on the representations contained in the brochure was not barred.

Moreover, to impose strict liability on the manufacturer under the circumstances of this case, it was not necessary for plaintiff to establish an express warranty as defined in section 1732 of the Civil Code. A manufacturer is strictly liable in tort when an article he places on the market, knowing that it is to be used without inspection for defects, proves to have a defect that causes injury to a human being. Recognized first in the case of unwholesome food products, such liability has now been extended to a variety of other products that create as greater hazards if defective.

Although in these cases strict liability has usually been based on the theory of an express or implied warranty running from the manufacturer to the plaintiff, the abandonment of the requirement of a contract between them, the recognition that the liability is not assumed by agreement but imposed by law, and the refusal to permit the manufacturer to define the scope of its own responsibility for defective products make clear that the liability is not one governed by the law of contract warranties but by the law of strict liability in tort. Accordingly, rules defining and governing warranties that were developed to meet the needs of commercial transactions cannot properly be invoked to govern the manufacturer's liability to those injured by their defective products unless those rules also serve the purposes for which such liability is imposed.

We need not recanvass the reasons for imposing strict liability on the manufacturer. . . . The purpose of such liability is to insure that the costs of injuries resulting from defective products are borne by the manufacturers that put such products on the market rather than by the injured persons who are powerless to protect themselves. Sales warranties serve this purpose fitfully at best. In the present case, for example, plaintiff was able to plead and prove an express warranty only because he read and relied on the representations of the Shopsmith's ruggedness contained in the manufacturer's brochure. Implicit in the machine's presence on the market, however, was a representation that it would safely do the jobs for which it was built. Under these circumstances, it should not be controlling whether plaintiff selected the machine because of the statements in the brochure. . . . (Civ. Code, § 1735.) "The remedies of injured consumers ought not to be made to depend upon the intricacies of the law of sales." To establish the manufacturer's liability it was sufficient that plaintiff proved that he was injured while using the Shopsmith in a way it was intended to be used as a result of a defect in design and manufacture of which plaintiff was not aware that made the Shopsmith unsafe for its intended use.

?

. . . .
The judgment is affirmed.

Case Questions:

1. How does this case expand the concept of strict liability in the product context?

2. What is it about certain products that justifies the imposition of strict liability?

3. What problems did the court see with confining the notion of strict liability to the law of sales?

How much risk should a pharmaceutical firm assume in producing a drug? Surely, the risk that a person assumes when he or she takes a pharmaceutical to remedy a medical problem should not be greater than the risk of living with the condition. Realistically, no risk at all is impossible, but the issue of risk becomes an ethical as opposed to logical question when one asks whether the manufacturer has properly advised consumers about the level of risk involved in using a product at a time when they can make the decision. In the INTERNATIONAL ENVIRONMENT box in this chapter, this issue is addressed in the context of global marketing.

Legal Policy: Consumer Protection

The courts have recognized and responded to the harsh business realities that often obtain in the producer-consumer relationship. To compensate for the relative powerlessness of consumers in the modern marketing system, they have tried to improve the legal position of the injured consumer relative to that of the corporation. This preference for *consumer protection* is one reason for the continuing evolution of product-liability theories, and at present, legal policy follows the broader social trend toward consumer protection.

This trend in policy has meant a shift away from traditional analysis in terms of *negligence*. One reason is the practical difficulty of proving negligence on the part of the manufacturer. In turn, this shift in focus makes the negligence standard of "reasonably careful behavior" somewhat less important than it has been in the past. The courts have increasingly turned instead to the "strict liability in tort" to set limits on behavior in the marketplace.

PRODUCT-LIABILITY POLICY: AN INTERNATIONAL PERSPECTIVE. One of the basic problems in settling product-liability disputes in the international arena is jurisdiction. As in most litigation, of course, both parties will seek the most favorable forum, and on the international level, the problem is compounded by the fact that the burden of proving such charges as product defectiveness may vary from country to country. We will examine more closely the principles of strict liability and negligence later in the chapter, but for the present purpose, we will point out that while the principle of strict liability eases the burden of proof for the plaintiff, the principle of negligence requires that the defendant must be shown to be at fault. This distinction is the basis of the "categorization" summarized in Table 11-1—an admittedly broad distinction between "progressive" (strict-liability) and "traditionalist" (negligence) countries.

Recall the case of *International Shoe Company v. State of Washington*, discussed in Chapter 5. In that case, the Supreme Court laid down the test of *minimum contacts*, holding that a court may claim jurisdiction over an out-of-state defendant only when the defendant has had at least "minimum contacts" with

As businesses in the 1990s enter an era of intense competition and declining profits, they are coming more and more to recognize the overriding importance of the quality of both products and services in keeping them viable—and, indeed, in making them successful. Thinking in terms of quality must become a way of life. In the 1980s, the U.S. automobile industry lost a high percentage of market share to Japanese imports of perceived higher quality, and the automotive industry, although a highly visible case in point, is just one among many industries that must learn the rules of the new quality-control game.

The components of quality and the means by which one corporation—Motorola—focused on improvement and came out a winner are the subjects here. Quality means total customer satisfaction. It includes both defect-free products and service to customers. This view is held across industries and specifically by Motorola, the manufacturer of semiconductors, cellular phones, and other electronics goods, whose CEO and president, George Fisher, has argued that "product quality is not the biggest problem. Mistakes in billing, credit, back ordering and delivery are more likely to keep us from our objective." This recognition is actually an expansion of Motorola's original goal—now close to being met—of reducing significantly the company's product-defect rate.

In order to provide better quality, firms must first analyze what they are doing currently. The analysis must proceed in terms of what their customers require. One powerful customer-focused diagnostic tool is called quality functional deployment (QDF), which translates customer needs into product design during development instead of after the fact through such responses as complaint letters. In fact, both the complaint section and the inspection team are now virtual throwbacks because they do not acknowledge what is paramount, namely, the credo that "quality is everyone's responsibility."

Measuring the level of quality is another important step in attaining total customer satisfaction. This goal can largely be achieved through such personal measures as the quality audit and employee suggestions and through such management measures as assessing the total cost of quality, focusing on long-term market share, and shortening cycle times.

Finally, when problem areas have been identified, there are operational and human-resources techniques that can be employed to improve quality over the long run. Motorola has used many of the means aforementioned to turn around their quality and even win the prestigious Malcolm Balridge Quality Award.

Motorola's sales and market share in the semiconductor industry fell sharply from the early to mid-1980s—the problem being uneven quality and delivery delays to customers increasingly dissatisfied with a company unresponsive to their needs. Although it was thought that the company might never regain its lead in the semiconductor business, by 1988 Motorola's management had taken matters in hand, and the present outlook remains good for other products. Corporate focus is now on total customer satisfaction.

Motorola began with the goal of reducing the rate of component defects, setting some steep targets in 1987—targets that the company has already come close to meeting. By the end of 1991, for example, Motorola had lowered the companywide defect rate to an average of 40 per million units from 6000 per million in 1986. What is so interesting about Motorola's success is its attempt to extend such exacting standards to everything from basic research to routine meetings, including functions not easily isolated into separate tasks. For instance, Motorola has been able to reduce the number of days needed to close the corporate books from 12 to four and to bring service-center average repair time for communications products down to seven from 12 days. In addition, while attending to quality, the company has also been active in product innovation.

One interesting technique that Motorola has used to improve quality is the concept of "next operation as customer"—that is, whether you are an internal department or an external customer, if you receive the product or service, you are considered a customer. In any conflicts over requirements, the needs of the external customer take precedence. These requirements are then written as internal specifications and placed on flow-charts, with the requirements offering the greatest potential for improvement given the highest priority. In this way, such benefits as improved knowledge, communication, and cooperation can be achieved in pursuit of total customer satisfaction.

For its successes, in 1988 Motorola was given one of the first Balridge Awards, which recognize the delivery of high-quality products and services. The award criteria met by Motorola include strong management leadership, clear goals, and a commitment by everyone in the firm to reach for "perfection."

a plaintiff within the court's jurisdiction. Although the "minimum-contacts" test is not clearly defined in case law, it is widely applied and generally governs the jurisdiction of U.S. courts over nonresidents.

In *World-Wide Volkswagen Corp. v. Woodson* (100 S.Ct. 559, 62L. Ed. 2d 490 [1980]), the Court denied jurisdiction to an Oklahoma court in a product-liability case because the defendants—a New York-based Audi retailer and wholesaler—had established no "minimum contacts" with the state of Okla-

The pharmaceutical industry is a truly international business. Drug companies and their products cross boundaries limited only by marketing strategies and the drug-approval procedures of individual nations. In some cases, for instance, drugs used widely in European countries cannot be made or sold in the United States; in other cases, the reverse is true.

The sleep remedy Halcion, a product of the Upjohn Company, has been marketed in over 90 countries and has annual sales of over $250 million ($100 million in the United States). Despite its success for over 15 years, however, the drug remains controversial. At issue are its benefits versus the risk of its dangerous side effects, the ethical dilemma of marketing a profitable but possibly unsafe drug, and the international dimensions of global pharmaceutical marketing.

In 1982, Halcion was licensed by the U.S. Food and Drug Administration for sale in the United States in doses up to .5 mg. Halcion was applauded by clinicians and users because it acted fast and left the system quickly, without the extended grogginess of barbiturates or other benzodiazepines (the class to which Halcion belongs). However, even three years before FDA approval, Halcion had been withdrawn from the Dutch market because of such side effects as depression and chronic anxiety.

FDA approval did not come smoothly. There was always concern about Halcion's side effects, and the FDA medical officer who handled the drug's review, citing the Dutch case and Upjohn's own trials, concluded that Halcion had a "narrower margin of safety" than other benzodiazepines and was "associated with a greater number of adverse affects." Various physicians and drug researchers have concluded that the FDA and Upjohn have both been irresponsible regarding Halcion. They ask whether profitability has not overtaken concern for public health as the ultimate value.

Questions about the drug's safety have continued, culminating in several lawsuits against Upjohn, including some in which Halcion's adverse reactions were alleged to have caused criminal behavior. For example, although one woman taking Halcion became agitated and paranoid and then murdered her mother, the case was dismissed when the court concluded that she had not acted voluntarily. She then sued Upjohn for negligence in not providing proper warning about the drug's side effects, maintaining that they had adversely influenced her behavior. The suit also maintained that Upjohn had "falsified and fraudulently misrepresented, concealed, and omitted data in its Halcion submissions to the FDA." Although Upjohn denied the allegations and refused to accept responsibility, the company nonetheless settled with the woman in 1991. At the same time, Upjohn moved to keep the record confidential both on the details of the settlement and on its own unpublished side-effects data on the drug.

Complaints about the drug's adverse reactions to the nervous system, such as aggression and personality changes, were gathered in the United States through the FDA's spontaneous-reporting system, which goes into effect after a drug is approved. Moreover, international reports were similar, and by 1988, France, Italy, and Germany had blocked the sale of the .5 mg dosage.

In the United Kingdom, the Committee on Safety of Medicines (CSM), the regulatory authority for drugs, followed closely the 1991 settlement described above. In October of that year, the CSM suspended sales of Halcion, citing allegations of incomplete safety disclosures. Norway and Finland also banned Halcion. The European community has demanded that Halcion be prescribed for a period of only three weeks (treatment to then be reviewed), and then only when sleep problems are severe.

In the United States, however, sales continue while the FDA reviews the CSM ban. Upjohn states that no scientific or medical data exist to support withdrawing the drug from the market.

Using the same basis as the CSM, should the FDA also suspend sales? Clearly, different standards apply in each country—a fact which, in the case of pharmaceuticals, makes international marketing more than just a business issue.

What is the risk to the user of Halcion? Compared to the benefits, is it at an acceptable level? Ideally, people who take Halcion because they are having sleeping problems should be at no risk at all. Realistically, however, as one analyst puts it, "If you take medication, you are implicitly accepting a risk." Still, Upjohn and the FDA have been slow to decrease that risk. The company, it seems, should at the very least have promoted greater caution in prescribing Halcion—after all, the drug is recommended only for very short-term use. In addition, according to other industry observers, the FDA should have enforced a warning procedure as well as making sure that Upjohn told the public about the drug's dangers.

In terms of the categories in the risk matrix in Figure 11-1, Halcion users have in the past fallen into the "consumer's-risk" group, where they assumed all the risks associated with Halcion. However, the latest developments have changed the picture, and now Upjohn's "manufacturer's risk" may be the greatest, as the company stands to lose business because of its failure to inform the public properly.

homa—for example, they had never sought any privileges or protections of Oklahoma law. In *Oswalt v. Scripto, Inc.*, however, a Texas "long-arm statute" (*see* Chapter 4) was allowed to extend to a Japanese manufacturer of butane lighters who dealt exclusively with a U.S. distributor: The distributorship agreement was deemed sufficient to satisfy the "minimum-contacts" requirement.

TABLE 11-1	Product-Liability Policy: Selected "Strict-Liability" and "Negligence" Countries	
"STRICT LIABILITY" COUNTRIES (WHERE THE BURDEN OF PROOF IS EASED FOR THE PLAINTIFF)	**"NEGLIGENCE" COUNTRIES (WHERE FAULT MUST BE SHOWN)**	
United States	England	
France	Commonwealth Countries	
Belgium	Latin America	
Luxembourg	Japan	
Switzerland	Italy	
Scandinavian Countries	Austria	
Holland	Greece	
Germany	Spain	
New Zealand	Portugal	
	Turkey	

Source: Adapted from Frank A. Orban, III, "Product Liability: A Comparative Legal Restatement—Foreign Law and the ECC Directive," *Georgia Journal of International and Comparative Law* 8:2 (1978).

The phrase *lex loci delictic* refers to the "place of the wrong," and the classical rule in product-liability and other cases was once that the place where the tort was committed determined the tort law that was applied. However, because some case law holds that the "policies of interested states be recognized" or that "the most significant relationship" of states to involved parties be considered, the classical doctrine has been modified. Foreign plaintiffs, for example, may choose to bring suit in the United States because of the strict-liability provisions of U.S. law.

In general, although the place where the injury occurred is still a primary consideration in the choice of law, a factor of growing importance is the trend toward applying the law that is most favorable to the plaintiff. Finally, as a very general point of comparison between respective legal practices, the key differences in the development of product liability in the United States and Europe are summed up by one scholar in the field in Table 11-2.

Concluded in 1972, the Hague Convention on the Law Applicable to Products Liability attempted to impart some uniformity to the choice of product-liability law in the international arena. Basically, the Hague Convention is a comprehensive report on important factors to be considered in the selection and application of law to cases involving product liability, and it is important to remember that although it was agreed upon by all countries of the Hague Conference of Private International Law, it has not been *ratified* by many of those countries (including the United States). The key guidelines of the Hague Convention—contained in Articles 4, 5, and 6 and qualified by Article 7—are summarized in Table 11-3.

■ Concept Check 11-1 Policy Bases of Product Liability

- Describe the principle of *risk management* as it applies to business policy regarding product liability.
- Explain the developing legal response to the business policies of *quality control* and *risk management*.

TABLE 11-2   *Product Liability in U.S. and European Law*

- *The lawyer's contingent fee.* Outside of the United States such a fee arrangement is usually prohibited [a contingent fee is one that a claimant's lawyer arranges to be paid if he wins the case for the client]. Consequently, plaintiffs must finance any litigation from their own pocket as well as run the risk of possibly having to pay the defendant's legal fees, if the defendant prevails.

- *Inadequate workers-compensation payments and absence of national health insurance.* In Europe the well-developed schemes absorb all medical expenses and there is less of a discrepancy between what Europeans can obtain by way of workers compensation and what they can obtain through a civil suit.

- *The high degree of technical expertise and specialization within the American plaintiff's bar.* In Europe, lawyers for various reasons have not developed specialized nonlegal know-how enabling them to bring compelling product-liability actions, especially where design defects are involved.

- *Discovery and deposition procedures.* In Europe no directly analogous procedures exist which can get the plaintiff "into the defendant's operations," except to an extent in the United Kingdom.

- *The availability in the public domain of extensive safety, accident and other information critical to developing product liability cases.* In Europe both government and companies are much more secretive about information they collect. Nongovernmental information-gathering institutions do not exist in the same number and strength as in the United States.

- *Juries.* In Europe there are no civil juries as Americans understand them which can bring community values and perspectives to a product-liability case, including perceptions of what is "adequate" compensation.

- *Consumer awareness.* In Europe for various sociohistorical reasons, consumerism is not as well developed or organized as in the United States.

- *The tendency of European lawyers and writers to focus on compensation as the sole purpose of product liability.* American lawyers, especially the plaintiff's bar, have long seen product liability as also a device for law and industrial reform. Product litigation, particularly in the design defect area, has done much to *prevent* future injuries in addition to compensating the victim in the case at hand.

Source: Frank A. Orban, III, "Product Liability: A Comparative Legal Restatement—Foreign Law and the ECC Directive," *Georgia Journal of International and Comparative Law* 8:2 (1978), p. 393.

■ THE EVOLUTION OF PRODUCT LIABILITY

The landmark case in the early history of product liability shows how this area of law is historically based in the law of contract: *Winterbottom v. Wright* (10 Mees & W 109, 11 L.J. Ex. 415 [1842].[1] In 1840, a royal mail coach overturned, and the coachman was injured because the wheels of the coach were not securely bolted to the axles. The coachman sued the man under contract to the Postmaster-General to keep the coaches in good repair. Reflecting the social policy of the times (that is, to promote and protect industry), the court rules against the coachman on the grounds that he was not a party to the contract.

Tort Principles and Case Law

As social policy changed, the courts developed exceptions to this strict interpretation of contract law. Over the last half of the nineteenth century, sellers were held liable to third parties for negligence in the preparation or sale of

---

[1] The history of product liability is drawn from Kimble and Lesher, *Products Liability* (Minneapolis, MN: West Publishing Co., 1979).

TABLE 11-3	*The Hague Convention on Product Liability: Selected Guidelines*

Article 4

The applicable law shall be the internal law of the state of the place of injury, if that state is also:

a. the place of the habitual residence of the person directly suffering damage, or
b. the principal place of business of the person claimed to be liable, or
c. the place where the product was acquired by the person directly suffering damage.

Article 5

Notwithstanding the provisions of Article 4, the applicable law shall be the internal law of the state of the habitual residence of the person directly suffering damage, if that state is also:

a. the principal place of business of the person claimed to be liable, or
b. the place where the product was acquired by the person directly suffering damage.

Article 6

Where neither of the laws designated in Articles 4 and 5 applies, the applicable law shall be the internal law of the state of the principal place of business of the person claimed to be liable, unless the claimant bases his claim upon the internal law of the state of the place of injury.

Article 7 qualifies the three previous articles somewhat by establishing a "foreseeability" test; that is, that a defendant must have been able to foresee the availability of that product in those states:

Article 7

Neither the law of the state of the place of injury nor the law of the state of the habitual residence of the person directly suffering damage shall be applicable by virtue of Articles 4, 5 and 6 if the person claimed to be liable establishes that he could not reasonably have foreseen that the product or his own products of the same type would be made available in the state through commercial channels.

Source: Wills L.M. Reese, "Further Comments on the Hague Convention on the Law Applicable to Products Liabilty," *Georgia Journal of International and Comparative Law* 8:2 (1978).

goods "imminently" or "inherently" dangerous to human safety, such as food, beverages, drugs, firearms, and explosives.[2] The courts argued that even though the producers had no contractual relationship with users, they owed a "duty" to users to exercise reasonable care in the manufacturing process.

MACPHERSON V. BUICK MOTOR CO. This line of argument led ultimately to the application of tort principles to product liability in the case of *MacPherson v. Buick Motor Co.* (111 N.E. 1050 [1916]). In this case, an auto manufacturer who sold a car to a dealer was liable to the ultimate purchaser of that car for any negligence in the manufacture or inspection of the vehicle. Although the court still relied on the traditional concept of "inherently dangerous goods," it explicitly shifted the analysis from contract to *negligence* (tort) principles—that is, the requirement of the producer to exercise "due care" in the marketing of goods to users (*see* Chapter 10). This approach has been accepted by all American courts and adopted by the *Restatement (Second) of Torts*. Over time, the restrictive concept of "inherently dangerous" products was abandoned and the concept of negligence was expanded to include labeling, installation, inspection,

> **goods "imminently" (or "inherently") dangerous to human safety** In cases of *product liability*, the concept that the producer of certain goods has a duty to users to exercise reasonable care in manufacturing although there is no contract with product users

---

[2] *Thomas v. Winchester*, 6 N.Y. 397 (1852); *Huset v. J.I. Case Threshing Machine Co.* 120 F. 865 (1903). Kimble & Lesher, note 1 *supra* at p.6.

and design as well as production. (The case of *MacPherson v. Buick Motor Co.* is excerpted below in our discussion of NEGLIGENCE.)

There is, however, a weakness in the negligence approach to product liability: It burdens the plaintiff with the difficult task of proving the defendant's negligence. To avoid this problem, courts turned to the concept of *warranty*—that is, an assurance made by the producer to the user. This approach, however, was also limited: Only the *original* purchaser of an item could bring an action, and he could sue only the person who sold the product to him. Because most merchandise passes through many hands on the way from producer to consumer, this theory was very restrictive.

Once again, therefore, the courts began to make exceptions to the rule. First, publicity about substandard sanitary conditions resulted in a burst of hysteria about the adulteration and misbranding of foods during the early twentieth century. In order to protect the public interest, the courts ruled that food businesses should be held to an *absolute* duty to produce and distribute unadulterated food products. This exception was then expanded to include drugs, beverages, and cosmetics. This principle followed a long common-law tradition of holding food marketers to special responsibilities.

HENNINGSEN V. BLOOMFIELD MOTORS. The breakthrough case in this line of argument also involved a defective car. In *Henningsen v. Bloomfield Motors* (161 A.2d 69 [1960]), the court held that even though the car passed through a dealer, an automobile manufacturer was liable to the ultimate buyer of a car under the terms of the warranty: The manufacturer did not have to be in *direct* contact with the ultimate buyer. The court decided that it was an accepted part of modern marketing that manufacturers sell to dealers, who then resell the goods to consumers. In recognition of this system, manufacturers direct their marketing efforts towards consumers, not dealers. Manufacturers, not middlemen, put goods on the market, solicit their use, and advertise their safety and quality.

ESCOLA V. COCA-COLA BOTTLING. Product-liability law then turned to the theory of *strict liability in tort*—that is, the principle whereby a user must demonstrate simply that injury was caused by a defective product. As early as 1944, Justice Traynor of California introduced these principles in a concurring opinion in the case of *Escola v. Coca-Cola Bottling Co.* (150 P.2d 436 [1944]). In this case, a waitress was injured when a bottle of soda broke in her hand either because of a defect in the glass of the bottle or because of over-charging with carbon dioxide. While the majority based its decision on the negligence of the bottler, Traynor insisted that proving negligence was unnecessary: He argued that in order to discourage manufacturers from marketing defective products, manufacturers should be liable for any injuries caused by defective products.

GREENMAN V. YUBA POWER PRODUCTS. Justice Traynor's argument for strict liability was applied by the majority in *Greenman v. Yuba Power Products, Inc.* (377 P.2d 897 [1963] (*see* p. 381). Here, the plaintiff, injured by a power tool, sued both for negligence and for breach of warranty. The California Supreme Court rejected these arguments but found for the plaintiff on a theory of strict liability:

> A manufacturer is strictly liable in tort when an article he places on the market, knowing that it is to be used without inspection for defects, proves to have a defect that causes injury to a human being. . . . The purpose of such liability is to

insure that the costs of injuries resulting from defective products are borne by the manufacturers that put such products on the market rather than by the injured persons who are powerless to protect themselves.

Most states and the *Restatement (Second) of Torts* have now adopted this doctrine.

The Expansion of Manufacturer Liability

There are many reasons why public policy should place the responsibility for injuries caused by defective products on manufacturers. First, the manufacturer can (1) promote safe design, production, and packaging; (2) anticipate and warn against known dangers; and (3) eliminate defects that have already caused injuries. Second, assigning responsibility to the manufacturer makes the most sense economically: The manufacturer is usually the largest concern in the chain of production and distribution and so can best absorb losses. In addition, the manufacturer can pass on the costs of product liability to its customers by raising prices; this practice effectively distributes the costs among the wider community. Third, holding manufacturer responsible corresponds to the manufacturers' own practice of *indemnifying* or *insuring* dealers who handle their products.

Nevertheless, the expansion of manufacturers' liability for injuries associated with their products is not without social costs. For one thing, product-liability suits generally exert an upward pressure on both the company's general expenses (particularly if a recall is necessary) and the costs of products themselves. Second, the expansion of liability has led to the increasing cost (and sometimes the complete unavailability) of product-liability insurance. Small businesses have a particularly difficult time handling this burden. For example, a 1986 U.S. Chamber of Commerce Study found that forty percent of the small businesses that it represents had experienced insurance rate increases of between 100 and 500 percent.[3]

■ *Concept Check 11-2 The Evolution of Product Liability*

- Describe the weaknesses in the *negligence* approach to product liability.
- Explain the role played by the case of *MacPherson v. Buick Motor Co.* in the evolution of public policy on product liability.
- Discuss some of the reasons why public policy often places the responsibility for injuries caused by defective products on manufacturers.

■ NEGLIGENCE

As discussed in Chapter 10, the four elements of a *negligent tort* remain exactly the same when applied to product-liability cases:

1. a *duty* owed by the particular defendant to the particular plaintiff to act as a reasonably prudent person under the same or similar circumstance
2. a *breach* of such a duty by the defendant—that is, a failure to act reasonably

---

[3] Stephanie Goldberg, "Manufacturers Take Cover," 72 *ABA Journal* 52 (July 1, 1986).

3. *injury*, including personal injury or property damage
4. a *causal link* between defendant's breach of duty and injuries sustained by plaintiff

Negligent Torts and Product Liability

The landmark case of *MacPherson v. Buick Motor Co.* first applied the theory of negligence to product liability. The opinion, written by Judge Cardozo of the New York Court of Appeals, had both an immediate and widespread effect on the state of the law. The principles laid down in *MacPherson* are now accepted throughout the country.

MacPHERSON v. BUICK MOTOR CO.
New Court of Appeals, 217 N. Y. 382, 111 N. E. 1050 (1916)

MacPherson, who was injured as a result of being thrown from his car after one of its wheels collapsed, brought a negligence action against Buick Motor Co. in New York trial court. Buick had purchased the defective wheel from another manufacturer, incorporated it into the automobile, and passed it on to the retail dealer. The case is now being resolved in New York's highest court after an appeal by the defendant to determine the legal issue of whether Buick's duty is capable of being extended to parties beyond those with which it has a contractual relationship.

The foundations of this branch of the law, at least in this state, were laid in Thomas v. Winchester. A poison was falsely labeled. The sale was made to a druggist, who in turn sold to a customer. The customer recovered damages from the seller who affixed the label. "The defendant's negligence," it was said, "put human life in imminent danger." A poison, falsely labeled, is likely to injure any one who gets it. Because the danger is to be foreseen, there is a duty to avoid the injury.

. . . .

. . . [E]arly cases suggest a narrow construction of the rule. Later cases, however, evince a more liberal spirt. . . . [We] turn to the latest case in this court in which Thomas v. Winchester was followed. The case is Statler v. Ray Mfg. Co. The defendant manufactured a large coffee urn. It was installed in a restaurant. When heated, the urn exploded and injured the plaintiff. We held that the manufacturer was liable. We said that the urn "was of such a character inherently that, when applied to the purposes for which it was designed, it was liable to become a source of great danger to many people if not carefully and properly constructed."

. . . The defendant argues that things imminently dangerous to life are poisons, explosives, deadly weapons—things whose normal function it is to injure or destroy. But whatever the rule in Thomas v. Winchester may once have been, it has no longer that restricted meaning. . . . A large coffee urn (Statler v. Ray Mfg. Co., supra) may have within itself, if negli-

gently made, the potency of danger, yet no one thinks of it as an implement whose normal function is destruction. . . .

We hold, then, that the principle of Thomas v. Winchester is not limited to poisons, explosives, and things of like nature, to things which in their normal operation are implements of destruction. If the nature of a thing is such that it is reasonably certain to place life and limb in peril when negligently made, it is then a thing of danger. Its nature gives warning of the consequences to be expected. If to the element of danger there is added knowledge that the thing will be used by persons other than the purchaser, and used without new tests, then, irrespective of contract, the manufacturer of this thing of danger is under a duty to make it carefully. That is as far was we are required to go for the decision of this case. There must be knowledge of a danger, not merely possible, but probable. . . . The proximity or remoteness of the relation is a factor to be considered. We are dealing now with the liability of the manufacturer of the finished product, who puts it on the market to be used without inspection by his customers. If he is negligent, where danger is to be foreseen, a liability will follow.

. . . .

. . . Beyond all question, the nature of an automobile gives warning of probable danger if its construction is defective. This automobile was designed to go 50 miles an hour. Unless its wheels were sound and strong, injury was almost certain. It was as much a thing of danger as a defective engine for a railroad. The defendant knew the danger. It knew also that the car would be used by persons other than the buyer. This was apparent from its size; there were seats for three persons. It was apparent also from the fact that the buyer was a dealer in cars, who bought to resell. . . . The dealer was indeed the one person of whom it might be said with some approach to certainty that by him the car would not be used. Yet the defendant would have us say that he was the one person whom it was under a legal duty to protect. The law does not lead us to so inconsequent

---

PART THREE   REGULATING PRIVATE BUSINESS CONDUCT AND CRIME

a conclusion. Precedents drawn from the days of travel by stagecoach do not fit the conditions of travel to-day. The principle that the danger must be imminent does not change, but the things subject to the principle do change. They are whatever the needs of life in a developing civilization require them to be.

. . . .

In this view of the defendant's liability there is nothing inconsistent with the theory of liability on which the case was tried. It is true that the court told the jury that "an automobile is not an inherently dangerous vehicle." The meaning, however, is made plain by the context. The meaning is that danger is not to be expected when the vehicle is well constructed. The court left it to the jury to say whether the defendant ought to have foreseen that the car, if negligently constructed, would become "imminently dangerous." Subtle distinctions are drawn by the defendant between things inherently dangerous and things imminently dangerous, but the case does not turn upon these verbal niceties. If danger was to be expected as reasonably certain, there was a duty of vigilance, and this whether you call the danger inherent or imminent. In varying forms that thought was put before the jury. We do not say that the court would not have been justified in ruling as a matter of law that the car was a dangerous thing. If there was any error, it was none of which the defendant can complain.

We think the defendant was not absolved from a duty of inspection because it bought the wheels from a reputable manufacturer. It was not merely a dealer in automobiles. It was a manufacturer of automobiles. It was responsible for the finished product. It was not at liberty to put the finished product on the market without subjecting the component parts to ordinary and simple tests. Under the charge of the trial judge nothing more was required of it. The obligation to inspect must vary with the nature of the thing to be inspected. The more probable the danger the greater the need of caution.

. . . .

The judgment should be affirmed, with costs.

Case Questions:

1. What is the most important result of the *MacPherson* decision?

2. Why, on the facts of *MacPherson*, would it have been illogical to limit the analysis to contract law?

3. How might the extension of liability for faulty products beyond contract to that of tort be construed as a necessary development?

The *MacPherson* decision carried legal thinking beyond previous rulings on inherently dangerous goods. The decision established the idea that because manufacturers knowingly put products on the market that affect the interests of consumers, they owe a legal duty of care and vigilance to consumers. Because the manufacturers are in a position to foresee the potentially harmful effects of their products, they are responsible for trying to minimize such harm. By creating a legal duty between the manufacturer and the consumer, the court in *MacPherson* made it possible for plaintiffs to argue the negligent breach of that duty.

SCOPE AND APPLICATION. This concept of negligence applies to all of the activities that precede a product's reaching the market. Thus, there can be negligence in product design, the inspection and testing of materials, the manufacture and assembly of the product, the packaging, the accompanying instructions and warnings, or the inspection and testing of the final product. Because negligence can arise from *omission* as well as *commission*, failing to discover a flaw is as negligent as creating one. Likewise, failing to warn about potential dangers in the intended and foreseeable uses of a product is a breach of duty.

However, the application of negligence theories to testing and inspection procedures has created problems for managers. In the *MacPherson* case, for example, Buick was judged negligent in not inspecting wheels purchased from an outside supplier. Thus, the manufacturer becomes responsible for materials and components produced by others as well as its own work. The question is, how much testing is enough? Consider a drug with adverse effects. If the adverse effects appear only after a long period of time or affect only a small number of users, even extensive drug trials may not pick them up.

The Reasonable-Behavior Standard. Consumers, however, may find it difficult to prove negligence in product liability cases. Manufacturers—like other defendants—need only meet the general standard of reasonable behavior: Their conduct is judged against the behavior of a reasonably careful manufacturer of similar products—that is, one that possesses the skills and expertise standard in the industry. In practice, a manufacturer need only demonstrate that, no matter what defects exist, it has used "ordinary care under the circumstances" to escape liability for negligence. It is easier for manufacturers to show that they have met industry standards than for consumers to find evidence to the contrary.

PENDING APPLICATION: THE CASE OF CIGARETTES.

Increasingly, the courts have also found it necessary to address the potential liability of manufacturers for products with lengthy histories of common use. The most dramatic of these lawsuits have been for the damages caused by cigarettes, which have undoubtedly been the most profitable consumer product ever marketed. Because cigarettes have proved so lucrative to the tobacco industry for so many years, the stakes are very high.

Required by the federal Cigarette Labeling and Advertising Act, warnings have appeared on cigarette packages since 1966, but tens of millions of people have continued to smoke, and many millions more have begun, all ignoring posted warnings of the danger to their health. At the same time, cigarette advertising, although banned on television since 1971, has portrayed smoking as a benign way to "be cool" (for youngsters) and relieve tension. The issue of tobacco-industry negligence for the harm done—and thus their liability—is now in the courts.

The most important case thus far in which a plaintiff has tried to collect damages from a tobacco company is *Cipollone v. Liggett Group, Inc.* A lifelong cigarette smoker diagnosed with lung cancer (who later died from it) maintained that despite compliance with the federal labeling law, the manufacturer had failed in its duty to warn her about the health hazards of smoking and was thus negligent. Moreover, in *Cipollone* and other cases, plaintiffs have also charged tobacco companies with unethical conduct—for example, that they have not revealed research findings showing the dangers of tobacco and that their advertising undermines package warnings. The ruling of the Supreme Court in *Cipollone* which is excerpted below, was delivered in the summer of 1992.

CIPOLLONE v. LIGGETT GROUP, INC.
United States Supreme Court, 60 U.S.L.W 4703 (1992)

Thomas Cipollone filed an action against Liggett Group, Inc., a cigarette manufacturer, alleging that the company should be held liable for the 1984 death from lung cancer of his mother, who had been a smoker since 1942. Cipollone's claims, which were based on New Jersey law, cited several theories of liability, including negligence, strict liability, breach of express warranty, and intentional tort. Specifically, Cipollone claimed that Liggett had breached express warranties in its advertising; had failed to warn consumers about smoking's hazards; had fraudulently misrepresented the dangers of smoking to consumers; and had conspired to deprive the public of scientific information about adverse health effects. In response, Liggett asserted that Cipollone's action was preempted by the Federal Cigarette Labeling and Advertising Act, which was enacted in 1965 and amended in 1969. The District Court agreed with Liggett and dismissed Cipollone's case, and the Court of Appeals affirmed.

Cipollone brought his cause to the Supreme Court to determine whether federal statute barred his state-based tort action.

JUSTICE STEVENS delivered the opinion of the Court.

"WARNING: THE SURGEON GENERAL HAS DETERMINED THAT CIGARETTE SMOKING IS DANGEROUS TO YOUR HEALTH." A federal statute enacted in 1969 requires that warning (or a variation thereof) to appear in a conspicuous place on every package of cigarettes sold in the United States. The questions presented to us by this case are whether that statute, or its 1965 predecessor which required a less alarming label, pre-empted petitioner's common law claims against respondent cigarette manufacturers. . . .

On August 1, 1983, Rose Cipollone and her husband filed a complaint invoking the diversity jurisdiction of the Federal District Court. Their complaint alleged that Rose Cipollone developed lung cancer because she smoked cigarettes manufactured and sold by the three respondents. After her death in 1984, her husband filed an amended complaint. After trial, he also died; their son, executor of both estates, now maintains this action.

Petitioner's third amended complaint alleges several different bases of recovery, relying on theories of strict liability, negligence, express warranty, and intentional tort. These claims, all based on New Jersey law, divide into five categories. The "design defect claims" allege that respondents' cigarettes were defective because respondents failed to use a safer alternative design for their products and because the social value of their product was outweighed by the dangers it created. The "failure to warn claims" allege both that the product was "defective as a result of [respondents'] failure to provide adequate warnings of the health consequences of cigarette smoking" and that respondents "were negligent in the manner [that] they tested, researched, sold, promoted, and advertised" their cigarettes. The "express warranty claims" allege that respondents had "expressly warranted that smoking the cigarettes which they manufactured and sold did not present any significant health consequences." The "fraudulent misrepresentation claims" allege that respondents had wilfully "through their advertising, attempted to neutralize the [federally mandated] warnin[g]" labels, and that they had possessed, but had "ignored and failed to act upon" medical and scientific data indicating that "cigarettes were hazardous to the health of consumers." Finally, the "conspiracy to defraud claims" allege that respondents conspired to deprive the public of such medical and scientific data.

As one of their defenses, respondents contended that the Federal Cigarette Labeling and Advertising Act, enacted in 1965, and its successor, the Public Health Cigarette Smoking Act of 1969, protected them from any liability based on their conduct after 1965. In a pretrial ruling, the District Court concluded that the federal statutes were intended to establish a uniform warning that would prevail throughout the country and that would protect cigarette manufacturers from being "sub-

jected to varying requirements from state to state," but that the statutes did not pre-empt common law actions. Accordingly, the court granted a motion to strike the pre-emption defense entirely.

The Court of Appeals rejected respondents' contention that the federal Acts expressly pre-empted common law actions, but accepted their contention that such actions would conflict with federal law. Relying on the statement of purpose in the statutes, the court concluded that Congress' "carefully drawn balance between the purposes of warning the public of the hazards of cigarette smoking and protecting the interests of the national economy" would be upset by state law damages actions based on noncompliance with "warning, advertisement, and promotion obligations other than those prescribed in the [federal] Act." Accordingly, the court held:

> "the Act pre-empts those state law damage[s] actions relating to smoking and health that challenge either the adequacy of the warning on cigarette packages or the propriety of a party's actions with respect to the advertising and promotion of cigarettes. [W]here the success of a state law damage[s] claim necessarily depends on the assertion that a party bore the duty to provide a warning to consumers in addition to the warning Congress has required on cigarette packages, such claims are pre-empted as conflicting with the Act."

The court did not, however, identify the specific claims asserted by petitioner that were pre-empted by the Act. . . . Complying with the Court of Appeals mandate, the District Court held that the failure to warn, express warranty, fraudulent misrepresentation, and conspiracy to defraud claims were barred to the extent that they relied on respondents' advertising, promotional, and public relations activities after January 1, 1966 (the effective date of the 1965 Act). The court also ruled that while the design defect claims were not pre-empted by federal law, those claims were barred on other grounds. Following extensive discovery and a four-month trial, the jury answered a series of special interrogatories and awarded $400,000 in damages to Rose Cipollone's husband. In brief, it rejected all of the fraudulent misrepresentation and conspiracy claims, but found that respondent Liggett had breached its duty to warn and its express warranties before 1966. It found, however, that Rose Cipollone had "voluntarily and unreasonably encounter[ed] a known danger by smoking cigarettes" and that 80% of the responsibility for her injuries was attributable to her. For that reason, no damages were awarded to her estate. However, the jury awarded damages to compensate her husband for losses caused by respondents' breach of express warranty. . . .

In 1964, the advisory committee issued its report, which stated as its central conclusion: "Cigarette smoking is a health hazard of sufficient importance in the United States to warrant appropriate remedial action." Relying in part on that report, the Federal Trade Commission (FTC), which had long regulated unfair and deceptive advertising practices in the cigarette industry, promulgated a new trade regulation rule. That rule, which was to take effect January 1, 1965, established that it would be a violation of the Federal Trade Commission Act "to fail to disclose, clearly and prominently, in all advertising and on every pack, box, carton, or container [of cigarettes] that cigarette smoking is dangerous to health and may cause death from cancer and other diseases." . . .

Section 2 of the Act declares the statute's two purposes: (1) adequately informing the public that cigarette smoking may be hazardous to health, and (2) protecting the national economy from the burden imposed by diverse, nonuniform and confusing cigarette labeling and advertising regulations. In furtherance of the first purpose, §4 of the Act made it unlawful to sell or distribute any cigarettes in the United States unless the package bore a conspicuous label stating: "CAUTION: CIGARETTE SMOKING MAY BE HAZARDOUS TO YOUR HEALTH." In furtherance of the second purpose, §5, captioned "Preemption," provided in part:

"(a) No statement relating to smoking and health, other than the statement required by section 4 of this Act, shall be required on any cigarette package.
"(b) No statement relating to smoking and health shall be required in the advertising of any cigarettes the packages of which are labeled in conformity with the provisions of this Act."

Although the Act took effect January 1, 1966, §10 of the Act provided that its provisions affecting the regulation of advertising would terminate on July 1, 1969.

As that termination date approached, federal authorities prepared to issue further regulations on cigarette advertising. . . .

It was in this context that Congress enacted the Public Health Cigarette Smoking Act of 1969, which amended the 1965 Act in several ways. First, the 1969 Act strengthened the warning label, in part by requiring a statement that cigarette smoking "is dangerous" rather than that it "may be hazardous." Second, the 1969 Act banned cigarette advertising in "any medium of electronic communication subject to [FCC] jurisdiction." Third, and related, the 1969 Act modified the pre-emption provision by replacing the original §5(b) with a provision that reads:

"(b) No requirement or prohibition based on smoking and health shall be imposed under State law with respect to the advertising or promotion of any cigarettes the packages of which are labeled in conformity with the provisions of this Act."

. . .

[t]he narrowing of the pre-emption provision to prohibit only restrictions "imposed under State law" cleared the way for the FTC to extend the warning-label requirement to print advertisements for cigarettes.

Article VI of the Constitution provides that the laws of the United States "shall be the supreme Law of the Land; . . . any Thing in the Constitution or Laws of any state to the Contrary notwithstanding."

. . .

Consideration of issues arising under the Supremacy Clause "start[s] with the assumption that the historic police powers of the States [are] not to be superseded by . . . Federal Act unless that [is] the clear and manifest purpose of Congress." Accordingly, "'[t]he purpose of Congress is the ultimate touchstone'" of pre-emption analysis.

In the absence of an express congressional command, state law is pre-empted if that law actually conflicts with federal law . . . or if federal law so thoroughly occupies a legislative field "'as to make reasonable the inference that Congress left no room for the States to supplement it.'"

In our opinion, the pre-emptive scope of the 1965 Act and the 1969 Act is governed entirely by the express language in §5 of each Act. When Congress has considered the issue of pre-emption and has included in the enacted legislation a provision explicitly addressing that issue, and when that provision provides a "reliable indicium of congressional intent with respect to state authority," . . . "there is no need to infer congressional intent to pre-empt state laws from the substantive provisions" of the legislation. . . . In this case, the other provisions of the 1965 and 1969 Acts offer no cause to look beyond §5 of each Act. Therefore, we need only identify the domain expressly pre-empted by each of those sections.

In the 1965 pre-emption provision regarding advertising (§5(b)), Congress spoke precisely and narrowly: "No *statement* relating to smoking and health shall be required *in the advertising* of [properly labeled] cigarettes." Section 5(a) used the same phrase ("No *statement* relating to smoking and health") with regard to cigarette labeling. As §5(a) made clear, that phrase referred to the sort of warning provided for in §4, which set forth verbatim the warning Congress determined to be appropriate. Thus, on their face, these provisions merely prohibited state and federal rule-making bodies from mandating particular cautionary statements on cigarette labels (§5(a)) or in cigarette advertisements (§5(b)).

Beyond the precise words of these provisions, this reading is appropriate for several reasons. First, as discussed above, we must construe these provisions in light of the presumption against the pre-emption of state police power regulations. This presumption reinforces the appropriateness of a narrow reading of §5. Second, the warning required in §4 does not by its own effect foreclose additional obligations imposed under state law. That Congress requires a particular warning label does not automatically pre-empt a regulatory field. Third, there is no general, inherent conflict between federal pre-emption of state warning requirements and the continued vitality of state common law damages actions. . . . All of these considerations indicate that §5 is best read as having superseded only positive enactments by legislatures or administrative agencies that mandate particular warning labels.

This reading comports with the 1965 Act's statement of purpose, which expressed an intent to avoid "diverse, nonuniform, and confusing labeling and advertising *regulations* with respect to any relationship between smoking and health." Read against the backdrop of regulatory activity undertaken by state legislatures and federal agencies in response to the Surgeon General's report, the term "regulation" most naturally refers to positive enactments by those bodies, not to common law damages actions.

The regulatory context of the 1965 Act also supports such a reading. As noted above, a warning requirement promulgated by the FTC and other requirements under consideration by the States were the catalyst for passage of the 1965 Act. These regulatory actions animated the passage of §5, which reflected Congress' efforts to prevent "a multiplicity of State and local regulations pertaining to labeling of cigarette packages," and to "pre-empt [all] Federal, State, and local authorit[ies] from requiring *any statement* . . . relating to smoking and health in the advertising of cigarettes."

Compared to its predecessor in the 1965 Act, the plain language of the pre-emption provision in the 1969 Act is much broader. First, the later Act bars not simply "statements" but rather "requirement[s] or prohibition[s] . . . imposed under State law." Second, the later Act reaches beyond statements "in the advertising" to obligations "with respect to the advertising or promotion" of cigarettes.

. . .

The 1969 Act worked substantial changes in the law: rewriting the label warning, banning broadcast advertising, and allowing the FTC to regulate print advertising. In the context of such revisions and in light of the substantial changes in wording, we cannot accept the parties' claim that the 1969 Act did not alter the reach of §5(b). . . .

Although portions of the legislative history of the 1969 Act suggest that Congress was primarily concerned with positive enactments by States and localities, the language of the Act plainly reaches beyond such enactments. In this case there is no "good reason to believe" that Congress meant less than what it said; indeed, in light of the narrowness of the 1965 Act, there is "good reason to believe" that Congress meant precisely what it said in amending that Act.

Moreover, common law damages actions of the sort raised by petitioner are premised on the existence of a legal duty and it is difficult to say that such actions do not impose "requirements or prohibitions." It is in this way that the 1969 version of §5(b) differs from its predecessor: Whereas the common law would not normally require a vendor to use any specific *statement* on its packages or in its advertisements, it is the essence of the common law to enforce duties that are either affirmative *requirements* or negative *prohibitions*. We therefore reject petitioner's argument that the phrase "requirement or prohibition" limits the 1969 Act's pre-emptive scope to positive enactments by legislatures and agencies. . . .

Although the presumption against pre-emption might give good reason to construe the phrase "state law" in a pre-emption provision more narrowly than an identical phrase in another context, in this case such a construc-

tion is not appropriate. As explained above, the 1965 version of §5 was precise and narrow on its face; the obviously broader language of the 1969 version extended that section's pre-emptive reach. Moreover, while the version of the 1969 Act passed by the Senate pre-empted "any State *statute or regulation* with respect to . . . advertising or promotion," the Conference Committee replaced this language with "State *law* with respect to advertising or promotion." In such a situation, §5(b)'s pre-emption of "state law" cannot fairly be limited to positive enactments.

That the pre-emptive scope of §5(b) cannot be limited to positive enactments does not mean that that section pre-empts all common law claims. . . .

Nor does the statute indicate that any familiar subdivision of common law claims is or is not pre-empted. We therefore cannot follow petitioner's passing suggestion that §5(b) pre-empts liability for omissions but not for acts, or that §5(b) pre-empts liability for unintentional torts but not for intentional torts. Instead we must fairly but—in light of the strong presumption against pre-emption—narrowly construe the precise language of §5(b) and we must look to each of petitioner's common law claims to determine whether it is in fact pre-empted. The central inquiry in each case is straightforward: we ask whether the legal duty that is the predicate of the common law damages action constitutes a "requirement or prohibition based on smoking and health . . . imposed under State law with respect to . . . advertising or promotion," giving that clause a fair but narrow reading.

We consider each category of damages actions in turn. In doing so, we express no opinion on whether these actions are viable claims as a matter of state law; we assume *arguendo* that they are.

Failure to Warn

To establish liability for a failure to warn, petitioner must show that "a warning is necessary to make a product . . . reasonably safe, suitable and fit for its intended use," that respondents failed to provide such a warning, and that that failure was a proximate cause of petitioner's injury. In this case, petitioner offered two closely related theories concerning the failure to warn: first, that respondents "were negligent in the manner [that] they tested, researched, sold, promoted, and advertised" their cigarettes; and second, that respondents failed to provide "adequate warnings of the health consequences of cigarette smoking."

Petitioner's claims are pre-empted to the extent that they rely on a state law "requirement or prohibition . . . with respect to . . . advertising or promotion." . . . The Act does not, however, pre-empt petitioner's claims that rely solely on respondents' testing or research practices or other actions unrelated to advertising or promotion.

Breach of Express Warranty

. . . Petitioner's evidence of an express warranty consists largely of statements made in respondents' advertising. . . .

A manufacturer's liability for breach of an express

warranty derives from, and is measured by, the terms of that warranty. Accordingly, the "requirements" imposed by an express warranty claim are not "imposed under State law," but rather imposed *by the warrantor.* While the general duty not to breach warranties arises under state law, the particular "requirement . . . based on smoking and health . . . with respect to the advertising or promotion [of] cigarettes" in an express warranty claim arises from the manufacturer's statements in its advertisements. In short, a common law remedy for a contractual commitment voluntarily undertaken should not be regarded as a "requirement . . . *imposed under State law"* within the meaning of §5(b).

. . . .

Accordingly, to the extent that petitioner has a viable claim for breach of express warranties made by respondents, that claim is not pre-empted by the 1969 Act.

Fraudulent Misrepresentation

Petitioner alleges two theories of fraudulent misrepresentation. First, petitioner alleges that respondents, through their advertising, neutralized the effect of federally mandated warning labels. Such a claim is predicated on a state-law prohibition against statements in advertising and promotional materials that tend to minimize the health hazards associated with smoking. Such a *prohibition,* however, is merely the converse of a state law *requirement* that warnings be included in advertising and promotional materials. Section 5(b) of the 1969 Act pre-empts both requirements and prohibitions; it therefore supersedes petitioner's first fraudulent misrepresentation theory.

Regulators have long recognized the relationship between prohibitions on advertising that downplays the dangers of smoking and requirements for warnings in advertisements. . . .

Long-standing regulations of the Food and Drug Administration express a similar understanding of the relationship between required warnings and advertising that "negates or disclaims" those warnings: "A hazardous substance shall not be deemed to have met [federal labeling] requirements if there appears in or on the label . . . statements, designs, or other graphic material that in any manner negates or disclaims [the required warning]." In this light it seems quite clear that petitioner's first theory of fraudulent misrepresentations is inextricably related to petitioner's first failure to warn theory, a theory that we have already concluded is largely pre-empted by §5(b).

Petitioner's second theory, as construed by the District Court, alleges intentional fraud and misrepresentation both by "false representation of a material fact [and by] conceal[ment of] a material fact." . . .

Section 5(b) pre-empts only the imposition of state law obligations "with respect to the advertising or promotion" of cigarettes. Petitioner's claims that respondents concealed material facts are therefore not pre-empted insofar as those claims rely on a state law duty to disclose such facts through channels of communication other than advertising or promotion. . . .

Moreover, petitioner's fraudulent misrepresentation

claims that do arise with respect to advertising and promotions (most notably claims based on allegedly false statements of material fact made in advertisements) are not pre-empted by §5(b). Such claims are not predicated on a duty "based on smoking and health" but rather on a more general obligation—the duty not to deceive. This understanding of fraud by intentional misstatement is appropriate for several reasons. First, in the 1969 Act, Congress offered no sign that it wished to insulate cigarette manufacturers from longstanding rules governing fraud. . . . This indicates that Congress intended the phrase "relating to smoking and health" (which was essentially unchanged by the 1969 Act) to be construed narrowly, so as not to proscribe the regulation of deceptive advertising.

Moreover, this reading of "based on smoking and health" is wholly consistent with the purposes of the 1969 Act. State law prohibitions on false statements of material fact do not create "diverse, nonuniform, and confusing" standards. Unlike state law obligations concerning the warning necessary to render a product "reasonably safe," state law proscriptions on intentional fraud rely only on a single, uniform standard: falsity. Thus, we conclude that the phrase "based on smoking and health" fairly but narrowly construed does not encompass the more general duty not to make fraudulent statements. Accordingly, petitioner's claim based on allegedly fraudulent statements made in respondents' advertisements are not pre-empted by §5(b) of the 1969 Act.

Conspiracy to Misrepresent or Conceal Material Facts

Petitioner's final claim alleges a conspiracy among respondents to misrepresent or conceal material facts concerning the health hazards of smoking. The predicate duty underlying this claim is a duty not to conspire to commit fraud. For the reasons stated in our analysis of petitioner's intentional fraud claim, this duty is not pre-empted by §5(b) for it is not a prohibition "based on smoking and health" as that phrase is properly construed. Accordingly, we conclude that the 1969 Act does not pre-empt petitioner's conspiracy claim.

To summarize our holding: The 1965 Act did not pre-empt state law damages actions; the 1969 Act pre-empts petitioner's claims based on a failure to warn and the neutralization of federally mandated warnings to the extent that those claims rely on omissions or inclusions in respondents' advertising or promotions; the 1969 Act does not pre-empt petitioner's claims based on express warranty, intentional fraud and misrepresentation, or conspiracy.

The judgment of the Court of Appeals is accordingly reversed in part and affirmed in part, and the case is remanded for further proceedings consistent with this opinion.

Case Questions

1. Which state law theories did the court hold were pre-empted by the federal statute, and which theories

were not? What do you think Congress intended in enacting the Federal Cigarette Labeling and Advertising Act? Do you believe that Congress intended to pre-empt actions for tort damages against cigarette companies for smoking-related deaths?

2. Is it fair to hold a cigarette manufacturer liable for smoking-related injuries, or are smokers themselves ultimately responsible?

3. What public-policy considerations underlie the federal statute? Does the statute strike the right balance between these competing interests? Does the court's decision strike the proper balance between them?

Failure to Warn

[handwritten: LOOK FOR : STRICT LIABILITY. WORDS CONSUMER EXPECTATIONS]

Many products—even the most ordinary—pose some level of risk and the law recognizes that it is often not possible to design a totally safe product. However, manufacturers are legally obligated to warn consumers about *known* dangers. Manufacturers may be found negligent if: (1) they fail to warn users about a recognized risk, (2) the warning is too vague to be adequate, or (3) the warning is not brought to the user's attention. There is no duty to warn against misuse that is so rare or unusual that it cannot be foreseen.

This last point poses a special difficulty for manufacturers: They must not only supply warnings but must communicate them in such a way that a reasonable person will read and understand them. Thus, a warning buried in an instruction manual may be judged inadequate; in other instances, a warning sticker on the product is sufficient.

WARNING: THE CASE OF PHARMACEUTICALS. Much current legislation in this field concerns toxic and allergic reactions to cosmetics, drugs, and vaccines. The courts have taken two different approaches to such over-the-counter items. Some courts impose a duty to warn users of adverse effects only when an appreciable number of people will be affected. Other courts have rejected this strictly quantitative approach in favor of a more qualitative judgment: They weigh the benefits of providing a warning (the risks that are avoided) against its costs (discouraging the beneficial use of the product).

Because an expert (a physician) selects the product, prescription drugs are unique. Both prescription and nonprescription drugs are marketed after thorough testing and approval by the Food and Drug Administration. In general, the pharmaceutical company's duty is limited to warning physicians of the potential hazards of prescription drugs. However, the company is required to warn physicians of even the rarest and most infrequent risks of serious injury. There is no duty to warn consumers directly except in mass-inoculation and similar projects that involve routine administration without a physician's supervision. There can be no breach of the duty to warn until the company knows, or should have known, of the existence of the hazard.

■ *Concept Check 11-3 Negligence*

- What are the elements of a *tort* when applied to product-liability cases?
- Describe the current scope of the concept of *negligence* as it applies to a producer's activities.
- Explain how a manufacturer may be held liable for *failure to warn* consumers about product dangers.

■ STRICT PRODUCT LIABILITY

strict liability In tort law, principle that liability is based on a product itself being defective, not on a defendant's *negligence*

Strict liability is the most recent evolution in tort law. Because it eliminates the whole question of *negligence* and, in a sense, *fault*, its introduction into the field of product liability has transformed the very nature of the inquiry. Proving strict liability is a matter of demonstrating that a product caused an injury because it was defective; the reason for the defect is irrelevant. The product itself, rather than the defendant's conduct, is under scrutiny. (The PERSONAL PROFILE box in this chapter is devoted to Ralph Nader, the well-known advocate of the expansion of strict liability in the area of consumer safety.)

defective product Under *strict liability*, a substantial product that causes injury because the manufacturer violated a legal duty to the user

Under strict liability, it is not the manufacturer's unreasonable or negligent conduct that triggers liability; rather, as a matter of public policy, the manufacturer is held liable for allowing a **defective product** to enter the marketplace. When a producer introduces a defective product into the marketplace, each member in the product's *distribution channel* may become liable for negligence. Figure 11-2 illustrates the key difference in potential liability between potential strict-liability and negligence litigation.

The theory of strict liability holds manufacturers liable on three counts:

1. They have the greatest *control* over the quality of their products.
2. They can *distribute the cost* by raising prices.
3. They have *special responsibilities* in their role as sellers.

The following case was the first to apply this approach to a product-liability dispute.

GRIMSHAW v. FORD MOTOR CO.
California Court of Appeals, 119 Cal. App. 3d 757 (1981)

The Pinto was Ford Motor Co.'s attempt to produce a compact one-ton car that could be marketed for less than $2,000. Unfortunately, however, Ford was willing to sacrifice public safety for corporate profits. In order to fulfill Ford's objective, the Pinto was designed and manufactured with various structural defects, the most significant of which was the location of the gas tank behind the rear axle, rather than above the rear axle as was standard practice for compact cars. In addition, the bumper was extraordinarily weak and protrusions in the automobile's differential housing increased the possibility that rear impact would cause the gas tank to rupture. The dangers of these defects manifested themselves during pre-production testing, when the Pinto failed to meet the industry standard for crashes in excess of 20 miles per hour. Nevertheless, Ford, faced with redesigning and retesting costs, decided to go ahead with production.

The plaintiffs, Richard Grimshaw and the heirs of Lillian Gray, brought this action against Ford for severe injuries sustained when the 1972 Pinto in which Gray and Grimshaw were driving burst into flames after being rear-ended by another vehicle.

The trial court ruled in favor of the plaintiffs, awarding Gray's heirs $500,000 in compensatory damages and Grimshaw over $.5 million in compensatory damages and $3.5 million in punitive damages. Ford appeals.

. . . Harley Copp, a former Ford engineer and executive in charge of the crash testing program, testified that the highest level of Ford's management made the decision to go forward with the production of the Pinto, knowing that the gas tank was vulnerable to puncture and rupture at low rear impact speeds creating a significant risk of death or injury from fire and knowing that "fixes" were feasible at nominal cost. He testified that management's decision was based on the cost savings which would inure from omitting or delaying the "fixes."

. . . .

Ford contends that the court erroneously admitted irrelevant documentary evidence highly prejudicial to Ford. We find the contention to be without merit.

(1) *Exhibit No. 125:*

Exhibit No. 125 was a report presented at a Ford production review meeting in April 1971, recommending action to be taken in anticipation of the promulgation of federal standards on fuel system integrity. The report recommended, *inter alia,* deferral from 1974 to 1976 of the adoption of "flak suits" or "bladders" in all Ford cars, including the Pinto, in order to realize a savings of $20.9 million. The report stated that the cost of the flak suit or bladder would be $4 to $8 per car. . . . A reasonable inference may be drawn from the evidence that despite management's knowledge that the Pinto's fuel system could be made safe at a cost of but $4 to $8 per car, it decided to defer corrective measures to save money and enhance profits. The evidence was thus highly relevant and properly received.

. . . .

Ford contends that its motion for judgment notwithstanding the verdict should have been granted because the evidence was insufficient to support a finding of malice or corporate responsibility for such malice. The record fails to support the contention.

. . . .

Through the results of the crash tests Ford knew that the Pinto's fuel tank and rear structure would expose consumers to serious injury or death in a 20 to 30 mile-per-hour collision. There was evidence that Ford could have corrected the hazardous design defects at minimal cost but decided to defer correction of the shortcomings by engaging in a cost-benefit analysis balancing human lives and limbs against corporate profits. Ford's institutional mentality was shown to be one of callous indifference to public safety. There was substantial evidence that Ford's conduct constituted "conscious disregard" of the probability of injury to members of the consuming public.

Ford's argument that there can be no liability for punitive damages because there was no evidence of corporate ratification of malicious misconduct is equally without merit. . . .

There is substantial evidence that management was aware of the crash tests showing the vulnerability of the Pinto's fuel tank to rupture at low speed rear impacts with consequent significant risk of injury or death of the occupants by fire. There was testimony from several sources that the test results were forwarded up the chain of command. . . .

While much of the evidence was necessarily circumstantial, there was substantial evidence from which the jury could reasonably find that Ford's management decided to proceed with the production of the Pinto with knowledge of test results revealing design defects which rendered the fuel tank extremely vulnerable on rear impact at low speeds and endangered the safety and lives of the occupants. Such conduct constitutes corporate malice.

. . . .

In *Richard Grimshaw v. Ford Motor Company,* the judgment and the order denying Ford's motion for judgment notwithstanding the verdict on the issue of punitive damages are affirmed.

Case Questions:

1. What did the court find most offensive about Ford's decision to go ahead with production of the Pinto?

2. Do you think that the high punitive-damages award was warranted? Why?

FIGURE 11-2 Potential Litigation: Strict Liability versus Negligent Liability

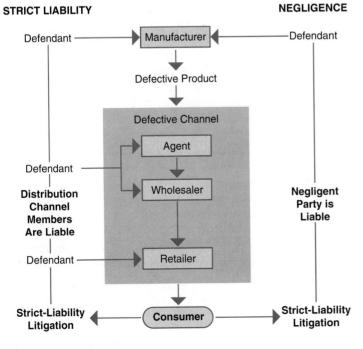

STRICT LIABILITY   NEGLIGENCE

Defendant — Manufacturer — Defendant

Defective Product

Defective Channel

Agent

Wholesaler

Retailer

Defendant / **Distribution Channel Members Are Liable**

Negligent Party is Liable

Consumer

Strict-Liability Litigation ← Consumer → **Strict-Liability Litigation**

Defining Defectiveness

While the tort of negligence imposes the added burden of proving that the defendant was negligent, it at least provides the reasonable person a standard by which to measure negligence. Although strict liability eases the plaintiff's burdens and improves chances for recovery, it does not provide a universally accepted standard for measuring *defectiveness*.

Section 402A of the *Restatement (Second) of Torts* relies on what has become known as the **"consumer-expectations" test:**

"consumer-expectations" test
In *tort law*, principle that a plaintiff is subject to liability for physical harm caused by a product if its defective condition is unreasonably dangerous to the user

1. One who sells any product in a defective condition unreasonably dangerous to the user or consumer or to his property is subject to liability for physical harm thereby caused to the ultimate user or consumer, or to his property if
   (a) the seller is engaged in the business of selling such a product, and
   (b) the product is expected to and does reach the user or consumer without substantial change in the condition in which it is sold.
2. The rule stated in Subsection (1) applies although
   (a) the seller has exercised all possible care in the preparation and sale of his product, and
   (b) the user or consumer has not bought the product from or entered into any contractual relation with the seller.

"Unreasonably dangerous" means a product that is "dangerous to an extent beyond that which would be contemplated by the ordinary consumer who purchases it, with the ordinary knowledge common to the community as to its characteristics."[4]

Although the *Restatement (Second) of Torts* definition has had great influence, it is not universally accepted. A California court, for example, has rejected the need to prove unreasonable danger, arguing that this defeats the purpose of strict liability by imposing a negligence-like burden of proof on the plaintiff.

TESTS FOR DEFECTIVENESS. The Minnesota Supreme Court has made a move to replace product-oriented standards of design defect with a conduct-oriented test. In *Bilotta v. Kelly Co.* (346 N.W.2d 616 [1984]), the plaintiff's injuries resulted when a mechanical dock-board suddenly fell to its lowest position after a truck pulled away. Concerned about arbitrary and sometimes conflicting decisions based on the consumer expectations test of the *Restatement (Second) of Torts*, the court proposed a new standard that takes into account certain business realities. The court argued that in many design-defect cases like the *Bilotta* case, the manufacturer knows and appreciates the risks but consciously chooses a less safe design. For example, defendant Kelly Co. offered a safety device on its top-of-the-line dockboard to prevent precisely the kind of accident that took place. However, it chose to market less expensive models without the safety device in order to remain competitive. The court argued that in this type of situation, the manufacturer's conduct is as much an issue as the product itself.

The *Bilotta* jury was instructed to balance the likelihood and the gravity of the harm inflicted on the plaintiff against the feasibility and the burden of taking effective precautions to avoid that harm. Although this test merges strict liability with some aspects of negligence, the court deliberately avoided making the plaintiff prove actual negligence.

---

[4] *Restatement (Second) of Torts*, Section 402A, Comment g.

Due to the efforts of many people over the past twenty-five years, the movement for consumer rights in the United States has become a force in politics and industry. Few would argue, however, that its current successes and influence—and the generally high level of awareness enjoyed by consumer issues in the public mind—result in large measure from the efforts of one man—Ralph Nader. Since the landmark publication of Unsafe at Any Speed in 1965, Nader has assumed the public interest as his mandate on many fronts—from auto safety to insurance reform to industrial pollution. Along the way, he has, predictably, angered entrenched corporate players who view his attacks on the one hand, as self-interested publicity ploys and, on the other hand, as misguided "left-wing" attacks on the system. Despite the criticism, however, Nader's accomplishments are so visible that the virtual folk-hero mantle that he wears is understandable.

Born in 1934 into a Connecticut family of Lebanese immigrants, Nader was raised on a diet of social justice. Interested in muckraking from an early age, he received degrees from Princeton (in government and economics) and Harvard Law School, where he began writing on issues of social reform. His first article on auto safety was published in the Harvard Law Review in 1958; called "American Cars: Designed for Death," it dramatically pictured the corporate negligence that he saw as the cause of needless highway carnage. Working in Washington in the mid-1960s, Nader compiled a report on highway safety for the Department of Labor and began developing the media contacts that would help to make his later work so successful.

That government report became Unsafe at Any Speed, whose influence on public policy and corporate liability would be hard to underestimate. With careful documentation, Nader targeted General Motors and the Chevrolet Corvair, maintaining that the manufacturer's design and production, not drivers themselves or the quality and condition of roads, were responsible for highway deaths. Legislation followed in the Traffic and Motor Vehicle Safety Act of 1966. Harassment of Nader by General Motors only provided public sympathy for him, and the publicity undoubtedly helped to get the law passed.

Nader's personal goal was to become a "people's lawyer," and, as his activism and reputation grew, he built an infrastructure to demand corporate and government accountability for consumer protection in a variety of fields. Nader's strategy includes legal means as well as lobbying efforts to achieve results. Thus, his associates (sometimes called "Nader's Raiders") are usually lawyers whose task is to influence and shape legislation as well as to challenge corporations. The organizations that Nader has built have become an interlocking system of legal and lobbying groups, such as the Center for Study of Responsive Law, the Corporate Accountability Research Group, and the Public Interest Research Group. Many of these groups operate both at federal and state and local levels.

By becoming a sort of traveling salesman for consumerism, zealously campaigning and speaking to groups nationwide, Nader has over the years exposed industrial hazards, bureaucratic inefficiencies in enforcing government safety standards, and the continuing failure of the automobile industry to build safe cars.

In the last few years, Nader has put his efforts behind expanding the tort system, maintaining that this step must be taken so that plaintiffs can "combat industrial violence." It is Nader's position that proposed tort reforms would only dismantle the civil jury system and thus restrict a consumer's ability to sue corporations whose products are unsafe or environmentally damaging. Although it is generally accepted that the courts are hopelessly backlogged, Nader contends that instituting a victim-compensation system similar to the workers-compensation fund (rather than suing in court) would make fund payment an exclusive remedy. According to Nader, tort suits are more effective "because they are not predictable."

On another front, Nader has taken on the cable-television business, launching a citizens-awareness project in 1991. Nader is arguing for more federal regulation of the cable TV industry, including a drive to make it responsive to its initial promise of community and educational programming. The "people's lawyer" wants to see people more deeply involved in shaping a powerful communications force in their lives.

As we noted earlier, Nader's career has never been free from attack; he has ruffled a lot of powerful feathers, and he is no saint. In 1990, for example, in an article entitled "Ralph Nader Inc.," Forbes magazine sought to shatter some of the myths surrounding the man. One of the magazine's main assertions was that Nader receives financial support from plaintiffs' attorneys—lawyers who would benefit from precisely the kinds of consumer suits that he supports—and that these trial lawyers might have some influence on him. Regarding what they called the "Ralph Nader Trust"—the combined organizations that have grown around his original nucleus—Forbes also questions his "sainthood," pointing out that the nonprofit, tax-exempt status of his organizations is "loosely policed" even as Nader crusades for strong regulation for others; that his organizations tend to be quite secretive, especially about funding; and that Nader groups are not democratically run.

UNAVOIDABLY UNSAFE PRODUCTS. The *Restatement (Second) of Torts* recognizes the impossibility of making entirely safe some products that are beneficial to society. Prescription drugs and vaccines are prime examples. Thus, the *Restatement* does not hold drug companies strictly liable for a product that is properly manufactured and accompanied by appropriate directions and warnings. Such a product is not defective simply because of its unavoidable hazards; there must be something wrong with it in addition (Section 402A, comment k). In other words, although drugs are excluded from design defects, they remain subject to manufacturing defects. As we saw earlier, drug companies must warn the medical profession, but not necessarily patients, of the potential dangers.

Kearl v. Lederle Laboratories (218 Cal. Rptr. 453 [1985]) provides a good example of how this principle works. *Kearl* concerned a child who developed paralysis about four weeks after taking an oral polio vaccine. The child's parents alleged both that the vaccine's design was defective and that the warning they had read and signed noting the risk of contracting polio was inadequate. The appeals court exempted the vaccine from design liability on the grounds that it was unavoidably unsafe and judged the warning to be adequate.

The State-of-the-Art Defense

state-of-the-art defense In tort cases, the argument that design defects or other flaws not known when the product was made are acceptable, and that the manufacturer is responsible only for knowledge current at the time of manufacture

The so-called **state-of-the-art defense,** which has profound implications for business executives, lies on the frontiers of strict liability. The central argument is that a manufacturer should not be held responsible for design defects and other flaws that were not known to be dangerous at the time the product was marketed. Instead, manufacturers should be judged by whatever level of knowledge was "state of the art" when the product was manufactured.

Even though recognized by many jurisdictions, this defense remains controversial. Thus, there are wide variations throughout the country, not only in whether the state-of-the-art defense is recognized but in how it is defined and applied. One approach emphasizes cost and practicability: State-of-the-art knowledge is interpreted as a mixture of current industry standards and technical and economic feasibility. A second approach limits the defense more strictly by equating state-of-the-art knowledge with current scientific wisdom and technological understanding. Under this approach, defects are acceptable only if it was technologically *impossible* to remedy them or scientifically *impossible* to discover them at the time. The following case illustrates how the courts apply this latter approach.

BESHADA v. JOHNS-MANVILLE PRODUCTS CORPORATION
New Jersey Supreme Court, 447 A.2d 539 (1982)

The plaintiffs, workers suffering from asbestos-related illnesses and survivors of stricken workers, sued the defendants, manufacturers and distributors of asbestos products, on a theory of strict product liability. In essence, the plaintiff's claim alleged a failure to give any warning of the adverse health effects of exposure to asbestos prior to the 1960's. In response, the defendants asserted the state-of-the-art defense on the basis that the U.S. medical community did not perceive asbestos as a health hazard until the 1960's. The trial court denied the plaintiffs' motion to have the defense stricken from the record. This subsequent appeal by the plaintiffs in the New Jersey Supreme Court focuses on the validity of the traditional state of the art defense.

. . . .

Plaintiffs based their motion on *Freund v. Cellofilm Properties, Inc.* (1981), our most recent case concerning product liability. In Freund, Justice Handler elaborated the difference between negligence and strict liability in a failure to warn case. He explained that in strict liability cases knowledge of the dangerousness of the product is imputed to defendants. Plaintiff need not prove that defendant knew or should have known of its dangerousness. The only issue is whether the product distributed by defendant was reasonably safe. Plaintiffs urge that *Freund* disposed of the state-of-the-art issue. Since defendant's knowledge of the dangers of the product is presumed, it is irrelevant whether the existence of such dangers was scientifically discoverable. Defendants respond that *Freund* imputes to defendants only "existing knowledge, the technical knowledge available at the time of manufacture."

. . . .

. . . Defendants argue that the question of whether the product can be made safer must be limited to consideration of the available technology at the time the product was distributed. Liability would be absolute, defendants argue, if it could be imposed on the basis of a subsequently discovered means to make the product safer since technology will always be developing new ways to make products safer. Such a rule, they assert, would make manufacturers liable whenever their products cause harm, whether or not they are reasonably fit for their foreseeable purposes.

. . . .

. . . [T]he principles laid down in *Freund* and our prior cases contradict defendants' position. Essentially, state-of-the-art is a negligence defense. It seeks to explain why defendants are not culpable for failing to provide a warning. They assert, in effect, that because they could not have known the product was dangerous, they acted reasonably in marketing it without a warning. But in strict liability cases, culpability is irrelevant. The product was unsafe. That it was unsafe because of the state of technology does not change the fact that it was unsafe. Strict liability focuses on the product, not the fault of the manufacturer. . . .

. . . .

The most important inquiry, however, is whether imposition of liability for failure to warn of dangers which were undiscoverable at the time of manufacture will advance the goals and policies sought to be achieved by our strict liability rules. We believe that it will.

Risk Spreading. One of the most important arguments generally advanced for imposing strict liability is that the manufacturers and distributors of defective products can best allocate the costs of the injuries resulting from those products. The premise is that the price of a product should reflect all of its costs, including the cost of injuries caused by the product. This can best be accomplished by imposing liability on the manufacturer and distributors. Those persons can insure against liability and incorporate the cost of the insurance in the price of the product. In this way, the costs of the product will be borne by those who profit from it: the manufacturers and distributors who profit from its sale and the buyers who profit from its use. . . .

Defendants argue that this policy is not forwarded by imposition of liability for unknowable hazards. Since such hazards by definition are not predicted, the price of the hazardous product will not be adjusted to reflect the costs of the injuries it will produce. Rather, defendants state, the cost "will be borne by the public at large and reflected in a general, across the board increase in premiums to compensate for unanticipated

risks." There is some truth in this assertion, but it is not a bad result.

First, the same argument can be made as to hazards which are deemed scientifically knowable but of which the manufacturers are unaware. . . .

Second, spreading the costs of injuries among all those who produce, distribute and purchase manufactured products is far preferable to imposing it on the innocent victims who suffer illnesses and disability from defective products. . . .

Finally, contrary to defendants' assertion, this rule will not cause the price and production level of manufactured products to diverge from the so-called economically efficient level. Rather, the rule will force the price of any particular product to reflect the cost of insuring against the possibility that the product will turn out to be defective.

Accident Avoidance. In *Sutter* [*v. San Angelo Foundry & Machine Company* (1979)], we stated:

"Strict liability in a sense is but an attempt to minimize the costs of accidents and to consider who should bear those costs. . . . Using this approach, it is obvious that the manufacturer rather than the factory employee is "in the better position both to judge whether avoidance costs would exceed forseeable accident costs and to act on that judgment."

Defendants urge that this argument has no force as to hazards which by definition were undiscoverable. Defendants have treated the level of technological knowledge at a given time as an independent variable not affected by defendants' conduct. But this view ignores the important role of industry in product safety research. The "state-of-the-art" at a given time is partly determined by how much industry invests in safety research. By imposing on manufacturers the costs of failure to discover hazards, we create an incentive for them to invest more actively in safety research.

Fact finding process. . . . The vast confusion that is virtually certain to arise from any attempt to deal in a trial setting with the concept of scientific knowability constitutes a strong reason for avoiding the concept altogether by striking the state-of-the-art defense.

Scientific knowability, as we understand it, refers not to what in fact was known at the time, but to what *could have been known* at the time. . . . Proof of what could have been known will inevitably be complicated, costly, confusing and time-consuming. . . .

The concept of knowability is complicated further by the fact, noted above, that the level of investment in safety research by manufacturers is one determinant of the state-of-the-art at any given time. Fairness suggests that manufacturers not be excused from liability because their prior inadequate investment in safety rendered the hazards of their product unknowable.

. . . .

For the reasons expressed above, we conclude that plaintiffs' position is consistent with our holding in *Freund* and prior cases underlying strict liability. . . .

Defendants have argued that it is unreasonable to impose a duty on them to warn of the unknowable. Failure to warn of a risk which one could not have known existed is not unreasonable conduct. But this argument is based on negligence principles. We are not saying what defendants should have done. That is negligence. We are saying that defendants' products were not reasonably safe because they did not have a warning. Without a warning, users of the product were unaware of its hazards and could not protect themselves from injury. We impose strict liability because it is unfair for the distributors of a defective product not to compensate its victims. As between those innocent victims and the distributors—and the public which consumes their products—which should bear the unforeseen costs of the product.

The judgment of the trial court is reversed; the plaintiff's motion to strike the state-of-the-art defense is granted.

Case Questions:

1. What does the decision find problematic with regard to allowing "state of the art" as a defense to strict liability?

2. What is the primary difference between negligence and strict liability?

3. How strongly do the traditional policies behind strict liability play into the court's decision?

In 1983, two other courts were more hospitable to the state-of-the-art defense in design-defect cases. A New Jersey court, while emphasizing that evidence on the state of the art was not an absolute defense in strict-liability cases, did allow state-of-the-art considerations to influence the risk-utility test used to determine design defects (*O'Brien v. Muskin Corp.*, 463 A.2d 298 [1983]). An Oregon court embraced the state-of-the-art defense even more enthusiastically, requiring the plaintiff to establish that an alternative, safer design was technologically and commercially feasible at the time when the product was manufactured (*Appel v. Standex International Corp.*, 660 P.2d 686 [1983]).

■ *Concept Check 11-4 Strict Product Liability*

- In what key ways does *strict liability* differ from *negligence* as a criterion?
- Describe the *"consumer expectations" test* for product defectiveness.
- Explain the *state-of-the-art defense*. What is the central argument of this defense?

■ WARRANTY

warranty A guarantee or assurance made to the purchaser of a product

The warranty provisions of the Uniform Commercial Code (UCC) provide alternative grounds of recovery for people who are injured by the products they use. To understand warranties, we turn from tort analysis to contracts. A **warranty** is essentially a guarantee or an assurance that is made to the purchaser of a product. Although there are many types of warranties, we will cover only the three most important forms here: (1) *express warranties* (2) the *implied warranty of merchantability* and (3) the *implied warranty of fitness for a particular purpose*. Finally, we will examine the concept of *privity*.

 ### Express Warranties

express warranty Affirmations of fact or premises made about a product by a seller to a buyer

Express warranties are defined and governed by Section 2-313 of the UCC: They are affirmations of fact or promises made by the seller that relate to the goods and become part of the basis of the bargain. Express warranties are frequently created by oral or written statements about the nature of a product, although they need not include the words "guarantee" or "warranty." They can also be created when a seller uses a sample or model as part of the bargain. A real-life example is the statement of a book salesman that the cover of a particular book is made of genuine leather.

A description of the goods may also be interpreted as a claim about their characteristics and thus an express warranty. For example, the description of a truckload of apples as "Grade-A MacIntosh" is an express warranty. Express warranties may also be created by blueprints, technical specifications, standards set by past deliveries, advertisements, statements, illustrations made in brochures, or the display of a model or sample.

Although the oral comments made by a salesperson may be as binding as the written statements composed by the manufacturer, not every salesperson's claim is an express warranty. Section 2-313 of the UCC clearly states that "an affirmation merely of the value of the goods or a statement purporting to be merely the seller's opinion or commendation of the goods does not create a warranty." This provision recognizes the reality of sales "puffing": It is an accepted part of our market system that salespeople try to present products in the best possible light in order to make a deal. When a stereo salesperson says, "In my opinion that is one heck of a stereo system," it is clearly an opinion and not a warranty. When the salesman says, "This system has a new set of Panasonic speakers," however, an express warranty is created.

SAMPLES AND MODELS. When sellers use a sample or model of goods for sale as part of the basis of the bargain, they guarantee by law that the bulk of the lot being sold will conform to the quality of that sample or model. This principle creates problems with nonmanufactured goods subject to natural variations— for example, coal or catered food.[5] In addition, the sample itself sometimes creates ambiguities. For instance, a firm selling cherries once sent a sizing card with a circular hole 54/56 inches in diameter to a buyer to indicate the size of the cherries. A dispute arose over whether this meant that the average size or the minimum size of the cherries would be 54/56 inches. The court avoided that particular problem by holding that the size card was not a model or sample (*Washington Fruit & Produce Co. v. Ted. Mirski Co.*, 3 UCC Rep. Serv. 175 [1965]).

Implied Warranties

In contrast to express warranties, **implied warranties** are created by law as a matter of public policy. They do not arise from any agreement between the parties to a sale. In order to protect buyers, the courts tend to construe implied warranties.

MERCHANTABILITY. The implied **warranty of merchantability** is governed by Section 2-314 of the UCC. This warranty is limited to *merchants*—that is, professional sellers with some special skills or knowledge about their goods. Isolated sales by nonmerchants are not subject to this implied warranty.

At the heart of the UCC's approach is the idea that merchantable goods must be "fit for the ordinary purposes for which such goods are used." For example, if you buy an AM-FM radio, you rightfully expect it to receive AM and FM radio stations. Likewise, refrigerators are supposed to keep food cold and lightbulbs should give light. Other UCC clauses, however, imply that the standards of merchantability are relative rather than absolute. Goods are judged

implied warranty A guarantee of assurance to a purchaser which is created by law as a matter of public policy and which does not arise from any agreement between buyer and seller

warrant of merchantability *Implied warranty* given by a seller that a product is fit for the ordinary purposes for which it is used

---

[5] *Sylvia Coal Co. & Coke Co.*, 156 S.E. 2d 1 (1967), and *Graulich Caterer, Inc. v. Hans Holterbosch, Inc.*, 243 A.2d 253 (1968).

against industry standards, so that products which are equal in quality to other brands on the market are normally merchantable. Those goals must, however, conform strictly to any trade descriptions used in the contract. For example, Grade-A butter has a specific meaning in the food business; Grade-B butter sold as Grade-A would not pass the merchantability test. (The YOU DECIDE feature in this chapter examines the application of the "consumer-expectation" test to the implied warranty of merchantability.)

YOU DECIDE
The Implied Warranty

An implied warranty means that consumers will receive goods that are merchantable—that is, they will receive what they are led to expect they will get, goods that will perform safely when used in an intended or reasonably foreseeable manner. On the surface, the concept seems unambiguous. However, when examined carefully, the concept of "consumer expectations" is neither simple nor clear. Whose expectations, for example, and for what kinds of goods? Is an injured plaintiff the determinant for the expectation or is some community standard? Can a jury be expected to decide objectively what a reasonable expectation is? Or might a jury decision be subjective because jurors are either unaware of community expectations or unfamiliar with a product?

If you purchase an item—for example, an electric pencil sharpener—it must, according to the UCC, be "fit for ordinary purposes for which such goods are used." Thus, you can reasonably expect it to sharpen pencils—probably faster and to a sharper point than a mechanical one. However, if it turns your pencil into a mass of splinters which then become embedded in your hand, you might argue that the item was defective and, if you are injured, press a product-liability lawsuit accordingly. The jury might be instructed by the judge to apply the "consumer expectation" test in your case.

Some products, however, do not easily fit this description, and questions like those noted above may arise. Areas in which it is difficult to use the consumer-expectations test often involve potentially dangerous design characteristics or toxic ingredients that the ordinary consumer—plaintiff or juror—is unlikely to know about or expect. If the defective product is a fork-lift truck, for instance, a jury made up of ordinary community members would probably not know what a consumer's expectations should be regarding this complex piece of equipment. Would jurors thus be able to render an objective judgment? Would the consumer expectation test, deriving as it does from the implied warranty of fitness and merchantability, be appropriate?

In the case of Webster v. Blue Ship Tea Room (198 N.E.2d 309 [1964]), we encounter the case of an implied warranty as applied to New England fish chowder served to a customer in a Boston restaurant. (UCC 2-315, which covers merchantability, specifically states that "the serving for value of food or drink . . . is a sale.") Webster, the plaintiff and a native New Englander, suffered serious injury to her throat from an unexpected bone in the fish chowder. Should her "consumer expectations" have included chowder without bones (fish chowder is not clam chowder)? Was there an implied warranty that fish chowder which is "fit for the ordinary purpose" would be bone-free? As the judge sitting on this case, would you have found for the plaintiff? For further discussion, see p. 412.

warranty of fitness for a particular purpose *Implied warranty that applies only when a seller knows a buyer's particular purpose in purchasing the goods and when a buyer depends heavily on a seller's skill or expertise in selecting the goods*

FITNESS FOR A PARTICULAR PURPOSE. The implied **warranty of fitness for a particular purpose** is governed by Section 2-315 of the UCC. This warranty applies only when the buyer is especially dependent on the seller's expertise. To establish the warranty, the buyer must indicate to the seller both (1) his particular needs and (2) his reliance on the seller's advice to select the proper item. If the seller then supplies the wrong product—even if that product is properly made and merchantable—for the buyer's purposes, the warranty of fitness for a particular purpose is breached.

For example, in *Lewis v. Mobil Oil Corp.* (438 F.2d 500 [1971]), a sawmill was damaged when the wrong oil was added to the hydraulic system. The buyer told the salesperson that he did not know what kind of oil to buy and that he was depending on the salesperson to make the right choice for him. He then explained that the oil was for a specific kind of hydraulic system at his sawmill. Because this explanation established an implied warranty, the seller was responsible for the damages caused by the wrong oil; because companies often buy goods that must be specially selected, manufactured, or assembled to fit into their operations, implied warranties of this kind are especially important for business.

Privity ⬿O

A complex issue that runs through the whole history of product liability, **privity** is a relationship or connection between contracting parties. At common law, a plaintiff had to have privity with the defendant in order to bring an action against that defendant. Manufacturers could thus use their lack of privity with the ultimate consumers of their products as a defense against product-liability suits of all kinds. A major theme in the history of product liability is the erosion of the privity defense.

Privity considerations are important in actions for breach of warranty. Suppose, for example, that you purchase a defective lawnmower from a retailer and wish to sue on a warranty theory. Although there is a direct contract between you and the retailer, you wish to reach further up the distribution chain and sue the manufacturer. Is there sufficient privity of contract between you and the manufacturer? What if someone other than yourself—perhaps a member of your family—is hurt by the lawnmower? Is there still sufficient privity of contract to support a suit? These two examples illustrate the two different dimensions of privity (*see* Fig. 11-3). **Horizontal privity** refers to all the people who use a product. **Vertical privity** refers to a product's chain of distribution.

Privity retains its importance only in cases involving implied warranties. The public-policy rationale for eliminating privity requirements in express-warranty cases was stated as far back as 1932 (*Baxter v. Ford Motor Co.*, 12 P.2d 409 [1932]). The reasoning is that manufacturers reach out directly to consumers both in creating a demand for their products and in creating express warranties through advertising. Therefore, the manufacturers, not the intermediary channels of distribution, should be responsible for the breach of those warranties.

We will examine horizontal and vertical privity in more detail and then discuss the increasingly important privity theory of *market-share liability*.

HORIZONTAL PRIVITY. Section 2-318 of the UCC addresses the problem of horizontal privity. There are three alternative definitions from which states adopting the UCC must choose. Even the most restrictive option extends horizontal

privity In *product liability*, a direct relationship between seller and buyer that may serve as the standard for such actions as *breach of warranty* (*see also* Chapter 10)

horizontal privity In actions for *breach of warranty*, the relationships among all people who use a product

vertical privity In actions for *breach of warranty*, the relationships constituting a product's chain of distribution

FIGURE 11-3 The Chain of Privity

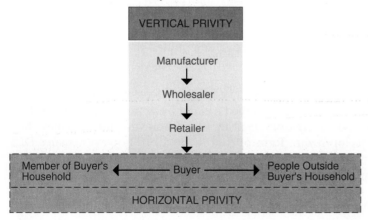

privity to household and family members and to guests. The other options eliminate all restrictions on the relationship to the buyer, allowing anyone "who may reasonably be expected to use, consume or be affected by the goods" to sue for breach of warranty. At least 16 states have adopted a less restrictive rule.

The three versions of the UCC provision also vary in their limitations on the types of losses covered. Two limit the expansion of horizontal privity to personal injury; the third extends it to property damage. Only economic losses remain uncovered.

VERTICAL PRIVITY. The UCC leaves the question of vertical privity to the courts to resolve. Because consumers often find that the retailers from whom they purchase defective items do not offer them any recourse, the issue comes up frequently. Either the retailer has since gone out of business or lacks the financial resources to cover losses. Currently, the courts are divided over whether to extend vertical privity to manufacturers.

Vertical privity is most important when the losses involved are strictly economic—when personal injury or property damage are involved, a plaintiff can sue in tort. For economic damages, there is no such alternative.

The case of *Nobility Homes of Texas, Inc. v. Shivers* (557 S.W.2d 77 [1977]) addressed just this problem. The case concerned the purchase of a mobile home from an independent retailer who later went out of business. The home was so defective that it was not habitable, and the buyer's only recourse was to sue the manufacturer under the implied warranty of merchantability. In its decision to award the buyer his economic losses, the Texas Supreme Court carved out an exception to the common-law idea of privity: The court argued that despite the lack of privity, consumers should be protected from devastating economic losses caused by defective products.

MARKET-SHARE LIABILITY. In cases involving large numbers of victims injured by certain pharmaceuticals, the concept of **market-share liability** has been examined as a remedy. This theory is based on the idea of *collective liability* and maintains in general that an entire industry is liable for the injuries caused by a certain product. Liability is apportioned according to a manufacturer's market-share size for that product. Market-share liability applies specifically to cases in which the plaintiff cannot determine exactly which manufacturer produced the pharmaceutical that caused the injury. Figure 11-4 illustrates the relationship among producers, distribution-channel members, and consumers in a case to which the doctrine of market-share liability may apply.

market-share liability In actions with many victims of a product whose exact specific manufacturer cannot be determined, the principle that *collective liability* exists for which the entire industry is responsible

Although market-share liability thus deviates from the traditional tort concept that a plaintiff must clearly be able to identify the manufacturer of the product causing the injury, the courts have determined that only under certain unique circumstances can it be used—namely, in suits involving the pharmaceutical known as DES.

This theory of liability was critical in *Sindell v. Abbott Laboratories* (607 P.2d 924 [1980]), a California case that involved a claim by women that DES, a drug that their mothers had taken from 1947 to 1971 to prevent miscarriages, had caused them to develop a rare form of cancer. By 1980, however, many DES manufacturers were out of business. Moreover, the plaintiffs had to prove that the remaining manufacturers had actually marketed the drug that their mothers had used—an almost impossible task. Recognizing the plaintiffs' difficulty in obtaining a remedy, the court allocated liability to DES manufacturers in

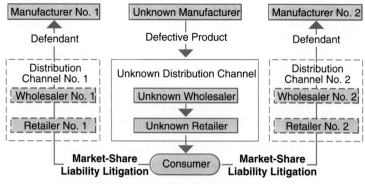

FIGURE 11-4 Potential Litgation: Market-Share Liability

proportion to the share of the DES market that they held at the time. A manufacturer will subsequently be held liable unless it can prove that it did *not* market DES for use during pregnancy.

Court findings in more recent cases involving DES, other pharmaceuticals, and consumer and industrial products have indicated that market-share liability should be applied only in very specific occurrences of product liability. For instance, in *Shackil v. Lederle Laboratories* (561 A.2d 511 [N.J. 1989]), market-share liability was rejected for an injury resulting from a children's DPT vaccine; the court determined that the product was used as part of a national health program, that there was no latent-effects problem (as with DES), and that vaccines are not generic. In addition, the courts have stated that if all potentially negligent defendants can be identified, then market-share liability should not be applied. (*See* the ETHICAL ENVIRONMENT box for further discussion of court determinations in a variety of cases—and the appropriateness of linking liability to market shares.)

Warranty Disclaimers

Merchants sometimes try to sell goods without any warranties—for example, by posting a sign saying, "This product is sold without any warranties express or implied." The UCC allows sellers to disclaim warranties and to limit the buyer's remedies for breach of warranty, but only within strict limits. In addition, the UCC offers the courts a great deal of leeway in sinking down such exculpatory clauses. Because merchants hold far stronger bargaining positions than buyers, the courts have not looked favorably upon attempts to disclaim liability.

Express Warranties. Although it may seem illogical to be able to disclaim express warranties, the UCC accepts the possibility as long as the language of the disclaimer and the express warranties can be interpreted as consistent with each other. This question of consistency is tried as an issue of fact—a procedure that gives the courts a good deal of flexibility. In general, the courts have struck down disclaimers contained in the same written agreement as express warranties.

Implied Warranties. More often, disclaimers seek to eliminate implied warranties. Although the warranty of merchantability may be disclaimed verbally or in writing, the disclaimer must in both cases mention the word "merchantability." By contrast, a valid disclaimer of fitness for a particular purpose does not require any particular wording but must be in writing. Written disclaimers of any kind must be *conspicuous*—that is, printed in a way that

Because it seems to contradict traditional tort law, the concept of market-share liability occupies a unique position within the broader arena of product-liability suits and awards. Although the principle arose as the solution to a DES suit (Sindell v. Abbott Laboratories), in the thirteen years since that decision, the concept has been reevaluated, its application more narrowly defined, and its fairness questioned. Particularly instructive is Hymowitz v. Eli Lilly & Co., a 1989 case also involving DES, which provided an innovative development to the ruling in Sindell.

In Sindell, the court determined that because the cancer that arose in the daughters of DES users who had taken the drug during pregnancy did not appear until the women were teenagers, finding and identifying the manufacturer who caused a specific woman's disease was virtually impossible. Over a period of 24 years, over 300 companies had made and sold the generic product, a synthetic hormone whose efficacy in preventing miscarriages was discovered in 1947; over three million pregnant women took the drug. In order to provide a remedy for the plaintiffs, the court devised market-share as a type of collective liability, observing that modern society produces "fungible goods which may harm consumers and which cannot be traced to any specific producer. The response of the courts can be . . . denying recovery to those injured by such products, or to fashion remedies to meet these changing needs" (607 P.2d at 936).

As part of the remedy, the court provided two means by which the liability of potential defendants would be kept reasonable: (1) the plaintiff had to sue a substantial share of the DES market; and (2) the defendant manufacturer could exculpate itself by establishing that it had not produced and marketed the injury-causing drug. Both of these means addressed the unfairness either of allocating liability to a firm that had not caused the injury or of allocating too great a share of the damages burden to a specific manufacturer. It was not until later DES cases, however, that this principle was refined and some assumptions about market-share liability questioned.

In one DES case, Smith v. Eli Lilly & Co. (137 Ill. 2d 222, 560 N.E.2d 324 [1990]), the court rejected market-share liability as a flawed concept, stating that because reliable market information was unavailable, damages apportioned on the basis of market share would result in arbitrary variations in awards. The judgment here made it clear that it would not be fair to make a firm pay damages out of proportion to its liability—that liability could not accurately be determined.

In product-liability cases outside the DES arena, the market-share liability solution was rejected. For example, although asbestos-related injuries share with DES illnesses a long latency period, asbestos products, which are produced in thousands of different forms with different asbestos content, are not fungible. Without a generic product, the manufacturers did not pose the same risk to the sufferers.

Other liability cases involve vaccines. In one example, (Sheffield v. Eli Lilly & Co., 144 Cal. App. 3d 583, 192 Cal. Rptr. 870 [1983]), Sindell was rejected because it was found that negligence occurred in manufacturing rather than design (remember, DES was a generic—everyone's formula was the same), so not all producers shared the blame. There were also the social ramifications of such a liability finding—for example, would it deter pharmaceutical companies from developing new drugs, inhibiting a process that ultimately benefits the public? In a 1989 case involving DPT, Shackil v. Lederle Laboratories (561 A.2d 511 N.J. [1989]), market-share liability was also rejected, in part on a similar public-policy basis. The court also noted that, unlike DES victims, those injured by the vaccine had an alternative remedy in the National Childhood Vaccine Injury Act of 1986, which would compensate them even if they could not prove who the manufacturer of the vaccine was.

A New York case, Hymowitz v. Eli Lilly & Co. (73 N.Y.2d 487, 539 N.E.2d 1069, 541 N.Y.S.2d 941, cert. denied, 110 S. Ct. 350 [1989]), provided that although market-share liability, as determined in Sindell, applies, the preferable method for determining the market share for DES was to use a national rather than a local market. The court ruled that the role of an individual manufacturer's product in causing the injuries of any particular plaintiff is irrelevant to the market-share theory; rather, each manufacturer's liability should be based on the overall risk produced by the product. A drug manufacturer can avoid being held liable for DES injuries only if it can prove that it did not market DES for use during pregnancy.

The idea that liability is to be measured by the risk to the public at-large, and not to a specific plaintiff, is the current status of market-share liability. This principle represents a broader awareness of social responsibility than did the earlier finding in Sindell. It also has the benefit of providing a uniform standard applicable to all DES cases, thus easing burdens to both the parties and the courts. However, many analysts point out that even with its advances, Hymowitz still leaves open the question of whether, in pursuit of goals of social benefit and fairness to those who cannot find remedy elsewhere, we are penalizing those who bear no responsibility for the problem.

ought to be noticed by a reasonable person (say, in bold-face capital letters in a contrasting color). Disclaimers cannot be made *subsequent to* the contract for sale. Thus, disclaimers printed on delivery tables, invoices, or manuals are not valid.

On the other hand, the phrases "as is" and "with all faults" provide the merchant with broad, powerful, and valid disclaimers. Under Section

2-316(3)(a) of the UCC, such "terms in ordinary commercial usage are understood to mean that the buyer takes the entire risk as to the quality of the goods involved." Thus, it is possible for a used-car salesman legitimately to disclaim all warranties on a vehicle by displaying a sign saying "as is." Even an "as is" clause is not a valid disclaimer, however, if "the circumstances indicate otherwise."

The case of *Lee v. Peterson*, 716 P.2d 1373 (1986), shows how the UCC rules governing disclaimers are applied. The dispute concerned a used copier machine that produced copies too light to be worthwhile. The acceptance form stated that the 30-day express warranty (limited to the replacement of parts worn and broken during normal use and excluding photoconductor drums) was "in lieu of all other warranties and/or representations. . . . " In fact, the machine did need a new photoconductor drum. The court ruled that the disclaimer could not apply to the warranty of merchantability because it neither mentioned the word "merchantability" nor contained an "as is" statement. The buyer prevailed.

The Magnuson-Moss Warranty Act ☆ *KNOW* ☆

Statutes like the **Magnuson-Moss Warranty Act** provide yet a third approach to product liability. This act, effective since 1975, deals with consumer-product warranties and it is enforced by the Federal Trade Commission. This act provides the kind of express protection for consumers that the UCC does not. It does not require warranties, but if a warranty is offered, it must comply with the statute's requirements. Although Magnuson-Moss changes the substance of warranties very little, it has forced manufacturers to improve the way in which warranty information is communicated to consumers. The act itself declares that its purposes are "to improve the adequacy of information available to consumers, prevent deception, and improve competition in the marketing of consumer products."

There are three key substantive changes made by the Magnuson-Moss Act:

1. The emphasis is shifted from refunds to repair or replacement.
2. Warranties cannot be made conditional on the use of approved suppliers or replacement parts unless they are provided for free.
3. It is impossible to disclaim implied warranties totally. Even in limited warranties, implied warranties must run as long as the written warranty.

Magnuson-Moss Warranty Act A federal law protecting users of all tangible consumer products made or sold in the U.S. by requiring *warranties* to comply with statutory requirements

CONSUMER / PROTECTION NOT professionals

Scope of Magnuson-Moss. Magnuson-Moss covers all tangible consumer products made or sold in the United States that are "normally used for personal, family, or household purposes." Thus, it covers a car bought for a family but not a bulldozer purchased by a construction firm. In addition, some housing components, such as replacement siding, sump pumps, and furnaces, are covered. It applies only to consumers—that is, people who do not buy for resale—and to products over a certain price ($5 to $15, depending on the provision).

The scope of the Magnuson-Moss Act is limited to written warranties offered in conjunction with the sale of an item. This provision excludes all the implied warranties and many of the express warranties established by the UCC. Because there is no requirement to offer written warranties, however, a manufacturer can easily avoid the act's mandate.

The broadest of the act's requirements is that warrantors must "fully and conspicuously disclose in simple and readily understood language" the terms and conditions of any warranty offered. FTC rules have enlarged upon this stipulation by requiring that sellers of products costing more than $15 make the text of written warranties available to consumers before they make a purchase.

***Recovering Damages under* Magnuson-Moss.** Consumers with relatively large claims may bring suit in state or federal court. If victorious, they may be awarded costs and attorney's fees. When large numbers of plaintiffs are involved, class-action suits may be brought by the FTC or by private parties. Plaintiffs may also bring actions under state "Littel FTC Acts." Finally, the FTC can obtain cease-and-desist orders against warrantors or impose fines of $10,000 per violation.

■ *Concept Check 11-5* Warranty

- Define *express* and *implied warranties* and explain the key differences between them.
- Explain how the principles of *merchantability* and *fitness for a particular purpose* apply to *implied warranties*.
- Define the concept of *privity* and explain the principle of *market-share liability* as a theory of privity.
- In what ways might a merchant be able to sell a product without *warranty?*
- Explain how the *Magnuson-Moss Act* provides an alternative approach to product-liability law.

YOU DECIDE: ANSWER/DISCUSSION
The Implied Warranty

The judge in Webster v. Blue Ship Tea Room *rendered the following judgment: The fish bone "lurking" in the chowder did not break the implied warranty of the UCC, and the restaurant was not found liable for Ms. Webster's injuries. Fish chowder being what it is in the long tradition of New England cooking, no chef could be expected to break the fish up into such small pieces that bones could be located and removed. The judge made a point of the woman's origin as a New Englander, the implication being that, with her knowledge of the tradition, she should not have expected a chef to go to that length.*

If you had approached the case as an issue of "consumer expectation," you might have rendered the same judgment. However, one might also consider that there was a "foreign substance" in the chowder—the bone. Did this make the food unwholesome and unfit to eat—that is, not "fit for the ordinary purposes"? Would you then have decided in the plaintiff's favor on the basis that the merchantability test had not been passed?

Interpreting each case on the relative standard of merchantability is difficult and becomes even more so with the complex products in today's world. Although the consumer-expectation test does offer some guidance, as we have seen, it is not always appropriate. Still, if you were the judge in a case of potential liability when a lawnmower malfunctions and the plaintiff is injured as opposed to the potential liability over a bone in fish chowder, you would need all the help you could get.

SUMMARY

- In their efforts to improve the legal position of consumers injured by defective and dangerous products, the courts have employed a growing number of legal theories. Today, plaintiffs in product liability cases can turn to tort and contract analyses.
- The tort of *negligence* rests on the concept that manufacturers owe a legal duty of care to consumers. In contrast, *strict liability* in tort grows out of public-policy concerns that individuals harmed by defective products be compensated. The law of negligence requires that the plaintiff prove that the defendant used less than ordi-

nary care and so is at fault, while proof of strict liability requires only a demonstration that the product was defective and did indeed cause the injury. Both torts apply to all a manufacturer's activities, including design, inspection, packaging, instructions, and warnings, as well as production.

- *Breach of warranty* is a matter of contract law and is governed by the *Uniform Commercial Code. Express warranties* are created when sellers make assertions about a product's characteristics orally, in writing, or in demonstrations. *Implied warranties* are obligations imposed by the law. All goods are required to be *merchantable* or *fit for ordinary purposes,* while items selected by sellers to fit a buyer's needs must also be fit for that particular purpose. Breach of warranty has one major legal obstacle for plaintiffs—*privity.* This is the (gradually eroding) requirement that plaintiffs have a certain kind of legal, contractual relationship with defendants in order to sue them. Although limited in its application, the privity theory of *market-share liability* has been used in certain cases: For example, when the manufacturer of a certain pharmaceutical has been unidentified, the industry as a whole has been deemed liable.

- A wide variety of government agencies deal with consumer protection and product-liability issues. The most important contribution is made by the Federal Trade Commission, which enforces the *Magnuson-Moss Warranty Act.* While this legislation does not make many substantive changes in warranty law, it does promote fuller disclosure of warranty terms to consumers.

QUESTIONS AND PROBLEMS

1. A customer goes into a local hardware store to buy paint with which to renovate his house. He tells the salesperson the quantity and color of paint he wants, but does not say which paint is to be used for what purposes. Later, it turns out the bathroom paint peels because it cannot withstand the constant moist atmosphere, the paint used on the ceilings was too thin to be used for that purpose and damaged the carpet when it dripped, and the paint used for the outside shutters was not weatherproof and quickly came off. The customer sues the store for breach of implied warranties of merchantability and fitness for a particular purpose. Who wins and why?

2. Chuck and Cindy Jones, newly married, win several prizes on a television game show. They sell some of their wedding gifts to make room for the prizes. Their next door neighbor buys their microwave oven. Unfortunately, he receives a severe shock and is injured when he tries to use it. He sues the Joneses for breach of warranty of merchantability, claiming that the microwave does not do what a microwave is meant to do. Who wins and why?

3. Terry Cohen, a tax collector, took a break from his work and went to a vending machine to purchase an orange soda supplied by Allendale Bottling Company. He returned to his office and opened the soda. After taking a few swallows, plaintiff discovered an insect at the bottom of the bottle. When he saw the insect he became nauseated, went to the restroom, vomited, and had diarrhea. Is Allendale liable for breach of warranty? Explain. [*Cohen v. Allendale Coca-Cola Bottling Co.,* 351 SE 2d 897 (1986)]

4. Stemfitters Silk Flower Manufacturing Co. bought several pieces of flower-making machinery from ABC Machine Co. All of the machines were covered by full written warranties. An employee is seriously injured when one of the machines malfunctions. The employee and Stemfitters sue ABC Machine Co., claiming violation of the Magnuson-Moss Act. What is ABC Machine Co's best defense?

5. Plaintiff, Dr. Crisostomo, was diagnosed by his doctor as having an acute case of gout and was prescribed the drugs Zyloprim and Colchicine. Plaintiff's doctor said Colchicine could cause stomach upset but mentioned no other side effects. Five days later, Crisostomo developed mouth sores and chills and decided to take some pencillin he had in the house. Feeling worse each day, he went back to his

doctor, who diagnosed him as having Stevens-Johnson Syndrome, which is characterized by skin lesions spread over the whole body. Due to lesions that scarred plaintiff's eyes, his tear ducts are damaged, his eyesight is now 20:200/20:100. Plaintiff cannot tolerate bright light and his eyes are always painful. He sued the manufacturer under strict liability and failure to warn, alleging that the manufacturer knew or should have known that the combination of penicillin and Zyloprim would increase the risk of Stevens-Johnson syndrome and the warnings given to doctors are inadequate. Who will prevail? [*Crisostomo v. Stanley*, 857 F. 2d. 1146 (1988)]

6. Scott Borden takes his friend's car for a "joy ride" without her permission. While he is driving the car, the brake malfunctions, causing him to lose control of the car and receive serious injuries. It is discovered that the brake malfunction was caused by a manufacturing defect in the car. Borden sues the manufacturer for breach of the implied warranty of merchantability, arguing that a car of fair and average quality is supposed to be able to brake safely. In most jurisdictions, who wins?

7. Horace DuBois supplied John Manly's Automotive Paint and Body Shop with Imron polyurethane enamel and other Kenron Chemical Corp. products. Customers began returning cars painted in the body shop because of tiny bubbles in the finish, and John had to repaint the cars several times. Kenron representatives diagnosed the problem as "solvent popping" and directed John's attention to a dented drum of Kenron paint thinner purchased from Mr. DuBois in June. The bubble problem continued until December, when Mr. Manly returned all salvageable materials to his supplier and obtained supplies elsewhere. Chemical analysis showed that the thinner was undeniably polluted. Is there sufficient cause to bring an action in strict product liability? [*E.I. Du-*

pont De Nemours & Co. v. Dillaha, 659 S.W.2d 756 (Ark. 1983)]

8. Puppy Palace sold a defective metal ring on a dog collar to a dog owner. The dog, an excessively playful German Shepherd, escapped and caused injury to plaintiff, Mrs. Oehler. The plaintiff would now like to sue the Puppy Palace because of her injuries, claiming that were it not for the defective collar, the injuries would never have occurred. Decide. [*Oehler v. Davis and Puppy Palace Enterprises, Inc.*, 298 A. 2d. 895 (1973)]

9. The Chocolate Co. purchases a large order of whey from Meadow Creamery. Chocolate Co.'s order specified that the whey be "extra grade," "guaranteed salmonella negative," and "tested salmonella negative before shipment to Chocolate Co." Extra grade whey is understood in the trade as being free from salmonella. Meadow shipped contaminated whey to Chocolate Co. As a result, several hundred thousand pounds of chocolates manufactured by Chocolate Co. were contaminated with salmonella. Did Meadow Creamery make an express warranty to Chocolate Co.? [*Bloomer Chocolate Co. v. Bongards Creameries, Inc.*, 635 F. Supp. 911 (N. D. Ill. 1985)]

10. Sara Connelly, an Avon group sales leader, receives a Uniden extend-a-phone from Avon as a prize during a promotional scheme. The phone has two parts, a base and a handset. The handset has a label attached to it which states "Caution—Loud ring. Move switch to 'talk' position before holding receiver to ear." The phone is installed according to the instuctions provided and used on several occasions without incident. Later, the phone rings and Ms. Connelly answers it for the first time. She forgets to move the switch to "talk," however, and permanently impairs her hearing. She sues the phone manufacturer for breach of express and implied warranties. Can she recover? [*Watson v. Uniden Corp. of America.* 775 F.2d 1514 (11th Cir. 1985)]

BUSINESS CRIME AND CRIMINAL PROCEDURE

In Chapter 10, we compared torts and crimes. A *tort* occurs when a person injures another by violating his or her duty to that person. Tort law defines the duties that members of society owe each other and provides a mechanism by which the injured party can obtain a remedy from the wrongdoer by bringing a lawsuit in civil court. Lawsuits involving torts are private affairs involving only the injured person and the alleged wrongdoer.

Crimes are offenses against society as a whole. The state represents society in criminal proceedings by prosecuting the alleged criminal. The person who has been injured by the crime is not a party to the action but usually appears as a witness for the prosecution. The penalty for violating a criminal law is usually either a fine, payable to the state, or imprisonment.

Often, an act that causes an injury is both a tort and a crime. Suppose, for example, that Jones punches Smith in the nose. If Smith suffers a broken nose and incurs doctor bills, he has a *civil* action for the *tort* of battery against Jones. The purpose of the civil action is to provide a remedy for Smith, and that remedy will likely be monetary. At the same time, society as a whole is offended by Jones's action: Therefore, society as an entity prosecutes Jones through its representative (the state prosecutor) for *criminal battery*, which is usually a misdemeanor.

All societies must define the acts that are considered offensive and therefore criminal. Although the legal concepts discussed in this chapter have a much broader application, we will examine the criminal law as it exists within the context of business relations.

■ PHILOSOPHY AND GOALS OF PUNISHMENT

Penologists and criminal law experts have recognized five specific goals of punishment.

DETERRENCE. The goal of **general deterrence** suggests that the threat of punishment for committing certain acts is intended to discourage members of society in general from committing those acts. By promising punishment for committing certain acts, criminal law seeks to instill a sense of acceptable and unacceptable behavior in society as a whole.

The objective of *special deterrence* is to dissuade those who have previously broken the law from committing additional crimes. The hope is that a person who has committed a crime and been punished for it will refrain from that behavior in the future in order to avoid unpleasant consequences of the act. Unfortunately, the high rate of repeated crime, or *recidivism*, demonstrates that imprisonment—at least in its current form—is not a particularly effective method of preventing criminals from committing future crimes.

REHABILITATION AND INCAPACITATION. Some people believe that punishment should reform the criminal by such means as counseling, education, and job training in prison. This approach is known as the objective of *rehabilitation*. Over the past decade, however, our commitment to rehabilitating criminals has waned, in part because rehabilitation programs in prisons require the expenditure of substantial tax dollars. *Incapacitation* or **restraint** is another objective of punishment. Its purpose is to remove proven criminals from society, thereby preventing them from committing additional crimes.

RETRIBUTION. The perspective of **retribution** is almost exclusively concerned with notions of what is right and wrong, just and unjust, moral and immoral. Retributionists believe that human beings are responsible moral agents who can choose between right and wrong. This view seeks to impose punishment that is commensurate with the crime as a way to redeem society's values.

To a certain degree, this approach holds that punishing criminals "cleanses" the public of anger and vengefulness while strengthening the belief in the rule of law. Moreover, punishment allows the public to extract its "pound of flesh" from those who have threatened society by running afoul of its accepted codes of behavior. The ultimate retribution for committing a crime is the death penalty.

Corporate Crime. Later in this chapter, we will examine more closely the imposition of criminal sanctions for the commission of corporate crimes—a practice that challenges traditional theories of the purposes and goals of punishment. Is it reasonable, for example, to expect corporations to behave like individuals when weighing the advantage of committing a crime against the likelihood of a penalty? How can society impose retribution on a corporation? For example, should corporate executives be put to death if a product causes the death of a consumer? What penalties can criminal law impose that will rehabilitate corporations that commit crimes?

■ CRIMINAL PROCEDURE

Both criminal and civil law apply when one person commits a wrongful act that causes injury to another person. Despite this overlapping jurisdiction, however, civil and criminal proceedings are not identical, primarily because each body of law allows for the imposition of different penalties. Suppose, for example, that your neighbor drives his car negligently and that your front lawn and the surrounding fence are damaged as a result. Although the civil-justice sys-

---

general deterrence Principle that members of a society will be discouraged from committing criminal acts by the threat of *punishment*

restraint Goal of *punishment* whereby proven criminals are removed from society to prevent them from committing further crimes

retribution Concept that *punishment* commensurate with a crime is a way to protect social values

---

tem will require your neighbor to pay you for the damage to your property, the neighbor is not likely to be jailed for the offenses.

By contrast, criminal penalties are only imposed for "serious" crimes. Indeed, in some states, people who are convicted of committing serious crimes can be divested of certain civil rights—(for example, the right to vote). If the crime is serious enough, they may even be executed. Because of the significant differences between civil and criminal cases in the United States, different *procedures* are used for the two kinds of cases.

In light of the seriousness of the penalties for violating a criminal law, both the Constitution and statutory law—federal and state codes (*see* Chapter 1)—impose strict sets of procedural rules to ensure that persons who are accused of criminal acts are tried fairly and convicted only if guilt has been established beyond a reasonable doubt. The substantive and procedural aspects of criminal proceedings are discussed below.

Constitutional Requirements

The underlying premise of all criminal law is that a person who has been accused of committing a crime is presumed innocent until proven guilty. This common-law tenet places the burden of proving the defendant's guilt squarely on the shoulders of the state. The accused is not required to establish his innocence. In addition to the presumption of innocence, the following constitutional amendments pertain to criminal proceedings and establish protections intended to deter the government from unreasonably invading citizens' privacy and civil rights.

THE FOURTH AMENDMENT. The Fourth Amendment protects people from being detained *unreasonably*; it also prohibits the *unreasonable search* of persons and their homes, papers, and personal effects. It requires that there be *probable cause* before any search warrant is issued. *Black's Law Dictionary* defines **probable cause** in part as "having more evidence for than against": An investigation must reveal facts that would lead a reasonably intelligent and prudent person to believe that the suspect had indeed acted as charged.

probable cause Facts such that a reasonable person would believe that an offense has been committed and the accused has committed it

THE FIFTH AMENDMENT. The Fifth Amendment states in part that "no person shall . . . be subject for the same offense to be twice put in jeopardy of life or limb, nor shall be compelled in any criminal case to be a witness against himself, nor be deprived of life, liberty, or property, without due process of law." The Fifth Amendment thus protects Americans against *double jeopardy*—that is, being tried twice for the same crime. It also prohibits the police from requiring the accused to incriminate himself either before or during a trial.

THE SIXTH AMENDMENT. The Sixth Amendment guarantees the accused's right to speedy and public jury trial in criminal cases. It requires that the defendant be permitted to confront his accusers and be given access to an attorney.

THE EIGHTH AMENDMENT. The Eighth Amendment states that "excessive bail especially shall not be required, nor excessive fines imposed, nor cruel and unusual punishments inflicted." The term "excessive," however, is subject to debate—as is the term "cruel and unusual punishment." Consider, for example, the case of *Clemmons v. Bohannon* (88-2730, 10th Cir. [1990]). The case centered on the civil rights of prisoners in a prison system that did not consider tobacco smoking as a factor in cell assignments. Nonsmoking prisoners concerned about the health hazards of secondary smoke brought a lawsuit contending that their civil rights were being violated. They felt that smokers should be housed with smokers, nonsmokers with nonsmokers. The court agreed, concluding that it was "cruel and unusual punishment" to put a smoker and a nonsmoker in the same cell.

Steps in the Criminal Justice System

Although specific procedures vary from jurisdiction to jurisdiction, the criminal justice system comprises a sequence of stages through which a suspected criminal's case passes. As you can see in Figure 12-1, the process involves the police, courts, and corrections institutions.

FIGURE 12-1 Criminal-Justice Process: The Movement of Cases through the Criminal Justice System   *Source:* President's Commission on Law Enforcement and Administration of Justice, *The Challenge of Crime in a Free Society* (Washington, DC: Government Printing Office, 1967).

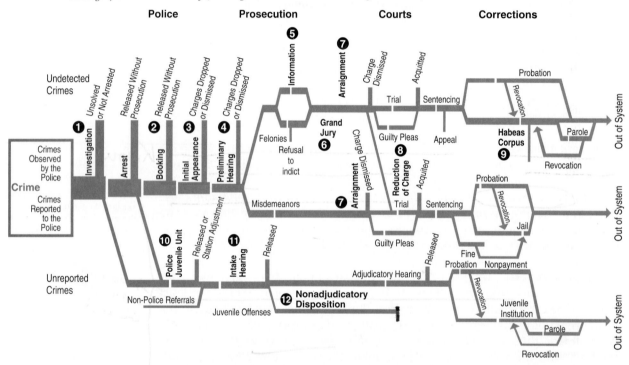

1. May continue until trial.
2. Administrative record of arrest. First step at which temporary release on bail may be available.
3. Before magistrate, commissioner, or justice of peace. Formal notice of charge, advice of rights. Bail set. Summary trials for petty offenses usually conducted here without further processing.
4. Preliminary testing of evidence against defendant. Charge may be reduced. No

separate preliminary hearing for misdemeanors in some systems.
5. Charge filed by prosecutor on basis of information submitted by police or citizens. Alternative to grand jury indictment. Often used in felonies, almost always in misdemeanors.
6. Reviews whether government evidence sufficient to justify trial. Some states have no grand jury system; others seldom use it.

7. Appearance for plea. Defendant elects trial by judge or jury (if available). Counsel for indigent usually appointed here in felonies, often not at all in other cases.
8. Charge may be reduced at any time prior to trial in return for plea of guilty or for other reasons.
9. Challenge on constitutional grounds to legality of detention. May be sought at any point in process.
10. Police often hold informal

hearings or dismiss or adjust many cases without further processing.
11. Probation officer decides desirability of further court action.
12. Welfare agency, social services, counseling, medical care, etc., for cases where adjudicatory handling not needed.

ARREST. When the police learn that a crime has been committed, either because they observed it directly or received a report, an investigation to identify the offender begins. Once the suspect has been identified, the police may make an arrest if they (1) obtain an arrest warrant from a magistrate or (2) possess sufficient knowledge of the facts and circumstances to lead a reasonable person to conclude that the suspect committed or is in the process of committing the crime. Most arrests are made without a warrant because of the likelihood that the delay of obtaining a warrant would allow the suspect to escape.

[handwritten margin note: You can be arrested w/out warrant Know ★]

CUSTODY. The accused's constitutional right to counsel and right against self-incrimination are triggered when he is taken into custody by the police. In *Miranda v. Arizona* (384 U.S. 436 [1966]), the U.S. Supreme Court ruled that arresting officers must inform suspects of these rights before they are questioned. To satisfy this requirement, police read suspects the so-called *Miranda* warnings (*see* Table 12-1). The suspect is *booked*—that is, charged with the commission of specific criminal offenses—upon arrival at the police station.

PRETRIAL PROCEDURES. After the arrest, the officer files a *criminal complaint*. Shortly thereafter, the accused is brought before a magistrate for an initial appearance. The purpose of this appearance is to determine whether the police have obtained sufficient evidence to warrant a trial. At this first appearance, one of the following events will generally occur:

1. The case may be dismissed if the magistrate finds that there was no probable cause for the arrest.
2. If the offense is minor and the accused pleads guilty, the magistrate may dispose of the case immediately, usually by imposing a fine.
3. If the offense is serious and the accused pleads not guilty, the magistrate will appoint a lawyer to represent the suspect and set bail.

Bail is an amount of money established by the court to be paid by the accused to ensure that he will return for trial. The Eighth Amendment protects the accused from excessive bail, and many courts have systems of releasing people on personal recognizance or in another's custody without monetary bail. However, the system of bail may be unfair to poor people who cannot raise money even with the help of friends or bail-bond companies; Since all

---

TABLE 12-1	The *Miranda* Warnings

The following warnings must be given to the subject before the interrogation begins:

1. "You have the right to remain silent and refuse to answer questions."
2. "Anything you do say may be used against you in a court of law."
3. "You have the right to consult an attorney before speaking to the police and to have an attorney present during any questioning now or in the future."
4. If you cannot afford an attorney, one will be appointed for you before questioning begins."
5. "If you do not have an attorney available, you have the right to remain silent until you have had an opportunity to consult with one."
6. "Now that I have advised you of your rights, are you willing to answer questions without an attorney present?"

[handwritten margin note: Know]

people are presumed innocent until proven guilty they should not be placed behind bars simply because they cannot raise bail. The following case discusses the issue of preventive detention when there is no reason to believe that the defendant will flee the court.

UNITED STATES v. SALERNO
United States Supreme Court, 107 S. Ct. 2095 (1987)

Respondents Anthony Salerno and Vincent Cafaro were arrested after being charged with various Racketeer Influenced and Corrupt Organizations Act (RICO) violations, mail and wire fraud offenses, extortion, and various criminal gambling violations. At respondents' arraignment, the Government moved to have Salerno and Cafaro detained. The District Court held a hearing at which the Government made a detailed charge showing that Salerno was the "boss" and Cafaro a "captain" in the Genovese crime family of La Cosa Nostra. The Government also offered testimony by two trial witnesses, who would assert that Salerno personally participated in two murder conspiracies. The District Court granted the Government's detention motion, concluding that the Government had established by clear and convincing evidence that no condition or combination of conditions of release would ensure the safety of the community or any person. Respondents appealed, contending that the Bail Reform Act of 1984 is unconstitutional to the extent that the Act permits pretrial detention on the ground that the arrestee is likely to commit future crimes. The United States Court of Appeals for the Second Circuit agreed and concluded that the Government could not, consistent with due process, detain persons who had not been accused of any crime merely because they were thought to present a danger to the community.

Chief Justice Rehnquist delivered the Opinion of the Court.

The Bail Reform Act of 1984 allows a federal court to detain an arrestee pending trial if the government demonstrates by clear and convincing evidence after an adversary hearing that no release conditions "will reasonably assure . . . the safety of any other person and the community." The United States Court of Appeals for the Second Circuit struck down this provision of the Act as facially unconstitutional, because, in the court's words, this type of pretrial detention violates "substantive due process." . . .

The Due Process Clause of the Fifth Amendment provides that "No person shall . . . be deprived of life, liberty, or property, without due process of law. . . ." This Court has held that the Due Process Clause protects individuals against two types of government action. So-called "substantive due process" prevents the government from engaging in conduct that "shocks the conscience," or interferes with rights "implicit in the concept of ordered liberty." When government action depriving a person of life, liberty, or property survives substantive due process scrutiny, it must still be implemented in a fair manner. This requirement has traditionally been referred to as "procedural" due process.

Respondents first argue that the Act violates substantive due process because the pretrial detention it authorizes constitutes impermissible punishment before trial. The Government, however, has never argued that pretrial detention could be upheld if it were "punishment." The Court of Appeals assumed that pretrial detention under the Bail Reform Act is regulatory, not penal, and we agree that it is.

As an initial matter, the mere fact that a person is detained does not inexorably lead to the conclusion that the goverment has imposed punishment. To detemine whether a restriction on liberty constitutes impermissible punishment or permissible regulation, we first look to legislative intent. Unless Congress expressly intended to impose punitive restrictions, the punitive/regulatory distinction turns on " 'whether an alternative purpose to which [the restriction] may rationally be connected is assignable for it, and whether it appears excessive in relation to the alternative purpose assigned [to it].' "

We conclude that the detention imposed by the Act falls on the regulatory side of the dichotomy. The legislative history of the Bail Reform Act clearly indicates that Congress did not formulate the pretrial detention provisions as punishment for dangerous individuals. Congress instead perceived pretrial detention as a potential solution to a pressing societal problem. There is no doubt that preventing danger to the community is a legitimate regulatory goal.

Nor are the incidents of pretrial detention excessive in relation to the regulatory goal Congress sought to achieve. The Bail Reform Act carefully limits the circumstances under which detention may be sought to the most serious of crimes. The arrestee is entitled to a prompt detention hearing, and the maximum length of pretrial detention is limited by the stringent time limitations of the Speedy Trial Act. . . . We conclude, therefore, that the pretrial detention contemplated by the Bail Reform Act is regulatory in nature, and does not constitute punishment before trial in violation of the Due Process Clause.

. . . .

The government's interest in preventing crime by arrestees is both legitimate and compelling. . . .

On the other side of the scale, of course, is the individual's strong interest in liberty. We do not minimize the importance and fundamental nature of this right. But, as our cases hold, this right may, in circumstances where the government's interest is sufficiently weighty, be subordinated to the greater needs of society. We think that Congress' careful delineation of the circumstances under which detention will be permitted satisfies this standard. When the government proves by clear and convincing evidence that an arrestee presents an identified and articulable threat to an individual or the community, we believe that, consistent with the Due Process Clause, a court may disable the arrestee from executing that threat. Under these circumstances, we cannot categorically state that pretrial detention "offends some principle of justice so rooted in the traditions and conscience of our people as to be ranked as fundamental."

. . . .

The judgment of the Court of Appeals is therefore reversed.

Justice Marshall, with whom Justice Brennan joins, dissenting.

This case brings before the Court for the first time a statute in which Congress declares that a person innocent of any crime may be jailed indefinitely, pending the trial of allegations which are legally presumed to be untrue, if the Government shows to the satisfaction of a judge that the accused is likely to commit crimes, unrelated to the pending charges, at any time in the future. Such statutes, consistent with the usages of tyranny and the excesses of what bitter experience teaches us to call the police state, have long been thought incom-

patible with the fundamental human rights protected by our Constitution. Today a majority of this Court holds otherwise. . . .

. . . .

. . . The majority proceeds as though the only substantive right protected by the Due Process Clause is a right to be free from punishment before conviction. The majority's technique for infringing this right is simple: merely redefine any measure which is claimed to be punishment as "regulation," and, magically, the Constitution no longer prohibits its imposition. . . .

. . . .

Our society's belief, reinforced over the centuries, that all are innocent until the state has proved them to be guilty, like the companion principle that guilt must be proved beyond a reasonable doubt, is "implicit in the concept of ordered liberty," and is established beyond legislative contravention in the Due Process Clause.

Case Questions

1. Upon what basis did the majority conclude that the detention imposed upon the respondents by the Bail Reform Act was not unconstitutional?

2. What standard was used by the Court to determine whether a restriction on liberty constitutes impermissible punishment or permissible regulation?

3. Explain how the dissent views the motive behind the majority's ruling?

GRAND JURY INDICTMENT. The Fifth Amendment forbids any person from being tried for a serious federal crime without an indictment by a grand jury. Although some states also use the grand jury system, the severity of the offenses that must go before the grand jury varies. A grand jury, which is made up of ordinary citizens, is charged with determining whether there is probable cause to believe that the accused committed the crime in question. If the grand jury accepts the evidence presented by the prosecutor, it hands up an **indictment**. The accused is then **arraigned**—that is, brought to the trial court, informed of the charges, and required to enter a plea.

In states that do not use a grand jury system, the prosecutor files an **information**—that is, a statement of the crime of which the person is accused. Arraignment then follows.

As the comparison in Table 12-2 shows, there is a significant difference between the information filed for a preliminary hearing and the information filed for a grand jury.

PLEA BARGAINING. Prior to the commencement of a trial, the accused may enter into a deal with the prosecution—to plead guilty to a lesser offense than he was originally charged with—a **plea bargain**. The accused benefits by being punished for a lesser crime; the prosecution saves the time and expense, as well as the uncertainty of the outcome of a jury trial. As this chapter's YOU DECIDE feature indicates, however, plea bargaining has been criticized, among other things, for permitting criminals to serve insufficient sentences.

grand jury A panel of citizens charged with determining whether there is *probable cause* to believe that an accused person has committed the crime in question

indictment Formal charge by a *grand jury* accusing a person of a crime

arraignment Following *indictment*, the bringing of an accused person to trial court, informing him of the charges, and requiring him to enter a *plea*.

information Filing by a prosector in states without grand juries stating the crime of which a person is accused

plea bargain Accused person's agreement with the prosecution to plead guilty to an offense lesser than that with which he or she has been charged

Know

TABLE 12-2 *Information Filing: Preliminary Hearing and Grand Jury*

PRELIMINARY HEARING	GRAND JURY
1. Determination of probable cause.	1. Determination of probable cause.
2. Decision by magistrate [one person [a professional.	2. Decision by grand jurors [a group [laypersons.
3. Prosecution testimony.	3. Prosecution testimony.
4. Public.	4. Secret.
5. Accused present.	5. Accused not present.
6. Right of accused to assistance of counsel.	6. No right to counsel for accused.
7. Right of accused to cross-examine.	7. No right to cross-examine by accused.
8. Defense testimony permitted.	8. No defense testimony.
9. Accused's counsel may record.	9. No recording by accused.
10. Transcript required.	10. Transcript often not permitted.
11. Waiverable (with exceptions).	11. Waiverable (with exceptions).
12. Miranda warnings required.	12. No Miranda warnings required.
13. Suppression of illegally secured evidence.	13. Exclusionary rule not applicable.
14. Self-incriminating testimony not required.	14. Grant of immunity possible to secure incriminating testimony.

Source: *Kolasa and Meyer*, The American Legal System.

YOU DECIDE
Plea Bargaining

Despite the long tradition of the practice, the issue of plea bargaining is a controversial one. Even though a majority of plea-bargained cases in this country end in guilty pleas, many people still regard it as unfair. Although different critics have different reasons for feeling this way, almost all of them contend that the process is not in the best interests of the general public.

Some critics charge, for example, that the lesser sentences generally imposed in such instances are actually a kind of reward for saving the state the time and money involved in a trial: They argue that plea bargaining shields criminals from the full impact of the penalties that can be imposed for their crimes. For instance, is it fair for a mobster who admits to cold-blooded murder to plea bargain for a lesser penalty than a life term with no parole in exchange for his testimony against other mob figures? Is it fair for a rapist to plead guilty in exchange for a shorter jail term?

Still other critics argue that the mere fact that plea bargaining is available as an alternative makes it more likely that someone will commit a crime. For example, someone who is caught shoplifting may simply offer to pay the store for the stolen merchandise in exchange for not being arrested. In effect, the availability of such "slap-on-the-wrist" punishment may tip the balance in a would-be wrong doer's

decision to commit or not commit the crime. Although this example involves a relatively minor nonviolent crime, the same logic can be applied to other crimes.

The question of whether an alleged criminal who engages in plea bargaining is deprived of his right to due process is a different kind of issue: After all, the criminal is deprived, or deprives himself, of the right to a trial before a jury of his peers. Is it ethical to trade off someone's constitutionally guaranteed right to a trial for an economic benefit? Does it matter whether the person can be proven guilty by the evidence?

One case that turned on the issue of due process was Bordenkircher v. Hayes (434 US 357 (1978), in which a prosecutor threatened the accused during a plea bargaining. The prosecutor stated that he would have Hayes reindicted on more serious charges if he did not plead guilty to the original charge. Was this approach an instance of plea bargaining or coercion? Would your opinion change if you knew that Hayes actually committed both crimes and was a habitual offender? Whether or not your opinion changes, does the latter bit of information make you feel that the prosecutor should have tried to get an indictment on the more serious charge? (For further discussion, see p. 447.)

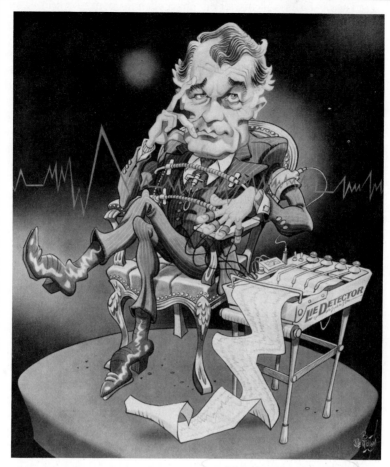

Inadmissible Evidence In 1983, celebrated criminal-defense attorney F. Lee Bailey, a champion of the use of the *polygraph* or "lie detector" in criminal investigations, launched a short-lived television program entitled *Lie Detector*, on which he invited guests to "prove" the truth or falsehood of their claims in personal disputes. The "lie" detector is actually an *emotion* detector: It measures certain physiological activities—heart rate, blood pressure, galvanic skin response—related to emotional states in order to record changes due to such "stressful" feelings as guilt and lying. It is, of course, less than dependable. Beyond the fact that considerable expertise is required to interpret the resultant chart, factors other than lying can cause the same physiological changes. Because interpretation of the polygraph depends on *changes* in established "neutral" baseline readings, habitual liars often exhibit no physiological changes because they experience no measurable emotional changes; similarly, a guilty person can induce stress by focusing on his or her crime during the initial period of neutral questioning—a high baseline can make subsequent comparisons meaningless. Tranquilizers have been shown to improve "cheating," as have simple exercises in not paying attention to the questions—one study achieved a significant cheat rate among subjects who concentrated on counting backwards from seven instead of listening to the operator. Although results are generally inadmissible in court, lie detectors can have more limited applications in aiding investigations—the FBI, for example, uses them to probe leads and verify facts. Perhaps more important, although no research has validated lie-detection procedures for employment screening, about one-third of this country's largest corporations still use them for such purposes as detecting drug use.

TRIAL. Unless a suspect is charged with a minor crime, such as those punishable by less than six months in prison, the Constitution guarantees the right to a jury trial. However, many suspects voluntarily waive that right either by accepting a plea bargain or by pleading guilty. If the suspect chooses to go to trial, the prosecution bears the burden of proving guilt beyond a reasonable doubt. If convicted, the defendant has the right to appeal. (For *civil and criminal court procedures, review* Chapters 4 and 5.)

■ Concept Check 12-1 *Philosophy and Goals of Punishment & Criminal Procedure*

- Explain the traditional rationale behind *deterrence, rehabilitation,* and *retribution* as goals of criminal punishment.
- Define and explain the principle of *probable cause.*
- Describe the key steps in criminal *pretrial procedures.*
- Explain the processes of *indictment* and *arraignment.*

■ CATEGORIES OF CRIME

The acts that we view as antisocial, and therefore criminal, cover a broad spectrum of severity. Crimes which cause the greatest damage to their victims—and which therefore pose the greatest risk to society—are punished most severely. Statutes defining criminal acts usually divide them into three categories: *violations, misdemeanors,* and *felonies.* These categories reflect both the severity of the crime and the punishment that is meted out for its commission.

violation (or infraction) *Crime considered a petty offense and carrying no legal disadvantage*

VIOLATIONS AND INFRACTIONS. A petty offense, such as a parking or a speeding ticket, is a **violation** or **infraction.** The Model Penal Code[1] states that violations may be punished only by fines, forfeitures, or other civil penalties. Violations are not considered crimes as such, and no *legal* disadvantage—such as the loss of the right to vote—can be based on conviction for a violation.

misdemeanor *Crime less serious than a felony and punishable by imprisonment up to a year and/or a fine*

MISDEMEANORS. Crimes like simple assault are **misdemeanors.** The punishment for misdemeanors is imprisonment for a period up to one year and/or a fine. Those who commit misdemeanors serve their time in penal facilities other than penitentiaries. Federal law and most state statutes declare that those offenses which are not felonies are misdemeanors.

felony *The most serious kind of crime including such acts as murder, arson, and rape, generally punishable by prison terms determined by the nature of the crime*

FELONIES. The most serious kind of crime is a **felony.** Examples of felonies include murder, rape, and arson. The Model Penal Code, for example, divides felonies into *capital offenses* and *first-* through *third-degree felonies.* Capital offenses are punishable by death. First-degree felonies are punishable by a maximum term of life in federal prison. Second-degree felonies are punishable by a maximum of ten years in federal prison. Third-degree felonies are punishable by no more than five years in federal prison.

---

[1] In Chapter 9, we saw an example of a model law in the Uniform Commercial Code. The Model Penal Code was drafted by the American Law Institute. Although it has been adopted only in part and by a few states, it is widely influential.

Although the U.S. penal system is beyond the scope of this book, the business of punishment is not. For an interesting development in penal practice, see the ORGANIZATIONAL PROFILE box below.

ORGANIZATIONAL PROFILE
Wackenhut Corporation

Does crime ever pay? Wackenhut Corporation, one of a handful of companies that build, manage, and/or operate private prisons, is out to prove that it does.

As Wackenhut sees it, the rising crime rate, coupled with the pressures on the U.S. penal system to house more and more prisoners in roughly the same space, is a business opportunity. Unless things change radically in the next few years, about four million Americans will be in prison by the year 2000. In many states, the largest item in the budget will be corrections. In addition, approximately 80 percent of all prisons are medium- or maximum-security facilities. As of 1990, Arizona, California, Florida, Kentucky, New Mexico, Texas, and Tennessee have awarded contracts to private prison businesses. Wackenhut wants to provide facilities for minimum- and medium-security prisons. In essence, it wants to privatize the prison system. To date, the company runs eleven correction or detention facilities, including one medium-security jail.

So far, although the company has not made much money from its venture, but about twenty-five percent of the company's overall growth comes from prisons—Wackenhut also provides security and investigative services, security training, and institutional food and health services, and designs and sells electronic security devices. Wackenhut intends to pursue private prisons as a potential profit center, and it may yet hit gold in this area. For one thing, because prison-

ers' rights are in the spotlight, it is impressive that private jails offer each prisoner his own bed when many federal and state jails cannot make that claim.

The issue of cost is also a much more important factor in the question of privatization. Wackenhut has stated that the per-prisoner cost in one of its Texas-based prerelease facilities is $35.50 per day. The state pays $40 per day. On first examination, a saving of $4.50 does not seem like much. However, if a state housed 1000 prisoners in private prisons, the savings would be impressive: $1000 \times \$4.5 = \$4500$ per day. This equation translates into a savings for the state of $1,642,500 per year.

On the face of it, these positive points are impressive. There are, however, other questions to consider: Can private prisons do a better job at providing housing, food, and security than government-run prisons, and can they do it for less money and still make a profit? Should the authority to administer the punishments meted out by federal and state courts be handed over to private contractors? Might such contractors abuse their power? Might they start cutting corners to increase profit margins?

Whatever the answers to such questions, Wackenhut and the other companies in this fledgling industry have a worthwhile idea that may ultimately be accepted by the government and the courts. It remains to be seen whether such an idea can succeed profitably.

■ PRINCIPLES OF CRIMINAL RESPONSIBILITY

As we noted previously, the objective of criminal law is to deter and punish the commission of acts that threaten society's safety and order. The critical concept is that a crime is committed when a person engages in forbidden *conduct*— neither bad thoughts alone nor mere action, or inaction where there is a duty to act, are criminal. Instead, the law requires the existence of *both* a bad act (*actus reus*) and a bad state of mind (*mens rea*) as a basis for the imposition of criminal responsibility.

Note that two other conditions must also exist for a crime to have been committed. First, the person's act must have caused a harmful result. Second, state or federal law must define the conduct as criminal.

The Criminal Act

The Model Penal Code states that "a person is not guilty of an offense unless his liability is based on conduct that includes (1) a voluntary act or (2) the omission to perform an act of which he is physically capable." In other words, a de-

actus reus *Wrongful act that, along with criminal intent, is the basis for a crime*

fendant must have done something illegal or failed to do something legally required. We require a wrongful act, or **actus reus**, because we would otherwise have a system of criminal justice that punishes on the basis of *intent*. Thus, the mere thought of shooting a professor for assigning a poor grade is not held to be criminal.

Failure to Act. In some circumstances, the *failure* to act may fulfill the actus reus element. The determining factor is whether there is a *legal duty* to act, not just a *moral* one. In most circumstances, people are not under a legal duty to warn others that harm may befall them. For example, someone who overhears a murder threat is not legally required to warn the intended victim. However, individuals have a legal duty to file an annual income-tax return. Thus, individuals are legally responsible for completing the task even if they are unable to file the return themselves.

Vicarious Liability. Vicarious liability is a no-fault liability that omits the personal *actus reus* requirement: In vicarious liability, the defendant is held liable for the wrongdoing of another person. As we saw in Chapter 7, a *principal* may be held responsible for the wrongful act of an *agent* when the agent acts within the scope of the agency. This question often arises in an employer-employee context.

The Mental Element

No

mens rea *Criminal intent that, along with a wrongful act, is the basis for a crime*

Exception to "Innocent until proven Guilty"

Know This

Criminal intent, or **mens rea,** refers to the actor's state of mind. It is different from the perpetrator's *motive* for the action. The Model Penal Code defines four mental states that apply to the commission of crimes: (1) *intent* (or purpose) to perform the act or cause the result, (2) *knowledge* of the act's nature or outcome, (3) *recklessness,* and (4) *negligence.*

Strict Liability. The *mens rea* requirement is omitted in some circumstances. Thus, criminal liability can be imposed if a legislature has defined a certain behavior as criminal even if fault cannot be proven—that is, strict liability. Penalties for these offenses, however, are usually less severe than for offenses in which *mens rea* is present. Note that strict liability is not the same as vicarious liability.

■ *Concept Check 12-2   Categories of Crime & Principles of Criminal Responsibility*

- Define and give examples of *violations, misdemeanors,* and *felonies.*
- Define *vicarious* and *strict liability* as principles applied to criminal responsibility.
- Define *mens rea* and describe each of the four mental states applied by the *Model Penal Code* to the commission of a crime.

■ BUSINESS-RELATED CRIMES

For most people, business-related crime means "white-collar" crime. In turn, the phrase "white-collar crime" conjures up images of impeccably dressed executives performing illegal activities. Criminologists, however, use the phrase to describe a wide range of illegal economic activity, including the following:

425

(A)

(B)

A Question of Coercion Kidnapped in 1973 and held hostage by a terrorist organization calling itself the "Symbionese Liberation Army," media heiress Patricia Hearst resurfaced in a bank-surveillance photograph taken during an armed robbery on 15 April 1974 (A). Observing that other photos revealed "a gun held by another person on her," an FBI spokesman speculated that Hearst appeared to be acting "under duress and coercion." When the principle of *mens rea* also requires proof of *specific intent*, it must be shown that a criminal act was performed both *knowingly* and *willingly*—an individual may knowingly commit an illegal act even though under coercion. When Hearst was finally rescued, she was also arrested and tried for bank robbery in the spring of 1976. (B). The defense, headed by the well-known criminal lawyer F. Lee Bailey, cited specific intent and claimed that Hearst had been coerced into robbing banks by her captors (most of whom had been killed by the FBI the previous summer). The jury declined to believe Hearst, and she was convicted.

Violation of one of the many laws regulating the conduct of business. For example, the Occupational Health and Safety Act (OSHA) makes it a crime to expose employees to specified levels of known carcinogens.

Failure to adhere to the reporting requirements of a statute. For example, a stockbroker's willful failure to report the details of stock transactions to the Securities and Exchange Commission (SEC) may result in the imposition of criminal penalties.

Criminal conduct, such as perjury, conspiracy, or mail fraud.

Violation of the Racketeer Influenced and Corrupt Organizations Act (RICO), which states that a person is guilty of racketeering if he engages in *one or more* acts that are prohibited by federal or state criminal laws.

Computer Crime

Computer crime is one of the most rapidly growing types of white-collar crime. Estimates of computer theft range from $100 to $300 million a year. Even more startling, the United States Chamber of Commerce estimates that 100 computer crimes go undetected for every one that is discovered.

Computer crime is not really a new breed of crime. Rather, it consists largely of old crimes committed in new ways. Modern technology makes the act more inventive and, often, more difficult to detect and prosecute. Such crimes frequently involve **conversion**—the use of the computer by the thief to gain the use or control of something that belongs to another. For example, two employees who take their employer's computer programs are guilty of criminal conversion.

conversion *Crime* increasingly committed by use of computers, by which one takes control of another person's property

Criminals also use computers in a criminal manner when they use someone else's hardware without permission. Although some courts have refused to find that the wrongful use of a computer amounts to a conversion because nothing tangible has been taken, others have reached a different result. The following case illustrates a conversion activity.

STATE v. McGRAW
Indiana Court of Appeals, 459 N.E.2d 61 (1984)

Defendant McGraw was employed as a computer operator for the Indianapolis Department of Planning and Zoning. The city leased the computer service, and its employees were not authorized to use the computers for private business matters. Nevertheless, McGraw used the computer in his business of selling Naturslim, a dietary product. He used the computer for client lists, inventory control, client birthdates, customer solicitation, and other business-related material. He had been previously reprimanded for selling his product on office time and was subsequently discharged. After being discharged, McGraw requested that a fellow employee, who was also a computer operator, print out his Naturslim data and then erase it from the computer's memory bank. Instead of complying, the fellow employee informed his supervisor, and an investigation revealed McGraw's activities. The state charged McGraw with two counts of theft. McGraw was found guilty on both counts. The trial court sustained McGraw's motion to dismiss the counts of theft on the grounds that the facts stated did not constitute an offense and therefore the court had no jurisdiction. The state appeals.

Neal, Presiding Judge

. . . .

The sole issue on appeal is whether . . . the unauthorized use of another person's computer for private business is theft under the statute as a matter of law.

Theft is defined by Ind. Code 35-43-4-2(a) as follows:

"A person who knowingly and intentionally exerts unauthorized control over property of another person with intent to deprive the other person of any part of its value or use, commits theft, a Class D felony."

Ind. Code 35-41-1-2 defines property:

'Property' means *anything of value; and includes a gain or advantage or anything that might reasonably* be regarded as such by the beneficiary; real property, personal property, money, labor, *and services;* intangibles; commercial instruments; written instruments concerning labor, services, or property; written instruments otherwise of value to the owner, such as a public record, deed, will, credit card, or letter of credit; a signature to a written instrument; extension of credit; trade secrets; contract rights, . . . and other interests in or claims to wealth; electricity, gas, oil, and water; captured or domestic animals, birds, and fish; food and drink; and human remains.

The State essentially argues that the theft statute comprehends a broad field of conduct and a wide range of activities, and is sufficiently broad to prohibit McGraw's acts here. . . .

McGraw's initial arguments involve a close examination of the pertinent statutory language. The theft statute, he argues, is divided into a conduct portion "knowingly and intentionally exerting unauthorized control over the property of another person" and the intent portion, "with the intent to deprive the other person of any part of its value or use." The word use does not appear in the conduct portion; therefore, the unauthorized control must be over the property itself. Further, he argues, Ind. Code 35-41-1-2 which defines property does not include the word "use" as such, and Ind. Code 35-43-4-1(a) which defines "exert control over property," does not employ the term "use." Additionally, he contends that "services" as used in Ind. Code 35-41-1-2 is limited to the context of labor.

In addition to the above construction argument, McGraw asserts that to be guilty of the offense, a specific prohibition of his conduct must exist. He contends that he could not deprive the city of the "use" of the computer unless his data caused an overload on the computer memory banks, or that he used the computer for his private business at a time which interfered with city use. He argues that the value of the services was de minimus. He finally claims that his activities were no more than personal use of an office phone, calculator, or copy machine.

Inasmuch as the evidence clearly supports the fact that McGraw knowingly and intentionally used the city leased computer for his own monetary benefit, the only real question is whether "use" of a computer is a property subject to theft. . . .

. . . .

We deem McGraw's interpretation of the statutes overly restrictive. In short, he is arguing old common law precepts pertaining to larceny. In our view his contentions are inapposite to the plain meaning of the statutory sections involved herein.

Computer services, leased or owned, are a part of our market economy in huge dollar amounts. Like cable television, computer services are ". . . anything of value." Computer time is "services" for which money is paid. Such services may reasonably be regarded as valuable assets to the beneficiary. Thus, computer services are property within the meaning of the definition of property subject to theft. When a person "obtains" or "takes" those services, he has exerted control under Ind. Code 35-43-4-1(a). Taking without the other person's consent is unauthorized taking. Depriving the other person of any part of the services' use completes the offense.

Property must be shown to have a value, however slight, but the monetary value of property is of no concern, and the jury may under proper instructions infer some value. The theft statute comprehends a broad field of conduct, and does not limit the means or methods by which unauthorized control of property may be obtained. We disagree that specific prohibition to exerting control is necessary to support the conviction theft. . . . Further, we disagree that it is a defense to exerting unauthorized control that the owner was not using the property at the time.

We are of the opinion that Counts VIII and IX of the information states an offense. The judgment of the trial court dismissing Courts VIII and IX is reversed, the convictions are ordered reinstated, and the trial court is ordered to sentence McGraw pursuant thereto.

Case Questions

1. What was the property in this case?

2. Explain how the Indiana Court of Appeals found McGraw guilty of theft.

3. Under what circumstances might an employee use work computers for his or her own personal benefit but not be guilty of theft?

Computer thieves have also made entry into computerized payroll and accounts-payable systems. The easiest way into such systems is for the thief to substitute his name for the proper payee's name on a computer-generated check.

THE 1984 FEDERAL COMPUTER CRIME STATUTE. It is often difficult to fit computer crimes within statutory definitions of such crimes as theft, alteration, and larceny. As a result, many people who clearly committed wrongful acts with computers have been acquitted.

In response to the vulnerability of both computer owners and the computer industry, as well as to the inadequacy of existing statutes, Congress finally developed the counterfeit Access Device and Computer Fraud and Abuse Act of 1984, which was enacted as part of the Comprehensive Crime Control Act. This statute forbids the knowing use or access of computers without authorization in six areas:

1. The unauthorized use or access of a computer to glean classified military or foreign-policy information with intent to harm the United States or benefit a foreign country is a felony.
2. The unauthorized use of a computer to collect credit or financial information protected under federal privacy laws is a misdemeanor.
3. The unauthorized access to a federal government computer and the use, modification, destruction, or disclosure of data that it contains or the prevention of others from using it is a misdemeanor.
4. The alteration or modification of data in financial computers causing a loss of $1000 or more is a misdemeanor.
5. The modification of data that impairs medical treatment to individuals is a misdemeanor.
6. The fraudulent transfer of computer passwords or similar information that could aid unauthorized computer access that either (a) affects interstate commerce or (b) permits access to a government computer is a misdemeanor.

Conspiring or attempting to commit any of the preceding offenses is also illegal. The penalties attached to computer crimes range from fines to imprisonment.

It is important to realize, however, that neither the Computer Fraud and Abuse Act of 1984 nor the updated act of 1986 addresses the alteration or destruction of computer programs when the action does not fit into the categories listed above. Someone who has acted with fraudulent intent but who has not technically violated the law has a good chance of being acquitted. Such activities include computer "hacking" and planting computer "viruses."

Computer Hackers. The first computer hackers were often students fascinated with the idea of circumventing the few computer systems on line at the time. However, as simple computer hardware evolved into complicated computer networks, hackers soon developed techniques for accessing various systems. Those hackers who had criminal intent when they "cracked the system" became the target of government campaigns against computer crime.

Computer Viruses. Computer viruses are "bugs" planted in a computer's instructions and then spread to other computer systems or programs by copying themselves over and over again. A virus may not infect the stored data, but it can affect parts of host programs. The result can be benign—for example, a benign virus embedded in a program of the TV show *Jeopardy* may play a tune other than the *Jeopardy* theme—or destructive—the Michelangelo virus that was programmed to wipe out all the data in any infected personal computer on March 6, 1992.

Several types of antiviral programs have been developed to prevent, detect, or identify computer viruses. New programs, however, must be developed for each new virus that is identified.

At the heart of all such problems is one basic—and as yet unresolved—question: Do the protections of the First and Fourth Amendments extend to computers, or are they limited to the traditional print media? It is likely to be some time before this issue is adequately answered.

Mail and Wire Fraud

Federal law makes it illegal to use the mail or any interstate electronic communications network to perpetrate a fraudulent scheme. The statute, which is very broad, is used by prosecutors to combat virtually any criminal activity that entails even peripheral use of the postal system. Such diverse activities as illegal drug sales through the mail, phony credit-card schemes, and selling useless hair-growing tonic by mail can all be indictable offenses under mail- and wire-fraud statutes. The following case illustrates the application of mail- and wire-fraud statutes to fight fraudulent practices in commodities trading.

UNITED STATES v. DIAL
U.S. Court of Appeal, Seventh Circuit, 757 F.2d 163 (1985)

Defendant Donald Dial, an experienced silver trader, was the manager of a branch office of the Clayton Brokerage Company. Horace Salmon was the company's president. By extensive use of the telephones and the mail, Dial solicited his customers to participate in commodity futures block orders. His conduct in so doing involved misrepresentation and breach of his fiduciary duty. Dial and Salmon were found guilty by a jury of mail and wire fraud (18 U.S.C. ##1341 and 1343) in connection with the trading of silver futures on the Chicago Board of Trade. Defendants appeal.

Posner, Circuit Judge

. . .

In 1978 Dial was looking for a very large investor to make a multi-million dollar purchase of silver futures through Clayton Brokerage. In preparation for the appearance of such an investor Salmon arranged for Dial to control a trading account at Clayton Brokerage in the name of Multi-Projects (Cayman), Ltd., a Cayman Islands corporation. An "equity raiser" named Kirst located on Dial's behalf the putative grand investor in the person of Nasrullah Khan, who said he represented a group of investors organized as the International Monetary Corporation (IMC). While negotiations between Khan and Dial's son were proceeding, Dial began buying silver futures for the Multi-Projects account. But he put up no cash or cash equivalent for these purchases. To understand the significance of this omission, recall that a futures contract commits each of the contracting parties to buy or sell the underlying commodity at a date in the future at whatever the market price then is. Since the brokerage house (here, Clayton Brokerage) is responsible for the undertakings in its customers' futures contracts, it wants to be sure that each customer has the financial wherewithal to make good on his obligation under his futures contract should the price move in the opposite direction from his expectations. To this end, the brokerage house requires each of its customers to put up "margin"—cash or a cash equivalent such as a Treasury bill—as a guarantee of solvency. The required margin is a (small) percentage of the contract price and fluctuates as the price fluctuates.

. . . [W]hen Dial bought silver futures for the Multi-Projects account without putting up any cash or cash equivalent—bought a lot of silver futures, 200 in all, worth $5 million—Clayton Brokerage Company's computer department notified its margin department that margin calls amounting to $100,000 should be issued to Multi-Projects, and they were. But Salmon instructed the director of the computer department to delete the Multi-Projects account from its computer programs and as a result the margin calls (which were never met) stopped.

On the weekend of November 10, 1978, . . . negotiations with Khan were successfully concluded and Kirst was dispatched to London to pick up IMC's check for $25 million. On the same weekend Dial engaged in intensive solicitation of his regular customers to create a block order for silver futures to put in for execution on Monday, November 13. Kirst as directed deposited IMC's check—drawn on the Oxford International Bank in the Turks and Caicos Islands, and not certified—on Monday morning in Clayton Brokerage Company's account in a Chicago bank. Between 8:43 a.m. and 12:15 p.m. Salmon transmitted to the floor of the Board of Trade an order to buy 12 February (1979) silver futures contracts, and Dial transmitted orders on behalf of Multi-Projects, himself, his son, and Kirst and other associates, including two secretaries, for a total of 262 February futures. During this period the price of February silver fluctuated between $5.83 and $5.86 an ounce. At 12:40 p.m. Dial put in the block order, which was to buy 583 February futures, at higher prices—between $5.88 and $5.90. At 12:59 (two minutes after having bought 2,000 December futures for IMC), Dial bought 1,192 February futures for IMC at $5.92. Later that afternoon Salmon sold 10 of his 12 February futures at $5.91, seven cents more than he had bought them for that morning. The price kept on rising as the afternoon wore on, until it reached its limit—a 20 cent rise from the opening price. . . .

At some point during the day, Dial and Salmon learned that Khan's check had not been certified. Yet Dial, authorized by Salmon, continued in the following days to buy silver futures heavily for IMC's account, even as it became increasingly likely from communications with the Oxford Bank that the check would never clear. On November 28 Dial decided the price of silver was now too high. He placed an order to sell 200 February silver futures contracts for the Multi-Projects account at $6.13. . . .

. . . .

The question for decision is whether the conduct we have described amounts to a fraud; if so, the defendants are guilty of federal wire and mail fraud, as there is no dispute that the telephone and the mails were used extensively. . . .

. . . [W]e think there was a scheme to defraud in a rather classic sense, which is obscured only because commodity futures trading is an arcane business—though not to these defendants. Fraud in the common law sense of deceit is committed by deliberately misleading another by words, by acts, or, in some instances—notably where there is a fiduciary relationship, which creates a duty to disclose all material facts—by silence. . . . The essence of a fiduciary relationship is that the fiduciary agrees to act as his principal's alter ego rather than to assume the standard arm's length stance of traders in a market. Hence the principal is not armed with the usual wariness that one has in dealing with strangers; he trusts the fiduciary to deal with him as frankly as he would deal with himself—he has bought candor.

As a broker, and therefore . . . a fiduciary of his customers, Dial, when he solicited his customers to participate in block orders, implicitly represented to them that he would try to get the best possible price. He could have gotten a better price by putting their orders in ahead of the orders he placed for his own accounts and those of his friends. In trading ahead of his customers without telling them what he was doing, he was misleading them for his own profit, and conduct of this type has long been considered fraudulent.

. . . It is true that the Board of Trade has no express rule against trading ahead of a customer (other than by a floor broker) and that there is no other specific prohibition (relevant to this case) of insider trading on commodity futures exchanges. But it is apparent that such a practice, when done without disclosure to the customer, is both contrary to a broker's fiduciary obligations and harmful to commodity futures trading, because it means that a person wanting to engage in such trading can trade only through an agent who has a conflict of interest.

. . . .

. . . Dial and Salmon not only defrauded their own customers; they also defrauded the people from whom they bought silver futures contracts, and their employer, the Clayton Brokerage Company, by trading, without margin, the Multi-Projects and IMC accounts. Trading without margin gives a misleading signal, because it is a signal not backed by any cash.

. . . The defendants' failure to disclose to their employer what was going on was a breach of the defendant's fiduciary duty as employees. Although they owed no similar duty to people on the other side of their silver futures transactions, their trading an unmargined account was an active misrepresentation and hence actionable even without a breach of fiduciary duty.

It is true that no one "lost money," because silver prices were rising for reasons other than the defendants' unmargined trading. . . . But the analysis is incomplete. The defendants' customers did lose money—the additional profit they would have made if the defendants had placed their customers' orders ahead of rather than behind their own orders. And Clayton was subjected to the risk of having to make good what might have been $25 million in trading losses in the IMC account. The risk did not materialize, but just as it is embezzlement if an employee takes money from his employer and replaces it before it is missed, so it is fraud to impose an enormous risk of loss on one's employer through deliberate misrepresentation even if the risk does not materialize. Finally, the defendants confused the market by signaling the presence of big buyers who had not in fact put up any money (IMC and Multi-Projects); and to undermine the confidence on which successful futures trading depends is to harm the exchanges, and the society at large.

. . . .

Affirmed

Case Questions

1. Explain the fradulent scheme in which the court found defendants to have participated.

2. How did defendants defraud their customers and cause them to lose money?

3. How did defendants defraud the Clayton Brokerage Company?

4. How did defendants defraud the market as a whole?

Case: Accountant Criminal Liability

When people talk about misdeeds that accountants commit, they are generally referring to the civil aspects—the tort aspects discussed in Chapter 10. Sometimes, however, the facts of a particular case permit criminal prosecution under the federal mail-fraud statute, the federal false-statement statute, the federal

Securities Exchange Acts of 1933 and 1934, and various state laws. Part of the reason for the misconception is the fact that, until relatively recently, accountants themselves tended to assume that if they adhered to the professional standards promulgated by the American Institute for Certified Public Accountants (AICPA)—that is, generally accepted accounting principles (GAAP) and generally accepted auditing principles (GAAS)—they would be safe from criminal prosecution. The trend indicated by the result of several cases indicates that this is no longer so.

Perhaps the leading case in this area is one of the earliest, *United States v. Simon* (1969), commonly referred to as *Continental Vending.* The case involved three auditors who were being prosecuted for violating the Securities Exchange Act of 1934 by filing false statements with a government agency on behalf of a client, Continental Vending. After Continental Vending filed for bankruptcy, the auditing firm agreed to pay a $2-million settlement for civil liabilities in an out-of-court settlement.

The criminal suit was brought to determine whether the auditors were criminally liable for the inadequate reporting of a situation involving financial transactions between the president of Continental Vending and a company affiliate. More specifically, the auditors did not disclose the affiliate's inability to repay a loan from the president.

Eight expert witnesses testified for the auditing firm, stating that the auditors had complied with both GAAP and GAAS. Three of the experts added additional information: They indicated that full disclosure would have been preferable. An appeals court, however, upheld an original lower-court finding that the auditors were criminally liable: It found that the auditors did not give a *fair presentation* of the situation in the audited statements and they did not act in *good faith.*

Other cases that more or less followed the same logic include *Escott v. BarChris Construction Corp.* (283 F. Supp. 643 [1968]). In this case, the issue was whether GAAS is an appropriate measure of due care for professional auditors hired to perform a year-end audit and follow-up review. (A *follow-up review* is a review performed between the date of an audited balance sheet and the release of the financial statements.) Peat Marwick found material errors and omissions in the company's prospectus. The court ruled that although accountants should not be held to a higher standard of care than that recognized in their profession, Peat Marwick's review did not meet that standard. Unfortunately, however, the court never stated explicitly that GAAS compliance was *sufficient* to protect the auditors. In addition, because such a black-letter statement of the law is rarely, if ever, enforced in that way in malpractice cases, the court's language in this case cannot be heavily relied on.

EMS Government Securities v. Alexander Grant & Co. (1986) is yet another case in this area. This case involved audited financial statements that contained material misstatements. The errors were concealed by the partner in charge of the audit, who hoped that the misstatements would be straightened out over time. The partner was eventually convicted of sustaining the fraud and sentenced to 12 years in prison.

Ultimately, the thrust of such decisions seems to be that auditors must look at the big picture in order to avoid criminal prosecution: The part of each transaction in the corporation's overall financial picture must be examined. The auditor's true client—the public—must always be kept in mind.

The INTERNATIONAL ENVIRONMENT box in this chapter discusses auditor liability in England and Australia.

In British Commonwealth countries like England and Australia, the perspective on an auditor's potential criminal liability is quite different than the current view in this country. For example, the scandal surrounding the Luxembourg-based Bank of Credit and Commerce International (BCCI) was uncovered partly because of cooperation between the London office of Price Waterhouse (which was hired by BCCI to perform an audit) and the British government. The circumstances surrounding this debacle—including the amounts of money, famous people, and number of countries involved in concealing the frauds—were enormously complex.

The procedures that led to the uncovering of the fraud came about because the accounting firm documented the details of the apparent fraud at the end of its audit. The audit was performed at the request of Britain's chief bank regulator, the Bank of England. Ironically, British law permitted the accounting firm to bill BCCI for the time spent on the investigation.

British law works this way: Individual banks must submit any investigations or reports that they require to the proper regulatory authority. The Bank of England, the client bank, and the outside auditors also meet once a year in order to discuss the records. This practice gives auditors the opportunity to come forward without fear of reprisal if they discover some irregularity on the client's part. It is also why auditors can be criminally liable for not reporting errors to the authorities.

Australian law also leaves room for auditors to report frauds committed by their clients. An Australian auditor may be criminally liable: (1) as an auditor; (2) as an officer of the company; and (3) as a party to offenses committed by other persons. Liability as an auditor means failure to comply with statutory duties by willfully, recklessly, or negligently failing to disclose material errors or falsely disclosing such errors. Conviction on either of these grounds can result in imprisonment and/or a fine.

Australian law does not address the question of whether adhering to a set of professional standards is an adequate defense against criminal liability. However, both American and British courts have ruled against—or at least modified—such reasoning. Consequently, it is not unlikely that Australian courts will do the same, particularly because auditors may be deemed guilty of committing a criminal offense if they fail to report improprieties.

On the other hand, the question of whether an accountant who is acting as an officer of the corporation can be criminally liable for failing to report fraud or some other crime on the part of the company has not been adequately resolved under Australian law. Nevertheless, it is possible that auditors can be considered corporate officers for purposes of such actions as insolvency proceedings, winding-up proceedings, and furnishing false information.

In other words, auditors who are parties to the offenses of others may find themselves criminally liable for the acts of those parties. Under Australian law, auditors who (1) do not fulfill the common-law duty of reporting findings of fraud or other irregularities to senior management and/or the regulatory authorities may be found guilty of aiding and abetting the perpetrator(s); (2) conspire with the management of the company to commit an impropriety may be guilty of conspiracy; and (3) knowingly cover up offenses that they discover (by failing to report them) may be guilty of the same offenses.

The general obligations of auditors under various British Commonwealth laws seem to be imported into the United States. Recent court decisions, proposed legislation, and public sentiment are converging to require more of auditors of public companies. If errors are made in a company's published financial statements, and if those errors come to the attention of the shareholders, auditors may find themselves scrambling to document the fact that they exercised a high standard of due diligence. If they can't, they may find themselves in jail.

Racketeering and RICO

Racketeer Influenced and Corrupt Organizations Act (RICO) 1970 federal statute that prohibits the use of a business in a pattern of activity

In October 1970, as part of the Organized Crime Control act, President Richard M. Nixon signed the **Racketeer Influenced and Corrupt Organizations Act (RICO)** into law. Congress's original intention in enacting RICO was to stop the infiltration of organized crime into legitimate businesses by providing stiff civil and criminal penalties for engaging in an extremely wide range of racketeering activities. However, because Congress could not legally outlaw "membership" in organized crime, it drafted a law prohibiting the activities that are characteristic of organized crime.

racketeering Activities characteristic of organized crime and including, among others, crimes of violence, crimes involving illicit goods and services, and crimes involving commercial fraud

RACKETEERING. In essence, RICO prohibits the use of an "enterprise" in "a pattern of racketeering" activity. A "pattern of racketeering" requires evidence of two acts within ten years of each other. **Racketeering** includes crimes of *vio-*

lence (such as murder, kidnapping, robbery, arson, extortion, and obstruction of justice); crimes that involve *illicit services and goods* (such as narcotics, counterfeiting, gambling, pornography, theft, and trafficking in restricted goods); crimes that involve the *breach of fiduciary duties in the context of organized labor* (restrictions on loans and payments to labor organizations); and crimes involving *commercial fraud* (mail and wire fraud, securities fraud, and embezzlement). The statute also prohibits the use of money acquired from a pattern-of-racke-

The Dishonest Confidential Clerk.

Crime in the Financial Sector Although business-related crimes still run the gamut from intramural embezzlement to much more broad-reaching corporate statutory violations, their scope appears to have increased by quantitative leaps and bounds. Consider, for example, some of the numbers from the savings-and-loan scandals that first erupted in the late 1980s. In about 60 percent of the cases already investigated by the government, criminal fraud was discovered, with 237 financial institutions involved in 182 criminal indictments between October 1988 and July 1990. Although it was estimated at the time that perhaps as many as 350 institutions had been involved in about 20,000 cases of criminal wrongdoing, the Justice Department deemed it necessary to limit its prosecution to about 100 of the most serious violators. The total cost of the ongoing S&L bailout will ultimately cost the taxpayers some $300 billion; the annual cost of a crime like burglary is about $4.5 billion. The idea of the *financial-services industry* is relatively new, its rapid growth due in part to the globalization of financial markets and the technological acceleration of postindustrial economies. It is estimated, for example, that only 1 percent of the dollar amount of all transactions are financed by currency. At the same time, it has also been calculated that although each individual in the U.S. holds $111 in currency, the outstanding total of U.S. currency at the end of 1990—$246 billion— amounts to about $1000 for every man, woman, and child in the country. Where is all of this currency? It is being held, according to the Federal Reserve System and various financial theorists, in the so-called "underground economy": the collective resources of individuals and institutions engaged in such "currency crimes" as tax avoidance, illegal overseas investments, and organized crime. At present the underground economy may equal 25 percent of current GNP, and such episodes as Irangate and the BCCI scandal surfaced when underground currency was converted into *transaction deposits*—claims issued by depository institutions (e.g., banks) on funds controlled by primary institutions (i.e., the Federal Reserve).

teering activity to gain a financial stake in legitimate enterprises. This section permits prosecutions for money-laundering schemes and the acquiring of legitimate businesses with "dirty money"—for example, with profits from an illegal drug operation.

CRIMINAL AND CIVIL COMPONENTS OF RICO. RICO has both criminal and civil components. Under the criminal component, the federal government may prosecute any person or enterprise that violates its provisions. Possible criminal penalties include a fine of $25,000, twenty years in prison, and the forfeiture of property. Under the RICO civil provision, an individual or business can file a lawsuit against any enterprise for causing it injury by engaging in an activity covered by RICO. Successful plaintiffs may recover triple damages, attorneys' fees, and court costs.

However, attractive civil remedies have caused a rash of civil suits—from divorces to contract disputes—to be brought under RICO. All that is needed to bring such a lawsuit for breach of contract is a plaintiff who is willing to (1) plead fraud and (2) allege that the defendant used the mails or the telephone at least twice, either to form or breach a contract.

Moreover, the consequences of such actions can be harsh. Whether or not charges are well substantiated, RICO defendants are often branded racketeers. Consequently, defendants suffer loss of reputation, and even defendants who are later cleared of any wrongdoing can be faced with irreparable harm. The possibility of having to pay triple damages is also overwhelming to many alleged racketeers. People and businesses confronted with this dual threat often grasp at out-of-court settlements rather than deal with public trials.

Criticism of RICO. The potential for abuse under RICO has caused many critics to complain that the statute is being used in ways far beyond the scope of Congress's original intent. Many of their arguments are grounded in the statute's vague language. Some of these critics—including the American Civil Liberties Union, the U.S. Chamber of Commerce, the American Bar Association, and unions such as the A.F.L.-C.I.O.—have already urged Congress to clarify through further legislation the ways in which it intended RICO civil suits to be used.

In addition, the courts have already had a hand in trying to interpret RICO's loose language. In *Sedima, S.P.L.R. v. Imrex Co.* (473 U.S. 479 [1985]), for example, the Supreme Court was asked to decide whether a private civil suit could be brought under RICO. The case involved a Belgian corporation (Sedima) that had entered into a joint venture with the defendant corporation (Imrex). The plaintiff's role was to place orders from Belgian buyers with Imrex. Imrex was supposed to obtain the goods in the United States and ship them to the buyer. The companies had agreed to split the net proceeds from their business. After about $8 million in business had been completed, Sedima became convinced that Imrex was cheating it out of some of its profits. Both the district court and the second circuit court of appeals found that Sedima's complaint was defective because the company did not have standing to sue under RICO.

The Supreme Court disagreed, holding that even though Congress had drafted the legislation for the specific purpose of going after organized crime, the language of the statute does not prevent private civil suits. The appeals court was not required to rule on the particular facts of the case.

The Supreme Court further examined the issue in the following case.

Securities in the '80s (VI): RICO and Its Critics In September 1988, Rudolph Giuliani, U.S. Attorney for the Southern District of New York, raised the possibility of seeking a RICO indictment against the financial-investment firm of Drexel Burnham Lambert for its involvement in the securities-violation case that centered on its head of high-yield bonds, Michael Milken (see Chapter 8). Under RICO, for example, Drexel would have had to post bond of perhaps as much as $1 billion *before* trial; as a possible debt, money owed to the government as RICO bond payment would have taken precedence over all other debts owed by the firm, with all other lenders forced to take junior positions. Ultimately, RICO provisions were not tested in this case because Drexel settled with the government before going to trial. RICO figured prominently, however, in the 98-count indictment handed down against Milken in March 1989—an indictment which, theoretically, carried penalties of 520 years in prison and $11 billion in fines. Critics of the application of RICO to the Milken case point out that Milken ultimately pleaded guilty to only six crimes—only three of which resembled those described in the indictment. They also point out that Milken did *not* admit to such charges as racketeering, manipulation of the junk-bond market, or even insider trading—nor was he prosecuted under those charges. According to critics of Giuliani's decision, the issue in the Drexel and Milken cases was not so much the threat of the incorrect use of a law but the use of an inappropriate and ill-defined law; Giuliani, they argue, could have used the Securities Act of 1934 as the basis for all securities-fraud prosecutions.

H. J. INC. v. NORTHWESTERN BELL TELEPHONE
United States Supreme Court 109 S.Ct. 2893 (1989)

In 1986, customers of Northwestern Bell Telephone Co. filed a class-action suit under RICO and a Minnesota law outlawing bribery against the company and the Minnesota Public Utility Commission (MPUC), which is the agency responsible for setting the rates that the company could charge its customers. In essence, the complaint alleged that employees of Northwestern Bell had tried to bribe members of the public agency to set favorable rates. The District Court and the Court of Appeals

had dismissed the RICO claims on the ground that the complaint did not allege a "pattern" of racketeering. The Supreme Court addressed this issue.

Justice Brennan delivered the opinion of the Court. . . . RICO renders criminally and civilly liable "any person" who uses or invests income derived "from a pattern of racketeering activity" to acquire an interest in or to operate an enterprise engaged in interstate commerce, 1962(a); who acquires or maintains an interest in or control of such an enterprise "through a pattern of racketeering activity," 1962(b) who, being employed by or associated with such an enterprise, conducts or participates in the conduct of its affairs "through a pattern of racketeering activity," 1962(c); or, finally, who conspires to violate the first three subsections of 1962, 1962(d). RICO provides for drastic remedies: conviction for a violation of RICO carries severe penalties and forfeiture of illegal proceeds. . . . a person found in a private civil action to have violated RICO is liable for treble damages, costs, and attorney's fees, 1964(c).

Petitioners' 5-count complaint alleged that between 1980 and 1986 Northwestern Bell sought to influence members of the MPUC in the performance of their duties—and in fact caused them to approve rates for the company in excess of a fair and reasonable amount—by making cash payments to commissioners, negotiating with them regarding future employment, and paying for parties and meals, for tickets to sporting events and the like, and for airline tickets. Based upon these factual allegations, petitioners alleged in their first count a pendent state-law claim, asserting that Northwestern Bell violated the Minnesota bribery statute, as well as state common law prohibiting bribery. They also raised four separate claims under 1962 of RICO. Count II alleged that, in violation of a 1962(a), Northwestern Bell derived income from a pattern of racketeering activity involving predicate acts of bribery and used this income to engage in its business as an interstate "enterprise." Count III claimed a violation of 1962(b), in that, through this same pattern of racketeering activity, respondents acquired an interest or control of the MPUC, which was also an interstate "enterprise." In Count IV, petitioners asserted that respondents participated in the conduct and affairs of the MPUC through this pattern of racketeering activity, contrary to 1962(c). Finally, Count V alleged that respondents conspired together to violate 1962(a), (b), and (c), thereby contravening 1962(d).

The District Court granted respondents' Federal Rule of Civil Procedure 12(b)(6) motion, dismissing the complaint for failure to state a claim upon which could be granted. The Court found that "(e)ach of the fraudulent acts alleged by (petitioners) was committed in furtherance of a single scheme to influence MPUC commissioners to the detriment of Northwestern Bell's ratepayers." It held that dismissal was therefore mandated by the Court of Appeals for the Eighth Circuit's decision in Superior Oil Company v. Fulmer, 785 F.2d 252(1986), which the District Court interpreted as

adopting an "extremely restricitve" test for a pattern of racketeering activity that required proof of "multiple illegal schemes." The Court of Appeals for the Eighth Circuit affirmed the dismissal of petitioners' complaint, confirming that under Eighth Circuit precedent "(a) single fraudulent effort or scheme is insufficient" to establish a pattern of racketeering activity, 829 F.2d 648, 650 (1987) and agreeing with the District Court that petitioners' complaint alleged only a single scheme, ibid. Two members of the panel suggested in separate concurrences, however, that the Court of Appeals have rejected the Eighth Circuit's interpretation of RICO's pattern concept to require an allegation and proof schemes, and we granted certiorari to resolve this conflict.

Congress has done nothing. . . . to illuminate RICO's key requirement of a patttern of racketeering; and as the plethora of different views expressed by the Courts of Appeals since Sedima demonstrates, developing a meaningful concept of "pattern" within the existing statutory framework has proved to be no easy task.

It is, nevertheless, a task we must undertake in order to decide this case. Our guides in this endeavor must be the text of the statute and its legislative history. We find no support in those sources for the proposition, espoused by the Court of Appeals for the Eighth Circuit in this case, that predicate acts of racketeering may form a pattern only when they are part of separate illegal schemes. Nor can we agree with those courts that have suggested that a pattern is established merely by proving two predicate acts, or with amici in this case who argue that the word "pattern" refers only to predicates that are indicative of a perpetrator involved in organized crime or its functional equivalent. In our view, Congress had a more natural and commonsense approach to RICO's pattern element in mind, intending a more stringent requirement than proof simply of two predicates, but also envisioning a concept of sufficient breadth that it might encompass multiple predicates within a single scheme that were related and that amounted to, or threatened the likelihood of, continued criminal activity. . . .

The section of the statute headed "definitions," 18 U.S.C. 1961, does not so much define a pattern of racketeering activity as state a minimum necessary condition for the existence of such a pattern. Unlike other provisions in 1961 that tell us what various concepts used in the ACT "mean," 1961(5) says of the phrase "pattern of racketeeriing activity" only that it "requires at least two acts of racketeering activity, one of which occurred after (October 15, 1970) and the last of which occurred within ten years (excluding any period of imprisonment) after the commission of a prior act of racketeering activity." It thus places an outer limit on the concept of a pattern of racketeering that is broad indeed.

Section 1961(5) does indicate that Congress envisioned circumstances in which no more than two predicates would be necessary to establish a pattern of racketeering—otherwise it would have drawn a narrower boundary to RICO liability, requiring proof of a greater number of predicates. . . . Section 1961(5) concerns only the minimum number of predicates necessary to establish a pattern; and it assumes that there is something to a RICO pattern beyond simply the number of predicate acts involved. . . .

In addition to 1961(5), there is the key phrase "pattern of racketeering activity" itself from 1962. In normal usage, the word "pattern" here would be taken to require more than just a multiplicity of racketeering predicates. A "pattern" is an "arrangement or order of things or activity," 11 *Oxford English Dictionary* 357 (2d ed. 1989), and the mere fact that there are a number of predicates is no guarantee that they fall into any arrangement or order. It is not the number of predicate but the relationship that they bear to each other or some external organizing principle that renders them "ordered" or "arranged." The text of RICO conspicuously fails anywhere to identify, however, forms of relationship or external principles to be used in determining whether racketeering activity falls into a pattern for purposes of the Act.

It is reasonable to infer, from this absence of any textual identification of sorts of patterns that would satisfy 1962's requirement, in combination with the very relaxed limits to the pattern concept fixed in 1961(5), that Congress intended to take a flexible approach.

RICO's legislative history reveals Congress' intent that to prove a pattern of racketeering activity a plaintiff or prosecutor must show that the racketeering predicates are related and that they amount to or pose a threat of continued criminal activity.

For analytical purposes these two constituents of RICO's pattern requirement must be stated separately, though in practice their proof will often overlap. The element of relatedness is the easier to define.

We have no reason to suppose that Congress had in mind for RICO's pattern of racketeering component any more constrained a notion of the relationships between predicates that would suffice. . . .

To establish a RICO pattern it must also be shown that the predicates themselves amount to, or that they otherwise constitute a threat of continuing racketeering activity. It is this aspect of RICO's pattern element that has spawned the "multiple scheme" test adopted by some lower courts, including the Court of Appeals in this case.

But although proof that a RICO defendant has been involved in multiple criminal schemes would certainly be highly relevant to the inquiry into the continuity of the defendant's racketeering activity, it is implausible to suppose that Congress thought continuity might be shown only by proof of multiple schemes. The Eighth Circuit's test brings a rigidity to the available methods of proving a pattern that simply is not present in the idea of "continuity" itself; and it does so, moreover, by introducing a concept—the "scheme"—that appears nowhere in the language or legislative history of the Act. We adopt a less inflexible approach that seems to us to derive from a common-sense everyday understanding

of RICO's language and Congress' gloss on it. What a plaintiff or prosecutor must prove is continuity of racketeering activity, or its threat, simpliciter. This may be done in a variety of ways, thus making it difficult to formulate in the abstract and general test for continuity.

"Continuity" is both a closed- and open-ended concept, referring either to a closed period of repeated conduct, or to past conduct that by its nature projects into the future with a threat of repetition. It is, in either case, centrally a temporal concept—and particularly so in the RICO context, where what must be continuous, RICO's predicate acts or offenses, and the relationship these predicates must bear one to another, are distinct requirements. In such cases, liability depends on whether the threat of continuity is demonstrated.

Whether the predicates proved establish a threat of continued racketeering activity depends on the specific facts of each case.

The limits of the relationship and continuity concepts that combine to define a RICO pattern, and the precise methods by which relatedness and continuity or its threats may be proved, cannot be fixed in advance with such clarity that it will always be apparent whether in a particular case a "pattern of racketeering activity" exists. The development of these concepts must await future cases, absent a decision by Congress to revisit RICO to provide clearer guidance as to the ACT's intended scope. . . .

Various amici urge that RICO's pattern element should be interpreted more narrowly than as requiring relationship and continuity in the senses outlined above, so that as defendant's racketeering activities form a pattern only if they are characteristic either of organized crime in then traditional sense, or of an organized crime in the traditional sense, or of an organized-crime-type perpetrator, that is, of an association dedicated to the repeated commission of criminal offenses. . . .

It is argued, nonetheless, that Congress' purpose in enacting RICO . . . was to combat organized crime; and that RICO's broad language should be read narrowly so that the Act's scope is coextensive with this purpose. We cannot accept this argument for a narrowing construction of the Act's expansive terms.

We . . . decline the invitation to invent a rule that RICO's pattern of racketeering concept requires an allegation and proof of an organized crime nexus.

Under the analysis we have set forth above, and consistent with the allegations in their complaint, petitioners may be able to prove that multiple predicates alleged constitute "a pattern of racketeering activity," in that they satisfy the requirements of relationship and continuity. The acts of bribery alleged are said to be related by a common purpose, to influence Commissioners in carrying out their duties in order to win approval of unfairly and unreasonably high rates for Northwestern Bell. Furthermore, petitioners claim that the racketeering predicates occurred with some frequency over at least a 6-year period, which may be sufficient to satisfy the continuity requirement. Alternatively, a threat of continuity of racketeering activity might be established at trial by showing that the alleged bribes were a regular way of conducting Northwestern Bell's ongoing business, or a regular way of conducting or participating in the conduct of the alleged and ongoing RICO enterprise, the MPUC. . . .

Case Questions

1. RICO was enacted to give the government a new weapon in the fight against organizations wholly devoted to criminal activity. Is it fair to apply the law to criminal activity between legitimate businesses, like a telephone company, and a government agency like the MPUC?

2. What are the advantages for plaintiffs of bringing an action under RICO in federal court, as opposed to merely bringing an action in state court under a state's common law?

■ Concept Check 12-3   Business-Related Crimes

- Explain the principal articles of the *1984 Federal Computer Crime Statute*.
- Discuss a situation in which the activities of an auditing professional may result in criminal liability.
- Discuss the 1970 *Racketeer Influenced and Corrupt Organization Act* and explain its function in terms of its criminal and civil components. What are some of the primary criticisms of RICO?

■ CRIMINAL RESPONSIBILITY: CORPORATIONS AND MANAGERS

English common law did not hold corporations legally responsible for criminal actions. Instead, corporations were treated as artificial entities that could not be blamed for moral lapses or punished by imprisonment. As corporations proliferated in size and influence, however, courts began to express the opinion that such entities should be held liable under criminal law.

Corporate Mens Rea

The development of the tort concept of vicarious liability—that is, that a corporation is liable for the torts of its agents—helped to modify the view that only people, not corporations, could commit acts. By the mid-1800s, the law recognized that corporations could be held liable for torts and crimes that neither constituted felonies nor involved personal violence. Most early criminal prosecutions of corporations involved violations of regulatory statutes that did not include a mens rea component. In addition, judicial rulings began to emerge that recognized the notion that a corporation's failure to act where it had the legal duty to do so could also be criminal.

However, the concept that corporations could be found guilty of crimes requiring specific mental states did not emerge until the turn of the century, when corporations actually became defined as persons. At first, courts were willing to find corporations liable only for crimes requiring the *purposeful* commission of a criminal act. Later, however, the final impediment to full criminal liability fell as courts found corporations guilty of crimes requiring only *willfulness* and *knowledge*. In these decisions, the intent of the corporate agent who commits the wrongful action is transferred to the corporation as a whole.

Issues in Corporate Liability

Judicial acceptance of the view that corporations can be held criminally liable has raised these closely related issues:

- Who, in a corporation, should be treated as acting for the entity?
- What should happen if the company has done everything in its power to prevent a crime?
- Should a company's efforts to prevent the commission of crimes among its employees be a defense in prosecutions?

Is it appropriate to treat the activities of high-level officers as corporate action? Should corporate officers be held responsible for activities that occur at places far removed from corporate headquarters? Is it fair, however, to impose criminal liability in a corporation for the behavior of low-level employees who had no policy-making power? As it now stands, the wrongdoer's corporate status is essentially irrelevant: The criminal act of any employee acting within the scope of his employment may be imputed to the corporation as a whole.

THE ISSUE OF REMEDY. Because corporations cannot be incarcerated, the sentence following the conviction of a corporation for a crime may include compensation and restitution to the victim and a stiff fine. There is also some degree of social stigma that attaches to a corporation that is convicted of a crime. But are fines and social stigma effective in deterring corporations from committing future crimes? Fines are relatively ineffective, particularly for large corporations, because they can be passed on to consumers. Moreover, it is unlikely that imposing higher fines would solve the problem because this practice might threaten corporate solvency and thus hurt shareholders, employees, and the economy as a whole.

From a theoretical standpoint, the consummate criminal penalty for a corporation would be one that neither hurts innocent parties nor unnecessarily inhibits legitimate business activity. Nevertheless, many observers feel that only the responsible individuals should be prosecuted and that the imposition of criminal liability on corporations should be abandoned altogether.

Individuals in the Corporation

If convicted of a crime committed in the course of doing business, a corporate agent may be jailed or fined or both. In recent years, there has been an expansion in the law with respect to criminal prosecutions of upper-echelon corporate employees. For example, until recently, corporate managers were not expected, under the law, to provide employees with a hazard-free workplace. Now, however, managers face convictions for homicide if they are responsible for unsafe workplace conditions that cause an employee's death. In 1985, for example, three corporate agents were sentenced to 25-year prison terms following a homicide conviction involving a worker who died from cyanide exposure (*People v. O'Neill*, Cook Co. Cir. Ill [1985]).

Corporate officers have also been prosecuted for criminal mail fraud for breaching fiduciary duties to corporations. For example, executives have been convicted of mail fraud for using the mail system in the course of defrauding a corporation.

In addition, certain strict-liability statutes may attach criminal responsibility even if an executive does not have personal knowledge of a wrongful act: As shown in the following case, it may be enough for the executive to have a responsible position over the employee who actually committed the crime.

UNITED STATES v. PARK
United States Supreme Court, 421 U.S. 658 (1975)

Respondent Park is the president and chief executive officer of Acme Markets, Inc., a national retail food chain. Acme and respondent were charged with violations of the Federal Food, Drug, and Cosmetic Act. In its information, the Government alleged that the acts by defendants in receiving food through interstate commerce and holding the food in a building accessible to rodents and in exposing the food to contamination by rodents resulted in the food's being adulterated in violation of the Act. At trial, the jury found respondent guilty on all counts of the information. The Court of Appeals reversed the conviction and remanded for a new trial. The Government petitions for a certiorari.

Mr. Chief Justice Burger delivered the opinion of the Court.

. . .

Acme pleaded guilty to each count of the information. Respondent pleaded not guilty. . . . An FDA consumer safety officer testified concerning evidence of rodent infestation and other unsanitary conditions discovered during a 12-day inspection of the Baltimore warehouse in November and December 1971. He also related that a second inspection of the warehouse had been conducted in March 1972. On that occasion the inspectors found that there had been improvement in the sanitary conditions, but that "there was still evidence of rodent activity in the building and in the warehouses and we found some rodent-contaminated lots of food items."

. . . The Government's final witness, Acme's vice president for legal affairs and assistant secretary, identified respondent as the president and chief executive officer of the company and read a bylaw prescribing the duties of the chief executive officer. He testified that respondent functioned by delegating "normal operating duties," including sanitation, but that he retained "certain things, which are the big, broad, principles of the operation of the company," and had "the responsibility of seeing that they all work together."

. . . .

Respondent was the only defense witness. He testified that, although all of Acme's employees were in a sense under his general direction, the company had an "organizational structure for responsibilities for certain functions" according to which different phases of its operation were "assigned to individuals who, in turn, have staff and departments under them." . . . Respondent stated that he did not "believe there was anything

[he] could have done more constructively than what [he] found was being done."

. . . .

At the close of the evidence, respondent's renewed motion for a judgment of acquittal was denied. The relevant portion of the trial judge's instructions to the jury challenged by respondent is set out in the margin.* Respondent's counsel objected to the instructions on the ground that they failed fairly to reflect our decision in United States v. Dotterweich [1943], and to define "'responsible relationship.'" The trial judge overruled the objection. The jury found respondent guilty on all counts of the information, and he was subsequently sentenced to pay a fine of $50 on each count.

The Court of Appeals reversed the conviction and remanded for a new trial. . . . The Court of Appeals concluded that the trial judge's instructions "might well have left the jury with the erroneous impression that Park could be found guilty in the absence of 'wrongful action' on his part," and that proof of this element was required by due process. It held, with one dissent, that the instructions did not "correctly state the law of the case." . . .

The question presented by the Government's petition for certiorari in United States v. Dotterweich, *supra,* and

* "In order to find the Defendant guilty on any count of the Information, you must find beyond a reasonable doubt on each count.

. . . .

"However, you need not concern yourselves with the first two elements of the case. The main issue for your determination is only with the third element, whether the Defendant held a position of authority and responsibility in the business of Acme Markets.

. . . .

"The statute makes individuals, as well as corporations, liable for violations. An individual is liable if it is clear, beyond a reasonable doubt, that the elements of the adulteration of the food as to travel in interstate commerce are present. As I have instructed you in this case, they are, and that the individual had a responsible relation to the situation, even though he may not have participated personally.

"The individual is or could be liable under the statute, even if he did not consciously do wrong. However, the fact that the Defendant is pres[id]ent and is a chief executive officer of the Acme Markets does not require a finding of guilt. Though, he need not have personally participated in the situation, he must have had a responsible relationship to the issue. The issue is, in this case, whether the Defendant, John R. Park, by virtue of his position in the company, had a position of authority and responsibility in the situation out of which these charges arose."

the focus of this Court's opinion, was whether "the manager of a corporation, as well as the corporation itself, may be prosecuted under the Federal Food, Drug, and Cosmetic Act of 1938 for the introduction of misbranded and adulterated articles into interstate commerce." In *Dotterweich,* a jury had disagreed as to the corporation, a jobber purchasing drugs from manufacturers and shipping them in interstate commerce under its own label, but had convicted Dotterweich, the corporation's president and general manager. . . .

In reversing the judgment of the Court of Appeals and reinstating Dotterweich's conviction, this Court looked to the purposes of the Act and noted that they "touch phases of the lives and health of the people which, in the circumstances of modern industrialism, are largely beyond self-protection." It observed that the Act is of "a now familiar type" which "dispenses with the conventional requirement for criminal conduct awareness of some wrongdoing. In the interest of the larger good it puts the burden of acting at hazard upon a person otherwise innocent but standing in responsible relation to a public danger."

Central to the Court's conclusion that individuals other than proprietors are subject to the criminal provisions of the Act was the reality that "the only way in which a corporation can act is through the individuals who act on its behalf." . . .

. . . .

. . . *Dotterweich* and the cases which have followed reveal that in providing sanctions which reach and touch the individuals who execute the corporate mission—and this is by no means necessarily confined to a single corporate agent or employee—the Act imposes not only a positive duty to seek out and remedy violations when they occur but also, and primarily, a duty to implement measures that will insure that violations will not occur. The requirements of foresight and vigilance imposed on responsible corporate agents are beyond question demanding, and perhaps onerous, but they are no more stringent than the public has a right to expect of those who voluntarily assume positions of authority in business enterprises whose services and products affect the health and well-being of the public that supports them.

. . . .

Turning to the jury charge in this case, it is of course arguable that isolated parts can be read as intimating that a finding of guilt could be predicated solely on respondent's corporate position. But this is not the way we review jury instructions, because "a single instruction to a jury may not be judged in artificial isolation, but must be viewed in the context of the overall charge." Cupp v. Naughten (1973).

Reading the entire charge satisfies us that the jury's attention was adequately focused on the issue of respondent's authority with respect to the conditions that formed the basis of the alleged violations. Viewed as a whole, the charge did not permit the jury to find guilt solely on the basis of respondent's position in the corporation; rather, it fairly advised the jury that to find guilt it must find respondent "had a responsible relation to the situation," and "by virtue of his position . . . had . . . authority and responsibility" to deal with the situation. The situation referred to could only be "food . . . held in unsanitary conditions in a warehouse with the result that it consisted, in part, of filth or . . . may have been contaminated with filth."

. . . The record in this case reveals that the jury could not have failed to be aware that the main issue for determination was not respondent's position in the corporate hierarchy, but rather his accountability, because of the responsibility and authority of his position, for the conditions which gave rise to the charges against him.

We conclude that, viewed as a whole and in the context of the trial, the charge was not misleading and contained an adequate statement of the law to guide the jury's determination.

. . . .

Reversed.

Case Questions

1. Upon what basis did the jury determine Park's guilt?

2. What is the policy justification for holding a person who occupies a position of corporate authority, and who acts on behalf of the corporation, responsible for the liabilities of the corporation? Explain.

THE FAIRNESS OF PUNISHING CORPORATE AGENTS. Is the imposition of criminal responsibility upon individuals within a corporation consistent with the objectives of punishment discussed in the beginning of this chapter? In many ways, yes. First, it is harmonious with the common-law tradition of punishing the personally guilty wrongdoer. Second, it is an arguably more effective method of deterrence to punish individuals rather than the corporation: After all, people who are convicted of a crime face serious immediate negative consequences, such as damaged reputations and loss of employment. In addition, a conviction often sends a message throughout a corporation's decision-making structure that everybody had better abide by the law or face severe personal consequences.

Holding corporate agents criminally liable, however, is not without drawbacks. First, it is often difficult to identify which particular employee is to blame for a given policy or act. As a result, prosecutors may exhaust tremendous resources in investigations to determine just who is at fault. Second, the extent to which individual convictions prevent future crimes is questionable: The imprisonment of white-collar criminals is rare enough not to pose a serious threat to those considering the risks of breaking the law. Third, it is unlikely that the threat of punishment will deter crimes that are more a function of bad judgment than a conscious disregard for the law.

■ Concept Check 12-4   Criminal Responsibility: Corporations and Managers

- Explain the role played by the concept of *vicarious liability* in the concept of corporate tortious and criminal activity.
- Focusing on the question of *remedy*, discuss the key issues in corporate liability.

■ DEFENSES AGAINST CRIMINAL RESPONSIBILITY

Particularly in recent years, certain criminal defenses, such as the insanity defense and claims of self-defense, have received a great deal of public attention. These defenses are rarely relevant to criminal prosecutions involving businesses. Nevertheless, the following discussion briefly covers some of these defenses as well as others more closely related to business activities.

Insanity

The insanity defense is one of the most controversial defenses in criminal law. This defense essentially negates the actor's criminal responsibility by asserting that he was unable to control or understand his actions. But medical and legal definitions of insanity differ: A person may be medically insane but culpable under legal standards. Proof that a defendant was legally insane at the time of the criminal act is a *complete* defense to liability: If a person did not know what he was doing, he cannot be held legally responsible for his acts.

Identifying and defining legal insanity, however, is not easy. Nowhere is this difficulty more apparent than in its definitions under criminal law. Several definitions are used in different jurisdictions:

- The **M'Naughten Rule**, which was developed in the 1800s, holds that a person is considered insane if, at the time of the criminal act, he could not understand the nature of the act or distinguish whether the act was right and wrong because of a mental disability.
- The **Durham Rule** holds that a defendant is insane if he was suffering from a mental illness at the time the crime was committed and if the insanity was the cause of the act.
- The **Substantial Capacity Test**, which appears as Section 4.01 of the American Law Institute's Model Penal Code, holds that "a person is not responsible for criminal conduct if at the time of such conduct as a result of mental disease or defect he lacks substantial capacity whether to appreciate the criminality (wrongfulness) of his conduct or to conform his conduct to the requirements of the law."

M'Naughten Rule Definition used in the *insanity defense* that states that a defendant is insane if, at the time of the crime, he or she could not understand the nature of the act or distinguish if it was right or wrong.

Durham Rule Definition used in the *insanity defense* that states that a defendant is insane if he or she was suffering from mental illness when the crime was committed and if the illness caused the act

Substantial Capacity Test Definition used in the *insanity defense* that states that a person is not responsible for a crime if, when it was committed, as a result of mental disease or defect the accused was unable to appreciate wrongfulness or conform his conduct to the law

- The **Irresistible Impulse Rule** states that the defendant is not guilty if he committed a criminal act while under the influence of an insane impulse that controlled his will. This defense is available to those who are driven to commit a criminal act by a temporary or momentary surge of insanity as well as to those who suffer from a mental illness.

Irresistible Impulse Rule
Definition used in the *insanity defense* that states that a person is not guilty of a criminal act committed while under the influence of an insane impulse controlling his or her will

Criticism of the insanity defense usually runs along one of three lines of argument. First, many critics believe that a defendant can escape liability by faking insanity during interviews with court-appointed psychiatrists. Second, there is

Exhibit A On November 24, 1963, Dallas nightclub owner Jack Ruby (with gun) shot and killed Lee Harvey Oswald, who was suspected of having assassinated President John F. Kennedy two days earlier. The killing took place in the basement of the Dallas, Texas, police station and was seen over live television cameras by millions. Invoking the *M'Naughten rule* in his appeal of Ruby's death sentence, attorney Melvin Belli (see the PERSONAL PROFILE in Chapter 10) argued insanity: According to Belli, Ruby had acted while suffering from "some kind of blackout" brought on by a bout of "psychomotor epilepsy." History records, of course, that the judge rejected Belli's argument; Ruby was judged legally sane and died in prison. Guidelines on the insanity defense proposed by the American Law Institute in 1962 have met with increased acceptance. In 1983, however, the acquittal by reason of insanity of John W. Hinckley, who had tried to assassinate President Ronald Reagan, called those guidelines into public question. For one thing, the barrage of "expert" testimony delivered at the trial severely damaged the principle of psychiatric evidence. Some critics now argue that only testimony bearing on mental abnormality and *conscious intent* should be permitted at the guilt stage of the trial; testimony regarding more subtle impairments would be restricted to the sentencing stage. Another proposal involves a pool of disinterested experts called neither by the defense nor the prosecution, but rather by the court; meeting as a panel, these experts would seek a consensus regarding the defendant's mental state at the time of the crime.

concern that the defense relies too heavily on expert psychiatric testimony. Finally, legal scholars charge that the defense—that is, establishing beyond a reasonable doubt that the defendant was sane when the act was committed—places an impossible burden upon the prosecution.

John W. Hinckley's attempt to assassinate President Ronald Reagan in 1981 highlighted these issues. As you will recall, Hinckley was found not guilty by reason of insanity (*United States v. Hinckley*, 525 F. Supp. 1342 [1982]). Congress subsequently changed the federal definition of insanity to state that a defendant has an affirmative defense if he had been unable, because of severe mental defect or disease, to appreciate the nature, quality, or wrongfulness of his acts.

Infancy

According to common law, children are conclusively presumed to be devoid of criminal capacity between birth and seven years of age. Although children between seven and 14 years of age are presumed to be incapable of criminal intent, this presumption can be rebutted if the prosecution shows that the child knew what he was doing and knew that it was wrong. With defendants over 14, incapacity is not presumed but may be demonstrated.

Under the federal Juvenile Delinquency Act, juveniles can be tried as adults for felonies if the crimes were committed after their sixteenth birthday. Many state statutes, however, place juveniles who exclusively commit such crimes in juvenile court, even for offenses that would be considered murder if committed by an adult.

Entrapment

Law enforcement investigations often involve undercover operations. Upon receiving information about an upcoming criminal activity or an ongoing illegal enterprise, a law enforcement official may seek to infiltrate the scheme in order to gather evidence. For example, if the government has reason to suspect that certain company executives routinely engage in bribing public officials, it might place agents in government positions where they can offer favors in exchange for illegal bribes.

If such a law-enforcement technique results in the prosecution of the executives, defendants may seek to avoid liability by asserting the defense of *entrapment*. **Entrapment** exists when the commission of the crime is a result of the law-enforcement agent's inducement, not the wrongdoer's criminal predisposition. As you will recall, our criminal law is grounded on the objective of imposing responsibility for moral blameworthiness. The defense of entrapment is aimed at discouraging the government from luring a person into committing a crime that he or she was not otherwise inclined to commit.

entrapment *Defense* against criminal responsibility holding that the commission of a crime resulted from the inducement of a law enforcement agent

Mistake of Fact

As you will recall, our legal system does not impose criminal responsibility upon individuals unless they possessed the requisite mental state at the time the crime was committed. Both ignorance and mistake of fact or law may be defenses to crimes if they outweigh this requirement.

A **mistake of fact** occurs when a person commits an act that would have been lawful if the facts had actually been as the actor reasonably assumed they

mistake of fact Defense against criminal responsibility holding that the crime committed would have been lawful had the facts been as the actor reasonably assumed they were

were. Suppose a foreman in charge of shipping crates of microchips places a crate in his car, honestly believing that it contained a set of encyclopedias the boss had promised him several weeks earlier. In such a case, the defendant may assert a defense of mistake of fact.

Perhaps you have heard the overused adage, "A mistake of law is no defense." This axiom is true to the extent that it is used to mean that a person need not be aware of the existence of a certain law to be convicted of breaking it. For example, a clerk in a department store who makes a habit of skimming five percent off the top of every cash sale could not assert a mistake of laws: He could not successfully claim that he intended to keep the money but did not know that embezzlement was a crime. As long as the clerk's act and mental state correspond with those required for embezzlement, he is criminally liable.

■ **Concept Check 12-5   Defenses against Criminal Responsibility**

- Explain the four principal rules or tests used to define *insanity* as a criminal defense.
- Define *entrapment* and *mistake of fact* as defenses against criminal liability.

You Decide: Answer/Discussion

Plea Bargaining

To punish a person because he has done what the law allows him to do is a violation of due process. In the give-and-take of plea bargaining, however, there is no such provision as long as the accused is free to accept or reject a prosecutor's offer.

In Bordenkircher v. Hayes, the defendant was free to decide not to take the plea bargain. Moreover, the Court did not regard the element of coercion in the prosecutor's threat as the guiding factor in the case. Although the Court's decision was split 5-4, the majority of the justices felt the fact that the prosecutor was fairly certain that both charges could be proven beyond a reasonable doubt before he made the offer carried more weight: In other words, because the prosecutor had probable cause to believe that Hayes committed both crimes, it was within his discretion to decide which charge to file or to bring before a grand jury. The conscious exercise of selective law enforcement is not a violation of the Constitution as long as the selectivity was not deliberately grounded on an illegal standard—for example, race or religion—or some other arbitrary classification.

In this case, it seems that the prosecutor used fairly straightforward reasoning in offering Hayes the opportunity to plead to a lesser charge. Hayes's "reward" for not costing the state the time and expense of the trial was a shorter term in prison and a less serious charge on his conviction record. The prosecutor merely played to the defendant's fear that a jury trial might lead to a harsher result.

SUMMARY

- A *criminal act* is a behavior that society defines as an intolerable threat to the social order. Torts, as we learned in an earlier chapter, involve the breach of duties between private individuals that culminates in private litigation. *Crimes,* however, are prosecuted by the state, which represents all the people.

- Penologists and criminal law experts have identified five specific goals of *punishment.* These are *general deterrence, special deterrence, rehabilitation, incapacitation (restraint),* and *retribution.* Each form of punishment, ranging from monetary fines to the death penalty, satisfies some of these goals and fails to achieve others.

- Because crimes are punished by depriving a person of property (when a fine is imposed) or freedom (when a jail term is imposed), the Constitution and the statutes have established a set of procedural rules to ensure that those accused of committing crimes are treated fairly. The Constitution protects people from *unreasonable searches and seizures, double jeopardy, excessive bail,* and *cruel and unusual punishment,* while guaranteeing the right to a fair trial and an attorney. Additionally, the federal government and each state has established a system of stages through which those suspected of committing crimes pass. For purposes of punishment, crimes are categorized by severity. *Felonies* are the most severe, *misdemeanors* fall in the middle, and *violations* are the least serious.

- The necessary elements of each crime are defined by federal and state statutes. Each crime requires the commission of, or failure to commit, an act and a specified state of mind.

- Within the business world, crimes generally fall into one of several categories of *"white-collar" crimes.* Such crimes involve (1) violating a statute that regulates a business, (2) neglecting a statute's disclosure requirements, or (3) committing an act that has been specifically made illegal by a statute. The statutes that are most frequently used to prosecute business crimes are: The 1984 *Federal Computer Crime Statute,* which outlaws computer crimes; the *mail-* and *wire-fraud laws,* which prohibit the use of the postal system and electronic communications networks to commit a fraud; and *RICO,* which makes it illegal to use a legitimate business for a pattern of *racketeering* activity. In addition to being a criminal law, RICO has a civil component that permits private suits against businesses or individuals that have engaged in racketeering.

- *Corporate crime* presents a challenge to traditional notions of criminal responsibility. At common law, corporations were not considered distinct entities, and were thus considered incapable of acting or formulating a state of mind. Instead, they acted only through agents. Today, however, courts deem corporations persons under the law. In addition to holding a corporate entity criminally liable, agents of a corporation, such as corporate officers, may be held personally liable and prosecuted criminally.

- Although rarely relevant in criminal proceedings involving businesses, the most frquently invoked *criminal defenses* are: *insanity, infancy, entrapment,* and *mistake of fact.*

QUESTIONS AND PROBLEMS

1. An employee stole money from his employer for several weeks. He had checks issued to fictitious people and then cashed them. After the theft was discovered, and as part of the routine investigation, the police asked the employee if he knew anything about the missing funds. The employee blurted "I know you know that I did it, but I just needed the money." He is taken into custody and given his *Miranda* warnings. At the trial the employee's attorney requests the court to suppress his client's confession because it was given without proper *Miranda* warnings. Will the judge throw out the confession?

2. While Marcus Lawrence is carving meat for the buffet at a posh local restaurant, he is suddenly seized with a violent pain in his chest. His knife flies out of his hand and kills a nearby patron while he is reacting to the pain. As it turns out, Mr. Lawrence suffered a massive heart attack. He had no history of heart disease and no warning signals that the attack was imminent. Is he guilty of murdering the patron?

3. Peter Taylor, a meat cutter at a local meat butchering and processing plant, is responsible for sliding the sides of beef along the hanging rack to prepare them for cutting. When one of the sides of beef seems to be stuck, he gives it a tug to get it moving. Later, he discovers a body with a rope around its neck atop the rack. It is discovered to be the night security guard, who had been placed there by thieves. The guard, although unconscious, was alive until the tug at the side of beef caused the rope to strangle him. Has Peter Taylor committed a crime?

4. The defendant, Marion Black, entered her home to find a male acquaintance waiting for her. The acquaintance verbally attacked her, causing her to run

upstairs to her room. When the defendant discovered that her friend was about to leave the premises, she called out to him, approached, shot, and killed him. The defendant claimed self-defense because she thought that he was reaching for a knife in his pocket. At trial defendant contends she was insane at the time of the killing because she suffered from schizophrenia. Defendant also asserted that because of her mental illness, all the signed statements she gave to police after she received her Miranda warnings were inadmissible. Discuss defendant's defenses and how successful she will be. [*Commonwealth of PA v. Marion Black*, 411 A.2d 767 (1979)]

5. A pharmacy clerk at the Esquire Drug Stores entered into contracts with General Mills and Eastern Coupon Clearing House without the knowledge or authority of Esquire Drug Stores. The clerk would mail coupons to the two companies in his employer's name, obtain the reimbursement checks, endorse his employer's name on the back of the checks, then deposit the checks in his personal account. The checks totaled $4,663.20. When defendant was arrested, there was no cash missing from the Esquire Stores, but charges were filed. What were the charges? [*Commonwealth of PA v. Jerry Rosenzweig*, 522 A.2d. 1088 (1987)]

6. Sylvester Carthon was riding with friends when their car ran out of gas. Sylvester walked to the gas station and bought gas, but when he returned the car and his friends were gone. He then walked to his girlfriend's apartment and put the can on her kitchen table. The can rolled off, spilling gasoline on the floor. As Sylvester reached for a mop to clean it up, there was an explosion and a fire. Sylvester screamed that "He was sorry, he didn't mean it," and asked someone to call the fire department. Sylvester was arrested and charged with arson. Will he be convicted? Explain. [*Commonwealth v. Carthon*, 354 A.2d 557 (1976)]

7. Ray Lambert was involved in several post office robberies of money orders. Police, en route to his house with a warrant, encountered him in the street, arrested him, and read him the *Miranda* warnings. He indicated that he understood the warnings and proceeded to answer questions. The police wanted to find the stolen money orders, but Mr. Lambert asked for his attorney. The police ceased their interrogation, but began talking among themselves about how it would be a shame to have to involve his girlfriend and family. Ray Lambert then led the police to the money orders. Later, however, the defendant's attorney makes a motion to suppress his confession, claiming that Mr. Lambert was coerced into confessing after police threatened to involve his girlfriend. Is his confession voluntary? [*U.S. v. Thierman*, 678 F.2d 1331 (1982)]

8. Special agent Homer Banks of the Bureau of Alcohol, Tobacco, and Firearms meets with a confidential informant. The informant tells him that a third party, Byron Kennedy, has firearms to sell. He introduces them, and tells Mr. Kennedy that the agent is a narcotics dealer. During the meeting, Byron Kennedy indicates that he is willing to exchange firearms for cocaine. The parties agree that Mr. Kennedy will make a sample delivery of firearms. The next day, they meet and exchange firearms for $600. More business is discussed—50 firearms for 2 ounces of cocaine and $1,000. After several more meetings, the agent initiates contact and another exchange is discussed. Was Byron Kennedy entrapped by the agent? [*U.S. v. Hawkins*, 823 F.2d 1020 (1987)]

9. After making a car sale, the salesman is told by management to collect an additional $300 from the buyer and have the buyer obtain a cosignor. He traveled to the buyer's home and received the document and the additional money. Upon returning to work, he hands over the document—but not the money—to management. When asked about the $300, the salesman says the buyer gave it to him for doing such a good job on the sale. Is he guilty of embezzlement?

10. Johnson, who had been involved in organized crime, moved out of state and began living under an assumed name. He engaged an attorney, Peluso, to handle the purchase of some land. Eventually, Johnson's past caught up with him when he was indicted for having transported and

pledged stolen securities during the period of his involvement with the syndicate. He asked Peluso to defend him against the securities charges. According to Johnson, Peluso told him that if he pleaded guilty, Peluso would arrange a plea bargain whereby Johnson would receive only a three-year sentence. Johnson signed a guilty plea, but in fact no plea bargain had been arranged, and Johnson was sentenced to 25 years. Peluso died soon afterward. Johnson moved that his sentence be vacated, claiming that he pleaded guilty only on the advice of counsel and did so knowing that the statements he signed were false. He also requested the court to acknowledge that the plea bargain process was "a charade" and asked that his guilty pleas be vacated for that reason. Did Johnson win? [*Browder v. United States*, U.S. District Court, District of Oregon, 398 F. Supp. 1042 (1975)]

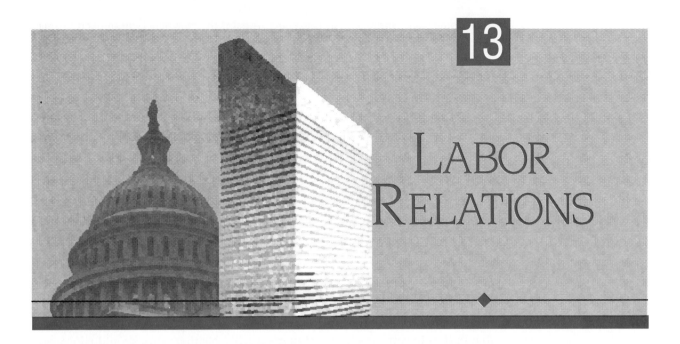

LABOR RELATIONS

Most workers are employees rather than employers. Employees must agree to certain wages, hours, and other conditions and terms of employment. In many cases, however, groups of employees can negotiate better deals for themselves than can employees acting alone, if the firm is large. The employer may also find group negotiation helpful—it is generally more efficient to negotiate and administer one agreement rather than hundreds. A small firm, of course, may be easily able to negotiate a separate bargain with each employee. In addition, people with special needs or skills may require special agreements with their employers. For example, a shop foreman with a weak back might insist that the company buy him a particular kind of chair.

Unions are made up of groups of employees with similar employment goals who agree to have one organization represent them in negotiations with their employer (or employers if the union represents an entire industry). These goals might include better and/or safer working conditions, higher wages, or greater benefits, among other things.

This chapter will examine the public policies that regulate employment agreements and union-management relations. In order to help counter the destructive results of conflict, American labor law provides a framework that permits employers, unions, and nonunionized employees to cooperate. Most of the discussion will center on the legal aspects of private and public bargaining between unions and employers.

■ THE EMPLOYMENT-AT-WILL DOCTRINE *NO*

Under the common-law **employment-at-will doctrine**, any employment agreement can be ended by either party at any time and for any reason—as long as doing so does not violate the Constitution, a contract, or a statute. Today, however, there are numerous exceptions to this doctrine:

employment-at-will doctrine
The common-law concept that either party to an employment agreement can end it at any time for any reason as long as there is no violation of a contract or statute or the Constitution

- Some states stipulate that firings are illegal if they violate (1) an implied promise of fair dealing or *good faith* made when the worker was hired, or (2) *public policy* according to which courts have carved out further exceptions.
- Unionized employees are protected by formal written contracts.
- Government employees are protected by civil-service laws.
- Some federal statutes—for example, Title VII of the Civil Rights Act of 1964, the National Labor Relations Act of 1935 (NLRA), or the Occupational Safety and Health Act of 1970 (OSHA)—specifically out law certain reasons for dismissal.

The number of wrongful dismissals in the United States is difficult to calculate. Evidence from the unionized workplace suggests that such dismissals may well constitute an important social problem that is exacerbated by the fact that employers are usually reluctant to hire someone who has been fired by someone else. One advantage of union membership is that union contracts often call for an independent arbitrator to judge whether an employee has been fired unfairly. Historically, labor arbitrators have overturned the employer's decision in more than half of all cases.

The Good-Faith Doctrine

Section 1-203 of the Uniform Commercial Code (UCC) (*see* Chapter 9) states that parties to contracts must act in good faith: Neither party should take action designed to deny the other party the benefits of the contract. Although the UCC does not apply to labor agreements, many courts have extended the concept of good faith to such agreements. A dismissal may therefore be judged unlawful because it violates an implicit covenant of good faith in a verbal or written labor agreement. The following case illustrates this issue.

FORTUNE v. NATIONAL CASH REGISTER CO.
Massachusetts Supreme Judicial Court, 364 N.E. 2d. 1251 (1977)

Oliver Fortune worked for National Cash Register as a salesman under a contract allowing termination of the employment relationship at the behest of either himself or NCR and also providing a bonus for all sales made within his "territory" for supervision or coverage purposes. Fortune received a termination notice in January 1969, shortly after helping NCR secure a $5 million account with First National, a company within his territory, for the delivery of a new line of cash registers to take place over four years. Despite being allowed to stay with NCR for an additional 1.5 years, largely due to his successful sales history with First National, Fortune was fired in June 1970 and denied all bonus payments on subsequent First National orders.

Fortune, the plaintiff, sued NCR for breach of contract in the trial court. The trial court ruled in Fortune's favor, awarding him the bonus payments denied by NCR. NCR appealed to the Appeals Court, which reversed. Fortune appeals to the Supreme Judicial Court of Massachusetts.

At the close of the plaintiff's case, the defendant moved for a directed verdict, arguing that there was no

evidence of any breach of contract. . . . Ruling that Fortune could recover if the termination and firing were in bad faith, the trial judge . . . submitted this issue to the jury. NCR then rested and, by agreement of counsel, the case was sent to the jury for special verdicts on two questions:

1. Did the Defendant act in bad faith . . . when it decided to terminate the Plaintiff's contract as a salesman by letter dated December 2, 1968, delivered on January 6, 1969?
2. Did the Defendant act in bad faith . . . when the Defendant let the Plaintiff go on June 5, 1970?

The jury answered both questions affirmatively, and judgment entered in the sum of $45,649.62.

. . . .

The contract at issue is a classic terminable at will employment contract. It is clear that the contract itself reserved to the parties an explicit power to terminate the contract without cause on written notice. It is also clear that under the express terms of the contract Fortune has received all the bonus commissions to which he is entitled. Thus, NCR claims that it did not breach

---

the contract, and that it has no further liability to Fortune. According to a literal reading of the contract, NCR is correct.

However, Fortune argues that, in spite of the literal wording of the contract, he is entitled to a jury determination on NCR's motives in terminating his services under the contract and in finally discharging him. We agree. We hold that NCR's written contract contains an implied convenant of good faith and fair dealing, and a termination not made in good faith constitutes a breach of the contract.

We do not question the general principles that an employer is entitled to be motivated by and to serve its own legitimate business interests; that an employer must have wide latitude in deciding whom it will employ in the face of the uncertainties of the business world; and that an employer needs flexibility in the face of changing circumstances. We recognize the employer's need for a large amount of control over its work force. However, we believe that where, as here, commissions are to be paid for work performed by the employee, the employer's decision to terminate its at will employee should be made in good faith. NCR's right to make decisions in its own interest is not, in our view, unduly hampered by a requirement of adherence to this standard.

. . . .

In the instant case, we need not . . . speculate as to whether the good faith requirement is implicit in every contract for employment at will. It is clear, however, that, on the facts before us, a finding is warranted that a breach of the contract occurred. Where the principal seeks to deprive the agent of all compensation by terminating the contractual relationship when the agent is on the brink of successfully completing the sale, the principal has acted in bad faith and the ensuing transaction between the principal and the buyer is to be re-garded as having been accomplished by the agent. The same result obtains where the principal attempts to deprive the agent of any portion of a commission due the agent. . . . In our view, the Appeals Court erroneously focused only on literal compliance with payment provisions of the contract and failed to consider the issue of bad faith termination.

NCR argues that there was no evidence of bad faith in this case; therefore, the trial judge was required to direct a verdict in any event. We think that the evidence and the reasonable inferences to be drawn therefrom support a jury verdict that the termination of Fortune's twenty-five years of employment as a salesman with NCR the next business day after NCR obtained a $5,000,000 order from First National was motivated by a desire to pay Fortune as little of the bonus credit as it could. The fact that Fortune was willing to work under these circumstances does not constitute a waiver, or estoppel; it only shows that NCR had him "at their mercy.". . . .

We think that NCR's conduct in June, 1970 permitted the jury to find bad faith.

. . . .

Judgment of the Superior Court affirmed.

Case Questions:

1. Explain the good faith exception to the employment-at-will doctrine.

2. What legal remedy is the employee able to invoke by virtue of the implied obligation of good faith that he would otherwise not be able to if his employment terms were literally construed?

3. What interests are balanced by the court in determining whether to imply good faith into a contract?

The Public-Policy Exception

Clearly, firings on certain grounds would interfere with the public's best interest. For example, you cannot legally be fired for (1) refusing to break the law, (2) accusing your company of breaking the law, (3) exercising a statutory right (such as engaging in union activity or voting), or (4) fulfilling a legal duty (serving on a jury).

The term "law" in this context is broadly interpreted to include administrative agency rules. Thus, you cannot be fired for reporting violations of rules, filing charges of discrimination, cooperating with investigations by regulatory agencies, or refusing to do work that you believe dangerous.

In general, the "public-policy" argument rests on the idea that a firing is unlawful if it punishes an employee for acting in line with public policy. The argument is a broad one that offers the courts ample opportunity to overturn a dismissal. Although some employers may view it as a *carte blanche* approach, decisions are generally made on a case-by-case basis.

There is also debate as to which sources of public policy bear on cases of wrongful dismissal. Some states, for example, only consider those policies stated in laws or the state's constitution. Other states consider judicial decisions (*see* Chapter 4). Still other states allow the jury to decide whether a policy ought to be taken into account in a particular suit.[1] The case of *Flesner v. Technical Communications Corp.* concerns an employee who was terminated for performing "an important public deed."

[1] W. H. Daughtrey Jr., "Another Exception Under the Employment-at-Will Doctrine: *Bowman v. State Bank,*" 24 *American Business Law Journal* 246 (1986).

FLESNER v. TECHNICAL COMMUNICATIONS CORPORATION

Massachusetts Supreme Court, 410 Mass. 805 (1991)

Jeffrey Flesner asserts that he was discharged by his former employer, Technical Communications Corporation (TCC), in retaliation for his cooperation in a United States Customs Service investigation of TCC. Flesner was a salesperson with defendant TCC. Defendants Arnold McCalmont and his son, James McCalmont, are president and sales manager, respectively. TCC is a Massachusetts corporation that sells, internationally, communications systems. In July, 1983, Flesner planned a sales trip to Argentina. He claims that prior to leaving for Argentina, he repeatedly asked James McCalmont whether a temporary export license was necessary. He was told that because he was only demonstrating security equipment to potential buyers, he would not need a license. Although TCC had applied for a temporary export license for Argentina, the application had been returned with no action taken. At the airport, a TCC employee gave Flesner the equipment and a manila envelope containing Customs documents. Flesner checked the equipment through to Argentina and was detained by Customs officials in Boston. He handed them the manila envelope but was told that he would be handcuffed and arrested if he did not cooperate. The equipment was seized and Flesner cooperated. He was instructed not to tell TCC that he was cooperating with Customs unless asked directly. Flesner related the events to the McCalmonts and Wolz, a TCC manager. Later, when he was summoned to a meeting with Arnold McCalmont and TCC's attorney, he informed them that he was cooperating with Customs. On August 31, 1983, after his job duties had been restricted, he asked Wolz about his future with TCC. Wolz said he should resign so that he would receive severance pay or be fired the next day. Flesner resigned on September 1, 1983.

Justice Abrams delivered the opinion of the court.
. . .

A Superior Court judge awarded summary judgment in favor of TCC. Flesner now appeals, contending that the judge erred in dismissing his claims for (1) wrongful discharge; (2) misrepresentation; (3) invasion of privacy; and (4) violation of the Massachusetts Civil Rights Act, G. L. c. 12, § 11I (1990 ed.). In addition, the defendants claim that Flesner is precluded from recovering damages by his own misrepresentations. We

transferred the case to this court on our own motion. We reverse the summary judgment on the wrongful discharge and misrepresentation claims. We affirm on the other claims. . . .

1. *Motion for summary judgment.* Where a moving party properly asserts that there is no genuine issue of material fact, "the judge must ask himself not whether he thinks the evidence unmistakably favors one side or the other but whether a fair-minded jury could return a verdict for the plaintiff on the evidence presented." . . .

In cases where motive, intent, or other state of mind questions are at issue, summary judgment is often inappropriate. . . . In such cases, "[m]uch depends on the credibility of the witnesses testifying as to their own states of mind. In these circumstances, the jury should be given an opportunity to observe the demeanor, during direct and cross-examination, of the witnesses whose states of mind are at issue." . . .

With these principles in mind, we consider the merits of Flesner's arguments.

2. *Wrongful discharge.* Flesner claims that TCC constructively discharged him in violation of public policy because of his cooperation with the Customs officials. We have recognized an exception to the traditional doctrine that at-will employees may be discharged for any reason or no reason at all, where the discharge is for reasons that violate public policy. We have held, for example, that a cause of action will lie when an employee is fired for disobeying the employer's instruction to testify falsely at a trial or for enforcing safety regulations for which she was responsible.

In *Smith-Pfeffer v. Superintendent of the Walter E. Fernald State School,* 404 Mass. 145, 149-150 (1989), we stated that redress is available for employees who are terminated "for asserting a legally guaranteed right (e.g., filing workers' compensation claim), for doing what the law requires (e.g., serving on a jury), or for refusing to do that which the law forbids (e.g., committing perjury)." Flesner claims he was discharged for cooperating with the Customs officials. The law did not *require* him to cooperate; he had the right to remain silent. Nevertheless, it is the public policy of this Commonwealth to encourage cooperation with ongoing criminal investigations. . . .

We think that the reasons for imposing liability in the categories of cases set forth in *Smith-Pfeffer* also justify legal redress in certain circumstances for employees terminated for performing important public deeds, even though the law does not absolutely require the performance of such a deed. In such a situation, as in the *Smith-Pfeffer* categories, allowing the employer to terminate employees for reasons that directly contradict the public policy of the Commonwealth would seriously impair that policy.

Cooperating with an ongoing governmental investigation is an important public deed which fits this category. . . . The judge, however, granted summary judgment because "TCC never urged Flesner not to cooperate with Customs officials or otherwise hamper an investigation." This assertion does not demonstrate an absence of evidence on an essential element of the claim. Flesner's claim is that the discharge itself was motivated by a desire to interfere with or retaliate for his cooperation with the investigation. Such intentional interference, if found by a jury, would constitute a wrongful discharge in violation of public policy.

Moreover, the judge asserted that, while "Flesner may be said to have been fired for participating in an illegal scheme in which the employer was involved, . . . such a termination does not fall within the public policy exception." Although a reasonable jury may conclude that such was the cause for Flesner's termination, it would not be required to so conclude. Where a jury can draw opposite inferences from the evidence, summary judgment is improper. Flesner's deposition asserts that he asked about export licenses and TCC told him they were not necessary. Thus, it is permissible to conclude that Flesner left on his trip completely unaware that he was acting in violation of the law. He describes his ongoing cooperation with Customs authorities and a corresponding deterioration in his working relationship with TCC. He asserts that he was told to resign with two weeks' pay or be fired. This evidence sufficiently raises a question of material fact as to whether Flesner was discharged in retaliation for this cooperation with a law enforcement investigation. The defendants contend that Flesner was discharged, if at all, for other legitimate business reasons. Thus, the motive for the discharge is a primary contested issue of fact. In such circumstances, the grant of summary judgment on these claims was improper.

3. *Damages.* In addition to economic damages, Flesner claims damages for emotional distress and mental anguish as well as punitive damages. Punitive damages are not allowed in this Commonwealth unless expressly authorized by statute. Because no such legislative authorization applies to this case, Flesner's claim for punitive damages cannot stand. . . .

The parties focused on liability in the motion for summary judgment. Therefore, the factual background on damages is undeveloped. Indeed, no facts alleged in the complaint or submitted on summary judgment evidence any suffering by Flesner of mental anguish due to the defendant's conduct in wrongfully discharging him. We decline to adopt a hard and fast rule on whether tort damages in general and emotional distress damages in particular are recoverable in wrongful discharge cases in the absence of a well-developed factual record. If at trial no facts are brought out supporting damages for emotional distress due to the defendant's intentional conduct, then the question need not be reached. We therefore decline to address this issue.

The judge also granted summary judgment on Flesner's misrepresentation claim because the complaint did not allege damages independent of those alleged in connection with the termination of his employment. "Therefore," according to the judge, the "plaintiff's cause of action, if one lies, must be for Wrongful Discharge."

Even if the judge were correct that the only damages Flesner alleges are those arising out of his termination, a point we do not decide, the overlap does not justify dismissal of the claim. Flesner, of course, cannot recover double damages for the two claims, but he is entitled to proceed on more than one theory of recovery. The judge does not conclude that Flesner insufficiently alleged or supported his claim of misrepresentation. Summary judgment should not have been allowed on the misrepresentation claim.

5. *Flesner's alleged misrepresentation.* The defendants argue that Flesner is precluded from recovering damages because he misrepresented several facts on his résumé and in his job interview leading to his employment with TCC. According to the defendants, TCC would not have hired Flesner had they known these representations were not true. Therefore, they conclude that even though they did not discover these misrepresentations until after Flesner resigned, he cannot recover any damages because TCC would have been justified in firing him even absent any wrongful motives. Because the judge ordered summary judgment for the defendants on all counts, he did not reach this issue.

The defendants cite a line of Federal wrongful discharge and employment discrimination cases in support of their argument. These cases all deal with the question of the appropriate *remedy* once discrimination or a wrongful discharge has been established. In *Mt. Healthy,* a teacher was fired, in part because of his exercise of rights secured him by the First Amendment to the United States Constitution. Several other permissible reasons *could* have supported the discharge, however. The Supreme Court remanded the case to the District Court to determine whether the school board in fact *would* have fired the plaintiff even absent the impermissible reason. The court reasoned that the plaintiff should not be put in a better position than he would have been in had the wrong not been committed. Later cases extended this principle to allow employers to show that other legitimate reasons would have justified their conduct even though those reasons were not discovered until after the fact.

Even if the defendants are correct that they may show that their "after the fact" discovery of legitimate reasons for discharging Flesner precludes recovery, resolution of this issue is not appropriate at the summary judgment stage. The parties dispute whether Flesner actually made some of the misrepresentations. As for other misrepresentations, although Flesner concedes he made them, he disputes their effect. Flesner argues that TCC did not rely on these statements in hiring him. At the very least, it is certainly disputed whether TCC would have *discharged* Flesner (as opposed to not hiring him) had they discovered the misrepresentations during the course of employment. The cases cited by the defendants in which a court found that the employee was unqualified and would not have been hired absent the discrimination involved wrongful conduct in the hiring stage, not the discharge stage. . . .

6. *Invasion of privacy.* Flesner alleges that TCC "monitored" his personal telephone calls and made anonymous telephone calls to his friends and family inquiring about him. He asserts a claim for damages for invasion of privacy pursuant to G. L. c. 214, § 1 B (1990 ed.). The judge ruled that the evidence was insufficient to support these allegations and ordered summary judgment for the defendants. We agree with the judge's holding.

Because Flesner would bear the burden of proving his claim of invasion of privacy at trial, the defendants, as the parties moving for summary judgment, had the burden of demonstrating at least that there was an absence of evidence in the record supporting Flesner's claim. If the evidence is insufficient to support his claim, "a trial would be useless and [the defendants are] entitled to summary judgment as a matter of law."

We agree with the defendant that, accepting Flesner's statement of evidence on the claim of invasion of privacy as accurate, the evidence was insufficient as a matter of law. The only evidence cited by Flesner that TCC telephoned his family and friends was his own deposition testimony that his family and friends told him that they had received such calls. The sole evidence that Flesner offers to support his claim that TCC monitored his calls was his testimony regarding Herman Wolz's admitted conduct. Flesner stated that Wolz admitted that he called Flesner's insurance company to verify that reimbursement claimed by Flesner for a call to the company was justified. Flesner asserts that the fact that Wolz verified this one call "leads me to believe that they were monitoring my [tele]phone calls. Personal as well as professional." This unsupported statement of belief also is insufficient to survive a summary judgment motion. The judge was correct in his disposition of this claim.

7. *The Massachusetts Civil Rights Act claim.* Finally, Flesner claims that he is entitled to relief under the Massachusetts Civil Rights Act, G. L. c. 12, § 11I (1990 ed.) (MCRA). The MCRA provides a remedy to a person whose secured rights under the Constitution or laws of the United States or the Commonwealth have

been interfered with by threats, intimidation, or coercion. Flesner has not clearly identified any "secured right" with which TCC interfered. In his complaint he mentions rights under the Fourteenth Amendment of the United States Constitution and unspecified rights under the Massachusetts Declaration of Rights which he characterizes as the "freedom to use [one's] faculties in all lawful ways to live and work where he will; to earn his livelihood in any lawful calling; to pursue any livelihood or avocation; and for that purpose to enter into all contracts, which may be proper, necessary, and essential to his carrying out to a successful conclusion the purposes mentioned above." The essence of his argument on appeal appears to be based on a right to contract for personal employment. The cases in which he purports to find such a constitutional right date from 1929 and earlier. Whatever may be the validity of those cases today, they do not support the contention that Flesner has a secured constitutional right to retain his at-will employment contract. He has failed to identify a secured right within the meaning of the MCRA. Summary judgment was properly granted.

8. *Conclusion.* The judgment is affirmed with respect to Flesner's claims of invasion of privacy and violation of the Massachusetts Civil Rights Act. It is reversed with respect to the wrongful discharge and misrepresentation claims.

So ordered.

Case Questions

1. What factors did the court consider in adopting the flexible standard for determining wrongful-discharge cases in which an employee is fired for cooperating with an investigation even though his job does not require him to do so?

2. Would it be more or less workable to apply a rigid standard like the three categories for redressing terminations under *Smith-Pfeffer* so that employers and employees both know the parameters of their legal rights regarding employment discharge and why?

3. The court ruled that Flesner's testimony regarding what his family told him and what Wolz admitted to him were insufficient to defeat a motion for summary judgment. What evidence should an employee be required to show in order to prove that his privacy rights have been violated?

■ *Concept Check 13-1   The Employment-at-Will Doctrine*

- Explain *employment at will* as a common-law doctrine.
- Describe at least one exception to the employment-at-will doctrine.
- Explain the principle of *good faith* as an article in labor agreements.

■ UNION STRUCTURE TODAY

In order to understand the larger concept of labor and employment law, we must, of course, understand something about the organizations whose relationships give rise to the need for regulations and policies to deal both with organizational conflict and cooperation. In this section, we will provide an overview of labor organizations in the United States, touching upon the history of such organizations as we explain their development, functions, and role in shaping public policy.

Figure 13-1 provides a picture of union membership in terms of the country's largest unions. Table 13-1 gives figures for overall United States union membership for selected years between 1900 and 1990. As you can see, membership has been declining steadily: Between 1975 and 1990, for example, union membership among American workers on wages or salaries dropped from twenty-three to just over thirteen percent.

Why the decline? For one thing, foreign competition in heavily unionized industries has taken a toll: Industries such as automobile and steel manufacturing have reduced their labor forces, and some companies have succeeded in demanding labor concessions—"givebacks"—as the price of providing continued employment. Meanwhile, other companies have maintained nonunionized facilities by developing employee-relations programs, launching aggressive nonunion campaigns, and, in some instances, transferring operations to areas less congenial to unionization.

Perhaps most important, however, the makeup of the work force has changed: Whereas union membership is still mostly white, male, and blue-collar, the work force now includes many more women and minorities. For example, compare the raw numbers indicated in Figure 13-1 with the comparative statistics in Table 13-2: The structure of employment in the United States

FIGURE 13-1 Largest U.S. National Unions

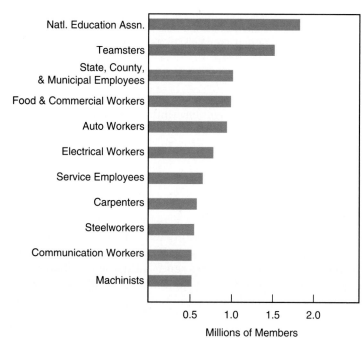

Millions of Members

TABLE 13-1   *U.S. Union Membership, 1900-1990*

YEAR	TOTAL MEMBERSHIP (IN THOUSANDS)	CIVILIAN LABOR FORCE* (IN THOUSANDS)	UNIONIZED PERCENT OF CIVILIAN LABOR FORCE
1900	868	28,376	3.1
1920	5,048	41,340	12.2
1933	2,973	50,882	5.8
1939	8,763	55,218	15.7
1945	14,332	53,860	26.6
1953	16,940	63,015	26.9
1960	17,049	69,629	24.5
1970	19,381	82,715	23.4
1975	22,207	96,613	23.0
1980	20,968	104,719	20.0
1981	20,647	106,393	19.4
1982	19,763	110,204	17.9
1983	17,717	111,551	15.8
1984	17,340	113,544	15.3
1985	16,996	115,463	14.7
1986	16,975	117,834	14.4
1987	16,913	119,865	14.1
1988	17,002	121,669	14.0
1989	16,960	123,869	13.7
1990	16,740	124,787	13.4

Civilian labor force = 14 years and older for 1900-45, 16 years and older, 1946-present.

Sources: E. Edward Herman, Joshua L. Schwarz, and Alfred Kuhn, *Collective Bargaining and Labor Relations*, 3rd. ed. (Englewood Cliffs, NJ: Prentice Hall, 1992). Data from U.S. Bureau of the Census, *Historical Statistics of the United States* (Washington, DC: Government Printing Office, 1975); U.S. Bureau of Labor Statistics, *Employment and Earnings* (Washington, DC: Government Printing Office, 1982-1990).

has shifted toward demographic groups (women), industries (clerical and service), and geographic areas (the south) that are all less heavily unionized sectors of the economy.

The AFL-CIO

In 1886, the American Federation of Labor (AFL) was founded for skilled craft workers. The Congress of Industrial Organization (CIO) was formed in 1937 to organize workers on an industry-by-industry basis. By 1940, these two unions were competing for members in most trades and industries. When they merged in 1955, the ground rules for resolving the kinds of conflicts in which both unions were involved were established (although, as this chapter's PERSONAL PROFILE shows, at least one form of internal conflict—racial—took even

TABLE 13-2 *U.S. Union Membership, 1990*

CATEGORY	PERCENT UNION
Total over 15 years old	16.1
Sex	
Female	12.6
Male	19.3
Race	
Black	21.1
Hispanic	14.8
White	15.5
Industry	
Manufacturing	20.6
Construction	21.0
Transportation, communication, and utilities	31.6
Trade	6.3
Finance, insurance, and real estate	2.5
Government workers	36.5
Occupation	
Blue collar	26.4
Clerical	13.6
Service	13.8
Managerial and professional speciality	14.3
Sales, technical and related support	10.4
Region	
South	9.2
Non-South	19.2

Source: Herman, Schwarz, and Kuhn, *Collective Bargaining and Labor Relations.* Data from Department of Labor, Bureau of Labor Statistics, *Employment and Earnings* (Jan. 1991).

longer to resolve). The AFL-CIO is the single best-known union organization in the United States today. It is important to realize, however, that a *federation* is merely a *group* of unions—it is not a union itself. A **labor union** refers to a national or international association of workers organized to protect member rights, interest, and welfare, primarily through collective bargaining.

labor union National or international association of workers organized to protect members' rights, interests, and welfare

Union Locals

Union members elect officers to act for them. The local is controlled by majority vote. The local's meetings are usually held monthly. Like clubs, service organizations, and other groups, local unions may host social activities, political functions, and fundraisers. However, their most important job is to bargain with their members' employers about wages, hours, terms, conditions of employment, and job-related grievances. Often, locals look to national headquarters for professional help in collective-bargaining matters.

The most important task of the union is to organize the unorganized. Early local unions were formed by workers without the help of a larger organization. However, most locals formed since the 1940s were first created by par-

(A)

(B)

(C)

Gompers, Lewis, and the AFL and the CIO An ex-socialist, Samuel Gompers (A) was cofounder of the American Federation of Labor (AFL) in 1886 and served continuously as its president until 1924. Gompers (1850–1924) guided the early AFL away from broad utopian goals and toward practical organizing activities—the union focused, for example, on skilled workers who were less easily fired and better equipped to insist on a collective-bargaining agent. Although encouraging labor support for labor's political friends, Gompers nevertheless steered organized labor toward a pragmatic accommodation with the capitalist system: "As we get 25 cents a day wage increase," he argued, "it . . . brings us nearer the time when a greater degree of social justice and fair dealing will obtain among men." By 1914, the AFL claimed 2 million of the 2.7 million U.S. labor-union members. Because the AFL, however, generally left its organizing as a federation to its constituent unions, semiskilled workers like those in the country's mass-production industries received little attention from the giant labor federation. In 1935, unions dissatisfied with their treatment by the AFL formed a Committee for Industrial Organization (CIO), first chaired by United Mine Workers president John L. Lewis (B). Charging the CIO with the cardinal sin of splitting labor, the AFL suspended the CIO in 1936 and then expelled the satellite organization in 1938. At the same time, however, the AFL responded to CIO pressure to unionize mass-production workers, and equally intense organizing drives by both sides ultimately swelled union ranks from 3.6 million in 1934 to 8 million in 1939 and 17 million in 1955—the year in which the two unions merged. The symbolic joint gavel is shared (C) by new AFL-CIO president George Meany (left) and CIO-United Automobile Workers president Walter Reuther. Lewis (1880–1969) was president of the CIO (reorganized as the Congress of Industrial Organizations in 1938) from 1935 to 1940 and head of the United Mine Workers from 1920 until 1960.

ent unions. Creating new locals is a long, hard, and costly process that often requires the efforts of paid organizers over a period of years. A local cannot be established until enough workers at a plant or in an area vote for it. Even after it is set up, the local may need the union to bargain with both the employers and the National Labor Relations Board (NLRB).

There are two kinds of locals: *craft* and *industrial*. The members of a craft local do the same kind of work in the same geographic area; the members of an industrial local include many different kinds of workers serving the same employer.

CRAFT LOCALS. Craft unions are important in such industries as publishing, printing, and building construction. Unions, employers, and the government recognize about 800 detailed trades or crafts. Anyone practicing one of these lines of work would consider joining the craft local in a particular area. For instance, carpenters in Albuquerque, New Mexico, might join that city's union. Carpenters' helpers and apprentices still in training might be able to join as well. If one employer has a large, stable force of people practicing a particular craft, those workers may organize their own craft local. Generally, however, the members of a craft local do not work regularly for the same employer. For example, a carpenter might go from one construction job to another and work for several building contractors.

In addition to the union functions outlined above, craft unions are responsible for (1) overseeing apprenticeship programs and (2) hearing complaints and backing up agreements on wages, hours, and working conditions negotiated with employers.

Organization and Procedure. Craft unions employ full-time **business agents** to negotiate agreements with organizations representing employers in an area. The business agent will try to persuade every employer in the area who might hire the union's members to agree to the same terms. The agreement—known as a **collective-bargaining agreement**—must be ratified by a vote of the local's membership. At that point, it becomes the authority for terms of employment for the local and for any employers who sign it. Business agents usually have another duty as well: They send union members to work on projects as requests come in from employers who are party to the document.

By custom, either the first worker whom the business agent picks for a project or the member with the most seniority becomes the *steward*. The steward keeps the business agent in touch with the work site. In either case, the steward is responsible for getting information from the business agent to the workers and vice versa. The steward also reports violations of the agreement to the manager in charge. If necessary, he may also report them to the business agent. If the employer does not correct the violation, the business agent may call the union's workers off the job.

INDUSTRIAL LOCALS. The manufacturing, transportation, finance, and mining industries are all thoroughly organized into union locals representing factories or worksites. Typically, an industrial local tries to attract all the many employees representing a wide variety of occupations at a workplace.

Agreement Procedure. Industrial locals do not usually employ full-time business agents. Rather, they rely on elected officers who are employed at the plant. Thus, the agreement is worked out between a bargaining committee, elected officers, and plant management. A bargaining agent from the national

business agent *Craft-union* employee whose function is to negotiate agreements with organizations representing employers in a given area

collective-bargaining agreement Contract, resulting from negotiations between an employer and a *labor union*, that states terms and conditions of employment

PERSONAL PROFILE
A. Philip Randolph

A unique chapter in the American labor movement was written by the black union and civil-rights leader, A. Philip Randolph. From his early days as a socialist activist, to his fight for rights for black workers, to his contribution to the 1963 march on Washington, D.C. for jobs and freedom, Randolph combined persuasive dignity with total commitment to his cause.

The son of a Florida minister, Randolph (1889-1979) headed north to study at the City College of New York. During World War I, he founded and coedited The Messenger, a monthly magazine promoting black militancy and a kind of democratic socialism. The magazine communicated the belief that blacks should join trade unions because working-class solidarity was in their best interest; it also worked to persuade unions to end racial discrimination.

In 1925, Randolph organized the Brotherhood of Sleeping Car Porters. Due to a pattern of discrimination in the rail-way industry, the union was all black: Its 15,000 members worked 400 hours a month for the Pullman company for wages from $67 to $94, from which the cost of uniforms and meals was deducted. Unfortunately, these were considered "good" jobs—and often the only ones available to black college graduates. Randolph's efforts at organization were countered by Pullman's establishment of a company union.

It was not until 1937, after 12 years of tough battling, that the union was able to get to the bargaining table with Pullman. The contract that was signed was the first between a white employer and a black union. Although Randolph and other union leaders were treated condescendingly by Pullman representatives, Randolph used the tactic that was his ultimate weapon in achieving his successes, "deliberate dignity"—what Bayard Rustin called the dignity that served strong purposefulness.

With the beginning of World War II, Randolph's goal

A. Philip Randolph Randolph took advantage of the upsurge in organizing activities by the CIO in the late 1930s to force the Pullman Company to the bargaining table with his Brotherhood of Sleeping Car Porters. From this point of contact with the country's largest and most powerful labor organizations, he carried the fight against racist union practices to the AFL, where he raised the issue of black workers' rights throughout the 1940s and 1950s. Although censured two years later for his strident criticism of union racial policies, Randolph was made vice-president and member of the AFL-CIO executive council in 1957. It was from his conviction that economic justice must be a primary goal of the civil-rights movement that Randolph played a key role in organizing the August 1963 March on Washington.

union might assist. The agreement must be ratified by members of the local. In
some industries, however, the union works out one agreement for all of its
locals.

Union agreements negotiated for industrial workers are much more complex than those negotiated for craft workers. One reason is that they cover the
terms of employment for many more kinds of work. Another reason is that
craft workers traditionally control the speed at which they work, while industrial workers must negotiate about the production process with employers.

Organization. The internal organization of an industrial local generally
reflects the structure of the workplace. Industrial **shop stewards** are elected by
the union members in a particular department or "shop." Stewards collect dues
and try to recruit any workers who are new to the plant. Stewards also meet in
steward councils to coordinate their work and elect a *chief steward.* If the workplace has many levels of management, there may be many stewards—for example, a chief steward for each division as well as a steward for each shop
within it. Night shifts may have their own stewards and division chiefs as well.

shop steward *Industrial-union
member in a particular
department who collects dues
and recruits new members*

National and International Unions

Both craft and industrial locals usually (but not necessarily) belong to national
or international unions. A national union represents locals nationwide; typically, an international union also represents locals in Canada or Mexico.

Although these "umbrella" organizations are typically focused on a particular craft or industry, they may also extend their reach. For instance, **amalgamated craft unions,** like the Brotherhood of Boilermakers, Iron Ship
Builders, Blacksmiths, Forgers, and Helpers unite the craft workers of related
trades. In the same way, industrial unions may be *multiindustrial.* You may be
surprised to learn, for example, that the full name of the famous
"autoworkers" union, the UAW, is the United Automobile, Aircraft and Agri-

amalgamated craft union
*Umbrella organization that unites
craft workers of related trades*

cultural Implement Workers and that the Teamsters Union also represents chauffeurs, warehouse workers, brewery workers, and clerks in retail stores. Some unions represent both industrial and craft locals. The International Brotherhood of Electrical Workers, for example, includes both industrial locals in electrical manufacturing and craft locals in the building trades.

NATIONAL-LOCAL ORGANIZATION. The formal links between a national union and its locals vary from one to another. Normally, locals pay dues to the national (or international) and abide by its constitution and bylaws. Such laws are passed at annual or biannual conventions attended by delegates who represent a certain number of members. These delegates choose an executive board which may, in turn, choose an executive committee whose members act as full-time officers; executives may hire full-time staff to fill several offices. Figure 13-2 shows the organizational structure of the AFL-CIO.

All locals stand to gain if the union can create and maintain a strong presence in its field of action: Employers will be less cooperative if they must compete with a great many nonunionized rivals that may pay lower wages or spend less on maintaining good working conditions. Thus, employers often rely on a national or international union's expert negotiators.

In addition, unions provide a range of services, including legal advice and counsel, pension and health insurance plans, union-supported medical centers, special payments for strikers, and political lobbying both for local and national concerns. The service and lobbying activities of the International Ladies's Garment Workers' Union are detailed in this chapter's ORGANIZATIONAL PROFILE.

■ *Concept Check 13-2   Union Structure Today*

- Discuss one or two instances of employer-labor agreements in the last decade that reflect the changing functions and influence of U.S. labor unions.
- Describe the differences in making *collective-bargaining agreements* between *craft* and *industrial locals*.

■ UNIONS AND THE LAW

Four federal laws specifically govern union efforts by providing the base for a web of rules, regulations, and decisions. The first two, the *Norris-LaGuardia Act* of 1932 and the *Wagner Act* of 1935 (also known as the *National Labor Relations Act* of 1935), served to help unions. After World War II, however, Congress was convinced that employers needed safeguards against unfair union practices, and in 1947 enacted the *Taft-Hartley Act* (formally known as the *Labor Management Relations Act*), as an amendment to the Wagner Act. This measure created a whole new code of conduct for union agents. The last law, the *Landrum-Griffin Act*, was enacted in 1959 to clean up corruption among union officials and to guarantee certain civil rights for union members. A summary of these acts appears in Table 13-3.

The Norris-LaGuardia Act

In 1932, Congress was not yet ready to forbid employers from interfering with union efforts, as it would do just three years later. Rather, it limited the ways in which judges could intervene in labor disputes. Such disputes became pri-

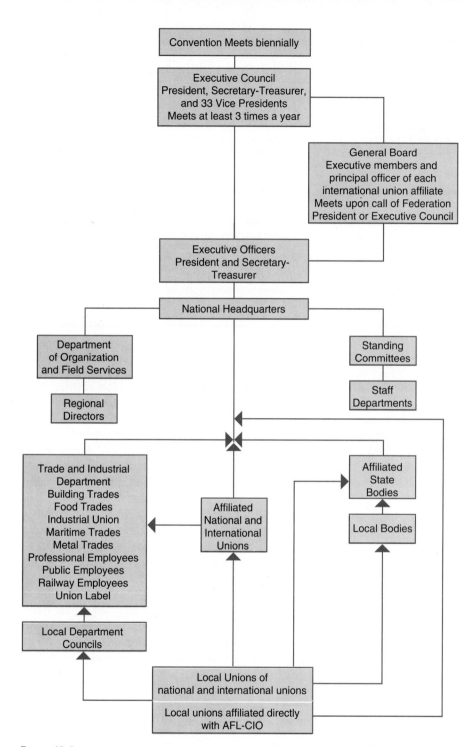

FIGURE 13-2 Organizational Structure of the AFL-CIO   *Sources:* Herman, Schwarz, and Kuhn, *Collective Bargaining and Labor Relations;* Courtney D. Gifford, ed., *Directory of U.S. Labor Organizations* (Washington, DC: The Bureau of National Affairs, Inc., 1989).

vate matters rather than grist for the courts, which tended to favor employers. In effect, the **Norris-LaGuardia Act** stripped employers of two legal devices commonly used to prevent workers from forming unions. However, in order to understand the importance of these two devices, it is first necessary to know something about legal responses to labor disputes prior to Norris-LaGuardia.

Norris-LaGuardia Act 1932 federal statute prohibiting employers from enforcing *yellow-dog contracts* and making it more difficult to get *injunctions* against union activities

| **TABLE 13-3** | *Major U.S. Labor-Relations Legislation* |

Norris-LaGuardia (1932)	Restricted the right of courts to issue injunctions against unions engaging in various activities such as strikes; forbade yellow-dog contracts.
National Labor Relations Act ["Wagner Act"] (1935)	Established rights of workers to form unions, to bargain collectively, and to strike; forbade employers from engaging in unfair labor practices; established National Labor Relations Board to administer the Act.
Fair Labor Standards Act (1938)	Established a minimum wage and maximum work week; outlawed child labor
Taft-Hartley Amendments (1947)	Amended the National Labor Relations Act to prohibit unfair union practices; established right-to-work law provisions. Established national emergency dispute resolution procedures.
Landrum-Griffin Act (1959)	Amended the National Labor Relations Act; required that unions hold democratic elections; required that unions annually make financial disclosures to the Department of Labor.

Source: Ricky W. Griffin and Ronald J. Ebert, *Business,* 2nd ed. (Englewood Cliffs, NJ: Prentice Hall, 1991).

THE CRIMINAL AND CIVIL CONSPIRACY DOCTRINES. Before the Norris-LaGuardia Act, union efforts were badly hampered by courts adopting the **criminal conspiracy doctrine** and, later, the **civil conspiracy doctrine**. The first labor case was heard in 1806, when a group of Philadelphia shoemakers were fined $8 each for creating an illegal criminal conspiracy aimed at raising their wages. Amid much public protest, courts in Pennsylvania, Maryland, New York, and Massachusetts continued to rule against union efforts on the ground that they were criminal conspiracies.

It was not until the next century that the Supreme Judicial Court of Massachusetts virtually needed the criminal conspiracy doctrine. In *Commonwealth v. Hunt* (1842), Justice Shaw declared that an association of workers could serve "useful and honorable purposes": In other words, unions were not illegal unless their purposes and methods were illegal.

The courts then developed the civil conspiracy doctrine, which held that a group of employees could be restrained from activities that harmed others even if the group's purpose was legal. Thus, in *Vegelahn v. Gunther* (1896), a Massachusetts court issued an injunction forbidding the union to picket even though the union's goals of obtaining higher wages and shorter hours were legal. The court decided that the employer deserved relief from a union tactic that could lead to more serious harm.

YELLOW-DOG CONTRACTS AND INJUNCTIONS. The two devices effectively denied to employers by the Norris-LaGuardia Act were *yellow-dog contracts* and *injunctions*. **Yellow-dog contracts** were cards that employers required workers to sign. These cards stated that the worker was not a union member and would not become one while working for that employer. Workers who refused to sign were fired. Those who signed the cards, or so the saying went, felt like "yellow dogs—with their tails between their legs."

Weakened by the Erdman Act of 1898 (which dealt with the railroad industry) and their constitutionality questioned by the courts as early as 1908

---

criminal conspiracy doctrine Concept formerly used by the courts to hamper union activities, arguing that such activities were illegal

civil conspiracy doctrine Concept formerly used by the courts to hamper union activities by arguing that a union could be restrained from activities that harmed others even if the union's purpose was legal

yellow-dog contract Card that an employer required a worker to sign as a condition of employment, stating the worker was not a union member and would not become one while working for the employer

"If you don't come in Sunday, don't come in Monday." These ringing words reflect the status and treatment of the predominantly immigrant workers in the ladies garment industry at the turn of the century. Exploitation in the sweatshops meant fifteen-hour-plus workdays, low wages, dangerous working conditions, child labor abuses, and more.

Enter the International Ladies's Garment Workers's Union (ILGWU). Founded in 1900 to combat these abuses, the union's first line of attack was the strike. In 1909, 20,000 shirtwaist makers left their jobs and picketed for two months. This work force, consisting overwhelmingly of women and young girls, endured arrests and beatings but were successful in winning a work reduction to 52 hours weekly and a wage increase.

As conditions changed, so the issues facing the ILGWU have evolved. The major challenge for the ILGWU in the 1990s is stemming the rise of imported clothing as well as fighting the problems wrought by imports for domestic workers. Due in large measure to imports from countries with low wage levels, clothing manufacture in the United States has fallen dramatically since the 1970s. From 1979 to 1988 domestic output declined by one-third, and employment in one key area—the women's dress sector—went from 184,000 in 1973 to just 68,000 in 1988. For those garment workers still on the job, imports have contributed to downward pressure on wages, exploitation of undocumented immigrant workers, new "sweatshops" in an "underground" economy, and obstacles to union organizing efforts.

In order to fight this trend, ILGWU has mounted major legislative efforts to regulate imports and has supported grass-roots campaigns to help members preserve jobs. To protect workers against sweatshops and industrial homework (where safety and wages cannot be monitored), the union has joined a coalition with other apparel-related industries and testified on numerous occasions before the Department of Labor, as well as working on the state level. In addition, the ILGWU works on the political front, supporting those candidates pledged to the union's goals of limiting imports, full employment, and increasing the minimum wage.

A major goal of the ILGWU has always been what the union refers to as "social unionism"—that is, improving the lives of its members as whole persons, not just as factory workers. This goal has entailed an ongoing commitment to improving health and education beyond the workplace. Starting with the establishment of the Union Health Center in 1914 and continuing with its current health-maintenance program, which provides such services as comprehensive exams and mammography, the ILGWU has worked toward improving workers' health. The union offers comprehensive hospital and medical coverage and maintains a health service plan that allows workers to purchase prescription drugs at low cost.

In addition, it provides social services like the Friendly Visiting Program, in which homebound or institutionalized retirees are provided with companionship and help with Social Security benefits and other matters. The ILGWU also offers counseling services for problems related to alcohol and drug abuse under its Member Assistance Program.

Historically, the ILGWU has been a union of immigrants, its membership changing over the years from largely Italians and Jews to Eastern Europeans to Hispanics and Asians. To keep members informed, the ILGWU publishes *Justice*, its monthly newspaper, in English, Spanish, and Chinese. (Reflecting its changing membership, it ceased its Italian edition in 1986, after 67 years.) Educational projects currently include teaching English and preparing members for citizenship tests, as well as offering classes in history, politics, and trade-union principles.

At no time has education been a greater priority than in the last few years, with the Worker-Family Education Project, which offers classes in English as a Second Language (ESL), basic education, skills for earning a high school equivalency diploma, and upgrading workplace skills. This last project is innovative in that it combines language with learning new job-related skills.

The ILGWU was also a strong supporter of the 1986 Immigration Reform and Control Act, which provided amnesty to undocumented aliens living illegally in the United States since before January 1, 1982. After passage of the law, the ILGWU established a two-part strategy, called the Immigration Project, to help its workers fulfill the requirements of the legalization process and then learn the basic English and citizenship skills needed for naturalization. The union has also worked with civil-rights groups to monitor discrimination against workers.

(*Adair v. U.S.*), yellow-dog contracts were nullified by Norris-LaGuardia as legally unenforceable.

Preliminary injunctions are orders from a judge to prevent actions that may cause permanent harm. After issuing an injunction, the court has time to consider claims on both sides. It may then lift the order or issue a **permanent injunction**. Prior to the Norris-LaGuardia Act, injunctions were often granted on slight pretexts to stop or prevent strikes that arguably threatened to damage a business. Although judges did not forbid strikes outright, they issued orders requiring unions to meet so many conditions that the results were the same.

preliminary injunction Court order to prevent, temporarily, actions that might cause harm (*see also* Chapter 4)

permanent injunction Court order to prevent, permanently, actions that might cause harm (*see also* Chapter 4)

The Norris-LaGuardia Act made the terms for granting such requests for injunctions so stiff that they were effectively ruled out.

The Wagner and Taft-Hartley Acts

Wagner Act 1935 federal law that protects the rights of workers to form, join, or assist *labor unions* and to bargain collectively

National Labor Relations Board (NLRB) Independent federal agency established by the *Wagner Act* to enforce labor law, certify the results of certain union elections, and conduct elections among employees to choose unions

Taft-Hartley Act 1947 amendment to the *Wagner Act* that outlaws *unfair labor practices* by unions

In 1935, Congress moved actively to encourage the growth of unions. The **Wagner Act** protected the right of workers to form, join, or assist unions and to bargain with employers about wages, hours, and terms and conditions of employment as a group.

The original Wagner Act set up the **National Labor Relations Board (NLRB)** to enforce labor law and certify the results of certain kinds of union elections. The NLRB is an independent federal agency that conducts elections among employees to establish which union shall represent the employees or to dismiss a union that workers no longer want to represent them.

As amended by the **Taft-Hartley Act**, the Wagner Act also outlaws a number of union practices. In addition, it governs decisions as to which issues should be subject to collective bargaining and which kinds of employees may be represented by unions.

The provisions of the Wagner and Taft-Hartley Acts fall under three general categories: *unfair labor, employer,* and *union practices.*

UNFAIR LABOR PRACTICES. The major practices forbidden by the amended Wagner Act fall into two groups: unfair practices by *employers* and unfair practices by *unions.* Thus, a firm may not (1) refuse to negotiate in good faith with someone who represents a majority of its workers or (2) interfere with employees in the exercise of their collective bargaining rights. (*See* Table 13-4 *for some unfair labor practices.*) The firm will be subject to an unfair labor-practice charge if it discriminates against employees exercising their rights, tries to influence union elections, or seeks to influence union management.

In turn, union agents may not interfere with an employee's exercise of protected rights, including the right to oppose or refrain from union activities. In addition, certain kinds of strikes and boycotts are forbidden. Like employers, unions have a duty to bargain in good faith. This duty will be discussed later in this chapter.

Unfair Employer Practices. To decide whether an employer activity is unfair, the NLRB uses a *reasonable likelihood test*: Does the activity tend to interfere with, restrain, or coerce employees exercising protected rights? The union need not prove an actual instance of interference for a practice to be found illegal. However, if there is a possibility that the employer did not foresee the effect of the practice, proof of hostile intent may be required.

Because such activity unduly influences employees in the free exercise of their rights, the promising or granting of benefits in order to discourage unionization or union activities is illegal. By the same token, reducing or withholding benefits as a way of fighting a union organizational drive is also illegal. For example, it is illegal for employers to threaten to close a plant, discharge workers, impose harsher working conditions, or threaten violence. Firms also risk unfair labor practice charges if they poll or interrogate employees about their union sympathies. To avoid such charges, firms must institute certain safeguards (a secret ballot) in order to free employees from fear of discrimination. Employers

TABLE 13-4   *Unfair Labor Practices*

BY EMPLOYERS	BY UNIONS
• Interfering with, restraining, or coercing workers who are exercising their rights to organize. *Example:* Promising wage increases if a certification election fails. • Refusing to bargain with union agents or bargaining in bad faith. *Example:* Failing to attend bargaining sessions or to back up claims with information. • Discriminating against workers who join or favor a union. *Example:* Firing or demoting shop stewards because of their positions. • Trying to control the union or interfering with union affairs. *Example:* Helping a candidate in an election for union office. • Discriminating against workers who help enforce labor law. *Example:* Firing or demoting workers who report unfair labor practices to the NLRB.	• Restraining or coercing workers in exercising their rights to join or not join a union (unless the union and employer have previously agreed that workers must join). *Example:* Preventing nonunion workers from entering a worksite. • Refusing to bargain or bargaining in bad faith with employers. *Example:* Striking without warning the employer. • Leading employers to discriminate against workers (except for nonpayment of dues). *Example:* Suggesting demotions of nonmembers. • Charging members discriminatory or very high dues and entrance fees. • Forcing employers to pay for unnecessary workers or services (i.e., featherbedding). • Encouraging or threatening strikes to pressure an employer or self-employed person to join a union or employer organization, stop doing business with a person or business, recognize an uncertified union, or pressure others to recognize a union. *Example:* Threatening to strike if employer contracts work to a nonunionized firm.

may, however, put forth general views about unions and make predictions about the effect of a new union on the firm if the predictions involve consequences that the employer could not prevent (*NLRB v. Gissel Packing Co.*, 395 U.S. 575 [1969]).

In addition, employers have the right to establish rules for the work environment. One area of recent controversy within this provision revolves around the right of employers to require employees to be tested for drug use. Although such testing has become generally accepted as a condition for being *hired*, it continues to be debated hotly in union halls and argued frequently in the courts as a condition of *continued* employment. The YOU DECIDE feature in this chapter examines some of the fundamental issues involved in workplace drug testing.

Because the employer's right to establish workplace rules may conflict directly with employees' rights to organize unions, the NLRB regulates when and where employees can engage in campaign activities. For instance, the board has established rules for the distribution of literature. Most employees may only solicit votes orally on the work premises at breaks, lunch, or other nonworking times. However, if other kinds of oral solicitations are permitted during worktimes, the NLRB may decide that a particular employer is discriminating unfairly against union activity. Because literature could clutter the workplace, many employees may distribute union literature only at nonworking times and in nonworking areas. Again, the rule cannot be applied solely to

Very few people at either end of the political spectrum would disagree that illegal drug use—and substance abuse in general—is a social problem of monumental proportions in the United States. One issue that has arisen in the last decade is how to identify, treat, and/or punish abusers—punishment being a method of deterrence. Depending on their jobs, some workers both in the private and public sectors are now subject to various kinds of screening.

However, whether and how to administer drug tests remains an issue that resounds with constitutional implications. The most basic question is: Does a mandatory drug test, whose purpose is to uncover evidence of abuse, violate one's Fourth Amendment right to be "secure . . . against unreasonable searches"? The test of reasonableness must be determined in light of society's need to counteract the plague of drug abuse, which is as dangerous in the workplace as it is on the streets.

The federal government entered the picture in 1988, when it passed the Drug-Free Workplace Act, mandating that firms seeking federal contracts make good-faith efforts to rid their workplaces of drugs. However, although its strong language called for such action, the law did not mandate the legally uncertain measure of drug testing itself—thus leaving employers in a quandary.

Clearly, questions of public safety motivate the use of drug testing. In the wake of the Exxon Valdez accident, for example, the Coast Guard moved quickly to enforce drug testing. In addition, nuclear-plant workers are required to undergo testing; obviously, any impairments caused by drug use in such a workplace invite disaster. Not all instances, however, whether in the public or private sector, are that clear cut.

The recent case of Policemen's Benevolent Association of N.J. vs. Washington Township, 672 F.Supp. 779 (D.N.J.1987), highlights not only the constitutional issues involved but many others as well. The municipal township promulgated a plan to implement urinalysis drug testing for its police force as well as for its other employees. The testing was to be of two types: mandatory annual testing as part of scheduled physical exams and random testing.

Although sympathetic to the township's need to have a drug-free police force, the Policemen's Benevolent Association—the police officers' union—challenged the plan on several grounds. It maintained that there was no reasonable suspicion of drug use among the members of the force (or even in the township) and that the mandatory test thus intruded on the officers' privacy. They stated moreover that the random test is a so-called mass test of the sort that had been struck down in the courts as unreasonable. For its part, the township argued that because a police officer's job permits limited privacy rights, the mandatory test involved minimal intrusion. Town officials also stated their plan for random testing was both efficient and focused within detailed guidelines.

As the judge in the case, would you issue an injunction against the testing? In your deliberations, you must balance these questions: Is there a significant issue of public safety here? Does the plan violate Fourth Amendment rights? For further discussion, see p. 496.

---

union literature. A similar ban would have to be in effect for all handouts—such as United Way pamphlets or brochures about social events.

Although wearing union buttons or insignias is a protected activity, it may be limited if it interferes with the employer's right to conduct business. An insignia may be prohibited if it might cause a disturbance, present a safety hazard, distract workers, damage a product, or offend customers.

In general, seemingly legal employer rules may be held unfair if the employer has a pattern of hostility to union efforts, or the rule is instituted at a time of great union activity. In the case of *Lechmere v. NLRB*, however, the Supreme Court held that an employer did not commit an unfair labor practice when it barred nonemployee union organizers from placing leaflets on windshields in an employer-owned parking lot. (The case begins on page 471.)

Unfair Union Practices. The Taft-Hartley Act specified six unfair union practices. First, it is illegal for union agents to coerce or restrain an employee in the exercise of protected rights, such as voting in union elections or presenting a grievance. In addition, employees have a right to work during a strike and to vote down unionization without restraint. Mass picketing that restricts lawful entry or exit from a worksite is one example of illegal interference in an employee's right to disagree with a union.

LECHMERE v. NATIONAL LABOR RELATIONS BOARD
United States Supreme Court, 60 LW 4145 (1992)

Local 919 of the United Food and Commercial Workers Union, AFL-CIO, made repeated efforts to organize employees at a retail store in Newington, Connecticut, owned and operated in the Lechmere Shopping Plaza by petitioner, Lechmere, Inc. The store is located to the Plaza's south end, with the main parking lot to the north. A strip of thirteen smaller stores not owned by Lechmere runs along the west side of the Plaza, facing the parking lot. The parking lot is jointly owned by Lechmere and the developer of the smaller stores. A forty-two-foot-wide grassy strip of public property borders the parking lot and is broken only by the Plaza's entrance. A four-foot-wide section of the grassy strip adjoins the parking lot and is owned by Lechmere. None of the 200 employees of the store were represented by the union. Nonemployee union organizers began placing handbills on the windshields of cars parked in a corner of Lechmere's parking lot, which was used mostly by employees. They were told that Lechmere prohibited solicitation or handbilling on parked cars and left upon request. On several subsequent occasions, they returned to place handbills. They later relocated to the public grassy strip, where they handbilled cars before opening and after closing hours. They picketed for one month and then intermittently for the next six months. They recorded license-plate numbers, and with the help of the Connecticut Department of Motor Vehicles, they obtained the names and addresses of roughly 20 percent of the store's nonsupervisory employees. After mailings, phone calls, and home visits, only one employee had signed a union authorization card. The union filed an unfair labor practice charge with respondent National Labor Relations Board (Board) for Lechmere's barring the nonemployee organizers from its property in violation of the National Labor Relations Act. An administrative law judge ruled in the union's favor, and the Board adopted an order to post signs in the store proclaiming that Lechmere would not prohibit Local 919 representatives or others from distributing literature to employees in the parking lot. Lechmere's petition for review was denied by the Court of Appeals and the Board's order enforced. The Supreme Court granted certiorari.

No. 90-970

JUSTICE THOMAS delivered the opinion of the Court.

This case requires us to clarify the relationship between the rights of employees under §7 of the National Labor Relations Act, 49 Stat. 452, as amended, 29 U. S. C. §157, and the property rights of their employers. . . .

II
A

. . . .

Section 7 of the NLRA provides in relevant part that "[e]mployees shall have the right to self-organization, to form, join, or assist labor organizations." Section 8(a)(1) of the Act, in turn, makes it an unfair labor practice for an employer "to interfere with, restrain, or coerce employees in the exercise of rights guaranteed in [§7]." By its plain terms, thus, the NLRA confers rights only on *employees,* not on unions or their nonemployee organizers. In *NLRB* v. *Babcock & Wilcox Co.,* 351 U.S 105 (1956), however, we recognized that insofar as the employees' "right of self-organization depends in some measure on [their] ability . . . to learn the advantages of self-organization from others," §7 of the NLRA may, in certain limited circumstances, restrict an employer's right to exclude nonemployee union organizers from his property. It is the nature of those circumstances that we explore today.

Babcock arose out of union attempts to organize employees at a factory located on an isolated 100-acre tract. The company had a policy against solicitation and distribution of literature on its property, which it enforced against all groups. Almost all employees drove to work in private cars and parked in a company lot that adjoined the fenced-in plant area. The parking lot could be reached only by a 100-yard-long driveway connecting it to a public highway. This driveway was mostly on company-owned land, except where it crossed a 31-foot-wide public right-of-way adjoining the highway. Union organizers attempted to distribute literature from this right-of-way.

The union successfully challenged the company's refusal to allow nonemployee organizers onto its property before the Board. While acknowledging that there were alternative, nontrespassory means whereby the union could communicate with employees, the Board held that contact at the workplace was preferable. "[T]he right to distribute is not absolute, but must be accommodated to the circumstances. Where it is impossible or unreasonably difficult for a union to distribute organizational literature to employees entirely off of the employer's premises, distribution on a nonworking area, such as the parking lot and the walkways between the parking lot and the gate, may be warranted." Concluding that traffic on the highway made it unsafe for the union organizers to distribute leaflets from the right-of-way, and that contacts through the mails, on the streets, at employees' homes, and over the telephone would be ineffective, the Board ordered the company to allow the organizers to distribute literature on its parking lot and exterior walkways.

The Court of Appeals for the Fifth Circuit refused to enforce the Board's order and this Court affirmed.

While recognizing that "the Board has the responsibility of 'applying the Act's general prohibitory language in the light of the infinite combinations of events which might be charged as violative of its terms,'" we explained that the Board had erred by failing to make the critical distinction between the organizing activities of employees (to whom §7 guarantees the right of self-organization) and nonemployees (to whom §7 applies only derivatively). Thus, while "[n]o restriction may be placed on the employees' right to discuss self-organization *among themselves,* unless the employer can demonstrate that a restriction is necessary to maintain production or discipline," "no such obligation is owed nonemployee organizers." As a rule, then, an employer cannot be compelled to allow distribution of union literature by nonemployee organizers on his property. As with many other rules, however, we recognized an exception. Where "the location of a plant and the living quarters of the employees place the employees beyond the reach of reasonable union efforts to communicate with them," employers' property rights may be "required to yield to the extent needed to permit communication of information on the right to organize."

Although we have not had occasion to apply *Babcock's* analysis in the ensuing decades, we have described it in cases arising in related contexts. Two such cases, *Central Hardware Co.* v. *NLRB,* 407 U. S. 539 (1972), and *Hudgens* v. *NLRB,* 424 U. S. 507 (1976), involved activity by union supporters on employer-owned property. Having decided the cases on constitutional grounds, we remanded them to the Board for consideration of the union supporters' §7 claims under *Babcock.* In both cases, we quoted approvingly *Babcock's* admonition that accommodation between employees' §7 rights and employers' property rights "must be obtained with as little destruction of the one as is consistent with the maintenance of the other." There is no hint in *Hudgens* and *Central Hardware,* however, that our invocation of *Babcock's* language of "accommodation" was intended to repudiate or modify *Babcock's* holding that an employer need not accommodate nonemployee organizers unless the employees are otherwise inaccessible.

If there was any question whether *Central Hardware* and *Hudgens* changed §7 law, it should have been laid to rest by *Sears, Roebuck & Co.* v. *San Diego County District Council of Carpenters,* 436 U.S. 180 (1978). As in *Central Hardware* and *Hudgens,* the substantive §7 issue in *Sears* was a subsidiary one; the case's primary focus was on the circumstances under which the NLRA pre-empts state law. Among other things, we held in *Sears* that arguable §7 claims do not pre-empt state trespass law, in large part because the trespasses of nonemployee union organizers are "far more likely to be unprotected than protected," permitting state courts to evaluate such claims, therefore, does not "create an unacceptable risk of interference with conduct which the Board, and a court reviewing the Board's decision, would find protected," . . .

We further noted that, in practice, nonemployee organizational trespassing had generally been prohibited except where "unique obstacles" prevented nontrespassory methods of communication with the employees.

B

Jean Country sets forth a three-factor balancing test:

"[I]n all access cases our essential concern will be [1] the degree of impairment of the Section 7 right if access should be denied, as it balances against [2] the degree of impairment of the private property right if access should be granted. We view the consideration of [3] the availability of reasonably effective alternative means as especially significant in this balancing process." . . .

Citing its role "as the agency with responsibility for implementing national labor policy," the Board maintains in this case that *Jean Country* is a reasonable interpretation of the NLRA entitled to judicial deference. It is certainly true, and we have long recognized, that the Board has the "special function of applying the general provisions of the Act to the complexities of industrial life." Like other administrative agencies, the NLRB is entitled to judicial deference when it interprets an ambiguous provision of a statute that it administers.

Before we reach any issue of deference to the Board, however, we must first determine whether *Jean Country*—at least as applied to nonemployee organizational trespassing—is consistent with our past interpretation of §7. "Once we have determined a statute's clear meaning, we adhere to that determination under the doctrine of *stare decisis,* and we judge an agency's later interpretation of the statute against our prior determination of the statute's meaning." *Babcock's* teaching is straightforward: §7 simply does not protect nonemployee union organizers *except* in the rare case where "the inaccessibility of employees makes ineffective the reasonable attempts by nonemployees to communicate with them through the usual channels." Our reference to "reasonable" attempts was nothing more than a commonsense recognition that unions need not engage in extraordinary feats to communicate with inaccessible employees—*not* an endorsement of the view (which we expressly rejected) that the Act protects "reasonable" trespasses. Where reasonable alternative means of access exist, §7 guarantees do not authorize trespasses by nonemployee organizers, *even* (as we noted in *Babcock,* "under . . . reasonable regulations" established by the Board.

Jean Country, which applies broadly to "all access cases," misapprehends this critical point. Its principal inspiration derives not from *Babcock,* but from the following sentence in *Hudgens:* "[T]he locus of th[e] accommodation [between §7 rights and private property rights] may fall at differing points along the spectrum depending on the nature and strength of the respective §7 rights and private property rights asserted in any given context." From this sentence the Board concluded that it was appropriate to approach every case by balancing §7 rights against property rights, with alternative means of access thrown in as nothing more than an "especially significant" consideration. As explained above, however, *Hudgens* did not purport to modify *Babcock*, much less to alter it fundamentally in the way *Jean Country* suggests. To say that our cases require accommodation between employees' and employers' rights is a true but incomplete statement, for the cases also go far in establishing the *locus* of that accommodation where nonemployee organizing is at issue. So long as nonemployee union organizers have reasonable access to employees outside an employers' property, the requisite accommodation has taken place. It is *only* where such access is infeasible that it becomes necessary and proper to take the accommodation inquiry to a second level, balancing the employees' and employers' rights as described in the *Hudgens* dictum. At least as applied to nonemployees, *Jean Country* impermissibly conflates these two stages of the inquiry—thereby significantly eroding *Babcock*'s general rule that "an employer may validly post his property against nonemployee distribution of union literature." We reaffirm that general rule today, and reject the Board's attempt to recast it as a multifactor balancing test.

C

The threshold inquiry in this case, then, is whether the facts here justify application of *Babcock*'s inaccessibility exception. The ALJ below observed that "the facts herein convince me that reasonable alternative means [of communicating with Lechmere's employees] *were* available to the Union." Reviewing the ALJ's decision under *Jean Country*, however, the Board reached a different conclusion on this point, asserting that "there was no reasonable, effective alternative means available for the Union to communicate its message to [Lechmere's] employees,"

We cannot accept the Board's conclusion, because it "rest[s] on erroneous legal foundations." As we have explained, the exception to *Babcock*'s rule is a narrow one. It does not apply wherever nontrespassory access to employees may be cumbersome or less-than-ideally effective, but only where "the *location of a plant and the living quarters of the employees* place the employees *beyond the reach* of reasonable union efforts to communicate with them." Classic examples include logging camps, mining camps, and mountain resort hotels. *Babcock*'s exception was crafted precisely to protect the §7 rights of those employees who, by virtue of their employment, are isolated from the ordinary flow of information that characterizes our society. The union's burden of establishing such isolation is, as we have explained, "a heavy one," and one not satisfied by mere conjecture or the expression of doubts concerning the effectiveness of nontrespassory means of communication.

The Board's conclusion in this case that the union had no reasonable means short of trespass to make Lechmere's employees aware of its organizational efforts is based on a misunderstanding of the limited scope of this exception. Because the employees do not reside on Lechmere's property, they are presumptively not "beyond the reach," of the union's message. Although the employees live in a large metropolitan area (Greater Hartford), that fact does not in itself render them "inaccessible" in the sense contemplated by *Babcock*. Their accessibility is suggested by the union's success in contacting a substantial percentage of them directly, via mailings, phone calls, and home visits. Such direct contact, of course, is not a necessary element of "reasonably effective" communication; signs or advertising also may suffice. In this case, the union tried advertising in local newspapers; the Board said that this was not reasonably effective because it was expensive and might not reach the employees. Whatever the merits of that conclusion, other alternative means of communication were readily available. Thus, signs (displayed, for example, from the public grassy strip adjoining Lechmere's parking lot) would have informed the employees about the union's organizational efforts. *Access* to employees, not *success* in winning them over, is the critical issue—although success, or lack thereof, may be relevant in determining whether reasonable access exists. Because the union in this case failed to establish the existence of any "unique obstacles," that frustrated access to Lechmere's employees, the Board erred in concluding that Lechmere committed an unfair labor practice by barring the nonemployee organizers from its property.

* * *

The judgment of the First Circuit is therefore reversed, and enforcement of the Board's order denied.

It is so ordered.

Case Questions

1. Why does the Court distinguish between nonemployee organizers who are attempting to unionize employees and employees who are attempting to unionize themselves?

2. Is the adherence to cases in such locations as logging camps, mining camps, and mountain resort hotels were held to be inaccessible for unionizing employees a practical standard in situations in which the parking lot and the store are both owned by the same person?

3. The Court points out that, after mailing and visits, only one employee signed a union authorization card. Explain whether the governing factor regarding accessibility should be the opportunity to receive information or the amount of success that a union has in gaining membership.

It should be noted that the prohibition against unfair union pressure is not as broadly worded as the prohibition against unfair employer pressure. Peer pressure and union propaganda are not unfair labor practices. Threats of violence, or other clearly intimidating behavior, are.

Second, it is illegal for union agents to pressure employers to discriminate against certain employees in order to encourage or discourage union membership. A union is required to serve the interests of all members of the bargaining unit in good faith. Thus, a union may not refuse to pursue a member's grievance because of his race, sex, or politics. Bad faith, arbitrary, or discriminatory treatment of a member is an unfair union practice.

Third, refusing to bargain in good faith with an employer regarding wages, hours, terms, and conditions of employment is an unfair union practice.

Fourth, certain types of strikes and boycotts are illegal if they are intended to (1) force an employer or self-employed person to join a labor or employer organization, (2) force an employer or self-employed person not to deal with another employer, (3) compel an employer to recognize the union and bargain with it without first obtaining NLRB certification of the proposed bargaining unit (we will have more to say about NLRB certification later in this chapter), or (4) force an employer to assign work to a particular craft.

Fifth, unions may be found guilty of an unfair union practice if the NLRB finds that their initiation fees or dues are excessive or discriminatory.

Finally, it is illegal for unions to require employers to pay for services that were not actually performed—for instance, by insisting on including unnecessary employees in certain assignments (a practice called *featherbedding*).

The Landrum-Griffin Act

One barrier to the merger of the AFL and the CIO was perceived corruption among leaders of certain AFL unions. In 1957, two years after the federations merged, a congressional committee led by Senator John L. McClellan of Arkansas began an investigation of union corruption.

The investigation lasted until 1959. It produced impressive evidence of crime and corruption in a few of the older AFL unions, notably the Longshoremen of the East Coast and the Teamsters. Congress responded quickly with the *Labor-Management Reporting and Disclosure Act* of 1959 (commonly referred to as the **Landrum-Griffin Act**). Its goal was to provide standards for union democracy and honesty by detailing the rights of union members, the responsibilities of union officers, and the proper uses of union funds.

A Union Workers "Bill of Rights." The Taft-Hartley Act tried to protect workers from undemocratic or corrupt unions by denying unions any say in who was hired or fired. The idea was to prevent workers from cooperating with corrupt unions in order to get a job or for fear of losing one. In effect, the Landrum-Griffin Act provided a "bill of rights" for union members. Under this act:

- All union members have equal rights to nominate candidates for union elections, attend membership meetings, and vote on union business.
- Dues and initiation fees can be increased only if certain procedures are followed.
- Any member may bring a court or agency action against the union after making a reasonable effort to exhaust the methods of protest offered by the union itself.

Landrum-Griffin Act (also known as the *Labor-Management Reporting and Disclosure Act*) 1959 federal statute that provides a bill of rights for union members and imposes safeguards on the use of union funds in order to eliminate union corruption

Members are entitled to a full and fair hearing whenever they are disciplined by a union office (unless the charge is failure to pay dues).

Misuse of Funds. Along with a bill of rights for union members, the Landrum-Griffin Act imposes safeguards meant to prevent the corrupt use of union funds. Therefore, this act (1) forbids anyone from using the union's property or money except to benefit the union or its members; (2) makes stealing or embezzling union funds a federal crime; (3) prevents union officers, agents, shop stewards, and union employees from holding or acquiring financial interests that conflict with the union's interests; and (4) prohibits union funds from being used to support candidates for union office. In addition, felons may not hold union office until either five years after they are convicted or they are released from prison after conviction.

Election Procedures. Union election procedures are also mandated. Locals must hold elections of officers by secret ballot at least every three years. All candidates must have a chance to see lists of eligible voters, and members may petition the secretary of labor or the courts to declare an improper election invalid after union remedies have been exhausted. Officers guilty of misconduct may be removed by a secret ballot of the membership unless a union constitution provides an alternative method of removal that the secretary of labor deems adequate.

■ Concept Check 13-3   Unions and the Law

- Define *preliminary injunction* and *yellow-dog contract* and describe the basic purpose of the *Norris-LaGuardia Act.*
- Explain the primary goals of the *Taft-Hartley Act* amendments to the *Wagner Act.*
- Describe an *unfair labor practice* and give examples both of an *unfair employer* and *unfair union practice.*
- Explain the principal goals of the *Landrum-Griffin Act.*

■ COLLECTIVE BARGAINING

Employers may wish that they were dealing with different unions—or with no union at all; unions may wish that they were dealing with different employers. Like it or not, however, unions and employer are, of course, stuck with each other. They must bargain in good faith. If the bargaining process fails, they resort to economic warfare. Collective-bargaining agreements have been described as a kind of "peace treaty"[2] meant to prevent economic warfare. Unlike sales contracts, however, the relationship outlined by such agreements represents one of a series of compromises over time rather than the conclusion to a process. The single most important benefit that employers seek from an agreement is the assurance that plants and projects will operate without strikes. Job security is the primary issue for workers.

---

[2] T. Kennedy, "Freedom to Strike Is in the Public Interest," 48 *Harvard Business Review* 45 (July-August, 1970).

The Collective-Bargaining Process

The aim of collective bargaining is to agree upon terms of employment that both parties can accept for the duration of the agreement. Bargaining does not necessarily arrive at terms that are truly fair or just—only at terms that both sides can accept. The union and the employer typically start by setting their sights high. The employer, for example, may want to reduce benefits or wages. More often, however, the union presents a list of demands. A few of these are usually "throwaway" items presented to test the water and give the employers notice of a future agenda. As a rule, both sides will retreat from their starting positions in search of a compromise.

Continuous bargaining, though rare, has attracted increased interest as one way to avoid stalled negotiations and strikes in industrial bargaining. Under this procedure, a joint committee is formed to continue bargaining on problems that either arise or are anticipated *between agreements*. This type of bargaining has helped industries deal with problems connected with changes in technology.

Collective-Bargaining Issues

UNION SECURITY.   One major issue of collective bargaining is **union security**— that is, the right of a union to exist and its right to represent a particular group of workers. The first right is guaranteed by law. The second right is typically secured by clauses in collective-bargaining agreements. About 85 percent of all workers covered by labor agreements with private industry are bound by one of the following forms of union-security clauses:

- A **union-shop clause** requires all employees to join the union. New workers must join soon after they are hired. In a **modified union shop**, although workers who are already union members must continue to be members while working for that employer, employees who were not union members at the time of the agreement need not become members.
- **Maintenance-of-membership clauses** require only that workers who voluntarily join the union cannot leave it except during a periodic "window of opportunity"— usually 10 or 15 days—before the agreement expires.
- **Agency-shop clauses** require all employees to pay fees to the union even if they do not become members. This provision forces nonmembers to share the cost of benefits that the union brings to all workers covered by the agreement. Unions, however, may exact fees only for "performing the duties of an exclusive representative of an employee on labor-management issues." They may not exact fees for such activities as support of union political lobbying (*Communication Workers v. Beck*, U.S. Supreme Court, June 29, 1988, No. 86-637).
- **Check-off clauses** require employers to deduct union dues from the wages of those workers who ask for this service and pay those dues to the union.

Twenty-one states, mainly in the South and Midwest, have enacted **right-to-work laws** that make it illegal to require union membership to get a job (*see* Figure 13-3).

MANAGEMENT SECURITY.   Naturally, management wants security as much as unions do. **Management-security clauses** give employers the right to run their firms. Some such clauses state generally that the power to make decisions about a business belongs solely to its management as long as decisions are not

---

continuous bargaining Method to avoid stalled negotiations and strikes by forming joint labor-management committees to discuss problems that arise or are anticipated between agreements

union security The right, guaranteed by law, of a union to exist, and its right, secured by clauses in *collective-bargaining agreements*, to organize a particular group of workers

union-shop clause *Union-security clause* requiring all employees, including new ones, to join the union

modified union-shop clause *Union-security clause* guaranteeing that employees who were not union members at the time of an agreement need not join, although workers who are already union members must maintain membership while working for that employer

maintenance-of-membership clause *Union-security clause* allowing workers who voluntarily join a union to leave only during a short period just before the agreement expires

agency-shop clause *Union-security clause* requiring all employees, union members and non-members, to pay fees in order to share the costs of the benefits provided by the union

check-off clause *Union-security clause* requiring employers to deduct union wages from the wages of employees requesting the deduction and to pay those dues to the union

right-to-work laws Statutes enacted in a number of states that make it illegal to require union membership as a condition of employment

management-security clause Clause in a *collective-bargaining agreement* stating that employers have the sole power to run their firms as long as their decisions are not illegal or contrary to labor agreements

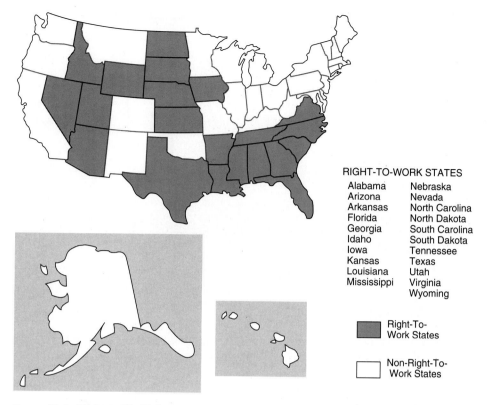

RIGHT-TO-WORK STATES

Alabama	Nebraska
Arizona	Nevada
Arkansas	North Carolina
Florida	North Dakota
Georgia	South Carolina
Idaho	South Dakota
Iowa	Tennessee
Kansas	Texas
Louisiana	Utah
Mississippi	Virginia
	Wyoming

Right-To-Work States

Non-Right-To-Work States

FIGURE 13-3 "Right-to-Work" States *Source: Human Resource Management* (Chicago: Commerce Clearing House, Inc., 1990). Reprinted with permission.

contrary to law or labor agreements. Others list management functions with which unions may not interfere—for example, hiring or assigning work. (This chapter's INTERNATIONAL ENVIRONMENT box examines a unique European approach to worker participation in organizational functions normally reserved for management.)

WAGES. The clauses covering wages in labor agreements are more diverse: Among other matters, they cover special wages for learners and apprentices, cost-of-living increases, and increases for workers who become more productive. For the most part, employers want to pay no more in wages and benefits than other employers are paying on the average, to fill a particular job. Unions seek to make wage levels the same for particular jobs throughout an industry or area: If one employer is paying less, others will also want to pay less.

Wages thus depend on factors in which both management and labor have a stake. One important factor, for example, is productivity: The more a company produces, the more resources it has for compensating the workforce that contributes to production.

Just how much impact do unions have on wages?[3] Because the answer to this question depends on numerous variables—for example, differences in competitive and noncompetitive markets, differences across occupations, differences due to region, age, and race—it is difficult to supply a simple quantified answer. Figure 13-4 shows the *average differential* between union and

---

[3] See E. Edward Herman, Joshua L. Schwarz, and Alfred Kuhn, *Collective Bargaining and Labor Relations*, 3rd ed. (Englewood Cliffs, NJ: Prentice Hall, 1992), pp. 269-78.

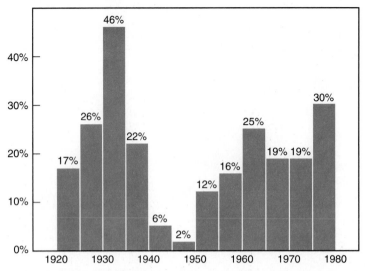

FIGURE 13-4 Union-Nonunion Wage Differential, 1920–1990 *Source:* Richard B. Freeman and James L. Medoff, *What Do Unions Do?* (New York: Basic Books, 1989).

nonunion wages over a 60-year period. The high of 46 percent during the Great Depression suggests that labor agreements, particularly long-term contracts, help to shield union workers against economic fluctuations.

Figure 13-5 shows the changes in the differential over the next decade. The gap has been closing since 1983—in fact, nonunion wages have risen faster than union wages since 1980. Analysts cite such factors as increased foreign competition, declining union membership and power, and the growth of nonunionized sectors in the economy.

JOB SECURITY. Job security is another important union goal. Labor agreements, for example, usually require employers to lay off workers in slack times on the basis of seniority—recently hired workers are laid off first and senior (long-time) workers are laid off last. The rules of such provisions are often complex. Unions also seek to avoid layoffs through work-sharing provisions that require employers to rotate employment or reduce the hours that each employee works each week in slack periods.

FIGURE 13-5 Changes in Union-Nonunion Wages, 1980–1989 *Source: American Workers in the 1990s* (Washington, DC: AFL-CIO Department of Economic Research, 1990). Data from U.S. Bureau of Labor Statistics, *Employment Cost Indexes and Levels, 1975–1989* (Washington, DC: Government Printing Office, 1989).

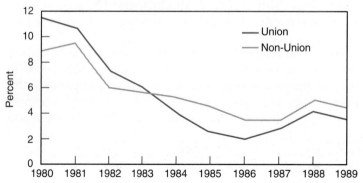

Participation by workers in the decision-making processes of corporations is not part of the traditional model of labor-management relations in the United States. Historically, management has held all authority and workers have followed orders. Labor organizations, meanwhile, provide collective bargaining for wages and improved working conditions but do not directly affect the running of the business. However, in light of the need for U.S. corporations to become more competitive and efficient, it has become increasingly useful for them to examine the Dutch model of works councils, in which employees help to design the kinds of policies normally reserved only to management and shareholders in the United States.

The Dutch works council is mandated by corporation law, which also provides that a company have a management board, full-time employees who run and represent the firm, and a supervisory board appointed by the shareholders. The role of the council is to consult on a wide range of subjects affecting the corporation, to advise on a variety of other decisions, and to help determine a third group. It is only on this last set that the workers are involved in decisions regarding the more traditional labor-management issues. The first two categories have to do with running the business. As the 1979 law updating previous works-councils statutes puts it: The council's purpose is "to promote consultation with and representation of persons employed in the enterprise . . . in the interest of the proper functioning of the enterprise in all its objectives."

The works council is a legal entity that is to be made up solely of employees who represent various groups in the firm, from production to clerical; there is no seat for management on the council. Because this group may conflict with the management board, the law sets up outside industrial committees; established according to industry, these committees have the power to resolve conflicts between the council and the board.

Specific stipulations govern works-council functions. For example, the company must allow councils to meet during work hours and must pay them regular salaries for time spent in meetings and other council-related activities. The company must cooperate with the council by providing all information that it requests in order to fulfill its consultative function. This procedure may involve such things as providing names and addresses of executives, financial statements, future plans, and policies regarding employees. The council, however, is expected to comply with the requirement preventing the disclosure of sensitive knowledge learned in the course of their duties.

On certain matters, the management board cannot make a decision unless the works council's advice has been sought and rendered. These are major issues to the firm and include:

1. substantial capital investments
2. transfer of control of all or part of the firm
3. takeovers of or large investments in other firms
4. expansion, reduction, discontinuation, or other changes in the firm's activities
5. management-board membership changes

If, after having met with the council and provided it with all requested information, the board then makes a decision that counters the council's advice, the decision cannot be implemented for 30 days. If negotiations do not result in a satisfactory decision, the council has the statutory right to appeal to the "Enterprise Chamber" in the Dutch court system.

In areas regarding labor and management, the works council codetermines policies. Unless a collective-bargaining agreement already applies, the council must be asked for its consent on the following: remuneration systems; hours and vacation rules; performance-review rules; pension plans; handling of grievances; and rules regarding hiring, firing, or promotion. Without the council's consent, management-board decisions cannot be put into effect. In this case, the board can request the industrial committee to approve its decision. Without this approval, or that of the council, the decision is null and void.

Although this system's social benefit as a means of improving the quality of life for workers while enhancing the concept of democracy seems clear, such a participation plan would no doubt encounter a variety of legal and policy obstacles in the United States. Under U.S. labor law, for example, a works council might be viewed as an employer-sponsored body and thus prohibited. It would certainly be challenged by unions, who might regard it as a throwback to the days before unions protected workers. Employers, on the other hand, while not wanting to give up power, might view such a participation plan as a way to further disarm powerful unions. Although both sides might agree that there is mutual gain when the firm prospers, the idea of worker participation based on the successful Dutch model would undoubtedly need to be revised to work here.

GRIEVANCES. Finally, all labor agreements provide a process for handling grievances.

Exclusive Representation

The union selected by the majority of the members of a unit represents it *exclusively* in collective bargaining. Indeed, one union per bargaining unit is a basic principle of labor law. There is a simple reason for this rule: If a firm were to bargain with multiple representatives, it might adopt a divide-and-conquer policy, playing favorites and harming the employees' interests.

The Duty to Bargain

Once the Wagner Act was passed, employees no longer had to rely solely on economic action, or the threat of it, to influence decisions shaping their work lives. The employer was now legally compelled to bargain. The Taft-Hartley Act, together with thousands of NLRB and court decisions, spells out the *duty to bargain*.

Under Section 8(d) of the Taft-Hartley Act, employers must meet with certified representatives of their employees "at reasonable times, to confer in good faith with respect to *wages, hours, and other terms and conditions of employment*" as well as any questions arising under previous agreements. These topics are *mandatory*: If the other side places it on the bargaining table, neither the employer or the union can refuse to discuss any question or decision relating to wages, hours, terms, or conditions of employment.

Refusal to bargain is an unfair labor practice: If a firm refuses to meet for a bargaining session or refuses to discuss a mandatory issue, it will be guilty of a violation of the law. The firm's intentions, reasons, or past history of cooperation are irrelevant. Other violations include refusing to carry out a written agreement or failing to consult the union before changing a condition subject to bargaining.

GOOD-FAITH BARGAINING. Beyond avoiding such violations, both sides must demonstrate good faith in bargaining conduct. In general, *good faith* is the willingness to provide the information necessary to back up claims. For example, an employer must supply a certified union with information on the wages of all workers who will be covered by an agreement. Without such information, how could the union back up claims that workers should be paid more? Management need not (1) provide information about a firm's profits unless it is basing its own arguments and claims on that data nor (2) discuss topics that are not mandatory.

BAD-FAITH BARGAINING. Some topics may not be discussed. For example, a proposal to bar an employer from hiring workers who have not already joined the union is illegal. If either side brings up illegal topics, it is bargaining in bad faith. **Permissive topics** may or may not be discussed at the discretion of both sides. For instance, an employer might refuse or agree to discuss a union's request that products have a union label or a proposal for a joint fund to promote the interests of the industry as a whole.

permissive topics Subjects which, left to the discretion of both sides, may or may not be discussed in *collective bargaining*

Note that bad-faith bargaining is different than "tough" bargaining—that is, refusing to compromise while bargaining. Some decisions by the NLRB and the courts hold that a "take-it-or-leave-it" position amounts to bad faith. Other decisions uphold the right of parties to stand their ground. Table 13-5 summarizes some of the actions, whether those of management, labor, or both, that have been found to constitute bad-faith bargaining.

Bargaining Units

bargaining unit Designated group of employees represented by a union

Decisions about *bargaining units* affect the outcome of bargaining. A **bargaining unit** is the designated group of employees represented by a union. The NLRB supervises and certifies the results of union elections, thus mandating that em-

TABLE 13-5	Bad-Faith Bargaining Practices

Refusal to respond to a request for a bargaining conference

Refusal to send to bargaining conferences representatives having power to negotiate

Constantly changing regotiating positions

Determination not to come to an agreement

Deliberate delaying or hampering of progress in negotiations

Unilateral granting of concessions to employees during negotiations with the union

Engaging in a campaign to undermine the union

Insisting on a contract with the employees rather than with the union

Rejecting demands without making a counterproposal

Refusal to sign a written contract embodying agreed-upon terms.

Source: Herman, Schwarz, and Kuhn, *Collective Bargaining and Labor Relations; Labor Law Course* (Chicago: Commerce Clearing House, 1987).

ployers bargain with representatives chosen by workers. One of its tasks in this process is to approve bargaining units. Units must meet several requirements determined by the NLRB.

For example, unless an employer agrees to a one-person unit, the unit must include at least two employees. For instance, a craft union can only negotiate an agreement for a single worker on a construction job if the employer chooses to recognize the union. The NLRB might examine the history and previous types of organizations at a plant, and it may also consider employees' wishes in the matter.

Community of Interests. More importantly, the bargaining group must define a *community of interests*. For example, the grouped employees might perform similar kinds of work, have similar training and skills, share a worksite, talk to each other regularly, or be supervised by the same managers. The more a group of workers has in common, the better the chance that it will be accepted as a bargaining unit. However, a set of groupings will not be rejected simply because another division would produce units with stronger common interests. For instance, a bargaining unit made up both of production and maintenance workers at a plant will not be rejected simply because production workers have more in common with each other than with maintenance workers. The NLRB's job is to determine that the units adopted are *at least suitable*, not that they are the *most suitable* units that could possibly be adopted.

The NLRB assumes that certain traditional groupings, called *presumptively appropriate units*, represent a community of interest. These groupings will almost certainly be approved. For example, the production and maintenance workers of a manufacturing plant nearly always form an appropriate unit, as do an employer's clerical workers. (The production and maintenance workers' unit, however, would include shipping clerks or other clerical employees who work in a production area at a particular plant.) In some industries, certain departments traditionally have their own bargaining units—for example, the bindery department of a printing shop. To break with precedent, a union must convince the NLRB that the usual rule does not apply.

Note that the NLRB will not accept a unit simply because a group of workers have joined a union and wish it to represent them. That would be only one factor in the NLRB's decision. Industry precedents are probably more important.

■ Concept Check 13-4   Collective Bargaining

- What is the single most important benefit that employees seek from a *collective-bargaining agreement*?
- Define and contrast *maintenance-of-membership* and *union-shop clauses*.
- Explain *good-faith* and *bad-faith bargaining* and describe a hypothetical situation in which one or more instances of either occurs.
- Discuss the criteria outlined by the NLRB for an appropriate *bargaining unit*.

■ GRIEVANCES AND ARBITRATION

As a group of labor-relations experts once put it, collective bargaining has created a kind of "industrial jurisprudence."[4] Few, if any, agreements have been so clear and complete that no conflicts between the union or a worker on the one hand and management on the other arise during the period that they cover. Such disputes are usually settled through a *grievance* procedure in much the same way the court system clarifies the meaning of the law. Nearly every agreement spells out a process for handling grievances. An independent mediator or arbitrator—an unbiased outsider—is usually called to settle any such matters. Unless a worker's health or safety is in danger, work goes on while the dispute is being settled. Supervisors' orders must be obeyed—even if they are contrary to the agreement—until the grievance process overturns them.

Grievances

grievance process Procedure by which conflicts between employees and employers are resolved

Generally, the **grievance process** may be used only to resolve conflicts over the meaning of the agreement—for example, when one side claims that the other is not complying with the agreement and the other side argues that the agreement does not rule out the conditions or actions inspiring the complaint.

Grievance processes serve many functions. First, they protect the individual worker from unfair treatment. Second, they are a means of settling problems peacefully and fairly, thus preventing interruptions of work. Next, each case that is settled prevents other cases disputing the same issue from arising and provides guidance for settling those that do arise. Finally, in the best circumstances, the process promotes better understanding on both sides.

The Grievance Process. The typical grievance process, which begins when a worker brings a written complaint to a supervisor, has four steps. Most complaints can be settled at the first stage, perhaps with the help of an officer representing the union local. Those matters that cannot be resolved are discussed by the head of a department at a factory and by the union grievance committee. If no decision is made, the dispute is taken to the next stage—a meeting of the company's personnel director and a representative of the national or international union. If the conflict is still unresolved, an impartial arbitrator is usu-

---

[4]Independent Study Group for the Committee for Economic Development, "The Public Interest in National Labor Policy" (1961), p. 32 in A. Cox, D. C. Bok, and R. A. Gorman, *Cases and Materials on Labor Law*, 8th ed. (Foundation Press, 1977), p. 570.

ally called in. The arbitration process is discussed in the next section. In industries with a great many employees, there may be more intermediate stages for appeals. Figure 13-6 illustrates the grievance procedure.

Arbitration ☆ KNOW

The vast majority of collective-bargaining agreements call for **arbitration**. They almost always limit the arbitrator's power to some extent, usually to disputes about the application or interpretation of the agreement. In addition, some agreements state that the arbitrator may not settle disputes on certain subjects. An arbitrator bound by this language may decide that the matter at hand is not covered by the agreement and is therefore *nonarbitrable*.

The two sides may be able to choose an arbitrator together. If not, they may ask the American Arbitration Association or the Federal Mediation and Conciliation Service either to name candidates or to pick an arbitrator. The person chosen will make a final and binding decision after hearing arguments on both sides, usually in an informal proceeding.

arbitration Method of dispute resolution, required in most *collective-bargaining agreements*, whereby the decision of a neutral third party chosen in advance by both sides must be accepted for arbitrable matters

ARBITRATION AND THE *STEELWORKERS* TRILOGY. Arbitration, as we saw in Chapter 5, is an alternative to a lawsuit. However, the courts have often been asked to enforce an arbitrator's decision and to decide when a matter is arbitrable. Over thirty years ago, the first group of a series of decisions involving arbitration was handed down by the U.S. Supreme Court. This 1960 group of legal decisions, sometimes known as the "*Steelworkers* Trilogy" cases, involved arbitration and the United Steelworkers and set the foundation for the labor-arbitration process as well as the finality of arbitration awards. Although these cases put the authority of arbitrators on firm ground, in the years since, litigation has continued regarding judicial review of labor arbitration.

Steelworkers *I and II.* Two of the Trilogy cases concerned whether a question was arbitrable. In the first, *United Steelworkers v. Warrior & Gulf Navigation Company* (363 U.S. 574 [1960]), the union was asking for an arbitrator to consider whether the firm had violated a labor agreement when it subcontracted

FIGURE 13-6 Typical Grievance Procedure *Source:* Adapted from John H. Jackson and Vermon A. Musselman, *Business: Contemporary Concepts of Practices* (Englewood Cliffs, NJ: Prentice Hall, 1987).

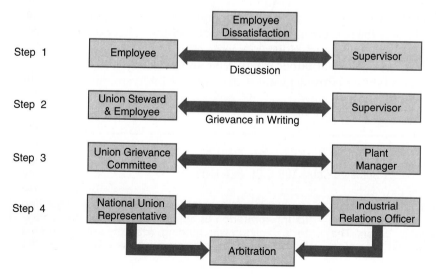

maintenance and dock repair work. The subcontract had cut Warrior & Gulf's maintenance and repair workers from forty-two to twenty-three—clearly grounds for union concern. However, a clause in the union's agreement with the employer excluded from arbitration matters that are "strictly a function of management." Subcontracting, the firm maintained, was such a function. The Court decided that the subcontracting question was arbitrable because the agreement did not explicitly exclude it. This ruling ultimately became an important guideline.

In the second case, *United Steelworkers v. American Manufacturing Company* (363 U.S. 564 [1960]), the firm had refused to reinstate an employee who was partially disabled and drawing workers' compensation. The lower court had ruled the grievance frivolous and not arbitrable. In reversing this decision, the Supreme Court ruled that the collective-bargaining contract had stated that *all* grievances would go to arbitration and that the courts should not decide which cases had merit.

The Enterprise Wheel *Principles*. In the third of these cases, *United Steelworkers v. Enterprise Wheel & Car Corporation* (363 U.S. 593 [1960]), the Court stated that "the refusal of courts to review the merits of an arbitration award is the proper approach to arbitration under collective bargaining agreements." In the years since this statement of judicial restraint, several exceptions were created that allow judicial review of arbitration decisions.

One exception occurs when enforcement of the decision threatens to violate public policy. In *Alexander v. Gardner-Denver* (415 U.S. 36 [1974]), for example, the Supreme Court held that a person who had lost a case in arbitration regarding a grievance alleging racial segregation could still seek recourse under the 1964 Civil Rights Act. This decision provided the opportunity to relitigate an arbitration award in court.

The Grace *and* Misco *Cases*. The public-policy issue is also a factor in *W. R. Grace & Co. v. International Union of Rubber Workers, Local 759* (461 U.S. 757 [1983]). In this case, the Court, pursuing the thinking behind the trilogy cases, stated again that the courts could not "second-guess" an arbitration award. Significantly, however, the court also held that courts could not enforce an award "contrary to public policy."

Although the decision in *W. R. Grace* would seem to leave open the question of just what constitutes public policy—and thus to provide an opening for judicial review—the Court's decision in *United Paperworkers International Union v. Misco* (108 S. Ct. 364 [1987]), which is excerpted below, narrowed the public-policy exception for overturning an arbitration decision. This exception can be used only when the award violates a very clear and dominant policy, not merely an interpretation of public interest. From the trilogy cases to *Misco*, the Court has reached its current position that judicial intervention in arbitration decisions should be restrained.

UNITED PAPERWORKERS INTERNATIONAL UNION v. MISCO
United States Supreme Court 108 S.Ct. 364 (1987)

Misco, Inc., which operated a Louisiana paper plant, had a collective bargaining agreement with the United Paperworkers International Union. The Agreement stated that the company and the union could arbitrate any grievance that arose regarding its interpretation or application and that the arbitrator's decision was binding. After the police arrested Isiah Cooper, an employee whose job involved the

---

484

operation of dangerous equipment, for the illegal possession of marijuana, Misco fired him pursuant to a company rule prohibiting employees from bringing controlled substances onto its premises. Cooper was arrested in his car, which was parked in the company's parking lot. An arbitrator overturned the discharge after finding that the company had not proved that Cooper had possessed marijuana on its property. The company moved in federal court to vacate the arbitrator's decision on the ground that it violated public policy. Both the District Court and the Court of Appeals agreed with the company. On Cooper's behalf, the union appealed to the Supreme Court.

Justice WHITE delivered the opinion of the Court.

The issue for decision involves several aspects of when a federal court may refuse to enforce an arbitration award rendered under a collective-bargaining agreement.

. . .

The Union asserts that an arbitral award may not be set aside on public policy grounds unless the award orders conduct that violates the positive law, which is not the case here. But in the alternative, it submits that even if it is wrong in this regard, the Court of Appeals otherwise exceeded the limited authority that it had to review an arbitrator's award entered pursuant to a collective-bargaining agreement. Respondent, on the other hand, defends the public policy decision of the Court of Appeals but alternatively argues that the judgment below should be affirmed because of erroneous findings by the arbitrator. We deal first with the opposing alternative arguments.

A

[1] Collective-bargaining agreements commonly provide grievance procedures to settle disputes between union and employer with respect to the interpretation and application of the agreement and require binding arbitration for unsettled grievances. In such cases, and this is such a case, the Court made clear almost 30 years ago that the courts play only a limited role when asked to review the decision of an arbitrator. The courts are not authorized to reconsider the merits of an award even though the parties may allege that the award rests on errors of fact or on misinterpretation of the contract. "The refusal of courts to review the merits of an arbitration award is the proper approach to arbitration under collective bargaining agreements. The federal policy of settling labor disputes by arbitration would be undermined if courts had the final say on the merits of the awards." As long as the arbitrator's award "draws its essence from the collective bargaining agreement," and is not merely "his own brand of industrial justice," the award is legitimate.

"The function of the court is very limited when the parties have agreed to submit all questions of contract interpretation to the arbitrator. It is confined to ascertaining whether the party seeking arbitration is making a claim which on its face is governed by the

contract. Whether the moving party is right or wrong is a question of contract interpretation for the arbitrator. In these circumstances the moving party should not be deprived of the arbitrator's judgment, when it was his judgment and all that it connotes that was bargained for.

"The courts, thererfore, have no business weighing the merits of the grievance, considering whether there is equity in a particular claim, or determining whether there is particular language in the written instrument which will support the claim."

[2–7] The reasons for insulating arbitral decisions from judicial review are grounded in the federal statutes regulating labor-management relations. These statutes reflect a decided preference for private settlement of labor disputes without the intervention of government: The Labor Management Relations Act of 1947, 61 Stat. 154, 29 U.S.C. § 173(d) provides that "[f]inal adjustment by a method agreed upon by the parties is hereby declared to be the desirable method for settlement of grievance disputes arising over the application or interpretation of an existing collective-bargaining agreement." The courts have jurisdiction to enforce collective-bargaining contracts; but where the contract provides grievance and arbitration procedures, those procedures must first be exhausted and courts must order resort to the private settlement mechanisms without dealing with the merits of the dispute. Because the parties have contracted to have disputes settled by an arbitrator chosen by them rather than by a judge, it is the arbitrator's view of the facts and of the meaning of the contract that they have agreed to accept. Courts thus do not sit to hear claims of factual or legal error by an arbitrator as an appellate court does in reviewing decisions of lower courts. To resolve disputes about the application of a collective-bargaining agreement, an arbitrator must find facts and a court may not reject those findings simply because it disagrees with them. The same is true of the arbitrator's interpretation of the contract. The arbitrator may not ignore the plain language of the contract; but the parties having authorized the arbitrator to give meaning to the language of the agreement, a court should not reject an award on the ground that the arbitrator misread the contract. So, too, where it is contemplated that the arbitrator will determine remedies for contract violations that he finds, courts have no authority to disagree with his honest judgment in that respect. If the courts were free to intervene on these grounds, the speedy resolution of grievances by private mechanisms would be greatly undermined. Furthermore, it must be remembered that grievance and arbitration procedures are part and parcel of the ongoing process of collective bargaining. It is through these processes that the supplementary rules of the plant are established. As the Court has said, the arbitrator's award settling a dispute with respect to the interpretation or application of a labor agreement must draw its essence from the contract and cannot simply reflect the arbitrator's own notions of industrial justice. But as long as the arbitrator is even arguably construing or applying the contract and acting within the scope of his authority, that a court is convinced he committed serious error does not suffice to overturn his decision. Of course, decisions procured by the parties through fraud or through the arbitrator's dishonesty need not be enforced. But there is nothing of that sort involved in this case.

B

[8] The Company's position, simply put, is that the arbitrator committed grievous error in finding that the evidence was insufficient to prove that Cooper had possessed or used marijuana on company property. But the Court of Appeals, although it took a distinctly jaundiced view of the arbitrator's decision in this regard, was not free to refuse enforcement because it considered Cooper's presence in the white Cutlass, in the circumstances, to be ample proof that Rule II.1 was violated. No dishonesty is alleged; only improvident, even silly, factfinding is claimed. This is hardly sufficient basis for disregarding what the agent appointed by the parties determined to be the historical facts.

[9] Nor was it open to the Court of Appeals to refuse to enforce the award because the arbitrator, in deciding whether there was just cause to discharge, refused to consider evidence unknown to the Company at the time Cooper was fired. The parties bargained for arbitration to settle disputes and were free to set the procedural rules for arbitrators to follow if they chose. Section VI of the agreement, entitled "Arbitration Procedure," did set some ground rules for the arbitration process. It forbade the arbitrator to consider hearsay evidence, for example, but evidentiary matters were otherwise left to the arbitrator. App. 19. Here the arbitrator ruled that in determining whether Cooper had violated Rule II.1, he should not consider evidence not relied on by the employer in ordering the discharge, particularly in a case like this where there was no notice to the employee or the Union prior to the hearing that the Company would attempt to rely on after-discovered evidence. This, in effect, was a construction of what the contract required when deciding discharge cases: an arbitrator was to look only at the evidence before the employer at the time of discharge. As the arbitrator noted, this approach was consistent with the practice followed by other arbitrators. And it was consistent with our observation in *John Wiley & Sons, Inc. v. Livingston*, 376 U.S. 543, 557, 84 S.Ct. 909, 918, 11 L.Ed.2d 898 (1964), that when the subject matter of a dispute is arbitrable, "procedural" questions which grow out of the dispute and bear on its final disposition are to be left to the arbitrator.

Under the Arbitration Act, the federal courts are empowered to set aside arbitration awards on such grounds only when "the arbitrators were guilty of misconduct . . . in refusing to hear evidence pertinent and material to the controversy." If we apply that same standard here and assume that the arbitrator erred in refusing to consider the disputed evidence, his error was not in bad faith or so gross as to amount to affirmative misconduct. Finally, it is worth noting that putting aside the evidence about the marijuana found in Cooper's car during this arbitration did not forever foreclose the Company from using that evidence as the basis for a discharge.

Even if it were open to the Court of Appeals to have found a violation of Rule II.1 because of the marijuana found in Cooper's car, the question remains whether the court could properly set aside the award because in its view discharge was the correct remedy. Normally, an arbitrator is authorized to disagree with the sanction imposed for employee misconduct. In *Enterprise Wheel*, for example, the arbitrator reduced the discipline from discharge to a 10-day suspension. The Court of Appeals refused to enforce the award, but we reversed, explaining that though the arbitrator's decision must draw its essence from the agreement, he "is to bring his informed judgment to bear in order to reach a fair solution of a problem. *This is especially true when it comes to formulating remedies.*" The parties, of course, may limit the discretion of the arbitrator in this respect; and it may be, as the Company argues, that under the contract involved here, it was within the unreviewable discretion of management to discharge an employee once a violation of Rule II.1 was found. But the parties stipulated that the issue before the arbitrator was whether there was "just" cause for the discharge, and the arbitrator, in the course of his opinion, cryptically observed that Rule II.1 merely listed causes for discharge and did not expressly provide for immediate discharge. Before disposing of the case on the ground that Rule II.1 had been violated and discharge was therefore proper, the proper course would have been remand to the arbitrator for a definitive construction of the contract in this respect.

C

The Court of Appeals did not purport to take this course in any event. Rather, it held that the evidence of marijuana in Cooper's car required that the award be set aside because to reinstate a person who had brought drugs onto the property was contrary to the public policy "against the operation of dangerous machinery by persons under the influence of drugs or alcohol." 768 F.2d, at 743. We cannot affirm that judgment.

[10, 11] A court's refusal to enforce an arbitrator's award under a collective-bargaining agreement because it is contrary to public policy is a specific application of the more general doctrine, rooted in the common law, that a court may refuse to enforce contracts that violate law or public policy. That doctrine derives from the basic notion that no court will lend its aid to one who founds a cause of action upon an immoral or illegal act, and is further justified by the observation that the public's interests in confining the scope of private agreements to which it is not a party will go unrepresented unless the judiciary takes account of those interests when it considers whether to enforce such agreements.

In the common law of contracts, this doctrine has served as the foundation for occasional exercises of judicial power to abrogate private agreements.

In *W.R. Grace,* we recognized that "a court may not enforce a collective-bargaining agreement that is contrary to public policy," and stated that "the question of public policy is ultimately one for resolution by the courts." We cautioned, however, that a court's refusal to enforce an arbitrator's *interpretation* of such contracts is limited to situations where the contract as interpreted would violate "some explicit public policy" that is "well defined and dominant, and is to be ascertained 'by reference to the laws and legal precedents and not from general considerations of supposed public interests.'" In *W.R. Grace*, we identified two important public policies that were potentially jeopardized by the arbitrator's interpretation of the contract: obedience to judicial orders and voluntary compliance with Title VII. We went on to hold that enforcement of the arbitration award in that case did not compromise either of the two public policies allegedly threatened by the award. Two points follow from our decision in *W.R. Grace.* First, a court may refuse to enforce a collective-bargaining agreement when the specific terms contained in that agreement violate public policy. Second, it is apparent that our decision in that case does not otherwise sanction a broad judicial power to set aside arbitration awards as against public policy. Although we discussed the effect of that award on two broad areas of public policy, our decision turned on our examination of whether the award created any explicit conflict with other "laws and legal precedents" rather than an assessment of "general considerations of supposed public interests." At the very least, an alleged public policy must be properly framed under the approach set out in *W.R. Grace,* and the violation of such a policy must be clearly shown if an award is not to be enforced.

[12] As we see it, the formulation of public policy set out by the Court of Appeals did not comply with the statement that such a policy must be "ascertained 'by reference to the laws and legal precedents and not from general considerations of supposed public interests.'" The Court of Appeals made no attempt to review existing laws and legal precedents in order to demonstrate that they establish a "well defined and dominant" policy against the operation of dangerous machinery while under the influence of drugs. Although certainly such a judgment is firmly rooted in common sense, we explicitly held in *W.R. Grace* that a formulation of public policy based only on "general considerations of supposed public interests" is not the sort that permits a court to set aside an arbitration award that was entered in accordance with a valid collective-bargaining agreement.

[13] Even if the Court of Appeals' formulation of public policy is to be accepted, no violation of that policy was clearly shown in this case. In pursuing its public policy inquiry, the Court of Appeals quite properly considered the established fact that traces of marijuana had been found in Cooper's car. Yet the assumed connection between the marijuana gleanings found in Cooper's car and Cooper's actual use of drugs in the workplace is tenuous at best and provides an insufficient basis for holding that his reinstatement would actually violate the public policy identified by the Court of Appeals "against the operation of dangerous machinery by persons under the influence of drugs or alcohol." 768 F.2d, at 743. A refusal to enforce an award must rest on more than speculation or assumption.

[14] In any event, it was inappropriate for the Court of Appeals itself to draw the necessary inference. To conclude from the fact that marijuana had been found in Cooper's car that Cooper had ever been or would be under the influence of marijuana while he was on the job and operating dangerous machinery is an exercise in fact-finding about Cooper's use of drugs and his amenability to discipline, a task that exceeds the authority of a court asked to overturn an arbitration award. The parties did not bargain for the facts to be found by a court, but by an arbitrator chosen by them who had more opportunity to observe Cooper and to be familiar with the plant and its problems. Nor does the fact that it is inquiring into a possible violation of public policy excuse a court for doing the arbitrator's task. If additional facts were to be found, the arbitrator should find them in the course of any further effort the Company might have made to discharge Cooper for having had marijuana in his car on company premises. Had the arbitrator found that Cooper had possessed drugs on the property, yet imposed discipline short of discharge because he found as a factual matter that Cooper could be trusted not to use them on the job, the Court of Appeals could not upset the award because of its own view that public policy about plant safety was threatened. In this connection it should also be noted that the award ordered Cooper to be reinstated in his old job or in an equivalent one for which he was qualified. It is by no means clear from the record that Cooper would pose a serious threat to the asserted public policy in every job for which he was qualified.

The judgment of the Court of Appeals is reversed.
So ordered.

Case Questions

1. The Court refused to uphold the Court of Appeals decision because it did not demonstrate a "well defined and dominant policy against the operation of dangerous machinery while under the influence of drugs." If you were re-arguing the case, on what sources could you rely in order to establish such a policy?

2. What were the competing public-policy issues at stake in this case? Which policy took precedence? Do you agree with the decision?

- Explain the functions served by the *grievance process*.
- Under what circumstances may a judge overrule or refuse to enforce an arbitrator's interpretation of a contract?
- Discuss the evolution and status of the Supreme Court's position on *arbitrable questions* and public policy through the *"Steelworkers Trilogy"* and *Misco*.

■ WHEN BARGAINING FAILS

Labor experts say that a union and employer have come to an *impasse* when an agreement is about to expire, a long series of bargaining sessions have been held, and there are no signs that another agreement will be entered into soon. This situation may arise if (1) there is no ground for compromise without sacrificing important interests, (2) bargaining agents have missed a chance to settle, (3) the union membership has voted down a settlement, or (4) one or both parties may want it.

THE BARGAINING ZONE.   According to some analysts, an impasse can best be explained as a failure of the parties to bring their respective demands into a *bargaining zone*. (*See* Figure 13-7.) One party (in this instance, the union) makes a demand that is unacceptable to the other, which has established an upper limit on a tolerable compromise. If the union's *expectation*—as opposed to its *demand*—actually falls into a zone that satisfies the employer's *expectation* (as opposed to the employer's *desired result*), and if the employer's expectation does not drop below the limit of union expectation, an impasse can be resolved.

Faced with an unresolved impasse, both sides may agree to extend an old agreement. Sometimes, union members settle for whatever wages and benefits the employer gives them and continue working without any agreement at all.

"NO CONTRACT, NO WORK."   However, the tradition in heavily unionized American industries is "no contract, no work": An impasse signals the beginning of eco-

FIGURE 13-7 The Bargaining Zone   *Source:* Frederick E. Schuster, *Human Resource Management: Concepts, Cases and Readings,* 2nd ed. (Reston, VA: Reston Publishing Co., 1985).

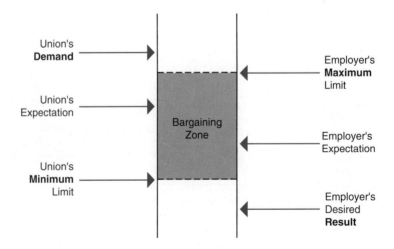

(A)

(B)

(C)

Labor Disputes in the Gilded Age Between the end of the Civil War and the mid-1870s, a thriving economy and a peak in workers' power combined to channel union activism into efforts at political and economic reform. With the Depression of 1873, however, an expanded labor pool increased employers' power, and union membership declined from 300,000 in 1873 to a mere 50,000 in 1878. The mid- and late 1870s then witnessed a period of intensely bitter labor strife. In 1877, for example, rioters in Pittsburgh responded to wage cuts by the railroads by looting, burning freight cars and the Union Railroad Round-House (A), and exchanging fire with local militia. Signs of an impending "red revolution" were detected by officials in Pennsylvania and surrounding states. In the spring of 1886, when the McCormick Harvester Co. locked out 1400 unionized workers in Chicago and attempted to replace them with strikebreakers, protesting workers were fired on by police. A protest meeting called for the Haymarket began peacefully enough, but when a bomb exploded injuring about 70 policemen, the famous Haymarket Riot erupted (B). "Labor agitators" were cited among the guilty parties, and four "anarchists" were hanged for conspiracy to commit murder. The Homestead Strike (C) erupted when the Carnegie steel plant at Homestead, Pennsylvania, introduced new machinery and cut wages. Locked-out strikers belonging to the Amalgamated Association of Iron and Steel Workers blocked access to the plant by strikebreakers, and management called out 300 armed Pinkerton agents. After a preliminary battle in which several men on both sides were beaten, 8000 state militiamen were dispatched to the plant. Bargaining got under way with concessions likely until a young anarchist tried to assassinate factory co-owner Henry Clay Frick; public opinion turned against the strikers and hopes of compromise disappeared. The Pullman strike of 1894, led by the black labor activist A. Philip Randolph, is discussed in this chapter's PERSONAL PROFILE box.

nomic warfare. Workers go on strike when the agreement expires and stay on strike until a new one is concluded.

Both workers and employers are almost always hurt by strikes. Workers lose wages and possibly their jobs; employers lose business. Why, then, would anyone want to engage in economic warfare? The answer varies from case to case. An employer may be trying to break the back of a union by emptying its strike fund or undermining its leaders. If union leaders think the coming agreement will be hard for the membership to swallow, they may decide that a strike is needed to vent frustration or convince both members and the employer that the union will be aggressive in its stance.

Types of Strikes

economic strike Union strike after which members are not entitled to reinstatement if they have been replaced

unfair labor-practices strike Union strike after which members must be reinstated even if their jobs have been filled

The Wagner Act recognizes two kinds of strikes: **economic strikes** and **unfair labor-practice strikes**. Workers who participate in either of these types of strikes retain their legal status as employees—they are entitled to the protection that the Wagner Act offers employees. Participants in a strike protesting unfair labor practices must be reinstated after the strike even if their jobs are already filled. Participants in an economic strike are not entitled to reinstatement if they have been replaced.

In addition to economic and unfair labor-practice strikes, there are several other kinds of strikes. Although we will briefly describe them here, they are not important in the United States today. *Political strikes* are common in countries where unions are affiliated with political parties (for example, France and Italy); strikers hope to influence government action. *Organizational strikes* are intended to force an employer to recognize a union. The goal of the *jurisdictional strike* is to force an employer to assign work to the members of one union rather than another. Such conflicts are now resolved by the NLRB, by the unions themselves, or by arbitration.

As the name suggests, *grievance strikes* are organized to protest day-to-day problems arising under an agreement. As we saw earlier, most agreements now provide for grievance procedures and arbitration to solve such problems. However, some industries, including construction, trucking, and coal mining, do not usually require arbitration in their agreements. Note that workers have also been known to violate arbitration clauses by holding *wildcat strikes*—work stoppages without the approval of union leaders.

Aspects of Strikes

Once a strike is underway, both labor and management may use a number of tactics to strengthen their positions. Among these activities are worker *picket lines* and employer *lockouts*, two of the most typical strategies.

picket line Protest activiity of striking workers that takes place around the work site to get publicity, boost employee morale, and discourage customers and suppliers from entering

PICKET LINES. Strikes of all kinds typically include **picket lines** made up of several or many strikers and their supporters gathered around worksites holding protest signs and chanting slogans. The purpose of such activities is to publicize strikes, encourage employees to join, or discourage customers and suppliers from entering facilities.

Industrial strikes often maintain large, noisy lines to discourage strikebreakers from working. Craft unions, however, often maintain only small lines of one or two people. The purpose is basically to inform other craft workers that a strike is in progress.

KNOW

LOCKOUTS. In a strike, workers resist the employer's demands or pursue their own demands by withholding work. In a **lockout**, employers resist a union's demands or force it to make concessions by withholding employment. Lockouts may involve either shutting down a plant entirely or laying off workers and bringing in temporary nonunion workers. When a plant is shut down, a lockout poses the same costs and possible benefits to an employer as a strike.

The Wagner Act forbids lockouts designed to avoid bargaining or to prevent workers from forming a union. However, lockouts, like strikes, may be used to pressure the other side during an impasse. *Defensive lockouts* preempt a threatened strike: By shutting down operations before the strike, employers gain the advantage of control; employers, not the union, decide when the stoppage begins and which plants or operations close. By shutting out some workers and not others, employers can divide local membership and possibly discourage striking among those workers who have not been shut out.

No-Strike, No-Lockout Clauses. Collective-bargaining agreements often contain **no-strike, no-lockout clauses** that pledge both sides to avoid such tactics for the duration of the agreement. Instead, the parties agree to rely on the grievance process to resolve disputes.

A no-strike clause may be absolute or it may permit strikes on certain issues or in certain circumstances. For instance, auto workers are permitted to strike against company-imposed production standards if the grievance process fails to resolve the dispute. Other agreements permit strikes when a grievance process that does not include arbitration fails or when employers refuse to honor an arbitrator's decision.

Penalties stated in the agreement may be invoked if one side violates a no-strike, no lockout clause. Examples of such penalties include (1) automatic cancellation of either the union-security clause or the entire agreement, (2) the legal firing of wildcat strikers and their leaders, and (3) the court-ordered payment of damages to unions and employers who bring violation suits.

Since the Supreme Court's *Boys Markets v. Retail Clerks* decision (398 U.S. 235 [1970]) federal courts may issue injunctions against strikes that violate labor agreements containing both a no-strike clause and a mandatory arbitration procedure. Such injunctions are powerful employer tools because they force striking employees back to work.

Disputes and National Emergencies ✈✈✈✈✈✈

TAFT-HARTLEY PROVISIONS. At the end of World War II, many Americans felt that the nation's health and safety could be threatened by strikes that shut down most or all of a vital industry. The Taft-Hartley amendments address this issue by providing a procedure to intervene in strikes that may threaten national security.

Presidential Board of Inquiry. The president may appoint a board of inquiry if he determines that a strike may create a national emergency. This step has been taken on thirty-five occasions since 1947. The board's job is to research the facts of the dispute and present a report to the president. The board need not assign blame, nor is it empowered to make recommendations to the president to mediate between union and management unless the president makes a special request.

Injunctions. Once the board has reported the facts, the president must then decide whether to petition one or more U.S. district courts with jurisdiction over the parties to issue injunctions forbidding a strike or lockout. There have been only five cases in which a president decided not to ask for an injunction. Although judges do not have to honor the president's request, they have done so in all but one case.

By law, such injunctions require employees to go back to work or, if the injunction precedes a strike, to continue working under prestrike wages and working conditions for up to 80 days. With the help of the Federal Mediation and Conciliation Service, the parties must continue to bargain in good faith during that period. Critics of this procedure say that the injunction prevents real bargaining because employers benefit from prestrike wages—that in fact employers may have created the original impasse with the hope that the president and the courts would intervene.

Board Mediation. Should the dispute remain unsettled after 60 days, the board would make a second report to the president, which includes a statement of the employer's last offer to settle. Then, during the next 15 days, the NLRB would poll the employees to find out whether or not they will accept that offer. (Such an offer was rejected in all 17 of the cases in which employees were polled under this provision.) It should be noted that (1) the employer might not have been making its best offer at that time and that (2) union members might hurt their own organization by accepting the offer in a way that would reflect badly on their leaders.

In most cases, agreements were concluded during the presidential injunction period. In other cases, agreements were made after the injunction period but without a strike. Since a strike could arise at the end of the injunction period—there have been six strikes already that have threatened the national security—the president could petition Congress to pass legislation requiring employees to return to their jobs. In 1972, Congress actually did impose such a law on the west coast longshore workers, who settled with their employers before the date the new law would have summoned them back to work.

■ *Concept Check 13-6   When Bargaining Fails*

- Give a hypothetical example of a dispute and its resolution according to the theory of the *bargaining zone.*
- Define and explain the difference between *economic* and *unfair labor-practice strikes.*
- Give an example of a labor dispute that was considered a national emergency under the *Taft-Hartley* amendments.

■ UNIONS IN THE PUBLIC SECTOR

sovereignty doctrine Principle that the federal government is the ultimate source of power and legal rights in the U.S., as extended to mean that government employers should not be required to bargain collectively

The labor laws discussed so far deal with employees in the private sector; the laws that deal with government employees are quite different. The main difference lies in the **sovereignty doctrine**, which points out that the federal government is the ultimate source of power and legal rights throughout the United States. State, county, and city governments also have authority that private employers do not have. Many critics believe that, in the public sector, this authority should not be limited by a requirement to subject decision making to collective bargaining.

Labor Laws in the Public Sector

The Civil Service Reform Act of 1978 was enacted to clarify earlier executive orders that attempted to establish both grievance procedures for public employees and procedures to negotiate disputes. The newly created Federal Labor Relations Authority was authorized both to hear complaints about unfair labor practices and appeals and to make issues subject to bargaining.

With the exception of postal workers, federal employees cannot bargain collectively over wages, fringe benefits, or hours. However, agencies may bargain with unions as to (1) the numbers, types, and grades of positions; (2) the use of technology; (3) procedures for performing work or exercising authority; and (4) the alternatives open to employees who are in some way hurt by management decisions.

THE RIGHT TO STRIKE. Both the federal government and most states forbid public employees to strike. Seven states permit only certain kinds of public-employee strikes. Some analysts contend that the right to strike lies behind the success of collective bargaining: If employers did not see bargaining as a way of avoiding strikes, they would probably be much less cooperative than they have been. In fact, the right to strike is considered necessary for real bargaining to take place.

Like all rights, however, the right to strike must be weighed against the need to protect public health and safety. There has been much debate as to which public services are so essential that they may not be disrupted even briefly. In any case, many laws that prohibit strikes by public employees do not distinguish between essential and nonessential services. The rationale for these laws is the sovereignty doctrine.

Laws forbidding public employees to strike have not had total success. Teachers, firefighters, police, sanitation workers, and postal employees have all gone on strike. In fact, the number of public-sector strikes has increased since the 1960s. The ETHICAL ENVIRONMENT box in this chapter weighs the issue of the public-sector right to strike from the perspective of an important historical episode—the 1919 Boston police strike.

CASE: THE PATCO STRIKE. In July 1981, a majority of members of the Professional Air Traffic Controllers Organization (PATCO) decided to hold an illegal strike. President Ronald Reagan's response was to give the strikers two days to return to work or lose their jobs permanently. In February, a U.S. Court of Appeals had already heard a case concerning whether a district court could issue an injunction against this strike by federal workers. The case follows.

UNITED STATES v. PROFESSIONAL AIR TRAFFIC CONTROLLER'S ORGANIZATION
U.S. Court of Appeals, Seventh Circuit, 653 F.2d 1134 (1981)

Air Traffic employees at O'Hare Airport, members of the Professional Air Traffic Controllers Organization (PATCO) Local #316, conducted a unified slowdown of airport traffic between August 6 and August 15, 1980, greatly stifling the flow of travel and causing numerous delays. This action was taken in response to the Federal Aviation Adminis- tration's failure to meet PATCO's demands for an upgrading of the O'Hare tower and tax-free bonuses of $7,500 to each controller.

On August 18, 1980, the United States sought an injunction in U.S. District Court to prevent any further work stoppages by PATCO. The court dismissed the action on the grounds that a district court has no authority to enjoin a strike because such power is the province of the Federal Labor Relations Authority. The United States appeals.

Prior to the enactment of Title VII of the Civil Service Reform Act of 1978, federal labor-management relations were regulated by Executive Order 11491, as amended. Section 19(b)(4) of the order made it an unfair labor practice for a labor organization to "call or engage in a strike, work stoppage, or slowdown . . . or condone any such activity by failing to take affirmative action to prevent or stop it." . . .

. . . .

Title VII of the Civil Service Reform Act of 1978 was enacted to provide a comprehensive statutory scheme for the regulation of federal labor-management relations. The statute created a new, independent agency, the Federal Labor Relations Authority (FLRA), which was to be primarily responsible for carrying out the purposes of Title VII. . . .

. . . .

. . . When Congress enacted Title VII, it adopted the language of section 19(b)(4) of the Executive Order in section 7116(b)(7), making it an unfair labor practice for a union "to call, or participate in, a strike, work stoppage, or slowdown." . . .

We find additional support for our conclusion in both the language of the statute itself and the congressional debates prior to its enactment. Section 7101(b) of the Civil Service Reform Act of 1978 provides that "[t]the provisions of this chapter should be interpreted in a manner consistent with the requirement of an effective and efficient Government." . . . While the Government is waiting for the FLRA to follow this procedure, the employees could be out on strike. Such a result is not consistent with the goal of "an effective and efficient Government." The reason for Congress's prohibition of strikes by federal employees was reiterated during the congressional debates on Title VII:

The primary reason for Government services is to supply the public with certain essentials of life which cannot reasonably be supplied by the average citizen himself, or to him by private enterprise. . . . Because these services are essential to the health, welfare and safety of the public, . . . it becomes intolerable that they be interrupted.

. . . .

Although we agree with the statement that Congress intended the FLRA to parallel the NLRB in many respects, . . . Congress, by exempting federal employees from the NLRA and enacting Title VII, indicated that it intended private and public employees to be treated differently under the law. . . .

The district court's analysis of the parallel to the NLRB is further undercut by a provision in the National Labor Relations Act that authorizes a district court to enjoin a strike upon a petition of the Attorney General when the strike "will imperil the national health or safety." Congress recognized that in certain critical situations, district courts must have jurisdiction to enjoin threatened or actual strikes immediately, without waiting for the NLRB to act. . . .

. . . .

. . . [It is suggested] that the district court viewed the criminal penalty of 18 U. S. C. § 1918 and the termination of employment implicit in the terms of 5 U. S. C. § 7311 as the exclusive remedies for engaging in the prohibited conduct. We disagree with that conclusion.

. . . In the case at bar, dismissing or indicting the air traffic controllers involved in the slowdown would not be a viable remedy for the Government. First, terminating a substantial number of controllers would seriously impair the FAA's ability to provide the public with this essential service; this is precisely the sort of result that the statutory provisions were intended to prevent. Second, indicting or terminating the controllers after a strike does nothing to prevent the strike and the serious consequences that would surely follow. Thus, the only remedy available to the Government that can prevent a strike is an injunction.

. . . we conclude that an injunction is an available remedy under section 7311.

. . . .

For the reason stated herein, the order of the district court dismissing the action is reversed and the cause is remanded for further proceedings.

Case Questions:

1. Why should employees be able to strike in the private sector but not in the public sector?

2. How does the NLRB differ from the FLRA?

3. Why was an injunction the most appropriate remedy in the PATCO case?

■ *Concept Check 13-7   Unions in the Public Sector*

- Define the *sovereignty doctrine* and explain its application to the issue of the public-sector right to strike.
- Explain the arguments both for and against the public-sector right to strike.

The Current State of Work Stoppage Supporters of striking Professional Air Traffic Controllers (PATCO) rally in Boston, August 1981, shortly after President Ronald Reagan fired the 11,000-member PATCO workforce. According to official statistics, there were 4000-5000 strikes per year in the U.S. during the 1950s and 1960s. By the 1980s, the figure had dropped to 2300-3800, with perhaps as many as 2 million workers involved per year. Because data since 1981 reflects only strikes involving 1000 or more workers, most state and local strikes are no longer reflected in the official figures. The number of covered major strikes peaked at 424 in 1974 before dropping dramatically to less than 50 per year in the late 1980s. Not surprisingly, the drop in the number of work stoppages by federal-government employees beginning in 1982 (the year following the PATCO strike) has been drastic—from 11,400 affected workers and 650,500 idle days to zero in each year since. Strikes by local-government employees have been similarly affected: The number of workers involved decreased from 87,000 in 1981 to 7400 in 1988. Interestingly, public-opinion polls conducted in the late 1980s showed increased public support for the right of government employees to strike.

The question of whether public employees have the right to strike can be looked at first from an historical perspective. In the city of Boston in 1919, police officers joined the AFL through the Boston Social Club, the affiliation's rank-and-file organization. Their objective was to present their economic and job-related requests to the city through what is now sanctioned as a union. However, the now infamous police commissioner, Edwin U. Curtis, ordered the officers to abandon their union, citing department rules that they could join no group outside the department made up of members of the force. When the officers refused, Curtis filed charges on 19 for failing to follow orders. The police threatened to strike. The mayor's response was a special panel that made recommendations to avert the walkout. Curtis, however, overruled the mayor and suspended the men. The result: a strike—the first in U.S. law enforcement—on September 9, 1919.

Curtis labeled the strikers "deserters," refusing to negotiate with them. Following rioting and looting, he insured city safety by enlisting volunteer police and the army and then fired the entire department. Public opinion was on his side, having been helped by Governor Calvin Coolidge's statement that "there is no strike against the public safety by anyone, anywhere, any time."

In Curtis's own words, in his report to the Commonwealth of Massachusetts two months after the strike: "The sole issue involved in the 'strike' . . . was whether the Boston police force as a body should be allowed to affiliate with the American Federation of Labor." His position, in other words, was that there could be no union. He went on to say that "the question of wages was not an issue, because wages of patrolmen are fixed by the concurrent action of the mayor and Police Commissioner." That is, no collective bargaining.

In the aftermath of the Boston strike, public sentiment was so negative to labor organizations in law enforcement that it was many years before police unions were started

again. In fact, even New Deal President Franklin Roosevelt declared in 1937 that strikes were actually a "military" tactic used to obstruct the functions of government until demands were met and that their use by federal employees was "unthinkable and intolerable."

Although police unions are now a familiar feature of the public employee-management landscape, the issues regarding in cases strikes by public employees are still unresolved—especially where public safety is involved. The right to strike depends in part on whether one views public- and private-sector employees as essentially similar or essentially different. In addition, the question arises as to whether a strike by public employees—for instance, police officers—will endanger the public welfare. Finally, are strikes allowable by certain groups of public employees but not by others?

Opponents of legalized public-employee strikes argue that the two sectors are quite different and that such strikes would erode government authority, increase taxes and inflation, and endanger the public safety, especially that of innocent third parties. Moreover, they contend that because allowing strikes for only "nonessential" public workers—such as clerks in the Department of Agriculture—is inequitable, strikes should be illegal for all public employees.

Given the reality that public employees do strike, advocates of legalization have offered several counter-arguments. For one thing, legalization would provide parity for public workers with those in the private sector doing comparable jobs—for instance, nurses or bus drivers—who enjoy the legal right to strike. This argument maintains that the two sectors are similar and that public workers deserve the same rights as those in the private sector. This side also contends that by legalizing strikes, the air can be cleared and all parties to a dispute can concentrate on the substantive issues. Moreover, the threat of a strike can be used to bring about resolution of conflicts that will not disappear simply because the law does not permit them to be acted upon.

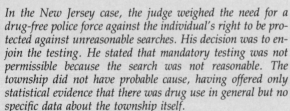

In the New Jersey case, the judge weighed the need for a drug-free police force against the individual's right to be protected against unreasonable searches. His decision was to enjoin the testing. He stated that mandatory testing was not permissible because the search was not reasonable. The township did not have probable cause, having offered only statistical evidence that there was drug use in general but no specific data about the township itself.

Moreover, the judge stated that although "public employees, such as police officers, may have a lessened expectation of privacy with respect to their employment . . . they do

not surrender all of their constitutional rights when they accept a public position" (672 F.Supp 787 [D.N.J. 1987]). Testing was deemed an intrusion when carried out in absence of any reasonable suspicion that a police officer had been using illegal drugs.

Not even this judge, of course, would argue against society's right to be protected by law-enforcement officers (or airline pilots), whose performance is nothing less than optimum, and to demand this protection. However, in his argument and elsewhere in the courts, we come against this constitutional issue repeatedly.

In two cases that reached the Supreme Court (Skinner v. Railroad Labor Executives Association 109 S.Ct. 1402 [1989]) and National Treasury Employees Union v. Von Raab 109 S.Ct. 1384 [1989]), it was held that, under the Fourth Amendment, urinalysis drug testing was an unreasonable "search" because the federal regulations in neither case led to a finding of probable cause. However, the Court also applied a balancing test that superseded the requirements of probable cause: Drug testing could occur without a particular suspicion of drug use (1) when drug abuse would cause a clear hazard and (2) when the testing would reduce the hazard. Because these cases were decided before the PBA case, they did not offer a final resolution: No clear "hazard" was evident in the New Jersey situation.

Current thinking, then, is that there must be some threshold at which we say that based on a reasonable suspicion, society or fellow workers or the environment are at risk from a given person. Determining the reasonable suspicion in individual cases from objective facts would seem to be the only way to justify a "probable cause" for a drug test— that is, a search—under the Fourth Amendment.

SUMMARY

- Under the common-law *employment-at-will doctrine*, employers are free to fire a worker for any reason or no reason at all, so long as they do not violate a contract, statutory right, or civil right. However, judges have ruled firings illegal if they violate public policy or an implied covenant of good faith.

- Today's labor organizations focus on day-to-day working conditions, wages, and terms of employment. In 1940, the CIO and the AFL were competing for members in most trades and industries. When the AFL and CIO became one federation in 1955, their new constitution forbade raiding and established a structure of self-government with three levels: the *local*; the *national* or *international* union; and the federation's headquarters and executive boards.

- The most important job of *locals* is to bargain with employers and handle job-related grievances. The members of a *craft local* do the same kind of work in the same geographic area. The members of an *industrial local* include many different kinds of workers serving the same employer. Typically, an industrial local tries to attract all the eligible employees at a workplace to become members.

- *National* or *international unions* organize the unorganized—a task that often requires the efforts of paid organizers over years. The *federation* acts as the voice of labor in American politics, pooling funds and influence. Its members avoid the expense of fighting off raids. They also gain the benefits of legal and other services provided by the federation.

- Four federal laws govern unions, providing the base for a web of rules, regulations and decisions. In 1932, the *Norris-LaGuardia Act* took courts out of the business of helping employers block union organizing. In effect, it overruled the *criminal* and *civil conspiracy doctrines*. The *Wagner Act* of 1935 protected the right of workers to form unions and bargain collectively. As amended by the *Taft-Hartley Act* in 1947, the law outlines *unfair labor practices* by both unions and employers. The Taft-Hartley Act provides a procedure to intervene in strikes that threaten the nation. The *Landrum-Griffith Act* of 1959 aimed to clean up corruption in unions and guarantee their members certain rights.

- The *National Labor Relations Board (NLRB)* supervises union elections. One of its tasks is to approve *bargaining units*, each of which must represent *community of interests* among its members. They may not include supervisors, managers, or confidential workers, none of whom has a legally protected right to bargain collectively.

- Legally, employers and unions must bargain, but if the bargaining process reaches an impasse, they may resort to *strikes* and *lockouts*. *Collective bargaining* aims at terms of employment that both parties can accept for a given period. As a rule, both sides retreat from their starting positions in search of a compromise. A typical agreement includes some form of *union-security clause*, clauses covering *wages* and *job security*, a "no-strike, no-lockout" clause, and a *grievance process* ending in arbitration.

- Workers who participate in strikes protesting unfair labor practices usually are entitled to their jobs after the strike. However, participants in an *economic strike* are not entitled to their jobs if they have been replaced. Organizational, jurisdictional, political, and grievance strikes are no longer important in the United States.

- Unions of government employees are governed by different laws than those governing private-sector unions. The federal government and most state governments forbid their workers to strike. Yet despite the use of mediation, fact-finding, and compulsory arbitration to settle impasses, the number of *public-sector strikes* increased during the 1960s and 1970s, followed by a period of marked decrease in the 1980s and into the 1990s.

QUESTIONS AND PROBLEMS

1. When Alex Cameron came to work at Orange Brands, he signed a contract stating that he would not join a union while he worked for the company. Six months later he joined a union, and the company sued him for breach of contract. What was the outcome? Why?

2. Cafeteria Workers Union Local 72 held elections. The candidates were permitted to see lists of eligible voters beforehand. The vote was taken by a show of hands, the candidates having the most votes winning. A local member challenges the election. Why? Explain.

3. The president of International Desk Makers, Local 69, appoints a nominating committee to decide upon a slate of candidates for the next union election. The committee meets in closed session and decides on a slate of nominees, checks with the nominees to be certain they will run for office, and then presents the slate for elections. A local member challenges this procedure. Why?

4. American District Telegraph is engaged in furnishing protective services by means of electric devices that are installed and maintained by its servicemen. The company also operates a one-man division responsible for selling, installing, and repairing background music systems. There are three types of employees: S-1s and S-3s who install and repair the electric devices and the S-2s, who are charged with protecting the customer's premises. All want to be represented by a union. What would be the appropriate bargaining unit(s)? [*American District Telegraph*, 160 NLRB No. 82 (1966)]

5. Grocery Mart, Inc., is a chain of 10 supermarkets in New York State. Although the store is a chain, the working conditions in each store vary because each is located in a different physical setting. In addition, employees are paid on the basis of local market considerations. The union would like to establish a company-wide unit for collective bargaining purposes. Management would prefer storewide bargaining units. What will the NLRB probably decide?

6. Lamoureux was an employee at the Wright Line Company. He worked there ten years and was considered a better than average employee but was discharged for falsifying time cards in violation of a plant rule. The plant rule allowed an employee to be discharged if he or she knowingly altered or falsified production time reports, payroll records, or time cards. Other employees had committed the same offense but were not fired. At a NLRB hearing, evidence was presented that Lamoureux had become a leading union advocate. He was known as a "union kingpin," who solicited union support from his fellow employees and brought about a successful union election. Will Lamoureux's discharge be upheld? Explain. [*Wright Line*, 251 NLRB No. 150 (1980)]

7. A minority of the employees of a large corporation have been represented by a bargaining unit (Unit 1) for over 40 years. The unit, which has not been recognized or certified as the exclusive bargaining agent or unit under the NLRA, regularly meets with management to discuss employee concerns. Eventually, a group of minority employees form their own unit (Unit 2)

because they feel that Unit 1 is unresponsive to the company's discriminatory practices. Management meets with Unit 2, but refuses to discuss individual member grievances or to acknowledge the status of the employees who accompany the Unit 2 members to grievance meetings under the procedure for non-Unit 1 members. (The company has one grievance procedure for Unit 1 employees and another for everyone else.) The company's motivation for denying equal status to Unit 2 is (1) its desire to have all grievances formally processed through one group and (2) its hesitance to deal with racially segregated employee organizations. Do the company's actions 'interfere with, restrain or coerce its employees in organizing, forming, joining or assisting" Unit 2 in violation of the NLRA? [*Black Grievance Committee, v. NLRB*, 749 F.2d 1972 (3d Cir. 1984)]

8. When union members became dissatisfied with their exclusive bargaining agent, the chair of the worker's committee which processed grievances and met regularly with management asked the supervisor of employee relations how to stop the automatic deduction for union dues. The union also asked the supervisor to find out, for employees' information, what management did in a nonunion shop. The supervisor told management executives of the conversation with the union, gave the union representatives copies of the nonunion agreement, and posted it in several visible places. The supervisor, after further discussions with management, told the union that (1) the best way to get out of paying dues was to cancel the entire collective bargaining agreement and (2) the present chairman must stay on as chairman of the employees.

    The supervisor then provided a memo cancelling the present collective bargaining agreement and met with the union to discuss the plan. The supervisor created the withdrawal petition for the employees and allowed members to leave their work stations to collect signatures. Since the union initiated this state of affairs, do management's actions constitute interference with the union? [*Texaco, Inc. v. NLRB*, 722 F.2d 1226 (5th Cir. 1984)]

9. One section of a plant was not profitable. The union began organizing the section employees. The necessary cards were signed and elections were set. Prior to the election, management discussed the union with the section employees several times. During a conversation with an employee concerning a promotion, management asked her to discuss the union with employees. The day before the election, management held a meeting with section employees and told them that ratification of the union would result in a cost increase, followed by a loss of customers, followed by employees losing their jobs. Among other things, management also said that those who planned to vote yes could stay home the next day and those who planned to vote no could come to work. The union won the election. One week later management closed the section, citing financial reasons and denying that the union played a part in its decision. Is management's decision to close the section a violation of the NLRA? [*Purolator Armored, Inc. v. NLRB*, 764 F.2d 1423 (11th Cir. 1985)]

10. Charlotte applied for a sales position at a local department store. At the interview, Charlotte was told that she was being hired as a permanent employee. Charlotte took the job but was fired three months later. She sued claiming the company's actions violated public policy and good faith and fair dealing. Is Charlotte correct? Explain.

14

LABOR STANDARDS

Since the depression of the 1930s, Congress has passed numerous laws regulating the compensation of employees and providing for workers' continued health and safety. Federal and state laws apply to workers who are on the job, recovering from job-related injuries, fired, laid off, or retired. Compensation administrators must comply with this complex web of government labor standards. In this chapter, we will discuss some of the most important pieces of government regulation that protect workers. The Fair Labor Standards Act (FLSA) is probably the most well-known of these regulations because it contains the minimum wage laws.

Other regulations include (1) worker's compensation, which protects people who are hurt on the job or who develop work-related illnesses, (2) Social Security, which provides income and medical benefits to many retirees and to survivors of workers who have died, (3) unemployment compensation, which temporarily supports workers who lose their jobs, and (4) the Occupational Safety and Health Act (OSHA), which tries to assure workers of a safe work environment.

■ THE FAIR LABOR STANDARDS ACT

Fair Labor Standards Act (FLSA) 1938 federal statute that sets standards for minimum wages, maximum hours, child labor, and equal pay for equal work regardless of sex

President Franklin D. Roosevelt, who was committed to controlling wages and hours from the start of his tenure in office (1933), first attempted to set fair-labor standards in the National Industrial Recovery Act. However, the act was invalidated by the Supreme Court. The **Fair Labor Standards Act** represented Roosevelt's second attempt to introduce these labor standards. There was a fierce legislative battle before the final passage of the FLSA in 1938.

The constitutionality of the FLSA was a major issue for its drafters. They grounded the FLSA on the commerce clause, arguing that the federal government has the power to prevent goods produced under unfair standards from entering the channels of commerce controlled by Congress—that is, interstate in producing goods for such commerce. Its coverage was gradually expanded

500

REST PERIODS-REST ROOMS

'Isn't it great!
A place to let go for a minute or two'

Getting away from the steady grind
to music a book or talk

A five minute rest
four times a day
in the workroom

Flagging energies
are built up by

a ten minute rest

during each
working period

'Setting up' exercises
are a relief
from constant sitting'

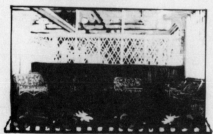

Simple comfortable
and only a step from the workroom

Small inexpensive but with big returns
to employer and employee

Standard Labor Theories The state of the art in labor standards, *circa* 1910. Studies in worker motivation and job satisfaction have traditionally identified two theories of management-employee relations. The classical *Theory X* holds that because people regard work as an unpleasant necessity, they respond basically only to tangible rewards—monetary compensation or other equally valuable consideration. The more optimistic *Theory Y* (sometimes called the *human-resources model*) assumes that because work is a natural outlet for people's personal-fulfillment needs, such approaches as "participative management," in appealing to the individual employee's willingness and ability to work, take advantage of the worker's own potential and initiative. Contemporary theories of organizational behavior favor some variation on the *contingency approach*: the theory that work-setting behavior results from such interacting factors as personal characteristics, corporate culture, situational factors, and the history (past and present) of a company's individual and group relationships. This company's commitment to "setting up exercises," by the way, appears to be an early step in the right direction. *Employee fitness programs* have become increasingly common because they have been shown to be effective in enhancing stress resistance—and in increasing positive attitudes, attendance, and productivity.

to all employees of enterprises involved in interstate commerce and to many public employees.

The FLSA has been amended several times. It now addresses four major issues: *minimum wages, maximum hours, child labor*, and *equal pay* for equal work regardless of sex. The goals of the FLSA were to put more people to work and to eliminate labor abuses. The courts have interpreted these goals to be public purposes. Because employees are not allowed to waive their rights under the FLSA, this interpretation has enhanced the effectiveness of the law.

Because this law has relatively clear terms, one might assume that it would be relatively uncontroversial. To the contrary, it continues to generate more litigation than any other area of labor-relations law at the federal district-court level. The Department of Labor conducts tens of thousands of compliance investigations annually, disclosing in one recent year over $130 million in unpaid wages.[1]

Minimum Wage and Maximum Hours

The following discussion defines the scope of the FLSA provisions concerning minimum wages and maximum hours. The first part focuses on the coverage of the Act. The next section centers on the FLSA's stipulations concerning work hours. Finally, we will examine some of the effects of the Act's minimum-wage provisions.

---

[1] CCH Editorial Staff, *Minimum Wages and Overtime Pay: The Answer Book in Federal Law* (Commerce Clearing House, 1985), p. 3.

PERSONAL PROFILE
Louis D. Brandeis

Louis D. Brandeis was one of the most influential justices ever to sit on the bench of the U.S. Supreme Court. Brandeis was born in Louisville, Kentucky, on November 13, 1856, and entered Harvard Law School without a college degree in 1875. In 1877, the university had to hold a special vote permitting Brandeis to receive his degree because he had not yet reached the required age of 21. After practicing law briefly in St. Louis, Brandeis returned to Boston and opened a practice there. He remained with his Boston firm until his appointment to the Supreme Court in 1916. His tenure on the High Court lasted for 23 years, until 1939. Brandeis was the first Jewish person to be named to the Supreme Court.

During the years that Brandeis practiced law, Brandeis often worked without pay to argue for causes that he believed in, including consumer protection and the support of labor unions. One such case resulted in "savings bank life insurance," which is available at savings banks in Massachusetts, Connecticut, and New York, and which put the cost of life insurance within the reach of the general population.

For all of Brandeis's important work, perhaps his most enduring contribution was in the area of labor relations. He worked unflaggingly to correct misunderstandings between labor and management and to use collective bargaining (see Chapter 13) to solve industrial disputes. His support of the

constitutionality of state minimum-wage and maximum-hour laws changed the face of workers' rights in this country forever.

Brandeis's belief that power brought social responsibility was at least part of the reason that he worked so diligently to promote his views of fairness and classlessness in the application of the law. Typically, he examined each case according to a set formula. First, he analyzed the facts of each case very carefully—no matter how complicated they were—until he had a complete understanding of the problem. Next, he looked at the social, economic, and historical significance of the case and examined expert opinion in the matter. Finally, he sought a long-range solution. This method of basing arguments in supportive data (for example, statistical information) became known as the "Brandeis brief." In essence, the analysis took the abstract concepts set out in the Fifth and Fourteenth Amendments to the Constitution and placed them in the "real" world. Brandeis detailed this method of analysis in his book Other People's Money, and How the Bankers Use It, *which was published in 1914. That book was an antimonopoly treatise which described banking's role in corporate America and which influenced the passage of the Clayton and Federal Trade Commission Acts.*

Brandeis was essentially a turn-of-the-century liberal who was able to turn idealistic concepts of social change into concrete suggestions for implementing such change. This approach was particularly valuable during a time when the social repercussions of the industrial revolution were first being woven into the fabric of American society. Brandeis was known for his ability not only to formulate such ideas and plans in great detail but could also garner public support for them.

Perhaps most important, Brandeis's knowledge of how economic organizations work, coupled with his deep sense of social responsibility, helped him devise reasonable solutions for the problems of the time. His belief in ethical individualism (that is, social responsibility on the part of industry) and in economic competition that serves social ideals played an important role in his decision making as a jurist. Guaranteeing the rights of individuals in an industrial society was his primary goal.

Louis Brandeis, Associate Justice of the United States Supreme Court, 1916–39. Mustering statistical support from the areas of economics, sociology, and even physiology, Brandeis the trial lawyer argued successfully before the Supreme Court in *Muller v. Oregon* (1908) that minimum-hours statutes for women were neither unreasonable nor unconstitutional. This approach to the presentation of a case—which came to be known as the "Brandeis brief"—is perhaps Brandeis' most enduring contribution to the practice of law in the U.S.

COVERAGE. The FLSA provides for two different forms of coverage: *individual* and *enterprise* coverage. *Individual coverage* depends on a particular employee's duties—that is, whether he is personally "engaged in interstate commerce or engaged in the production of goods for interstate commerce." Thus, in some companies, only some workers will be covered. Employees are considered to be engaged in commerce if their work is indispensable to the movement of goods or people across state lines—for example, unloading goods received from out of state, keeping records of goods shipped to other states, or even using the telephone or the mail for interstate communication. Likewise, the production of goods for interstate commerce has been broadly interpreted to include all the tasks needed to put goods into commerce, including supervising, packing, labeling, and the like, as well as manufacturing.

Enterprise coverage extends to every employee of a business that is engaged in interstate commerce or in the production of goods for such commerce. This category includes businesses that receive and use materials that have been shipped across state lines (for example, a hospital that uses drugs, medical supplies, and other equipment from out of state). Although some businesses (for example, hospitals, construction companies, and laundries) need meet only this commerce test to be covered by the FLSA, most enterprises must also have gross annual sales that are greater than a specified minimum.

Exemptions. In order to satisfy the special needs of certain industries, Congress exempted some categories of workers from these provisions:

- employees in a variety of transportation businesses, including airlines, trucking, railroads, and taxicabs are fully exempted from overtime requirements;
- outside salespersons, some agricultural workers, and employees of seasonal recreation businesses are exempt from both the wages and overtime provisions;
- executive, administrative, and professional employees (that is, "white-collar workers" who meet certain tests of responsibilities and salary) are exempt.

The last category is the most important. Because the intention of the law is that these exemptions be interpreted narrowly, categories are strictly defined. All exempted categories, however, share the use of discretion and judgment in performance of jobs. *Executives,* for example, have the authority to hire, fire, and promote, and spend most of their time managing the business and directing the work of employees.

The Public Sector. Originally, the FLSA applied only to private employers. However, a 1974 amendment broadened its scope to include state and local government employers. The Supreme Court at first held that Congress lacked the constitutional power to apply FLSA requirements to state and local governments in "areas of traditional government functions." However, it reversed itself in the following landmark case.

GARCIA v. SAN ANTONIO METROPOLITAN TRANSIT AUTHORITY
United States Supreme Court, 469 U.S. 528 (1985)

The San Antonio Metropolitan Transit Authority, a public mass transit system, refused to grant its employees overtime pay, citing its immunity from the Federal Labor Standards Act. Several SAMTA employees, including Garcia, commenced an action in U.S. District Court for overtime pay arguing that SAMTA was subject to the FLSA. The district court refused to apply the FLSA to SAMTA, agreeing with SAMTA that under the *National League of Cities* case, laws made by Congress pursuant to its Commerce Clause power do not reach traditionally inte-

gral functions of the state. The U.S. Supreme Court considers the validity of the "traditional governmental functions" approach to determining state immunity from the FLSA.

Justice Blackmum delivered the opinion of the Court.

We revisit in these cases an issue raised in *National League of Cities v. Usery* (1976). In that litigation, this Court, by a sharply divided vote, ruled that the Commerce Clause does not empower Congress to enforce the minimum-wage and overtime provisions of the Fair

Labor Standards Act (FLSA) against the States "in areas of traditional governmental functions." . . .

Our examination of this "function" standard applied in these and other cases over the last eight years now persuades us that the attempt to draw the boundaries of state regulatory immunity in terms of "traditional governmental function" is not only unworkable but is also inconsistent with established principles of federalism and, indeed, with those very federalism principles on which *National League of Cities* purported to rest. The case, accordingly, is overruled.

. . . .

The prerequisites for governmental immunity [from federal regulation] under *National League of Cities* were summarized by this Court in *Hodel* [v. *Virginia Surface Mining & Recl. Assn* (1981)]. Under that summary, four conditions must be satisfied before a state activity may be deemed immune from a particular federal regulation under the Commerce Clause. . . .

The controversy in the present cases has focused on the third *Hodel* requirement—that the challenged federal statute trench on "traditional governmental functions." . . .

. . . .

We believe, however, that there is a . . . fundamental problem at work here. . . . Any rule of state immunity that looks to the "traditional," "integral," or "necessary" nature of governmental functions inevitably invites an unelected federal judiciary to make decisions about which state policies it favors and which ones it dislikes. . . .

We therefore now reject, as unsound in principle and unworkable in practice, a rule of state immunity from federal regulation that turns on a judicial appraisal of whether a particular governmental function is "integral" or "traditional." Any such rule leads to inconsistent results at the same time that it disserves principles of democratic self-governance, and it breeds inconsistency precisely because it is divorced from those principles. . . .

. . . One approach to defining the limits on Congress' authority to regulate the States under the Commerce Clause is to identify certain underlying elements of political sovereignty that are deemed essential to the States' "separate and independent existence." . . . In *National League of Cities* itself, for example, the Court

concluded that decisions by a State concerning the wages and hours of its employees are an "undoubted attribute of state sovereignty." The opinion did not explain what aspects of such decisions made them such an "undoubted attribute," and the Court since then has remarked on the uncertain scope of the concept. The point of the inquiry, however, has remained to single out particular features of a State's internal governance that are deemed to be intrinsic parts of state sovereignty.

. . . .

The States unquestionably do "retai[n] a significant measure of sovereign authority." They do so, however, only to the extent that the Constitution has not divested them of their original powers and transferred those powers to the Federal Government. . . .

. . . .

Insofar as the present cases are concerned, then, we need go no further than to state that we perceive nothing in the overtime and minimum-wage requirements of the FLSA, as applied to SAMTA, that is destructive of state sovereignty or violative of any constitutional provision. SAMTA faces nothing more than the same minimum-wage and overtime obligations that hundreds of thousands of other employers, public as well as private, have to meet.

. . . .

This analysis makes clear that Congress' action in affording SAMTA employees the protection of the wage and hour provisions of the FLSA contravened no affirmative limit on Congress' power under the Commerce Clause. The judgment of the District Court therefore must be reversed.

Case Questions:

1. What in the Court's view is problematic with the "traditional governmental functions" classification?

2. What important effect does *Garcia* have on the scope of the application of the FLSA?

3. What in the Constitution gives Congress the power to regulate SAMTA?

Extending the wage and hour provisions of the FLSA to the public sector is extremely costly. For example, an Ohio survey estimated that first-year costs of compliance were $625,000 for Akron, $4,650,000 for Cleveland, and $1,700,000 for Toledo. The total of all of Ohio's cities was $20-25 million a year.[2] In addition, compliance with the FLSA can disrupt longstanding collective-bargaining agreements.

These problems were so great that within nine months of the *Garcia* decision, Congress had introduced and adopted legislation to soften its effects.

---

[2] T.P. Pappas, "The Aftermath of *Garcia*: Will Justice Blackmun's Analysis Continue to Work?" 15 *Capital University Law Review* 522 (Spring 1986).

This legislation reinstated compensatory time, excluded volunteers from FLSA coverage, allowed moonlighting, and delayed the date the decision became effective.

HOURS. The FLSA does not limit the number of hours that people may work: It merely stipulates that employees must be paid for all hours worked and that they must be paid one and a half times their regular rate for any hours over 40 worked during the week. Recognizing that this requirement raises special problems in some industries, the law provides special rules for calculating overtime for hospital and nursing home employees, firefighters, and law-enforcement officers.

The Definition of "Work." *Work* includes not only the principal activities of a job but incidental activities which are somehow indispensable or integral to the job and which infringe on the employee's freedom of action. For example, employers must compensate employees for coffee breaks, fire drills, and brief rest periods. They need not pay workers for sick leaves, holidays, and vacation time. If meal breaks are longer than a half hour and if employees are free to leave their post at that time, they need not be compensated. Meal periods that are shorter or that have to be spent at a work post must be compensated because they do not allow any real freedom from work.

Activities immediately before or after work are analyzed the same way. For example, employers must pay for the time that retail salespeople spend arranging merchandise before work and putting it away afterwards, for the time spent by bank tellers in waiting for an audit to be completed, and for the time spent by workers in the chemical industry showering and changing clothes. In each case, the activity is a required part of the job. Time spent changing clothes for the employee's convenience or for checking in and out of a plant need not be compensated because it is not integral to the job.

Overtime. Overtime requirements raise a general managerial issue: Should businesses pay overtime to existing workers or instead hire more workers? For the most part, the law has succeeded in discouraging overtime by making it expensive. The general trend today is toward less than a 40-hour week, and workers usually want more overtime than employers make available. However, some businesses have irregular workloads: Accountants, for example, must face the tax season and retailers must work the Christmas rush. These employers must weigh the cost of overtime pay against the costs of recruiting, screening, and training temporary workers during seasons of peak demand.

MINIMUM WAGE. The goal of the minimum-wage law is to keep workers who occupy low-paid and less productive jobs out of poverty. The federal minimum wage was first set at 25 cents an hour in 1938; in 1991, it was $4.25 (*see* Table 14-1 for federal minimum-wage rates from 1938 to 1991). At $4.25 an hour, annual earnings for a minimum-wage job are less than $8,000. Although this sum may be sufficient for a single person, it is only 60 percent of the poverty level for a family of four. Forty-one states also have minimum wage laws covering employees exempt from the FLSA. Sixteen of these states have minimums above the federal level.

Tips are counted towards the minimum wage if employees routinely receive over $30 a month in tips. The FLSA allows employers to take credit of up to 40 percent against the hourly minimum wage for these employees. This means, for example, that restaurants can pay waiters and waitresses as little as

TABLE 14-1 *Minimum-Wage Rates, 1938–1991*

| DATE OF CHANGE | NONFARM WORKERS | | FARM WORKERS |
	COVERED	NEWLY COVERED	
October 24, 1938	$0.25	$—	$—
October 24, 1939	0.30	—	—
October 24, 1945	0.40	—	—
January 25, 1950	0.75	—	—
March 1, 1956	1.00	—	—
September 3, 1961	1.15	1.00	—
September 3, 1963	1.25	—	—
September 3, 1964	—	1.15	—
September 3, 1965	—	1.25	—
February 1, 1967	1.40	1.00	1.00
February 1, 1968	1.60	1.15	1.15
February 1, 1969	—	1.30	1.30
February 1, 1970	—	1.45	—
February 1, 1971	—	1.60	—
May 1, 1974	2.00	1.90	1.60
January 1, 1975	2.10	2.00	1.80
January 1, 1976	2.30	2.20	2.00
January 1, 1977	—	2.30	2.20
January 1, 1978	2.65	2.65	2.65
January 1, 1979	2.90	2.90	2.90
January 1, 1980	3.10	3.10	3.10
January 1, 1981	3.35	3.35	3.35
April 1, 1990	3.80	3.80	3.80
April 1, 1991	4.25	4.25	4.25

Source: U.S. Department of Labor, Employment Standards Administration.

$2.47 an hour. However, employers cannot take the credit unless the tips are actually received.

The impact of the minimum wage on employment levels has been a source of continuing concern—after all, the minimum wage has a ripple effect throughout the economy. Some economists argue that raising the minimum wage eventually leads to increases for everyone else in order to preserve the wage differentials between skill levels. Theoretically, such a rise in wages might increase unemployment because businesses could respond by hiring fewer people or automating in order to reduce labor costs. The result might be to force inexperienced and unskilled workers out of the work force altogether or to push them into the unregulated part of the economy where they can be paid less.

The Subminimum Wage. Several studies have in fact shown that the minimum wage increased teenage unemployment. Since the late 1960s, Congress has considered—but never passed—many proposals for a lower so-called *sub-minimum wage* for workers under age 19. Proponents have argued that it would provide teenagers with the work experience and work habits needed to get full time jobs as adults. Dissenters have countered that any increase in teenage employment would come at the expense of older workers. They have also argued that it was not inadequate wages, but rather the inaccessibility of entry-level jobs, combined with a deplorable lack of basic academic and work-readiness skills, that caused high levels of teenage unemployment among minorities.

As demography eases the youth-unemployment problem in the 1990s, the arguments in favor of a subminimum wage are rapidly losing force. Because of low birth rates in the late 1960s and 1970s, there is now a shortage of teenage workers. Fast-food chains, for example, are finding it difficult to fill minimum wage jobs and are turning to older retired workers.

Case: Minimum Wages and Equity for the 1990s. The question of whether there should be a set minimum wage has always been grounded in the concepts of *equity* and *fairness*—that is, the right of all U.S. citizens to earn a living wage.[3] Debates surrounding these concepts are generally ethical and political in nature and have relatively little to do with economics or law. Such has been the case since a federal wage floor was first initiated under the FLSA more than 50 years ago.

As we have seen, certain classes of employees are exempt from the minimum-wage law. They include agricultural workers, domestic workers, certain outside salespeople, certain jobs in low-volume retail trades and services, certain seasonal amusement concerns, learners and apprentices, messengers, full-time students, and handicapped workers. Ostensibly, these provisions are intended to open the job market to workers who would otherwise have difficulty obtaining employment. In reality, they have had an unbalanced racial impact.

Today, the debate over minimum wages is largely concerned with issues of social policy such as the following:

1. The effect of legislation on various groups (namely, teenagers, women, illegal aliens, and minorities).
2. How federal law is affected by state minimum-wage legislation.
3. Whether the trend toward two-income families adversely affects the intent of the law.
4. How the decline in union membership affects the intent of the legislation.
5. Whether the international trend away from government intervention in wage setting is making the United States less competitive by forcing U.S. employers to pay their employees higher wages. (The INTERNATIONAL ENVIRONMENT box in this chapter discusses the issue of wages and "job exporting" in countries like Mexico.)

Today, proponents of a minimum wage contend that it is the best way to bring workers out of poverty. They argue that a decent minimum wage makes welfare benefits less attractive and encourages the work ethic. Opponents argue that the best way to set a wage rate is through the marketplace: They contend that a minimum wage increases the cost of labor without a corresponding increase in productivity.

Forty-two states, plus Puerto Rico, Guam, and the U.S. Virgin Islands,

---

[3] This discussion is based in part on C. N. O'Brien, "Revising the Minimum Wage for the 1990s," 12 *Loy L. A. Int'l L. J.* 217 (1990).

have passed minimum-wage laws that set floor rates higher than the federal government's rate. Some of these statutes are very specific (for example, "X rate for A jobs" and "Y rates for B jobs") while others are general ("always 50 cents per hour above the federal rate"). The adoption of such provisions may eventually render the federal law meaningless. Nevertheless, during a period when the trend is away from higher-paying manufacturing jobs and toward lower-paying service jobs, many observers believe that the federal government still continues to have a duty to protect workers from the inequities of the marketplace.

THE INTERNATIONAL ENVIRONMENT
Wages in Mexico

Foreign competition has forced many U.S. manufacturers to move production outside the country in an effort to cut costs. For example, many U.S. companies now ship American-made parts and materials across the Mexican border to so-called maquiladora *("handwork") plants for assembly by lower-paid Mexican workers. When this practice first began in the late 1960s, the workers in these plants were paid as little as $4–$5 per day. By the 1980s, some of these plants had evolved into full-fledged factories. The workers in these plants now move between third-world living conditions and modern factory conditions.*

Some people in the United States—especially organized labor—have criticized what they liken to the practice of "exporting" jobs. They claim that agreements like the maquiladora *take jobs away from American workers. Proponents of these factories respond that the high cost of labor in the United States makes it impossible to keep certain kinds of jobs in this country. Naturally, various third-world countries, including South Korea and Hong Kong as well as Mexico, benefit from these jobs. However, the jobs that move to Mexico, especially those in the automobile industry, cause the most resentment among U.S. workers. The high pitch of feelings may be due, at least in part, to the fact that the United States and Mexico share a border that is 2,000 miles long.*

Mexico in fact has become a sort of mecca to the automobile industry. Mexican automobile workers are emerging as a low-cost, high-quality work force. A typical worker in a Mexican factory makes about $1.75 per hour—or $70 for a 40-hour week. Compare that to a U.S. worker who is paid at the minimum wage: That worker would make about $170 for the same 40-hour week. Remember, too, that worker benefits are not included in these figures. There is also another, more subtle difference. The automobile industry in the United States is stagnant. Due to the power of the United Auto Workers Union, the most senior workers at U.S. auto plants are the ones who get to keep their jobs in a shrinking market. They are also the workers who are least likely to adapt to new technology and compensation packages that include givebacks.

Auto workers and manufacturers seem to be faced with a classic dilemma. Can the United States remain competitive in the world market—particularly the automobile market—if manufacturers keep jobs within the country's borders and are required to pay U.S. wages and benefits? Can the United States morally and ethically afford to give up jobs within its borders in order to remain competitive in the world market?

Child Labor Laws

In order to prevent "oppressive" child labor, the FLSA has set a minimum age of 16 for most work and 18 for hazardous occupations. Children between ages 14 and 16 are permitted to work at certain specified occupations that do not interfere with their education, health, or well-being—for example, newspaper delivery, acting, and some agricultural jobs. Employers who violate these laws face civil penalties of up to $1,000 for each violation.

The states also have child labor laws. State laws take precedence over the federal standards if they are stricter. Many state laws, for example, regulate street trades (peddling, and newspaper selling) by requiring special permits for minors. The states have generally coped with the problems posed by child actors, dancers, musical performers, and models by requiring parental permission. Some states also demand releases from civic and school authorities.

The Child-Labor Picture Lewis Hine, *Young Boys Working at Midnight in Indiana Glassworks*, 1908. It is estimated that children once formed about one third of the industrial workforce in the United States. Photos like those taken by Hine were enlisted in efforts to limit child labor—efforts that led, in 1916, to the Keating-Owens Act, which sought to discourage child labor by prohibiting interstate commerce in any goods manufactured by children under 16 years of age. Progressive—and somewhat optimistic—opinion held that because very few producers could afford to limit sales to the confines of markets in their own states, child labor would soon disappear altogether.

The Equal Pay Act of 1963

This amendment to the FLSA concerns sex discrimination: It is illegal to pay employees of one sex less than the other for jobs requiring equal skill, effort, and responsibility. However, differential rates based on merit, seniority, or incentive plans are allowed. The Equal Pay Act also prohibits employers from correcting existing illegal differentials by lowering wages. Chapter 15 discusses equal opportunity in detail and puts the Equal Pay Act into fuller perspective.

- Compare and contrast some of the different forms of coverage under the *Fair Labor Standards Act*.
- What are the basic goals of *minimum-wage laws*? What are some of the arguments for and against them?
- How do minimum-wage laws define *work*?
- Explain some of the arguments for and against the idea of a *subminimum wage*.

■ WORKERS' COMPENSATION

Workers' compensation addresses the financial and medical problems of workers injured on the job. Its two primary objectives are:

workers' compensation System of state and federal programs in which the lost wages and medical expenses of employees with job-related injuries and illnesses are paid

1. to pay for any medical expenses incurred in the treatment and rehabilitation of injured employees, and
2. to compensate employees for most short- or long-term losses in earnings.

The system was designed as a no-fault system based on insurance principles rather than tort litigation. The costs of workers' compensation are paid by employers on the basis of their actual injury records.

However, confusion over the modern workers'-compensation system and its tort-law origins persists. The current system, for example, still combines both tort-law and social-insurance principles. From tort law comes its complete reliance on employer liability: Neither employees nor the government makes any contribution to the benefits paid out; employers shoulder the entire financial burden. From insurance comes its no-fault principles: Every injured worker receives support from the system, no matter how the injury was caused. Liability depends solely on the injury's connection with work; negligence and fault are irrelevant.

Over the course of this century, state legislatures have continually expanded the coverage of workers-compensation laws to include more workers, more employers, and more types of injuries. Workers' compensation has also become mandatory in more states.

Worker Coverage

FEDERAL COVERAGE.   Some workers are covered by federal rather than state workers-compensation laws. The earliest of these laws, the Federal Employers' Liability Act of 1908, did not replace the tort-law system: It merely limited the common-law defenses that employers could use. It was followed in 1916 by the Federal Employee's Compensation Act, which established a workers-compensation program for all civil employees of the United States government. The Longshoremen's and Harbor Workers' Compensation Act of 1927 was designed to fill a gap in the state programs. It covers workers who are traditionally subject to maritime law and are therefore ineligible for state workers-compensation benefits.

However despite federal legislation supplementing the state workers-compensation programs, there remain many employees who are not covered by either state or federal law. Their only recourse is state employers' liability and tort law.

STATE COVERAGE.   Although the percentage varies widely from state to state, the vast majority of the U.S. labor force is covered by state workers-compensation laws. Coverage is least complete for farmworkers, household and casual workers, state and local government employees, and employees of small businesses or charities.

Three states share a unique situation: Their statutes make workers' compensation optional for private employers. However, employers who choose not to join the state workers'-compensation program can be sued under tort law and cannot avail themselves of certain standard defenses (for example, employee contributory negligence).

Covered Injuries

This issue of covered injuries has provoked a substantial amount of litigation over the years. Generally, the courts apply a four-part test to determine whether an injury is covered by workers-compensation law. To receive benefits, an employee must have received (1) a *personal injury* (2) as the result of *an accident* (3) that arose out of and (4) in *the course of employment*.

The first two clauses are relatively uncontroversial. The courts have defined *personal injury* quite broadly so that it includes diseases and mental disabilities as well as physical trauma to the body. *Accidents* are events which result from something unexpected and which can be traced to a particular time, place, occasion, or cause.

THE ISSUE OF CAUSAL CONNECTION.   There is, however, much greater difference of opinion over the interpretation of the third part of the test, which examines the *causal connection* between the job and the injury. Initially, the courts awarded compensation only when the source of an injury was peculiar to the worker's usual occupation. For example, a laborer whose foot froze while he was working outside all night in very cold weather was excluded from coverage: Because all laborers at the same job were exposed to the same weather, the court ruled that the frostbite did not result from a purely occupational hazard (*Robinson's Case*, 198 N.E. 760 [1935]).

This doctrine was eventually replaced by a more generous test: Even if the hazard was shared by the public, a worker could claim compensation if his job increased the risk involved. For example, everyone is at risk of being struck by lightning. However, a worker successfully claimed compensation when his job increased his risk of exposure to lightning by putting him on top of an exposed hill, in wet clothes, near an iron bed and electrical wiring (*Bauer's Case*, 49 N.E.2d 118 [1943]).

The Actual-Risk and Positional-Risk Tests. Some states are even more liberal, applying an *actual-risk test* that eliminates all consideration of whether a job hazard is also common to the public. This test would compensate injured employees for all kinds of "acts of God" taking place while on the job. Under the *positional-risk test*, injuries are compensated as long as it is *some condition of employment* that puts the worker in a position to be injured. For example, being struck by lightning while on the job is compensable simply because the job caused the worker to be in a certain place at a certain time. It does not matter whether that place and time *increased* the workers's probability of being struck by lightning.

The final part of the test usually refers both to the time and place of an injury and to what the worker was doing at the time. For inside employees (those who routinely work on their employers' premises), this provision covers the whole time they are on those premises. For outside employees (for example, traveling salesmen or truck drivers), it covers the entire period between their leaving home to go to work and their return home.

When an occupational disease, rather than an accident, is involved, this portion of the test poses a problem: Many occupational diseases have obscure causes and are contracted only after a long period of exposure. Thus, when a coal miner develops black-lung disease after working 30 years in several different mines, it is impossible to say exactly when and where the disease was contracted.

Benefits and Administration

BENEFIT CATEGORIES. There are five categories of workers-compensation benefits. They are determined by the nature of injuries incurred (from common medical needs to death on the job), and they differ in the allotment of benefits for *expenses* and *wages lost*.

Medical Benefits. The first category, which covers only medical expenses, accounts for about 80 percent of all work-related injuries and more than one-third of the money spent on workers-compensation benefits. Because employees are not put out of work, there is no need to replace lost income, only to pay for medical services. Both the amount and duration of these benefits are unlimited in 45 states.

Temporary Total Disability. The second category, *temporary total disability*, applies to employees whose injuries temporarily prevent them from working but who can later return to their old jobs. After a waiting period of two to seven days, these workers are eligible for benefits replacing part of their wages as well as paying for their medical expenses. Although benefits vary from state to state, most give the injured worker about two-thirds of the wages lost. Both the duration and the total amount of benefits may be limited. The majority of all workers-compensation claims that require income-replacement benefits fall into this category.

Permanent Partial Disability. *Permanent partial disability* covers workers who are permanently disabled and unable to return to their old jobs but who can still hold some other kind of regular employment. The amount of benefits depends both on wages lost and on the severity of the physical impairment. Schedules fix the compensation awarded for many injuries—for example, the loss of an arm, hand, eyesight, or hearing. Permanent partial disabilities account for a disproportionate amount of benefits: They comprise just over a quarter of all compensable injuries but absorb more than 60 percent of all nonmedical benefits paid.

Permanent Total Disability. *Permanent total disability* includes only about 0.1 percent of all cases. These workers have injuries that are both permanent and totally disabling. Either they cannot perform any available work, or they have a major physical impairment like blindness. Benefits usually amount to about two-thirds of the worker's wages, with a ceiling on weekly benefits.

Death on the Job. The fifth and final category covers workers who are killed on the job. In this situation, income-replacement benefits are paid to the worker's spouse and children. Benefits continue until the children come of age and the spouse dies or remarries.

Levels of compensation vary enormously from state to state. Benefits are generally several times greater in the most generous state than in the least generous one. Federal programs award the largest amounts: The Federal Employees' Compensation Act (FECA) hands out benefits 10 or even 20 times as large as the smallest of the state awards.

In the case that follows the courts attempt to determine the death-benefit award. As you will see, it is sometimes difficult to determine compensable weekly wage.

MORRISON-KNUDSEN CONSTRUCTION COMPANY v. DIRECTOR, WORKERS' COMPENSATION PROGRAMS
United States Supreme Court, 469 U.S. 624 (1983)

James Hilyer was killed in the course of his employment with the Morrison-Knudsen Construction Company. Due to his coverage under the Longshoremen's and Harbor Workers' Compensation Act, Hilyer's family was paid two-thirds of his average weekly wage by Morrison-Knudsen. However, the plaintiff-respondent, Mrs. Hilyer, believed that amounts paid by her husband as contributions to a union trust fund under the terms of a collective-bargaining agreement between his union and the company should have been included in the weekly compensation figure. After the refusal of the Benefits Review Board to include the contribution amounts in "wages," Mrs. Hilyer appealed to the Court of Appeals. The Court of Appeals having found merit to the plaintiff's claim, Morrison-Knudsen's appeal to the Supreme Court involves the issue of whether the subject contributions may properly be deemed as "wages" within the meaning of the Longshoremen's and Harbor Workers' Compensation Act.

Chief Justice Burger delivered the opinion of the Court.
. . . .

This case involves the meaning of 33 U.S.C. § 902(13), a definitional section that was part of the Compensation Act in 1927, when it became law, and that has remained unchanged through 10 revisions of the Act. The section provides:

"Wages" means the money rate at which the service rendered is recompensed under the contract of hiring in force at the time of the injury, including the reasonable value of board, rent, housing, lodging, or similar advantage received from the employer, and gratuities received in the course of employment from others than the employer.

We begin with the plain language of the Compensation Act. Since it is undisputed that the employers' contributions are not "money . . . recompensed" or "gratuities received . . . from others," the narrow question is whether these contributions are a "similar advantage" to "board, rent, housing, [or] lodging." We hold that they are not. Board, rent, housing, or lodging are benefits with a present value that can be readily converted into a cash equivalent on the basis of their market values.

The present value of these trust funds is not, however, so easily converted into a cash equivalent. . . .

Nor can the value of the funds be measured by the employee's expectation interest in them, for that interest is at best speculative. . . . The value to the Hilyer family of the Health and Welfare Fund depends on its need for the services the Fund provides; the value of the Pension and Disability Fund depends on whether Hilyer's interest vested. And the value of the Training Fund, which was established to insure "adequate trained manpower," and not for the benefit of the individual workers, is even more amorphous.

. . . .

Respondent Hilyer argues that . . . the remedial policies underlying the Act authorize the agency and require us to expand the meaning of the term to reflect modern employment practices. It is argued that fringe benefits are advantageous to both the worker, who receives tax-free benefits that he otherwise would have to buy with after-tax dollars, and do the employer, who reduces payroll costs by providing his workers with services that they could not on their own purchase with equivalent dollars. Respondent Hilyer contends that the incentive to trade salary for benefits should not be diluted by failing to consider the value of the benefits in determining survivorship and disability rights.

There is force to this argument, but a comrehensive statute such as this Act is not to be judically expanded because of "recent trends." . . .

. . . [R]einterpretation of the term "wages" would significantly alter the balance achieved by Congress. As noted above, employer-funded benefits were virtually unknown in 1927 [the year Congress passed the statute]; as a result, employers have long calculated their compensation costs on the basis of their cash payroll. Since 1927, however, the proportion of costs attributable to fringe benefits has increased significantly. In 1950, these benefits constituted only 5% of compensation costs: their value increased to 10% by 1970 and is over 15% presently. According to some projections, they could easily constitute more than one-third of labor costs by the middle of the next century. This shift in the relative value of take-home pay versus fringe benefits dramatically alters the cost factors upon which employers and their insurers have relied in ordering their affairs. If these reasonable expectations are to be altered, that is a task for Congress.

. . . .

. . . Accordingly, the judgment of the Court of Appeals is Reversed.

Case Questions:

1. What problem does the Supreme Court have with including the contributions in the respondent's death benefit award?

2. How does the Court reject the respondent's primary argument?

3. How does the Court define "wages" for purposes of the Compensation Act?

INSURANCE PAYMENTS. Funds for workers'-compensation benefits come from employers' insurance policies. Although some employers have self-insurance plans, most purchase insurance from private companies or state funds. Because premiums for large companies depend on individual accident experience, they have a financial incentive to try to prevent accidents. This is not true, however, for small firms: Because their premiums are based on the accident experience of the industry as a whole, any safety steps that they take will not necessarily reduce premiums.

Administration of Claims

The first step in a workers-compensation case is the filing of an injury report with the state agency administering the system. The employer's insurance company then processes the claim and, in most cases, reaches an agreement with the employee. In these uncontested cases, the state agency plays only a passive role.

Workers who are dissatisfied with insurance-company offers can file claims with the state workers'-compensation agency. Filing begins a quasi-judicial review process administered by the agency to decide the complaint. Unresolved cases proceed through a series of informal, formal, and review-board hearings. If either party remains unsatisfied, it can appeal to the state courts.

Criticism of the Workers-Compensation System

Many people object to the way the workers-compensation system works. They contend, for example, that delay, confusion, and mistrust have taken the place of a system that is supposed to provide quick and efficient medical treatment and wage replacement on a no-fault basis. The issue ultimately involves workers, employers, and service providers. The result is that many cases wind up in court. Disputed claims take an average of two years to resolve, and workers making those claims are often reduced to poverty before a resolution is reached. And even if a claim is paid, the payment rate may be so low that the injured worker cannot possibly make ends meet. In some states, benefits also stop after a certain amount of time. Employers who are critical of the current workers-compensation system focus on such issues as *cost containment*, the *burden of proof*, and the complexities of *litigation*.

Cost Containment. One of the major criticisms of the system is that costs should be contained. The term *cost containment*, however, is sometimes a euphemism for *fewer benefits*. Employers argue that they must view the problem from the perspective of the bottom line; critics contend that the "human" costs are more important. For example, if the cost-cutting method adopted by a given state involves taking away cost-of-living raises, then injured workers are really being forced to take a cut in real benefits.

Burden of Proof. Another frequent criticism is the charge that claimants have a diminished burden of proof, especially in cases of mental disorder (including stress), cumulative injury, and occupational disease. In cases of partial disability, workers' compensation must pay the costs associated with the injury. Social security disability provisions only apply in certain cases of total disability.

Litigation. The frequency and difficulty of litigation is another criticism voiced by critics of the system. For one thing, U.S. society as a whole is generally more litigious. In addition, it is difficult to categorize some injuries as work-related without a close examination of the facts of the particular case.

Legislation for Occupational Disease

In addition, the workers-compensation system has not dealt adequately with the problem of occupational diseases such as asbestosis and black-lung disease. Coverage has been far less complete than for accidents. For one thing, state reluctance to cover such illnesses is philosophical: Because occupational diseases do not fit into traditional *negligence* doctrines, they appear to be a health-insurance issue rather than a workers-compensation problem. In addition, there are practical considerations. As we saw earlier, assigning responsibility for benefits to any single employer is difficult for many diseases because they are caused by exposure over a prolonged period of time. Finally, the heavy incidence of particular diseases in certain industries may pose a ruinous financial burden for employers engaged in them.

The modern workers-compensation system grew out of a social philosophy which believed that victims of work-related injuries not only deserved medical and financial benefits, but deserved to have them delivered in a dignified fashion. It is now becoming clear that a similar system must be developed for the victims of work-related disease.

COVERAGE. Workers-compensation statutes in a few states have always defined occupational injury to include disease. Other states have followed the precedent set by New York in 1920, when it specified diseases covered by workers' compensation in a schedule. Most states have since given up schedules in favor of general coverage.

Defining "Occupational Disease." General coverage, however, raises the problem of distinguishing between occupational disease and non-job-related disease. The definitions of *occupational disease* adopted by most states contrast sharply with recent, more liberal approaches to defining job-related injuries. States, for example, have stressed that occupational disease must be peculiar to a particular occupation and caused by its special conditions. Some examples are silicosis, radiation diseases, and the loss of hearing due to prolonged exposure to noise.

Job-related stress poses another controversial issue in this area. Stress can lead to a variety of physical ailments, including heart attack, ulcers, and mental disturbances. The YOU DECIDE feature in this chapter illustrates how the courts determine whether an employee's stress-related injury truly is also job-related.

FEDERAL LAWS. Some occupational diseases are so serious or so common that they call for special intervention by the federal government. The first case led to the *Federal Coal Mine Health and Safety Act* of 1969. Among its provisions were monthly cash benefits for coal miners totally disabled because of black-lung disease. In 1972, full medical benefits were added. The goal was to shift the cost of miners' disabilities to the mine operators and coal consumers who benefited from their labor.

Case: The Problem of Asbestos. At present, the courts and Congress are wrestling with the problems posed by massive exposure to asbestos over the past 40 years. Over 20 million people in asbestos, shipbuilding, auto maintenance, and other industries have been exposed and may develop asbestos-related disease. Workers' compensation has provided relatively small benefits to only a few of these workers. Therefore, tens of thousands of workers have filed lawsuits against manufacturers and third parties. Asbestos companies like Johns-Manville have declared bankruptcy to establish a procedure whereby all claimants will have an equal opportunity to obtain recovery; the company has argued that its only other option would be to expend all of its assets paying some people and leave nothing for everyone else. However, long delays and enormous litigation costs have once again proven that the tort system has severe drawbacks for dealing with occupational-injury cases.

Legislative Response. In response to the asbestos problem, Congress considered two bills in 1985 that attempted to provide fast, fair, and efficient com-

YOU DECIDE
Stress and Compensation

The issue of work-related stress has become pressing in recent years. There are many reasons for increased concern including the increasing number of two-wage-earner families who must cope with the everyday pressures of both home and office and the decreased stigma attached to mental problems.

In other types of worker's-compensation claims, the employee must be able to prove that the injury was caused by his or her employment and occurred in the course of that employment. In stress cases, only the causal relationship has to be shown. Even this requirement, however, can be a problem if the stress was caused by a combination of employment and personal factors. Consequently, proving that the stress was totally—or even primarily—work-induced is particularly difficult.

The courts have responded to this dilemma by devising two tests for proving mental injury. The so-called subjective test is met if the employee can prove that he or she "honestly perceived" that a mental injury occurred in the course of employment. The objective test is more strenuous: It examines the type, duration, and intensity of the stress. In some states, the standard is "normal daily" stress; in others, it is stress that is "extraordinary." Unfortu-

nately, differing standards make it impossible for the courts to reach a consensus definition of work-related mental injury.

Consider the facts in Decker v. Oklahoma State University (766 P.2d 1371 [1988]). A college instructor whose duties included teaching five classes in data processing each weekday, attending faculty meetings, and going to graduation exercises became extremely stressed by his job. For approximately three years, he had received consistently good performance reviews. At that point, he was asked by a fellow employee to work overtime, without compensation, to help develop a new data-processing curriculum. It was unclear whether the employee had jurisdiction to make this request. When the instructor refused to perform the additional work, his relationship with his fellow employee became strained, and he began to suffer from anxiety and insomnia. An unsatisfactory job-performance evaluation followed, making him even more upset. Eventually, the instructor suffered a heart attack while he was in his office.

Should the instructor be permitted to get worker's compensation? Was his injury work-related? For further discussion, see p. 535.

pensation for the victims of occupational disease. Although both the Asbestos Workers' Recovery Act (H. R. 1626) and the Occupational Disease Compensation Act (H. R. 3090) died in Congress, they showed a possible way out of a difficult problem.

The proposed legislation followed the precedents set by other workers-compensation schemes in awarding benefits on a no-fault basis and in shifting much of the cost to employers (although asbestos manufacturers and suppliers would also have contributed). The Asbestos Workers' Recovery Act essentially

The Spectrum of Industrial Disease Warehouse, United Carbon Company, Liberal, Kansas, 1956. It is estimated that 4000 coal miners die each year from the disease known as *black lung*, which is generated by coal dust. The disease has been directly responsible for well over 100,000 deaths, and the number of disabled has reached at least another 265,000. According to the Center for Disease Control, approximately 19 million U.S. workers have been exposed to dangerous toxic substances in the workplace over the last 20 years alone. Respiratory diseases run the spectrum from black lung to brown lung (textile-fiber dust) and red lung (iron dust) to white lung (asbestos fibers), and the National Institute of Environmental Health Services estimates that 40 percent of all cancers in the U.S. result from workplace exposure to hazardous substances. As for coal mines, another 100,000 miners have been killed *in* the mines since 1900. In 1968, for example, an explosion at a West Virginia mine killed 78 miners—one of a number of incidents that led to the passage of the Coal Mine Safety Act in 1969.

provided rules to decide which of the existing workers-compensation laws should control in each case and then provided for a supplemental benefit in addition to the regular workers-compensation remedy.

The second bill provided for special, extremely generous benefits for the injured while preserving their right to sue third parties. This proposal also set up a Surgeon General's Risk Assessment panel to designate additional toxic substances to be covered by the law and to provide needed medical guidance to compensation administrators.

■ Concept Check 14-2   Workers' Compensation

- What are the chief differences between *workers-compensation laws* and the tort laws in which they originate?
- Explain the major conditions that must be demonstrated for coverage under most workers-compensation laws.
- Define and distinguish between the *actual-risk* and *potential-risk tests* for workers-compensation coverage.
- Describe the five *benefit categories* under workers-compensation statutes.
- Explain the criteria by which stress qualifies as an *occupational disease*.

■ INCOME-MAINTENANCE PROGRAMS

The Three-Tiered System

For most Americans, earnings from regular work are their major source of income. When they retire and that income stops, they may be hard-pressed financially. There are thus a variety of programs, both public and private, designed to provide an income for the retired worker. According to a model developed by Alicia Munnell, the United States has a three-tiered system of retirement-income maintenance.[4] First, there are *welfare programs* designed to provide a minimum guaranteed income to the elderly who are in need. Second, there is a *public program* (*Social Security*) that provides wage-related retirement benefits from mandatory employer and employee contributions. Third, there are *private retirement plans*, such as company pensions and individual savings plans, which are regulated and promoted by public policies. However, because there is little coordination between these programs, they overlap and may even work at cross-purposes. Here we shall discuss the second and third tiers of the system, both of which are directly supported by business.

Social Security and Other Public Retirement Programs

The **Social Security Act** of 1935 was a direct response to the hardships of the Depression and the reality that even the most responsible and hard-working individuals can be ruined by forces beyond their control. It compromised conservative American traditions of self-reliance with radical ideas about government intervention in social problems. The law built on the accepted practices of federal-state cooperation and of pooling individual risks for insurance purposes

Social Security Act 1935 federal law providing social-insurance benefits to individuals under eleven different programs

---

[4] A. H. Munnell, *The Future of Social Security* (Brookings Institution, 1977), p. 5.

to accomplish new and different ends. It was shaped, in part, by the need to survive the constitutional review of a conservative Supreme Court that was suspicious of federal provision of social services.

SOCIAL SECURITY: BENEFITS AND BENEFICIARIES. The Social Security Act includes eleven different programs, the largest of which is the **Old Age, Survivors, Disability, and Hospital Insurance Program (OASDHI)**. Commonly called "Social Security," this program is the keystone in a broad range of public-benefits and income-assistance programs. We will examine Social Security as a *social insurance program*, but other programs may be characterized as *cash-income assistance* (for example, Aid to Families with Dependent Children) or *in-kind assistance* (Medicaid and food stamps).

Table 14-2 provides a breakdown of the estimated number of U.S. workers who are covered under Social Security and other public-benefit or "social-insurance" plans. From 1960 through the mid-1980s, the number of workers covered under such plans increased by about 75 percent; in the same period, the workforce itself grew by about 60 percent. By 1985, approximately 117 million people—over 90 percent of the total workforce—was covered by public benefit and retirement plans.

By 1986, almost 23 million retired workers were receiving Social Security benefits, which accounted for 42 percent of all income to persons over 65.[5] The average monthly benefit to retired individuals was $488 and $831 for retired couples. Table 14-3 shows federal expenditures for Social Security benefits, by

TABLE 14-2	*Workers Covered under Public-Benefits Programs, 1960–1985 (in millions)*				
EMPLOYMENT AND COVERAGE STATUS	**1960**	**1970**	**1975**	**1980**	**1985**
Total labor force	73.1	86.2	96.2	109.1	117.5
Paid civilian population	64.6	77.6	86.0	98.9	107.7
Unpaid family workers	1.4	.8	.7	.6	.4
Unemployed	4.5	2.6	7.3	7.4	7.7
Armed Forces	2.5	3.4	2.2	2.1	1.7
Civilian population covered by					
Public retirement programs	60.9	75.3	83.7	96.4	106.9
OASDHI	55.4	69.2	77.0	89.3	99.7
Unemployment insurance	43.7	55.8	69.7	87.2	98.2
Workers' compensation	44.6	59.0	68.6	79.1	87.0
Temporary disability insurance	11.3	14.6	15.7	18.4	19.8

Source: Adapted from Judah Matras, *Dependency, Obligations, and Entitlements* (Englewood Cliffs, NJ: Prentice Hall, 1990). Data from U.S. Bureau of Labor Statistics and U.S. Bureau of the Census, *Statistical Abstract of the United States 1988* (Washington, DC: Government Printing Office, 1987).

---

[5] Andrew Achenbaum, *Social Security: Visions and Revisions* (Cambridge Univ. Press, 1986), p. 4.

TABLE 14-3	Social Security Benefits Payments, 1970–1986 (in millions of dollars)				

TYPE OF BENEFICIARY	1970	1975	1980	1985	1986
	Benefit Payments During Year				
Total amount	**31,863**	**66,923**	**120,472**	**186,195**	**196,692**
Monthly benefits	31,570	66,586	120,118	185,988	196,489
Retired workers	18,437	38,078	70,359	116,823	123,584
Disabled workers	2,448	6,908	12,817	16,483	17,409
Wives and husbands	2,194	4,104	7,043	11,061	11,700
Children	3,517	6,643	10,514	10,710	10,899
Under age 18	2,701	4,823	7,374	8,502	8,687
Disabled children	250	537	1,048	1,760	1,961
Students	566	1,283	2,093	447	251
Of retired workers	303	634	1,142	1,140	1,166
Of deceased workers	2,760	4,888	7,389	7,762	7,843
Of disabled workers	454	1,121	1,982	1,809	1,890
Widowed mothers	574	1,009	1,572	1,474	1,457
Widows and widowers	4,055	9,596	17,638	29,330	31,345
Parents	39	50	55	51	48
Special benefits	306	198	119	57	47
Lump sum	294	337	355	207	203

Sources: Adapted from Matras, *Dependency, Obligations, and Entitlements*. Data from Social Security Administration, *Annual Statistical Supplement to the Social Security Bulletin* (Washington, DC: U.S. Department of Health and Human Services, 1987); U.S. Bureau of the Census, *Statistical Abstract of the United States 1988* (Washington, DC: Government Printing Office, 1987).

type of beneficiary, between 1970 and 1986. As you can see, benefit payments rose from almost $32 billion in 1970 to over $196 billion in 1986.[6]

Beginning in 1965, several new programs, including the Permanent Food Stamp Act and the Social Security Amendment that created Medicare and Medicaid, were enacted. The year 1965 thus marks a clear dividing line between moderate and higher growth rates in benefits payments. Figure 14-1 shows the growth in selected programs from 1970 to 1980. The food-stamp program, for example, increased by 490 percent during the decade. Compared to a 6.6-percent increase between 1961 and 1965, payments to individuals increased at a rate of 15.3 percent between 1966 and 1979.[7]

SOCIAL SECURITY COVERAGE. Initially, Social Security covered only retiring workers, but a 1939 amendment extended coverage to the family members of work-

---

[6] Judah Matras, *Dependency, Obligations, and Entitlements* (Englewood Cliffs, NJ: Prentice Hall, 1990), pp. 266-73.

[7] Michael E. Levy, "Federal Budget Policies of the 1970s: Some Lessons for the 1980s," *Stabilization Policies* (St. Louis, MO: Washington Univ. Center for the Study of American Business, 1980), pp. 169-70.

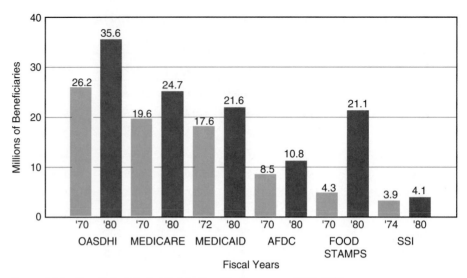

FIGURE 14-1 Growth in Selected Public-Benefits Programs, 1970–1980 *Sources*: L. Douglas Lee, "The Deficit Dilemma—and Its Solution," *The Journal Institute for Socioeconomic Studies*, 8 (Spring 1983). Data from Social Security Administration, *Annual Statistical Supplement to the Social Security Bulletin* (Washington, DC: U.S. Department of Health and Human Services, 1982).

ers who had died. Disability insurance was added in 1954 and medical insurance in 1965. Today, when workers retire, die, or become disabled, they or their families may receive Social Security benefits to replace lost income and to help pay for medical expenses. As the following case illustrates, however, the Social Security administration establishes guidelines for awarding benefits.

BOWEN v. YUCKERT
United States Supreme Court, 96 L.Ed. 2d 119 (1987)

Janet Yuckert, a travel agent, was denied Social Security benefits for alleged vertigo, headaches, and flat feet by the Washington Department of Health and Social Services. The district court affirmed the denial of these benefits because Yuckert had not passed a 5-step test determining the existence of a disability enacted by the Secretary of Health and Human Services under authority of the Social Security Act. Specifically, she had failed to show the second step, which requires a medically severe impairment. The U.S. Court of Appeals, construing the Social Security Act as not authorizing the Secretary to condition benefits on severe impairment, reversed on the basis that the Secretary had exceeded his authority under the SSA in so doing. The U.S. Supreme Court now reviews the Court of Appeals' interpretation of the SSA.

Justice Powell delivered the opinion of the Court.

Title II of the Social Security Act (Act) provides for the payment of insurance benefits to persons who have contributed to the program and who suffer from a physical or mental disability. Title XVI of the Act provides for the payment of disability benefits to indigent persons under the Supplemental Security Income (SSI) program. Both titles of the Act define "disability" as the "inability to engage in any substantial gainful activity by reason of any medically determinable physical or mental impairment which can be expected to result in death or which has lasted or can be expected to last for a continuous period of not less than 12 months. . . ." The Act further provides that an individual:

> shall be determined to be under a disability only if his physical or mental impairment or impairments are of such severity that he is not only unable to do his previous work but cannot, considering his age, education, and work experience, engage in any other kind of substantial gainful work which exists in the national economy, regardless of whether such work exists in the immediate area in which he lives, or whether a specific job vacancy exists for him, or whether he would be hired if he applied for work.

The Secretary has established a five-step sequential evaluation process for determining whether a person is disabled. 416.920 (1986). Step one determines whether the claimant is engaged in "substantial gainful activity." If he is, disability benefits are denied. If he is not, the decisionmaker proceeds to step two, that determines whether the claimant has a medically severe impairment or combination of impairments. That determination is governed by the "severity regulation" at issue in this case. The severity regulation provides:

> If you do not have any impairment or combination of impairments which significantly limits your physical or mental ability to do basic work activities, we will find that you do not have a severe impairment and are, therefore, not disabled. We will not consider your age, education, and work experience.

The ability to do basic work activities is defined as "the abilities and aptitudes necessary to do most jobs." Such abilities and aptitudes include "[p]hysical functions such as walking, standing, sitting, lifting, pushing, pulling, reaching, carrying, or handling"; "[c]apacities for seeing, hearing, and speaking"; "[u]nderstanding, carrying out, and remembering simple instructions"; "[u]se of judgment"; "[r]esponding appropriately to supervision, coworkers, and usual work situations"; and "[d]ealing with changes in a routine work setting."

If the claimant does not have a severe impairment or combination of impairments, the disability claim is denied. . . .

. . . .

. . . The severity regulation requires the claimant to show that he has an "impairment or combination of impairments which significantly limits" "the abilities and aptitudes necessary to do most jobs." On its face, the regulation is not inconsistent with the statutory definition of disability. The Act "defines 'disability' in terms of the effect a physical or mental impairment has on a person's ability to function in the workplace." The regulation adopts precisely this functional approach to determining the effects of medical impairments.

. . . .

. . . If a claimant is unable to show that he has a medically severe impairment, he is not eligible for disability benefits. In such a case, there is no reason for the Secretary to consider the claimant's age, education, and work experience.

The legislative history reinforces this understanding of the statutory language. Section 423(d)(2)(A) was intended to "reemphasize the predominant importance of medical factors in the disability determination." The 1967 amendments left undisturbed the longstanding regulatory provision that "medical considerations alone may justify a finding that the individual is not under a disability." . . .

. . . .

We have recognized that other aspects of the Secretary's sequential evaluation process contribute to the uniformity and efficiency of disability determinations. The need for such an evaluation process is particularly acute because the Secretary decides more than 2 million claims for disability benefits each year, of which more than 200,000 are reviewed by administrative law judges. The severity regulation increases the efficiency and reliability of the evaluation process by identifying at an early stage those claimants whose medical impairments are so slight that it is unlikely they would be found to be disabled even if their age, education, and experience were taken into account. . . .

. . . .

The judgment of the Court of Appeals for the Ninth Circuit is reversed. The case is remanded for the Court of Appeals to consider whether the agency's decision is supported by substantial evidence.

Case Questions:

1. What is the purpose of a requirement that impairment be severe as a precondition to receiving benefits?

2. Why does the Supreme Court find that the Secretary did not exceed his authority under the SSA?

BENEFIT STRUCTURE. Social Security benefits are not automatic: Beneficiaries must establish their eligibility after retirement, death, or disability. To be eligible, retirees first must have worked in a covered job for at least ten years—that is, they must have contributed to Social Security payroll taxes for a minimum of nine years. Second, retirees must be at least 62 years old to draw any benefits and at least 65 to draw full benefits. By the year 2000, full benefits will not be available until age 67. Workers who delay drawing Social Security benefits beyond age 65 receive an increased benefit. Third, if retirees earn more than a specified amount of money, their benefits are reduced.

Of course, Social Security benefits are not lavish. The goal of the program from the start has been only to provide a basic minimum of financial support. The assumption was that retirees would supplement social security with other sources of income. The amount of benefits awarded to individuals depends on average monthly earnings while working. A special minimum-benefit plan has also been established for low-wage earners. Dependents receive about half as much as retired workers. Since 1975, because Social Security benefits have been tied to the government consumer price index, they are not eroded by inflation. Further, for people with annual incomes over $25,000, half of Social Security benefits are federally taxable.

FUNDING THE PROGRAM. Social Security is financed by a payroll tax (the Federal Insurance Contributions Act [FICA]) split equally between employers and employees. When the bill was first enacted, this tax was set at 1 percent each for employer and employee, payable on the first $3,000 of a worker's annual earnings. In 1988, the tax was raised to 7.51 percent on the first $43,800 in earnings, and it is scheduled to go on rising.

Private Pensions: ERISA

There has been a rapid growth in private pensions since World War II. By 1974, 44 percent of the labor force was covered, workers and employers were contributing some $25 billion to the funds, and 6.4 million retirees and survivors were drawing benefits.[8] Congressional investigations, however, found that many private pension plans were underfunded and mismanaged and unfairly deprived employees of benefits. In response, Congress in 1974 passed the **Employee Retirement Income Security Act (ERISA)** to regulate private pension plans. Although the goals remain the same, these provisions were modified by the Tax Reform Act of 1986. The 1986 changes generally improve coverage and benefits for the average worker while limiting benefits for executives.

Vesting and Portability. ERISA also set minimum *vesting* and *portability* standards so that more employees could share in company pension benefits. **Vesting** refers to an employee's right to participate in a plan and to receive the money contributed to it by the company. Many plans require employees to work a minimum number of years in order to have a right to the pension—that is, to be *vested*.

Portability refers to employees' rights to take pensions with them as they change employers. ERISA permits, but does not require, employers to allow vested employees to transfer their assets in the company pension fund when they leave the company.

Pension-Plan Management. ERISA also regulates the financial management of company pension plans. It requires firms to set aside money for pensions in special funds that are either invested or used to purchase annuities. It has also established fiduciary responsibilities for pension-fund administrators to safeguard this money. According to the "prudent-man" rule, fiduciaries must make rational financial decisions consistent with the thinking of any prudent person. They are legally responsible for negligence and are prohibited from engaging in certain kinds of transactions.

The Pension Guaranty Corporation. To further protect employee pension rights, ERISA established the Pension Benefit Guaranty Corporation. This institution is funded by company contributions and insures pensions paid to vested employees in case an employer goes bankrupt. ERISA's reporting and disclosure requirements also ensure that employees know more about their pension rights.

Finally, because company pension plans are not available to all workers,

Employee Retirement Income Security Act (ERISA) 1974 federal law that regulates private pension plans

vesting *ERISA* provision that employees have the right to participate in pension plans and receive the money contributed to it by their employers

portability *ERISA* provision that employees have the right to take their pensions with them when they change employers

---

[8] Munnell, note 3 *supra* at p. 19.

ERISA also made provisions for individuals to set aside money for their retirement. Individual Retirement Accounts and Keough plans actually encourage workers to save for retirement by offering them immediate tax advantages.

Case: ERISA and Employer Liability. Ever since ERISA became law, important questions have been raised about employer liability. Employees won a major victory in the following case, in which the court held that the employer intentionally violated ERISA by firing employees before they became eligible for their pensions. The employer had maintained a "computerized liability avoidance program" to facilitate the firings.

McLENDON v. CONTINENTAL GROUP, INC.
749 F. Supp. 582 (D.N.J. 1989)

Plaintiffs claim that the Continental Group, Inc., implemented a nation-wide plan to avoid pension liabilities. Defendants faced a declining market for their product and recognized that they faced substantial layoffs and a potentially huge unfunded pension liability. In order to avoid this liability they developed a computer program to identify employees who had not yet qualified for pensions and who were therefore targeted for dismissal. The plan was shrouded in secrecy and executed company-wide at the direction of high level corporate management. The district court was asked to decide whether this scheme violated section 510 of ERISA.

SAROKIN, District Judge.

This is an action brought pursuant to Section 510 of the Employee Retirement Income Security Act of 1974 (ERISA), 29 U.S.C. § 1140 (1982). Section 510 provides, in pertinent part:

It shall be unlawful for any person to discharge, fine, suspend, expel, discipline, or discriminate against a participant or beneficiary for exercising any right to which he is entitled under the provisions of an employee benefit plan, . . . or for the purpose of interfering with the attainment of any right to which such participant may become entitled under the plan. . . .

Plaintiffs claim that defendants, through the implementation of a nation-wide scheme to avoid pension liabilities, prevented them from obtaining benefits under the pension plan in violation of § 510.

. . .

The . . . plan was intended to save hundreds of millions of dollars in unfunded pension liabilities. The evidence of the plan, its secrecy, and its execution comes from the files of the defendants themselves. The documents are more than a smoking gun; they are a fusillade.

The evidence in support of plaintiffs' claims has been known to and possessed by the defendants since the inception of this case. Nonetheless, defendants have denied the existence of the plan and its implementation. For a corporation of this magnitude to engage in a complex, secret and deliberate scheme to deny its workers

bargained-for pension benefits raises questions of corporate morality, ethics and decency which far transcend the factual and legal issues posed by this matter.

. . .

The documents which come from Continental's own files are replete with evidence not only of the creation and existence of Liability Avoidance Program but of its implementation throughout the company. The court in rendering its opinion in this matter, will make no effort to review the testimony of each and every witness or set forth each and every document which clearly supports the existence and operation of this program designed to deprive Continental employees of attaining the requirements necessary to entitle them to Magic Number pensions. Where the testimony of defendants' witnesses has purported to contradict the clear documentary evidence, the court specifically finds that the documents created at the time accurately reflect what transpired and clearly are more credible than the testimony of the witnesses many years after the events. No contemporaneous document has been produced by defendants which directly challenges either the existence, propriety, or implementation of the Liability Avoidance Program.

Liability avoidance was calculated by reference to the Bell System referred to above, which provided Continental with information as to who should be laid off and who should be kept on layoff in order to avoid the vesting of such liabilities. From the outset, this plan was devised and operated in secrecy. Indeed, the name Bell is a reverse acronym standing for "Lowest Level of Employee Benefits" or "Let's Limit Employee Benefits."

The fundamental principles of liability avoidance are set forth in the Bell User Manual (PX 754 at 185271) as follows:

Liability Avoidance

There are two fundamental principles contained in the concept referred to as avoidance. First, we must be very careful that our plans make every attempt to avoid, insofar as practicable, triggering liabilities already vested in 70–75 qualified employees. Secondly, we must, wherever appropriate, shrink and cap our work forces in order to prevent currently inexpensive D.V.B.'s (Deferred Vested Benefit) from migrating into the very expensive 70–75 category. (PX 754 at 185271)

Pursuant to the plan, the goal of avoiding these unfunded liabilities was a determinative factor, and usually the prime factor, in deciding what plants to close or continue open, what work to accept or reject, where that work was to be performed, what jobs should or should not be combined, and who should and who should not be retained or laid off. The proof in support of the plan and its implementation is so overwhelming that if plaintiffs were required to meet a beyond a reasonable doubt standard, they could have done so. Indeed, the court questions the good faith of Continental throughout this litigation in denying even the existence of the plan.

. . .

The court has found that Continental violated ERISA and set upon a deliberate course of conduct aimed at depriving employees of eligibility for bargained-for pensions. The evidence in support of that conclusion comes solely from the files of Continental. Therefore, defendants, unlike in most cases, began the defense of this action having in their possession, indeed, in their sole possession, all of the necessary facts upon which liability has now been predicated. In the face of this overwhelming and unequivocal documentary evidence, Continental chose to deny the existence of the program, deny its implementation *anywhere*, deny its effect upon *any* employee, and finally contend that if the program existed, and if it was implemented, *no* employees were injured thereby.

No one can fault any litigant for engaging in the defense of a claim, particularly one of this magnitude involving hundreds of millions of dollars, if there is a substantial basis to do so and where *bona fide* factual disputes exist. But in this case, despite the overwhelming evidence against them, evidence which has been in their possession since the commencement of this suit and certainly before, defendants have chosen to extend these proceedings, resist discovery, initiate appeals, and in general lengthen the proceeding and increase plaintiffs' expenses. There are times when a litigant must admit its guilt and make amends, rather than defend to the death the indefensible.

[But] Continental has indicated its intention to demand hearings as to each of the remaining plants in order to establish that either decisions for layoffs were made in each absent the intent to avoid liability, or if such was the intent and result, that said employees would have sustained the same loss in any event because of external economic conditions.

Accordingly, the court will appoint a special master for the specific purpose of assisting the parties in the settlement of the remaining issues in this matter and to expedite a determination of the amounts due to class members and the prompt payment of those amounts; or, absent a settlement, recommending a procedure to expedite the determination of those remaining issues and claims.

Case Questions

1. How did Continental Group, Inc. attempt to avoid paying ERISA benefits?
2. What did Continental mean by "liability avoidance"?

Unemployment Compensation

unemployment compensation System established by the 1935 *Social Security Act* to provide monetary benefits to people who are temporarily out of work

Today's nationwide system of **unemployment compensation** is yet another product of the Depression. Part of the Social Security Act of 1935 established a federal-state system to provide relief to people who normally hold steady jobs but are temporarily out of work. This system now covers about 97 percent of all wage and salary jobs. Jobs in agriculture and domestic household service are notable exceptions. Some other workers, such as railroad and federal government employees, have separate programs.

FUNDING. Unemployment benefits are funded in part by a federal tax on employers. The tax rate is 6.4 percent on the first $7,000 of each worker's wages, but up to 5.4 percent is offset by tax credits. This federal money pays for the administration of the program and part of the benefits paid out. The federal government also maintains a loan fund from which states can borrow to meet monthly compensation costs. Each state also collects unemployment taxes from employers. These taxes generally amount to about 1.3 percent of total wages. The greater the number of employees terminated, the more an employer must pay.

KEEP OFF THE GRASS

COXEY

STILL ASKS CONGRESS

... TO ...

EMANCIPATE LABOR.

Give Work to the Unemployed.

Improve the Highways.

Reduce Hours of Toil.

Put Children in School, not in Factories.

Issue Legal Tender Money, not Interest Bearing Bonds.

THE PEOPLE'S PARTY

Will elect a Congress to represent the People and not Wall Street.

Copyright 1894, by HENRY VINCENT.

Coxey's Army In the 30 years following the Civil War, some $400 million in federal currency ("greenbacks") issued during the war remained in circulation. That amount, however, remained fixed by law and was insufficient to fund an expanding economy. Most advocates of "soft money" argued that the situation could be eased if the banking system were reformed and allowed to increase its issue of money. One soft-money group, the so-called *Greenbackers,* identified the problem as a shortage of government-issued paper currency. In 1894, in the wake of a depression that hit the country in the spring of 1893, an ex-Greenbacker activist named Jacob S. Coxey proposed a federal-works program for the jobless to be funded by an issue of $500 million in paper money. To dramatize his scheme, Coxey organized a march of the unemployed on Washington. When "Coxey's Army" (about 400 threadbare men) arrived in Washington, they were arrested for trampling on the Capitol grass.

Because they are set by the states, the amount and duration of unemployment benefits vary widely. Generally speaking, benefits cover about half the worker's former weekly wage, within set minimums and maximums. The benefits themselves are charged against each recipient's ex-employer.

ELIGIBILITY. To be eligible for benefits, candidates must have left their jobs voluntarily, been terminated for gross misconduct, or become unemployed as a result of a labor dispute. In addition, the length of time that they have worked and their prior earnings must be greater than the minimum required. Once on the rolls, recipients must actively seek work and not refuse suitable employment. In the following case, the plaintiff was denied unemployment compensation because he refused a temporary job that would have required him to work on Sunday.

FRAZEE v. ILLINOIS DEPARTMENT OF EMPLOYMENT SECURITY et al.
United States Supreme Court, 489 U.S. 829 (1988)

Frazee refused a temporary retail position offered to him by Kelly Services because the job would have required him to work on Sunday, thus violating his personal religious beliefs. He applied for unemployment compensation but was denied benefits. The denial was affirmed by an administrative review board, the Illinois Circuit Court, and the State Appellate Court. Each court said the denial was on the grounds that his refusal to work was not based on the tenets of an established religion.

Justice White delivered the opinion of the Court.

. . .

We have had more than one occasion before today to consider denials of unemployment compensation benefits to those who have refused work on the basis of their religious beliefs. In *Sherbert* v. *Verner, supra,* at 410, the Court held that a State could not "constitutionally apply the eligibility provisions [of its unemployment-compensation program] so as to constrain a worker to abandon his religious convictions respecting the day of rest." *Thomas* v. *Review Bd. of Indiana Employment Security Div.,* supra, also held that the State's refusal to award unemployment compensation benefits to one who terminated his job because his religious beliefs forbade participation in the production of armaments violated the First Amendment right to free exercise. Just two years ago, in *Hobbie* v. *Unemployment Appeals Comm'n of Florida, supra,* Florida's denial of unemployment compensation benefits to an employee discharged for her refusal to work on her Sabbath because of religious convictions adopted subsequent to employment was also declared to be a violation of the Free Exercise Clause. In each of these cases, the appellant was "forced to choose between fidelity to religious belief and . . . employment," *id.,* at

144, and we found "the forfeiture of unemployment benefits for choosing the former over the latter brings unlawful coercion to bear on the employee's choice," *ibid.* In each of these cases, we concluded that the denial of unemployment compensation benefits violated the Free Exercise Clause of the First Amendment of the Constitution, as applied to the States through the Fourteenth Amendment.

It is true, as the Illinois court noted, that each of the claimants in those cases was a member of a particular religious sect, but none of those decisions turned on that consideration or on any tenet of the sect involved that forbade the work the claimant refused to perform. Our judgments in those cases rested on the fact that each of the claimants had a sincere belief that religion required him or her to refrain from the work in question. Never did we suggest that unless a claimant belongs to a sect that forbids what his job requires, his belief, however sincere, must be deemed a purely personal preference rather than a religious belief. Indeed, in *Thomas,* there was disagreement among sect members as to whether their religion made it sinful to work in an armaments factory; but we considered this to be an irrelevant issue and hence rejected the State's submission that unless the religion involved formally forbade work on armaments, Thomas' belief did not qualify as a religious belief. Because Thomas unquestionably had a sincere belief that his religion prevented him from doing such work, he was entitled to invoke the protection of the Free Exercise Clause.

There is no doubt that "[o]nly beliefs rooted in religion are protected by the Free Exercise Clause," *Thomas, supra,* at 713. Purely secular views do not suffice. *United States* v. *Seeger,* 380 U.S. 163 (1965); *Wisconsin* v. *Yoder,* 406 U.S. 205, 215-216 (1972). Nor do we underestimate the difficulty of distinguishing between religious and secular convictions and in determining whether a professed belief is sincerely held. States are clearly entitled to assure themselves that there is an ample predicate for invoking the free Exercise Clause. We do not face problems about sincerity or about the religious nature of Frazee's convictions, however. The courts below did not question his sincerity, and the State concedes it. Tr. of Oral Arg. 35. Furthermore, the Board of Review characterized Frazee's views as "religious convictions," App. 18, and the Illinois Appellate Court referred to his refusal to work on Sunday as based on a "personal professed religious belief," 159 Ill. App. 3d, at 475, 512 N.E. 2d, at 790. . . .

Frazee asserted that he was a Christian, but did not claim to be a member of a particular Christian sect. It is also true that there are assorted Christian denominations that do not profess to be compelled by their religion to refuse Sunday work, but this does not diminish Frazee's protection flowing from the Free Exercise Clause. *Thomas* settled that much. Undoubtedly, membership in an organized religious denomination, especially one with a specific tenet forbidding members to work on Sunday, would simplify the problem of identifying sincerely held religious beliefs, but we reject the notion that to claim the protection of the Free Exercise Clause, one must be responding to the commands of a particular religious organization. Here, Frazee's refusal was based on a sincerely held religious belief. Under our cases, he was entitled to invoke First Amendment protection. . . .

The State does not appear to defend this aspect of the decision below. In its brief and at oral argument, the State conceded that the Free Exercise Clause does not demand adherence to a tenet or dogma of an established religious sect. Instead, the State proposes its own test for identifying a "religious" belief, asserts that Frazee has not met such a test, and asks that we affirm on this basis. We decline to address this submission; for as the case comes to us, Frazee's conviction was recognized as religious but found to be inadequate because it was not claimed to represent a tenet of a religious organization of which he was a member. That ground for decision was clearly erroneous.

The State offers no justification for the burden that the denial of benefits places on Frazee's right to exercise his religion. . . .

As was the case in *Thomas* where there was "no evidence in the record to indicate that the number of people who find themselves in the predicament of choosing between benefits and religious beliefs is large enough to create 'widespread unemployment,' or even to seriously affect unemployment," 450 U.S., at 719, there is nothing before us in this case to suggest that Sunday shopping, or Sunday sporting, for that matter, will grind to a halt as a result of our decision today. And, as we have said in the past, there may exist state interests sufficiently compelling to override a legitimate claim to the free exercise of religion. No such interest has been presented here.

The judgment of the Appellate Court of Illinois for the Third District is therefore reversed, and the case is remanded for further proceedings not inconsistent with this opinion.

It is so ordered.

Case Questions

1. Does the Free Exercise of Religion Clause require a person to be part of a recognized religion or religious sect?
2. Are secular as well as religious beliefs protected by the Free Exercise Clause of the Constitution?

Because of limits on both eligibility and the duration of benefits, unemployment compensation helps only about one-third of the unemployed during periods of high employment and about one-half during recessions. According to a 1970 federal regulation, the duration of benefits must be extended by 50 percent—up to a 39-week maximum—during periods of high unemployment in a given state. Even when unemployed workers qualify for compensation, the amount of the benefits may be inadequate to support themselves and their dependents.

■ *Concept Check 14-3   Income-Maintenance Programs*

- Describe the *three-tiered system* of retirement-income maintenance in the United States.
- What are the primary purposes of *ERISA laws*?
- Define *vesting* and *portability* as employee rights under ERISA laws.

■ THE OCCUPATIONAL SAFETY AND HEALTH ACT

Occupational Safety and Health Act (OSHA) 1970 federal law requiring employers to provide safe workplaces free from known occupational hazards

During the 1960s, public attention began to be drawn more forcefully to the lack of safety in the workplace. There were 14,500 workers dying annually in industrial accidents and 100,000 dying annually from occupational diseases. In response, Congress passed the **Occupational Safety and Health Act (OSHA)** of 1970 "to assure so far as possible every working man and woman in the nation safe and healthful working conditions and to preserve our human resources." The law required employers to provide safe workplaces free from known occupational hazards and established the government apparatus needed to promulgate and enforce health and safety standards. Earlier workers-compensation laws had made financial provisions for the injured but were not designed to prevent accidents.

Safety in the Workplace

OSHA's goal is to reduce injuries and illness in the workplace. It is difficult, however, to determine how well OSHA has achieved that goal. Available statistics are both inconsistent and incomplete. For example, the National Institute for Occupational Safety and Health (NIOSH) has estimated that employers have reported only about half the on-the-job deaths that have actually occurred. In addition, there is no way to judge what current injury and illness rates would be if the law had never been passed. Because its standards currently cover only about one-quarter of workplace injuries, OSHA's impact must certainly be limited. However, the rate of workplace injuries and illnesses reported by the Bureau of Labor Statistics does show a drop during most of OSHA's history.

Cost-effectiveness studies of OSHA's operations are also inconclusive. They depend on controversial estimates of such factors as the economic benefits of the prevention of deaths and injuries, the rate of creation of new jobs, decreases in lost work time, and increased productivity. Business critics of OSHA have claimed that as much as one-third of compliance expenditures may be wasted.

Determining Risk

In a landmark 1980 decision (excerpted below), the Supreme Court raised the question of when government intervention and regulation are appropriate and when problems are better left to private resolution. Specifically, the Court challenged the way in which OSHA and other federal agencies set health and safety standards. OSHA policy had been to eliminate *all* health risks by setting standards that made the workplace *absolutely* free from dangers. However, in overturning an OSHA exposure limit to benzene, a toxic liquid used in making varnishes and dyes, the Supreme Court ruled that some risks were so small that they were acceptable: OSHA could regulate only when a hazard posed a *significant* health risk to workers. If a significant risk exists, however, the agency can demand compliance regardless of cost.

INDUSTRIAL UNION DEPARTMENT, AFL-CIO v. AMERICAN PETROLEUM INSTITUTE

United States Supreme Court, 448 U.S. 607 (1980)

In 1978, the Secretary of Labor, acting pursuant to the Occupational Safety and Health Act (OSHA), set new limits on worker exposure to benzene after some evidence revealed that the chemical could cause cancer. The new policy also required employers to invest substantial sums to protect employees from this suspected carcinogen. The American Petroleum Institute brought an action charging that the Secretary's actions had exceeded his authority.

Mr. Justice Stevens announced the judgment of the Court and delivered an opinion.

The Occupational Safety and Health Act of 1970 (Act), was enacted for the purpose of ensuring safe and healthful working conditions for every working man and woman in the Nation. This litigation concerns a standard promulgated by the Secretary of Labor to regulate occupational exposure to benzene, a substance which has been shown to cause cancer at high exposure levels. The principal question is whether such a showing is a sufficient basis for a standard that places the most stringent limitation on exposure to benzene that is technologically and economically possible.

The Act delegates broad authority to the Secretary to promulgate different kinds of standards. The basic definition of an "occupational safety and health standard" is found in § 3(8), which provides:

The term "occupational safety and health standard" means a standard which requires conditions, or the adoption or use of one or more practices, means, methods, operations, or processes, reasonably necessary or appropriate to provide safe or healthful employment and places of employment.

Where toxic materials or harmful physical agents are concerned, a standard must also comply with § 6 (b)(5), which provides:

The Secretary, in promulgating standards dealing with toxic materials or harmful physical agents under this subsection, shall set the standard which most adequately assures, to the extent feasible, on the basis of the best available evidence, that no employee will suffer material impairment of health or functional capacity even if such employee has regular exposure to the hazard dealt with by such standard for the period of his working life. Development of standards under this subsection shall be based upon research, demonstrations, experiments, and such other information as may be appropriate. In addition to the attainment of the highest degree of health and safety protection for the employee, other considerations shall be the latest available scientific data in the field,

the feasibility of the standards, and experience gained under this and other health and safety laws.

Whether the toxic material to be regulated is a carcinogen, the Secretary has taken the position that no safe exposure level can be determined and that § 6(b)(5) requires him to set an exposure limit at the lowest technologically feasible level that will not impair the viability of the industries regulated. In this case, after having determined that there is a causal connection between benzene and leukemia (a cancer of the white blood cells), the Secretary set an exposure limit on airborne concentrations of benzene of one part benzene per million parts of air (1 ppm), regulated dermal and eye contact with solutions containing benzene, and imposed complex monitoring and medical testing requirements on employers whose workplaces contain 0.5 ppm or more of benzene.

On pre-enforcement review pursuant to 29 U.S.C. § 655 (f), the United States Court of Appeals for the Fifth Circuit held the regulation invalid. The court concluded that the Occupational Safety and Health Administration (OSHA) had exceeded its standard-setting authority because it had not shown that the new benzene exposure limit was "reasonably necessary or appropriate to provide safe or healthful employment" as required by § 3(8), and because § 6 (b)(5) does "not give OSHA the unbridled discretion to adopt standards designed to create absolutely risk-free workplaces regardless of costs." . . .

I

. . . .

Industrial health experts have long been aware that exposure to benzene may lead to various types of non-malignant diseases. . . .

As early as 1928, some health experts theorized that there might also be a connection between benzene in the workplace and leukemia. . . .

. . . In an August 1976 revision of its earlier recommendation, NIOSH stated that these studies provided "conclusive" proof of a causal connection between benzene and leukemia. . . .

In October 1976, . . . NIOSH recommended that a 1 ppm exposure limit be imposed for benzene. . . .

. . . .

Public hearings were held on the proposed standard, commencing on July 19, 1977. The final standard was issued on February 10, 1978. . . .

. . . .

As presently formulated, the benzene standard is an expensive way of providing some additional protection for a relatively small number of employees. According to OSHA's figures, the standard will require capital investments in engineering controls of approximately $266 million, and recurring annual costs of approximately $34 million. The figures outlined in OSHA's explanation of the costs of compliance to various industries indicate that only 35,000 employees would gain any benefit from the regulation in terms of a reduction in their exposure to benzene. . . .

. . . .

II

The critical issue at this point in the litigation is whether the Court of Appeals was correct in refusing to enforce the 1 ppm exposure limit on the ground that it was not supported by appropriate findings.

. . . .

With respect to leukemia. evidence of an increased risk (*i.e.*, a risk greater than that borne by the general population) due to benzene exposures at or below 10 ppm was even sketchier. . . . [T]here was only one study that provided any evidence of such an increased risk. That study, conducted by the Dow Chemical Co., uncovered three leukemia deaths, versus 0.2 expected deaths, out of a population of 594 workers; it appeared that the three workers had never been exposed to more than 2 to 9 ppm of benzene. . . .

. . . .

In the end OSHA's rationale for lowering the permissible exposure limit to 1 ppm was based, not on any finding that leukemia has ever been caused by exposure to 10 ppm of benzene and that it will *not* be caused by exposure to 1 ppm, but rather on a series of assumptions indicating that some leukemias might result from exposure to 10 ppm and that the number of cases might be reduced by reducing the exposure level to 1 ppm. . . .

. . . .

III

Our resolution of the issues in these cases turns, to a large extent, on the meaning of and the relationship between § 3(8), which defines a health and safety standard as a standard that is "reasonably necessary and appropriate to provide safe or healthful employment," and § 6(b)(5), which directs the Secretary in promulgating a health and safety standard for toxic materials to "set the standard which most adequately assures, to the extent feasible, on the basis of the best available evidence, that no employee will suffer material impairment of health or functional capacity. . . ."

A

Under the Government's view, § 3(8), if it has any substantive content at all, merely requires OSHA to issue standards that are reasonably calculated to produce a safer or more healthy work environment. . . .

. . . .

B

By empowering the Secretary to promulgate standards that are "reasonably necessary or appropriate to provide safe or healthful employment and places of employment," the Act implies that, before promulgating any standard, the Secretary must make a finding that the workplaces in question are not safe. But "safe" is not the equivalent of "risk-free." There are many activities that we engage in every day—such as driving a car or even breathing city air—that entail some risk of accident or material health impairment; nevertheless, few people would consider these activities "unsafe." Similarly, a workplace can hardly be considered "unsafe" unless it threatens the workers with a significant risk of harm.

Therefore, before he can promulgate *any* permanent health or safety standard, the Secretary is required to make a threshold finding that a place of employment is unsafe—in the sense that significant risks are present and can be eliminated or lessened by a change in practices. . . .

. . . .

E

. . . .

In this case the record makes it perfectly clear that the Secretary relied squarely on a special policy for carcinogens that imposed the burden on industry of providing the existence of a safe level of exposure, thereby avoiding the Secretary's threshold responsibility of establishing the need for more stringent standards. In so interpreting his statutory authority, the Secretary exceeded his power.

Case Questions

1. In its opinion, the Court states that only a small number of employees will benefit from the reduction in exposure to benzene that was mandated by the new standards. Should a cost-benefit analysis be used when the issue is worker safety and health?

2. Do you agree with the Secretary's position that there is no safe level of workplace exposure to a known carcinogen?

3. How much scientific proof should be required before the Secretary may impose strict limitations on worker exposure to a substance on the ground that it causes cancer?

RISK ANALYSIS. OSHA responded to this decision by quantifying specific health risks in the workplace and comparing them to general levels of risk. For example, OSHA's 1983 proposal for an inorganic-arsenic standard estimated the lifetime risks of contracting cancer at existing exposure levels and at the proposed new level. It justified the new standard by comparing these risks to general occupational risk rates. The new arsenic standard was set so that it would reduce this particular risk of cancer to less than half the death rate in high-risk occupations like fire fighting and mining but to several times more than the death rate in average risk occupations.

In succeeding proposals for ethylene-oxide and asbestos standards, the agency refined its approach. For example, it compared the risks of contracting cancer after exposure to these toxic substances with other cancer risks in the workplace.

By 1987, OSHA had applied its new risk-analysis techniques to benzene and, under pressure from labor unions, was ready to revive the standard overturned by the Supreme Court seven years earlier. This time OSHA could point to a NIOSH study concluding that rubber workers exposed to benzene fumes at a level of 10 parts per million were 154 times as likely to develop leukemia as workers not exposed to the chemical. The new standard greatly reduces, although it does not completely eliminate, leukemia risks for workers exposed to benzene. In line with the philosophy expressed by the Supreme Court, exposed workers will still be 70 percent more likely to develop leukemia than other workers. Compliance with the new rules, affecting 240,000 workers, will cost business an estimated $24 million a year.

Proposals for OSHA Reform

As we will see in the ETHICAL ENVIRONMENT box at the end of this section, enforcement of OSHA provisions has been something less than successful. After a period of fewer problems, the incidence of worker injury, disease, and death has risen steadily over the past 10-15 years. One result of all such data has been a cry for reform of the agency and its procedures.

Many areas of change have been proposed. The call for a complete revision of the OSH Act will probably not happen because general consensus is that the Act serves its purpose. However, it is likely that OSHA will be revamped to strengthen its powers of enforcement.

Increased Civil Penalties. Among the new remedies available to the agency OSHA is likely to be able to increase the amount of the civil penalties that it assesses. A 1978 report, for example, revealed that the average fine for serious OSHA violations was only $800; between 1971 and 1976, the average fine for over 8000 citations had been a mere $33. In 1986, however, OSHA altered policy in response to a significant increase in violations of the federal record-keeping rules on which the agency typically based its inspections. Chrysler was fined $911,000 for failing to report 182 job-related injuries at a single assembly plant; the final settlement of $285,000 was the highest safety-violation fine ever paid by an American company. (The largest fines levied by OSHA are listed in Table 14-4.) Although OSHA has continued with its new policy, the remedy may turn out to be a two-edged sword: when employers hit with high fines may find it advantageous to contest citations, the resulting litigation could undermine the purpose of the penalty—a safer workplace.

Criminal Penalties. Another possibility is the imposition of severe criminal penalties on employers whose willful violation of OSHA standards results in death or serious injury. For example, one proposal calls for a jail term of between six months and 10 years for a first offense and from 1 to 20 years for a second offense if an employee death resulted from the violation. Imprisonment for 5 to 10 years has been suggested as punishment for a violation resulting in the serious injury of an employee.

| | TABLE 14-4 | *Largest Penalties Levied by OSHA* | |

DATE	COMPANY	REASON FOR PENALTY	PENALTY/SETTLEMENT (IN THOUSANDS OF DOLLARS)
2/11/88	Doe Run	Safety/health violation	$2,780/not settled
1/14/88	Kohler	Record keeping	$1,398/not settled
11/4/87	Bath Iron Works	Safety/health violation	$4,200/not settled
10/22/87	TPMI Macomber	Building collapse	$2,475/not settled
	Texstar Construction		$2,524/not settled
9/25/87	Scott Paper	Record keeping	$813/$475
7/21/87	IBP	Record keeping	$2,598/not settled
7/6/87	Chrysler (Newark, Delaware)	Safety/health violation	$1,576/not settled
11/5/86	Chrysler (Belvidere, illinois)	Record keeping	$911/$285
4/1/86	Union Carbide	Record keeping	$1,378/$409
2/27/80	Newport News Shipbuilding	Safety/health violation	$804/$121

Sources: Adapted from Rogene A. Buchholz, *Business Environment and Public Policy: Implications for Management and Strategy* (Englewood Cliffs, NJ: Prentice Hall, 1990). Data from Cathy Trost, "Occupational Hazard," *The Wall Street Journal* 22 Apr. 1988. Reprinted by permission. Copyright © 1988 Dow Jones & Co., Inc.

victims-rights legislation
Proposed reform to *OSHA* regulations giving injured workers and/or their families the right to participate in OSHA's investigations of their claims

Victims-Rights Legislation. **Victims-rights legislation** is yet another proposed avenue of reform. Injured parties—that is, the victim—and/or their families would have the right to participate in OSHA's investigations of their cases. In addition, the victim would have a say in the citation issued by OSHA. OSHA currently has a provision that permits the families of deceased employees to receive information about investigations. Families are not, however, allowed to participate in investigations. Injured employees are not given any such rights.

In 1990, the General Accounting Office (GAO) issued a report on the matter of victim's rights. The report makes several major suggestions, including:

- amendment of the OSH Act to make the standards-setting process more efficient (for example, a shortened public-notice and comment period for the revision of old standards);
- expansion of criminal penalties and the possible institution of a criminal-investigation function within OSHA; and
- elimination of the need for a court order to shut down a facility that an OSHA inspector deems hazardous.

■ *Concept Check 14-4   The Occupational Safety and Health Act*

- Explain the development and purpose of *risk-analysis techniques* in setting and enforcing OSHA standards.
- What are the most important proposals that have been made for reforming OSHA?

When the Occupational Safety and Health Act was first passed, although most analysts agreed that it was needed, not everyone agreed on how the Act should be administered. The result of the ensuing debate was the Occupational Safety and Health Administration (OSHA). OSHA was given responsibility for the rule-making, enforcement, and adjudication functions of the Act. The National Institute for Occupational Safety and Health (NIOSH) was created to do the research for the rule-making arm of the agency.

There were, however, many areas of dissent. The result was a series of compromises. For example, although employers do not have to be given advance notice of inspections, they can refuse to allow the inspector to enter the premises. OSHA inspectors do not have the authority to close plants that are in violation of the law without obtaining a court order.

At least for a while, OSHA worked well. Throughout the 1970s, the number of workplace injuries and fatalities declined. During the 1980s, however, this positive trend reversed itself, and an increase in workplace injuries has fueled a revival of the debate about OSHA's administrative policies.

Closer examination shows that the increase in job-related injuries corresponds with a relatively low level of enforcement during the Reagan and Bush administrations. The number of job-safety inspectors, for example, was reduced by nearly one-third; the number of prosecutions slowed to a trickle, and many announced sanctions appeared to be no more than token actions. In short, the policy of voluntary compliance with OSHA translated into an unpleasant concept: Worker death and injury, it seems, became accepted as part of the work environment.

This situation promoted several questions about the ethics of the agency's handling of its mandate. Can employers, for example, be expected to shoulder the entire blame for not complying with OSHA's rules and regulations when the agency operates according to the whim of the executive branch? What can be done to remedy the situation? Because it seems that traditional remedies (that is, workers' compensation, civil litigation, regulation, and the like) have not worked, should criminal sanctions be invoked?

It is obvious to many observers that some sort of overhaul is needed, and a number of solutions have been suggested in response to this need. Some concern major revision of the OSH Act, others involve fine-tuning the Act, and still others concern changes in its administration. The most likely scenario is that new provisions will be made in OSHA's enforcement and compliance procedures, workplace standards, and criteria for employer/employee rights and responsibilities. If and when such provisions are drafted, the question remains: Will they be drafted in the same spirit of compromise as the original provisions?

The college instructor-plaintiff in Decker v. Oklahoma State University was permitted to collect under worker's compensation. The court stated that although the Oklahoma law required an "accidental personal injury" before a claim could be granted, the term could be interpreted loosely so that a series of events—rather than one event—could meet the guideline. In this case, the plaintiff's anxiety was directly related to his relationships with both his fellow employee and the supervisor who gave him an unsatisfactory review. In addition, the heart attack occurred on the employer's premises. Medical testimony supported the plaintiff's contention that the injury arose out of and in the course of his employment.

Decker was thus able to prove that there was a causal relationship between the injury and the job. He was also able to show that the risk was reasonably related to his employment. The plaintiff asserted that his heart attack was due to "extraordinary conditions tantamount to tactical harassment [that] were created by an employment situation."

The court's determination hinged on whether the injury was the result of too much stress in general or too much stress concerning work. The court found that the plaintiff's stress was an outgrowth of dealing with work conditions that he found untenable. The distinction between these different types of stress meant the difference between winning and losing the case.

SUMMARY

- Over the course of the century, both state and federal governments have increasingly intervened in the relationship between employer and employee. Government regulation is aimed primarily at protecting workers from financial hardship and bodily harm, preventing abusive practices, and maximizing employment. Most of the legislation in force today grew out of President Roosevelt's efforts to cope with the devastation of the Great Depression of the 1930s. While some states recognized the existence of labor problems at an earlier date, the Depression effectively demonstrated just how outside forces could overwhelm even the best prepared and most responsible of families. Government intervention seemed an appropriate solution to many of the problems.

- The *Fair Labor Standards Act* established the basic labor standards that we take for granted today: the *minimum wage, overtime pay* for more than a 40-hour week, a *minimum age* for workers, and—in a later amendment—*equal pay* for the two sexes. This law has been supplemented by state minimum wage laws.

- The *workers-compensation system* is a network of state statutes that pays for the medical expenses of workers injured on the job and partially replaces lost wages. It is a no-fault system heavily influenced by insurance concepts that offers more universal and more efficient compensation than the common-law tort system. The federal government's role has been limited to extending coverage to some special categories of workers and to exerting pressure on states to expand their benefits.

- Despite attempts to broaden its coverage, workers' compensation has failed to cope adequately with occupational illness. There is as yet no effective system in place to help workers who develop illnesses after prolonged exposure to toxic substances on the job. The federal government has so far intervened only on behalf of coal miners suffering from black-lung disease, but the crisis with asbestos-related disease may prompt Congress to take more comprehensive action on work-related disease.

- A combined system of *welfare, social security,* and *private pensions* is designed to provide an adequate income to retirees and their dependents. Federal programs and policies guarantee minimal subsistence for the elderly in need, mandate individual contributions to social security retirement funds, and encourage both company pensions and individual savings for retirement. *Social Security benefits,* while nearly universal, are relatively low. The government's goal is not to provide full support for retired workers, but to supplement private sources of retirement income. The 1974 *Employee Retirement Income Security Act* (*ERISA*) regulates private pension plans.

- *Unemployment compensation* is a joint state and federal program which partially replaces a worker's earnings during temporary periods of unemployment. It provides a fallback for employees who lose their jobs involuntarily.

- The most recent legislation on labor standards is the *Occupational Safety and Health Act* (*OSHA*). This program tries to prevent injuries and occupational illness by promulgating and enforcing health and safety standards for the workplace. Employers are policed by a regular inspection program, backed up with fines for violations. OSHA's aims, while laudable, have proven difficult to implement, and attempts at reforming OSHA include *victims-rights legislation*. Business has criticized both the costs and the effectiveness of the program.

QUESTIONS AND PROBLEMS

1. Martha Clark was employed as a bookkeeper at the Benson Co. While employed there, the Controller resigned with no immediate replacement, and so Clark took over as the company's accountant, performing the Controller's usual duties. From the time the Controller left until a new one was hired, Clark worked in excess of 40 hours per week and was not paid overtime. She filed suit alleging a violation of the FASA. Decide. [*Clark v. J.M. Benson Co., Inc.,* 789 F 2d. 282 (1986)]

2. Stephen Hines falls from a scaffold and receives injuries when his scaffold-mate accidentally bumps into him while cleaning windows. He files his workers' compensation claim. The employer opposes it on the basis that the accident was the scaffold-mate's fault and the employer should therefore not have to pay. Does Mr. Hines collect his benefits?

3. John Bearse's wife, Mary, is killed on the job when she inhales toxic fumes which accidentally escaped in the foundry she worked for. He remarries within three months. Shortly thereafter, he finds out that surviving spouses may receive income replacement benefits and applies for them. His claim is denied. Does Mr. Bearse have a valid basis upon which to appeal the denial?

4. Randy Nichols retired from the Army at age 38, after 20 years of service. Upon retiring, he took a position as a manager in a communications company, telling Rita, his wife, that they would be able to retire in splendor at 65 since he would be drawing two retirement checks. Rita is nervous about this scheme because it seems illegal to her. Is it illegal?

5. Dorothe Stepp worked as a staff technician in a lab that performs chemical examinations on body fluids that are submitted by physicians. Some of the fluids come from people who have AIDS, but those vials have warnings attached to them. Stepp's supervisor had discussions with her regarding the AIDS specimens and the proper safety procedures to be used with them. On February 10, 1987, Stepp refused to perform a test on any possible AIDS specimen. On February 13, 1987, she was informed that a refusal would be considered insubordination and she would be subject to termination. Stepp again refused to do the test and was suspended. When Stepp returned she again refused to do the test, claiming, "AIDS is God's plague on man and performing the tests would go against God's will." She was fired and sought unemployment compensation, claiming that the company violated OSHA regulations for failing to provide a safe work place. Discuss. [Stepp v. Employment Security Division Review Board, 521 N.E. 2d. 350 (1988)].

6. Bruce Heins was a casual driver and dock worker at the Carolina Freight Carrier Company. He was asked by his employer to take an honesty test. After beginning the test, he stopped, claiming that the questions offended him. Heins' employer informed him that refusing to take the test would render his employment file incomplete and no more work would be given to him. Heins filed for unemployment compensation and was denied benefits on the basis that failing to take the honesty test was willful misconduct. Was the decision overturned? Explain. [Heins v. Unemployment Compensation Bd. of Review, Pa. Super., 534 A.2d. 592 (1987)]

7. During an OSHA inspection, Smith Co. was cited for certain relatively minor violations. Smith Co. defended against the citation by asserting that the reason for the citation was an employee's refusal to follow Smith Co.'s orders and Smith Co. had no knowledge of the refusal until OSHA found the violation. Will Smith Co.'s defense prevent liability from attaching to its violation? [OSHRC and Raymond Hendrix, d/b/a Alsea Lumber Co., 511 F.2d 1139 (9th Cir. 1975)]

8. At the end of her shift, Nina Campion, a nurse's aide, puts one arm into her overcoat. When she reaches to put her other arm in, she feels a "pop" in her shoulder joint and afterwards is unable to perform her lifting duties. Can Nina collect workers' compensation for her injuries? [Davis v. Houston General-Insurance Co., 233 S.E.2d 479 (1977)]

9. On July 25, Paul Patterson fell from the tracks of a pusher-tractor at the construction company where he worked. He sustained injuries to his back. He received total temporary workers' compensation benefits for his time off and returned to work on August 13. Mr. Patterson's doctor gave him permission to return to work with no limitations on his duties, even though he told the doctor he was still experiencing periodic dizzy spells. In December, Mr. Patterson is laid off and goes into business for himself as a tree trimmer. While trimming a tree, he experiences a dizzy spell and falls off a 40-foot ladder, sustaining serious injuries. He then files for workers' compensation based on the July 25 accident. Will the benefits be granted?

[*Williams Construction Co. v. Garrison,* 400 A.2d 22 (1979)]

10. Chuck Jackson brings an action against Chemical Co. for injuries he received when he fell from a ladder on Chemical Co.'s premises. At the time, he was employed by an independent contractor who was hired to remove machinery from Chemical Co.'s premises. Mr. Jackson claims that he fell from the ladder because the ladder did not meet OSHA standards. Chemical Co. argues that the OSHA standards are intended only to protect Chemical Co.'s employees, not independent contractors who come onto the premises. Which argument wins out? [*Teal v. E. I. DuPont de Nemours & Co.,* 728 F.2d 799 (6th Cir. 1984)]

15

EMPLOYMENT DISCRIMINATION

Affirmative action and equal employment opportunity are shaping everyday personnel practices as well as raising issues of substantial legal liability for employers. In this chapter, we will examine the laws and court decisions that affect equal employment opportunity today. The goals of these laws are to ensure that workers compete for job opportunities on the basis of merit and that there is no discrimination in the workplace on the basis of race, sex, religion, national origin, age, or handicap.

A wide variety of legislation and regulatory activity addresses discrimination in the workplace. In addition to such major pieces of federal legislation as the Civil Rights Act of 1964 and the Equal Employment Opportunity Act of 1972, there is antidiscriminatory language in such laws as the State and Local Fiscal Assistance Act of 1972 and the Vietnam Era Veterans Readjustment Assistance Act of 1979. There are also a host of presidential Executive Orders on the subject. Table 15-1 identifies some legislation in this area.

In this chapter, we will examine only federal measures against employment discrimination. However, employers must also be aware of state and local fair-employment practice laws. Some of these have more extensive coverage than the federal provisions—for example, they may outlaw discrimination based on marital status or apply to smaller employers. Finally, the vast majority of collective-bargaining agreements contain guarantees against discrimination by the employer, the union, or both.

CIVIL RIGHTS IN THE UNITED STATES

Slavery was accepted by and incorporated into U.S. law and society before the Civil War. By 1860, the census recorded that nearly 90 percent of the 4.4 million blacks in the country were slaves. It was even open to dispute whether blacks were legally human or just chattel property. In 1857, for example, the

TABLE 15-1 *Federal Equal Employment Laws and Orders*

Civil Rights Acts of 1866 and 1871	Entitles all citizens to equal treatment before the law
Equal Pay Act of 1963	Requires equal pay for equal work without regard to sex
Title VII of the Civil Rights Act of 1964 amended by Equal Employment Opportunity Act of 1972)	Prohibits discrimination on the basis of race, color, religion, national origin, and sex by private and public employers, employment agencies, and labor organizations
Executive Order 11141 (1964)	Prohibits age discrimination by federal contractors
Executive Order 11246 (1965) as amended by Executive Order 11375 (1967)	Prohibits discrimination by federal contractors on basis of race, color, religion, sex or national origin
Age Discrimination in Employment Act of 1967	Prohibits age discrimination against those aged 40 to 70
Executive Order 11478 (1969)	Prohibits discrimination against federal government employees based on race, color, religion, sex, national origin, political affiliation, marital status, or physical handicap
State and Local Fiscal Assistance Act of 1972	Prohibits discrimination on basis of race, color, national origin, sex, religion, age, and handicap in programs receiving federal revenue-sharing funds
Vocational Rehabilitation Act of 1973	Prohibits discrimination by federal contractors against the physically and mentally handicapped and requires affirmative action
Vietnam Era Veterans Readjustment Assistance Act of 1974	Requires federal contractors and the federal government to promote employment opportunities for Vietnam veterans, especially the disabled
Pregnancy Discrimination Act of 1978	Amended Title VII to prohibit sex discrimination on the basis of pregnancy

Supreme Court decided this issue in the landmark *Dred Scott* decision, declaring that blacks have "no rights which the white man was bound to respect" (*Dred Scott v. Sandford*, 19 How. 393 [1857]). This decision created a furor in the North. It also contributed to the election of Abraham Lincoln and, ultimately, to the secession of the southern states and the Civil War.

Reconstruction Legislation

After the Civil War, Congress amended the Constitution in order to override the *Dred Scott* decision and end slavery. The Thirteenth Amendment, ratified in 1865, banned slavery in the United States. Although the Thirteenth Amendment officially confirmed the Emancipation Proclamation of 1863, it did very little to extend the benefits of freedom to former slaves. Much of the legislation that affected the lives of the newly freed slaves—indeed, the lives of both black and white Southerners—in the years immediately following the Civil War was designed to give Congress control over the management of Reconstruction. We will focus here on the Fourteenth and Fifteenth Amendments and the Civil Rights Acts of 1866 and 1871.

THE FOURTEENTH AMENDMENT. The members of Lincoln's party who had pushed for the vigorous pursuit of both the war and the "reconstruction" of the South

Scott v. Sandford *(19 How. 393 [1857])* Dred Scott, who was owned by an army officer residing in the slave state of Missouri, accompanied his owner to Wisconsin Territory, which had been closed to slavery by the Congressional Missouri Compromise of 1820. Supported by abolitionist groups, Scott sued for his freedom on the ground that he had resided in free territory. The case reached the Supreme Court, which, according to most legal historians, embarked on a series of ill-advised decisions. First, the Court ignored the question of whether, as a slave, Scott had a right to sue in the federal courts; the justices also sidestepped the issue of whether Scott's suit was valid under Missouri law. Rather, the Court decided to rule on the constitutionality of the Missouri Compromise—and everything that the statute implied about the relationship of Congressional power to the Constitution itself. With eight of nine justices issuing separate opinions on different aspects of the case, Chief Justice Roger Taney nevertheless managed to forge a consensus in *Scott v. Sandford* (1857). According to six justices, Scott had "reverted" to slavery when he returned with his owner to Missouri. Five of those six justices then proceeded to base their argument on the Fifth Amendment guarantee against deprivation of private property without due process (*see Chapter 3*): Congress could not prohibit slaveowners from taking their property into federal territory. Congress, therefore, could not prohibit slavery anywhere—it could only protect it—and only state law could ban slavery in any part of the nation. Ultimately, then, Congress was effectively barred from participating in any compromise solution to the complex of slavery-related problems that contributed to the Civil War.

responded to Southern efforts to weaken the practical impact of the Thirteenth Amendment by passing the Fourteenth and Fifteenth Amendments. The goal of the Fourteenth Amendment, ratified in 1868, was to protect black civil rights, especially in the South. It stated that

> No state shall make or enforce any law which shall abridge the privileges or immunities of citizens of the United states; nor shall any State deprive any person of life, liberty, or property without due process of law; nor deny to any person within its jurisdiction the equal protection of the laws.

Once again, the intentions of the federal legislators were foiled. A series of court decisions over the next 30 years weakened the application of the Amendment. First, because it was applied for the most part to corporate "persons" in government regulation cases, the "due-process" clause did not offer individuals much protection. The "privileges-and-immunities" clause also lost its potential impact in an 1873 Supreme Court decision, when New Orleans butchers tried to use it to block a local slaughterhouse monopoly (*Slaughter-House Cases*, 16 Wall. 36). In its ruling, the Court distinguished between the rights afforded the people by virtue of national citizenship and those that came from state citizenship. Only *national* rights were protected by the Fourteenth Amendment, it said, and these were few: the right to travel between states, for instance, or the right to petition Congress. Most civil rights, the Court said, came from state citizenship and were therefore not protected by the Fourteenth Amendment.

Impact of the "Equal-Protection" Clause. The "equal-protection" clause had the greatest effect. It was drafted with the intention of providing relief for acts of group discrimination. Its impact, however, was limited by an 1883 Supreme Court ruling that it did not apply to actions by private businesses (*Civil Rights Cases*, 109 U.S. 3 [1883]).

In its 1896 decision in *Plessy v. Ferguson* (163 U.S. 537), the Court next considered the application of the clause to discrimination by state governments. At issue was a Louisiana law requiring blacks and whites to be seated separately on trains. In its decision, the Court created the **separate-but-equal doctrine**: As long as the seating provided on the train for the two groups was similar, separation need not imply inequality. Thus, separate-but-equal facilities were ruled a legitimate way to provide equal protection. The *Plessy* decision remained in force until it was overruled by a 1954 Supreme Court decision, *Brown v. Board of Education* (347 U.S. 483 [1954]). In this landmark case, concerning the segregated school system of Topeka, Kansas, the Court ruled that separate facilities are inherently unequal (*see* Chapter 3).

separate-but-equal doctrine 1896 Supreme Court ruling (*Plessy v. Ferguson*) that racial separation need not imply inequality as long as the races had similar facilities; overruled in 1954 (*Brown v. Board of Education*) with the finding that separate facilities are inherently unequal

THE FIFTEENTH AMENDMENT. When the Fourteenth Amendment failed to protect black voting rights, Congress passed the Fifteenth Amendment. This 1870 Amendment states that "The right of citizens of the United States to vote shall not be denied on account of race, color, or previous condition of servitude." Until 1877, it was enforced by federal supervision of elections in the South. After that time, it lost its effectiveness, as terrorist burnings and shootings were used to intimidate blacks.

THE CIVIL RIGHTS ACTS OF 1866 AND 1871. The Civil Rights Acts were based on the enabling clauses of the Thirteenth and Fourteenth Amendments. Because it protects the rights of all citizens to make contracts, and because employment is a contractual relationship, the 1866 Act is directly relevant to employment discrimination. The 1871 Act prohibits racial discrimination by state and local governments. These two Reconstruction Acts had little impact at the time they were passed because the courts interpreted them extremely narrowly.

A century later, however, they were revived and given a broader meaning. Beginning with a 1968 decision, the courts have applied these Reconstruction laws—since codified as Sections 1981 and 1982 of Title 42 of the U.S. Code—to modern cases of employment discrimination. These laws offer plaintiffs two advantages over later civil rights laws:

- their procedural requirements are not as strict, and
- they allow plaintiffs to seek punitive damages.

In two 1987 decisions, the Supreme Court further broadened the use of these two laws by ruling that they applied to discrimination not just against blacks but against any ethnic group.

THE END OF RECONSTRUCTION. The effect of the Reconstruction legislation and constitutional amendments was short-lived. Once the Republican party lost interest in the black minority, Southern states began to evade the law: By the 1890s, they were imposing literacy tests, poll taxes, and other requirements on would-be voters in order to exclude blacks. Discrimination issues remained out of the social and legal spotlight for the next half century.

The Civil Rights Movement

By the 1950s, however, the country was once more prepared to consider the issue of discrimination. Blacks had migrated to northern cities in large numbers and increased their political influence with the growth of organizations like the National Association for the Advancement of Colored People (NAACP) and a black press. Initially, black organizations channeled their civil rights efforts through the courts, sponsoring litigation that struck a responsive chord in the Supreme Court of the 1950s. The Court began to interpret the Fourteenth and Fifteenth Amendments more broadly and overturned a number of discriminatory state laws and programs. At the same time, the federal government moved to enforce existing civil rights laws more strictly and to put a halt to segregation in the South.

Blacks next began a well-publicized program of organized, nonviolent protests such as boycotts, sit-ins, freedom rides, and mass demonstrations. These efforts, which culminated in a 1963 March on Washington, were designed to politically pressure local businesses and public facilities to desegregate.

■ *Concept Check 15-1   Civil Rights in the United States*

- Describe the intent and effect of the *Thirteenth, Fourteenth*, and *Fifteenth Amendments* in extending constitutional civil rights.
- Explain the intent and effect of the *due-process, privileges-and-immunities*, and *equal-protection clauses* of the Fourteenth Amendment.
- What is the primary importance of the *Civil Rights Acts of 1866 and 1871*?

■ TITLE VII OF THE CIVIL RIGHTS ACT OF 1964

In response to the civil rights movement, President John F. Kennedy submitted a broad civil rights bill to Congress. Congress initially refused to pass it, but after Kennedy's assassination, President Johnson, who personally gave civil rights legislation the highest attention, shepherded it through Congress. He signed it into law in 1964.

Although the Civil Rights Act of 1964 was not the first federal law addressing discrimination, it was certainly the most comprehensive. It provided for equal access to public facilities, outlawed discriminatory voter registration tests and employment discrimination, and denied federal money to segregated programs and organizations. **Title VII** is that part of the Act which deals with employment discrimination and thus concerns us.

Title VII, which was amended by the Equal Employment Opportunity Act of 1977, prohibits discrimination in employment on the basis of race, sex, color, religion, or national origin. Discrimination based on age and handicap has required additional legislation. The law applies to all public and private employers with 15 or more employees. Note that even though federal employees are excluded, Section 717 "requires nondiscrimination in federal employment." It applies to all employment practices, including recruitment and selection, training, compensation, and promotion.

We will begin by examining legal definitions of *discrimination* that apply generally to groups protected by the provisions of Title VII. In discussing the administration of Title VII and the Equal Employment Opportunity Commission, we will look more closely at discrimination on the bases of *national origin* and *sex*, including EEOC guidelines on *sexual harassment*.

Defining Discrimination: Disparate Treatment and Disparate Impact

The definition of *discrimination* is the crux of Title VII. What first leaps to mind—and was first employed by the courts—is *prejudicial treatment*: taking harmful action against an individual because of hostility toward some group to which that person belongs. Because prejudice is really a matter of motivation, it is not easy to prove. As a result, the courts have since developed and employed two other legal theories of discriminatory behavior: *disparate treatment* and *disparate impact.* We will cover both of these theories, including grounds for discrimination claims and defenses against such claims, in the following sections. Because disparate-impact theory has led to a series of important rulings in employment-discrimination cases, we will examine in some detail the evolution of litigation involving tests of disparate impact and the passage of the Civil Rights Act of 1991.

DISPARATE TREATMENT.   **Disparate treatment** refers to intentional discrimination in which different groups are treated differently. Generally, the courts infer intent from the employer's use of different standards for various groups. For example, an employer who hires male job applicants with young children but systematically rejects female applicants in the same situation is guilty of disparate treatment, which is the most obvious and easily understood form of discrimination.

The Supreme Court has stated that in order to prove disparate treatment, the plaintiff must demonstrate that "discrimination was the company's standard operating procedure—the regular rather than the unusual practice" (*International Brotherhood of Teamsters v. United States*, 431 U.S. 324, 335 n.15 [1977]). Thus, the law is concerned with class-wide discrimination, not just individual injustice.

"Pattern and Practice." This kind of case, commonly known as a **"pattern-and-practice" claim**, also requires the plaintiff to prove a discriminatory motive. More often than not, the motive is inferred from the *actual* disparity in the treatment of the different groups. It thus becomes a question of num-

---

Title VII   *1964 Civil Rights Act section that prohibits employment discrimination on the basis of race, sex, color, religion, or national origin*

disparate treatment   Intentional *employment discrimination* in which different groups are treated differently

"pattern-and-practice" claim   As the basis for an *employment-discrimination claim*, the actual disparity in an employer's treatment of different groups as standard policy

bers and statistics. The courts, however, have ruled that only gross disparities justify the inference of a discriminatory motive.

Defenses against Charges of Disparate Treatment. Employers can defend against pattern-and-practice claims either by refuting the existence of a disparity or by offering a legitimate explanation for it. The first approach generally means an attack on the plaintiff's statistics. The second demands that the employer have a nondiscriminatory reason for the disparity. Employers need not prove their good intentions: They must merely raise a genuine question about discriminatory intent. The plaintiff may still prevail, however, if he can show that the employer's so-called legitimate reasons were simply a pretext for international discrimination (*Texas Department of Community Affairs v. Burdine*, 450 U.S. 248 [1981]).

DISPARATE IMPACT. **Disparate impact** ignores the whole issue of intent and simply examines the *consequences* of an employer's personnel practices. The issue is whether a single standard has different consequences for different groups. For example, some common job prerequisites, such as requiring a high-school diploma or a passing grade on an employment test, may screen out more blacks than whites. Minimum-height and -weight requirements screen out more women, Orientals, and Hispanics than white males. Standards with disparate impact are justified only if they are either necessary to the safe and efficient operation of the business or inherently work-related.

disparate impact Principle that in *employment discrimination*, a single standard has different consequences for different groups

Statistical Approaches to Establishing Claims. There are three statistical approaches to establishing disparate impact: *comparative, demographic,* and *concentration statistics.* While recognizing the weaknesses of the approach, the courts have nevertheless repeatedly upheld the use of such statistics in proving the existence of employment discrimination.

Comparative statistics are based on the idea that *rates* of hiring, firing, promoting, transferring, and demoting people should be approximately the same for all groups. Thus, if employers hire half of all white male job applicants, they should hire approximately half of all black or female applicants. In practice, the courts have held that hiring rates for women and minorities should be at least 80 percent of that for white men.

Demographic statistics contend that each employer's workforce should reflect the racial, ethnic, and gender composition of the general labor market. Thus, if there are many Hispanics in the local population, there should be a large number of Hispanics working for a company located in that community. The difficulty is in deciding what population group to use as the comparison standard: In other words, where is the geographical boundary of the local market? Skilled jobs pose another problem: Should the composition of workers holding skilled jobs be compared to the general labor pool or to the pool of skilled workers?

demographic statistics Statistical approach proving *employment discrimination* according to the principle that each employer's workforce should reflect the racial, ethnic, and gender composition of the general labor market

Concentration statistics hold that discrimination exists if all the members of a group are in the same job category. For example, discrimination exists when even though a company has equal numbers of male and female entry-level employees, most of the women hold only secretarial jobs.

concentration statistics The statistical approach to proving *employment discrimination* according to the principle that discrimination exists if all members of a group are in the same job category

Defenses against Charges of Disparate Impact. Although the defense in disparate-impact cases follows the same lines as disparate-treatment cases, the employer is held to somewhat stricter standards. First, the employer can challenge the existence of a disparity by attacking the plaintiff's statistics. However, while a disparity in treatment must be gross, a disparity in impact need only be appreciable because there is no question of intent.

Second, an employer may demonstrate that the disputed employment practice is either job-related or justified by some business necessity. For instance, the courts have ruled that an airline's paramount interest in safety justifies a policy transferring flight attendants to ground duty when they become pregnant. The airline industry has successfully argued that it is impossible to predict which pregnant flight attendants would be subject to illnesses like morning sickness and fatigue and so might compromise safety in an emergency (*Levin v. Delta Air Lines, Inc.* [1984]). The defense, however, is not foolproof: The plaintiff can still prevail by demonstrating that an employer satisfy legitimate business needs with nondiscriminatory personnel practices.

Discrimination and the Evolution of Disparate Impact

The disparate-impact theory has undergone a considerable degree of change since it was first established by the Supreme Court in *Griggs v. Duke Power Co.* (401 U.S. 424) in 1971. In this section, we will examine how this theory has evolved, assess the impact of these changes on the ways in which employment-discrimination cases are litigated, and examine the ultimate effect that new rules will have on the ways that businesses hire and promote employees.

GRIGGS V. DUKE POWER CO. *Griggs* was the first case to define how workers can prove that a *facially neutral rule*—one that seems or claims to make a legal distinction among groups—can nevertheless be found to violate the Civil Rights Act because it has the *effect* of unlawfully discrimination against a protected class.

The issue in this case concerned whether a power plant in North Carolina could legally require that all employees possess high-school educations or pass a standardized intelligence tests before being hired or transferred to better jobs. Black employees of Duke, who were generally employed in the lowest-paying positions in the company, claimed that the rule had the effect of preventing their transfer into higher-paying jobs. They also claimed not only that prior to the adoption of the Civil Rights Act of 1964, the company openly discriminated on the basis of race, but that the rule—which went into effect on the day the Act became effective—was adopted for the implicit purpose of perpetuating the practice of keeping blacks out of higher-paying positions. The company argued that transfer requirements were intended to screen out applicants who did not possess the skills needed to perform higher-paying jobs.

In assessing the plaintiff's allegations, the court noted that the Civil Rights Act was intended to root out both overt discrimination and policies that have the *effect* of discrimination. According to the court, the key to distinguishing between legal and illegal racially neutral rules is determining whether they are *job-related*. If, for example, a hiring requirement is designed to screen out applicants who do not possess the skills necessary to do a job, it is legal under the Act. If, on the other hand, a rule requires an applicant to possess skills that are not required to perform the job, an inference arises that it was adopted for the purpose of unlawful discrimination. Under *Griggs*, the burden of proof with respect to job-relatedness rested squarely with the employer.

In applying this rule to Duke's requirement that an employee could not transfer jobs without a high-school education, the court found that it was *not* sufficiently related to job performance. In this regard, the court noted that a number of white employees who had not completed high school were performing satisfactorily in higher-paying positions. Therefore, the court held, the Duke rule constituted unlawful discrimination on the basis of race.

WARDS COVE V. ATONIO. Eighteen years later, in the case of *Wards Packing Cove Co. v. Atonio*, 490 U.S. 642 (1989), the Supreme Court revisited the issue of disparate-impact discrimination. The resulting opinion significantly changed the application of the theory by imposing additional burdens of proof on plaintiffs alleging that they have been victimized by racially neutral rules and thereby lessening employers' burden of proof.

Plaintiff's Burden of Proof. With respect to plaintiff's burden of proof, the court held that employees, who were alleging that several workplace rules had the effect of unlawful discrimination, must specifically identify *which* of the rules resulted in disparate impact. For example, assume that an employer required that employees have a college degree and ten years of experience in the field and pass a psychological test as a condition for being promoted to a high-level management position. To prove that these requirements were unlawful under a disparate-impact test, the court held in *Wards Cove* that a plaintiff must specifically identify which of the three requirements had the effect of undue discrimination against a protected class.

The Business-Justification Defense. Second, the court decreased the burden of proof for employers charged with disparate-impact discrimination. Rather than proving that a requirement was job-related, as required under *Griggs*, an employer could justify the use of a policy merely by asserting a "business justification." Under the newly created **business-justification defense**, a rule is acceptable if it serves any legitimate goals of the employer—that is, it need not bear a specific relationship to job performance. If an employer succeeds in establishing that a policy is justified under this defense, the burden shifts back to the plaintiff to prove that the policy is not in fact justified for the reasons put forth by the employer.

An excerpt from the *Wards Cove* decision appears below.

business-justification defense
Defense against *disparate-impact discrimination* charging that an employer's policy is justified if it serves legitimate goals of the employer

---

WARDS COVE PACKING CO., INC. v. ATONIO
United States Supreme Court, 109 S.Ct. 2114 (1989)

Former salmon cannery workers brought a class action against their employer alleging discrimination on the basis of race. The complaint alleged that noncannery jobs were filled by predominantly white workers, while lower-paying cannery jobs were filled by predominantly nonwhite workers. Additionally, during salmon runs, the primarily nonwhite cannery workers and the primarily white noncannery workers were housed by the company in separate dormitories and ate in separate dining facilities. The complaint charged that the company's hiring, promotion practices, and segregated living and dining facilities violated Title VII of the Civil Rights Act of 1964. The District Court rejected the workers' disparate-treatment and disparate-impact claims. On appeal, however, the Court of Appeals affirmed the lower court's ruling with respect to the disparate-treatment claim but reversed the dismissal of the disparate-impact claim. The employer appealed to the U.S. Supreme Court, seeking clarity on the party's respective burdens of proof in a disparate-impact claim under Title VII.

Justice WHITE delivered the opinion of the Court.
Title VII of the Civil Rights Act of 1964, 42 U.S.C. § 2000e–2(a) makes it an unfair employment practice for an employer to discriminate against any individual with respect to hiring or the terms and condition of employment because of such individual's race, color, religion, sex, or national origin; or to limit, segregate or classify his employees in ways that would adversely affect any employee because of the employee's race, color, religion, sex, or national origin. *Griggs v. Duke Power Co.*, 401 U.S. 424, 431, 91 S.Ct. 849, 853, 28 L.Ed.2d 158 (1971), construed Title VII to proscribe "not only overt discrimination but also practices that are fair in form but discriminatory in practice." Under this basis for liability, which is known as the "disparate impact"

theory and which is involved in this case, a facially neutral employment practice may be deemed violative of Title VII without evidence of the employer's subjective intent to discriminate that is required in a "disparate treatment" case. . . .

In holding that respondents had made out a prima facie case of disparate impact, the court of appeals relied solely on respondents' statistics showing a high percentage of nonwhite workers in the cannery jobs and a low percentage of such workers in the noncannery positions. Although statistical proof can alone make out a prima facie case, the Court of Appeals' ruling here misapprehends our precedents and the purposes of Title VII, and we therefore reverse. . . .

It is clear to us that the Court of Appeals' acceptance of the comparison between the racial composition of the cannery work force and that of the noncannery work force, as probative of a prima facie case of disparate impact in the selection of the latter group of workers, was flawed for several reasons. Most obviously, with respect to the skilled noncannery jobs at issue here, the cannery work force in no way reflected "the pool of *qualified* job applicants" or the "*qualified* population in the labor force." Measuring alleged discrimination in the selection of accountants, managers, boat captains, electricians, doctors, and engineers—and the long list of other "skilled" noncannery positions found to exist by the District Court, by comparing the number of nonwhites occupying these jobs to the number of nonwhites filling cannery worker positions is nonsensical. If the absence of minorities holding such skilled positions is due to a dearth of qualified nonwhite applicants (for reasons that are not petitioners' fault), petitioners' selection methods or employment practices cannot be said to have had a "disparate impact" on nonwhites.

One example illustrates why this must be so. Respondents' own statistics concerning the noncannery work force at one of the canneries at issue here indicate that approximately 17% of the new hires for medical jobs, and 15% of the new hires for officer worker positions, were nonwhite. If it were the case that less than 15–17% of the applicants for these jobs were nonwhite and that nonwhites made up a lower percentage of the relevant qualified labor market, it is hard to see how respondents, without more, would have made out a prima facie case of disparate impact. Yet, under the Court of Appeals' theory, simply because nonwhites comprise 52% of the cannery workers at the cannery in question, respondents would be successful in establishing a prima facie case of racial discrimination under Title VII.

Such a result cannot be squared with our cases or with the goals behind the statute. The Court of Appeals' theory, at the very least, would mean that any employer who had a segment of his work force that was—for some reason—racially imbalanced, could be haled into court and forced to engage in the expensive and time-consuming task of defending the "business necessity" of the methods used to select the other members of his work force. The only practicable option for many employers will be to adopt racial quotas, insuring that no portion of his work force deviates in racial composition from the other portions thereof; this is a result that Con-

gress expressly rejected in drafting Title VII. The Court of Appeals' theory would "leave the employer little choice . . . but to engage in a subjective quota system of employment selection. This, of course, is far from the intent of Title VII."

The Court of Appeals also erred with respect to the unskilled noncannery positions. Racial imbalance in one segment of an employer's work force does not, without more, establish a prima facie case of disparate impact with respect to the selection of workers for the employer's other positions, even where workers for the different positions may have somewhat fungible skills (as is arguably the case for cannery and unskilled noncannery workers). As long as there are no barriers or practices deterring qualified nonwhites from applying for noncannery positions, if the percentage of selected applicants who are nonwhite is not significantly less than the percentage of qualified applicants who are nonwhite, the employer's selection mechanism probably does not operate with a disparate impact on minorities. Where this is the case, the percentage of nonwhite workers found in other positions in the employer's labor force is irrelevant to the question of a prima facie statistical case of disparate impact. As noted above, a contrary ruling on this point would almost inexorably lead to the use of numerical quotas in the workplace, a result that Congress and this Court have rejected repeatedly in the past.

Moreover, isolating the cannery workers as the potential "labor force" for unskilled noncannery positions is at once both too broad and too narrow in its focus. Too broad because the vast majority of these cannery workers did not seek jobs in unskilled noncannery positions; there is no showing that many of them would have done so even if none of the arguably "deterring" practices existed. Thus, the pool of cannery workers cannot be used as a surrogate for the class of qualified job applicants because it contains many persons who have not (and would not) be noncannery job applicants. Conversely, if respondents propose to use the cannery workers for comparison purposes because they represent the "qualified labor population" generally, the group is too narrow because there are obviously many qualified persons in the labor market for noncannery jobs who are not cannery workers. . . .

Consequently, we reverse the Court of Appeals' ruling that a comparison between the percentage of cannery workers who are nonwhite and the percentage of noncannery workers who are nonwhite makes out a prima facie case of disparate impact. . . .

Since the statistical disparity relied on by the Court of Appeals did not suffice to make out a prima facie case, any inquiry by us into whether the specific challenged employment practices of petitioners caused that disparity is pretermitted, as is any inquiry into whether the disparate impact that any employment practice may have had was justified by business considerations. Because we remand for further proceedings, however, on whether a prima facie case of disparate impact has been made in defensible fashion in this case, we address two other challenges petitioners have made to the decision of the Court of Appeals.

First is the question of causation in a disparate-impact case. . . .

Our disparate-impact cases have always focused on the impact of *particular* hiring practices on employment opportunities for minorities. Just as an employer cannot escape liabiity under Title VII by demonstrating that, "at the bottom line," his work force is racially balanced (where particular hiring practices may operate to deprive minorities of employment opportunities), a Title VII plaintiff does not make out a case of disparate impact simply by showing that, "at the bottom line," there is racial *imbalance* in the work force. As a general matter, a plaintiff must demonstrate that it is the application of a specific or particular employment practice that has created the disparate impact under attack. Such a showing is an integral part of the plaintiff's prima facie case in a disparate-impact suit under Title VII.

Here, respondents have alleged that several "objective" employment practices (*e.g.,* nepotism, separate hiring channels, rehire preferences), as well as the use of "subjective decision making" to select noncannery workers, have had a disparate impact on nonwhites. Respondents base this claim on statistics that allegedly show a disproportionately low percentage of nonwhites in the at-issue positions. However, even if on remand respondents can show that nonwhites are underrepresented in the at-issue jobs in a manner that is acceptable under the standards set forth in Part II, *supra,* this alone will *not* suffice to make out a prima facie case of disparate impact. Respondents will also have to demonstrate that the disparity they complain of is the result of one or more of the employment practices that they are attacking here, specifically showing that each challenged practice has a significantly disparate impact on employment opportunities for whites and nonwhites. To hold otherwise would result in employers being potentially liable for "the myriad of innocent causes that may lead to statistical imbalances in the composition of their work forces."

Some will complain that this specific causation requirement is unduly burdensome on Title VII plaintiffs. But liberal civil discovery rules give plaintiffs broad access to employers' records in an effort to document their claims. Also, employers falling within the scope of the Uniform Guidelines on Employee Selection Procedures, are required to "maintain . . . records or other information which will disclose the impact which its tests and other selection procedures have upon employment opportunities of persons by identifiable race, sex, or ethnic group[s.]" This includes records concerning "the individual components of the selection process" where there is a significant disparity in the selection rates of whites and nonwhites. Plaintiffs as a general matter will have the benefit of these tools to meet their burden of showing a causal link between challenged employment practices and racial imbalances in the work force; respondents presumably took full advantage of these opportunities to build their case before the trial in the District Court was held. . . .

If, on remand, respondents meet the proof burdens outlined above, and establish a prima facie case of disparate impact with respect to any of petitioners' employment practices, the case will shift to any business justification petitioners offer for their use of these practices. This phase of the disparate-impact case contains two components: first, a consideration of the justifications an employer offers for his use of these practices; and second, the availability of alternate practices to achieve the same business ends, with less racial impact. We consider these two components in turn.

Though we have phrased the query differently in different cases, it is generally well-established that at the justification stage of such a disparate impact case, the dispositive issue is whether a challenged practice serves, in a significant way, the legitimate employment goals of the employer. The touchstone of this inquiry is a reasoned review of the employer's justification for his use of the challenged practice. A mere insubstantial justification in this regard will not suffice, because such a low standard of review would permit discrimination to be practiced through the use of spurious, seemingly neutral employment practices. At the same time, though, there is no requirement that the challenged practice be "essential" or "indispensable" to the employer's business for it to pass muster: this degree of scrutiny would be almost impossible for most employers to meet, and would result in a host of evils we have identified above.

In this phase, the employer carries the burden of producing evidence of a business justification for his employment practice. The burden of persuasion, however, remains with the disparate-impact plaintiff. . . .

We acknowledge that some of our earlier decisions can be read as suggesting otherwise. But to the extent that those cases speak of an employers' "burden of proof" with respect to a legitimate business justification defense, they should have been understood to mean an employer's production—but not persuasion—burden. The persuasion burden here must remain with the plaintiff, for it is he who must prove that it was "because of such individual's race, color," etc., that he was denied a desired employment opportunity.

Finally, if on remand the case reaches this point, and respondents cannot persuade the trier of fact on the question of petitioners' business necessity defense, respondents may still be able to prevail. To do so, respondents will have to persuade the factfinder that "other tests or selection devices, without a similarly undesirable racial effect, would also serve the employer's legitimate [hiring] interest[s];" by so demonstrating, respondents would prove that "[petitioners were] using [their] tests merely as a 'pretext' for discrimination." If respondents, having established a prima facie case, come forward with alternatives to petitioners' hiring practices that reduce the racially-disparate impact of practices currently being used, and petitioners refuse to adopt these alternatives, such a refusal would belie a claim by petitioners that their incumbent practices are being employed for nondiscriminatory reasons. . . .

Of course, any alternative practices which respondents offer up in this respect must be equally effective as petitioners' chosen hiring procedures in achieving petitioners' legitimate employment goals.

For the reasons given above, the judgment of the

Court of Appeals is reversed, and the case is remanded for further proceedings consistent with this opinion.

It is so ordered.

Case Questions

1. As part of their *prima facie* case, plaintiffs must identify the specific hiring practices that result in a racially imbalanced workforce—it is not enough simply to establish a statistical disparity. Is this requirement needed to protect employers from frivolous lawsuits, or does it impose a hardship upon plaintiffs, who typically have considerably less resources than defendants?

2. Should the law infer that a workforce that is grossly imbalanced on the basis of race is the product of discrimination?

3. Should our country's history of widespread racism and segregation play any part in determining whether a racially imbalanced workforce in a particular company is the product of discrimination?

THE CIVIL RIGHTS ACT OF 1991. Congress enacted the *Civil Rights Act of 1991* both to reverse the tighter restrictions that the Supreme Court placed upon plaintiff-employees in *Wards Cove* and other opinions and to strengthen the remedies available to prevailing plaintiffs.

Rejection of the Business-Justification Defense. With respect to altering *Wards Cove*, the Civil Rights Act of 1991 explicitly rejects the business-justification defense and reinstates the job-related test first set down in *Griggs*. In addition, the Act reinstates the burdens of proof with respect to job-relatedness under *Griggs*. For employers, it is not enough merely to *assert* that a rule is justified—they must *prove* it.

Changes in Burden-of-Proof Guidelines. Much of the debate about the Civil Rights Act of 1991 concerns whether or not its changes in burden of proof in disparate-impact cases would ultimately lead to quotas. To address this concern, which has been repeatedly voiced by the Bush Administration, the Act does not suspend the *Wards Cove* requirements that plaintiffs specifically identify which of a number of an employer's selection criteria has a disparate impact.

Business lobbyists also succeeded in keeping out a proposal to change this requirement by arguing that employers, who often use numerous criteria for job selection, would simply adopt strict racial and gender quotas to avoid costly litigation. Even without this provision, however, some business leaders are still worried that the Act's reinstatement of *Griggs'* disparate-impact test will result in increased litigation against employers. An employer's best defense, they contend, may simply be to hire a certain number of members of protected classes in order to avoid the appearance of having a racially or sexually imbalanced work force.

Administration of Title VII

As the previous discussion indicates, some members of Congress opposed fair-employment laws, and during the drafting of Title VII, some legislators demanded compromises to weaken the impact of the law. For example, the law included special provisions to protect established seniority systems and to prevent the use of hiring quotas or preferential treatment. Even more importantly, Congress failed to give the agency administering the law—the Equal Employment Opportunity Commission—any real enforcement powers.

These handicaps, however, did not severely cripple Title VII: The courts gave it very supportive treatment by avoiding the procedural technicalities written into the Act, promoting class-action suits, accepting EEOC guidelines

THE EEOC. In addition to administering Title VII, the **Equal Employment Opportunity Commission (EEOC)** administers other federal employment-discrimination laws, oversees affirmative-action plans to eliminate discriminatory practices, handles the employment-discrimination complaints of federal employees, and coordinates all federal equal-employment activities. The EEOC's five commissioners are appointed by the President and approved by the Senate. They serve five-year terms.

The Equal Employment Opportunity Act. The EEOC got off to a poor start. Not only was it handicapped by a lack of enforcement powers, it was not well managed. The **Equal Employment Opportunity Act** of 1972 remedied the first problem: It gave the agency the authority to file lawsuits, issue rules and regulations, and require reporting. Later in the 1970s, management reforms streamlined the ways in which the agency handled complaints and reduced the backlogs. The federal government also consolidated all of its equal-employment activities under the EEOC.

Filing Charges. Disgruntled workers must first file equal-employment complaints with the appropriate state or local agency, if one exists, and give it 60 days to resolve the problem. Only then may workers file a charge with the EEOC. They may do this at the nearest EEOC field office or at a state or local fair employment-practice agency that has been contracted to handle initial charges. The investigator decides whether the charge falls under EEOC jurisdiction and draws up a formal complaint. The field officer can route the complaint either for rapid processing aimed at a quick settlement or for extended processing aimed at litigation.

The next step is to inform the employer of the charge and request the pertinent information. If necessary, a subpoena may be used. The EEOC field office may then hold a fact-finding conference attended by both parties. If the case has been slated for rapid processing, the agency will try to reach a settlement during this conference.

If there is no settlement, the EEOC then undertakes a formal investigation during which it interviews witnesses, makes field visits, and examines documents. The investigator consults with an attorney to decide whether the charge has merit under the law. At this point, the agency makes an effort to reach a settlement through conciliation among the parties.

If there is still no settlement, the case is referred upward through the hierarchy for a final decision about whether to take the employer to court. When the EEOC decides against litigation, it issues claimants a *right-to-sue notice*, allowing them to sue on their own behalf. Claimants who wish to reach the courts as soon as possible may expedite the proceedings by requesting a right-to-sue letter at a much earlier stage.

Remedies. When the EEOC wins a case, the court has broad discretion to frame a remedy appropriate to the circumstances. It may (1) order back pay for victims of discrimination (a potentially expensive remedy in class-action suits involving a lot of people), (2) issue decrees terminating testing programs and ordering the immediate promotion of discrimination victims, (3) revise a seniority system by retroactively awarding seniority to individuals who were either not hired at all or not promoted because of discrimination, or (4) choose a preferential remedy, such as ordering an organization to establish an

Equal Employment Opportunity Commission (EEOC) Federal agency that administers *Title VII of the 1964 Civil Rights Act* and other federal *employment-discrimination laws* and oversees *affirmative-action plans*

Equal Employment Opportunity Act 1972 federal law that strengthened the *EEOC*, giving it the authority to file lawsuits, issue rules and regulations, and require reporting

Korematsu v. U.S. *(323 U.S. 214* [*1944*]*)* In January of 1983, Fred Korematsu (left) was among the Japanese-Americans who filed petitions with the Commission on Wartime Relocation and Internment of Civilians (CWRIC), which was established by Congress in 1980 to investigate the internment, in 1942–43, of more than 110,000 citizens of Japanese descent in West Coast Relocation Centers. As we noted in *Chapter 3,* in only one instance has a legal classification been affirmed by the Supreme Court under the language of the *strict-scrutiny test*—the test requiring the classifying government body to demonstrate compelling interest in support of a classification. That case concerned Fred Korematsu, who had tried to avoid internment and was tried for violating Executive Order 9066, which excluded Japanese-Americans from designated "military areas" on the West Coast (those "special areas" included the whole state of California and most of Oregon and Washington). Given a suspended sentence and probation, Korematsu was thus under the authority of the courts and not, pursuant to Order 9066, the Army. When the Army interned him anyway, his case reached the Supreme Court—one of the three cases known collectively as the "Japanese-American cases." In *Korematsu v. U.S.* (1944), the Court—with three justices dissenting—ruled that Korematsu's exclusionary classification was a result of military urgency and not any ethnic hostility or discrimination. In 1983, the CWRIC declared that a "grave injustice" had been done to Japanese-Americans and recommended that Congress appropriate funds to pay $20,000 in damages to each survivor of the relocation program. Legislation has been introduced but so far has not been acted on.

affirmative-action program to expedite hiring, training, and promotion of protected-group members. The latter remedy will be discussed in detail later in the chapter.

Discrimination on the Basis of National Origin

✗ KNOW

As we have seen, Title VII prohibits discrimination on the basis of *race* (which includes such broad categories as "black," "Asian," and "Native American"), *color* (which refers literally to skin color), and *national origin* (which refers either to the country of one's ancestors or to cultural characteristics). National origin has accounted for a relatively small number of the fair-employment cases and an even smaller proportion of plaintiff victories. The results have favored the plaintiffs in only a quarter of the cases brought.

This form of discrimination will remain a problem, however, as long as immigration to the United States continues. In addition, there is always the potential for international events to target national-origin groups for discrimination. German- and Japanese-Americans, for example, suffered such discrimination during World War II. More recently, Iranians in the United States were singled out during the hostage crisis of 1980.

EEOC Guidelines. The EEOC's definition of discrimination on the basis of national origin is quite broad, "including, but not limited to, the denial of equal employment opportunity because of an individual's, or his or her ancestor's, place of origin; or because an individual has the physical, cultural, or linguistic characteristics of a national origin group" (29 C.F.R. Section 16501.1 [1984]). Thus, it can apply to people from another state as well as another country, or to whites as well as nonwhites. Employers may discriminate even when they do not know exactly where workers come from and simply label them as "foreign." (The question of discrimination on the basis of language is raised in this chapter's International Environment box.)

In a 1980 case, an employer fired a Mexican-American from his job in a department store ostensibly because of a "lack of good business sense." The court ruled this an instance of national-origin discrimination because the worker possessed adequate qualifications and had received good job evaluations. Evidence of ethnic jokes and slurs also supported the employee's claim (*Whatley v. Scaggs*, 27 Fair Empl. Prac. Cas. 1202 [1980]). The most important limit on national-origin discrimination—that employers may hire only U.S. citizens without violating Title VII—was set by the Supreme Court in the following case.

Review

ESPINOZA v. FARAH MANUFACTURING CO.
United States Supreme Court, 414 U.S. 86 (1973)

The Petitioner, Cecilia Espinoza, a citizen of Mexico living in Texas, brought an action for employment discrimination under Title VII against the Farah Manufacturing Co. for its refusal to hire her because she was not a U.S. citizen. Following a decision by the trial court in favor of Espinoza, the Court of Appeals reversed, ruling for Farah. The sole issue before the U.S. Supreme Court on this appeal by Espinoza is whether Title VII can be interpreted as permitting an employer to consider citizenship in the hiring decision.

Mr. Justice Marshall delivered the opinion of the Court.
Section 703 makes it "an unlawful employment prac-

tice for an employer . . . to fail or refuse to hire . . . any individual . . . because of such individual's race, color, religion, sex, or national origin." Certainly the plain language of the statute supports the result reached by the Court of Appeals. The term "national origin" on its face refers to the country where a person was born, or, more broadly, the country from which his or her ancestors came. The statute's legislative history, though quite meager in this respect, fully supports this construction. . . .

There are other compelling reasons to believe that Congress did not intend the term "national origin" to embrace citizenship requirements. Since 1914, the Federal Government itself, through Civil Service Commission regulations, has engaged in what amounts to discrimination against aliens by denying them the right to enter competitive examination for federal employment. But it has never been suggested that the citizenship requirement for federal employment constitutes discrimination because of national origin, even though since 1943, various Executive Orders have expressly prohibited discrimination on the basis of national origin in Federal Government employment.

. . . .

. . . Suffice it to say that we cannot conclude Congress would at once continue the practice of requiring citizenship as a condition of federal employment and, at the same time, prevent private employers from doing likewise. . . .

The District Court drew primary support for its holding from an interpretative Equal Employment Opportunity Commission which provides:

Because discriminatioin on the basis of citizenship

has the effect of discriminating on the basis of national origin, a lawfully immigrated alien who is domiciled or residing in this country may not be discriminated against on the basis of his citizenship. . . .

. . . .

It is equally clear, however, that these principles lend no support to petitioners in this case. . . . It is conceded that Farah accepts employees of Mexican origin, provided the individual concerned has become an American citizen. Indeed, the District Court found that persons of Mexican ancestry make up more than 96% of the employees at the company's San Antonio division, and 97% of those doing the work for which Mrs. Espinoza applied. . . . [Mrs. Espinoza] was denied employment, not because of the country of her origin, but because she had not yet achieved United States citizenship.

. . . .

We agree with the Court of Appeals that neither the language of the Act, nor its history, nor the specific facts of this case indicate that respondent has engaged in unlawful discrimination because of national origin. Affirmed.

Case Questions:

1. The *Espinoza* opinion provides a good example of statutory interpretation. How does the Court go about achieving its result?

2. How was the Court assured that Farah was not basing its decision on national origin?

THE IMMIGRATION REFORM AND CONTROL ACT OF 1986. Discrimination against job applicants on the basis of national origin or citizenship is also prohibited by the Immigration Reform and Control Act of 1986. Under this Act, employers are required to examine papers that establish the identity of a job applicant and whether that person is authorized to work in the United States. A Social Security card, a U.S. birth certificate, a U.S. passport, a certificate of naturalization, and various other papers may serve this purpose. Employers are not required to investigate whether an applicant's papers are genuine.

Employers may be fined if they fail to keep records showing compliance with these provisions. Employers who hire illegal aliens are fined from $250 to $2,000 per illegal employee for a first offense. Repeat offenders can be fined up to $10,000 per illegal employee.

Discrimination on the Basis of Sex

Employment discrimination against women has become increasingly important as more women have joined the labor force. Entrenched social patterns have been hard to overcome: Although their presence in traditionally male jobs has increased substantially since the passage of the Equal Employment Act, women still earn on average significantly less than men.

As Table 15-2 shows, part of the problem results from the fact that

TABLE 15-2 — Women in Major Occupational Categories

	PERCENTAGE OF WOMEN
Engineers	7.3%
Lawyers and judges	19.5
Librarians	85.4
Physicians	20.0
Dentists	9.3
Registered nurses	94.6
Elementary, secondary teachers	72.9
Managers, administrators	44.7
Sales workers, retail and personal service	68.6
Secretaries, stenographers, typists	98.2
Precision production, craft, and repair	8.7
Transportation and material moving	9.0
Food service workers	61.6
Private household (maids, servants)	96.3

Source: U.S. Bureau of Labor Statistics, Employment and Earnings *(January 1989).*

women workers remain concentrated in occupation categories that are traditionally lower-paying than many of those dominated by men. It is sometimes argued that both occupational concentration and inequality of pay stem from the same fact—namely, that women are generally less qualified. As Table 15-3 illustrates, however, at no income level do women earn more than 71 percent of what men earn regardless of educational level.

Essentially, the types of discrimination that we have already seen applied to groups protected by Title VII also apply to women, as do tests for discrimination and defenses against charges of discrimination. The issue of pay inequality and the principle of *comparable worth* fall under the Equal Pay Act of

TABLE 15-3 — *Education and Median Income for Men and Women*

	MEDIAN INCOME FOR MEN	MEDIAN INCOME FOR WOMEN	WOMEN'S PERCENTAGE OF MEN'S INCOME
Elementary			
Less than 8 years	$14,903	$ 9,227	66.6%
8 years	18,939	12,174	64.2
High School			
1–3 years	21,269	12,940	60.8
4 years	25,394	16,461	64.8
College			
1–3 years	29,536	19,843	67.2
4 years	35,244	23,406	66.4
5+ years	41,691	29,694	71.2

Source: U.S. Bureau of the Census, Money Income and Poverty Status in the United States: 1987 *(Washington, DC: Government Printing Office, 1988).*

One result of the internationalization of the world economy has been an increase in the number of American workers who are foreign-born and for whom English is not their native language. Indeed, it is expected, for example, that Hispanics, most of whom speak Spanish as a primary language, will be the largest ethnic group in the U.S. by the year 2000. It is also projected that by the year 2000, one out of ten employees in the U.S. will be Hispanic.

In response to the increasingly international character of many workforces, a growing number of employers have adopted "English-only" rules that forbid employees from speaking any language other than English within their workplace. Employers have argued that such rules are needed for several reasons. First, some employers have claimed that tensions often arise within a workplace when some employees are speaking a language among themselves that other employees cannot understand.

Second, employers have also asserted that English-speaking employees get distracted by overhearing conversations among coworkers that are not in English, and that this situation can in turn lower overall productivity. Some employers have also claimed that permitting employees to speak different languages interferes with the creation of a harmonious workforce. Others have argued conversations between employees that are not in English interfere with the ability of English-speaking supervisors to monitor the quality of work. Finally, employers have defended English-only rules on the ground that they are needed to maintain a safe work environment: A multiplicity of languages within a workplace, they assert, may adversely affect the level of communication that is needed to eliminate certain potentially hazardous conditions.

The courts have not been generally sympathetic to these arguments for imposing English-only rules. Indeed, a number of courts have ruled that such language prohibitions violate the Title VII ban against discrimination on the basis of national origin.

Title VII does not explicitly define the term "national origin." The courts, however, have historically interpreted this phrase to mean country of origin. They have applied both disparate-treatment and disparate-impact tests to cases involving English-only rules. In the context of cases alleging disparate-treatment discrimination on the basis of national origin, courts look for workplace policies and practices that treat workers whose ancestors came from a particular country different than other workers whose ancestors hailed from other parts of the world. Some courts have applied a disparate-treatment test to assess the actual legality of English-only rules.

Under a disparate-impact test, on the other hand, courts have examined whether English-only rules have a disparate impact on people whose ancestors come from a particular country. Courts have in some cases held that such rules are unlawful because they have a disparate impact on workers who were born in non-English-speaking countries.

Although courts are generally hostile to English-only rules that apply to all workers in a workplace, some opinions indicate a willingness to accept the rule if it is narrowly tailored to a particular group of workers in order to promote a specific business goal. For example, English-only rules may be justified only when they are needed to insure worker safety: A rule requiring that the use of English only by all workers engaged in the operation of dangerous equipment would probably be upheld as a business necessity needed to insure a safe environment for workers.

1963, which is discussed below. In this section, we will discuss certain of the most important issues that have been raised in Title VII sex-discrimination litigation: *sex stereotyping, pregnancy,* and *sexual harassment.*

SEX STEREOTYPING. Much Title VII litigation on sex discrimination concerns sex stereotyping—that is, the assumption that women are suited for only certain kinds of work. For example, employers have traditionally assumed that women lacked the strength and stamina to do heavy labor. The courts have ruled for the most part that employers cannot limit women's work assignments on the basis of such *group* stereotypes. Rather, employers must judge each woman's abilities on an individual basis.

bona fide occupational qualification (BFOQ) In *employment-discrimination litigation,* the principle that gender, religion, or national origin can be used as a basis to limit jobs to one group only if the nature of the job makes these proper occupational conditions

Bona Fide Occupational Qualification. Limiting jobs to one sex is legitimate only if gender is a **bona fide occupational qualification (BFOQ).** Thus, most height and weight requirements have been struck down because the employer has not been able to prove their relationship to the job. Rules prohibiting the employment of both members of a married couple have been upheld, as courts have accepted the reasoning that marriage interferes with the execution of work. However, gender was not held to be a BFOQ for salespeople dealing with foreign customers who were said to be prejudiced against women (*Fernandez v. Wynn Oil Co.*, 653 F.2d 1275 [1981]).

In the following case, the Supreme Court ruled that a major accounting firm had engaged in sexual stereotyping and that the practice had played an unwarranted role in evaluating a woman's candidacy for a partnership.

PRICE WATERHOUSE v. HOPKINS
United States Supreme Court, 109 S.Ct. 1775 (1989)

Ann Hopkins, a senior manager at Price Waterhouse, a large accounting firm, was the only woman proposed for partnership in 1982. As part of the process, all partners in the firm were invited to submit comments on Hopkins. Several partners made comments that reflected a stereotyped view of women. For example, one comment suggested that Hopkins' chances for becoming a partner would improve if she dressed and acted in a more "feminine" manner. After Price Waterhouse decided to place Hopkins' application on hold, she filed a complaint alleging that the decision was illegal sex discrimination. Both the lower and appellate courts sided with Hopkins after finding that Price Waterhouse had failed to prove that the sexist comments did not cause it to place Hopkins' application on hold. Price Waterhouse brought the case to the Supreme Court in order to obtain clarification on an employer's burden of proof in a case where some permissible and some impermissible criteria play a role in an employment decision.

Justice BRENNAN announced the judgment of the Court and delivered an opinion, in which Justice MARSHALL, Justice BLACKMUN, and Justice STEVENS join.

. . . .

The specification of the standard of causation under Title VII is a decision about the kind of conduct that violates that statute. According to Price Waterhouse, an employer violates Title VII only if it gives decisive consideration to an employee's gender, race, national origin, or religion in making a decision that affects that employee. On Price Waterhouse's theory, even if a plaintiff shows that her gender played a part in an employment decision, it is still her burden to show that the decision would have been different if the employer had not discriminated. In Hopkins' view, on the other hand, an employer violates the statute whenever it allows one of these attributes to play any part in an employment decision. Once a plaintiff shows that this occurred, according to Hopkins, the employer's proof that it would have made the same decision in the absence of discrimination can serve to limit equitable relief but not to avoid a finding of liability. We conclude that, as often happens, the truth lies somewhere in-between.

In passing Title VII, Congress made the simple but momentous announcement that sex, race, religion, and national origin are not relevant to the selection, evaluation, or compensation of employees. Yet, the statute does not purport to limit the other qualities and characteristics that employers *may* take into account in making employment decisions. The converse, therefore, of "for cause" legislation, Title VII eliminates certain bases for distinguishing among employees while otherwise preserving employers' freedom of choice. This balance between employee rights and employer prerogatives turns out to be decisive in the case before us.

Congress' intent to forbid employers to take gender into account in making employment decisions appears on the face of the statute. In now-familiar language, the statute forbids an employer to "fail or refuse to hire or to discharge any individual, or otherwise to discriminate with respect to his compensation, terms, conditions, or privileges of employment," or to "limit, segregate, or classify his employees or applicants for employment in any way which would deprive any individual of employment opportunities or otherwise adversely affect his status as an employee, *because of* such individual's . . . sex." We take these words to mean that gender must be irrelevant to employment decisions. To construe the words "because of" as colloquial shorthand for "but-for causation," as does Price Waterhouse, is to misunderstand them.

But-for causation is a hypothetical construct. In determining whether a particular factor was a but-for cause of a given event, we begin by assuming that that factor was present at the time of the event, and then ask whether, even if that factor had been absent, the event nevertheless would have transpired in the same way. The present, active tense of the operative verbs of § 703(a)(1) ("to fail or refuse"), in contrast, turns our attention to the actual moment of the event in question, the adverse employment decision. The critical inquiry, the one commanded by the words of § 703(a)(1), is whether gender was a factor in the employment decision *at the moment it was made*. Moreover, since we know that the words "because of" do not mean "*solely* because of," we also know that Title VII meant to condemn even those decisions based on a mixture of legitimate and illegitimate considerations. When, therefore, an employer considers both gender and legitimate factors at the time of making a decision, that decision was "because of" sex and the other, legitimate considerations—even if we may say later, in the context of litigation, that the decision would have been the same if gender had not been taken into account. . . .

We need not leave our commonsense at the

doorstep when we interpret a statute. It is difficult for us to imagine that, in the simple words "because of," Congress meant to obligate a plaintiff to identify the precise causal role played by legitimate and illegitimate motivations in the employment decision she challenges. We conclude, instead, that Congress meant to obligate her to prove that the employer relied upon sex-based considerations in coming to its decision. . . .

To say that an employer may not take gender into account is not, however, the end of the matter, for that describes only one aspect of Title VII. The other important aspect of the statute is its preservation of an employer's remaining freedom of choice. We conclude that the preservation of this freedom means that an employer shall not be liable if it can prove that, even if it had not taken gender into account, it would have come to the same decision regarding a particular person. The statute's maintenance of employer prerogatives is evident from the statute itself and from its history, both in Congress and in this Court. . . .

In saying that gender played a motivating part in an employment decision, we mean that, if we asked the employer at the moment of the decision what its reasons were and if we received a truthful response, one of those reasons would be that the applicant or employee was a woman. In the specific context of sex stereotyping, an employer who acts on the basis of a belief that a woman cannot be aggressive, or that she must not be, has acted on the basis of gender. . . .

As to the existence of sex stereotyping in this case, we are not inclined to quarrel with the District Court's conclusion that a number of the partners' comments showed sex stereotyping at work. As for the legal relevance of sex stereotyping, we are beyond the day when an employer could evaluate employees by assuming or insisting that they matched the stereotype associated with their group, for " '[i]n forbidding employers to discriminate against individuals because of their sex, Congress intended to strike at the entire spectrum of disparate treatment of men and women resulting from sex stereotypes.' " An employer who objects to aggressiveness in women but whose positions require this trait places women in an intolerable and impermissible Catch–22: out of a job if they behave aggressively and out of a job if they don't. Title VII lifts women out of this bind.

Remarks at work that are based on sex stereotypes do not inevitably prove that gender played a part in a particular employment decision. The plaintiff must show that the employer actually relied on her gender in making its decision. In making this showing, stereotyped remarks can certainly be *evidence* that gender played a part. In any event, the stereotyping in this case did not simply consist of stray remarks. On the contrary, Hopkins proved that Price Waterhouse invited partners to submit comments; that some of the comments stemmed from sex stereotypes; that an important part of the Policy Board's decision on Hopkins was an assessment of the submitted comments; and that Price Waterhouse in no way disclaimed reliance on sex-linked evaluations. This is not, as Price Waterhouse suggests, "discrimination in the air"; rather, it is, as

Hopkins puts it, "discrimination brought to ground and visited upon" an employee. Brief for Respondent 30. . . .

As to the employer's proof, in most cases, the employer should be able to present some objective evidence as to its probable decision in the absence of an impermissible motive. Moreover, proving "that the same decision would have been justified . . . is not the same as proving that the same decision would have been made." An employer may not, in other words, prevail in a mixed-motives case by offering a legitimate and sufficient reason for its decision if that reason did not motivate it at the time of the decision. Finally, an employer may not meet its burden in such a case by merely showing that at the time of the decision it was motivated only in part by a legitimate reason. The very premise of a mixed-motives case is that a legitimate reason was present, and indeed, in this case, Price Waterhouse already has made this showing by convincing Judge Gesell that Hopkins' interpersonal problems were a legitimate concern. The employer instead must show that its legitimate reason, standing alone, would have induced it to make the same decision.

. . .

The District Court found that sex stereotyping "was permitted to play a part" in the evaluation of Hopkins as a candidate for partnership. Price Waterhouse disputes both that stereotyping occurred and that it played any part in the decision to place Hopkins' candidacy on hold. In the firm's view, in other words, the District Court's factual conclusions are clearly erroneous. We do not agree. . . .

It takes no special training to discern sex stereotyping in a description of an aggressive female employee as requiring "a course at charm school." Nor, turning to Thomas Beyer's memorable advice to Hopkins, does it require expertise in psychology to know that, if an employee's flawed "interpersonal skills" can be corrected by a soft-hued suit or a new shade of lipstick, perhaps it is the employee's sex and not her interpersonal skills that has drawn the criticism.

Nor is the finding that sex stereotyping played a part in the Policy Board's decision undermined by the fact that many of the suspect comments were made by supporters rather than detractors of Hopkins. A negative comment, even when made in the context of a generally favorable review, nevertheless may influence the decisionmaker to think less highly of the candidate; the Policy Board, in fact, did not simply tally the "yes's" and "no's" regarding a candidate, but carefully reviewed the content of the submitted comments. The additional suggestion that the comments were made by "persons outside the decisionmaking chain" (Brief for Petitioner 48)—and therefore could not have harmed Hopkins— simply ignores the critical role that partners' comments played in the Policy Board's partnership decisions.

. . .

We hold that when a plaintiff in a Title VII case proves that her gender played a motivating part in an employment decision, the defendant may avoid a finding of liability only by proving by a preponderance of the evidence that it would have made the same decision even if it had not taken the plaintiff's gender into account. Because the courts below erred by deciding that the defendant must make this proof by clear and convincing evidence, we reverse the Court of Appeals' judgment against Price Waterhouse on liability and remand the case to that court for further proceedings.

It is so ordered.

Case Questions

1. Do you agree with the court's decision to impose the "preponderance of evidence" standard, which is the lowest burden of proof, upon employers in "mixed motive" cases? Should an employer have to disprove discrimination by "clear and convincing evidence," or even "beyond a reasonable doubt," when a plaintiff proves that gender or race played a role in an employment decision?

2. If you represented Price Waterhouse, how could you actually prove, by a preponderance of the evidence, that Hopkins' application would have been put on hold even if it had not received sexist comments regarding her candidacy? What kind of evidence would you offer?

PREGNANCY. The continuing controversy about pregnancy benefits ended with the enactment of the 1978 Pregnancy Disability Amendment to Title VII. This amendment broadened the definition of sex discrimination to include discrimination based on pregnancy, childbirth, and related medical conditions. By law, employers must treat pregnant women in the same way as other disabled workers. Thus, pregnant women cannot be discharged or required to take sick leave at a specified time. In addition, they must be reinstated after taking leave. If employers provide disability or paid sick leave to other employees, they must do so for pregnant women. However, a pregnant woman who decides to leave work longer than is medically necessary receives no benefits.

KNOW

A related issue is raised by the question of employment and fetal protection: Can employers discriminate against workers who are at greater risk of injury when the worker is a woman and the greater risk is risk to her unborn baby? This question is the subject of the YOU DECIDE feature in this chapter.

YOU DECIDE

Employment and Fetal Protection

The proliferation of potentially dangerous substances in many workplaces, plus concern about possible liability for related injuries, has led a number of employers to adopt policies banning workers who, for one reason or another, are more at risk of injury. One of the most controversial of these policies prohibits women who have not ruled out childbirth as a life choice from working in areas that could endanger fetal health. In addition to raising questions about whether such policies discriminate on the basis of sex, fetal-protection rules have triggered many of the issues and heated emotions that have characterized our country's debate about abortion—that is, issues revolving around a woman's right to control her body and make decisions about her life ought to take precedence over the rights of a fetus.

A recent Supreme Court decision raised serious questions about the legality of fetal-protection policies. The case of International union, UAW v. Johnson Controls, Inc., 111 S.Ct. 1196 (1991) involved a fetal-protection policy adopted by Johnson Controls, Inc., a manufacturer of batteries, in 1982. Under the policy, women who could not document that they were medically incapable of bearing children were barred from manufacturing jobs that exposed them to lead, which is a known cause of fetal defects. The company adopted the policy after eight female employees who had worked in jobs that exposed them to lead became pregnant and showed dangerous levels of the substance in their blood.

Two years later, the union representing the workers at Johnson filed a lawsuit alleging that the company's fetal-protection policy violated Title VII of the Civil Rights Act of 1964 because it discriminated on the basis of sex and pregnancy. Both the federal district and circuit courts that considered the case before it made its way to the Supreme Court upheld the policy on the ground that it was justified as a "business necessity"—namely, the need to protect the health of fetuses of female workers.

Is a policy like Johnson Control's fetal-protection policy a valid way to protect the health of fetuses who have yet to be conceived? Should all women be barred from certain jobs because they may at some point in the future have a child? If fetal-protection policies are not permitted, how can employers protect themselves from liability for damages if a female worker who was exposed to a harmful substance gives birth to an injured infant? For further discussion, see p. 585.

SEXUAL HARASSMENT. The issue of sexual harassment in the workplace has received unprecedented attention in the wake of the confirmation hearings for Supreme Court Justice Clarence Thomas, during which Anita Hill, a law professor, charged that Thomas sexually harassed her while she was under his supervision at the Equal Employment Opportunity Commission. Even though Professor Hill's charges did not abort Justice Thomas' quest for a seat on the Supreme court, they did succeed in bringing into the forefront of public consciousness a relatively new area of the law. Cases date back only to 1977, EEOC guidelines to 1980 (*see* Fig. 15-1). There are two kinds of *sexual harassment*. The first and most blatant form is the exchange of sexual favors for employment opportunities. The second form is *environmental sexual harassment*, in which a worker is subjected to unwanted sexual comments, innuendos, jokes, physical contacts, and the like.

The legal approach to sexual harassment was transformed by a 1986 Supreme Court decision. The Court ruled that an employer may be held liable for sex discrimination even though the worker does not use an established grievance procedure or otherwise notify the employer of the problem. The Court did not set any general rule about employer liability but did indicate that it depended on the circumstances of the case (*Meritor Savings Bank v. Vinson,* 106 S. Ct. 2399 [1986]).

This decision implies that explicit policies and procedures regarding sexual harassment may offer businesses some legal protection from liability. Thus, it is not surprising that corporations are increasingly issuing written policies against sexual harassment. This chapter's ORGANIZATIONAL PROFILE details the efforts of one U.S. corporation to establish company policies and practices for dealing with sexual harassment in the workplace.

Defenses to Charges of Discrimination

There are four critical defenses to discrimination charges under Title VII: *no adverse impact, business necessity, seniority systems,* and *bona fide occupational qualifications.*

FIGURE 15-1 EEOC Rules on Sexual Harassment
Source: Equal Employment Opportunity Commission

Harassment on the basis of sex is a violation of Section 703 of Title VII of the Civil Rights Act of 1964. The Equal Employment Opportunity Commission (EEOC) has provided specific definitions of what constitutes sexual harassment: unwelcome sexual advances, requests for sexual favors, and other verbal or physical conduct of a sexual nature when (1) submission to such conduct is made, either explicitly or implicitly, a term or condition of an individual's employment, (2) submission to or rejection of such conduct by an individual is used as the basis for employment decisions affecting such individual, or (3) such conduct has the purpose or effect of substantially interfering with an individual's work performance or creating an intimidating, hostile, or offensive working environment.

In determining whether alleged conduct constitutes sexual harassment, the commission looks at the record as a whole and at the totality of the circumstances, such as the nature of the sexual advances and the context in which the alleged incidents occurred. The determination of the legality of a particular action is made from the facts, on a case-by-case basis.

Applying general Title VII principles. EEOC states that an employer, employment agency, joint apprenticeship committee, or labor organization is responsible for its acts and those of its agents and supervisory employees with respect to sexual harassment regardless of whether the specific acts complained of were authorized or even forbidden by the employer and regardless of whether the employer knew or should have known of their occurrence.

In the minds of many experts on programs for dealing with sexual harassment in the workplace, Corning Inc. is a model. The upstate New York company, which manufactures glassware, first addressed the issue in the 1970s by holding workshops to sensitize supervisors. Despite such early efforts, however, Corning's female employees complained in the early 1980s that the work environment remained hostile; in fact, the attrition rates for female employees at Corning were quite high.

To address this problem, the company embarked on a campaign in the mid-1980s to root out sexual harassment and sex discrimination and to increase the diversity of its workforce. The company implemented an affirmative-action program which called for the hiring and promotion of certain numbers of women and minorities at every level of the company. In addition, the company surveyed its female employees to assess their complaints, which included unequal pay, lack of child-care programs, and charges about sexual harassment.

In addition to establishing a child-care program and addressing inequities in pay, the company adopted a formal policy reflecting a twofold approach to sexual harassment. First, Corning required that employees—especially supervisors—attend workshops to increase their awareness of how their own behavior could be interpreted as sexual harassment. Although most people, for example, understand that

it is sexual harassment when a supervisor penalizes an employee for rejecting sexual advances, fewer people understand another form of harassment called "hostile-environment" harassment. Under this theory, an employer can be liable under Title VII if it fails to eliminate conduct in the workplace that creates a demeaning environment for a protected group. Conduct that can contribute to creating a hostile environment includes lewd gestures and sexually explicit or demeaning remarks.

Corning thus implemented a strict program to deal with this form of discrimination. Under written policy, the first step for a woman who feels harassed is to inform the harasser that she finds the conduct offensive. If the behavior does not cease, the next step is to inform management. Finally, the policy provides for a formal investigation mechanism.

Although Corning does not claim to have put an end to sexual harassment and discrimination of every kind, its progress is clear. Its workforce has diversified, and greater numbers of women and minorities are receiving higher salaries and being promoted to management positions. Corning's aggressiveness in this area reflects more than just concern about getting slapped with lawsuits: The company believes that it is good business to have a diversified workforce in which all employees feel encouraged to reach their highest potential and that such efforts will be rewarded.

NO ADVERSE IMPACT.   This defense is essentially a war of statistics: The employer challenges the data on discrimination presented by the worker and provides a statistical demonstration that employment practices have not adversely affected women or minorities.

BUSINESS NECESSITY.   A **business necessity** is defined as a practice that is necessary for the safe and efficient operation of the business, such as the airline rule grounding pregnant flight attendants for safety reasons. When applied to recruitment and hiring, it means that selection techniques must be correlated with job performance. Thus, any test for hiring and recruitment must be able to predict the candidate's ability to perform the job.

business necessity Defense against *employment-discrimination charges* on the ground that recruitment or hiring practices are necessary for the safe and efficient operation of a business

SENIORITY SYSTEMS.   Seniority represents a tension in the law between Title VII rights and rights that are negotiated as part of collective-bargaining agreements. **Seniority systems** generally perpetuate past patterns of discrimination because they were negotiated on behalf of white male incumbents. As a group, women and minorities have less seniority because they have until recently been the targets of discriminatory employment practices. As the last hired, they are the first to be fired when firms are in trouble.

seniority systems Defense against *employment-discrimination charges* on the ground that policies regarding compensation and promotion have been negotiated in collective-bargaining agreements (*see also* Chapter 13)

Initially, courts declined to protect seniority systems against allegations of discrimination: They reasoned that seniority systems perpetuated the effects of past discrimination and frequently awarded additional seniority to individuals and groups victimized by past discrimination.

The **Firefighters Local** *Case.* The tide has turned since 1977, however, as the courts have increasingly upheld seniority systems against Title VII challenges. In a 1984 decision, for example, the Supreme Court ruled against black firemen protesting the last-hired, first-fired effect of the department's seniority system (*Firefighters Local Union No. 1784 v. Stotts*, 467 U.S. 501 [1984]). The case was complicated by the existence of a consent decree issued to resolve prior allegations of racial discrimination. Most of the blacks hired or promoted under that decree were fired or demoted during layoffs a few years later. The Supreme Court ruled that the layoffs were proper because the consent decree did not mention layoffs and the seniority system, which was never intended to discriminate, was bona fide and thus protected by Title VII. Although the Court recognized that the layoffs were frustrating the purpose of the consent decree, it felt that ". . . it is inappropriate to deny an innocent employee the benefits of his seniority in order to provide a remedy in a pattern or practice suit such as this."

Lorance v. AT&T. A recent case, which is excerpted below, also reflects the unwillingness of the courts to interfere with seniority systems even when they ensure the continuation of inequality in a workforce. In *Lorance v. AT&T Technologies, Inc.* (109 S.Ct. 2261 [1989]), the Supreme Court upheld the validity of a system that had been adopted by AT&T in 1982. This system determined seniority by calculating the amount of time spent *in a particular job.* Prior to this agreement, seniority at the company had been calculated by totaling the amount of time that an employee had spent *in any job in the plant.* The suit was filed by women who had only recently been promoted to higher-paying "tester" jobs and who, as a result of the change in the way seniority was calculated, wound up lower on the seniority scale for those positions.

LORANCE v. AT&T TECHNOLOGIES, INC.
United States Supreme Court, 109 S.Ct. 2261 (1989)

Three female employees of AT&T Technologies, Inc. (AT&T) brought an action challenging the company's seniority system as discriminatory. All three petitioners had worked as hourly-wage employees in AT&T's Montgomery Works plant since the early 1970s and have been represented by respondent Local 1942, International Brotherhood of Electrical Workers, AFL-CIO. Until 1979, all hourly-wage earners accumulated competitive seniority on the basis of years worked, and a worker promoted to the more highly skilled and better-paid "tester" positions retained this plantwide seniority. A July 23, 1979 collective-bargaining agreement executed by respondents changed the manner in which tester seniority was calculated: It was no longer determined by how many years one had worked at the plant, but rather by the time actually spent as a tester. The present action arises from this contractual modification. It was possible to regain full plantwide seniority after spending five years as a tester and completing a training program. Petitioners became testers between 1978 and 1980. In 1982, an economic downturn caused them to be de-

moted due to lower seniority under the new seniority system. They would not have been demoted had the former plantwide seniority system been in effect. Petitioners filed complaints with the Equal Employment Opportunity Commission (EEOC) and then filed a lawsuit in district court claiming that the new system was the product of intentional sexual discrimination. The petitioners wished to file as class representatives for women employees of the company's plant who lost plantwide seniority or who were deterred from seeking promotions to tester positions due to the new system. The United States District Court for the Northern District of Illinois granted the employer's motion for summary judgment on the ground that petitioners had not filed their complaints with the EEOC within the limitation period of 180 days from the time of the unfair practice. The Court of Appeals affirmed. The Supreme Court granted certiorari to resolve the conflict over when the limitations period begins in a lawsuit that arises out of a seniority system that is not alleged to be discriminatory on its face or as presently applied.

Justice SCALIA delivered the opinion of the Court. . . .

Section 706(e) of Title VII of the Civil Rights Act of 1964, provides that "[a] charge . . . shall be filed [with the EEOC] within [the applicable period] after the alleged unlawful employment practice occurred." Assessing timeliness therefore "requires us to identify precisely the 'unlawful employment practice' of which [petitioners] complai[n]." Under § 703(a) of Title VII, it is an "unlawful employment practice" for an employer

"(1) . . . to discriminate against any individual with respect to his compensation, terms, conditions, or privileges of employment, because of such individual's race, color, religion, sex, or national origin; or

"(2) to limit, segregate, or classify his employees or applicants for employment in any way which would deprive or tend to deprive any individual of employment opportunities or otherwise adversely affect his status as an employee, because of such individual's race, color, religion, sex, or national origin." § 2000e–2(a).

Petitioners' allegation of a disparate impact on men and women would ordinarily suffice to state a claim under § 703(a)(2), since that provision reaches "practices that are fair in form, but discriminatory in operation," "[S]eniority systems," however, "are afforded special treatment under Title VII," by reason of § 703(h), which states:

"Notwithstanding any other provision of this subchapter, it shall not be an unlawful employment practice for an employer to apply different standards of compensation, or different terms, conditions, or privileges of employment pursuant to a bona fide seniority . . . system, . . . provided that such differences are not the result of an intention to discriminate because of race, color, religion, sex, or national origin. . . ."

We have construed this provision to mean that "absent a discriminatory purpose, the operation of a seniority system cannot be an unlawful employment practice even if the system has some discriminatory consequences." Thus, for liability to be incurred "there must be a finding of actual intent to discriminate on [statutorily proscribed] grounds on the part of those who negotiated or maintained the [seniority] system."

Petitioners do not allege that the seniority system treats similarly situated employees differently or that it has been operated in an intentionally discriminatory manner. Rather, they claim that its differential impact on the sexes is unlawful because the system "ha[d] its genesis in [sex] dsicrimination." Specifically, the complaint alleges that respondents "conspired *to change* the seniority rules, in order to protect incumbent male testers," and that the resulting agreement effected a *"manipulation of* seniority rules" for that "purpose." This is in essence a claim of intentionally discriminatory *alteration* of their contractual rights. . . . Under the collective-bargaining agreements in effect prior to 1979, each petitioner had earned the right to receive a favorable position in the hierarchy of seniority among testers (if and when she became a tester), and respondents elimi-

nated those rights for reasons alleged to be discriminatory. Because this diminution in employment status occurred in 1979—well outside the period of limitations for a complaint filed with the EEOC in 1983—the Seventh Circuit was correct to find petitioners' claims time-barred under § 706(e).

We recognize, of course, that it is possible to establish a different theoretical construct: to regard the employer as having been guilty of a continuing violation which "occurred," for purposes of § 706(e), not only when the contractual right was eliminated but also when each of the concrete effects of that elimination were felt. Or it would be possible to interpret § 703 in such fashion that when the proviso of § 703(h) is not met ("provided that such differences are not the result of an intention to discriminate because of race, color, religion, sex, or national origin") and that subsection's protection becomes unavailable, nothing *prevents* suits against the later effects of the system *on disparate impact grounds* under § 703(a)(2). The answer to these alternative approaches is that our cases have rejected them. . . .

. . .In holding that, when a seniority system is nondiscriminating in form and application, it is the allegedly discriminatory *adoption* which triggers the limitations period, we respect not only § 706(e)'s general "'value judgment concerning the point at which the interests in favor of protecting valid claims are outweighed by the interests in prohibiting the prosecution of stale [claims],'" but also the considerations underlying the "special treatment" accorded to seniority systems under § 703(h). This "special treatment" strikes a balance between the interests of those protected against discrimination by Title VII and those who work—perhaps for many years—in reliance upon the validity of a facially lawful seniority system. There is no doubt, of course, that a facially discriminatory seniority system (one that treats similarly situated employees differently) can be challenged at any time, and that even a facially neutral system, if it is adopted with unlawful discriminatory motive, can be challenged within the prescribed period after adoption. But allowing a facially neutral system to be challenged, and entitlements under it to be altered, many years after its adoption would disrupt those valid reliance interests that § 703(h) was meant to protect. In the context of the present case, a female tester could defeat the settled (and worked-for) expectations of her co-workers whenever she is demoted or not promoted under the new system, be that in 1983, 1993, 2003, or beyond. Indeed, a given plaintiff could in theory sue successively for not being promoted, for being demoted, for being laid off, and for not being awarded a sufficiently favorable pension, so long as these acts—even if nondiscriminatory in themselves—could be attributed to the 1979 change in seniority. Our past cases, to which we adhere today, have declined to follow an approach that has such disruptive implications.

For the foregoing reasons, the judgment of the Court of Appeals is
Affirmed.

Case Questions

1. Why is it necessary to have a time limit in bringing employment-discrimination cases?

2. Prior cases have rejected the theory that would hold an employer liable for the late discriminatory effects of an uncontested, facially neutral seniority system. Does the Court's concern that a female tester could defeat the valid expectations of coworkers whenever she is demoted or not promoted support this hesitancy to acknowledge the prior sexual discrimination?

3. Section 703(h) of Title VII of the Civil Rights Act of 1964 states that such a change in a seniority system is not unlawful unless it is the result of an intent to discriminate. The Court interpreted this to mean that if a discriminatory purpose is absent, the fact that the system has a discriminatory effect does not make it unlawful. How could a class of individuals prove an intent to discriminate based on the Court's analysis?

BONA FIDE OCCUPATIONAL QUALIFICATION. In some cases, the very nature of a job makes gender, religion, or national origin a proper occupational qualification. (Race and color are never valid BFOQs.) Thus, it is legal to hire only male actors to play male roles.

The courts and the EEOC have devised several tests to determine when gender is a BFOQ. In a 1969 case concerning the ability of women to lift heavy weights in a telephone switchman's job, the court ruled that an employer must prove that "all or substantially all women would be unable to perform safely and efficiently the duties of the job involved" (*Weeks v. Southern Bell Telephone and Telegraph Co.*, 408 F.2d 228 [1969]). The case excerpted below, however, laid out a different test.

DIAZ v. PAN AMERICAN WORLD AIRWAYS, INC.
U.S. Court of Appeals, Fifth Circuit, 442 F.2d 385 (1971)

Celio Diaz was denied the position of flight attendant by Pan Am due to that company's long-standing policy of hiring only females for the job. As a result, Diaz brought a class action in U.S. District Court claiming impermissible gender discrimination in violation of Title VII. Because Pan Am admitted to discrimination on the basis of gender, the only question was whether gender is a BFOQ for the job of flight attendant. The district court resolved this question in favor of Pan Am. Diaz appeals.

Tuttle, Circuit Judge:
. . . §703(e) . . . states:

(e) Notwithstanding any other provision of this subchapter,
(1) it shall not be an unlawful employment practice for an employer to hire and employ employees . . . on the basis of his religiion, sex, or national origin in those certain instances where religion, sex, or national origin is a bona fide occupational qualification reasonably necessary to the normal opertion of that particular business or enterprise. . . .

Since it has been admitted that appellee has discriminated on the basis of sex, the result in this case, turns, in effect, on the construction given to this exception.

. . . In attempting to read Congress' intent in these circumstances, however, it is reasonable to assume, from a reading of the statute itself, that one of Congress' main goals was to provide equal access to the job market for both men and women. . . .

Attainment of this goal, however, is , as stated above, limited by the bona fide occupational qualification exception in section 703(e). . . . [W]e adopt the EEOC guidelines which state that "the Commission believes that the bona fide occupational qualification as to sex should be interpreted narrowly." . . .

. . . .

. . . [T]he trial court found that Pan Am's current hiring policy was the result of a pragmatic process ". . . designed to yield under Pan Am's current operating conditions better *average* performance for its passengers than would a policy of mixed male and female hiring." (emphasis added) The performance of female attendants was *better* in the sense that they were *superior* in such non-mechanical aspects of the job as "providing reassurance to anxious passengers, giving courteous personalized service and, in general, making flights as pleasurable as possible within the limitations imposed by aircraft operations."

The trial court also found that Pan Am's passengers overwhelmingly preferred to be served by female stewardesses. Moreover, on the basis of the expert testimony of a psychiatrist, the court found that . . . an air carrier is required to take account of the special psychological needs of its passengers. These psychological needs are better attended to by females. . . .

. . . .

. . . [W]e do not feel that these findings justify the discrimination practiced by Pan Am.

. . . [T]he use of the word "necessary" in section 703(e) requires that we apply a business *necessity* test, not a business *convenience* test. . . .

The primary function of an airline is to transport passengers safely from one point to another. . . . No one has suggested that having male stewards will so seriously affect the operation of an airline as to jeopardize or even minimize its ability to provide safe transportation. . . .

We do not mean to imply, of course, that Pan Am cannot take into consideration the ability of *individuals* to perform the non-mechanical functions of the job. What we hold is that because the non-mechanical aspects of the job of flight cabin attendant are not "reasonably necessary to the normal operation" of Pan Am's business, Pan Am cannot exclude *all* males simply because *most* males may not perform adequately.

. . . .

Appellees also argue, and the trial court found, that . . . it was simply not practicable to find the few males that would perform properly.

We do not feel that this alone justifies discriminating against all males. Since, as stated above, the basis of exclusion is the ability to perform non-mechanical functions which we find to be tangential to what is "reasonably *necessary*" for the business involved, the exclusion of *all* males because this is the *best* way to select the kind of personnel Pan Am desires simply cannot be justified. Before sex discrimination can be practiced, it must not only be shown that it is impracticable to find the men that possess the abilities that most women possess, but that the abilities are *necessary* to the business, not merely tangential.

. . . .

The judgement is reversed and the case is remanded for proceedings not inconsistent with this opinion.

Case Questions:

1. What test does the court use to determine when gender is a BFOQ?

2. How is the test similar to the Supreme Court's disparate-impact analysis in *Griggs*?

3. Explain how BFOQs are an exception to the general rule of Title VII.

■ *Concept Check 15-2   Title VII of the Civil Rights Act of 1964*

- Explain the primary intent of *Title VII* of the 1964 Civil Rights Act.
- Explain *disparate treatment* and *disparate impact* as tests for determining discriminatory behavior. What is a *pattern-and-practice claim*?
- Describe the three *statistical approaches* to establishing disparate impact.
- Describe the application of the disparate-impact test in *Griggs v. Duke Power* and *Wards Cove v. Antonio*. Explain the *business-justification defense*. What are the most important provisions of the *Civil Rights Act of 1991*?
- What are the main functions of the *Equal Employment Opportunity Commission*? Explain the EEOC guidelines defining discrimination on the basis of *national origin*.
- Define the principle of the *bona fide occupational qualification* and explain its application to charges of discrimination based on *sex stereotyping*.
- Explain *business necessity* and *seniority systems* as defenses against charges of discrimination under Title VII.

■ AFFIRMATIVE ACTION AND EXECUTIVE ORDER 11246

Executive Order 11246 (the Order), issued by President Lyndon Johnson in 1965, forbids employment discrimination by federal contractors and subcontractors. It follows government tradition in using the power of federal contracts to influence private business. Businesses comply both in order to avoid legal action and to retain profitable government contract work. Because about forty percent of the civilian workforce in the United States is employed by compa-

Executive Order 11246 Issued by President Johnson in 1965, order forbidding *employment discrimination* by federal contractors and subcontractors

nies receiving federal contracts, the impact of Executive Order 11246 is substantial.[1]

EXTENSION OF COVERAGE. Coverage of the Order has been deepened and broadened by repeated amendments. President Johnson extended its protection to women just two years later in Executive Order 11375. Section 503 of the Rehabilitation Act of 1973 applied its principles to the physically and mentally handicapped. In 1974, Section 402 of the Vietnam Era Readjustment Assistance Act added preferential provisions for Vietnam veterans, especially the disabled.

THE ORDER AND AFFIRMATIVE ACTION. The Order marked a drastic departure from the passive approach to discrimination taken by Title VII: The Order demanded that contractors not simply refrain from discriminating but also take **affirmative action** to promote the employment of protected groups in order to correct past wrongs. In 1974, the EEOC made affirmative-action plans a requirement for all employers.

Revised Order No. 4, issued by President Nixon in 1971, provided the specifics on compliance with the prior Executive Orders. It required all federal contractors and subcontractors with contracts over $50,000 and 50 or more employees to have written affirmative-action plans. State and local governments with 15 or more employees—susceptible to the order because of federal revenue-sharing funds—had to meet the same requirement. This provision was a positive obligation for all contractors and local governments, regardless of an employer's past record on discrimination.

> **affirmative action** Under *Executive Order 11246*, the active promotion of the employment of protected groups in order to correct past wrongs

Affirmative-Action Programs

Creating and administering an affirmative-action program is a complex, time-consuming endeavor. The company's chief executive officer must issue a written policy statement declaring that the organization will not discriminate. This policy must be widely disseminated to recruiters and employment offices, subcontractors and suppliers, and unions and employees. There is also a positive obligation to show women and minorities in nonstereotyped jobs in company advertising and publications.

Although they are not asked to treat minority hiring as a matter of satisfying "quotas," employers are expected to make good-faith efforts to reach goals like those published by the EEOC in Figure 15-2.[2] Responsibility for implementing policy is usually delegated to a high-level manager, who plans, implements, coordinates, and evaluates the affirmative-action program over the long term.

The personnel department is also charged with certain responsibilities in implementing both government guidelines and company policy. Because it is difficult to demonstrate that they are bias-free, formal tests have been abandoned by many employers. Certain seemingly general job-interview questions may also be unlawful. For example, the question "Do you have a picture you can send us?" may be interpreted as sex-related. Instead of asking, "Do you have a disability?" interviewers must rephrase the question: "Do you have any

---

[1] See James E. Jones, William P. Murphy, and Robert Belton, *Cases and Materials on Discrimination in Employment* (Minneapolis, MN: West, 1987), p. 595.

[2] See Murray L. Weidenbaum, *Business, Government, and the Public*, 4th ed. (Englewood Cliffs, NJ: Prentice Hall, 1990), pp. 116-24.

EEOC AFFIRMATIVE-ACTION PROGRAM GUIDELINES

AFFIRMATIVE ACTION - RESULTS

The most important measure of an Affirmative-Action Program is its RESULTS.

Extensive efforts to develop procedures, analyses, data collection systems, report forms and fine written policy statements are meaningless unless the end product will be measurable, yearly improvement in hiring, training and promotion of minorities and females in all parts of your organization.

Just as the success of a company program to increase sales is evaluated in terms of actual increases in sales, the only realistic basis for evaluating a program to increase opportunity for minorities and females is its actual impact upon these persons.

The essence of your Affirmative-Action Program should be:

- *Establish strong company policy and commitment.*
- *Assign responsibility and authority for program to top company official.*
- *Analyze present work force to identify jobs, departments and units where minorities and females are underutilized.*
- *Set specific, measurable, attainable hiring and promotion goals, with target dates, in each area of underutilization.*
- *Make every manager and supervisor responsible and accountable for helping to meet these goals.*
- *Re-evaluate job descriptions and hiring criteria to assure that they reflect actual job needs.*
- *Find minorities and females who qualify or can become qualified to fill goals.*
- *Review and revise all employment procedures to assure that they do not have discriminatory effect and that they help attain goals.*
- *Focus on getting minorities and females into upward mobility and relevant training pipelines where they have not had previous access.*
- *Develop systems to monitor and measure progress regularly. If results are not satisfactory to meet goals, find out why, and make necessary changes.*

FIGURE 15-2 Sample EEOC Affirmative-Action Program Guideline *Source: Equal Employment Opportunity Commission*

physical impairments that might interfere with your ability to do this job?" Table 15-4 lists several potentially discriminatory interview subjects along with questions that may and may not be asked about them.

PROCEDURES FOR COMPLIANCE. EEOC guidelines establish procedures for implementing and evaluating the practical effect of affirmative-action programs. These include *support programs, audit and reporting systems,* and, most importantly, *utilization analyses.*

Support Programs. Affirmative-action regulations require employers to develop supportive programs within the business and the community. For instance, they might institute special training in affirmative action for supervisors, offer more extensive employee counseling, set up day-care programs, or solve employee-transportation and housing problems.

Internal Audit and Reporting Systems. The employer is also required to establish an internal audit and reporting system to monitor the progress of the affirmative-action program on a continuing basis. If needed, the employer can then take prompt corrective action.

Utilization Analyses. The basis of an affirmative action program is the **utilization analysis** carried out by the employer. This is a detailed analysis of the composition of the company's employees as compared to that of the general labor force. The number and percentage of minorities and women in each job category in the company is measured and then weighed against the number of qualified and potentially qualified minorities and women in the labor market as a whole.

utilization analysis Used as the basis of an *affirmative-action program*, review of the composition of a firm's employees as compared to the general labor force

Regulations provide some guidelines for deciding what group the company workforce should be compared against. For example, the analysis must consider the minority population and unemployment levels in the local area,

	TABLE 15-4	*Antidiscrimination Rules for Employment Interviews*

SUBJECT	WHAT EMPLOYERS CAN ASK	WHAT EMPLOYERS CANNOT ASK
Age	Are you between 18 and 65? If not, state your age.	How old are you? What is your date of birth?
Religion	Nothing	Which church do you belong to? What religious holidays do you observe?
Race	Nothing	What is your skin color or complexion?
Sex	Nothing (unless directly job related)	Do you have a picture you can send us?
Disability	Do you have any physical impairments that interfere with your ability to do the job?	Do you have a disability?
Name	Have you ever worked for this company under a different name?	State other names under which you have worked.
Citizenship	Are you a citizen of the United States?	Of what country are you a citizen?
Character	Have you been convicted of a crime?	Have you ever been arrested?
National origin	Nothing	What nationality are you or your parents?
Education	Where did you go to school?	
Experience	What kind of jobs have you held?	
Relatives	Do you have any relatives working for the company?	Are you married? Do you have children?
Organization memberships	Are you a member of any organization (exclude those indicating race, creed, color or national origin)?	List all societies to which you belong.

Source: Murray L. Weidenbaum, Business, Government, and the Public, *4th ed. (Englewood Cliffs, NJ: Prentice Hall, 1990).*

the availability of skilled minorities and women, the availability of promotable and transferable minority employees, and the ability of the employer or nearby institutions to offer training.

Corrective Action. If the utilization analysis shows that a company has fallen short in employing any or all of the target groups, the employer must take steps to correct the deficiency. This process involves setting a numerical goal for the employment of each group within each job classification. In addition, the employer must draw up a timetable for meeting these goals. The timetable must set both intermediate annual targets and a final date for achieving a long-range goal.

Although employers are not legally obligated to meet established dates, they must make good-faith efforts to honor them. Such efforts include changing existing personnel policies to eliminate discriminatory barriers and developing new programs to encourage the hiring and promotion of women and minorities. For example, a company might find new recruitment sources, eliminate certain job requirements, change applications and testing procedures,

568

PART FOUR   EMPLOYMENT AND THE LAW

review wage and salary programs, improve in-house training programs to encourage upward mobility, extend maternity leaves, or modify layoff and recall policies.

ENFORCEMENT: THE OFCCP. The *Office of Federal Contract Compliance Program (OFCCP)* in the Department of Labor is responsible for enforcing all federal contract provisions. This agency's efforts have a greater impact than those of the EEOC because they reach more employers.

Review Procedure. When contracts are large, the OFCCP may review bidders even before contracts are awarded. Mostly, however, the agency carries out regular audits of firms already holding contracts. These firms are generally audited no more frequently than once every two years. Large contractors, contractors with greater career opportunities, contractors with poor EEO records, and contractors located in areas with high concentrations of minority workers are all audited more frequently. The OFCCP also conducts audits in response to complaints about specific companies.

An OFCCP review begins with a desk audit of documents and is often followed by onsite inspection. The inspector examines personnel records and practices, giving special attention to affirmative-action policies and procedures. Once the audit is complete, the agency issues a letter accepting the affirmative-action program, accepts a letter of commitment from the employer to remedy minor violations, or negotiates a conciliation agreement to correct major deficiencies.

Affirmative Action and Reverse Discrimination

Affirmative-action programs have led to allegations of *reverse discrimination* against "majority" workers—that is, white males. The use of *numerical quotas* in hiring and promotion has been especially controversial. At the heart of the debate lies a moral judgment: Does past discrimination against certain groups justify present preferential treatment in compensation?

Such *group* justice, it is argued, may not be fair to *individuals.* Affirmative action, for example, does not benefit the individual black who suffered from discrimination fifty years ago. Rather, it offers a better job to blacks entering the work force today. Likewise, affirmative action does not penalize the white male worker of the last generation who unfairly benefited from discrimination. Instead, it weakens the employment chances of innocent white men now holding jobs.

In this section, we will trace the evolution of law on the controversial issue of affirmative action to see how the courts have struggled to improve opportunities for minorities without unduly impinging upon the rights of non-minorities.

SUPREME COURT DECISIONS. In a 1976 case, two white employees accused their employer of discrimination after the company fired them for stealing from a company shipment but retained a black employee also charged with the theft. The Supreme Court ruled the employer's action illegal, stating that Title VII and the Civil Rights Act of 1866 banned employment discrimination against whites as well as blacks (*McDonald v. Sante Fe Transportation Co.*, 427 U.S. 273 [1976]).

University of California v. Bakke: *Reverse Discrimination (I):* Two years later, another case alleging reverse discrimination reached the Supreme Court.

In *Regents of the University of California v. Bakke*, the court was faced with the issue of whether a medical school's admission criteria, which favored minority group members, violated the constitutional rights of a white male whose application had been rejected even though he had better credentials that some successful minority applicants. The decision in this case, portions of which appear below, split the court and left the issue of reverse discrimination unresolved.

REGENTS OF THE UNIVERSITY OF CALIFORNIA v. BAKKE

United States Supreme Court, 438 U.S. 265 (1978)

The admissions program at the Medical School at the University of California–Davis reserved 16 seats in each new class of 100 for disadvantaged minority groups, allowing only Blacks, Chicanos, Asians, and American Indians to vie for these spots. Each application submitted by one of these groups was reviewed by a special admissions committee, using similar rating methods as the general admissions committee but without applying the normal 2.5 grade point average minimum.

Allan Bakke, a white applicant whose grade point average and MCAT scores were higher than some of the students accepted for the special program, was denied admission and proceeded to sue the University of California under the Fourteenth Amendment of the Constitution, alleging a violation of equal protection. Bakke prevailed in all the California courts. The University of California now appeals to the U.S. Supreme Court.

Mr. Justice Powell announced the judgment of the Court.

. . . .

. . . The parties do disagree as to the level of judicial scrutiny to be applied to the special admissions program. . . .

. . . .

Nevertheless, petitioner argues that the court below erred in applying strict scrutiny to the special admissions program because white males, such as respondent, are not a "discrete and insular minority" requiring extraordinary protection from the majoritarian political process. This rationale, however, has never been invoked in our decisions as a prerequisite to subjecting racial or ethnic distinctions to strict scrutiny. . . . Racial and ethnic distinctions of any sort are inherently suspect and thus call for the most exacting judicial examination.

. . . .

We have held that in "order to justify the use of a suspect classification, a State must show that its purpose or interest is both constitutionally permissible and substantial, and that its use of the classification is 'necessary . . . to the accomplishment' of its purpose or the safeguarding of its interest." The special admissions

program purports to serve the purposes of: (i) "reducing the historic deficit of traditionally disfavored minorities in medical schools and in the medical profession"; (ii) countering the effects of societal discrimination; (iii) increasing the number of physicians who will practice in communities currently underserved; and (iv) obtaining the educational benefits that flow from an ethnically diverse student body. It is necessary to decide which, if any, of these purposes is substantial enough to support the use of a suspect classification.

If petitioner's purpose is to assure within its student body some specified percentage of a particular group merely because of its race or ethnic origin, such a preferential purpose must be rejected not as insubstantial but as facially invalid. Preferring members of any one group for no reason other than race or ethnic origin is discrimination for its own sake. This the Constitution forbids.

. . . .

Hence, the purpose of helping certain groups whom the faculty of the Davis Medical School perceived as victims of "societal discrimination" does not justify a classification that imposes disadvantages upon persons like respondent, who bear no responsibility for whatever harm the beneficiaries of the special admissions program are thought to have suffered. To hold otherwise would be to convert a remedy heretofore reserved for violations of legal rights into a privilege that all institutions throughout the Nation could grant at their pleasure to whatever groups are perceived as victims of societal discrimination.

Petitioner identifies, as another purpose of its program, improving the delivery of health-care services to communities currently underserved. . . .

Petitioner simply has not carried its burden of demonstrating that it must prefer members of particular ethnic groups over all other individuals in order to promote better health-care delivery to deprived citizens. . . .

The fourth goal asserted by petitioner is the attainment of a diverse student body. This clearly is a constitutionally permissible goal for an institution of higher education. . . .

. . . .

. . . But petitioner's argument that this is the only effective means of serving the interest of diversity is seriously flawed. . . . Petitioner's special admissions program, focused *solely* on ethnic diversity, would hinder rather than further attainment of genuine diversity.

. . . .

In [a properly devised] admissions program, race or ethnic background may be deemed a "plus" in a particular applicant's file, yet it does not insulate the individual from comparison with all other candidates for the available seats. . . .

This kind of program treats each applicant as an individual in the admissions process. The applicant who loses out on the last available seat to another candidate receiving a "plus" on the basis of ethnic background will not have been foreclosed from all consideration for that seat simply because he was not the right color or had the wrong surname. . . .

. . . .

The fatal flaw in petitioner's preferential program is its disregard of individual rights as guaranteed by the Fourteenth Amendment. . . . For this reason, that portion of the California court's judgment holding petitioner's special admissions program invalid under the Fourteenth Amendment must be affirmed.

In enjoining petitioner from ever considering the race of any applicant, however, the courts below failed to recognize that the State has a substantial interest that legitimately may be served by a properly devised admissions program involving the competitive consideration of race and ethnic origin. For this reason, so much of the California court's judgment as enjoins petitioner from any consideration of the race of any applicant must be reversed.

With respect to respondent's entitlement to an injunction directing his admission to the Medical School, petitioner has conceded that it could not carry its burden of proving that, but for the existence of its unlawful special admissions program, respondent still would not have been admitted. Hence, respondent is entitled to the injunction, and that portion of the judgment must be affirmed.

Case Questions:

1. What does the decision say about the constitutionality of the university's special admissions program?

2. What is strict scrutiny and when is a court to apply it?

3. What was the University of California trying to achieve through its special admissions program?

United Steelworkers v. Weber: *Reverse Discrimination (II):* In 1979, the Supreme Court was faced once again with a case of reverse discrimination, this time in an employment context. In dispute was an affirmative-action program that formed part of the collective-bargaining agreement between the Kaiser Aluminum and Chemical Corporation and the United Steelworkers of America. According to the agreement, Kaiser would admit at least 50 percent blacks into a skilled training program until 39 percent of its Louisiana plant's skilled workers were black—a figure matching the proportion of blacks in the local workforce. When the agreement was signed in 1974, just two percent of the plant's skilled workers were black. The case was brought by a white Kaiser employee who was not accepted into the training program.

Reversing the decisions of lower courts, the Supreme Court endorsed the use of affirmative-action programs in a five-to-two decision. Justice Brennan wrote that the Kaiser program "falls within the area of discretion left by Title VII to the private sector voluntarily to adopt affirmative action plans designed to eliminate conspicuous racial imbalance in traditionally segregated job categories." The decision was narrowed by the Court's emphasis that the Kaiser program did not demand the firing of white employees, did not totally bar white employees from training, and was a temporary measure designed to eliminate an existing racial imbalance (*United Steelworkers of America v. Weber*, 443 U.S. 193 [1979]).

United States v. Paradise: *Strict Quota Systems.* In 1987, the Supreme Court considered a promotion system using strict numerical quotas. The system was imposed on the Alabama state police by a federal court order. It required the force to promote one black trooper for every white promoted to each rank—if there were qualified blacks available—until they formed 25 percent of that rank. Portions of the Court's decision appear below.

UNITED STATES v. PARADISE

United States Supreme Court, 107 S.Ct. 1053 (1987)

In response to an NAACP complaint regarding its past history of overt discrimination against black trooper applicants, a mandatory policy was imposed by a 1972 Federal District Court order upon the Alabama Police Department. When the plaintiffs, Paradise and a class of black plaintiffs also parties to the 1972 action, sought relief from the district court regarding the Department's discriminatory promotions practices, the parties consented to an arrangement allowing the Department to fashion its own fair promotion procedure. However, due to the parties' inability to agree on any procedure proposed by the Department and in response to a pressing departmental need to promote 15 troopers to corporal, the district in 1983 issued an interim mandatory quota policy, similar to that of the 1972 order. This time, the Department was required to ensure that at least 50 percent of all promotions to corporal were given to black troopers until 25 percent of all troopers were black. The Court of Appeals affirmed the District Court's order on a challenge by the United States. The United States next makes its appeal to the U.S. Supreme Court.

Justice Brennan announced the judgment of the Court and delivered an opinion in which Justice Marshall, Justice Blackman, and Justice Powell join.

The United States maintains that the race-conscious relief ordered in this case violates the Equal Protection Clause of the Fourteenth Amendment to the Constitution of the United States.

. . . [W]e conclude that the relief ordered survives even strict scrutiny analysis: it is "narrowly tailored" to serve a "compelling governmental purpose."

. . . .

In determining whether race-conscious remedies are appropriate, we look to several factors, including the necessity for the relief and the efficacy of alternative remedies, the flexibility and duration of the relief, including the availability of waiver provisions; the relationship of the numerical goals to the relevant labor market; and the impact of the relief on the rights of third parties. . . .

. . . .

The options proffered by the Government and the Department would not have served the court's purposes. The Department proposed, as a stop-gap measure, to promote four blacks and eleven whites and requested additional time to allow the Department of Personnel to develop and submit a nondiscriminatory promotion procedure. . . .

. . . The Department's ad hoc offer to make one round of promotions without an adverse impact ignored the court's concern that an acceptable procedure be adopted with alacrity. . . .

Moreover, the Department's proposal ignored the in-jury to the plaintiff class that resulted from its delay in complying with the terms of the 1972 order and the 1979 and 1981 Decrees. . . . To permit ad hoc decisionmaking to continue and allow only four of fifteen slots to be filled by blacks would have denied relief to black troopers who had irretrievably lost promotion opportunities. . . .

. . . .

By 1984 the District Court was plainly justified in imposing the remedy chosen. Any order allowing further delay by the Department was entirely unacceptable. . . .

. . . .

The features of the one-for-one requirement and its actual operation indicate that it is flexible in application at all ranks. The requirement may be waived if no qualified black candidates are available. . . . [I]f external forces, such as budget cuts, necessitate a promotion freeze, the Department will not be required to make gratuitous promotions to remain in compliance with the court's order.

. . . The requirement endures only until the Department comes up with a procedure that does not have a discriminatory impact on blacks—something the Department was enjoined to do in 1972 and expressly promised to do by 1980. . . .

. . . .

The one-for-one requirement did not impose an unacceptable burden on innocent third parties. As stated above, the temporary and extremely limited nature of the requirement substantially limits any potential burden on white applicants for promotion. . . . Nor has the court imposed an "absolute bar" to white advancement. In the one instance in which the quota was employed, 50% of those elevated were white.

. . . .

Finally, the basic limitation, that black troopers promoted must be qualified, remains. Qualified white candidates simply have to compete with qualified black candidates. To be sure, should the District Court's promotion requirement be applied, black applicants would receive some advantage. But this situation is only temporary, and is subject to amelioration by the actiion of the Department itself.

. . . .

. . . [We] conclude that the District Judge properly balanced the individual and collective interests at stake, including the interests of the white troopers eligible for promotion, in shaping this remedy. . . .

. . . .

The race-conscious relief imposed here was amply justified, and narrowly tailored to serve the legitimate and laudable purposes of the District Court. The judgment of the Court of Appeals, upholding the order of the District Court, is affirmed.

1. Why did the United States argue that the District Court order was a violation of equal protection?

2. Why was the Alabama Police Department a good target for affirmative action?

3. Is the strict quota system proposed by the District Court completely rigid? How does the answer to this question affect the Supreme Court's analysis?

Johnson v. Transportation Agency: *Sex Discrimination.* In 1987, the Supreme Court finally extended explicit support for affirmative-action programs aimed at women (*Johnson v. Transportation Agency*, No. 85-1129). A male employee of the Santa Clara Transportation Agency sued when a woman was promoted over him to road dispatcher. The woman had less seniority and had scored marginally lower on the employment test. The Transportation Agency was committed to filling thirty-six percent of its traditionally skilled male jobs with women as part of an affirmative-action program. The Court emphasized that sex was just one of many factors considered in the promotion decision and that, once again, there had been "no absolute bar" to the advancement of male employees.

In a scathing dissent, however, Justice Anton Scalia argued that the decision "effectively replaced the goal of a discrimination-free society with the quite incompatible goal of proportionate representation by race and by sex in the workplace." He felt the courts should distinguish between the correction of prior discrimination by employers and the correction of employment imbalances based on "long-standing social attitudes" about what is desirable work for women. These social attitudes, he argued, were not imposed on women, but rather were voluntarily espoused by them. Scalia concluded that ". . . it is the alteration of social attitudes, rather than the elimination of discrimination, which today's decision approves as justification for state-enforced discrimination."

Martin v. Wilks: *Consent Decrees.* In the most recent affirmative-action case, the Supreme Court called into question the validity of a consent decree establishing an affirmative-action program. *Consent decrees* are voluntary agreements between parties to a lawsuit—approved by a court—to settle disputes before they are ruled on by judges or juries.

This case concerned the legal effect of a consent degree between the city of Birmingham, Alabama, and the NAACP, which settled a lawsuit alleging that the city had discriminated on the basis of race in the hiring and promotion of firefighters. The consent decree, which had been approved by a federal district court in the early 1980s, provided for specific goals for the hiring and promotion of blacks.

In *Martin v. Wilks*, a group of white firefighters brought suit against the city alleging that they were denied hiring and promotion opportunities. In its defense, the city claimed that the plaintiffs' claim of discrimination was barred by the consent decree. The Supreme Court, however, disagreed and held that the legality of the consent decree could be attacked by the white firefighters.

Many civil rights experts have expressed strong misgivings about the *Martin* decision, which is excerpted below. They fear that it threatens to undo every existing affirmative-action plan established by consent decree. Moreover,

Bakke: *Quotas and the Burden of Proof* Protestors demonstrate against the Supreme Court's decision in *Regents of the University of California v. Bakke* in June 1978. Allan Bakke's controversial case began in a California trial court, which ruled in his favor by defining the University's minority-admissions program as a racial quota system. However, although the trial court rejected race as an admissions criterion, it did not order Bakke's admission to medical school at the University of California at Davis: When the University's minority-admissions program was discounted as a factor, the court did not find sufficient proof of Bakke's admissability. Bakke thus took his case to the California Supreme Court, which made a significant modification in the trial-court ruling: Finding the standard of *strict scrutiny* applicable to the case, that court ruled that the University admissions program violated the equal-protection clause of the Fourteenth Amendment. In addition, the burden of proof thus shifted to the University; because that burden had not been satisfied, according to the court, Bakke should be admitted. Despite the concern of several major civil-rights groups, the University pressed the case to the U.S. Supreme Court. The Court issued no opinion but announced a judgment that granted both sides some portion of victory. First, Justice Lewis Powell spoke for five justices in declaring the University's minority-admissions program in violation of the due-process clause of the Fourteenth Amendment. Second, however, the four other justices—each of whom disagreed in some part with the majority's description of the admissions program—agreed with Justice Powell's opinion that race may indeed be considered as one of a number of criteria in admissions judgments.

they foresee the decision having a chilling effect on employers' willingness to enter into voluntary agreements with women and minorities to redress past discrimination.

MARTIN v. WILKS
United States Supreme Court, 109 S.Ct. 2180 (1989)

White firefighters sued the City of Birmingham, Alabama (City), and the Jefferson Personnel Board (Board) alleging that they were denied promotions in favor of less-qualified black firefighters. They claimed decisions were being made on the basis of race in reliance on certain consent decrees that violated the Constitution and federal statute. The decrees were a result of litigation by the NAACP and seven black individuals against the City and the Board for racial discrimination in violation of the Civil Rights Act of 1964 by means of certain hiring and promoting practices of various public-service jobs. Among the goals of the decrees were the interim and long-term hiring of black firefighters. At a fairness hearing, the Birmingham Firefighters Association (BFA) objected to the decrees. The decrees were later approved. Seven white BFA firefighters filed a complaint and were denied the right to intervene as parties. A new group of white firefighters, the Wilks respondents, brought suit against the City and Board, alleging denial of promotions on account of race. A group of black firefighters, the Martin petitioners, were allowed to intervene to defend the decrees. The District Court held that because the promotions were made pursuant to the consent decrees, the City was not guilty of racial discrimination. The Court of Appeals reversed the decision and held that because the white Wilks respondents were not parties or privies to the consent decrees, their independent claims of racial discrimination were not precluded.

Chief Justice REHNQUIST delivered the opinion of the court.

    . . . .

"[I]t is a principle of general application in anglo-American jurisprudence that one is not bound by a judgment *in personam* in a litigation in which he is not designated as a party or to which he has not been made a party by service of process." This rule is part of our "deep-rooted historic tradition that everyone should have his own day in court." A judgment or decree among parties to a lawsuit resolves issues as among them, but it does not conclude the rights of strangers to those proceedings. . . .

Petitioners argue that, because respondents failed to timely intervene in the initial proceedings, their current challenge to actions taken under the consent decree constitutes an impermissible "collateral attack." They argue that respondents were aware that the underlying suit might affect them and if they chose to pass up an opportunity to intervene, they should not be permitted to later litigate the issues in a new action. The position has sufficient appeal to have commanded the approval of the great majority of the federal courts of appeals, but we agree with the contrary view expressed by the Court of Appeals for the Eleventh Circuit in this case. . . .

Petitioners also urge that the congressional policy favoring voluntary settlement of employment discrimination claims, also supports the "impermissible collateral attack" doctrine. But once again it is essential to note just what is meant by "voluntary settlement." A voluntary settlement in the form of a consent decree between one group of employees and their employer cannot possibly "settle," voluntarily or otherwise, the conflicting claims of another group of employees who do not join in the agreement. . . .

For the foregoing reasons we affirm the decision of the Court of Appeals for the Eleventh Circuit. That court remanded the case for trial of the reverse discrimination claims. . . .

Affirmed.

Case Questions

1. The Court rejects the great majority of the federal courts of appeals which had taken the position that if a person fails to intervene in a proceeding in which he is aware that the decision may effect him personally, he is not permitted to litigate the issue later in a new action. In what circumstances does the Court's contrary view seem valid, if at all?

2. The Court states that a voluntary settlement between an employer and a group of employees cannot possibly settle the conflicting claims of another group of employees. Should employment discrimination be eradicated or perpetuated on a permanent basis by binding all employees to the first agreement that is reached? Is it better to leave open the possibility of subsequent suits that may serve to counter or reinforce employment discrimination?

- What is the primary focus of *Executive Order 11246?*
- Explain *utilization analysis* as an affirmative-action procedure.
- Describe the procedure followed by the *Office of Federal Compliance Program* in enforcing federal-contract provisions.
- Describe the role of *numerical quotas* in charges that *reverse discrimination* is unfair.
- Compare the Supreme Court's ruling on reverse discrimination in *Bakke* and *United Steelworkers v. Weber.*
- Discuss the Supreme Court's decision regarding *consent decrees* in *Martin v. Wilks.*

■ AGE AND DISABILITY DISCRIMINATION

The Age Discrimination in Employment Act

Some years after the passage of Title VII, advocacy groups finally succeeded in convincing Congress that older workers also constitute a minority group suffering from adverse stereotypes and discrimination. The **Age Discrimination in Employment Act** of 1967 **(ADEA)** prohibits discrimination against workers aged 40 to 65.

Older workers are often more costly than younger workers, partly because the cost of medical benefits is tied to age and partly because older workers generally have more seniority. As a result, companies are less likely to hire older workers and may either pressure older workers already on the payroll into early retirement or fire them to reduce costs.

ENFORCEMENT. ADEA basically follows Title VII rules. The courts apply the same disparate-treatment/disparate-impact analysis to prove the existence of discrimination. It is administered by the EEOC and is subject to the same enforcement procedures as Title VII. The agency tries first to reach a settlement through conciliation. If these efforts fail, either the EEOC or the aggrieved individual may file suit. The remedies employed by the courts include mandatory employment, reinstatement, promotion, and back pay.

PROVISIONS. ADEA applies to employers with 20 or more employees, labor unions with more than 25 members, and public employees. A 1978 amendment extended its coverage to workers aged 40 to 70, raised the minimum mandatory retirement age to 70, and eliminated any mandatory retirement age for the federal civil service. High-level executives and policy-makers who are entitled to pensions of more than $27,500 per year are excluded from retirement provisions; they may still be forced to retire at age 65.

Compulsory Retirement. Compulsory early retirement is permitted if age is a BFOQ because of the physical demands of a job. Thus, air-traffic controllers, airline pilots, and FBI agents are all subject to early retirement. The courts generally apply the same BFOQ tests developed for Title VII cases: In other words, the employer must show that either (1) substantially all older workers cannot perform the duties of the job, (2) it would be difficult to distinguish which older individuals were capable, or (3) older workers would jeopardize the business's paramount function.

Age Discrimination in Employment Act (ADEA) 1967 federal law that, as amended, prohibits discrimination against workers ages 40 to 70

Aging, Ageism, and the Workforce Congressman Claude Pepper, Chairman of the House Committee on Aging and longtime advocate of elderly rights, meets with a group of centenarians on issues
of age discrimination in America. *Ageism* may be defined as a form of prejudice that leads to discrimination on the basis of actual or perceived chronological age. This attitude has had a long-
standing—and often paradoxical—effect on perceptions of the elderly as images in the socioeconomic picture in this country and elsewhere. With the advent of wage labor and the decline of
agriculture, for example, the traditional advantages of the elderly workforce—leverage, knowledge, experience—declined; the extension of formal education and the introduction of new technologies furthered that decline. Up until about World War I, that decline was a matter mostly of
perceptions—not of the actual socioeconomic status of the elderly. In the first two decades of this
century, however, that decline in status became not only more real but more visible, especially as
increases in the number of the impoverished elderly contributed to the perception of a "social
problem." That perception, in turn, led to such responses as the Social Security Act of 1935 (*see
Chapter 14*), which was supplemented by the spread throughout American industry of such programs as mandatory-retirement and pension plans. In reality, such programs also encouraged the
principle of *age grading* in employment—that is, the advantage (to employers and labor unions
alike) of favoring workers aged about 30 to 55 over both younger and older workers. The combination of all these factors has ultimately made it virtually impossible for the elderly to affect their socioeconomic status by means of employment and earning power, and as a result, their plight has
become all the more visible.

The Rehabilitation Act of 1973

Until the passage of the Americans with Disabilities Act of 1990, disabled people had fewer safeguards against discrimination than other groups. Prior to the ADEA, the *Rehabilitation Act* of 1973 was the only federal law prohibiting discrimination against the disabled, and it applied only to private employers with government contracts in excess of $2,500 and public programs that received federal financial assistance. Under the Rehabilitation Act, disabled employees of private employers who did not do business with the federal government were not protected by federal law.

DEFINING "HANDICAPPED." Because its language is not specific, there is much confusion over just what disabilities are covered by this Act. Section 7(B)(i) defines a *handicapped* individual as someone who "has a physical or mental impairment which substantially limits one or more of such person's major life activities." The courts have agreed that this provision includes drug and alcohol abuse and mental retardation but excludes repeated or chronic illnesses. Sensitivity to tobacco smoke is questionable. The courts generally base their decision on the number and type of jobs from which an impairment disqualifies a person. Fear of heights and an inability to lift heavy weights are insufficient, for example, because there are still many jobs open to individuals suffering from these conditions.

A case with potentially wide-ranging applications is the 1987 Supreme Court ruling that contagious diseases fall under the terms of the Act. This decision, which appears below, offers some hope to those who have been dismissed from their jobs despite the fact that they do not pose a real health threat to their colleagues.

SCHOOL BOARD OF NASSAU COUNTY v. ARLINE
United States Supreme Court, 197 S.Ct. 1123 (1987)

Gene Arline, an elementary school teacher, brought suit against the School Board of Nassau County in Federal District Court alleging a violation of the Rehabilitation Act of 1973 after being discharged following her third relapse of tuberculosis in two years. The district court dismissed the plaintiff's claim, reasoning that a person with a contagious disease is not "handicapped" within the meaning of the Rehabilitation Act. The Court of Appeals reversed, taking a broader interpretation of the statute. The School Board appeals to United States Supreme Court.

Justice Brennan delivered the opinion of the Court.

Section 504 of the Rehabilitation Act of 1973 prohibits a federally funded state program from discriminating against a handicapped individual solely by reason of his or her handicap. This case presents the questions whether a person afflicted with tuberculosis, a contagious disease, may be considered a "handicapped individual" within the meaning of § 504 of the Act, and, if so, whether such an individual is "otherwise qualified" to teach elementary school.

. . . Section 504 of the Rehabilitation Act reads in pertinent part:

No otherwise qualified handicapped individual in the United States, as defined in section 706(7) of this title, shall, solely by reason of his handicap, be excluded from participation in, be denied the benefits of, or be subjected to discrimination under any program or activity receiving Federal financial assistance. . . .

In 1974 Congress expanded the definition of "handicapped individual" for use in § 504 to read as follows:

[A]ny person who (i) has a physical or mental impairment which substantially limits one or more of such person's major life activities, (ii) has a record of such an impairment, or (iii) is regarded as having such an impairment.

. . . "Physical impairment" is defined [by the Department of Health and Human Services] as follows:

"[A]ny physiological disorder or condition, cosmetic

---

disfigurement, or anatomical loss affecting one or more of the following body systems: neurological; musculoskeletal; special sense organs; respiratory, including speech organs; cardiovascular; reproductive, digestive, genitourinary; hemic and lymphatic; skin; and endocrine."

In addition, the regulations define "major life activities" as:

"functions such as caring for one's self, performing manual tasks, walking, seeing, hearing, speaking, breathing, learning, and working."

. . . According to the testimony of Dr. McEuen, Arline suffered tuberculosis "in an acute form in such a degree that it affected her respiratory system," and was hospitalized for this condition. Arline thus . . . had a "physiological disorder or condition . . . affecting [her] . . . respiratory [system]." This impairment was serious enough to require hospitalization, . . . [meaning] that one or more of her major life activities were substantially limited by her impairment. . . . Arline's hospitalization . . . [is] . . . a "record of . . . impairment" within the meaning of 29 U.S.C. § 706(7)(b)(ii), and is therefore a handicapped individual. . . . Petitioners maintain, however, Arline's record of impairment is irrelevant in this case, since the School Board dismissed Arline not because of her diminished physical capabilities, but because of the threat that her relapses of tuberculosis posed to the health of others.

We do not agree with petitioners that, in defining a handicapped individual under § 504, the contagious effects of a disease can be meaningfully distinguished from the disease's physical effects on a claimant in a case such as this. Arline's contagiousness and her physical impairment each resulted from the same underlying condition, tuberculosis. It would be unfair to allow an employer to . . . use that distinction to justify discriminatory treatment.

. . . .

Allowing discrimination based on the contagious effects of a physical impairment would be inconsistent with the basic purpose of § 504, which is to ensure that handicapped individuals are not denied jobs or other benefits because of the prejudiced attitudes or the ignorance of others. By amending the definition of "handicapped individual" to include not only those who are actually physically impaired, but also those who are regarded as impaired and who, as a result, are substantially limited in a major life activity, Congress acknowledged that society's accumulated myths and fears about disability and disease are as handicapping as are the physical limitations that flow from actual impairment. . . . The fact that *some* persons who have contagious diseases may pose a serious health threat to others under certain circumstances does not justify excluding from the coverage of the Act *all* persons with actual or perceived contagious diseases. Such exclusion would mean that those accused of being contagious would never have the opportunity to have their condition evaluated in light of medical evidence and a determination made as to whether they were "otherwise qualified." Rather, they would be vulnerable to discrimination on the basis of mythology . . . .

We hold that a person suffering from the contagious disease of tuberculosis can be a handicapped person within the meaning of the § 504 of the Rehabilitation Act of 1973, and that respondent Arline is such a person. We remand the case to the District Court to determine whether Arline is otherwise qualified for her position. The judgment of the Court of Appeals is affirmed.

. . . .

Case Questions:

1. How does the Court deal with the possibility that employees with contagious diseases may present a public threat?

2. What factors contributed to the Court's liberal interpretation of the meaning of "handicapped individual"?

3. Would Arline have had a cause of action under the Rehabilitation Act if she were a private school teacher?

REASONABLE ACCOMMODATION. The employer is obligated to make **reasonable accommodations** for handicapped workers. Although there is some dispute over what accommodations are "reasonable," such accommodations typically include widening doorways for wheelchairs or revising assembly-line techniques. The issue often comes down to how much money an employer should be required to spend on such modifications. Sometimes, as in *Arline*, another type of accommodation will be deemed reasonable (recall that the Court determined that finding another job for a teacher who could no longer perform classroom duties was reasonable).

reasonable accommodation
The requirement, under the Rehabilitation Act of 1973, that employers make modifications in the workplace for handicapped workers

WEAKNESS OF PROTECTION. Overall, the Rehabilitation Act actually offers the handicapped relatively poor protection. Not only does it lack the general coverage of Title VII, but the provision applying to organizations receiving federal funds has been disputed. It is not clear what activities fall under the provisions of the law—*all* the activities of such an organization or just the *specific* programs receiving funds.

Enforcement is also extremely limited. Cases involving federal contractors must be left strictly to the OFCCP; there is no private right of action. In practice, this means that cases are settled quite slowly. There is also some dispute over whether a private right of action exists in cases concerning organizations receiving federal funds. Even if such a right exists, it may be limited to injunctive relief. Thus, there is no hope for individual compensation.

Most state statutes offer broader coverage than the federal law because they apply to the majority of private employers. However, they are more restrictive in their definitions of a *handicap* and more exacting in their demands that the handicapped individual be able to perform all job functions.

✗ Americans with Disabilities Act of 1990

Americans with Disabilities Act (ADA) 1990 federal law providing that a disabled worker cannot be denied employment if he or she is a "qualified individual"

The **Americans with Disabilities Act** of 1990 (**ADA**) offers considerably more protection to disabled workers than the Rehabilitation Act. Beginning in July 1992, all businesses with 25 or more employees must comply with the ADA. As of July 1994, all employers with 15 or more employees will become subject to the Act.

Under the ADA, a disabled worker cannot be denied employment if he or she is a "qualified individual"—if he or she can perform the essential functions of a job with or without "reasonable accommodation." The only way to avoid the requirement of reasonable accommodation is for employers to prove that such measures would impose an "undue hardship" upon them. In assessing the validity of an undue-hardship defense, the courts will examine the employer's size and wealth.

The remedies available to successful litigants under the ADA are also considerably tougher than those obtainable under the Rehabilitation Act. Prevailing plaintiffs, for example, are entitled to back pay, attorney's fees, compensatory damages for pain and suffering, and, in cases of extreme discrimination, punitive damages.

■ *Concept Check 15-4* *Age and Disability Discrimination*

- What are the major provisions of the *Age Discrimination in Employment Act*?
- How does the *Rehabilitation Act* of 1973 define "handicapped"?
- Explain the concept of *reasonable accommodations* as applied by the Rehabilitation Act and the *Americans with Disabilities Act* of 1990.

■ DISCRIMINATION IN PAY

The Equal Pay Act of 1963

Equal Pay Act (EPA) 1963 amendment to the Fair Labor Standards Act making it illegal to pay employees of one sex less than the other for jobs requiring equal skill, effort, and responsibility

The **Equal Pay Act (EPA)**, a 1963 amendment to the Fair Labor Standards Act (*see* Chapter 14), provides an alternative source of relief for some victims of sex discrimination. It makes it illegal to pay employees of one sex less than the other for jobs requiring equal skill, effort, and responsibility. Differential rates based on merit, seniority, or incentive plans are permitted. The law states that no employer having employees subject to any provision of this section shall discriminate within any establishment in which such employees are employed, between employees on the basis of sex by paying wages to employees in such establishment at a rate less than the rate at which he pays wages to employees of the opposite sex in such establishment for equal work on jobs the performance of which requires equal skill, effort, and responsibility, and which are performed under similar working conditions.

INCOME DISPARITY. As Table 15-5 shows, the gap between the median annual incomes of men and women has remained between 57 and 65 percent over about the last 40 years.[3] According to the Census Bureau, over the course of a lifetime, men will earn approximately twice as much women with the same education. Between 1947 and 1980, although the number of women in the workforce increased 173 percent, the salaries of full-time female workers had dropped from 60.2 to 59.7 percent of men's salaries. For women in management positions, the decline was even greater—from 58 to 55 percent.

Another means of calculating the disparity between women's and men's salaries is suggested by Figure 15-3.[4] In 1979, full-time women workers earned,

TABLE 15-5	Median Annual Earnings, Men and Women, 1955–1987		
YEAR	WOMEN	MEN	WOMEN'S EARNINGS AS % OF MEN'S
1955	$ 2,719	$ 4,252	63.9%
1960	3,293	5,417	60.8
1965	3,823	6,375	60.0
1970	5,323	8,966	59.4
1973	6,335	11,186	56.6
1976	8,099	13,455	60.2
1979	10,151	17,014	59.7
1980	11,197	18,612	60.2
1981	12,001	20,260	59.2
1982	13,014	21,077	61.7
1983	13,915	21,881	63.6
1984	15,607	24,517	63.7
1985	15,926	24,644	64.6
1986	16,232	25,256	64.3
1987	17,504	26,722	65.5

Sources: Adapted from Buchholz, Business Environment and Public Policy. *Data from U.S. Department of Labor, Bureau of Labor Statistics; U.S., Department of Commerce,* Statistical Abstract of the United States 1989 *(Washington, DC: Government Printing Office, 1988).*

---

[3] These figures are compiled by Rogene A. Buchholz, *Business Environment and Public Policy: Implications for Management Strategy,* 4th ed. (Englewood Cliffs, NJ: Prentice Hall, 1992), pp. 333-36.

[4] See Weidenbaum, *Business, Government, and the Public,* pp. 127-34.

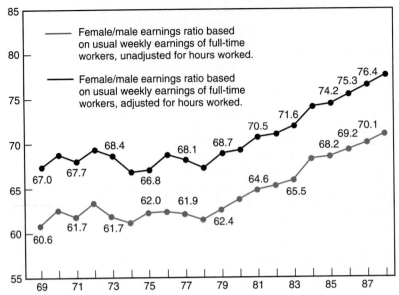

FIGURE 15-3 Difference in Male and Female Pay, 1969–1988   *Source: Adapted from Weidenbaum, Business, Government, and the Public. Data from U.S. Department of Labor.*

on average, 62 percent of the wages earned by men; by 1986, that figure had risen to 70 percent. Adjustments for hours worked brings the figure up to 75 percent. Further adjustments can be made for education and work experience—factors that bring the ratio up to 86 percent. When some portion of the remaining 14-percent difference is attributed to discrimination, the question of "equal pay for equal work" becomes an issue.

PROVING A CASE.   In order to prove a prima facie case of a violation of the Equal Employment Act, however, the plaintiff must demonstrate the existence of four distinct factors: namely, that there are two workers of the opposite sex who are employed

- in the same establishment
- receiving unequal pay
- on the basis of sex
- for work that is equal

Let's examine each of these criteria in more detail.

The Same Establishment. The first requirement—that the workers be employed in the *same establishment*—is not as clear-cut as it may first appear. The term "establishment" refers to a physically separate place of business, not to an employer or a company. Thus, a single employer can have many establishments—for example, multiple retail outlets or multiple plants and warehouses. It is not a violation of the law for there to be sex-based disparities in pay among these various locations.

Unequal Pay. The second requirement, *unequal pay,* raises the issue of whether "pay" refers to every possible kind of compensation and benefit. For example, in one equal-pay case, female employees asserted that their employer violated the EPA by lodging them in double-occupancy hotel accommodations while male employees received single rooms. No disparity in wages or insurance benefits was alleged (*Laffey v. Northwest Airlines, Inc.,* 12 Empl. Prac.

Dec., Section 11,216 [1976]). Obviously, it is very difficult to quantify and compare some benefits.

The Basis of Sex. The third requirement, that pay differences be *based on sex*, may be satisfied simply by demonstrating that there is a single person of the opposite sex receiving greater wages for equal work in the same establishment. A broad pattern of sex discrimination in pay should be shown, however, because defendants can easily challenge this kind of evidence by offering some explanation for the differential in pay other than gender.

Equal Work. The fourth requirement, *equal work*, is both the most important and most difficult part of the case. Jobs, after all, are rarely identical. The EPA itself describes equal work in terms of skill, effort, responsibility, and working conditions. According to the courts, the jobs compared must be "substantially equal"—that is, more than similar but less than identical. In practice, the inexactness of this test has led to contradictory court decisions. For example, various courts have disagreed over whether a male hospital orderly's job is equal to that of a female nurse's aide.[5]

It is clear, however, that this requirement refers solely to the work actually done, not to employees' qualifications. Thus, if the day-to-day work carried out by men and women is the same, their pay must be the same.

DEFENSES AND REMEDIES. Defendants can avoid liability by refuting any one of the four requirements discussed above. In addition, the EPA itself sets forth some specific exceptions to the law. For example, there is no liability if the wage differential is based on a seniority system, a merit system, a piecework system, or on any factor other than sex. For the most part, the case law revolves around the application of these exceptions. When the EPA has been violated, however, the following remedies are available:

- the Secretary of Labor may sue for injunctive relief;
- both individual employees and the Secretary of Labor may sue for damages; and
- the Justice Department may seek criminal penalties.

The Concept of Comparable Worth

Title VII also prohibits sex-based discrimination in rates of pay. Its application, however, is potentially much broader because a 1981 Supreme Court decision ruled that workers could successfully claim sex discrimination in pay under Title VII without meeting the equal-work standard of EPA. Thus, the decision implied that employers could be liable for sex discrimination in pay for jobs that were not strictly "equal" (*County of Washington v. Gunther*, 452 U.S. 161 [1981]).

Women's groups, disappointed in the limited impact of the EPA on women's wages, have seized on this decision in order to promote the concept of **comparable worth**. The idea behind comparable worth is that wages should be based on the *intrinsic value of a job* rather than market forces. If, for example, teaching elementary school requires as much skill, effort, and responsibility as driving a truck, then the teacher's salary should be the same as the truck driver's. The key issues in the debate over comparable worth are summarized in this chapter's ETHICAL ENVIRONMENT box.

comparable worth Concept that wages should be based on the intrinsic value of a job

---

[5] *Brennan v. Owesboro-Davies County Hosp.*, 523 F.2d 1013 (1975); *Brennan v. Prince William Hosp. Corp.*, 503 F.2d 282 (1974); *Hodgson v. Golden Isles Convalescent Home, Inc.*, 468 F.2d 1256 (1972).

The idea of comparable worth was created after studies in the 1970s and 1980s revealed that jobs that have been traditionally held by women were compensated at lower rates than those traditionally held by men. The disparity was found even when the positions required equivalent skills, training, and responsibility. For example, clerical workers, who are usually women, typically receive lower salaries than assembly-line employees, who are usually men, even though these jobs are often comparable in terms of the necessary skills, training, and responsibility. According to advocates of comparable worth, traditionally female jobs are lower-paying because of sexism, not because the work performed is any less valuable to an employer. The goal of comparable worth is to set compensation rates within a company on the basis of the skills and training, thereby eliminating differentials based on sex.

Some economists, however, have criticized the doctrine of comparable worth on the ground that its underlying assumptions are wrong. Women have historically received lower salaries, they assert, because they have made different employment choices and because the jobs that they have traditionally held have, in fact, produced less for the company than traditionally male jobs. According to critics of comparable worth, women could enter higher-paying "men's jobs" if they chose to. The labor market, they say—and not some vague value-assessment scheme—should determine the wages assigned to positions within a company.

On the other hand, proponents of comparable worth believe that sex discrimination is the only viable explanation for the widespread salary differentials between men and women. Women, they argue, have many fewer "choices" than critics of comparable worth are willing to acknowledge. According to supporters of comparable worth, sex discrimination in the hiring process channels women into lower-paying jobs, and sex discrimination in the promotion and transfer process keeps them there. Intervention by means of comparable-worth assessments and adjustments, they contend, is needed to eliminate such obstacles to gender equality in the labor market.

Critics of comparable worth can find solace in the fact that courts have not been particularly hospitable to the concept. Although the Supreme Court has yet to address this issue, several lower courts have rejected comparable-worth claims by holding that wage discrimination on the basis of sex could not be proven without evidence that the employer was motivated by the desire to treat women worse than men. It is not enough, under these decisions, to show merely that jobs held by women are compensated at lower rates than jobs held by men.

Both sides of the comparable worth debate are waiting to see the impact of recent Title VII cases and civil-rights legislation. Of most interest is the Supreme Court's decision in *Wards Cove*, which raised plaintiffs' burden of proof, and the Civil Rights Act of 1991, which lowered it.

While proponents of comparable worth see it as a necessary policy to close the earnings gap between men and women, its detractors feel that it would upset the whole labor market and economy. In practice, applying comparable worth raises major problems:

- How does one decide which jobs are comparable?
- Assuming the courts did mandate a rise in women's wages rather than a reduction in men's, where would the money come from?

These issues are potentially more difficult than deciding which jobs are equal.

Comparable worth may eventually be decided in the state legislatures rather than the courts. Minnesota led the way by adopting a comparable-worth plan for state employees in 1983. By 1987, more than half of the states had begun or finished studies of their workforces that included considerations of comparable worth. Twenty states had already set aside funds to make pay adjustments based on the studies' findings.

■ Concept Check 15-4 Discrimination in Pay

- Discuss the criteria for proving a violation of the *Equal Pay Act*.
- Define and discuss the doctrine of *comparable worth*.

A majority of the Supreme Court rejected Johnson Controls' argument that its fetal-protection policy was a valid way to protect fetal health and insulate itself from potential liability. According to the court, women workers have a right both to be fully informed of the risks associated with a particular job and to decide for themselves whether to assume those risks.

The majority written by Justice Harry Blackmun, who wrote the historic opinion in Roe v. Wade, held that the policy violated Title VII on several grounds. First, the court held that the Johnson policy applied only to women despite evidence that exposure to lead is harmful to the male reproductive system. Second, the court rejected the company's argument that the policy was justified under the "BFOQ" exception. Johnson Controls argued that, for safety reasons, being a man was a BFOQ for performing manufacturing jobs entailing exposure to dangerous levels of lead that posed a danger to fetal health. The court, however, stated that it had in the past upheld use of the BFOQ defense only when the safety of other workers or customers were at issue. Protection of unconceived fetuses, according to the court, did not warrant discrimination against all female workers:

> The unconceived fetuses of Johnson Controls' female employees, however, are neither customers nor third parties whose safety is essential to the business of battery making. No one can disregard the possibility of injury to future children: the BFOQ, however, is not so broad that it transforms this deep social concern into an essential aspect of batterymaking.

Justice Blackmun also dismissed dissenting justices' concerns about employer's potential liability for injuries caused to fetuses by exposure to lead. If employers comply with lead standards issued by the Occupational Safety and Health Administration (OSHA), and fully informing workers of the risks, liability should not be found.

SUMMARY

- Racial discrimination was a central issue of the Civil War and its legal aftermath. The Constitutional amendments and civil rights acts pushed through Congress to protect the black minority at that time had a surprisingly limited impact, however. Unsympathetic courts interpreted them narrowly and federal enforcement activities were temporary.

- The Civil Rights Movement of the 1950s and 1960s produced more far-reaching results. The courts and the presidency began to reinterpret and enforce existing civil rights laws, while Congress passed the most sweeping single piece of antidiscrimination legislation, the *Civil Rights Act of 1964*. This Act prohibits discrimination based on color, sex, national origin, and religion. *Title VII* of that Act, which is administered by the *Equal Employment Opportunity Commission*, deals with *employment discrimination*.

- In applying Title VII, the courts developed two definitions of discrimination. Each relies on statistical proofs. In cases of *disparate treatment*, the employer discriminates intentionally, applying different standards to different groups of workers. In cases of *disparate impact*, the employer has a single standard which has different consequences for different groups. Employers can defend against charges of discrimination by disproving the existence of a disparity, by providing an alternate explanation for it, or by claiming a *bona fide occupational qualification, business necessity*, or a *seniority system*.

- A series of Executive Orders during the late 1960s and early 1970s radically changed the direction of federal antidiscrimination efforts. While Title VII simply requires employers to refrain from discriminating, these later regulations demand *affirmative action*: that is, an active attempt to overcome the effects of past discrimination by promoting the employment of women and minorities. Employers must compare the composition of their workforce with that of the local labor pool. When minorities and women are underrepresented, they must establish numerical goals and timetables to correct the deficiency and change personnel practices in an effort to achieve those goals.

- In practice, employers have often used preferential hiring and even rigid quotas to satisfy the demands of affirmative-action regulations. This strategy led to countercharges of reverse discrimination against white males. The courts have generally upheld the concept of affirmative action, while questioning some specific practices such as quotas.

- Other federal legislation has added older and handicapped workers to the list of protected groups. The *Age Discrimination in Employment Act* prohibits discrimination based on age and has increased the mandatory retirement for most workers to age 70. The *Rehabilitation Act of 1973* demands that employers hire and make *reasonable accommodations* for handicapped workers who are otherwise qualified for a job. The 1990 *Americans with Disabilities Act* further extends protection to disabled workers and provides that a "qualified individual," even if disabled, cannot be denied employment.

- *Sex discrimination* raises a whole set of controversial issues, including, *sex stereotyping, pregnancy benefits,* and *sexual harassment.* Currently, women's advocates are pressing for *comparable worth*: That is, they want the courts to demand that employers pay men and women equal wages for jobs that are "comparable" in value even if their duties and tasks are in no way similar. The law already specifies that men and women receive equal pay for "equal" work.

QUESTIONS AND PROBLEMS

1. Su Chang is of Chinese origin. She applied at Mama Ferrilli's Italian Restaurant for a position on the early morning cleaning crew. The job was advertised in the newspaper. At the interview she was told that her qualifications and experience fit the position but since the restaurant was an Italian one, they wanted to employ only Italians to keep the atmosphere as authentic as possible. Su is very disappointed when she sees the same "want ad" in the newspaper the following week. Does Su have a case against Mama Ferrilli's Italian Restaurant?

2. Fred O'Malley, who is blind, applied for a position teaching physical education at a local high school which receives federal funds for various programs. When Fred was not hired, he sues, alleging handicap discrimination. Who wins and why? [*Zorick v. Tynes*, 372 So.2d 133 (1979)]

3. Dr. Jones, a family practice physician with an active private practice, has a vacancy for a nurse and receptionist on her eight-person staff. Dr. Jones refuses to hire a male as a secretary for either position. What is her legal position?

4. Charmaine Jennings and Mark Giordano are the two final applicants for a position as a school administrator. Both applicants are qualified for the position. Mr. Carter, the school superintendent responsible for the ultimate hiring decision, calls both in for separate interviews. Through questioning, Mr. Carter discovers that Ms. Jenning's husband is a high-level business executive and the two have no children. Mr. Giordano's wife suffers from a debilitating illness and is unable to work. Mr. Carter chooses to hire Mr. Giordano for the job, theorizing that he needs the income since he is the sole breadwinner for his family. Does Ms. Jennings have a basis upon which to sue the school system?

5. Mark Feldstein, a recent college graduate, applied for a job as a reporter for *The Christian Science Monitor*. On the employment application there were several questions relating to religion, such as "Are you a member of the Mother Church? Are you free from the use of liquor, tobacco, drugs, medicine?" The application closed with the following: "The First Church of Christ, Scientist, may by law apply the test of religious qualification to its employment policies. Those who meet this requirement and are otherwise qualified will be hired, promoted, and transferred without regard to their race, national origin, sex, color, or age."
Feldstein filed his application with his resume and letters of recommendation, etc. He was qualified for the job, but he was rejected. He alleged religious discrimination. Under what theory did the District Court found in favor of *The Christian Science Monitor*? [*Feldstein v. The Christian Science Monitor*, United States District Court, 30 FEP 1842 (E. D. Mass. (1983)]

6. Susan Tepper, employed as a receptionist for a large realty company, is required to wear a uniform. In commemoration of the country's bicentennial, the company has uniforms designed which look like American flags made into ponchos. Because the uniform is short and provocative on her, she is the subject of improper attention by males coming onto the premises when she wears it. She complains to her supervisor and changes are made, but the uniform is still revealing. When Ms. Tepper reverts to wearing her previous uniform, she is fired. What will the result be if she sues? Why? [*EEOC v. Sage Realty Corp.*, 507 F. Supp. 599 (S.D.N.Y. 1981)]

7. At the Pierre Advertising Agency there is a frequent and longstanding policy of top executives actively seeking out the creative ideas of "younger" employees (those in their twenties and thirties) and casting aside the ideas of those considered "older" (forties and fifties). This practice has resulted in ten older employees leaving the company. Their positions have been filled by men and women in their early to late thirties. The ten employees filed suit alleging age discrimination. The company defends on the grounds that it is their right to choose the best advertising ideas to sell its clients' products. The company also asserts that it has never fired anyone due to age and that each of these employees left on their own accord. Do the ten employees have any basis on which to sue? Explain.

8. Arthur Wolfson, 5 ft. 6 inches, 249 lbs., accepted an offer from Copier Corp. for a position as a computer programmer contingent upon passing a physical. The examining physician found Arthur to be 100 lbs. overweight and therefore obese. The applicant was otherwise qualified for the position and had experience performing as a computer programmer. In the doctor's opinion, Mr. Wolfson's weight posed a significant risk to the short- and long-term disability and life insurance programs administered by Copier. He was not given the job. What will probably happen if he sues Copier? [*State Division of Human Rights v. Xerox Corp.*, 480 N.E. 2d 695 (1985)]

9. Betsy Lawson and Lisa Crawford, both female operators with the telephone company, file suit alleging that the telephone company discriminated against them, and eventually fired them, because of their known lesbian relationshp. [*Desantis v. Pacific Telephone & Telegraph Co., Inc.*, 608 F.2d 327 (9th Cir. 1979)]

10. Hank Grant, a male with long blond hair, is not hired by a newspaper company which asserts that Hank's hair length is not in keeping with its employee grooming code. That code requires male or female employees who come in contact with the public to be neatly dressed and groomed in accordance with the standard customarily accepted in the business community. Mr. Grant argues that the company is discriminating against him on the basis of sex because if he were a female, his hair length would be acceptable. How will the issue be decided? [*Willingham v. Macon Telegraph Publishing Co.*, 507 F.2d 1084 (1975)]

ANTITRUST AND THE SHERMAN ACT

A free-market economy revolves around the idea that unfettered competition among private businesses is the most efficient means of distributing goods and services to the population. Thus, *competition* is a cornerstone of our economic system. In its purest, most idealistic form, competition has the following characteristics.

- There are no restrictions on entry into or exit from a market.
- There is no single firm big enough to dominate a market or have any appreciable influence over market prices.
- Because the products produced by competing firms are essentially identical, consumers are indifferent as to which seller they buy from.
- Consumers base their decisions on price.
- Firms determine the quantity of goods that they produce on consumer demand.
- Demand is based on market price.

This model, of course, is not very realistic. There is, however, a good deal of legislation in the United States that is geared toward making such a theoretical model work. These laws seek to encourage competition by outlawing specific unfair practices, such as collusive price fixing and pricing intended to drive others out of business. At the same time, however, the economic environment of the times greatly affects how strictly laws can be enforced. For example, in the 10 years following the enactment of the Sherman Act, only 18 cases were tried. In part, this was due to the reasoning of the era: Big business was efficient and effective. By the 1930s, however, antitrust legislation was invoked much more often. Such was the general policy up through about 1983, when the American Telephone and Telegraph Company (AT&T) was broken up by the courts.

Today, the prevailing view seems to be more permissive of mergers and acquisitions. It is largely thought that consumer protection should be the focus of the legislation—that is, there should be no restrictions on business mergers unless the result is market control or domination by one or a few firms. It is important to note that the various trends in enforcement of the antitrust laws are due largely to shifting political, economic, and historical attitudes and philosophies. Many people, for example, like the current view—the larger the better. Others blame the consolidation of production and marketing capacity for the elimination of jobs.

■ MARKET COMPETITION

In order to understand the nature and impact of legislation directed at market activities, it is necessary to understand something about the characteristics of markets and the ways in which they are organized. **Perfect competition**, for example, refers to the pure-competition model just described. Because farmers have no direct say in the price charged for their products, agriculture is an example of an industry with many of the characteristics of a perfectly competitive industry. The farmers' control is limited to the amount they plant, how they plant it, and how much they reap.

perfect competition In a free-market economy, the theoretical model of exchange of goods and services

The direct opposite of perfect competition, **monopoly**, refers to a market in which there is only one supplier of a product for which there are no close substitutes. Entry into the market is restricted. In many cases, the government does the restricting—for example, public utilities are generally privately owned companies shielded by regulation from competition. In other cases, the restriction is the outgrowth of a patent on a product or long-term market-share growth and domination.

monopoly *Market* in which there is only one supplier of a product with no close substitutes and to which market entry is restricted and price controls self-imposed

Monopolistic competition covers a hybrid in which many firms supply substantially similar products. Items usually falling into this group include soaps, detergents and cleaning supplies, cosmetics, and certain first-aid products (band-aids, iodine, cotton balls and swabs). Monopolistic competition is the category in which public perception and brand loyalty play the biggest part. For example, if Johnson & Johnson can make consumers think that their band-aids adhere better than store-brand band-aids, consumers are likely to buy more of the product. The underlying perception is that the *quality* of J&J's product is better. Because there are many other similar products available, setting prices in this type of business environment is somewhat limited. For example, if J&J decides to take advantage of its popularity in the band-aid market by imposing a price increase, it is likely that some consumers will switch to another brand.

Although products may be differentiated (automobiles) or standardized (aluminum and steel), an **oligopoly** is an industry with relatively few competing firms. Most American industries are increasingly oligopolistic—that is, a few large firms control the lion's share of the market. An oligopolistic industry can be controlled by one large firm or by several firms with relatively equal size and power. In the United States, the most visible oligopolies are the automobile industry, which has three major competitors (Chrysler, Ford, and General Motors), and the airline industry. Entry into this type of competitive environment, although technically possible, is quite difficult.

oligopoly *Market* with relatively few competitors of about equal size and to which market entry is difficult

In most cases, price structure is the result of strategic plans in which each competitor tries to anticipate and preempt its rivals. The constant price wars in the airline industry and the competitive rebates given for the purchase of new automobiles are good examples of this feature of oligopolistic competition. Companies that cannot afford to keep up with the competition are either put out of business or absorbed by larger firms. Over time, this process further consolidates the economic power of the giants in a market.

	Number of firms	Products differentiated or homogeneous	Price a decision variable	Free entry	Distinguished by	Examples
Perfect competition	Many	Homogeneous	No	Yes	Price competition only	Wheat farmer Textile firm
Monopoly	One	A single unique product	Yes	No	Still constrained by market demand	Public utility Beer in Taiwan
Monopolistic competition	Many	Differentiated	Yes, but limited	Yes	Price and quality competition	Restaurants Hand soap
Oligopoly	Few	Either	Yes	Limited	Strategic behavior	Automobiles Aluminum

FIGURE 16-1   Characteristics of Market Organizations   *Source: Adapted from Karl E. Case and Ray C. Fair, Principles of Economics (Englewood Cliffs, NJ: Prentice Hall, 1989).*

Figure 16-1 summarizes the basic characteristics of the major types of market organizations.

No one seriously believes that there ever will be "pure" competition. Instead, the goal is the maintenance of a system of *workable competition* characterized by markets in which a reasonable number of firms compete fairly for market share. Antitrust policy has sought to maintain workable competition by addressing *conduct* and *market structure* of business organizations rather than by direct regulation of corporate decision making or performance. This focus reflects our country's goal, as Justice Hugo Black put it, of preserving "free and unfettered competition as the rule of trade."

This chapter discusses the Sherman Act of 1890, Chapter 17 examines the Clayton Act of 1914 and the legislation that amends it, and Chapter 18 examines the Federal Trade Commission Act of 1914. When analyzing the specific provisions of these laws, think about whether they are intended to influence conduct or structure and the type of corporate performance that they seek to promote or discourage.

A summary chart of antitrust legislation appears in Table 16-1.

■ OVERVIEW OF THE SHERMAN ACT

Sherman Act   1890 federal law outlawing contracts or combinations that restrained interstate trade and providing that anyone who *monopolized*, or attempted to monopolize, any part of interstate commerce or U.S. foreign trade was guilty of a felony

trust   Association formed by owners of competing businesses to control *competition* in their industry

In 1890, Congress passed the **Sherman Act,** this country's first piece of antitrust legislation. The Sherman Act had two sections. Section 1 outlawed contracts or combinations that restrained interstate trade. **Trusts**—that is, legal devices whereby the owners of competing businesses join together as members of an aggregation in order to control competition in their commodity—were included in this legislation. Section 2 made it a felony for any person to monopolize or attempt to monopolize any part of the interstate commerce or foreign trade of the United States.

PENALTIES.   The Sherman Act permits both the Justice Department and private parties whose businesses have been injured to sue. For several decades after their enactment, antitrust laws carried relatively minor penalties for both corporations and individuals. The year 1974, however, marked a turning point in antitrust enforcement policy. Violations are now felony actions; fines of up to $1 million and prison terms of up to three years can now be imposed. The

TABLE 16-1   *U.S. Antitrust Legislation*

Sherman Act (1890)	
Section 1	Outlawed all contracts or combinations in restraint of interstate trade.
Section 2	Provided that any person who monopolized any part of the interstate commerce or foreign trade of the United States, or who attempted to do so, was guilty of a felony.
Clayton Act (1914)	
Section 2	Made it illegal for a business to offer different prices to different customers "where the effect . . . may be substantially to lessen competition."
Section 3	Outlawed exclusive dealing "where the effect . . . may be substantially to lessen competition."
Section 7	Made it illegal for corporations to acquire the stock of other companies where "the effect may be substantially to lessen competition."
FTC Act (1914)	Created the Federal Trade Commission (FTC).
Section 5	Outlawed "unfair methods of competition in commerce."
Robinson-Patman Act (1936)	Rewrote Section 2 of the Clayton Act to make it more specific.
Wheeler-Lea Act (1938)	Amended Section 5 of the FTC Act so that it outlaws not only "unfair methods of competition in commerce" but also "unfair or deceptive acts or practices in commerce."
Celler-Kefauver Amendment (to the Clayton Act) (1950)	Amended Section 7 of the Clayton Act to bring the sale and purchase of assets within its scope.

Sherman Act also has civil as well as criminal components, and private parties may sue for up to three times the monetary damages actually suffered. Civil suits may result in either dissolution of or divestiture by the defendant.

CASE: STANDARD OIL AND THE RULE OF REASON. Standard Oil of New Jersey was the first large corporation to be successfully prosecuted under the Sherman Act. In the course of reviewing a lower court ruling, the U.S. Supreme Court fashioned the standards by which it would assess whether a corporation's actions constituted a violation of the statute. Essentially, the Court held that it would apply a **rule-of-reason test** in determining violations under Section 1 of the Sherman Act: The reasonableness or unreasonableness of a company's behavior will be determined on a case-by-case basis. The courts must thus balance the negative and positive economic effects of an **exclusionary practice**—that is, any practice designed to exclude or limit competitive access to a market. If the positive effects outweigh the negative, there is no violation of the Sherman Act. This rule recognizes that some exclusionary practices are acceptable because they actually foster competition. The rule, therefore, examines and evaluates practices and is not applied to actions judged illegal in themselves—actions discussed later in the chapter.

    On the whole, however, the Court was less accepting of attempts to form monopolies: It ordered the dissolution of both Standard Oil and American Tobacco because they ran afoul of Section 2 of the Sherman Act by intending to form monopolies.

rule-of-reason test Examination on a case-by-case basis of business practices to determine if they violate Section 1 of the Sherman Act

exclusionary practice Any practice designed to exclude or limit competitive access to a market

"THAT'S RIGHT, WILLIE; YOU AND TEDDY MUST ALWAYS KEEP STEP TO PAPA'S FIDDLE!"

Theodore Roosevelt and the Progressive Agenda In 1904, financial analyst John Moody (later co-founder of Standard and Poor) identified 318 major trusts, dominating "every line of productive industry in the United States" with over $7 billion in combined capital. As in this contemporary cartoon—which depicts President William McKinley and Vice-President Theodore Roosevelt dancing to the tune of "The Trusts"—many observers were already becoming wary of the inordinate influence of organized capital on the political process. Succeeding McKinley in 1901, Roosevelt attempted to bring a progressive agenda to the task of big-business regulation. In 1902, he secured the establishment of the Bureau of Corporations to inspect the financial records of all businesses engaged in interstate commerce. In the same year, he revived the nearly forgotten Sherman Antitrust Act by successfully suing the Northern Securities Company, a mammoth railroad trust assembled by J. P. Morgan, John D. Rockefeller, and others. Given the stature of the opponents that he had challenged in the Northern Securities case, Roosevelt immediately garnered immense popular support, and in the next seven years, his administration filed another 43 major "trust-busting" suits. The passage of the Pure Food and Drug Act and the Meat Inspection Act (both 1906) laid the groundwork for consumer-protection regulation, and the Hepburn Act (also 1906), which gave the Interstate Commerce Commission the power to set maximum railroad rates, created the first government regulatory commission.

■ *Concept Check 16-1 Market Competition & Overview of the Sherman Act*

- Describe a model of *pure competition.*
- Define the following forms of market competition: *monopoly, monopolistic competition,* and *oligopoly.*
- What is the purpose of the *rule-of-reason test* when applied under Section 1 of the Sherman Act?
- Give an example of an *exclusionary practice* and explain how it falls under the provisions of the Sherman Act.

■ THE SHERMAN ACT: SECTION 2

As we observed previously, the Sherman Act comprises two sections. The second section, prohibits three things: (1) monopolization (2) attempts to monopolize and (3) conspiracy to monopolize any part of interstate or foreign commerce.

Monopolization

Under Section 2 of the Sherman Act, the offense of monopoly has two elements: (1) the possession of monopoly power in the relevant market and (2) the willful acquisition or maintenance of that power as distinguished from growth or development as a result of a superior product, business acumen, or historic accident.

One of the most difficult problems facing the courts and antitrust policy-makers is defining a *monopoly.* As an aid to understanding market power, economists have developed the model of pure monopoly that we described earlier. A pure monopoly is characterized by the following conditions: (1) a single seller (2) a lack of substitutes for the seller's product and (3) significant restrictions upon entry into the seller's industry.

In the real world, public-policy decisions have caused governments to grant the utility industry the status of a pure monopoly. Most industries, however, are not pure monopolies. It is the court's job to differentiate between an acceptable level of market *dominance* and an unacceptable level of market *control.* This analysis is akin to the application of the rule-of-reason test described above.

LEGAL APPROACHES TO DEFINING A MONOPOLY. Monopoly power can be broadly characterized as *market power*—that is, the power to control prices and exclude competitors. In order to identify the practice of wielding monopolistic market power, the courts have approached corporate activity from two perspectives: *size* and *conduct.* The first perspective is known as the *structural approach,* the second as the *conduct approach.*

The Structural Approach. Perhaps the primary measure of market power is the market share enjoyed by a company or a group of companies. Courts often treat a very high market share as a sign of monopoly power.

When they do so, they use the two-stage **structural analysis** devised by Judge Learned Hand in *United States v. Aluminum Company of America* (Alcoa)

structural analysis Two-stage procedure to decide if a firm has *monopolistic power,* stage 1 defining the market that the firm is said to have dominated and stage 2 calculating the percentage of the market held by the firm

(148 F.2d 416 [1945]). The first stage of this analysis defines the market that a company is said to have dominated. The second stage calculates the percentage of that market enjoyed by the company in question.

The Alcoa *Case.* A brief examination of the *Alcoa* case illustrates how the steps in structural-approach analysis are implemented. Formed in 1888, Alcoa specialized at first in the production of virgin aluminum ingots made from the ore of aluminum, bauxite. As late as 1937, when the *Alcoa* case first came to courts, the company was still the sole domestic producer of virgin aluminum ingots, with more than 90 percent of that market. By this time, however, the company had also entered another business—the fabrication of aluminum ingots into various goods. There was much more competition in this business. In addition, some aluminum ingots are made from recycled aluminum rather than raw ore. The production of secondary ingots was also more competitive than the virgin ingot business.

Defining Alcoa's market was difficult, however. If the manufacture of all secondary ingots and those virgin ingots that Alcoa itself did not fabricate into other products were included, Alcoa had only one-third of the market. However, it had almost 65 percent of the market if the definition included all of Alcoa's ingots—regardless of whether they were fabricated into other products—as well as secondary and imported ingots.

Alcoa denied that the latter description was valid. It also pointed to some competition from imported and secondary ingots, argued that it had not engaged in aggressively monopolistic practices since 1913, and contended that its overall rate of profit (ten percent) was not unusually high.

Judge Hand rejected these arguments. He defined Alcoa's market as the market for virgin ingot, which it dominated to a high degree, and pointed out that the overall profit rate of ten percent included profits from the relatively competitive fabrication business. Profits from the virgin-ingot business, in which Alcoa had no domestic competition, may well have been much higher. He also ruled that even if Alcoa had not engaged in aggressively monopolistic practices for a long time, it had still acted monopolistically. His reasoning was and is controversial. He suggested, for example, that because it is illegal for rival companies to engage in price fixing, it would be illogical to let a single dominant firm set prices.

In addition, at least two problems often make it hard to apply the structural approach: (1) One goal of a competitive business is to eliminate competitors, and (2) Bigness can have positive effects—big companies can often produce goods much more efficiently than their smaller rivals.

The Conduct Approach. Until the *Alcoa* case, the dominant philosophy of enforcement was the **conduct approach**, which stresses the *behavior* of companies rather than their size: In other words, the primary consideration in evaluating whether a firm has monopolistic power is what it *does*, not how big it *is*. Predatory pricing, reciprocal dealing, and tie-in arrangements—all of which will be discussed in some detail later—are examples of behavior that may be treated as monopolistic under the conduct approach. Furthermore, the courts must find otherwise legal conduct wrongful if the *overall* behavior of the firm demonstrates the use of monopolistic power. Thus, certain kinds of actions—notably deceptive acts and behavior—can be prosecuted only under the conduct approach. This view has not found much favor in the 1980s.

conduct approach Legal perspective to decide if a firm has *monopolistic power* by evaluating its behavior rather than its size

GENERAL RULE FOR DEFINING A MONOPOLY. The U.S. Supreme Court set forth a general rule defining monopolies in its 1966 ruling *United States v. Grinnell Corpora-*

tion. The rule embodies both the structural and conduct approaches. Portions of the decision in this case follow.

UNITED STATES v. GRINNELL CORPORATION
United States Supreme Court, 384 U.S. 563 (1966)

The United States brought an antitrust action against Grinnell Corporation, which manufactures plumbing supplies and fire sprinkler systems; American District Telegraph Co. (ADT), which sold both burglary and fire-protection services; Holmes Electric Protective Co. (Holmes), which sold only burglary protection; and Automatic Fire Alarm Co. of Delaware (AFA), which sold only fire-protection services. Grinnell owned 76 percent of ADT's stock, 89 percent of ADT's stock, and 100 percent of Holmes' stock. The security services offered by these companies worked in the same way: In the event of a burglary or fire, hazard-detecting devices, which were installed on the protected premises, automatically sent signals to a central service station. The federal government's suit alleged that these defendants violated the Sherman Antitrust Act by entering into agreements that gave each company the exclusive right to sell its services within specified geographic regions.

Mr. Justice Douglas delivered the opinion of the Court.

. . . .

In 1961 accredited companies in the central station service business grossed $65,000,000. ADT, Holmes, and AFA are the three largest companies in the business in terms of revenue: ADT (with 121 central stations in 115 cities) has 73% of the business; Holmes (with 12 central stations in three large cities) has 12.5%; AFA (with three central stations in three large cities) has 2%. Thus the three companies that Grinnell controls have over 87% of the business.

. . . .

. . . After Grinnell acquired control of the other defendants, the latter continued in their attempts to acquire central station companies—offers being made to at least eight companies between the years 1955 and 1961, including four of the five largest nondefendant companies in the business. When the present suit was filed, each of those defendants had outstanding an offer to purchase one of the four largest nondefendant companies.

In 1907 Grinnell entered into a series of agreements with the other defendant companies and with Automatic Fire Protection Co. to the following effect:

AFA received the exclusive right to provide central station sprinkler supervisory and waterflow alarm and automatic fire alarm service in New York City, Boston and Philadelphia, and agreed not to provide burglar alarm service in those cities or central station service elsewhere in the United States.

Automatic Fire Protection Co. obtained the exclusive right to provide central station sprinkler supervisory and waterflow alarm service everywhere else in the United States except for the three cities in which AFA received that exclusive right, and agreed not to engage in burglar alarm service.

. . . .

Grinnell agreed to furnish and install all sprinkler supervisory and waterflow alarm actuating devices used in systems that AFA and Automatic would install, and otherwise not to engage in the central station protection business.

The agreements remained substantially unchanged until 1949 when ADT purchased all of Automatic Fire Protection Co.'s rights under it for $13,500,000. After these 1907 agreements expired in 1954, AFA continued to honor the prior division of territories; and ADT and AFA entered into a new contract providing for the continued sharing of revenues on substantially the same basis as before. In 1954 Grinnell and ADT renewed an agreement with a Rhode Island company which received the exclusive right to render central station service within Rhode Island at prices no lower than those of ADT and which agreed to use certain equipment supplied by Grinnell and ADT and to share its revenues with those companies. ADT had an informal agreement with a competing central station company in Washington, D. C., "that we would not solicit each other's accounts."

ADT over the years reduced its minimum basic rates to meet competition and renewed contracts at substantially increased rates in cities where it had a monopoly of accredited central station service. ADT threatened retaliation against firms that contemplated inaugurating central station service. And the record indicates that, in contemplating opening a new central station, ADT officials frequently stressed that such action would deter their competitors from opening a new station in that area.

The District Court found that the defendant companies had committed *per se* violations of § 1 of the Sherman Act as well as § 2 and entered a decree. . . .

. . . .

. . . In United States v. E. I. du Pont De Nemours & Co. (1956), we defined monopoly power as "the power to control prices or exclude competition." The existence of such power ordinarily may be inferred from the predominant share of the market. . . . In the present case, 87% of the accredited central station service business leaves no doubt that the congeries of these defendants have monopoly power—power which, as our discussion of the record indicates, they did not hesitate to wield—if that business is the relevant market. The only remaining question therefore is, what is the relevant market?

. . . .

The District Court treated the entire accredited central station service business as a single market and we think it was justified in so doing. Defendants argue that the different central station services offered are so diverse that they cannot under *du Pont* be lumped together to make up the relevant market. For example, burglar alarm services are not interchangeable with fire alarm services. They further urge that *du Pont* requires that protective services other than those of the central station variety be included in the market definition.

But there is here a single use, i.e., the protection of property, through a central station that receives signals. It is that service, accredited, that is unique and that competes with all the other forms of property protection. We see no barrier to combining in a single market a number of different products or services where that combination reflects commercial realities.

. . . .

We also agree with the District Court that the geographic market for the accredited central station service is national. The activities of an individual station are in a sense local as it serves, ordinarily, only that area, which is within a radius of 25 miles. But the record amply supports the conclusion that the business of providing such a service is operated on a national level. . . .

. . . [T]his monopoly was achieved in large part by unlawful and exclusionary practices. The restrictive agreements that pre-empted for each company a segment of the market where it was free of competition of the others were one device. Pricing practices that contained competitors were another. The acquisitions by Grinnell of ADT, AFA, and Holmes were still another. Grinnell long faced a problem of competing with ADT. That was one reason it acquired AFA and Holmes. Prior to settlement of its dispute and controversy with ADT, Grinnell prepared to go into the central station service business. By acquiring ADT in 1953, Grinnell eliminated that alternative. Its control of the three other defendants eliminated any possibility of an outbreak of competition that might have occurred when the 1907 agreements terminated. By those acquisitions it perfected the monopoly power to exclude competitors and fix prices.

. . . .

The judgment below is affirmed. . . .

Mr. Justice Fortas, with whom Mr. Justice Stewart joins, dissenting.

. . . .

We have here a case under both § 1 and § 2 of the Sherman Act, which proscribe combinations in restraint of trade, and monopolies and attempts to monopolize. The judicial task is not difficult to state: Does the record show a combination in restraint of trade or a monopoly or attempt to monopolize? If so, what are its characteristics, scope and effect? And, finally, what is the appropriate remedy for a court of equity to decree?

Each of these inquiries depends upon two basic referents: definition of the geographical area of trade or commerce restrained or monopolized, and of the products or services involved. . . . In the present case . . . the essence of the offense is monopolization, achieved or attempted, and the major relief is divestiture. For these purposes, "market" definition is of the essence, just as in § 7 cases the kindred definition of the "line of commerce" is fundamental. We must define the area of commerce that is allegedly engrossed before we can determine its engrossment; and we must define it before a decree can be shaped to deal with the consequences of the monopoly, and to restore or produce competition.

In this case, the relevant geographical and product markets have not been defined on the basis of the economic facts of the industry concerned. They have been tailored precisely to fit defendants' business.

. . . .

The geographical market is defined as nationwide. But the need and the service are intensely local. . . . The premises protected do not travel. They are fixed locations. They must be protected where they are. Protection must be provided on the spot. It must be furnished by local personnel able to bring help to the scene within minutes. Even the central stations can provide service only within a 25-mile radius. . . .

But because these defendants, the trial court found, are connected by stock ownership, interlocking management and some degree of national corporate direction, and because there is some national participation in selling as well as national financing, advertising, purchasing of equipment, and the like, the court concluded that the competitive area to be considered is national. This Court now affirms that conclusion.

This is a non sequitur. It is not permissible to seize upon the nationwide scope of defendants' operation and to bootstrap a geographical definition of the market from this. The purpose of the search for the relevant geographical market is to find the area or areas to which a potential buyer may rationally look for the goods or services that he seeks. The test . . . is "the geographic structure of supplier-customer relations." . . .

. . . .

Here, there can be no doubt that the correct geographic market is local. The services at issue are intensely local: they can be furnished only locally. The business as it is done is local—not nationwide. . . .

. . . .

The trial court's definition of the "product" market even more dramatically demonstrates that its action has been Procrustean—that it has tailored that market to the dimensions of the defendants. . . .

. . . .

. . . Its definition of the "relevant market" is not merely confined to "central station" protective services, but to those central station protective services which are "accredited" by insurance companies.

There is no pretense that these furnish peculiar services for which there is no alternative in the market place, on either a price or a functional basis. The court relies solely upon its finding that the services offered by accredited central stations are of better quality, and upon its conclusion that the insurance companies tend to give "noticeably larger" discounts to policyholders who use accredited central station protective services.

This Court now approves this strange red-haired, bearded, one-eyed man-with-a-limp classification.

. . . .

I believe this approach has no justification in economics, reason or law. . . .

. . . [T]he court should have defined the relevant market here to include all services which, in light of geographical availability, price and use characteristics, are in realistic rivalry for all or some part of the business of furnishing protective services to premises.

. . . .

I do not intend by any of the foregoing to suggest that, on this record, the relief granted by the trial court and the substantially more drastic relief ordered by this Court would necessarily be unjustified. . . . Since I am of the opinion that defendants and the courts are entitled to a reappraisal of the liability consequences as

well as the appropriate provisions of the decree on the basis of a sound definition of the market, I would reverse and remand for these purposes.

Case Questions

1. In determining the relevant market, the majority applied a national-market analysis, while the dissent opted for a local-market approach. What are the implications of each perspective? Which better serves the underlying policy of antitrust legislation?

2. How does the majority define the "product" at issue in this case? How does this differ from the dissent's definition? What are the respective pros and cons of adopting a broad or narrow approach to defining a product?

DEFINING THE RELEVANT MARKET. As we have already seen, the structural approach requires the court to determine the relevant market. Markets may be defined by products or by geographical areas. As we saw in the *Alcoa* case, this determination is not always easy. For example, corporate defendants are most likely to want a broad definition of the market, making the likelihood of proving monopolistic actions more difficult.

In order to describe the market in which monopolistic practice may be taking place, the courts may look at two different criteria: the nature of the *product* in the market and the nature of *geographic demand* in the market.

Product Markets. A *product market* includes goods or services that can be substituted for one another—that is, competing products. The courts use the economic concept of *cross-elasticity of demand* as a device to pinpoint a product market. In the *Alcoa* case, for example, the demand was relatively inelastic because there was only a small possibility of product substitution. Consequently, Alcoa controlled the price of virgin aluminum ingots. Other products, however, are much more vulnerable to substitution, and several other prominent cases have been decided on the basis of product market. Among the most important are the so-called "Cellophane case" (*United States v. E. I. du Pont De Nemours & Company*, 351 U.S. 377 [1956]), which is the subject of the You DE-CIDE issue in this chapter, and *Telex Corporation v. International Business Machines Corporation* (510 F.2d 894 [1975]), which is excerpted below.

TELEX CORPORATION v. INTERNATIONAL BUSINESS MACHINES CORPORATION
U.S. Court of Appeals, Tenth Circuit, 510 F.2d 894 (1975)

Plaintiff-appellee, Telex Computer Products, Inc. (Telex), alleged that defendant-appellant, International Business Machines Corporation (IBM), violated Sections 1 and 2 of the Sherman Act, and Section 2 of the Clayton Act, in that IBM had monopolized and attempted to monopolize the manufacture, distribution, sale, and leasing of electronic data processing equipment. The District Court found and concluded that IBM had violated

the anti-trust laws and awarded damages to Telex. IBM appeals.

Per curiam
. . .At the outset it is necessary to distinguish between the general systems portion of the industry which encompasses the manufacture of the basic electronic data processing system, the essential equipment being a central processing unit. . . . In the segment of the in-

dustry involving the manufacture of the central processing units, IBM did not have monopoly power, although it was estimated by the court that its market share was about thirty-five percent.

In addition to the central processing unit, a data processing system also has a number of so-called peripheral devices which are connected with the central processing unit and which perform various special functions in the data processing system. These include information storage components like magnetic tape drives, magnetic disk drives, magnetic drums and magnetic strip files; terminal devices such as printers; memory units, which are specialized storage units, and other similar types of peripheral components. Sometimes these devices are included in the central processing unit, that is, do not exist as external components. It is these peripheral components with which we are primarily concerned in this lawsuit. . . . The term "plug compatible peripheral device" . . . refers to a component which is functionally equivalent to the manufacturer's peripheral device and can be readily plugged into that central processing unit. Undoubtedly it is the wide use of the IBM central processing unit that caused Telex and others to market peripheral devices which were plug compatible with the IBM unit and which could replace IBM peripheral devices which had been made for the IBM central system.

The Relevant Market:

The District Court found that there existed a definable market for all peripheral devices plug compatible with IBM processing units. The court further found that there were individual submarkets for each particular type of peripheral product.

. . . The number of manufacturers of IBM peripherals [rose] from two or three in 1966 to approximately 100 as of the time of trial. Telex and some eleven others were the major manufacturers of IBM plug compatible products.

Originally, of course, IBM, being the only manufacturer of peripheral products plug compatible with its system, had 100 percent of the market. The court found that as other manufacturers entered the plug compatible market with IBM, the IBM share became substantially eroded. . . .

. . . .

During this period of time, Telex was gaining considerably in connection with the plug compatible printers and Telex offered a price advantage in that their product could be used without limit.

. . . .

The Fixed Term Plan was adopted as a result of this (on May 25, 1971).

Effect of the Fixed Term Plan:

The plan called for prices of the competition to be undercut to a considerable extent. At the same time, IBM was to face a reduction in its profits, at least for the first two years. A very considerable increase was contemplated in 1975.

. . . .

[T]he [district] court considered it necessary to analyze IBM's adoption of a long-term lease program solely in the light of IBM's dominant market position. . . .

. . . .

The court concluded that:

"IBM's Fixed Term Plan was generated and implemented at the time it was with the primary intent and purpose of suppressing plug compatible competition and to maintain its monopoly power in the plug compatible disk, tape and printer markets and the general plug compatible market for peripheral devices."

. . . .

The main quarrel of IBM with the court's determination of the relevant market is that it is limited mainly to peripheral products plug compatible with IBM's equipment. It encompasses only part of the peripheral equipment marketed by Telex and the other plug compatible manufacturers. It fails to include the peripheral equipment market by systems manufacturers other than IBM.

. . . .

In support of its contention that it did not have monopoly power, IBM cites that its share of the computer systems industry amounted to 35.1 per cent and that its share of computer hardware was limited to 36.7 per cent. Further, that its share of total peripheral equipment was limited to 45.6 per cent of the tape market, 38.3 per cent of the printer market, and 30.3 per cent of the disk and memory market. IBM points out that the court's finding as to the possession of IBM of monopoly power is inconsistent with its findings that there existed substantial competition between IBM and other manufacturers in the area of peripheral products. . . .

. . . .

The threshold issue is whether the court erred in its findings as to the scope and extent of the relevant product market for determination whether there existed power to control prices or to exclude competition, that is, whether there was monopoly power. . . .

. . . .

We recognize that market definition is generally treated as a matter of fact and that findings on this subject are not to be overturned unless clearly erroneous. Our question is, therefore, whether it was clearly erroneous for the court to exclude peripheral products of systems other than IBM such as Honeywell, Univac, Burroughs, Control Data Corp. and others, together with peripheral products plug compatible with the systems and, indeed, whether the systems themselves manufactured by the companies are to be taken into account. It is significant, of course, that peripheral products constitute a large percentage of the entire data processing system, somewhere between 50 and 75 per cent.

Inasmuch as IBM's share of the data processing industry as a whole is insufficient to justify any inference or conclusion of market power in IBM, the exclusion from the defined market of those products which are not plug compatible with IBM central processing units has a significant impact on the court's decision that IBM possessed monopoly power.

Manufacturers of peripherals were not limited to those which were plug compatible with IBM CPUs. These manufacturers were free to adapt their products through interface changes to plug into non-IBM systems. It also followed that systems manufacturers could modify interfaces so that their own peripheral products could plug into IBM CPUs. Factually, then, there existed peripheral products of other CPU manufacturers which were competitive with IBM peripherals and unquestionably other IBM peripherals were capable of having their interfaces modified so that their peripheral products would plug into non-IBM's CPU.

The fact that Telex had substantially devoted itself to the manufacture of peripheral products which were used in IBM CPUs and which competed with IBM peripheral products cannot control in determining product market since the legal standard is whether the product is reasonably interchangeable.

This standard was laid down by the Supreme Court in the famous case of United States v. E. I. DuPont de Nemours & Co. (1956). In this case, as in the case at bar, the scope of the products market was crucial. The Supreme Court determined that if one product may substitute for another in the market it is "reasonably interchangeable."

. . . .

It seems clear that reasonable interchangeability is proven in the case at bar and hence the market should include not only peripheral products plug compatible with IBM CPUs, but all peripheral products, those com-

patible not only with IBM CPUs but those compatible with non-IBM systems. This is wholly justifiable because the record shows that these products, . . . may be interchanged with minimal financial outlay, and so cross-elasticity exists within meaning of the *DuPont* decision.

The court's very restrictive definition of the product market in the face of evidence which established the interchangeable quality of the products in question, together with the existence of cross-elasticity of demand, must be regarded as plain error.

. . . .

The judgment of the trial court against IBM must be reversed because it is based upon an erroneous determination of a fundamental element in the case. . . .

Case Questions

1. What did the district court determine the relevant product market to be in this case?

2. Upon what grounds did the court of appeals disagree? Explain the standard laid down in *United States v. E. I. Du Pont de Nemours & Co.* (cited in the case).

Geographical Markets. In order to determine whether a monopoly exists, it is also necessary to look at the geographical nature of demand for a product. An alleged monopolist's competitors include all companies that sell the same kind of product within the area in which potential customers are willing to search for substitutes or other sources of supply. If potential buyers are willing to obtain product substitutes from other geographic regions, no single firm can exercise power over a product in a particular market or area.

Consider, for example, the market for cornflakes, which includes a number of producers located throughout the country. If one major producer raised its prices, customers could readily substitute cornflakes made by another manufacturer. Therefore, the entire nation is the relevant geographical market for cornflakes. Cornflake producers compete with breakfast-cereal producers nationwide.

But what about the geographical nature of demand for cement? If the Topeka Cement Company raises its prices, customers will find it difficult to substitute cement obtained from companies in other regions—transportation costs will quickly exceed the actual cost of the locally produced cement. Thus, in determining the Topeka Cement Company's degree of monopolistic control, the relevant market should include only those competitors who do business within the same geographical region.

MEASURING MARKET POWER. The Shell Oil Company is one of the biggest businesses in the United States—indeed, in the whole world. By contrast, a general store in a small town of northeastern Vermont is not even among the biggest stores in Vermont, let alone in New England or the United States. Such stores have small sales and still smaller earnings. Shell, however, is not a monopoly, and the general store might be.

At first glance, this prospect may sound unreasonable. However, the gen-

A good deal of legal action surrounds competing products— products that can be substituted for one another. The term elasticity *refers to ease of substitution. For example, the market for cotton swabs is highly* elastic *because there is little difference between swabs carrying the brand name "Q-tip" and those carrying the private label of a chain of discount stores (such as K-Mart). In the Alcoa case already examined, the demand was relatively inelastic because there was only a small possibility of product substitution and the Alcoa company controlled the price of virgin aluminum ingots.*

By contrast, United States v. E. I. du Pont De Nemours & Co. *(351 U.S. 377 [1956]), the so-called "Cellophane case," involved a product that was relatively* elastic. *The case centered on the following facts: In the 1950s, E. I. du Pont De Nemours & Company produced about seventy-five percent of all of the cellophane wrap produced in the United States during the years in question. The government charged the company with operating a monopoly. Du Pont countered with the argument that because consumers could use products such as aluminum foil and wax paper for the same purpose, the relevant market consisted of all flexible wrapping materials—not just cellophane wrap. Du Pont had only about a 20-percent market share of all flexible wraps during the same period. Consequently, Du Pont contended that if it raised its price, consumers could easily switch to a different product. The Supreme Court accepted Du Pont's view of the situation.*

The Court's decision, however, raised a great deal of con-troversy. Some critics, for example, wondered whether there is a difference between "market power" and "monopoly power." Others asked if the difference should hinge on whether a company restricts its own output or that of its rivals.

In the context of the Cellophane case, the question would take the following form: Did the fact that Du Pont had a relatively small market share of all flexible wraps change the fact that it had a virtual monopoly in the market for cellophane wrap? Should the Court have considered how broad the market was for each type of wrap? Should it have further studied the differences among the various markets? For example, while a person wrapping vegetables at home might choose to use either cellophane wrap or aluminum foil, a supermarket would almost be forced to use the cellophane wrap because it is unlikely that consumers would purchase produce that they could not first inspect by sight.

As far as price was concerned, the Court defined market power as "the power to control prices or exclude competition." The same basic issue arises: Was the crux of the matter Du Pont's inability to control the price of all flexible wraps—or was it the fact that the company could control the price of cellophane wrap? Remember, any company can raise its price. The objective is to do so without losing so many customers that the price rise becomes unprofitable.

Should Du Pont's control of the cellophane-wrap market have been considered a monopoly? Was the Supreme Court wrong when it equated all related wraps? For further discussion, see p. 619.

---

eral store may be the only store of any kind in the towns of that region while Shell Oil Co. has a good deal of competition. In other words, monopolies are monopolies by virtue of their *relative* positions in the markets that they dominate. Although size may be a factor, it is not the only one. Similarly price cutting is a perfectly legitimate business strategy in markets that are truly competitive. However, in an industry dominated by a monopolist, price cutting might be viewed solely as an attempt to undercut competition.

In a market analysis, the court first selects the relevant market and then determines what share of it is held by the alleged monopoly. There is no clear dividing line as to how much of a market a company must control in order to be treated by the courts as a monopoly. However, a company that has 70–90 percent generally will not be considered monopolistic even if the company has the power to influence prices by changing its output. If the federal government wants to bring Sherman Act Section 2 charges against a company with market share below 50 percent, it will usually accuse that company of *"attempting* to monopolize" an industry.

IDENTIFYING THE EXERCISE OF MARKET POWER.   A problem area for the judiciary is how to avoid penalizing firms that have *fairly* attained a monopoly position because of their special knowledge or insights about an industry. According to the Supreme Court's decision in *United States v. Grinnell Corporation*, which was discussed earlier in this chapter, the charge of illegal monopolization requires (1) only the existence of a monopoly and (2) conduct by which monopolists exercise their power to exclude competition from a market. Let's consider certain kinds of market conditions and conduct that may have a bearing on whether the Sherman Act has been violated.

Thin Markets. A *thin market* lacks the customers necessary to support more than a single supplier. It is not monopolistic merely to enter a thin market. In order to violate Section 2 of the Sherman Act, a company must commit some other, specifically exclusionary action.

Horizontal Mergers. A merger between two or more competing companies that creates a monopoly violates Section 2 of the Sherman Act. Monopolies created through **horizontal mergers**—that is, through the expansion of a single company—may be legitimate, especially if the expansion was unavoidable. (Horizontal mergers are discussed in much more detail in Chapter 17.)

horizontal merger *Merger between competing or potentially competing firms (see also Chapter 17)*

Selection of Customers. An old common-law principle holds that a company must conduct its business in a manner that does not arbitrarily discriminate against particular customers. Monopolies have the market power to discriminate.

Predatory Behavior. There is no precise, objective legal definition of **predatory behavior.** However, such behavior has two hallmarks: (1) it seems jarring or unnatural; and (2) it targets particular competitors, groups of competitors, or possible competitors. For example, a monopoly that purchased controlling interest in a potential competitor and then voted at the shareholders' meeting to stay out of its own market would probably be convicted of predatory behavior. Similarly, one newspaper publisher was found to have acted predatorily when he refused to sell advertising space to any company that placed advertisements on a radio station.

predatory behavior *Market activity which seems jarring or unnatural and which targets a particular competitor, group of competitors, or possible competitors*

Concerted Action. Suppose that instead of merging, two or more separate companies acted together to preclude competition. They would still be guilty of violating Section 2 of the Sherman Act through **concerted action**. In the nineteenth century, for example, it was common for the large companies in many industries to form cartels that divided markets among themselves. Today, companies are periodically accused of cooperating to fix prices and of dividing territories among themselves.

concerted action *Practice whereby two or more separate firms act jointly to preclude competition*

Many of the issues discussed above arose in the case of *Berkey Photo, Inc. v. Eastman Kodak Co.* In that case, which is excerpted below, Berkey, a film-finishing company, accused Kodak of acting monopolistically by creating a new film and then refusing to tell other photofinishers how to process it. When the case came before the court, Kodak held about 64 percent of the U.S. market for amateur cameras and 88 percent of the film market.

BERKEY PHOTO, INC. v. EASTMAN KODAK CO.
U.S. Court of Appeals, Second Circuit, 603 F.2d 263 (1979)

Plaintiff Berkey Photo, Inc. (Berkey), a film-finishing company, accused Eastman Kodak Co. (Kodak), its competitor in the photofinishing services market, of acting monopolistically in violation of Section 2 of the Sherman Act by creating a new film and then refusing to tell others how to process it. Kodak had long been the dominant firm in the "amateur con- ventional still camera" market. The market consists of small, simple, and relatively inexpensive cameras, the direct descendants of the popular "box" camera, the best known of which was Kodak's "Brownie." When the case came before the court, Kodak held about 64 percent of the U.S. market for amateur cameras and 88 percent of the film market.

Berkey contends that Kodak illicitly gained an advantage in the markets for photofinishing equipment or services by leveraging its power over film and cameras. The jury below found that Kodak's monopoly in the film market had been used to disadvantage rivals in cameras, photofinishing, and photofinishing equipment markets. Kodak appeals.

Irving R. Kaufman, Chief Judge:

. . . .

. . . [T]he use of monopoly power attained in one market to gain a competitive advantage in another is a violation of § 2, even if there has not been an attempt to monopolize the second market. It is the use of economic power that creates the liability. But, as we have indicated, a large firm does not violate § 2 simply by reaping the competitive rewards attributable to its efficient size, nor does an integrated business offend the Sherman Act whenever one of its departments benefits from association with a division possessing a monopoly in its own market. So long as we allow a firm to compete in several fields, we must expect it to seek the competitive advantages of its broad-based activity—more efficient production, greater ability to develop complementary products, reduced transaction costs, and so forth. These are gains that accrue to any integrated firm, regardless of its market share, and they cannot by themselves be considered uses of monopoly power.

. . . .

We turn now to the events surrounding Kodak's introduction of the 110 photographic system in 1972.

. . . .

. . . On March 16, 1972, amid great fanfare, the system was announced. Finally, said Kodak, there was a "little camera that takes big pictures." Kodacolor II was "a remarkable new film"—indeed, the best color negative film Kodak had ever manufactured. There had long been other small cameras, Kodak explained: "But they weren't like these. Now there are films fine enough, and sharp enough, to give you big, sharp pictures from a very small negative."

In accord with Kodak's 1967 plan, Kodacolor II was sold only in the 110 format for eighteen months after introduction. It remains the only 110-size color print film Kodak has ever sold.

As Kodak had hoped, the 110 system proved to be a dramatic success. In 1972—the system's first year— the company sold 2,984,000 Pocket Instamatics, more than 50% of its sales in the amateur conventional still camera market. The new camera thus accounted in large part for a sharp increase in total market sales, from 6.2 million units in 1971 to 8.2 million in 1972.

. . . .

Berkey contends that the introduction of the 110 system was both an attempt to monopolize and actual monopolization of the camera market. It also alleges that the marketing of the new camera constituted an impermissible leveraging of Kodak's film monopoly into the two photofinishing markets, services and equipment.

. . . .

There is little doubt that the evidence supports the jury's implicit finding that Kodak had monopoly power in cameras. The principal issues presented to us regarding the effect of the 110 introduction in the camera market are whether Kodak engaged in anticompetitive conduct and, if so, whether that conduct caused injury to Berkey.

Through the 1960s, Kodak followed a checkered pattern of predisclosing innovations to various segments of the industry. Its purpose on these occasions evidently was to ensure that the industry would be able to meet consumers' demand for the complementary goods and services they would need to enjoy the new Kodak products. But predisclosure would quite obviously also diminish Kodak's share of the auxiliary markets. It was therefore, in the words of Walter Fallon, Kodak's chief executive officer, "a matter of judgment on each and every occasion" whether predisclosure would be for or against Kodak's self-interest. . . . [I]n 1963, when Kodak came out with Kodacolor X and the 126 Instamatic, it kept its own counsel until the date of introduction.

As early as 1968, some Kodak employees urged that advance warning of the P-30 system would be needed, at least to film processors and manufacturers of photofinishing equipment, to give them time to prepare for Kodacolor II and the new high-temperature finishing process, which was eventually labeled C-41. . . . Nevertheless, Kodak decided not to release advance information about the new film and format. The decision was evidently based on the perception of Dr. Louis K. Eilers, Kodak's chief executive officer at that time, that Kodak would gain more from being first on the market for the sale of all goods and services related to the 110 system than it would lose from the inability of other photofinishers to process Kodacolor II.

. . . .

Withholding from others advance knowledge of one's new products ordinarily constitutes valid competitive conduct. Because, as we have already indicated, a monopolist is permitted, and indeed encouraged, by § 2 to compete aggressively on the merits, any success that it may achieve through "the process of invention and innovation" is clearly tolerated by the antitrust laws.

. . . .

Moreover, enforced predisclosure would cause undesirable consequences beyond merely encouraging the sluggishness the Sherman Act was designed to prevent. . . . Berkey postulates that Kodak had a duty to disclose limited types of information to certain competitors under specific circumstances. But it is difficult to comprehend how a major corporation, accustomed though it is to making business decisions with antitrust considerations in mind, could possess the omniscience to anticipate all the instances in which a jury might one day in the future retrospectively conclude that predisclosure was warranted. And it is equally difficult to discern workable guidelines that a court might set forth to aid the firm's decision. For example, how detailed must the information conveyed be? And how far must research have progressed before it is "ripe" for disclosure? These inherent uncertainties would have an inevitable chilling effect on innovation. They go far, we believe, towards explaining why no court has ever imposed the duty Berkey seeks to create here.

An antitrust plaintiff urging a predisclosure rule, therefore, bears a heavy burden in justifying his request. Berkey recognizes the weight of this burden. It contends that it has been met. Kodak is not a monolithic monopolist, acting in a single market. Rather, its camera monopoly was supported by its activity as a film manufacturer. Berkey therefore argues that by not disclosing the new format in which it was manufacturing film, Kodak unlawfully enhanced its power in the camera market. Indeed, Kodak not only participates in but monopolizes the film industry. The jury could easily have found that, when Kodak introduced a new film format, rival camera makers would be foreclosed from a substantial segment of the market until they were able to manufacture cameras in the new format. Accordingly, Berkey contended that Kodak illegitimately used its monopoly power in film to gain a competitive advantage in cameras. Thus Berkey insists that the jury was properly permitted to consider whether, on balance, the failure to predisclose the new format was exclusionary. We disagree.

. . . .

. . . The first firm, even a monopolist, to design a new camera format has a right to the lead time that follows from its success. The mere fact that Kodak manufactured film in the new format as well, so that its customers would not be offered worthless cameras, could not deprive it of that reward. Nor is this conclusion altered because Kodak not only participated in but dominated the film market. Kodak's ability to pioneer formats does not depend on it possessing a film monopoly. Had the firm possessed a much smaller share of the film market, it would nevertheless have been able to manufacture sufficient quantities of 110-size film—either Kodacolor X or Kodacolor II—to bring the new camera to market. It is apparent, therefore, that the ability to introduce the new format without predisclosure was solely a benefit of integration and not, without more, a use of Kodak's power in the film market to gain a competitive advantage in cameras.

. . . .

. . . We have held that Kodak did not have an obligation, merely because it introduced film and camera in a new format, to make any predisclosure to its camera-making competitors. Nor did the earlier use of its film monopoly to foreclose format innovation by those competitors create of its own force such a duty where none had existed before. In awarding Berkey $15,250,000, just $828,000 short of the maximum amount demanded, the jury clearly based its calculation of lost camera profits on Berkey's central argument that it had a right to be "at the starting line when the whistle blew" for the new system. The verdict, therefore, cannot stand.

Case Questions

1. Does the fact that a company is large and has monopoly power mean that it is violating the Sherman Act? Explain.

2. Upon what basis did the court hold that Kodak did not act monopolistically?

3. Why does the court hold that it is a legitimate business practice to keep new developments secret? What might be the consequence if there were a duty placed upon a company to disclose these secrets?

Attempts and Conspiracies to Monopolize

In addition to prohibiting actual monopolies, Section 2 of the Sherman Act forbids any "*attempt* to monopolize" and any effort to "combine or *conspire* to monopolize" foreign and interstate commerce. These two offenses will be considered separately.

ATTEMPTS TO MONOPOLIZE. In 1905, in *Swift and Company v. United States* (196 U.S. 375), the Supreme Court distinguished "attempts to monopolize" both from conspiracies to monopolize and from actual monopolization. There are, the Court ruled, two elements to the crime of attempting to monopolize. First, the person or persons accused must intend to create a monopoly. Second, there must be a "dangerous probability" that it will succeed.

Predatory Pricing. Because intentions are not physical objects that can be examined directly, we must infer intent from actions. The action that most obviously suggests an intent to monopolize is **predatory pricing**, which occurs when a large company temporarily cuts prices below production costs to drive competitors from the market. After the competitors are gone, the large company can raise its prices.

Not every price reduction is predatory, however: It is the likelihood that

predatory pricing Practice whereby a large firm temporarily cuts prices below production costs to drive competitors from the market (*see also* Chapter 17)

the predator will eventually raise prices that makes a very low price predatory. How can the courts decide whether a low level of prices evidences a predatory intent to drive competitors out of business and raise prices down the line? Economic theory provides a fairly easy answer: When prices fall below a company's marginal costs—that is, the cost of producing and marketing any additional unit of output—it is very likely that the company will raise prices to recover its losses. In practice, however, many companies do not know their own marginal costs of production, and courts are ill-equipped to make such calculations.

CONSPIRACIES TO MONOPOLIZE. Conspiring to monopolize is a separate crime under Section 2 of the Sherman Act. The differences between conspiring and attempting to monopolize are not always clear. Often, companies are charged with both offenses.

There are two elements to the charge of conspiring to monopolize foreign or interstate trade. First, there must be evidence of some *planned collective action* intended to create a monopoly by two or more entities. (As with attempts to monopolize, intentions can be inferred from actions.) Second, the alleged conspirators must have committed *at least one overt action* in furtherance of a plan to monopolize.

In the case of *Matsushita Electric*, the Supreme Court was asked to decide a charge of conspiring to monopolize the U.S. market for television sets through predatory pricing.

MATSUSHITA ELECTRIC INDUSTRIAL CO. v. ZENITH RADIO CORPORATION
United States Supreme Court, 106 S.Ct 1348 (1986)

Petitioners are 21 Japanese corporations or Japanese-controlled American corporations that manufacture and/or sell "consumer electronic products" (CEPs)—primarily television sets. Respondents are Zenith Radio Corporation (Zenith) and National Union Electric Corporation (NUE), American corporations that manufacture and sell television sets. Respondents brought an action in Federal District Court, alleging that over a 20-year period, petitioners had illegally conspired to drive American firms from the American CEP market by engaging in a scheme to fix and maintain artificially high prices for television sets sold by petitioners in Japan and, at the same time, to fix and maintain artificially low prices for the sets exported to and sold in the United States.

The District Court found that the evidence did not support an inference of conspiracy and granted summary judgment in petitioners' favor. The Court of Appeals reversed. Based on inferences drawn from the evidence, the Court of Appeals concluded that a reasonable factfinder could find a conspiracy to depress prices in the American market in order to drive out American competitors, which conspiracy was funded by excess profits obtained in the Japanese market. Matsushita appeals to the U.S. Supreme Court.

Justice Powell delivered the opinion of the Court.

. . .

We begin by emphasizing what respondents' claim is *not*. Respondents cannot recover antitrust damages based solely on an alleged cartelization of the Japanese market, because American antitrust laws do not regulate the competitive conditions of other nations' economies. . . .

. . . The thrust of respondents' argument is that petitioners used their monopoly profits from the Japanese market to fund a concerted campaign to price predatorily and thereby drive respondents and other American manufacturers of CEPs out of business. Once successful, according to respondents, petitioners would cartelize the American CEP market, restricting output and raising prices above the level that fair competition would produce. The resulting monopoly profits, respondents contend, would more than compensate petitioners for the losses they incurred through years of pricing below market level.

. . . .

A predatory pricing conspiracy is by nature speculative. Any agreement to price below the competitive level requires the conspirators to forego profits that free competition would offer them. The foregone profits may be considered an investment in the future. For the investment to be rational, the conspirators must have a reasonable expectation of recovering, in the form of later monopoly profits, more than the losses suffered. . . . The success of any predatory scheme depends on *maintaining* monopoly power for long enough both to recoup the predator's losses and to harvest some additional gain. Absent some assurance that the hoped-for monopoly will materialize, *and* that it can be sustained for a significant period of time, "[t]he predator must make a substantial investment with no assurance that it will pay off."

For this reason, there is a consensus among commentators that predatory pricing schemes are rarely tried, and even more rarely successful.

. . . .

Finally, if predatory pricing conspiracies are generally unlikely to occur, they are especially so where, as here, the prospects of attaining monopoly power seem slight. In order to recoup their losses, petitioners must obtain enough market power to set higher than competitive prices, and then must sustain those prices long enough to earn in excess profits what they earlier gave up in below-cost prices. Two decades after their conspiracy is alleged to have commenced, petitioners appear to be far from achieving this goal: the two largest shares of the retail market in television sets are held by RCA and respondent Zenith, not by any of the petitioners. . . . The alleged conspiracy's failure to achieve its ends in the two decades of its asserted operation is strong evidence that the conspiracy does not in fact exist. . . .

. . . .

As our discussion . . . shows, petitioners had no motive to enter into the alleged conspiracy. To the contrary, as presumably rational businesses, petitioners had every incentive not to engage in the conduct with which they are charged, for its likely effect would be to generate losses for petitioners with no corresponding gains. The Court of Appeals did not take account of the absence of a plausible motive to enter into the alleged predatory pricing conspiracy. It focused instead on whether there was "direct evidence of concert of action." The Court of Appeals erred in two respects: (i) the "direct evidence" on which the court relied had little, if any, relevance to the alleged predatory pricing conspiracy; and (ii) the court failed to consider the absence of a plausible motive to engage in predatory pricing.

The "direct evidence" on which the court relied was evidence of *other* combinations, not of a predatory pricing conspiracy. Evidence that petitioners conspired to raise prices in Japan provides little, if any, support for respondents' claims: a conspiracy to increase profits in one market does not tend to show a conspiracy to sustain losses in another. Evidence that petitioners agreed to fix *minimum* prices (through the "check price" agreements) for the American market actually works in petitioners' favor, because it suggests that petitioners were seeking to place a floor under prices rather than to lower them. . . .

. . . Here, the conduct in question consists largely of (i) pricing at levels that succeeded in taking business away from respondents, and (ii) arrangements that may have limited petitioners' ability to compete with each other (and thus kept prices from going even lower). This conduct suggests either that petitioners behaved competitively, or that petitioners conspired to *raise* prices. Neither possibility is consistent with an agreement among 21 companies to price below market levels. Moreover, the predatory pricing scheme that this conduct is said to prove is one that makes no practical sense: it calls for petitioners to destroy companies larger and better established than themselves, a goal that remains far distant more than two decades after the conspiracy's birth. Even had they succeeded in obtaining their monopoly, there is nothing in the record to suggest that they could recover the losses they would need to sustain along the way. In sum, in light of the absence of any rational motive to conspire, neither petitioners' pricing practices, nor their conduct in the Japanese market, nor their agreements respecting prices and distribution in the American market, suffice to create a "genuine issue for trial."

. . . .

The decision of the Court of Appeals is reversed, and the case is remanded for further proceedings consistent with this opinion.

Case Questions

1. Respondents in this case argue that petitioners engaged in predatory pricing practices. Explain predatory pricing.

2. Upon what basis did the Supreme Court reverse the decision of the court of appeals? Explain.

3. Can American companies recover antitrust damages based on anticompetitive practices in another country? Why or why not?

Conspiracy and International Antitrust Law. The question of just how far U.S. antitrust law can reach is an issue that is receiving increasing attention in an era of international economic merger—for example, the European Community—and turmoil—the dilemmas over trade with Mexico and imports from Japan. American antitrust law specifically indicates that it has some form of jurisdiction over international commerce. One noteworthy case in this area is *Timberlane Lumber Co. v. Bank of America* (549 F.2d 597 9th Cir. [1976]), which involved an international conspiracy to prevent the import of timber into the

United States. The INTERNATIONAL ENVIRONMENT box in this chapter examines the application of the legal theories on which the case was based.

■ Concept Check 16-2   The Sherman Act: Section 2

- Explain the two elements that must be demonstrated in order to show *monopolization* under Section 2 of the Sherman Act.
- Define *market power*. Explain and contrast the *structural* and *conduct approaches* to determining market power.
- Discuss *product* and *geographical markets* as criteria for determining the relevant market in a case of alleged monopolization. Explain the role of the concept of *cross-elasticity of demand* in defining a product market.
- Explain and give examples of the types of market conditions and conduct that have a bearing on whether or not Section 2 of the Sherman Act has been violated.
- Define and give an illustration of *predatory pricing*.
- Distinguish between *attempts* and *conspiracies* to monopolize and construct a hypothetical illustration of each.

■ THE SHERMAN ACT: SECTION 1

The first section of the Sherman Act reads as follows:

> Every contract, combination in the form of trust or otherwise, or conspiracy, in restraint of trade or commerce among the several states, or with foreign nations, is declared to be illegal. Every person who shall make any contract or engage in any combination or conspiracy hereby declared to be illegal shall be deemed guilty of a felony, and, on conviction thereof, shall be punished by fine not exceeding one million dollars if a corporation, or, if any other person [corporations were then regarded as "corporate persons"], $100,000 or by imprisonment not exceeding three years, or by both said punishments, in the discretion of the court.

In this section, we will look more closely at the concept of *restraint of trade* as it is defined by Section 1 of the Sherman Act and interpreted by the courts. Examining such practices as *price fixing* and *price maintenance*, we will consider the legal criteria for identifying violations and distinguish between *horizontal* and *vertical* restraint.

Per Se Violations

per se violation Inherently anticompetitive practice that is presumed by the courts to be an unreasonable restraint of trade

Although Section 1 of the Sherman Act deals with every restraint of trade, the courts have examined primarily conduct that *unreasonably* restrains trade. As we have seen, the law treats some practices as **per se violations**: Certain practices that are inherently antithetical to competition are presumed by the courts to constitute an unreasonable restraint upon free trade. Defendants charged with per se violations are not permitted to introduce evidence that justifies their actions. Much like the concept of strict liability in tort, commission of a per se antitrust violation subjects a defendant to punishment regardless of mitigating circumstances.

LEGAL JUDGMENT AND ANTICOMPETITIVE ACTION.   There are other types of anticompetitive actions that sometimes, but not always, result in an unreasonable restraint upon trade. When examining this type of conduct, the courts cannot merely presume that the consequences of activities are unreasonable. Instead, they

Although U.S. antitrust law permits actions to be brought against foreign nations, enforcement is not required. In fact, it is sometimes expedient not to enforce applicable provisions. The key question is how enforcing U.S. antitrust law against a foreign country will affect both countries. To a certain extent, the American company that supplied the impetus for the action must take a back seat to the national interest of this country. In other words, the bottom line is how other trade agreements between the United States and the other foreign country involved will be affected. If the ultimate result will be detrimental to the interests of the United States, the company's case may not be upheld by U.S. courts regardless of its merits.

The Timberlane Lumber case is an example of how this logic works. The case involved a conspiracy that directly affected the foreign commerce of the United States in violation of the Sherman Act. These are the facts of the case: Officials of the Bank of America in the United States and Honduras conspired to prevent Timberlane's Honduran subsidiaries from milling and exporting lumber. The Honduran timber export industry remained in the hands of the individuals whom the bank selected and financed.

The Supreme Court agreed that it might have jurisdiction to hear the case. Nevertheless, it devised the following six-point test to determine whether the effects of the foreign

action sufficiently affected U.S. commerce to warrant enforcement of the law's "extraterritorial authority":

1. *the nationality, allegiance, or principal locations of the parties*
2. *the relative importance of their conduct*
3. *the relative effects on the countries involved in the activity*
4. *the absence or presence of (a) intent to harm the United States or (b) forseeability that such harm would be the result*
5. *the degree of conflict between U.S. law and the law of the foreign country*
6. *compliance problems.*

The Court found that the facts in Timberlane failed to support an action under the Sherman Act.

The approach taken by the Court is extremely interesting because it required the interests of each of the parties to the action to be weighed and balanced against the interests of the other parties. Although this view advocates something less than a strict letter-of-the-law philosophy, it is still regarded as a fair—and practical—consideration of all nations involved in international antitrust disputes.

must apply the rule of reason, which requires an inquiry into the circumstances and actual consequences of the conduct. Defendants charged with committing these violations have the opportunity to present evidence justifying their conduct and showing that it did not result in an unreasonable restraint upon trade.

Price Fixing. For the past 30 years, courts have struggled with the issue of applying the per se rule or rule of reason to various anticompetitive actions, including price fixing. **Price fixing** results when two or more competing firms collaborate to establish a price or price range for a particular product. Price-fixing arrangements can be horizontal or vertical. *Horizontal price fixing* is characterized by an agreement among competitors, while *vertical price fixing* arises between buyers and sellers, usually manufacturers and retailers.

price fixing Practice, usually considered a *per se violation*, whereby two or more competitors establish a price or price range for a product

Historically, the courts have tended to treat horizontal price-fixing arrangements as per se violations. Recently, however, they appear to be moving away from this approach. The rule of reason was applied in the following case.

NATIONAL COLLEGIATE ATHLETIC ASSOCIATION v. BOARD OF REGENTS OF THE UNIVERSITY OF OKLAHOMA
United States Supreme Court 468 U.S. 85 (1984)

The NCAA adopted a plan under which all televised football games of NCAA member institutions must follow prescribed guidelines. Under the plan, the **rights to negotiate and contract for the telecasting of college football games of NCAA members were awarded to two "carry networks," ABC and CBS.**

The College Football Association (CFA) was formed to promote the interest of major football-playing schools within the NCAA structure. Respondents, the Universities of Oklahoma and Georgia, are members of the CFA. Thereafter, CFA developed an independent plan and contracted with NBC—a contract that violated certain limitations under the NCAA plan.

In response, the NCAA announced that it would take disciplinary action against any CFA member that complied with the CFA–NBC contract. Respondents commenced this action in the United States District Court and obtained a preliminary injunction preventing the disciplinary action sought by NCAA. The NCAA appeals to the U.S. Supreme Court.

Justice Stevens delivered the opinion of the Court.

Since its inception in 1905, the NCAA has played an important role in the regulation of amateur collegiate sports. It has adopted and promulgated playing rules, standards of amateurism, standards for academic eligibility, regulations concerning recruitment of athletes, and rules governing the size of athletic squads and coaching staffs. . . . With the exception of football, the NCAA has not undertaken any regulation of the televising of athletic events.

. . . .

CFA was to promote the interests of major football-playing schools within the NCAA structure. The Universities of Oklahoma and Georgia, respondents in this Court, are members of the CFA.

. . . .

The [NCAA television] plan adopted in 1981 for the 1982–1985 seasons is at issue in this case. This plan, like each of its predecessors, recites that it is intended to reduce, insofar as possible, the adverse effects of live television upon football game attendance. . . .

In separate agreements with each of the carrying networks, ABC and the Columbia Broadcasting System (CBS), the NCAA granted each the right to telecast the 14 live "exposures" described in the plan, in accordance with the "ground rules" set forth therein. Each of the networks agreed to pay a specified "minimum aggregate compensation to the participating NCAA member institutions" during the four-year period in an amount that totaled $131,750,000. In essence the agreement authorized each network to negotiate directly with member schools for the right to televise their games. . . .

The plan also contains "appearance requirements" and "appearance limitations" which pertain to each of the two-year periods that the plan is in effect. The basic requirement imposed on each of the two networks is that it must schedule appearances for at least 82 different member institutions during each two-year period. Under the appearance limitations no member institution is eligible to appear on television more than a total of six times and more than four times nationally, with the appearances to be divided equally between the two carrying networks. The number of exposures specified in the contracts also sets an absolute maximum on the number of games that can be broadcast.

. . . .

Beginning in 1979 CFA members began to advocate that colleges with major football programs should have a greater voice in the formulation of football television policy than they had in the NCAA. CFA therefore investigated the possibility of negotiating a television agreement of its own, developed an independent plan, and obtained a contract offer from the National Broadcasting Co. (NBC). This contract, which it signed in August 1981, would have allowed a more liberal number of appearances for each institution, and would have increased the overall revenues realized by CFA members.

. . . .

There can be no doubt that the challenged practices of the NCAA constitute a "restraint of trade" in the sense that they limit members' freedom to negotiate and enter into their own television contracts. In that sense, however, every contract is a restraint of trade, and as we have repeatedly recognized, the Sherman Act was intended to prohibit only unreasonable restraints of trade.

It is also undeniable that these practices share characteristics of restraints we have previously held unreasonable. . . . By restraining the quantity of television rights available for sale, the challenged practices create a limitation on output; our cases have held that such limitations are unreasonable restraints of trade. Moreover, the District Court found that the minimum aggregate price in fact operates to preclude any price negotiation between broadcasters and institutions, thereby constituting horizontal price fixing, perhaps the paradigm of an unreasonable restraint of trade.

Horizontal price fixing and output limitation are ordinarily condemned as a matter of law under an "illegal per se" approach because the probability that these practices are anticompetitive is so high; a per se rule is applied when "the practice facially appears to be one that would always or almost always tend to restrict competition and decrease output." *Broadcast Music, Inc. v. Columbia Broadcasting System, Inc.* (1979). In such circumstances a restraint is presumed unreasonable without inquiry into the particular market context in which it is found. Nevertheless, we have decided that it would be inappropriate to apply a per se rule to this case. . . . [W]hat is critical is that this case involves an industry in which horizontal restraints on competition are essential if the product is to be available at all.

. . . What the NCAA and its member institutions market in this case is competition itself—contests between competing institutions. . . . Moreover, the NCAA seeks to market a particular brand of football—college football. The identification of this "product" with an academic tradition differentiates college football from and makes it more popular than professional sports to which it might otherwise be comparable, such as, for example, minor league baseball. In order to preserve the character and quality of the "product," athletes must not be paid, must be required to attend class, and the like. . . . Thus, the NCAA plays a vital role in enabling college football to preserve its character, and as a result enables a product to be marketed which might otherwise be unavailable. In performing this role, its actions widen consumer choice—not only the choices available to sports fans but also those available to athletes—and hence can be viewed as procompetitive.

. . . .

Per se rules are invoked when surrounding circumstances make the likelihood of anticompetitive conduct so great as to render unjustified further examination of the challenged conduct. But whether the ultimate finding is the product of a presumption or actual market analysis, the essential inquiry remains the same—whether or not the challenged restraint enhances competition. Under the Sherman Act the criterion to be used in judging the validity of a restraint on trade is its impact on competition.

Because it restrains price and output, the NCAA's television plan has a significant potential for anticompetitive effects. The findings of the District Court indicate that this potential has been realized. The District Court found that if member institutions were free to sell television rights, many more games would be shown on television, and that the NCAA's output restriction has the effect of raising the price the networks pay for television rights. Moreover, the court found that by fixing a price for television rights to all games, the NCAA creates a price structure that is unresponsive to viewer demand and unrelated to the prices that would prevail in a competitive market. And, of course, since as a practical matter all member institutions need NCAA approval, members have no real choice but to adhere to the NCAA's television controls.

The anticompetitive consequences of this arrangement are apparent. Individual competitors lose their freedom to compete. Price is higher and output lower than they would otherwise be, and both are unresponsive to consumer preference. . . . At the same time, the television plan eliminates competitors from the market, since only those broadcasters able to bid on television rights covering the entire NCAA can compete. Thus, as the District Court found, many telecasts that would occur in a competitive market are foreclosed by the NCAA's plan.

. . . .

The District Court did not find that the NCAA's television plan produced any procompetitive efficiencies which enhanced the competitiveness of college football television rights; to the contrary it concluded that NCAA football could be marketed just as effectively without the television plan.

. . . .

Our decision not to apply a *per se* rule to this case rests in large part on our recognition that a certain degree of cooperation is necessary if the type of competition that petitioner and its member institutions seek to market is to be preserved. It is reasonable to assume that most of the regulatory controls of the NCAA are justifiable means of fostering competition among amateur athletic teams and therefore procompetitive because they enhance public interest in intercollegiate athletics. The specific restraints on football telecasts that are challenged in this case do not, however, fit into the same mold as do rules defining the conditions of the contest, the eligibility of participants, or the manner in which members of a joint enterprise shall share the responsibilities and the benefits of the total venture.

. . . .

Perhaps the most important reason for rejecting the argument that the interest in competitive balance is served by the television plan is the District Court's unambiguous and well-supported finding that many more games would be televised in a free market than under the NCAA plan. The hypothesis that legitimates the maintenance of competitive balance as a procompetitive justification under the Rule of Reason is that equal competition will maximize consumer demand for the product. The finding that consumption will materially increase if the controls are removed is a compelling demonstration that they do not in fact serve any such legitimate purpose.

. . . .

Accordingly, the judgment of the Court of Appeals is affirmed.

Case Questions

1. Explain the rule of reason. Compare that with the per se test.

2. What factors led the Supreme Court to apply a rule of reason, not a per se test, to the horizontal price fixing arrangement issue in this case?

3. Since every contract involves some restraint of trade, what does the Sherman Act purport to prohibit?

Trade and Professional Associations

Professions are represented by associations like the National Society of Professional Engineers, the American Medical Association, and the bar associations of the 50 states. Similar associations exist in just about every manufacturing and service industry. Like their professional counterparts, trade associations promote the interests of the industries that they represent. Like their professional counterparts, they sometimes identify their interests with the public interest.

TRADE ORGANIZATIONS. One of the purposes for which trade organizations exist is the collection of information about production and prices in the industry. Not surprisingly, information of this sort can be used to fix prices indirectly. If, for example, a company knew that all its competitors were going to cut back production and raise prices, it would feel safe in doing so itself. For this reason, trade associations usually do not publish information about the plans of individual companies.

However, even if an association publishes only aggregate data about production and prices in the industry as a whole, individual companies can still use that information in forming their own plans. Within limits, moreover, it would not be desirable to prevent them from doing so. Although rational planning is socially and economically desirable, it should be done on an *individual*, not a *collective*, basis. When plans are formulated by members acting collectively, they may be in violation of antitrust laws.

The Hardwood *Case.* A trade organization that formally fixed prices would be a classic cartel and thus clearly illegal. But the price-fixing practices of most trade associations are much more subtle. For example, in an industry with few firms, trial and error will sooner or later teach them the most mutually profitable level of prices. Members of a trade association can easily benefit from this process, but when member activities become too "harmonious," they may be in violation of the Sherman Act.

The landmark antitrust decision affecting trade associations is *American Column and Lumber Company v. United States* (257 U.S. 377 [1921]), usually known as the *Hardwood* case. The case involved a trade association of hardwood retailers that sent each member daily information about sales among all members (actually naming customers) as well as monthly information about production, inventories, and prices. Hardwood retailers never *agreed* to fix prices nor did they actually fix them in any formal way. Nevertheless, the court decided that the association's attempt "to procure 'harmonious' individual action" violated Section 1 of the Sherman Act.

PROFESSIONAL ASSOCIATIONS. Antitrust law was not applied to professional associations until the 1970s. There was a tradition of regarding the learned professions as somehow "different" from trade associations—an attitude that some critics attribute to the fact that most legislators and judges are lawyers who are themselves members of a learned profession.

Until the mid-1970s, for example, the medical profession had strict rules against solicitation and advertising. The American Medical Association claimed that "the employment of advertising is the clearly defined difference between a reputable physician and a quack."[1] This position changed, however, in 1975, when the Federal Trade Commission overturned these rules on the ground that they violated Section 5 of the Federal Trade Commission Act. The minimum fee schedules and similar devices the medical profession had used to prevent price competition, such as "relative value scales," were also eliminated. (Such a scale might indicate that a doctor ought to charge three times as much for one procedure as for another.)

The legal profession has also been brought within the reach of antitrust law. Rules prohibiting advertising were invalidated in the 1977 decision *Bates v. State Bar of Arizona* (433 U.S. 350). Price fixing by lawyers had been considered

---

[1] American Medical Association, *Judicial Council Opinions and Report*, 1971, cited in Marshall C. Howard, *Antitrust and Trade Regulation* (Englewood Cliffs, NJ: Prentice Hall, 1983), p. 92.

two years earlier in *Goldfarb v. Virginia State Bar*, which is excerpted below. A case involving the National Society of Professional Engineers is discussed in this chapter's ETHICAL ENVIRONMENT box.

GOLDFARB v. VIRGINIA STATE BAR
United States Supreme Court 421 U.S. 773 (1975)

Respondent Fairfax County Bar Association published a minimum-fee schedule that quoted prices at which various legal services should be rendered. Petitioners, husband and wife, contracted to buy a home in Fairfax County, Va., and were required to obtain a title examination. Petitioners solicited numerous lawyers to perform the service but could not find any lawyer who would charge less than the rate fixed by the schedule. Petitioners allege that the operation of the minimum fee schedule constitutes price fixing in violation of the Sherman Act.

Mr. Chief Justice Berger delivered the opinion of the Court.

. . . The financing agency required (petitioners) to secure title insurance; this required a title examination, and only a member of the Virginia State Bar could legally perform that service. Petitioners therefore contacted a lawyer who quoted them the precise fee suggested in a minimum-fee schedule published by respondent . . . the lawyer told them that it was his policy to keep his charges in line with the minimum-fee schedule which provided for a fee of 1% of the value of the property involved . . . (petitioners) sent letters to 36 other Fairfax County lawyers requesting their fees. Nineteen replied, and none indicated that he would charge less than the rate fixed by the schedule; several stated that they knew of no attorney who would do so . . .

Because petitioners could not find a lawyer willing to charge a fee lower than the schedule dictated, they had their title examined by the lawyer they had first contacted. They then brought this class action against the State Bar and the County Bar alleging that the operation of the minimum-fee schedule, as applied to fees for legal services relating to residential real estate transactions, constitutes price fixing in violation of § 1 of the Sherman Act. Petitioners sought both injunctive relief and damages.

After a trial solely on the issue of liability the District Court held that the minimum-fee schedule violated the Sherman Act. . . .

. . . .

The Court of Appeals reversed as to liability. . . . There has long been judicial recognition of a limited exclusion of "learned professions" from the scope of the antitrust laws, the court said; that exclusion is based upon the special form of regulation imposed upon the professions by the States, and the incompatibility of certain competitive practices with such professional regulation. It concluded that the promulgation of a minimum-fee schedule is one of "those matters with respect to which an accord must be reached between the necessities of professional regulation and the dictates of the antitrust laws." The accord reached by that court was to hold the practice of law exempt from the antitrust laws.

. . . .

We granted certiorari, and are thus confronted for the first time with the question of whether the Sherman Act applies to services performed by attorneys in examining titles in connection with financing the purchase of real estate.

The County Bar argues that because the fee schedule is merely advisory, the schedule and its enforcement mechanism do not constitute price fixing. Its purpose, the argument continues, is only to provide legitimate information to aid member lawyers in complying with Virginia professional regulations. Moreover, the County Bar contends that in practice the schedule has not had the effect of producing fixed fees. The facts found by the trier belie these contentions, and nothing in the record suggests these findings lack support.

. . . Here a fixed, rigid floor arose from respondents' activities: every lawyer who responded to petitioners' inquiries adhered to the fee schedule, and no lawyer asked for additional information in order to set an individualized fee. . . . The fee schedule was enforced through the prospect of professional discipline from the State Bar, and the desire of attorneys to comply with announced professional norms. . . . [T]he motivation to conform was reinforced by the assurance that other lawyers would not compete by underbidding. This is not merely a case of an agreement that may be inferred from an exchange of price information, . . . for here a naked agreement was clearly shown, and the effect on prices is plain.

Moreover, in terms of restraining competition and harming consumers like petitioners the price-fixing activities found here are unusually damaging. A title examination is indispensable in the process of financing a real estate purchase, and since only an attorney licensed to practice in Virginia may legally examine a title, consumers could not turn to alternative sources for the necessary service. All attorneys, of course, were practicing under the constraint of the fee schedule. . . . The County Bar makes much of the fact that it is a voluntary organization; however, the ethical opinions issued by the State Bar provide that any lawyer, whether or not a member of his county bar association, may be disciplined for "*habitually* charg[ing] less than the suggested minimum fee schedule adopted by his local bar Association. . . . " These factors coalesced to create a pricing system that consumers could not realistically escape. On this record respondent's activities constitute a classic illustration of price fixing.

. . . .

The County Bar argues that Congress never intended to include the learned professions within the terms "trade or commerce" in § 1 of the Sherman Act, and therefore the sale of professional services is exempt from the Act. No explicit exemption or legislative history is provided to support this contention. . . .

In arguing that learned professions are not "trade or commerce" the County Bar seeks a total exclusion from antitrust regulation. Whether state regulation is active or dormant, real or theoretical, lawyers would be able to adopt anticompetitive practices with impunity. We cannot find support for the proposition that Congress intended any such sweeping exclusion. The nature of an occupation, standing alone, does not provide sanctuary from the Sherman Act . . . nor is the public-service aspect of professional practice controlling in determining whether § 1 includes professions. . . . Congress intended to strike as broadly as it could in § 1 of the Sherman Act, and to read into it so wide an exemption as that urged on us would be at odds with that purpose.

The language of § 1 of the Sherman Act, of course, contains no exception. "Language more comprehensive is difficult to conceive." . . . Whatever else it may be, the examination of a land title is a service; the exchange of such a service for money is "commerce" in the most common usage of that word. It is no disparagement of the practice of law as a profession to acknowledge that it has this business aspect. . . .

In the modern world it cannot be denied that the activities of lawyers play an important part in commercial intercourse, and that anticompetitive activities by lawyers may exert a restraint on commerce. Reversed and remanded.

Case Questions

1. How does the publication of minimum fees by the Virginia County Bar constitute price fixing? Explain.

2. Why is it significant that only an attorney licensed to practice in Virginia may legally examine a title?

3. Upon what basis does the Court disagree with the County Bar that "learned professionals" were not intended to be covered by Section 1 of the Sherman Act? Explain.

THE ETHICAL ENVIRONMENT
National Society of Professional Engineers v. United States

The case of National Society of Professional Engineers v. United States *(435 U.S. 679 [1978]) involved an unusually restrictive code of ethics—one that actually prevented members from discussing fees for their services until potential clients had agreed to engage them. Although the code did not set prices as such, it completely prevented price competition. The Justice Department charged that the organization's prohibition against competitive pricing was actually an unfair restraint of free trade that violated Section 1 of the Sherman Act. The society, which refers to each of the edicts in its code as a "canon," countered this argument by stating that (1) the rule of reason protected its actions because it was acting for the public good—engineers were discouraged from cutting corners in order to ensure low bids, and that (2) it was entitled to preferential treatment under the law because it was one of the so-called "learned professions."*

The Supreme Court used its decision in this case to redefine the rule of reason, finding that the term "rule of reason" did not translate to "rule of reasonable." In other words, the reasonableness of a given action was not the heart of the case. Rather, the primary issue was whether an action that is illegal per se under the Sherman Act—that is, an anticompetition provision—is subject to the rule of reason. The Court found that it is not.

The question of whether the underlying reasons for the society's canon were good was not an issue in the decision. Instead, the Court determined that the key question was whether the canon promoted or suppressed competition. However, no specific rules concerning the application of the new rule-of-reason standard were laid out. On some levels, this omission left an ethical void because the Court had refused to analyze the society's actions in light of its specialized knowledge. Is the public good, for example, not supposed to take priority in such situations? Could competitive bidding between engineers not be contrary to this stated goal?

In finding that the rule of reason should not be applied to this case, the Court relieved the government of its duty to prove that the agreement was anticompetitive. In turn, this ruling precluded the society from presenting evidence to support contentions unrelated to the anticompetitive nature of its code.

The results of this case left the society with only one alternative if it felt that its ethical position had to be upheld: It could petition Congress for an exemption from the Sherman Act. The fact that the organization did not file such a petition may leave us with another question: Does the society's failure to pursue the matter further lay the burden of public safety at its door?

Vertical Restraints of Trade

Most of the actual practices examined in this chapter have been **horizontal restraints of trade**—agreements among firms in the same line of business. Now we will consider some **vertical restraints of trade**—agreements between companies at different stages of producing and distributing some good or service. Some vertical restraints have horizontal effects—that is, effects on other companies in the same line of trade. An attempt by a company to prevent its customers from buying its rivals' goods is an example.

The law tends to view vertical restraints more favorably than horizontal ones. Nonetheless, the Sherman Act and other antitrust laws also protect the right of each business to make its own choices about how to compete in any market, free of coercion from suppliers or customers.

RESALE PRICE MAINTENANCE. Vertical restraints, like horizontal ones, may call for either per se or rule-of-reason analysis. In general, vertical price restraints like **resale price maintenance** are now illegal per se. Other vertical restraints, such as vertical territorial divisions, are governed by the rule of reason. Many legal observers think that all vertical restrictions ought to be treated in the same way.

Fair-Trade Laws. Resale price maintenance *within a state*, however, has not always been illegal. In 1937, Congress passed the Miller-Tydings Amendment to the Sherman Act. This amendment permitted the states to pass **fair-trade laws** permitting resale price maintenance within their borders, even for businesses involving interstate commerce. Forty-six states eventually accepted the invitation. Under these laws, it was legal for companies to insist upon contracts fixing the price at which their customers resold their goods.

Fair-trade laws, however, have always been controversial. During the period of high inflation of the 1970s, prices in states that had passed fair-trade laws appeared to be higher than elsewhere, and in 1975, Congress repealed the Miller-Tydings Amendment. Since then, all efforts to impose resale price maintenance in interstate commerce have been illegal per se under the Sherman Act.

TERRITORIAL RESTRICTIONS. Resale price maintenance is purely vertical in nature. Territorial restrictions on trade, which occur when a market is divided between firms, can be either horizontal or vertical. They are horizontal when different companies in the same line of business agree to grant one another exclusive territories. Such horizontal agreements are illegal per se.

Exclusive Rights to Sell. Vertical territorial restrictions, which grant dealers exclusive rights to sell manufacturers' products in certain areas, are much more complex. They are not always illegal, however, because they may promote competition among different brands. Companies grant exclusive territories to dealers chiefly in hopes of getting them to develop markets for brands more thoroughly than they would if they were selling many brands. Other dealers in the same area would be selling those other brands—perhaps also under exclusive arrangements. If so, the total effect would be to intensify interbrand competition. Because interbrand competition is exactly what antitrust law aims to promote, territorial restrictions usually get rule-of-reason treatment in the courts.

The Sealy *Case.* Sometimes, however, the relation between a company

horizontal restraint of trade Agreement among firms in the same line of business to restrain trade

vertical restraint of trade Agreement between firms at different stages of producing and distributing some good or service to restrain trade

resale price maintenance *Vertical restraint of trade* whereby a firm fixes the price at which its customers can resell its products

fair-trade laws State laws that at one time permitted resale price maintenance, even for businesses involved in interstate commerce

The Standard in Operating Systems Described as history's youngest self-made billionaire, William H. (Bill) Gates founded Microsoft Corp., the world's largest computer software company, in 1975. Almost twice as large as its nearest competitor in PC software, Lotus Development Co., Microsoft's size and power derive largely from its "Microsoft disk operation system" (MS-DOS). In 1981, IBM, the world's largest manufacturer of personal computers, selected MS-DOS as the operating system for its line of PCs. As a result, the Microsoft system directs the inner workings of virtually all of the 40 million IBM and IBM-compatible PCs in the world. With MS-DOS the undisputed standard in PCs (many manufacturers simply install the system and pay royalties), Microsoft enjoys not only a steady flow of profits but a significant advantage in the market for application programs: Unless a program can communicate with MS-DOS, it is of no use to the owner of IBM and IBM-sytle PCs. Some analysts have seen in this set of circumstances at least the right conditions for a monopoly in the making. MS-DOS, for example, is so pervasive in its compatibility requirements that Microsoft seems, at least theoretically, to be in a position to influence a broad range of manufacturing decisions that would only strengthen the industry's reliance on the Microsoft operating system. Steep barriers to market entry face small software makers, and those already in business are having trouble finding room in distribution channels. On the other hand, IBM itself has taken steps to loosen its alliance with Microsoft, developing software in ventures with other companies and entering licensing agreements with other suppliers. Although a proposed merger between Lotus and Novell fell through in 1990, alliances among other companies like Hewlett-Packard and Sun Microsystems have been formed to challenge Microsoft on such fronts as standardized data-sharing systems that would make it easier to link different programs.

practicing territorial restrictions and the companies given exclusive territorial rights is so close as to have horizontal effects. Sealy, a company that markets mattresses, granted licenses to a number of manufacturing companies that produced and sold mattresses under the Sealy label. Each of these companies had an exclusive territory. The problem resulted when each of these producers held stock in Sealy itself—and when each person on Sealy's board of directors had been nominated by the shareholders, including the company's licensees. Through Sealy, these manufacturers had in effect established horizontal links. In *United States v. Sealy, Inc.* (388 U.S. 350[1967]), this arrangement was declared illegal per se.

Exclusive Distribution Rights. Another kind of common territorial restriction occurs when a manufacturer grants exclusive territories to distributors. For example, assume that a particular bicycle manufacturer sells its bikes to only one retailer in each geographical area of a state. Because customers have no other place to shop for bikes within the area, this practice allows each retailer to charge high prices for them. The practice, therefore, destroys *intrabrand* competition. It does not, however, affect *interbrand* competition—customers can choose to purchase a different brand that is priced lower.

The following case examines the question of whether the type of territorial restriction described in the case above should be subject to the rule of reason or the per se rule. Note that in deciding this case, the court had to contend with an earlier decision, *United States v. Arnold, Schwinn & Co.* (388 U.S. 365 [1967], that focused upon whether title to the goods was held by the manufacturer or the distributor. This factor was regarded as irrelevant by many legal scholars.

CONTINENTAL T.V., INC. v. GTE SYLVANIA, INC.
United States Supreme Court 433 U.S. 36 (1977)

Respondent GTE Sylvania, Inc. (Sylvania) manufactures and sells television sets. Sylvania adopted a franchise plan under which it limited the number of franchises granted for any given area and required each franchise to sell its Sylvania products only from the location(s) at which it was franchised. Petitioner, Continental T.V., Inc. (Continental), was one of the most successful Sylvania franchisees. This suit is the result of the rupture of a franchiser-franchisee relationship that had previously prospered under the Sylvania plan.

Mr. Justice Powell delivered the opinion of the Court . . .

. . . Dissatisfied with its sales in the city of San Francisco, Sylvania decided in the spring of 1965 to franchise Young Brothers, an established San Francisco retailer. The proposed location of the new franchise was approximately a mile from a retail outlet operated by petitioner Continental. . . . Continental protested that the location of the new franchise violated Sylvania's marketing policy, but Sylvania persisted in its plans. Continental then canceled a large Sylvania order and placed a large order with Phillips, one of Sylvania's competitors.

During this same period, Continental expressed a desire to open a store in Sacramento, Cal., a desire Sylvania attributed at least in part to Continental's displeasure over the Young Brothers decision. Sylvania believed that the Sacramento market was adequately served by the existing Sylvania retailers and denied the request. In the face of this denial, Continental advised Sylvania in early September 1965, that it was in the process of moving Sylvania merchandise from its San Jose, Cal., warehouse to a new retail location that it had leased in Sacramento. Two weeks later, allegedly for unrelated reasons, Sylvania's credit department reduced Continental's credit line from $300,000 to $50,000. . . . Shortly thereafter, Sylvania terminated Continental's franchises. . . .

. . . .

We turn first to Continental's contention that Sylvania's restriction on retail locations is a *per se* violation of § 1 of the Sherman Act as interpreted in *Schwinn* [*United States v. Arnold, Schwinn & Co.* (1967)].

. . . .

. . . [In *Schwinn*,] the Court proceeded to articulate the following "bright line" *per se* rule of illegality for vertical restrictions: "Under the Sherman Act, it is unreasonable without more for a manufacturer to seek to restrict and confine areas or persons with whom an article may be traded after the manufacturer has parted with dominion over it." . . . But the Court expressly stated that the rule of reason governs when "the manufacturer retains title, dominion, and risk with respect to the product and the position and function of the dealer in question are, in fact, indistinguishable from those of an agent or salesman of the manufacturer."

. . . .

In the present case, it is undisputed that title to the television sets passed from Sylvania to Continental. Thus, the *Schwinn per se* rule applies unless Sylvania's restriction on locations falls outside *Schwinn's* prohibition against a manufacturer's attempting to restrict a "retailer's freedom as to where and to whom it will resell the products." . . . As the Court of Appeals conceded, the language of *Schwinn* is clearly broad enough to apply to the present case. Unlike the Court of Appeals, however, we are unable to find a principled basis for distinguishing *Schwinn* from the case now before us.

. . . .

Sylvania argues that if *Schwinn* cannot be distinguished, it should be reconsidered. Although *Schwinn* is supported by the principle of *stare decisis* . . . , we are convinced that the need for clarification of the law in this area justifies reconsideration. *Schwinn* itself was an abrupt and largely unexplained departure from *White Motor Co. v. United States* (1963), where only four years earlier the Court had refused to endorse a *per se* rule for vertical restrictions. Since its announcement, *Schwinn* has been the subject of continuing controversy and confusion, both in the scholarly journals and in the federal courts. The great weight of scholarly opinion has been critical of the decision, and a number of the federal courts confronted with analogous vertical restrictions have sought to limit its reach. In our view, the experience of the past 10 years should be brought to bear on this subject of considerable commercial importance.

The traditional framework of analysis under § 1 of the Sherman Act is familiar and does not require extended discussion. Section 1 prohibits "[e]very contract, combination . . . , or conspiracy, in restraint of trade or commerce." Since the early years of this century a judicial gloss on this statutory language has established the "rule of reason" as the prevailing standard of analysis. *Standard Oil Co. v. United States* (1911). Under this rule, the factfinder weighs all of the circumstances of a case in deciding whether a restrictive practice should be prohibited as imposing an unreasonable restraint on competition. *Per se* rules of illegality are appropriate only when they relate to conduct that is manifestly anticompetitive. As the Court explained in *Northern Pac. R. Co. v. United States* (1958), "there are certain agreements or practices which because of their pernicious effect on competition and lack of any redeeming virtue are conclusively presumed to be unreasonable and therefore illegal without elaborate inquiry as to the precise harm they have caused or the business excuse for their use."

. . . In essence, the issue before us is whether *Schwinn's per se* rule can be justified under the demanding standards of *Northern Pac. R. Co.* . . .

. . . .

The market impact of vertical restrictions is complex because of their potential for a simultaneous reduction of intrabrand competition and stimulation of interbrand competition. . . .

. . . .

Vertical restrictions reduce intrabrand competition by limiting the number of sellers of a particular product competing for the business of a given group of buyers. Location restrictions have this effect because of practical constraints on the effective marketing area of retail outlets. Although intrabrand competition may be reduced, the ability of retailers to exploit the resulting market may be limited both by the ability of consumers to travel to other franchised locations and, perhaps more importantly, to purchase the competing products of other manufacturers. None of these key variables, however, is affected by the form of the transaction by which a manufacturer conveys his products to the retailers.

Vertical restrictions promote interbrand competition by allowing the manufacturer to achieve certain efficiencies in the distribution of his products. These "redeeming virtues" are implicit in every decision sustaining vertical restrictions under the rule of reason. Economists have identified a number of ways in which manufacturers can use such restrictions to compete more effectively against other manufacturers. . . . For example, new manufacturers and manufacturers entering new markets can use the restrictions in order to induce competent and aggressive retailers to make the kind of investment of capital and labor that is often required in the distribution of products unknown to the consumer. Established manufacturers can use them to induce retailers to engage in promotional activities or to provide service and repair facilities necessary to the efficient marketing of their products. Service and repair are vital for many products, such as automobiles and major household appliances. The availability and quality of such services affect a manufacturer's goodwill and the competitiveness of his product. Because of market imperfections such as the so-called "free rider" effect, these services might not be provided by retailers in a purely competitive situation, despite the fact that each retailer's benefit would be greater if all provided the services than if none did.

. . . .

We conclude that the distinction drawn in *Schwinn* between sale and nonsale transactions is not sufficient to justify the application of a *per se* rule in one situation and a rule of reason in the other. The question remains whether the *per se* rule stated in *Schwinn* should be expanded to include non-sale transactions or abandoned in favor of a return to the rule of reason. We have found no persuasive support for expanding the *per se* rule. As noted above, the *Schwinn* Court recognized the undesirability of "prohibit[ing] all vertical restrictions of territory and all franchising. . . . " And even

Continental does not urge us to hold that all such re- strictions are *per se* illegal.

In sum, we conclude that the appropriate decision is to return to the rule of reason that governed vertical re- strictions prior to *Schwinn*. When anticompetitive ef- fects are shown to result from particular vertical restric- tions they can be adequately policed under the rule of reason, the standard traditionally applied for the major- ity of anticompetitive practices challenged under § 1 of the Act. Accordingly, the decision of the Court of Ap- peals is affirmed.

Case Questions

1. How does the vertical restriction reduce *intrabrand* competition? Location restrictions? What effect does each of these restrictions have on *interbrand* competi- tion?

2. Explain the *per se rule* articulated in *Schwinn*. Why did the Court refuse to distinguish *Schwinn*?

3. How was the result in this case justified under the rule of reason? Explain.

■ *Concept Check 16-3 The Sherman Act: Section 1*

- Define the concept of a *per se violation* and explain the conditions under which *price fixing* may be considered such a violation.
- In being subject to the provisions of Section 1 of the Sherman Act, how do *trade associations* differ from other forms of business organization such as a corporation?
- Define and distinguish between *horizontal* and *vertical restraints* of trade.
- Define *resale price maintenance* and explain how *fair-trade laws* encourage the prac- tice.

■ ANTITRUST EXEMPTIONS

Competition has costs as well as benefits—costs that are greater in some indus- tries than in others. The benefits of competition also vary from industry to in- dustry. Some are "natural monopolies"; others benefit from the greatest possi- ble amount of competition. That is why some industries and activities are exempt from antitrust laws. Over the years, both Congress and the courts have exempted certain industries from antitrust law because other agencies have been set up to regulate them. Other industries or activities have been ex- empted for public-policy reasons.

REGULATED INDUSTRIES. The first ground for exemption concerns firms in indus- tries regulated by agencies assumed to have special expertise in those indus- tries. For example, motor carriers (chiefly busses) are regulated by the Inter- state Commerce Commission. Insurance companies are similarly exempt. Airlines were once exempt because they were regulated by the Civil Aeronau- tics Board (CAB). However, the Airline Deregulation Act of 1978 deregulated the industry and phased out the operation of the CAB (which no longer exists). The question of whether antitrust law now applies to the airline industry has not yet been decided.

EXEMPTIONS FOR THE PUBLIC GOOD. The other ground for exemption from antitrust law is the belief that the public as a whole benefits when certain industries or activities are exempted. Labor unions and *natural monopolies* fall into this cate- gory.

Labor Unions. Labor unions can be seen as monopolies because they aim to control the labor supply in a given industry. Moreover, their ultimate weapon—the strike—amounts to a concerted "refusal to deal"—an action that would be treated as a monopolistic practice in other contexts. Nonetheless, labor unions are believed to promote the generally recognized public policy favoring peaceful labor-management relations. As a result, the Norris-LaGuardia Act of 1932 exempts unions from antitrust law to the extent that they act by themselves to promote the welfare of their own members. Of course, unions cannot perform their main function—negotiating contracts governing wages, hours, and conditions—by themselves: Such contracts must be negotiated with employers. In certain circumstances, therefore, a contract might be viewed as a violation of antitrust law.

natural monopoly Good or service best provided by a single supplier because competition is impossible, impractical, or antiethical to the public interest

Natural Monopolies. A **natural monopoly** is a good or service whose unit cost falls with each additional unit of output and which is best provided by a single supplier because competition is impossible, impractical, or not in the public interest. Public utilities are natural monopolies: Because it would be inefficient to have three providers of water or electricity or telephone wires in the same town, providers of these services have been given monopolies but are regulated by government.

state action doctrine The exemption from federal antitrust laws of anticompetitive conduct required by government regulation

THE STATE ACTION DOCTRINE. The **state action doctrine** exempts from the federal antitrust laws anticompetitive conduct that is required by government regulation. Governments often adopt regulations that have an anticompetitive effect. Farmers, for instance, have been forced by marketing regulations to limit the size of their crops and to sell them at set prices. Although limitations on exemptions have been defined by numerous cases, such regulations have been upheld by the courts on the ground that the Sherman Act does not apply to state governments (*Parker v. Brown*, 137 U.S. 341 [1943]).

CASE: PROFESSIONAL BASEBALL. In Chapter 4 we discussed the principle of *stare decisis*, which has provided the basis for professional baseball's exemption from antitrust law. The original theory behind the exemption was that professional baseball is a sport, not a business, engaged in interstate commerce. It is fair to say that this is not the strongest of arguments: No other professional sport is so protected (see the ORGANIZATIONAL PROFILE box below). However, the decision stands for reasons discussed in Chapter 4, in the case of *Flood v. Kuhn* (407 U.S. 258 [1972]).

ORGANIZATIONAL PROFILE
The National Football League

Some observers contend that federal labor laws are the government's way of keeping out of disputes between employees and their employers by encouraging parties to reach mutually acceptable agreements—and allowing them to get around the antitrust laws. The courts have concluded that the protection of labor and labor unions is one of the primary protections offered by the antitrust laws. Consequently, court injunctions against union activity are virtually precluded by the combined power of Section 2 of the Clayton Act (see Chapter 17) and the Norris-LaGuardia Act.

In addition, the courts have determined that the distinctions outlined between these laws and certain labor laws—

particularly the collective-bargaining portions of the National Labor Relations Act—prevent suits charging antitrust violations in most labor-relations cases. The statutes themselves do not prevent antitrust actions between labor and management—a concept referred to as the nonstatutory labor exemption.

The Eighth Circuit went to what some critics characterize as bizarre lengths to promote this view in the case of Powell v. National Football League (888 F.2d 559, 8th Cir. [1989]). In Powell, professional football players and the National Football League Players Association brought an antitrust action against the National Football League and its member clubs. The case involved the issue of free agency.

The background of the current action is as follows:

- The 1982 NFL/NFLPA Collective Bargaining Agreement included a right of first refusal/compensation system that prevented players from moving between teams and kept their salaries down. Under that system, players had a short window of opportunity in which to negotiate with other teams. If a player received another offer, the original team could opt to (1) match the compensation package offered by the new team or to (2) receive draft-choice compensation from the player's new team. Draft-choice compensation was calculated on a formula that included the number of years that the player was with the NFL and the actual dollar amount offered by the new team.

  This system put veteran players at a disadvantage because their price was too high for most teams. Players who refused to comply with these rules were free to choose to take an unpaid leave for the season. The few players who chose this alternative often found themselves in a worse position the next year: Not only were they a year older, but their teams had gotten along without them.

- The 1982 Collective Bargaining Agreement expired on August 31, 1987, and the parties were unable to come to a new agreement.

- In 1989, the agreement was modified by management. The new agreement—in which the players had no say—stipulated that 37 players would be protected under essentially the same terms as those defined in the old agreement. The rest of the players ("unrestricted players") became free agents—that is, they were able to negotiate new deals without the old restrictions on their movements.

The court was asked in this action to determine whether the nonstatutory labor exemption from the antitrust laws was applicable to an expired agreement. The court found that it was. The court's holding seems to imply that the parties give up their right to bring an antitrust suit once they enter into collective bargaining. The decision, critics charge, is particularly odd because on the face of it the free-agency system appears to violate antitrust laws. It would seem, they add, that an impasse reached after about two years of collective bargaining indicates an absence of union consent. Because the nonstatutory labor exemption requires such consent, the court should, at the very least, be required to consider how the antitrust laws affect the situation.

■ *Concept Check 16-4 Antitrust Exemptions*

- Explain the primary reasons behind the antitrust-exemption status of labor unions.
- Define a *natural monopoly* and give an example of a good or service whose antitrust-exemption status under such conditions is debatable.
- Explain the *state action doctrine*.

You Decide: Answer/Discussion
The Cellophane Case

According to many critics, the Supreme Court's verdict in the Cellophane case was probably wrong. Although the Court properly looked at the interchangeability issue, it did not seem to give enough weight to the matter of market share and earnings.

The Court's definition of market power as "the power to control prices or exclude competition" is only accurate as far as it goes. It does not, for example, consider that the exclusion of competition may in itself be a way of gaining market share. Similarly, raising prices without losing market share is a commonly held business goal. It is not a definition of market power.

These same critics pose the following scenario: Nearly all of the locally grown strawberries in a region are bought up by the only large supermarket in a ten-mile area. Five mom-and-pop markets also located in the area sued the supermarket under the Sherman Act because they could not get any of the fresh produce to sell. Once in court, the supermarket argued that while it did have eighty percent of the retail strawberry market, consumers could easily buy blueberries, blackberries, or raspberries at the mom-and-pop stores. The court agreed, stating that fruit is fruit and that one berry can certainly be substituted for another.

The example may be oversimplistic and farfetched, but critics point out that it does highlight a flaw in the Supreme Court's reasoning in the Cellophane case: No court can determine whether there is a monopoly if it expands the relevant market to a point that makes the comparison irrelevant.

SUMMARY

- The central idea of a *free-market economy* is *competition*. Until the Civil War, most businesses were small and local. Vertical and horizontal integration of industries became common after that. Competition was at risk.

- Congress responded, in 1890, by passing the *Sherman Act.* In 1911, the Supreme Court construed it according to a *rule of reason:* Instead of finding certain lines of conduct illegal in all circumstances, the Court decided that the legality of *agreements restraining trade* should be determined by the reasonableness of their results. In 1914, Congress again attempted to restrain monopolies by passing the *Clayton* and *FTC Acts.*

- The Sherman Act comprises two sections. *Section 2* prohibits *monopolization*, attempts to monopolize, and combining or conspiring to monopolize any part of interstate or foreign commerce. The courts use a *structural analysis* to determine if firms have *monopoly power.* The first step of this analysis is defining the market that a company has dominated; the second is calculating the percentage of that market which it enjoys.

- *Section 1* of the Sherman Act prohibits *combinations, contracts, and conspiracies in restraint of trade.* It differs from Section 2 in that action can be prosecuted if the intent was monopolistic. Such an attempt need not be successful to be illegal. The most common antitrust offense under Section 1 is *price fixing,* which involves the collusive setting of prices by competitors.

- The courts sometimes examine the consequences of price fixing to determine if they are desirable enough to override its basic illegality. Many *professional associations* have tried—mostly without success—to justify price fixing by arguing that unrestrained competition is not desirable in such learned professions as medicine and engineering.

- Price fixing and other *horizontal restraints* affect a number of enterprises in the same line of trade. *Vertical restraints* tend to affect businesses upstream or downstream from the companies that insist upon them. Thus, for example, a company might demand that its customers sell its products at specified prices. This practice, called *resale price maintenance,* is purely vertical in nature. In contrast, territorial restrictions on trade can be either horizontal or vertical. They are horizontal—and thus *per se violations*—when different companies in the same line of business agree to grant one another exclusive territories. Vertical territorial restrictions are not always illegal because they may promote competition among different brands. These arrangements are examined by the courts on a case-by-case basis.

- In some industries, the costs of competition may be greater than the benefits. As a result, regulated industries like insurance and public utilities are exempt from antitrust law.

QUESTIONS AND PROBLEMS

1. The government brings suit against the Baby Products Manufacturing Co. for having a monopoly when it discovers that Baby Products is the sole manufacturer of a backpack baby carrier sold in the United States. Baby Products introduces documents indicating it is the sole patentholder for the carrier and moves to dismiss the suit. What will the outcome be?

2. Ledco, a multinational corporation, is in the business of manufacturing leather briefcases. When Ledco first started its business, it merely manufactured and sold briefcases. Over the years, Ledco has considered it more efficient to purchase the livestock breeding farms and tanners for its leathers, the cloth factories for its linings, and fastener companies for its briefcase closures. Has Ledco engaged in vertical or horizontal expansion? Explain how this might be of legal significance.

3. Three years ago, NFL teams established six-player developmental squads, paying each player $16,000 for the 16-week season, compared with

the $50,000 season minimum for a full-fledged player. The practice players, who never appear in actual games, complained that the NFL teams violated the Sherman Act's prohibition against restraint of trade by conspiring to rob them of the ability to negotiate for their salaries. A class action suit was filed by 235 players. What was the result? [*Anthony Brown et al. v. Pro Football Inc.*; U.S. District Court, Washington, No. 90-1071]

4. Ludlow is a college town. It houses a regional university and has few non-university-related businesses. Ludlow has sixteen pizza parlors, which serve mainly college students. Competition is so fierce between the pizza parlors that the owners come together to discuss it. The owners recognize that because of competition among them, no one is making much money. All but a few of the owners agree to divide the potential business by agreeing to direct their advertising and promotions only to certain segments of the student population—that is, one agrees to serve pizzas only on a take-out and delivery basis, one discounts prices for first-year students, one provides free sodas for juniors, etc. Students not in the groups the parlor caters to are not encouraged to patronize the establishment. It was agreed by the parlor owners who participated in the plan that there would be no relationship between them and the nonparticipating parlors. The participating parlors would also attempt to have the nonparticipants' suppliers drop their contracts with the nonparticipant parlors. The arrangement works well, with each participating pizza parlor owner gaining a larger share of the total market and additional revenue. Is the agreement permissible?

5. The American Medical Association had a longstanding practice of refusing to allow its members to accept patients on referral from chiropractors or to refer patients to chiropractors. Chiropractors filed suit, contending that the AMA used its Principal 3, which prohibits medical physicians from associating professionally with unscientific practitioners, to prevent, among other things, chiropractors from obtaining access to hospital diagnostic services and membership on hospital staffs. The court found the relevant market to be the American public nationwide, who receive health care services. The court also found that the AMA members received a greater portion of fees paid to health care providers. Based on the above, was there an antitrust violation by the AMA? If so, what type of relief was sought by the chiropractors? Explain. [*Wilk v. AMA*, 895 F. 2d 352 (1990)]

6. A famous designer is currently manufacturing blue jeans, which are so popular that it is difficult for stores to keep them stocked. The designer wants the jeans sold only at a high price in order to maximize profits and to prevent the designer's image from being, in the designer's eyes, "cheapened" by the jeans being made affordable to "the masses." The designer requires that all retailers who order the much demanded jeans agree to sell them for $85 per pair. A retailer who sells clothing at a discount outlet complains about this requirement. Is the designer's requirement legal?

7. A soft drink bottling company provides free maintenance on its vending machines if its products are the only ones used in the machines. Will competitor bottling companies be successful in asserting that this is exclusionary activity in violation of antitrust laws? [*Bayou Bottling, Inc. v. Dr. Pepper Co.*, 725 F.2d 300 (5th Cir. 1984)]

8. The United States filed suit against DuPont, claiming that the company has a monopoly in the cellophane market in violation of Section 2 of the Sherman Act. During the time in question, DuPont produced almost 75 percent of the cellophane sold in the United States. Cellophane constituted less than 20 percent of all packaging materials sold in the U.S. What did the Supreme Court find as the relevant market? Was there a violation of the Sherman Act? [*United States v. E. I. Du Pont de Nemours & Co.*, 351 U.S. 377 (1955)]

9. A skiing area in Aspen has four resorts. Three of the resorts are owned by one company. The resorts decided to offer skiiers passes good at all four resorts and revenues distributed to the resorts were decided based on yearly surveys of use. Eventually, the solo resort owner was offered a fixed revenue share which he felt was too

low. He offered several plans to monitor ticket sales, but all were rejected. The three-resort owner discontinued use of the interchangeable pass and offered instead a pass for its own resorts. It changed its four-resort pass advertising to three resorts and took other actions which made it difficult for the solo owner to market its own package. The solo owner brings suit alleging violation of Section 2 of the Sherman Act in that the three-resort owner has monopolized skiing at Aspen. The three-resort owner says it is not a violation of the Sherman Act for a firm with monopoly power not to cooperate with a smaller rival in a marketing arrangement. Is this correct? [*Aspen Skiing Co. v. Aspen Highlands Skiing Corp.*, 105 S. Ct. 2847 (1985)]

10. Topps Co. is the owner of thousands of contracts with major and minor league baseball players for the exclusive right to publish a players' name, picture, signature, and biographical sketch on baseball cards. Under a 1968 agreement with the Major League Baseball Players Association, all then existing individual agreements with the players were modified. If the association was presented with a competitive licensing proposal that might infringe on Topps' exclusive right to baseball cards sold with or without gum, Topps was to notify the association whether it released its rights. In addition, Topps reserved a right of first refusal on any merchandising proposal which included a player's picture larger than $5'' \times 7''$. Fleer presents the association with a proposal to market $5'' \times 7''$ patches, stickers, cards, iron-ons, and photographs, for sale with or without gum. Topps did not exercise its right of first refusal, but told the association that its prior experience in the business showed that the proposal was probably not worthwhile because such items tend to stay on the shelves and thereby inhibit retailers from purchasing other baseball-related items. Topps also said that the proposal might depress the sale of trading cards and decrease players' royalties. The association unanimously rejected Fleer's proposal, fearing a decrease in royalties. Fleer sued the association as a coconspirator with Topps in a suit for unreasonable restraint of trade in violation of Sections 1 and 2 of the Sherman Act. Is the 1968 agreement between Topps and the association a combination between two horizontal competitors designed to foreclose entry into the trading-card market in violation of the Sherman Act? [*Fleer Corp. v. Topps Chewing Gum, Inc.*, 658 F. 2d 139 (3d Cir. 1981)]

17

THE CLAYTON AND ROBINSON-PATMAN ACTS

The history of antitrust legislation is replete with shifts in public policy and opinion. For example, two early Supreme Court decisions limited the scope of the Sherman Act of 1890. The first ruling exempted manufacturers from the law. The second rejected the application of absolute rules to many kinds of monopolistic conduct and made them subject instead to the *rule of reason*, which requires the weighing of the consequences of challenged actions. This approach made the Sherman Act less powerful than it would have been had the Court held that certain practices were illegal in every case.

To correct some of the uncertainty generated by judicial interpretation of the Sherman Act, Congress passed the **Clayton Act** in 1914. The Clayton Act forbids specific practices such as tying arrangements, exclusive dealing, and price discrimination. It also contains language intended to slow the trend of corporate mergers, which had markedly increased during the early 1900s (Figure 17-1 shows the rise in U.S. corporate mergers over the last 100 years). In 1936, Congress passed the Robinson-Patman Act, which amended and strengthened the Clayton Act's ban against price discrimination. This chapter will examine these laws and the shifts in antitrust policy that have surrounded their interpretation.

> **Clayton Act** 1914 federal law forbidding such practices as *tying arrangements, exclusive dealing,* and *price discrimination*

■ MERGERS: TYPES, REGULATION, AND MERITS

Types of Mergers

A **merger** is the absorption of one company by another through the acquisition of its assets. The acquiring company retains its name and identity. The absorbed company ceases to exist as a separate business entity, even though it may retain its former name as a subsidiary of the acquiring company. Consumers often do not know that companies with whom they deal are sub-

> **merger** Absorption of one company by another through the acquisition of its assets

623

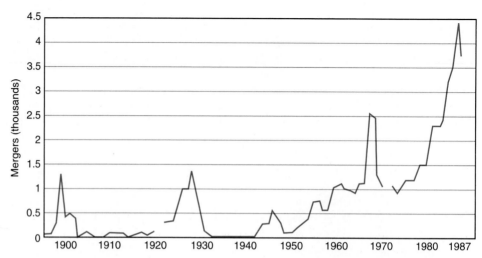

FIGURE 17-1 Growth in Corporate Mergers, 1895–1987   *Sources*: Robert L. Heilbroner and James K. Galbraith, *Understanding Macroeconomics*, 9th ed. (Englewood Cliffs, NJ: Prentice Hall, 1990). Data from Lawrence J. White, "Mergers and Acquisitions in the U.S. Economy: Aggregate and Historical Overview," in *Mergers and Acquisitions*, ed. Alan J. Auerbach (Chicago: University of Chicago Press, 1988).

sidiaries or to which other companies those subsidiaries belong. For example, how many customers of Budget Rent-A-Car know that they are doing business with Transamerica Corporation? Even though merged firms present separate faces to the public, the same top-level executives make decisions for both companies.

There are three kinds of mergers:

horizontal merger Merger between *competing* or *potentially competing* firms (*see also* Chapter 16)

vertical merger Merger between firms that do business as supplier and buyer

conglomerate merger Merger between firms that are in different lines of business

1. A **horizontal merger** occurs between competing or potentially competing companies. They offer interchangeable goods to the same potential customers, often within a geographic area. This kind of merger is most likely to be challenged under antitrust law.

2. A **vertical merger** occurs between firms in a position to do business with each other, usually as supplier and buyer. Firms with perfect vertical integration have subsidiaries or divisions representing every link of the chain, from raw materials to production to sales.

3. A **conglomerate merger** involves firms that are not in the same line of business. Often, conglomerate mergers occur to permit corporations to diversify by entering new markets or geographic regions. For example, Gulf & Western's purchase of Paramount Pictures put it in the entertainment business; its purchase of Simon and Schuster made it a major player in the publishing industry.

Regulating Mergers

Mergers are regulated under Section 7 of the Clayton Act as amended in 1950. This section prohibits mergers that "substantially lessen competition or [that] tend to create a monopoly." This language was intended to give the government the power to prevent mergers without evidence of intent to *monopolize*.

The Celler-Kefauver Amendment. The 1950 *Celler-Kefauver Amendment* to the Clayton Act also made it clear that horizontal, vertical, and conglomerate mergers were all subject to regulation. During the 1970s, many companies discovered that it was easier to expand by purchasing other companies than by investing in new facilities. A high inflation rate made it possible for them to buy companies on credit and pay back their loans with money that was worth less than the money that they had borrowed. Top executives also sought to protect their companies by investing in many unrelated businesses, thus freeing them from dependency on any one industry or set of economic conditions.

MERGERS AND DEREGULATION. The 1980s were a period of intense merger activity. Table 17-1 lists the fifteen largest corporate mergers in a decade characterized by a "big-is-better" attitude. Encouraged in part by the Reagan administration's support for relaxed application of antitrust legislation, corporate mergers experienced a boom in the 1980s. By 1984, for example, over 2500 deals totaled over $120 billion, and in 1986, more than 4000 mergers were valued at $190 billion. Nineteen-eighty-eight was a banner year for mergers and acquisitions (*see* Table 17-2), both "friendly" and "hostile": In the first half of the year alone, more deals were announced than had taken place in all of 1987 and at a value greater than that of all deals made in 1984. Nineteen-eighty-nine featured the leveraged buyout of RJR Nabisco for the record sum of $24.7 billion.

It should be noted, however, that although deregulation promoted by the Reagan administration contributed to the merger trend of the 1980s, there were also larger financial factors involved. For example, slow growth and expensive capital in the early to mid-1980s had caused the value of both corporate shares and assets to drop to the point at which aggressive buyers could take over companies by buying up their undervalued assets—that is, existing assets (such as current supplies of natural gas) that were cheaper than assets that would have to be created through new investments (exploration for new natural-gas fields). Later, when the stock market became healthier, speculators began buying companies that ultimately could be sold in a higher market.

TABLE 17-1   *Largest Corporate Mergers, 1981–1991*

BUYER	COMPANY BOUGHT	VALUE (in billions)	DATE
KKR	RJR Nabisco	$24.7	1989
Time	Warner Communications	13.9	1989
Socal	Gulf	13.4	1984
Philip Morris	Kraft	12.6	1988
Bristol-Meyers	Squibb	12.5	1989
Texaco	Getty	10.1	1984
British Petroleum	Sohio	7.6	1987
Du Pont	Conoco	7.4	1981
AT&T	NCR	7.4	1991
U.S. Steel	Marathon Oil	6.5	1981
Campeau	Federalled Stores	6.5	1988
Matsushita	MCA	6.5	1990
General Electric	RCA	6.4	1986
BCI Holdings	Beatrice Cos.	6.2	1986
GTE	Contel	6.2	1990

Sources: Data from The Wall Street Journal, *7 March 1984; Fortune, 21 Jan. 1985 and 20 Jan. 1986; and* Business Week, *15 Jan. 1990; The World Amanac 1992 (New York: Phoros Books, 1992).*

TABLE 17-2 *Largest Corporate Mergers, 1988*

BUYER	TARGET	PRICE (Billions)
R. H. Macy	Federated Department Stores	$6.2
Eastman Kodak	Sterling Drug	5.1
Bat Industries	Farmers Group	4.3
Bernard F. Brennan	Montgomery Ward	3.8
Black & Decker	American Standard	2.3
Desert Partners	USG	1.9
Mesa	Homestake Mining	1.9
Pirelli	Firestone Tire & Rubber	1.9
Dun & Bradstreet	IMS International	1.8
Barris Industries	Media General	1.6
Beazer	Koppers	1.3
Kohlberg Kravis Roberts	Stop & Shop	1.2
American Brands	E-II Holdings	1.1
Forstmann Little	AFG Industries	1.1
New England Electric	Public Service of New Hampshire	1.0

Sources: Heilbroner and Galbraith, Understanding Macroeconomics. *Data from* Business Week *and* M&A Data Base, Mergers Acquisitions Magazine. *Reprinted by permission, McGraw-Hill © 1988.*

In any case, the resulting economic concentration has been the subject of wide public-policy debate. Free-market advocates, for example, have argued that mergers have not had an adverse effect on efficiency and that antitrust policy should not therefore be used to discourage or undo them. We will examine pro-merger arguments in the next section. (U.S. policy toward antitrust enforcement is compared to that of Japan in this chapter's INTERNATIONAL ENVIRONMENT box.)

The Merits of Mergers

THEORETICAL APPROACHES. The public debate about the merits of mergers—a debate that has been reflected in numerous important court decisions—has been quite intense for the past fifteen years. In particular, it has centered on a disagreement over whether mergers should be evaluated solely on the basis of their effect on the economy—*economic analysis*—or whether their social and political effects should be considered as well—*multivalued analysis.*

This section will summarize policy guidelines established by the government for calculating the impact of merger activity on the economies of the industries involved—in particular, the *Herfindahl-Hirschman Index.* This section will also examine the issue of antitrust restraints on U.S. businesses in light of the increasingly competitive international environment by focusing on the *joint venture* as a business-growth strategy and on the *National Cooperative Research Act* of 1984, which was designed to encourage cooperative enterprise in areas of research and development.

Multivalued Analysis. Advocates of a *multivalued analysis,* who generally oppose mergers, contend that the accumulation of assets is dangerous even if it

Many international economists credit Japan's Ministry of International Trade and Industry (MITI) with orchestrating the country's meteoric climb from economic disaster after World War II to its current status as the industrial and technological envy of the world. MITI is led by an administrative vice-minister who is in charge of policy making and personnel decisions. To promote innovation, the vice-minister's tenure is limited to less than two years, after which he usually becomes a director of one or more private companies. In total, MITI employs about 12,000 employees, many of whom are top graduates of Japan's business, engineering, and law schools.

Although MITI cannot compel a corporation to take any particular direction or action, it derives its substantial power from two sources. First, 12,000 MITI technical officers consult directly with corporate heads about long-term planning, marketing, and research and development. It is not uncommon for an MITI officer to advise a corporation to invest in a particular foreign company or to branch out domestically into a new field. Second, many laws that are eventually adopted by Japan's legislative body are conceived of and drafted by MITI personnel. In this way, the agency determines, shapes, and coordinates both the country's industrial policy and the laws that regulate it.

Much of MITI's success has come as a result of the successful targeting of certain domestic and foreign industries for investment. On the domestic side, MITI's success is largely attributable to its creation of a series of cartels in certain industries in the 1950s and its restructuring of specific industrial sectors through the exercise of sweeping economic measures, such as imposing tariffs and quotas, controlling foreign exchange, and granting land subsidies. For example, it was MITI that decided to make Japan a leader in comput-

ers and semiconductors. Additionally, MITI championed the Japanese automobile industry by sponsoring a twenty-year policy of imposing strict quotas on car imports and encouraging mergers between large automotive producers.

MITI has also been aggressive in promoting international investment. Several years ago, for example, MITI created a "New Aid Plan" designed to develop certain sectors of foreign economies by contributing financial assistance toward rebuilding a country's infrastructure, providing Japanese expertise, and promoting direct investment and joint ventures. In Malaysia, for instance, MITI fostered investment in ceramics, electronics, and rubber footwear.

In developing its strategies for industrial growth, MITI has not had to worry much about violating Japanese antitrust laws. Compared to U.S. laws, Japan's antitrust laws have relatively no bite and are rarely enforced. Indeed, unlike Americans, the Japanese do not generally view cartels, conglomerates, and mergers as economic evils.

Some U.S. economists have advocated the creation of an American incarnation of MITI. Otherwise, they say, the American economy will develop haphazardly and without the investment in technological research and development that is the key to successful international competition in the next century.

There are, however, strong cultural and political forces within the United States that are hostile to the creation of a MITI-style agency. First, in the minds of many American economists and regular citizens, the notion of state economic planning is reminiscent of the now-defunct Soviet Union. Second, Americans have always had a distaste for corporate conglomerates, a deeper commitment than the Japanese to the enforcement of antitrust laws, and a stronger commitment to the notion of free-market competition.

poses no immediate danger of noncompetitive pricing. They charge that because assets are merely transferred from one set of hands to another, mergers do not contribute to economic growth as a whole. They also fear that the trend toward consolidation will result in the eventual extinction of small, locally owned businesses. Proponents of a multivalued analysis argue that vertical and conglomerate mergers are particularly destructive of competition because they reduce the number of players in a market while increasing the difficulty of market entry.

Economic Analysis. Advocates of purely *economic analysis* maintain that competition does not depend on any particular balance of large and small businesses. Thus, they are unconcerned with protecting small firms. Furthermore, economic-analysis proponents contend that an unregulated, or minimally regulated, market fosters the most efficient allocation of resources while maximizing productivity.

The goal of the Reagan administration, which adhered to economic analysis, was to increase productive efficiency and maximize wealth without regard to distribution. Consequently, Reagan economists argued that bigness is not inherently bad and that corporate mergers should not be discouraged. If a company had acquired enough money to purchase another, the theory goes, it must have done so by being more efficient or offering better products. Furthermore, mergers actually promote competition and overall economic efficiency by leading to the better use of capital and by lowering the cost of transportation, production, management, and research and development.

GUIDELINES FOR BUSINESS. We saw in Chapter 6 that uncertainty about government policy discourages business activity. Uncertainty about merger policy is no exception. In order to reduce uncertainty, the Justice Department publishes guidelines for legal mergers. Although these guidelines are not regulations and do not bind either the department or the courts, they are designed to make antitrust policy more predictable.

The Herfindahl-Hirschman Index. The department's 1984 guidelines measure market concentration with the **Herfindahl-Hirschman Index (HHI).** First, the department defines the *post-merger market*. Second, it identifies the share that every firm in that market (including the companies contemplating merger) will have after the merger. The formula is to square each firm's market share and add up the squares. For example, the formula for a market in which twenty firms each have a premerger share of five percent is:

$$20 \times 5^2 = 500$$

If two firms in this market were to merge, the new formula would be:

$$18 \times 5^2 = 450$$
$$1 \times 10^2 = 100$$
$$450 + 100 = 550$$

For a market in which five firms each have a premerger share of twenty percent, the formula is:

$$5 \times 20^2 = 2000$$

If two of *these* firms were to merge, the new formula would be:

$$3 \times 20^2 = 1200$$
$$1 \times 40^2 = 1600$$
$$1200 + 1600 = 2800$$

The final step in using HHI is to compare the postmerger HHI with the guidelines described in Table 17-3. Note that in concentrated markets "additional factors" are likely to be considered. If the market is one that is difficult to enter, a merger of two existing firms is likely to be challenged. If present market conditions tend to promote collusion, a challenge is also likely. The Justice Department also looks at the history and present state of the market and at the firms involved in the merger. Has the market suffered from collusion in the past? Is it competitive now? How has the acquiring firm generally influenced competition?

Although these guidelines do affect the Justice Department's prosecution decisions, they have not been adopted by any court. They are not laws—they are simply agency guidelines. In addition to profiling Bob Allen, the chairman and CEO of American Telephone & Telegraph Co., this chapter's PERSONAL PROFILE box shows that by exercising foresight and business savvy, a company can retain its economic potential and vitality even after being prosecuted for antitrust violations by the Justice Department.

Herfindahl-Hirschman Index (HHI) Justice Department's 1984 index of market concentration used to help determine the legality or illegality of mergers

| TABLE 17-3 | *Justice Department Merger Guidelines* |

POSTMERGER HHI	RESPONSE
Below 1,000	Unconcentrated market; mergers ordinarily will not be challenged
1,000–1,800	Only mergers increasing the market's HHI by more than 100 points are likely to be challenged
Over 1,800	Concentrated market; mergers increasing the market's HHI by less than 50 points are unlikely to be challenged; mergers causing increases of between 50 and 100 points are evaluated according to their probable impact, taking into account additional factors, such as barriers to entry (see below); mergers causing increases of more than 100 points are likely to be challenged.

CASE: ANTITRUST LAW AND JOINT VENTURES. As we have seen, many critics of antitrust laws argue that they hinder our international competitiveness. If it were not for antitrust laws, they assert, domestic competitors could collaborate more readily on research endeavors and other joint efforts to help them meet and beat foreign competition.

For example, Section 7 of the Clayton Act, which prohibits the acquisition of another corporation's assets if less competition or a monopoly would result,

PERSONAL PROFILE
Bob Allen of AT&T

In 1979, James Olson, then chairman and CEO of American Telephone & Telegraph Co., called upon his old friend and trusted adviser Robert E. Allen, an AT&T vice-president, to head up a project that was as important as any other in the company's history—to prepare a downsizing plan that would both satisfy the saber rattlers at the Justice Department's antitrust division and preserve the firm's strong economic base. Thirty days later, Allen presented a specific plan that called for minimizing monopolistic practices in exchange for retaining an involvement in both providing communications services and manufacturing related equipment like computers and telephones. Three years later, AT&T's consent decree with the Justice Department reflected Allen's plan, which agreed to give up local phone companies that comprised seventy-seven percent of the company's assets, preserving its right to continue operations both in communications services and manufacturing.

In 1988, when Allen took over as AT&T's CEO and chairman after Olson's death, he assumed responsibility for making his risky plan work. He began by restructuring management in order to decentralize decision making. Specifically, the firm was divided into 20 separate units headed by presidents with substantial independence on questions of policy. Allen's biggest move came in 1990, when he spearheaded a $7.4 billion acquisition of NCR, a competing manufacturer of computer equipment. The acquisition—which made AT&T the fifth-largest producer of computer equipment in the United States—was needed to bolster the computer-production end of the firm's business, which could

not compete with giants like IBM. AT&T created a number of innovative marketing programs and a high-power advertising campaign to maintain dominance in the communications-services market, in which it now competes with startup firms like MCI and Sprint.

Interestingly, AT&T's aggressiveness in the marketplace is not mirrored in Allen's personality. A soft-spoken Midwesterner, Allen began working for Indiana Bell at the age of twenty-two and has since worked his way up through AT&T ranks. The job at Indiana Bell was not Allen's first—he joined the work force when he was eight. A series of jobs during junior and senior high school enabled Allen to pay for his own education at Wabash College, where he studied political science and economics and played football. Allen planned to attend law school after graduation but decided instead to take a job as a traffic engineer at Indiana Bell. Allen's road to the top included stints at Pennsylvania Bell, Illinois Bell, and the Chesapeake & Potomac Telephone Companies. Finally, he wound up in the upper echelons of AT&T corporate hierarchy, where he was groomed for AT&T's top job.

Although Allen has exercised a firm hand over AT&T and charted an innovative course, the next few years remain critical for the giant company. Corporate observers are most interested in whether Allen's decision to risk such a large portion of the firm's fortunes on the high-stakes, roller-coaster computer-manufacturing business will ultimately pay off and whether he can continue to overcome increasing competition in the communications-services market.

has been held by the courts to apply to some **joint ventures**—partnerships between two or more corporations or a corporate and a government entity (*see* Chapter 21). Thus, if a plaintiff can show that a joint venture will lessen competition in a certain market, the partnership can be ruled illegal under the Clayton Act. Critics of antitrust have asserted that the looming threat of the Clayton Act violation has had a chilling effect on the same research-and-development joint ventures that are needed to keep the U.S. competitive in an increasingly competitive world market.

The National Cooperative Research Act. Such concern led Congress to enact the **National Cooperative Research Act (NCRA)** of 1984.[1] The statute was meant to encourage research-and-development joint ventures by spelling out more clearly which joint ventures were illegal and which were not. Sponsors of the legislation hoped that by clarifying this area, corporate fear of antitrust litigation would diminish and an increasing number of joint ventures would result. In addition, many legislators believed the NCRA was necessary because such competitors as Japan, Germany, and South Korea permit—and even assist in—the formation of joint ventures in research and development.

Application of the NCRA. The NCRA specifically applies to research-and-development joint ventures. In a nutshell, the act defines such an agreement as a combination of two or more entities joining together for the purpose of experimentation, analysis, or testing of engineering techniques, the practical application of methods, or the collection and exchange of research information. The act specifically excludes from joint ventures involved in such blatantly anticompetitive activities as the exchange of pricing and cost information and the making of agreements to restrict the sale or licensing of inventions. The NCRA also does not cover joint ventures engaged in such classic antitrust activities as price fixing and territorial restraints.

Provisions of the NCRA. The NCRA seeks to encourage joint ventures in three ways. First, it requires that courts apply the *rule of reason* to antitrust litigation involving research-and-development joint ventures—a less stringent standard than the per se rule applied in cases involving other types of combinations. Under the rule of reason, a court must consider the reasonableness of the activity and a wide variety of factors to determine whether an agreement is impermissibly anticompetitive.

Second, the amount of damages available to a party bringing a successful action under the NCRA is limited to actual losses—not the usual treble damages that are typically available under antitrust laws.

Finally, the NCRA authorizes courts to award attorney fees to joint ventures that have successfully defended themselves in antitrust litigation. This provision is intended to make those contemplating antitrust action against research-and-development joint ventures think long and hard about the wisdom of doing so: If they lose, they must pay often huge amounts of their opponent's attorneys fees.

Critics of the NCRA, however, complain that the act does not go far enough either in deterring antitrust litigation or in providing sufficient confidence for those who want to establish costly international joint ventures. Some critics have thus called for a more aggressive activity in encouraging in-

---

[1] This section is based on Tania Isenstein, "Increasing the International Competitiveness of the United States through Its Joint Venture Laws: A Lesson to Be Learned from South Korea," *American University Journal of International Law and Policy* 435 (1991); and Christopher Wright, "The National Cooperative Research Act of 1984; A New Antitrust Regime for Joint Research and Development Ventures," 1 *High Technology Law Journal* 133 (1986).

ternational joint ventures in research and development—activity that might include a national registry and even government involvement in planning. Spurred by growing realization that the United States is lagging behind in research and development, more debate—and perhaps even amendments to the NCRA—are expected.

■ Concept Check 17-1 Mergers: Types, Regulation, and Merits

- Explain and contrast *horizontal, vertical,* and *conglomerate mergers.*
- Explain the differences between *multivalued* and *economic analysis* as approaches to the merits of mergers.
- Describe the *Herfindahl-Hirschman Index* and give an example of how an HHI formula can reveal an anticompetitive merger.
- What are the key provisions of the *National Cooperative Research Act?*

■ MERGERS AND THE COURTS

Competing firms are those that operate in the same geographic area and whose products serve the same or substantially overlapping functions and may be used interchangeably. This section will examine horizontal, vertical, and conglomerate mergers as aspects of market-expansion strategy on the part of competing firms. In particular, it will focus on the various criteria for defining market-expansion agreements as mergers subject to the provisions of the Clayton Act, and will discuss some of the more important ways in which the courts have used those criteria in applying the provisions of the act.

competing firms Corporate entities which operate in the same geographic area and whose products are interchangeable

Horizontal Mergers

One obvious goal of a horizontal merger is to eliminate a competitor. There are, however, other possible goals. For instance, two small companies may merge to challenge a larger operation or a large company may merge with a small one that offers special advantages. Because the resulting company is bigger than either firm that formed it, a horizontal merger may also produce economies of scale.

In addition, management can be centralized, perhaps lowering overhead costs. With more plants under a centralized management, there is the possibility of increased flexibility in production, perhaps lowering unit costs. Distribution costs may also be lowered when spread over a wider network.

MARKET CRITERIA.   It is often difficult for the courts to decide which mergers are in fact horizontal. As we have seen, the distinctions between vertical and horizontal mergers are not always clear. Mergers described as horizontal have included the joining of a firm making metal cans and a firm making glass bottles, a strip-mining company and a deep-mining company, a company making dry table wine and a company making sweet and fruity wine, and a grocery chain in northeast Los Angeles and a grocery chain in southwest Los Angeles.[2]

   Price and Profitability. Buyers and sellers define markets by their re-

---

[2] *United States v. Continental Can Co.,* 378 U.S. 441 (1964); *United States v. General Dynamics Corp.,* 415 U.S. 486 (1974); In re *Coca-Cola Bottling Co.,* 93 FTC 110 (1979); *United States v. Von's Grocery Co.,* 384 U.S. 270 (1966).

sponses to *prices* and *opportunities for sales*. Buyers often switch from one product to a slightly different one (from metal cans to glass bottles) or abandon a nearby store in favor of one farther away in order to obtain a lower price. You will recall from Chapter 16 that if buyers are reluctant to change products or places of purchase, a low *cross-elasticity of demand* is said to exist between the two products or geographic areas. The difference in price would have to be enormous before many buyers would make the change.

In order to define a market, the courts try to determine whether one of the two firms involved in a merger could conceivably have made a profit at prices low enough to capture the other firm's customers. If the answer is yes, the firms were rivals and the merger is horizontal. Cross-elasticity of supply is also relevant: If suppliers can readily switch from one product to another in response to price changes, the two products may be part of one market.

undue concentration Result of a *horizonal merger* in which the new firm has an inordinate percentage share of the relevant market

Undue Concentration. Once a merger has been defined as horizontal, the plaintiff seeks to prove that the merger produces **undue concentration** in the relevant market. *Brown Shoe Co. v. United States* (370 U.S. 322 [1962]), the first Supreme Court decision under the amended Section 7 of the Clayton Act, concluded that the impact of a merger depends upon "the particular market—its structure, history and probable future." A year later, in *United States v. Philadelphia National Bank* (374 U.S. 363 [1963]), the Court defined an illegal merger as one that gives a firm "an undue percentage share of the relevant market, and results in a significant increase in the concentration of the firms in that market. . . ." This decision set the course of subsequent case law.

failing-company defense Legal position that a firm without a reasonable prospect of survival may *merge horizontally* with a competitor even if the merger may threaten competition

THE FAILING-COMPANY DEFENSE. Judges have long recognized that a firm with no reasonable prospect of survival may legally merge with a competing firm even if the merger threatens competition. For example, although the 1987 merger of the Greyhound and Trailways bus lines reduced intercity bus competition in parts of the country, Trailways would probably have failed had it not occurred. Defendants in horizontal merger cases can thus adopt the **failing-company defense.**

The failing-company defense draws upon congressional debate over the Celler-Kefauver Act in 1950. It is clear that the lawmakers wished to exempt any purchases of companies that would otherwise close their doors. Congress apparently hoped to help protect small-business owners or stockholders, creditors, and workers from the consequences of bankruptcy. But how should a court decide if a company is failing?

Citizen Publishing Company v. United States (394 U.S. 131 [1969]) answered this question. The defense had to demonstrate that:

1. The acquired firm was almost certain to declare bankruptcy and could not have been successfully reorganized (*see* Chapter 19).
2. The firm would have disappeared entirely after the bankruptcy.
3. The acquired firm did not have the option of another merger that would have had less effect on competition.

Justice Department guidelines, therefore, state that the failing-company defense applies only after the acquired firm has made "unsuccessful good faith efforts to elicit reasonable alternative offers . . . that would . . . pose a less severe danger to competition than does the proposed merger."[3] A reasonable

---

[3] 49 *Federal Register* at 26,837.

alternative offer might be from a competitor smaller than the proposed buyer. The Justice Department also recognizes a "failing-division" defense under similar circumstances.

Challenged mergers have succeeded through means other than the failing-business defense. For example, it has sometimes been possible for a firm to proceed with a challenged agreement by altering its terms. In *White Consolidated Industries, Inc. v. Whirlpool Corp.*, there had been an injunction against the proposed merger.

WHITE CONSOLIDATED INDUSTRIES, INC. v. WHIRLPOOL CORPORATION
U.S. Court of Appeals, Sixth Circuit, 781 F.2d 1224 (1986)

The parties in this antitrust action are competitors in the household appliance market. Plaintiffs, White Consolidated Industries, Inc., and Magic Chef, Inc., manufacture and distribute major household appliances nationwide, as does the defendant, Whirlpool Corporation. Defendant Dart & Kraft is a diversified food and consumer products company that acquired defendant Hobart Corporation. Hobart Corporation primarily manufactures kitchen equipment through its KitchenAid Division, which is known in particular for producing top-of-the-line dishwashers. Defendant Emerson Electric Company, mainly noted for its broad range of electrical and electronic products, manufactures and nationally distributes a line of garbage disposals and dishwashers.

Plaintiffs filed suit in the United States District Court for the Northern District of Ohio alleging that Whirlpool's proposed acquisition of KitchenAid violated Section 7 of the Clayton Act and Sections 1 and 2 of the Sherman Act. Plaintiffs sought to preliminarily and permanently enjoin defendant Whirlpool from acquiring the KitchenAid Division from defendants Dart & Kraft and Hobart Corporation.

Keith, Circuit Judge.
. . . .

Under the proposed acquisition agreement, Whirlpool would purchase from Dart & Kraft all of Hobart's KitchenAid stock, including the manufacturing assets of the dishwasher facility held by a Hobart subsidiary. Upon acquiring KitchenAid, Whirlpool proposed tendering a "curative divestiture" designed to defuse the anticompetitive effects of the transaction. The curative divestiture entailed Whirlpool selling KitchenAid manufacturing assets to defendant Emerson. After this partial divestiture, Whirlpool would keep the KitchenAid brand name and garbage disposer manufacturing assets and Emerson would agree to supply Whirlpool's quota of the KitchenAid Model KD21 dishwashers, compactors and service parts for a guaranteed twenty percent net profit. Aside from providing Whirlpool's inventory, Emerson would be allowed to market a differentiated Model KD21 only through its own "In-Sink-Erator" brand name and distribution network.

. . . The district court determined that, despite the "curative divestiture" provisions of the proposed acquisition, the small number of top appliance manufacturers would garner even larger shares of the dishwasher market after the acquisition, and that the combination of Whirlpool and KitchenAid in an already highly concentrated market would substantially reduce competition. Specifically, the trial court expressed concern that the curative divestiture provisions of the agreement failed to accord Emerson sufficient latitude in marketing the Model 21 dishwasher for it to freely compete against other dishwasher distributors. Moreover, the divestiture provisions failed to eradicate agreement restrictions on Emerson's ability to private label and distribute the Model 21, factors which in the district court's view, precluded Emerson from independently competing with Whirlpool and replacing KitchenAid in the market.

. . . .

The district court thereupon concluded the defendants had failed to overcome the plaintiffs' prima facie case showing that the transaction would substantially reduce competition by affording Whirlpool an increasing ability to control Emerson, restrict dishwasher output and raise prices. The preliminary injunction thereafter issued.

The defendants immediately amended the agreement to incorporate the curative measures suggested in the district court opinion and moved to vacate the injunction. In considering defendants' motion to vacate the preliminary injunction, the court determined that the amendments allowed post-transaction Emerson to (1) manufacture, distribute and market the Model 21 dishwasher under any name not similar to KitchenAid's; (2) distribute the Model 21 through any system Emerson chose; and (3) issue the Model 21 under private label. With these changes, the court determined that Emerson gained complete control from Whirlpool over its own dishwasher production and distribution as well as the ability to replace KitchenAid as a willing and viable competitor in the dishwasher market. The court concluded the amendment eliminated the anticompetitive effects of Whirlpool's proposed acquisition and ordered the preliminary injunction vacated. . . .

. . . .

On appeal the plaintiffs first contend that the district

court abused its discretion in vacating the preliminary injunction because the amended agreement fails to sufficiently ensure Emerson's ability to replace KitchenAid as a viable competitor. Specifically, plaintiffs argue that the amended agreement still leaves Whirlpool in control of Emerson's production levels and that Emerson's marketing ability is limited because Emerson is not an integrated household appliance business with a recognized brand name, distribution network and experienced sales personnel. We do not agree. The district court expressly found that the amendments rendered Emerson an independent force in the market and that Emerson is an experienced and capable manufacturing company. The district court also determined that under the amended agreement Emerson had been freed to transcend entry barriers and compete in the dishwashing business as it had succeeded in entering other businesses in the past:

> It is important to recognize that Emerson is not entering the market faced with traditional entry barriers. Along with its history of successful private labelling, Emerson will begin with a fully tooled plant, ready to produce a state-of-the-art machine. In addition, Emerson will have a guaranteed profits contract to supply dishwashers to Whirlpool for at least five years, which it can maintain or abandon depending upon its other successes. Emerson has a strong relationship with potential customers to which it already sells private label goods, and Emerson will be a new private labeller in the industry, replacing KitchenAid, a manufacturer unwilling to private label.
>
> In addition, Emerson is free to expand, using its expertise, industry contacts, and other resources. If it chooses, it may develop new dishwashers to replace the Model 21 when it becomes obsolete. Emerson is also free to enter other product markets, using In-Sink-Erator, or whatever name it develops for its

dishwashers. The fact is that the independent, viable Emerson created by this transaction may be able to become, if it chooses, a substantial player in more than just the dishwasher market; it may be able to take on a key role in other white goods markets, too. A KitchenAid with unenthusiastic ownership simply cannot compare to the post-transaction Emerson.

. . . .

We agree with the district court that the relevant injury is whether the amended curative divestiture does in fact leave Emerson as a willing, independent competitor capable of effective production in the dishwasher market. Upon review of the record as a whole, we are unable to conclude that the district court's findings above or its conclusion that plaintiffs failed to show a substantial likelihood of lessened competition from the amended transaction are clearly erroneous. Nor, in our view, did the district court clearly err in discrediting plaintiff's claims that the predation and leverage of the defendants could cause irreparable injuries to themselves or substantial harm to others. Finally, since Whirlpool's proposed acquisition of KitchenAid will probably increase competition, no public interest is served by enjoining the proposed transaction. We, therefore, conclude the district court did not abuse its discretion in vacating the preliminary injunction.

Case Questions

1. Explain the "curative divestiture" proposal made by Whirlpool.

2. Upon what basis did the court determine that this measure eliminated the anticompetitive effects of Whirlpool's proposed acquisition?

3. In what market position is Emerson left as a result of the amended curative divestiture?

Vertical Mergers

In a vertical merger, a firm buys either a customer ("forward vertical integration") or a supplier ("backward vertical integration"). The goal may be to make dealings with suppliers and sales outlets more efficient or simply more dependable. For instance, a manufacturer need not worry that a store will favor another company's products if the manufacturer owns the store. The risk for the company is that the new subsidiary or division may not be profitable.

To the extent that the acquiring firm dominates the business of its new subsidiary, vertical mergers affect the competition within three markets: (1) the acquiring firm's market (2) the supplier's market and (3) the customer's market. Suppose, for example, that a shoe manufacturer bought a chain of retail shoe stores and arranged to sell all its shoes in that chain and that the chain then sold only its parent company's shoes. The merger has cut off both other shoe manufacturers from a group of sales outlets and a source of supply for competing retail stores.

THE FORECLOSURE THEORY. Under the *foreclosure theory*, a vertical merger threatens competition if it blocks a third firm from a market. This condition generally arises if one of the merging firms is a monopolist. If the purchased shoe chain is the only one in town, no independent manufacturer can sell there after the merger. Courts also speak of degrees of foreclosure—that is, the blockage of firms from a certain percentage of a market. To determine whether there is a violation of Section 7 of the Clayton Act, courts begin by defining the relevant market. Then they calculate the degree to which the supplier or customer market is foreclosed following the vertical merger.

In the *Brown Shoe* Case, the proposed merger joined a shoe manufacturer, whose market share was about five percent, and a retailer, whose market share was about one percent in the same market. Both firms were too small to raise fears about concentration of that particular market. Nevertheless, the Court condemned the merger, citing two trends: (1) a market trend toward this kind of merger and (2) a tendency for parent manufacturers to monopolize retailers' sales.

When firms find large sections of a market foreclosed to them, they tend to buy dependable access through mergers of their own. Another shoemaker buys its own chain, and other shoemakers follow suit. Over time, independent shoe stores or manufacturers lacking their own sales outlets might disappear, and anyone interested in either making or retailing shoes in that geographic area would be forced to do both to compete.

Conglomerate Mergers

There are three kinds of conglomerate mergers: *product-extension*, *market-extension*, and *pure conglomerate* mergers. Although the goals of each are different, they all represent expansion for the acquiring firm.

EXTENDING PRODUCT LINES. In a **product-extension merger**, the products of the merging companies are related. It may be that the products can be distributed and marketed together or that they can be produced with the same equipment. The goal is generally to offer customers a line of products (such as a variety of canned foods) and to take advantage of any production or marketing economies of scale that may result. For example, once a firm like Del Monte is set up to produce and sell canned corn, it can do the same with canned green beans, tomatoes, and other vegetables at very little extra cost. It uses the same or similar methods to can, store, and ship all types of vegetables—an economy of scale in both production and distribution.

> **product-extension merger**
> *Conglomerate merger* in which the merging firms market related products

It also uses the same network of grocery stores and supermarkets—another economy of scale in distribution. In addition, it advertises all of its products whenever it advertises the Del Monte name—an economy of scale in marketing. A smaller or less diversified firm may thus have to spend more per product on advertising (or any of the other business functions) than does Del Monte.

EXTENDING GEOGRAPHIC REACH. In a **market-extension merger**, a firm acquires another firm that sells the same product in a different geographic area. Because economies of scale depend upon a large pool of customers, spreading the operation over a large area, perhaps several states, may be more efficient than having separate firms in each of those states. A firm cannot make a profit by pro-

> **market-extension merger**
> *Conglomerate merger* in which the merging firms sell the same product in different geographic areas

ducing more goods for less cost per unit unless it also increases sales. One way to do that is to make its goods available over a larger geographic area.

pure-conglomerate merger
Conglomerate merger in which the goal is to diversify and spread risk because the merging firms sell unrelated products

SPREADING RISK. A **pure-conglomerate merger** involves two firms whose products are unrelated. The purpose of such a merger is to diversify and spread risks. If the company fails in one market, it will not disappear entirely. Weaker divisions or subsidiaries of a conglomerate may be bailed out by other, stronger divisions or subsidiaries for some period of time.

CHALLENGES TO CONGLOMERATE MERGERS. Before the focus of antitrust enforcement shifted to horizontal mergers, conglomerate mergers were successfully challenged on three grounds: *potential competition*, *entrenchment*, and *reciprocal dealing*.

Potential Competition. In 1966, the Supreme Court ruled against Procter & Gamble's 1957 purchase of Clorox Chemical because the purchase destroyed a possibility for a more competitive market: The merger removed **potential competition**. Procter & Gamble's purchase was a product-extension merger: Although this highly diversified firm made a variety of household products, it did not make liquid bleach—the only product of Clorox. The Court was convinced that P&G would have set up its own bleach-manufacturing operation if it had not been able to obtain one through a merger. Had P&G actually done so, the market would have had one more competitor and would therefore have been less concentrated than it was after the merger.

potential competition Legal challenge that *conglomerate mergers* harm the possibility for a more competitive market

---

FEDERAL TRADE COMMISSION v. PROCTER & GAMBLE CO.
U.S. Supreme Court, 386 U.S. 568 (1966)

Petitioner, the Federal Trade Commission, initiated this proceeding charging that respondent, Procter & Gamble Co., had acquired the assets of Clorox Chemical Co. in violation of Section 7 of the Clayton Act as amended by the Celler-Kefauver Act. The charge was that Procter's acquisition of Clorox might substantially lessen competition or tend to create a monopoly in the production and sale of household liquid bleaches.

Mr. Justice Douglas delivered the opinion of the Court.
. . . .

As indicated by the Commission in its painstaking and illuminating report, it does not particularly aid analysis to talk of this merger in conventional terms, namely, horizontal or vertical or conglomerate. This merger may most appropriately be described as a "product-extension merger," as the Commission stated. The facts are not disputed, and a summary will demonstrate the correctness of the Commission's decision.

At the time of the merger, in 1957, Clorox was the leading manufacturer in the heavily concentrated household liquid bleach industry. It is agreed that household liquid bleach is the relevant line of commerce. . . . The relevant geographical market is the Nation and a series of regional markets. Because of high shipping costs and low sales price, it is not feasible to ship the product more than 300 miles from its point of manufacture. Most manufacturers are limited to competition within a single region since they have but one plant. Clorox is the only firm selling nationally; it has 13 plants distributed throughout the Nation. Purex, Clorox's closest competitor in size, does not distribute its bleach in the northeast or mid-Atlantic States; in 1957, Purex's bleach was available in less than 50% of the national market.

At the time of the acquisition, Clorox was the leading manufacturer of household liquid bleach, with 48.8% of the national sales—annual sales of slightly less than $40,000,000. Its market share had been steadily increasing for the five years prior to the merger. . . .

. . . .

Since all liquid bleach is chemically identical, advertising and sales promotion are vital. In 1957 Clorox spent almost $3,700,000 on advertising, imprinting the value of its bleach in the mind of the consumer. In addition, it spent $1,700,000 for other promotional activities. The Commission found that these heavy expenditures went far to explain why Clorox maintained so high a market share despite the fact that its brand, though chemically indistinguishable from rival brands, retailed for a price equal to or, in many instances, higher than its competitors.

Procter is a large, diversified manufacturer of low-price, high-turnover household products sold through grocery, drug, and department stores. Prior to its acquisition of Clorox, it did not produce household liquid bleach. . . .

. . . .

. . . In 1957, Procter was the Nation's largest advertiser, spending more than $80,000,000 on advertising and an additional $47,000,000 on sales promotion. Due to its tremendous volume, Procter receives substantial discounts from the media. As a multiproduct producer Procter enjoys substantial advantages in advertising and sales promotion. . . .

Prior to the acquisition, Procter was in the course of diversifying into product lines related to its basic detergent-soap-cleanser business. Liquid bleach was a distinct possibility since packaged detergents—Procter's primary product line—and liquid bleach are used complementarily in washing clothes and fabrics, and in general household cleaning. . . .

. . . .

The decision to acquire Clorox was the result of a study conducted by Procter's promotion department designed to determine the advisability of entering the liquid bleach industry. The initial report noted the ascendancy of liquid bleach in the large and expanding household bleach market, and recommended that Procter purchase Clorox rather than enter independently. Since a large investment would be needed to obtain a satisfactory market share, acquisition of the industry's leading firm was attractive. "Taking over the Clorox business . . . could be a way of achieving a dominant position in the liquid bleach market quickly, which would pay out reasonably well." 63 F.T.C. . . . A few months later, Procter acquired the assets of Clorox in the name of a wholly owned subsidiary, the Clorox Company, in exchange for Procter stock.

. . . .

Section 7 of the Clayton Act was intended to arrest the anticompetitive effects of market power in their incipiency. The core question is whether a merger may substantially lessen competition, and necessarily requires a prediction of the merger's impact on competition, present and future. The section can deal only with probabilities, not with certainties. And there is certainly no requirement that the anticompetitive power manifest itself in anticompetitive action before § 7 can be called into play. If the enforcement of § 7 turned on the existence of actual anticompetitive practices, the congressional policy of thwarting such practices in their incipiency would be frustrated.

All mergers are within the reach of § 7, and all must be tested by the same standard, whether they are classified as horizontal, vertical, conglomerate or other. As noted by the Commission, this merger is neither horizontal, vertical, nor conglomerate. Since the products of the acquired company are complementary to those of the acquiring company and may be produced with similar facilities, marketed through the same channels and in the same manner, and advertised by the same media, the Commission aptly called this acquisition a "product-extension merger." . . .

The anticompetitive effects with which this product-extension merger is fraught can easily be seen: (1) the substitution of the powerful acquiring firm for the smaller, but already dominant, firm may substantially reduce the competitive structure of the industry by raising entry barriers and by dissuading the smaller firms from aggressively competing; (2) the acquisition eliminates the potential competition of the acquiring firm.

The liquid bleach industry was already oligopolistic before the acquisition, and price competition was certainly not as vigorous as it would have been if the industry were competitive. Clorox enjoyed a dominant position nationally, and its position approached monopoly proportions in certain areas. . . .

The acquisition may also have the tendency of raising the barriers to new entry. The major competitive weapon in the successful marketing of bleach is advertising. Clorox was limited in this area by its relatively small budget and its inability to obtain substantial discounts. By contrast, Procter's budget was much larger; and, although it would not devote its entire budget to advertising Clorox, if could divert a large portion to meet the short-term threat of a new entrant. Procter would be able to use its volume discounts to advantage in advertising Clorox. Thus, a new entrant would be much more reluctant to face the giant Procter than it would have been to face the smaller Clorox.

Possible economies cannot be used as a defense to illegality. Congress was aware that some mergers which lessen competition may also result in economies but it struck the balance in favor of protecting competition.

The Commission also found that the acquisition of Clorox by Procter eliminated Procter as a potential competitor. The Court of Appeals declared that this finding was not supported by evidence because there was no evidence that Procter's management had ever intended to enter the industry independently and that Procter had never attempted to enter. The evidence, however, clearly shows that Procter was the most likely entrant. . . . Procter was engaged in a vigorous program of diversifying into product lines closely related to its basic products. Liquid bleach was a natural avenue of diversification since it is complementary to Procter's products, is sold to the same customers through the same channels, and is advertised and merchandised in the same manner. . . . Procter had considered the possibility of independently entering but decided against it because the acquisition of Clorox would enable Procter to capture a more commanding share of the market.

It is clear that the existence of Procter at the edge of the industry exerted considerable influence on the market. First, the market behavior of the liquid bleach industry was influenced by each firm's predictions of the market behavior of its competitors, actual and potential. Second, the barriers to entry by a firm of Procter's size and with its advantages were not significant. There is no indication that the barriers were so high that the price Procter would have to charge would be above the price that would maximize the profits of the existing firms. Third, the number of potential entrants was not so large that the elimination of one would be insignificant. Few firms would have the temerity to challenge a firm as solidly entrenched as Clorox. Fourth, Procter was found by the Commission to be the most likely entrant. These findings of the Commission were amply supported by the evidence.

The judgment of the Court of Appeals is reversed and remanded with instructions to affirm and enforce the Commission's order.

Case Questions

1. Why is the merger by Procter & Gamble termed a "product-extension merger"?

2. What are the anticompetitive effects that result from this product-extension merger?

3. Specifically, how does this acquisition raise the barriers to new entry into the market?

---

entrenchment Legal challenge to the purchase of a dominant firm by another in which the purchaser uses its assets to secure dominance and make the market harder to enter

Entrenchment. When Procter & Gamble purchased Clorox Chemical in 1957, it had assets of $500 million. Clorox had 49 percent of the bleach market and assets of $12 million. According to the theory of **entrenchment**, Procter & Gamble might in these circumstances use its greater assets to secure—"entrench"—Clorox's dominance. Eventually, such entrenchment would threaten to make the liquid-bleach market more difficult to enter. Note that this theory applies only to purchases of a dominant firm; if the purchased firm has bigger rivals, the parent firm's efforts to help it should make the market more competitive, not less. In any case, there is no evidence that conglomerates subsidize one product at the expense of others.

reciprocal dealing Legal challenge to the business practice in which one firm will buy goods from another only if the seller buys something in return

Reciprocal Dealing. Suppose that a large clothing retailer purchased a manufacturer of boys' sporting wear which, with one competitor, controlled 60 percent of the market for these products. If the retailer then required its wholesalers to purchase boys' sporting wear from its new acquisition, the merger may be ruled illegal because of **reciprocal dealing**. In fact, conglomerate mergers have been declared illegal because they made reciprocal dealing more likely. Reciprocal dealing makes a purchase a two-way street: The seller must also buy from the buyer. Section 3 of the Clayton Act outlaws such arrangements.

How do reciprocal deals threaten competition? Suppose one of the firms involved is a large buyer and uses its bargaining power to pressure its suppliers to buy its products. Although the products may be overpriced or shoddy, the suppliers must buy them to keep a substantial customer.

■ *Concept Check 17-2* *Mergers and the Courts*

- Explain mergers as market-expansion strategies on the part of *competing firms*. What *market criteria* are used to define a horizontal merger?
- Explain the reasoning behind the *failing-firm defense*.
- Discuss *foreclosure theory* as a criterion for defining a vertical merger.
- Discuss the three forms of conglomerate merger and give hypothetical illustrations of *geographic extension* and *risk spreading*.
- Explain *potential competition*, *entrenchment*, and *reciprocal dealing* as grounds for challenging conglomerate mergers.

■ Tie-Ins and Exclusive Dealing

In addition to mergers, the Clayton Act covers other potentially anticompetitive activities. According to Section 3, contracts or sales on terms that prevent customers from using products offered by a seller's competitors are illegal if their effect "may be to substantially lessen competition or tend to create a monopoly." This language is similar to the provisions concerning mergers.

However, it includes *reciprocal dealing, tie-ins*, and *exclusive dealing*. Note that Section 3 of the act applies only to tying and exclusive dealing involving goods and commodities, not services. Section 1 of the Sherman Act bars tying and exclusive dealing involving both services and goods and commodities.

Tie-Ins

Suppose that a storekeeper selling a one-of-a-kind item that you want insists that you may buy it only if you buy a different item along with it. The sale is a **tie-in**.

The problem with such sales is that customers may be forced to buy a product that they do not want in order to buy one that they do. This situation is a real possibility, however, only if the seller "has the power, within the market for the tying product, to require purchasers to accept burdensome terms that could not be exacted in a completely competitive market" (*United States Steel Corp. v. Fortner Enterprises, Inc.*, 429 U.S. 610 [1977] at 620). In other words, if the seller does not have some degree of market power, customers will simply take their business elsewhere. In the example above, the storekeeper has a kind of monopoly power because the item is unique and thus available only in that shop. Such a sale or contract may violate Section 3 of the Clayton Act even if it does not include a stated condition of the kind described in the law. Because you probably will not buy *both* the tied product and any substitutes for it, the tie has the effect of barring customers of the tying product from using products made by other firms. If competition in the market for the tied product may be reduced because of the loss of potential customers for better substitutes, the tie-in is illegal.

tie-in Type of sale in which a seller with market power requires a purchaser to buy a product that it does not want to order to buy one that it does

THE CURRENT STANDARD. As we noted previously, tie-ins involving goods and commodities are also illegal under Section 1 of the Sherman Act—that is, the provision against "restraint of trade." Congress outlawed tie-ins again in the Clayton Act in order to make prosecutions of tie-ins and exclusive dealing easier by banning those that constituted a *possible*, not only *actual*, restraint of trade.

In interpreting and applying the Clayton Act, the federal courts developed a three-prong test to determine whether a tie-in is illegal. Under the test, a tie-in is per se illegal under the following conditions: (1) the defendant has enough power in the tying product's market to restrain free competition in the tied product's market, (2) a degree of coercion is present, and (3) a "not insubstantial" amount of interstate commerce is affected. If this test is satisfied, the arrangement is per se illegal and the defendant is not permitted to introduce evidence justifying the tie-in.

In 1984, however, four of the nine Supreme Court justices rejected the notion that a tie-in could be declared illegal per se without considering its actual effects on a market.

JEFFERSON PARISH HOSPITAL DISTRICT NO. 2 v. HYDE
United States Supreme Court, 466 U.S. 2 (1984)

Respondent Edwin G. Hyde, a board-certified anesthesiologist, applied for admission to the medical staff of East Jefferson Hospital. Despite approval recommended by both the credentials committee and the medical staff executive committee, the hospital board denied the application because the hos-

---

pital was a party to a contract providing that all anesthesiological services required by the hospital's patients be performed by Roux & Associates, a professional medical corporation. Respondent then commenced this action seeking a declaratory judgment that the contract is unlawful and an injunction ordering petitioners to appoint him to the hospital staff. After trial, the District Court denied relief, finding that the anticompetitive consequences of the Roux contract were minimal and outweighed by benefits in the form of improved patient care. The Court of Appeals reversed because it was persuaded that the contract was illegal per se. Jefferson Parish Hospital appeals to the U.S. Supreme Court.

Justice Stevens delivered the opinion of the Court.

. . . .

There are at least 20 hospitals in the New Orleans metropolitan area and about 70 percent of the patients living in Jefferson Parish go to hospitals other than East Jefferson. Because it regarded the entire New Orleans metropolitan area as the relevant geographic market in which hospitals compete, this evidence convinced the District Court that East Jefferson does not possess any significant "market power"; therefore it concluded that petitioners could not use the Roux contract to anticompetitive ends. The same evidence led the Court of Appeals to draw a different conclusion. Noting that 30 percent of the residents of the parish go to East Jefferson Hospital, and that in fact "patients tend to choose hospitals by location rather than price or quality," the Court of Appeals concluded that the relevant geographic market was the East Bank of Jefferson Parish. . . .

The Court of Appeals held that the case involves a "tying arrangement" because the "users of the hospital's operating rooms (the tying product) are also compelled to purchase the hospital's chosen anesthesia service (the tied product)." Having defined the relevant geographic market for the tying product as the East Bank of Jefferson Parish, the court held that the hospital possessed "sufficient market power in the tying market to coerce purchasers of the tied product." . . . [T]he tying arrangement was therefore illegal "per se."

Certain types of contractual arrangements are deemed unreasonable as a matter of law. . . . A price-fixing agreement between competitors is the classic example of such an arrangement. . . .

. . . .

Our cases have concluded that the essential characteristic of an invalid tying arrangement lies in the seller's exploitation of its control over the tying product to force the buyer into the purchase of a tied product that the buyer either did not want at all, or might have preferred to purchase elsewhere on different terms. . . .

Accordingly, we have condemned tying arrangements when the seller has some special ability—usually called "market power"—to force a purchaser to do something that he would not do in a competitive market. When "forcing" occurs, our cases have found the tying arrangement to be unlawful.

. . . .

Per se condemnation—condemnation without inquiry into actual market conditions—is only appropriate if the existence of forcing is probable. . . . When the seller's share of the market is high, or when the seller offers a unique product that competitors are not able to offer, the Court has held that the likelihood that market power exists and is being used to restrain competition in a separate market is sufficient to make per se condemnation appropriate. . . . When, however, the seller does not have either the degree or the kind of market power that enables him to force customers to purchase a second, unwanted product in order to obtain the tying product, an antitrust violation can be established only by evidence of an unreasonable restraint on competition in the relevant market.

. . . .

The question remains whether this arrangement involves the use of market power to force patients to buy services they would not otherwise purchase. Respondent's only basis for invoking the per se rule against tying and thereby avoiding analysis of actual market conditions is by relying on the preference of persons residing in Jefferson Parish to go to East Jefferson, the closest hospital. A preference of this kind, however, is not necessarily probative of significant market power.

Seventy percent of the patients residing in Jefferson Parish enter hospitals other than East Jefferson. Thus East Jefferson's "dominance" over persons residing in Jefferson Parish is far from overwhelming. The fact that a substantial majority of the parish's residents elect not to enter East Jefferson means that the geographic data do not establish the kind of dominant market position that obviates the need for further inquiry into actual competitive conditions. . . .

. . . The record therefore does not provide a basis for applying the per se rule against tying to this arrangement.

In order to prevail in the absence of per se liability, respondent has the burden of proving that the Roux contract violated the Sherman Act because it unreasonably restrained competition. That burden necessarily involves an inquiry into the actual effect of the exclusive contract on competition among anesthesiologists. . . . There is, however, insufficient evidence in this record to provide a basis for finding that the Roux contract, as it actually operates in the market, has unreasonably restrained competition. . . . The evidence indicates that some surgeons and patients preferred respondent's services to those of Roux, but there is no evidence that any patient who was sophisticated enough to know the difference between two anesthesiologists was not also able to go to a hospital that would provide him with the anesthesiologist of his choice.

In sum, all that the record establishes is that the choice of anesthesiologists at East Jefferson has been limited to one of the four doctors who are associated with Roux and therefore have staff privileges. . . . Without a showing of actual adverse effect on competition, respondent cannot make out a case under the antitrust laws, and no such showing has been made.

. . . Accordingly, the judgment of the Court of Appeals is reversed, and the case is remanded to that court for further proceedings consistent with this opinion.

. . . .

Justice O'Connor, with whom The Chief Justice, Justice Powell, and Justice Rehnquist join, concurring in the judgment.

. . . I concur in the Court's decision to reverse but write separately to explain why I believe the hospital-Roux contract, whether treated as effecting a tie between services provided to patients, or as an exclusive dealing arrangement between the hospital and certain anesthesiologists, is properly analyzed under the rule of reason.

. . . .

. . . In practice, a tie has been illegal only if the seller is shown to have "sufficient economic power with respect to the tying product to appreciably restrain free competition in the market for the tied product. . . ." Without "control or dominance over the tying product," the seller could not use the tying product as "an effectual weapon to pressure buyers into taking the tied item," so that any restraint of trade would be "insignificant." The Court has never been willing to say of tying arrangements, as it has of price fixing, division of markets, and other agreements subject to *per se* analysis, that they are always illegal, without proof of market power or anticompetitive effect.

The *"per se"* doctrine in tying cases has thus always required an elaborate inquiry into the economic effects of the tying arrangement. As a result, tying doctrine incurs the costs of a rule-of-reason approach without achieving its benefits: the doctrine calls for the extensive and time-consuming economic analysis characteristic of the rule of reason, but then may be interpreted to prohibit arrangements that economic analysis would show to be beneficial. . . .

The time has therefore come to abandon the *"per se"* label and refocus the inquiry on the adverse economic effects, and the potential economic benefits, that the tie may have. . . .

. . . .

The ultimate decision whether a tie-in is illegal under the antitrust laws should depend upon the demonstrated economic effects of the challenged agreement. It may, for example, be entirely innocuous that the seller exploits its control over the tying product to "force" the buyer to purchase the tied product. For when the seller exerts market power only in the tying-product market, it makes no difference to him or his customers whether he exploits that power by raising the price of the tying product or by "forcing" customers to buy a tied product. On the other hand, tying may make the provision of packages of goods and services more efficient. A tie-in should be condemned only when its anticompetitive impact outweighs its contribution to efficiency.

. . . .

. . . [T]ying here cannot increase the seller's already absolute power over the volume of production of the tied product, which is an inevitable consequence of the fact that very few patients will choose to undergo surgery without receiving anesthesia. The hospital-Roux contract therefore has little potential to harm the patients. On the other side of the balance, the District Court found, and the Court of Appeals did not dispute, that the tie-in conferred significant benefits upon the hospital and the patients that it served.

The tie-in improves patient care and permits more efficient hospital operation in a number of ways. From the viewpoint of hospital management, the tie-in ensures 24-hour anesthesiology coverage, aids in standardization of procedures and efficient use of equipment, facilitates flexible scheduling of operations, and permits the hospital more effectively to monitor the quality of anesthesiological services. . . . Such an arrangement, which has little anticompetitive effect and achieves substantial benefits in the provision of care to patients, is hardly one that the antitrust law should condemn. This conclusion reaffirms our threshold determination that the joint provision of hospital services and anesthesiology should not be viewed as involving a tie between distinct products, and therefore should require no additional scrutiny under the antitrust law.

Case Questions

1. What are the essential characteristics of an unlawful tying arrangement?

2. Under what circumstances would applying the *"per se"* rule to a tying arrangement be justified?

3. Upon what basis did the majority conclude that this arrangement did not violate the antitrust laws?

4. In what instances would the concurring justices find that an arrangement was an illegal tying arrangement?

Exclusive Dealing

In **exclusive dealing,** a supplier and a buyer (either a wholesaler or retailer) agree that the latter will not buy certain kinds of products from anyone else. One kind of exclusive dealing is a *requirements contract,* in which customers agree to fill all or part of their buying needs through a particular supplier, who agrees in turn to meet those needs. The dangers of exclusive dealing are similar

exclusive dealing Agreement between buyer and seller that the buyer will not purchase certain kinds of products from any other firm, thus foreclosing access to other suppliers

to those of tie-ins: Suppliers may force buyers to purchase more than they need or may deny competing suppliers access to potential buyers.

The effect on competition of exclusive dealing is similar to that of vertical mergers: It threatens third parties by foreclosing access to suppliers or sales outlets. As early as 1949, however, Justice Felix Frankfurter noted that exclusive dealing offered benefits to the public, in contrast to ties (*Standard Oil Co. of California v. United States*, 337 U.S. 293). It can, for example, promote competition by lowering costs, and it can also protect suppliers from "interbrand free riding"—that is, the practice of making one brand benefit from the facilities or promotion efforts of a competing brand. Suppose, for example, that a firm which does not have an exclusive deal with its sales outlets advertises their locations in a particular area. Nothing prevents customers attracted to the stores by the ad from buying a competing brand.

Like tie-ins, exclusive deals may violate Section 1 of the Sherman Act, Section 3 of the Clayton Act, or both. They are also covered by Section 5 of the Federal Trade Commission Act (*see* Chapter 18). The question is whether, under the Clayton Act, the dealing lessens competition or, under the Sherman Act, is an unreasonable restraint of trade.

THE CURRENT STANDARD. The current standard in exclusive-dealing cases has arguably been established by the FTC in its unanimous 1982 opinion upholding the exclusive dealing between Beltone Electronic Corporation and seven to eight percent of the nation's hearing-aid retailers. The decision called for full-fledged market analysis. According to the Court, the degree to which the exclusive dealerships foreclosed competition was only "one of several variables to be weighed." The other factors were "market definition, . . . the duration of the contracts, the extent to which entry is deterred, and the reasonable justifications, if any, for the exclusivity."

COURT DECISIONS. Like tie-ins, exclusive dealing is possible only if the seller has the power to impose it. In 1922, for instance, forty percent of all stores selling patterns for women's and children's clothing had agreed to exclusive contracts with Standard Fashion Co., whose patterns were in special demand. The contracts stated that the stores would not carry competing patterns.

The Supreme Court argued that the contracts tended to create a monopoly: In a town with a single store selling patterns, no brand other than Standard Fashion would be available if the store agreed to the exclusive contract. Competing brands were foreclosed access to forty percent of the stores buying patterns—and possibly to the most desirable stores. The Court predicted a snowball effect: Shops would feel compelled to sign exclusive contracts because Standard would be more widely available—and therefore familiar—than other brands; the more stores that signed such contracts, the more other stores would feel forced to follow suit.

In *Tampa Electric Company v. Nashville Coal Company* (365 U.S. 320 [1961]), the Court reaffirmed the market-analysis approach by upholding a twenty-year requirement contract for coal (even though $120 million was involved), because the contract foreclosed less than one percent of the coal market. Eventually, *Tampa* led to general use of a rule-of-reason approach and the requirement that at least fifteen percent of the market must be foreclosed by an exclusive-dealing arrangement before it should be legally condemned.

■ **Concept Check 17-3   Tie-Ins and Exclusive Dealing**

- What is the current legal standard for defining *tie-ins* involving goods and commodities?

- Describe an *exclusive-dealing contract*. What factors do the courts currently consider in defining such a contract?

- In what sense can an exclusive-dealing contract contribute to the creation of a monopoly?

■ PRICE DISCRIMINATION:
THE ROBINSON-PATMAN ACT

Section 2 of the Clayton Act is a separate provision that deals with **price discrimination**. Its purpose is to prevent sellers from charging different customers different prices for the same commodity as part of a scheme to lessen competition.

Price discrimination, like tie-ins and exclusive dealing, can often be attacked either as an attempt to monopolize under the Sherman Act or as an unfair method of competition under the FTC Act. However, the antitrust law that addresses it most directly is Section 2 of the Clayton Act as amended by the **Robinson-Patman Act** of 1936.

The main forces behind the 1936 Robinson-Patman Act were small-business groups concerned about competition at the buyer's level. Before it was amended, the Clayton Act permitted prices to reflect "differences in the grade, quantity or quality of the commodity *sold*." This provision may sound reasonable when considering grade (as in grades of maple syrup from A to C or grades of meat) or quality. However, the reference to "quantity" meant that *bulk rates* could act as camouflage for discriminatory pricing. Although there are good reasons for bulk rates if a supplier's marginal costs are related to the size of a sale, the Clayton Act, as written, permitted differences in price that were not so justified.

Congress thus amended Section 2(a) to declare it unlawful to discriminate in price if the effect would be to "injure, destroy or prevent competition with any person . . . who receives the benefit of such discrimination, or with customers of either of them." Such discrimination becomes a prima facie violation of the act.

Competitive Injury

Illegal price discrimination injures competition at two levels. Injury among sellers is the *primary-line effect*. Injury among buyers is the *secondary-line effect*.

PRIMARY-LINE INJURY.   An injury to competition at the seller's level is usually inflicted by a large seller on a small one. Typically, it also involves a *seller* who charges different prices in different geographic market areas. **Predatory pricing**, which was once considered quite common, usually occurred when a national firm targeted certain geographic markets for cut rates intended to hurt local competition. Because the large firm had "deep pockets," it could absorb losses longer than small local firms.

price discrimination   Scheme to lessen competition by charging different customers different prices for the same commodity

Robinson–Patman Act   1936 amendment to the *Clayton Act* that outlaws specific practices relating to *price discrimination*

predatory pricing   Practice whereby a firm with a strong market position cuts rates in certain geographic markets in order to hurt local competition (*see also* Chapter 16)

Examine the relationship illustrated in Figure 17-2. Suppose that Smith Soap Co. sells its soap to Iowa distributors for 50 cents a bar. Jones Soap Co., trying to break into the Iowa market, may offer Iowans soap at 40 cents while selling the same soap in Nebraska (a place where Smith and Jones do not compete) for 50 cents a bar. In a predatory-pricing suit, Smith would probably be the plaintiff.

Jones has not broken the law by underselling Smith: Competition is legal. Jones, however, may have broken the law by charging Nebraska distributors unfairly. You may argue that Nebraskans have not been injured unless they are competing with Iowans. But if Jones has market power in Nebraska, the company may raise the price of soap there to 60 cents in order to pay for temporary losses in Iowa.

Predatory pricing of this kind probably will not benefit Iowans for long. For example, if Smith Soap Co. fails or merges with Jones, the predator may obtain market power in Iowa, especially if the Iowa market presents significant barriers to entry. To make up for its former loss (if any) and take advantage of its power, Jones may then raise the price of soap in Iowa to 55 cents. This kind of predatory pricing, therefore, can be prosecuted under the Sherman Act as an attempt to *monopolize*.

Another form of predatory pricing is *underselling* a rival's price to one customer at the same time that you are charging another customer a higher price for the same product. A predatory firm may also *subsidize* one product at the expense of other products it produces, with the goal of driving single-product firms out of the market. However, as long as this practice does not involve selling the same product at different prices to different customers, the firm is safe from prosecution under the Clayton Act.

The **Utah Pie** *Case.* So far, there is no clear decision setting forth the proper standard for judging when competition among buyers has been damaged by price differences. Not surprisingly, the problem has been to distinguish between legal price competition and illegal predatory pricing. One of the most significant—and most hotly criticized—decisions awarded damages to a Salt Lake City frozen-pie manufacturer who charged three nationally based rivals with predatory pricing. Despite the injury claimed, the plaintiff had doubled its sales and net worth and remained the leader in the market. Excerpts from this decision follow. Issues in predatory pricing that have arisen in the wake of the *Utah Pie* case are discussed in this chapter's ETHICAL ENVIRONMENT box.

FIGURE 17-2 Discriminatory Pricing (I)

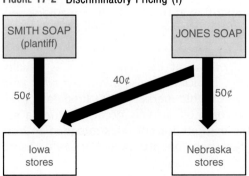

The Standard in Predatory Pricing A contemporary caricature suggests the power wielded by John D. Rockefeller and the Standard Oil Company over the U.S. oil-refining industry. In 1870, Rockefeller and his partners founded the Standard Oil Company of Ohio—proprietor of drilling, storage, and pipeline facilities and soon one of the largest refining companies in the country. What Rockefeller perceived were conditions of fierce competition not only in the oil-refining industry but in the railroad industry as well. He thus began reaching agreements with certain railroads to transport huge shipments of Standard Oil products in return for rebates that actually reduced the rates paid by Standard below those published by the railroad carriers. As Standard prospered and competitors floundered and disappeared, Rockefeller's competitive advantage naturally increased. Two years after its founding, Standard controlled about a fourth of the nation's entire refining capacity. By 1880, that figure had skyrocketed to almost 95 percent, and two years later, when Standard Oil had consolidated ownership of the securities of all its subsidiaries, the company had literally satisfied the definition of a *trust*. The courts of Ohio dissolved the Rockefeller trust on the ground that it was a monopoly constructed to control prices, but Rockefeller reorganized in New Jersey, where the law permitted the formation of "holding companies." In 1911, the U.S. Supreme Court finally ordered the Standard Trust dissolved into competing business units.

UTAH PIE CO. v. CONTINENTAL BAKING CO.
Uunited States Supreme Court, 386 U.S. 685 (1967)

Petitioner Utah Pie Company brought this suit for treble damages and injunction under Sections 4 and 16 of the Clayton Act against respondent Continental Baking Company. The complaint charged a conspiracy under Sections 1 and 2 of the Sherman Act, and violations of Section 2(a) of the Clayton Act as amended by the Robinson-Patman Act. The jury found for respondent on the conspiracy charge and for petitioner on the price discrimination charge. Judgment was entered for petitioner for damages and attorneys' fees. The Court of Appeals reversed, holding that the evidence against respondent was not sufficient to support a finding of probable injury to competition within the meaning of § 2(a). Certiorari was granted to petitioner.

Mr. Justice White delivered the opinion of the Court.

. . . .

The product involved is frozen dessert pies—apple, cherry, boysenberry, peach, pumpkin, and mince. The period covered by the suit comprised the years 1958, 1959, and 1960 and the first eight months of 1961. Petitioner is a Utah corporation which for 30 years has been baking pies in its plant in Salt Lake City and selling them in Utah and surrounding States. It entered the frozen pie business in late 1957. It was immediately successful with its new line and built a new plant in Salt Lake City in 1958. The frozen pie market was a rapidly expanding one. . . . Utah Pie's share of this market in those years was 66.5%, 34.3%, 45.5%, and 45.3% respectively, its sales volume steadily increasing over the four years. Its financial position also improved. . . . Its net worth increased from $31,651.98 on October 31, 1957, to $68,802.13 on October 31, 1961. . . .

. . . [Respondent] is a large company and . . . is a major factor in the frozen pie market. . . .

. . . .

The major competitive weapon in the Utah market was price. The location of petitioner's plant gave it natural advantages in the Salt Lake City marketing area and it entered the market at a price below the then going prices for [respondent's] comparable pies. For most of the period involved here its prices were the lowest in the Salt Lake City market. It was, however, challenged by . . . [respondent] at one time or another and for varying periods. There was ample evidence to show that . . . [respondent] contributed to what proved to be a deteriorating price structure over the period covered by this suit, and . . . in the course of the ongoing price competition sold frozen pies in the Salt Lake market at prices lower than it sold pies of like grade and quality in other markets considerably closer to its plants. . . .

. . . .

Petitioner's case against Continental is not complicated. Continental was a substantial factor in the market in 1957. But its sales of frozen 22-ounce dessert pies, sold under the "Morton" brand, amounted to only 1.3% of the market in 1958, 2.9% in 1959, and 1.8% in 1960. . . . Effective for the last two weeks of June it offered its 22-ounce frozen apple pies in the Utah area at $2.85 per dozen. It was then selling the same pies at substantially higher prices in other markets. The Salt Lake City price was less than its direct cost plus an allocation for overhead. . . . Continental's total sales of frozen pies increased from 3,350 dozen in 1960 to 18,000 dozen in 1961. Its market share increased from 1.8% in 1960 to 8.3% in 1961. The Court of Appeals concluded that Continental's conduct had had only minimal effect, that it had not injured or weakened Utah Pie as a competitor, that it had not substantially lessened competition and that there was no reasonable possibility that it would do so in the future.

We . . . differ with the Court of Appeals. Its opinion that Utah was not damaged as a competitive force apparently rested on the fact that Utah's sales volume continued to climb in 1961 and on the court's own factual conclusion that Utah was not deprived of any pie business which it otherwise might have had. But this retrospective assessment fails to note that Continental's discriminatory below-cost price caused Utah Pie to reduce its price to $2.75. . . . [The jury could] have reasonably concluded that a competitor who is forced to reduce his price to a new all-time low in a market of declining prices will in time feel the financial pinch and will be a less effective competitive force.

. . . We think there was sufficient evidence from which the jury could find a violation of § 2(a) by Continental.

. . . .

Section 2(a) does not forbid price competition which will probably injure or lessen competition by eliminating competitors, discouraging entry into the market or enhancing the market shares of the dominant sellers. But Congress has established some ground rules for the game. Sellers may not sell like goods to different purchasers at different prices if the result may be to injure competition in either the sellers' or the buyers' market unless such discriminations are justified as permitted by the Act. This case concerns the sellers' market. In this context, the Court of Appeals placed heavy emphasis on the fact that Utah Pie constantly increased its sales volume and continued to make a profit. But we disagree with its apparent view that there is no reasonably possible injury to competition as long as the volume of sales in a particular market is expanding and at least some of the competitors in the market continue to operate at a profit. Nor do we think that the Act only comes into play to regulate the conduct of price discriminators when their discriminatory prices consistently undercut other competitors. . . . In this case, the evidence shows a drastically declining price structure which the jury could rationally attribute to continued or sporadic price discrimination. The jury was entitled to conclude that "the effect of such discrimination" by [respondent], "may be substantially to lessen competition . . . or to injure, destroy, or prevent competition with any person who either grants or knowingly receives the benefit of such discrimination. . . ." The statutory test is one that necessarily looks forward on the basis of proven conduct in the past. Proper application of that standard here requires reversal of the judgment of the Court of Appeals.

Case Questions

1. Can there be damage or injury to competition even though the volume of sales in a market is expanding and some competitors continue to operate at a profit?

2. How was Utah Pie damaged as a competitive force by Continental's conduct?

3. How does illegal predatory pricing differ from legal price competition?

THE ETHICAL ENVIRONMENT
Predatory Pricing after Utah Pie

Predatory pricing is a tactic designed to achieve market dominance and higher profits in the long term through short-term price reductions that are intended to drive existing competitors out of the market, to dissuade potential competitors from entering the fray, or both. Thus, a predator will sustain an economic loss in the hope that, after a certain period of time, it will be the only remaining player in a market—a player who is thereafter free to raise prices without having to worry about being undercut by competitors.

True predatory pricing is clearly anticompetitive and, as a result, arguably falls within the scope of antitrust laws. Indeed, companies believing themselves to be victims of predatory pricing have sued alleged predators both under Section 2 of the Sherman Antitrust Act, which is aimed at attempts to monopolize, and the Robinson-Patman Act, which bars pricing designed to lessen competition or promote monopolization.

It is often quite tricky, however, to determine when a firm's pricing reduction is good business and fair competition and when it is unfair competition intended to eliminate competitors and gain market control. Although the Supreme Court sought in Utah Pie to make this task easier by creating an intent-based standard, some observers have argued that the decision made the situation more problematic by giving juries the impossible task of trying to read the minds of companies accused of predatory pricing. To make matters even worse, critics have charged that judicially created rules designed to simplify the situation after Utah Pie have actually made it easier for firms to get away with predatory pricing.

Since Utah Pie, courts have generally employed more clear-cut methods to determine whether a firm has engaged in predatory pricing. Several of these methods begin by calculating a baseline cost for a commodity: Pricing above this figure is presumed to be legal, while pricing below it is presumed to be illegal unless the accused predator can prove otherwise.

A particularly controversial method, which was created by the Seventh Circuit Court of Appeals, requires that a plaintiff alleging predatory pricing prove that a defendant has a market share of at least thirty percent. In the absence of such evidence, according to the appeals-court judge, there is inadequate proof that a defendant has the market power needed to recoup the short-term losses resulting from a price reduction. This guideline rejects entirely the relevance of evidence related to the defendant's intent.

Not surprisingly, many law and economic theorists think that the court's approach is a step in the right direction because it reaches only those situations in which monopolization is truly a threat: Proponents of such an approach contend that predatory pricing can sometimes result in more efficient markets and that the goal of antitrust law should only be to promote economic efficiency.

Critics at the other end of the spectrum have charged that the court's method is unsound from the standpoint of economics and public policy. First, they charge that firms with less than thirty-percent market dominance can benefit from predatory pricing—and that the rule, therefore, irrationally reaches only those firms with a greater market share. Second, critics complain that the appeals-court ruling favors defendants by saddling plaintiffs with difficult and costly burdens of proof with respect to market share. Finally, this guideline, according to its critics, is inconsistent with the underlying public-policy goals of antitrust law—namely, to maintain diverse markets comprised of many small businesses even if it means higher prices for consumers.

SECONDARY-LINE INJURY. The plaintiffs in secondary-line injury cases are buyers who are charged more than their rivals, as illustrated in Figure 17-3: Because Wiggins, who pays less for soap than Thompson, can afford to undercut Thompson, Thompson's business begins to fail. The injury is done both to Thompson, as an unfavored buyer, and to Thompson's customers.

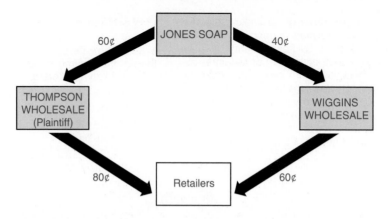

FIGURE 17-3 Discriminatory Pricing (II)

Price Discrimination: The Plaintiff's Burden

Recall that a *prima facie case* is one in which the facts are presumed to be true unless disproved. Pursuant to both statute and case law, in order to make out such a case in a civil action for price discrimination, the plaintiff must prove the following facts:

1. There must be actual sales made to at least two different customers. Offers to sell, licenses, leases, consignments, and loans are not "sales" in the legal sense of the word.
2. The sales must be nearly simultaneous. The fourth proviso of Section 2(a) states that price changes in response to "changing conditions in the market for or marketability" of the product are legal.
3. Tangible goods must be sold, not services nor something intangible like television signals.
4. Both the sales must involve goods of like grade or kind and quality in the same amounts. However, superficial differences (such as labeling or trademarks) are not relevant. Thus, it is illegal for the same canned evaporated milk to be sold at different prices under different labels (*FTC v. Borden Co.*, 383 U.S. 637 [1966]).
5. Both the sales must involve direct differences in price, or indirect differences in areas such as credit terms, accompanying services like delivery, or return privileges.[4]

Price Discrimination: Defenses

The Robinson-Patman Act outlines two defenses that, if proven by a defendant, will result in a finding of no price discrimination: (1) the price meets that of a competitor and (2) the price is justified by differences in costs.

MEETING THE COMPETITION. According to Section 2(a), sellers may refute a prima facie case of price discrimination by showing that they sought "in good faith to meet an equally low price of a competitor." In short, sellers may compete, as in

---

[4] This description of the prima facie case is based on Lawrence A. Sullivan, *Antitrust* (West, 1977), p. 680.

the example illustrated in Figure 17-4. Jones Soap is charging Nebraskans more than Iowans, but only in order to meet Smith's price in Iowa.

Defining "Good Faith." In applying this provision, however, the courts must define and identify discriminating "in good faith." In 1945, for example, the Supreme Court declared that the seller pleading a meeting-the-competition defense must have "first-hand" knowledge of an offer of a lower price from a rival (*FTC v. A.E. Staley Manufacturing Co.*, 324 U.S. 746). In 1951, the Court held that the defense is absolute, even if competition has been lessened by the defendant's action (*Standard Oil Co. v. FTC*, 340 U.S. 231). In 1963, it held that a low price to meet the competition is legal if a customer's *rival* has obtained this price either through vertical integration or from its supplier (*FTC v. Sun Oil Co.*, 371 U.S. 505). Finally, in 1983, the Court set forth a long list of rules outlining conditions under which the defense applies. The most important point was that it may be used in cases involving efforts either to gain new customers or to keep current customers (*Falls City Industries, Inc. v. Vanco Beverage, Inc.*, 460 U.S. 428). In the example above, Jones is trying to gain a customer. (The question of the meeting-the-competition defense and public policy is addressed in this chapter's YOU DECIDE feature.)

MEETING ONE'S COSTS. According to Section 2(b) of the Robinson-Patman Act, differences in price may be justified by differences in the seller's costs associated with the two separate sales. For instance, delivery costs will probably vary depending on distance and the size of shipments. Such variation can be reflected in prices for individual sales.

The cost-justification defense does not apply to charges made under Sections 2(c), 2(d), and 2(e) regarding brokerage payments, promotional allowances, or other special services favoring certain buyers. When the defense does apply, however, it is difficult to prove. The Supreme Court has permitted customers to be classed into narrowly defined groups for cost analysis. The defense also is more likely to succeed if a cost study was conducted *before* prices were set rather than after. As a practical matter, the cost justification defense is unlikely to serve as a cover-up for attempts to monopolize or lessen competition.

In the following case a gasoline retailer sued Texaco for unlawful price discrimination, which is a secondary-line injury under the Robinson-Patman Act. In response, Texaco did not dispute that it charged different prices. Rather, it asserted that it did not "discriminate" in price within the meaning of the act.

FIGURE 17-4 Pricing to Meet the Competition

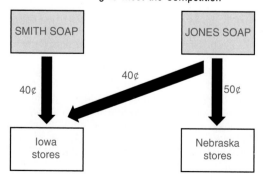

The case of Gerber Products Co. v. Beech-Nut Life Savers, Inc., *which was decided by a New York federal district court in the 1950s, both illustrates how the "meeting-the-competition defense" operates and highlights some interesting questions about the desirability of this defense from the standpoint of public policy.*

Gerber *involved a baby-food price war in California between Gerber, the largest manufacturer of baby foods in the United States, and Beech-Nut, its chief national competitor. In 1949, Beech-Nut entered the California baby-food market, which had been dominated by Gerber since the late 1920s. Beech-Nut's strategy to make a dent in Gerber's share of the California market consisted of a single packaging strategy—glass containers. Gerber's baby food came in tin containers. However, because glass was slightly more expensive than tin, Beech-Nut's baby food entered the market priced slightly higher than Gerber's product.*

Beech-Nut's strategy, however, did not work out as planned: By 1957, the company's share of the market was less than five percent, compared with Gerber's 73 percent, and showed signs of declining even further. In an effort to woo consumers away from Gerber, Beech-Nut bolstered its advertising campaign and reduced its prices to meet those charged by Gerber. Several months later, Gerber reduced its prices to restore the differential that had historically existed between its product, in tin containers, and Beech-Nut's, in the more desirable glass containers. Again, Beech-Nut

dropped its price to meet Gerber's. The second round of price reductions by the two companies meant that both were taking a loss on the sales of their product in California.

Gerber brought an action under Section 2(a) of the Robinson-Patman Act charging that Beech-Nut was selling at unreasonably low prices to destroy competition between the two companies and to eliminate Gerber as a competitor. Beech-Nut invoked the meeting-the-competition defense, asserting that the sole purpose of its price reductions was economic survival in the California baby-food market. Gerber countered that Beech-Nut should not be permitted to hide behind the "meeting-the-competition" defense because, given Beech-Nut's use of higher-priced glass containers, its price reductions were actually designed to undercut Gerber's prices.

The issue before the court was one of good faith: Was Beech-Nut acting in good faith by reducing its prices to meet Gerber's and survive in the California market, or was Beech-Nut's strategy an unfair attempt to drive Gerber out of the market and achieve long-term market domination by temporarily selling at a short-term loss?

The case raises an even deeper question about the meeting-the-competition defense. Does this defense help maintain oligopolies by permitting the few players in a given market to charge the same price for the same product? If so, should we repeal the Robinson-Patman Act or the defense? For further discussion, see p. 655.

TEXACO v. HASBROUCK
United States Supreme Court., 110 S.Ct. 2535 (1990)

Texaco sold gasoline directly to a number of independent retailers in Spokane, Washington, at a certain price, which was referred to as the "retail tank wagon" price (RTW). At the same time, however, Texaco sold gasoline to two distributors at considerable discounts. Between 1972 and 1981, the stations that were supplied by these two distributors experienced dramatic increases in sales, while the retailers supplied by Texaco lost business. These retailers filed an action against Texaco under the Robinson-Patman Act. The district court found in favor of the retailers and awarded treble damages. This award was affirmed on appeal. Texaco brought the matter to the Supreme Court, arguing that its discounts to distributors did not violate the Act because it was not responsible for these distributors' pricing decisions.

Stevens, J., delivered the opinion of the Court. . . .
   Justice STEVENS delivered the opinion of the Court.
   Given the jury's general verdict in favor of respon-

dents, disputed questions of fact have been resolved in their favor. There seems, moreover, to be no serious doubt about the character of the market, Texaco's pricing practices, or the relative importance of Texaco's direct sales to retailers ("through put" business) and its sales to distributors. The principal disputes at trial related to questions of causation and damages.

   Respondents are 12 independent Texaco retailers. They displayed the Texaco trademark, accepted Texaco credit cards, and bought their gasoline products directly from Texaco. Texaco delivered the gasoline to respondents' stations.

   The retail gasoline market in Spokane was highly competitive throughout the damages period, which ran from 1972 to 1981. Stations marketing the nationally advertised Texaco gasoline competed with other major brands as well as with stations featuring independent brands. Moreover, although discounted prices at a nearby Texaco station would have the most obvious impact on a respondent's trade, the cross-city traffic patterns and relatively small size of Spokane produced a city-wide competitive market. Texaco's through put sales in the Spokane market declined from a monthly volume of 569,269 gallons in 1970 to 389,557 gallons in 1975. Texaco's independent retailers' share of the market for Texaco gas declined from 76% to 49%. Seven of the respondents' stations were out of business by the end of 1978.

The respondents tried unsuccessfully to increase their ability to compete with lower priced stations. Some tried converting from full service to self-service stations. Two of the respondents sought to buy their own tank trucks and haul their gasoline from Texaco's supply point, but Texaco vetoed that proposal.

While the independent retailers struggled, two Spokane gasoline distributors supplied by Texaco prospered. Gull Oil Company (Gull) had its headquarters in Seattle and distributed petroleum products in four western States under its own name. In Spokane it purchased its gas from Texaco at prices that ranged from six to four cents below Texaco's RTW price. Gull resold that product under its own name; the fact that it was being supplied by Texaco was not known by either the public or the respondents. In Spokane, Gull supplied about 15 stations; some were "consignment stations" and some were "commission stations." In both situations Gull retained title to the gasoline until it was pumped into a motorist's tank. In the consignment stations, the station operator set the retail prices, but in the commission stations Gull set the prices and paid the operator a commission. Its policy was to price its gasoline at a penny less than the prevailing price for major brands. Gull employed two truck drivers in Spokane who picked up product at Texaco's bulk plant and delivered it to the Gull stations. It also employed one supervisor in Spokane. Apart from its trucks and investment in retail facilities, Gull apparently owned no assets in that market. At least with respect to the commission stations, Gull is fairly characterized as a retailer of gasoline throughout the relevant period.

The Dompier Oil Company (Dompier) started business in 1954 selling Quaker State Motor Oil. In 1960 it became a full line distributor of Texaco products, and by the mid-1970's its sales of gasoline represented over three-quarters of its business. Dompier purchased Texaco gasoline at prices of 3.95¢ to 3.65¢ below the RTW price. Dompier thus paid a higher price than Gull, but Dompier, unlike Gull, resold its gas under Texaco brand names. It supplied about eight to ten Spokane retail stations. In the period prior to October 1974, two of those stations were owned by the president of Dompier but the others were independently operated. In the early 1970's, Texaco representatives encouraged Dompier to enter the retail business directly, and in 1974 and 1975 it acquired four stations. Dompier's president estimated at trial that the share of its total gasoline sales made at retail during the middle 1970's was "probably 84 to 90 percent."

Like Gull, Dompier picked up Texaco's product at the Texaco bulk plant and delivered directly to retail outlets. Unlike Gull, Dompier owned a bulk storage facility, but it was seldom used because its capacity was less than that of many retail stations. Again unlike Gull, Dompier received from Texaco the equivalent of the common carrier rate for delivering the gasoline product to the retail outlets. Thus, in addition to its discount from the RTW price, Dompier made a profit on its hauling function.

The stations supplied by Dompier regularly sold at retail at lower prices than respondents'. Even before Dompier directly entered the retail business in 1974, its customers were selling to consumers at prices barely above the RTW price. Dompier's sales volume increased continuously and substantially throughout the relevant period. Between 1970 and 1975 its monthly sales volume increased from 155,152 gallons to 462,956 gallons; this represented an increase from 20.7% to almost 50% of Texaco's sales in Spokane.

There was ample evidence that Texaco executives were well aware of Dompier's dramatic growth and believed that it was attributable to "the magnitude of the distributor discount and the hauling allowance." In response to complaints from individual respondents about Dompier's aggressive pricing, however, Texaco representatives professed that they "couldn't understand it."

. . . Texaco contended that the special prices to Gull and Dompier were justified by cost savings, were the product of a good faith attempt to meet competition, and were lawful "functional discounts."

. . . It is appropriate to begin our consideration of the legal status of functional discounts by examining the language of the Act. Section 2(a) provides in part:

> "It shall be unlawful for any person engaged in commerce, in the course of such commerce, either directly or indirectly, to discriminate in price between different purchasers of commodities of like grade and quality, where either or any of the purchases involved in such discrimination are in commerce, where such commodities are sold for use, consumption, or resale within the United States or any Territory thereof or the District of Columbia or any insular possession or other place under the jurisdiction of the United States, and where the effect of such discrimination may be substantially to lessen competition or tend to create a monopoly in any line of commerce, or two injure, destroy, or prevent competition with any person who either grants or knowingly receives the benefit of such discrimination, or with customers of either of them. . . ."

The Act contains no express reference to functional discounts. It does contain two affirmative defenses that provide protection for two categories of discounts—those that are justified by savings in the seller's cost of manufacture, delivery or sale, and those that represent a good faith response to the equally low prices of a competitor. As the case comes to us, neither of those defenses is available to Texaco.

In other to establish a violation of the Act, respondents had the burden of proving four facts: (1) that Texaco's sales to Gull and Dompier were made in interstate commerce; (2) that the gasoline sold to them was of the same grade and quality as that sold to respondents; (3) that Texaco discriminated in price as between Gull and Dompier on the one hand and respondents on the other; and (4) that the discrimination had a prohibited effect on competition. Moreover, for each respondent to recover damages, he had the burden of proving the extent of his actual injuries.

The first two elements of respondents' case are not disputed in this Court, and we do not understand Texaco to be challenging the sufficiency of respondents' proof of damages. Texaco does argue, however, that although it charged different prices, it did not "discriminate in price" within the meaning of the Act, and that, at least to the extent that Gull and Dompier acted as wholesalers, the price differentials did not injure competition. We consider the two arguments separately.

Texaco's first argument would create a blanket exemption for all functional discounts. Indeed, carried to its logical conclusion, it would exempt all price differentials except those given to competing purchasers. The primary basis for Texaco's argument is the following comment by Congressman Utterback, an active sponsor of the Act:

> "In its meaning as simple English, a discrimination is more than a mere difference. Underlying the meaning of the word is the idea that some relationship exists between the parties to the discrimination which entitles them to equal treatment, whereby the difference granted to one casts some burden or disadvantage upon the other. . . . But where no such relationship exists, where the goods are sold in different markets and the conditions affecting those markets set different price levels for them, the sale to different customers at those different prices would not constitute a discrimination within the meaning of this bill."

We have previously considered this excerpt from the legislative history, and have refused to draw from it the conclusion which Texaco proposes. Although the excerpt does support Texaco's argument, we remain persuaded that the argument is foreclosed by the text of the Act itself. In the context of a statute that plainly reveals a concern with competitive consequences at different levels of distribution, and carefully defines specific affirmative defenses, it would be anomalous to assume that the Congress intended the term "discriminate" to have such a limited meaning. . . .

In *FTC v. Morton Salt Co.,* we held that an injury to competition may be inferred from evidence that some purchasers had to pay their supplier "substantially more for their goods than their competitors had to pay." Texaco, supported by the United States and the Federal Trade Commission as *amici curiae,* (the Government), argues that this presumption should not apply to differences between prices charged to wholesalers and those charged to retailers. Moreover, they argue that it would be inconsistent with fundamental antitrust policies to construe the Act as requiring a seller to control his customers' resale prices. The seller should not be held liable for the independent pricing decisions of his customers.

After observing that suppliers ought not to be liable for the independent pricing decisions of their buyers, and that without functional discounts distributors might go uncompensated for services they performed, the Committee wrote:

> "The Committee recommends, therefore, that suppliers granting functional discounts either to single-function or to integrated buyers should not be held responsible for any consequences of their customers' pricing tactics. Price cutting at the resale level is not in fact, and should not be held in law, 'the effect of' a differential that merely accords due recognition and reimbursement for actual marketing functions. The price cutting of a customer who receives this type of differential results from his own independent decision to lower price and operate at a lower profit margin per unit. The legality or illegality of this price cutting must be judged by the usual legal tests. In any event, consequent injury or lack of injury should not be the supplier's legal concern.

> "On the other hand, the law should tolerate no subterfuge. For instance, where a wholesaler-retailer *buys* only part of his goods as a wholesaler, he must not claim a functional discount on all. Only to the extent that a buyer *actually* performs certain functions, assuming all the risk, investment, and costs involved, should he legally qualify for a functional discount. Hence a distributor should be eligible for a discount corresponding to any part of the function he actually performs on that part of the goods for which he performs it."

We generally agree with this description of the legal status of functional discounts. A supplier need not satisfy the rigorous requirements of the cost justification defense in order to prove that a particular functional discount is reasonable and accordingly did not cause any substantial lessening of competition between a wholesaler's customers and the supplier's direct customers. The record in this case, however, adequately supports the finding that Texaco violated the Act.

The hypothetical predicate for the Committee's entire discussion of functional discounts is a price differential "that merely accords due recognition and reimbursement for actual marketing functions." Such a discount is not illegal. In this case, however, both the District Court and the Court of Appeals concluded that even without viewing the evidence in the light most favorable to the respondents, there was no substantial evidence indicating that the discounts to Gull and Dompier constituted a reasonable reimbursement for the value to Texaco of their actual marketing functions. Indeed, Dompier was separately compensated for its hauling function, and neither Gull nor Dompier maintained any significant storage facilities.

Despite this extraordinary absence of evidence to connect the discount to any savings enjoyed by Texaco, Texaco contends that the decision of the Court of Appeals cannot be affirmed without departing "from established precedent, from practicality, and from Congressional intent." Brief for Petitioner 14. This argument assumes that holding suppliers liable for a gratuitous functional discount is somehow a novel practice. That assumption is flawed.

[10] As we have already observed, the "due recognition and reimbursement" concept endorsed in the Attorney General's Committee's study would not countenance a functional discount completely untethered to either the supplier's savings or the wholesaler's costs. The longstanding principle that functional discounts provide no safe harbor from the Act is likewise evident from the practice of the Federal Trade Commission, which has, while permitting legitimate functional discounts, proceeded against those discounts which appeared to be subterfuges to avoid the Act's restrictions. . . .

Nor should any reader of the commentary or functional discounts be much surprised by today's result. Commentators have disagreed about the extent to which functional discounts are generally or presumptively allowable under the Robinson–Patman Act. They nevertheless tend to agree that in exceptional cases what is nominally a functional discount may be an unjustifiable price discrimination entirely within the coverage of the Act. . . .

Both Gull and Dompier received the full discount on all their purchases even though most of their volume was resold directly to consumers. The extra margin on those sales obviously enabled them to price aggressively in both their retail and their wholesale marketing. To the extent that Dompier and Gull competed with respondents in the retail market, the presumption of adverse effect on competition becomes all the more appropriate. Their competitive advantage in that market also constitutes evidence tendng to rebut any presumption of legality that would otherwise apply to their wholesale sales.

The evidence indicates, moreover, that Texaco affirmatively encouraged Dompier to expand its retail business and that Texaco was fully informed about the persistent and marketwide consequences of its own pricing policies. Indeed, its own executives recognized that the dramatic impact on the market was almost entirely attributable to the magnitude of the distributor discount and the hauling allowance. Yet at the same time that Texaco was encouraging Dompier to integrate downward, and supplying Dompier with a generous discount useful to such integration, Texaco was inhibiting upward integration by the respondents: two of the respondents sought permission from Texaco to haul their own fuel using their own tankwagons, but Texaco refused. The special facts of this case thus make it peculiarly difficult for Texaco to claim that it is being held liable for the independent pricing decisions of Gull or Dompier. . . .

"The competitive injury component of a Robinson–Patman Act violation is not limited to the injury to competition between the favored and the disfavored purchaser; it also encompasses the injury to competition between their customers." This conclusion is compelled by the statutory language, which specifically encompasses not only the adverse effect of price discrimination on persons who either grant or knowingly receive the benefit of such discrimination, but also on "customers of either of them." Such indirect competitive effects surely may not be presumed automatically in every functional discount setting, and, indeed, one would expect that most functional discounts will be legitimate discounts which do not cause harm to competition. At the least, a functional discount that constitutes a reasonable reimbursement for the purchasers' actual marketing functions will not violate the Act. When a functional discount is legitimate, the inference of injury to competition will simply not arise. Yet it is also true that not every functional discount is entitled to a judgment of legitimacy, and that it will sometimes be possible to produce evidence showing that a particular functional discount caused a price discrimination of the sort the Act prohibits. When such anticompetitive effects are proved—as we believe they were in this case—they are covered by the Act.

Case Questions

1. The Court accepted Texaco's argument that it is not illegal price discrimination to grant "functional discounts" to a buyer who is unrelated to a supplier who reaps some savings from the arrangement. Why then did the Court not find in Texaco's favor?

2. It is curious that Texaco was giving a discount to two independent distributors while charging higher rates to its own retailers. What might explain this practice?

Price Discrimination: Per Se Violations

The Robinson-Patman Act also defines three kinds of *per se* violations in Sections 2(c), 2(d), and 2(e). These involve unfair practices other than direct rebates or discounts on price: *brokerage allowances, promotional allowances,* and *special services* or *side items.*

BROKERAGE ALLOWANCES. Brokers charge a fee or commission, most often to the seller, for arranging a sale. In the early 1930s, large buyers who made purchases without using brokers had been demanding brokerage allowances for doing their own brokering. These allowances were more or less than a broker's fee would have been, depending upon the buyer's bargaining power. Section 2(c) outlaws brokerage allowances, without exception, regardless of the effects on competition.

PROMOTIONAL ALLOWANCES. Buyers who sold retail in the 1930s were also receiving allowances from sellers to cover the costs of promoting the seller's products in advertisements or through store displays and demonstrations. The practice was unfair because only *some* buyers benefited. In addition, when allowances exceeded the costs of the promotion, they acted as indirect rebates. Section 2(d) requires that all payments for services rendered by the buyer be available to *all* buyers on equal terms.

SPECIAL SERVICES. Section 2(e) states that services, or "side items" like displays, must be "accorded to all purchasers on proportionally equal terms"—that is, in proportion to quantity bought. Failure to do so is a violation of the Robinson-Patman Act.[5] Suppose, for example, that some buyers received services from sellers that others did not: The privileged buyers would in effect be getting an indirect rebate equal to the cost of the services.

Evaluating the Robinson-Patman Act

During the 1936 debate in Congress over the Robinson-Patman Act, Representative Emmanuel Celler predicted that "the courts will have the devil's own job to unravel the tangle."[6] He was right. Indeed, Justice Robert Jackson once noted that an appellate court seemed to have thought the law "almost beyond understanding."[7] Nor are judges alone in their confusion. A veritable chorus of scholars has criticized the act as overly technical, poorly written, and hostile to competition. Critics charge that it is hard to interpret and illogical: A law intended to preserve free markets condemns many reasonable forms of price-competition.

Defenders of the Act answer that it is devoted to protecting small businesses even at the expense of competition. According to Robinson-Patman, sameness in prices throughout a market is safe. Any differences must be explained and justified—a provision that discourages active price wars. As attorney Harry L. Shniderman put it, "The act results in 'Dullsville' rather than 'High Noon' in the marketplace."[8]

AWARDS UNDER THE ACT. Price-cutting firms in general most fear expensive civil-damages suit brought by buyers as a way of delaying or avoiding payment for goods delivered. In the past, damages awarded were three times the demonstrated difference in price—regardless of the actual costs, if any, suffered by the plaintiff.[9] Not surprisingly, the prospect of treble-damages suits has had a significant dampening effect on competition. The more unusual the seller's prices, the more vulnerable it will be to these suits. As a result, sellers risk aggressive pricing only when under pressure to do so.

---

[5] Howard, *supra* at n. 2, p. 181.

[6] 80 *Congressional Record* 9419 (1936).

[7] In *FTC v. Ruberoid Co.*, 343 U.S. 470 at 483 (1952).

[8] Harry L. Shniderman, "The Robinson-Patman Act: A Critical Appraisal," 55 *Antitrust Law Journal* 152 (Spring 1986).

[9] *Bruce's Juices, Inc. v. American Can Co.*, 330 U.S. 743 (1947). The formula did not require the plaintiff to prove that the discrimination had actually caused any losses.

However, recent court decisions may go far to check Robinson-Patman's dampening effect on competition. For instance, in *J. Pruett Payne Co. v. Chrysler Motors Corp* (451 U.S. 557 [1981]), the Court unanimously agreed not to apply automatic-damages guidelines.

Given the fundamental change since 1936 in public attitudes toward the giant corporations and chains that were the original targets of Robinson-Patman, such changes may have been inevitable. Giant corporations are no longer the inevitable villains in price discrimination suits. Large firms like Sears, Procter & Gamble, and General Foods have built up substantial good will.

■ *Concept Check 17-4 Price Discrimination: The Robinson-Patman Act*

- Why were the provisions of Robinson-Patman deemed necessary to supplement the Clayton Act?
- Discuss *primary-line* and *secondary-line injury* by giving hypothetical examples of each.
- What criteria must be met in order to establish a prima facie case of *price discrimination*?
- Explain the *meeting-the-competition defense* and the role of *good faith* in the courts' determination of its validity.

You Decide: Answer Discussion
The Baby Food Wars

The court in Gerber v. Beech-Nut *was not persuaded by the plaintiff's claim that Beech-Nut's price reductions were designed to drive it from the California market in order to achieve a monopoly for itself. In reaching the decision, the court relied on several facts. First, it noted that Beech-Nut's price reductions had not resulted in substantial losses for Gerber and that the company still controlled over 70 percent of the market. Second, the court stated that Gerber was unlikely to be driven from the California market by Beech-Nut's pricing moves because it had vast financial resources and was the leading manufacturer of baby food nationwide. Finally, the court did not accept Gerber's argument that Beech-Nut should have to charge more for its product because it came in glass containers. Acceptance of this argu-*ment, the court noted, would discourage companies from improving packaging. Finally, the court stated that Gerber had failed to show that Beech-Nut's price reductions would cause any lessening in competition or that Gerber would be eliminated from the market.*

Thus, it is clear from the court's decision that, in the end, Gerber's size and dominant position in the California baby-food market undercut the plausibility of its argument that Beech-Nut's price reductions were intended to create a monopoly. However, the decision also reveals how the meeting-the-competition defense permits—and might even encourage—the oligopolistic-pricing practices that were one of the evils that the Robinson-Patman Act was intended to address.

SUMMARY

- The *Clayton Act* sought to prohibit *mergers* insofar as they tended to lessen competition. But it said nothing about purchases of some company's assets, rather than its stocks, by another company. In 1950, however, the *Celler-Kefauver Amendment* to the Act targeted purchases of assets as well.
- *Mergers* often create economies of scale. *Horizontal mergers* enlarge firms by joining former competitors. *Vertical mergers* link separate stages in the manufacture or marketing of a product or service. *Conglomerate mergers* link firms in different lines of business and thus help them bear risk through diversification. Often, it is not

obvious how to classify any particular merger. Courts must determine cross-elasticity of supply and demand to define the outer limits of the relevant markets.

- In a horizontal-merger case, the plaintiff seeks to prove that the merger produces *undue concentration* in the relevant market. Under the *foreclosure theory*, a vertical merger threatens competition by blocking third parties' access to suppliers or sales outlets. Conglomerate mergers have been successfully challenged on three grounds: *potential competition, entrenchment,* and *reciprocity.*

- The Clayton Act also outlaws *tie-ins, exclusive dealing,* and *reciprocal deals.* All three potentially harm competition by interfering with the buyer's or seller's freedom of choice. For a tie-in to be illegal, the tied products must be distinct, the seller must have market power in the tying product's market, and the tie-in must affect more than a minimal amount of commerce.

- There have been two very different approaches to merger policy. Advocates of *economic analysis* regard most mergers favorably, insisting that the competitiveness of a market does not depend upon any particular balance of large and small firms. Advocates of *multivalued analysis* regard the accumulation of gigantic assets as suspicious even if there is no immediate threat of noncompetitive pricing.

- Adopting the economic approach, the Reagan Administration Justice Department focused on *market concentration,* setting forth the conditions that lead to collusion or monopoly. Its revised 1984 guidelines measured market concentration with the *Herfindahl-Hirschman Index (HHI),* which takes account of the variation in market share among the firms in a market. Promoted by the FTC and other regulatory bodies, mergers proliferated in the 1980s. The 1984 *National Cooperative Research Act* was enacted to spur the development of research-and-development *joint ventures* but may require further legislation to advance U.S. competitiveness in this area.

- *Price discrimination* can cause injury to competition among sellers or buyers. *Predatory pricing* typically occurred when a national firm targeted certain geographic markets for cut rates that were intended to hurt local competition. The main force behind the 1936 *Robinson-Patman Act* was small-business groups concerned about competition at the buyer's level from chain stores. Sellers may rebut a charge of price discrimination by showing that they sought to meet a rival's low price. Differences in price may also be justified by differences in the seller's costs associated with the two sales.

- Under the Robinson-Patman Act, an amendment to the Clayton Act, a *prima facie price discrimination case* requires actual, nearly simultaneous sales of tangible goods of "like grade and quality," to at least two different customers, at directly or indirectly different prices. A finding of no price discrimination will result only if the price meets that of competitors and if it is justified by cost differences. The Act specifically outlaws *brokerage allowances, promotional allowances,* and *special services* or side items provided to some buyers and not others.

- Many scholars have charged that the Robinson-Patman Act is overly technical, poorly written, and hostile to competition. The prospect of treble-damages suits under the Act has had a dampening effect on competition, but courts, and public opinion, are becoming increasingly tolerant of competitive pricing.

QUESTIONS AND PROBLEMS

KEY TERMS

1. Define the following terms:

   1. Horizontal merger

   2. Vertical merger

   3. Conglomerate merger

   4. Robinson-Patman Act

   5. Multivalued analysis

   6. Predatory pricing

   7. Primary-line injury

2. The Tatum Corporation, an electronics manufacturing firm with total assets of $125 million, seeks a merger with the Bledsoe Corporation. The Bledsoe Corporation is a computer manufac-

turing firm with total assets of $8.75 million. Must the proposed merger be reported to the FTC and Justice Department?

3. Dino's Sandwich Shop, Inc., has a string of 46 sandwich shops in New York. Barry's Pastry Shop, Inc., has 27 bakery shops in New Mexico. If Dino's and Barry's merge, is it a horizontal merger?

4. Benton Corporation is a large computer manufacturing firm. Benton merges with the Colco Food Corporation, a major food industry snack producer and food processor. Benton proposes to its computer-manufacture suppliers that they use Colco snacks in their snack machines at all their premises. Is there anything wrong with this arrangement?

5. Ken McNamara is the only retailer in the entire New England area who has GCB infant seats for sale. The seats are much in demand. He also has a stockpile of expensive bunting outfits that he has not been able to sell. In order to reduce his bunting inventory to make room for necessary items, Mr. McNamara will only sell the GCB infant seat if the buyer also purchases a bunting outfit. An irate infant seat customer who does not want or need a bunting outfit complains that this is illegal. Is it?

6. Perkins entered the oil and gasoline business in 1928 as the operator of a single service station in the State of Washington. By the mid 1950s, he had become one of the largest independent distributors of gasoline and oil in both Washington and Oregon. He was both a wholesaler, operating storage plants and trucking equipment, and retailer through his own Perkins stations. From 1945 to 1957 Perkins purchased almost all his gasoline from Standard. From 1955 to 1957 Standard charged Perkins a higher price for its gasoline and oil than Standard charged its own dealers, independent operators of Standard Signal and Chevron stations who marketed gasoline and oil under Standard's brand names. They also charged less to Signal Oil and Gas Co., a wholesaler, whose gas eventually reached the pumps of a major competitor of Perkins. Standard contends that the price differential did not affect competition, but Perkins contends a price discrimination that caused serious harm, forcing him to sell his business in 1987. Decide. [*Perkins v. Standard Oil Co. of Calif.*, 395 US 642 (1969)]

7. ICC is a coffee roaster located in Pittsburgh, Pa., which has marketed its brand of coffee locally for more than 50 years. Its brand was second only to Maxwell House in market share. In 1968 it expanded to Cleveland, Ohio, where it competed with several different roasters. In 1971 Folger's began marketing its coffee in Pittsburgh. ICC charges that when Folger's entered the Pittsburgh market area, it sold coffee to retailers at prices significantly lower than the prices it charged in other areas. ICC tried to match prices for a while, but because it was a local company, it could not subsidize its losses with profits derived from other geographic markets and was forced out of business. Folger's says it merely made available coupons which redeeming consumers could use to obtain price cuts and redeeming retailers could use as credits against invoices. The trial court holds that these price reductions were not to "purchasers," but to consumers—that is, the buying public—and therefore Folger's act is not proscribed by the antitrust laws. On appeal, how will the court decide? [*Indian Coffee Corp. v. Procter & Gamble Co.*, 752 F.2d 891 (3d Cir. 1985)]

8. The International Salt Co., the country's largest producer of salt for industrial users, also owned patents on two machines that utilize salt products. The "Lixator" dissolves rock salt into a brine that is used in various industrial processes. The other, "Saltomat," injects salt tablets into canned products during the canning process. Other businesses could lease these machines but were required by the lease agreement to use only the International Salt Co's unpatented salt and salt tablets. No one could use the machine without buying the salt. Was this illegal? Explain. [*International Salt Co. v. US*, 332 US 392 (1947)]

9. Plaintiffs, Jim and Bill Beam, regularly bought asphalt products from Monsanto. Plaintiffs were assured by defendants that they were buying materials at as low a price as the materials were being sold to anyone else, which

plaintiffs found not to be true. Plaintiffs found that there were differences in prices charged to purchasers for like-grade and quantity of asphalt products. Because of the higher prices, plaintiffs allege they were forced out of business with the consequent loss of their equipment and real estate and are asking for actual damages of $765,000 and treble damages of $2,295,000. Was there a violation of the Robinson-Patman Act? [*Beam v. Monsanto*, 414 F. Supp. 570 (1970)]

10. When McDonald's sells franchises, it requires the franchisee to lease the premises from McDonald's and give a $15,000 security deposit note. A franchisee complains that the requirements constitute an illegal tying arrangement because the lease and the security deposit note are actually tied to the McDonald's franchise. McDonald's argues that the aggregation of the three requirements is an essential ingredient of the franchised system's formula for success and there is but a single product, so no tie-in exists. In support of its argument McDonald's asserts, among other things, that it has the requirements because (1) it approaches the problem of restaurant selection site systematically to insure the success of each franchise; and (2) its policy of owning all its own restaurants and leasing them to the franchisees assures that the stores remain a part of the system so there is never the problem of the franchisee vacating the premises and having the restaurant taken over by another type of business, thereby having a negative effect on its goodwill. Will this reasoning be sufficient to rebut the tying arrangement charge? [*Principe v. McDonald's Corp.*, 631 F.2d 303 (1980)]

11. In the retail grocery market in Los Angeles, third-ranked Store A wants to acquire the capital stock and assets of sixth-ranked Store B. Together, their sales would put them in second place, with 7.5% of the $2.5 billion yearly retail grocery market in Los Angeles. Both companies have enjoyed rapid growth and success. During this time, there has been a steady decline in the number of single-store owners due to mergers with larger chain stores. The Federal Trade Commission brings action to stop the merger, alleging that it would violate Section 7 of the Clayton Act. The lower court permits the merger and the government appeals the decision. Store A defends by asserting that the merger is not prohibited under the Clayton Act because the Los Angeles grocery market was competitive before the mergers, has been since, and may continue to be in the future. Who wins and why? [*United States v. Von's Grocery Co.*, 384 U.S. 270 (1966)]

TRADE PRACTICES AND INTELLECTUAL PROPERTY

Federal antitrust legislation exists to protect the public against certain "evils," as legislators put it. The term "public" includes both corporate entities (*see* Chapter 7) and consumers.

Corporations are protected through the *patent system*, which safeguards intellectual property, and through the Lanham Act, which regulates the use of trade names. The Clayton Act and Section 5 of the Federal Trade Commission Act (FTC Act) protect corporations by shielding them from unfair competition.

Companies, however, can take actions that may harm their own customers. To protect customers from such practices, Congress passed the Wheeler-Lea Act in 1938, which expanded the scope of Section 5 of the FTC Act to forbid unfair or deceptive acts against either competing companies or consumers. The Federal Trade Commission (FTC) administers this legislation. In doing so, it performs the dual function of protecting both competing businesses and consumers.

This chapter, examines the critical role of the FTC in protecting consumers and promoting fair business practices, and defines and discusses *deceptive practices* in terms of key legislation. The chapter also discusses the effect of antitrust legislation on intellectual property.

■ THE FTC AND UNFAIR PRACTICES

Unfair trade practices are regulated through state and federal legislation as well as through case law. The focus here is on federal regulation, especially that of the FTC. Because most state laws resemble the FTC Act, state and federal regulations usually complement each other.

The Federal Trade Commission

The **Federal Trade Commission (FTC),** which regulates trade practices in the United States, was created in 1914. Because its efforts to maintain a system of free and competitive enterprise—regulating takeovers, antitrust suits, fair-

Federal Trade Commission (FTC) Federal agency, created in 1914, that regulates trade practices in the U.S. through bureaus of consumer protection, competition, and economics

credit laws, labeling, and advertising—have a direct impact on the legal environment of business, the FTC could easily have a greater impact on a business career than any other federal agency. The FTC's three arms are the bureaus of *consumer protection, competition,* and *economics.* (The organizational structure of the FTC is shown in Figure 18-1.)

The FTC is run by five commissioners who are nominated by the president of the United States and confirmed by the Senate. Each commissioner serves a seven-year term, and terms overlap. Because only three commissioners can belong to any one political party, presidents cannot always appoint commissioners from their own parties. The president chooses one commissioner to act as chairman.

FTC FUNCTIONS.   The FTC has the power to issue *trade-regulation rules* forbidding or requiring certain practices. By and large, it enforces these rules through voluntary compliance. Companies that wish to know whether a proposed course of action will be permitted can ask the FTC for an "advisory opinion."

In addition, the FTC also investigates industries and particular companies. When the results of an investigation indicate the need for action, the FTC attempts to negotiate an agreement. If these efforts fail, the FTC may bring cases before an administrative judge or go to federal court. In either event, the case may end up before the Supreme Court.

The FTC and Consumer Protection. Over the years, the FTC has been regarded as a consumer-protection agency. In this role, it defends the public from false advertisements and inaccurate or misleading packages and labels. One notable case in 1931 in which the FTC established itself as a consumer protection agency was *FTC v. Keppel,* 291 U.S. 304. Therein, the United States Supreme Court ruled that charges of unfair practices could be brought under the FTC Act only against a firm whose actions harmed competitors, not its own

FIGURE 18-1   Organization of the Federal Trade Commission

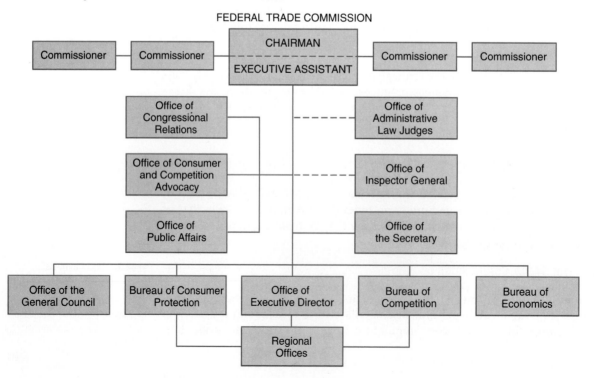

consumers. The FTC, however, has since argued that *unfair* practices—not just *deceptive* ones—may involve customers. The FTC first acted on this view in 1964, when it ruled that cigarette packages, cartons, and advertisements must bear labels advising consumers that cigarettes may be injurious to health. The "Cigarette Rule," as it is called, put the country on notice that the FTC would judge the fairness of commercial practices according to the following criteria: (1) whether the practice, even though not unlawful, offends public policy; (2) whether the practice is immoral, unethical, oppressive, or unscrupulous; and (3) whether it causes substantial injury to consumers or competitors or other businessmen.

Unfair Practices

FTC v. SPERRY & HUTCHINSON.   The first test of the new standard began in June 1968, when the FTC commission used it as the basis for a cease-and-desist order against the Sperry & Hutchinson Company (S&H). S&H sold S&H Green Stamps to supermarkets and other retail businesses which gave them to customers. The customers could take the stamps to S&H redemption centers to be exchanged for gifts. S&H was by far the largest company in the trading-stamp business.

S&H regulated the rate at which retailers gave stamps to customers. (This rate generally was one stamp for each dime's worth of purchases.) It also regulated the rate at which S&H redemption centers exchanged stamps for gifts. In other words, consumers had to have at least two books of S&H Green Stamps for almost any gift. If a customer did not have enough S&H green stamps, however, but did have trading stamps issued by another company, the customer could take the other stamps to an independent trading-stamp exchange and swap them for S&H Green Stamps. In this way, S&H attempted to close down independent trading-stamp exchanges. The FTC's 1968 cease-and-desist order required the company to stop the practice.

S&H appealed the order to the federal courts, arguing that the amended Section 5 of the FTC Act prohibited nothing but actions that broke the antitrust laws or were deceptive or immoral: The company argued that "unfair" practices harmed competitors, not customers, and that its attempts to suppress independent exchanges were not unfair. The Federal Court of Appeals for the Fifth Circuit upheld this argument.

In 1972, the U.S. Supreme Court overruled that decision. In doing so, however, it clearly reaffirmed the FTC's claim of power to deal with unfair acts when it said: "The FTC does not abrogate excessive power to itself if . . . it . . . considers public values beyond those enshrined in the letter . . . of the antitrust laws" (*FTC v. Sperry & Hutchinson Co.*, 405 U.S. 233 at 244 [1972]).

Throughout the 1970s, the FTC tried to develop a standard for deciding which commercial practices were unfair to consumers. But these criteria (and the rules issued under them) were quite controversial. In 1980, the FTC tried to deal with charges that its definition of unfairness to consumers was too broad. It thus issued a policy statement that set forth three criteria for deciding whether a practice was actually unfair:

1. The injury must be substantial, usually but not always involving monetary harm.
2. The consumer injury must not be outweighed by other countervailing benefits to consumers or competition.
3. The injury must be one that consumers, acting in a reasonable manner, could not have avoided.

In short, "unjustified consumer injury" became the "primary focus" of the FTC Act. "Immorality" and "public policy," both of which figured in the S&H criteria, were no longer to be used as independent grounds for a finding of unfairness.

■ *Concept Check 18-1   The FTC and Unfair Practices*

- How has the definition of *deceptiveness* evolved since the enactment of the FTC Act?
- Explain the principal functions of the *Federal Trade Commission*.
- What are the essential FTC criteria for an *unfair practice*?

■ DECEPTIVE PRACTICES

Deceptive acts, which can be committed against both competitors and consumers, arise mainly in connection with advertising. Under common law, it was difficult to sue advertisers who made false or misleading claims, no matter how false or misleading they were. Only people who claimed to have been *deceived* by the advertisements could sue the companies that placed them; the government was otherwise powerless to act. In fact, plaintiffs had to show that advertisers had intended to deceive—which is almost impossible to prove. They also had to show that *actions* on their part had been inspired by these advertisements—which is also very difficult to prove. In addition, deception had to be the "probable" result of the ad. In effect, these requirements meant that advertisers were subject to almost no restraints at all. (Key U.S. advertising legislation is summarized in Table 18-1.)

Defining Deception

THE TRADITIONAL STANDARD.   Although the Wheeler-Lea Act clearly affirmed the FTC's right to act against *deception*, it did not define the term. Over the years, the FTC and the courts defined it. The traditional definition, which held sway until 1980, had three parts.

First, a deceptive act or practice had to have a *tendency or capacity to mislead*. Such acts or practices could involve writing (as in written advertisements) or speech (as in television commercials). They could be misleading because of the information that they included or the information that they omitted. For an ad to be found misleading, it was not necessary to prove that anyone had actually been misled by it—tendency or capacity to mislead was enough for conviction.

Second, a deceptive act or practice had to be one that could *potentially mislead substantial numbers of people*. Unless an act or practice was clearly aimed at a specific group, such as children, the FTC would examine its effect upon consumers of all kinds (sophisticated and naïve, wary and unwary, young and old).

Third, a deceptive act or practice had to be *capable of misleading people in an important way*. Once again, however, it was not necessary to show that anyone had actually been misled, only that this was possible.

TABLE 18-1	*Key U.S. Advertising Legislation*

Pure Food and Drug Act (1906)
Forbids the manufacture, sale, or transport of adulterated or fraudulently labeled foods and drugs in interstate commerce. Supplanted by the Food, Drug, and Cosmetic Act of 1938; amended by Food Additives Amendment in 1958 and Kefauver-Harris Amendment in 1962.

Federal Trade Commission Act (1914)
Establishes the commission, a body of specialists with broad powers to investigate and to issue cease-and desist orders to enforce Section 5, which declares that "unfair methods of competition in commerce are unlawful."

Wheeler-Lea Amendment (1938)
Prohibits unfair and deceptive acts and practices regardles of whether competition is injured; places advertising of foods and drugs under FTC jurisdiction.

Lanham Act (1947)
Provides protection for trademarks (slogans and brand names) from competitors and also encompasses false advertising.

Magnuson-Moss Warranty/FTC Improvement Act (1975)
Authorizes the FTC to determine rules concerning consumer warranties and provides for consumer access to means of redress, such as the "class action" suit. Also expands FTC regularoty powers over unfair or deceptive acts or practices.

FTC Improvement Act (1980)
Provides the House of Representatives and Senate jointly with veto power over FTC regulation rules. Enacted to limit FTC's powers to regulate "unfairness" issues.

THE NEW STANDARD. Ronald Reagan and those he appointed to office believed that our economy should be regulated primarily by the marketplace, not by the government. Not surprisingly, the commissioners that Reagan appointed to the FTC felt that it had too much freedom to define acts and practices as deceptive. At first, Reagan's appointees hoped that Congress itself would adopt a narrower definition of deception. The narrower definition of FTC suggested at this time would have required "evidence that consumers are indeed injured" by an act or practice before it could be condemned as deceptive.

Congress, however, refused to adopt this new definition. In 1983, therefore, the commission issued a policy statement outlining the basis on which it proposed to act in the future. The new standard, like the old one, has three elements:

1. There must be a representation, omission, or practice that is likely to mislead the consumer.
2. The practice must be examined from the perspective of a consumer acting reasonably in the circumstances.
3. The representation, omission, or practice must be material.[1]

As you can see from Table 18-2, the standards differ in two main ways. First, under the new standard, actions must be "likely to deceive," whereas under the old one they had to have merely "a tendency or capacity to mislead." The FTC itself claims that the new wording, though "more informative" than the old does not change its basic meaning. Critics charge that the new wording represents an attempt to return to the old common-law standard.

Second, an act or practice must mislead a "consumer acting reasonably" rather than "a substantial number of consumers" in order to be considered de-

[1] 55 *Trade Reg. Rep.* (CCH) 50,455, at 56,701 n. 3 (1983).

TABLE 18-2 Traditional and New Standards for Defining Deceptiveness

TRADITIONAL STANDARD	NEW STANDARD
(1) "A tendency or capacity to mislead"	(1) "Likely to mislead"
(2) "A substantial number of consumers"	(2) "A consumer acting reasonably"
(3) "In a material way"	(3) "Practice must be material"

ceptive. The problem with the *reasonable-consumer standard* is that experience shows that many people do not behave reasonably. The new standard might leave these consumers, who need protection more than anyone else, without it. One recent case in which the FTC applied the reasonable-consumer standard involved a manufacturer of over-the-counter drugs.[2]

---

[2] M. Pertschuk and P. P. Bailey, "The Law of Deception: The Past as Prologue," 33 *American University Law Review* (1984).

BRISTOL-MYERS CO. v. FEDERAL TRADE COMMISSION
U.S. Court of Appeals, Second Circuit, 738 F.2d 554 (1984)

The Federal Trade Commission (the Commission or the FTC) upheld findings by its Administrative Law Judge (ALJ) that Bristol-Myers Company (Bristol) had engaged in a variety of deceptive practices in advertising its non-prescription or "over-the-counter" (OTC) internal analgesics, Bufferin and Excedrin. The Commission found that consumers viewing Bristol's ads would believe them to be making claims supported by a reasonable basis and that, lacking such basis, the ads were deceptive. The Commission ordered that Bristol refrain from making certain claims concerning the OTC analgesics unless it had a reasonable basis for making the claim.

Bristol petitions for review of the Commission's order on the ground that the order violates the First Amendment in the light of the protection due commercial speech.

Oakes, Circuit Judge:
. . . In concluding that Bristol and its advertising agencies had deceptively advertised Excedrin and Bufferin [from 1960 o 1973], the Commission found that Bristol had misrepresented that the analgesic superiority of Excedrin and Bufferin over competing products was scientifically proved, or "established," by the artful use of certain phrases such as "scientific tests" and "medically endorsed," as well as by the use of visual images. Bristol was found to have made seven false and deceptive claims of this nature, concerning both the efficacy and the freedom-from-side-effects of its non-prescription internal analgesic products. . . .

In addition, the Commission found that Bristol had claimed, without a reasonable basis, that both Bufferin, which is a form of buffered aspirin, and Excedrin, a

combination of aspirin, salicylamide, acetaminophen and caffeine, relieved tension and that physicians recommend Bufferin more frequently than they recommend any other OTC internal analgesic. Finding that such unsubstantiated claims were deceptive, the Commission in Part II of its Order requires Bristol not to make "any therapeutic performance or freedom-from, -side-effects claim" for any OTC internal analgesic unless it has a "reasonable basis for making that claim [consisting of] competent and reliable scientific evidence supporting that claim." . . .

. . .

The Commission further found that Bristol falsely represented that doctors recommend Bufferin more than any other OTC internal analgesic, Part IIIB of the Order prohibits Bristol from representing "that any group, body or organization endorses or recommends [the use of a Bristol OTC drug] unless at the time such statement or representation is made, [Bristol] has a reasonable basis for such statement or representation." . . .

Bristol argues that Part II violates the first Amendment in the light of the protection due commercial speech. But, as we have pointed out, deceptive advertising enjoys no constitutional protection and it may be regulated. Even in the absence of a finding of actual deception, agencies may properly regulate speech that is merely potentially deceptive. . . .

Nor is the prior substantiation doctrine as applied here in violation of the First Amendment. Bristol contends that the FTC is not entitled to presume that consumers expect all supportable product claims to possess a reasonable basis to support the claims. It therefore wishes us to reject whole series of FTC cases allegedly relying on such a presumption.

Whatever the merits of the argument that the use of

such a presumption violates the First Amendment, it is clear that in this case the FTC made a factual finding, based on its investigation of Bristol's ads, that consumers viewing the ads would believe them to be making claims supported by a reasonable basis. It then found that lacking such a basis the ads were deceptive. A conclusion of this nature is "in the very realm of the Commission's greatest expertise - what constitutes deception in advertising. As such the reviewing court must give the commissioner's findings "'great weight.'" We find the conclusion amply supported in this case.

. . .

Bristol advertised for a time that doctors recommended Bufferin more than any other "leading brand" of OTC internal analgesic. . . .

In interpreting advertisements the Commission may rely on its own expertise in this area and need not resort to surveys and consumer testimony. In this case the FTC's finding that the ads indicate that doctors recommend Bufferin more than any other OTC internal analgesic is clearly supported by substantial evidence on the record. The video portion of the Bristol advertisement unqualifiedly and explicitly says "doctors specify Bufferin more," which would plainly be understood to mean that Bufferin was preferred to all other OTC internal analgesics. The fact that the audio was qualified by the reference to "all leading brands of pain reliever" does not take the effect on the consumer of the full ad into account.

. . .

We have considered all of Bristol's claims but find that the Commission quite carefully crafted its remedial order to suit the violations. The Order is broad enough to protect the public while narrow enough to permit compliance without undue burden.

Order enforced.

Case Questions

1. What deceptive practices in advertising its analgesic did Bristol engage in?

2. Why did the Commission find that a reasonable consumer would be deceived by Bristol's advertising of its OTC internal analgesics?

3. What factors are relevant in determining whether a drug manufacturer has a reasonable basis for its claims concerning its OTC products?

Deception in Practice

The FTC has prosecuted a wide variety of deceptive practices. Some were found deceptive as a result of things that were *not* done rather than things that *were* done. For example, a weight-loss clinic that ran advertisements which failed to say that its treatment involved the use of a drug that the government had never certified as effective for losing weight was found to have acted deceptively (*Simeon Management Corp. v. FTC*, 579 F.2d 1137 [1978]).

In another case, a sugar company's advertisement falsely implied that its product was in some way unique. The implication was ruled deceptive under Section 5 of the amended FTC Act (*Amstar Corp.*, 83 FTC 659 [1973]). The Colgate-Palmolive company was successfully prosecuted for deceptive advertising when it ran a television commercial that ostensibly showed Rapid Shave shaving cream being used to shave a piece of "sandpaper." The sandpaper was really a sheet of glass covered with sand. (Colgate argued unsuccessfully that it had used a sheet of glass covered with sand because TV would have obscured the grainy surface of real sandpaper and that in fact Rapid Shave *would* shave sandpaper.) (*FTC v. Colgate-Palmolive Co.*, 380 U.S. 374 [1965]).

Another banned practice is called *bait and switch*: This practice lures customers into the store by advertising a product with a low price. However, once the customer speaks to a salesman, he discovers that the advertised product is unavailable and is directed toward a higher-priced item.

■ Concept Check 18-2   Deceptive Practices

- Explain the policy distinction between *unfair* and *deceptive practices.*
- Explain the different definitions of *deception* under the traditional and new standards applied by the FTC.
- Explain the *reasonable-consumer standard.*

■ THE LANHAM ACT

Lanham Trademark Act 1946 federal law that regulates the use of *trademarks*, making illegal any false representation of goods and services in interstate commerce

Section 5 of the amended FTC Act is not the only legal basis for prosecuting false advertisements. The other is the **Lanham Trademark Act** of 1946. As its name indicates, the Lanham Act deals mainly with trademarks. However, Section 43(a) makes it illegal to use "any false description or representation" of goods or services entering interstate commerce. It also allows "any person who believes that he is or is likely to be damaged by the use of any such false description or representation" to sue.

Scope of the Lanham Act

Despite the Act's broad language, the courts have tended to limit the right to sue under Section 43(a) to competitors of businesses making allegedly "false descriptions or representations."

COMPARATIVE ADVERTISING. A high proportion of cases falling under the provisions of the Lanham Act have dealt with *comparative* advertisements—that is, ads that make explicit or implicit comparisons between an advertised product and its competitors. In the 1970s, for example, American Home Products Corporation ran an advertisement for one of its over-the-counter remedies, Anacin. The ad claimed that American consumers regarded Anacin as superior to various rival products. Several of them, including Tylenol and Datril, were shown in the ad itself.

Johnson & Johnson is the manufacturer of Tylenol and Datril. Its lawyers persuaded a federal court that general references to Anacin's alleged superiority in the minds of consumers, without proof that they regarded Anacin as superior to Tylenol and Datril in particular, were a "false description or representation" within the meaning of Section 43(a) (*American Home Products Corp. v. Johnson & Johnson*, 577 F.2d 160 [1978]).

However, not every company whose products are mentioned in comparative advertisements brings a suit under Section 43(a), and not every company that brings suit carries it through to trial. For one thing, rival companies whose products are belittled in an ad often feel that the ad does not really harm their interests. In other cases, rival manufacturers may decide that the cost of litigation is higher than any benefit that could be had from it.

In fact, most companies bringing suit under Section 43(a) are really seeking a preliminary injunction against an ad, not to have it thrown out at the end of a trial. For one thing, trials sometimes last so long that by the time they have ended, the ad would in any case have been replaced by a new one. As a result, the history of Section 43(a) litigation includes relatively few full trials: If the plaintiff fails to secure a preliminary injunction, the case is usually abandoned. (It should also be noted that, as Table 18-3 shows, the American Association of Advertising Agencies has established its own guidelines for responsible comparative advertising.)

In addition, many comparative ads mention or show many competing products, not just one. As a result, rival manufacturers may feel that any harm these ads might do is shared among too many products to do any one of them much individual harm. Sometimes, of course, a maligned rival does react. Vidal Sassoon Incorporated, for example, brought suit against Bristol-Myers Company even though the Bristol-Myers ad mentioned products made by other manufacturers as well.

666

TABLE 18-3   *Comparative Advertising Guidelines*

1. The intent and connotation of the ad should be to inform and never to discredit or unfairly attack competitors, competing products, or services.

2. When a competitive product is named, it should be one that exists in the marketplace as significant competition.

3. The competition should be faily and properly identified but never in a manner or tone of voice that degrades the competitive product or service.

4. The advertising should compare related or similar properties or ingredients of the product, dimension to dimension, feature to feature.

5. The identification should be for honest comparison purposes and not simply to upgrade by association.

6. If a competitive test is conducted, it should be done by an objective testing service.

7. In all cases the test should be supportive of all claims made in the advertising that are based on the test.

8. The advertising should never use partial results or stress insignificant differences to cause the consumer to draw an improper conclusion.

9. The property being compared should be significant in terms of value or usefulness of the product to the consumer.

10. Comparisons delivered through the use of testimonials shoud not imply that the testimonial is more than one individual's thought unless that individual represents a sample of the majority viewpoint.

Source: American Association of Advertising Agencies

VIDAL SASSOON, INC. v. BRISTOL-MYERS CO.
U.S. Court of Appeals, Second Circuit, 661 F.2d 272 (1981)

Defendant, Bristol-Myers Co. ("Bristol"), is a pharmaceutical manufacturer. In an advertising campaign on behalf of its shampoo "Body on Tap," Bristol claimed that 900 women preferred Body on Tap shampoo to shampoo competitors when, in fact, only 200 women tested any one particular brand of shampoo and approximately one third of the "women" tested were between 13 and 18 years old. Plaintiff, Vidal Sassoon, Inc. ("Sassoon"), is a competitive shampoo manufacturer. Sassoon claimed that several of these advertisements violated the prohibition of the Lanham Trademark Act against false and misleading advertisements.

Sassoon submitted a consumer perception study prepared for it by ASI Market Research, Inc. ("ASI") which revealed that consumers, after viewing the television advertisements, would incorrectly believe that 900 women made product-to-product comparisons among two or more shampoos and that consumers would assume that Body on Tap was competitively superior. On the basis of the evidence, the district court found that Sassoon had demonstrated a probability of success on the merits and a possibility of irreparable injury if the dissemination of the advertisements by Bristol did not

cease. Accordingly, the court ordered that Bristol be preliminarily enjoined from disseminating its misleading advertisements. Bristol appeals.

Irving R. Kaufman, Circuit Judge:
. . . Bristol began in June [1980] to broadcast on national television a commercial "starring" the high-fashion model Cristina Ferrare. The commercial depicts a turbaned Miss Ferrare, apparently fresh from shampooing her hair, holding a bottle of Body on Tap. She claims: "[I]n shampoo tests with over nine hundred women like me, Body on Tap got higher ratings than Prell for body. Higher than Flex for conditioning. Higher than Sassoon for strong, healthy looking hair." As is well known to the consuming public, Prell, Flex, and Sassoon are shampoo competitors of Body on Tap. . . . As Miss Ferrare refers in turn to each of the shampoos, the product is flashed on the television screen. The commercial ends as Miss Ferrare, now brushing her dry hair, states: "Now I use Body on Tap for fuller body and clean, strong, beautifully conditioned hair. Body on Tap. It's a great shampoo."

The "Ferrare-900 women" commercial, although the prototype, was only the first in a series developed for a complex sales campaign. Bristol played variations on the same theme in newspaper advertisements and in brochures which it intended to mail to over ten million households.

The shampoo tests mentioned in all the advertisements were conducted for Bristol in 1978 and 1980 by an independent market research firm, Marketing Information Systems, Inc. ("MISI"). It is undisputed that 900 women did not, after trying both shampoos, make product-to-product comparisions between Body on Tap and Sassoon, or, for that matter, between Body on Tap and any of the other shampoos mentioned in the advertisements. Rather, groups of approximately 200 women, in what the advertising trade terms "blind monadic testing," each tested one shampoo and rated it on a qualitative scale ("outstanding," "excellent," "very good," "good," "fair," or "poor") with respect to 27 attributes, such as body and conditioning. Thus, no woman tried more than one shampoo. . . . Following this procedure, MISI determined that 36% of the women who tested Body on Tap found it "outstanding" or "excellent" with relation to "strong, healthy looking hair," whereas only 24% of the separate group of women who tested Sassoon gave it such ratings. These results are the basis of Bristol's advertising claim that the women preferred Body on Tap to Sassoon. When the "very good" and "good" ratings are combined with the "outstanding" and "excellent" ratings, however, there is only a statistically insignificant difference of 1% between the ratings of the two shampoos respecting "strong, healthy looking hair."

. . .

In September, 1980 Sassoon commenced this action, claiming that the several "Ferrare-900 women" advertisements violated the prohibition of § 43(a) of the Lanham Trademark Act, 15 U.S.C. § 1125(a). Sassoon charged that Bristol had made false and misleading representations since, *inter alia*: (a) only about 200 women, not "over 900 women," tested each shampoo; (b) the women tested only one shampoo, without making product-to-product comparisons; (c) only two-thirds of the test participants were adult women; (d) the advertisements failed to portray the test results accurately, because Bristol used only the top two qualitative rating categories; and (e) the methodology of the tests was flawed. Sassoon sought damages and a permanent injunction forbidding the broadcast or publication of the advertisements.

Following pretrial discovery Sassoon requested a preliminary injuction prohibiting the dissemination of the advertisements. . . .

Participants in the ASI test were asked to view the "Ferrare-900 women" commercial twice, following a screening of entertainment and other advertisement materials. . . . Answering the open-ended question, "This commercial described the results of shampoo tests. What did these tests show?", 62% of the participants indicated that the tests showed that Body on Tap was competitively superior, either in a general way (38%), or as specifically compared with one or more other brands (24%). In answer to another question, 53% stated that the primary message of the commercial was Body on Tap's competitive superiority.

. . .

Whether or not the statements made in the advertisements are literally true, § 43(a) of the Lanham Act encompasses more than blatant falsehoods. It embraces "innuendo, indirect intimations, and ambiguous suggestions" evidenced by the consuming public's misapprehension of the hard facts underlying an advertisement. Based largely on his evaluation of the ASI test results, Judge Stewart properly concluded, therefore, that Sassoon had made a showing of a probable § 43(a) violations. We also note that at least one statement made by Bristol, that 900 "women like" Cristina Ferrare tried the shampoo (when in fact only two-thirds of the sample were adult women), appears to be facially false, and may therefore be enjoined without regard to consumer reaction.

. . .

one of the principal purposes of the 1946 revisions of the Lanham Act was "[t]o modernize the trade-mark statutes so that they will conform to legitimate present-day business practice." We are therefore reluctant to accord the language of § 43(a) a cramped construction, lest rapid advances in advertising and marketing methods outpace technical revisions in statutory language and finally defeat the clear purpose of Congress in protecting the consumer. . . . But where depictions of consumer test results or methodology are so significantly misleading that the reasonably intelligent consumer would be deceived about the product's inherent quality or characteristics, and action under § 43(a) may lie.

. . .

Accordingly, we affirm the order of the district court.

Case Questions:

1. Why was Judge Stewart correct in concluding that Bristol's advertisements were in violation of § 43(a) of the Lanham Act? How do the results of the ASI test indicate that Bristol's advertisements were ambiguous and misleading to consumers?

2. How is it relevant to the outcome in this case that § 43(a) of the Lanham Act embraces "innuendo, indirect intimations, and ambiguous suggestions" as well as blatant falsehoods?

3. How is the Congressional purpose under the Lanham Act in protecting the consumer served by the injunction ordered against Bristol?

Relief under the Lanham Act

The Lanham Act focus on trademarks has had a powerful impact on the way the courts apply Section 43(a). Any case brought under that section must be concerned with the defendant's false representations regarding his own goods or services.[3] A company convicted under Section 43(a) may be punished either by fines or (as we have already seen) by injunctions that order the company to remove the false advertising from public circulation.

Skil Corp. v. Rockwell International Corp. (375 F. Supp. 777 [1974]) is the case that provided the current test for deciding whether to grant relief. In order to recover under the Lanham Act, plaintiffs must show that all five of the following conditions exist.

1. The defendants made false claims about the plaintiff's products.
2. The claims are capable of deceiving substantial numbers of people.
3. The claims must concern matters of sufficient importance to influence whatever decision is made.
4. The goods that are so advertised must have entered interstate commerce.
5. The plaintiffs must show that they have been hurt by the advertisement.

Many companies that bring suit under Section 43(a) believe that they have been injured by comparative advertising. Nonetheless, unflattering comparisons between a product being advertised and other products do not violate Section 43(a) unless the *advertised* product is set forth in some false or misleading way.

Note that both actual falsehoods and deliberate attempts to create false impressions are illegal. In evaluating the impressions created by ads, judges and juries must bear in mind the interpretation that would be made by an "average individual" or the "buying public" in general.

CORRECTIVE ADVERTISING Corrective advertising is an innovative remedy used by the FTC to protect consumers against deceptive advertising. What constitutes illegality in advertising was purposely left vague by Congress so that the FTC could fashion the most effective and encompassing remedies. When the FTC finds that a company has engaged in false and deceptive advertising with regard to a particular product, it has the power to order a company to include in its advertisements of the product in question a message containing corrective advertising. A corrective-advertising order can also direct a company to stop advertising a product for a specified period of time unless it devotes a specific percentage of subsequent advertising to a corrective advertising message. Finally, an order may also require corrective advertising to be run by the offender until a designated amount of money has been expended or certain number of corrective advertisements run.

Corrective advertising seeks to surpass protections provided by cease-and-desist orders—the primary, more traditional remedy for unfair or deceptive advertising. Unlike the cease-and-desist order, which is used to induce the advertiser to enter voluntarily into a consent order—and which may take years to go into effect—corrective advertising seeks to combat deceptive advertising more efficiently and effectively.

Proponents of corrective advertising argue that it has the potential to solve the problem of the so-called "delay profit." Under this view, the profit earned by continuation of deceptive advertising during FTC proceedings will be offset by the costs of ultimately complying with the corrective order. Another argument advanced on behalf of corrective advertising is that the remedy

---

[3] G. Schuman, "False Advertising: A Discussion of a Competitor's Rights and Remedies," 515 *Loyola University Law Journal* (1983).

is not *retrospective*: It focuses on the misleading nature of *future* advertising. Perhaps the best justification for corrective advertising is based on the recognition that the FTC Act prohibits not only *deceptive* acts and practices but also *unfair* acts and practices.

Each of these last two arguments would seem to be born out in a famous case involving the manufacturer of the mouthwash Listerine. A U.S. Court of Appeals for the District of Columbia affirmed an FTC order requiring that the manufacturer cease and desist from advertising that its product prevents, cures, or alleviates the common cold. The court also held that the FTC had the authority to order corrective advertising because there was factual data supporting the contention that the advertisements played a substantial role in reinforcing in the public's mind a false belief about the mouthwash. The court reasoned that because this belief would linger after false advertising ceased, corrective advertising was an appropriate remedy.

■ *Concept Check 18-3 The Lanham Act*

- Discuss the scope of *Lanham Act* regulatory power.
- What conditions must exist to merit relief under the Lanham Act?
- What are the chief arguments in favor of *corrective advertising* as a remedy under the Lanham Act?

■ INTELLECTUAL PROPERTY

intellectual property Creative activity that results in a *patent*, *copyright*, or *trademark* and confers a limited monopoly on the holder

Intellectual property is creative activity that results in *patents, copyrights,* and *trademarks.* Such properties confer limited monopolies upon their holders. The government restricts competition in this area much more than it does in other areas of economic activity.

The area, however, is by no means clear cut. For example, it is not always clear what is entitled to protection as intellectual property. Nor is it always clear how to divide the profits from such property between its creators on the one hand and those who commercialize their inspirations, on the other.

This section discusses *patents*, including patent law and types of *commercial patents* that qualify for protection under legal guidelines; *copyrights*, including both national and international copyright law; and *trademarks* and *service marks*, an area of increasing importance in an era of international marketing.

Patents

Ideas themselves cannot be patented: Only inventions and processes that put ideas into practice can be patented. Once a patent is granted, a person has the right to exclude others from selling, making, or even using the invention for a fixed period of time.

Patents and the Pace of Technology. In 1988, the United States Patent and Trade Office approved a patent for a genetically altered mouse that had been developed by scientists at Harvard University. Although plants and bacteria have been patented for many years, the Harvard patent was the first issued for an animal. The mouse, which was the product of over a half dozen years of experiments, was intended to create an animal that was highly susceptible to breast cancer so that the complexities of the disease could be studied. Scientists

"The Workhorse of Modern Electronic Devices" The invention of the *transistor* (promoted here by its developer, Bell Laboratories, on the occasion of its 30th birthday) was announced by AT&T in 1947. Smaller and requiring less power than the vacuum tubes then used in radios and other electronic equipment, the transistor promised to make sophisticated electronics available for a variety of consumer products. In 1954, Masaru Ibuka, cofounder of a small Japanese consumer-electronics company called Sony, signed a licensing agreement with AT&T to develop, among other products, a radio small enough to be carried in the pocket and used even in areas without electric power. Although warned by AT&T that the transistor was far too inadequate to handle the high frequencies required by radio, Sony was prepared to take advantage of its own research developments in improved high-frequency output for tape recorders. In 1957, Sony introduced the TR-63, the world's first pocket-size radio. Although its dominance in the transistor-radio market was short-lived (about two years), the company's place in the overall consumer-electronics field has, of course, been secure ever since. By the summer of 1992, for example, Sony had combined transistor and computer-chip technology to introduce such products as a minidisc player—a portable CD player about the size of a deck of cards which not only plays for as long as conventional CD players but which records as well. Similarly, the NT-1 digital microrecorder contains 1.8 million transistors in integrated-circuit chips; the NT-1 is about the size and thickness of a checkbook and uses a cassette only slightly larger than a postage stamp.

were able to inject mice embryos with a naturally occurring gene to make the mice more sensitive to cancer-causing agents. Mice that are genetically predisposed to developing cancer are expected to aid in testing not only the effects of heredity and environment on the disease but also new therapies. The Harvard patent, therefore, could open up a large new market for genetically altered animals for use in drug research and development.

Deciding what is and what is not patentable has become a complex issue, largely as a result of *biotechnology*—genetic engineering to produce either altered or entirely new organisms. Organisms that have been changed through selective breeding cannot be patented, and although biotechnology uses other methods for changing organisms, there was for a time some question as to whether these methods and their products would be patentable even in principle. If they were not, however, no company would bear the expense of developing products that others could easily copy and sell much more cheaply.

Although it is now clear that the courts will treat organisms created through biotechnology as patentable, new problems are certain to arise. For example, biotechnology changes so quickly that it is possible to argue that one researcher's work rests wholly or partly on the work of a researcher in another company. In such a case, who gets the patent? This issue can become especially thorny if one firm regards the work as an obvious extention of something that already exists.

GUIDELINES FOR PATENTABLE INVENTIONS AND PROCESSES. Patent applications are lengthy and complicated. An inventor should hire a patent attorney to assist in obtaining a patent for the invention. In order to be patentable, an invention or process must meet each of six conditions:

1. It must fill a useful purpose that cannot be illegal or immoral.
2. It must be a machine, a manufacturing process, a manufactured article, or a substance.
3. It must have been devised by the person who is seeking to patent it; only the inventor can apply for it.
4. It must be truly novel, not a mere reformulation of something that already exists. No patent can be issued for any product or process that has been described or patented before, either in the United State or in any other country.
5. It cannot be an obvious extension of something that exists already. For example, if you invented a new color, you would not be able to patent the fabric dyed with it because the "<u>new</u>" product would be an obvious extension of something that already existed.
6. Its inventor must have made efforts to ensure that the product or process is novel and must pursue the patent application in the manner prescribed by law.

COMMERCIAL PATENTS. In 1952, Congress enacted the Federal Patent Statute in order (1) to provide an incentive for inventors to invent and make their inventions public, and (2) to protect patented inventions from infringement. Any party can challenge either the issuance of a patent or the validity of an existing patent. There are no state patent laws; federal patent law is exclusive. Patents cannot be renewed. There are three types of commercial patents.

Utility patents cover new machines, manufacturing processes, manufactured articles, and substances ("compositions of matter"). It is possible to patent a *process* for making an object, as distinct from the object itself. Utility patents last for 17 years. Applications for about 100,000 utility patents are filed with the U.S. Patent Office annually, and about 75,000 are ultimately granted.

utility patent *Commercial patent covering a new machines, manufacturing processes, and manufactured articles or substances*

Some 25 percent of all utility patents ever issued in the United states are currently in effect. About one-third of all new patents in the United States are issued to foreigners. The second type of commercial patent is the **design patent**, which covers ornamentation—that is, the physical appearance of objects. These patents run for 14 years. **Plant patents** cover plants that have been reproduced by asexual means such as grafting, the rooting of cuttings, and biotechnology. About 100 plant patents have been issued annually in recent years. They run for 17 years.

RELIEF FROM INFRINGEMENT. Requests for relief from infringement of patents, like requests for patents, can be appealed to the federal courts. After such cases have been tried in federal district court, any appeal must be heard in the U.S. Court of Appeals for the Federal Circuit. Congress created this specialized body in hopes that it would be more competent than ordinary courts to consider questions of great legal and technological difficulty. (For the story behind the largest patent-infringement suit in history—and the man behind the patent—see the PERSONAL PROFILE of Edwin H. Land in this chapter.)

PATENT-SYSTEM REFORM. Many U.S. companies believe that the current patent system is in desperate need of revamping. Critics charge, among other things, that the patent system is bogged down in litigation, confusion over patent rights, and bureaucratic delay.

The Pressure of Foreign Competition. While U.S. patents are issued at a snail's pace, some U.S. executives worry that foreign competitors are gaining an edge by winning more and more patents that foreign companies can then use to establish dominance in a world market. Not surprisingly, Japan currently offers the most competition for American industry. Japanese companies have sharply increased domestic patent filings over the past five years and much of Japan's success may be attributed to its sophisticated electronic patent system. The system, which cost close to $1 billion, allows both instant filing of patent applications and speedy retrieval of the more than 30 million patents already on file.

Differences in the U.S. and Japanese systems may also explain shortfalls in the U.S. patent system. The United States, for example, uses a "first-to-invent" standard: Under U.S. law, a patent is granted to the person who can prove he or she had the idea first, no matter when application was filed for the patent. Under this system, patent applications are secret until the patent is granted—a process that takes 18 months on the average, but that can take years. By contrast, both Japan and Europe employ more expedient "first-to-file" systems and make patent applications public 18 months after filing. The U.S. system has thus been criticized as impeding competition and fostering redundant research.

Ironically, changes in U.S. patent laws instituted only ten years ago may have caused this legacy of delay and confusion. The United States Court of Appeals for the Federal Circuit was set up by Congress to hear all patent appeals at a time when U.S. technology was faltering against other highly industrialized nations. Because the court was adamantly propatent holder, patents and the rights of patent holders were cautiously protected. This protection, however, is a double-edge sword: The protective measures set in place may now be eroding U.S. competitiveness rather than fortifying it. This tendency is perhaps evidenced by the fact that patent litigation has risen by 52 percent during the decade between 1980 and 1990.

THOMAS A. EDISON
Copyright 1905 By Irving Underhill
New York

Mr. Edison and the Movies (I): The Motion Picture Patents Co. Thomas Edison demonstrates his film projector at his West Orange, New Jersey, laboratory. Contrary to popular history, Thomas Edison did not singlehandedly invent motion-pictures—either their technology or their commercial apparatus. The world took relatively little notice of various early patents in Germany, France, and England, as well as the U.S., until production companies—producers badly needing filmmaking equipment—sprang up immediately after the first successful screenings in 1895 and 1896. With a new industrial market eager to buy or lease equipment—or to pirate it—patent protection became a priority in corporate warfare being waged as early as the late 1890s. Edison patented his *kinetoscope* in 1893—a machine capable of displaying a sequence of unenlarged 35mm pictures for about 90 seconds; his first large-scale projection machine, the *Vitascope*, was actually marketed under contract to its real developers. Relying on both his prestige and resources, Edison worked to consolidate control over the U.S. motion-picture industry, but his effort to gain complete dominance was rebuffed in cases like *Edison v. American Mutoscope Co.* (1902), a patent-infringement suit filed by Edison against the American Mutoscope and Biograph Co.: "It is obvious that Mr. Edison was not a pioneer," announced a Federal District Court judge, who granted Edison's claim only to improvements of other people's inventions. When litigation failed against Mutoscope again in 1906 and 1907, Edison invited Mutoscope and seven other producing companies to join him in the Motion Picture Patents Co., which was formed in 1908. Controlling 16 crucial patents, the so-called "Trust" then entered into an exclusive agreement with Eastman Kodak, the only producer of raw film stock in the U.S., and established tightly controlled arrangements with distributors and exhibitors. Independent producers and distributors, however, continued to find ample room to operate in the burgeoning industry, almost equaling the Trust in output by 1912. In the same year, the federal government charged the Motion Picture Patents Co. with violations of the Sherman Antitrust Act *(see Chapter 16)*, and in 1915, a federal court declared the Trust an illegal conspiracy in restraint of trade.

U.S. management is also worried that overseas competitors will use U.S. patent laws against them. This fear may not be unfounded: Foreign companies are not only being awarded nearly 50 percent of all new U.S. patents annually but are enjoying the willingness of U.S. courts to grant injunctions in patents

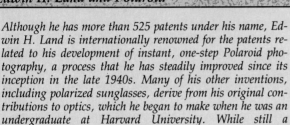

Although he has more than 525 patents under his name, Edwin H. Land is internationally renowned for the patents related to his development of instant, one-step Polaroid photography, a process that he has steadily improved since its inception in the late 1940s. Many of his other inventions, including polarized sunglasses, derive from his original contributions to optics, which he began to make when he was an undergraduate at Harvard University. While still a teenager, Land had begun the experiments that resulted in the first synthetic sheet polarizer, a major achievement in the field of polarized light that has been widely applied in science and industry.

Instead of remaining at Harvard to graduate, Land joined a Harvard physics instructor in setting up a partnership in 1932. Five years later, the Polaroid Corporation was founded by Land in Cambridge, Mass., with the financial backing of a number of Wall Street businessmen, including W. Averell Harriman and Lewis Strauss.

Polaroid prospered during World War II as Land invented a number of weapons improvements, including night-vision instruments for the military. Unlike many companies bound to wartime contracts, however, Polaroid did not suffer a prolonged decline when the war ended. In fact, the return of peace enabled Land to realize an idea that had preoccupied him since 1943. That year, while on vacation in New Mexico, he had taken a picture of his three-year-old daughter, who asked him why she had to wait to see the picture. As a result of this query, Land designed a camera and film that would produce an immediate photograph.

In February 1947, Land demonstrated his revolutionary process with a working model of his camera at the American Optical Society. The four-pound camera made its debut with the American public in time for the Christmas of 1948. The Land camera proved to be an immediate commercial success, bringing in about $5,000,000 in its first year. Although some professional photographers dismissed the camera as a high-priced toy, it soon found many applications in science, industry, the military, and medicine. It was adapted to X-rays, for example, and improved and sophisticated models became available for use in aerial photography, real-estate photography, and commercial and press photography.

Beginning in the early 1950s, the Eastman Kodak Company had supplied Polaroid's needs for negative materials, and in 1957 Polaroid and Kodak entered into an agreement whereby Polaroid shared certain instant-color technology so that Kodak could develop and supply negative material to Polaroid. Polaroid continued to disclose refinements and improvements in instant photography technology through the

1960s, and in early 1969, Kodak launched several enormously costly projects to develop instant photography based on Polaroid technology.

Polaroid's sophisticated SX-70 camera, which went on sale in late 1972, required almost a decade to develop because of its technological innovations and elaborate design. Its popularity was enhanced by several developments. Color film was not nearly a decade old, and in previous Polaroid cameras a layer of paper had to be peeled away from the picture. In this "no-garbage" SX-70, however, seventeen layers of chemical compounds were built into a single sheet that became the finished photo. The self-developing print was ejected from the camera instantly after exposure and was gradually processed within minutes. The Land camera eventually became a best seller and is today still a standard.

At the same time that Polaroid's SX-70 became commercially available, Kodak purchased large quantities of SX-70 cameras and film, and several Kodak departments were ordered to familiarize themselves with the SX-70 and test it. Motivated by Polaroid's success, Kodak increased its efforts to develop instant photography, and in September 1973, Kodak's Development Committee suggested to company employees that "development should not be constrained by what an individual feels is potential patent infringement." In 1976 Kodak introduced an integrated one-step camera and film.

In April 1974, Polaroid brought an action, alleging that Kodak had infringed several of its patents relating to the art and technology of the SX-70 camera and film. The parties engaged in five years of pretrial conferences, motions, and discovery. After a 75-day trial, the district court issued a 110-page memorandum and decision. The court held that Kodak had infringed seven of Polaroid's patents and issued a permanent injunction prohibiting Kodak from selling its instant-photography camera and film. Kodak made a motion requesting a stay of the injunction pending appeal of the patent-infringement claim, arguing that it would suffer irreparable injury if the stay was not granted. The decision was upheld on appeal, and Polaroid sought triple damages—an amount that could have resulted in a $12 billion award.

There was no immediate resolution to all of this litigation. In 1990, 14 years after the lawsuit was brought, a federal court in Boston ordered Eastman Kodak to pay Polaroid $910 million in damages—the largest patent-infringement award in history. The court later amended the award to $925 million with interest. Many experts viewed the ruling as a modest victory for Kodak, which might have been forced to sell off assets had the award exceeded $1 billion.

cases—often against their U.S. competitors. Figure 18-2 represents the corporate top-ten holders of patents granted in the U.S. in 1990.

Efforts led by the World Intellectual Property Organization and trade negotiators are currently aimed at imparting more uniformity to the world's patent laws. The United States will undoubtedly be a willing participant in any reforms that may help to regain its technological competitiveness.

Another issue in international patent law—patent piracy—is examined in the INTERNATIONAL ENVIRONMENT box in this chapter.

Copyrights

copyright Statutory protection given to the work of writers and artists

Article I, Section 8, clause 8 of the U.S. Constitution also provides the basis for copyright protection. Whereas patents protect the work of industrial innovators, **copyrights** protect the work of artists and authors. The term "work" includes books (both fiction and nonfiction), cartoons, greeting cards, leaflets, maps, movies, musical compositions, sound recordings, lectures, magazine articles, paintings, pamphlets, photographs, plays, prints, and sculptures. The work may be a typescript, printed material, or a tape. It does not have to be published.

Both patent and copyright protection extends to the tangible expression of an idea rather than to the idea itself. Thus, although you could not copyright the idea of a novel about childhood horrors that continue to haunt adults who grew up in a small town in Maine, Stephen King could copyright his novel *It*, which embodies that idea in a tangible form.

INTERNATIONAL COPYRIGHT LAWS. In 1988, nearly 102 years after the creation of the Berne Convention for the Protection of Literary and Artistic Works, the United States became a signatory to the treaty created to set minimum copyright standards.

FIGURE 18-2 Companies Granted U.S. Patents, FY 1990   *Source: Business Week,* Dec. 2, 1991. Data from U.S. Patent and Trademark Office.

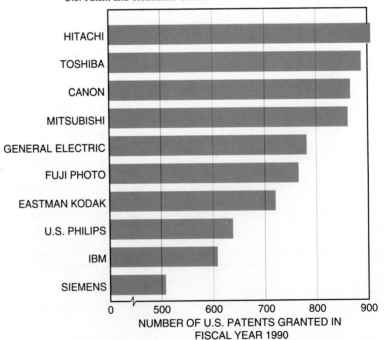

NUMBER OF U.S. PATENTS GRANTED IN
FISCAL YEAR 1990

The Berne Convention. The **Berne Convention**, also known as the International Union for the Protection of Literary and Artistic Works, now has nearly 80 member nations. Under the tenets of the Berne Convention, member nations must extend the protection of its own laws both to nationals of other member nations and to works that were published originally in a member nation. Participation in the Berne Convention helps protect copyrighted works from international pirates who steal them and then sell the creative accomplishments of others.

Berne Convention International treaty that sets minimum *copyright standards* and protects copyrighted work from international pirates

THE INTERNATIONAL ENVIRONMENT
Patent Piracy

Patent "pirates" are causing some of the United States' most competitive industries up to $17 billion in global sales annually. Patent piracy is stealing the copyrighted work of another. Drugmakers and producers of copyrighted software, movies, sound recordings, and books have all lost sales due to such theft.

Among the hardest hit have been multinational pharmaceutical companies. Their products are a form of intellectual property, the result of years of scientific research and costly development. It is estimated that in 1991 alone $4 billion in foreign sales were lost to piracy. For example, Pfizer, Inc., the maker of the patented antiinflammatory drug Feldene, has been victimized in Mexico by patent pirates. Pfizer sold Mexican retail druggists its capsules for 31 cents apiece only to discover that imitations were being introduced to consumers under different names at wholesale prices ranging from 25 to 67 cents per capsule!

Today's corporations must consider the problems that may arise when they seeks patent protection in the United States and abroad. Although each country has its own laws and rules governing the processing and granting of patent applications, the filing of a patent application in one country may have a significant effect on a corporation's ability to obtain corresponding patents in other countries. In addition, in today's world market, the components of a patented product may be produced in one country, assembled in a second, and sold in yet another. Thus, in the international scheme by which many products are produced and marketed, the commercialization of an invention in one country may have implications that affect the enforcement of patent rights granted in any number of other countries.

Countries disagree about how patent piracy should be addressed. In many developing nations, for example, nationalists and industrialists believe that they are entitled to copy existing patented products. Some Brazilian companies have even urged the compulsory licensing of patented drugs to local producers on the basis that patients should have the option to choose the most feasible medication.

Efforts to stem the rising trade deficit and the perceived injustice of patent piracy by foreign manufacturers led the United States Congress to include provisions in the Omnibus Trade and Competitiveness Act of 1988 that greatly strengthened remedies under the U.S. law. One provision, for example, facilitates the patentee's recourse before the International Trade Commission in seeking exclusion of offending products from the United States. Another provision amends patent laws to make the unauthorized importation, sale, and use of products in this country produced by a process patented in the United States an act of infringement. This provision remedies a prior problem faced by the holder of a U.S. process patent. Before the Trade Act, a U.S. process patent was not infringed upon when a foreign manufacturer used the process and then exported the resulting product to the United States. A process patent, which may be granted for any new and useful manufacturing process, gave the patentee only the right to exclude others from using his process within the United States for the duration of the U.S. patent. When a product patent was not or could not be obtained to supplement the process patent, the U.S. process-patent holder had no remedy against unauthorized importation.

In many countries, statutory protection of intellectual-property rights is weak or nonexistent. Recently, however, the United States has undertaken a nation-by-nation campaign to combat piracy. As of 1992, complying nations include Mexico, which has agreed to 20-year patent protection and 50-year software protection; Canada, which has agreed to the end of compulsory licensing of drugs to generic manufacturers in Canada; Argentina, where an intellectual-property law is expected to be passed by mid-1992; and, under threat of U.S. trade reprisals, China, which has agreed to strengthen copyright and patent protection.

The nation-by-nation approach, however, is only one way in which the United States and other countries are joining efforts to fight patent piracy. There are currently 102 nations involved in the General Agreement on Tariffs and Trade (GATT), which represents a promising worldwide effort to curb intellectual piracy. To date, the deepest inroads have been made in Mexico, which is being hailed as a model for Latin America. Brazil is of special concern to multinationals who covet Latin America's single largest market.

Action to protect intellectual property is expected both to spur investment by U.S. companies to export more patented and copyrighted products and to increase protection measures abroad. In particular, initiatives will also be monitored with great interest by European drug companies who also have a lot at stake.

The convention features the highest internationally recognized standards for the protection of works of authorship. Participation by the United States will also establish copyright relations with 24 new countries and will help enforce the most stringent level of international copyright protection for U.S. artists, authors, and other copyright holders. This fact is especially important for U.S. works protected by copyright—for example, books, recordings, movies and computer software—that have up until now been at high risk because of the differences between U.S. law and the protections of the Berne convention. Lastly, participation in Berne will put an end to the need for U.S. companies to develop separate arrangements with foreign countries in order to secure protection for their works.

The United States declined to join Berne when it was created in 1886, favoring instead participation in the Universal Copyright Convention, which was a multinational copyright treaty. At that time, foreign works were not protected in the United States under our copyright law. There was a major obstacle preventing the United States from joining the convention. Under United States law, authors could be protected only if they carried out certain administrative formalities, such as registering their work with the U.S. copyright office. This legislation was similar to industrial property laws that recognized an inventor's rights only if his or her invention had been registered. This requirement stood in the way of following Berne tenets, reflecting the idea that a work should be protected merely because it has been created.

During the 1920s and 1930s, increasing use of American copyrighted works fueled strong support by private organizations for participation by the United States in Berne. When the treaty came before the Senate in 1935, it was ratified but rescinded the following day.

By the 1980s, international piracy had fueled Congressional debate once again. Minor changes were made in the United States copyright law so that it conformed to Berne requirements. For example, architectural plans are now included among the pictorial, graphic or sculptural works entitled to protection. In addition, while creators of works in the United States must register with the United States Copyright Office before filing any lawsuit claiming infringement, this requirement is not applied to works from foreign countries. Although many artists argued for a change in U.S. copyright law to protect their "moral rights" in a work, such provisions were not provided in the bill.

The Universal Copyright Convention. United States participation in the Berne Convention is predated by membership in the **Universal Copyright Convention.** The Universal Copyright Convention is an international organization created shortly after World War II under the auspices of the United Nations Economic Security Council (UNESCO). (*See Chapter 21.*) It was established to devise a legal common denominator among member nations that would encourage both respect for the creators of literary, scientific, and artistic works and their international circulation.

The Universal Copyright Convention protects "literary, scientific and artistic works." This description has been interpreted to include most of the works included in Section 102 of the U.S. Copyright Act of 1976 except photographic works, works of applied art, and sound recordings. Member nations must accord the same protection to foreign works protected under the Universal Copyright Convention. Unlike the Berne convention, the Universal Copyright Convention places few substantive requirements on member nations. Under the Universal Copyright Convention, members must provide a minimum copyright term of twenty-five years from the death of the author or from first

Universal Copyright Convention
International organization to establish uniform legal standards to encourage the protection of copyrighted works

publication or registration. Finally, in order to protect the integrity of both the Berne Convention and Universal Copyright Convention, the Universal Copyright Convention provides that no Berne member may withdraw from Berne and subsequently rely on the Universal Copyright Convention in its relations with other Berne members.

Table 18-4 summarizes the provisions of the Berne Convention, Table 18-5 those of the Universal Copyright Convention.

COPYRIGHT TERMS. The Copyright Office of the Library of Congress, which is our national library, administers this country's copyright system. Its basic principles are set forth in the Copyright Revision Act of 1976, which became effective in 1978. Under this act, copyright protection is granted for the life of the author (or of the last surviving author in case of joint authorship) plus an additional fifty years. (Works published before 1978 received protection for twenty-seven years from the original date of publication, renewable for forty-seven years.)

If the copyright is owned by a corporation, copyright protection lasts for seventy-five years from the original date of the work's publication or 100 years from its creation, whichever comes first.

COPYRIGHT REGISTRATION. Authors of unpublished works can *register* them by depositing a copy of the work, an application, and a fee with the copyright office. Registration of published work, however, is more complicated. The work itself must bear a copyright notice—that is, the word "copyright" or some abbreviation of it (such as ©) along with the name of the copyright holder and the date of first publication. With the exception of motion pictures and computer pro-

TABLE 18-4	*The Berne Convention*

Background
- Also known as "The International Union for the Protection of Literary and Artisitc Works."
- Created in 1886.
- Currently has approximately 80 member nations.
- United States became signatory nation in 1989.
- Promotes "national treatment" protection for copyrighted works—each member nation must extend protection of its own laws to nationals of other nations, and to works originally published in a member nation.

Works Protected
- Protects literary and artistic works—"every production in the literary, scientific and artistic domain, whatever be the mode or form of its expression." Works include books, cinematographic works, paintings, maps, and architecture. Member nations can require works are fixed in some material form.

Requirements for Protection
- Automatic proteciton to copyrightable works originating in other member countries.

Length of Protection
- Protection for the life of the author plus fifty years but member nations may provide for a longer term. Photographs and work of applied art must be protected at least 25 years, and cinematographic works must be protected at least 50 years after their making. Anonymous works must be protected at least 50 years after publication.

Extent of Protection
- Beme requires member nations to protect right of translation, adaptation, public performance, public recitation, right of broadcasting, the film right and right of reproduction. Member nations must protect moral rights of attribution and integrity.

TABLE 18-5   *The Universal Copyright Convention*

Background

- Created shortly after World War II.
- Originally a means of including United States in a multinational copyright treaty because United States had refused to join Berne.
- Promotes "national treatment" approach as in Berne—member nations must accord same protection to foreign works protected under U.C.C. as they give domestic work.

Works Protected

- Protects "literary, scientific and artistic works"—this is interpreted to include most works included in Section 102 of U.S. Copyright Act of 1976, except photographic works, works of applied art and sound recordings.

Length of Protection

- Member nations must provide a minimum copyright term of 25 years from the death of the author or from first publication or registration. Photographic works or works of applied art, however, if protected at all, must only be protected for 10 years.

Extent of Protection

- U.C.C. as revised in Paris in 1971 states that member nations shall provide "adequate and effective protection" for the "basic rights ensuring the author's economic interests, including the exclusive right to authorize reproduction by any means, public performance and broadcasting."
- There is no provision for "moral rights."
- Authors have exclusive right to translate their works for a period of seven years. Thereafter, the member nation may provide for compulsory licenses for translation.

Notice Requirement

- U.C.C. notice afforded that a work in one member nation will satisfy formalities prerequisite to copyright protection under other U.C.C. members' domestic law.
- "U.C.C. notice" is an encircled "c," with the name of the copyright owner and the year of first publication on all copies published with the copyright owner's authorization.

grams, two copies of the work must be sent to the copyright office, along with the usual application and fee.

Note that works need not be registered to receive copyright protection. However, registration is desirable because without it, one cannot sue for infringement of copyright. Moreover, when authors register works within five years of original publication, the copyright is ordinarily presumed to be valid—a claim that would otherwise have to be proved.

INFRINGEMENT AND FAIR USE.   No one would go to the trouble and expense of registering publications if no benefit resulted. What, then, are the benefits of copyright protection to the person who holds the copyright? Copyright gives an individual (or business) exclusive rights to that publication. These exclusive rights are spelled out in Section 106 of the Copyright Revision Act. However, two exclusive rights have particular importance: (1) only copyright holders (or people acting with their permission) can *reproduce* protected works and (2) only copyright holders (or people acting with their permission) can *distribute* copies of the work.

Infringement. **Infringement of copyright** means the unauthorized use of these rights by someone other than the copyright holders or people chosen by them. Not everyone, however, must notify copyright holders and secure permission for using any part of a protected work.

Fair Use. The right to use brief, fully identified portions of a protected work without permission is called **fair use**. For example, students are permitted to quote from protected works in term papers. The limits of "fair use" are

infringement of copyright Unauthorized use of the rights of reproduction and distribution of copyrighted works by someone other than the copyright holder or designee

fair use Right to use brief, fully identified portions of copyright-protected work without permission

not always clear, but footnoting the source of copyrighted passages is not the same thing as getting permission to use them.

The Copyright Revision Act describes four criteria for deciding when any particular use of a protected work is and is not fair:

1. *The purpose and character of the use.* A distinction is made, for instance, between commercial use and educational use, and book reviewers are assumed to have a real need to quote from the works they are reviewing.

2. *The nature of the copyrighted work.* Some works, such as reference books, are clearly meant to be used by others.

3. *The amount and substantiality of the material quoted in relation to the protected work as a whole.* To quote 150 words from a one-page magazine article is not the same thing as to quote 150 words from a 500-page book.

4. *The effect of the use upon the potential market for, or value of, the copyrighted work.* If a magazine quoted, without permission, a small but sensational portion of a book before the book's publication, it might become impossible for the book's publisher to sell excerpts from the book to another magazine (*Harper & Row, Publishers v. Nation Enterprises,* 105 S. Ct. 2218 [1985]).

The issues of fair use and infringement are examined more fully in this chapter's YOU DECIDE feature.

CASE: COPYRIGHTS AND THE VISUAL ARTS. Although most art collectors would probably flinch at the idea of altering, mutilating, or destroying a coveted work of art, it does happen. A sculpture by artist David Smith, for example, was stripped of its paint without his consent. An even more notorious case involved a painting by Pablo Picasso: A pair of Australian entrepreneurs cut a Picasso painting into hundreds of small pieces that they then marked as original works of art!

"Moral Rights." The Visual Artists Rights Act, which became law on June 1, 1991, was enacted as an amendment to the federal copyright law in response to complaints by visual artists who were not given credit or control over their work. Under the new law, Congress has for the first time included "moral rights" within the U.S. copyright statute. Moral rights afford protection for the artists' personal, noneconomic interests both in receiving attribution for their work and in preserving it in the form in which it was created, even after its sale or licensing.

The concept of "moral rights" is rooted in European history. Moral rights were first enacted in France in the early part of this century. The underlying philosophy of these rights is to give artists their rightful recognition and integrity in the community for the *legacy* that they created rather than simply monetary return.

The 1991 act draws on tenets of the Berne Convention of 1886, which provided artists with moral rights in their work. In 1988, the United States became a signatory nation and in so doing agreed to adhere to a minimum standard of moral rights for U.S. artists. Congress, however, did not at this time change the Copyright Act to comply with the language of the Berne Convention, which reads in part:

Independently of the author's economic rights, and even after the transfer of said rights, the author shall have the right to claim authorship of the work and to object to any distortion, mutilation or other modification of, or other derogatory action in relation to, the said work, which would be prejudicial to his honor or reputation.

Mr. Edison and the Movies (II): Motion-Picture Copyrights Thomas Edison examines a film strip from his Home Projecting Kinetoscope. The single most important contribution to motion-picture technology produced by the Edison Laboratories was film strip perforated at equal intervals so that it would run smoothly through a projection machine and past the lens. Edison's *kinetoscope*, a "peep-show" viewing machine, was introduced in 1893 and superseded by large-scale projectors in 1896. Almost instantly, the motion-picture industry became party to ongoing—and increasingly urgent—disputes over the patent and copyright protections to be afforded the arts and technologies that fueled popular mass entertainment. In media like theatre, vaudeville, and motion pictures, for example, the issue of *performance* versus *publication* had to be raised. Until 1909, dramatic and musical compositions could be copyrighted only if supported by some notational system that was necessary to perform a given piece; in *White-Smith v. Apollo* (1908), it was thus ruled that a player piano did not infringe on a composer's copyright because the piano roll did not resemble the notational system—the score—originated by the composer. Less than reputable performance media like vaudeville and burlesque might be denied copyright protection because they did not qualify as "dramatic compositions" (a judgment which, in many cases, reflected the opinion that they were not "decent" or socially useful). Film, however, was regarded as establishing its own notational system simply by virtue of being visually understandable *as a complete recorded performance.* In *Edison v. Lubin* (1903), film became exempt from the "dramatic composition" criterion when the 1870 protection granted to photographs was extended; in the same case, the court held that the *film as a whole*—not just its individual photographs—could be protected. With such copyrightable advantages over competitors in the mass-entertainment industry, motion pictures gained popular dominance over both vaudeville theatres (where motion-picture performances first gained attention) and legitimate theatres (many of which were forced to convert to film theatres).

Rather, Congress claimed that moral rights were already sufficiently protected in the United States to permit adherence to the Berne Convention. Advocates of more stringent protection, however, voiced opposition that ultimately led to the 1991 legislation.

Beyond Reproduction. The 1991 act departs from prior copyright laws under which artists had authority to control only the *reproduction* of their work—a right that was lost upon resale. Now, paintings, drawings, prints, sculpture, and photographs created for exhibition must bear authorship credit under certain conditions. In addition, those works cannot be modified without permission and modified works cannot contain authorship credit without permission. What this means to the practicing artist is that someone who buys a piece of artwork does not have the right to cut it down to fit a smaller frame. Furthermore, the new law prevents publishers from altering works of art, reproducing them without giving the artist's name, or using an artist's name in connection with a modified version of an original creation.

Protection of the Artist's Name. The new law also allows artists to prevent the use of their names on works they did not create; to prevent the use of

---

YOU DECIDE

Fair Use

The Copyright Act of 1976 codified the judicially developed defense doctrine of fair use. In essence, the statute reflects both congressional recognition of "a defense in innumerable copyright actions over the years" and Congress's desire to "restate the present judicial doctrine of fair use." Under the statute, fair-use analysis requires assessment of the following factors: (1) the nature of the alleged infringing work, (2) the nature of the copyrighted work, (3) the extent of the taking, and (4) the economic injury caused by the taking. In some cases, the courts have analyzed other factors, such as bad faith on the part of the infringer and whether the public interest is promoted by the unauthorized taking of another's work.

Perhaps it was best stated by the distinguished jurist Learned Hand when he said, "The issue of fair use . . . is the most troublesome in the whole law of copyright." Some 50 years later, this observation remains accurate. The definition of fair use most often given by courts is ". . . a privilege in others than the owner of the copyright to use the copyrighted material in a reasonable manner without his consent."

Consider the thesis that was offered earlier—namely, that no one would go to the trouble and expense of registering publications if no benefit resulted. Commonly, however, teachers photocopy articles or portions of textbooks for distribution in class without so much as paying a royalty to the author. Where do we draw the line between fair use and cheating an author? In 1982, nine publishing companies charged that certain members of the faculty at New York University had violated U.S. copyright law by copying and selling to their students "substantial portions" of copyrighted works. The case was resolved by consent decree that provided that the university would follow a set of guidelines proposed by the Association of American Publishers. The

guidelines give college teachers an essentially unlimited right to make single copies for their own personal use. College teachers can also make multiple copies and distribute them to students if the material is short, if there is no real opportunity to ask the publisher for permission, and if the material has been copied for the use of a single class. Under these guidelines, no college teacher can make multiple copies more than nine times during any one semester. Clearly, however, this agreement does not address existing and potential abuses of the copyright law.

Congress has also attempted to provide for meeting desirable ends, such as the spread of useful knowledge. Clearly, fair-use considerations may be applicable to promoting these objectives. Copyright law that is too stringent may not only interfere with the law's intent to foster creativity but may also impede the spread of information that is of public interest. Copyright law may also implicate First Amendment concerns.

A recent case dealt with many of these issues. Eight major publishing houses sued Kinko's Graphics Corporation, the giant copying chain, alleging copyright infringement pursuant to the Copyright Act of 1976. More specifically, the publishers alleged that Kinko's, through 200 shops nationwide, infringed copyrights when it copied excerpts from books whose rights are held by the publishers without permission and without payment of required fees. Excerpts varied in length from 14 to 110 pages and were sold to students attending schools including New York University and Columbia University. Although this practice no doubt advanced educational objectives, did Kinko's overstep the parameters of the copyright law? Was the company's use of the excerpts a "fair use" specifically provided for in the Copyright Act of 1976? For further discussion, see p. 693.

---

their names on visual works if those works have been distorted, mutilated, or otherwise modified in a way that would prejudice their reputations as artists; to prevent distortion, mutilation, or modification of works in ways that would prejudice their reputations as artists; and to prevent the destruction of works that are of "recognized stature."

Exceptions to Coverage. As with any legislation, however, there are some serious gaps in the Visual Artists Rights Act of 1990. For example, the act excludes works made for hire, films, video and material not copyrighted, and it seeks to create a fundamental legal distinction between what is a work of visual art and what is not. Moreover, the protection provided by the act applies only to those works sold by an artist after June 1991—the effective date of the legislation—regardless of when the work was created.

Public art such as mobiles and sculptures displayed in prominent spaces, usually outdoors, have proven especially difficult to protect under the act. One such controversy, involving Richard Serra's "Tilted Arc," culminated in 1989. In 1979, the federal government commissioned the American sculptor to create a work of art for placement in lower Manhattan. The sculpture was installed in 1981 amidst controversy over its minimalist style and provocative subject matter. Serra believed that his commissioned piece would remain at its designated placement permanently. However, federal employees who did not appreciate the work spearheaded an effort to relocate the piece despite the artist's protest. After lengthy court battles, "Tilted Arc" was scheduled for dismantling in March 1989. Serra ultimately abandoned the legal recourse that he felt derived from the moral-rights clause of the Berne Convention, and "Tilted Arc" was removed several days later.

Under the new act, site-specific works like Serra's would still fall between the cracks of this new legislation, suggesting the possibility of more controversy in the future.

CASE: COMPUTER PROGRAMS. Another question that has been much discussed in the last two decades is whether computer programs can be copyrighted. When computers first appeared on the market in the 1940s and 1950s, there was a tendency to regard them as mere sets of mathematical instructions and thus outside existing copyright regulations. Today, as confirmed in cases like the following, computer programs can indeed be copyrighted.

BRODERBUND SOFTWARE, INC. v. UNISON WORLD, INC.,
U.S. District Court, Northern District of California, 648 F.Supp.
1127 (1986)

Plaintiffs, Broderbund Software, Inc. ("Broderbund"), and Pixellite Software ("Pixellite"), are the exclusive licensee and the copyright holder, respectively, of a computer software printing program called "The Print Shop" ("Print Shop"). Defendant, Unison World, Inc. ("Unison"), is engaged in the business of converting other publishers' software to make it adaptable with different computers. Unison markets a computer software printing program called "The Printmaster" ("Printmaster"). Both "Print Shop" and "Printmaster" are menu-driven programs that enable their users to create customized greeting cards, signs, banners, and posters.

Broderbund and Unison embarked on negotiations toward converting "Print Shop" to make it adaptable to IBM computers. Unison began to develop an identical version of "Print Shop" adaptable to IBM computers. After Unison had made considerable progress toward the conversion of "Print Shop," negotiations between the parties broke down. In March 1985, Unison released its program

"Printmaster," with features substantially similar to "Print Shop." Plaintiffs bring this suit against Union claiming that the overall appearance, structure, and sequence of the audiovisual displays in "Printmaster" infringe plaintiffs' copyright on "Print Shop."

Orrick, District Judge.

. . . David Balsam and Martin Kahn, the principals of plaintiff Pixellite Software, began developing "Print Shop" in the spring of 1983. . . .

. . . [W]ith the help of Broderbund artists, [Balsam and Kahn] spent almost an entire year developing what was to become "Print Shop." Broderbund obtained from Pixellite an exclusive license to distribute "Print Shop" worldwide and began marketing the product in May 1984. At the time of its introduction onto the market, "Print Shop" could be operated only on Apple computers. The product was a success, selling approximately 500,000 copies (to date of trial) at a manufacturer's suggested retail price of $49.95.

Unison rarely, if ever, develops entirely original programs. In May 1984, the president of Unison, Hong Lu, approached the president of Broderbund, Douglas Carlston.

. . .

. . . Unison personnel met with Balsam and Kahn to discuss whether it was really possible in three months to create an IBM version that was faithful to the original. Broderbund made it clear that if Unison were to receive the IBM rights to "Print Shop," it had to produce an exact reproduction of the original. Balsam very briefly showed the source code (the text that is translated into an "object code" and then directs the computer to perform its functions) to one of Unison's programmers, MacDuff Hughes, to give Hughes a feel for the depth and complexity of "Print Shop." Balsam also gave Unison personnel some commercially available copies of "Print Shop" to show to Japanese producers.

For the next four to six weeks, programmer Hughes was under orders from both Lu and David Lodge, Unison's products manager, to develop a program as identical to "Print Shop" as possible - to "imitate" it. . . . Hughes set out to recreate "Print Shop" as closely as possible.

After Hughes had made considerable progress toward a faithful reproduction of "Print Shop," however, negotiations for the IBM rights broke down. . . . Lu now told Hughes to stop copying "Print Shop" because the negotiations had failed. Instead, Lu instructed Hughes to finish developing their *enhanced* version of "Print Shop" as soon as possible. Hughes was no longer to feel "constrained" by the actual structure or appearance of "Print Shop" - he was now free to improve on it. This enhanced version would then be released by Unison as its own creations. . . .

Lu's order to stop any further copying of "Print Shop" did not include copying that had already been incorporated into Hughes' work in progress. . . .

After Hughes finished his part of the project, other programmers at Unison added a "calendar" function to the IBM version, streamlined the method by which the user could select ready-made designs, and provided for the memorization of designs. The Unison-IBM version otherwise remained the same as Hughes had designed it.

In March 1985, Unison released its program under the name "Printmaster." On May 28, 1985, plaintiffs brought this action for copyright infringement, trademark infringement, and unfair competition. In November 1985, Broderbund released its IBM version of "Print Shop." It is to these facts that the Court now applies the law applicable to audiovisual copyrights.

Are the Audiovisual Displays Protected under the Copyright Laws?

The dichotomy between ideas and expression. It is axiomatic that copyright protects only the expression of ideas and not the ideas themselves. Thus, if an idea is indistinguishable from its expression, that is, if the idea is "merged" into its expression, the expression cannot be protected under the copyright laws. . . .

Defendant herein argues that the idea underlying the menu screens, input formats, and sequencing of screens in "Print Shop" is indistinguishable from its expression. Any menu-driven computer program that allows its users to print greeting cards, signs, banners, and posters will have a user interface substantially similar to that in "Print Shop," defendant contends, because there is no other conceivable way to structure such a program. The evidence at trial disproved defendant's contention. Plaintiffs introduced a program titled "Sticky-bear Printer," marketed by Weekly Reader Family Software, that allows its users to print greeting cards, signs, banners, and posters with variable combinations of user-dictated text, graphics, and borders. The functions of "Stickybear Printer" are substantially the same as the functions of "Print Shop"; thus, it can be said that the ideas underlying "Stickybear Printer" and "Print Shop" are the same. Yet the expressions of those ideas are very different. The menu screens and sequence of screens in the two programs are different. The entire structure and organization of the user interfaces are different. In short, the existence of "Stickybear Printer" proves that there do exist other, quite different ways of expressing the ideas emboided in "Print Shop." The Court rejects defendant's contention that the idea and expression of "Print Shop" are indistinguishable from one another.

. . .

Mechanical or utilitarian constraints. . . .

[C]opyright protection extends only to the artistic aspects, and not the mechanical or utilitarian features, of a protected work. . . .

In the present case, it is clear that the structure, sequence, and layout of the audiovisual displays in "Print Shop" were dictated primarily by artistic and aesthetic considerations, and not by utilitarian or mechanical ones. Repeatedly, the testimony of David Balsam showed that, in creating the screens of "Print Shop," he based textual and graphic decisions on the basis of aesthetic and artistic preferences. On the "Now Type Your Message" screen of "Print Shop," for instance, no mechanical or practical constraint forced Balsam to make the "Stencil" typeface smaller on the display than the "Alexia" typeface. The choice was purely arbitrary. . . . Thus, the Court cannot accept defendant's argument that the audiovisual displays of "Print Shop" fall outside the scope of "pictorial" or "graphic" works as set forth in 101.

. . .

Did Defendant copy plaintiff's work? Having determined that the overall structure, sequence, and arrangement of the screens, text, and artwork (i.e., the audiovisual displays in general) are protected under the copyright laws, the Court now turns to the question of whether defendant in fact copied protected portions of "Print Shop."

. . .

. . . Plaintiffs produced sufficient direct evidence of copying to establish infringement. The uncontradicted testimony at trial was that both Hong Lu and David Lodge ordered Unison's programmers to copy "Print Shop." The programmers evidently executed these orders to the best of their ability. Some of the copying was done so carelessly that it left unmistakable traces. For example, in the "Custom Layout" screen of "Print Shop," the user is instructed to press the "Return" key on the Apple keyboard. . . .

The testimony of Hughes also provided probative direct evidence of copying. . . . He was hurrying to finish the project so that he could get back to school on time. In particular, Hughes copied the screens in the "Greeting Card," "Sign," and "Picture Editor" functions. . . .

Based on the foregoing, the Court finds that plaintiffs have adduced sufficient direct evidence of copying to prove infringement of the protected portions of "Print Shop."

. . .

Substantial similarity. The leading case in this area is *Arnstein v. Porter* (1947). There, the court established a two-step test for determining substantial similarity. . . . [T]he Ninth Circuit, albeit with some modification, adopted the *Arnstein* test and interpreted it to require the application of (1) an "extrinsic" test aimed at determining whether there exists a substantial similarity in underlying ideas; and (2) an "intrinsic" test to ascertain whether there exists a substantial similarity in the expression of the underlying idea. . . .

. . .

Application of the extrinsic test. . . . There is no question but that "Print Shop" and "Printmaster" share the same underlying idea. . . . [I]t is obvious that the purpose and uses of "Printmaster" and "Print Shop" are virtually identical. Both programs allow their users to create greeting cards, signs, banners and posters with various, user-selected combinations of text, graphics, and borders. Both operate in conjunction with dot-matrix printers. . . .

Application of the intrinsic test. In applying the intrinsic test, the finder of fact (in this case the Court) is to determine whether an "ordinary reasonable person" would find the expression of the subject works to be substantially similar. . . .

The ordinary observer could hardly avoid being struck by the eerie resemblance between the screens of the two programs. In general, the sequence of the screens and the choices presented, the layout of the screens, and the method of feedback to the user are all substantially similar. . . . Other similarities are too numerous to list.

. . . The application of the intrinsic test in the present case compels the finding that their expression is substantially similar.

IT IS HEREBY ORDERED THAT:

Defendant, Unison World, Inc., is adjudged to have infringed the copyright of plaintiff, Pixellite Software, on the audiovisual displays of the computer program known as "Print Shop."

Case Questions:

1. How would the outcome be different if there were no other conceivable way to structure the audiovisual displays embodied in "Print Shop"?

2. Since the functions of "Print Shop" and "Printmaster" are virtually identical, what is the protection afforded to "Print Shop" under the copyright laws?

3. How could Unison have avoided liability for infringement of plaintiff's copyright on "Print Shop"?

In 1988, the Copyright Office ruled that the copyright of a software program protects the screen displays as well as the computer code.

The Semiconductor Chip Act of 1984. A chip or integrated circuit is a collection of transistors in a single structure that work together to perform an electronic function, such as processing, memory, or logic. They are found in many places, including computers, watches and automobiles. A *semiconductor chip* is defined by statute as "any product having two or more layers of metallic, insulating, or semiconductor material, deposited or otherwise placed on, or etched away or otherwise removed from, a piece of semiconductor material in accordance with a predetermined pattern; and intended to perform electronic circuitry."

By enacting the *Semiconductor Chip Protection Act (SCPA)* in 1984, the

United States was the first country to protect chip designs. It is the first enactment of an intellectual-property law devised specifically to meet the legal needs of a new technology in the semiconductor industry. The SCPA is neither a patent nor a copyright law; rather, it is a hybrid form of intellectual-property law that combines some aspects of patent and copyright law with new elements of its own.

The interests at stake under the SCPA are industrial-property interests, which are generally more like those of the patent system than they are like those of the traditional subject matter of copyright. In other words, the interests seeking protection and advancement under the SCPA are primarily economic and material. A further interest, which is largely a means of accomplishing material progress, is that of promoting and encouraging technological progress in the semiconductor-electronics field. Investment in technology and the security of that investment, as well as related business concerns, thus assume more importance under the SCPA than under copyright law.

A case which illustrates the problem of copying of American computer-chip technology and which broke new legal ground involved Intel. Corp., a leading manufacturer of chips, and NEC Corp., the large Japanese computer company. At issue was the alleged copying of Intel's copyrighted "microcode"—a piece which is located inside a silicon-chip microprocessor and which is considered an interest protectable under U.S. copyright laws. The case began in 1984, when NEC filed an action seeking a declaratory judgment that Intel's copyrights on two sets of microcode were invalid and/or not infringed by NEFC. This action prompted Intel to file a counterclaim for infringement of its copyrights on those microcodes. The alleged copyright violations stemmed from a 1983 agreement between the two companies.

NEC, the alleged infringer, succeeded in proving the originality of its work. The court found (1) that a microcode fell within the congressional definition of a computer program under the Copyright Act of 1980 and that (2) it possessed protectable originality "fixed in any tangible medium of expression." Intel was unable to make a prima facie case of infringement, which entailed establishing: (1) a valid copyright on the microcodes, (2) access by NEC to the microcodes, and (3) substantial similarity between Intel's microcodes and NEC's microcodes. Despite its finding that a valid copyright existed to which NEC had access, the court held that NEC's microcodes were not substantially similar to Intel's.

Trademarks and Service Marks

All businesses must somehow distinguish themselves from their rivals. One way of doing this is to adopt a name. In fact, if a business does not adopt one, its customers probably will. For example, there is a fish restaurant in Boston that has no name. People refer to it as "the No-Name Restaurant." It is unavoidable.

A **trademark**, also called a **brand name**, identifies a product. "IBM," "Gillette," and "Levis," are all trademarks. Service marks identify services rather than products. "IBM" is also a *service mark*, and so are the names of retail stores like "Macy's" and "Tower Records" in addition to rock-and-roll bands and professional organizations. Trademarks and service marks permit companies to develop "good will" among customers by making them more aware of the firms they patronize.

trademark (or brand name)
Word, name, or symbol used to identify a product that can be registered and thus protected

TRADEMARK REGISTRATION. The common law gives a certain amount of protection to trademarks and service marks in the localities where they are actually used. If a trademark or service mark is used in a wider geographical area, it must be protected through either state or federal registration. The United States Patent and Trademark Office administers the federal registration process.

State systems for registering trademarks and service marks vary. On the federal level, trademarks and service marks can be registered for 20 years. If the mark has been in continuous use, the federal registration can be renewed for further 20-year terms. Companies must show that they actually use their trademark and service marks by filing affidavits to the effect at some point five to six years after the original registration. Without such an affidavit, the registration ceases to be valid.

"Use in Commerce." Trademarks can be registered with the federal government only if they are "used in commerce." Trademarks must be affixed to the goods that they identify or placed close to those goods (as in a point-of-sale display). The goods themselves must be sold or transported. Service marks must be used in advertisements, posters, and the like. The advertisement must appear when the service that it publicizes is actually available to the public; an announcement that a store will open in two weeks' time does not qualify as "use" of the service mark.

In addition, some services, such as dry cleaning or shoe repair, are too local in nature to qualify for federal, though not for state, registration. Local restaurants do, however, qualify for federal registration because they fall within the scope of the Civil Rights Act. The superscript symbol "R" enclosed by a circle denotes federal registration; the superscript symbol "TM" within a circle denotes state registration.

TRADEMARK INFRINGEMENT. When a company registers trademarks or service marks, it acquires the exclusive right to use them within the area of registration. If the registration is federal, the trademark is valid in the whole of the United States. Should another company then use the mark in question, the first company's rights would be infringed.

Sometimes, the first company will succeed in getting the other one to stop using the trademark or service mark by pointing out that it has been registered already. In other cases, stronger steps are needed. Infringement suits dealing with federally registered trademarks or service marks can be brought in either federal or state courts. Those dealing with trademarks or service marks registered in any of the 50 states must be brought in the courts of that state.

Protectability. When the suit is first heard by a judge, the plaintiff usually asks for an injunction preventing the defendant from using the trademark or service mark until the case can be tried. At the trial, the plaintiff must first show that the mark can be protected. As Figure 18-3 shows, marketing studies have discovered that protectability varies according to the *type* of trademark or brand name.

Suppose, for example, you started a successful store called "World-Famous George's Bike Shop." Another person might want to set up his own "World-Famous George's Bike Shop." If so, you would no doubt wish to sue for infringement of your service mark. Your lawyer would argue that the name had become so well established as to be associated specifically with your store. Note that if your rival had called his store "George's Bike Shop" you would not have a case—"George's Bike Shop" is just a simple description.

The standard for determining what terms can be protected is called the **primary significance test**, which was set forth in *Kellogg Co. v. National biscuit Co.*, the so-called *Shredded Wheat* case (305 U.S. 111 [1938]): "To establish a trade name in the term 'shredded wheat,'" the Supreme Court ruled then, "the plaintiff must show more than a subordinate meaning which applies to it. It must show that the primary significance of the term in the minds of the con-

primary significance test Legal standard for protectable *trademark* based on whether the producer or the product is dominant in the consumer's mind

Logo Logistics Procter & Gamble—which was then a Cincinnati manufacturer of soaps and candles—developed its once-famous moon-and-stars logo in about 1851. As the company grew and adopted a marketing philosophy around products of uniform quality, the trademark became more important as a means of identifying P&G goods, especially in an era before advertising had taken on the function of increasing product recognition. In 1875, P&G successfully sued a Chicago soapmaker who had introduced a look-alike logo, and the moon-and-stars emblem was registered as a trademark in 1882. One hundred years later, the P&G symbol faced another test of a much different kind: Perpetuating a rumor that a high-level P&G executive had admitted on *The Phil Donahue Show* that a percentage of the company's profits was "given to the devil," some Christian fundamentalist groups cited the moon-and-stars trademark as evidence of "satanic" devices and practices. As the rumors gained renewed strength in 1985, P&G resorted to press conferences and even a toll-free hotline—all to no avail. Although the logo still appears on the company building and letterhead (and, beginning in 1991, on a few product packages), it has been withdrawn as the company's general marketing trademark.

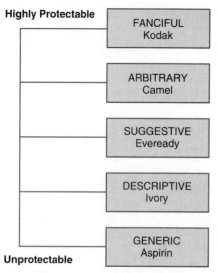

Highly Protectable

FANCIFUL
Kodak

ARBITRARY
Camel

SUGGESTIVE
Eveready

DESCRIPTIVE
Ivory

GENERIC
Aspirin

Unprotectable

FIGURE 18-3   Trademark Types and Protectability

Source: Dorothy Cohen, "Trademark Strategy," *Journal of Marketing* (Jan. 1986).

suming public is not the product but the producer." If the mark is protectable, plaintiffs must then demonstrate a "superior right" in the mark—that is, that they used it before the defendant did.

After these preliminary issues have been settled, the plaintiff must prove that the defendant's use of the mark creates a likelihood of confusion between the two businesses. Because it is much easier to prove that this has happened than to prove that it has not, if the case gets this far, the odds favor the plaintiff. Successful plaintiffs can win both permanent injunctions barring defendants from using the marks and actual and punitive damages for past usage. Federal courts can actually award treble damages and attorney's fees. The following trademark-infringement case involves one of the best-known trademarks in the United States.

LOIS SPORTSWEAR, U.S.A., INC. v. LEVI STRAUSS & CO.
U.S. District Court 631 F.Supp. 735 (1985)

Plaintiff, Lois Sportswear, U.S.A., Inc. ("Lois"), is an importer and distributor of wearing apparel, including jeans. Defendant is Levi Strauss & Company ("Levi"). Levi uses a stitching design mark (the "Levi arcuate mark") on the rear pockets of Levis jeans. Levi has procured and presently owns federal trademark registrations for the Levi's arcuate mark. Lois jeans and trousers exhibit a highly similar back pocket stitching design mark (The "Lois arcuate") on the jeans. These consolidated actions were commenced on December 14, 1982, when Lois filed a complaint seeking a declaratory judgment that the Lois arcuate does not violate the trademark rights of Levi in Levi's arcuate. Levi counterclaimed for injunctive and monetary relief, charging Lois with trademark infringement under the Lanham Act, violations of common-law trademark infringement

and unfair competition, and trademark dilution in violation of New York law.

Sweet, District Judge.

. . .

The Lois arcuate design was first used on the rear pocket of the Dylan brand jeans and has been used continuously on Lois brand jeans and trousers since 1961. The Lois arcuate consists of two curved arches intercepting at midpoint. The mark extends approximately three-quarters of an inch further towards the bottom pocket from the arcs intercept than the Levi arcuate. . . .

. . . .

Levi's jeans feature a permanently affixed red or orange pocket tab with the name Levi on the right rear pocket and a leather label (the Two Horse Brand label) sewn above the right pocket, as well as sewn-in labels and buttons bearing the Levi name. . . .

. . . .

Levi has submitted a consumer survey conducted by the market research firm of Bruno & Ridgway which Levi contends measures the degree to which consumers misassociated Lois' jeans with Levi jeans when the jeans were viewed in a simulated post-sale context. . . .

A total of 637 interviews, equally divided between males and females in the age range of 14 to 35, were conducted in six interviewing locations in different sections of the country. Respondents in each segment were intercepted in shopping malls and after being asked a series of screening questions, including whether or not they had purchased a pair of jeans in the last 12 months, were shown three videotaped segments, either Lois, Wrangler and [a] triangle design, or Levi, Wrangler and [a] triangle design. The respondents then were asked if they associated each pocket with a particular brand of jeans. Seventy-nine percent of respondents correctly identified the Levi arcuate and sixty-nine percent correctly recognized the Wrangler mark. Forty-three percent misassociated the Lois arcuate with Levi jeans. There were no identifications of the Lois arcuate with Lois jeans. . . . Lois contests the validity and admissibility of the survey and its results.

Levi has also submitted numerous exhibits and affidavits in support of its contention that the Levi arcuate has achieved a very high level of recognition and consumer association with Levi Strauss and has taken on its own meaning as a symbol. . . .

To sustain a claim of trademark infringement under 15 U.S.C. § 1114(1)(a), a plaintiff is required to demonstrate that the defendants' use of the same or similar mark is likely to cause confusion among potential consumers as to the source of its product. Likelihood of confusion is also an essential element of an unfair competition claim based on section 43(a) of the Lanham Act, as well as a common law claim of unfair competition. In order to prevail on its claims of infringement and unfair competition, Levi must demonstrate that its arcuate mark is deserving of protection and that there is a likelihood of confusion between the marks.

. . . .

In *Polaroid Corp. v. Polarad Electronics Corp.* (1961), the Second Circuit noted the factors that must be examined in making a determination as to the likelihood of confusion:

> [The] strength of [the] mark, the degree of similarity between the two marks, the proximity of the products, the likelihood that the prior owner will bridge the gap, actual confusion, and the reciprocal of defendant's good faith in adopting its own mark, the quality of defendant's product, and the sophistication of the buyers. Even this extensive catalogue does not exhaust the possibilities—the court may have to take still other variables into account.

. . . .

The Second Circuit has held that:
[t]he term "strength" as applied to trademarks refers to the distinctiveness of the mark, or more precisely, its tendency to identify the goods sold under the mark as [emanating] from a particular, although possibly anonymous, source.

Arbitrary and fanciful marks which are nondescriptive and non-suggestive are by their very nature distinctive and strong trademarks. A registered mark is also accorded the highest degree of protection. . . .

Based on the above analysis, Levis arcuate mark is a strong mark that qualifies for a high degree of protection. In addition to its status as an incontestable registered mark, the Levi's arcuate mark is a fanciful design which has no function other than as a source indicator. Furthermore, assuming Levi needed to establish secondary meaning, Levi has presented evidence of widespread advertising and promotion of Levi's jeans featuring the Levi's arcuate mark, continuous use of the mark for more than a century, and sales of more than 800 million pairs of jeans bearing the Levi's mark since 1971. Evidence of sales success, advertising expenditures, and length and exclusivity of use are factors relevant to a determination of the strength of a mark.

. . . .

A visual inspection of the two marks reveals that although there are distinguishing factors the marks are essentially identical. Both marks consist of two curved arches intercepting at midpoint. The marks are of the same general size, and from any distance it would be difficult to accurately distinguish them. Both marks appear at precisely the same location on similar pairs of jeans. The Lois mark extends approximately three-quarters of an inch further towards the bottom pocket from the arcs intercept, thus creating it to a limited extent an impression of a letter "Y" as compared to the "V" impression of the Levi design. However, absent any other markings, the marks are visually extremely similar and create "the same general overall impression."

. . . .

. . . Lois contends, however, that despite any literal similarity between the marks, the existence of other indicia of origin on the jeans completely obviates the likelihood of any confusion among purchasing consumers. As noted above, in many instances, "[t]he presence of [defendants'] name on the product goes far to eliminate confusion of origin."

Courts have held, however, that where a strong mark is involved the addition of identifying labelling may be insufficient to eliminate the likelihood of confusion. *See, e.g., Polo Fashions, Inc. v. Extra Special Products, Inc.* (1978) (mark "POLO" by Ralph Lauren infringed by "Polo by Marco Polo" despite distinguishing phrase); *A. T. Cross Co. v. Jonathan Bradley Pens, Inc.* (1972) ("LaCross By Bradley" confusingly similar to "Cross"). . . . [T]he fact that a plaintiff always uses a mark in conjunction with its name does not necessarily mean that a competitor is free to use that mark or a similar one on its own or in conjunction what that competitor's own name.

In this case, the mark is likely to be viewed frequently in a non-sale setting after point of sale labels are removed and cause confusion among both prospective customers and the general public. Even if the likelihood that a consumer might accidentally purchase a pair of Lois jeans under the mistaken impression that they were manufactured by Levi were small, any general confusion as to the source of jeans viewed by potential customers outside of stores may be actionable. . . . Although "permanent" markings bearing the Levi and Lois names remain on the products after the point of sale, the limited degree to which they would be visible in a public setting obviates any ability they might have to reduce the possibility of confusion. . . . In post-sale context, the marks are sufficiently similar so as to create a strong possibility of confusion among prospective purchasers as to the source of the respective products.

This conclusion is, of course, supported by the findings of the Bruno & Ridgway survey. As noted above, the fact that the survey did not duplicate market conditions at the point of sale does not render it irrelevant, since in the circumstances of this case post-sale confusion may be actionable. Although courts have frequently rejected surveys which were not conducted under actual marketing conditions, the degree of confusion created among the general public is sufficiently relevant to make such a survey probative. . . .

. . .

For the reasons discussed above, Lois's motion for summary judgment is denied and Levi's motion for summary judgment and an injunction is granted.

Case Questions:

1. How do Lois jeans, off the rack or in post-sale context, cause confusion among prospective customers and the general public?

2. Examine how Levi can show the strength of its arcuate mark.

3. How could Lois have prevented a likelihood of confusion between their jeans and Levi's jeans?

---

gray market goods Goods manufactured in one country, bearing valid *trademarks* in another, and imported without the trademark owner's consent

CASE: THE GRAY MARKET. **Gray market goods** are goods that are manufactured in a foreign country, bear valid U.S. trademarks, and are imported without the trademark owner's consent. They compete—usually at a lower price—with trademarked goods distributed by the producer's authorized U.S. distributors. Trademark owners contend that consumers often are being sold a second-rate version of the product; they contend that discounters are getting a free ride on the marketing and service associated with the real thing and that the value of the trademark owner's investment thus depreciates.

In what is generally considered a victory for discount shoppers and the stores catering to them, the U.S. Supreme Court narrowly upheld U.S. Customs Service regulations barring international companies from preventing imports of the same trademarked goods in *K-mart Corp. v. Cartier Inc.* (1987). In *K-mart*, the dispute centered around the practices of U.S. discounters who buy *authentically* trademarked cameras, perfumes, electronics, and apparel abroad and then sell these items in U.S. stores at prices below those of products manufactured by U.S. trademark holders. K-mart argued that U.S. law does not permit the owner of a trademark to prevent resale of his own goods.

Trademark holders, on the other hand, argued that the Tariff Act of 1922 allows a manufacturer to bar the import of trademarked goods that will compete with goods produced by a holder of a U.S. trademark. They also challenged the way in which the Customs Service interpreted the Tariff Act of 1930, which prohibits importation of any goods that bear trademarks owned by U.S. citizens or corporations. The court upheld Customs Service rules that let stores such as K-mart buy cameras, perfume, and other consumer products overseas and sell them in the United States without the permission of the American trademark owner.

The court held that gray market items are not copies of trademarked goods, but rather authentic products—for example, cameras, perfumes, watches, or electronic items—trademarked by multinational corporations with subsidiaries in several countries that own local trademarks. The Court's reliance on the Tariff Act of 1930 allows imports to be blocked only in limited situations. For instance, when a foreign company gives exclusive distribution rights to an unaffiliated U.S. company and then competes with it in the United States, Customs can bar the foreign company's goods. The decision also made it clear that if a U.S. trademark owner authorizes an unaffiliated foreign concern to make or distribute its products overseas, the American company can keep those products out of the United States.

However, about 90 percent of the current gray market—which totals as much as $10 billion a year—will not be inhibited by the ruling. Indeed, the decision could lead to an expansion of the market if national retail chains start selling gray market goods now that their legality is no longer questioned.

■ Concept Check 18-4   Intellectual Property

- Explain the nature of *patents*, *copyrights*, and *trademarks* as *intellectual property*.
- Discuss the principal criteria for *patentable* inventions or processes.
- Explain the differences in *copyright* applications to books (fiction and nonfiction), paintings, and computer software.
- Describe the *Berne* and *Universal Copyright Conventions* and discuss the evolution of U.S. copyright regulation in terms of these international agreements.
- Describe a hypothetical situation in which a dispute may arise over *fair use* and copyright *infringement*.
- Under what conditions is a *trademark* or *service mark* eligible for federal *registration*?

YOU DECIDE: ANSWER/DISCUSSION
Fair Use

In what has been hailed a landmark decision, Kinko's Graphics Corporation was found guilty of copyright infringement and was ordered to pay $510,000 in statutory damages to the eight publishers who brought suit. The judge also issued an injunction prohibiting Kinko's from continuing the practice. This case squarely pitted publishers against students, with the copying industry caught in the middle. At issue was an exception to the copyright law that deems copying permissible "fair use" when it strives to fulfill educational ends.

The court found that Kinko's practices did not conform to three of the four factors in the Copyright Act used to analyze what is fair use: (1) the purpose, whether commercial or not, of the taking; (2) the amount and substantiality of the taking; and (3) the effect on the market value of the copyrighted work. The copy chain did prevail on one prong of the test—that is the factor that deals with the nature of the copyrighted work: The Court ruled that the scope of fair use is greater with respect to factual than nonfactual works.

SUMMARY

- In 1938, Congress expanded the *Federal Trade Commission Act* so as to prohibit "unfair or deceptive acts or practices," in addition to "unfair methods of competition." An *unfair practice* can clearly hurt competitors. The FTC began developing standards for identifying commercial practices that are unfair to consumers as well. An act or practice was traditionally regarded as *deceptive* if it *tended* to mislead or damage substantial numbers of consumers. Under President Ronald Reagan, the FTC suggested that for deception, the misrepresentation must be *likely* to mislead *reasonable* consumers. *Deceptive practices* such as *bait and switch* have been prosecuted and banned.

- Another important basis for prosecuting false advertisements is Section 43(a) of the *Lanham Act*, which outlaws "any false description or representation" of goods or services in interstate commerce. Only competitors of the firm that made the false description have the right to sue under this section. A high proportion of Section 43(a) cases deal with *comparative advertisements*, which contrast the advertised product and its competitors. This practice does not violate the Lanham Act unless the advertised product is itself set forth in a misleading way. One remedy under the Act is *corrective advertising*.

- To promote creativity, the government has created the concept of *intellectual property:* limited monopolies in the form of *patent, copyright,* and *trademark* protection are extended to the tangible expression of ideas, although to ideas themselves. Even under established guidelines, deciding what is and is not patentable has been quite complex, largely as a result of the rapid developments in technology. In copyright law, a major change came with the enactment of the *Visual Artists Rights Act,* which for the first time gave artists credit and control over their work based on their "moral rights."

- Internationally, increased foreign competition has brought pressure to reform the U.S. patent system, which is regarded as too slow. In 1988, the U.S. signed the *Berne Convention,* a treaty that sets international copyright standards.

QUESTIONS AND PROBLEMS

1. A mouthwash company's television commercials depict people coming in out of the rain and being told by a family member that they might catch cold and should gargle with the mouthwash. The implication is that the mouthwash is beneficial in preventing colds. In fact, the mouthwash has nothing harmful in it, but neither is it effective as a cold preventive or remedy. The FTC brings suit to have the mouthwash company halt its advertising. What will the result be? [*Warner-Lambert Company v. FTC,* 562 F. 2d 749 (D.C. Cir. 1977)]

2. A & B Ice Cream Co. advertises that it has the "best ice cream in the universe." Does A & B's advertisement violate federal law?

3. A tire company advertises that each of the tires it manufactures is safe and individually constructed. In reality, while the company exercises its best efforts to use the best manufacturing procedures, tests, and quality control, the technology is unable to insure that there are no defects in each tire. The company asserts that its advertisement is only puffing and that any reasonable consumer knows that nothing can be manufactured to be entirely safe. Is the advertisement puffing? Explain.

4. A carpet store advertises a sale of its best "family" carpeting. In fact, the carpeting is of poor quality and not at all appealing. When customers come into the store, the salespersons shows them the sale carpet, but talks "confidentially" in disparaging terms about it and directs the customers to higher-priced, better-quality carpeting. Customers invariably purchase the higher-quality carpeting after comparing the two. Is the carpet store's practice illegal?

5. The plaintiff, who does business under the trade name Franklin Survey Company, is a map publisher. In 1932, he published and copyrighted a map of Delaware County, PA. He did no actual surveys or investigations of roads, creeks, or rivers. He obtained his information from other maps in his possession or in the possession of the township and municipal authorities. The defendant, a newspaper, printed the map in an article without plaintiff's permission. The defendant agrees that he copied the map but asserts that the map was not copyrightable. Was he right? [*Amsterdam v. Triangle Publications, Inc.,* 189 F. 2d. 104 (1951)]

6. Beginning on December 25, 1967, and continuing for five months, Firestone made the following assertion in an advertising compaign:

   The safe tire. Firestone.
   When you buy a Firestone tire . . . you get a safe tire . . . Firestone tires are custom-built one by one . . . And they're personally inspected for an extra margin of

694

safety. Every new Firestone design goes through rugged tests of safety and strength far exceeding any driving condition you'll ever encounter . . . All Firestone tires meet or exceed the new Federal Government testing requirements.

The state of tire manufacturing is such that the best manufacturing procedures and test and quality control techniques known in the industry cannot insure that each tire produced is free from any defects in workmanship or material. In another advertisement, Firestone claimed its tires "stop 25% quicker" based on one test it conducted. The Federal Trade commission filed suit and issued a cease and desist order for both campaigns. What did the FTC find wrong with the ads and will the cease and desist order stand? [*Firestone Tire & Rubber Co. v. F.T.C.*, 481 F. 2d. 246 (1973)]

7. Film company A brings action against film company B claiming that the movie *Starman* was a copyright infringement of company A's movie *Wavelength*. The claim is that the alien characters, as well as other parts of the film, are sufficiently similar to raise the copyright issue. Compare the information below on the alien issue. Was there a copyright infringement? Why or why not? Explain.

Starman
One alien

Alien is 35 years old

Alien falls in love and has sex with protagonist

Alien speaks 52 languages.

Scenes take place throughout U.S.

Alien restores life to dead things

Spacecraft emitted a large beam to earth

Wavelength
Three aliens

Aliens are nine years old

Aliens are protagonist's children

Aliens never speak; they use telecommunication

Scenes take place in California

Aliens kill humans

Spacecraft emitted lighting bolts

8. The Mary Carter Paint Company manufactures and sells paint and related products. The company has no history of selling single cans—it customarily sells twins. One day it decided to sell paint on a "buy 1 get 1 free" basis, pricing one can at the price of two and advertising the second as free. The FTC filed suit. What was the result? [*Federal Trade Commission v. Mary Carter Paint Co. et. al.*, 382 US 46 (1965)]

9. Mary Campanella wants to register the word "canyon" for candy bars. There is already a word mark "canyon" registered for fresh citrus fruit. The two are different in lettering design, but the word marks are identical. The U.S. Patent and Trademark Office has a rule that in borderline cases of "likelihood of confusion," the cases should be resolved against the newcomers. How will this case be decided? [*In re Mars, Inc.*, 741 F. 2d 395 (1984)]

10. Plaintiff published the novel *Looking for Mr. Goodbar* in 1975, and it stayed on the best-seller list for twenty-seven weeks. The book was based on an actual murder of a woman by a man she met in a bar. Plaintiff sold to Paramount Studios the rights to use the novel, its title, and any similar title for a movie, and a movie was subsequently made based on the novel. After the plaintiff's book was published, several factual accounts of the murder were published in magazines and a book, using the word "goodbar" in the title. Plaintiff did not take any legal action because she thought they were clearly distinguishable from her novel. Because of all the publications, the murder has been referred to by the media as the "Goodbar murder," and "goodbar" has taken on the vernacular meaning of the singles scene or a dangerous pickup. Defendant agreed to produce a television movie based on the factual murder investigation. The name of the TV movie was "Trackdown: Finding the Goodbar Killer." Plaintiff sues defendant alleging that the use of the word "Goodbar" in the title of the TV movie was trading in on plaintiff's reputation and good will generating from her novel and constituted a false designation of origin in violation of the Lanham Act, Section 1125(a). Under the Lanham Act there is protection for a creative work when the title has acquired a secondary meaning such that

the public identifies the title with the plaintiff and her work and there is a likelihood of confusion because the public will be misled into believing the defendant's work is sponsored by plaintiff since both bear similar titles.

Based on this, is it likely that plaintiff will be able to establish that the title has acquired secondary meaning? Explain. [*Rossner v. CBS, Inc.*, 612 F. Supp. 334 (1985)]

19

DEBTOR-CREDITOR RELATIONS

In the past 40 years, there has been a virtual revolution in the United States economy with respect to the volume and uses of credit. As a result, traditional attitudes about the way individuals and corporations borrow, manage, and repay funds are being abandoned. Evidence of this transformation is plentiful: Automatic teller machines let people do their banking day and night; stores and restaurants welcome half a dozen national credit cards; news stories report the bankruptcies of some major corporations and the record profits of others. Our borrowing habits are reflected by the high percentage of the population that holds credit cards—and by the increase in personal bankruptcies.

In response to these new developments, Congress has assumed the task of protecting citizens from the worst abuses that have developed in the new credit economy. Prior to 1968, only bankruptcy was subject to federal regulation. Between 1968 and 1978, however, Congress passed laws affecting borrowing, installment buying, credit cards, billing, discrimination in lending, reporting of personal financial data, bill-collecting, and bankruptcy. The enactment of these laws seems to indicate that Congressional sympathy lies with the indebted consumer rather than the creditor. This attitude is reflected in the legislation's language—for example, the new bankruptcy act mentions only "debtors," not "bankrupts," and the Fair Credit Reporting Act refers to borrowers as "consumers."

■ CREDIT

Have citizens actually benefited from this legislative revolution? Can such legislation compensate for ignorant or irresponsible credit management by individual consumers or irresponsible consumer behavior? Has the legislation achieved its objectives, or are we all subject to the ultimate and unpredictable "law of unintended consequences"? This chapter will examine the products of that remarkable decade of legislation, related judicial developments, and corporate decisions, in addition to discussing the growth of credit.

The Growth of Credit

The use of credit has so permeated our personal and business affairs that it is difficult to imagine life without it. On a personal level, our homes would be equipped with only pay telephones, and coin-operated devices would control our use of water and electricity. In other words, utility companies extend credit by allowing customers to receive service now and pay for it later. This is a form of credit called **service credit**.

service credit Form of credit in which one receives service now—for example, electricity—and pays for it later

CREDIT CARDS. When most people think of personal credit, they think of its most familiar symbol, the credit card, and of the power it gives us to postpone payment. Bank **credit cards**, principally MasterCard and Visa, have become the most popular form of credit card since their introduction some 30 years ago. Today, over 75 million Americans collectively carry more than 200 million such cards—and owe more than $80 billion at any given time. Prior to the introduction of these cards, most credit cards were offered by oil companies and retail stores. National retailers like Sears, with over 60 million cards, Penney's, and Federated Department Stores still constitute a major segment of the market.

credit card Type of personal credit that allows individuals, through arrangements with banks, retailers, and travel and entertainment firms, to purchase goods and services and receive cash advances up to a credit limit

The first *travel and entertainment (T&E) cards* were issued by Diners Club in 1950. American Express, whose card first appeared in 1958, now issues three times as many cards as Diners Club. T&E cards differ from bank and retail cards in their charges and billing practices. The customer generally pays an annual fee for a T&E card and is expected to pay the full balance due in each 30-day period. Interest is generally not charged on such cards. Bank credit cards charge interest—frequently 18 percent or more—but not necessarily a membership fee. The customer need not pay in full every month but may make a partial or minimum payment and be charged interest on the unpaid balance. The customer can charge additional purchases up to his or her credit limit.

debit card Bank-issued card that enables individuals to reduce bank balances immediately by the amount of a purchase or cash advance

Another form of card is the **debit card** offered by banks for use in automatic teller machines or in retail establishments. Whenever a consumer uses a debit card, his or her bank balance is immediately reduced by the amount of the purchase or cash advance. The Sears Discover card is a combined credit and debit card, depending on the way a consumer uses it.

Although credit cards are the most popular way to obtain credit, many other sources are also available. These include loans from commercial banks, savings and loan associations, consumer finance corporations, and credit unions. Money may also be borrowed against assets already held, such as stocks, bonds, and insurance policies. The basic types of consumer credit are summarized in Table 19-1.

CREDIT AND CONSUMER DEBT. To what extent have Americans taken advantage of expanding avenues of credit? According to the Federal Reserve System, individual debt in the United States rose from $621 billion in 1970 to $2.04 trillion in 1980 and $4.47 trillion by 1988—a sevenfold increase in just under 20 years. As Figure 19-1 illustrates, the same period witnessed an almost parallel increase in the number of consumer bankruptcy cases filed under the Bankruptcy Code of 1978: Between June 1981 and June 1990, the number of cases filed increased from just over 300,000 to over 660,000, and as Figure 19-1 shows, the rates of indebtedness and bankruptcy filings have been virtually parallel since 1985. (It should be noted, however, that credit levels are not the only factor in the increase in bankruptcy filings; interest rates and unemployment are also contributing factors. At the same time, levels of change in these areas have not

TABLE 19-1　*Types of Consumer Credit*

TYPE OF CREDIT	BASIC OPERATION
Open-End Credit	Balances owed on such cards usually require payment in full within thirty days. Such arrangements are not considered installment credit. Travel and entertainment cards, such as American Express and Diners Club, operate this way, as do most charge accounts with local businesses.
Installment Credit	Consumer agrees to repay a fixed amount in equal installments over a definite period of time. Automobile loans are usually of this type, as are personal loans.
Revolving Credit	The consumer has options of paying off the entire outstanding balance, only a specified minimum, or something in between. Bank credit cards and those issued by major retail establishments and gasoline companies usually work this way.

Source: American Bar Association, *You and the Law* (Lincolnwood, IL: Publications International, 1990). Data from the Federal Trade Commission.

been as great as those in the area of consumer debt, which seems to bear most of the responsibility.)[1]

CASE: LETTERS OF CREDIT.　It is important for a merchant who agrees to ship goods to a buyer to feel that payment for such goods is guaranteed. This is particularly important if goods are being shipped to a foreign buyer. In most cases, this "security" is accomplished with a bank-issued letter of credit. Such **letters of credit** are a form of contract between the parties. They are governed by Article 5 of the Uniform Commercial Code. A sample international letter of credit is appears in Figure 19-2.

Letters of credit act as guarantes of payment even though they are not

letter of credit　Form of security issued by a buyer's bank to a merchant affirming that payment for goods is guaranteed

FIGURE 19-1　Household Debt and Consumer Bankruptcy　*Source:* Robert M. Viles, "The Mainstreaming of Bankruptcy in American Life and Law," *New Hampshire Bar Journal* (March 1991). Data from Administrative Office of the U.S. Courts, *Bankruptcy Statistical Information* (Sept. 1990); U.S. Department of Commerce, *Statistical Abstract of the United States, 1990* (1991); and Board of Governors of the Federal Reserve System, *Annual Statistical Digest, 1988* (Nov. 1989).

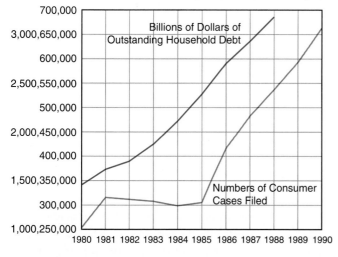

---

[1] Robert M. Viles. "The Mainstreaming of Bankruptcy in American Life and Law," *New Hampshire Bar Journal* (March 1991), pp. 7-14.

4

The First National Bank of Chicago
INTERNATIONAL BANKING DEPARTMENT
One First National Plaza/Chicago, Illinois 60670

ORIGINAL ☐ 7

Cable address: NATIONAL CHICAGO — Telex number: 2-53801 — Date of issue: JAN. 1, 19--

Irrevocable Documentary Letter of Credit Advising Bank	ISSUING BANK'S NUMBER	ADVISING BANK'S NUMBER
	cc. 123456	

Applicant

BANCO ESPANOL DE CREDITO
BARCELONA, SPAIN

LEATHER GOODS INC.
CHICAGO, ILLINOIS

Beneficiary

FABRICAS MAJORCA S.A.
(COMPLETE ADDRESS)

Amount

US$100,000.00 (ONE HUNDRED THOUSAND U.S. DOLLARS)

Expiry

Draft must be presented for negotiation or presented to the drawee on or before: JUNE 30, 19--

Dear Sir(s),

We hereby issue in your favor this documentary letter of credit which is available by negotiation of your draft(s) at -----180 DAYS SIGHT----- on THE FIRST NATIONAL BANK OF CHICAGO, CHICAGO, ILLINOIS, U.S.A., accompanied by the following documents:

DISCOUNT CHARGES ARE FOR ACCOUNT OF THE APPLICANT.
1. COMMERCIAL INVOICE IN TRIPLICATE,
2. U.S. CUSTOMS INVOICE IN TRIPLICATE,
3. FULL SET OCEAN CARRIERS CLEAN BILLS OF LADING, DATED ON BOARD, ISSUED IN AT LEAST TWO ORIGINALS PLUS ONE NON-NEGOTIABLE COPY TO ORDER OF SHIPPER, BLANK ENDORSED, MARKED FREIGHT COLLECT NOTIFY ABC FORWARDING CO., 38 S. DEARBORN ST., CHICAGO, ILLINOIS 60670.

NOTE: ALL BANK CHARGES OTHER THAN THOSE OF THE FIRST NATIONAL BANK OF CHICAGO, CHICAGO, ILLINOIS ARE FOR BENEFICIARY'S ACCOUNT.

Covering:

2,000 LEATHER COATS AT $50.00 EACH.   1,000 EACH OF STYLE NUMBER 95 AND 96.
TERMS: F.O.B. VESSEL, SPAIN.

Dispatch/shipment from	Partial shipments	Transhipments
SPAIN (ANY PORT)	PROHIBITED	PROHIBITED
To	INSURED BY ☒ Buyer ☐ Seller	
CHICAGO, ILLINOIS VIA THE GREAT LAKES		

Special conditions: NEGOTIATING BANK MUST AIRMAIL ONE ORIGINAL COMMERCIAL INVOICE, CUSTOMS INVOICE AND BILL OF LADING TO ABC FORWARDING CO., 38 S. DEARBORN STREET, CHICAGO, ILLINOIS 60670, FOR OUR ACCOUNT, AND A CERTIFICATE TO THIS EFFECT MUST BE SUBMITTED WITH THE REMAINING DOCUMENTS.

DRAFT MUST BEAR THE CLAUSE "DRAWN UNDER DOCUMENTARY CREDIT NO. 123456 OF THE FIRST NATIONAL BANK OF CHICAGO"

We hereby engage with drawers and/or bonafide holders that drafts drawn and negotiated in conformity with the terms of this credit will be duly honored on presentation and that drafts accepted within the terms of this credit will be duly honored at maturity.

Advising bank's notification

The amount of each draft must be endorsed on the reverse of this credit by the negotiating bank.

SPECIMEN

Yours faithfully,
THE FIRST NATIONAL BANK OF CHICAGO

JOHN DOE *John Doe*   DAVID DOE *David Doe*
Authorized Signature   Authorized Signature   Signature of Official of Advising Bank

FIGURE 19-2 Sample International Letter of Credit   *Source:* Reprinted by permission of First Chicago Bank.

truly guarantees. The process works this way:

1. The seller asks the buyer for a letter of credit.
2. The buyer asks his bank (the *opening* or *issuing bank*) to issue a letter of credit in accordance with the seller's terms.
3. Once the buyer's bank agrees to extend the amount of credit the buyer requests, it notifies the seller's bank (the *paying bank*) that it will issue a letter of credit.
4. The seller's bank can then opt either (1) to add confirmation (to guarantee payment to the seller) or (2) to simply inform the seller that the letter was issued.
5. The seller ships the goods in accordance with the terms of the letter of credit.
6. The seller's bank inspects and approves the documents and sends them to the buyer's bank. Note that if the seller's bank opted to confirm the letter of credit, the seller would be paid at this point.

7. The buyer's bank examines and approves the documents. If everything is in order, the buyer's account is debited and payment is wired to the seller's bank.

8. The seller's bank credits the seller's account.

It is important to note that the bank is obligated to pay on the letter of credit once the documents are presented. The bank need *not* confirm that the conditions of the letter were met. Although letters of credit are sometimes used in domestic transactions, they are nearly always used in international trade (see the INTERNATIONAL ENVIRONMENT box in this chapter).

■ Concept Check 19-1   Credit

- Describe the usage of *credit* and *debit cards*.
- Explain the process whereby a *letter of credit* is issued and approved.

■ CONSUMER-PROTECTION AND TRUTH-IN-LENDING LEGISLATION

The dramatic rise in credit usage increased the federal government's interest in seeing that consumers are treated in a fair and nondiscriminatory manner. Congressional policies in this area were first enacted in the *Consumer Credit Protection Act* of 1968. As Table 19-2 illustrates, that act, divided into several *titles* and amended several times, covers numerous legislative policies covering *truth in lending*, including the *Truth-in-Lending Act of 1968*; the *Truth-in-Lending Simplification Act of 1980*; and the *Fair Credit and Charge Card Disclosure Act of 1988*.

The Truth-in-Lending Act

Title I of the **Consumer Credit Protection Act**, which is known as the **Truth-in-Lending Act**, explicitly endorsed greater consumer awareness of the costs of credit. The Supreme Court further clarified the legislative intent in *Mourning v. Family Publications Service, Inc.* (411 U.S. 356 [1973]). The Court said that the act

Consumer Credit Protection Act 1968 federal law providing that consumers seeking credit are treated in a fair and nondiscriminatory way

Truth-in-Lending Act Title I of the *Consumer Credit Protection Act*, specifying disclosure of the terms under which consumers receive credit

TABLE 19-2	*The Consumer Credit Protection Act*

TITLE	COVERAGE
Truth-in-Lending Act (Title I, 1968) Truth-in-Lending Simplification and Reform Act (Title I, 1980)	Specifies disclosure of terms under which consumers obtain credit, including annual percentage rate
Fair Credit Billing Act (Title I, 1974)	Regulates billing practices on credit cards and other credit accounts
Garnishment of Wages (Title III, 1968)	Sets guidelines and limits on prejudgment collection efforts
Fair Credit Reporting Act (Title VI, 1970)	Protects consumer's privacy and insures accuracy of information in consumer credit reports
Equal Credit Opportunity Act (Title VII, 1974)	Guarantees equal access to credit
Fair Debt Collection Practices Act (Title VIII, 1977)	Protects consumers against unwarranted harassment by bill collectors

promoted consumer awareness by shifting the traditional view of caveat emptor (let the buyer beware) to a philosophy of "let the seller disclose."

SCOPE OF THE ACT. The Truth-in-Lending Act is concerned primarily with disclosure of the terms on which consumers obtain credit. It leaves the function of determining what *rates* may be charged to the states.

It is important to note that the act's scope is restricted to the most common loans acquired by private citizens. Specifically, the act applies to all mortgages and loans of $25,000 or less made to individuals for their personal use. In addition, the act applies only to creditors who are in the business of offering loans. Thus, loans involving friends or family members, for example, are not covered.

ENFORCING THE ACT. While the Federal Trade Commission is responsible for enforcing the Truth-in-Lending Act, the **Federal Reserve Board** is given the power to create its rules and procedures for applying its provisions. The board has thus promulgated **Regulation Z**, which, among other things, requires creditors to specify the loan finance charges, including any fees, and *annual percentage rates (APR)* as a percentage of total credit extended. The board regularly publishes interpretations of Regulation Z to clarify various issues.

The Truth-in-Lending Simplification Act

As cases arose under the Truth-in-Lending legislation, it became clear that certain features of the act were cumbersome, confusing, unclear, or open to abuse—in other words, debtors discovered that it was easy, and often remunerative, to go into debt and then sue for damages under the Truth-in-Lending Act. The regulations affecting disclosure were both complex and detailed, and any mistake or deviation that a creditor made, even if inadvertent or minor, could form the basis of a suit.

To remedy these problems, Congress enacted the **Truth-in-Lending Simplification Act** of 1980 (the **Simplification Act**), which took effect in 1982. Under the original Truth-in-Lending Act, any violation of the specifications of the statute, even if it concerned a very minor or technical point, was actionable. For example, a consumer could sue a creditor and collect a statutory penalty for each deviation if the sequence of required information on a billing form differed from the specific order. The Simplification Act accomplished several things: (1) prioritizing the kinds of information that are needed by consumers; (2) eliminating separate damages for all cosigners to a loan contract; and (3) easing certain disclosure rules for open-end accounts (revolving charge accounts and credit cards).

REQUIREMENTS FOR DISCLOSURE. Upon entering into an **open-end account**, a consumer must receive a statement of the finance charge, any other charges, any security interest (collateral or retention of right to repossess goods purchased but not paid for) retained by the creditor, and a statement of billing rights. The statement of billing rights must be sent annually for as long as the account remains open.

At periods corresponding with the billing cycle, the consumer must be supplied with a statement that discloses such things as the previous balance, transactions, credits, periodic rates, the balance on which the finance charge is

---

Federal Reserve Board Independent federal agency with the power to promulgate rules and procedures for applying the provisions of the *Truth-in-Lending Act*

Regulation Z *Federal Reserve Board* requirements for compliance with the *Truth-in-Lending Act*, including the condition that creditors specify loan finance charges, including any fees, and APR as a percentage of total credit extended

Truth-in-Lending Simplification Act (or Simplification Act) 1980 federal law that simplified regulations affecting disclosure by creditors

open-end account A consumer credit account such as a *credit card* or revolving charge account

computed, the amount of finance charges, and the outstanding balance on the closing date of the billing cycle.

Another amendment to the Truth-in-Lending law limits the cardholder's liability for unauthorized use of his or her card to $50. (Note that the cardholder must pay for a lesser unauthorized charge if it was made before the card issuer was notified of the cardholder's loss.) Figure 19-3 summarizes more fully FTC recommendations for the legal protection of credit-card rights.

The Simplification Act also made adjustments to the **rule of recission**. Recission is basically the "unmaking" of a contract. For example, a homeowner who signs a home-improvement contract has three business days to decide whether he actually wants the work done. If the contract involves a loan, the three-day period begins when the lender gives the borrower (the homeowner) the *right of recission*. Thus, if construction supplies are delivered to the house before the three-day period expires and the homeowner notifies the lender of recission, the lender (or contractor) must reclaim the material within a specified period of time or risk forfeiting it.

Certain disclosure requirements have been deemed by the courts to be

rule of rescission Law specifying the time at the beginning of a loan agreement that the borrower can unmake the contract

FIGURE 19-3 Guidelines for Credit Card Protection   *Source:* American Bar Association, *You and the Law.* Data from the Federal Trade Commission.

1. In a safe place, keep a list of your credit-card numbers, expiration dates, and the phone number of each card issuer.

2. Credit-card issuers offer a wide variety of terms (annual percentage rate, methods of calculating the balance subject to the finance charge, minimum monthly payments, and actual membership fees). When selecting a card, compare the terms offered by several card issuers to find the card that best suits your needs.

3. When you use your credit card, keep an eye on your card after you give it to a clerk. Take your card back promptly after the clerk is finished with it, and make sure it is yours.

4. Tear up the carbons when you take your credit-card receipt.

5. Never sign a blank credit-card receipt. Draw a line through any blank spaces above the total when you sign receipts.

6. Open credit-card bills promptly, and compare them with your receipts to check for unauthorized charges and billing errors.

7. Write the card issuer promptly to report any questionable charges. Written inquiries should not be included with your payment. Instead, check the billing statement for the correct address for billing questions. The inquiry must be in writing, and it must be sent within sixty days to guarantee your rights under the Fair Credit Billing Act.

8. Never give your credit-card number over the telephone unless you made the call. Never put your credit-card number on a postcard or on the outside of an envelope.

9. Sign new credit cards as soon as they arrive. Cut up and throw away expired credit cards. Cut up and return unwanted credit cards to the issuer.

10. If any of your credit cards are missing or stolen, report the loss as soon as possible to the card issuer. Check your credit-card statement for a telephone number for reporting stolen credit cards. Follow up your phone calls with a letter to each card issuer. The letter should contain your credit-card number, the date the card was missing, and the date you called in the loss.

11. If you report the loss before a credit card is used, the issuer cannot hold you responsible for any subsequent unauthorized charges. If a thief uses your card before you report it missing, the most you will owe for unauthorized charges on each card is $50.

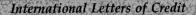

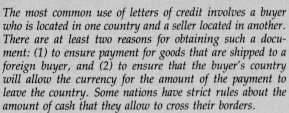

THE INTERNATIONAL ENVIRONMENT
International Letters of Credit

The most common use of letters of credit involves a buyer who is located in one country and a seller located in another. There are at least two reasons for obtaining such a document: (1) to ensure payment for goods that are shipped to a foreign buyer, and (2) to ensure that the buyer's country will allow the currency for the amount of the payment to leave the country. Some nations have strict rules about the amount of cash that they allow to cross their borders.

To prevent any problems, the bank officer assigned to inspect the letter of credit must examine the following information:

- Is the right amount of money set out in the letter of credit? For instance, if a letter of credit states that a French buyer will pay a Mexican seller $16,000 for 5000 pairs of huaraches, the bank may pay the seller that amount (if the rest of the documentation is correct) even though the parties actually intended the payment to be $6000.
- Can the shipment be made to the place and by the date named in the letter of credit? If not, an alternate route should be arranged and an amended letter should be obtained stipulating this route. For example, suppose the

original letter of credit states that the goods are to be shipped by air freight directly from New York to Moscow. The shipper cannot find a carrier to perform the contract—the best he can find is a flight to Paris, where the goods will be moved to another plane for the last leg of the trip to Moscow. If the new shipping plan is not expressly stated, the bank can refuse to honor the letter of credit.

- What is the date on which the letter of credit expires and, what is the last date on which the bank will honor it?
- Can documentation (for example, a bill of lading) be obtained that will show exactly where the goods were loaded and unloaded?

There is at least one red flag concerning the use of letters of credit: The bank need not verify that the shipment actually took place. Its only obligation is to examine the documentation that is presented to it for any discrepancies. Most errors occur in the areas of time of delivery and shipping instructions. However, there is the possibility that although a misspelled name can cause a letter to be rejected, payment for a missing shipment may be made if all of the documentation is correct.

---

fundamental to all consumer credit transactions. One important rule, involving a proper statement of the terms "finance charge" and "annual percentage rate," was the subject of the following case.

DIXEY v. IDAHO FIRST NATIONAL BANK
U.S. Court of Appeals, Ninth Circuit, 677 F.2d 749 (1982)

Appellee is the Idaho First National Bank (the "Bank"). The Bank made loans to Appellant Jim Dixey and appellants Ramon and Maria Martinez using the Bank's standard Sale and Loan Agreement. Appellants contend that the disclosures made by the Bank in connection with their loans failed to comply with the Truth-in-Lending Act (the "Act") and Federal Reserve Board Regulation Z, which implements the Act. The district court found that the Bank had committed three violations of the Act, but declined to award statutory damages for the "technical violations." Accordingly, the district court granted summary judgment for the Bank. Appellants appeal.

Kennedy, Circuit Judge:

. . . The district court found that the standard form contained three defects. First, the Bank violated the requirement of Regulation Z that "where the terms 'finance charge' and 'annual percentage rate' are required to be used, they shall be printed more conspicu-

ously than other terminology required by this part. . . ." The Bank printed the terms, "Finance charge" and "Annual percentage rate," in bold fact type, but also printed several other headings and disclosures in the same type, so that the two terms were not more conspicuous than other items. Second, the Bank included in the agreement a notice regarding the consumer's limited right to cancel a home solicitation sale, which is not required by the Act. This additional information was not delineated from the required disclosures as specified in Regulation Z. The purpose of the rule is to call attention to the required information. Third, the Bank placed the required prepayment penalty charge and delinquency charge disclosures on the back of the agreement. The customer's signature appeared on the front. Under 12 C.F.R. § 226.8(a) (1981), disclosures must be made on the same side of the page as, and above, the place for the customer's signature.

Although it found that the Bank had failed to satisfy the Act and Regulation Z in the above three respects, the district court characterized the discrepancies as "technical defects," and "minor, technical violations." Relying upon its power in equity, the trial court decided that because there was no evidence in the record that Appellants had been misled or confused by the flaws, the damage provisions of the Act should not avail the consumer in this particular case. . . . On appeal, the Bank neither disputes the finding that it committed three violations of the Act nor contends that it has any statutory defense. [We determine that the district court erred in withholding the statutory penalty, and we reverse].

Section 130 of the Act mandates civil penalties as follows: a creditor who fails to comply with any requirement of the Act "with respect to any person is liable to such person in an amount equal to the sum of" actual damages sustained plus twice the amount of any finance charge in connection with the transaction, provided the doubled charge "shall not be less than $100 nor greater than $1,000." Some courts have interpreted this provision as requiring strict compliance with the disclosures and terminology dictated by the Act, and have awarded the statutory penalty for all violations of the Act, however minor, because the first violation found by the district court was not de minimus and entitles appellants to the statutory penalty.

The Truth-in-Lending Act was passed to achieve "the informed use of credit," which "results from an awareness of the costs thereof by consumers." The Act requires disclosure of credit terms to consumers so that potential borrowers will be able to compare the available costs of credit. The most important disclosures mandated by the Act are those upon which consumers should compare competing loans, the finance charge and annual percentage rate. . . . Regulation Z, which the Federal Reserve Board drafted to specify disclosures helpful to informed borrowing, reflects the Act's concern with the cost of credit by requiring the annual percentage rate and finance charge to be printed more conspicuously than other terms. The rule facilitates comparison shopping for credit and stresses the cost of credit for the consumer.

The Bank failed to give required emphasis to these factors. . . . We disagree with the district court's characterization of this defect as "technical." . . .

. . .

We might have been more receptive to the district court's approach had the Act not been amended by the Truth-in-Lending Simplification and Reform Act of 1980, which, as the name suggests, was passed to simplify the information provided to consumers and to limit creditor civil liability to significant violations. The new civil liability provisions of the Act impose penalties for violating only those disclosures which are "of material importance in credit shopping," and not various "technical" violations. Suits to impose penalties for minor violations may no longer arise, as the amendments became fully effective on April 1, 1982. It should be noted, however, that under the amended Act, the finance charge and annual percentage rate are among the material terms affecting credit shopping and protected by civil liability. More importantly, the amendments also incorporate the requirements that the "annual percentage rate" and "finance charge" be more conspicuous in section 122(a) of the Act.

The parties shall bear their own costs on appeal. Reversed and remanded.

Case Questions:

1. Why did the Ninth Circuit disagree with the characterization of the Bank's failure to give conspicuous emphasis to the terms "finance charge" and "annual percentage rate" as "technical"?

2. What was the purpose of the Federal Reserve Board in drafting Regulation Z? What is the Act's concern?

REMEDIES FOR FAILURE TO DISCLOSE. A creditor who is found to have violated the disclosure provisions of the Truth-in-Lending Act may be either civilly or criminally liable. Criminal liability is based on a finding of willful action; it carries a fine of up to $5,000 and/or imprisonment for up to a year. Civil liability to the debtor is set at twice the creditor's finance charge payable to the debtor plus the cost of bringing the action; there is a minimum penalty of $100 and a maximum of $1000.

The Fair Credit Reporting Act

The **Fair Credit Reporting Act** states that its purpose is to ensure that agencies which evaluate and disseminate information about consumers' credit histories operate in a fair, impartial, and unintrusive manner. The FTC has primary enforcement power in the *public interest* (although not for individual consumers). Other agencies entrusted with enforcement include the Federal Deposit Insurance Corporation (FDIC), the Federal Reserve Board, the Interstate Commerce Commission (ICC), and the Secretary of Agriculture. Recently, a good deal of attention has come to rest on the rights of individual consumers under

Fair Credit Reporting Act Part of the *Consumer Credit Reporting Act*, ensuring the fair, impartial, and unintrusive evaluation and dissemination of information about consumers' credit histories by *credit-reporting agencies*

the act, especially its right-to-know provisions and the rights of consumers in their dealings both with lenders and credit-reporting agencies.

CONSUMER REPORTING AGENCIES.   Key terms in the Fair Credit Reporting Act include *consumer* and **consumer reporting agency**. The courts have interpreted this focus on the individual consumer to mean that credit reports on *businesses* are exempt from the act. Therefore, if a business is applying for a loan, and the commercial credit report on that business makes derogatory statements about an individual who has some involvement with the business, that person has no recourse under the Fair Credit Reporting Act. Other protections and provisions of this act have also been narrowly interpreted by the courts, thus perhaps reducing the scope that Congress intended. The ETHICAL ENVIRONMENT box below explores some additional issues involving consumer reporting agencies—namely, the issues of institutional information gathering and individual rights to privacy.

THE CONSUMER'S RIGHT TO KNOW.   The consumer's right to know who prepared a report and what it contains—as well as the right to correct any inaccurate infor-

> **consumer reporting agency**
> Private firm that investigates and reports on individual credit histories

THE ETHICAL ENVIRONMENT
Credit, Technology, and Privacy

Consumer credit bureaus—those omnipresent agencies that collect information on individual credit users—have been the target of consumer complaints for years. Among other things, consumer advocates have been trying hard to get credit bureaus to take responsibility for the following:

- the accuracy of their information
- correcting mistakes in a timely fashion
- giving consumers automatic annual updates on their records
- ensuring that consumers who choose to do so can prevent their names from being included on mailing lists that are sold to others

These same groups are also pushing to strengthen the Federal Trade Commission's powers of enforcement over these agencies.

The goals announced by various consumer groups stem from the privacy issues surrounding the collection and use of the information gathered about individuals. These issues have been catapulted into front page news by the continual emergence of new computer technology. Advances in this area permit various databases compiled by the government (such as tax returns), private industry records of charge-card purchases, supermarket-scanner readouts, etc.), and other institutions such as medical insurance carriers to be merged into fairly complete pictures of individuals. Think about it this way: Nearly 90 percent of all American adults have credit files. Under current federal law, anyone with a "legitimate business need" can see those records. Not surprisingly, this practice can cause immense problems for consumers—particularly if their records are incorrect.

Several questions are raised by consumer groups:

- Is it ethical for credit information to be supplied to others without the express consent of the subject? In other words, should a car dealer be permitted to check the credit rating of anyone who walks into the showroom, or should the sales person be required to wait until a deal is at least proposed?

- Is it fair that a consumer has no recourse if a credit bureau mistakenly damages his or her credit reputation? For example, suppose someone named "Robert Smith" declares bankruptcy, but the credit bureau accidentally enters this information into "Robert Smyth's" file. As long as the report was not purposely misfiled, Robert Smyth can be forced to bear the stigma of bankruptcy until the error is corrected.

- If someone charges a particular item in a department store, should the store be allowed to sell the purchaser's name to other vendors? Suppose Jane Doe buys a pair of skis. Can the vendor then sell her name to other suppliers of skiing gear or to a vacation packager who specializes in ski trips to Vermont?

These are only some of the complex consequences of the fact that there has been no new federal legislation in this area since the enactment of the Fair Credit Reporting Act. Consumer advocates continue to argue more and more forcefully that the ethics (and the constitutionality) of the privacy issues raised by the dual explosions of technology and credit use must be addressed through new legislation and new regulatory policy.

mation—is fundamental to the Fair Credit Reporting Act. Thus, when a lender or creditor rejects a consumer's application on the basis of an adverse credit report, the applicant must be notified of the name and address of the report's issuer. Then, if the consumer requests, the reporting agency must reveal to the consumer "the nature and substance" of all information in its files concerning that consumer. Although the consumer may not examine the files directly or get a verbatim transcript, he must receive enough data to be able to confirm or dispute the accuracy of the information.

The agency must also disclose its sources of information and the identities of those who have received reports on the consumer within the past six months (or two years for employment reports). If the consumer notifies the agency that any item is inaccurate, the agency must reinvestigate that information and update it or delete it from the file. If the consumer still disputes the information, he may write an explanatory statement that must be included in subsequent reports.

CONSUMER REMEDIES. A consumer who believes that a credit reporting agency has disobeyed any provision of the Fair Credit Reporting Act may sue that agency. There are basically two types of actionable violations of the act: (1) those that are *intentional* or *willful*, and (2) those that result from *negligence* or *ignorance*.

The Equal Credit Opportunity Act

In its original form, the **Equal Credit Opportunity Act** of 1974 required that credit must be made equally available to all creditworthy customers. Neither sex nor marital status could be considered as an aspect of such creditworthiness. Thus, women were the first beneficiaries of this act. This statute covers both individual and business borrowers, thus providing an important protection.

Equal Credit Opportunity Act
Section of the federal *Consumer Credit Reporting Act (CCRA)* requiring that credit be made equally available to all creditworthy customers without regard to race, color, religion, national origin, age, receipt of public assistance, or exercise of rights under the CCRA

ANTIDISCRIMINATION PROVISIONS. In 1976, however, the Equal Credit Opportunity Act was amended to expand its scope. Credit could no longer be denied on the basis of race, color, religion, national origin, age (*see* Chapter 9), receipt of public-assistance benefits, or the exercise of rights under the Consumer Credit Protection Act. Thus the Equal Credit Opportunity Act is both a consumer-protection statute and an antidiscrimination statute. As such, it is distinctive from all other sections of the Consumer Credit Protection Act.

Coverage of the act extends into every area of credit activity: Creditors are prohibited from discriminating throughout any aspect of the credit transaction "including solicitations of prospective applicants, information requirements, standards of creditworthiness, terms of credit, and collection practices."[2] It must be remembered that the Equal Credit Opportunity Act does not create a legal right to credit, but rather a legal right of *equal access* to credit.

In addition to broadening coverage beyond credit discrimination against women to other "protected classes," the 1976 amendments strengthened the enforcement provision by (1) requiring creditors to give written reasons for an applicant's rejection and (2) substantially increasing the damages available in class action suits.

---

[2] Gail R. Reizenstein, "A Fresh Look at the Equal Credit Opportunity Act," 14 *Akron Law Review* 223-225 (Fall 1980).

Nevertheless, Congress failed to set a minimum statutory recovery amount like the one in the Truth-in-Lending Act. The absence of such a provision may be one reason that consumers have not vigorously asserted claims under the Equal Credit Opportunity Act.

ADMINISTERING THE ACT. Although the language of the Equal Credit Opportunity Act itself is quite simple, its governing regulations are quite complicated. Indeed, certain regulations appear to be contradictory. For example, even though age discrimination is unlawful, creditors are permitted to consider the age of an applicant if it is used in the applicant's favor.

Other regulatory provisions prohibit creditors from using information gathered about an applicant's race, sex, or religion to discriminate on that basis in extending credit. Creditors may not disregard part-time income, ask whether income is derived from alimony, or require a newly married woman to reapply for a charge account under her spouse's name.

In addition, a creditor who opts to deny credit to an applicant must do so in accordance with regulations issued under the Equal Credit Opportunity Act. These regulations spell out the specific reasons that a creditor may use to reject a credit application. A federal court ruled on the basis of these provisions in the following case.

HIGGINS v. J.C. PENNEY, INC.
United States District Court, E.D. Missouri, 630 F.Supp. 722

In September 1984, Sara Higgins applied for a J.C. Penney credit card. Her application was denied because of information revealed by a credit agency's report. In response to Higgins' request to J.C. Penney for more specific information about the reasons for the rejection, she received a letter stating that her credit rating was too low because of "credit bureau/delinquent history," "type of bank accounts," and "type of credit references." Higgins sued J.C. Penney, alleging that their response did not satisfy the disclosure of the Equal Credit Opportunity Act.

Laimbaugh, District Judge

This case is before the Court on the parties cross-motions for summary judgment . . . The parties agree that there is no genuine issue of material fact and consequently, the sole issue for the Court is the application of the relevant law. . . .

In passing the Equal Credit Opportunity Act, Congress addressed what it viewed as inequities in the consumer credit system. It also included in the legislation a provision designed to make the credit application process more open by requiring creditors to provide applicants specific reasons for any adverse actions taken. This portion of the legislation has an important educational purpose.

The requirement that creditors give reasons for adverse action . . . is a strong and necessary adjunct to

the antidiscrimination purpose of the legislation, for only if creditors know they must explain their decisions will they effectively be discouraged from discriminatory practices. Yet this requirement fulfills a broader need: rejected credit applicants will not be able to learn where and how their credit status is deficient and this information should have a pervasive and valuable educational benefit. . . . S. Rep. No. 94-589, 94th Cong. 2d Sess., reprinted in 1976 U.S. Code Cong. & Admin. News, p. 406.

The reasons given by Penney, viewed in the abstract, are arguable not informative enough to satisfy Congressional intent. But, Congress, in passing the ECOA, directed the Federal Reserve Board to issue regulations implementing and refining the statutory language. . . . The Federal Reserve compiled a list of hypothetical reasons that in most cases would satisfy the specificity requirement of the Act's notice provisions, and also established some written guidelines for interpretation of the Act. Although it is a close question, the Court finds that the reasons given by Penney satisfy the statutory requirement of specificity as interpreted in accordance with the Federal Reserve regulations. In the absence of these regulations . . . the Court would probably find that Penney violated the ECOA notice provisions.

The first reason given for the credit denial was "credit bureau report/delinquency history." Plaintiff's correspondence with Penney does not bear out her allegation that this reason is not specific enough to satisfy the policies underlying the ECOA. . . . The language and tenor of the letters suggests the reason given by Penney enabled the plaintiff to focus her efforts in a particular area and to investigate the propriety of the company's decision. . . .

The second and third reasons . . . "type of bank accounts" and "type of credit references," are less obviously sufficient. Plaintiff contends that Penney could not reasonably expect her to know that the company's credit rating system considers applicants with checking accounts better credit risks than applicants with just savings accounts. . . .

Similarly, plaintiff contends that the reason "type of credit reference" did not adequately inform her that her credit application score was low was because she did not have a major bank card or gas card. . . .

The second and third reasons provided to plaintiff by Penney resemble, in their degree of specificity, those intended in the exemplary list of reasons included in the Federal Reserve regulations. While Penney's response required some degree of deductive reasoning by plaintiff, the Boards' interpretive regulation states that this is not impermissible. These regulations represent the Federal Reserve Board's view as to the amount of specificity necessary to comply with the statute. While the reasons given by plaintiff might have required her to exert more investigative effort than some might think is appropriate, the Court cannot say that the application of the regulations here frustrates the policies underlying the ECOA.

Plaintiff obviously knew she had only a savings account. The reason given by Penney, "type of bank account," when considered within the context of this knowledge, directed plaintiff to the appropriate area of inquiry. Further, plaintiff knew she did not have the type of credit experience other applicants might have. She should have reasonably suspected . . . that a creditor would look with disfavor on her relatively unsophisticated financial background. . . .

It is hereby ordered that the plaintiff's motion for summary judgment is denied and the defendant's motion for summary judgment is sustained.

It is further ordered that judgment is entered in favor of defendant and against the plaintiff, with both parties to bear their costs of suit.

Case Questions:

1. What are the competing interests between businesses and consumers that are affected by the Equal Credit Opportunity Act? Do you think that the court struck the right balance between these interests in this case?

2. The court stated that in the absence of the regulations promulgated by the Federal Reserve, it probably would have found that J.C. Penney's disclosure to Higgins was inadequate. Does this suggest the existence of a conflict between Congressional intent in enacting the Equal Credit Opportunity Act and the Federal Reserve's regulations? Should the court decision's be governed by the regulations or by Congressional intent?

The Fair Debt Collection Practices Act

Congressional hearings in 1976 and 1977 revealed many abusive debt-collection practices, including threatening or embarrassing letters, repeated harassing telephone calls, and visits from collectors at debtors' places of employment. In the same hearings, experts concurred that only a small proportion of debtors should be considered "deadbeats" who did not intend to pay what they owed. Although opponents of federal debt-collection legislation claimed that there would be conflict with state statutes, proponents cited the number of states with no such laws.

The result of the hearings was the **Fair Debt Collection Practices Act**, which was enacted in 1977 to eliminate abusive debt-collection practices. Only consumer transactions are protected. The language of the act makes it clear that the law was designed primarily to regulate *independent* collection agencies. Institutions whose business is to extend credit—for example, banks and credit unions—and "in-house" collectors are exempt. These exemptions permit a creditor, such as a home-improvement retail store that collects its own debts, to use methods forbidden to professional collectors.

Fair Debt Collection Practices Act 1977 federal law protecting consumers from abusive debt-collection practices by independent agencies

CATEGORIES OF FORBIDDEN PRACTICES. In contrast to the fairly general applications of the Truth-in-Lending Act and the Equal Credit Opportunity Act, Congress was extremely specific in drafting the Fair Debt Collection Practices Act. The legislation explicitly forbids three main categories of debt-collector practices: *harass-*

ment or abuse, false or misleading representations, and *unfair or unconscionable practices.*

According to the statute, harassment or abuse (threats, repeated frequent telephone calls, or abusive language) can be directed toward the debtor or toward a third party. For example, a friend or relative who knows the whereabouts of a debtor might be the target of agency harassment.

There are basically four categories of false or misleading representations prohibited under the law: those involving the collector, those relating to documents about the debt, those concerning the consumer, and those identifying documents in the collection process. Thus, collectors may not engage in any of the following activities:

- misrepresent their occupation—for example, claiming to be court officers, government agents, or lawyers
- spread false information about the debtor
- send false notices or subpoenas
- tell third parties that a debtor owes them money
- post-date debtors' checks to collect extra interest
- threaten to seize property unrelated to the debt.

The prohibition of unfair or unconscionable practices includes such abuses as threatening to seize property from the debtor when the property is exempt from seizure or when the creditor has no intention of seizing it, and communicating with the debtor in any way that illegally lets third parties know that collection procedures are occurring—for example, by open-faced postcard.

In the case that follows, the court considered the legal standard to be used in determining whether a communication from a debt collector is deceptive.

JETER v. CREDIT BUREAU, INC.
U.S. Court of Appeals, Eleventh Circuit, 760 F.2d 1168 (1985)

Defendant, Credit Bureau, operates a debt collection agency subject to the Fair Debt Collection Practices Act (FDCPA). One of Credit Bureau's clients during the time period preceding this lawsuit was Associated Consumers Club ("Associated Consumers"). Plaintiff, Jeter, is an alleged debtor of Associated Consumers. Associated Consumers referred Jeter's account to Credit Bureau for collection. Credit Bureau sent letters to Jeter which threatened adverse legal action unless payment was made.

Jeter sued Credit Bureau claiming violations of the FDCPA. The district court granted summary judgment to Credit Bureau on all issues. Jeter appeals.

R. Lanier Anderson, III, Circuit Judge:
...Sometime prior to October 25, 1982, Jeter incurred what Associated Consumers believed was a valid legal debt with Associated Consumers. On October 25, 1982, Jeter's account was referred by Associ-

ated Consumers to Credit Bureau for collection. On March 4, 1983, Credit Bureau sent Jeter a letter which reads as follows:

Take notice that the above creditor claims you are indebted to him as shown.

. . . .

Therefore, you are hereby notified that unless satisfactory arrangements are made within five (5) days from this date, we will recommend to our client, suit and subsequent action (judgment, garnishment, levy, and/or attachment proceedings) may be instigated against you by their attorneys.

. . . .

After March 4, and prior to April 7, 1983, neither Credit Bureau nor Associated Consumers took any further action with regard to Jeter's account. . . . On April 7, 1983, Credit Bureau sent Jeter another letter which reads as follows:

This is our final notice to you before recommending

that our client give the account to their attorney for legal action.

Although it may cause you embarrassment, inconvenience and further expense, we will do so if the entire balance is not in this office within the next five days.

. . . .

Attend to it now—This is a final notice.

Neither Credit Bureau nor Associated Consumers took any action with regard to Jeter's account subsequent to the April 7, 1983, letter.

Sometime prior to May 11, 1983, Jeter hired a lawyer, Elizabeth Leonard. On May 11, 1983, Ms. Leonard sent a letter on Jeter's behalf to Credit Bureau stating Jeter's position that she owed no money to Associated Consumers. A copy of the letter was sent to Associated Consumers. Thereafter, Credit Bureau determined that the collection of Jeter's account was impractical, closed its files, and made no further contact with Jeter.

On June 16, 1983, Jeter sued Credit Bureau in the federal district court for the Northern District of Georgia claiming violations of the FDCPA. First, Jeter claimed that as a consequence of Credit Bureau's letters and its subsequent inaction, Credit Bureau had violated 15 U.S.C.A. § 1692e(5) for "threat[ening] to take any action that cannot legally be taken or that is not intended to be taken" and § 1692e(10) for using "any false representation or deceptive means to collect or attempt to collect any debt. . . ." Second, Jeter claimed that Credit Bureau had "engage[d] in . . . conduct the natural consequence of which [was] to harass, oppress, or abuse any person in connection with the collection of a debt" in violation of 15 U.S.C.A. § 1692d.

. . . .

II. Applicable Legal Standard

The district court held that in determining whether the FDCPA has been violated the court was obligated to "decide whether a 'reasonable consumer' would be deceived, mislead [sic], or harassed by the letters at issue in this case." Relevant administrative adjudications and case law under the Federal Trade Commission Act "FTC Act"), upon which we rely by analogy, and persuasive authority under the FDCPA lead us to the conclusion that the district court applied an improper standard.

Section 5 of the FTC Act declares unlawful all "unfair or deceptive acts or practices in commerce." An act or practice is deceptive or unfair under § 5 if it has the tendency or capacity to deceive. The FTC Act was enacted to protect unsophisticated consumers, not only "reasonable consumers" who could otherwise protect themselves in the market place. . . .

. . . .

Because we believe that Congress intended the standard under the FDCPA to be the same as that enunciated in the relevant FTC cases, and because we believe that "[t]he FDCPA's purpose of protecting [consumers] . . . is best served by a definition of 'deceive' that looks to the tendency of language to mislead

the least sophisticated recipients of a debt collector's letters and telephone calls," *Wright v. Credit Bureau of Georgia* [1982], we adopt the . . . standard of "least sophisticated consumer" as previously followed by the federal courts. . . .

III. False or Misleading Representations?

Jeter claims that the letter sent by Credit Bureau violated 15 U.S.C.A. § 1692e(5) and (10). These subsections provide:

A debt collector may not use any false, deceptive, or misleading representation or means in connection with the collection of any debt. Without limiting the general application of the foregoing, the following conduct is a violation of this section:

. . . .

(5) The threat to take any action that cannot legally be taken or that is not intended to be taken.

. . . .

(10) The use of any false representation or deceptive means to collect or attempt to collect any debt or to obtain information concerning a consumer.

. . . .

Claim Under Subsection (10)

. . . .

. . . Under subsection (10), we must consider whether the "least sophisticated consumer" would be deceived by Credit Bureau's letters, *i.e.,* whether the letters were a "deceptive means" to collect alleged debts, valid or invalid, by the use of false or deliberately ambiguous threats to recommend legal action. It may be, although we doubt it, that a "reasonable consumer" would have taken Credit Bureau's letters as empty threats to recommend legal action at some undisclosed time in the distant future; however, the fact that Jeter hired a lawyer and responded to the second letter seems to support the opposite view. In any event, we are confident that whether the "least sophisticated consumer" would construe Credit Bureau's letter as deceptive is a question for the jury.

IV. Harassment or Abuse?

Jeter argues that the district court erred in granting summary judgment in favor of Credit Bureau on her claim under § 1692d. Section 1692d reads [in part] as follows:

A debt collector may not engage in any conduct the natural consequence of which is to harass, oppress, or abuse any person in connection with the collection of a debt. . . .

. . .

. . . The district court decided . . . that it was inappropriate to characterize Credit Bureau's conduct as violative of § 1692d:

The defendant in the present case merely threatened to institute legal action against the plaintiff. The sentence that the plaintiff objects to is the one that stated that the institution of such proceedings could possibly cause her "embarrassment, inconvenience, and further expense." The Court feels that this language would not oppress or harass a reasonable consumer. . . .

. . . .

That a lawsuit might cause a consumer "embarrassment, inconvenience, and further expense" is a true statement. Such consequences of a debt collection (or any other) lawsuit are so commonplace that even a consumer susceptible to harassment, oppression, or abuse would not have been harassed, oppressed, or abused by the statement *in and of itself*. A simple warning of "embarrassment, inconvenience, and further expense" does not create a "tone . . . of intimidation. . . ."

. . . .

. . . [E]ven when judged by the consumer protective standard we adopt today, § 1692d does not as a matter of law proscribe Credit Bureau's conduct in this case.

Thus, the district court's grant of summary judgment in favor of Credit Bureau on this issue is affirmed.

Case Questions:

1. Why did the district court decide that Credit Bureau's conduct did not cause Jeter harassment, oppression, or abuse pursuant to the FDCPA?

2. Under which standard would it be easier for a plaintiff to prove violative conduct by a collection agency under the FDCPA, the district court's "reasonable consumer" standard, or the Ninth Circuit's "least sophisticated consumer" standard?

3. How might the conduct of an independent collection agency in connection with the collection of a debt violate the FDCPA?

The One-Contact Rule. To do his job, of course, the debt collector must be able to find the presumed debtor. To prevent collectors' harassment of third parties while searching for debtors, the Fair Debt Collection Practices Act creates the *one-contact rule,* under which the debt collector may speak only once to a third party. The rule also stipulates that once the debtor is located, the collector may not communicate with any additional third parties except the consumer's lawyer. If the debtor has no lawyer, the collector may communicate with the debtor directly, but only during reasonable hours (that is, 8 A.M. to 9 P.M.) and not at work.

AFFIRMATIVE REQUIREMENTS. While most of the provisions of the Fair Debt Collection Practices Act involve prohibitions, there are two affirmative requirements. First, the collector must *validate* the debt by giving the consumer written notice of the amount and the identity of the creditor. If the consumer disputes any of the information, the collector must verify the accuracy of the debt. Such disclosure requirements protect consumers who do not owe any money at all. Second, if multiple debts are involved, any single payment to a collector must be distributed among creditors according to the consumer's instructions.

ENFORCEMENT OF THE ACT. The Fair Debt Collection Practices Act provides both for civil suits and administrative enforcement. In civil suits, although both actual and statutory damages are recoverable, there is no minimum amount of damages. Unlike most other consumer protection legislation, the Fair Debt Collection Practices Act allows a collection agency to recover legal fees if an unsuccessful suit brought by a consumer is found either to have been brought in bad faith or to harass the collection agency.

At the same time, a consumer whose suit against a collection agency is successful may also collect attorney's fees. This provision can help individuals who could otherwise not afford a lawyer or whose claims would not normally be large enough to bear the expense of a court case. This provision provides an avenue for consumers to challenge even small collection firms who violate the act's requirements.

Limited Remedies for Creditors

The collection methods described thus far do not involve lawsuits against debtors. Indeed, most creditors and collection agencies do not sue debtors unless all other methods have proven fruitless or the case involves a substantial debt that exceeds the cost of litigation. Creditors generally pursue collection methods through judicial action. Title III of the Consumer Credit Protection Act also provides limited remedies for debt collection.

JUDICIAL COLLECTION METHODS. The chief advantage of suing to collect an unpaid debt is the availability of judicial collection methods. *Garnishment, replevin,* and *attachment* are the most common forms of these remedies.

Garnishment. **Garnishment** is directed at a third party—called a *garnishee*—who owns or possesses something of value to the debtor. When a court sanctions garnishment, the third party is notified that the debtor's property should be withheld from the debtor so that it may be given to the creditor in order to satisfy the outstanding debt. Debtors' employers are the most common garnishees. Upon receipt of a garnishment notice, an employer is placed on notice that a creditor has a claim on the debtor's wages. If the creditor prevails in court, the money will be paid directly to the creditor.

Replevin. **Replevin** refers to a court proceeding to recover specific property in the debtor's possession. As a remedy, however, replevin is available only to **secured creditors**—that is, creditors who retain title to or a lien on the property in question. For example, assume that Smith agrees to lend $5000 to Jones so that she can purchase a new car. A condition of the loan is that Smith retains a lien on the car until the debt is paid off. Because Smith is a secured creditor, he can obtain a court order to replevy, or repossess, the car if Jones defaults on the debt.

Attachment. **Attachment** is the seizure of any of the debtor's property that is not exempted by statute. An order of attachment authorizes a court officer to seize and hold property pending the resolution of a lawsuit. Assume that Green defaults on a $25,000 business loan from Marks. Marks knows that Green owns a BMW worth $30,000. When Marks sues Green on the $25,000 debt, she might ask the court to order the pretrial attachment of his car—the only asset which he has that could satisfy the debt. If Marks wins, she's entitled to recover the outstanding amount on the debt from the sale of the car by the court.

Prejudgment Remedies. Orders of garnishment and replevin may be issued either before or after a trial. Attachment, however, is only a **prejudgment remedy**. The purpose of a prejudgment remedy is to preserve debtors assets that could be seized after a trial to pay off an obligation. Prejudgment remedies have themselves been the subject of much litigation because they raise issues of fairness: Specifically, they deprive the debtor of property before any court has determined whether the creditor is entitled to any money. As such, prejudgment remedies run the risk of depriving a person of property without due process—a constitutional violation.

Should a debtor be given notice and a hearing before a writ of garnishment is issued? The following case addresses this issue.

garnishment *Judicial debt-collection method* in which a third party who has something of value to the debtor is directed to withhold it in order that it may be paid to a creditor

replevin *Judicial debt-collection method* to recover specific secured property in a debtor's possession

attachment *Judicial debt-collection method* in which any of the debtor's property not exempted by statute is seized pending resolution of a lawsuit

prejudgment remedy *Judicial debt-collection method,* such as *attachment,* that holds property prior to a trial in order to preserve so that it may be used to pay a debt

SNIADACH v. FAMILY FINANCE CORPORATION OF BAY VIEW
United States Supreme Court, 395 U.S. 337 (1969)

Respondents instituted a garnishment action against petitioner as defendant and Miller Harris Instrument Co., her employer, as garnishee. The complaint alleged a claim of $420 on a promissory note. The garnishee filed its answer stating it had wages of $63.18 under its control earned by petition and unpaid, and that it would hold half of this amount subject to the order of the court in the garnishment proceeding.

Petitioner moved that the garnishment proceedings be dismissed as violative of the due process requirement of the Fourteenth Amendment. The Wisconsin Supreme Court sustained the lower state court in approving the procedure. The case is here on a petition for writ of certiorari.

Mr. Justice Douglas delivered the opinion of the Court.

The Wisconsin statute gives a plaintiff 10 days in which to serve the summons and complaint on the defendant after service on the garnishee. In this case petitioner was served the same day as the garnishee. She nonetheless claims that the Wisconsin garnishment procedure violates that due process required by the Fourteenth Amendment, in that notice and an opportunity to be heard are not given before the *in rem* seizure of the wages. What happens in Wisconsin is that clerk of the court issues the summons at the request of the creditor's lawyer; and it is the latter who by serving the garnishee sets in motion the machinery whereby the wages are frozen. They may, it is true, be unfrozen if the trial of the main suit is ever had and the wage earner wins on the merits. But in the interim the wage earner is deprived of his enjoyment of earned wages without any opportunity to be heard and to tender any defense he may have, whether it be fraud or otherwise.

Such summary procedure may well meet the requirements of due process in extraordinary situations. But in the present case no situation requiring special protection to a state or creditor interest is presented by the facts; nor is the Wisconsin statute narrowly drawn to meet any such unusual condition. Petitioner was a resident of this Wisconsin community and *in personam* jurisdiction was readily obtainable.

The question is not whether the Wisconsin law is a wise law or unwise law. Our concern is not what philosophy Wisconsin should or should not embrace. We do not sit as a superlegislative body. In this case the sole question is whether there has been a taking of property without that procedural due process that is required by the Fourteenth Amendment. . . .

A prejudgment garnishment of the Wisconsin type is a taking which may impose tremendous hardship on wage earners with families to support. Until a recent Act of Congress, § 304 of which forbids discharge of employees on the ground that their wages have been garnished, garnishment often meant the loss of a job. Over and beyond that was the great drain on family income. . . .

The leverage of the creditor on the wage earner is enormous. The creditor tenders not only the original debt but the "collection fees" incurred by his attorneys in the garnishment proceedings. . . .

Apart from those collateral consequences, it appears that in Wisconsin the statutory exemption granted the wage earner is "generally insufficient to support the debtor for any one week."

The result is that a prejudgment garnishment of the Wisconsin type may as a practical matter drive a wage-earning family to the wall. Where the taking of one's property is so obvious, it needs no extended argument to conclude that absent notice and a prior hearing this prejudgment garnishment procedure violates the fundamental principles of due process. Reversed.

. . . .

Mr. Justice Black, dissenting.

The Court here holds unconstitutional a Wisconsin statute permitting garnishment before a judgment has been obtained against the principal debtor. The law, however, requires that notice be given to the principal debtor and authorizes him to present all of his legal defenses at the regular hearing and trial of the case. The Wisconsin law is said to violate the "fundamental principles of due process." Of course the Due Process Clause of the Fourteenth Amendment contains no words that indicate that this Court has power to play so fast and loose with state laws. The arguments the Court makes to reach what I consider to be its unconstitutional conclusion, however, show why it strikes down this state law. It is because it considers a garnishment law of this kind to be bad state policy, a judgment I think the state legislature, not this Court, has power to make.

Case Questions:

1. How did the prejudgment garnishment procedure in this case deprive the employee of due process under the Fourteenth Amendment?

2. Why is notice and a prior hearing required under the Constitution before there can be a taking of property?

3. On what basis does Justice Black disagree with the majority of the Court in finding that the Wisconsin law violated the "fundamental principles of due process"?

In general, courts have conditioned the use of prejudgment remedies upon the provision of due process to the debtor. To satisfy this requirement, the debtor must be given a hearing and the right to be heard; in addition,

many prejudgment seizures do meet the constitutional requirements of due process.

Nevertheless, lawmakers have recognized the potential harshness of judicial-collection remedies and limited their use. States, for example, have enacted laws providing exemptions to these remedies for certain kinds of property, such as "homestead," life insurance, and "tools of the trade." Further, garnishment proceedings must follow constitutional due-process requirements.

TITLE III. Title III of the Consumer Credit Protection Act also restricts garnishment. Title III specifies that a creditor may garnish no more than 25 percent of a wage earner's disposable income, or no more than that portion of the wage earner's after-tax income which exceeds 30 times the minimum hourly wage. In addition, all creditors must divide the amount among themselves. The sole creditor exempt from this maximum is the government. Thus, debts owed for taxes may be garnished at a higher level. A much larger percentage of wages may also be garnished for alimony or child-support payments.

Title III also protects employees from being fired for indebtedness. Employers are forbidden from discharging an employee as a result of having his wages garnished "for any one indebtedness." However, this provision has been construed to mean "only *one* indebtedness": If multiple creditors pursue the debtor by judicial means, Title III will not protect him.

■ *Concept Check 19-2   Consumer-Protection and Truth-in-Lending Legislation*

- What are the principal purposes of the *Truth-in-Lending Act*? What are the requirements of *Regulation Z*?
- What provisions does the *Simplification Act* add to the Truth-in-Lending Act? Define the *rule of recission*.
- What requirements does the *Fair Credit Reporting Act* place on *consumer reporting agencies*?
- Describe the antidiscrimination provisions of the *Equal Credit Opportunity Act*.
- Give examples of practices forbidden by the *Fair Debt Collection Practices Act*. Explain the *one-contact rule*.
- Describe instances in which each of the following *judicial collection remedies* might be applied in the collection of a debt: *garnishment, replevin,* and *attachment*.

■ BUSINESS AND PERSONAL BANKRUPTCY

When a consumer becomes so burdened with debt that repayment seems impossible, or when a business fails to pay its suppliers and employees, the resolution is often bankruptcy. Figure 19-4 shows the number of bankruptcy petitions in the United States between 1981 and 1989. Article I, Section 8 of the Constitution gives Congress the power to establish uniform bankruptcy laws.

Bankruptcy is a legal proceeding whereby the debtor cancels all or a part of his debt and is enabled to start over with a clean slate. Bankruptcy proceedings allow all creditors to receive equal treatment within their class: That is, secured creditors are paid before *priority unsecured creditors* (those with administrative expense claims), who, in turn, are paid before unsecured creditors. The topic of *debt priority* is discussed in more detail later in this chapter.

bankruptcy Legal proceeding whereby a debtor's assets are liquidated and distributed to creditors, the remainder of his or her obligations are canceled, and the party starts over unencumbered by present debts

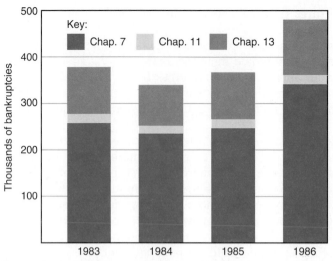

FIGURE 19-4 U.S. Bankruptcy Petitions, 1981-1989   *Source:* Administrative Office of the U.S. Courts, *Annual Report of the Director* (1990).

The first comprehensive bankruptcy statute was the Nelson Act, which was enacted in 1898. The Nelson Act was revised in 1938 with the enactment of the Chandler Act. The next, and most current, revision to this body of law was the 1978 **Bankruptcy Reform Act,** which went into effect on October 1, 1979, and was amended in 1984 and 1986. Currently, there is a movement interested in overhauling the entire bankruptcy statute.

Perhaps it is fortunate that bankruptcy law came into its own when it did: The courts now are hard-pressed to keep up with the rash of business and personal filings caused by the overspending of the 1980s and the recession of the 1990s. The number of personal and business filings in the system increased approximately sevenfold between the early 1970s and the late 1980s. This astounding rise is due partly to the open-credit environment of our society, partly to the "fresh-start" provisions of the bankruptcy law itself, and partly to growing social acceptance of bankruptcy as a way to manage out-of-control expenses.

The following discussion explains the structure of the Bankruptcy Reform Act of 1978. We will then focus on the ways in which this law works in both personal and business bankruptcies.

Personal Bankruptcy

The provisions of the Bankruptcy Reform Act of 1978 are intended to be attractive to personal debtors. They permit such debtors to keep some assets, such as their homes, under specific circumstances. In addition, married couples can file one action. Most consumer debtors file under Chapter 13 (repayment plans). The general recessionary economy, various regional influences—for example, the devastating loss of jobs in a particular area of the country—and changes in the demographics of families (more single-parent households, more fathers failing to pay child support) are among the reasons for the current rise in the number of personal bankruptcies.

Business Bankruptcy

The entire bankruptcy process is directed toward swift resolution. In the case of a liquidation proceeding, this means the payment of creditors as quickly and fairly as possible. In the context of business reorganization, this means allowing the debtor's business to continue in as normal a manner as possible while a repayment plan is worked out.

VALUATION. Both types of bankruptcy require the procedure of **valuation**—that is, establishing a value for every one of the business's assets. Once valued, assets must be (1) sold item by item (selling a store's entire inventory), (2) sold as an on-going part of a business (selling the financing arm of an automobile manufacturer), or (3) used in the reorganized portion of the business (using the showcases in a store).

valuation Procedure, required in personal and business bankruptcy, of establishing a value for the assets of bankrupt businessess

Valuation is difficult on many levels, but perhaps the most complicated aspect of the process is accounting for claims against the business (product- and environmental-liability claims) which cannot be assessed accurately at a given time and which would normally be discharged in bankruptcy.

Consider the following scenarios:

1. A manufacturer of children's pajamas goes bankrupt. Six months after the company goes out of business, a child is injured when the pajamas he is wearing go up in flames. Is the manufacturer still liable?
2. A paint manufacturer cited by the Environmental Protection Agency for illegal dumping that polluted the land behind the factory goes bankrupt. While the cleanup is on hold, the drinking water in nearby neighborhoods is contaminated. Who is responsible for the resulting injuries?

These illustrations point out the conflict between the fresh-start aspects of the Bankruptcy Code and the responsibility-of-the-perpetrator policies found in most other statutes. Although this discrepancy is causing a clamor for the reexamination of the existing bankruptcy law, it is unlikely that this issue will be decided through legislation. It is more probable that negotiations will address these matters on a case-by-case basis.

The Bankruptcy Reform Act of 1978

Title I of the 1978 Bankruptcy Code consists of eight chapters. The focus here is on those chapters that are most directly related to business management and family farms. Although Title I of the code has been amended twice—in 1984 and 1986—the changes were largely procedural in nature; the underlying concepts of the legislation remain the same.

CHAPTER 11: REORGANIZATIONS. The principal objective of Chapter 11 is to enable financially distressed corporations to return to profitable operations. A bankruptcy under Chapter 11 begins with a petition filed with the court. The case is considered a *voluntary* rehabilitation if the troubled corporation files for reorganization; the filing is *involuntary* if the firm's major creditors initiate the proceedings. If, following a hearing, a bankruptcy judge grants the petition for reorganization, the court may either (1) appoint an independent trustee to manage the company or (2) allow its current principals to remain in charge. In any event, the debtor is protected against collections, foreclosures, and judicial proceedings during the reorganization period.

The court or the trustee then appoints a committee of unsecured creditors, such as suppliers, employees, and commercial creditors, to participate in the reorganization. Other creditors, or *parties in interest*, may request that the court appoint additional committees. Thus, in reorganizations of large corporations, there may also be committees of major stockholders and such secured creditors as banks, insurance companies, and pension funds.

A workable plan for retiring the company's debt and returning to solvency is fundamental to reorganization. A typical reorganization plan may include selling off certain assets to repay creditors, an extension of maturity dates on loans, the transfer of the company's stock to creditors, a merger, or, in some cases, a transfer to Chapter 7 for total liquidation. If the debtor cannot gain creditor approval of a reorganization plan, any party in interest may present an alternative plan to the court.

When the plan is presented to the bankruptcy court, the judge decides if it is "fair and feasible." If so, it is submitted to the creditors for acceptance. Although unanimity among creditors is not required, approval must be given by a simple majority of at least one class of secured or unsecured creditors. This class must also hold at least two-thirds of the dollar amount of allowed claims. Even if some creditors veto the plan, it may still be confirmed by the court if creditors are treated fairly and equitably.

Ranking of Claims. A ranking of claims has always been required by law in either a bankruptcy or reorganization. The law mandates "absolute priority"—that is, one class of creditors must be completely compensated before the next receives anything. However, in practice, with the permission of the court of trustee, many plans offer partial payments to both higher- and lower-ranked creditors in hopes of securing general acceptance of the plan. The priority of claims specified in Chapter 11 is as follows:

- administrative expenses
- unsecured claims such as wages and salaries
- secured debts
- senior debts such as loan agreements
- equity holders of both preferred and common stock.

The plan must treat all claims within a class equally. It must provide details for its execution, such as payment schedules, merger plans, and the selection of officers and directors. When enough creditors approve the plan, the court holds a confirmation hearing and discharges the debtor.

Corporate Objectives for Reorganization. Most corporations filing for reorganization do so because they are in substantial financial difficulties. However, since the Bankruptcy Reform Act of 1978 became law, corporations with healthy balance sheets have petitioned for reorganization in order to avoid impaired credit, to escape obligations to pension plans, to minimize difficulties in the selling of assets, to undo burdensome labor contracts, or to avoid anticipated future liability.

The Manville Case. A firestorm of controversy was touched off in 1982, when the Manville Corporation, a Fortune 500 company in apparent financial health, filed a petition for reorganization. Manville, once the world's largest producer of asbestos products, faced a certain future of costly liability suits by victims (usually former employees) of asbestos-related diseases. By filing for reorganization, Manville attempted to (1) protect itself from additional lawsuits while developing a plan to be discharged from liability for all future claims, and to (2) guard against both the loss of jobs and income for Manville's workers and the general diminution of the industry.[3]

---

[3] Daniel G. Hilson, "The Genesis of a New Trend: Chapter 11, Avoiding or Managing Future Liability in Mass Tort Actions?" 15 *Capital University Law Review* 251, 256, 259 (Winter 1986).

The process was made possible by the definition of *claim* in the amended Bankruptcy Law, which broadened the category of claims to include those that might be owed at some time in the future but which arose before the date of filing. In Manville's case, this new definition seemed to mean that by gaining approval of a Chapter 11 reorganization plan—which would set aside a certain amount of funds to pay off future liability suits—the company could limit its ultimate liability to victims of asbestos.

Although commentators have criticized Manville's strategy as "cold-hearted," "dubious," and "shoddy," victims of asbestosis may ultimately benefit. A Chapter 11 reorganization could well be more protective of the victims' interest than straight bankruptcy, which might very well have resulted in the corporation's liquidation and left no money at all for liability claims. The reorganization plan offered some compensation both to victims who sued and to Manville's other creditors. In other words, *pro rata* compensation for asbestosis victims may be a better choice than no compensation at all.

In a different management strategy, Continental Airlines refused to recognize a collective-bargaining agreement that had been in force at Texas International Airlines before the two airlines merged. When the unions countered with an application to the National Mediation Board for new union elections, Continental declared Chapter 11 and sought to stay the election. In this situation, the district court allowed the election to proceed (*In re Continental Airlines Corp.*, 50 Bankr. 342 [S.D. Tex. 1985]). The Supreme Court, however, reached an opposite conclusion in the following case.

NATIONAL LABOR RELATIONS BOARD v. BILDISCO & BILDISCO
United States Supreme Court, 465 U.S. 513 (1984)

On April 14, 1980, respondent, Bildisco and Bildisco ("Bildisco"), a New Jersey distributor of building supplies, filed a voluntary petition in bankruptcy for reorganization under Chapter 11 of the Bankruptcy Code. At the time of the filing of the petition in bankruptcy, Bildisco was a party to a three-year collective-bargaining agreement with the representative of Bildisco's labor force, Local 408 of the International Brotherhood of Teamsters, Chauffeurs, Warehousemen and Helpers of America ("Union"). The agreement expressly provided that it was binding on the parties and their successors even though bankruptcy should supervene.

In December 1980, Bildisco requested permission from the Bankruptcy Court, pursuant to 11 U.S.C. § 365(a), to reject the collective-bargaining agreement. The Bankruptcy Court granted Bildisco permission to reject the collective-bargaining agreement. The District Court upheld the order of the Bankruptcy Court and the Union appealed to the Court of Appeals for the Third Circuit. During midsummer 1980, the Union had filed unfair labor charges against Bildisco with the National Labor Relations Board (the "Board"). The Board ultimately found that Bildisco had violated § 8(a) (5) and § 8(a) (1) of the National Labor Relations Act

(NLRA) and ordered Bildisco to make the pension, health, and welfare contributions and to remit dues to the Union, as required under the collective-bargaining agreement. The Board petitioned the Court of Appeals for the Third Circuit to enforce its order. The Third Circuit refused to enforce the Board's order. The Board petitions for certiorari.

Justice Rehnquist delivered the opinion of the Court.

Two important and related questions are presented by these petitions for certiorari: (1) under what conditions can a Bankruptcy Court permit a debtor-in-possession to reject a collective-bargaining agreement; (2) may the National Labor Relations Board find a debtor-in-possession guilty of an unfair labor practice for unilaterally terminating or modifying a collective-bargaining agreement before rejection of that agreement has been approved by the Bankruptcy Court. . . .

. . . The Board found that Bildisco had violated § 8(a) (5) and § 8(a) (1) of the NLRA by unilaterally changing the terms of the collective-bargaining agreement and by refusing to negotiate with the Union. . . . The Board petitioned the Court of Appeals for the Third Circuit to enforce its order [it issued against Bildisco].

That court held that a collective-bargaining agreement is an executory contract subject to rejection by a debtor-in-possession under § 365(a) of the Bankruptcy Code. . . .

. . . Because rejection relates back to the filing of a petition, the Court of Appeals held that if Bildisco were permitted to reject the contract, the Board was precluded from premising an unfair labor practice on Bildisco's rejection of the labor contract.

. . .

Section 365(a) of the Bankruptcy Code provides in full:

(a) Except as provided in sections 765 and 766 of this title and in subsections (b), (c), and (d) of this section, the trustee, subject of the court's approval, may assume or reject any executory contract or unexpired lease of the debtor.

This language by its terms includes all executory contracts except those expressly exempted, and it is not disputed by the parties that an unexpired collective-bargaining agreement is an executory contract. Any inference that collective-bargaining agreements are not included within the general scope of § 365(a) because they differ for some purpose for ordinary contracts, is rebutted by the statutory design of § 365(a) and by the language of § 1167 of the Bankruptcy Code. . . .

None of the parties to these cases dispute the foregoing proposition. But the Board contends that the standard by which the Bankruptcy Court must judge the request of a debtor-in-possession to reject a collective bargaining contract must be stricter than the traditional "business judgment" standard applied by the courts to authorize rejection of the ordinary executory contract. . . .

. . .

The Union and the Board argue that in light of the special nature of rights created by labor contracts, Bildisco should not be permitted to reject the collective-bargaining agreement unless it can demonstrate that its reorganization will fail unless rejection is permitted. This very strict standard was adopted by the Second Circuit in *Brotherhood of Railway, Airline and Steamship Clerks v. REA Express, Inc.* [(1975)], decided under the former Bankruptcy Act three years before § 365(a) was passed by Congress. . . .

. . .

The standard adopted by the Court of Appeals for the Second Circuit in *REA Express* is fundamentally at odds with the policies of flexibility and equity built into Chapter 11 of the Bankruptcy Code. The rights of workers under collective-bargaining agreements are important, but the *REA Express* standard subordinates the multiple, competing considerations underlying a Chapter 11 reorganization to one issue: whether rejection of the collective-bargaining agreement is necessary to prevent the debtor from going into liquidation. The evidentiary burden necessary to meet this stringent standard may not be insurmountable, but it will present difficulties to the debtor-in-possession that will interfere with the reorganization process.

We agree with the Court of Appeals below, and with the Court of Appeals for the Eleventh Circuit in a re-

lated case, *In re Brada Miller Freight System, Inc.* [(1983)], that the Bankruptcy Court should permit rejection of a collective-bargaining agreement under § 365(a) of the Bankruptcy Code if the debtor can show that the collective-bargaining agreement burdens the estate, and that after careful scrutiny, the equities balance in favor of rejecting the labor contract. The standard which we think Congress intended is a higher one than that of the business judgment rule, but a lesser one than that embodied in the *REA Express* opinion of the . . . Second Circuit. . . .

Since the policy of Chapter 11 is to permit successful rehabilitation of debtors, rejection shoud not be permitted without a finding that that policy would be served by such action. The Bankruptcy Court must make a reasoned finding on the record why it had determined that rejection should be permitted. Determining what would constitute a successful rehabilitation involves balancing the interests of the affected parties—the debtor, creditors, and employees. . . . In striking the balance, the Bankruptcy Court must consider not only the degree of hardship faced by each party, but also any qualitative differences between the types of hardship each may face.

. . .

The second issue raised by these cases is whether the NLRB can find a debtor-in-possession guilty of an unfair labor practice for unilaterally rejecting or modifying a collective-bargaining agreement before formal rejection by the Bankruptcy Court. . . .

. . .

While all parties to these cases ultimately concede that the Bankruptcy Court may authorize rejection of a collective-bargaining agreement, the Board and the Union nonetheless insist that a debtor-in-possession violates § 8(a) (5) and § 8(d) of the NLRA if it unilaterally changes the terms of the collective-bargaining agreement between the date of filing the bankruptcy petition and the date on which the Bankruptcy Court authorizes rejection of the agreement. But acceptance of such a contention would largely, if not completely, undermine whatever benefit the debtor-in-possession otherwise obtains by its authority to request rejection of the agreement. . . .

. . .

Section 8(d) applies when contractual obligations are repudiated by the unilateral actions of a party to the collective-bargaining agreement. We have recognized that Congress' central purpose in enacting § 8(d) was to regulate the modification of collective-bargaining agreements and to facilitate agreement in place of economic welfare. In a Chapter 11 case, however, the "modification" in the agreement has been accomplished not by the employer's unilateral action, but rather by operation of law. Since the filing of a petition in bankruptcy under Chapter 11 makes the contract unenforceable, § 8(d) procedures have no application to the employer's unilateral rejection of an already unenforceable contract.

. . .

... Nevertheless, it is important to note that the debtor-in-possession is not relieved of all obligations under the NLRA simply by filing a petition for bankruptcy. A debtor-in-possession is an "employer" within the terms of the NLRA, and is obligated to bargain collectively with the employees' certified representative over the terms of a new contract pending rejection of the existing contract or following formal approval of rejection by the Bankruptcy Court. But while a debtor-in-possession remains obligated to bargain in good faith under NLRA § 8(a) (5) over the terms and conditions of a possible new contract, it is not guilty of an unfair labor practice by unilaterally breaching a collective-bargaining agreement before formal Bankruptcy Court action.

Accordingly, the judgment of the Court of Appeals is affirmed.

Case Questions:

1. Upon what basis did the Court of Appeals conclude that Bildisco could reject the collective bargaining agreement?

2. What standard did the Supreme Court use in determining whether Bildisco should be allowed to reject the collective bargaining agreement? Contrast the standard advanced by the Board.

3. Why did the Court of Appeals and the Supreme Court refuse to find Bildisco guilty of an unfair labor practice in rejecting the existing contrast pending a formal approval by the Bankruptcy Court? How would the outcome differ if Bildisco failed to bargain collectively over the terms of a new contract pending formal rejection of the existing contract?

CHAPTER 7: LIQUIDATIONS. If a corporation's prospects for future earnings are too limited to allow for reorganization, liquidation under Chapter 7 is often the only alternative. Such liquidations may be voluntary—by petition of the debtor—or involuntary—by petition of unsecured creditors. To a certain extent, the process under Chapter 7 is much like the process under Chapter 13 (*see* Fig. 9-5). Until creditors elect a trustee, an interim trustee is appointed by a majority vote. If no trustee is elected, the interim trustee continues as trustee during the liquidation. The trustee is responsible for converting the company's assets into cash and distributing it to creditors. (The case of a trustee for a bankrupt company whose "assets" included a toxic landfill is the center of this chapter's YOU DECIDE feature.)

Creditor Ranking. The Bankruptcy Code specifies the priority in which creditors are to receive the money; ranking is important because there are often insufficient funds to pay off every entity. Not surprisingly, secured creditors who hold valid liens top the priority list. Seven classes of priority creditors follow: (1) administrative expenses associated with collecting the debtor's estate;

FIGURE 19-5 Chapter 7 Liquidation Procedures

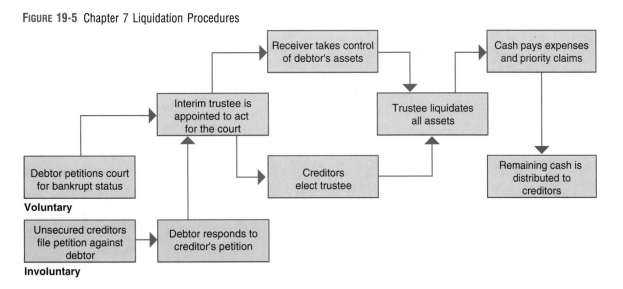

In the course of defending companies faced with multimillion dollar losses from product-liability lawsuits, lawyers have come up with a new tactic—filing bankruptcy. The strategy, for example, was used by A. H. Robins, a pharmaceutical manufacturer, to avoid liability for thousands of product liability cases involving the Dalkon Shield, a contraceptive device. It was also used by the Johns-Manville Corporation: The company filed a petition for bankruptcy to avoid liability to employees who had developed asbestosis from working with asbestos. Lately, companies have been filing for bankruptcy in an effort to avoid liability for the costs associated with environmental cleanups mandated under the two laws known collectively as the Superfund. (One of the most important environmental cases involving the bankruptcy strategy is Midlantic National Bank v. New Jersey (474 U.S. 494 [1986]), which is discussed below in more detail.)

Considerable controversy has been generated by what many feel is a lack of both ethics and morality behind this development in product-liability litigation. Plaintiffs' attorneys and consumer groups consider the tactic wholesale abuse of the bankruptcy laws intended to skirt responsibility to innocent people who have been injured by hazardous products. These groups are particularly concerned over the fact that by filing for Chapter 11 reorganization, solvent companies may avoid paying full compensation to injured consumers or employees while continuing to do business. Meanwhile, many companies involved in such lawsuits feel that they are simply availing themselves of the "fresh start" offered by the bankruptcy laws.

Midlantic National Bank v. New Jersey is a good example of both points of view. First, some background information about environmental law: In general, environmental laws are geared toward the cleanup of polluted property. The responsible party bears the cost of the cleanup. The Environmental Protection Agency has the power to undertake the cleanup if the responsible party does not do so. The party is then billed for the work.

Next, the facts about the case: A company that processed waste oil at facilities located in New York and New Jersey was cited by the New Jersey Department of Environmental Protection because it accepted oil contaminated with a toxic carcinogen. Later, an investigation of the New York facility revealed that contaminated oil had been accepted there as well. In the meantime, the company filed for liquidation under Chapter 7. The trustee informed the bankruptcy court that it intended to abandon the New York site and the personal property (that is, 400,000 gallons of contaminated oil located in deteriorating drums) at the New Jersey location under Section 554(a) of the Bankruptcy Code, which permits abandonment of any property that "is burdensome to the estate or that is of inconsequential value to the estate."

This brings up two important questions:
Can a debtor abandon contaminated property?
Can a Superfund claim be discharged in bankruptcy?

In the case of property abandonment, the question may be one of public policy. Suppose, for example, that the hazardous material in question is oil contaminated with PCBs (a cancer-causing substance) that is stored in drums located at the site to be abandoned. Whose interests should come first, the bankrupt company that is entitled under the bankruptcy laws to abandon property that is worthless or burdensome, or the public, whose exposure to the hazard would be greatly increased?

If the court determines that the property must be cleaned up and cannot be abandoned, who will pay for the cleanup? Remember, the automatic stay prevents a bankrupt company from being pursued by its debtors except under certain circumstances. Should environmental claims be dismissable in bankruptcy? Should it matter whether the polluting occurred before or after the bankruptcy was filed? For further discussion, see p. 725.

(2) tradespeople in the ordinary course of business; (3) employee salaries and benefits; (4) contributions to benefit plans; (5) certain claims of grain producers and fishermen; (6) consumers' claims for services not rendered or goods not delivered; and (7) federal, state, and local taxes. Unsecured nonpriority claims come next. Stockholder's claims are at the bottom of the list.

Asset Distribution. The payoff is accomplished as follows: If liquidation produces enough assets, secured creditors are paid in full. Then, each of the seven categories of unsecured creditors receives the same percentage share of the remaining assets. If they, too, are paid in full, remaining assets are distributed to the unsecured nonpriority claimants.

Under previous bankruptcy legislation, both partnerships and corporations could be discharged in liquidations. Under the new code, however, discharge is granted only if the debtor is an individual. **Discharge** is the legal step that ordinarily concludes a bankruptcy case: It signifies that the debts are no longer owed by the petitioner. A discharge allows the debtor to reenter busi-

discharge Last legal step in individual *bankruptcy proceedings*, signifying that the petitioner no longer owes the debts ness and be free of former debts. However, discharge does not cover debts for taxes, debts incurred fraudulently or illegally, debts not listed in the bankruptcy schedules, alimony and child support, fines, and government education loans.

CHAPTER 13: REPAYMENT PLANS. In order to file for protection under Chapter 13, a debtor must be a U.S. citizen, have a regular income, and owe less than $100,000 in unsecured debt and less than $350,000 in secured debt. Stock and commodities brokers may not file Chapter 13. The 1978 Bankruptcy Reform Act repealed the former Chapter XIII and rewrote and expanded its provisions. What had been a "wage earner's plan," originally containing an income ceiling, is now available to any "individual with regular income." By this definition, the act was expanded to include sole proprietorships and small businesses.

The Repayment Plan. When a debtor files a petition, an automatic stay is imposed on all creditors' actions against him, his property, and any codebtors. The petitioner must also file a *repayment plan*, including a monthly budget showing how repayment will be accomplished within three to five years. Unsecured creditors have no opportunity to vote on the plan, although secured creditors may object to it. When filed with the plan, a list of assets is subjected to the same exemptions as those of Chapter 7 liquidations.

A trustee is always named by the court, not elected by the creditors. Although the debtor remains in possession of assets, a reasonable proportion of his monthly income must be turned over to the trustee for distribution to creditors. If the debtor has a small business, he may continue to run it, overseen and advised by the trustee.

Plans vary widely. In some cases, repayment, as apportioned among all creditors, can be as little as one percent of the amount owed, although the bankruptcy court will normally require at least ten percent to be repaid. When the amount has been determined, the balance of a petitioner's debt is wiped out, and in the process, the debtor need not surrender any assets once repayment has been made.

Individual Filings under Chapter 13 and Chapter 7. Additional benefits of filing under Chapter 13 for both the individual and small business owner include the relative simplicity of filing, the fact that Chapter 13 does not allow for involuntary petitions, the lack of any creditors' committee, and more liberal discharge provisions than under Chapter 11 reorganizations; however, such debts as mortgages, alimony, and child support are nondischargeable.

There are even greater benefits to filing for individual bankruptcy under Chapter 11, and filings for liquidation have increased primarily because Chapter 7 exempts more properties from sale than did previous statutes. For example, certain values of equity in a home, interest in a car, household goods and furnishings, jewelry, and tools used in trade are among the items that typically cannot be liquidated.

Table 19-3 categorizes the primary differences in the Chapter 13 and Chapter 7 provisions for individual bankruptcy.

CHAPTER 12: THE FAMILY FARM BANKRUPTCY ACT OF 1986. This new chapter of the Bankruptcy Reform Act was written because the debt limits in Chapter 13 were too low for many family farms and Chapter 11 was unnecessarily complex. Like Chapter 13, the Family Farmer Bankruptcy Act includes protection for codebtors and few safeguards for creditors. For example, although the creditor's interest may attach to the proceeds of the sale, a Chapter 12 trustee may

FEATURE	CHAPTER 13 PAYMENT PLAN FOR PEOPLE WITH REGULAR INCOME	CHAPTER 7 STRAIGHT BANKRUPTCY LIQUIDATION
Basic Operation	File bankruptcy petition and proposed payment plan with court. Payment plan makes payments over a maximum of three to five years. Payments are made from disposable income (i.e., whatever is left over after necessities [food, shelter, etc.] have been allowed for), while debtor retains assets.	File bankruptcy petition with court. Trustee appointed to administer bankruptcy. All nonexempt assets sold. Debtor retains only exempt assets. Money is split among creditors, according to priority established by the Bankruptcy Code.
Limitations on Availability	For less than $100,000 in unsecured debt and less than $350,000 in secured debt.	No monetary limitations. Not available if debtor was discharged in bankruptcy within past six years.
Percentage of Consumer Filings under Bankruptcy Code	About twenty percent	About eighty percent
Availability	Can be used repeatedly.	Can be used only if not used during previous six years.
Effect on Debts	All or a portion of debts paid off over a period of time under a specific plan. With exceptions noted in text, debts are discharged. Liability to creditors ends when plan successfully carried out.	With exceptions noted in text, most debts are discharged (extinguished) upon bankruptcy. Liability to creditors ends with discharge order from court.
Effect on Home	Home will be preserved if plan successfully carried out. If not, home may be preserved under homestead exemption or marital ownership law.	Home may be preserved under homestead exemption or marital ownership law.
Effect on Automobile	Auto will be preserved if plan successfully carried out. If not, it might be taken by creditors (unless arrangements are made to pay off lien).	Auto might be taken by creditors (unless necessary for work and arrangements are made to pay off lien).
Affect on Nonexempt Assets	No effect if plan carried out successfully. If not, nonexempt assets can be sold to pay creditors, as in Chapter 7 bankruptcy.	All nonexempt assets will be sold.
Time to Repay	Usually up to three years, sometimes up to five years.	Not applicable.
Payments	All "disposable income" is available for payments; that is, whatever remains after necessities (food, shelter, etc.) are taken care of.	Most forms of debt discharged; however, other debts, such as taxes and child support, will have to be paid.
Portion of Debt Repaid	May allow payments for less than actual debts.	Will depend on the value of nonexempt assets sold to pay off debts.
Result at Conclusion of Bankruptcy Proceedings	Borrower is no longer liable for most debts if plan successfully carried out.	Bankruptcy court enters a discharge order, ending enforceability of all debts that can be discharged in bankruptcy.
Requirement for Bankruptcy Proceedings to End	Borrower must have made all payments in accordance with court-approved plan.	Court must have entered a discharge order.
Effect on Credit	Record of bankruptcy may remain on credit record for up to ten years. Creditors may prefer to see this form of bankruptcy, since successful completion of plan may pay more debts than will be paid under Chapter 7 filing.	Record of bankruptcy may remain on credit record for up to ten years.

Source: American Bar Association, *You and the Law.*

The issues presented in the first part of this discussion are difficult because there are no easy answers. The basic tenets of the bankruptcy law contradict those of the environmental laws. After all, how can a company be given a fresh start if its new beginning includes a huge debt? Conversely, can the public be expected to live with and/or pay for a company's environmental mistakes? The primary conflict, then, is between financial pressure and the public good.

This dilemma is being faced by an entire generation of environmentally conscious individuals and companies. At the same time, the same people and corporate entities are faced with equally real financial problems. Is there a middle ground? Should the government be asked to assume the cost of cleanup for bankrupt companies? If so, will this increase the number of bankruptcies? If not, who will pay?

In the Midlantic National Bank case, the bankruptcy court permitted the abandonment at both sites. All of the property was left unguarded. The oil in the hazardous drums, therefore, could be accessed by anyone who happened by. The Supreme Court reversed the decision and held that the lower court did not have the right to authorize the abandonment without some assurance that the public health and safety would be guaranteed.

The Court did not address any other issues in Midlantic. However, other courts have spoken to other issues in the bankruptcy/environmental liability arena. The decisions seem to indicate that the automatic stay of bankruptcy, which prevents creditors from pursuing their claims during the bankruptcy proceeding, does not apply to these cases: Once it is determined that the property poses sufficient danger and abandonment has been disallowed, debtors must fully comply with the provisions of the environmental laws. This exception has permitted environmental agencies to continue to cite violations and require corrective measures. There is, however, a subtle distinction here: Although agencies may not attempt to collect money from debtors, they can make the debtor spend money.

Other courts have also addressed the issue of the priority of claims against bankrupt estates. They have distinguished, for example, between pre- and post-petition debt. For example, the courts have generally held that if a bankrupt party either cannot or refuses to remedy a situation, the government will undertake the cleanup and charge the estate for a post-petition "administrative expense." The claims of the government, in other words, will have priority over other debtors. However, if the expense is incurred before the bankruptcy petition is filed, the government will be treated as an unsecured creditor.

Finally, the courts have addressed the issue of the dischargeability of environmental claims. Only a trend—not a policy—has emerged from these cases. The courts have tried to stipulate clearly that prepetition claims for money are dischargeable but that injunctions prohibiting illegal conduct are not; outcomes, however, have not been uniform because the latter part of the "rule" may require the debtor to incur a substantial debt.

It will take a lot more court rulings—and perhaps even new legislation—to resolve the issue of the treatment of bankruptcies that are initiated for the specific purpose of avoiding financial penalties.

---

sell the debtor's property without the consent of a creditor who has an interest in the property.[4]

As with Chapter 13, a debtor may voluntarily convert to a liquidation. However, unlike Chapter 13 provisions, Chapter 12 plans permit the sale of any or all of the debtor's property and payment of secured creditors over a longer period of time than the plan will be in force.

■ Concept Check 19-3   Business and Personal Bankruptcy

- Define *bankruptcy* and briefly describe the evolution of bankruptcy law in the United States.
- Explain the procedure of *valuation*.
- Explain the difference between *voluntary* and *involuntary reorganization* under Chapter 11 of the Bankruptcy Code. Describe the proceedings involved in a *Chapter 11* bankruptcy.
- Describe the proceedings involved in a *Chapter 7* bankruptcy. How are assets distributed?
- Explain the *repayment plan* required under a *Chapter 13* bankruptcy.

---

[4] Elizabeth Marston-Moore, "Family Farmer Bankruptcy Act of 1986," *Ohio State Bar Association Report*, March 2, 1987, pp. 299–300.

SUMMARY

- The transformation of our economy from a cash-payment system to its present credit dependency has created new challenges for our society. *Credit managing* for both businesses and consumers is increasingly necessary. Federal legislation in the 1970s broke new ground in protecting consumers from unscrupulous lending practices. The *Truth-in-Lending Act* established new regulations under which citizens may be better informed of credit terms before they borrow money from banks, finance companies, and similar institutions. The *Fair Credit Reporting Act* protects the privacy of consumers. The *Equal Credit Opportunity Act* was adopted to ensure all citizens equal access to credit.

- To protect consumers from unwanted harassment, badgering, and embarrassment by bill collectors, Congress enacted the *Fair Debt Collection Practices Act*. Garnishment, a long-established remedy for creditors, became more circumscribed by Title III of the *Consumer Credit Protection Act*.

- In tandem with Congress's consumer-protection efforts, the federal bankruptcy laws were revised in 1978. Under the *Bankruptcy Code*, debtors, whether they seek reorganization or liquidation, are treated more equitably and generously than under any previous bankruptcy laws. Furthermore, a new provision, *Chapter 13*, expands the choices of individuals and small business owners in the management of debt, and a recent amendment, *Chapter 12*, offers the same relief to owners of family farms. In the business climate of the 1980s and 1990s, business and personal filings increased dramatically.

QUESTIONS AND PROBLEMS

1. When Betty Simons purchases her brother's home, she borrows $24,000 from her boyfriend, Mark Wilson, for the down-payment. By the time she is to begin repaying the loan, the couple has broken up. Eventually, she tells her ex-boyfriend that she is suing him for damages because he did not disclose to her the interest and terms upon which she was to repay the loan. What should his response be?

2. Stanley Juras attended Montana State University from 1972 to 1976 with the help of several student loans to finance his education. After graduating Juras moved to California and subsequently defaulted on his loans. The university turned the delinquent account over to Aman Collection Services, a South Dakota collection agency. Aman obtained a judgment against Juras for $8,540. Juras appealed, citing, among other things, that the debt collector called him before 8:00 a.m., which constituted harassment and abuse under the Fair Labor Standards Act. Decide. [*Juras v. Aman Collection Services, Inc.*, 829 F.2d. 739 (1987)]

3. On January 1, Jeff Casey contracts with Ace Home Improvement Co. to enclose his back porch. He pays for the work by securing a loan with Ace. The Ace representative draws up the proper documents and drops them by Mr. Casey's house on January 5. In reading over the documents, Mr. Casey discovers that he has the right to rescind the contract. On January 7, he notifies Ace of his recission. Ace aserts that the contract could not be rescinded after January 4. Ace intends to sue for breach of contract. Who will win and why?

4. American Future Systems, Inc. sells china, cookware, crystal, and tableware, with 95 percent of those sales being financed by the company's own credit. AFS has what it calls a "winter program," where it separates applicants for credit into two groups. The first comprises: single, white, upper-class people in four-year colleges or nursing schools. The second is made up of minorities, males, and married people attending college or vocational school. Those in the first group are given immediate credit and shipment. Those in the second group must make three consecutive monthly payments—if a payment is not made, AFS retains the goods along with any prior payments made. AFS claims both programs meet the "special social needs" for credit shared by 18 to 21-year-olds.

Decide. [*US v. American Future Systems, Inc.* 743 F.2d. 169 (1984)]

5. Mr. Jacks enters into a contract to rent a TV at $17 per week. The contract read in boldface at the top, "This is a rental agreement with an option to purchase." Thus, Mr. Jacks was to become the owner of the TV if he paid the weekly fee for seventy-eight consecutive weeks. Is this rental agreement with the option to purchase a credit sale under the Truth-in-Lending Act? Explain. [*Clark v. Rent-It Corp.*, 685 F.2d 245 (8th Cir. 1982)]

6. The Credit Bureau prepared an allegedly erroneous credit report on Mr. Edwards with information supplied by Lacey's, a large department store. The store stated that Mr. Edwards had the worst possible credit rating assigned to consumers. Mr. Edwards claims that the store is a credit reporting agency within the Fair Credit Reporting Act. Is it? Explain. [*Rush v. Macy's New York, Inc.*, 596 F. Supp. 1540 (1984)]

7. Determine whether a credit-collection agency is liable under the Truth-in-Lending Act for performing the following acts in attempting to collect an overdue loan: (1) making continuous phone calls to the debtor; (2) calling the debtor's attorney; (3) using threats of violent crimes; (4) sending letters informing debtor of the collection agency now being responsible for the debt's collection; and (5) telling the debtor that he/she is a deadbeat for not paying debts due. (*Venes v. Professional Services Bureau*, 353 N.W.2d 671 (1984)]

8. Bayo Company has been steadily losing revenue over the past several years. Finally, hopelessly mired in debt, it files for Chapter 11 reorganization under the Bankruptcy Reform Act of 1978. Among the debts listed by Bayo Company's trustee are employee wages, three secured loans Bayo received for plant renovation and new machinery, one unsecured loan, and administrative expenses arising from the bankruptcy petition. In addition, Bayo has several thousand preferred and common stockholders. What is the priority of the payment of Bayo's claims?

9. Suppose that Bayo also has two years back taxes to pay, an off-the-record unsecured loan not included in the bankruptcy schedule, which Bayo received to help keep the company afloat, and a loan it received after providing the lender with financial statements which had been made to look as if Bayo was in much better financial condition than it actually was. Are these debts included with the debts above for discharge priority?

10. The Tracey Service Company was in the business of installing heating and air conditioning units in residential housing before it was involuntarily petitioned into Chapter 7 bankruptcy by one of its major debtors. Within three weeks, Tracey petitioned the court to convert the case into a Chapter 11 reorganization. At the hearing the debtor testified that he had $50,000 in accounts receivable awaiting collection efforts, but he had no equipment, no employees, and no business phone. What ruling do you think the judge made? [*In Re Tracey Service Co., Inc.*, Bkrtcy., 17 B.R. 405 (1982)]

20

PROPERTY, LAND-USE, AND ENVIRONMENTAL LAW

There would be no such thing as business law, or even business, if there were no such thing as *property*. Some property is *tangible*, such as land and movable objects. Other forms of property, such as copyrights, are *intangible*. Some property can be both. For example, an author who has written a book "owns" the manuscript and can keep it in his desk. In this case, although the property right in the manuscript would be real both in the legal and practical sense, it would not be very valuable in the legal sense. In that sense, a more valuable *right* would be the right to copy and distribute the book or make it into a movie. These rights are forms of property that are separate from the book itself. Thus, they may be bought and sold separately. Property law, of course, is an important area in the world of business.

The things that can and cannot be treated as property change. So do the rights attached to property, especially as the scope of laws related to urban planning and environmental protection broadens. These laws constantly reshape established property rights in an effort to protect the public from various dangers associated with the use of land and natural resources. This chapter discusses the legal definitions of property, including zoning laws, and then proceeds to discuss one of the most important aspects of property law—environmental protection.

■ DEFINING PROPERTY

property Rights over movable objects, land, and intangibles established as a relationship between individuals or organizations holding those rights and all others whose interest in that property is legally enforceable

When people hear the word "property," they generally think of *real property* (real estate) or *personal property* like objects that can easily be moved (for example, television sets and clothing). Legally, however, the term "property" refers neither to land nor objects alone. "Property" also includes rights over the use of land and objects as well as other exclusive rights over them. In fact, **property** is actually a *relationship*—namely, between the individual or organization holding rights over something that can be used and disposed of and everyone else whose interest in that something that can be enforced by law.

In order to understand the legal issues surrounding the concept of "property," we will begin with a brief discussion of property *rights*, including the right of *ownership*. We will then clarify the definition of *property* by drawing two important distinctions about the nature of property: between *fixed* and *movable* property and between *tangible* and *intangible* property.

The Basis of Property Rights: Ownership and the Law

The everyday use of the term "private property" suggests a realm where the owner is the supreme authority—a kind of private state, as in the expression "a man's home is his castle." **Ownership** generally includes the following rights:

- the right to *possess* property
- the right to *dispose* of property (to give it away, sell it, or bequeath it)
- the right to *enjoy* property or put it to *use*
- the right to *alter the nature* of property
- and even the right to *destroy* property.

ownership Rights including the right to possess, dispose of, enjoy or use, alter, and, in certain circumstances, destroy property

As we indicated earlier, "property" is actually a relationship among rights. Ownership, too, is a series of rights *protected by law*: Without law, neither property nor ownership, strictly speaking, exists.

It is important to remember that ownership is also *exclusive*: If someone else could move into your house or build one on your land without your permission, it would not be your house or your land. *Exclusivity* means that other parties are excluded from exercising your ownership rights as listed above. However, people often think of property rights as *absolute*—as unlimited or unrestricted. Property rights are not absolute: The public, for example, has certain rights over all private property.

For instance, you have the right to live in your house, and no one else has that right. Nevertheless, the law imposes conditions on that right, including duties that you must fulfill and limits on what you can do with the house and its lot. Zoning laws, for example, may prevent you from either selling an oil company the right to dig for oil in your backyard or from building a swimming pool there.

Fixed versus Movable Property

The earliest distinction between different kinds of property was between *real* and *personal* property. **Real property** (also called **real estate**) is land and everything attached to it, including the air above it and the minerals below its surface. A tree, for example, is real property when the right of ownership attaches to it.

Once it is cut up into logs, however, that tree becomes **personal property**—movable property, whether tangible or intangible, other than real property; **chattel** (derived from the French word for *"cow"*, once considered a particularly valuable form of personal property) is the legal term for tangible physical property (for example, furniture or an automobile) that can be moved easily. The distinction between real and personal property is important because the two kinds of property have been—and, to some extent, still are—treated quite differently under common law (*see* Chapter 1). For example, whereas each piece of real estate can be considered *unique*, chattel may not be.

real property (or **real estate**) *Property* consisting of land and all *fixtures* attached to it, as well as the air above it and the minerals beneath its surface

personal property *Movable property*, whether tangible or intangible, other than *real property*

chattel Tangible personal property, either *personal* (for example, an automobile) or *real* (a partnership in land) that can be moved or transferred

Reasonable people may differ about what is and is not easily *movable*. For example, although area rugs are chattel, what about wall-to-wall carpeting? In some states, wall-to-wall carpeting is indeed chattel; in most, however, it is a **fixture**—that is, an item of personal property that has been attached to real estate so permanently that the law considers it part of the real estate. When you buy a house, you automatically buy all its fixtures, such as the toilets, the sink, and the boiler. If you move in and find that the toilets have been removed, you can sue. However, you cannot sue to recover the former owner's furniture or clothing unless these items of personal property were specifically named in the deed of sale. In the following case, homeowners argued in the Arkansas Supreme Court that their wall-to-wall carpeting was a fixture for purposes of collecting under a fire insurance policy.

fixture An item of *personal property* so permanently attached to *real property* that the law considers part of that real property

---

COX v. STATE FARM FIRE & CASUALTY CO.
Arkansas Supreme Court, 398 S.W. 60 (1966)

Plaintiff-appellants are homeowners. This action by appellants is upon a fire insurance policy issued by the appellee, State Farm Fire & Casualty Co. Appellants contend that a wall-to-wall carpet was a fixture, so that its loss falls within the fire insurance coverage upon the dwelling. The trial court held that the carpet was personal property, for the loss of which the insurance company had discharged its maximum possible liability. Homeowners appeal.

George Rose Smith, J.

. . . All the facts were stipulated. When the plaintiffs bought the house the downstairs floors were covered with wall-to-wall carpeting that had worn out. About a month before the fire the plaintiffs moved this carpeting upstairs and replaced it with new carpeting downstairs. The new carpet was specially cut to fit the house; its effect in enhancing the value of the house was greater than its resale value. It was attached to the floor with tacks around the edges and could have been removed without damage to the house.

The hardwood floor under the carpet had been patched with unfinished boards. It was stipulated that the plaintiffs (if permitted to do so) would have testified: (a) That if they had removed the carpet to use the bare floor they would have relaid and refinished parts of the floor; (b) that in laying the carpet they meant for it to become part of the house; and (c) that if they should sell the house it would be their intention to sell the carpeting along with the building.

. . .

Here the question was plainly one of fact. It is agreed that the carpeting could have been removed without any damage to the floors. Such ready removability supports the conclusion that the article is not a fixture. On the other hand, the carpeting was cut to fit this particular house — a circumstance that led the plaintiffs to regard it as so much a part of the dwelling that they would only have sold the house and carpeting as a unit. . . .

Whether wall-to-wall carpeting is a fixture has been considered in a number of other states. The decided majority of the cases have concluded that such carpeting is not a fixture.

As an alternative argument the appellants contend that, regardless of its character as a fixture, the carpeting should be held to fall within this language in the insurance policy: "This policy covers: dwelling building described in the Declarations, including its additions and extensions, building equipment, fixtures and outdoor equipment pertaining to the service of the premises (if the property of the owner of the dwelling), while located on the premises of the described dwelling or temporarily elsewhere, and all materials and supplies on such premises or adjacent thereto incident to the construction, alteration or repair of such dwelling."

The appellants stress this part of the quoted clause: ". . . dwelling building described in the Declarations, including its . . . fixtures . . . while located on the premises of the described dwelling or temporarily elsewhere." It is argued that the reference to the "dwelling building" is in itself sufficient to encompass everything that is defined by the law as a fixture. Hence, the appellants insist, the further reference to "fixtures" indicates an intention on the part of the parties to refer to something in addition to what the law regards as a fixture. We are cited to the case of *Cosgrove v. Troescher* (1901), where the court said that "carpets, window shades, gas fixtures are movables, and not fixtures."

This argument does not reach the situation presented here. It is true that one may refer, in everyday speech, to an electrical fixture or to a gas fixture without intending to employ the technical legal definition of a fixture. Hence if this case involved such a removable electrical or gas appliance the appellants' argument might be persuasive. But we are not aware of any usage in everyday speech that refers to a "carpet fixture" or to a "wall-to-wall carpet fixture." A carpet could at best be called a fixture only in the legal sense, and, as we have

seen, the record does not compel us to reach that conclusion of fact.
Affirmed.

Case Questions:

1. Contrast the arguments advanced by plaintiff and defendant concerning whether the wall-to-wall carpet was a fixture.

2. On what basis did the court find that plaintiff's wall-to-wall carpeting was not a fixture?

3. Why did the court reject the alternative argument that the wall-to-wall carpet fell within the language in the insurance policy?

Tangible versus Intangible Property

Under common law, *property* can be strictly construed to consist in rights in objects or land. Thus, **tangible property** would include rights in sneakers, stereo systems, and flower beds. The concept of property, however, has broadened to include rights in **intangible property** that is connected with sources of income or wealth other than literal "things" (for example, copyrights or patents). Authors, for instance, do not own every copy of the books they write and copyright. However, they do have property rights that restrict the ways in which people who do own those copies can use them. For example, it is illegal to sell photocopies of a copyrighted book without the copyrighter's permission. Other forms of intangible property include stocks and bonds that represent rights of ownership in corporations.

> **tangible property** *Property rights* in physical objects or land
>
> **intangible property** Rights connected with property which has no value of its own but which represents income or wealth other than *tangible property*

■ *Concept Check 20-1   Defining Property*

- Define *property*.
- Explain the distinction between *real* and *personal property*. What is a *fixture*?
- Explain the difference between *tangible* and *intangible property*.

■ PUBLIC VERSUS PRIVATE INTERESTS

Considering all the limitations on what you may or may not do with your house, you might conclude that the law serves to *restrict* your property rights rather than to *protect* them. But whom do you call when a trespasser refuses to get off your property? The police, of course. In a hypothetical "state of nature," without law or police or some other means of controlling social interaction and the conflicting desires of individuals, anyone might be able to overpower you and take over your house by force.

In a very real sense, then, there could be no private property without government. By the same token, if private property were absolute—that is, if the government (or some other body responsible for social cooperation) did not retain basic rights over it—there could be no government. For example, governments must obtain revenue through taxation, a claim on citizens' pocketbooks. Because private property is exclusive but not absolute, it thus has two sides—an "individual side" and a "social side"—that go together.[1]

---

[1] Richard T. Ely, *Property and Contract in Their Relation to the Distribution of Wealth*, Vol. 1 (1914), pp. 135-37, in John E. Cribbet and Corwin W. Johnson, eds., *Cases and Materials on Property* (Indianola, IA: Foundation Press, 1984), p. 38.

We will discuss this dual nature of private property by describing three aspects of governmental power to control the use of property in order to insure social survival and protect the public interest: the doctrine of *eminent domain*, the *zoning* authority, and the principle of *taking*. Finally, we will discuss an aspect of property law that has both public and private dimensions, especially as it concerns the environment as property: *nuisance law*.

Eminent Domain: Seizing Private Property for Public Use

The government's power to tax is only one expression of the concept that a society's survival and development sometimes require that the public's interest take precedence over an individual's rights. Another expression of this doctrine is **eminent domain**, which refers to the government's right, upon payment of just compensation, to seize private property for public use. The government exercises its power of eminent domain every time it takes private property to expand a highway or string new utility wires.

> **eminent domain** A government's right, upon payment of *just compensation*, to seize private property for public use

The Fifth and Fourteenth Amendments to the U. S. Constitution, which grant the power of eminent domain to the federal and state governments, respectively (*see* Chapter 3), provide that private property may be taken for public use as long as the owner is justly compensated. The power of eminent domain may be delegated by the federal and state governments to municipalities and municipal or private corporations involved in such diverse activities as distributing electricity and building and maintaining roads, telephone and telegraph lines, rapid-transit systems, canals, ports, parks, and game reserves.

The government's right to exercise eminent domain does not depend upon the consent of the property owner: You cannot refuse to sell your house or land to a federal agency that is authorized to build a highway over your property. The power of eminent domain is preeminent to that of individual rights of ownership.

It is unconstitutional, however, for the government to seize private property without justly compensating owners and affording them due process. A **condemnation proceeding**—a court action for the purpose of taking private property for public use—accomplishes both of these constitutional requirements by (1) ensuring that the entity that seeks to take the property has the right to do so; and (2) by establishing **just compensation** for the property—that is, an amount equal to the property's fair market value at the time of taking.

> **condemnation proceeding** Court action for the purpose of *taking* private property for public use
>
> **just compensation** An amount equal to private property's fair market value at the time of its *taking* for public use

Zoning: Restrictions on Land Use

Zoning laws limit or impose conditions on the *use* of specific pieces of land or certain other forms of property, such as buildings of historic value. The right of a state to enact zoning laws flows from its inherent *police power* (*see* Chapter 3): Recall, for example, that a state's police power includes the duty to protect the safety, health, morals, and general welfare of citizens.

> **zoning laws** Regulations limiting or imposing conditions on the use of specific pieces of land or other forms of *real property*

Although both zoning and eminent domain involve governmental encroachment upon private-property rights, it is important to understand how the two principles differ. Eminent domain involves the *complete* appropriation of private property for public use—the owner is left with no property. Zoning laws, however, merely *regulate the ways* in which owners may use property to which they retain ownership. For example, a zoning law may prohibit commercial activities on land in a specified section of a city regardless of the owner's desire to use his or her property for commercial purposes.

All zoning regulation seeks to balance private and public interests, and input at the local level is crucial if private interests are not to be ignored. In fact, states generally give cities and counties partial or complete power to write zoning laws and to approve development projects. Consequently, most land-use regulation is contained in local ordinances.

Some states, however, retain a veto power over local plans or impose requirements in addition to those they set. In Vermont, for example, building or development permits must be obtained both from a state and a local agency. Other states divide land into classes and allow local governments to establish guidelines for each class. In Hawaii, the State Land-Use Commission classifies real estate as urban, rural, agricultural, or conservation. With the exception of conservation land, the county—not the state—enforces state restrictions on development. Still other states and some local governments have created regional agencies to oversee land use. California, for instance, requires developers of the San Francisco Bay coastline to obtain permits from both local governments and the Bay Conservation Development Commission.

While the federal government does not directly regulate the use of private land, it does so indirectly through laws protecting the environment. For instance, state and local government plans to improve air quality may rest on the locations of shopping centers that attract car traffic or the locations of sewer lines and factories. The federal Clean Air Act (discussed below) requires these plans to be submitted to the Environmental Protection Agency. Proposals to dredge or fill in part of the nation's waters must often be approved by the Army Corps of Engineers. The federal government also directly regulates certain nonprivate land, such as national forests and American Indian trust land.

The Issue of Taking

A frequent subject of litigation involving the government's power of eminent domain, and its corresponding duty of just compensation, concerns the action known as **taking of property**: Generally speaking, a government *takes* private property when, for the public benefit, it *destroys the value* of the property for the owner.

taking of property Government action depriving private *ownership* rights to property appropriated for public use

Because the regulation of land use derives from the states' police power rather than the constitutional power of eminent domain, zoning laws do not require compensation for property owners. People can and do disagree, however, about whether a zoning regulation can also be said to take away property from owners for public ends. Remember, in discussing *property*, we are discussing a bundle of *rights*. Under certain circumstances, for example, the government might use various regulations to deprive you of part of your bundle of property rights in your house without actually buying it, kicking you out into the street, or otherwise directly affecting your ownership or possession rights. Property owners who suffer great costs because of land-use regulations can and do sue the government for damages on the ground that the regulation was an unconstitutional "taking" of property without just compensation.

Until the 1970s, in part because of concern that governments might be subject to large damage awards, many lawmakers were thus reluctant to enact environmental-protection laws that could result in litigation on the grounds of unconstitutional taking. Property owners may indeed win suits if the public benefit enhanced by the regulation seems slight when compared to the loss to the owner or if the regulation actually serves only the interest of a few people. In order to decide whether owners must be compensated, courts usually weigh public benefit against private cost.

A classic example of the balancing test applied to zoning authority is *Penn Central Transportation Company v. City of New York* (438 U.S. 104 [1978]). In this case, the Supreme Court found that the public benefit derived from preserving the beauty and historic value of a New York City beaux-arts train station outweighed the cost imposed on the owner when New York City rejected the owner's plan to build a 53-story building on top of the station.

TAKING AND THE LEGAL SCOPE OF ZONING. The scope of legal zoning ordinances is limited to the powers delegated by the state. Therefore, the goals of an ordinance must be reasonably close to or implied in the goals set forth in a delegating statute. They must also conform to a master plan, if one exists. In addition, they must meet a three-part judicial test associated with the police power:

1. If a judge cannot find at least a plausible reason for believing that a zoning ordinance will accomplish its stated end, it can be ruled *arbitrary*.
2. If classifications contained in the ordinance do not plausibly serve that end, the ordinance can be found *discriminatory*.
3. If an ordinance rules out all reasonably suitable uses of property, it may be struck down as *confiscatory*.

The U.S. Supreme Court first declared that zoning was not a "taking" without compensation in the landmark case *Village of Euclid v. Ambler Realty Co.* (1926). Since this case, the type of general zoning that it approved has become known as *Euclidian zoning*.

VILLAGE OF EUCLID v. AMBLER REALTY CO.
United States Supreme Court, 272 U.S. 365 (1926)

The Village of Euclid is an Ohio municipal corporation. Appellee is the owner of a tract of land containing 68 acres. Adjoining this tract on the east and west are restricted residential tracts upon which residences have been erected. On November 13, 1922, an ordinance was adopted by the Village Council, establishing a comprehensive zoning plan for regulating and restricting the location of trades, industries, apartment houses, two-family houses, single family houses, etc.

Appellee seeks an injunction restraining the enforcement of the ordinance and all attempts to impose or maintain any of its restrictions upon appellee's property, claiming that the ordinance is unconstitutional. The court below held that the ordinance was unconstitutional and void, and enjoined its enforcement. The Village of Euclid appeals.

Mr. Justice Sutherland delivered the opinion of the Court.

. . . The ordinance is assailed on the grounds that it is in derogation of § 1 of the Fourteenth Amendment of the Federal Constitution in that it deprives appellee of liberty and property without due process of law and denies it the equal protection of the law. . . .

Before proceeding to a consideration of the case, it is necessary to determine the scope of the inquiry. The bill alleges that the tract of land in question is vacant and has been held for years for the purpose of selling and developing it for industrial uses, for which it is especially adapted, being immediately in the path of progressive industrial development; that for such uses it has a market value of about 10,000 per acre, but if the use be limited to residential purposes the market value is not in excess of $2,500 per acre; that the first 200 feet of the parcel back from Euclid Avenue, if unrestricted in respect of use, has a value of $150 per front foot, but if limited to residential uses, and ordinary mercantile business be excluded therefrom its value is not in excess of $50 per front foot.

It is specifically averred that the ordinance attempts to restrict and control the lawful uses of appellee's land so as to confiscate and destroy a great part of its value;

that it is being enforced in accordance with its terms; that prospective buyers of land for industrial, commercial and residential uses in the metropolitan district of Cleveland are deterred from buying any part of this land because . . . the ordinance constitutes a cloud upon the land, reduces and destroys its value, and has the effect of diverting the normal industrial, commercial and residential development thereof to other and less favorable locations.

. . .

The question is . . . as stated by appellee: Is the ordinance invalid in that it violates the constitutional protection "to the right of property in the appellee by attempted regulations under the guise of the police power, which are unreasonable and confiscatory?"

Building zone laws are of modern origin. They began in this country about twenty-five years ago. Until recent years, urban life was comparatively simple; but with the great increase and concentration of population, problems have developed, and constantly are developing, which require, and will continue to require, additional restrictions in respect of the use and occupation of private lands in urban communities. . . . Such regulations are sustained, under the complex conditions of our day, for reasons analogous to those which justify traffic regulations, which, before the advent of automobiles and rapid transit street railways, would have been condemned as fatally arbitrary and unreasonable. . . .

The ordinance now under review, and all similar laws and regulations, must find their justification in some aspect of the police power, asserted for the public welfare. The line which in this field separates the legitimate from the illegitimate assumption of power is not capable of precise delimitation. It varies with circumstances and conditions. . . . Thus the question whether the power exists to forbid the erection of a building of a particular kind or for a particular use, like the question whether a particular thing is a nuisance, it to be determined, not by an abstract consideration of the building or of the thing considered apart, but by considering it in connection with the circumstances and the locality. A nuisance may be merely a right thing in the wrong place—like a pig in the parlor instead of the barnyard. If the validity of the legislative classification for zoning purposes be fairly debatable, the legislative judgment must be allowed to control.

There is no serious difference of opinion in respect of the validity of laws and regulations fixing the height of buildings within reasonable limits, the character of materials and methods of construction, and the adjoining area which must be left open, in order to minimize the danger of fire or collapse, the evils of overcrowding, and the like, and excluding from residential sections offensive trades, industries and structures likely to create nuisances.

Here, however, the exclusion is in general terms of all industrial establishments, and it may thereby happen that not only offensive or dangerous industries will be excluded, but those which are neither offensive nor dangerous will share the same fate. But this is no more than happens in respect of many practice-forbidding laws which this Court has upheld although drawn in general terms so as to include individual cases that may turn out to be innocuous in themselves. The inclusion of a reasonable margin to insure effective enforcement, will not put upon a law, otherwise valid, the stamp of invalidity.

. . .

We find no difficulty in sustaining restrictions of the kind thus far reviewed. The serious question in the case arises over the provisions of the ordinance excluding from residential districts, apartment houses, business houses, retail stores and shops, and other like establishments. This question involves the validity of what is really the crux of the more recent zoning legislation, namely, the creation and maintenance of residential districts, from which business and trade of every sort, including hotels and apartment houses, are excluded. Upon that question this Court has not thus far spoken. . . .

. . .

The matter of zoning has received much attention at the hands of commissions and experts, and the results of their investigations have been set forth in comprehensive reports. These reports, which bear every evidence of painstaking consideration, concur in the view that the segregation of residential, business, and industrial buildings will make it easier to provide fire apparatus suitable for the character and intensity of the development in each section; that it will increase the safety and security of home life; greatly tend to prevent street accidents, especially to children, by reducing the traffic and resulting confusion in residential sections. . . . With particular reference to apartment houses, it is pointed out that the development of detached house sections is greatly retarded by the coming of apartment houses, which has sometimes resulted in destroying the entire section for private house purposes; that in such sections very often the apartment house is a mere parasite, constructed in order to take advantage of the open spaces and attractive surroundings created by the residential character of the district. Moreover, the coming of one apartment house is followed by others . . . bringing, as their necessary accompaniments, the disturbing noises incident to increased traffic and business, and the occupation, by means of moving and parked automobiles, or larger portions of the streets, thus detracting from their safety and depriving children of the privilege of quiet and open spaces for play, . . . until, finally, the residential character of the neighborhood and its desirability as a place of detached residences are utterly destroyed. Under these circumstances, apartment houses, which in a different environment would be not only entirely unobjectionable but highly desirable, come very near to being nuisances.

If these reasons, thus summarized, do not demonstrate the wisdom or sound policy in all respects of those restrictions which we have indicated as pertinent to the inquiry, at least, the reasons are sufficiently cogent to preclude us from saying, as it must be said before the ordinance can be declared unconstitutional, that such provisions are clearly arbitrary and unreasonable, having no substantial relation to the public health, safety, morals, or general welfare.

Nuisance Law

William A. Prosser, a leading authority on tort law (*see* Chapter 10), has observed that "there is perhaps no more impenetrable jungle in the entire law than that which surrounds the word 'nuisance.' It has meant all things to all men, and has been applied indiscriminately to everything from an alarming advertisement to a cockroach baked in a pie."[2]

nuisance Unreasonable interference with the use and enjoyment of another individual's or organization's interest in *real property*

For our purposes, a private **nuisance** can be defined as unreasonable interference with the use and enjoyment of another's interest in real property. Nuisance requires *substantial* harm resulting from the interference. In addition to being substantial, the interference must be *unreasonable*. To determine whether interference is unreasonable, courts balance the *social utility of the activity*—that is, the value of a defendant's conduct to society at large—against the amount of harm to the plaintiff. Note also that the difference between a private and public nuisance is basically one of degree: While a *private* nuisance affects a single individual or a small number of people, a public nuisance affects a substantial number of people or an entire community.

The law of nuisance has played a significant and long-standing role in environmental protection. In the sixteenth century, for example, cases were brought to eliminate pollutants such as odors emanating from free-roaming swine. In more recent years, tort actions for nuisance have provided remedies for personal injury and property damage caused by environmental pollution. Odors, noise, toxic substances, and air and water pollution created by industry have all been held to be both public and private nuisances.

The use of nuisance law to eliminate environmental irritants reached a height in the United States during the 1920s and 1930s, when landowners invoked it to control both actual and threatened noxious gases in their neighborhoods. Gas stations and funeral parlors generated the greatest volume of cases. In virtually all of these cases, the plaintiffs asked only for *injunctions*—court orders compelling defendants to cease permanently the conduct occasioning the complaint. (*See* Chapter 4 *for a more complete explanation of injunctions*). Monetary damages were sought from defendants against whom the courts were unlikely to issue injunctions, such as government entities, charities, and public utilities.

Although the use of nuisance complaints as a weapon against environmental damage increased during the 1960s—the decade that gave birth to to-

---

[2] See William L. Prosser and W. Page Keeton, *Prosser and Keeton on Torts*, 5th ed. (St. Paul, MN: West, 1984).

day's environmental movement—the effectiveness of such complaints was also questioned. For one thing, proving private nuisance was gradually becoming more difficult because many industrial pollutants did not warrant **special damages**—damages that can be collected only if the plaintiff has suffered some unique harm from defendant activities differing from other activities in the area.

special damages Monetary compensation that can be awarded and collected only as the result of harm unique to the activities of the defendant

There are other problems with using nuisance law to fight environmental destruction. For example, nuisance litigation by private parties is frequently unsuccessful because of equitable and other defenses available to the defendant. Under the doctrine of "coming to the nuisance," for instance, plaintiffs are precluded from claiming nuisance if they voluntarily chose to move into areas in which a defendant's activity was ongoing. If a defendant proves one or more of these equitable defenses, the plaintiff cannot prevail.

Despite these difficulties, however, nuisance actions have been brought against a great number of major industries and municipalities. Activities complained about include those of chemical plants, sewage-treatment plants, oil refineries, and many other manufacturing ventures. In the following case, the Illinois Supreme Court was faced with the question of whether a waste-disposal site was a nuisance. The court postulated a *balancing test* that it found useful in reaching a decision.

■ Concept Check 20-2   Public versus Private Interests

- Explain the *rights* that are generally included under the *ownership* of *property*.
- Describe the doctrine of *eminent domain* and the principle of *zoning* and explain the key differences between them.
- Explain the concept of *taking of property* and distinguish it from the principles underlying zoning laws. Why do zoning laws not require *just compensation* to the property owner?
- Explain how *nuisance* laws may be used to deal with environmental problems.

■ LAND-USE PLANNING

In 1928, the U.S. Chamber of Commerce developed a national model for state laws delegating zoning powers to local governments. Under these guidelines, state and local governments may use **land-use planning** to "regulate and restrict the height, number of stories, and size of buildings and other structures; the percentage of a [building] lot that may be occupied by the building; the size of the [building's] yard, courts, and other open spaces; the density of population; and the location and use of buildings, structures, and land for trade, industry, residence or other purposes."[3] This provision has perhaps become the most widely accepted of all American-model acts.

land-use planning Principles for establishing regulations, primarily at the state and local levels, to control activities affecting the use of public and private land

In addition to zoning laws, land-use planning includes state or regional master plans, which are usually separate from delegating statutes empowering local governments to zone. These plans set forth general goals for an area. There are also planning commissions made up of private citizens appointed by local officials to recommend changes in local ordinances. These commissions often work together with a professional planning department.

---

[3] The Standard State Zoning Act, cited in Roger Bernhardt, *Real Property* (St. Paul, MN: West, 1984), p. 395.

The Purpose of Planning

Although planning power comes from police power, it is not equally broad. Only certain traditional purposes related to the health, safety, morals, and the general welfare of citizens are appropriate for zoning ordinances or master plans. Moreover, the odds that any unusual ordinance will be challenged have proved to be quite high.

Not surprisingly, numerous attempts to protect the public from eyesores have been controversial. For example, zoning laws that regulate or outlaw billboards and satellite dishes have implicated First-Amendment rights allowing for freedom of expression. Accordingly, courts have balanced First-Amendment rights against the state's right to exert its police power to protect the appearance of roads and neighborhoods. Thus, because *zoning* is both a highly visible instance of land-use planning, and because disputes about land-use planning highlight ongoing tensions between traditional American ideals of private choice and community interests, we will survey several of the most important and common purposes for which such planning has been used. Basically, these uses are divided into two general categories: the *protection* of the public interest and the *prevention* of conditions that are detrimental to the public interest.

PROTECTION OF REAL ESTATE VALUES. One purpose of planning is to conserve and enhance the value of buildings. Generally speaking, zoning aims to promote orderly development, which should enhance the real estate of the area as a whole and thus enhance the community's tax base. A common way of meeting this goal is to create areas where buildings look alike and serve similar purposes. For example, ordinances that restrict building in certain areas to single-family houses are fulfilling this goal.

PROTECTION OF BEAUTY OR HISTORIC VALUE. Zoning may also aim to preserve the beauty or historic value of buildings, neighborhoods, or scenic areas. Often, this step is taken to protect a tourist industry. In New Orleans, for example, owners of buildings in the historic Vieux Carré district cannot alter facades or designs without the approval of a special commission.

PROTECTION OF ENVIRONMENTAL VALUES. Planners have recently come to realize that zoning can also be used to protect sensitive lands.[4] Like most zoning regulations, environmental zoning laws seek to foster orderly development, and some communities allow trade-offs in the application of permits. San Francisco, for example, requires developers to compensate for the loss of open spaces in one area by constructing a new park in another. Montgomery County, Maryland, relieves the tax pressure to sell undeveloped farmland: Farmers who do not wish to sell such farmland may sell "rural development rights" to builders in nearby locales like Washington, D.C.; although the undeveloped land can no longer be sold for housing, it is taxed on farm values and not on subdivision rates.

Table 20-1 summarizes certain categories of sensitive lands threatened by urban development and also suggests some compatible alternatives for their use.

---

[4] This section is based on William P. Cunningham and Barbara Woodworth Cunningham, *Environmental Science: A Global Concern* (Dubuque, IA: Wm. C. Brown, 1990), pp. 521–22.

TABLE 20-1	*Types of Sensitive Land and Recommended Uses*
Surface waters and riparian lands	Ports, harbors, marinas, parks and open space, industry requiring water access
Marshes and wetlands	Water storage, recreation, wildlife habitat
Fifty-year flood plain	Agriculture, forestry, recreation, some development not sensitive to flooding
Scenic, historic, and cultural areas	Parks, recreation, greenbelts, open space, wildlife habitat
Aquifer recharge zone	Agriculture, forestry, open space, low-density housing, industry that produces no toxic effluents; restricted fertilizer pesticide, solvent, and herbicide use
Steep, erodable land	Forestry, recreation, open space; maximum housing density: one house per three acres with careful erosion control
Prime agricultural land	Agriculture; housing density not more than one house per 25 acres

Source: William P. Cunningham and Barbara Woodworth Cunningham, *Environmental Science: A Global Concern* (Dubuque, IA: Wm. C. Brown, 1990). Adapted from Ian McHarg, *Design with Nature* (Philadelphia: Natural History Press, 1969).

PREVENTION OF OVERCROWDING. Some regulations aim at keeping streets uncrowded or otherwise easing transportation—for instance, by requiring buildings to have parking lots or driveways. All kinds of limits on the size of buildings or the number of buildings on a piece of land serve to lessen traffic and insure adequate air and light. However, because these limits also generally keep the price of land and housing high, they tend to exclude lower-income people from an area. In itself, then, demographic regulation may not be considered a reasonable purpose of zoning: Such zoning laws have been known to disguise hidden agendas—namely, keeping minority groups that tend to be relatively poor out of selected neighborhoods.

■ Concept Check 20-3   Land-Use Planning

- Describe the primary purposes of *land-use planning*.
- Why have the courts ruled that *zoning* does not constitute *taking* without compensation?

■ PROTECTING THE ENVIRONMENT

The National Debate about Our Environment

There is a long-standing debate between those who favor heavy governmental regulation of environmental matters and those who favor a more moderate or even hands-off approach. For example, critics of strict controls on air, water, and noise pollution contend that the price of a "clean" environment is too high because of detrimental effects to the economy and employment. According to these critics, corporations, which are saddled with high costs related to environmental protection, will merely pass them on to consumers and/or reduce the size of their work force to cut costs. (*See* this chapter's ORGANIZATIONAL PRO-

FILE box for a discussion of one major corporation's response to environmental challenges.)

Proponents of government regulation, on the other hand, believe that time is of the essence in saving our environment after so many years of neglect. The dangers are too serious, they argue, to leave the issue in the hands of a business sector whose economic interests are often opposed to environmental protection.

While the debate continues about whether and how much government should be involved in mandatory regulation, a large federal environmental-regulation bureaucracy has developed during the past several decades. The Council on Environmental Quality and the Environmental Protection Agency (EPA) are the primary federal agencies concerned with the environment. The Council on Environmental Quality, which is under the executive office, develops and recommends policies to the president and Congress; the EPA promulgates and enforces federal environmental laws and regulations. Both of these agencies conduct research and establish controls. Additionally, both agencies have assisted states in developing and implementing their own pollution-control programs. The Department of the Interior, the Food and Drug Administration, and the Department of Energy and Transportation also play significant roles in promulgating regulations aimed at environmental protection. Figure 20-1 shows not only the EPA, which is discussed in more detail below, but several other key federal agencies responsible for environmental protection and management.

Environmental activism in the 1960s led to legislative action intended to strengthen environmental-protection laws. During this period, existing laws were amended and new statutes enacted to protect the environment and regulate the use of our nation's natural resources. One of these statutes is the National Environmental Policy Act, which is also examined more fully later in this chapter.

Environmental Problems

Properly understood, the term *environment* includes both natural and urban settings. For example, limiting the right of owners to change historic buildings is a kind of environmental protection. Nuclear radiation from accidents at nuclear power plants, depletion of the ozone layer of the earth's atmosphere, soil erosion, pollution of groundwater with farm chemicals, and the extinction of various plant and animal species are also environmental problems.

These problems are difficult to solve for several reasons. First, they tend to have many, varied, and interrelated causes and effects. The effects of pollution, for example, have often been shifted by the effects of regulation, either from air to water or land or from one location to another. Second, the solutions to environmental problems often require action across political boundaries. This means that separate units of government, representing people who may not all be affected by the problem to the same degree, must cooperate. Third, although it is always costly to leave environmental problems unchecked, it is also expensive to solve them. It is a challenge to determine which costs are greater, who should pay, and how payment should be made. As a rule, the group of people who pay for prevention or cleanup is not the same as the group that suffers the costs of environmental damage. In general, in order to relieve the public of pollution-related costs, both now and in the future, environmental protection imposes immediate costs on industry and the users of industrial products. Meanwhile, environmental groups often find themselves representing otherwise voiceless "future generations."

Whatever the scope of these problems—and whatever the prospect of future generations—it seems obvious today that improvements in our shared environment must be coordinated at a high level of social organization. For most environmental activists, only government can take appropriate action to insure both for current and future generations the benefits of a form of "property" that is sometimes called **commons** (or **common-property resources**): resources which belong at once to everyone and to no one and to which individuals have essentially unmanaged access. In the sections that follow, we will survey some key legislative, regulatory, and policy steps taken by the U.S. government in its role in managing common-property resources in the public interest: the *National Environmental Policy Act*, the *Environmental Protection Agency*, the *Clean Air Act*, and the *Clean Water Act*. We will touch briefly on some issues in chemical

commons (or common-property resources) Resources, such as off-coast fishing waters, belonging at once to everyone and no one and to which individuals have essentially unmanaged access

FIGURE 20-1 Federal Executive Agencies Responsible for Resource Management and Environmental Protection *Source:* William P. Cunningham and Barbara Woodword Cunningham, *Environmental Science: A Global Concern* (Dubuque, IA: Wm. C. Brown, 1990). Data from U.S. General Accounting Office.

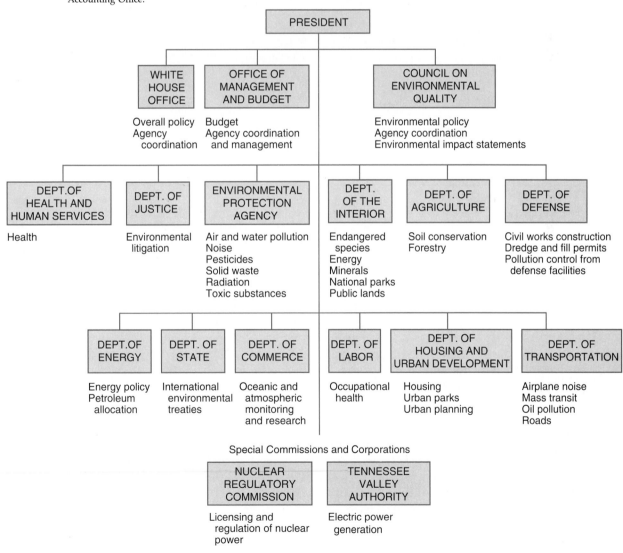

The safety, health, and environmental managers at DuPont usually spend their days at one of the corporation's facilities dressed in protective glasses and hardhats. Recently, however, the giant chemical company asked these managers to participate in formulating a corporate environmental policy. The policy, which DuPont refers to as its "vision," sets out the goals that the company hopes to achieve during the 1990s. The DuPont "vision" describes how the company will conduct its affairs in key areas of business and policy with respect to safety, health, and the environment. Its drafters have tried to anticipate and respond to increasing public awareness and concern about the environmental impact of the company's numerous facilities, which are engaged in a variety of activities worldwide.

The DuPont vision also seeks to promote the ideal of ethical conduct in environmental matters and to make this commitment central to the concerns of those who occupy every level of corporate management. For example, it reflects the view that profitability and environmental responsibility are not mutually exclusive. In addition, as a statement of the company's ethical priorities, DuPont environmental policy commits the firm to making technical resources available for environmental improvement. Similarly, the company has committed itself to responding to public concerns in communities in which its plants are located. This policy reflects DuPont's view that a company's right to operate within a community necessarily includes the obligation to consider that community's needs and interests.

Much of DuPont's emphasis in environmental matters has been on manufacturing. Annually, for example, the Na-tional Wildlife Federation publishes its Toxic 500 list, which identifies the 500 U.S. industrial plants with the most emissions of harmful substances. In 1989, fourteen of those plants belonged to DuPont. DuPont responded by working aggressively to reduce the level of material emitted from cited plants. DuPont's environmental awareness also extends to its products. As a leading manufacturer of plastic and polymer materials, DuPont has the expertise—and perhaps the obligation—to develop ways to recover and recycle plastic waste. In acknowledging this challenge, the company has embarked on a major venture to establish a worldwide business in this technology.

Environmental protection has also given DuPont a competitive advantage in the global marketplace. In West Germany, for example, improper disposal of used motor oil by consumers is a serious pollution concern. In one of DuPont's European affiliates, an ingenious program was developed to recover and recycle used automobile oil. The program succeeded not only in preventing pollution from used oil, but in conserving natural resources through recycling. It thus helped to improve West Germany's environment while increasing DuPont's profits.

Also of major importance is DuPont's policy with respect to the production of chlorofluorocarbon, a chemical that is harmful to the layer of ozone that protects the earth from potentially carcinogenic solar rays. DuPont has decided to phase out production of these compounds by the end of the decade—a commitment exceeding that of most other producers in the chemical industry.

and waste pollution and in energy conservation and conclude with some comments about developments in international environmental law.

The National Environmental Policy Act

National Environmental Policy Act (NEPA) Comprehensive legislation, enacted by Congress in 1969, for establishing and enforcing federal environmental policy

In 1969, a blowout of an oil well off the coast of Santa Barbara, California, killed thousands of fish and wild birds and flooded miles of beaches with oil. Congress responded to the nation's growing sense of crisis over the environment with its first broad statement of environmental policy, the **National Environmental Policy Act** (NEPA) of 1969. NEPA was intended to usher in a decade of federal laws and regulations designed to protect the environment. It outlined six goals:

1. to promote the idea that the present generation is the "trustee" of the environment for future generations;
2. to assure Americans "safe, productive, and . . . pleasing surroundings";
3. to allow the environment to be used in as many ways as possible without unwanted or unexpected results;
4. to maintain environmental diversity;
5. to ensure that population growth does not put too much stress on natural resources; and

6. to maintain the quality of resources and promote recycling (the reuse of materials) in order to minimize the use of resources that could become scarce.

To accomplish these difficult but necessary goals, NEPA created a three-member Council on Environmental Quality (CEQ). The officials of CEQ are nominated by the president and confirmed by the Senate. CEQ advises the president on how current and proposed national policies and programs will affect the environment. It also keeps track of changes or trends in the field, resolves conflicts among agencies over policies affecting the environment, and sets the rules for agencies so that they can meet the goals of NEPA.

ENVIRONMENTAL IMPACT STATEMENTS. All federal agencies are required by NEPA to take the environment into account when making decisions. Specifically, section 102(2)c requires a "detailed statement" of the environmental impact of every proposed federal law or action that would significantly affect the environment. Other agencies may comment on these statements while they are being prepared. The final statement about a project, which is called the **environmental impact statement (EIS)**, is released to the president, the council, and the public. The EIS must make three points. It must:

environmental impact statement (EIS) Project statement, required by the *National Environmental Policy Act*, of the environmental effects of any projected federal program

1. specifically discuss any harmful effects of the action and weigh the short-term benefits of the action against all long-term needs or costs;
2. identify any aspect of the action that cannot be reversed (for example, the extinction of a species or permanent damage to an area); and
3. present options other than the proposed action and discuss their environmental impact as well.

(See *Baltimore Gas and Electric Co. v. Natural Resources Defense Council, Inc.* [1983], Chapter 6, *pp. 191–92, for an example of such a statement.*)

The object of the EIS is to make sure that agency officials, other parts of the government, and the public understand the consequences of actions *before* they are taken. The purpose of environmental impact statements has been defined by the courts as "environmental full disclosure" (*Environmental Defense Fund, Inc. v. Corps of Engineers*, 325 F. Supp. 749 [1971]). The statements should be thorough, simple, and clear enough to inform people without special training. Too much technical language or too many minute details will only get in the way of decision making.

The particular usefulness of an EIS, of course, varies from case to case. Nevertheless, there are at least three general questions about the value of an EIS that pertain to a broad range of decisions that can be made about legislative or policy actions affecting the environment: Is a *cost-benefit analysis* feasible as a feature of an EIS? Under what circumstances is an EIS really necessary? How practical is the provision requiring *research* into the "worst-case" scenario entailed by an action?

Inclusion of a Cost-Benefit Analysis. There has been some disagreement about whether an EIS should include a cost-benefit analysis. Those who think it should not often criticize cost-benefit analysis itself. After all, it can be difficult, if not impossible, to reduce factors like life and health to dollar amounts.

The argument in favor of using cost-benefit analysis is that NEPA requires federal agencies to seek ways of quantifying the value of damage to the environment so that such damage not be ignored when decisions are made. If an EIS includes a cost-benefit analysis, a court reviewing it can easily see which factors the agency considered and the importance that it gave to each of them. Therefore, the EIS should include documentation of how the agency reached its conclusions.

The EIS: Pro and Con. The courts have consistently resisted arguments that environmental impact statements were unnecessary in particular cases. So far, there are only two kinds of exceptions. Congress has expressly cleared the way for certain projects. The trans-Alaska oil pipeline, for instance, was exempted by law from judicial review under NEPA.[5] In addition, the U.S. Supreme Court ruled in 1981 that the U.S. Navy did not have to prepare an EIS before storing nuclear weapons in Hawaii (*Weinberg v. Catholic Action of Hawaii,* 454 U.S. 139 [1981]). The justices argued that because information about storage of nuclear weapons was exempt from disclosure under the Freedom of Information Act (*see* Chapter 6), it should be exempt under NEPA as well. An EIS would be necessary only if (1) the navy actually stored weapons at that site and (2) the need to protect national security prevented the navy from revealing the location of stored weapons.

The "Research and Worst-Case" Regulation. The effects of an action may be far from clear. When faced with gaps in information, for example, agencies cannot merely report failure. They must meet the requirements of the "research and worst-case" regulation developed by the CEQ. Barring undue costs, every effort must be made to research the facts. If the research would be too costly or if there is no known way to establish the facts, the agency must imagine the worst possible outcome of an action and decide the likelihood that this outcome will occur. In practice, it is probably necessary to include a worst-case scenario even if a projected worst-case outcome is extremely unlikely. The Sierra Club, for example, won a case on that ground; it is excerpted below.

---

[5] The Trans-Alaska Pipeline Authorization Act, 43 U.S.C. 1652(d) (1976), in Frank F. Skillern, *Environmental Protection: The Legal Framework* (Colorado Springs, CO: Shepard's-McGraw, 1981), p. 43.

SIERRA CLUB v. SIGLER
U.S. Court of Appeals, Fifth Circuit, 695 F.2d 957 (1983)

Galveston Bay is part of a system of estuarine bays along the Texas coast. It is Texas' largest estuary and serves as nursery and habitat for vast numbers of wildlife, including fish and migratory birds. However, the bay also has served for many years as a commercial waterway for the ports of Galveston, Houston, and Texas City. Galveston Wharves ("Wharves") is a utility of the City of Galveston that filed a permit application with the Army Corps of Engineers to extend and deepen the channel into Galveston Bay to facilitate the traffic in large ships. This project will be the first in the United States to permit oil tankers to operate in a wildlife estuary. The primary focus of the controversy has been on the effects of a major oil spill in a waterway that serves as a breeding ground for much of Texas' wildlife population.

The Environmental Impact Statement ("EIS") was prepared as required by the National Environmental Policy Act of 1969 (NEPA), and a final EIS ("FEIS") was issued in September of 1979. Based upon the FEIS and federal law, the Galveston District Engineer of the U.S. Army Corps of Engineers issued five permits authorizing the deepening of the channel and construction of the oil terminal, tank farm, and pipeline system.

The Sierra Club and four other plaintiffs brought suit against the Corps and other federal defendants, challenging the adequacy of the FEIS and the issuance of the permits. The Court of Appeals for the Southern District of Texas denied all challenges to the FEIS and upheld the issuance of the permits. The Sierra Club appeals.

Gee, Circuit Judge:

. . . The nation's largest concentration of refineries and petrochemical plants is found on the western shores of the Texas Gulf Coast stretching from Freeport in the south to Beaumont in the north. Between these two points lies the City of Galveston, which is located on the Galveston Island flanking the main channel into Galveston Bay.

. . . In September [1974], the project [to extend and deepen the channel into the Bay] was revised by the Wharves and the Pelican Terminal Company ("PELCO"), who plan to build the project without federal participation. The Wharves and PELCO proposal contemplated building an oil terminal to offload very large crude carriers (VLCC's or "supertankers") of up to 320,000 dwt [dead weight tons] and to deepen and lengthen the channels into the Bay and the Port of Galveston to accommodate them. The proposed location of this "superport" oil terminal is Pelican Island, which is inside the Bay and adjacent to Galveston City. . . .

. . .

Preparation of the FEIS was governed by NEPA and by the regulations enforcing it promulgated by the Council on Environmental Quality (CEQ) because CEQ regulations implementing NEPA are binding on all federal agencies. . . .

. . .

. . . One of those regulations requires that under certain conditions an EIS contain a "worst case" analysis.

When an agency is evaluating significant adverse effects on the human environment in an environmental impact statement and there are gaps in relevant information or scientific uncertainty, the agency shall always make clear that such information is lacking or that uncertainty exists.

. . .

(b) If (1) the information relevant to adverse impacts is essential to a reasoned choice among alternatives and is not known and the overall costs of obtaining it are exorbitant or (2) the information is relevant to adverse impacts, is important to the decision and the means to obtain it are not known (e.g., the means for obtaining it are beyond the state of the art) the agency shall weigh the need for the action against the risk and severity of possible adverse impacts were the action to proceed in the face of uncertainty. If the agency proceeds, it shall include a worst case analysis and an indication of the probability or improbability of its occurrence.

40 C. F. R. § 1502.22 (1981).

. . .

The Corps first argues that the catastropic "worst case" oil spill analysis urged by the Sierra Club—involving a total cargo loss by a supertanker in the Bay—is beyond the statutory minima of NEPA and therefore need not be performed. . . .

. . .

The CEQ's interpretation of its worst case regulation makes it quite clear that the Sierra Club's catastrophic worst case is precisely what the CEQ intended.

NEPA requires that impact statements, at a minimum, contain information to alert the public and Congress to *all know possible* environmental consequences of agency action. Thus, one of the federal government's most important obligations is to present to the fullest extent possible the spectrum of consequences that may result from agency decisions and the details of their potential consequences for the human environment. . . .

(Forty Most Asked Questions Concerning CEQ's NEPA Regulations (1981).

. . .

Nonetheless, the trial court held and the Corps argues that a worst case analysis is not required for remote consequences. Here the trial court's legal analysis and the Corps' argument are incorrect.

. . .

The trial court and the corps also misunderstand the role of "speculation" in preparing a worst case analysis. The trial court acknowledged that a worst case analysis is "somewhat speculative" by nature. Yet, despite the fact that NEPA permits, even demands, "reasonable speculation," the trial court proceeded to require that the plaintiffs demonstrate a method for performing an "accurate" analysis that can support a "detailed discussion" of alternatives. Based on this demand, the court labeled the worst case analysis mere "guesswork" based on "uninformed speculation and conjecture." . . . The preparation of a worst case analysis is not intended to and therefore cannot be held to the exacting standards imposed by the trial court because it goes beyond existing knowledge and methods of acquiring knowledge. . . . The record reveals that the Sierra Club in this case adequately established the base of information upon which a worst case analysis could be premised.

As the Sierra Club claims, this case presents precisely the type of situation for which the worst case regulation was designed. All parties agree that a total cargo loss *could* occur and *could* wreak catastrophic environmental damage in the Bay. While this damage is a "significant adverse effect," there is considerable uncertainty about its likelihood, scope, and consequences; information on it is certainly important, if not essential, to the Corps' decision, yet that information is beyond the state of the art. However, there is a body of data with which a reasonable worst case analysis can be made that is not unreasonably speculative. Remoteness does not bar a worst case analysis so founded and should instead be weighed by the Corps when it applies the worst case analysis in its decisionmaking process. The Corps must at least consider information relevant to a "significant" effect of a proposal, if that information is both "important" to that decision and not based on "unreasonable speculation."

The Corps, however, may not hide behind its ignorance of the worst case consequences and avoid confronting the costs of proceeding in the face of uncertainty. If the Corps decides to proceed with the issuance of these permits despite the uncertainty caused by this lack of information, the FEIS must be rewritten by the Corps to include a worst case analysis.

Case Questions:

1. Explain the worst-case scenario presented by the Sierra Club.

2. Did it matter to the Court of Appeals that concrete and determinative data concerning the probability and effect of the worst-case scenario was not available? Explain.

3. Why is it necessary to require a government agency to include a worst-case analysis of an action in the Environmental Impact Statement?

The Environmental Protection Agency

Environmental Protection Agency (EPA) Independent agency established to protect resources and encourage resource conservation

The **Environmental Protection Agency (EPA),** an independent agency in the executive branch, was established about a year after the passage of National Environmental Policy Act to protect various species, natural systems, and resources and to encourage resource conservation. Like members of CEQ, the EPA's top officials are nominated by the president and confirmed by the Senate. However, unlike CEQ, which sets broad *policy* goals, the EPA is a *regulatory* body (*see* Chapter 6).

The EPA has grown rapidly. In the beginning, it was a group of offices that administered existing programs. From 1970 to the early 1980s, however, Congress both expanded the EPA's original programs and created new ones. The result is not only one of the largest of all federal regulatory agencies but an agency that has available to it one of the widest ranges of federal enforcement actions. Like other regulatory agencies, the EPA issues permits and licenses. It also sets standards and rules on a huge variety of subjects and enforces its rules through formal and informal proceedings.

THE STRUCTURE OF THE EPA. The EPA is a five-tier organization headed by an administrator and deputy administrator who are responsible for various bureaus, including the science and advisory board, administrative law judges, the regional operations for state and local relations and for congressional and legislative affairs. The second tier of the organization includes the offices of the general counsel and enforcement and compliance monitoring. The offices of the inspector general and research and development are located in the agency's third tier.

In the fourth tier are the administration offices for water, pesticides, air, and radiation. The last tier consists of ten regional offices that monitor the environment from Seattle to Boston. The agency's overall structure enables it to wage an integrated, coordinated attack on environmental pollution in conjunction with state and local governments. The basic structure of the EPA is outlined in Figure 20-2.

EPA ENFORCEMENT. The EPA's enforcement action depends on the law that gives it authority to act in a particular case. For example, it can bring administrative actions. A record 4,100 EPA administrative actions were initiated in 1989—a figure that represents a fourfold increase in just ten years. This figure, which was the second highest in agency history, yielded penalties totalling $34.9 million. Table 20-2 summarizes major EPA actions taken between Fiscal Year 1972 and Fiscal Year 1989. If necessary, the EPA can also ask the Department of Justice to take a case to federal court.

In keeping with the EPA's many gains over the past several years, its office of enforcement has drafted a five-year strategy to insure the agency's continued effectiveness. Agency officials realize that environmental regulations cannot succeed without credible, effective enforcement. Therefore, as part of its five-year strategy, the EPA will concentrate on enforcement. The goals are twofold: to identify significant noncompliance violators and to deal with these violations quickly and forcefully.

To streamline the often difficult process of identifying violators, the EPA has improved its ability to cut through the jungle of regulations for determining exactly who owns and controls a given corporation. In addition to its own data on corporate ownership and control, the EPA will now have access to Dunn and Bradstreet's Marketing Index, which provides up-to-date information on corporate parentage and activities. These two databases will enable the agency to obtain information about corporate structure, pollutants used, and the geographic location of facilities. With this data, the EPA can more easily de-

FIGURE 20-2 Administrative Structure of the Environmental Protection Agency   *Source: The United States Government Manual, 1990/91.*

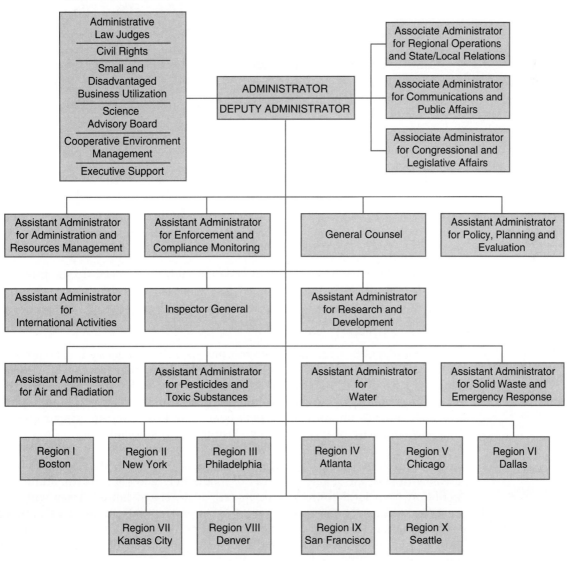

TABLE 20-2   *Actions Initiated by the EPA, Fiscal Year 1972-FY 1989*

	FY72	FY73	FY74	FY75	FY76	FY77	FY78	FY79	FY80
Clean Air Act	0	0	0	0	210	297	129	404	86
Clean Water Act/Safe Drinking Water Act	0	0	0	738	915	1,128	730	506	569
Resource Conservation and Recovery Act	0	0	0	0	0	0	0	0	0
Comprehensive Environmental Response, Compensation, and Liability Act	0	0	0	0	0	0	0	0	0
Federal Insecticide, Fungicide, and Rodenticide Act	860	1,274	1,387	1,614	2,488	1,219	762	253	176
Toxic Substances Control Act	0	0	0	0	0	0	1	22	70
Totals	860	1,274	1,387	2,352	3,613	2,644	1,622	1,185	901

	FY81	FY82	FY83	FY84	FY85	FY86	FY87	FY88	FY89
Clean Air Act	112	21	41	141	122	143	191	224	336
Clean Water Act/Safe Drinking Water Act	562	329	781	1,644	1,031	990	1,214	1,345	2,146
Resource Conservation and Recovery Act	159	237	436	554	327	235	243	309	453
Comprehensive Environmental Response, Compensation, and Liability Act	0	0	0	137	160	139	135	224	220
Federal Insecticide, Fungicide, and Rodenticide Act	154	176	296	272	236	338	360	376	443
Toxic Substances Control Act	120	101	294	376	733	781	1,051	607	538
Totals	1,107	864	1,848	3,124	2,609	2,626	3,194	3,085	4,136

Source: "EPA's Environmental Enforcement in the 1990s," *Environmental Law Reporter* 20 (August 1990). Data from Environmental Protection Agency, *FY 1989 Enforcement Accomplishments Report*.

termine whether a corporation is in violation and, if so, speed up the prosecution process.

Clean Air Act

Clean Air Act Legislation, enacted by Congress in 1963 and revised in 1970 and 1990, permitting the *Environmental Protection Agency* to set air-quality standards, limit the release of air pollutants, and establish controls over sources of air pollution

The **Clean Air Act** dates from 1963 but has since been amended to its present form, first in 1970 and then in 1977 and 1990. The act permits the EPA to set national air-quality standards for some pollutants, to limit the release into the air of other pollutants, to set standards for new sources of air pollution, and to establish controls on automotive emissions. The EPA also protects air quality by approving state plans controlling existing sources of pollution.

In cooperation with the states, the EPA also classifies the United States into one of three groups according to air quality. National standards apply to areas with poor air quality. In areas of moderately good air quality, additional pollution from local sources is permitted up to stated limits. Areas with the best air, such as national parks, get the most protection from new local sources of air pollution. A permit to build a new plant in a clean-air area must be approved by county, regional, and state air-pollution boards, a regional EPA office, and the EPA's main office in Washington, D.C.

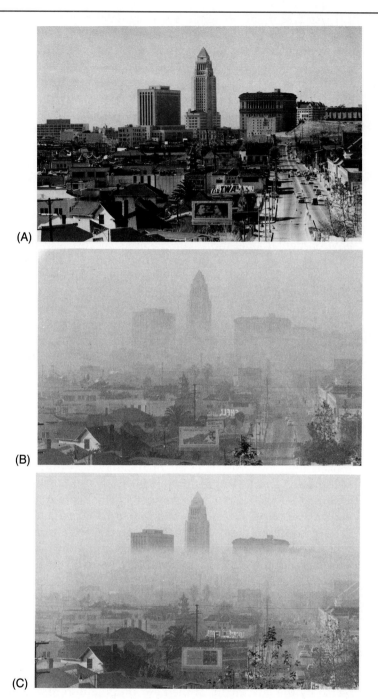

(A)

(B)

(C)

A Clogged and Present Danger The *inversion layer* is a layer of warm air above a stratum of cool air near the ground; it prohibits the natural dispersion of air contaminants into the upper atmosphere. These three photos were taken by the Los Angeles County Air Pollution Control District. Photograph A was taken on a clear day in L.A. (which occurs about 50 days per year); the sun is shining (although not too brightly), the wind is blowing at about 7 to 8 mph, and the inversion layer is *above* 1,500 feet—thereby allowing contaminants to disperse. In Photograph B, the optimal conditions recorded in Photograph A are reversed—the sun (believe it or not) is brilliant, winds are weak, and the inversion-layer temperature is low, causing the inversion layer to drop to just below 1,500 feet. In Photograph C, the upper portion of L.A. City Hall is visible because smog has been entrapped by an inversion layer only 300 feet above the ground. In 1989, California's South Coast Air Quality Management District proposed some 160 new rules for cleaning the air in the L.A. Basin—rules which would reduce smog-causing emissions by 70 percent and the number of days per year on which the air is considered "hazardous" from 150 to 0.

As you might imagine, such regulations place a considerable burden of delay and expense on private industry. Thus, the EPA has recently adopted two approaches to ease the burden. One is to set allowable air-pollution standards for a plant as a whole rather than for each process that takes place within it. The other is to allocate the permissible amount of pollution within an area through free-market processes. The agency grants pollution "credits" to companies that reduce the pollution that they cause. These credits can be sold to a bank and bought by another company that finds the credits cheaper than actually decreasing pollution at its own plants. Thus, one company or plant can pollute more if another company or plant pollutes less.

THE CLEAN AIR ACT: 1990 REVISIONS. The 1990 landmark revisions to the Clean Air Act of 1977 significantly strengthened and broadened this important piece of environmental legislation. For example, by the year 2003 passenger cars must emit sixty percent less nitrogen oxide, and pollution-control equipment must last ten years. Additionally, chemicals that damage the ozone layer must be phased out by the year 2000. Moreover, the amendment seeks to curtail the use of industrial pollutants that contribute to the problem of acid rain (which is the subject of this chapter's YOU DECIDE feature).

These most recent revisions to the Clean Air Act add teeth to an already tough piece of legislation. The act now permits the EPA to set national air-quality standards for new sources of pollution and to establish emission controls on automobiles. In addition, unlike prior statutes, the Clean Air Act vests enforcement with a single administrative agency and permits citizens to sue the EPA itself if it fails to do its job.

However, both the initial enactment of the act and subsequent efforts to amend it have generated a great deal of controversy. For example, one of the most contentious aspects of the original law was the emphasis that it placed on substituting public transportation for the use of automobiles: Although most U.S. citizens realize the environmental gains that can be made with more widespread use of public transportation, few have actually changed their lifestyles.

In addition, many businesses have resisted the law, including its most recent revisions. It is projected, for example, that the bill for the provisions in the latest amendment to the act will cost between $25 to $35 billion a year once the act fully goes into effect. Because of corporate concerns—and those of some economists—the law permits companies developing new products to pass research-and-development costs on to consumers. For example, it is expected that oil companies will add six to ten cents to the price of a gallon of gas to cover R&D costs associated with producers' new responsibilities for environmental protection. Additionally, cars will cost about $600 more because of required antipollution devices. To safeguard against layoffs in industries most affected by the law, many of the new antipollution regulations will be phased in over the next fifteen years.

Although environmentalists would have preferred requiring corporations to absorb the costs of assuming more environmental responsibility, they nevertheless felt triumphant about passage of the 1990 amendments. With the revised law in place, they can now turn their attention to impressing upon individuals the numerous ways in which their conduct as consumers affects the environment. Activists hope that the law will play a decreasingly important role as individuals and corporations alike become more environmentally sensitive and unwilling to make choices that harm the planet.

POLLUTION CONTROL: COSTS AND BENEfiTS. Clearly, air-pollution control is expensive. But what are the *benefits* in terms of the same dollars spent on control?[6] Today, the annual cost of pollution control is estimated to be about one percent of the gross national product, and not only do these costs contribute to higher prices in affected industries, but they lead, in turn, to reduced consumer demand; this cycle, of course, results in lost jobs. However, look at Figure 20-3: Air-pollution control also creates (new) jobs, and in fact, the EPA estimates that with half a million people working in the pollution-control industry by the mid-1980s, the net impact of pollution-control programs will be an *increase* in employment. During the same period, private-industry expenditures on pollution control of $8.5 billion resulted in $19.3 billion in sales, $2.6 billion in profits, and 167,000 new jobs.

Such figures notwithstanding, however, calculating pollution-control costs in terms of dollars is relatively easy; it is calculating the overall benefits of such programs that remains much more difficult. Two seminal studies have nevertheless attempted to calculate air-pollution control programs in terms of

FIGURE 20-3 Unemployment Rate With and Without Pollution Control *Source:* Charles E. Kupchella and Margaret C. Hyland, *Environmental Science: Living within the System of Nature*, 2nd ed. (Boston: Allyn and Bacon, 1989). U.S. Environmental Protection Agency; data from Data Resources, Inc.

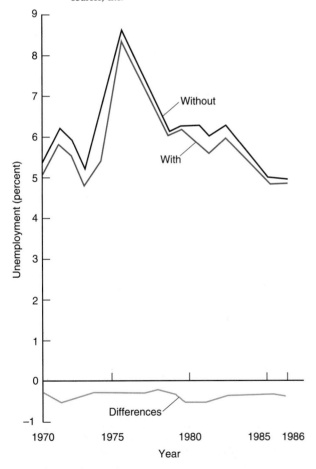

---

[6] This section is based on Charles E. Kupchella and Margaret C. Hyland, *Environmental Science: Living within the System of Nature*, 2nd ed. (Boston: Allyn and Bacon, 1989), pp. 354–60.

dollars and cents: In 1973, L. B. Barrett and T. E. Waddell prepared a report entitled *The Cost of Air Pollution Damage: A Status Report for the EPA*, and in 1979, CEQ issued a report by A. M. Freeman called *The Benefits of Air and Water Control*. Both studies had to make numerous assumptions about such factors as the costs of being ill and missing work and the relationship between pollution and both sickness and physical-materials damage. Both, however, were able to draw some reasonable conclusions.

The two pie-charts in Figure 20-4 illustrate one of Barrett and Waddell's key findings about the cost of *not* controlling air pollution. Figure 20-4A is broken down by costs attributable to major pollutants, Figure 20-4B by the cost in damages to various affected categories: Rounded off, the total impact on vegetation, materials and property, and health was $16.1 billion.

Ten years later, Freeman attempted to estimate the *benefits* of air pollution-control programs. Assuming the dollar value of a decade later and a 10-year improvement in air quality of 20 percent, Freeman calculated the annual economic benefit of the Clean Air Act 10 years later to be $23.3 billion (*see* Figure 20-5).

FIGURE 20-4A The Cost of Not Controlling Air Pollution: Economic Impact of Selected Pollutants

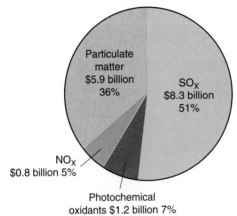

FIGURE 20-4B The Cost of Not Controlling Air Pollution: Economic Impact by Category   *Source: Charles E. Kupchella and Margaret C. Hyland, Environmental Science: Living within the System of Nature, 2nd ed. (Boston: Allyn and Bacon, 1989). L.B. Barrett and T.E. Waddell, Cost of Air Pollution Damage: A Status Report (Triangle Park, NC: National Environmental Research Center, Environmental Protection Agency, 1973), Publication No. AP-85.*

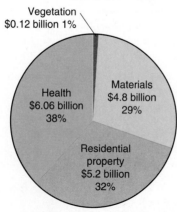

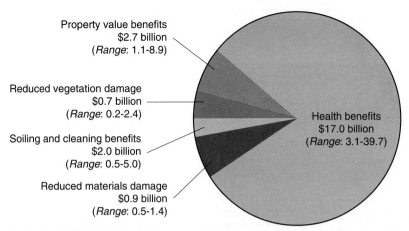

Property value benefits
$2.7 billion
(*Range*: 1.1-8.9)

Reduced vegetation damage
$0.7 billion
(*Range*: 0.2-2.4)

Soiling and cleaning benefits
$2.0 billion
(*Range*: 0.5-5.0)

Reduced materials damage
$0.9 billion
(*Range*: 0.5-1.4)

Health benefits
$17.0 billion
(*Range*: 3.1-39.7)

FIGURE 20-5 The Benefits of Controlling Pollution   *Source:* Charles E. Kupchella and Margaret C. Hyland, *Environmental Science: Living within the System of Nature*, 2nd ed. (Boston: Allyn and Bacon, 1989). Adapted from A.M. Freeman, *The Benefits of Air and Water Pollution Control: A Review and Synthesis of Recent Estimates*. A Report Prepared for the Council on Environmental Quality (Brunswick, ME: Bowdoin College, 1979).

Admittedly, the data collected from these and various studies does not always agree, nor is it as precise as eventually it will be. It is fairly safe to conclude, however, that not only is there a definite cost associated with polluted air but that the cost is significant.

Clean Water Act

As amended in 1977, the 1972 **Clean Water Act** makes it a national goal to end the practice of discharging pollutants into navigable waters; among other things, it provides for federal funding of sewage-treatment plants nationwide. The Act aims to achieve a level of water quality that (1) protects fish, shellfish, and other forms of wildlife and (2) allows people to swim and sail boats near beaches. In 1987, Congress extended the scope of the act over President Reagan's veto: The president had argued that the act was a piece of "pork-barrel" legislation (an appropriation for political patronage); Congress argued that the public has long been willing to pay the price to keep both the air and water clean.

Under the act, each state must decide what kinds of uses are permitted on each of its major bodies of water and then set pollution standards accordingly for each body. Thus, rivers used for swimming or commercial fishing must be cleaner than rivers used only for transportation. The EPA sets nationwide standards for industrial discharges into water for each type of industry and pollutant. Plants must have discharge permits from the EPA or a state agency that maintains the EPA's standards.

The Clean Water Act allows private citizens to sue a company for violating the act if (1) the violation involves a standard or limitation that is either embodied in the act or issued by a state pursuant to it and (2) the federal or state government is not diligently pursuing an action against the company to enforce the law. The following case illustrates this type of lawsuit.

Clean Water Act Legislation, enacted by Congress in 1972 and amended in 1977, to protect fish and other wildlife and to control the discharge of pollutants into navigable waters

SIERRA CLUB v. SCM CORPORATION

U.S. District Court, Western District of New York 572 F.Supp.
828 (1983)

Defendant, SCM Corporation, operates a potato and onion processing plant. In operating its plant, defendant discharges treated waste into Wolcott Creek in Wayne County. A permit authorizing the discharge of limited amounts of pollutants was issued to SCM by the New York State Department of Environmental Conservation ("DEC"). However, SCM violated their DEC permit by discharging nonconforming pollutants into the creek. DEC initiated an administrative enforcement proceeding against SCM for violating the permit standards. On May 4, 1982, after extensive negotiations, SCM and DEC entered into a consent order in settlement of the administrative enforcement proceeding.

On November 11, 1982, pursuant to the citizens suit provision of the Clean Water Act, plaintiff, Sierra Club, commenced this action alleging various violations of the Federal Clean Water Act as well as noncompliance with the pollutant discharge permit issued by DEC. SCM filed this motion to dismiss the complaint.

Telesca, District Judge.

. . . The consent order imposed a Ten Thousand Dollar fine on SCM (Nine Thousand Dollars of which was suspended unless SCM violated the consent order), established a schedule of compliance with permit specifications, and required SCM to immediately implement several other steps in order to improve the quality of their waste discharge.

. . .

Section 505 of the Clean Water Act confers jurisdiction on Federal District Court over lawsuits initiated by private citizens against any person who is alleged to be in violation of (1) an effluent standard or limitation under the Clean Water Act or (2) an order issued by a State with respect to such standard or limitation. However, Section 505 goes on to provide that no such action may be commenced:

If the Administrator or State has commenced and is *diligently prosecuting a civil or criminal action in a court of the United States, or a State* to require compliance with the standard, limitation, or order, but in any such action in a court of the United States any citizen may intervene as a matter or right (emphasis added).

Defendant SCM argues that the consent order obtained in the DEC enforcement proceeding constitutes "diligent prosecution in a court of the United States or a State," and therefore contends that this Court lacks jurisdiction over the instant lawsuit. I disagree.

In determining whether the DEC administrative enforcement proceeding in this case should be deemed the functional equivalent of a court, and thereby erect a bar to federal court jurisdiction, I am guided by the importance Congress placed upon the private citizen's right to participate in the *actual enforcement* of the Clean Water Act.

A high degree of informed public participation in the control process is essential to the accomplishment of the objectives we seek—a restored and protected natural environment. . . . [T]he manner in which these measures are implemented will depend, to a great extent, *upon the pressures and persistence which an interested public can exert upon the governmental process.* The Environmental Protection Agency and the State should actively encourage and assist the involvement and participation of the public in the process of setting water quality requirements and in their *subsequent implementation and enforcement.* Sen. Report on the Clean Water Act, Legis. Hist. of the Water Pollution Control Act, at 1430 (emphasis added).

Accordingly, Section 505 of the Act was included to ensure that interested citizens either had the right themselves to commence an enforcement proceeding in federal court, or, if that enforcement proceeding had already been initiated, the right to intervene in that proceeding in order to actively participate in the enforcement effort.

In the instant case, plaintiff lacked the opportunity to participate in the DEC administrative enforcement proceeding which resulted in the consent order. Plaintiffs claim they were unaware of the on-going negotiations between SCM and DEC administrative enforcement proceeding which resulted in the consent order. Plaintiffs claim they were unaware of the on-going negotiations between SCM and DEC concerning permit violations. Furthermore, it appears that no notice of an impending order of consent was published and the DEC did not afford the plaintiffs the right of formal intervention in the enforcement proceedings. . . .

My holding is thus a limited one. Under the *particular facts presented here,* where settlement of permit violations is achieved as a result of enforcement proceedings in which plaintiffs, as interested members of the public, lacked the opportunity to be heard on the merits of the proposed consent order, a citizens suit pursuant to 33 U.S.C. Section 1365 (a) (1) may properly be entertained by a federal district court.

. . .

. . . [T]he defendant's motion to dismiss the complaint is, in all respects, denied.

CHEMICAL AND WASTE POLLUTION AND ENERGY CONSERVATION Consider the following facts:[7]

- Because *synthetic chemicals* like metals and pesticides have not evolved as part of the ecosystem, biological systems do not possess the enzymes necessary to break them down; these *persistent chemicals* are thus likely to enter living organisms through food intake; lead and mercury poisoning in humans are among the more familiar results of this process.

- The phenomenon of *biomagnification* means that, as organisms assimilate persistent chemicals, their accumulation in organic systems increases the amount of those chemicals that are passed on at each stage in the food chain; biomagnification is a major factor in the disappearance of predatory carnivores like eagles and game fish from large sections of their ranges.

- Although the pesticide DDT was banned in the United States in the 1970s, a 1985 study by the National Institute of Environmental Health Sciences showed that 100 percent of subjects tested still retained detectable DDT residues in their bodies.

- Of the four billion tons of waste produced annually in the United States, 300 million tons come from mining, 475 million tons from agriculture, 380 million tons from industry, and 145 million tons from municipalities; according to some estimates, every American generates about 1,500 pounds of domestic waste per year, and at the current rate, the amount of such waste in the year 2000 will be twice that of 1975.

- About 50 million tons of waste is dumped in the ocean every year; of 26,000 abandoned hazardous-waste sites in the United States, over 1,100 were on the national priority list for cleanup by 1988, and the General Accounting Office estimates that the cleanup cost will be about $100 billion; according to the EPA, about 90 percent of all hazardous waste handled by private contractors in the United States is dumped illegally.

- Each person in the United States uses about seven tons of oil per year; in countries like Sweden and Denmark, which have standards of living at least as high as ours, long-standing energy-conservation programs have kept usage at about half that rate; at the current consumption rate of 20 billion barrels per year, *proven* (as opposed to *estimated*) oil reserves will last only about 35 years.

- In 1975, 53 nuclear power plants were operational in the U.S., and official estimates called for about 1,000 by the turn of the century; the last plant to be ordered and not canceled in the United States was ordered in 1974, and it now appears that there will be only about 124 plants (generating about 16 percent of our electricity) in the United States in the 1990s; although there are now about 400 plants operating outside the United States, only France and Japan are still committed to nuclear-energy programs.

---

[7] This data is drawn from these sources: Kupchella and Hyland, *Environmental Science: Living within the System of Nature*, pp. 516–21, 560–65, 466–68, 531–32; Cunningham and Cunningham, *Environmental Science: A Global Concern*, pp. 200–01, 256–64, 482–86, 334–44; and Bernard J. Nebel, *Environmental Science: The Way the World Works*, 3rd ed. (Englewood Cliffs, NJ: Prentice Hall, 1990), pp. 356–64.

Concern about the environmental crisis facing our planet is shared by governments, businesses, and most citizens. There is, however, much less agreement on the issue of who should be held accountable for environmental hazards and pollutants.

The problem of acid rain, which is reasonably traceable to industry, is a perfect example. Acid rain—any precipitation, rain, fog, mist, or snow that is more acidic than normal—has been recognized as a problem in and around the industrial centers of North America and most of Europe for over 100 years. Chemical analysis of acid rains reveals the presence of sulfuric and nitric acid, both of which are commonly found in the emissions of electrical utilities, coal-burning power plants, automotive vehicles, and industrial facilities.

There are those who favor holding industry accountable for acid rain because industry clearly contributes to the problem. One proponent of this viewpoint, for example, notes that all environmental crises go through four stages. During the first stage, the problem is discovered by science. The second stage is marked by public acknowledgment that a pollutant is in fact causing a problem. In the third stage, concerned technicians and economists place increasing emphasis on the overall social cost of the problem. The final stage is reached when the public is finally persuaded that it will cost society far more to continue ignoring the problem than to do something about it.

According to many analysts, the problem of acid rain has reached the third stage. Acid rain, which was first described in England in 1852, has now been acknowledged as a problem by a majority of the scientific community. At this point, scientists, economists, and technicians are debating the social costs of the problem, what can be done about it, and who should pay.

Reaching the final stage, however, has been hindered by public and governmental skepticism about whether anything at all can really be done about acid rain. As recently as the early 1980s, for example, EPA administrators indicated that they were actually doubtful about the existence of acid rain and called for more research rather than spending more money to control the problem.

On the other hand, critics of this wait-and-see approach charge that the time has come to move forward on eradicating acid rain. Holding industry accountable, they assert, is the best place to start. Meanwhile, opponents of holding industry accountable for the acid-rain problem are equally vocal and indignant. They question whether science is even correct in asserting that acid rain poses any danger at all. Instead, they assert that pollutants in the rain are only a minor contributor to the high level of acidity found in some Eastern lakes and streams; that the acidity is mostly natural, not industrial, in origin; and that acid rain does not, as has been charged, threaten forests in the Eastern United States.

Obviously, these assumptions have very different policy implications than the findings of a 1981 government study, which recommended a major reduction in sulfur-dioxide emissions as a means of countering a very real acid-rain problem. Although those who oppose holding industry accountable are not opposed to Clean Air Act emission controls, they still suggest that fears about industrial emissions may prove largely unwarranted.

Opponents of holding industry accountable also believe that our developing understanding of the earth's natural ecosystems is likely to reveal additional evidence suggesting that acid rain is not a significant problem. For example, some environmentalists trace the high level of acid in some lakes to acid rain. Critics of this theory suggest, however, that many lakes are naturally high in acidity. Opponents of holding industry accountable also claim that because the rain in the area is so diluted, acid rain poses an insignificant threat to the future of forests in the Eastern United States.

In sum, those who oppose any moves to hold industry accountable for acid rain caution that more research is needed before any company should be compelled to spend any money.

To what extent do you believe that acid rain is a significant environmental problem? To what extent should industry be held accountable for this problem? For further discussion, see p. 763.

Not surprisingly, laws dealing with waste, pollution, and energy, both in the United States and abroad, are numerous and complex. Enacted in 1947, for example, the Federal Insecticide, Fungicide, and Rodenticide Act (FIFRA) dealt only with pesticides shipped across state lines. Amended in 1972 and 1975, however, FIFRA now extends regulations to all pesticides and requires the EPA to designate *restricted-use pesticides*—those whose use must be supervised by applicators who have passed specific certification requirements. Regardless of place of production, all pesticides intended for sale in the United States must now be registered. The EPA can inspect private usage sites either by permission or with a warrant and may recall products and seize those that are used illegally.

The disciplines of environmental science and environmental law have grown rapidly in the last few decades; so, too, have developments in the areas of *chemicals and toxic waste* and *energy.*

CHEMICALS AND TOXIC WASTE. The EPA may forbid or limit the production, use, sale, or disposal of dangerous chemicals. It may specify the ways a chemical may be used or require special labeling by manufacturers. The agency's policy about a potentially dangerous chemical depends upon how well it performed in tests to uncover its potential to cause cancer, birth defects, and other diseases.

Pesticides, the chemicals that most farmers and gardeners depend upon to kill insects, must be registered with the agency, which reviews the accompanying instructions and warning labels. Some pesticides, such as DDT, have been banned outright. Others can be applied only to certain crops, applied only at certain times, or applied only by people who have been certified under the EPA's training program.

A major source of chemical pollution is the waste produced by industrial processes. For example, when a flood spread deadly dioxin-contaminated waste in Times Beach, Missouri, all 2,400 residents of the town were evacuated, and state and federal governments had to buy their homes for a total of $36.5 million.

Although the states are primarily responsible for waste disposal, the EPA oversees state plans. The agency also monitors the movement of poisonous and radioactive waste, called *toxic wastes,* from their sources—for example, factories, gas stations, and dry cleaners—to disposal sites. Sites themselves are monitored as well. About 900 are leaking now; thousands more may also threaten underground water sources.[8]

Under the 1980 "Superfund" Act, the EPA may either (1) obtain judicial orders that force chemical companies to clean up their toxic waste sites or (2) bring suit to recover the costs after cleaning up a site itself. Most of the superfund for this purpose comes from taxes on chemical companies.

ENERGY. In 1973, during the Yom Kippur War between Egypt and Israel, Arab oil suppliers put an embargo on the export of their oil, and Americans found themselves lining up for hours at gas stations. After the embargo, these suppliers joined the other members of the Organization of Petroleum Exporting Countries (OPEC) to raise the price of oil.

These events prompted Americans to be much less wasteful of energy and to look for ways of producing more energy domestically. Other than domestic oil, the obvious alternatives were coal, which is plentiful but dirty to burn, and nuclear power, which is both expensive and controversial. Because of heavy coal usage in the northeastern corridor of the United States and along the Great Lakes by Canada, acid rain, which is caused by wind-blown emissions from coal plants, is causing friction between the two countries, each side claiming that the other is not doing all that it should to protect its neighbor. Meanwhile, nuclear power not only poses the danger of meltdowns at power plants but also produces radioactive waste that no state or community wants buried on its turf. In short, balancing the need for a safe, clean environment

---

[8] "19th Environmental Quality Index," *National Wildlife,* February-March, 1987.

The Best-Laid Plans . . . *Memo from Metropolitan Edison Co. (1970):* "These 372-foot natural-draft cooling towers will serve the first unit at Metropolitan Edison Company's Three Mile Island Nuclear Station located on the Susquehanna River south of Harrisburg, Pa. The towers, which will operate like huge chimneys, will prevent any significant change in the temperature of the Susquehanna. Water in the cooling-tower cycle will be used to remove heat from the steam-generating system. Water trickles down the wooden baffles around the base of the tower while the heat escapes up the tower. The cooled water is reused over and over, and water is taken from the Susquehanna only to replace that lost through evaporation." On March 28, 1979, a malfunctioning valve caused an out-of-control reaction that melted about twenty percent of the Three Mile Island reactor core and released radioactive water into the Susquehanna River, where bacteria proliferated in contaminated residue. Although no "excess deaths" have yet been reported, one radiation-health team has estimated that the 100-plus hours of low-level radiation received by Harrisburg residents may result in 300 to 900 cases of fatal cancer and leukemia.

against the need for energy is difficult. (The ETHICAL ENVIRONMENT box chronicles some of the concerted efforts being made for a safe environment by a combination of forces from the business sector.)

The United States, of course, still enjoys substantial domestic energy sources. Many of them, in fact, are found on federally owned lands and waters. There is coal in the American West; oil and gas near the coast along the Gulf of Mexico, the Atlantic Ocean, and the Pacific Ocean; oil shale in Colorado and Utah; and uranium elsewhere. However, the environmental cost of digging into these resources is potentially enormous, and wind, water, and solar power are arguably both cleaner and, in the long run, cheaper sources of energy than oil, coal, and nuclear power. Nevertheless, research, investment, and political might will be needed to make these sources major contributors to American energy supplies.

THE ETHICAL ENVIRONMENT
The Valdez Principles

The environmental tragedy in Alaska's Prince William Sound in 1989 has spawned a national debate about corporate responsibility for preventing and protecting our environment. Internationally broadcast, television images of blackened waterways and wildlife covered with Exxon crude oil left a lasting impression on viewers, which led to a worldwide call for action. In addition to damaging Exxon's public image, the Alaskan oil-spill generated litigation that broke new ground in setting standards for a corporation's criminal and civil liability for causing environmental damage.

The disaster also gave birth to the Coalition for Environmentally Responsible Economies (CERES)—an organization comprised of investors, financial-service brokers, and environmental groups. Because its members control more than $150-billion in pension and mutual funds, CERES is a force to be reckoned with. The organization's goal is to attract corporate support for the "Valdez Principles"—a ten-point code of governance for corporate conduct that articulates broad standards for evaluating corporate activities directly and indirectly affecting the environment. Corporations that sign on to the principles agree to implement its policies and procedures.

Because CERES's success depends upon corporate acceptance of the Valdez Principles, the organization has developed a three-part strategy for convincing firms to adhere to those principles and thereby assume a greater degree of environmental responsibility. First, the organization targeted Fortune 500 corporations to be the first to adopt the principles: The assumption was that if the campaign was successful with the nation's biggest corporations, smaller firms would surely follow. Unfortunately, however, not one of the Fortune 500 companies agreed to be held to the Valdez Principles.

As its next line of attack, CERES appealed to 54 of the nation's largest companies by placing resolutions calling for adherence to the principles before corporate shareholders. Although none of these companies formally adopted the resolutions, spirited discussions about environmental concerns took place at virtually every shareholder meeting.

The third prong of the CERES campaign will try to enlist the support of the public to put pressure on companies to adhere to the Valdez Principles. CERES plans to conduct and publicize compliance assessments both of corporations that have and have not adopted the principles.

In addition to this three-prong strategy, and despite early setbacks, CERES activities already boast some positive effects. For example, some corporations have voluntarily adhered to the Valdez Principles, primarily in the hopes of improving public images and reducing the potential for costly litigation. In addition, there has been an unprecedented increase in dialogue among corporate-management personnel about how to make ethical and environmentally responsible decisions. As a by-product of many of these discussions, many corporations have adopted formal policies on environmental protection.

International Environmental Law

Transboundary and global environmental problems have become serious issues in the 1990s, and international law has become critical in addressing these problems. Table 20-3, for example, summarizes a list of 22 fundamental principles for the establishment and development of laws to protect the global environment as recommended in 1986 by an international panel of experts in environmental law. In the spring of 1992, world leaders at the United Nations Conference on the Environment and Development (UNCED) discussed issues that may guide future international cooperation on the environment.

UNCED participants will be guided by principles that were enumerated two decades ago at the historical United Nations Stockholm Conference on the Human Environment. Of particular import is Principle 21, which is the focal point for many international treaties intended to eliminate transboundary pollution. It provides in part that:

> . . . States have, in accordance with the Charter of the United Nations and the principles of international law, the sovereign right to exploit their own resources pursuant to their own environmental policies, and the responsibility to ensure that activities within their own jurisdiction or control do not cause damage to the environment of other states or of areas beyond the limits of national jurisdiction. . . .

| TABLE 20-3 | *International Environmental Protection Principles* |

FUNDAMENTAL RIGHTS

Article 1 stipulates that the "first and keystone" principle is the "fundamental right of all human beings to an environment adequate for their health and well-being;"

Article 2 stipulates that states [nations] shall conserve and use the environment and natural resources for the benefit of present and future generations;

Article 3 specifies that states shall maintain ecosystems and ecological processes essential for the functioning of the biosphere, preserve biological diversity, and observe the principle of optimum sustainable yield in the use of living natural resources and ecosystems;

Article 4 requires states to establish adequate environmental protection standards and to monitor changes in and publish relevant data on environmental quality and resource use;

Article 5 requires states to make or require environmental assessments of proposed activities that may significantly affect the environment or use of a natural resource;

Article 6 obliges states to inform in a timely manner all persons likely to be significantly affected by a planned activity and to grant them equal access and due process in administrative and judicial proceedings;

Article 7 requires states to ensure that conservation is treated as an integral part of the planning and implementation of development activities and to provide assistance to other states, especially to developing countries, in support of environmental protection and sustainable development;

Article 8 affirms that states shall cooperate in good faith with other states in implementing the preceding rights and obligations;

Article 9 requires states to use transboundary natural resources in a reasonable and equitable manner;

Article 10 requires states to prevent or abate any transboundary environmental interference that could or does cause significant harm, although some exceptions would be provided under Articles 11 and 12;

Article 11 allows states to carry out or permit certain dangerous but beneficial activities, provided they take all reasonable precautions to limit the risk and to ensure that compensation is provided should substantial transboundary harm occur, and requires states to ensure that compensation is provided for substantial transboundary harm resulting from activities that were not known to be harmful when they were undertaken;

Article 12 requires states that plan to carry out or permit activities causing transboundary harm that is substantial but far less costly than the cost of prevention to negotiate with the affected state on the equitable conditions under which the activity could be carried out;

Article 13, with regard to transboundary natural resources and environmental interferences, requires states to apply at least the same standards for environmental conduct and effects that are applied domestically;

Article 14 affirms that states shall cooperate in good faith with other states to achieve optimal use of transboundary natural resources and effective prevention or abatement of transboundary environmental interferences;

Article 15 obliges states of origin to provide timely and relevant information to the other concerned states regarding transboundary natural resources or environmental interferences;

Article 16 requires that states must provide prior and timely notification and relevant information to the other concerned states and make an environmental assessment of planned activities that may have significant transboundary effects;

Article 17 stipulates that states of origin shall consult at an early stage and in good faith with other concerned states regarding existing or potential transboundary interferences with their use of a natural resource or the environment;

Article 18, with regard to transboundary natural resources and environmental interferences, specifies that states shall cooperate with the concerned states in monitoring, scientific research, and standard setting;

Article 19 obliges states to develop contingency plans regarding emergency situations likely

TABLE 20-3   *Continued*

to cause transboundary environmental interferences and to give prompt warnings, relevant information, and cooperation to concerned states when such emergencies occur;

    Article 20 requires states to grant all persons who are and may be affected by transboundary interferences with equal access, due process, and equal treatment in administrative and judicial proceedings;

    Article 21 obliges states to cease activities that breach an international obligation regarding the environment and to provide compensation for the harm caused; and,

    Article 22 affirms that states shall settle environmental disputes by peaceful means, and require that, if mutual agreement is not reached within 18 months on a solution or on other dispute settlement arrangements, the dispute shall be submitted to conciliation and, if unresolved, thereafter to arbitration or judicial settlement at the request of any of the concerned states.

Source: Charles E. Kupchella and Margaret C. Hyland, *Environmental Science: Living within the System of Nature*, 2nd ed. (Boston: Allyn and Bacon, 1989). Reprinted from *Environment Reporter, Current Developments* 17:1501–02 (The Bureau of National Affairs, Inc., 1987).

However, a major weakness in solving international environmental problems may be the inability of a governing body to monitor and enforce policies once they are enacted in the global arena. To help redress this problem, those who attend the future conferences will be asked to make assurances for "global environmental security"—a concept that likens the threat of danger to our common environment to that of the inherent dangers posed by nuclear capability. The assurances of global environmental security may, however, prove to be untenable in efforts to orchestrate the ideologies of various and numerous world powers. This problem promises to be just one among the many difficulties in creating an effective international legal regime.

In addition, despite the existence of more than 100 treaties that address international environmental issues, existing international environmental law is perceived by many as soft and ineffective. For example, failure in one case to ratify a popular civil-liability convention that would provide compensation for injury from nuclear power plants left victims of the Soviet Chernobyl disaster in 1986 unable to benefit from the convention's compensation scheme. International institutions have also been criticized for inadequately addressing incidents involving multinational corporations. In an effort to address this problem following the 1984 Union Carbide disaster in Bhopal (*see* the INTERNATIONAL ENVIRONMENT box in Chapter 10), the Indian government tried to elicit support for a policy of *nondelegation of duty* for corporations engaged in harmful activities: **Delegation of duty** refers to the act of transferring to another party all or part of a corporation's contractual duties, and the Indian proposal would thus impute liability, without exception, to the parent corporation.

delegation of duty   Act of transferring to another party all or part of a party's contractual duties or legal obligations

    The case of *Volkswagenwerk Aktiengesellschaft v. Schlunk* (1987) illustrates another problem: the failure of companies to adhere to international standards, even those that have been ratified and are in place. In this controversial case, the U.S. Supreme Court ruled that Michigan's "long-arm" jurisdiction, which enables a state to bring a foreign defendant before its courts (*see* Chapter 4), could be used to effect service of process on a German corporation by serving of process on a domestic subsidiary. This decision, however, undermined diplomatic efforts on the federal level—several countries had already joined the United States in ratifying a treaty governing foreign service of process in cases like *Volkswagenwerk*. Interestingly, the Michigan decision may also adversely affect U.S. citizens: Foreign courts may be allowed to permit service on U.S. de-

The Tall-Stack Strategy Smokestacks like these in the Saar industrial region of the Federal Republic of Germany proliferated in the 1960s and 1970s as a result of the *tall-stack strategy*: the theory that tall smokestacks would lift pollutants up and over surrounding populations to be sufficiently diluted before returning to earth. There is, however, at least one hard-and-fast rule in environmental science: *everything—and there are no exceptions—must go somewhere*. Reliance on the combustion of fossil fuels has resulted in an increase in atmospheric carbon dioxide in the last century, North American and European forests are now receiving about 30 times more acidity than would fall from precipitation in clean air, and in West Germany alone, nitrogen oxide emissions have risen 50 percent since 1966. The United Nations convened the first Scientific Conference on the Conservation and Utilization of Resources in 1949; in 1972, representatives of 114 nations promulgated a Declaration on the Human Environment, and a follow-up conference 10 years later produced the "World Campaign for the Biosphere." Perhaps the first and most crucial step toward global environmental governance occurred in 1986, when experts in environmental law reported to the World Commission on Environment and Development a comprehensive list of principles to protect the environment and promote viable development. Twenty-two "Fundamental Rights" articles are listed in Table 20-3.

fendants by foreign citizens even if it means applying law that is less stringent than U.S. law.

Despite many shortcomings in establishing an international legal regime to protect the environment, there are grounds for some hope. The United Nations, for instance, could conceivably play a critical role in providing relief in ecological disputes. Currently, however, the United Nations lacks an executive environmental agency: Originally hailed as a "coordinator and catalyst for environmental action," its only agency dedicated solely to the environment, United Nations Environmental Program (UNEP), is, in reality, a paper tiger. Accordingly, UNEP will be a critical target for revision during the upcoming UNCED convention. Some analysts suspect that convention participants may propose the creation of a "United Nations EPA" empowered to prevent violations of international standards.

Other proposals seek to increase access to the International Court of Justice, which is the most suitable forum for these matters, and to create adjudicatory mechanisms to handle transboundary disputes. Separate United States initiatives are also underway. For example, recent amendments to the Clean Air Act include several internationally oriented provisions, including a provision calling for the examination of stratospheric-ozone and other climate-change issues.

In sum, experts now agree that the resolution of transboundary environmental issues will require a cooperative world community that will adhere to a conflict-resolution capability of laws international that are in scope. The United Nations will undoubtedly play a key role in helping to promote compliance by developing nations, as well as in providing sources of funding and technology to allow nations to abide by standards once they are in place.

■ Concept Check 20-4   Protecting the Environment

- Describe the key terms in the ongoing debate about the environment, especially as they relate to business rights and obligations.
- Describe the basic goals of the *National Environmental Policy Act.*
- Explain the primary functions of the *environmental impact statement.* Explain the debate over the *cost-benefit analysis* and "research and worse-case" provisions of the EIS.
- Describe the enforcement procedures of the *Environmental Protection Agency.* What are the main differences between the EPA and the *Council on Environmental Quality?*
- What are the main goals of the *Clean Air Act?* What are the most important provisions of the 1990 revisions to the Act?
- Describe the guidelines advanced by the *United Nations Conference on the Environment and Development.* What is the major weakness of this program?

YOU DECIDE: ANSWER/DISCUSSION
Industry and Acid Rain

No judicial decision has yet ordered a company to pay damages for causing acid rain. However, it is expected that if and when such a case reaches the courts, the issue will be analyzed like all other environmental issues: Specifically, scientific, economic, and ethical concerns will be weighed to strike a balance between competing interests.

Despite many sophisticated scientific advances, there is still widespread uncertainty about what causes ecosystems to thrive or perish. Some analysts even believe that there is no direct relationship between pressure on the environment— through pollution and deforestation, for example—and environmental damage. Similarly, the issue of the causes and cures for acid rain has left scientists in a quandary.

Improving the environment always costs jobs and money, but, in the balance, will the benefits of protection outweigh the costs? Finally, values are important. For some, nature is valuable for reasons that have nothing to do with commerce. Aesthetic enjoyment of the environment, they assert, is not a dollars-and-cents proposition.

With such divergent and strongly held beliefs about whether acid rain is indeed a problem (and, if so, who should be responsible for remedying it), it is certain that this issue will be the subject of a great deal of litigation in the future.

SUMMARY

- Definitions of *property rights* hinge on the balance of power between individuals and the government. Without government and law, there could be no private property. At the same time, if *private-property* rights were absolute, there could be no government or organized society. The public interest encroaches upon the right of private property in the areas of taxation, *eminent domain,* and zoning measures enacted pursuant to the state's police powers.

- *Zoning* regulations balance private and public interests. Most land-use regulation is contained in local ordinances. Property owners who suffer substantial costs through land-use regulations can and do sue the government for damages, arguing that the regulation is an unconstitutional *taking* of property without *just compensation.*

- *Land-use regulation* need not provide for the compensation of property owners if the regulation satisfies a recognized purpose under the police power. One such purpose is the conservation (and perhaps the enhancement) of the value of buildings. Even small cities typically have 20 to 25 types of zones. To protect the public from eyesores, zoning laws have regulated or outlawed billboards and satellite dishes—perhaps interfering with the free expression of opinion. The courts have thus had to balance the public's First Amendment rights against its right to protect the appearance of roads and neighborhoods.

- The public asserts control over private property through laws protecting the quality and safety of our environment. *Environmental law,* which is grounded in *nuisance law,* has been an emerging field over the past two decades. In general, *environmental protection* imposes immediate costs on industry and on the users of industrial products in order to prevent costs to the public, now and in the future. The *National Environmental Policy Act* (NEPA) of 1969 ushered in a decade of federal laws and regulations designed to protect the environment. It requires all federal agencies to prepare *environmental impact statements.* The courts have defined the purpose of such statements as "environmental full disclosure." Recent amendments and revisions to the *Clean Air Act* will be phased in over the next decade. Consumers will bear the added expenses, however, of many of the controls that will be put in place.

- The *Environmental Protection Agency* (EPA) is one of the largest federal regulatory agencies, with among the widest ranges of action. It has the power to set national air-quality standards for some pollutants, to limit the release into the air of other pollutants, to set standards for new sources of air pollution, and to establish controls on emissions from cars. The EPA designates areas where dumping is permitted, grants permits, and fines violators. It also sets national standards for the safety of drinking water and may forbid or limit the production, use, sale, or disposal of dangerous chemicals. The agency has grown significantly over the past decade, and it recently adopted a five-year strategy to insure its continued effectiveness.

- Corporate America has also taken a more active role in environmental protection. Motivated in part by the Valdez oil tanker disaster in Alaska at the beginning of the decade, corporations have started to examine how they may reduce the use of environmental pollutants. Increasingly, ethical behavior on the part both of individuals and corporations will be required to attack the pollution problem and promote a healthy environment. Dialogue among corporate management, environmental activists, shareholders, and consumers will be a key element in making environmental protection a concern and benefit for all.

- Wastes produced by industrial processes are a major source of chemical pollution. Cleaning up *toxic-waste* sites is a huge task. So, too, is balancing our need and desire for a safe, clean environment against our need for *energy.* In the United States, coal is plentiful but dirty. Nuclear power is expensive and extremely controversial. Wind, water, and solar power are arguably both cleaner and, in the long run, cheaper sources of energy. However, they are not yet major sources.

QUESTIONS AND PROBLEMS

1. Urbana, a densely populated urban area, enacted an ordinance which required that all new housing have a minimum floor space of 1,800 feet and be built on lots no smaller than two acres. The existing housing consists of units averaging 1,000 square feet on lots of 1/8 acre. Urbana sought to jus-

tify its ordinance on the basis of a study showing that minimum house sizes were related to health problems. Is this reason legally sufficient for the city to justify increasing the size of houses and lots? Explain.

2. Peter Kempton operated a pig farm in an area zoned nonresidential for thirty-five years. Over that period, the area had changed into nearly an all residential area with single family homes being predominant. The area had since been rezoned residential, but the pig farm was grandfathered in. The town previously attempted to secure immediate termination of the pig farm under a zoning ordinance but failed because the use was held to be a protected nonconforming use. The town then passed a nonzoning regulation which was so strict that it rendered the continued use of the pig farm all but impossible. Mr. Kempton goes to court claiming that passage of the ordinance was taking of property in violation of the Fifth Amendment. Was the ordinance a taking and can the business be terminated without a reasonable period of amortization? Explain.

3. An organization representing the interests of Asian Americans challenges the constitutionality of a zoning resolution which allegedly displaces low-income Chinese persons from Chinatown in New York City in favor of upper-income families. The group alleges that New York City, in exercising its delegated zoning powers for the general welfare of the community, is constitutionally obligated to affirmatively afford a realistic opportunity for the construction of low- and moderate-income housing for the many present and future low- and moderate-income residents of Chinatown needing decent and affordable housing and that the city has failed to do so. Does the *Mount Laurel* holding directly square with this situation? Explain your answer. [*Asian Americans for Equality v. Koch*, 492 N.Y.S.2d 837 (1985)]

4. The citizens of a township allege their well water was contaminated by toxic pollutants leaching into the local aquifer from a landfill established and operated by the township. The citizens allege that because of their exposure to chemicals, they have an increased risk of cancer and other illnesses. They seek to recover the expenses of annual medical exams to monitor their physical health. Should such damages be awarded under a statutory provision for recovery from a public entity? If so, what needs to be known to make the determination? [*Ayers v. Jackson Township*, 525 A. 2d 287 (1987)]

5. Plaintiffs entered into an agreement to purchase a condominium unit which they planned to occupy as their residence. Ten days before plaintiffs took title, the city adopted an ordinance prohibiting the owner of an individual condominium from recovering possession of his unit from a tenant who had continuously occupied it since before the master-condominium deed was recorded. The tenants occupying plaintiff's unit had continuously occupied it since before the master deed was recorded, so plaintiffs were precluded from recovering possession of their unit until the present tenant died or left voluntarily. The plaintiffs collected $521 per month rent from the present tenants. They sued the city on the ground that the new ordinance is a compensable taking without due process. How does the court decide? [*Loeterman v. Town of Brookline*, 524 F. Supp. 1325 (1981)]

6. The City of New York enacted an ordinance requiring licensed taxicabs to use gasoline containing no more than the specified low levels of lead and after January 1, 1974, to use only nonleaded gasoline. The ordinance also required pre-1970 taxicabs to be equipped with omission control devices that complied with the 1970 taxi and limousine federal standards. Later models had to be equipped with such emission control devices as may be specified in the New York City and Limousine Commission. The taxicab drivers sued, claiming that the Federal Clean Air Act prohibited states or their subdivisions from regulating fuel and fuel additives if the federal administrator finds that no control is necessary, and prohibited states or their subdivisions from creating standards for exhaust emission control devices for new motor vehicles and new motor vehicle engines. Based on the above, will an injunction be issued against the city? Decide. [*Allway Taxi,*

Inc. v. City of New York, 340 F. Supp. 1120 (1972)]

7. Lois Connelly kept a pet lion in her home. The county passed an ordinance prohibiting people from keeping certain dangerous animals, including lions, without a permit. Plaintiff was denied a permit because she did not meet the requirements for receiving such a permit, that is, that the animal be kept for purpose of education, reproduction, or research. Ms. Connelly, who was not compensated for the loss of the lion, argues that the ordinance violated the equal protection clause by treating people who kept lions as pets different from people keeping them for research, reproduction, or educational purposes. Is this a violation of the Fifth and Fourteenth Amendment prohibition against taking without due process of law and denial of equal protection? Why or why not? [*Kent v. Polk County Board of Supervisors*, 391 N.W.2d 220 (1986)]

8. The Nollans entered into a lease purchase agreement to buy a beachfront property. They had plans to build a three-bedroom home in place of the dilapidated bungalow that presently sat on the property. Before construction could begin the Nollans needed a coastal development permit. When they applied, they were informed that the permit would be given subject to the condition that they allow the public an easement to pass across a portion of their property that allowed access to a public beach. The Nollans refused claiming eminent domain. Were they correct? Explain. [*Nollan v. California Coastal Com'n*, 107 S.CT. 3141, 1987)]

9. Charles Baxter, a building developer, formed a not-for-profit corporation named Baxter's Place to operate a hospice for AIDS patients. Baxter applied to the City of Belleville for a special case permit but was refused based on the negative effect and health hazard an AIDS facility would have on the city and on the neighborhood, especially with a junior high school so close in proximity to the building. Is the city's zoning action valid because of its concern for the public good? [*Baxter v. City of Elleville, Illinois*, 720 F.Supp. 20 (1989)]

10. Central City enacted an ordinance prohibiting the importation of any spent nuclear fuel or other radioactive waste for the purpose of storage within the township. The purpose of its ordinance is to protect the public good based on a local legislative finding that an acceleration of nuclear-waste storage is contrary to the welfare of its inhabitants. Plant Corporation was the owner of Oyster Creek Nuclear Generating Station located in the township. Oyster Creek was not only a nuclear power plant, but also a federally licensed utilization facility as defined by the Atomic Energy Act of 1954. It was therefore authorized to generate nuclear energy and to retrieve and store on-site special nuclear material, including spent nuclear fuel. The corporation wanted to return 224 spent nuclear-fuel assemblies originally stored at an out-of-state facility to Oyster Creek's facility. Does the Atomic Energy Act preempt the local ordinance and permit the fuel to be returned? Why or why not? [*Jersey Central Power and Light Co. v. Township of Lacey*, 772 F.2d 1103 (3d Cir. 1985)]

21

INTERNATIONAL BUSINESS LAW

Not surprisingly, the legal environment of business has become more complex as it has become more international. International trade is an extremely important component of the U.S. economy. Products, services, and people routinely cross national boundaries. Today, in fact, it would be difficult to imagine any business that does not have some contact with international trade. One business, for example, may want to hire foreign-born employees. A manufacturing firm may make a product using supplies or parts from another country. A company may try to get a loan from a local bank that is in fact owned by a foreign country. Although a firm may sell its product in the United States, the product may then be shipped to a foreign country. Without even trying, the U.S. company is, in each instance, engaging in an international business transaction.

In order to get a better understanding of the complex nature of the international business environment, consider the two illustrations in Figure 21-1.[1] Figure 21-1A shows the *flows* involved in the conduct of business on an international scale; these "flows" include not only commercial products (goods and services), but other factors like personnel, technology, and capital. In this schematic, flows are theoretically "free" of interference. Figure 21-1B, however, introduces two elements that affect the free flow of international business activity. First, there are certain *barriers*—that is, primarily governmental barriers such as trade controls, tariffs, and controls over capital and technology. Second, there are *international institutions,* including such multinational organizations as the United Nations, the International Monetary Fund, and the European Community, that affect the flow of international business through their influence on various aspects of international commerce—for example, the international monetary system and foreign-exchange and financial markets as well as the policies of individual nations or blocs of nations.

As a result of exposure to international business, U.S. companies must be aware of the legal complexities that they face. This chapter will examine the

---

[1] See Christopher M. Korth, *International Business: Environment and Management* (Englewood Cliffs, NJ: Prentice Hall, 1985), pp. 12-17.

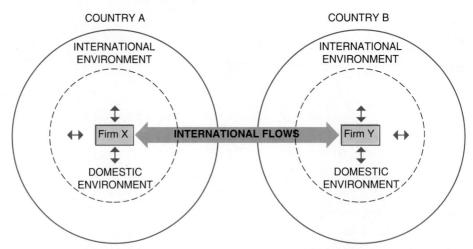

FIGURE 21-1A The Flow of Business Activity in the International Environment

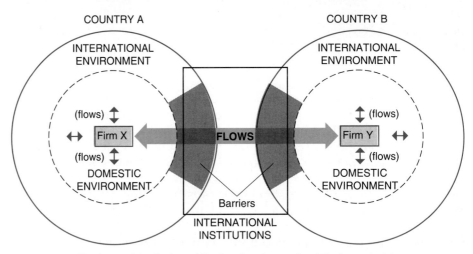

FIGURE 21-1B Barriers and Institutions Affecting Free International Business Activity *Source: Christopher M. Korth,* International Business: Environment and Management *(Englewood Cliffs, NJ: Prentice Hall, 1985).*

major participants and issues in the legal environment of international business. It will examine the different types of trading relationships that are commonly found in international transactions, and will look at multinational corporations and the Foreign Corrupt Practices Act of 1977. In addition, the chapter will examine international organizations and agreements which affect international transactions and which raise questions about trade and trade restrictions, and will discuss certain issues in antitrust policy that arise during the conduct of business on an international scale.

■ TRADING RELATIONSHIPS

International trading relationships take many forms. First, a business need not be a corporation to be engaged in international trade, nor does it have to be a certain size or have several offices. Actually, an *international trading relationship* can be any movement of goods, services, capital, or people across national boundaries. Types of relationships include *import-export*, *sales*, and *licensing* agreements.

Import-Export Relationships

The simplest trading relationship is a basic *import-export relationship*, in which only goods or products cross national boundaries. A company can *import* a product, or bring a product into its own country, simply by placing an order with a firm in a foreign country and taking delivery at home. Similarly, a company can receive an order for a product and *export* it by shipping it to a customer in the foreign country.

In many cases, it is not necessary for either importers or exporters to leave their offices at all. Although this type of transaction may be fairly straightforward, there are a variety of legal constraints that may affect it. For instance, import quotas, export controls, and laws governing product liability in both the buyer's country and the seller's country may have a constraining effect. (One practice that is widely illegal but, according to many observers, widely practiced—*dumping*—is the subject of this chapter's YOU DECIDE feature.)

Sales Representatives and Sales Agents

A business may want an individual or another company to represent it in a foreign country. A sales representative or a sales agent can be responsible for promoting and selling the product, providing information about it, and looking after the reputation of the company and the product in the foreign country.

A *sales representative* takes orders for a product and transmits those orders back to the manufacturer. A sales representative is not an employee of the company, does not take title to the goods, and cannot bind the company contractually. The decision to enter into a contract with the ultimate purchaser is left to the manufacturer, and shipping is usually made directly to the ultimate purchaser. The sales representative generally receives a commission.

A **sales agent,** however, is an employee who can contractually bind the firm for which he or she works. Some countries require that all business be done through appointed sales agents. In addition, there may be restrictions concerning the termination of a relationship between a firm and its sales representatives or sales agents.

sales agent Manufacturer's representative in a foreign country who takes and transmits orders and can contractually bind the firm by which he or she is employed

Licensing

Licensing is based on a contract allowing a foreign individual, firm, or country to use a foreign-based company's intellectual properties. Such a contract gives permission to another company to use the first company's patents, trademarks, or copyrights in the foreign country (*see* Chapter 18). The contract may allow the foreign firm to manufacture the other firm's goods and sell them in its own country. In return, the manufacturing firm receives payments known as *royalties*.

licensing Contract that gives an individual, firm, or country permission to use the patents, trademarks, or copyrights of a company in another country

A licensing arrangement is useful in that it allows a firm to enter a foreign market without making a substantial investment. Some foreign countries do not have the same protection for patents, copyrights, or trademarks that are found in the United States. Other countries restrict licensing arrangements or the amount of royalties that can be paid to firms based in other countries.

How would you feel if you discovered that you were paying extra for your running shoes because their American manufacturer was selling them much more cheaply abroad? What if you found that your favorite brand of stereo equipment was affordable to you only because consumers in its country of origin were being overcharged?

Dumping *is the practice of selling products abroad for less than the price charged at home. A firm might choose to dump goods for several reasons—to get rid of excess inventory quickly, to gain share in a foreign market, or even to drive competitors from the market. The selling firm can avoid losing money in the long term by subsidizing its foreign sales through high domestic prices, by receiving government subsidies that allow it to continue producing while profits suffer, or from low prices eventually eliminating competition and—its hold on the market assured—raising prices abroad. Although dumping is illegal in the United States, opinions vary widely as to when it occurs and who is harmed by it.*

If a firm claims that its market share or position have been damaged by dumping, what criteria should be applied in resolving the issue? When is below-cost pricing unfair, and when has the "injured" firm simply lost a competitive battle? If consumers benefit from low prices and weak firms go out of business, has any harm been done at all?

In *Zenith v. Matsushita (475 U.S. 574 [1986]), the American electronics firm, Zenith, charged that several Japanese manufacturers had engaged in a long-term conspiracy to capture the American television market by overcharging for their product at home in order to subsidize below-cost or "predatory" prices charged in the United States. If, in fact, the Japanese firms failed to dominate the American market in the twenty years of sales competition described in the suit, did a "conspiracy" exist? If they failed to recoup the losses they incurred by selling below cost, did they in fact engage in dumping and predatory pricing?* For further discussion, see p. 797.

Direct Investment

As a strategy for entering the markets of foreign countries, *investment* is one of the most important means by which companies expand globally. Figure 21-2 tells an interesting story about the role of the United States as an investor in international business. In 1984, the United States was the world's number-one creditor nation, with foreign investments increasing nearly threefold, from $434 billion to $1.2 trillion, between 1970 and 1987. During the same period, however, foreign investment in U.S. assets increased even more rapidly—from $280 billion in 1970 to $1.5 trillion in 1987. As a result, by 1987, the United States was also the world's number-one debtor nation, with foreign investments in the United States surpassing U.S. investment abroad for the first time.

FIGURE 21-2 The United States in International Investment, 1970-1988 (in constant 1982 dollars)

Sources: Adapted from Rogene A. Buchholz, Business Environment and Public Policy: Implications for Management and Strategy, *4th ed. (Englewood Cliffs, NJ: Prentice Hall, 1992). Data from Richard McKenzie,* The Global Economy and Government Power *(St. Louis, MO: Washington University Center for the Study of American Business, 1989); Department of Commerce, Bureau of Economic Analysis,* Economic Report of the President), *Washington, DC: Government Printing Office, 1990).*

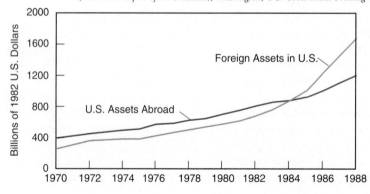

Table 21-1 lists the results of a Department of Commerce survey into the major reasons for the kind of corporate investment that produces figures like these. This section will look at a few of the more common forms taken by this strategy: making *direct investments*, opening *branches* and *subsidiaries*, and entering *joint ventures*.

PORTFOLIO INVESTMENTS. A **portfolio investment** is the investment of money in the *securities* of a foreign company. Many countries restrict the ability of foreigners to invest in such securities. While some of these restrictions prohibit any person who is not a national of that country from purchasing securities, others restrict such purchases to securities of companies in specified industries. Other types of regulations include restrictions on the ability to transfer currency into or out of the country.

portfolio investment Investment of money in the securities of a foreign company

BRANCHES. A **branch** of a U.S. company may perform the same services, manufacture similar products, or sell the same goods in a foreign country as it does in the United States. A branch is merely an arm or an extension of the U.S. firm in the foreign country. It does not take on any special form in the foreign country, nor does it have any separate identity. A U.S. firm would be directly liable for any contracts entered into by one of its branches, and lawsuits brought against foreign branches would be deemed lawsuits against the U.S. firm.

branch Extension of a U.S. firm in a foreign country that may manufacture similar products, perform the same services, or sell the same goods as in the U.S.

SUBSIDIARIES. A **subsidiary** does business according to a *form* specified by the laws of a foreign country. A U.S. subsidiary's identity is separate from that of its U.S.-based parent corporation. Usually, a subsidiary is a corporation incorporated under the laws of the foreign country, with the U.S. firm owing at least 51 percent of its stock. Under some regulations, however, a foreign entity may be deemed a subsidiary if the U.S. firm has "effective control" over the

subsidiary Unit of a firm in a foreign country which does business in a form specified by that country's laws and which has a corporate identity separate from that of its domestic parent company

TABLE 21-1	*Reasons for Foreign Investment*	

	MENTIONED BY NUMBER OF COMPANIES
1. Maintain or increase market share locally	33
2. Unable to reach market from United States because of tariffs, transportation costs, or nationalistic purchasing policies	25
3. Meet competition	20
4. Meet local content requirements and host government pressure	18
5. Faster sales growth than in the United States	15
6. To obtain or use local raw materials or components	13
7. Low-wage costs	13
8. Greater profit prospects abroad	11
9. Follow major customers	10
10. Inducements connected with host government investment promotion programs	8

Sources: Adapted from Buchholz, Business Environment and Public Policy. *Data from Department of Commerce, Domestic and International Business Administration,* The Multinational Corporation: Studies on U.S. Foreign Investment, *Vol. 2 (Washington, DC: Government Printing Office, 1973).*

subsidiary. *Effective control* may mean actually controlling the day-to-day operations of the subsidiary or providing the materials needed to manufacture the product.

JOINT VENTURES. A **joint venture** in this context is usually defined as a partnership between two corporations or a partnership between a corporation and a governmental entity. A joint venture is normally set up for a specific purpose or function and for a limited period of time. Some countries, while encouraging the use of the joint venture as a way of benefiting from a foreign firm's expertise but establish rules that the resulting company must eventually revert to nationals only. Some joint ventures are truly international in scope. For example, a Japanese car company and a U.S. car company have formed a joint venture to manufacture automobiles in Mexico.

■ Concept Check 21-1   Trading Relationships

- Describe a hypothetical *licensing* relationship between two businesses located in different countries.
- Give three examples of *direct-investment* relationships that a U.S. firm can enter into with international firms.
- What is a *joint venture* in the international business context?

■ MULTINATIONAL CORPORATIONS

Typically, a business that is interested in foreign investment begins with a simple export operation and expands to include licensing arrangements, distributors, sales agents, or sales representatives. Only after sales have reached a level at which it becomes profitable to manufacture products in the foreign jurisdictions do businesses generally set up branches or subsidiaries. It is these large business entities with production capabilities in more than one country that we speak of as **multinational corporations.**

Some people, however, prefer to describe such businesses as *multinational enterprises,* recognizing that it is not only corporations that do business internationally—partnerships, joint ventures with foreign governments, and even sole proprietorships may produce goods in more than one country. On some occasions, a further distinction is made: *Multinational corporations* are those with parent corporations that have more than one national identity. Other corporations are often called *transnational corporations.*

Whatever they have been called, multinational corporations have received a good deal of criticism. This section will focus both on the nature of the criticism leveled at such businesses and the response of the corporations in question—in particular, the advantages offered by multinational enterprise to host countries—and will examine the nature of the regulatory controls faced by corporations doing business in foreign countries.

Criticisms of Multinational Corporations

There are three areas of criticism faced by multinational corporations: the charges of excessive market control, excessive political control, and profit maximization as an over-arching agenda. True or not, such criticisms result frequently in the host countries exercising control over or regulating the activities of multinational corporations in various ways.

EXCESSIVE MARKET CONTROL.   The perception that multinational corporations exercise market control is really a restatement of the reasons why multinational corporations set up subsidiaries in foreign markets. Multinational corporations seek to take advantage of existing markets, whether for raw materials, labor and capital, or finished products. If none of these markets in a foreign jurisdiction was more favorable than those in the home country, multinational corporations would never seek to do business outside home markets. If, however, the multinational corporation seeks to take full advantage of the markets that it finds in a foreign jurisdiction, then it may be faced with accusations of exploiting the foreign market. For example, if the multinational corporation can hire a worker in a foreign jurisdiction for $5 an hour when it would be paying $10 in the home-country jurisdiction, there is an incentive to set up a manufacturing plant in the foreign jurisdiction. If the going market rate in the foreign jurisdiction is $5 an hour and the multinational corporation offers $6 an hour, then it is charged that the multinational corporation is seeking advantage in the host-country labor market. Competitors in the foreign jurisdiction will either have to raise wages or find themselves at a competitive disadvantage.

EXCESSIVE POLITICAL INFLUENCE.   A second area of criticism concerns political power. Much of this criticism stems from U.S. activity in Latin America during the 1970s and from more recent disclosures linking United States covert actions with business organizations.

This criticism is also based on the fact that in some less-developed countries, governments encourage multinational investment by offering corporate incentives. This situation may thus create a certain dependency between the government and the multinational. If the operation proves to be unsuccessful, or if the multinational corporation decides to leave the country, negative political consequences often follow.

Similarly, some multinational corporations enter into joint ventures with foreign governments. This type of relationship also has definite positive or negative political consequences. The multinational corporation seeks favorable treatment from the foreign government, and the government wants to make sure of the positive consequences that flow from the investment.

PROFIT-MAXIMIZATION STRATEGY.   The third area of criticism revolves around the multinational corporation's strategy for maximizing profits from *global* enterprise. Large multinational corporations make direct investments in several foreign countries. The multinational corporation measures its performance according to the capacity of its worldwide operations to maximize profits. If *overall* performance goals are not being met, the corporation may seek to improve profitability by cutting the cost of doing business. Although a particular operation—for example, a subsidiary located in a foreign country—may be profitable, ceasing its operations may still cut corporate costs and maximize profits in the long run. In addition, political and/or public-relations considerations may influence the decision to close a foreign rather than a domestic operation, but the multinational corporation is, in either case, weighing such factors against long-run profit forecasts and trying to use its resources as efficiently as possible. The benefits of a foreign operation to a host country will be considered primarily within the context of profit maximization, and multinational corporations have thus gained a reputation of being more concerned with global profit than with local needs and benefits.

Corporate Response to Criticism

The problem areas just discussed have had a powerful impact, resulting sometimes in host-country demands for stronger regulation of multinationals. Understandably, multinationals themselves consider such criticisms unfair at best. They point out, for example, the benefits that their companies provide to host nations. They argue that the operations of multinational corporations offer the following advantages:

- provide employment
- train managers
- provide products and services that raise the standard of living
- introduce and develop new technical skills
- introduce new managerial and organizational techniques
- provide greater access to international markets
- lift the gross national product
- increase productivity
- help to build foreign-exchange reserves
- serve as a point of contact between host-country businesspeople and politicians in the home country
- encourage the development and/or spin-off of new industries
- assume investment risks that might not otherwise have been undertaken
- mobilize for productive purposes capital that might otherwise have gone for less productive uses.[2]

■ Concept Check 21-2   Multinational Corporations

- Define a *multinational corporation* and describe some of the activities that qualify companies for the designation.
- In what ways can the business activities of multinational corporations be translated into *political* influence in a host country?
- Cite a few examples in support of the claims of multinational corporations that their activities benefit host countries.

■ HOST-COUNTRY REGULATORY CONTROL

Host countries control the activities of multinational corporations in a variety of ways. The following list illustrates the types of regulations that can exist:

1. *Exclusionary restrictions upon entry.* A host country can keep multinational corporations out of specific industries or out of the country altogether.
2. *Conditional entry.* A host country may set certain conditions on the multinational corporation before allowing it to invest. For example, only joint ventures may be allowed or a factory may have to be turned over to the nationals of that country

---

[2] George A. Steiner and John F. Steiner, *Business, Government, and Society: A Managerial Perspective*, 4th ed. (New York: Random House, 1985), p. 593.

within a certain period of years. Sometimes, conditional entry may give the multinational corporation favorable tax treatment or financial incentives.

3. *Control over capital movement.* The host country may restrict the ability of the multinational corporation to capitalize its investment by restricting the flow of currency into or out of the country, or by making it difficult for the multinational corporation to obtain loans or sell securities to raise capital.

4. *Tax legislation.* Unfavorable tax treatment can have a negative impact on multinational corporations. Conversely, favorable tax laws may attract multinational corporations.

5. *Disclosure legislation.* An effective method of controlling the activities of such a multinational corporation is the use of *disclosure legislation.* Such legislation can include (1) reporting requirements in the form of annual or quarterly reports; (2) reports about hiring practices, future plans, or secret processes; or (3) requirements that native workers be represented on the board of directors of multinational corporations.

6. *Merger legislation.* Merger legislation, which is similar to U.S. antitrust laws, may be used to restrict the amount of stock in a national company a multinational can purchase or to limit its ability to take over or merge with an existing firm.

7. *Nationalization.* One of the most effective controls that host countries have over multinational corporations is the **nationalization** of property. When property is nationalized, it is taken over by the host-country government. If adequate compensation is paid for the property, the action is known as an **expropriation;** if adequate compensation is not paid, it is known as **confiscation.** Aside from being an effective means of controlling a multinational corporation, nationalization is also one of the greatest risks that multinational corporations face. Closely connected to this problem is "creeping expropriation," which occurs when a host country puts severe restrictions on the activities of a multinational corporation without actually nationalizing its property.

nationalization Taking of the property of a *multinational corporation* by the host-country government

expropriation *Nationalization* of the property of a *multinational corporation* with adequate compensation paid by the host-country government

confiscation *Nationalization* of the property of a *multinational corporation* without just compensation by a host-country government

The Act of State Doctrine

When foreign-owned property is confiscated—that is, taken without just compensation—by a host government, the foreign business usually seeks to recover its property, either in its own or in a third country. The **act of state doctrine,** however, prevents the courts of one state from challenging the validity of public acts that a recognized foreign sovereign commits within its own territory.

Because it is the duty of the executive branch to carry out foreign affairs with other nations, the judicial branch is reluctant to interfere on the ground of separation of powers. Therefore, courts will usually implement the act of state doctrine even when it may seem to lead to inequitable results. This practice means, however, that *all* state acts may be implemented—even when these acts are abhorrent to our own notions of justice.

The **Bernstein** *Exception.* In order to deal with such a situation, the *Bernstein exception* to the act of state doctrine was introduced. In 1937, Bernstein, a German Jew, was forced to transfer his property to a Nazi agent. After the war, he sought return of his property from the third party then in control of its proceeds. Although a New York court first applied the act of state doctrine, after a State Department letter was delivered to the appeals court, the court amended the doctrine to allow review and jurisdiction of the matter.

The **First National City Bank** *Case.* One influential application of the act of state doctrine resulted from Fidel Castro's rise to power in Cuba in 1960. Two years earlier, First National City Bank, an American institution, had lent $15 million to Banco Nacional de Cuba, secured by a pledge of United States Government bonds. By 1960, $5 million had been repaid and the collateral re-

act of state doctrine Legal principle preventing the courts of one country from challenging the validity of public acts, such as *confiscation*, that a recognized foreign government commits within its own country

duced accordingly. In the meantime, however, Castro had come to power, and his army had seized all of First National's Cuban branches. The bank then sold the remaining bonds of collateral to repay the loan, realizing a profit of about $1.8 million in the process. Castro's government sued in Federal District Court to recover the $1.8 million, and First National countersued, claiming the money as damages resulting from the takeover of its Cuban property. The Supreme Court held that the act of state doctrine did not prevent First National from pursuing its counterclaim "on the merits."

■ Concept Check 21-3   Host-Country Regulatory Control

- Give some examples of the means by which the United States, as a *host country* to foreign investors, regulates their activities in this country.
- Define *nationalization* and give examples to distinguish between the practices of *expropriation* and *confiscation*.
- Explain the *act of state doctrine* and the *Bernstein* exception to that doctrine.

■ THE FOREIGN CORRUPT PRACTICES ACT

Foreign Corrupt Practices Act (FCPA)   1977 federal law that prohibits bribery of foreign officials by domestic firms and requires issuers of securities to keep records accurately reflecting financial transactions

The **Foreign Corrupt Practices Act** of 1977 (**FCPA**) was passed in response to revelations of corporate payments of bribes to officials of foreign governments. The shock waves of these disclosures were felt by foreign government officials, corporate management, and the U.S. government, and public reaction to these revelations was quite strong.

Because it seeks to regulate conduct that takes place outside the boundaries of the United States, the Foreign Corrupt Practices Act is still viewed as controversial. Some experts complain that it puts U.S. businesses at a competitive disadvantage. They argue further that the act regulates conduct that may in fact be perfectly legal in the host country. On the other hand, because questionable payments may put U.S. firms that do not engage in such practices at a competitive disadvantage, they may result in injury that takes place in the United States.

This section will discuss both the reporting requirements and the activities that the FCPA prohibits, as well as the revisions to the FCPA made in the Omnibus Trade and Competitiveness Act of 1988.

Reporting Requirements

Under the reporting requirements of the Foreign Corrupt Practices Act, which are enforced by the SEC, any "issuer" of securities, as defined by the Securities Exchange Act of 1934 (*see* Chapter 8), must keep its books and records in such a way that they accurately reflect the issuer's financial transactions. The issuer must also establish internal accounting systems that accurately reflect its assets. The purpose of these requirements is to make it more difficult for firms to hide questionable payments to foreign government officials.

Prohibited Conduct

The second section of the FCPA is the more controversial. It prohibits giving anything of value to a foreign government official in order to influence a discretionary decision. The term *"anything of value"* includes money, gifts, or other items that would be deemed of value in that particular culture. The term *"foreign government official"* refers to individuals acting in official capacities. Note that the law is violated if something is given to a third party and there is a *reasonable expectation* that it will be given in turn to a foreign official. The term *"discretionary decision"* refers to the making of a decision that will assist the firm in obtaining or retaining business.

The ETHICAL ENVIRONMENT box in this chapter deals with two cases of conduct under the Foreign Corrupt Practices Act: one concerning the successful prosecution of a violator and one concerning a corporate code for compliance.

The Grease Payment Exception. One important exception to the Foreign Corrupt Practices Act is the so-called *grease payment exception.* This exception allows firms to make payments in order to expedite functions that do not require discretionary decisions. If a foreign government official, such as a clerk, has the job of stamping documents or processing paperwork, it is possible to make a payment that will *expedite* the matter. This provision holds especially if delay would cause merchandise to be destroyed or damaged.

1988 Revisions to the FCPA: The Omnibus Trade and Competitiveness Act

Challenges to the ambiguity of the Foreign Corrupt Practices Act arose quickly. And after much debate and controversy, several revisions were passed that either clarify or alter the intentions of the original statutes. The **Omnibus Trade and Competitiveness Act** of 1988 (**Trade Act**) amends the accounting and antibribery provisions of the FCPA. Although substantially increasing penalties for violation, the Trade Act amendments generally give corporations more latitude in dealing with foreign countries.

Omnibus Trade and Competitiveness Act (Trade Act) 1988 federal statute amending the controversial accounting and antibribery provisions of the FCPA

Case: Agent Liability. Among the bribery statutes of the FCPA altered or rescinded by the Trade Act is the "Eckhardt Amendment," which blocked the prosecution of corporate agents when the company itself was not found to have violated the FCPA. The following case illustrates the application of the Eckhardt provisions of the FCPA.

UNITED STATES v. McLEAN
U.S. Court of Appeals, Fifth Circuit, 738 F.2d 655 (5th Cir. 1984)

In 1979, grand juries were impanelled to investigate whether American businessmen had bribed Mexican officials in violation of the Foreign Corrupt Practices Act (FCPA). Three years later, the grand juries returned a 49-count indictment charging Crawford Enterprises, Inc. (CEI), which was a broker and lessor of gas-compression systems, and nine individuals with violating the FCPA. Specifically, the indictment charged that CEI and George S. McLean and Luis A. Uriate, two employees of International Harvester Co., conspired to bribe officials of Petroleos Mexicanos (Pemex), the national petroleum company of Mexico.

W. Eugene Davis, Circuit Judge:
We are presented for the first time with the question of whether the Foreign Corrupt Practices Act (FCPA) permits the prosecution of an employee for a substantive offense under the Act if his employer has not and cannot be convicted of similarly violating the FCPA. We conclude that the Act prohibits such a prosecution and affirm the district court.

During the late 1970s Petroleos Mexicanos (Pemex) purchased larger quantities of turbine compressor equipment to capture and pump to processing plants a high volume of natural gas. The Solar division of International Harvester Company (Harvester) was the dominant worldwide supplier to such equipment. George S. McLean was its vice-president and Luis A. Uriarte was its Latin American regional manager; both were Harvester employees. Crawford Enterprises, Inc. (CEI) was a broker and lessor of gas compression systems which

---

frequently purchased equipment from Harvester for resale or lease. Harvester, as prime contractor, had supplied Pemex with equipment in the mid-Seventies; during the period of accelerated development in the late 1970s, however, Harvester acted as a subcontractor for CEI, which had contracted with Pemex to build complete compression plants.

. . . Although McLean and Uriarte's employer, Harvester, was not charged in the forty-nine count indictment, the government concedes that all acts of McLean and Uriarte were committed within the scope of their employment with Harvester. . . .

Both McLean and Uriarte filed motions to dismiss the charges pending against them on grounds that the failure of the government to convict Harvester of a violation under the FCPA barred their prosecution. . . .

The substantive violations of the Act are established in two sections. Section 78dd-1 makes it unlawful for an issuer (defined as an entity subject to the securities registration requirements of § 78l and 78o of Title 15), its officers, directors, employees or agents, to use the mails or other instrumentality of interstate commerce to bribe foreign officials for various purposes including to obtain business. Section 78dd-2 provides generally the same prohibition for a domestic concern, its officers, directors, shareholders and employees. Domestic concern is broadly defined to include any United States citi-

zen, national or resident; or any corporation (other than an issuer), partnership or other entity subject to United State jurisdiction and control. . . .

A major objective of the Eckhardt amendment is to allow the employee the benefit of the superior resources of the corporation in presenting a defense in the criminal proceeding; a closely related objective is to prevent the employer from making its employee a scapegoat. . . .

. . . .

We hold that in order to convict an employee under the FCPA for acts committed for the benefit of his employer, the government must first convict the employer. Because the government failed to convict Harvester and under the plea agreement will be unable to indict Harvester and try it with McLean, the Act bars McLean's prosecution. Affirmed.

Case Questions

1. One goal of criminal statutes is to deter criminal conduct in the future. Do you think that the court's ruling dismissing the charges against the Harvester officials will deter international corporate crime?

2. Can you postulate any explanation for why Harvester, Inc. was not named in the indicatment?

According to some critics, this change in the 1977 FCPA raises the possibility of a so-called "scapegoat" scenario whereby employees might be prosecuted for violations mandated by senior management. Congressional opponents of the Trade Act have charged that, in general, its amendments have severely compromised the original intentions of the 1977 FCPA.[3]

Routine Payments. Permitted under the revisions to the FCPA are payments for "routine governmental action" such as issuing permits and visas, providing police protection or phone service, and inspecting, loading and unloading, and protecting cargo. It is still illegal to make payments for actions that award or continue business with a firm.

Affirmative Defenses. If a payment is lawful in the country in which it was made, the Trade Act makes it permissible for U.S. firms. In addition, it is lawful to pay for foreigners' travel and lodging for the purpose of promoting a firm's products or services.

Remaining Ambiguities. It is still unclear what is meant by the term "corruptly" under the FCPA. Because liability can also be difficult to determine, particularly with the repeal of the Eckhardt Amendment, firms and individuals are not advised to act conservatively with respect to FCPA provisions. This is particularly true when foreign agents are employed to act on a firm's behalf. The Department of Justice can review any prospective transaction and issue in advance an opinion on its legality.

---

[3] See Bartley A. Brennan, "The Foreign Corrupt Practices Act Amendments of 1988: 'Death' of a Law," *N.C.J. International Law and Commercial Regulation* 15 (1990), pp. 229-47.

In the first test of the FCPA against a major corporation (SEC v. Ashland Oil, Inc.), Ashland Oil was accused of paying millions of dollars for a majority interest in Midlands Chrome, Inc., which was controlled by an official of the Omani government, for the purpose of obtaining a highly profitable crude oil contract in Oman. In settling the case, Ashland agreed to avoid future violations of FCPA provisions.

The Ashland case demonstrates that even business transactions that appear legitimate will be scrutinized for compliance with the FCPA. Some firms have taken steps to avoid trouble in advance. The following state of corporate policy regarding the FCPA has been issued by Chevron.

> Chevron conducts its business in more than ninety countries around the world. And each of these countries has a unique set of mores, customs, and business practices, along with its own distinctive laws and regulations. To compete effectively and harmoniously, and to satisfy the expectations and needs of our customers, the Chevron companies in these countries have been tailored to respect and conform to the local environment.
>
> We realize that special problems can come up when business transactions involve more than one country. In those instances, care must be taken to assure that in complying with the laws of one country we do not violate the laws of another.

The U.S. Foreign Corrupt Practices Act makes it a crime for a U.S. company, or its employees or agents, to make or authorize corrupt payments to foreign officials for the purpose of obtaining or retaining business. While in some instances payments of this nature may be acceptable in the country where made, they are strictly against our policy even though the refusal to make them may cause the company to lose business.

To assure compliance with the Foreign Corrupt Practices Act, the company has issued detailed guidelines governing, and in some cases prohibiting, such matters as foreign political contributions, foreign consulting arrangements, agency, contractor, and joint-venture agreements, rebates, expediting payments, split payments, and entertainment of or gifts to government officials or employees. Such guidelines are set forth in the company's Manual of Compliance Procedures and Guidelines. All employees who have any contact with foreign operations must be familiar with and strictly observe these guidelines. It is essential that any contract, payment, or practice that could possibly run afoul of the act, or the related disclosure requirements of U.S. securities laws, be reviewed in advance by the Comptroller of the parent company.

■ Concept Check 21-4   The Foreign Corrupt Practices Act

- Explain the major provisions of the *Foreign Corrupt Practices Act* of 1977. What actions are prohibited under the FCPA?
- What are the basic terms of the controversy surrounding the FCPA?
- Describe some of the major changes in the FCPA made by the *Omnibus Trade and Competitiveness Act* of 1988.

■ INTERNATIONAL CONTRACTS

International business transactions often involve a variety of contracts. These might include contracts for the leasing of office space, employment contracts, licensing contracts, distributorship contracts, sales representative contracts, or agency contracts. Contracts may also be for the purchase of raw materials or the sale of finished products. Such contracts may also include joint-venture contracts or contracts for the purchase or sale of goods between a branch or subsidiary and the parent company.

As a general rule, parties to international business contracts must deal with many of the same considerations that they would with a domestic contract. However, because the parties are dealing with different legal systems, customs, and languages, additional terms must be negotiated. Some contract clauses to be considered in an international contract include (1) choice of language, (2) terms of payment, (3) force majeure clause, (4) government approval, (5) arbitration clause, (6) choice of forum, and (7) choice of law. Each of these clauses is discussed below.

In negotiating these various contract clauses, the U.S. firm must of course be sensitive to the laws and customs of foreign countries. As with all contracts, it is the *relationship* and not the *document* that is important. Although a contract need not include any of the following provisions, an international business entity must be aware of the issues raised in these types of clauses.

TERMS-OF-PAYMENT CLAUSE. A **terms-of-payment clause** is common to most contracts. In an international contract, however, this clause should designate the *currency* to be used in payment as well as the location of payment. Designating currency makes it possible to limit the risk of currency fluctuations through the purchase of futures contracts. The location of payment is important because some currencies cannot be *repatriated*—that is, cannot leave the particular foreign country. Similarly, if payment is to be made in the local currency, the party to be paid must make sure that the local currency can be taken back to the home country.

Letters of Credit and Bills of Lading. One major risk in any contract is that the goods shipped will not be paid for. In order to avoid the expense and time of enforcing the seller's contract rights to payment, the transaction could be structured to use a *letter of credit* (*see* Chapter 19). A **letter of credit** is a promise made by a bank located in the buyer's country to make payments under conditions specified in a contract. Thus, the effect of a letter of credit is to substitute the bank's credit for the buyer's. Usually, the issuing bank will authorize payment of the specified amount upon presentation of a *bill of lading* covering the shipped merchandise. A **bill of lading** is a receipt indicating that the shipping company has actually received the goods (*see* Fig. 21-3). This receipt also serves the function of a negotiable title document for the goods.

If a letter of credit is labeled "irrevocable," it cannot be revoked during the transaction. If it is "confirmed," a bank in the seller's country adds its guarantee of payments to that of the issuing bank. Letters of credit are governed in the United States by the Uniform Commercial Code (*see* Chapter 9) and also by the international principles stated in the Uniform Customs and Practice for Documentary Credits.

FORCE-MAJEURE CLAUSE. The term "force majeure" refers to a "superior power." A **force-majeure clause** is similar to the common-law concept of impossibility of performance and the UCC concept of commercial impracticability. Typically this clause excuses performance under certain specified circumstances. A force-majeure clause may designate natural disasters such as floods, storms, earthquakes, or "acts of God" as excuses for nonperformance. Such clauses may also designate political unrest, including war, riots, police actions, or strikes, to excuse performance. They may even include runaway inflation, drastic currency devaluations, or stock-market collapses.

In a force-majeure clause, it is important to establish a standard such as the length of time or severity of the occurrence necessary to bring the clause into force. It is also important to include a provision for recourse in the case of partial performance.

terms-of-payment clause *International-contract clause* designating the currency to be used in payment and the location of payment

letter of credit In *international contracts*, promise made by a buyer's bank in one country to make payments under specified conditions (*see also* Chapter 19)

bill of lading Receipt indicating that a shipping company has actually received the goods being sold and serving as a negotiable title document for those goods

force majeure clause *International-contract clause* excusing performance under certain specified circumstances such as natural disasters, political unrest, and economic turmoil

SEA-LAND SERVICE, INC.

INTERNATIONAL BILL OF LADING
NOT NEGOTIABLE UNLESS CONSIGNED "TO ORDER"
(SPACES IMMEDIATELY BELOW FOR SHIPPERS' MEMORANDA)

(2) SHIPPER/EXPORTER (COMPLETE NAME AND ADDRESS)

(5) BOOKING NO.

(5A) BILL OF LADING NO.

(6) EXPORT REFERENCES

(3) CONSIGNEE (COMPLETE NAME AND ADDRESS)

(7) FORWARDING AGENT, F.M.C. NO.

(8) POINT AND COUNTRY OF ORIGIN

(4) NOTIFY PARTY (COMPLETE NAME AND ADDRESS)

(9) ALSO NOTIFY-ROUTING & INSTRUCTIONS

(12) INITIAL CARRIAGE BY (MODE) *

(13) PLACE OF INITIAL RECEIPT *

(14) VESSEL VOY. FLAG

(15) PORT OF LOADING

(10) LOADING PIER/TERMINAL

(10A) ORIGINAL(S) TO BE RELEASED AT

(16) PORT OF DISCHARGE

(17) PLACE OF DELIVERY BY ON-CARRIER *

(11) TYPE OF MOVE (IF MIXED, USE BLOCK 20 AS APPROPRIATE)

PARTICULARS FURNISHED BY SHIPPER

SEA-LAND-U.S. CUSTOMS CONTAINER BOND IIT 145

MKS. & NOS./CONTAINER NOS.	NO. OF PKGS.	HM * *	DESCRIPTION OF PACKAGES AND GOODS	GROSS WEIGHT	MEASUREMENT
(18)	(19)		(20)	(21)	(22)

(23) Declared Value $ ________ If shipper enters a value, carriers "package" limitation of liability does not apply and the ad valorem rate will be charged.

RATE OF EXCHANGE

(24) FREIGHT PAYABLE AT/BY

ITEM NO.		RATED AS	PER	RATE	PREPAID		COLLECT		LOCAL CURRENCY
		TOTAL CHARGES							

If this box is checked, goods have been loaded, stowed and counted by Shipper. Carrier has NOT done so and is not responsible for accuracy of count, condition or nature of goods described in PARTICULARS FURNISHED BY SHIPPER.

THE RECEIPT, CUSTODY, CARRIAGE AND DELIVERY OF THE GOODS ARE SUBJECT TO THE TERMS APPEARING ON THE FACE AND BACK HEREOF AND TO CARRIER'S APPLICABLE TARIFF.

In witness whereof three (3) original bills of lading all the same tenor and date one of which being accomplished the others to stand void have been issued by Sea-Land Service, Inc. or its designated agent on behalf of itself, other participating carriers, the vessel, her master and owners or charterers.

* APPLICABLE ONLY WHEN USED FOR MULTIMODAL OR THROUGH TRANSPORTATION.
* * INDICATE WHETHER ANY OF THE CARGO IS HAZARDOUS MATERIAL UNDER DOT, IMCO OR OTHER REGULATIONS AND INDICATE CORRECT COMMODITY NUMBER IN BOX 20.

AT ....

BY ....

SL 2265 5/82 BILL OF LADING NO. DATE FOR SEA-LAND SERVICE, INC.

FIGURE 21-3 Sample International Bill of Lading *Source: Reprinted by permission of Sea-land Service, Inc.*

GOVERNMENT-APPROVAL CLAUSE. An international contract involves governmental regulations at several levels. As a result, it is important to include a clause dealing with government approval. Such a clause should specify which party is responsible for getting the necessary licenses, permits, or government permission for the transaction.

ARBITRATION CLAUSE. **Arbitration clauses** are regularly used in international contracts. A *mandatory arbitration clause* may specify that arbitration is required before the filing of any lawsuit with respect to the contract. A *binding arbitration clause* may specify that the parties will be bound by any arbitration decision.

arbitration clause
International-contract clause specifying mandatory or binding arbitration or applicable arbitration

Arbitration clauses could also specify which arbitration rules will apply and where arbitration will take place.

Arbitration Bodies. There are several bodies that deal with international arbitration. For example, the American Arbitration Association has rules and facilities for international arbitration. The International Center for the Settlement of Investment Disputes has arbitration rules and facilities for certain kinds of arbitrations, as does the United Nations Commission on International Trade Law (UNCITRAL). There are, however, some practitioners who believe that an arbitration clause merely adds another layer of expense and time in resolving contract disputes. Others believe that arbitration provides an efficient and cost-effective means of resolving disputes. The following case illustrates how U.S. courts enforce arbitration clauses in international contracts. It should be read in connection with the case of *Shearson/American Express, Inc. v. McMahon* (1987) on securities regulation, excerpted in Chapter 8.

SCHERK v. ALBERTO-CULVER CO.
United States Supreme Court, 417 U.S. 506 (1974)

In February 1969, Alberto-Culver Co., a large Illinois-based manufacturer and distributor of toiletries and hair products, entered into a contract with Fritz Scherk, who owned several cosmetic companies in Germany and Liechtenstein. Under the agreement, which was signed in Vienna, Austria, Scherk transferred the ownership of his companies to Alberto-Culver, along with the unencumbered ownership of trademarks for the cosmetic products manufactured by his companies. In the event that a dispute arose between the parties, the contract required arbitration before the International Chamber of Commerce in Paris, France, but required the arbitrator to apply the law of Illinois to resolve the conflict.

Mr. Justice Stewart delivered the opinion of the Court. . . .

The closing of the transaction took place in Geneva, Switzerland, in June 1969. Nearly one year later Alberto-Culver allegedly discovered that the trademark rights purchased under the contract were subject to substantial encumbrances that threatened to give others superior rights to the trademarks and to restrict or preclude Alberto-Culver's use of them. Alberto-Culver thereupon tendered back to Scherk the property that had been transferred to it and offered to rescind the contract. Upon Scherk's refusal, Alberto-Culver commenced this action for damages and other relief in a Federal District Court in Illinois, contending that Scherk's fraudulent representations concerning the status of the trademark rights constituted violations of § 10 (b) of the Securities Exchange Act of 1934, and Rule 10b-5 promulgated thereunder.

In response, Scherk filed a motion to dismiss the action for want of personal and subject-matter jurisdiction

as well as on the basis of *forum non conveniens,* or alternatively, to stay the action pending arbitration in Paris pursuant to the agreement of the parties. . . . On December 2, 1971, the District Court denied Scherk's motion to dismiss, and, on January 14, 1972, it granted a preliminary order enjoining Scherk from proceeding with arbitration. . . . The Court of Appeals for the Seventh Circuit, with one judge dissenting, affirmed. . . .

The United States Arbitration Act, reversing centuries of judicial hostility to arbitration agreements, was designed to allow parties to avoid "the costliness and delays of litigation," and to place arbitration agreements "upon the same footing as other contracts. . . ." Accordingly, the Act provides that an arbitration agreement such as is here involved "shall be valid, irrevocable, and enforceable, save upon such grounds as exist at law or in equity for the revocation of any contract.". . .

. . . .

. . . Alberto-Culver's contract to purchase the business entities belonging to Scherk was a truly international agreement. . . . [M]ost significantly, the subject matter of the contract concerned the sale of business enterprises organized under the laws of and primarily situated in European countries, whose activities were largely, if not entirely, directed to European markets.

. . . In this case, . . . in the absence of the arbitration provision considerable uncertainty existed at the time of the agreement, and still exists, concerning the law applicable to the resolution of disputes arising out of the contract.

Such uncertainty will almost inevitably exist with respect to any contract touching two or more countries, each with its own substantive laws and conflict-of-laws rules. A contractual provision specifying in advance the forum in which disputes shall be litigated and the law to be applied is, therefore, an almost indispensable precondition to achievement of the orderliness and predictability essential to any international business transaction. Furthermore, such a provision obviates the danger that a dispute under the argeement might be submitted to a forum hostile to the interests of one of the parties or unfamiliar with the problem area involved.

. . . .

An agreement to arbitrate before a specified tribunal is, in effect, a specialized kind of forum-selection clause that posits not only the situs of suit but also the procedure to be used in resolving the dispute. The invalidation of such an agreement in the case before us would not only allow the respondent to repudiate its solemn promise but would, as well, reflect a "parochial concept that all disputes must be resolved under our laws and in our courts. . . . We cannot have trade and commerce in world markets and international waters exclusively on our terms, governed by our laws, and resolved in our courts." *The Bremen* v. *Zapata Off-Shore Co.*

. . . .

Accordingly, the judgment of the Court of Appeals is reversed and the case is remanded to that court with directions to remand to the District Court for further proceedings consistent with this opinion.

Case Questions

1. What would have been the impact upon international business of a Supreme Court ruling that the arbitration clause was not binding?

2. What are the pros and cons of including a mandatory arbitration clause in an international business contract?

3. What do you think Alberto-Culver wanted to litigate this dispute in federal court instead of arbitrating the case in Paris?

CHOICE-OF-FORUM CLAUSE. Parties to an international contract have some flexibility in designating *where* a lawsuit will be brought in the case of a contract dispute. This option is known as a **choice-of-forum clause.** The parties may choose a country for convenience, for familiarity with the legal process, or for the efficiency of its legal system. If the choice of forum has a rational relationship to the contract or to the contracting parties, these clauses are generally enforceable.

choice-of-forum clause
International-contract clause designating where a lawsuit will be brought in case of a contract dispute

CHOICE-OF-LAW CLAUSE. The parties in an international contract can also designate that a particular country's laws will apply to any dispute arising out of the contract. This option is known as a **choice-of-law clause.** Choice-of-forum and choice-of-law clauses need not designate the same country. A contract can specify, for example, that any dispute arising out of the contract will be tried in the United States but that the law of another country will apply. In the United States, the laws of foreign countries are considered issues of fact, and evidence is introduced as to the law of that particular country. As a practical matter, however, courts are usually better equipped to apply the laws of their own countries to contract disputes. (See this chapter's INTERNATIONAL ENVIRONMENT box for a discussion of the legal system in the People's Republic of China.)

choice-of-law clause
International-contract clause designating that a particular country's laws will apply in a contract dispute

When No Contract Exists

There are times when parties may enter into a sale of goods without negotiating a contract and times when certain terms are omitted in a contract. In these cases, if a dispute arises the outcome is far from certain. The United Nations Convention on Contracts for the International Sale of Goods is an attempt to provide some certainty in these instances. The Convention on Contracts for the International Sale of Goods is a type of Uniform Commercial Code for international transactions. It will be discussed in detail in the next section of this chapter.

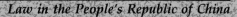

The product of thousands of years of tradition and culture with the powerful addition of communist ideology, the Chinese legal system functions to serve the interests of the many over those of the individual, although its structure bears at least superficial resemblances to the court systems of many Western countries. As highly refined as it is, however, the judicial process in the People's Republic is usually considered a last resort in a vast nation that values mediation as the ideal means of conflict resolution. Mediation and litigation are both conducted within the Chinese court system (see the chart below for an overview).

The court system in the Peoples' Republic of China is hierarchical, with two branches presided over by the Supreme People's Court. One branch, the Special People's Courts, hears cases dealing with the military, the railway system, and conservation issues. The other branch, consisting of three levels—local, intermediate, and higher—tries civil and criminal cases. Although the intermediate, higher, and supreme courts can each hear appeals from the lower courts, litigants can appeal only once before a court's decision becomes binding—except in instances where capital punishment may be imposed (these cases are referred to the Supreme People's Court for examination and approval).

With a few exceptions, such as cases dealing with state secrets, all trials are public and verdicts publicly pronounced. Defendants in criminal cases have the right to defend themselves; they may also hire lawyers, use court-appointed lawyers, or ask close relatives or guardians to argue in their favor.

All but the simplest cases are heard by a collegiate bench consisting either of several judges or a judge and elected jury whose voting rights are equal; decisions are based on the principle of majority rule, although the minority opinion is duly recorded. Justices are appointed by the state; they must be at least 23 years of age and have studied law. Particularly important or difficult cases are decided by judicial committees composed of highly qualified members; rulings are carried out by the collegiate bench.

Thousands of People's Conciliation Committees throughout China are used to resolve disputes without recourse to the court system (although any party to a disagreement can appeal a mediated decision to the courts for satisfaction). Based on a longstanding social tradition, mediation as now employed is a means of serving the nation's interests and raising political consciousness more than as an individual right or safeguard. Still, most cases are heard by Conciliation Committees before or instead of a hearing before the court.

Many labor disputes—and even personal matters between workers—are resolved within the labor unions, which are controlled by Communist Party members whose decisions are designed to further party interests over all others. Strikes are not permitted, and collective bargaining is unknown.

Disputes with foreigners arising in the course of international trade and exchange are settled by the Foreign Economic and Trade Arbitration Commission or the Maritime Arbitration Commission. These agencies usually rely on mediation to resolve problems.

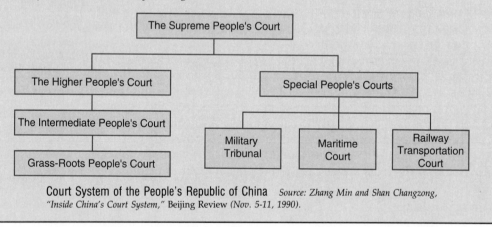

Court System of the People's Republic of China *Source: Zhang Min and Shan Changzong, "Inside China's Court System," Beijing Review (Nov. 5-11, 1990).*

■ Concept Check 21-5 International Contracts

- Briefly describe each of the major types of clauses that are often included in international business contracts. Explain and distinguish between *choice-of-forum* and *choice-of-law* clauses.
- May individuals enter into a sale of goods without negotiating a written contract? Explain.

■ International Agreements and Forums

International law refers to the body of rules and regulations, usually in the form of treaties and conventions, regulating relationships among nations. International law is sometimes referred to as the "law of war and peace." Many people engaged in international business view international law as something of interest to academics but with little practical business application. There are, however, areas of international law that directly affect the activities of international business entities.

A Law of Consent. Because international law is a law of *consent*—that is, it only applies to those who agree to be bound by it—codes of conduct are important. Many observers would argue that international law has no force because there is no mechanism for enforcement, such as a police force or an international army. In this sense, however, international law can be compared with domestic contract law, which is also a law of consent.

International law rarely speaks clearly. Nor is it effective in areas in which one nation is required to impair its vital interests. In other areas, such as setting standards for weights and measures, setting international standards for telecommunications, regulating international aviation, and other matters dealing with health and safety, international treaties and international law have proven to be effective.

International Organizations. Regional and international organizations are also important participants in the legal environment of international business. These organizations provide a forum for discussing issues of trade regulation and governmental relationships with international business. Three international organizations of specific importance to international business are the United Nations, the General Agreement of Tariffs and Trade (GATT), and the European Economic Community (EEC). The structure and general functions of the United Nations are discussed in this chapter's Organizational Profile box. United Nations activities in international law are discussed below. Ralph Bunche, one of the principal architects of the U.N., is the subject of the Personal Profile in this chapter.

The United Nations and International Law

Of particular interest to international business is the **U.N. Convention on Contracts for the International Sale of Goods**, to which the U.S. Senate gave its advice and consent in 1987. The Convention is a type of international Uniform Commercial Code; in fact, the UCC was used as a model. The Convention applies to sales transactions between two parties in different countries if each country has ratified the Convention. It does not apply to the sale of goods to consumers. Although the two parties to the transaction can agree that the Convention will not apply to the transaction, if they do not reach such an agreement the Convention is applicable. The Convention deals with issues of contract formation as well as the obligations and remedies available to the parties to the transaction.

The Convention provides choice-of-forum or choice-of-law clauses if parties cannot agree; because the unfamiliar rules of a foreign jurisdiction do

U.N. Convention on Contracts for the International Sale of Goods International commercial code that applies to sales transactions between two businesses in different member nations

The United Nations is a multinational organization that was established to replace the defunct League of Nations. Its goals and organization were decided over the course of four years of meetings and discussions and its charter signed by 50 nations in San Francisco on June 26, 1945. The U.N. Charter permits the organization to change and grow according to the needs of the times. All member nations are regarded as having sovereign equality.

The primary goal of the U.N. is achieving world peace and security through cooperation and international law. Other goals include human rights for all people, social progress, and a better quality of life for citizens of every country. Member nations are required to pursue these goals and objectives.

The huge tasks that the U.N. established for itself could not be undertaken—let alone accomplished—without some

sort of system. The U.N. system—sometimes referred to as a "family" of organizations—is comprised of six main organs (see **Figure 21-4**). The first three organs described below are empowered to establish subsidiary organs to help them achieve their mandates.

- **The General Assembly** *Charged with discussing and making recommendations about any topic that falls within the scope of the U.N. Charter, approving the U.N. budget, and determining at least part of the composition of the other main organs, including the Security Council. All member nations have an equal vote in the General Assembly.*
- **The Security Council** *Responsible for insuring international peace and security, especially in times of crisis. The Security Council is comprised of 15 members.*

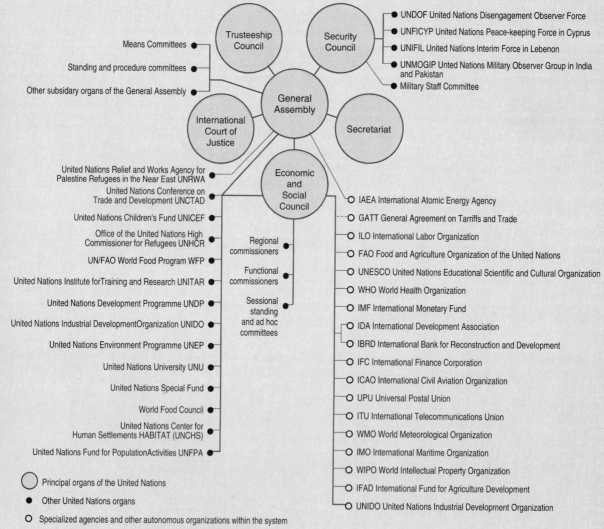

The United Nations System *Source:* Basic Facts about the United Nations *(New York: United Nations, 1987).*

FIGURE 21-4

Five members—China, France, the United Kingdom, the United States, and the Soviet Union, whose seat has now been taken by the independent Russian republic—are permanent. The other ten members are elected by the General Assembly for two-year terms. All member nations of the U.N. are bound by the decisions made by the Security Council.

- The Economic and Social Council *Responsible for U.N. work in the areas of economics, human rights, and social matters. It is comprised of 54 members elected by the General Assembly for three-year terms. There are no permanent members.*

- The Trusteeship Council *Responsible for operating the U.N. trusteeship system and is comprised of the five permanent members of the Security Council. The United States has sole responsibility for administration.*

- The International Court of Justice (ICJ) *The judicial arm of the U.N. It consists of 15 judges elected by the General Assembly and the Security Council. The court can hear only disputes between nations—for example, territorial disputes. Cases cannot be brought by or against individuals, corporations, or other entities. However, a nation can bring a case on behalf of an individual. The court can also be asked to issue advisory opinions or appoint an umpire or arbitrator. Most countries still decline to acknowledge the compulsory jurisdiction of the ICJ. Even when a decision is rendered in a case (and not all cases lead to decisions), disputing parties can disregard that decision, as did Iran in the case of U.S. diplomatic hostages in 1979-81. In the realm of international law, political considerations will outweigh judicial considerations.*

- The Secretariat *Responsible for administration. The Secretary-General is appointed by the General Assembly upon the recommendation of the Security Council and serves as the chief executive officer of the U.N. for a set term of years.*

Among the subsidiary organs established by the General Assembly, the Security Council, and the Economic and Social Council are the United Nations Children's Fund (UNICEF), the International Atomic Energy Commission (IAEA), The International Labor Organization (ILO), The United Nations Educational, Scientific, and Cultural Organization (UNESCO), and the World Health Organization (WHO). (Figure 21-4 illustrates the major subsidiary agencies, some of which function more autonomously than others.)

One of the most difficult issues facing the United Nations remains that of human rights. The General Assembly passed a resolution known as the Universal Declaration of Human Rights in 1948. Since then, the U.N. has been working toward meeting the main concept of this resolution—equality and dignity for citizens of all nations regardless of "race, sex, language, religion, political or other opinion, national origin, property, birth or other status." Two covenants reinforce this concept: the International Covenant on Civil and Political Rights *and the* International Covenant on Economic, Social, and Cultural Rights. *Violations are considered annually in public sessions. Ongoing investigations include alleged violations in Chile, Afghanistan, Bolivia, El Salvador, Equatorial Guinea, Guatemala, Iran, Poland, and South Africa. In addition, the rights of women have recently come under much closer scrutiny.*

At public sittings on March 18, 19, and 20, 1980, the International Court of Justice, meeting at its headquarters at the Hague in the Netherlands, hears oral arguments on the question of its jurisdiction in the case of *United States of America v. Iran.* As Agent of the United States, Robert B. Owen presents the argument of the U.S. concerning its diplomatic and consular staff in Teheran, Iran.

not apply, it can lend certainty to the business transaction. In addition, it could reduce the necessity of proving the foreign law in a domestic court if a dispute should arise.

General Agreement on Tariffs and Trade

General Agreement on Tariffs and Trade (GATT) International agreement that provides a framework for multilateral tariff-reduction negotiations

Another major international institution that affects international business is the **General Agreement on Tariffs and Trade (GATT).** GATT was set up in 1947 as a temporary arrangement pending the formation of an International Trade Organization. However, it has remained as an important instrument for the liberalization of international trade policies. The purpose of GATT is to reduce or eliminate trade barriers, such as tariffs, quantity restrictions, and nontariff barriers to trade. The process is one of multilateral tariff-reduction negotiations.

An important point to bear in mind is that although GATT is a formal international agreement, its basic purpose is to provide a framework within which nations can defend themselves against pressure applied by their own special-interest groups. For example, one of the biggest problems in the international trade system is the tendency of governments to support domestic exporters with various types of assistance; in turn, countries targeted by subsidized foreign industries often react to protect their own domestic industries against "unfair competition." Practices in both situations are often fostered by internal industry pressure. GATT encourages governments to protect domestic industries within guidelines established by international agreement—for example, by providing remedies for such practices as dumping. GATT, therefore, functions as part of each nation's *domestic* legal system.

Finally, several other key institutions work to encourage cooperation and foster development in international finance and foreign exchange. Four of the most important are described in Table 21-2.

Influential not only in shaping international business law but also in establishing and maintaining peaceful relations among many countries, the United Nations met for the first time in London in 1946 and is now headquartered in New York. Among its first architects was the American Ralph J. Bunche, who is remembered for many notable accomplishments—including being the first black person to receive the Nobel Prize for Peace.

Born in 1904 to a working-class family in Detroit, Bunche was raised by his grandmother. After working his way through college while excelling in a number of sports and academic activities, he graduated in 1927, the only black in his class. During the next few years he completed both his MA and his PhD at Harvard (he was the first black person to receive a Doctor of Philosophy at Harvard) and taught at Howard University, where he organized and chaired its first political science department. His efforts to end segregation,

his academic training in government and international relations, and such personal qualities as integrity, pragmatism, and perseverance made him ideally suited for the government appointments that soon began to come his way.

The early 1940s saw Bunche involved in the work of the Office of Strategic Services, where he headed the Africa Section. In 1944, he joined the State Department, where colonial matters became an enduring commitment. The following year, he was appointed to the preparatory committee of the United Nations. At its first session in 1946, he was a member of the U.S. delegation, and he remained an officer of the U.N. in one capacity or another until he retired shortly before his death in 1971. He was in fact the highest ranking American in the U.N. Secretariat, serving as principal adviser to three successive secretaries-general in the 1950s and 1960s.

Named Acting U.N. Mediator in the first Arab-Israeli

war following the assassination of his predecessor, Bunche achieved the United Nations's first success in its evolving role as international peacekeeper by negotiating an armistice between Israel and Egypt, Jordan, Syria, and Lebanon. It was this achievement that won him the Nobel Peace Prize in 1950; it was followed by his direction of U.N. peacekeeping efforts in the Middle East, the Congo, Cyprus, Yemen, and Pakistan.

Bunche remained an ardent opponent of segregation and racism at home, having suffered their effects in his early career. In 1953, he turned down the post of Assistant Secretary of State because he refused to return to the "Jim Crow" conditions of life in the nation's capital, and he was among the thousands who participated in the 1965 civil rights march in Selma, Alabama. His spectacular, if unsung, achievements in civil rights at home and human rights abroad represent a distinguished legacy. Modesty and realism combine in Bunche's perspective statement on the United Nations: "It is obvious that the problems of thousands of years could not be solved in a decade or two. . . . International organizations are only the beginning of a monumental task; their main work lay ahead."

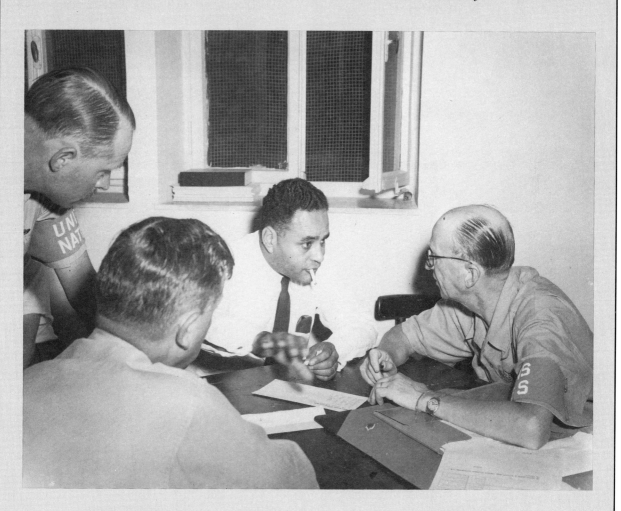

Haifa, Palestine, 1948: Ralph Bunche (center), Acting U.N. Mediator for Palestine confers with Gen. A. Lundgren, the U.N.'s Chief Military Observer. It was a member of the U.N. Secretarial staff that Bunche first became involved in the Palestinian conflict that erupted in 1947. Bunche was undoubtedly at the right place at the right time but he was also undoubtedly the right mediator. There was no precedent for his approach to working out an armistice between Israel and the neighboring Arab states of Egypt, Jordan, Syria, and Lebanon, and one of Bunche's procedural innovations turned out to be crucial: Rather than attempting to negotiate with the Arab allies as a unified group—an approach that has long proved to be an obstacle to Middle East mediation efforts—Bunche determined instead to pursue his efforts in one-on-one negotiations. The armistice that Bunche worked out was the U.N.'s first successful effort at military containment.

International Monetary Fund (IMF)	Chief regulatory agency for international finance and foreign exchange; since the early 1970s, a central clearing bank for noncommunist countries.*
International Bank for Reconstruction and Development (IBRD)	With its affiliate the International Finance Corporation referred to as the "World Bank"; extends financing to over 150 member-nations, with almost $20 billion in development loans currently approved.
International Finance Corporation (IFC)	Affiliated with the IBRD; provides risk capital rather than fixed-interest loans and invests in domestic industries backed by government guarantees.
International Development Association (IDA)	Also affiliated with the IBRD; provides loans at soft terms to least-developed nations for such basic projects as irrigation and road construction.

Since 1969, the IMF has extended loans through special drawing rights (SDRs), which supplement dollar and gold reserves. An SDR is actually an owned reserve asset created by the IMF to be loaned to member-nations according to a formula that takes into account such factors as the applicant's share of gross world product. Rates are adjusted to reflect fluctuations in the foreign-exchange market and take into account governments' efforts to influence exchange rates through their own monetary policies. In addition to short-term loans to help countries with balance-of-payment difficulties, the IMF has issued approximately $120 billion in SDR loans.

Sources: *Adapted from Theodore A. Couloumbis and James A. Wolfe,* Introduction to International Relations: Power and Justice, *4th ed. (Englewood Cliffs, NJ: Prentice Hall, 1990); Warren J. Keegan,* Global Marketing Management *4th ed. (Englewood Cliffs, NJ: Prentice Hall, 1989).*

The European Economic Community

The *European Economic Community (EEC)* provides regional governance for member nations. The EEC has a law-making body as well as its own court. Its antitrust rules and regulations (specifically Article 85 and Article 86 of the Treaty of Rome) have the most impact on international business entities. Some of the other areas of EEC concern include the freedom of movement of goods and workers between member states.

An example of the conflict that can arise between EEC regulation and a member state's laws is illustrated in the following case.

REGINA v. HM TREASURY, EX PARTE DAILY MAIL AND GENERAL TRUST PLC
Queens Bench Division (Crown Office List), Feb. 6, 1987

The following case concerns the attempt of a British company to transfer its residence from the United Kingdom to Holland because of more favorable tax regulations. The case raised the issue of whether England could hinder the company from leaving for this reason or whether such actions were prevented by a Treaty of the European Economic Community (EEC), which sought to make it easier for companies to establish themselves in any member country.

Mr. Justice Macpherson:
A company's freedom to transfer its residence, without Treasury consent, from the UK to another EEC country with less burdensome tax laws, is a matter which is open to doubt and which should be clarified by the European Court before it can finally be decided by the English court.

Mr. Justice Macpherson so held when referring a question to the European Court of Justice in an application by an investment company, Daily Mail and General

---

Trust plc, for judicial review of the Treasury's refusal to acknowledge that it could cease to reside in the UK without Treasury consent.

Article 52 of the Treaty of the European Economic Community (EEC) provides: "restrictions on the freedom of establishment of nationals of a member state in the territory of another . . . shall be abolished . . . 'Freedom of establishment shall include the right to . . . set up . . . companies. . . .' "

Section 2(1) of the European Communities Act 1972: "All . . . rights . . . under the Treaties . . . are without further enactment to be given legal effect . . . in the United Kingdom. . . ."

Section 482(1) of the Income and Corporation Taxes Act 1970: "all transactions of the following classes shall be unlawful unless carried out with the consent of the Treasury . . . : (a) for a body corporate resident in the United Kingdom to cease to be so resident."

His Lordship said that on March 1, 1984 the company submitted to the Treasury an application to cease to be resident in the UK. . . . The primary reasons were fiscal. It wished to escape from some of the more swingeing taxation provisions which applied to it when resident in the UK and from certain burdensome provisions concerning the stock market price of its shares.
. . .

The arguments of Mr. Vaughan for the company were:

He said that the combined forces of the Treasury and Inland Revenue were acting contrary to the letter and spirit of articles 52 and 58, and that the company was wrongly being prevented from establishing itself in Holland; . . . just as restrictions on emigration of nationals were barred, so were restrictions on corporations.

The freedom to leave, both for nationals and for companies or firms was, said Mr. Vaughan, a necessary component or corollary of the right to establish in another state.

Mr. Buxton for the Treasury stressed the continuing English nature of the company. He said that its ambition to avoid UK tax was solely the concern of English domestic law. . . .

The court's inclination was to doubt that section 482 should be allowed to prevent or fetter the voluntary movement of residence of a corporation which wished to take advantage of a better fiscal climate in another EEC state.

The aim was not to evade tax altogether, nor to remove to a foreign tax shelter, but to exchange one fiscal system for another. The object of the treaty was the removal of barriers and the creation of an economic community without protective barriers of any kind for persons or corporations, or for trade generally—the creation, in other words, of a true common market.

It was appropriate that the European Court should be asked to consider the matter. . . .

Case Questions

1. What policies are fostered by the court's decision?

2. What is the likely impact of the EEC treaty and the court's decision upon the business-tax rates among EEC member nations?

3. Should a country be able to enact legislation preventing a company from establishing residence in another country? What competing interests are at stake?

Today, the EC is properly known as the *European Community* (EC), an organization still grounded in the terms of the 1958 treaty, which eliminated numerous trade barriers across European borders and laid the groundwork for a common European market. On December 31, 1992, almost all such barriers were removed, and the EC is now on its way to becoming—at least in theory—"One Europe."[4] Some of the articles of the Treaty of Rome dealing with the establishment of a European "Common Market" are cited in Table 21-3.

Codes of Conduct

Several other international bodies seek to control the activities of international business entities through the use of "codes of conduct." It could be argued that these codes of conduct have no binding effect on the activities of international business entities. However, the negotiation process itself does lead to increased sensitivity to the issues involved on the part of all negotiating parties.

---

[4] The twelve member nations of the EC are Belgium, Denmark, France, Germany, Greece, Ireland, Italy, Luxembourg, the Netherlands, Portugal, Spain, and the United Kingdom.

TABLE 21-3	*Selected Articles of "Common Market" Legislation*

Article 2 "By establishing a common market and progressively approximating the economic policies of member states, to promote throughout the Community a harmonious development of economic activities."

Article 3(c) "The abolition, as between member states, of obstacles to freedom of movement for persons, services, and capital."

Article 3(b) "The approximation of the laws of member states to the extent required for the proper functioning of the common market."

Article 85 "Agreements and practices of any kind between undertakings or associations of undertakings infringe competition rules if they restrict competition within the common market and affect interstate trade."

Article 86 Prohibits abuse (imposing trading conditions or limiting production to the detriment of consumers) by firms that are market leaders.

Article 90 Development of trade must be in the interests of the community.

The Tripartite Declaration. The *Tripartite Declaration of Principles Concerning Multi-National Enterprises and Social Policies* was adopted by the International Labor Organization. This declaration deals with issues of labor relations, including working conditions, training, and employment. It also deals with issues of social policy. The United Nations General Assembly passed a resolution adopting the *Restrictive Business Practices Code.* The purpose of the code is to protect competition as well as protect social welfare and consumer interests. The code covers price fixing, refusals to deal, mergers, and trademark protection.

U.N. Conference on Trade and Development. The *United Nations Conference on Trade and Development* is working on an international code of conduct for the transfer of technology. One purpose of this code is to set up standards for technology transfer with respect to the interests of developing nations.

The OECD. The Organization of Economic Cooperation and Development has issued *Guidelines for International Investment and Multinational Enterprises.* The member governments of the OECD adopted guidelines regarding disclosure of information by international business entities, competition, employment and industrial relationships, financing, and taxation. These guidelines set standards for international business entities that include refraining from restrictive business activities, respecting the rights of employees to be represented by trade unions, and providing information regarding a firm's activities and policies.

GUIDELINES FOR MULTINATIONAL CORPORATIONS. Finally, the United Nations Commission on Transnational Corporations is drafting a code of conduct. This is one of the broadest and most comprehensive codes of conduct dealing with the activities of multinational corporations. The code contains provisions regarding the disclosure of information, respect for human rights, and injunctions against corrupt practices and sets guidelines for ownership and control, taxation, consumer protection, environmental protection, and transfer of technology.

The OECD Guidelines, the Tripartite Declaration, and the proposed United Nations Code of Conduct on Transnational Corporations all deal directly with the activities of multinational corporations. Three other agreements—the *United Nations Universal Declaration of Human Rights* (1948), the *European Convention on Human Rights* (1950), and the *Helsinki Final Act*

(1975)—focus primarily on human rights and environmental protection but, in so doing, touch upon several areas of international business activity.[5]

■ Concept Check 21-6 International Forums and Agreements

- Explain international law as a *law of consent* and the importance of *codes of conduct* in its enforcement.
- Describe the basic provisions and functions of the *General Agreement on Tariffs and Trade*.

■ TRADE RESTRICTIONS AND ANTITRUST ISSUES

Import Regulation

A continuing conflict between governments and international businesses is the issue of open markets or free trade. As we saw earlier, the purpose of GATT is to eliminate trade barriers. Import **tariffs**—taxes placed on imported products—and import **quotas**—limits on the quantity of imported products—are the most common types of restrictions. Other types of restrictions known as **nontariff barriers,** may exist as well. They include standards for safety or health that have the impact of restricting imports.

Some arguments in favor of such restrictions include the need to protect a country's (1) national security, (2) infant industries, and (3) domestic work force. These restrictions may also be used to retaliate against another country's restrictions.

tariff *Import regulation* in the form of a tax placed on imported products

quota *Import regulation* in the form of a limit on the quantity of imported products

nontariff barrier *Import regulation* in the form of a restriction imposed on imports according to such criteria as health or safety standards

IMPORT PRACTICES. As the value of the dollar fluctuates with respect to foreign currencies, the cost of foreign products imported into the United States changes. In some cases, however, the cost of imports is still much less than can be explained by merely the exchange rate. In some cases, for example, foreign manufacturers price their U.S. products below cost in order to capture a large market share; as we have seen, this practice is known as "dumping." In many cases, U.S. manufacturers are unable to compete against such low-priced imports.

The danger exists that once a foreign manufacturer has captured a sufficiently large market share, it will be able to raise the price of these products to an extremely high level, thereby injuring U.S. consumers. (*Matsushita Electric Industrial Co. v. Zenith Radio Corporation* [1986], excerpted in Chapter 16, is a case in which such a plan was alleged.) Although some relief from such activity can be found in antitrust laws, it is an extremely long and expensive process. Title VII of the United States Tariff Act provides some relief for U.S. manufacturers from this type of activity.

THE TARIFF ACT. The **United States Tariff Act** of 1930, as amended, provides for the imposition of "countervailing duties" or "antidumping duties" to counteract the effect of foreign goods being sold below "fair value." A U.S. manufacturer seeking relief must file a complaint both with the U.S. Department of

United States Tariff Act 1930 federal law, as amended, that provides for the imposition of *countervailing* or *antidumping duties* to counteract the effect of foreign goods being sold below fair value

---

[5] See Rogene A. Buchholz, *Business Environment and Public Policy: Implications for Management and Strategy*, 4th ed. (Englewood Cliffs, NJ: Prentice Hall, 1991), pp. 574-80.

Commerce's International Trade Administration and the International Trade Commission. The Department of Commerce makes a determination as to whether the goods were sold below "fair value." This determination may mean that the goods are being sold in the United States below the cost of production or below the price charged in the home market. The International Trade Commission then makes a determination as to whether this pricing has resulted in material injury to the U. S. industry involved. If only one or two U.S. manufacturers are being injured by these import practices, relief will not be given. Industrywide injury must be found.

If the Department of Commerce and the International Trade Commission determine that goods are being sold at an unfairly low price and that industry injury has occurred as a result of foreign government subsidies, they can impose **countervailing duties.** These duties are designed to counteract foreign government subsidies. Because this is an issue between two governments that may involve highly sensitive foreign-policy questions, both the procedure and the determination are taken out of the hands of the complaining U.S. manufacturer. If the unfairly low price is not a result of government subsidies, then relief takes the form of **antidumping duties.** A determination not to impose antidumping duties can be appealed by the complaining party.

The following case illustrates the method used by the International Trade Administration to calculate the fair value of products being sold in the United States.

countervailing duty Duty on imported goods being sold at unfairly low prices as a result of foreign-government subsidies

antidumping duty Duty on imported goods being sold at unfairly low prices for reasons other than foreign-government subsidies

---

SMITH-CORONA GROUP v. UNITED STATES
U.S. Court of Appeals, Fifth Circuit, 713 F.2d 1568 (5th Cir. 1983)

Smith-Corona was the last remaining manufacturer of portable typewriters in the United States. The other major producers of typewriters, which are Brother Industries, Ltd., Brother Corp., Silver Seiko, Ltd., and Silver Reed America, Inc., are all based in Japan. The following case involves a dispute between these companies under the Antidumping Act, which seeks to prevent foreign companies from driving domestic companies out of business by "dumping" products in foreign markets.

Edward S. Smith, Circuit Judge.

This appeal presents a challenge to various price adjustments granted to the foreign manufacturers and importers of the subject merchandise by the U.S. International Trade Administration (ITA) in determining antidumping duties under 19 U.S.C. §§ 1673 *et seq.* (Supp. V. 1981). . . .

The Antidumping Act provides that if foreign merchandise is sold or is likely to be sold in the United States at less than its *fair value* to the material injury of a United States industry, then an additional antidumping duty shall be imposed. The amount of the duty shall equal the amount by which the *foreign market value* exceeds the United States price for the merchandise.

. . .

United States price, as defined in section 1677a, is computed by one of two methods: purchase price or exporter's sales price. . . .

Where the importer is an unrelated independent party, purchase price is used. Purchase price is the actual or agreed-to price between the foreign producer and the independent importer, prior to the time of importation. Where the importer is related, an arm's length transaction does not occur until the goods are resold to a retailer or to the public. In that case, "exporter's sale price" is used. Exporter's sales price is the price at which the goods are eventually transferred in an arm's length transaction, whether from the importer to an independent retailer or directly to the public. . . .

On the other side of the scale, foreign market value is also computed on the basis of arm's length transactions by one of three methods: (1) home market sales; (2) third country sales; or (3) contructed value. The home market sales method is preferred. . . .

Thus, the ITA, using either purchase price or exporter's sales price, computes and adjusts the United States price of the merchandise. Additionally, the ITA, on the basis of either home market sales, or third country sales, or constructed value, computes and adjusts the foreign market value of the merchandise. These values, which *should* be on an equivalent basis after adjustment, are then compared and the amount by which foreign market value exceeds United States price is imposed as an additional antidumping duty. . . .

Our review of the statute reveals tremendous deference to the expertise of the Secretary of Commerce in administering the antidumping law. We find no specific limitation in the statute, nor do we find any evidence of

record, that would compel reversal of the ITA's determinations in this proceeding. . . . Affirmed.

Case Questions

1. From the standpoint of domestic companies, what are the pros and cons of the Antidumping Act?

2. From the standpoint of consumers, what are the pros and cons of the Antidumping Act?

Export Controls

EXPORT LICENSES. The United States government has a long history of controlling what goods are exported from the United States: In fact, it is not too much of an exaggeration to say that nothing can be sent out of the United States without government permission. In reality, "permission" takes the form of an **export license.** There are two types of export licenses. The first is called a *general license.* The exporter essentially issues the license to himself. Although the exporter must use the proper license designation for the type of goods to be exported and the country of destination, there is no special procedure for doing this. The second type of license, known as a *validated license,* is issued by the government according to a special procedure.

export license Permission by the U.S. government to export goods

THE EXPORT ADMINISTRATION ACT. Under the **Export Administration Act** of 1979, as amended in 1984, the president has the power to control the export of goods and commodities for one of the following four reasons: (1) national security, (2) foreign policy, (3) commodities in short supply, and (4) nuclear nonproliferation.

Under this authority, several administrative agencies restrict the export of certain commodities through the use of validated licenses. Validated licenses are issued based on two criteria: (1) the type of product and (2) the ultimate destination of the product. Certain types of products cannot be exported because of their high level of technology or their strategic or military purpose. The most extensive list of controlled or restricted commodities is the Commodities Control List, which is maintained by the Department of Commerce's Office of Export Administration. The list was developed by the COCOM (Coordinating Committee) countries, which include the United States, and other NATO countries except for Iceland, plus Japan, Australia, and New Zealand.

Although there are some countries for which there are few export restrictions, there are other countries to which virtually nothing can be exported. Countries to which goods are exported are divided into seven categories. The country with the least restrictions is Canada, to which almost anything can be exported. The most restricted countries include Cuba, Korea, Vietnam, and Kampuchea (formerly Cambodia).

"End-User's Certification." One controversial aspect of these export controls is known as **"end-user's certification":** In applying for a validated license, the exporter must "certify" both the ultimate end-user of the product and the

Export Administration Act 1979 federal law, amended in 1984, giving the president the power to control the export of goods and commodities for reasons of national security, foreign policy, commodities in short domestic supply, and nuclear nonproliferation.

end-user's certification Requirement in U.S. government *export licensing* that exporters designate both the end user of the product and the product's destination country

country of destination. For example, if an exporter sells a product to a customer in Canada and the Canadian customer reexports the product to an unauthorized end-user or destination, the U.S. exporter can be charged with violating the Export Administration Act: Although the U.S. exporter may have no further control over the product, the exporter is still responsible for the ultimate destination of the product. Criminal and civil penalties may apply to any violation. Although enforcement of this provision may seem difficult, it is not impossible. A violation may be reported by a disgruntled employee, a competitor, or even by the exporter.

International Antitrust Issues

As we saw earlier, one of the criticisms of multinational corporations is their perceived ability to control markets: Because of size and structure, large multinational corporations are often in a position to deal with their subsidiaries in ways that could result in competitive advantage. For example, a multinational corporation could use below-market pricing in transferring goods between the parent and the subsidiary. It could also allocate markets among subsidiaries.

Other types of international business may also be able to engage in practices that restrain trade. For example, a company may use licenses to restrict exports or hinder a certain country from gaining full technological benefits from a license. Some firms can enter joint ventures or acquire companies that may give them dominant market positions. Such restrictive practices or restraints of trade at the international level raise problems of jurisdiction and the enforcement of antitrust laws against activities or entities outside a country's territory.

As we saw in Chapter 16, the United States has an extensive system of antitrust laws. These laws apply to a company's activities both within the United States and in foreign countries. They can apply to a firm's foreign activities even if a foreign country's laws do not prohibit the conduct in question.

"THE RULE OF REASON." In 1979, the United States Department of Justice issued guidelines for antitrust enforcement for international business activities. Under these guidelines, it indicated that potential violations would be governed by the "rule of reason": The Department of Justice will look at particular conduct or activity in light of the entire business transaction, including any business justification or the availability of any less-restrictive alternatives. Furthermore, it will look to see what impact the conduct has in the United States.

The purpose of this type of enforcement is to protect U.S. consumers and other U.S. exporters. If the conduct of a company in the foreign country has an adverse impact on foreign firms that send goods into the United States, U.S. consumers, who benefit from the low cost of imported goods, could be injured. Similarly, if the actions of one U.S. exporter make it difficult or impossible for another U.S. exporter to enter the market, the other exporters may be injured.

The application of U.S. antitrust laws to activities that take place in foreign countries is controversial. The application of U.S. law to activities that take place outside of the United States is known as **extraterritoriality**: In enforcing antitrust laws, the United States bases jurisdiction on the citizenship of the firm, as well as on the adverse impact that takes place within U.S. borders.

extraterritoriality Application of U.S. law to activities that take place outside the U.S.

■ Concept Check 21-7 Trade Restrictions and Antitrust Issues

- Distinguish between *tariffs* and *nontariff barriers* and cite some specific examples of the latter.
- What are the principal provisions of the *United States Tariff Act* of 1930?
- What are the principal provisions of the *Export Administration Act* of 1979?
- Explain the principle of *end-user's certification*.
- Explain the *rule of reason* guideline for international antitrust enforcement.

YOU DECIDE: ANSWER/DISCUSSION
Dumping

In Zenith v. Matsushita, *the Supreme Court found for the defendants, ruling that predatory pricing did not occur and that Zenith could not recover damages resulting from its loss of market share. The majority opinion determined that there was insufficient evidence of conspiracy and that the Japanese firms had not gained enough market share to justify the claim of predatory pricing. In this decision, the Court upheld the opinion of the district court that had first rendered judgment.*

Consider, however, the finding of the Court of Appeals, which had earlier reversed the district court and which was subsequently overruled by the Supreme Court. The Court of Appeals found both direct and circumstantial evidence that some kind of conspiracy did exist and so found for the plaintiffs. In addition, the dissenting opinion of the Supreme Court argued that the Japanese firms clearly favored growth in market share over short-term profit, supporting Zenith's claim that they were engaged in dumping.

As national markets the world over merge into a single global economy, the definition of fair competition will continue to be challenged. American firms have undoubtedly suffered losses and setbacks in the 1980s and 1990s, but whether these result from their own management decisions or reflect the unfair actions of competitors is a question that will be considered in the courts—and in the marketplace—for years to come.

SUMMARY

- *International trade* is an important part of the U.S. economy. As our economy becomes more international, so do U.S. businesses. Most U.S. businesses will find themselves involved in the international environment at some point in their future, and they must be aware of the legal environment of international business.

- There are many forms that an international business can take. International business can be simply an *import/export operation*, it can hire *a sales representative* or *sales agent* to sell products in the foreign country, or a *licensing* arrangement may be used. These methods do not call for a significant investment. However, as the international business market share increases, it may be more effective to invest directly in the host country. This investment may take the form of setting up a *branch* or *subsidiary* to manufacture the product or provide the services in the host country. Some international business takes the form of a *joint venture*.

- *Multinational corporations* have manufacturing or service facilities in more than one host country. Because of their large size and unique character, special problems arise. These problems include the ability of the multinational corporation to gain a significant share of the markets for labor, raw materials, and finish products. Another issue of concern is the real or perceived political power of the multinational corporation, and the final issue involved is the worldwide profit-maximizing point of view of the multinational. Host countries therefore exercise control over multinationals' activities in a variety of ways.

- One way in which the United States has sought to regulate the conduct of multinational corporations in general, and U.S. companies in particular, is the *Foreign Corrupt Practices Act* of 1977. The FCPA (1) prohibits giving anything of value to a foreign official in order to influence a discretionary decision and (2) provides for accounting procedures for all U.S. companies governed by the Securities Exchange Act of 1934. The 1988 *Omnibus Trade and Competitiveness Act* amends the FCPA's accounting and antibribery provisions, increasing the penalties for violation.

- All international businesses deal with various aspects of *contract law*. An international business must be aware of the host country's different customs and legal systems. Of special concern are issues of *payment, choice of law,* and *choice of forum*. Although disputes involving contracts can be settled in a variety of ways, *international arbitration* is becoming increasingly important.

- At the international level, organizations seek to regulate the conduct of international businesses in a variety of ways. The *U.N. Convention on Contracts for the International Sale of Goods* is a uniform code for private international law. The *General Agreement on Tariffs and Trade* is an international body that seeks to eliminate trade restrictions between trading nations. An international body at the regional level is the *European Economic Community*.

- The debate continues over the ideals of free trade and the consequences of restrictions. *Import regulations* and *export controls* are viewed by the United States as necessary for protecting our domestic economy. These restrictions, however, affect the economic realities and benefits of free trade.

- One way the United States does seek to maintain free competition at the international level is through antitrust enforcement. Thus, the United States will enforce its antitrust laws outside the United States if the impact an be felt by U.S. consumers or other U.S. exporters.

QUESTIONS AND PROBLEMS

1. The members of the International Association of Machinists (IAM) were disturbed by the high price of oil and petroleum-derived products in the United States. They believed the actions of OPEC were the cause of the high prices. Therefore, the IAM sued OPEC's member countries in December 1978, alleging that their price-setting activities violated U.S. antitrust laws. On what basis did the IAM sue? Were they successful? [*International Association of Machinists and Aerospace Workers (IAM) v. The Organization of Petroleum Exporting Countries (OPEC)*, 649 F. 2d. 1354 (1981)]

2. Dr. Will Pirkey, an otolaryngologist, signed an employment contract in which he agreed to work for two years at the King Faisal Hospital in Saudia Arabia. Before his departure, Pirkey received his employment contract which contained a clause providing that the agreements would be construed in accordance with Saudi Arabian law. Because of the assassination of King Faisal as well as other reasons, Dr. Pirkey did not go to Saudi Arabia as agreed and contests the choice-of-law provision as unconscionable. He asks that his home state's law (Colorado) govern. Did the court agree? Discuss. [*Pirkey v. Hospital Corp. of America*, 483 F. Supp. 770 (1980)]

3. U.S. Company owned a subsidiary in France which had a contract to deliver compressors for use in the Soviet pipeline. The U.S. government banned the export of goods to the Soviet Union by U.S. companies or U.S.-controlled foreign companies. U.S. Company ordered its subsidiary to stop delivery of the compressors. The French government, however, ordered delivery of the compressors. Will U.S. Company be able to fulfill its contract obligations? What justification could be used to institute these export controls? [*Dresser Industries, Inc. v. Baldridge*, 549 F. Supp. 108 (D.C. 1982)]

4. Zenith manufactured consumer electronic products and brought an action requesting that countervailing duties be imposed on similar products being exported to the United States from Japan. Zenith contended that the products benefited from a "grant paid by the Japanese government" because of an indirect tax which the Japanese government imposes when the goods are sold in Japan but is rebated when

the products are exported." What are some of the reasons which can justify the imposition of countervailing duties? Would the remittance of a tax constitute a "bounty or grant" that would justify the imposition of such duties? [*Zenith Radio Corporation v. United States*, 437 U.S. 443]

5. Pfizer, Inc., a Delaware corporation, owned several foreign subsidiaries that had the exclusive right to sell Pfizer's product throughout Europe. A German corporation brought suit against Pfizer in the United States claiming violation of U.S. antitrust laws. Do U.S. antitrust laws apply to Pfizer's activities which take place entirely outside of the United States? Can they be applied if the injury is basically to a foreign corporation? [*Eurim-Pharm Gmbh v. Pfizer, Inc.*, 593 F. Supp. 1102 (1984)]

6. Zapata entered into a contract with a German corporation to use one of Zapata's oil-drilling rigs off the coasts of Italy. The contract stated, "Any dispute arising must be treated before the London Court of Justice." A severe storm damaged the oil rig as it was being towed through the Gulf of Mexico. Zapata filed suit in federal district court. Does the U.S. court have jurisdiction to decide the dispute? What is the purpose behind a choice-of-forum clause and should it be enforced? [*M/S Bremen v. Zapata Off-Shore Co.*, 407 U.S. (1972)]

7. M.N.C. sets up a clothing manufacturing plant in the Bahamas. In order to encourage M.N.C.'s investment, the Bahamian government offered M.N.C. a tax holiday for five years. Workers can be hired for $1.50 per hour, while the average wage in the U.S. is $8.50. What are the potential problems and criticisms M.N.C. will face with this investment? What are the ways that M.N.C. can lessen the impact?

8. Mitsubishi entered into a joint venture with Chrysler to distribute automobiles in Puerto Rico. When they entered into the agreement they specified that "All disputes . . . shall be finally settled by arbitration in Japan in accordance with the rules and regulations of the Japan Commercial Arbitration Association." Mitsubishi brought an action in the United States District Court to compel arbitration when a dispute arose regarding the contract. Can such a contract clause be enforced? On what bases will a court compel arbitration on such a claim? [*Mitsubishi Motors v. Soler Chrysler-Plymouth*, 105 S.Ct. 3346 (1985)]

9. The Bensalem Appliance Co. recently opened a subsidiary in Mexico City. Not only do the owners have to learn a new language and culture, they also have to do business differently than in the United States. In order to expedite receiving parts for their appliances, Bensalem must make payments of anything from television sets to substantial sums of money to shippers, sales clerks, or anyone else involved in selling or shipping parts. Bensalem has recently read about the FCPA and is worried that its activities violate the act. Advise them.

10. Nestle Corporation sold baby formula in less-developed countries using questionable marketing techniques. It was discovered that some mothers were watering the formula to make it go further. As a result, the babies were unable to get full nutritional value from the formula. Several church organizations exerted pressure on Nestle to change its marketing practices. What mechanisms are available to influence the conduct of multinational corporations? Are international controls or international codes of conduct effective to influence the conduct of multinationals?

APPENDIX

■ THE CONSTITUTION OF THE UNITED STATES OF AMERICA

We the people of the United States, in order to form a more perfect union, establish justice, insure domestic tranquility, provide for the common defense, promote the general welfare, and secure the blessings of liberty to ourselves and our posterity, do ordain and establish this Constitution for the United States of America.

Article 1

Section 1. All legislative powers herein granted shall be vested in a Congress of the United States, which shall consist of a Senate and House of Representatives.

Section 2. 1. The House of Representatives shall be composed of members chosen every second year by the people of the several States, and the electors in each State shall have the qualifications requisite for electors of the most numerous branch of the State legislature.

2. No person shall be a representative who shall not have attained to the age of twenty-five years, and been seven years a citizen of the United States, and who shall not, when elected, be an inhabitant of that State in which he shall be chosen.

3. Representatives and direct taxes[1] shall be apportioned among the several States which may be included within this Union, according to their respective numbers, which shall be determined by adding to the whole number of free persons, including those bound to service for a term of years, and excluding Indians not taxed, three

fifths of all other persons.[2] The actual enumeration shall be made within three years after the first meeting of the Congress of the United States, and within every subsequent term of ten years, in such manner as they shall by law direct. The number of representatives shall not exceed one for every thirty thousand, but each State shall have at least one representative; and until such enumeration shall be made, the State of New Hampshire shall be entitled to choose three, Massachusetts eight, Rhode Island and Providence Plantations one, Connecticut five, New York six, New Jersey four, Pennsylvania eight, Delaware one, Maryland six, Virginia ten, North Carolina five, South Carolina five, and Georgia three.

4. When vacancies happen in the representation from any State, the executive authority thereof shall issue writs of election to fill such vacancies.

5. The House of Representatives shall choose their speaker and other officers; and shall have the sole power of impeachment.

Section 3. 1. The Senate of the United States shall be composed of two senators from each State, chosen by the legislature thereof,[3] for six years; and each senator shall have one vote.

2. Immediately after they shall be assembled in consequence of the first election, they shall be divided as equally as may be into three classes. The seats of the senators of the first class shall be vacated at the expiration of the second year, of the second class at the expiration of the fourth year, and of the third class at the expiration of the sixth year, so that one third may be chosen every second year; and if vacancies happen by resignation, or otherwise, during the recess of the legislature of any

---

[1] See the Sixteenth Amendment.

[2] See the Fourteenth Amendment.
[3] See the Seventeenth Amendment.

State, the executive thereof may make temporary appointments until the next meeting of the legislature, which shall then fill such vacancies.[4]

3. No person shall be a senator who shall not have attained to the age of thirty years, and been nine years a citizen of the United States, and who shall not, when elected, be an inhabitant of that State for which he shall be chosen.

4. The Vice President of the United States shall be President of the Senate, but shall have no vote, unless they be equally divided.

5. The Senate shall choose their other officers, and also a president pro tempore, in the absence of the Vice President, or when he shall exercise the office of the President of the United States.

6. The Senate shall have the sole power to try all impeachments. When sitting for that purpose, they shall be on oath or affirmation. When the President of the United States is tried, the chief justice shall preside: and no person shall be convicted without the concurrence of two thirds of the members present.

7. Judgment in cases of impeachment shall not extend further than to removal from office, and disqualification to hold and enjoy any office of honor, trust or profit under the United States: but the party convicted shall nevertheless be liable and subject to indictment, trial, judgment and punishment, according to law.

Section 4. 1. The times, places, and manner of holding elections for senators and representatives, shall be prescribed in each State by the legislature thereof; but the Congress may at any time by law make or alter such regulations, except as to the places of choosing senators.

2. The Congress shall assemble at least once in every year, and such meetings shall be on the First Monday in December, unless they shall by law appoint a different day.

Section 5. 1. Each House shall be the judge of the elections, returns and qualifications of its own members, and a majority of each shall constitute a quorum to do business; but a smaller number may adjourn from day to day, and may be authorized to compel the attendance of absent members, in such manner, and under such penalties as each House may provide.

2. Each House may determine the rules of its proceedings, punish its members for disorderly behavior, and, with the concurrence of two thirds, expel a member.

3. Each House shall keep a journal of its proceedings, and from time to time publish the same, excepting such parts as may in their judgment require secrecy; and the yeas and nays of the members of either House on any question shall, at the desire of one fifth of those present, be entered on the journal.

4. Neither House, during the session of Congress, shall, without the consent of the other, adjourn for more than three days, nor to any other place than that in which the two Houses shall be sitting.

---

[4] See the Seventeenth Amendment.

Section 6. 1. The senators and representatives shall receive a compensation for their services, to be ascertained by law, and paid out of the Treasury of the United States. They shall in all cases, except treason, felony, and breach of the peace, be privileged from arrest during their attendance at the session of their respective Houses, and in going to and returning from the same; and for any speech or debate in either House, they shall not be questioned in any other place.

2. No senator or representative shall, during the time for which he was elected, be appointed to any civil office under the authority of the United States, which shall have been created, or the emoluments whereof shall have been increased, during such time; and no person holding any office under the United States shall be a member of either House during his continuance in office.

Section 7. 1. All bills for raising revenue shall originate in the House of Representatives; but the Senate may propose or concur with amendments as on other bills.

2. Every bill which shall have passed the House of Representatives and the Senate, shall, before it become a law, be presented to the President of the United States; If he approves he shall sign it, but if not he shall return it, with his objections, to that House in which it shall have originated, who shall enter the objections at large on their journal, and proceed to reconsider it. If after such reconsideration two thirds of that House shall agree to pass the bill, it shall be sent, together with the objections, to the other House, by which it shall likewise be reconsidered, and if approved by two thirds of that House, it shall become a law. But in all such cases the votes of both Houses shall be determined by yeas and nays, and the names of the persons voting for and against the bill shall be entered on the journal of each House respectively. If any bill shall not be returned by the President within ten days (Sundays excepted) after it shall have been presented to him, the same shall be a law, in like manner as if he had signed it, unless the Congress by their adjournment prevent its return, in which case it shall not be a law.

3. Every order, resolution, or vote to which the concurrence of the Senate and the House of Representatives may be necessary (except on a question of adjournment) shall be presented to the President of the United States; and before the same shall take effect, shall be approved by him, or being disapproved by him, shall be repassed by two thirds of the Senate and House of Representatives, according to the rules and limitations prescribed in the case of a bill.

Section 8. The Congress shall have the power

1. To lay and collect taxes, duties, imposts, and excises, to pay the debts and provide for the common defense and general welfare of the United States; but all duties, imposts, and excises shall be uniform throughout the United States;

2. To borrow money on the credit of the United States;

3. To regulate commerce with foreign nations, and among the several States, and with the Indian tribes;

4. To establish a uniform rule of naturalization, and uniform laws on the subject of bankruptcies throughout the United States;

5. To coin money, regulate the value thereof, and of foreign coin, and fix the standard of weights and measures;

6. To provide for the punishment of counterfeiting the securities and current coin of the United States;

7. To establish post offices and post roads;

8. To promote the progress of science and useful arts, by securing for limited times to authors and inventors the exclusive right to their respective writings and discoveries;

9. To constitute tribunals inferior to the Supreme Court;

10. To define and punish piracies and felonies committed on the high seas, and offenses against the law of nations;

11. To declare war, grant letters of marque and reprisal, and make rules concerning captures on land and water;

12. To raise and support armies, but no appropriation of money to that use shall be for a longer term than two years;

13. To provide and maintain a navy;

14. To make rules for the government and regulation of the land and naval forces;

15. To provide for calling forth the militia to execute the laws of the Union, suppress insurrections and repel invasions;

16. To provide for organizing, arming, and disciplining the militia, and for governing such part of them as may be employed in the service of the United States, reserving to the States respectively, the appointment of the officers, and the authority of training the militia according to the discipline prescribed by Congress;

17. To exercise exclusive legislation in all cases whatsoever, over such district (not exceeding ten miles square) as may, by cession of particular States, and the acceptance of Congress, become the seat of the government of the United States, and to exercise like authority over all places purchased by the consent of the legislature of the State in which the same shall be, for the erection of forts, magazines, arsenals, dockyards, and other needful buildings; and

18. To make all laws which shall be necessary and proper for carrying into execution the foregoing powers, and all other powers vested by this Constitution in the government of the United States, or any department or officer thereof.

Section 9. 1. The migration or importation of such persons as any of the States now existing shall think proper to admit, shall not be prohibited by the Congress prior to the year one thousand eight hundred and eight, but a tax or duty may be imposed on such importation, not exceeding ten dollars for each person.

2. The privilege of the writ of habeas corpus shall not be suspended, unless when in cases of rebellion or invasion the public safety may require it.

3. No bill of attainder or ex post facto law shall be passed.

4. No capitation, or other direct, tax shall be laid, unless in proportion to the census or enumeration hereinbefore directed to be taken.[5]

5. No tax or duty shall be laid on articles exported from any State.

6. No preference shall be given by any regulation of commerce or revenue to the ports of one State over those of another: nor shall vessels bound to, or from, one State be obliged to enter, clear, or pay duties in another.

7. No money shall be drawn from the treasury, but in consequence of appropriations made by law; and a regular statement and account of the receipts and expenditures of all public money shall be published from time to time.

8. No title of nobility shall be granted by the United States: and no person holding any office of profit or trust under them, shall, without the consent of the Congress, accept of any present, emolument, office, or title, of any kind whatever, from any king, prince, or foreign State.

Section 10. 1. No State shall enter into any treaty, alliance, or confederation; grant letters of marque and reprisal; coin money; emit bills of credit; make any thing but gold and silver coin a tender in payment of debts; pass any bill of attainder, ex post facto law, or law impairing the obligation of contracts, or grant any title of nobility.

2. No State shall, without the consent of the Congress, lay any imposts or duties on imports or exports, except what may be absolutely necessary for executing its inspection laws: and the net produce of all duties and imposts laid by any State on imports or exports, shall be for the use of the treasury of the United States; and all such laws shall be subject to the revision and control of the Congress.

3. No State shall, without the consent of the Congress, lay any duty of tonnage, keep troops, or ships of war in time of peace, enter into any agreement or compact with another State, or with a foreign power, or engage in war, unless actually invaded, or in such imminent danger as will not admit of delay.

Article II

Section 1. 1. The executive power shall be vested in a President of the United States of America. He shall hold his office during the term of four years, and, together with the Vice President, chosen for the same term, be elected, as follows:

2. Each State shall appoint, in such manner as the legislature thereof may direct, a number of electors, equal to the whole number of senators and representatives to which the State may be entitled in the Congress: but no senator or representative, or person holding any office of trust or profit under the United States, shall be appointed an elector.

---

[5] See the Sixteenth Amendment.

The electors shall meet in their respective States, and vote by ballot for two persons, of whom one at least shall not be an inhabitant of the same State with themselves. And they shall make a list of all the persons voted for, and of the number of votes for each; which list they shall sign and certify, and transmit sealed to the seat of the government of the United States, directed to the president of the Senate. The president of the Senate shall, in the presence of the Senate and House of Representatives, open all the certificates, and the votes shall then be counted. The person having the greatest number of votes shall be the President, if such number be a majority of the whole number of electors appointed; and if there be more than one who have such majority, and have an equal number of votes, then the House of Representatives shall immediately choose by ballot one of them for President; and if no person have a majority, then from the five highest on the list the said House shall in like manner choose the President. But in choosing the President, the votes shall be taken by States, the representation from each State having one vote; a quorum for this purpose shall consist of a member or members from two thirds of the States, and a majority of all the States shall be necessary to a choice. In every case after the choice of the President, the person having the greatest number of votes of the electors shall be the Vice President. But if there should remain two or more who have equal votes, the Senate shall chose from them by ballot the Vice President.[6]

3. The Congress may determine the time of choosing the electors, and the day on which they shall give their votes; which day shall be the same throughout the United States.

4. No person except a natural born citizen, or a citizen of the United States, at the time of the adoption of this Constitution, shall be eligible to the office of President; neither shall any person be eligible to the office who shall not have attained to the age of thirty-five years, and been fourteen years a resident within the United States.

5. In case of the removal of the President from office, or of his death, resignation, or inability to discharge the powers and duties of the said office, the same shall devolve on the Vice President, and the Congress may by law provide for the case of removal, death, resignation or inability, both of the President and Vice President, declaring what officer shall then act as President, and such officer shall act accordingly until the disability be removed, or a President shall be elected.

6. The President shall, at stated times, receive for his services a compensation which shall neither be increased nor diminished during the period for which he shall have been elected, and he shall not receive within that period any other emolument from the United States, or any of them.

7. Before he enter on the execution of his office, he shall take the following oath or affirmation:—"I do solemnly swear (or affirm) that I will faithfully execute the office of President of the United States, and will to the best of my ability, preserve, protect and defend the Constitution of the United States."

Section 2. 1. The President shall be commander in chief of the army and navy of the United States, and of the militia of the several States, when called into the actual service of the United States; he may require the opinion in writing, of the principal officer in each of the executive departments, upon any subject relating to the duties of their respective offices, and he shall have power to grant reprieves and pardons for offenses against the United States, except in cases of impeachment.

2. He shall have power, by and with the advice and consent of the Senate, to make treaties, provided two thirds of the senators present concur; and he shall nominate, and by and with the advice and consent of the Senate, shall appoint ambassadors, other public ministers and consuls, judges of the Supreme Court, and all other officers of the United States, whose appointments are not herein otherwise provided for, and which shall be established by law: but the Congress may by law vest the appointment of such inferior officers, as they think proper, in the President alone, in the courts of laws, or in the heads of departments.

3. The President shall have power to fill up all vacancies that may happen during the recess of the Senate, by granting commissions which shall expire at the end of their next session.

Section 3. He shall from time to time give to the Congress information of the state of the Union, and recommend to their consideration such measures as he shall judge necessary and expedient; he may, on extraordinary occasions, convene both Houses, or either of them, and in case of disagreement between them with respect to the time of adjournment, he may adjourn them to such time as he shall think proper; he shall receive ambassadors and other public ministers; he shall take care that the laws be faithfully executed, and shall commission all the officers of the United States.

Section 4. The President, Vice President, and all civil officers of the United States, shall be removed from office on impeachment for, and conviction of, treason, bribery, or other high crimes and misdemeanors.

Article III

Section 1. The judicial power of the United States shall be vested in one Supreme Court, and in such inferior courts as the Congress may from time to time ordain and establish. The judges, both of the Supreme and inferior courts, shall hold their offices during good behavior, and shall, at stated times, receive for their services, a compensation, which shall not be diminished during their continuance in office.

Section 2. 1. The judicial power shall extend to all cases, in law and equity, arising under this Constitution, the laws of the United States, and treaties made, or which shall be made, under their authority;—to all cases

---

[6] Superseded by the Twelfth Amendment.

affecting ambassadors, other public ministers and consuls;—to all cases of admiralty and maritime jurisdiction;—to controversies to which the United States shall be a party;[7]—to controversies between two or more States;—between citizens of different States;—between citizens of the same State claiming lands under grants of different States, and between a State, or the citizens thereof, and foreign States, citizens or subjects.

2. In all cases affecting ambassadors, other public ministers and consuls, and those in which a State shall be party, the Supreme Court shall have original jurisdiction. In all the other cases before mentioned, the Supreme Court shall have appellate jurisdiction, both as to law and fact, with such exceptions, and under such regulations as the Congress shall make.

3. The trial of all crimes, except in cases of impeachment, shall be by jury; and such trial shall be held in the State where the said crimes shall have been committed; but when not committed within any State, the trial shall be at such place or places as the Congress may by law have directed.

Section 3. 1. Treason against the United States shall consist only in levying war against them, or in adhering to their enemies, giving them aid and comfort. No person shall be convicted of treason unless on the testimony of two witnesses to the same overt act, or on confession in open court.

2. The Congress shall have power to declare the punishment of treason, but no attainder of treason shall work corruption of blood, or forfeiture except during the life of the person attainted.

Article IV

Section 1. Full faith and credit shall be given in each State to the public acts, records, and judicial proceedings of every other State. And the Congress may by general laws prescribe the manner in which such acts, records and proceedings shall be proved, and the effect thereof.

Section 2. The citizens of each State shall be entitled to all privileges and immunities of citizens in the several States.[8]

2. A person charged in any State with treason, felony, or other crime, who shall flee from justice, and be found in another State, shall on demand of the executive authority of the State from which he fled, be delivered up to be removed to the State having jurisdiction of the crime.

3. No person held to service or labor in one State under the laws thereof, escaping into another, shall, in consequence of any law or regulation therein, be discharged from such service or labor, but shall be delivered up on claim of the party to whom such service or labor may be due.[9]

Section 3. 1. New States may be admitted by the Congress into this Union; but no new State shall be formed or erected within the jurisdiction of any other State; nor any State be formed by the junction of two or more States, or parts of States, without the consent of the legislatures of the States concerned as well as of the Congress.

2. The Congress shall have power to dispose of and make all needful rules and regulations respecting the territory or other property belonging to the United States; and nothing in this Constitution shall be so construed as to prejudice any claims of the United States, or of any particular State.

Section 4. The United States shall guarantee to every State in this Union a republican form of government, and shall protect each of them against invasion; and on application of the legislature, or of the executive (when the legislature cannot be convened) against domestic violence.

Article V

The Congress, whenever two thirds of both Houses shall deem it necessary, shall propose amendments to this Constitution, or, on the application of the legislatures of two thirds of the several States, shall call a convention for proposing amendments, which in either case, shall be valid to all intents and purposes, as part of this Constitution, when ratified by the legislatures of three fourths of the several States, or by conventions in three fourths thereof, as the one or the other mode of ratification may be proposed by the Congress; Provided that no amendment which may be made prior to the year one thousand eight hundred and eight shall in any manner affect the first and fourth clauses in the ninth section of the first article; and that no State, without its consent, shall be deprived of its equal suffrage in the Senate.

Article VI

1. All debts contracted and engagements entered into, before the adoption of this Constitution, shall be as valid against the United States under this Constitution, as under the Confederation.[10]

2. This Constitution, and the laws of the United States which shall be made in pursuance thereof; and all treaties made, or which shall be made, under the authority of the United States, shall be the supreme law of the land; and the judges in every State shall be bound thereby, any thing in the Constitution or laws of any State to the contrary notwithstanding.

3. The senators and representatives before mentioned, and the members of the several State legislatures, and all executive and judicial officers, both of the United States and of the several States, shall be bound by oath

---

[7] See the Eleventh Amendment.

[8] See the Fourteenth Amendment, Sec. 1.

[9] See the Thirteenth Amendment.

---

[10] See the Fourteenth Amendment, Sec. 4

or affirmation to support this Constitution; but no religious test shall ever be required as a qualification to any office or public trust under the United States.

Article VII

The ratification of the conventions of nine States shall be sufficient for the establishment of this Constitution between the States so ratifying the same.

Done in Convention by the unanimous consent of the States present the seventeenth day of September in the year of our Lord one thousand seven hundred and eighty-seven, and of the independence of the United States of America the twelfth. In witness whereof we have hereunto subscribed our names.

[Names omitted]

*   *   *

Articles in addition to, and amendment of, the Constitution of the United States of America, proposed by Congress, and ratified by the legislatures of the several States, pursuant to the fifth article of the original Constitution.

Amendment I [first ten amendments ratified December 15, 1791]

Congress shall make no law respecting an establishment of religion, or prohibiting the free exercise thereof; or abridging the freedom of speech, or of the press; or the right of the people peaceably to assemble, and to petition the government for a redress of grievances.

Amendment II

A well regulated militia, being necessary to the security of a free State, the right of the people to keep and bear arms, shall not be infringed.

Amendment III

No soldier shall, in time of peace be quartered in any house, without the consent of the owner, nor in time of war, but in a manner to be prescribed by law.

Amendment IV

The right of the people to be secure in their persons, houses, papers, and effects, against unreasonable searches and seizures, shall not be violated, and no warrants shall issue, but upon probable cause, supported by oath or affirmation, and particularly describing the place to be searched, and the persons or things to be seized.

Amendment V

No person shall be held to answer for a capital or otherwise infamous crime, unless on a presentment or indictment of a grand jury, except in cases arising in the land or naval forces, or in the militia, when in actual service in time of war or public danger; nor shall any person be subject for the same offense to be twice put in jeopardy of life or limb; nor shall be compelled in any criminal case to be a witness against himself, nor be deprived of life, liberty, or property, without due process of law; nor shall private property be taken for public use, without just compensation.

Amendment VI

In all criminal prosecutions, the accused shall enjoy the right to a speedy and public trial, by an impartial jury of the State and district wherein the crime shall have been committed, which district shall have been previously ascertained by law, and to be informed of the nature and cause of the accusation; to be confronted with the witnesses against him; to have compulsory process for obtaining witnesses in his favor, and to have the assistance of counsel for his defense.

Amendment VII

In suits at common law, where the value in controversy shall exceed twenty dollars, the right of trial by jury shall be preserved, and no fact tried by a jury shall be otherwise reëxamined in any court of the United States, than according to the rules of the common law.

Amendment VIII

Excessive bail shall not be required, nor excessive fines imposed, nor cruel and unusual punishments inflicted.

Amendment IX

The enumeration in the Constitution of certain rights shall not be construed to deny or disparage others retained by the people.

Amendment X

The powers not delegated to the United States by the Constitution, nor prohibited by it to the States, are reserved to the States respectively, or to the people.

Amendment XI [January 8, 1798]

The judicial power of the United States shall not be construed to extend to any suit in law or equity, commenced or prosecuted against one of the United States by citizens of another State, or by citizens or subjects of any foreign State.

Amendment XII [September 25, 1804]

The electors shall meet in their respective States, and vote by ballot for President and Vice President, one of whom, at least, shall not be an inhabitant of the same State with themselves; they shall name in their ballots the person voted for as President, and in distinct ballots, the person voted for as Vice President, and they shall make distinct lists of all persons voted for as President and of all persons voted for as Vice President, and of the number of votes for each, which lists they shall sign and certify, and transmit sealed to the seat of the government of the United States, directed to the President of the Senate;—The President of the Senate shall, in the presence of the Senate and House of Representatives, open all the certificates and the votes shall then be counted;—The person having the greatest number of votes for President, shall be the President, if such number be a majority of the whole number of electors appointed; and if no person have such majority, then from the persons having the highest numbers not exceeding three on the list of those voted for as President, the House of Representatives shall choose immediately, by ballot, the President. But in choosing the President, the votes shall be taken by States, the representation from each State having one vote; a quorum for this purpose shall consist of a member or members from two thirds of the States, and a majority of all the States shall be necessary to a choice. And if the House of Representatives shall not choose a President whenever the right of choice shall devolve upon them, before the fourth day of March next following, then the Vice President shall act as President, as in the case of the death or other constitutional disability of the President. The person having the greatest number of votes as Vice President shall be the Vice President, if such number be a majority of the whole number of electors appointed, and if no person have a majority, then from the two highest numbers on the list, the Senate shall choose the Vice President; a quorum for the purpose shall consist of two thirds of the whole number of Senators, and a majority of the whole number shall be necessary to a choice. But no person constitutionally ineligible to the office of President shall be eligible to that of Vice President of the United States.

Amendment XIII [December 18, 1865]

Section 1. Neither slavery nor involuntary servitude, except as a punishment for crime whereof the party shall have been duly convicted, shall exist within the United States, or any place subject to their jurisdiction.

Section 2. Congress shall have power to enforce this article by appropriate legislation.

Amendment XIV [July 28, 1868]

Section 1. All persons born or naturalized in the United States, and subject to the jurisdiction thereof, are citizens of the United States and of the State wherein they reside. No State shall make or enforce any law which shall abridge the privileges or immunities of citizens of the United States; nor shall any State deprive any person of life, liberty, or property, without due process of law; nor deny to any persons within its jurisdiction the equal protection of the laws.

Section 2. Representatives shall be apportioned among the several States according to their respective numbers, counting the whole number of persons in each State, excluding Indians not taxed. But when the right to vote at any election for the choice of electors for President and Vice President of the United States, representatives in Congress, the executive and judicial officers of a State, or the members of the legislature thereof, is denied to any of the male inhabitants of such State, being twenty-one years of age, and citizens of the United States, or in any way abridged, except for participating in rebellion, or other crime, the basis of representation therein shall be reduced in the proportion which the number of such male citizens shall bear to the whole number of male citizens twenty-one years of age in such State.

Section 3. No person shall be a senator or representative in Congress, or elector of President and Vice President, or hold any office, civil or military, under the United States, or under any State, who having previously taken an oath, as a member of Congress, or as an officer of the United States, or as a member of any State legislature, or as an executive or judicial officer of any State, to support the Constitution of the United States, shall have engaged in insurrection or rebellion against the same, or given aid or comfort to the enemies thereof. But Congress may by a vote of two thirds of each House, remove such disability.

Section 4. The validity of the public debt of the United States, authorized by law, including debts incurred for payment of pensions and bounties for services in suppressing insurrection or rebellion, shall not be questioned. But neither the United States nor any State shall assume or pay any debt or obligation incurred in aid of insurrection or rebellion against the United States, or any claim for the loss or emancipation of any slave; but all such debts, obligations, and claims shall be held illegal and void.

Section 5. The Congress shall have the power to enforce, by appropriate legislation, the provisions of this article.

Amendment XV [March 30, 1870]

Section 1. The right of citizens of the United States to vote shall not be denied or abridged by the United States or by any State on account of race, color, or previous condition of servitude.

Section 2. The Congress shall have power to enforce this article by appropriate legislation.

Amendment XVI [February 25, 1913]

The Congress shall have power to lay and collect taxes on incomes, from whatever source derived, without apportionment among the several States, and without regard to any census or enumeration.

Amendment XVII [May 31, 1913]

The Senate of the United States shall be composed of two senators from each State, elected by the people thereof, for six years; and each senator shall have one vote. The electors in each State shall have the qualifications requisite for electors of the most numerous branch of the State legislature.

When vacancies happen in the representation of any State in the Senate, the executive authority of such State shall issue writs of election to fill such vacancies; *Provided,* That the legislature of any State may empower the executive thereof to make temporary appointments until the people fill the vacancies by election as the legislature may direct.

This amendment shall not be so construed as to affect the election or term of any senator chosen before it becomes valid as part of the Constitution.

Amendment XVIII[11] [January 29, 1919]

After one year from the ratification of this article, the manufacture, sale, or transportation of intoxicating liquors within, the importation thereof into, or the exportation thereof from the United States and all territory subject to the jurisdiction thereof for beverage purposes is thereby prohibited.

The Congress and the several States shall have concurrent power to enforce this article by appropriate legislation.

This article shall be inoperative unless it shall have been ratified as an amendment to the Constitution by the legislatures of the several States, as provided in the Constitution, within seven years from the date of the submission hereof to the States by Congress.

Amendment XIX [August 26, 1920]

The right of citizens of the United States to vote shall not be denied or abridged by the United States or by any State on account of sex.

Congress shall have the power to enforce this article by appropriate legislation.

---

[11] Repealed by the Twenty-first Amendment.

Amendment XX [January 23, 1933]

Section 1. The terms of the President and Vice President shall end at noon on the 20th day of January and the terms of Senators and Representatives at noon on the 3d day of January, of the years in which such terms would have ended if this article had not been ratified; and the terms of their successors shall then begin.

Section 2. The Congress shall assemble at least once in every year, and such meeting shall begin at noon on the 3d day of January, unless they shall by law appoint a different day.

Section 3. If, at the time fixed for the beginning of the term of President, the President-elect shall have died, the Vice President-elect shall become President. If a President shall not have been chosen before the time fixed for the beginning of his term, or if the President-elect shall have failed to qualify, then the Vice President-elect shall act as President until a President shall have qualified; and the Congress may by law provide for the case wherein neither a President-elect nor a Vice President-elect shall have qualified, declaring who shall then act as President, or the manner in which one who is to act shall be selected, and such person shall act accordingly until a President or Vice President shall have qualified.

Section 4. The Congress may by law provide for the case of the death of any of the persons from whom the House of Representatives may choose a President whenever the right of choice shall have devolved upon them, and for the case of the death of any of the persons from whom the Senate may choose a Vice President whenever the right of choice shall have devolved upon them.

Section 5. Sections 1 and 2 shall take effect on the 15th day of October following the ratification of this article.

Section 6. This article shall be inoperative unless it shall have been ratified as an amendment to the Constitution by the legislatures of three-fourths of the several States within seven years from the date of its submission.

Amendment XXI [December 5, 1933]

Section 1. The Eighteenth Article of amendment to the Constitution of the United States is hereby repealed.

Section 2. The transportation or importation into any State, Territory, or possession of the United States for delivery or use therein of intoxicating liquors in violation of the laws thereof, is hereby prohibited.

Section 3. This article shall be inoperative unless it shall have been ratified as an amendment to the Constitution by conventions in the several States, as provided in the

Constitution, within seven years from the date of the submission thereof to the States by the Congress.

Amendment XXII [March 1, 1951]

No person shall be elected to the office of the President more than twice, and no person who has held the office of President, or acted as President, for more than two years of a term to which some other person was elected President shall be elected to the office of the President more than once.

But this article shall not apply to any person holding the office of President when this article was proposed by the Congress, and shall not prevent any person who may be holding the office of President, or acting as President, during the term within which this article becomes operative from holding the office of President or acting as President during the remainder of such term.

This article shall be inoperative unless it shall have been ratified as an amendment to the Constitution by the legislatures of three-fourths of the several States within seven years from the date of its submission to the States by the Congress.

Amendment XXIII [March 29, 1961]

Section 1. The District constituting the seat of Government of the United States shall appoint in such manner as the Congress may direct:

A number of electors of President and Vice President equal to the whole number of Senators and Representatives in Congress to which the District would be entitled if it were a State, but in no event more than the least populous State; they shall be in addition to those appointed by the States, but they shall be considered, for the purposes of the election of President and Vice President, to be electors appointed by a State; and they shall meet in the District and perform such duties as provided by the twelfth article of amendment.

Section 2. The Congress shall have power to enforce this article by appropriate legislation.

Amendment XXIV [January 23, 1964]

Section 1. The right of citizens of the United States to vote in any primary or other election for President or Vice President, for electors for President or Vice President, or for Senator or Representative in Congress, shall not be denied or abridged by the United States or any State by reason of failure to pay any poll tax or other tax.

Section 2. The Congress shall have power to enforce this article by appropriate legislation.

Amendment XXV [February 10, 1967]

Section 1. In case of the removal of the President from office or of his death or resignation, the Vice President shall become President.

Section 2. Whenever there is a vacancy in the office of the Vice President, the President shall nominate a Vice President who shall take office upon confirmation by a majority of both Houses of Congress.

Section 3. Whenever the President transmits to the President pro tempore of the Senate and the Speaker of the House of Representatives his written declaration that he is unable to discharge the powers and duties of his office, and until he transmits to them a written declaration to the contrary, such powers and duties shall be discharged by the Vice President as Acting President.

Section 4. Whenever the Vice president and a majority of either the principal officers of the executive departments or of such other body as Congress may by law provide, transmit to the President pro tempore of the Senate and the Speaker of the House of Representatives their written declaration that the President is unable to discharge the powers and duties of his office, the Vice President shall immediately assume the powers and duties of the office as Acting President.

Thereafter, when the President transmits to the President pro tempore of the Senate and the Speaker of the House of Representatives his written declaration that no inability exists, he shall resume the powers and duties of his office unless the Vice President and a majority of either the principal officers of the executive departments or of such other body as Congress may by law provide, transmit within four days to the President pro tempore of the Senate and the Speaker of the House of Representatives their written declaration that the President is unable to discharge the powers and duties of his office. Thereupon Congress shall decide the issue, assembling within forty-eight hours for that purpose if not in session. If the Congress, within twenty-one days after receipt of the latter written declaration, or, if Congress is not in session, within twenty-one days after Congress is required to assemble, determines by two-thirds vote of both Houses that the President is unable to discharge the powers and duties of his office, the Vice President shall continue to discharge the same as Acting President; otherwise, the President shall resume the powers and duties of his office.

Amendment XXVI [June 30, 1971]

Section 1. The right of citizens of the United States who are eighteen years of age or older to vote shall not be denied or abridged by the United States or by any State on account of age.

Section 2. The Congress shall have power to enforce this article by appropriate legislation.

■ UNIFORM COMMERCIAL CODE (EXCERPTS)

Section 1-102. Purposes; Rules of Construction; Variation by Agreement

(1) This Act shall be liberally construed and applied to promote its underlying purposes and policies.
(2) Underlying purposes and policies of this Act are
   (a) to simplify, clarify and modernize the law governing commercial transactions;
   (b) to permit the continued expansion of commercial practices through custom, usage and agreement of the parties;
   (c) to make uniform the law among the various jurisdictions.
(3) The effect of provisions of this Act may be varied by agreement, except as otherwise provided in this Act and except that the obligations of good faith, diligence, reasonableness and care prescribed by this Act may not be disclaimed by agreement but the parties may by agreement determine the standards by which the performance of such obligations is to be measured if such standards are not manifestly unreasonable.

Section 1-203. Obligation of Good Faith

Every contract or duty within this Act imposes an obligation of good faith in its performance or enforcement.

Section 2-104. Definitions: "Merchant"; "Between Merchants"

(1) "Merchant" means a person who deals in goods of the kind or otherwise by his occupation holds himself out as having knowledge or skill peculiar to the practices or goods involved in the transaction or to whom such knowledge or skill may be attributed by his employment of an agent or broker or other intermediary who by his occupation holds himself out as having such knowledge or skill. . . .
(3) "Between merchants" means in any transaction with respect to which both parties are chargeable with the knowledge or skill of merchants.

Section 2-105. Definitions: "Goods"

(1) "Goods" means all things (including special manufactured goods) which are movable at the time of identification of the contract for sale other than the money in which the price is to be paid, investment securities (Article 8) and things in action. "Goods" also includes the unborn young of animals and growing crops and other identified things attached to realty as described in the section on goods to be severed from realty.

Section 2-302. Unconscionable Contract or Clause

(1) If the court as a matter of law finds the contract or any clause of the contract to have been unconscionable at the time it was made the court may refuse to enforce the contract, or it may enforce the remainder of the contract without the unconscionable clause, or it may so limit the application of any unconscionable clause as to avoid any unconscionable result.
(2) When it is claimed or appears to the court that the contract or any clause thereof may be unconscionable the parties shall be afforded a reasonable opportunity to present evidence as to its commercial setting, purpose and effect to aid the court in making the determination.

Section 2-313. Express Warranties by Affirmation, Promise, Description, Sample

(1) Express warranties by the seller are created as follows:
   (a) Any affirmation of fact or promise made by the seller to the buyer which relates to the goods and becomes part of the basis of the bargain creates an express warranty that the goods shall conform to the affirmation or promise.
   (b) Any description of the goods which is made part of the basis of the bargain creates an express warranty that the goods shall conform to the description.
   (c) Any sample or model which is made part of the basis of the bargain creates an express warranty that the whole of the goods shall conform to the sample or model.
(2) It is not necessary to the creation of an express warranty that the seller use formal words such as "warrant" or "guarantee" or that he have a specific intention to make a warranty, but an affirmation merely of the value of the goods or a statement purporting to be merely the seller's opinion or commendation of the goods does not create a warranty.

Section 2-314. Implied Warranty: Merchantability; Usage of Trade

(1) Unless excluded or modified (Section 2-316), a warranty that the goods shall be merchantable is implied in a contract for their sale if the seller is a merchant with respect to goods of that kind. Under this section the serving for value of food or drink to be consumed either on the premises or elsewhere is a sale.
(2) Goods to be merchantable must be at least such as

   (a) pass without objection in the trade under the contract description; and
   (b) in the case of fungible goods, are of fair average quality within the description; and

(c) are fit for the ordinary purposes for which such goods are used; and

(d) run, within the variations permitted by the agreement, of even kind, quality and quantity within each unit and among all units involved; and

(e) are adequately contained, packaged, and labeled as the agreement may require; and

(f) conform to the promises or affirmations of fact made on the container or label if any.

(3) Unless excluded or modified (Section 2-316) other implied warranties may arise from course of dealing or usage of trade.

Section 2-315. Implied Warranty: Fitness for Particular Purpose

Where the seller at the time of contracting has reason to know any particular purpose for which the goods are required and that the buyer is relying on the seller's skill of judgment to select or furnish suitable goods, there is unless excluded or modified under the next section an implied warranty that the goods shall be fit for such purpose.

Section 2-316. Exclusion or Modification of Warranties

(1) Words or conduct relevant to the creation of an express warranty and words or conduct tending to negate or limit warranty shall be construed wherever reasonable as consistent with each other; but subject to the provisions of this Article on parol or extrinsic evidence (Section 2-202) negation or limitation is inoperative to the extent that such construction is unreasonable.

(2) Subject to subsection (3), to exclude or modify the implied warranty of merchantability or any part of it in the language must mention merchantability and in case of a writing must be conspicuous, and to exclude or modify any implied warranty of fitness the exclusion must be by a writing and conspicuous. Language to exclude all implied warranties of fitness is sufficient if it states, for example, that "There are no warranties which extend beyond the description on the face hereof."

(3) Notwithstanding subsection (2)

(a) unless the circumstances indicate otherwise, all implied warranties are excluded by expressions like "as is," "with all faults" or other language which in common understanding calls the buyer's attention to the exclusion of warranties and makes plain that there is no implied warranty; and

(b) when the buyer before entering into the contract has examined the goods or the sample or model as fully as he desired or has refused to examine the goods there is no implied warranty with regard to defects which an examination ought in the circumstances to have revealed to him; and

(c) an implied warranty can also be excluded or modified by course of dealing or course of performance or usage of trade.

(4) Remedies for breach of warranty can be limited in accordance with the provisions of this Article on liquidation or limitation of damages and on contractual modification of remedy.

■ NATIONAL LABOR RELATIONS ACT (EXCERPTS)

Rights of Employees

Section 7. Employees shall have the right to self-organization, to form, join, or assist labor organizations, to bargain collectively through representatives of their own choosing, and to engage in other concerted activities for the purpose of collective bargaining or other mutual aid or protection, and shall also have the right to refrain from any or all such activities except to the extent that such right may be affected by an agreement requiring membership in a labor organization as a condition of employment as authorized in section 8(a)(3).

Unfair Labor Practices

Section 8. (a) It shall be an unfair labor practice for an employer—

(1) to interfere with, restrain, or coerce employees in the exercise of the rights guaranteed in section 7;

(2) to dominate or interfere with the formation or administration of any labor organization or contribute financial or other support to it; *Provided,* That subject to rules and regulations made and published by the Board pursuant to section 6, an employer shall not be prohibited from permitting employees to confer with him during working hours without loss of time or pay;

(3) by discrimination in regard to hire or tenure of employment or any term or condition of employment to encourage or discourage membership in any labor organization: *Provided,* That nothing in this Act, or in any other statute of the United States, shall preclude an employer from making an agreement with a labor organization (not established, maintained, or assisted by any action defined in section 8(a) of this Act as an unfair labor practice) to require as a condition of employment membership therein on or after the thirtieth day following the beginning of such employment or the effective date of such agreement, whichever is the later, (i) if such labor organization is the representative of the employees as provided in section 9(a), in the appropriate collective-bargaining unit covered by such agreement when made, and (ii) unless following an election held as provided in section 9(e) within one year preceding the effective date of such agreement, the Board shall have certified that at least a majority of the employees eligible to vote in such election have voted to rescind the authority of such labor organization to make such an agreement; *Provided further,*

That no employer shall justify any discrimination against an employee for nonmembership in a labor organization (A) if he has reasonable grounds for believing that such membership was not available to the employee on the same terms and conditions generally applicable to other members, or (B) if he has reasonable grounds for believing that membership was denied or terminated for reasons other than the failure of the employee to tender the periodic dues and the initiation fees uniformly required as a condition of acquiring or retaining membership;

(4) to discharge or otherwise discriminate against an employee because he has filed charges or given testimony under this Act;

(5) to refuse to bargain collectively with the representatives of his employees, subject to the provisions of section 9(a).

(b) It shall be an unfair labor practice for a labor organization or its agents—

(1) to restrain or coerce (A) employees in the exercise of the rights guaranteed in section 7: *Provided,* That this paragraph shall not impair the right of a labor organization to prescribe its own rules with respect to the acquisition or retention of membership therein; or (B) an employer in the selection of his representatives for the purpose of collective bargaining or the adjustment of grievances;

(2) to cause or attempt to cause an employer to discriminate against an employee in violation of subsection (a)(3) or to discriminate against an employee with respect to whom membership in such organization has been denied or terminated on some ground other than his failure to tender the periodic dues and the initiation fees uniformly required as a condition of acquiring or retaining membership;

(3) to refuse to bargain collectively with an employer, provided it is the representative of his employees subject to the provisions of section 9(a);

(4)(i) to engage in, or to induce or encourage any individual employed by any person engaged in commerce or in an industry affecting commerce to engage in, a strike or a refusal in the course of his employment to use, manufacture, process, transport, or otherwise handle or work on any goods, articles, materials, or commodities or to perform any services; or (ii) to threaten, coerce, or restrain any person engaged in commerce or in an industry affecting commerce, where in either case an object thereof is:

(A) forcing or requiring any employer or self-employed person to join any labor or employer organization or to enter into any agreement which is prohibited by section 8(e);

(B) forcing or requiring any person to cease using, selling, handling, transporting, or otherwise dealing in the products of any other producer, processor, or manufacturer, or to cease doing business with any other person, or forcing or requiring any other employer to recognize or bargain with a labor organization as the representative of his employees unless such labor organization has been certified as the representative of such employees under the provisions of section 9: *Provided,* That nothing contained in this clause (B) shall be construed to make unlawful, where not otherwise unlawful, any primary strike or primary picketing;

(C) forcing or requiring any employer to recognize or bargain with a particular labor organization as the representative of his employees if another labor organization has been certified as the representative of such employees under the provisions of section 9;

(D) forcing or requiring any employer to assign particular work to employees in a particular labor organization or in a particular trade, craft, or class rather than to employees in another labor organization or in another trade, craft, or class, unless such employer is failing to conform to an order or certification of the Board determining the bargaining representative for employees performing such work: *Provided,* That nothing contained in this subsection (b) shall be construed to make unlawful a refusal by any person to enter upon the premises of any employer (other than his own employer), if the employees of such employer are engaged in a strike ratified or approved by a representative of such employees whom such employer is required to recognize under this Act: *Provided further,* That for the purposes of this paragraph (4) only, nothing contained in such paragraph shall be construed to prohibit publicity, other than picketing, for the purpose of truthfully advising the public, including consumers and members of a labor organization, that a product or products are produced by an employer with whom the labor organization has a primary dispute and are distributed by another employer, as long as such publicity does not have an effect of inducing any individual employed by any person other than the primary employer in the course of his employment to refuse to pick up, deliver, or transport any goods, or not to perform any services, at the establishment of the employer engaged in such distribution;

(5) to require of employees covered by an agreement authorized under subsection (a)(3) the payment, as a condition precedent to becoming a member of such organization, of a fee in an amount which the Board finds excessive or discriminatory under all the circumstances. In making such a finding, the Board shall consider, among other relevant factors, the practices and customs of labor organizations in the particular industry, and the wages currently paid to the employees affected;

(6) to cause or attempt to cause an employer to pay or deliver or agree to pay or deliver any money or other thing of value, in the nature of an exaction for services which are not performed or not to be performed; and

(7) to picket or cause to be picketed, or threaten to picket or cause to be picketed, any employer where an object thereof is forcing or requiring an employer to recognize or bargain with a labor organization as the representative of his employees, or forcing or requiring the employees of an employer to accept or select such labor organization as their collective bargaining representative, unless such labor organization is currently certified as the representative of such employees:

(A) where the employer has lawfully recognized in accordance with this Act any other labor organization and a question concerning representation may not appropriately be raised under section 9(c) of this Act,

(B) where within the preceding twelve months a valid election under section 9(c) of this Act has been conducted, or

(C) where such picketing has been conducted without a petition under section 9(c) being filed within a reasonable period of time not to exceed thirty days from the commencement of such picketing: *Provided,* That when such a petition has been filed the Board shall forthwith, without regard to the provisions of section 9(c)(1) or the absence of a showing of a substantial interest on the part of the labor organization, direct an election in such unit as the Board finds to be appropriate and shall certify the results thereof: *Provided further,* That nothing in this subparagraph (C) shall be construed to prohibit any picketing or other publicity for the purpose of truthfully advising the public (including consumers) that an employer does not employ members of, or have a contract with, a labor organization, unless an effect of such picketing is to induce any individual employed by any other person in the course of his employment, not to pick up, deliver or transport any goods or not to perform any services.

Nothing in this paragraph (7) shall be construed to permit any act which would otherwise be an unfair labor practice under this section 8(b).

(c) The expressing of any views, argument, or opinion, or the dissemination thereof, whether in written, printed, graphic, or visual form, shall not constitute or be evidence of an unfair labor practice under any of the provisions of this Act, if such expression contains no threat of reprisal or force or promise of benefit.

(d) For the purposes of this section, to bargain collectively is the performance of the mutual obligation of the employer and the representative of the employees to meet at reasonable times and confer in good faith with respect to wages, hours, and other terms and conditions of employment, or the negotiation of an agreement or any question arising thereunder, and the execution of a written contract incorporating any agreement reached if requested by either party, but such obligation does not compel either party to agree to a proposal or require the making of a concession: *Provided,* That where there is in effect a collective-bargaining contract covering employees in an industry affecting commerce, the duty to bargain collectively shall also mean that no party to such contract shall terminate or modify such contract, unless the party desiring such termination or modification—

(1) serves a written notice upon the party to the contract of the proposed termination or modification sixty days prior to the expiration date thereof, or in the event such contract contains no expiration date, sixty days prior to the time it is proposed to make such termination or modification;

(2) offers to meet and confer with the other party for the purpose of negotiating a new contract or a contract containing the proposed modifications;

(3) notifies the Federal Mediation and Conciliation Service within thirty days after such notice of the existence of a dispute, and simultaneously therewith notifies any State or Territorial agency established to mediate and conciliate disputes within the State or Territory where the dispute occurred, provided no agreement has been reached by that time; and

(4) continues in full force and effect, without resorting to strike or lockout, all the terms and conditions of the existing contract for a period of sixty days after such notice is given or until the expiration date of such contract, whichever occurs later.

The duties imposed upon employers, employees, and labor organizations by paragraphs (2), (3), and (4) shall become inapplicable upon an intervening certification of the Board, under which the labor organization or individual, which is a party to the contract, has been superseded as or ceased to be the representative of the employees subject to the provisions of section 9(a), and the duties so imposed shall not be construed as requiring either party to discuss or agree to any modification of the terms and conditions contained in a contract for a fixed period, if such modification is to become effective before such terms and conditions can be reopened under the provisions of the contract. Any employee who engages in a strike within any notice period specified in this subsection, or who engages in any strike with the appropriate period specified in subsection (g) of this section, shall lose his status as an employee of the employer engaged in the particular labor dispute, for the purposes of sections 8, 9, and 10 of this Act, as amended, but such loss of status for such employee shall terminate if and when he is reemployed by such employer. Whenever the collective bargaining involves employees of a health care institution, the provisions of this section 8(d) shall be modified as follows:

(A) The notice of section 8(d)(1) shall be ninety days; the notice of section 8(d)(3) shall be sixty days; and the contract period of section 8(d)(4) shall be ninety days.

(B) Where the bargaining is for an initial agreement following certification or recognition, at least thirty days' notice of the existence of a dispute shall be given by the labor organization to the agencies set forth in section 8(d)(3).

(C) After notice is given to the Federal Mediation and Conciliation Service under either clause (A) or (B) of this sentence, the Service shall promptly communicate with the parties and use its best efforts, by mediation and conciliation, to bring them to agreement. The parties shall participate fully and promptly in such meetings as may be undertaken by the Service for the purpose of aiding in a settlement of the dispute.

(e) It shall be an unfair labor practice for any labor organization and any employer to enter into any contract or agreement, express or implied, whereby such employer ceases or refrains or agrees to cease or refrain from handling, using, selling, transporting or otherwise dealing in any of the products of any other employer, or to cease doing business with any other person, and any contract or agreement entered into heretofore or hereafter containing such an agreement shall be to such extent unenforceable and void: *Provided,* That nothing in this subsection (e) shall apply to an agreement between a labor organization and an employer in the construction industry relating to the contracting or subcontracting of work to be done at the site of the construction, alteration, painting, or repair of a building, structure, or other work: *Provided further,* That for the purposes of this subsection (e) and section 8(b)(4)(B) the terms "any employer," "any person engaged in commerce or in industry affecting commerce," and "any person" when used in relation to the terms "any other producer, processor, or manufacturer," "any other employer," or "any other person" shall not include persons in the relation of a jobber, manufacturer, contractor, or subcontractor working on the goods or premises of the jobber or manufacturer or performing parts of an integrated process of production in the apparel and clothing industry: *Provided further,* That nothing in this Act shall prohibit the enforcement of any agreement which is within the foregoing exception.

(f) It shall not be an unfair labor practice under subsections (a) and (b) of this section for an employer engaged primarily in the building and construction industry to make an agreement covering employees engaged (or who, upon their employment, will be engaged) in the building and construction industry with a labor organization of which building and construction employees are members (not established, maintained, or assisted by any action defined in section 8(a) of this Act as an unfair labor practice) because (1) the majority status of such labor organization has not been established under the provisions of section 9 of this Act prior to the making of such agreement, or (2) such agreement requires as a condition of employment, membership in such labor organization after the seventh day following the beginning of such employment or the effective date of the agreement, whichever is later, or (3) such agreement requires the employer to notify such labor organization of opportunities for employment with such employer, or gives such labor organization an opportunity to refer qualified applicants for such employment, or (4) such agreement specifies minimum training or experience qualifications for employment or provides for priority in opportunities for employment based upon length of service with such employer, in the industry or in the particular geographical area: *Provided,* That nothing in this subsection shall set aside the final proviso to section 8(a)(3) of this Act: *Provided further,* That any agreement which would be invalid, but for clause (1) of this subsection, shall not be a bar to a petition filed pursuant to section 9(c) or 9(e).*

(g) A labor organization before engaging in any strike, picketing, or other concerted refusal to work at any health care institution shall, not less than ten days prior to such action, notify the institution in writing and the Federal Mediation and Conciliation Service of that intention, except that in the case of bargaining for an initial agreement following certification or recognition the no-

tice required by this subsection shall not be given the expiration of the period specified in clause (B) of the last sentence of section 8(d) of this Act. The notice shall state the date and time that such action will commence. The notice, once given, may be extended by the written agreement of both parties.

■ CIVIL RIGHTS ACT OF 1964 (EXCERPT)

Discrimination Because of Race, Color, Religion, Sex, or National Origin

Section 703. (a) It shall be an unlawful employment practice for an employer:

(1) to fail or refuse to hire or to discharge any individual, or otherwise to discriminate against any individual with respect to his compensation, terms, conditions, or privileges of employment, because of such individual's race, color, religion, sex, or national origin; or

(2) to limit, segregate, or classify his employees or applicants for employment in any way which would deprive or tend to deprive any individual of employment opportunities or otherwise adversely affect his status as an employee, because of such individual's race, color, religion, sex, or national origin.

(b) It shall be an unlawful employment practice for an employment agency to fail or refuse to refer for employment, or otherwise to discriminate against, any individual because of his race, color, religion, sex, or national origin, or to classify or refer for employment any individual on the basis of his race, color, religion, sex, or national origin.

(c) It shall be an unlawful employment practice for a labor organization:

(1) to exclude or to expel from its membership, or otherwise to discriminate against, any individual because of his race, color, religion, sex, or national origin;

(2) to limit, segregate, or classify its membership, or applicants for membership or to classify or fail or refuse to refer for employment any individual, in any way which would deprive or tend to deprive any individual of employment opportunities, or would limit such employment opportunities or otherwise adversely affect his status as an employee or as an applicant for employment, because of such individual's race, color, religion, sex, or national origin; or

(3) to cause or attempt to cause an employer to discriminate against an individual in violation of this section.

(d) It shall be an unlawful employment practice for any employer, labor organization, or joint labor-management committee controlling apprenticeship or other training or retraining, including on-the-job training programs to discriminate against any individual because of his race, color, religion, sex, or national origin in admission to, or employment in, any program established to provide apprenticeship or other training.

---

* Sec. 8(f) is inserted in the Act by subsec. (a) of Sec. 705 of Public Law 86-257 (1959). Sec. 705(b) provides:

Nothing contained in the amendment made by subsection (a) shall be construed as authorizing the execution or application of agreements requiring membership in a labor organization as a condition of employment in any State or Territory in which such execution or application is prohibited by State or Territorial law.

(e) Notwithstanding any other provision of this title, (1) it shall not be an unlawful employment practice for an employer to hire and employ employees, for an employment agency to classify, or refer for employment any individual, for a labor organization to classify its membership or to classify or refer for employment any individual, or for an employer, labor organization, or joint labor-management committee controlling apprenticeship or other training or retraining programs to admit or employ any individual in any such program, on the basis of his religion, sex, or national origin in those certain instances where religion, sex, or national origin is a bona fide occupational qualification reasonably necessary to the normal operation of that particular business or enterprise, and (2) it shall not be an unlawful employment practice for a school, college, university, or other educational institution or institution of learning to hire and employ employees of a particular religion if such school, college, university, or other educational institution or institution of learning is, in whole or in substantial part, owned, supported, controlled, or managed by a particular religion or by a particular religious corporation, association, or society, or if the curriculum of such school, college, university, or other educational institution or institution of learning is directed toward the propagation of a particular religion. . . .

(h) Notwithstanding any other provision of this title, it shall not be an unlawful employment practice for an employer to apply different standards of compensation, or different terms, conditions, or privileges of employment pursuant to a bona fide seniority or merit system, or a system which measures earnings by quantity or quality of production or to employees who work in different locations, provided that such differences are not the result of an intention to discriminate because of race, color, religion, sex, or national origin, nor shall it be an unlawful employment practice for an employer to give and to act upon the results of any professionally developed ability test provided that such test, its administration or action upon the results is not designed, intended or used to discriminate because of race, color, religion, sex, or national origin. It shall not be an unlawful employment practice under this title for any employer to differentiate upon the basis of sex in determining the amount of the wages or compensation paid or to be paid to employees of such employer if such differentiation is authorized by the provisions of section 6(d) of the Fair Labor Standards Act of 1938, as amended (29 U.S.C. 206(d)).

(i) Nothing contained in this title shall apply to any business or enterprise on or near an Indian reservation with respect to any publicly announced employment practice of such business or enterprise under which a preferential treatment is given to any individual because he is an Indian living on or near a reservation.

(j) Nothing contained in this title shall be interpreted to require any employer, employment agency, labor organization, or joint labor-management committee subject to this title to grant preferential treatment to any individual or to any group because of the race, color, religion, sex, or national origin of such individual or group on account of an imbalance which may exist with respect

to the total number or percentage of persons of any race, color, religion, sex, or national origin employed by any employer, referred or classified for employment by any employment agency or labor organization, admitted to membership or classified by any labor organization, or admitted to, or employed in, any apprenticeship or other training program, in comparison with the total number or percentage of persons of such race, color, religion, sex, or national origin in any community, State, section, or other area, or in the available work force in any community, State, section, or other area.

■ THE SHERMAN ACT (EXCERPTS)

Section 1. Trusts, Etc., in Restraint of Trade Illegal; Penalty

Every contract, combination in the form of trust or otherwise, or conspiracy, in restraint of trade or commerce among the several States, or with foreign nations, is declared to be illegal. Every person who shall make any contract or engage in any combination or conspiracy declared by sections 1 to 7 of this title to be illegal shall be deemed guilty of a felony, and, on conviction thereof, shall be punished by fine not exceeding one million dollars if a corporation, or if any other person, one hundred thousand dollars, or by imprisonment not exceeding three years, or by both said punishments, in the discretion of the court.

Section 2. Monopolizing Trade a Felony; Penalty

Every person who shall monopolize, or attempt to monopolize, or combine or conspire with any other person or persons, to monopolize any part of the trade or commerce among the several States, or with foreign nations, shall be deemed guilty of a felony, and, on conviction thereof, shall be punished by fine not exceeding one million dollars if a corporation, or, if any other person, one hundred thousand dollars, or by imprisonment not exceeding three years, or by both said punishments, in the discretion of the court.

■ THE CLAYTON ACT (EXCERPTS)

Section 3. Sale, Etc., on Agreement Not to Use Goods of Competitor

It shall be unlawful for any person engaged in commerce, in the course of such commerce, to lease or make a sale or contract for sale of goods, wares, merchandise, machinery, supplies, or other commodities, whether patented or unpatented, for use, consumption, or resale within the United States or any Territory thereof or the District of Columbia or any insular possession or other place under the jurisdiction of the United States, or fix a price charged therefor, or discount from, or rebate upon, such price, on the condition, agreement, or understanding that the lessee or purchaser thereof shall not use or deal in the goods, wares, merchandise, machinery, supplies, or other commodities of a competitor or competitors of the lessor or seller, where the effect of such lease, sale, or contract for sale or such condition, agreement or understanding may be to substantially lessen competition or tend to create a monopoly in any line of commerce.

Section 4. Suits by Persons Injured; Amount of Recovery

Any person who shall be injured in his business or property by reason of anything forbidden in the anti-trust laws may sue therefor in any district court of the United States in the district in which the defendant resides or is found or has an agent, without respect to the amount in controversy, and shall recover threefold the damages by him sustained, and the cost of suit, including a reasonable attorney's fee.

Section 4A. Suits by United States; Amount of Recovery

Whenever the United States is hereafter injured in its business or property by reason of anything forbidden in the antitrust laws it may sue therefor in the United States district court for the district in which the defendant resides or is found or has an agent, without respect to the amount in controversy, and shall recover actual damages by it sustained and the cost of suit.

Section 4B. Limitation of Actions

Any action to enforce any cause of action under sections 15 or 15a of this title [§§ 4 and 4A of the Clayton Act] shall be forever barred unless commenced within four years after the cause of action accrued. No cause of action barred under existing law on the effective date of this section and sections 15a and 16 [§§ 4A and 5 of the Clayton Act] of this title shall be revived by said sections.

Section 6. Antitrust Laws Not Applicable to Labor Organizations

The labor of a human being is not a commodity or article of commerce. Nothing contained in the antitrust laws shall be construed to forbid the existence and operation of labor, agricultural, or horticultural organizations, instituted for the purposes of mutual help, and not having capital stock or conducted for profit, or to forbid or restrain individual members of such organizations from lawfully carrying out the legitimate objects thereof; nor shall such organizations, or the members thereof, be held or construed to be illegal combinations or conspiracies in restraint of trade, under the antitrust law.

Section 7. Acquisition by One Corporation of Stock of Another

No corporation engaged in commerce shall acquire, directly or indirectly, the whole or any part of the stock or other share capital and no corporation subject to the jurisdiction of the Federal Trade Commission shall acquire the whole or any part of the assets of another corporation engaged also in commerce, where in any line of commerce in any section of the country, the effect of such acquisition may be substantially to lessen competition, or to tend to create a monopoly.

No corporation shall acquire, directly or indirectly, the whole or any part of the stock or other share capital and no corporation subject to the jurisdiction of the Federal Trade Commission shall acquire the whole or any part of the assets of one or more corporations engaged in commerce, where in any line of commerce in any section of the country, the effect of such acquisition, of such stocks or assets, or of the use of such stock by the voting or granting of proxies or otherwise, may be substantially to lessen competition, or to tend to create a monopoly.

This section shall not apply to corporations purchasing such stock solely for investment and not using the same by voting or otherwise to bring about, or in attempting to bring about, the substantial lessening of competition. Nor shall anything contained in this section prevent a corporation engaged in commerce from causing the formation of subsidiary corporations for the actual carrying on of their immediate lawful business, or the natural and legitimate branches or extensions thereof, or from owning and holding all or part of the stock of such subsidiary corporations, when the effect of such formation is not to substantially lessen competition.

Section 8. Interlocking Directorates and Officers

No person at the same time shall be a director in any two or more corporations, any one of which has capital, surplus, and undivided profits aggregating more than $1,000,000, engaged in whole or in part in commerce, other than banks, banking associations, trust companies, and common carriers subject to the Act to regulate commerce, approved February fourth, eighteen hundred and eighty-seven, if such corporations are or shall have been theretofore, by virtue of their business and location of operation, competitors, so that the elimination of competition by agreement between them would constitute a violation of any of the provisions of any of the antitrust laws. The eligibility of a director under the foregoing provision shall be determined by the aggregate amount of the capital, surplus, and undivided profits, exclusive of dividends declared but not paid to stockholders, at the end of the fiscal year of said corporation next preceding the election of directors, and when a director has been elected in accordance with the provisions of this Act it shall be lawful for him to continue as such for one year thereafter.

BIBLIOGRAPHY

CHAPTER 1: WHAT IS LAW?

Bodenheimer, Edgar. "Jurisprudence," *Guide to American Law*. West, 1984.

Christie, George C. "Positive Law," *Guide to American Law*. West, 1984.

Feinberg, Joel, and Hyman Gross. *The Philosophy of the Law*. Wadsworth, 1986.

Friedman, Laurence M. *American Law*. Norton, 1984.

Fuller, Lon L. *The Morality of Law*. Yale University Press, 1964.

Gall, Gerald L. *The Canadian Legal System*, 2nd ed. Carswell, 1983.

Gutman, Israel, ed. *Encyclopedia of the Holocaust*. Vol. 3. Macmillan, 1990.

Llewellyn, Karl. "K.N. Llewellyn," in Joseph Bingham, Morris Cohen, Walter Cook et al., *My Philosophy of Law: Codes of 16 American Scholars*. Boston Law Book Co., 1941.

Loh, Wallace D. "Law and Social Science," in Robert Janosik, ed. *The Encyclopedia of the American Judicial System*. Scribner, 1987.

Murphy, Walter F., and C. Herman Pritchett. *Courts, Judges, and Politics*, 2nd ed. Random House, 1974.

Vago, Steven. *Law and Society*. Prentice Hall, 1981.

CHAPTER 2: ETHICS AND SOCIAL RESPONSIBILITY

Andrews, Kenneth R. "Ethics in Practice," *Harvard Business Review* 67 (1989).

Berle, A. A. "Corporate Powers as Powers in Trust," 44 *Harvard Law Review* 1049 (1931).

Baumhart, Raymond C. "How Ethical Are Businessmen?" *Harvard Business Review* 39 (July–August 1961).

Carroll, Archie B. "A Three-Dimensional Conceptual Model of Corporate Performance," *Academy of Management Review* (Oct. 1979).

Cavanaugh, Gerald F., and Arthur F. McGovern. *Ethical Dilemmas in the Modern Corporation*. Prentice Hall, 1988.

Churchill, Neil. "Toward a Theory of Social Accounting," *Sloan Management Review* 15:3 (1974).

Dodd, E. Merrick. "For Whom Are Managers Corporate Trustees?" *Harvard Law Review* 45 (1932).

Foote, Susan B. "Corporate Responsibility in a Changing Legal Environment," *California Management Review* 26:3 (1984).

Freeman, R. Edward. *Strategic Management: A Stakeholder Approach*. Pittman, 1984.

Freeman, R. Edward, and Daniel R. Gilbert, Jr. *Corporate Strategy and the Search for Ethics*. Prentice Hall, 1988.

Friedman, Milton. *Capitalism and Freedom*. University of Chicago Press, 1963.

Landes, David. *The Unbound Prometheus*. Cambridge University Press, 1969.

Pastin, Mark. "Business Ethics, By the Book," *Business Horizons* 28 (1986).

Preston, Lee E. *Social Issues and Public Policy in Business and Management: Retrospect and Prospect*. University of Maryland College of Business and Management, 1986.

Rawls, John. "Justice as Fairness," rpt. in Hoffman, W. Michael, and Jennifer Mills Moore. *Business Ethics*. McGraw-Hill, 1984.

Rawls, John. *A Theory of Justice*. Harvard Belknap, 1971.

Velasquez, Manuel G. *Business Ethics: Concepts and Cases*. Prentice Hall, 1982.

CHAPTER 3: THE CONSTITUTION AND BUSINESS

Brigham, John. *Civil Liberties and American Democracy.* Congressional Quarterly, 1984.

Burns, James MacGregor, J. W. Peltason, and Thomas E. Cronin. *Government by the People,* 13th ed. Prentice Hall, 1987.

"Constitutional Law—First Amendment—Protection of Commercial Speech," 32 *University of Kansas Law Review* 679 (1984).

"Constitutional Law—Interscholastic High School Athletics and the Right to Procedural Due Process," 17 *Suffolk University Law Review* 269 (1983).

"Constitutional Law—Obscenity— . . . the Determination of Obscenity Set Forth in *Miller v. California,*" 51 *University of Cincinnati Law Review* 669 (1982).

Greenwalt, Kent. "Free Speech Justifications," 89 *Columbia Law Review* 119 (1989).

Labunski, Richard. "The 'Collateral Bar' Rule and the First Amendment: The Constitutionality of Enforcing Unconstitutional Orders," 37 *American University Law Review* 323 (1988).

Lewis, Anthony. "*New York Times v. Sullivan* Reconsidered: Time to Return to 'The Central Meaning of the First Amendment,'" 83 *Columbia Law Review* 603 (1983).

Nowak, John E., Ronald D. Rotunda, and J. Nelson Young. *Handbook on Constitutional Law,* 2nd ed. West, 1983.

Pierce, Samuel R., Jr. "Anatomy of an Historic Decision: *New York Times Co. v. Sullivan,*" 43 *North Carolina Law Review* 315 (1965).

Pritchett, Charles Herman. *Constitutional Law of the Federal System.* Prentice Hall, 1984.

Rehnquist, William H. "A Plea for Help: Solutions to Serious Problems Currently Experienced by the Federal Judicial System," 28 *St. Louis University Law Journal* 1 (1984).

"The Standard of Review in Equal Protection and Due Process Challenges to Vermont's Blue Laws," 6 *Vermont Law Review* 173 (1981).

Stern, Robert L. "The Scope of the Phrase *Interstate Commerce,*" *American Bar Association Journal* (July 1955).

Stevens, John Paul. "Some Thoughts on Judicial Restraint," *Judicature* 66 (1982).

Stewart, David O. "Skeptical about Speech," *ABA Journal* (October 1991).

CHAPTER 4: THE COURT SYSTEM

Administrative Office of the United States Courts. *Federal Judicial Workload Statistics.* Government Printing Office, 1990.

Administrative Office of the United States Courts. *The United States Courts: Their Jurisdiction and Work.* Government Printing Office, 1989.

Bator, Paul M., et al. *Hart and Wechsler's Federal Courts and the Federal System.* West, 1981.

Black, Eugene F. "A Brief for Resurrection of Equity Jurisprudence," 60 *Michigan State Bar Journal* 381 (1981).

Burger, Warren E. "Annual Report on the State of the Judiciary," 69 *American Bar Association Journal* 442 (1983).

"Comments: Threat of Enforcement—Prerequisite of a Justiciable Controversy," 62 *Columbia Law Review* 106 (1962).

Frank, Jerome. "The Judging Process and the Judge's Personality," in John J. Bonsignore et. al., *Before the Law: An Introduction to the Legal Process.* 3rd ed. Houghton-Mifflin, 1984.

Frankfurter, Felix. "A Note on Advisory Opinions," 37 *Harvard Law Review* 1002.

Friedenthal, Jack H., Marykay Kane, and Arthur R. Miller. *Civil Procedure.* West, 1985.

Friedman, Lawrence. *American Law.* Norton, 1984.

Gale, Mary Ellen. "Retribution, Punishment, and Death," 18 *University of California, Davis Law Review* 973 (1985).

Geimer, William S. "Death at Any Cost: A Critique of the Supreme Court's Recent Retreat from Its Death Penalty Standards," 12 *Florida State University Law Review* 737 (1985).

Leonard, Arthur S. "Specific Performance of Collective Bargaining Agreements," 52 *Fordham Law Review* 193 (1983).

Levi, Edward H. *An Introduction to Legal Reasoning.* University of Chicago Press, 1948.

Newman, Ralph A. "The Place and Function of Pure Equity in the Structure of Law," 16 *Hastings Law Journal* 401 (1965).

O'Brien, David M. *Judicial Roulette: Report of the Twentieth Century Fund Task Force on Judicial Selection.* Priority Press, 1988.

Pritchett, C. Harman. *Constitutional Law of the Federal System.* Prentice Hall, 1984.

Re, Edward D. *Cases and Materials on Remedies* Foundation Press, 1982.

Schwartz, Alan. "The Case for Specific Performance," 89 *Yale Law Journal* 271 (1979).

Thompson, Robert S., and John A. Sebert, Jr. *Remedies: Damages, Equity, and Restitution.* Bender, 1983.

Tribe, Laurence H. *God Save This Honorable Court: How the Choice of Supreme Court Justices Shapes Our History.* Random House, 1985.

Weinstein, Jack B. "Rendering Advisory Opinions—Do We, Should We?" *Judicature* 54 (November, 1970).

CHAPTER 5: LITIGATION DISPUTE RESOLUTION

Charfoos, Lawrence S., and David W. Christensen. "Depositions: A Practical Guide," *Trial* (August 1986).

Clark, Lincoln, and Jane Orbeton. "Mandatory Mediation of Divorce: Maine's Experience," *Judicature* 69 (Feb.–Mar. 1986).

Conklin, Daral G. "Plain Talk about Pleadings," *Hawaii Bar Journal* 16 (1981).

Couric, Emily. "Jury Sleuths: In Search of the Perfect Panel," *National Law Journal,* (21 July 1986).

"Developments in the Law—State Court Jurisdiction," 73 *Harvard Law Review* 911 (1960).

James, Fleming, and Geoffrey Hazard. *Civil Procedure.* 3rd ed. Little, Brown, 1985.

Kasunic, David E. "One Day/One Trial: A Major Improvement in the Jury System," *Judicature* 67 (Aug. 1983).

Kennelly, John J. "Effective Discovery vis-a-vis Abuse of Discovery—Which Is Which?" *Trial Lawyer's Guide* 29 (1985).

Kirsch, Jonathan L. "Which Courthouse? What Advantage?" *California Lawyer* 6 (1986).

Kurland, Philip B. "The Supreme Court, the Due Process Clause, and the In Personam Jurisdiction of State Courts," 25 *University of Chicago Law Review* 569 (1958).

Outline of Japanese Judicial System. Supreme Court of Japan, 1987.

Phillips, Barbara Ashley, and Anthony C. Piazza. "Using Mediation to Resolve Disputes," *California Lawyer* 3 (1983).

Rosenberg, Maurice. "Can Court-Related Alternatives Improve Our Dispute Resolution System?" *Judicature* 69 (Feb.–Mar. 1986).

Tierney, Joan D. "Demonstrative Evidence," *Trial* (January 1986).

Weiner, Stephen A., "The Civil Jury Trial and the Law-Fact Distinction," 54 *California Law Review* 1867 (1966).

Wright, Charles Alan. *Handbook of the Law of Federal Courts.* 4th ed. West, 1983.

Wrightsman, Lawrence S. *Psychology and the Legal System.* Brooks/Cole, 1987.

CHAPTER 6: REGULATION AND ADMINISTRATIVE AGENCIES

Asbury, Carolyn H. "The Orphan Drug Act: The First Seven Years," *Journal of the American Medical Association* 265 (February 1991).

Benson, James S. "FDA Enforcement Activities Protect Public," *FDA Consumer* (January–February 1991).

Berger, Rauol. "Administrative Arbitrariness and Judicial Review," 65 *Columbia Law Review* 55 (1965).

Breyer, Stephen. *Regulation and Its Reform.* Harvard University Press, 1982.

Burros, Marian. "F.D.A. Plans to Take the Fantasy out of Food Labels," *The New York Times* (18 September 1991).

Dodd, Walter F. "Administrative Agencies as Legisla-

tors and Judges," *American Bar Association Journal* 25 (1939).

Edwards, David V. *The American Political Experience: An Introduction to Government.* 4th ed. Prentice Hall, 1988.

Federal Regulatory Directory. 5th ed. Congressional Quarterly, 1986.

Fine, Michael Ezra. "Rethinking the Nondelegation Doctrine," 62 *Boston University Law Review* 257 (1982).

Garner, Les. "Management Control in Regulatory Agencies: A Modest Proposal for Reform," 34 *Administrative Law Review* 465 (1987).

Gellhorn, Ernest, and Barry Boyer. *Administrative Law and Process.* West, 1981.

Gibbons, Ann. "Billion-Dollar Orphans: Prescription for Trouble," *Science* 24 (May 1990).

Lowi, Theodore J., and Benjamin Ginsberg. *American Government: Freedom and Power.* Norton, 1990.

Hysom, John and William Bolce. *Business and Its Environment.* West, 1983.

McFarland, Dalton E. *Management and Society: An Institutional Framework.* Prentice Hall, 1982.

McGarity, Thomas O. "Regulatory Reform in the Reagan Era," 45 *Maryland Law Review* 253 (1986).

Pierce, Richard J., et al. *Administrative Law and Process.* Foundation Press, 1985.

Rosenberg, Morton. "Beyond the Limits of Executive Power: Presidential Control of Agency Rulemaking Under Executive Order 12, 291," 80 *Michigan Law Review* 193 (1981).

Rosenstein, David. "Another Look at Rules of Evidence for Public Service Commission Proceedings," 34 *Administrative Law Review* 373 (1982).

Saks, Michael. "Holding the Independent Agencies Accountable: Legislative Veto of Agency Rules," 36 *Administrative Law Review* 41 (1984).

Shapiro, David L. "The Choice of Rulemaking or Adjudication in the Development of Administrative Policy," 78 *Harvard Law Review* 921 (1965).

Stewart, Richard B. "The Reformation of American Administrative Law," 88 *Harvard Law Review,* 1669 (1975).

Strauss, Peter L., and Cass R. Sunstein. "The Role of the President and OMB in Informal Rulemaking," 38 *Administrative Law Review* 181 (1986).

Warren, Kenneth. *Administrative Law in the American Political System.* West, 1982.

Weidenbaum, Murray L. *Business, Government, and the Public.* 4th ed. Prentice Hall, 1990.

CHAPTER 7: FORMS OF BUSINESS ORGANIZATION

Barker, Robert. "Prime Cut: Burger King's Master Limited Partnership," *Barron's* (28 April 1986).

Brenner, Gary, Joel Ewan, and Henry Custer. *The Complete Handbook for the Entrepreneur.* Prentice Hall, 1990.

Buchholz, Rogene A. *Business Environment and Public Policy.* 2nd ed. Prentice Hall, 1986.

Conard, Alfred F., Robert L. Knauss, and Stanley Siegal. *Enterprise Organization.* 3rd ed. Foundation Press, 1982.

Crane, Judson A., and Alan A. Bromberg. *Law of Partnership.* West, 1968.

Friedman, Lawrence M. *A History of American Law.* Simon & Schuster, 1985.

Hamilton, Robert W. *The Law of Corporations.* West, 1980.

Hamsmann, Henry B. "The Role of Non-Profit Enterprise," 89 *Yale Law Journal* 835 (1980).

Henn, Harry G., and John R. Alexander. *Law of Corporations.* West, 1983.

Hillman, Robert W. "Power Shared and Power Denied: A Look at Participatory Rights in the Management of General Partnerships," 4 *University of Illinois Law Review* 865 (1984).

Holstein, William J. "The Stateless Corporation," *Business Week* (14 May 1990).

Katz, Donald R. "The Big Store," *Esquire* (September 1987).

Siler, Julia Flynn. "Bolting the Boardroom Door at Sears," *Business Week* (31 May 1991).

Steffen, Roscoe T. *Agency-Partnership.* West, 1977.

Stewart, Thomas A. "How to Manage in the New Era," *Fortune* (15 January 1990).

Swasy, Alecia. "Procter & Gamble Fixes Aim on Tough Market: The Latin Americans," *The Wall Street Journal* (15 June 1990).

Veasy, E. Norman. "Further Reflections on Court Review of Judgments of Directors," *Business Lawyer* 40 (August 1985).

Worthy, J. C. *Shaping an American Institution: Robert E. Wood and Sears, Roebuck.* University of Illinois Press, 1984.

CHAPTER 8: SECURITIES REGULATION

Alsup, Roger. "A Peek under the Shell: Investment Bank's Equity Position in Tender Offer Should Trigger Disclosure Requirements of the Williams Act," 46 *Washington and Lee Law Review* 689 (1989).

Block, Dennis J., and Nancy E. Barton. "Section 16(b) of the Exchange Act: An Archaic Insider Trading Statute in Need of Reform," 12 *Securities Regulation Law Journal* 203 (1984).

Bloomenthal, Harold S. *Securities Law Handbook.* Clark Boardman, 1984.

Burns, Rita. "State Takeover Laws: The Third Generation," 21 *UWLA Law Review* 63 (1990).

Carter, John C. "Remedies Act: Revisions Will Limit the Impact," *National Law Journal* (July 1991).

De Toro, Anthony. "Market Manipulation of Penny Stocks," 17 *Securities Regulation Law Journal* 227 (1989).

Federal Regulatory Directory. 7th ed. Congressional Quarterly, 1989.

Henn, Harry G., et al. *Handbook of the Law of Corporations.* 3rd ed. West, 1983.

Jennings, Richard W., and Harold Marsh, J. *Securities Regulation: Cases and Materials.* 6th ed. Foundation Press, 1991.

Jiminez, Pamela. "International Securities Enforcement Cooperation Act and Memoranda of Understanding," 31 *Harvard International Law Journal* 295 (1990).

Ketchum, Richard G. "The Role of the Securities and Exchange Commission in Regulating International Securities Trading: Looking to the Future," 4 *Boston University International Law Journal* 33 (1986).

Kripke, Homer. "Fifty Years of Securities Regulation in Search of a Purpose," *Corporate Practice Commentator* (1984–85).

Langevoort, Donald C. "The Insider Trading Sanctions Act of 1984 and Its Effect on Existing Law," 37 *Vanderbilt Law Review* 1273 (1984).

Lazarow, Warren Todd. "The Misappropriation Theory in Light of *Carpenter* and the Insider Trading and Securities Fraud Enforcement Act," 17 *Pepperdine Law Review* 185 (1989).

Lidstone, Herrick K., Jr. "The Securities Enforcement Remedies and Penny Stock Reform Act of 1990," *Business Law Newsletter* (February 1991).

Long, Joseph C. *Blue Sky Law.* Clark Boardman, 1986.

Mahoney, Paul G. "Securities Regulation by Enforcement: An International Perspective," 7 *Yale Journal on Regulation* 149 (1990).

Ravech, Barry. "Securities Law—Application of Chapter 93A to Rule 10B-5 Violations—When Is a Note a Security Under Rule 10B-5?" 71 *Massachusetts Law Review* 145 (1986).

Shopkorn, Stanley B. "Global Trading: The Current and Future Impact on United States Markets and United States Portfolio Managers," 4 *Boston University International Law Journal* 25 (1986).

"Short-Swing Profits in Failed Takeover Bids—The Role of Section 16(b)," 59 *Washington Law Review* 895 (1984).

Skousen, K. Fred. *An Introduction to the SEC.* South-Western, 1980.

Sontag, Sherry R. "Regulators Fight a Cagey Foe," *National Law Journal* (14 May 1990).

Steinberg, Marc I. *Securities Regulation.* Law Journal Seminars-Press, 1986.

Stewart, James B. *Den of Thieves.* Simon and Schuster, 1991.

Stone, Dan G. *April Fools: An Insider's Account of the Rise and Collapse of Drexel Burnham.* Warner, 1991.

Tidwell, Gary L. "Here's a Tip—Know the Rules of Insider Trading," *Sloan Management Review* (Summer 1987).

Titus, Robert B., and Peter G. Carroll. "Netting the Outsider: The Need for a Broader Restatement of

Insider Trading Doctrine," 8 *Western New England Law Review* 127 (1986).

Van Horne, James C. *Financial Management and Policy.* 7th ed. Prentice Hall, 1986.

CHAPTER 9: CONTRACTS

Blum, Brian A., and Juliana B. Wellman. "Participation, Assent, and Liberty in Contract Formation," 26 *Arizona State Law Journal* 901 (1982).

Calamari, John D., and Joseph M. Perillo. *Handbook of the Law of Contracts.* West, 1977.

Edwards, Carolyn M. "Contract Formulation under Article 2 of the Uniform Commercial Code," 61 *Marquette Law Review* 215 (1977).

Eisenberg, Melvin A. "The Bargain Principle and its Limits," 95 *Harvard Law Review* 741 (1982).

Epstein, Richard A. "Unconscionability: A Critical Reappraisal," 18 *Journal of Law and Economics* 293 (1975).

Fuller, Lon L., and Melvin A. Eisenberg. *Basic Contract Law.* 4th ed. West, 1981.

Gabel, Peter, and Jay M. Feinman. "Contract Law as Ideology," in *The Politics of Law: a Progressive Critique,* David Kairys, ed. Pantheon, 1982.

Goldstein, Mark A. "U.N. Convention Demystifies International Sales Contracts," *Business Credit* (November–December 1990).

Goldstein, Mark A. "The U.N. Sales Convention: A New Tool to Help in Drafting International Sales Contracts," *Business America* (21 November 1988).

Kronman, Anthony T. "Contract Law and Distributive Justice," 89 *Yale Law Journal* 472 (1980).

Kronman, Anthony T. "Mistake, Disclosure, Information, and the Law of Contracts," *Journal of Legal Studies* 7 (1978).

Llewellyn, Karl N. "Why We Need the Uniform Commercial Code," 4 *University of Florida Law Review* 367 (1957).

Mentschikoff, Soia. "Reflections of a Drafter: Soia Mentschikoff," 43 *Ohio State Law Journal* 537 (1982).

Niehaus, James B. "Unconscionability and the Fundamental Breach Doctrine in Computer Contracts," 57 *Notre Dame Lawyer* 547 (1982).

Para, Noel J. "New Taboos on the International Sale of Goods," *Management Review* (July 1991).

Petit, Mark Jr. "Modern Unilateral Contracts," 63 *Boston University Law Review* 551 (1983).

Smyth, J., and D. Soberman. *The Law and Business Administration in Canada.* 5th ed. Prentice Hall, 1987.

Stern, Richard L., and Reed Abelson. "Franchise Hell," *Forbes* (2 September 1991).

Taylor, Graham R., and Maria L. Crisera. "Sales of Goods: U.N. Pact Has Wide Application," *National Law Journal* (23 December 1991).

Tiersma, Peter M. "The Language of Offer and Acceptance: Speech Acts and the Question of Intent," 74 *California Law Review* 189 (1986).

Travalio, Gregory M. "Clearing the Air After Battle: Reconciling Fairness and Efficiency in A Formal Approach to U.C.C. Section 2-207," 33 *Case Western Reserve Law Review* 327 (1983).

Twining, William. *Karl Llewellyn and the Realist Movement.* Wiedenfeld and Nicholson, 1985.

White, James J., and Robert S. Summers. *Handbook on the Uniform Commercial Code.* West, 1972.

Whittemore, Meg. "International Franchising," *Inc.* (April 1988).

CHAPTER 10: TORTS

Areno, Alvin, and James Loebbecke. *Auditing.* 4th ed. Prentice Hall, 1988.

Cassels, Jamie. "The Uncertain Lesson of Law: Lessons from Bhopal," 29 *Osgood Hall Law Journal* 1 (1991).

Chakravarty, Subrata N. "The Ghost Returns," *Forbes* (10 December 1990).

Conaway, Sharon E. "The Continuing Search for Solutions to the Drinking Driver Tragedy and the Problem of Social Host Liability," 82 *Northwestern University Law Review* 403 (1988).

Delgado, Richard. "Beyond *Sindell:* Relaxation of Cause-in-Fact Rules for Indeterminate Plaintiffs," 70 *California Law Review* 881 (1982).

Franklin, Marc A., and Robert L. Rabin. *Tort Law and Alternatives.* 3rd ed. Foundation Press, 1983.

Galanter, Marc. "Legal Torpor: Why So Little Has Happened in India after the Bhopal Tragedy," 20 *Texas International Law Journal* 269 (1985).

Jacob, Rahul. "Can You Trust That Audit?" *Fortune* (18 November 1991).

Laizer, Edwin C. "The Right to Be Left Alone—The Invasion of Privacy Tort in the Louisiana Jurisprudence," 30 *Loyola Law Review* 953 (1984).

Lowhurst, Daven G. "Intra-Corporate Communications: Sufficient Publication for Defamation or Mere Corporate Babbling?" 7 *Comm/Ent L.J.* 647 (1985).

Menzel, David L. "The Defense of Contributory Negligence in Accountant's Malpractice Actions," 13 *Seton Hall Law Review* 292 (1982).

Prosser, William L., and W. Page Keeton. *Prosser and Keeton on Torts.* 5th ed. West, 1984.

Reynolds, Osborne M., Jr. "Tortious Battery: Is I Didn't Mean Any Harm' Relevant?" 37 *Oklahoma Law Review* 717 (1984).

Seminara, Mary H. "When the Party's Over: *McGuiggan v. New England Telephone & Telegraph Co.* and the Emergence of a Social Host Liability Standard in Massachusetts," 68 *Boston University Law Review* 193 (1988).

Smolla, Rodney A. "Emotional Distress and the First Amendment: An Analysis of *Hustler v. Falwell,*" 20 *Arizona State Law Journal* 369 (1988).

"Tort Law—Conditional Privilege for Defamatory Statements in Legitimate Business Communication," 19 *Suffolk University Law Review* 176 (1985).

"Tort Law—Negligence—Assumption of Risk—Sports Injuries," 21 *Duquesne Law Review* 815 (1983).

"Torts—Injury-by-Animal Law Exception to Traditional Common Law Premises Liability," 24 *Washburn Law Journal* 676 (1985).

Wright, Richard W. "Causation in Tort Law," 73 *California Law Review* 1735 (1985).

CHAPTER 11: PRODUCT LIABILITY

Brahams, Diana. "Medicine and the Law: Drug-Company Data and the Public Interest," *The Lancet* (24 August 1991).

Brimelow, Peter, and Leslie Spencer. "Ralph Nader, Inc.," *Forbes* (17 September 1990).

Calnan, Alan. "Perpetuating Negligence Principles in Strict Products Liability: The Use of State of the Art Concepts in Design Cases," 36 *Syracuse Law Review* 797 (1985).

Campbell, Richard P. "The Protective Order in Products Liability Litigation: Safeguard or Misnomer?" 31 *Boston College Law Review* 771 (1990).

"Case Note: Torts—Minnesota Replaces the Restatement Standard with a Negligence Standard in Design Defect Cases," 11 *William Mitchell Law Review* 891 (1985).

Cohan, John Alan. "The Uniform Commercial Code as Applied to Implied Warranties of 'Merchantability' and 'Fitness' in the Sale of Horses," 73 *Kentucky Law Journal* 665 (1985).

Coll, J. Peter, Jr. "Market-Share Liability Limited to Cases Involving DES Claims," *National Law Journal* (6 November 1989).

Cowley, Geoffrey. "Sweet Dreams or Nightmare?" *Newsweek* (19 August 1991).

Goldblatt, Samuel, et al. "Products Liability: Annual Survey of Recent Developments," 26 *Torts & Insurance Law Journal* 420 (1990).

Grant, Jonathan E. "The 'Misuse' Defense in Drug Products Liability Cases," 8 *Pace Law Review* 535 (1988).

Hermann, Gary D. "The Consumer Expectation Test—Application of a Difficult Standard for Determining Product Defects," *Federation of Insurance and Corporate Counsel Journal* (Winter 1991).

Hurst, Robert D., and Henry J. Baily. *American Law of Products Liability*. 2nd ed. Lawyers Co-operative, 1974.

Jameson, James B. "Applying the No-Privity Exception to Express Warranties—Another Step toward Extending Strict Liability to Recover Solely Economic Losses," 24 *South Texas Law Journal* 243 (1983).

Krulwich, Andrew S. "Recalls: Legal and Corporate Responses to FDA, CPSC, NHTSA, and Product Liability Considerations," *The Business Lawyer* 39 (February 1984).

Lester, Paul A. "The Magnuson-Moss Warranty Act: The Courts Begin to Talk," *Uniform Commercial Code Law Journal* 16 (Fall 1983).

Marmorstein, Jerome. "Tobacco Politics in the American Culture," *The Center Magazine* (July–August 1986).

Masten, Patricia Kurp. "The Move toward a Negligence Standard in Strict Products Liability Failure to Warn Cases," 27 *Duquesne Law Review* 755 (1989).

Matlow, Susan Kim. "Market Share Liability: A Current Assessment of a Decade-Old Doctrine," 44 *Vanderbilt Law Review* 369 (1991).

National Synposium on Civil Justice Issues. *In Search of Proper Balance*. Conference Report, New York City, April 30–May 1, 1986.

Prosser, William L. "The Assault upon the Citadel (Strict Liability to the Consumer)," 69 *Yale Law Journal* 1099 (1960).

Razook, Nim R. "The Ultimate Purchaser's and Remote Seller's Guide through the Code Defenses in Product Economic Loss Cases," *American Business Law Journal* 23 (Spring 1985).

Sargent, Randy G. "Sales—A Warranty of Fitness for a Particular Purpose Is Based upon a Special Reliance by the Buyer on the Seller to Provide Goods That Will Perform a Specific Use Envisaged and Communicated by the Buyer," 34 *Drake Law Review* 577 (1985).

Siggins, Charlotte Smith. "Strict Liability for Prescription Drugs: Which Shall Govern—Comment K or Strict Liability Applicable to Ordinary Products?" 16 *Golden Gate University Law Review* 309 (1986).

Therrien, Lois. "Motorola and NEC: Going for the Glory," *Business Week/Quality 1991* (August 1991).

White, James J., and Robert S. Summers. *Handbook of the Law Under the Uniform Commercial Code*. 2nd ed. West, 1980.

CHAPTER 12: BUSINESS CRIME AND CRIMINAL PROCEDURE

Brickey, Kathleen F. "Corporate Criminal Accountability: A Brief History and an Observation," 60 *Washington University Law Quarterly* 393 (1982).

Brown, Harold. "RICO—The New Dimension," 89 *Commercial Law Journal* 396 (1984).

"The Computer Fraud and Abuse Act of 1986: a Measured Response to a Growing Problem," 43 *Vanderbilt Law Review* 453 (1990).

Ginger, Laura. "Business' Civil RICO Liability Goes Unchecked: No Previous Conviction Required," *American Business Law Journal* 24 (Summer 1986).

Hansen, Ann C. "Criminal Law—Theft of Use of Computer Services—*State v. McGraw*," 7 *Western New England Law Review* 823 (1985).

Hollinger, Richard C., and Lonn Lanza-Kaduce. "The Process of Criminalization: The Case of Computer Crime Laws," *Criminology* 26 (1988).

Kell, Walter G., and William C. Boynton. *Modern Auditing*. 5th ed. Wiley, 1989.

LaFave, Wayne R., and Jerold Israel. *Criminal Procedure*. West, 1984.

LaFave, Wayne R., and Austin W. Scott, Jr. *Criminal Law*. West, 1986.

Low, Peter W., John Calvin Jeffries, Jr., and Richard Bonnie. *Criminal Law: Cases and Materials*. Foundation Press, 1982.

McCormack, David R. "The Tightening White Collar: Expanding Theories of Criminal Liability for Corporate Executives, Directors, and Attorneys," *Texas Bar Journal* 49 (May 1986).

Metzger, Michael B. "Corporate Criminal Liability for Defective Products: Policies, Problems, and Prospects," 73 *Georgetown Law Journal* 1 (1984).

Miller, Henry T., "Recent Changes in Criminal Law: The Federal Insanity Defense," 46 *Louisiana Law Review* 337 (1985).

Morawetz, Thomas H. "Retributivism and Justice," 16 *Connecticut Law Review* 803 (1984).

Pickholz, Marvin G., Stephen Horn, and Justin D. Simon. *Guide to White Collar Crime*. Bureau of National Affairs, 1986.

Reimer, Douglas M. "Judicial and Legislative Responses to Computer Crimes," *Insurance Counsel Journal* 53 (July 1986).

Skadden, Arps, Slate, Meagher & Flom. *Guide to RICO*. Bureau of National Affairs, 1986.

Tompkins, Joseph B., Jr., and Linda A. Mar. "The 1984 Federal Computer Crime Statute: A Partial Answer to a Pervasive Problem," 6 *Computer/Law Journal* 459 (Winter 1986).

CHAPTER 13: LABOR RELATIONS

Adams, Roy J. "Should Works Councils Be Used as Industrial Relations Policy?" *Monthly Labor Review* (July 1985).

Alexander, Kenneth O. "Worker Participation and the Law Once Again: Overview and Evaluation," *Labor Law Journal* 39 (1988).

Allen, Robert, and Timothy Keaveny. *Contemporary Labor Relations*. Addison-Wesley, 1983.

Berlin, Philip E. "More State Laws Now Regulate Drug Testing in the Workplace," *National Law Journal* (8 July 1991).

Berlowe, Amanda J. "Judicial Deference to Grievance Arbitration in the Private Sector: Saving *Grace* in the Search for a Well-Defined Public Policy Exception," 42 *University of Miami Law Review* 767 (1988).

Burton, John F., Jr., and Charles Krider. "The Role and Consequences of Strikes by Public Employees," 79 *Yale Law Journal* 148 (1979).

Carrel, Michael R., and Christina Heavrin. *Collective Bargaining and Labor Relations: Cases, Practice and Law*. Merrill, 1985.

Daughtrey, William H. Jr. "Another Exception under the Employment-at-Will Doctrine: *Bowman v. State Bank*," 24 *American Business Law Journal* 243 (1986).

Feldacker, Bruce S. *Labor Guide to Labor Law*. Reston, 1983.

Fox, Neil. "PATCO and the Courts: Public Sector Labor Law as Ideology," 85 *University of Illinois Law Review* 245 (1985).

General Executive Board Report to the 40th Convention of the International Ladies' Garment Workers' Union (June 1989).

Goldman, Alvin L., *Labor Law and Industrial Relations in the United States of America*. 2nd ed. Bureau of National Affairs, 1984.

Gould, William B., IV. "Judicial Review of Labor Arbitration Awards—Thirty Years of the *Steelworkers Trilogy*: The Aftermath of *AT&T* and *Misco*," 64 *Notre Dame Law Review* 464 (1989).

Herman, E. Edward, Joshua L. Schwarz, and Alfred Kuhn, *Collective Bargaining and Labor Relations*. 3rd ed. Prentice Hall, 1992.

Holley, William H., Jr., and Kenneth M. Jennings. *The Labor Relations Process*. 2nd ed. Dryden, 1984.

Hoyman, Michele, and Lamont E. Stallworth. "The Arbitration of Discrimination Grievances in the Aftermath of *Gardner-Denver*," *The Arbitration Journal* 39 (1984).

Janssen, Judith M. "Substance Abuse Testing and the Workplace: A Private Employer's Perspective," 12 *George Mason University Law Review* 611 (1990).

Kelley, Kevin W. "United Paperworkers International Union v. Misco," 18 *Capital University Law Review* 141 (1989).

McMillion, Major Michael R. "Collective Bargaining in the Federal Sector: Has the Congressional Intent Been Fulfilled?" 127 *Military Law Review* 169 (1990).

Metlzer, Bruce D. "The Supreme Court, Arbitrability, and Collective Bargaining," 28 *Chicago Law Review* 464 (1961).

Mukamal, Stuart S., and Jay E. Grenig. "Collective Bargaining: The Exclusion of Confidential and Managerial Employees," 22 *Duquesne Law Review* 1 (1983).

Schuler, Randall. *Personnel and Human Resource Management*. West, 1987.

Sloane, Arthur A., and Fred Witney. *Labor Relations*. 5th ed. Prentice Hall, 1985.

Taylor, Douglas, and Margaret K. Taylor. "Random Drug Testing in the Mass Transit Industry," 12 *George Mason University Law Review* 587 (1990).

Thornicroft, Kenneth W. "The War on Drugs Goes to Work: Employer Drug Testing and the Law," 17 *Ohio Northern University Law Review* 771 (1991).

CHAPTER 14: LABOR STANDARDS

Anderson, Patrick M. "The Agricultural Employee Exemption from the Fair Labor Standards Act of 1938," 12 *Hamline Law Review* 649 (1990).

Achenbaum, W. Andrew. *Social Security: Visions and Revisions.* Cambridge University Press, 1986.

"Benzene Exposure is Curbed by U.S.," *The New York Times* (3 September 1987).

Bixby, Michael B. "Workplace Homicide: Trends, Issues, and Policy," 70 *Oregon Law Review* 333 (1991).

Blan, Ollie L., Jr. "ERISA—A Primer for the Insurance Trial Counsel," *Insurance Counsel Journal* 53 (January 1986).

Bowens, Greg. "Detroit South: Mexico's Auto Boom," *Business Week* (16 March 1992).

CCH Editorial Staff. *Minimum Wages and Overtime Pay: The Answer Book on Federal Law.* Commerce Clearing House, 1985.

Chelius, James Robert. *Workplace Safety and Health: The Role of Workers' Compensation.* American Enterprise Institute for Public Policy Research, 1977.

Clarke, Charles H. "Supreme Court Assault on the Constitutional Settlement of the New Deal: *Garcia* and *National League of Cities*," 6 *Northern Illinois University Law Review* 39 (1986).

Cohen, Wilbur J. "The Development of the Social Security Act of 1935: Reflections Some 50 Years Later," 68 *Minnesota Law Review* 379 (1983).

Cross, Frank B. "Beyond Benzene: Establishing Principles for a Significance Threshold on Regulatable Risks of Cancer," *Emory Law Journal* 35 (Winter 1986).

Goldsmith, Willis J. "Current Developments in Safety and Health: Upping the OSHA Enforcement Ante," 16 *Employee Relations Law Journal* 543 (1991).

Hasty, Keith N. "Worker's Compensation: Will College and University Professors Be Compensated for Mental Injuries Caused by Work-Related Stress?" 17 *Journal of College and University Law* 535 (1991).

Hogwood, Terry. "The Occupational Safety and Health Act of 1970," 25 *Baylor Law Review* 104 (1973).

Holzman, Sy. "The Occupational Safety & Health Act: Is It Time for a Change?" 17 *Northern Kentucky Law Review* 177 (1989).

Ivancevich, John M., and William F. Glueck. *Foundations of Personnel/Human Resources Management.* Business Publications, Inc., 1983.

Karr, Albert R. "U.S. Tightens Benzene Rule for Workplace," *The Wall Street Journal* (2 September 1987).

Larson, Arthur. *Workers' Compensation Law: Cases, Materials, and Text.* Matthew Bender, 1984.

Lerner, Max. *Mr. Justice Brandeis.* Yale Univ. Press, 1932.

McGovern, Peter J. "Children's Rights and Child Labor: Advocacy on Behalf of the Child Worker," 28 *South Dakota Law Review* 293 (1982).

Milkovich, George T., and Jerry M. Newman. *Compensation.* Business Publications, Inc., 1987.

Nordlund, Willis J. "A Brief History of the Fair Labor Standards Act," *Labor Law Journal* 39 (1988).

O'Brien, Christine Neylon. "Revising the Minimum Wage for the 1990s," 12 *Loyola of Los Angeles International and Comparative Law Review* 217 (1989).

Pappas, Thomas P. "The Aftermath of *Garcia:* Will Justice Blackmun's Analysis Continue to Work?" 15 *Capital University Law Review* 543 (1986).

Postol, Lawrence P. "The Federal Solution to Occupational Disease Claims—The Longshore Act and Proposed Federal Programs," *Tort and Insurance Law* 21 (1986).

"The Proposed Subminimum Wage for Youth: Pro and Con," *Congressional Digest* (April 1985).

Rossrow, James M. "Unemployment Insurance System Marks Its 50th Anniversary," *Monthly Labor Review* (September 1985).

Rothstein, Mark A. "OSHA after Ten Years: A Review and Some Proposed Reforms," 34 *Vanderbilt Law Review* 71 (1981).

Ruhga, Victoria L. "Mental Stress and Workers' Compensation in Nebraska," 69 *Nebraska Law Review* 842 (1990).

Schuler, Randall S. *Personnel and Human Resource Management.* 3rd ed. West, 1987.

U.S. Chamber of Commerce, *Analysis of Workers' Compensation Laws 1985.* U.S. Chamber of Commerce, 1985.

Willis, Robert N. "The Evolution of the Fair Labor Standards Act," 26 *University of Miami Law Review* 607 (1972).

CHAPTER 15: EMPLOYMENT DISCRIMINATION

Bell, Carolyn Shaw. "Comparable Worth: How Do We Know It Will Work?" *Monthly Labor Review* (December 1985).

Braun, Michelle M. "The Battle between Mother and Fetus: Fetal Protection Policies in the Context of Employment Discrimination: *International Union, UAW v. Johnson Controls, Inc.*," 14 *Hamline Law Review* 401 (1991).

Brooks, Roy L. "Use of the Civil Rights Acts of 1866 and 1871 to Redress Employment Discrimination," 62 *Cornell Law Review* 258 (1977).

Burnham, Walter Dean. *Democracy in the Making: American Government and Politics.* 2nd ed. Prentice Hall, 1986.

Casey, Robert P., and David B. Montgomery. "New Act Clarifies Disparate-Impact Law," *National Law Journal* (9 March 1992).

Cherrington, David J. *Personnel Management: The Management of Human Resources.* 2nd ed. Wm. C. Brown, 1987.

Cooper, Charles J. "*Wards Cove Packing Co. v. Atonio*: A Step toward Eliminating Quotas in the American Workplace," 14 *Harvard Journal of Law & Public Policy* 84 (1991).

Deale, Frank E. "*Martin v. Wilks*," *Journal of Human Rights* 7 (1990).

Eglit, Howard. "The Age Discrimination Act of 1975, As Amended: Genesis and Selected Problem Areas," 57 *Chicago-Kent Law Review* 915 (1981).

Fisher, Jeffrey M. "In the Wake of *AT&T Technologies, Inc.*: Interpreting Title VII's Statute of Limitations for Facially Neutral Seniority Systems," 33 *University of Illinois Law Review* 711 (1990).

Flaccus, Janet A. "Discrimination Legislation for the Handicapped: Much Ferment and the Erosion of Coverage," 55 *University of Cincinnati Law Review* 81 (1986).

Furnish, Hannah Arterian. "A Path through the Maze: Disparate Impact and Disparate Treatment under Title VII of the Civil Rights Act of 1964 after *Beazer* and *Burdine*," 23 *Boston College Law Review* 419 (1982).

Grossman, Alison E. "Striking Down Fetal Protection Policies: A Feminist Victory?" 77 *Virginia Law Review* 1607 (1991).

Hammonds, Keith H. "Corning's Class Act," *Business Week* (31 May 1991).

Harbrecht, Douglas. "Sexual Harassment: Out of the Shadows," *Business Week* (28 October 1991).

Hernandez, Berta E. "Title VII V. Seniority; The Supreme Court Giveth and the Supreme Court Taketh Away," 35 *American University Law Review* 339 (1986).

Johnson, Robert Charles. "Partnership and Title VII Remedies: *Price Waterhouse* Cracks the Glass Ceiling," 41 *Wisconsin Law Review* 787 (1991).

Jones, James E., William P. Murphy, and Robert Belton. *Cases and Materials on Discrimination in Employment*. West, 1987.

Keotahian, Avak. "National Origin Discrimination in Employment: Do Plaintiffs Ever Win?," *Employee Relations Law Journal* 11 (1985/1986).

Kerner, Benjamin. "The Americans with Disabilities Act of 1990: New Challenges for Labor and Management," 3 *Detroit College of Law Review* 891 (1991).

Kovacic-Fleischer, Candace S. "Proving Discrimination after *Price Waterhouse* and *Wards Cove*: Semantics as Substance," 39 *American University Law Review* 573 (1990).

Lacayo, Richard. "Replying in the Affirmative," *Time* (9 March 1987).

Larson, David A. "What Disabilities Are Protected Under the Rehabilitation Act of 1973?" *Labor Law Journal* 37 (Nov. 1986).

Maney, Mark. "Application of the Adverse Impact Analysis to Subjective Criteria in Title VII Employment Discrimination Cases," 38 *Baylor Law Review* 363 (1986).

Mealey, Linda M. "English-Only Rules and 'Innocent' Employers: Clarifying National Origin Discrimination and Disparate Impact Theory under Title IV," 74 *Minnesota Law Review* 371 (1989).

Milkovich, George T., and Jerry M. Newman. *Compensation*. 2nd ed. Business Publications, Inc., 1987.

Monat, Jonathan S., and Angel Gomez. "Sexual Harassment: The Impact of *Meritor Savings Bank v. Vinson* on Grievances and Arbitration Decisions," *The Arbitration Journal* 41 (Summer 1986).

Perea, Juan F. "English-Only Rules and the Right to Speak One's Primary Language in the Workplace," 23 *Journal of Law Reform* 2 (1990).

Peterson, Janice. "The Challenge of Comparable Worth: An Institutionalist View," *Journal of Economic Issues* 24 (1990).

Postol, Lawrence P., and David D. Kadue. "An Employer's Guide to the Americans with Disabilities Act: From Job Qualifications to Reasonable Accomodations," 24 *John Marshall Law Review* 693 (1991).

Ross, Julia C. "New Civil Rights Act," *ABA Journal* (January 1992).

Samowitz, Cary B. "Title VII, United States Citizenship, and American National Origin," 60 *New York University Law Review* 245 (1985).

Schiff, Martin. "Reverse Descrimination Re-Defined as Equal Protection: The Orwellian Nightmare in the Enforcement of Civil Rights Law," 8 *Harvard Journal of Law and Public Policy* 627 (1985).

Seymour, Richard T. "A Point of View: Why Executive Order 11246 Should Be Preserved," *Employee Relations Law Journal* 11 (1986).

Shaw, G. Jerry, and William L. Bransford. "From Disabled to Enabled: New Law Extends Rights of Handicapped in Employment," *ABA Journal* (February 1991).

Siniscalco, Gary R., and Cynthia Remmers. "Comparable Worth in the Aftermath of *AFSCME v. State of Washington*," *Employee Relations Law Journal* 10 (1984).

Sirota, Michael L. "Sex Discrimination: Title VII and the Bona Fide Occupational Qualification," 55 *Texas Law Review* 1025 (1977).

Sovereign, Kenneth L. *Personnel Law*. Reston, 1983.

Strickler, George M. "*Martin v. Wilks*," 64 *Tulane Law Review* 1557 (1990).

Sullivan, Charles A. "The Equal Pay Act of 1963: Making and Breaking a Prima Facie Case," 31 *Arkansas Law Review* 545 (1978).

Taylor, Benjamin T., and Fred Witney. *Labor Relations Law*. 6th ed. Prentice Hall, 1992.

Taylor, Susan H. "The Case for Comparable Worth," *Journal of Social Issues* 45 (1989).

Thomas, R. Roosevelt, Jr. "From Affirmative Action to

Affirming Diversity." In *Managing People and Organizations*. John J. Gabarro, ed. McGraw-Hill, 1991.

Tribe, Laurence H. "Dismantling the House That Racism Built: Assessing 'Affirmative Action,'" in *Constitutional Choices*. Harvard University Press, 1985.

Vogel, Michael S. "The Remains of Title VII after *Lorance v. AT&T Technologies*," 22 *Columbia Human Rights Law Review* 73 (1990).

Weiner, Eric S. "*Martin v. Wilks* and the Future of Consent Decrees as a Means of Settling Title VII Cases," *Civil Rights Journal* 1 (1990).

Wells, Jane May. "The Bona Fide Occupational Qualification Exception—Clarifying the Meaning of 'Occupational Qualification,'" 38 *Vanderbilt Law Review* 1345 (1985).

CHAPTER 16: ANTITRUST AND THE SHERMAN ACT

Areeda, Phillip, and Louis Kaplow. *Antitrust Analysis: Problems, Text, Cases*. 4th ed. Little, Brown, 1988.

Bartok, Richard E. "NFL Free Agency Restrictions under Antitrust Attack," 31 *Duke Law Journal* 503 (1991).

Bevan, Susan J. "Antitrust Per Se or Rule of Reason: The Right of Engineers to Formulate Bidding Policies as a Learned Profession—*National Society of Professional Engineers v. United States*," 28 *DePaul Law Review* 1141 (1979).

"Comments: Antitrust Law—Sherman Act, Section 2—A Monopolist Has No Duty to Predisclose Information on Innovations," 55 *Notre Dame Lawyer* 554 (1980).

Gellhorn, Ernest. *Antitrust Law and Economics*. West, 1981.

Graglia, Lino A. "One Hundred Years of Antitrust," *The Public Interest* (Summer 1991).

Hovenkamp, Herbert. *Economics and Federal Antitrust Law*. West, 1985.

Howard, Marshall C. *Antitrust and Trade Regulation*. Prentice Hall, 1983.

Johnson, Sam D., and A. Michael Ferrill. "Defining Competition: Economic Analysis and Antitrust Decisionmaking," 36 *Baylor Law Review* 585 (1984).

Kozik, Susan Marie. "*NCAA v. Board of Regents of Univ. of Okla et al.*," 61 *Chicago-Kent Law Review* 593 (1985).

Krattenmaker, Thomas G., Robert H. Lande, and Steven C. Salop. "Monopoly Power and Market Power in Antitrust Law," 76 *Georgetown Law Journal* 241 (1987).

Landes, William M., and Richard A. Posner. "Market Power in Antitrust Cases," 94 *Harvard Law Review* 937 (1981).

Lock, Ethan. "*Powell v. National Football League*: The Eighth Circuit Sacks the National Football League

Players Association," 67 *Denver University Law Review* 135 (1990).

Marcus, Philip. *Antitrust Law and Practice*. West, 1980.

Middleton, Martha. "'New Antitrust' Era Takes Shape," *National Law Journal* (January 1986).

"Notes: Unravelling the Current Rule for Applying the Per Se Rule: Explanations, Solutions, and a Proposal," 10 *Journal of Corporation Law* 1051 (1985).

Perkins, James Wilson. "*In re Japanese Electronic Products Antitrust Litigation*: Sovereign Compulsion, Act of State, and the Extraterritorial Reach of the United States Antitrust Laws," 36 *American University Law Review* 721 (1987).

Phillips, John R. "Things Your Mother Should Have Told You—A General Practitioner's Guide to U.S. Antitrust Law," 64 *Michigan Bar Journal* 25 (1985).

Shenefield, John H. "Thoughts on Extraterritorial Application of the United States Antitrust Laws," 52 *Fordham Law Review* 351 (1983).

Shepherd, William G. "Assessing 'Predatory' Actions by Market Shares and Selectivity," *Antitrust Bulletin* 31 (1986).

Thompson, Allen R. *Economics*. 2nd ed. Addison-Wesley, 1988.

Van Cise, Jerrold G. *The Federal Antitrust Laws*. 4th rev. ed. American Enterprise Institute, 1982.

Wertheimer, Barry. "Rethinking the Rule of Reason: From *Professional Engineers* to *NCAA*," 6 *Duke Law Journal* 1297 (1984).

CHAPTER 17: THE CLAYTON AND ROBINSON-PATMAN ACTS

Baker, Tyler A. "The Supreme Court and the Per Se Tying Rule: Cutting the Gordion Knot," 66 *Virginia Law Review* 1235 (1980).

Best, Michael H. *The New Competition: Institutions of Industrial Restructuring*. Harvard Univ. Press, 1990.

Brown, Donna. "Whither Japan's MITI?" *Management Review* (April 1991).

Cann, Wesley A., Jr. "Section 7 of the Clayton Act and the Pursuit of Economic 'Objectivity': Is There Any Role for Social and Political Values in Merger Policy?" 60 *Notre Dame Law Review* 273 (1985).

Coy, Peter. "Twin Engines: Can Bob Allen Blend Computers and Telecommunications at AT&T?" *Business Week* (20 January 1992).

Curran, William J., III. "Corporate Realities, Liberal Myths: Interpreting Section 7 of the Clayton Act," 30 *St. Louis University Law Journal* 171 (1985).

Doyle, Carol. "Reciprocity as a Basis for Challenging Conglomerate Mergers Under the Clayton Act," 12 *Loyola University Law Journal* 481 (1981).

Elzinga, Kenneth G. "The New International Economics Applied: Japanese Televisions and U.S. Consumers," 64 *Chicago-Kent Law Review* 941 (1988).

Goldstein, Jessica L. "Single Firm Predatory Pricing in Antitrust Law: The *Rose Acre* Recoupment Test and the Search for an Appropriate Judicial Standard," 91 *Columbia Law Review* 1757 (1991).

Howard, Marshall C. *Antitrust and Trade Regulation: Selection Issues and Case Studies.* Prentice Hall, 1983.

Isenstein, Tania. "Increasing the International Competitiveness of the United States through Its Joint Venture Laws: A Lesson to Be Learned from South Korea," 6 *American University Journal of International Law and Policy* 435 (1991).

Joskow, Paul L., and Alvin K. Klevorick. "A Framework for Analyzing Predatory Pricing Policy," 89 *The Yale Law Journal* 213 (1979).

Kramer, Victor H. "The Supreme Court and Tying Arrangements: Antitrust as History," 69 *Minnesota Law Review* 1013 (1985).

Kupfer, Andrew. "Bob Allen Rattles the Cages at AT&T," *Fortune* (19 June 1989).

LaRue, Paul H. "The Robinson-Patman Act: The Great Issues and Personalities," 55 *Antitrust Law Journal* 135 (1986).

Maher, John A., and Nancy J. LaMont. "National Cooperative Research Act of 1984: Cartelism for High-Tech Ventures (and Others?)," 7 *Dickinson Journal of International Law* 1 (1988).

Marcus, Philip. *Antitrust Law and Practice.* West, 1980, with 1983 Pocket Part.

Petty, Ross D. "Predatory Promotion: A Theory of Antitrust Liability Whose Time Has Come?" 27 *American Business Law Journal* 215 (1989).

Shniderman, Harry L. "The Robinson-Patman Act: A Critical Appraisal," 55 *Antitrust Law Journal* 149 (1986).

Simkovic, Martin S. "Judicial Tests to Determine Predatory Pricing before and after *Matsushita*," 44 *University of Miami Law Review* 839 (1990).

Steuer, Richard M. "Exclusive Dealing in Distribution," 69 *Cornell Law Review* 101 (1983).

Surdell, Steven M. "Mergers under the Reagan Justice Department: Redefining Section 7 of the Clayton Act," 11 *Journal of Legislation* 421 (1984).

Werden, Gregory J. "Challenges to Horizontal Mergers by Competitors under Section 7 of the Clayton Act," 24 *American Business Law Journal* 213 (1986).

Chapter 18: Trade Practices and Intellectual Property

"Apple 'Bytes' Back: Copyrightability of Computer Programs," 5 *Bridgeport Law Review* 363 (1984).

Bailey, Patricia P., and Michael Pertschuk. "The Law of Deception: The Past as Prologue," 33 *American University Law Review* 849 (1984).

Best, Arthur. "Controlling False Advertising: A Comparative Study of Public Regulation, Industry Self-Policing, and Private Litigation," 20 *Georgia Law Review* 1 (1985).

Burge, David A. *Patent and Trademark Tactics and Practice.* Wiley, 1984.

Coverdale, John F. "Trademarks and Generic Words: An Effect-on-Competition Test," 51 *University of Chicago Law Review* 868 (1984).

David, Bob, and David Stripp. "Patent for Genetically Altered Mouse Opens Era for Research, Spurs Protests," *The Wall Street Journal* (13 April 1988).

Evans, Lawrence E., Jr. "A Primer on Trademarks and Service Marks," 18 *St. Mary's Law Journal* 137 (1986).

Eveloff, Sheldon H., and Martin L. Faigus. "What Clients Need to Know about Software Piracy," *Journal of Accountancy* 170 (1990).

Field, Thomas G. "Brief Survey of the Proposal for Better Reconciliation of the Options in Patent, Trademark, Copyright, and Related Law," *Idea* 26 (1985).

Hobbs, Pamela. "Methods of Determining Substantial Similarity in Copyright Cases involving Computer Programs," 67 *University of Detroit Law Review* 393 (1990).

Hovenkamp, Herbert. "Technology, Politics, and Regulated Monopoly: An American Historical Perspective," 62 *Texas Law Review* 263 (1984).

Kaplow, Louis. "The Patent-Antitrust Intersection: A Reappraisal," 97 *Harvard Law Review* 1815 (1984).

Klitzke, Ramon A. "Patents and Monopolization: The Role of Patents under Section 2 of the Sherman Act," 68 *Marquette Law Review* 557 (1985).

McManis, Charles R. *The Law of Unfair Trade Practices.* West, 1983.

Middleton, Alan S. "A Thousand Clones: The Scope of Copyright Protection in the Look and Feel of Computer Programs," 63 *Washington Law Review* 195 (1988).

Miller, Arthur R., and Michael H. Davis, *Intellectual Property: Patents, Trademarks, and Copyright.* West, 1983.

"Notes: *Harper & Row, Publishers v. Nation Enterprises*—Rewriting the Fair Use Criteria?" 6 *Northern Illinois University Law Review* 379 (1986).

Raysman, Richard, and Peter Brown. "Copyright Protection Extended to a 'Total Concept' of Software," *National Law Journal* (January 1987).

Rice, David A. "Consumer Unfairness at the FTC: Misadventures in Law and Economics," 52 *George Washington Law Review* 1 (1984).

Rose, Lance. "End-User Licensees of Computer Programs—Are They Allowed to Compete with Their Licensors?" 13 *Rutgers Computer and Technology Law Journal* 297 (1987).

Rudnick, Rhoda L. "Window Dressing: Trademark Protection for Computer Screen Displays and Software," *Trademark Reporter* (July–August 1990).

Schechter, Roger E. *Unfair Trade Practices and Intellectual Property*. West, 1986.

Schulman, John. "Patents, Trademarks, and Copyrights—An Informal Comparative Analysis," 10 *New York Law Forum* 174 (1984).

Schuman, Gary. "False Advertising: A Discussion of a Competitor's Rights and Remedies," 15 *Loyola University Law Journal* 1 (1983).

Sorenson, Gail Paulus. "Impact of the Copyright Law on College Teaching," 12 *Journal of College and University Law* 509 (1986).

Sullivan, E. Thomas, and Brian A. Marks. "The FTC's Deceptive Advertising Policy: A Legal and Economic Analysis," 64 *Oregon Law Review* 593 (1986).

Ward, Peter. *Federal Trade Commission: Law, Practice, and Procedure*. Law Journal Seminars Press, 1986.

Westenberg, David A. "What's in a Name? Establishing and Maintaining Trademark and Service Mark Rights," *Business Lawyer* 18 (1986).

CHAPTER 19: DEBTOR-CREDITOR RELATIONS

Altman, Edward. *Corporate Financial Distress*. Wiley, 1983.

American Bar Association. *You and the Law*. Publications International, Ltd., 1990.

Barron, Paul. "An Introduction to the Fair Debt Collection Practices Act," 95 *Banking Law Journal* 500 (1978).

Beams, Floyd. *Advanced Accounting*. 4th ed. Prentice Hall, 1988.

Black, David F. "Truth in Lending after 'Simplification,'" 20 *Clearinghouse Review* 236 (1986).

Chatz, Robert B., John W. Costello, and Karen Gross. "An Overview of the Bankruptcy Code," *Commercial Law Journal* 34 (August/September 1979).

Dye, Harold V. "An Overview of Chapter 13—Its Uses and Abuses," 43 *Montana Law Review* 35 (1982).

Fensterstock, Blair C. "The Public and the Fair Credit Reporting Act," *Communications and the Law* 2 (1980).

Fisher, Paul, M., et al. *Advanced Accounting*. 3rd ed. Southwestern, 1986.

Fischer, L. Richard, Janice D. Lampinen, and Michael F. McEneney. "Consumer Credit: An Overview of New Credit and Charge Card Disclosure Requirements," 23 *Uniform Commercial Code Law Journal* 3 (1990).

Fox, Karla Harbin. "New Hope for Harassed Consumers: The Federal Fair Debt Collection Practices Act of 1977," 18 *American Business Law Journal* 19 (1980).

Griffith, Elwin. "Recent Developments in the Effort to Simplify Truth in Lending," 19 *Tulsa Law Journal* 30 (Fall 1983).

Haggard, Thomas R. "The Continuing Conflict Between Bankruptcy and Labor Law—The Issues that *Bildisco* and the 1984 Bankruptcy Amendments Did Not Resolve," 27 *Brigham Young University Law Review* 1 (1986).

Hilson, Daniel G. "The Genesis of a New Trend: Chapter 11, Avoiding or Managing Future Liability in Mass Tort Actions?" 15 *Capital University Law Review* 243 (1986).

Kaplan, Harold L. "Bankruptcy as a Corporate Management Tool," *ABA Journal* (January 1987).

Marston-Moore, Elizabeth. "Family Farmer Bankruptcy Act of 1986," *Ohio State Bar Association Report* (March 1987).

Matheson, John H. "The Equal Credit Opportunity Act: A Functional Failure," 21 *Harvard Journal on Legislation* 371 (1984).

Rasor, Paul B. "Privacy Implications of Consumer Credit Protection Laws," 19 *John Marshall Law Review* 941 (1986).

Schwartz, Evan I. "Credit Bureaus: Consumers Are Stewing—and Suing," *Business Week* (29 July 1991).

Taylor, Winnie F. "The Equal Credit Opportunity Act's Spousal Co-Signature Rules: Suretyship Contracts in Separate Property States," 48 *Albany Law Review* 382 (1984).

"What Price Privacy?" *Consumer Reports* (May 1991).

Winger, Bernard, and Frasca, Ralph, *Personal Finance* Charles Merrill, 1986.

CHAPTER 20: PROPERTY, LAND-USE, AND ENVIRONMENTAL LAW

"A Nation Troubled by Toxics," 19th Environmental Quality Index, *National Wildlife* (Feb.–Mar. 1987).

Albanese, Jay S. "Love Canal Six Years Later: The Legal Legacy," *Federal Probation* 48 (1984).

Beauchamp, Tom. *Case Studies in Business, Society, and Ethics*. Prentice Hall, 1983.

Bernhardt, Roger. *Real Property*. 2nd ed. West, 1981.

Boyer, Ralph E. *Survey of the Law of Property*. 3rd ed. West, 1981.

"The Council on Environmental Quality's Research and Worst Case Regulation: The Recent Litigation," 64 *Oregon Law Review* 547 (1986).

Cribbet, John E., and Corwin W. Johnson. *Property: Cases and Materials*. 5th ed. Foundation Press, 1984.

Frank, Robert P. "Delegation of Environmental Impact Statement Preparation: A Critique of NEPA's Enforcement," *Environmental Affairs* 13 (1985).

Gaba, Jeffrey M. "Federal Supervision of State Water Quality Standards Under the Clean Water Act," 36 *Vanderbilt Law Review* 1167 (1983).

Hagman, Donald G. *Urban Planning and Land Development Control Law*. West, 1971.

Kramer, Bruce M. "Transboundary Air Pollution and the Clean Air Act: An Historical Perspective," 32 *Kansas Law Review* 181 (1983).

Kratovil, Robert, and Raymond J. Werner. *Real Estate Law.* 9th ed. Prentice Hall, 1988.

Murchison, Kenneth M. "Does NEPA Matter?—An Analysis of the Historical Development and Contemporary Significance of the National Environmental Policy Act," 18 *University of Richmond Law Review* 557 (1984).

Rodgers, William H., Jr. *Handbook on Environmental Law.* West, 1977.

"The First Amendment 'Law of Billboards,'" 30 *Journal of Urban and Contemporary Law* 333 (1986).

Skillern, Frank F. *Environmental Protection: The Legal Framework.* Shepard's/McGraw-Hill, 1981.

Sturdivant, Frederick. *Business and Society: A Managerial Approach.* Irwin, 1981.

White, Harold M., Jr., and Rita Lauria. "The Evolving Legal Status of Home Satellite Earth Stations," *Communications and the Law* 8 (1986).

CHAPTER 21: INTERNATIONAL BUSINESS LAW

Alford, Roger P. "Why a Private Right of Action against Dumping Would Violate GATT," 66 *New York University Law Review* 696 (1991).

Barton, John H., and Bart S. Fisher. *International Trade and Investment: Regulating International Business.* Little, Brown, 1986.

Benz, Steven F. "Below-Cost Sales and the Buying of Market Share," 42 *Stanford Law Review* 695 (1990).

Brennan, Bartley A. "The Foreign Corrupt Practices Act of 1988: 'Death' of a Law," 15 *North Carolina Journal of International Law and Commerce Regulation* 229 (1990).

Buchholz, Rogene A. *Business Environment and Public Policy: Implications for Management and Strategy Formulation.* 2nd ed. Prentice Hall, 1986.

Clark, Lawrence S., and Peter D. Kinder. *Law and Business.* McGraw-Hill, 1988.

DeCosse, Stephen J., and Susan S. Katcher. "Newly Amended Foreign Corrupt Practices Act," *Wisconsin Lawyer* (July 1990).

Dowd, Raymond J. "Civil RICO Misread: The Judicial Repeal of the 1988 Amendments to the Foreign Corrupt Practices Act," 14 *Fordham International Law Journal* 947 (1990–1991).

Earle, Beverley H. "Foreign Corrupt Practices Act Amendments: The Omnibus Trade and Competitiveness Act's Focus on Improving Investment Opportunities," 37 *Cleveland State Law Review* 549 (1989).

Fisher, Franklin M. "*Matsushita*: Myth v. Analysis in the Economics of Predation," 64 *Chicago-Kent Law Review* 769 (1988).

Gold, Marc. "Managing Dumping in an International Economy," 21 *George Washington Journal of International Law and Economics* 503 (1988).

Gray, Whitmore, and Henry Ruiheng Zheng. "General Principles of Civil Law in the People's Republic of China," *Law and Contemporary Problems* 52 (1989).

Griffin, Joseph P., and Michael R. Calabrese. "The New Rules for International Contracts," *American Bar Association Journal* 74 (March 1988).

Naitao, Wu. "The Origin of the Chinese Legal System," *Beijing Review* (17–23 Sept. 1990).

Nanda, Ved P., ed. *The Law of Transnational Business Transactions.* Clark Boardman, 1987.

O'Hara, William T. "Dispute Resolution in the Union of Soviet Socialist Republics and the People's Republic of China," *Rhode Island Bar Journal* (Feb. 1985).

Parseghian, Lynn E. "Defining the 'Public Act' Requirement in the Act of State Doctrine," 58 *University of Chicago Law Review* 1151 (1991).

Rivlin, Benjamin, ed. *Ralph Bunche: The Man and His Times.* New York: Holmes and Meier, 1989.

Shaw, Bill. "Foreign Corrupt Practices Act: A Legal and Moral Analysis," *Journal of Business Ethics* 7 (1988).

Vagts, Detlev F. *Transnational Business Problems.* Foundation Press, 1986.

Wallace, Cynthia Day. *Legal Control of the Multinational Enterprise: National Regulatory Techniques and the Prospects for International Controls.* Martinus Nijhoff, 1983.

Wood, Diane P. "'Unfair' Trade Injury: A Competition-Based Approach," 41 *Stanford Law Review* 1153 (1989).

CASE INDEX

Names of cases excerpted in the text are printed in **boldface** type.

O'Brien v. Muskin Corp., 404
Oswalt v. Scripto, Inc., 384

Palsgraf v. Long Island Railroad Co., 371
Panama Refining Co. v. Ryan, 186, 187
Paradise, United States v., 571–73
Park, United States v., 442–43
Parker v. Brown, 618
Penn Central Transportation Company v. City of New York, 734
People v. O'Neill, 441
Philadelphia National Bank, United States v., 632
Planned Parenthood v. Casey, 133
Plessy v. Ferguson, 108, 110, 542
Polaroid Corp. v. Polarad Electronics Corp., 691
Policemen's Benevolent Association of N.J. v. Washington Township, 470
Polo Fashions, Inc. v. Extra Special Products, Inc., 691
Powell v. National Football League, 618–19
Price Waterhouse v. Hopkins, 557–59
Professional Air Traffic Controllers Organization, United States v., 493–94

Radovich v. National Football League, 111, 112
Raffles v. Wichelhaus, 331
Ramirez v. Superior Court, Santa Clara County, 157
Regents of the University of California v. Bakke, 569–71, 574
Regina v. HM Treasury, Ex Parte Daily Mail and General Trust PLC, 790–91
Reves v. Ernst & Young, 265–67
RI Hospital Trust National Bank v. Swartz, 369
Robinson v. Wieboldt Stores Inc., 354–55, 512
Rodgers v. Fisher Body Division General Motors Corporation, 115–16
Roe v. Wade, 105, 132, 133, 585
Rogers v. Loews L'Enfant Plaza Hotel, 359–60
Roginsky v. Richardson-Merrell, Inc., 118, 135
Rosenblum v. Adler, 28, 29–30, 367–68, 369
Rusch Factors v. Levin, 369
Rutter v. Northeastern Beaver County School District, 374

Sablosky v. Edward S. Gordon Co., Inc., 170–71
Salerno, United States v., 420–21
San Antonio School District v. Rodriquez, 94, 95
Scherk v. Alberto-Culver Co., 272, 782–83
School Board of Nassau County v. Arline, 578–79
Sealy, Inc., United States v., 613–15
Sears, Roebuck & Co. v. San Diego County District Council of Carpenters, 472
Securities and Exchange Commission v. Ralston Purina Co., 279–80

SEC v. Ashland Oil, Inc., 779
SEC v. Texas Gulf Sulphur, 289
Sedima, S.P.L.R. v. Imrex Co., 436
Sedmak v. Charlie's Chevrolet, Inc., 121–22
Seeger, United States v., 528
Shackil v. Lederle Laboratories, 409, 410
Shearson/American Express, Inc. v. Mc-Mahon, 272–73, 782
Sheffield v. Eli Lilly & Co., 410
Sherbert v. Verner, 528
Shewmaker v. Minchew, 360
Shlensky v. Wrigley, 58, 253
Shubert, United States v., 111
Sierra Club v. Morton, 104
Sierra Club v. SCM Corporation, 754–55
Sierra Club v. Sigler, 744–46
Simeon Management Corp. v. FTC, 665
Simmons v. Parkette National Gymnastic Training Center, 315–17
Simon, United States v., 366, 433
Sindell v. Abbott Laboratories, 408–9, 410
Sindle v. New York City Transit Authority, 354
Skil Corp. v. Rockwell International Corp., 699
Skinner v. Railroad Labor Executives Association, 497
Skinner v. Tober Foreign Motors Inc., 341
Slawek v. Commonwealth of Pennsylvania, 213–14
Smith-Corona Group v. United States, 794–95
Smith-Pfeffer v. Superintendent of the Walter E. Fernald State School, 456
Smith v. Eli Lilly & Co., 410
Smith v. Seven Springs Farm, Inc., 374
Smith v. Van Gorkom, 255–57
Smith v. Western Electric, 119–21
Sniadach v. Family Finance Corporation of Bay View, 714
Spano v. Perini Corporation, 375
Standard Oil Co. of California v. United States, 642
Standard Oil Co. v. FTC, 649
Standard Oil Co. v. United States, 616
State v. McGraw, 428–29
Statler v. Ray Mfg. Co., 290
Steinberg v. Chicago Medical School, 322, 343
Strauder v. West Virginia, 159
Superior Oil Company v. Fulmer, 438
Sutter v. San Angelo Foundry & Machine Company, 403
Swift and Company v. United States, 603
Sylvestre v. State of Minnesota, 311–12
Synar, Bowsher v., 67–68

Tampa Electric Company v. Nashville Coal Company, 642
Taylor v. Louisiana, 159
Telex Corporation v. International Business Machines Corporation, 597–99
Tennessee Electric Power Co. v. TVA, 104
Texaco v. Hasbrouck, 650–53
Texas Department of Community Affairs v. Burdine, 545
Texas v. Johnson, 17, 85, 98
Thomas v. Review Bd. of Indiana Employment Security Div., 528, 529

Thomas v. Winchester, 290, 387n
Thurmond v. Wieser, 320
Timberlane Lumber Co. v. Bank of America, 605–6, 607
Toole v. Richardson-Merrell, Inc., 116–17
TSC Industries, Inc. v. Northway, Inc., 297–98

UAW v. Johnson Controls, Inc., 559
Ultramares v. Touche, 369
United Paperworkers International Union v. Misco, 484–87
United States of America v. Iran, 787
United States Steel Corp. v. Fortner Enterprises, Inc., 639
U.S. v. SCRAP, 104
United States Workers v. Mitchell, 105
United Steelworkers v. American Manufacturing Company, 484
United Steelworkers v. Enterprise Wheel & Car Corporation, 484, 486
United Steelworkers v. Warrior & Gulf Navigation Company, 483–84
United Steelworkers v. Weber, 571
Utah Pie Co. v. Continental Baking Co., 644, 646–47

Valentine v. Christensen, 87
Vegelahn v. Gunther, 466
Vidal Sassoon, Inc. v. Bristol-Myers Co., 667–68
Village of Euclid v. Ambler Realty Co., 734–36
Virginia State Board of Pharmacy v. Virginia Citizens Consumer Council, 87
Volkswagenwerk Aktiengesellschaft v. Schlunk, 761
Von's Grocery Co., United States v., 631n

W.R. Grace & Co. v. International Union of Rubber Workers, Local 759, 474, 487
Wards Cove Packing Co., Inc. v. Atonio, 547–50
Washington Fruit & Produce Co. v. Ted. Mirski Co., 405
Webster v. Blue Ship Tea Room, 406, 412
Webster v. Reproductive Health, 133
Weeks v. Southern Bell Telephone and Telegraph Co., 564
Weinberg v. Catholic Action of Hawaii, 744
Whatley v. Scaggs, 553
Whirlpool Corporation v. Marshall, 205–7
White Consolidated Industries, Inc. v. Whirlpool Corporation, 633–34
White Motor Co. v. United States, 616
White-Smith v. Apollo, 682
White v. Guarante, 369
Wilko v. Swan, 272
Williamson v. Lee Optical of Oklahoma, Inc., 93
Winterbottom v. Wright, 386
Wisconsin v. Yoder, 528
World-Wide Volkswagen Corp. v. Woodson, 145, 383–84
Wright v. Credit Bureau of Georgia, 711
Wrightwood Dairy Co., United States v., 79

SUBJECT INDEX

Allen, Robert E., 628, 629
Allowances
    brokerage, 653–54
    promotional, 654
Amalgamated Association of Iron and
        Steel Workers, 489
Amalgamated craft unions, 463
Amendments, constitutional, 81–98
    First, 73, 83, 84–90, 357, 528–29, 738
    Second, 83
    Fourth, 83, 90–91, 417, 470, 497
    Fifth, 83, 91–98, 417, 420–21, 541,
        732
    Sixth, 159, 417
    Eighth, 417–18, 419
    Ninth, 83
    Tenth, 78, 83
    Eleventh, 124
    Thirteenth, 540, 541
    Fourteenth, 17, 83, 91–98, 540–42,
        543, 574, 732
    Fifteenth, 542, 543
    Sixteenth, 83
    Eighteenth, 83
    Twenty-first, 82
    Bill of Rights, 83, 91
    process of amending, 81–82
American Arbitration Association
        (AAA), 168, 169, 172, 483, 782
American Bar Association, Standing
        Committee on the Federal Judi-
        ciary of, 130
American Continental Corp. (ACC),
        296
American Federation of Labor (AFL),
        458, 460. See also AFL-CIO
American Institute of Certified Public
        Accountants (AICPA), 203, 371,
        433
American Law Institute, 223, 334, 348,
        444, 445
American Medical Association, 217,
        610
American Mutoscope and Biograph
        Co., 674
American Stock Exchange (AMEX), 267
Americans with Disabilities Act
        (ADA), 580
American system, 72
American Telephone and Telegraph
        Company (AT&T), 215, 588,
        629, 671
Amling, F., 268n
Amoroso, Anthony, 51
Amstar Corp., 665
Amtrak, 183, 184–85
Analytical jurisprudence (positivism),
        6–8, 9, 15
Ancient Roman law, 18
Annual percentage rates (APR), 702
Answer (to complaint), 151, 152
Anticompetitive action, legal judge-
        ment and, 606–9
Anti-Drug Abuse Act of 1988, 126
Antidumping duties, 794
Anti-Federalists, 74, 83
Antitrust Division of Department of
        Justice, 179
Antitrust law, 190, 588–622

exemptions to, 617–19
international, 796
joint ventures and, 629–31
market competition and, 589–90
Sherman Act of 1890, 78, 179, 190,
        590–617, 639, 642, 674
    on attempts to monopolize, 591,
        603–6, 644
    on conspiracy to monopolize,
        604–6
    on monopolization, 593–603
    overview of, 590–93
    penalties under, 590–91
    per se violations, 606–9
    Section 1, 590, 606–17
    Section 2, 590, 593–606
    trade and professional associations
        and, 609–12
    vertical restraints of trade, 613–17
summary of legislation, 591
See also Clayton Act (1914); Mergers;
        Robinson-Patman Act (1936)
Apparent authority, 226
Appeal, procedures and grounds for,
        165–66
Appellant, 123, 165
Appellate courts, 123, 165–66
Appellee, 123, 165
Apprehension, reasonable, 353
Aquinas, St. Thomas, 5, 54
Arbitrager, 284
Arbitrary agency actions, 205
Arbitration, 157, 167, 168–71, 482–88
    international-contract arbitration
        clauses, 781–83
Aristotle, 5
Arline, Gene, 578
Armed services, blacks in, 463
Army Corps of Engineers, 733
Arnal Corporation, 350–51
Arraignment, 421
Arrest, 419
Arthur Anderson, 371
Article I review, 186
Articles of Confederation, 68
Articles of incorporation, 241
Artist's name, protection of, 683–84
Asbestos cases, 402–4, 517–19, 718–19,
        722
Asbestos Workers' Recovery Act,
        518–19
Ashland Oil, Inc., 779
Assault, 353
Assent, 321–23
    manifestation of, 318
    mutual, 318
Asset distribution in Chapter 7
        bankruptcy, 722
Association of American Publishers,
        683
Assumption of risk doctrine, 374, 376
Atomic Energy Commission, 202
AT&T, 215, 588, 629, 671
Attachment, 713
AT&T Technologies Inc., 562–64
Auctions, offer and acceptance at, 340
Auditor liability, 434
Austin, John, 6
Australia, auditor liability in, 434

Authenticated copies, 162
Authority
    actual, 225
    of agent, 225–27
    apparent, 226
    corporate, 241–43
    defined, 63
    delegation from principal to agent,
        223
    express, 225
    extraterritorial, 607
    in federalism, flow of, 69–70
    implied, 225
Authorization of agency funding, con-
        gressional, 203–4
Automobile industry in Mexico, 509
Avoidable (speculative) damages, 114
Award, arbitration, 168, 169

B.C.C.I./First American scandal, 38,
        434, 435
Backward vertical integration, 634
Bad-faith bargaining, 480, 481
Bail, 417, 419–20
Bailey, F. Lee, 423, 427
Bail Reform Act of 1984, 420–21
Bait and switch, 665
Bakke, Allan, 570–71, 574
Bakke decision, 569–71, 574
Balanced-budget amendment, 82
Balance of payments, 248, 249
Balance of trade, 248, 249
Balancing test, due process, 207–9
Banco Nacional de Cuba, 775–76
Banking Act of 1933, 275
Bank of Credit and Commerce Interna-
        tional (BCCI), 38, 434, 435
Bank of England, 434
Bank of the United States, 71
Bankruptcy, 715–25
    business, 716–17
    defined, 715
    environmental liability and, 722, 725
    household debt and consumer, 698,
        699
    personal, 716
    petitions, in U.S. (1981–1989), 716
Bankruptcy courts, 125
Bankruptcy Reform Act (1978), 716,
        717–24
    Chapter 11 reorganization, 717–21,
        722
    Chapter 7 liquidation, 721–23, 724
    Chapter 13 repayment plans, 723,
        724
    Chapter 12 family farms bankruptcy,
        723–25
BarChris Construction Corporation,
        281–83
Bargaining
    bad-faith, 480, 481
    collective. See Collective bargaining
    good-faith, 480
Bargaining units, 480–82
Bargaining zone, 488
Barmash, Isidore, 303
Barrett, L.B., 752
Battery, 22, 351, 352–53
    criminal, 22, 415

Battle of the forms, 339, 340
Baumhart, R.C., 51n
Beauty of land, protection of, 738
Bell, Griffin, 202
Belli, Melvin M., 363, 364, 445
Bell Laboratories, 671
Belton, Robert, 566n
Beltone Electronic Corporation, 642
Bench trials, 123
Benefits, workers' compensation, 513–15
Benefits of Air and Water Control, The (Freeman), 752
Bentham, Jeremy, 47
Benzene exposure standard, 531–32
Berle, A.A., 41
Berne Convention for the Protection of Literary and Artistic Works, 676, 677–79, 681, 684
Bernstein exception to act of state doctrine, 775
Berring, Robert C., 25n
Best-evidence rule, 162
BFOQ defense, 556–57, 564–66, 576, 585
Bhopal, India, Union Carbide disaster in, 103, 365, 372, 761
Biddle, Nicholas, 72
"Big Six" accounting firms, 371
Bilateral contract, 310
Bildisco & Bildisco, 719–21
Bill of lading, 780, 781
Bill of Rights, 83, 91
   union workers', 474–75
Binding arbitration clause, 781
Binding contract, 318
Biomagnification, 755
Biotechnology, 672
Birmingham, Alabama, King's protests in, 55–56
Black, Hugo, 590
Black lung disease, 518. *See also* Asbestos cases
Blackmun, Harry, 585
Blacks
   in armed services, 463
   civil rights and, 539–43
   slavery, 539–40
Black's Law Dictionary, 371, 417
Black unions, 462
Blue laws, 95–98
Board of directors, corporate, 252, 253
   corporate-opportunity doctrine and, 254–55
   interested director, 257
   reforming role of, 259
   takeovers and, 300
Bodenheimer, Edgar, 3n
Boesky, Ivan, 284, 288
Boisjoly, Roger, 204
Bok, D.C., 482n
Bolce, William, 215n
Bona fide occupational qualification (BFOQ), 556–57, 564–66, 576, 585
Bond(s)
   defined, 263
   junk, 270, 301
   See also Securities

Borah, William E., 26
Boston police strike (1919), 496
Branch, foreign, 771
Brandeis, Louis D., 67, 276, 357, 502–3
Brand name. *See* Trademarks and service marks
Breach of contract. *See under* Contract(s)
Breach of duty of care, 363–69, 389
   remedies for, 119
Breach of fiduciary duties, 122
Brennan, Bartley A., 778n
Brennan, Edward, 231
Brennan, William, 98, 106, 571
Briefs, 123, 165
Bristol-Myers Company, 666, 667–68
British system of government, 61–62
Brokerage allowances, 653–54
Brokerage firms, 270
Brokers, 270–71
Brown, Linda, 110
Buchholz, Rogene A., 534, 581n, 770, 771, 793n
Budgetary control of administrative agencies, 202
Budgetary power of Congress, 203–4
Budgeting, zero-based, 217
Bunche, Ralph J., 788–89
Burden of proof, 161
   in disparate impact cases, 547, 550
   of price discrimination, 648
   workers' compensation and, 516
Bureaucracy, 180
Bureau of Corporations, 592
Bureau of Labor Statistics, 530
Burger, Warren, 128
Burger King Investor's Master Limited Partnership, 238–39
Burnett, Carol, 357
Burns, James M., 211
Bush, George, 130, 131, 201, 216–17, 550
Business agents, 461
Business bankruptcy, 716–17
Business-government environment, 39, 40
Business-judgment rule, 255–57, 258
Business-justification defense, 546, 547, 550
Business necessity defense, 561
Business of the Supreme Court, The (Frankfurter and Landis), 276
Business organization, forms of, 222–62
   agency law and, 222–28
      agency obligations, 223–28
      nature of agency relationship, 223
   corporations. *See* Corporations
   partnerships, 231–39, 243
      defined, 232
      dissolution and termination, 235
      liability, 235
      management, 235
      nature of, 232–34
      types of, 236–39
   sole proprietorships, 228–31, 243
Business-related crime, 38, 416, 426–40
   accountant criminal liability, 432–34
   computer crime, 428–30

mail and wire fraud, 431–32
racketeering and RICO, 293, 420, 428, 434–40
Bylaws, 252

Cabinet, 182
Calamari, John D., 320n, 321n
Calhoun, John C., 72
Canon law, 19
Capacity to contract, 315–18
Capital movement by multinational, control over, 775
Capital offenses, 424
Cardozo, Benjamin, 108, 376
Care, duty of, 255–57, 363, 389
Carnegie, Andrew, 254
Carroll, Archie B., 41–44, 349
Carroll, P.G., 290
Carrousel Motor Hotel, 352–53
Cartels, 601
Carter, Jimmy, 130, 131, 183, 201, 202, 216
Case, Karl E., 590
Case law, 24, 27, 67, 386–89
Case of the Speluncean Explorers, The (Fuller), 3, 4–5, 11–15
Cases, reading and briefing, 28–30
Cash-income assistance, 520
Castro, Fidel, 775, 776
Categorical imperative, 48–50
Causal connection, 390
   between injury and job, 512–13, 535
   negligent tort and, 369–72
Cause
   in fact, 370–71
   probable, 91, 417, 497
   proximate, 371–72
Cavanaugh, Gerald F., 37
Caveat emptor, 271, 702
Cease-and-desist orders, 669
Celler, Emmanuel, 654
Celler-Kefauver Amendment (1950), 591, 624–25, 632
Cellophane case, 595, 597, 599, 600, 619
Center for Disease Control, 518
Certiorari, writ of, 129, 134
Certo, Samuel C., 269
Chain franchise, 328
Challenger (space shuttle), 204
Chancery courts. *See* Courts of equity
Change
   law and facilitation of orderly, 3
   rules of, 8
Changzong, Shan, 784
Chapter 11 bankruptcy, 717–21, 722
Chapter 7 bankruptcy, 721–23, 724
Chapter 13 bankruptcy, 723, 724
Chapter 12 bankruptcy, 723–25
Charity principle, 254
Charlie's Chevrolet, Inc., 121–22
Charter Oak Fire Insurance Company, 236–37
Chattel, 729
Check-off clauses, 476
Checks and balances, 65–66
Chemical pollution, 755, 757
Chernobyl disaster, Soviet (1986), 761
Chevron, 779

Chief executive officer (CEO), 253
Chief steward, 463
Child labor laws, 78, 509–10
Children, capacity to contract, 315–17
Chilean Civil Code, 18
Chlorofluorocarbon, 742
Choice-of-forum clause, 783
Choice-of-law clause, 783
Christie, George C., 6n
Cigarette Labeling and Advertising
    Act, 392–97
Circuit courts, 125
Circumstantial evidence, 161
Citizenship, diversity of, 102
Civil action, 347. See also Torts
Civil Aeronautics Board (CAB), 617
Civil cases, jury in, 155–58
Civil conspiracy doctrine, 466
Civil disobedience, 54–57
Civilian Conservation Corps (CCC), 195
Civilian government employees, in-
    crease in (1950–1987), 211
Civilian Works Administration (CWA),
    195
Civil law, 2, 17–18
Civil penalties for OSHA violations,
    533, 534
Civil procedures, 21
Civil rights, 539–43
    civil rights movement, 88, 462–63,
        543, 789
    Reconstruction legislation, 540–43
Civil Rights Act (1866 and 1871), 540,
    542–43
Civil Rights Act (1964), 77, 539
    Title VII of, 540, 543–65
        administration of, 550–53
        defenses to discrimination
            charges, 560–66
        defining discrimination, 544–46
        disparate impact, 545–50, 556
        disparate treatment, 544–45
        national origin, discrimination on
            basis of, 553–54
        sex discrimination, 554–60, 585
Civil Rights Act (1991), 550
Civil rights movement, 88, 462–63,
    543, 789
Civil Service Reform Act (1978), 201,
    203, 493
Civil War, 540
Civil War Amendments, 109
Claims
    Chapter 11, ranking of, 718
    workers' compensation, administra-
        tion of, 515
Class-action suits, 104
Clayton Act (1914), 179, 190, 502, 591,
    623
    Celler-Kefauver Amendment (1950),
        591, 624–25, 632
    on exclusive dealing, 641–43
    joint ventures and, 629–30
    price discrimination and, 643–55
    on reciprocal dealing, 638
    on tie-ins, 639–41
    See also Mergers
Clean Air Act, 733, 748–53, 756, 763
    1990 revisions, 750

Clean Water Act, 753–59
"Clear and present" danger standard,
    84
Clorox Chemical, 636–38
Close corporation statutes, 246
Closely held corporation, 246
Closing arguments, 164
Coalition for Environmentally Respon-
    sible Economies (CERES), 759
Coal Mine Safety Act, 518
COCOM (Coordinating Committee)
    countries, 795
Code Civil, French, 18
Code of Federal Regulations (CFR),
    25–27
Codes, 25
    of conduct, 53–54, 791–93
    See also Ethics
Codex Justinianus, 18
Coercion, 427
Cohen, Morris L., 25n
Colgate-Palmolive Company, 665
Collection, debt, 701, 709–13
    judicial collection methods, 713–15
Collective bargaining, 461, 475–82, 502
    bargaining units, 480–82
    duty to bargain, 480, 481
    exclusive representation, 479–80
    impasse in, 488–92
        bargaining zone and, 488
        disputes and national emergen-
            cies, 491–92
        strikes, 488–96
    issues, 476–79
    process, 476
Collective-bargaining agreement, 461
    seniority system and, 561–64
Collective liability, 408
Command, 6
Commerce, Department of, 793–94
    International Trade Administration,
        794
    Office of Export Administration, 795
Commerce, interstate, 73–74, 500–511,
    666–70
Commerce Clause, 77–81, 280
"Commercial" income of nonprofits,
    247
Commercial patents, 672–73
Commercial speech, 84, 85, 87–90
Commission, acts of, 346. See also Torts
Commission on Wartime Relocation
    and Internment of Civilians
    (CWRIC), 552
Committee of Returned Volunteers,
    183
Commodities Control List, 795
Common law, 18–19, 107
    of contracts, Uniform Commercial
        Code and, 335–43
Common Law, The (Holmes), 16
Common needs, government and,
    64–65
Commons (common-property re-
    sources), 741
Common stock certificate, 264
Communication of offer, 319
Community of interests, 481–82
Comparable worth, 583–84

Comparative advertising, 666–68
Comparative negligence, 373
Comparative statistics, 545
Compelling state interest, 73
Compensation
    executive, 295
    just, 732
    workers'. See Workers' compensa-
        tion
    See also Wages
Compensatory damages, 114–16, 135,
    333
Competing firms, 631
Competition
    characteristics of pure, 588
    destructive, 190
    exclusive dealing and, 642
    foreign, 673–76
    interbrand, 615, 616
    intrabrand, 615, 616
    market, 589–90
    monopolistic, 589
    perfect, 589
    potential, 636
    pricing to meet, 648–49
    Robinson-Patman's dampening ef-
        fect on, 655
    workable, 590
Competitive injury, 643–48
    primary-line injury, 643–47
    secondary-line injury, 647–48
Complaint, 148–52
    criminal, 419
Comprehensive Crime Control Act,
    430
Compulsory retirement, 576
Computer crime, 428–30
Computer Fraud and Abuse Act of
    1984, 430
Computer hackers, 430
Computer programs, copyrighting,
    684–87
Computer viruses, 430
Concentration, undue, 632
Concentration statistics, 545
Concerted action, 601
Concurrent power, 70
Concurring opinion, 29
Condemnation proceeding, 732
Conditional privileges, 362
Conduct approach to defining
    monopoly, 594
Confederation, 69
Confiscation, 775
Conglomerate mergers, 624, 635–38
Congress, 67
    administrative agencies and, 186,
        202–5
    commerce powers of, 79
Congressional Research Service, 204
Congress of Industrial Organization
    (CIO), 458, 460. See also AFL-
    CIO
Consent
    as defense to intentional tort, 362
    informed, 362
    international law as law of, 785
    to jurisdiction, 142
Consent decrees, 573–75

letters of, 699–700
    international, 700, 704, 780
privacy and, 706
service, 698
types of, 699
See also Debtor-creditor relations
Credit cards, 698, 703
Creditors
    bankruptcy and, 615
    Chapter 7, ranking of, 721–22
    remedies for, 713–15
    secured, 713
    See also Debtor-creditor relations
Crime, 415–50
    business-related, 38, 416, 426–40
        accountant criminal liability,
            432–34
        computer crime, 428–30
        mail and wire fraud, 431–32
        racketeering and RICO, 293, 420,
            428, 434–40
    categories of, 424–25
    criminal procedure, 21, 416–24
        constitutional requirements,
            417–18
        steps in criminal justice system,
            418–24
    criminal responsibility, 440–47
        conditions required for, 425–26
        corporate, 440–44
        defenses against, 444–47
        principles of, 425–26
    defined, 347, 415
    punishment, philosophy and goals
        of, 415–16
    torts distinguished from, 347
Criminal act, 425–26
Criminal battery, 22, 415
Criminal complaint, 419
Criminal conspiracy doctrine, 466
Criminal justice system, steps in,
    418–24
Criminal law, 2
Criminal penalties for OSHA viola-
    tions, 533
Cronin, Thomas E., 211
Cross-elasticity of demand, 597, 632
Cross-elasticity of supply, 632
Cross-examination, 163
"Cross-section" principle, 159
Crown-jewel option, 300, 301
Cruel and unusual punishment,
    417–18
Cultural relativism, 43
Cumulative voting, 252
Cunningham, William P., 738n, 755n
Curtis, Edwin U., 496
Custody, 419
Customary law, 18
Customers, selection of, 601
Cutter Laboratories, 365

Dalkon Shield, 722
Damages
    under Magnuson-Moss, 412
    monetary, 114–18, 333–34
        compensatory, 114–16, 135, 333
        consequential, 114, 333
        liquidated, 114–15, 333–34

nominal, 118, 333
    punitive, 116–18, 135, 333
special, 737
Danger, abnormal, 375–76
Daughtrey, W.H., Jr., 454n
DDT, 755
Death on the job, workmens' compen-
    sation for, 513–14
Debit card, 698
Debt, credit and consumer, 698–99. *See
    also* Debtor-creditor relations
Debt-collection practices, 701, 709–13
    judicial collection methods, 713–15
Debtor-creditor relations, 697–727
    bankruptcy, 698, 699, 715–25
        Bankruptcy Reform Act of 1978,
            716, 717–24
        business, 716–17
        personal, 716
    Consumer Credit Protection Act
        (1968), 701–15
        Equal Credit Opportunity Act,
            701, 707–9
        Fair Credit Reporting Act, 701,
            705–7
        Fair Debt Collection Practices Act,
            701, 709–13
        limited remedies for creditors,
            713–15
        Truth-in-Lending Act, 701–2
        Truth-in-Lending Simplification
            Act, 701, 702–5
    credit and, 697–701, 706, 780
        growth of, 698–701
        types of, 699
Deceptive advertising, 87, 88, 662–65,
    669–70
Declaration on the Human Environ-
    ment, 762
Declaratory judgments, 105
Decrees of specific performance, 113,
    121–22
Decretals of Pope Gregory IX, 19
Defamation, 355–57
Default judgment, 151
Defective product, 398, 400–402
Defendant
    answer of, 151, 152
    defined, 148
    summons to appear in court, 142,
        148–52
Defense(s)
    affirmative, 152
    business-justification, 546, 547, 550
    against charges of disparate impact,
        545–46
    against charges of disparate treat-
        ment, 545
    contractual, 329–33
    against criminal responsibility,
        444–47
    in defamation case, 357
    to employment discrimination
        charges, 560–66
    under Equal Pay Act, 583
    to intentional torts, 361–62
    to negligent torts, 372–74
    against price discrimination, 648–53
    state-of-the-art, 402–4

Defense-contract fraud, 203
Defensive lockouts, 491
Delay profit, 669
Delegating statutes, 186
Delegation of duty, 761
Demand, cross-elasticity of, 597, 632
Democratic-Republican party, 76
Demographic statistics, 545
De novo, 205
Deontological theories of ethical be-
    havior, 46, 48–51
Deponents, 154
Depositions, 154
Depression of 1873, 489
Deregulation, 215–17
    mergers and, 625–26
Derivative action, 253
Derivative suit, 255
DES cases, 408–9, 410
Design patent, 673
Destructive competition, 190
Detention, preventive, 420–21
Deterrence, 416
Diners Club, 698
Direct-action environment, 39
Directed verdict, motion for, 163–64
Direct evidence, 161
Direct examination, 163
Direct investment, 770–72
Directors. *See* Board of directors, cor-
    porate
Direct oversight of agencies by Con-
    gress, 204–5
Disability
    discrimination based on, 578–80
    permanent partial, 513
    permanent total, 513
    temporary total, 513
Disability insurance, 522–23
Discharge, 722–23
    of environmental claims, 725
Disclaimers, warranty, 409–11
Disclosure
    failure to disclose, remedies for,
        705
    Fair Debt Collection Practices Act
        and, 712
    host-country legislation on, 775
    Truth-in-Lending Simplification Act
        and, 702–3
Discovery, 152–54
Discretion, 113
    judicial, 107–9
Discretionary responsibilities of busi-
    ness, 42, 44
Discrimination
    age, 540, 576–77
    on basis of language, 556
    defining, 544–46
    disability, 578–80
    employment. *See* Employment dis-
        crimination
    Equal Credit Opportunity Act to
        protect against, 707
    price. *See* Price discrimination
    racial, 10, 462–63
    reverse, 569–76
    sex, 94, 510, 554–60, 580–83, 585
Dismissal of case, grounds for, 151–52

Dismissals, wrongful employment, 451–58
Disobedience, civil, 54–57
Disparate impact, 545–50, 556
Disparate treatment, 544–45
Dispute resolution, 2–3, 167–72, 173
  adversarial system of, 139
  arbitration, 157, 167, 168–71, 482–88
  mediation, 167, 171–72, 173, 492
  methods of, 167
  See also Litigation
Dissenting opinion, 29, 165–66
Dissolution of partnership, 235
Distinguished precedent, 107
Distribution, primary and secondary, 283
Distribution channel, liability for negligence in product's, 398
Distribution rights, exclusive, 615
Distributorship, 328
District courts
  federal, 102, 125, 127
  Japanese, 140–41
Diversity of citizenship, 102
Dividend payments, 263
Divine law, 5
Documents, discovery and examination of, 154
Dodd, E. Merrick, 41
Dodd, Walter F., 189n
Dodge, John F. and Horace, 44
Dodge Motor Co., 240
"Doing business" standard, 143
Domestic corporation, 246
Domicile, 142
"Donative" income of nonprofits, 247
Double jeopardy, 417
Double taxation, 244
Douglas, Max E., 269
Douglas, William O., 276
DPT vaccine, injury resulting from, 409
Dramshop laws, 349
Drew, Daniel, 38
Drexel Burnham Lambert, 38, 270, 288, 289, 293, 296, 437
Drug-Free Workplace Act (1988), 470
Drug testing, workplace, 91, 469, 470, 496–97
Drunk drivers, social host liability and, 348–49
Dual federalism, 78
Due diligence, 280
Due process, 83, 91–93, 420–21
  defined, 92
  procedural, 92–93, 208, 420
  substantive, 93, 96, 420
  tests of, 94–95
    balancing test, 207–9
Due Process Clause
  Fifth Amendment, 91–93, 420–21
  Fourteenth Amendment, 91–93
Dumping, 769, 770, 794, 796
Duress, 331–32, 362
Durham Rule, 444
Dutch model of works councils, 479
Duties
  antidumping, 794
  countervailing, 794

Duty
  to bargain, 480, 481
  breach of, 363–69, 389
  of care, 255–57, 363, 389
  in contract, 309–10
  delegation of, 761

E.I. du Pont de Nemours & Co., 742
Eastman Kodak Company, 674, 675
Ebert, Ronald J., 268, 466
Ecenia, Stephen A., 197n
Eckhardt provisions of Federal Corrupt Practices Act, 777–78
Eclectic school, 7
Economic analysis of mergers, 627–28
Economic and Social Council, U.N., 787
Economic deregulation, 190, 216–18
Economic manager, presidential role of, 195
Economic order, necessity of contract law for, 308–9
Economic regulation, 190
Economic responsibility of business, 42, 44
Economic retaliation, 361
Economic strikes, 490
Economy
  global, 248
  underground, 435
Edison, Thomas, 674, 682
Education
  median income by gender and, 555
  state and local agencies responsible for, 211–12
Edward I, King, 107
Edwards, David V., 178
Edward S. Gordon Co., Inc., 170–71
Eighteenth Amendment, 83
Eighth Amendment, 417–18, 419
8K Report, 285
Eisenberg, Melvin A., 308n
Eisenhower, Dwight, 183
Elastic Clause, 71–72
Elbing, Alvar O., 39n
Election procedures, union, 475
Eleventh Amendment, 124
Eli Lilly & Co., 410
Ely, Richard T., 731n
Emancipation Proclamation, 540
Emergencies, national, 491–92
Emerson, Ralph Waldo, 54
Eminent domain, 732
Emotional distress, intentional infliction of, 358–60
Employee fitness programs, 501
Employee Retirement Income Security Act (ERISA), 524–26
Employer
  unfair employer practices, 468–70
  vicarious liability for employee, 228, 229
Employer-employee relationships, unilateral contracts in, 311–12. *See also* Labor relations
Employment-at-will doctrine, 451–54
Employment discrimination, 539–87
  affirmative action, 561, 565–76
    programs, 566–69
    reverse discrimination and, 569–76

age discrimination, 540, 576–77
civil rights in U.S. and, 539–43
  civil rights movement, 88, 462–63, 543, 789
  Reconstruction legislation, 540–43
disability, discrimination based on, 578–80
Executive Order 11246, 540, 565–66
in pay, 580–84
Title VII of Civil Rights Act of 1964, 540, 543–65
  administration of, 550–53
  defenses to discrimination charges, 560–66
  defining discrimination, 544–46
  disparate impact, 545–50, 556
  disparate treatment, 544–45
  national origin, discrimination on basis of, 553–54
  sex discrimination, 554–60, 585
En banc panel, 166
End-user's certification, 795–96
Energy and Transportation, Department of, 740
Energy conservation, 755
Energy supply, 757–58
"English-only" rules, 556
Enterprise Wheel principles, 484
Entities, corporate, 243–44
Entitlement, 92
Entrapment, defense of, 446
Entrenchment, 638
Entrepreneurial nonprofits, 247
Enumerated (express) powers, 69, 71
Environment
  business-government, 39, 40
  corporate stakeholder, 37–39
Environmental impact statement (EIS), 743–46
Environmental protection, 739–63
  bankruptcy and environmental liability, 722, 725
  Clean Air Act, 733, 748–53, 756, 763
  Clean Water Act, 753–59
  environmental problems, 740–42
  international environmental law, 759–63
  national debate about, 739–40
  National Environmental Policy Act (NEPA), 742–46
  nuisance law and, 736–37
Environmental Protection Agency (EPA), 722, 733, 740, 746–48
  actions initiated by (1972–1989), 748
  air-quality standards, 748–53
  enforcement by, 746–48
  structure of, 746, 747
Environmental sexual harassment, 560, 561
Environmental values, protection of, 738
EPA. *See* Environmental Protection Agency (EPA)
Equal Credit Opportunity Act, 701, 707–9
Equal Employment Opportunity Act
  of 1972, 539, 551
  of 1977, 544
  proving prima facie case of violation of, 582–83

Equal Employment Opportunity Commission (EEOC), 180, 215, 231, 551–53
  affirmative-action program guideline, 567–69
  filing charges with, 551
  guidelines on discrimination on basis of national origin, 553
  remedies, 551–53
  rules on sexual harassment, 560
Equal Pay Act (1963), 510, 540, 580–83
Equal protection of law, 91, 92, 93–95, 542
  challenge to blue laws, 96
  defined, 93
  tests of, 94–95
Equal Rights Amendment, 82
Equal work, 583
Equitable remedies, 118–22, 334
Equity
  courts of, 113
  defined, 113
  minimum wages and, 508–9
Equity jurisdiction, 156
Equity security. See Securities; Stock
Erdman Act of 1898, 466
ERISA, 524–26
Ernst & Young, 265–67
Estoppel, promissory, 325
Eternal law, 5
Ethical custom, 39–41
Ethical individualism, 503
Ethical responsibility of business, 42, 44
Ethics
  anticompetitive code of, 612
  approaches to ethical behavior, 46–52
    deontological theories, 46, 48–51
    teleological theories, 46–48
  defined, 33
  ethical standards for corporate decisions, 52–54
    codes of conduct, 53–54, 791–93
    personal standards, 52–53
    professional codes, 54
  quasi-contract and, 314
  torts and, 348–51
  of voir dire, 160
Euclidian zoning, 734
European Economic Community (European Community), 65, 790–91, 792
Evidence
  circumstantial, 161
  direct, 161
  hearsay, 162
  inadmissible, 423
  insubstantial, 205
  parol evidence rule, 332
  prima facie, 233
  psychiatric, 445
  real, 162
  rebuttal, 164
  rules of, 161–62
  testimonial, 162
Evidentiary hearing, 208–9
Excessive bail, 417, 419
Exchanges in contracts, 310

Exclusionary practice, 591
Exclusionary rule, 90
Exclusive dealing, 641–43
Exclusive distribution rights, 615
Exclusive representation, 479–80
Exclusive rights to sell, 613–15
Exculpatory clauses, 327
Executive action, 26
Executive agencies, 177, 183, 740, 741
Executive branch, reorganization of, 201–2
Executive compensation, 295
Executive control of administrative agencies, 201–2
Executive Order 9066, 552
Executive Order 11141, 540
Executive Order 11246, 540, 565–66
Executive Order 11375, 540
Executive Order 11478, 540
Executive orders, 25–27, 201–2
Executive privilege, 62
Exemplary (punitive) damages, 116–18, 135, 333
Exigent circumstance, 91
Expert witnesses, 153
Export Administration Act, 795–96
Export controls, 795
Export-import relationships, 769
Exporting firm, 249
Export license, 795
Express authority, 225
Express contract, 313–14
Express powers, 69, 71
Express warranty, 395–96, 404–5, 409
Expropriation, 775
Extended precedent, 107–8
Externalities, 191–92
Extraterritorial authority, 607
Extraterritoriality, 796
Exxon, 43, 759
Exxon Valdez accident, 470

Facially neutral rule, 546
Fact
  cause in, 370–71
  contracts implied in, 313
  mistake of, 446–47
Failing-company defense, 632–33
Failure to act, 426
Failure to warn, 391, 395, 397
Fair, Ray C., 590
Fair Credit Billing Act, 701, 703
Fair Credit Reporting Act, 701, 705–7
Fair Debt Collection Practices Act, 701, 709–13
Fair Employment Practices Committee, 463
Fair Labor Standards Act (FLSA), 466, 500–511
  child labor laws, 78, 509–10
  coverage of, 503–6
  Equal Pay Act amending, 510, 540, 580–83
  Equal Pay Act of 1963, 510, 540, 580–83
  minimum wages and maximum hours, 503–9
Fairness
  minimum wages and, 508–9

  of punishing corporate agents, 443–44
  See also Equity
Fair-play standard, 143
Fair-trade laws, 613
Fair use, 680–81, 683, 693
Fair value, determination of, 794
False advertising, 87, 88, 662–70
  FTC Act and, 662–65
  Lanham Act and, 663, 666–70
False Claims Act, 203
False imprisonment, 353–55
False or misleading representation, 710
Falwell, Jerry, 358
Family courts (Japanese), 141
Family Farm Bankruptcy Act of 1986, 723–25
"Family resemblance" approach, 265–66
Farah Manufacturing Co., 553–54
Fault, liability without reference to, 375–76
FDA, 179, 182, 189–90, 384, 397, 740
Featherbedding, 474
Federal Arbitration Act, 272
Federal Aviation Administration, 493
Federal Coal Mine Health and Safety Act (1969), 517
Federal contractors and subcontractors, employment discrimination by, 565–66
Federal Courts Improvement Act of 1982, 125
Federal court system, 124–33
  selection and makeup of, 129–33
    ideology and, 130–31, 132
    politics and, 130
    race and sex, 131–33
  venue in, 147
  workload of, 126–29
Federal Deposit Insurance Corporation (FDIC), 195
Federal district courts, 102, 125, 127
Federal Emergency Relief Administration (FERA), 195
Federal Employees' Compensation Act (FECA), 511, 514
Federal Employers' Liability Act (1908), 511
Federal equal employment laws and orders, 540
Federal Food, Drug, and Cosmetic Act, 442, 443
Federal Insecticide, Fungicide, and Rodenticide Act (FIFRA), 756
Federal Insurance Contributions Act (FICA), 524
Federalism, 68–77, 124
  arguments for, 70
  defined, 68–69
  dual, 78
  flow of authority in, 69–70
  key principles of U.S., 70–76
Federalists, 74, 76
Federal Labor Relations Authority, 493
Federal Mediation and Conciliation Service, 483, 492
Federal National Mortgage Association, 183

Federal Patent Statute (1952), 672
Federal Power Commission, 196
Federal-question jurisdiction, 125
Federal Register, 26, 194, 215
Federal Register Act (FRA), 27
Federal Regulation of Lobbying Act, 51
Federal Reporter, 27
Federal Reserve Board, 702
Federal Reserve System, 179, 435, 698
Federal Rules of Civil Procedure,
    152–53, 156
Federal Supplement, 27
Federal system, 65
Federal Trade Commission Act (1914),
    190, 502, 591, 642, 663, 670
Federal Trade Commission (FTC), 179,
    196, 199–200, 411, 610, 659–65
  corrective-advertising order, 669–70
  deceptive trade practices and,
    662–65, 669–70
  Fair Credit Reporting Act enforce-
    ment, 705
  on franchise, 327–28
  functions of, 660–61
  organization of, 660
  unfair trade practices and, 661–62
Federal Trade Commission Improve-
    ment Act (1980), 663
Felonies, 424
Fetal-protection rules, 559, 585
Fiduciary relationship
  breach of duties in, 122
  corporation-shareholder, 252, 253,
    254–55
  misappropriation theory and, 292
Fifteenth Amendment, 542, 543
Fifth Amendment, 83, 91–98, 417, 541,
    732
  Due Process Clause, 91–93, 420–21
"Fighting-words" doctrine, 84
Finality, principle of, 106
Financial-services industry, 435
Fines for OSHA violations, 533, 534
Finkelstein, Edward, 303
Fireman, Paul, 295
Firings, 451–54
First Amendment, 73, 83, 84–90
  freedom of the press, 357
  Free Exercise Clause of, 528–29
  zoning and, 738
First-degree felonies, 424
First Hundred Days, 195
First National City Bank case, 775–76
Fisher, George, 383
Fisher Body Division General Motors
    Corporation, 115–16
Fisk, James, 38
Fitness for a particular purpose, war-
    ranty of, 406–7
Fixture, 730–31
Flag burning, 98
Flag-desecration statutes, 85
Follow-up review, 433
Food and Drug Administration (FDA),
    179, 182, 189–90, 384, 397, 740
Food-stamp program, 521
Force-majeure clause, 780
Ford, Gerald, 216
Ford, Henry, 44, 240

Ford Motor Co., 44, 58, 240
Foreclosure theory, 635
Foreign affairs, government support of
    business in, 188
Foreign commerce, conspiracy and in-
    ternational jurisdiction in,
    605–6, 607
Foreign competition, 673–76
Foreign corporation, 246
Foreign Corrupt Practices Act (FCPA),
    768, 776–79
Foreseeability, proximate cause and,
    371
Formal adjudication hearings, 197–98
Formalistic jurisprudence (positivism),
    6–8, 9, 15
Formal rule making, 195–96
Forward vertical integration, 634
Fourteenth Amendment, 17, 83, 91–98,
    540–42, 543, 574, 732
  Equal Protection Clause, 91, 92,
    93–95
  Due Process Clause of, 91–93
Fourth Amendment, 83, 90–91, 417,
    470, 497
Franchise, 327–29, 330
Frankfurter, Felix, 276, 642
Fraud, 126–27, 292
  defense-contract, 203
  mail and wire, 431–32
  medicare, 203
Fraudulent misrepresentation, 331, 396
Free agency, 618–19
Freedman, Richard B., 478
Freedom(s)
  contract law and promotion of indi-
    vidual, 309
  First Amendment, 84, 85–90
Freedom of Information Act, 202, 744
Freedom-of-religion challenge to blue
    laws, 96
Free Exercise Clause, 528–29
Freeman, A.M., 752
Freeman, R. Edward, 39*n*, 43, 241
Free-market model of social responsi-
    bilities, 39–41, 50
Free speech, 98
French civil code, 18
Frick, Henry Clay, 489
Friedman, Lawrence M., 3*n*
Friedman, Milton, 38, 39–41
FTC. *See* Federal Trade Commission
    (FTC)
Fuller, Lon L., 1, 3, 6, 11, 308*n*
Future dispute arbitration clause, 170

Galbraith, John, 626
Gall, Gerald L., 17*n*
Gandhi, Mohandas K., 57
Garment workers, 467
Garnishment, 701, 713, 714, 715
Gates, William H. (Bill), 614
GATT, 677, 788–90, 793
GE Capital Corporation, 303
Gemarah, 19
General Accounting Office (GAO),
    204–5, 534
General Agreement on Tariffs and
    Trade (GATT), 677, 788–90, 793

General Assembly, U.N., 786
General deterrence, 416
General Electric, 203
General jurisdiction, courts of, 113
Generally accepted accounting princi-
    ples (GAAP), 433
Generally accepted auditing principles
    (GAAS), 433
General Motors Corporation, 43,
    239–40
General partner, 236
General trial courts. *See* Trial courts
Geographical markets, 599
Geographic reach, merger extending,
    635–36
Getty Oil, 360
Gilbert, Daniel R., Jr., 39*n*, 43
Gilded Age, labor disputes in, 489
Gillette, 250
Gilmore, Grant, 336
Ginsburg, Benjamin, 215*n*, 217
Giuliani, Rudolph, 437
Glass-Steagall Act (Banking Act of
    1933), 275
Glazer, Myron and Penin Migdal, 203
Global economy, 248
Global environmental security, 761
Global securities enforcement, 287
Goldberg, Stephanie, 389*n*
Golden Rule, 48
Gompers, Samuel, 460
Good faith, defining, 649, 650
Good-faith bargaining, 480
Good-faith doctrine, 340, 341, 452–53
Goods
  contracts for sale of, 332
  gray market, 692–93
  "imminently" or "inherently" dan-
    gerous to human safety, 387–88
  U.N. convention on contracts for in-
    ternational sale of, 338, 783,
    785–88
Good samaritans, 365
Gorman, R.A., 482*n*
Gospel of Wealth, The (Carnegie), 254
Gould, Jay, 38
Government, 63–81
  British vs. U.S., 61–62
  business-government environment,
    39, 40
  Commerce Clause, 77–81, 280
  federalism, 68–77, 124
  power to control use of property,
    732–37
  purpose of, 63–65
  types of systems of, 68–69
  U.S. system of, purpose of forming,
    65–68
Government-approval clause, 781
Government corporations, 177, 183–85
Government employees, civilian
    (1950–1987), 211
Government spending, support of
    business through, 188
Grand jury, 62, 155, 421, 422
Gratian, 19
Gray market goods, 692–93
Grease payment exception, 777
Great Britain

auditor liability in, 434
system of government, 61–62
Great Depression, 41, 78
Greenbackers, 527
Greenmail, 288, 300, 301
Gregory IX, Pope, 19
Grievances, 479, 482–83
Grievance strikes, 490
Griffin, Ricky W., 268, 466
Grotius, Hugo, 7
Guidelines for International Investment and Multinational Enterprises (OECD), 792

Hackers, computer, 430
Hague Conference of Private International Law, 385
Hague Convention on the Law Applicable to Products Liability, 385, 387
Halcion (drug), 384
Hamilton, Alexander, 76
Hand, Learned, 593, 594, 683
Handicapped, defining, 578–79
Hansmann, Henry B., 247
Harassment
debt collection and prohibition of, 710
sexual, 560, 561
Harding, Warren G., 26
Hardwood case, 610
Harlan, John, 110
Harriman, W. Averell, 675
Hart, H.L.A., 8
Harvard Business Review, 51
Harvard University, 670
Hatch Act, 105
Hayburn's Case, 106
Hayes, George E.C., 95
Haymarket Riot (1886), 489
Health, state and local agencies responsible for, 212
Health risk, determining, 530–33
Hearing(s)
agency, 196–97
evidentiary, 208–9
formal adjudication, 197–98
Hearsay evidence, 162
Hearst, Patricia, 427
Henry Ford & Son, 240
Hepburn Act, 592
Herfindahl-Hirschman Index (HHI), 626, 628
Herman, E. Edward, 455, 459, 465, 477n, 481
Hewlett-Packard, 614
High Courts (Japan), 140
Hill, Anita, 560
Hilson, Daniel G., 718n
Hinckley, John W., 445, 446
Hine, Lewis, 510
Historic value of property, protection of, 738
Hobbes, Thomas, 50
Hoffman, W. Michael, 39n
Holding companies, 645
Holmes, Oliver Wendell, Jr., 11, 16–17, 98
Holocaust, 9

Home Projecting Kinetoscope, 682
Homestead Strike, 489
Honda Motor Co., 250
Honeywell, 43
Hoover, Herbert, 41
Hopkins, Ann, 557–59
Horizontal mergers, 601, 624, 631–34
Horizontal price fixing, 607
Horizontal privity, 407–8
Horizontal restraints of trade, 613
Host-country regulatory control, 774–76
"Hostile-environment" harassment, 560, 561
Host liability, social, 348–49
Hours, maximum, 502–9
Hughes, Charles, 104
Human laws, 5
Human nature, 50
Husted, Stewart W., 269
Hyland, Margaret C., 751, 752, 753, 755n, 761
Hyson, John, 215n

IBM, 43, 250, 597–99
Ibuka, Masaru, 671
Icahn, Carl, 284
ICC, 179, 182, 196, 592
Ideology, federal court system and, 130–31, 132
Illegal agreements, 326–27
Illusory promises, 325
Immigration Reform and Control Act (1986), 467, 554
Immunities, intergovernmental, 71–72
Implied authority, 225
Implied consent, 142
Implied contract, 313–14
Implied power, 69–70
Implied warranty, 405–7, 409–11, 412
Import-export relationships, 769
Import regulation, 793–95
Imprisonment, false, 353–55
Improper agency procedures, 207
Inadequate information, 191
Inadmissible evidence, 423
Incapacitation, punishment for, 416
Income disparity by gender, 555, 581–82
Income-maintenance programs, 519–29
ERISA, 524–26
Social Security, 519–24
three-tiered system of, 519
unemployment compensation, 526–29
Incorporation, articles of, 241
Independent agencies, 177, 182–83
Independent contractors, 223
India, Gandhi's civil disobedience in, 57
Indiana, takeover statute in, 301–2
Indictment, 421
Indirect-action environment, 39
Indirect compensatory damages, 114
Individualism, ethical, 503
Individual Retirement Accounts, 525
Individual (sole) proprietorship, 228–31, 243
Individual transactions, necessity of contract law for, 308

Industrial committees, 479
Industrial locals, 461–63
Industrial Revolution, 348
Industry, acid rain and, 756, 763
Infancy, defense of, 446
Influence, undue, 332
Informal adjudication, 198
Informal rule making, 193–94, 198
Information
conveyance of, by agent, 224
filing, 421, 422
inadequate, 191
insider, 288–89, 304
Informed consent, 362
Infractions, 424
Infringement of copyright, 680
Infringement of trademark, 688–92, 693
Injunctions, 113, 119–21, 688
in nuisance cases, 736
permanent, 467
preliminary, 467
against strikes, 491–92
Injury(ies), 390
actual, 369
competitive, 643–48
covered under workers' compensation, 512–13
defined, 347
job-related, 535
mental, tests for proving, 517
See also Torts
In-kind assistance, 520
Insanity defense, 444–46
Insider information, 288–89, 304
Insider Trading and Securities Enforcement Act (1988), 292
Insider Trading Sanctions Act (1984), 292
Insider transactions, 287–98
in Japan, 287
the law and, 292–93
Section 10b/Rule 10B-5 of 1934 Act, 289–91
short-swing profits and, 293–94
solicitation of proxies, 294–98
Installment credit, 699
Institutes, 18
Institutions, international business activity and, 767, 768
Insubstantial evidence, 205
Insurance policies, workers' compensation benefits from, 515
Intangible property, 731
Intel Corp., 687
Intellectual property, 670–93
copyrights, 676–87
computer programs, 684–87
infringement and fair use, 680–81, 683, 693
international laws, 676–79
registration, 679–80
terms, 679
visual arts and, 681–84
patents, 659, 670–76
trademarks and service marks, 687–93
gray market goods, 692–93
infringement of, 688–92, 693

petit, 155
selection of, 158–61, 172
Jury trial, right to, 155–61, 417
Jury verdict, 164–65
Just compensation, 732
Justice
Rawls' theory of, 34–35, 50
standards for, 48
Justice, Department of, 196, 202
Antitrust Division of, 179
judicial bargaining process and, 130
merger guidelines, 627–28
Justice (ILGWU monthly newspaper),
467
Justices of the peace, 135
Justiciability, justiciable controversy,
101–2, 104–6
Justinian, 18
Juvenile Delinquency Act, 446

Kaiser Aluminum and Chemical Cor-
poration, 571
Kant, Immanuel, 48–50
Keating, Charles H., Jr., 296
Keating-Owens Act, 510
Keegan, Warren J., 790
Keene, John, 372
Keeton, W. Page, 736*n*
Kennedy, John F., 182, 276, 445, 463,
543
Kennedy, T., 475*n*
Keough plans, 525
Kerper, Hazel B., 3*n*
Kessler, David A., 189–90
Kinetoscope, 674, 682
King, Martin Luther, Jr., 55–56, 88
Kinko's Graphics Corporation, 683, 692
Kissinger, Henry, 357
Korematsu, Fred, 552
Korth, Christopher M., 767*n*
Kroc, Ray, 330
Kronman, Anthony T., 308*n*
Kuhn, Alfred, 455, 459, 465, 477*n*, 481
Kuhn, Bowie, 110, 111–12
Kupchella, Charles E., 751, 752, 753,
755*n*, 761

Labor, Department of, 502
Labor Management Relations Act of
1947, 485
Labor-Management Reporting and Disclosure Act of 1959 (Landrum-
Griffin), 464, 466, 474–75
Labor relations, 451–99
arbitration, 482–88
collective bargaining, 461, 475–82,
502
bargaining units, 480–82
duty to bargain, 480, 481
exclusive representation, 479–80
issues, 476–79
process, 476
employment-at-will doctrine, 451–54
grievances, 479, 482–83
impasse in bargaining, 488–92
bargaining zone and, 488
disputes and national emergencies, 491–92
strikes, 488–96

unions and the law, 464–75
Landrum-Griffin Act, 464, 466,
474–75
Norris-LaGuardia Act, 464–68, 618
Taft-Hartley Act, 464, 466, 468–74,
480, 491–92
Wagner Act, 79, 464, 466, 468–74,
480, 491, 618
unions in public sector, 492–97
union structure, 454–64
AFL-CIO, 458–59, 460, 463, 465
national and international unions,
463–64
U.S. union membership (1900–1990),
454–58, 459
union locals, 459–63
Labor standards, 500–538
Fair Labor Standards Act (FLSA),
466, 500–511
child labor laws, 78, 509–10
coverage of, 503–6
Equal Pay Act of 1963, 510, 540,
580–83
minimum wages and maximum
hours, 503–9
income-maintenance programs,
519–29
ERISA, 524–26
Social Security, 519–24
three-tiered system of, 519
unemployment compensation,
526–29
Occupational Safety and Health Act
(OSHA), 530–35
workers' compensation, 511–19
administration of claims, 515
benefits and administration,
513–15
covered injuries, 512–13
criticism of, 515–16
legislation for occupational disease, 516–19
worker coverage, 511–12
Labor unions, 459
antitrust exemption of, 617–18
See also Unions
Laissez-faire theories, 191
Land, contracts for sale of, 332
Land, Edwin H., 675
Landes, David, 36*n*
Landis, James M., 274, 276
Landrum-Griffin Act, 464, 466, 474–75
Land use
planning, 737–39
restrictions on (zoning), 732–36
types of sensitive land and recommended uses, 738
Language, discrimination on basis of,
556
Lanham Trademark Act (1946) and,
663, 666–70
Latin America, Procter & Gamble in,
250–51
Law
administrative regulations and executive orders, 25–27, 201–2
adversary system of, 21, 36, 101, 139
branches of, 21–24
case law, 24, 27, 67, 386–89

cases, reading and briefing, 28–30
contracts implied in, 313, 314
conventional, 5
courts of, 113
criminal law, 2
customary, 18
defining, 1
functions of, 2–3
legal traditions, 17–20
civil law, 2, 17–18
common law, 18–19, 107, 335–43
religion, influence of, 19–20
limits of, 54–57
morality and, 33–34. *See also* Ethics;
Social responsibility of business
nature of, 3–17
jurisprudence concepts, 3–5, 11–17
natural law perspective, 5–6, 15
positivist perspective, 6–8, 9, 15
social science perspective, 8–11
procedural vs. substantive, 21–22
public vs. private, 22–23
remedies at, 114–18
sources of, 24–25
See also Statutes
Lawyer's Edition, 27
Lawyer's work product, exemption
from discovery, 153
Layer-cake theory of federalism, 70
Layoffs, 478
League for Nonviolent Civil Disobedi-
ence Against Military Segregation, 463
League of Nations, 26
Lee, L. Douglas, 522
Legal codes, 18, 25. *See also* Statutes
Legal control of administrative agen-
cies, 202
Legality, contractual, 326–27
Legal realism, 8, 10–11, 15, 16
Legal-residuum rule, 197
Legal responsibility of business, 42, 44
Legal Training and Research Institute
(Japan), 141
Legislation, 24
administrative agencies' power of,
186–87
advertising, 663, 666–70
debtor-creditor. *See* Bankruptcy;
Consumer Credit Protection Act
(1968)
stare decisis and, 109–12
Legislative acts, 67
Legislative courts, 125
Letters of credit, 699–700
international, 700, 704, 780
Leveraged buyout (LBO), 300–301,
302, 303
Levine, Dennis, 284, 288
Levi Strauss & Co., 690–92
Levitt, Theodore, 51
Levy, Michael E., 521*n*
Lewis, John L., 460
Liability
accountant, 366–69, 370
criminal, 432–34
collective, 408
corporate, 441
livestock and, 375–76

market-share, 408–9, 410
of minors under contract, 315–17
of partnership, 235
product. *See* Product liability
professional, 366–69, 370
social host, 348–49
of sole proprietor, 230
vicarious, 228, 229, 426, 440
See also Torts
Libel, 355, 356, 357
Liberty, defined, 92
Library of Congress, Copyright Office
of, 679
License
export, 795
state, for sole proprietorship, 229
Licensing, 212–14
contractual legality and, 327
international relationship based on,
769
Lie detector, 423
Limited partners, 236
Limited partnerships, 236–37
master (MLP), 237–39
Lincoln Savings & Loan, 296
Lipson, Leslie, 63*n*
Liquidated damages, 114–15, 333–34
Liquidations, 721–23
Litigation, 139–76
alternatives to, 167–72
arbitration, 157, 167, 168–71,
482–88, 781–83
mediation, 167, 171–72, 173, 492
jurisdiction and, 140–47
over corporations, 140, 143–46
over natural persons, 140, 141–42
venue and, 103–4, 146–47
patent, 673
pretrial procedure, 147–55, 419–21
discovery, 152–54
pretrial conference, 154–55
summons and complaint, 142,
148–52
taking case to trial, 155–66
conduct of trial, 161–62
order of trial, 162–65
procedures and grounds for appeal, 165–66
trial by jury, right to, 155–61,
417
workers' compensation and, 516
Livestock, liability and, 375–76
Llewellyn, Karl, 10, 335, 336
Local administrative agencies, 211–15
Locals, union, 459–63
Locke, John, 50
Lockouts, 491
Lodge, Henry Cabot, 26
Loews Corporation, 303
Loews L'Enfant Plaza Hotel, 359–60
Logo, 689
Long-arm statutes, 102, 143–46, 384
Longshoremen's and Harbor Workers'
Compensation Act (1927), 511,
514
Los Angeles, air pollution in, 748
Lotus Development Co., 614
Lowi, Theodore J., 215*n*, 217

Loyalty
of agent, 224
undivided, rule of, 254
Lundgren, A., 789

McClellan, John L., 474
McCormick Harvester Co., 489
McDonald, Allan, 204
McDonald's Corporation, 330
McGovern, Arthur F., 37
McKenzie, Richard, 770
McKinley, William, 592
McMahon, Eugene and Julia, 272–73
Madison, James, 65, 66, 74
Magnuson-Moss Warranty Act,
411–12, 663
Mail fraud, 431–32
Maintenance-of-membership clause,
476
Majority, rule by, 55
Majority opinion, 165
Malcolm Balridge Quality Award, 383
Malice, 357
actual, 86–87, 88
Maloney Act (1938), 275
Management, 37
of partnership, 235
Management-employee relations, theo-
ries of, 501
Management-security clauses, 476–77
Manager
accountable, 38–39
criminal responsibility of, 441–44
economic, presidential role of, 195
Mandamus, writ of, 75
Mandatory arbitration clause, 781
Manifestation of assent, 318
Manner of acceptance, 339
Manufacturer liability, expansion of,
389
Manufacturer-retailer franchise, 328
Manufacturer-wholesaler franchise, 328
Maquiladora ("handwork") plants, 509
Marble-cake theory of federalism, 70
Marbury, William, 75
March on Washington (1963), 462, 463
Market(s)
geographical, 599
multinational corporations' control
of, 773
product, 597–99
relevant, defining, 597–99
securities, 267–74, 285
functions of, 268
investor protection, 271–74
mechanics of investing in, 269–71
thin, 601
Market competition, 589–90
Market-extension merger, 635–36
Market failure, regulation against,
190–93
Marketplace efficiency, contract law
and, 309
Market power, 593, 619
identifying the exercise of, 600–603
measuring, 599–600
Market Reform Act (1990), 275, 285
Market-share liability, 408–9, 410

Marshall, John, 71–72, 74, 76, 77–78
Marshall, Thurgood, 95, 96, 131
Massachusetts, blue laws in, 97
Massachusetts Civil Rights Act, 458
"Mass-disaster" cases, 118, 135
Mass media, judicial process and, 156
MasterCard, 698
Master limited partnership (MLP),
237–39
Material alterations, 339–40
Material terms under Convention on
Contracts for International Sale
of Goods, 338
Matras, Judah, 520, 521
Maximum hours, 502–9
Meany, George, 460
Meat Inspection Act, 592
Media
defamation cases brought against,
356, 357
judicial process and mass, 156
Mediation, 167, 171–72, 173, 492
Medicaid, 212, 521
Medical benefits (workmen's compen-
sation), 513
Medicare, 521
Medicare fraud, 203
Medoff, James L., 478
Meeting-the-competition defense,
648–49, 650, 655
Megatrends (Naisbett), 248
Mens rea, 425, 426
corporate, 440
Mental infirmity, capacity to contract
and, 317–18
Mental injury, tests for proving, 517
Mentschikoff, Soia, 336
Menzel, David L., 373*n*
Merchantability, warranty of, 405–6,
412
Mergers, 623–38
conglomerate, 624, 635–38
courts and, 631–38
defined, 623
growth in (1895–1987), 624
horizontal, 601, 624, 631–34
host-country legislation on, 775
largest corporate, 625, 626
merits of, 626–31
regulating, 624–26
statutory, 299
vertical, 624, 634–35
Messenger, The (magazine), 462
Metropolitan Edison Company, 758
Mexico, wages in, 509
Microsoft Corp., 614
Midlands Chrome, Inc., 779
Milken, Michael, 270, 284, 288, 293,
296, 437
Mill, John Stuart, 47
Miller-Tydings Amendment to Sherman Act, 613
Min, Zhang, 784
Minimum contacts, test of, 382–84
Minimum wage, 502–9
Ministry of International Trade and In-
dustry (MITI), 627
Minors, capacity to contract of, 315–17

Miranda warnings, 419
Mirror-image rule, 338, 339
Misappropriation theory, 292, 304
Misco, Inc., 484–87
Misdemeanors, 424
Mishnah, 19
Misrepresentation, 331, 367
   fraudulent, 331, 396
Missouri Compromise of 1820, 541
Mistake
   as contractual defense, 329–31
   of fact, 446–47
Mistranscription, 331
Misunderstanding, 331
MITI, 627
M'Naughten Rule, 444, 445
Mobil Corporation, 43
Model Business Corporation Act
   (MBCA), 241
Model Penal Code, 424, 425, 426, 444
Models, express warranty based on,
   405
Modified union shop, 476
Monetary damages, 114–18
   for breach of contract, 333–34
   compensatory, 114–16, 135, 333
   nominal, 118, 333
   punitive, 116–18, 135, 333
Monopolistic competition, 589
Monopoly, 589, 593–603
   attempts to monopolize, 591, 603–6,
      644
   conditions of pure, 596
   conspiracies to monopolize, 604–6
   defining, 594–97
      general rule for, 594–97
      legal approaches to, 593–94
   defining relevant market, 597–99
   market power and
      identifying exercise of, 600–603
      measuring, 599–600
   natural, 618
Montgomery Ward, 230
Moody, John, 592
Moore, Jennifer Mills, 39*n*
Mootness, 105
Morality, 33
   law and, 33–34
   values and, 34–36
   See also Ethics; Social responsibility
      of business
Morality of Law, The (Fuller), 6
Moral rights, 681–83, 684
Moral-rights standards, 48
Morton Thiokol, 204
Motion-picture copyrights, 682
Motion Picture Patents Co., 674
Motion to dismiss, 151–52
Motor Carrier Act of 1980, 216
Motorola, total quality management at,
   383
Movable property, 729, 730
Multinational corporations, 250,
   772–74, 792–93
   codes of conduct for, 792–93
   defined, 772
   host-country regulatory control of,
      774–76

Multivalued analysis of mergers,
   626–27
Munnell, Alicia, 519
Murphy, William P., 566*n*
Musselman, Vernon A., 134
Mutual assent, 318
Mutual mistake, 330
"Mutual" nonprofits, 247
Myers, Michael, 51

NAACP, 543, 573
Nabrit, James M., 95
Nader, Ralph, 203, 401
Naisbett, John, 248
Napoleonic Code, 18
NASA, 204
National Association for the Advance-
   ment of Colored People
   (NAACP), 543, 573
National Association of Securities
   Dealers Automatic Quotation
   System (NASDAQ), 268, 285
National Cash Register Co., 452–53
National Conference of Commissioners
   on Uniform State Law, 334
National Cooperative Research Act
   (NCRA) of 1984, 626, 630–31
National emergencies, 491–92
National Environmental Policy Act
   (NEPA), 742–46
National Football League, 618–19
National Football League Players Asso-
   ciation, 618
National Industrial Recovery Act
   (1933), 78, 186, 187, 500
National Institute for Occupational
   Safety and Health (NIOSH),
   530, 531, 533, 535
National Institute of Environmental
   Health Services, 518
Nationalization, 775
National Labor Relations Act (Wagner
   Act), 79, 464, 466, 468–74, 480,
   491, 618
National Labor Relations Board
   (NLRB), 179, 297, 461, 468–74
   bargaining unit requirements,
      480–82
   mediation, 492
National Oats Company, 342–43
National origin, discrimination on ba-
   sis of, 553–54
National Railroad Passenger Corpora-
   tion, 184
National Recovery Administration, 364
National Resources Defense Council,
   191–92
National Security Council (NSC), 201
National Taxpayers Union, 82
National unions, 463–64
Natural law perspective, 5–6, 15
Natural monopoly, 618
Natural persons, jurisdiction over, 140,
   141–42
Nature-of-transaction exemption from
   registration, 278
Nazi law, Holocaust and, 9
Nebel, Bernard J., 755*n*

NEC Corp., 687
Necessary-and-Proper Clause, 71–72
Necessities, children's contract liabilities for, 317
Needs, government and common,
   64–65
Negligence, 164
   accountant's liability in civil actions
      for, 366
   comparative, 373
   contributory, 372–73
   defined, 363
   potential litigation for strict vs. neg-
      ligent liability, 398, 399
   product liability and, 385, 387,
      389–97
      failure to warn, 391, 395, 397
      negligent torts, 389–97
      tobacco-industry, 392–97
Negligent torts. *See under* Torts
New Deal, 78, 131, 179, 195
New Frontier, 182
New York City Retirement System, 295
New Yorker, The, 86–87
New York State Law Revision Com-
   mission, 335
New York Stock Exchange (NYSE),
   267, 272
Ninth Amendment, 83
Nixon, Richard M., 62, 183, 566
NLRB. *See* National Labor Relations
   Board (NLRB)
No adverse impact defense, 561
Nominal damages, 118, 333
Nondisclosure, 331
Nonjudicial informal agency action,
   198
Nonprofit corporations, 246–48
Nontariff barriers, 793
Norris-LaGuardia Act, 464–68, 618
Northern Securities Company, 592
Northway, Inc., 297–98
Northwestern Bell Telephone, 437–40
No-strike, no-lockout clauses, 491
Notice-and-comment procedure,
   193–94, 198
Nuclear Regulatory Commission,
   196–97, 202
Nuisance law, 736–37
Nullification crisis of 1832, 72
Nuremberg Laws, 9
Nutrition Education and Labeling Act
   (1990), 189

Obedience of agent, 224
Objective test of mental injury, 517
Objective theory of assent, 321
Obligations, 8
O'Brien, C.N., 508*n*
O'Brien, David M., 130
Occidental Petroleum Corp., 294
Occupational disease, 530
   defining, 516–17
   legislation for, 516–19
Occupational Disease Compensation
   Act, 518, 519
Occupational Safety and Health Act
   (OSHA), 530–35

discretion and, 107–9
distinguished, 107
extended, 107–8
overruled, 108
stare decisis and, 107–12, 618
Predatory behavior, 601
Predatory pricing, 603–5, 643–47, 770, 797
Preemption doctrine, 73
Pregnancy Disability Amendment to Title VII (1978), 559
Pregnancy Discrimination Act of 1978, 540
Prejudgment remedies, 713–15
Prejudicial errors, 166
Prejudicial treatment. *See* Discrimination
Preliminary hearing, 421, 422
Preliminary injunctions, 119, 467
Presence, determining physical, 142
Presidential board of inquiry, 491
Press, the
constitutional privilege of, 357
freedom of, 85–87
Presumptively appropriate units, 481
Pretrial conference, 154–55
Pretrial procedures, 147–55, 419–21
Preventive detention, 420–21
Price and pricing
defining market by, 631–32
to meet competition, 648–49
predatory, 603–5, 643–47, 770, 797
resale price maintenance, 613
Price discrimination, 643–55
competitive injury and, 643–48
defenses against, 648–53
per se violations, 653–54
plaintiff's burden, 648
Price fixing, 607–9
trade and professional associations and, 610–12
Price wars, 650, 655
Price Waterhouse, 371
Prima facie case of price discrimination, 648
Prima facie evidence, 233
Primary distribution, 283
Primary-line injury, 643–47
Primary rules, 8
Primary significance test, 689–90
Prince William Sound, 1989 oil spill in, 759
Principal, 223
agent's obligations to, 224–25
obligations to agents, 223–24
obligations to third parties, 225–27
tort and vicarious liability of, 227–28
Prior restraint, 84
Prison system, 425
Privacy
credit information and issue of, 706
invasion of, 357, 457–58
Private law, 22, 23
Private offerings, 279
Private pensions, 524–26
Private property, seized for public use, 732
Privatization
of prison system, 425
proposals for, 217

Privilege(s)
in defamation cases, 357
as defense for intentional tort, 361–62
executive, 62
Privileged communications, exemption from discovery, 153
Privity, 407–9
Probable cause, 91, 417, 497
Procedural due process, 92–93, 208, 420
Procedural grounds for dismissal, 151–52
Procedural law, 21
Process patent, 677
Procter & Gamble, 250–51, 689
Product-extension merger, 635, 637
Product liability, 379–414
defined, 379
evolution of, 386–89
manufacturer liability, expansion of, 389
tort principles and case law, 386–89
filing bankruptcy over lawsuits on, 722
negligence approach to, 385, 387, 389–97
failure to warn, 391, 395, 397
negligent torts, 389–97
policy bases of, 380–85
business policy, 380–82
legal policy, 382–85, 386
in selected countries, 385
strict, 381, 385, 388–89, 398–404
defining defectiveness, 400–402
potential litigation for negligent liability vs., 398, 399
state-of-the-art defense, 402–4
in U.S. and European law, 386
warranty, 388, 404–12
defined, 404
disclaimers, 409–11
express, 395–96, 404–5, 409
implied, 405–7, 409–11, 412
Magnuson-Moss Warranty Act, 411–12, 663
privity, 407–9
Product markets, 597–99
Professional Air Traffic Controllers Organization (PATCO), 493–94, 495
Professional associations, 609, 610–12
Professional baseball, exemption from antitrust law, 618
Professional codes, 54
Professional responsibility, 371
Professionals, legal duty of, 365
Professional standards and liability, 366–69, 370
Profit, delay, 669
Profitability, defining market by, 631–32
Profit-maximization strategy of multinationals, 773–74
Profits, short-swing, 293–94
Program trading, 285
Promise(s)
defined, 309

illusory, 325
reciprocal, 310
Promissory estoppel, 325
Promissory notes, 162
Promotional allowances, 654
Proof. *See* Burden of proof; Evidence
Property, 728–31
commons (common-property resources), 741
defined, 728
fixed vs. movable, 729–31
due process protection of, 92
public vs. private interests in, 731–37
eminent domain and, 732
nuisance law and, 736–37
taking of property, 733–36
zoning and, 732–36
real, 729, 738
tangible vs. intangible, 731
Property law, decrees of specific performance, 121
Property rights, basis of, 729
Proprietorships, sole, 228–31, 243
Prospectus, 276–78
Prosser, William A., 736
Protectability of trademark, 688–90
Protectionism, 188
Protestant Work Ethic, 36
Proximate cause, 371–72
Proxy
solicitation of, 294–98
voting by, 252–53
Proxy statement, 295–97
Psychiatric evidence, 445
Public art, copyright protection for, 684
Public good, antitrust exemptions for, 617
Public Health Cigarette Smoking Act of 1969, 393, 394
Public law, 22–23
Publicly held corporation, 246
Public order, protection of, 2
Public-policy exception, 453–54
Public sector
Fair Labor Standards Act applied to, 504–6
right to strike, 493–96
unions in, 492–97
Public Service Commission of New York, 88–90
Public use, seizing private property for, 732
Pullman Company, 462
Pullman strike of 1894, 489
Punishment
of corporate agents, fairness of, 443–44
cruel and unusual, 417–18
philosophy and goals of, 415–16
See also Crime
Punitive damages, 116–18, 135, 333
Pure comparative negligence, 373
Pure-conglomerate merger, 636
Pure Food and Drug Act (1906), 592, 663

Quality control, product liability and, 380–82

Quality functional deployment (QDF), 383
Quantification, utilitarianism and problem of, 47
Quasi-contract, 313, 314, 317
Quid pro quo, 307
Quotas, import, 793
Quota systems, employment, 571–73

R. H. Macy & Co., 303
Race
 civil rights and civil rights movement, 88, 462–63, 539–43, 789
 "cross-section" principle and, 159
 federal court system and, 131
 jury selection and, 172
Racial discrimination, 10, 462–63
Racketeer Influenced and Corrupt Organizations Act (RICO), 293, 420, 428, 434–40
 criminal and civil components of, 436–40
 criticism of, 436, 437
 racketeering defined, 434–36
Raider, 301. See also Takeovers
Rail Passenger Service Act, 184
Ralston Purina Co., 279–80
Randolph, A. Philip, 462–63, 489
Ratification of constitutional amendment, 81, 82
Ratification of contract, 317
Rational bureaucrat model (rational-person model), 180
Rational relation test, 94
Rawls, John, 34–35, 46, 50, 56–57
Reagan, Ronald, 130, 131, 133, 201, 216, 445, 446, 493, 663
Reagan administration, 627
Real evidence, 162
Realism, legal, 8, 10–11, 15, 16
Real property (real estate), 729
 protection of value of, 738
Reason, rule of, 612, 613, 615, 616, 623, 630, 796
Reasonable accommodation, 579
Reasonable apprehension, 353
Reasonable-behavior standard, 392
Reasonable-consumer standard, 663–65
Reasonable likelihood test, 468
Reasonableness standard, 164
Reasonable or rational relation test, 72, 94
Reasonable person standard, 363
Reasonable search, 91
Reasonable suspicion, 497
Rebuttal evidence, 164
Recidivism, 416
Reciprocal dealing, 638
Reciprocal promises, 310
Recognition, rules of, 8
Reconstruction legislation, 540–43
Recruiting, truth in, 322, 343
Recycling, 742
Redeeming social value, 84
Red-herring (red-line) prospectus, 277
Redirect examination, 163
Reese, Wills L.M., 387

Reform
 of administrative agency action, 215–18
 of board of directors' role, 259
 corporate, 258–59
 of federal agency action, 215–18
 patent-system, 673–76
 penny-stock, 285–86
 regulatory, 217–18
Registration
 copyright, 679–80
 of securities
  under Securities Act of 1933, 274–78
  under Securities Exchange Act of 1934, 283
 trademark, 688
Registration statement, 274–76, 277
Regulated industries, antitrust exemption of, 617
Regulation
 administrative, 25–27
 debtor-creditor. See Consumer Credit Protection Act (1968)
 deregulation vs., 215–17
 economic, 190, 216–18
 growth of, 179–81
 host-country, 774–76
 import, 793–95
 against market failure, 190–93
 of mergers, 624–26
 reform and, 217–18
 securities. See Securities
 social, 181, 215–16
 See also Administrative agencies; Environmental protection
Regulation A, 278
Regulation D, 278
Regulation management, 216
Regulation Z, 702, 704, 705
Regulatory Analysis Review Group, 216
Rehabilitation, punishment for, 416
Rehabilitation Act of 1973, 566, 578–80
Rehnquist, William, 98, 128, 129, 358
Reich citizenship law, 9
Reizenstein, Gail R., 707n
Relativism, cultural, 43
Religion, influence of, 19–20
Remedies, 112–22
 for breach of contract, 333–34
 corporate liability and, 441
 in court system, 112–22
  defined, 113
  at equity, 118–22, 334
  at law, 114–18
 for creditors, limited, 713–15
 Equal Employment Opportunity Commission, 551–53
 under Equal Pay Act, 583
 for failure to disclose, 705
 under Fair Credit Reporting Act, 707
 judicial review after exhaustion of, 210
 for securities-laws violations, 285–86
Reorganization, Chapter 11, 717–21, 722

Reorganization of executive branch, 201–2
Repayment plans, 723
Replevin, 713
Reply (of plaintiff), 152
Reporters, 27
Reporting
 under Foreign Corrupt Practices Act, 776
 to SEC, 283–85
Representation
 exclusive, 479–80
 false or misleading, 710
Representatives, sales, 769
Requirements contract, 641
Resale price maintenance, 613
Rescission, rule of, 334, 703
Research and development, 188
 joint ventures in, 630–31
"Research and worst-case" regulation, 744
Res ipsa loquitor doctrine, 365
Respondeat superior, 227–28, 229
Respondent, 165
Responsibility
 criminal. See under Crime
 social. See Social responsibility of business
Responsiveness, philosophy of, 44
Restatement of Agency, 223
Restatement (Second) of Contracts, 309, 317, 321, 324, 331, 336, 341, 348, 353, 387, 400, 401
Restitution, 334
Restraining order, temporary, 119
Restraint, punishment for, 416
Restraint of trade
 horizontal, 613
 per se violations, 606–9
 vertical, 613–17
Restrictive Business Practices Code, 792
Restructuring power of Congress, 202
Retaliation, economic, 361
Retirement, compulsory, 576
Retirement-income maintenance, 519–26
Retribution, punishment for, 416
Reuther, Walter, 460
Reverse discrimination, 569–76
Reviewing (appellate) courts, 123, 165–66
Revised Uniform Limited Partnership Act (RULPA), 236
Revolving credit, 699
Richardson-Merrell, Inc., 116–17, 118, 135
RICO, 293, 420, 428, 434–40
Right(s)
 in contract, 309–10
 moral, 48, 681–83, 684
 property, basis of, 729
 states', 71
 to trial by jury, 155–61, 417
 See also Civil rights
Right to know, consumer's, 706–7
Right-to-work laws, 476, 477
Ripeness, 105, 210

Small Business Administration (SBA), 188
Small-claims courts, 135
Smith, David, 681
Smith, Kennedy, 156
Social control, law and maintenance of, 2
Social host liability, 348–49
Social insurance program, 520
Social order, necessity of contract law for, 308–9
Social performance model of social responsibility, 41–44
Social regulation, 181, 215–16
Social responsibility of business, 36–46, 254
    Brandeis' belief in, 502, 503
    corporate stakeholder environment and, 37–39
    legal perspectives on, 44–46
    models of, 39–44
    torts and, 348–51
Social science perspective, 8–11
Social Security Act, 519–24, 526, 577
    benefits and beneficiaries, 520–21
    benefit structure, 523–24
    coverage, 521–23
    funding of programs, 524
Social Security Amendment, 521
Sociological jurisprudence, 8, 10
Software program, copyright of, 684–86
Sole proprietorships, 228–31, 243
Solicitation of proxies, 294–98
Sony, 671
Sovereign, 6
Sovereignty doctrine, 492, 493
Soviet Chernobyl disaster (1986), 761
Special damages, 737
Special deterrence, 416
Special relationships, 332
Special services, 654
Specific intent, 427
Specificity of offer, 319
Specific performance, 334
    decrees of, 113, 121–22
Speculative (avoidable) damages, 114
Speech
    commercial, 84, 85, 87–90
    free, 98
    unprotected, 84–85
Speluncean Explorers, the Case of the (Fuller), 3, 4–5, 11–15
Sperry & Hutchinson Co., 661
Stakeholder environment, corporate, 37–39
Standard
    "doing business", 143
    fair-play, 143
    occupational safety and health, 531
    reasonable-behavior, 392
    reasonable-consumer, 663–65
    reasonableness, 164
    reasonable person, 363
    substantial-justice, 143
Standard Oil Company, 645
Standard Oil of New Jersey, 591

Standards
    ethical, for corporate decisions, 52–54
    for justice, 48
    labor. See Labor standards
    moral-rights, 48
    professional, 366–69, 370
    set by federal agencies, 189–90
    utilitarian, 48
Standing, 104–5, 209–10
Standstill agreement, 300
Stanford, Melvin J., 243
Staples, Sam, 54
Stare decisis, 107–12, 618
    Constitution and, 109
    legislation and, 109–12
State action doctrine, 618
State administrative agencies, 211–15
State and Local Fiscal Assistance Act of 1972, 539, 540
State concurrent jurisdiction, 125
State court system, 134–36
    common rules of venue in, 147
    jurisdiction of, 102
State license for sole proprietorship, 229
State-of-the-art defense, 402–4
States
    authority of, in federal system, 69–70
    Bill of Rights and, 83
    child labor laws, 509
    police power of, 73–74
States' rights, 71
State supreme courts, 123–24
State takeover statutes, 301–2
State workers' compensation laws, 512
Statistical approaches to establishing disparate impact, 545
Status quo, protection of, 3
Statute of Frauds, 332, 340
Statutes, 18, 24, 25
    close corporation, 246
    defined, 24
    delegating, 186
    long-arm, 102, 143–46, 384
    state takeover, 301–2
Statutes at Large, 25
Statutory consolidation, 299–301
Statutory merger, 299
"Steelworkers Trilogy" cases, 483
Steiner, George A., 774n
Steiner, John F., 774n
Steinsaltz, Adin, 19n
Stereotyping, sex, 556–59
Steward(s), 461
    shop, 463
Steward councils, 463
Stewardship principle, 254
Stewart, Potter, 56
Stock, 263, 264. See also Securities
Stockbroker, 270–71
Stock exchanges, 267–69
Stock-option plan, 295
Stock-parking scheme, 288
Stoner, James A.F., 241
Straight voting, 252

Strauss, Lewis, 675
Strauss, Peter L., 202n
Stress, job-related, 516–17, 535
Strict liability
    criminal, 426
    product liability, 381, 385, 388–89, 398–404
        defining defectiveness, 400–402
        potential litigation for negligent liability vs., 398, 399
        state-of-the-art defense, 402–4
    in torts, 375–76
Strict scrutiny, 94–95, 574
Strikes, 488–96
    aspects of, 490–91
    PATCO, 493–94, 495
    public-employee, 493–96
    Taft-Hartley provisions on, 491–92
    types of, 490
Structural approach to defining monopoly, 593–94
"Subchapter S" corporation, 246
Subcontractors, federal, 565–66
Subjective test of mental injury, 517
Subjective theory of assent, 321
Subject-matter limitations to judicial power, 124
Subject matter of case, jurisdiction and, 140
Subminimum wage, 507–8
Submission, arbitration, 168, 169
Subpoenas, 62, 154
Subsidiary, foreign, 771–72
Subsidization of business, 214–15
Substantial Capacity Test, 444
Substantial-justice standard, 143
Substantive due process, 93, 96, 420
Substantive ground for dismissal, 151–52
Substantive law, 21–22
Sugar Trust case of 1895, 78
Sullivan, L.B., 88
Sullivan, Lawrence A., 648n
Summary courts (Japanese), 141
Summary judgment, 152
Summons, 142, 148–52
    writs of, 348
Sunday-closing laws, 95–98
Sun Microsystems, 614
Sunset laws, 217
Sunstein, Cass R., 202n
"Superfund" Act (1980), 722, 757
Supplemental Security income (SSI), 522
Supply, cross-elasticity of, 632
Support programs, affirmative-action, 567
Supremacy Clause, 71, 74, 78
    preemption doctrine and, 73
Supreme court, Japanese, 140
Supreme Court, U.S., 67
    Article I review, 186
    on attempts to monopolize, 591
    Commerce Clause cases, 77–81
    on consent decrees, 573–75
    on conspiracy to monopolize, 604–5
    on consumer protection, 701–2

on disparate impact, 546–50
on disparate treatment, 544
on doing business standard, 143
Dred Scott decision, 75, 540, 541
dual federalism doctrine, 78
on equal protection, 542
expansion of federal commerce
  power and, 78–79
on flag burning, 98
on insider trading, 289–91
interpretation of Constitution, 62
Japanese-American cases, 552
jurisdiction, 129
justiciability cases, 104–6
on labor-arbitration process, 483–87
Marbury v. *Madison*, 74–75
on *Miranda* warnings, 419
overload of cases, 128
on peremptory challenges, 160, 161
procedural and substantive due process, 92–93
on racial segregation, 10
on reverse discrimination, 569–71,
  574
Roosevelt's court-packing scheme, 131
on seniority systems, 562–64
on sex discrimination, 573
on sexual harassment, 560
on strict quota systems, 571–73
on zoning, 734–36
See also specific cases
Supreme Court Reporter, 27
Supreme courts, state, 123–24
Surety contracts, 332
Suspect classes, 94
Suspicion, reasonable, 497
Sweatshops, 467
Swiss Civil Code, 18
Symbionese Liberation Army, 427

"Table S-3" rule, 191
Taft-Hartley Act, 464, 466, 468–74, 480,
  491–92
Takeovers, 288, 299–303
Taking of property, 733–36
Tall-stack strategy, 762
Talmudic law, 19
Taney, Roger, 541
Tangible items, discovery and exami-
  nation of, 154
Tangible property, 731
Tariff Acts (1922 and 1930), 692,
  793–94
Tariffs, 793
Taxation
  double, 244
  host-country tax legislation, 775
  unemployment compensation
    funded by, 526
Tax Reform Act of 1986, 524
Teamsters Union, 464
Technical Communications Corpora-
  tion (TCC), 455–58
Technology
  patents and pace of, 670–72
  state-of-the-art defense and under-
    standing of, 402–4

Teleological theories of ethical behav-
  ior, 46–48
Television cameras in courtroom, 156
Telling, Ed, 231
Temporary injunctions, 119
Temporary restraining order, 119
Temporary total disability, 513
Tender offers, 299–303
10K Report, 283–85
Tennessee Valley Authority (TVA),
  104, 195
10Q Report, 285
Tenth Amendment, 78, 83
Termination of offer, 320
Termination of partnership, 235
Terms-of-payment clause, 780
Territorial jurisdiction, 141–42
Territorial restrictions on trade, 613–17
Testimonial evidence, 162
Texaco, 360
Texas International Airlines, 719
Theory X, 501
Theory Y (human-resources model), 501
Thin markets, 601
Third-degree felonies, 424
Third parties, principal's obligations
  to, 225–27
Third-world countries, wages in, 509
Thirteenth Amendment, 540, 541
Thomas, Clarence, 131, 560
Thoreau, Henry David, 54–55
Three Mile Island Nuclear Station, 758
Tie-ins, 639–41
Tisch, Lawrence, 303
Title, 25
Title VII of Civil Rights Act of 1964.
  See under Civil Rights Act (1964)
Titus, R.B., 290
Tobacco-industry negligence, 392–97
Tocqueville, Alexis de, 118
Tombstone advertisement, 278
Tort law, 22, 346–47, 415
Torts, 346–78, 415
  application to product liability,
    386–89
  compensatory damages for, 114
  corporate responsibility and, 348–51
  defining, 347–51
  ethics and, 348–51
  history of, 348
  intentional, 346, 348, 351–62
    assault, 353
    battery, 22, 351, 352–53
    defamation, 355–57
    defenses to, 361–62
    defined, 351
    economic retaliation, 361
    false imprisonment, 353–55
    intentional infliction of emotional
      distress, 358–60
    interference with contractual rela-
      tions, 360
    invasion of privacy, 357, 457–58
    wrongful use of trade secrets, 361
  negligent, 346, 348, 362–75
    actual injury, 369
    breach of duty, 363–69

causal connection and, 369–72
  defenses to, 372–74
  duty of care, 363
  product liability, 389–97
  principal's liability for agent's,
    227–28
  strict liability in, 375–76
  See also Product liability
Toxic waste, 757
Trade
  balance of, 248, 249
  vertical restraints of, 613–17
Trade associations, 609–10
Trademarks and service marks, 687–93
  gray market goods, 692–93
  infringement of, 688–92, 693
  Lanham Trademark Act and, 663,
    666–70
  registration, 688
Trade name, 229
Trade practices, 659–70
  deceptive, 87, 88, 662–65, 669–70
  FTC and, 659–61
  Lanham Trademark Act (1946) and,
    666–70
  unfair, 661–62
Trade restrictions, 793–96
Trade secrets, wrongful use of, 361
Trading relationships, international,
  768–72
Transistor, invention of, 671
Transnational corporation. *See* Multi-
  national corporations
Transportation policy for intoxicated
  patron, 349
Travel and entertainment (T&E) cards,
  698
Treble-damages suits, 654
Trial
  criminal, 424
  taking case to, 155–66
    conduct of trial, 161–62
    order of trial, 162–65
    procedures and grounds for ap-
      peal, 165–66
    trial by jury, right to, 155–61, 417
Trial courts, 123
Tribe, Laurence H., 130*n*
Tripartite Declaration of Principles
  Concerning Multi-National En-
  terprises and Social Policies, 792
Trost, Cathy, 534
Truman, Harry, 463
Trust, 645
Trusteeship Council, U.N., 787
Trusteeship model of social responsi-
  bility, 41
Trusts, 590, 592
Truth-in-Lending Act, 701–2
Truth-in-Lending Simplification Act,
  701, 702–5
Truth in recruiting, 322, 343
Turkish Civil Code, 18
TVA, 104, 195
Twenty-First Amendment, 82
Type-of-security exemption from regis-
  tration, 278

Ultra vires, 242–43
Unauthorized agency actions, 205–7
Unclean hands, doctrine of, 119
Unconscionability, doctrine of, 171, 341–43
Unconstitutional agency actions, 205
Underground economy, 435
Undivided loyalty, rule of, 254
Undue concentration, 632
Undue influence, 332
Unemployment compensation, 526–29
Unemployment rate, pollution control and, 751
Unfair labor practices 468–74, 480
  employer, 468–70
  union, 469, 470–74
Unfair labor-practice strikes, 490
Unfair or unconscionable practices in debt collection, 710
Unfair trade practices, 661–62
Uniform Commercial Code, 334–43
  on acceptance, 338–40
  common law of contracts and, 335–43
  on contract modifications, 340–41
  on creation of contracts, 337
  firm offer under, 337–38
  good-faith doctrine, 452–53
  on privity, 407–8
  purpose of, 335
  unconscionability doctrine, 341–43
  on warranty disclaimers, 409–11
Uniform Franchise Offering Circular (UFOC), 328
Uniform Limited Partnership Act (ULPA), 236
Uniform Partnership Act (UPA), 232, 233
Unilateral contract, 310–12
Unilateral mistake, 331
Union Carbide disaster in Bhopal, India, 103, 365, 372, 761
Union Health Center (ILGWU), 467
Union-management relations. *See* Labor relations
Union Pacific Railroad, 38
Unions
  black, 462
  collective bargaining and, 461, 475–82, 502
    bargaining units, 480–82
    duty to bargain, 480, 481
    exclusive representation, 479–80
    issues, 476–79
    process, 476
  grievances and, 479, 482–83
  the law and, 464–75
    Landrum-Griffin Act, 464, 466, 474–75
    Norris-LaGuardia Act, 464–68, 618
    Taft-Hartley Act, 464, 466, 468–74, 480, 491–92
    Wagner Act, 464, 466, 468–74, 480, 491
  in public sector, 492–97
  structure, 454–64
    AFL-CIO, 458–59, 460, 463, 465
    national and international unions, 463–64

U.S. union membership (1900–1990), 454–58, 459
  union locals, 459–63
  unfair labor practices, 469, 470–74
Union security, 476
Union-shop clause, 476
Unique domicile, 142
Unitary system of government, 69
United Auto Workers (UAW) Union, 463–64, 509
United Mine Workers, 460
United Nations, 785–88
  goals of, 786
  International Court of Justice, 144, 763, 787
  system, 786–87
United Nations Commission on International Trade Law (UNCITRAL), 338, 782
United Nations Commission on Transnational Corporations, 792
United Nations Conference on the Environment and Development (UNCED), 759
United Nations Conference on Trade and Development, 792
United Nations Convention on Contracts for the International Sale of Goods, 338, 783, 785–88
United Nations Economic Security Council (UNESCO), 678
United Nations Environmental Program (UNEP), 762
United Nations Stockholm Conference on the Human Environment, 759
United States
  balance of payments (1960–1987), 249
  balance of trade (1976–1990), 249
  as world's number-one debtor nation, 770
U.S. Code, 129
U.S. Constitution. *See* Constitution, U.S.
U.S. Copyright Act of 1976, 678
U.S. Court of Appeals, 125–26
  appeals filed in, 126, 127–29
U.S. Department of the Navy, 215
United States Patent and Trademark Office, 670, 688
United States Reports, 27
U.S. Steel, 254
United Steelworkers, 483
Universal Copyright Convention, 678–79, 680
Universal Declaration of Human Rights, 787
Unocal Corp., 293
Unprotected speech, 84–85
Upjohn Company, 384
Utilitarianism, 46–48
Utilitarian standards, 48
Utilities, state and local agencies responsible for, 211
Utility, principle of, 47
Utility patents, 672–73
Utilization analyses, 567–68

Vago, Steven, 8*n*
"Valdez Principles," 759
Valid contract, 314–15
Valuation, 717
Value judgments, 348
Values, 34–36
  defined, 35
  morality and, 34–36
Vanderbilt, Cornelius, 38
Velasquez, Manuel G., 47*n*, 48
Venue, 103–4, 146–47
Verdict, 164–65
  motion for directed, 163–64
Vertical mergers, 624, 634–35
Vertical price fixing, 607
Vertical privity, 407, 408
Vertical restraints of trade, 613–17
Vesting, 524
Veto power of Congress, 202
Vicarious liability, 228, 229, 426, 440
Victims-rights legislation, 534
Vidal Sassoon Incorporated, 666
Vietnam Era Veterans Readjustment Assistance Act of 1979, 539, 540, 566
Vietnam War, 41, 183
Viles, Robert M., 699
Violations, 424
Visa, 698
Visual Artists Rights Act, 681, 684
Visual arts, copyright and, 681–84
Vitascope, 674
Vocational Rehabilitation Act (1973), 540
Voidable contract, 315
Void contract, 315
Voir dire, 159–61
Voting rights of shareholders, 252–53

Wackenhut Corporation, 424
Waddell, T.E., 752
Wages
  collective bargaining over, 477–78
  in Mexico, 509
  minimum, 502–9
  subminimum, 507–8
Wagner Act, 79, 464, 466, 468–74, 480, 491, 618
Wallace, Wanda A., 370
Wall Street Journal, 292, 304
Warn, failure to, 391, 395, 397
Warrantless searches, 91
Warranty, 364, 388, 404–12
  defined, 404
  disclaimers, 409–11
  express, 395–96, 404–5, 409
  implied, 405–7, 409–11, 412
    of fitness for a particular purpose, 406–7
    of merchantability, 405–6, 412
  Magnuson-Moss Warranty Act, 411–12, 663
  privity, 407–9
Warren, Earl, 128
Warren, Kenneth F., 194
Washington, George, 105
Waste, toxic, 757
Waste pollution, 755, 757
Watergate, 62

Water pollution, control of, 753–59
Weber, Max, 180
Webster, Daniel, 71
Weidenbaum, Murray L., 216, 301, 566n, 568, 581n, 582
Weinberg, Mel, 51
Welfare, state and local agencies responsible for, 212
Western Electric, 119–21
West reporting system, 27
Wheeler-Lea Act (1938), 591, 659, 662, 663
Whirlpool Corporation, 633–34
Whistleblowing, 39, 203
"White-collar" crime. See Business-related crime
White knight, 294, 301
Whitney, Richard, 276
Wholesaler-retailer franchise, 328
Wholesome Meat Act, 73
Wieboldt Stores Inc., 354–55
Wildcat strikes, 490
Williams Act (1968), 79, 299–300
Wilson, Charles E., 188
Wilson, James, 74
Wilson, Woodrow, 26, 180
Winans, R. Foster, 292, 304
Wire fraud, 431–32
Witnesses, 154
  expert, 153
Wolfe, James A., 790
Wolf packs, 301
Women
  discrimination on basis of pay, 580–84

employment discrimination against, 554–60
  in major occupational categories, 555
Wood, Arthur, 231
Wood, Robert E., 230
Woodworth, Barbara, 738n
Work
  equal, 583
  Fair Labor Standards Act definition of, 506
Workable competition, 590
Worker coverage under public-benefits programs (1960–1985), 520
Worker-Family Education Project (ILGWU), 467
Workers' compensation, 511–19
  administration of claims, 515
  benefits and administration, 513–15
  covered injuries, 512–13
  criticism of, 515–16
  legislation for occupational disease, 516–19
  worker coverage, 511–12
Working conditions, state and local agencies responsible for, 212
Workplace
  discrimination in. See Employment discrimination
  drug testing in, 91, 469, 470, 496–97
  employer's right to establish rules in, 469, 470
  safety in, 530–35
Works councils, Dutch model of, 479
Works Progress Administration (WPA), 195

Work stoppages, 493–95. See also Strikes
World Intellectual Property Organization, 676
World Wise Schools program, 183
Wright, Christopher, 630n
Wrigley, Philip K., 58
Writ(s), 113
  of certiorari, 129, 134
  of mandamus, 75
  of summons, 348

Xerox, 250

Yellow-dog contracts, 466–67
Yeltsin, Borin, 64
Yom Kippur War, 757
Youth, capacity to contract and, 315–17
Yuba Power Products, Inc., 381–82
Yugoslavia, civil war in, 64

Zenith Radio Corporation, 604–5, 770, 793, 797
Zero-based budgeting, 217
Zoning, 732–36
  Euclidian, 734
  land-use planning, 737–39
  purpose of, 738–39
  taking and legal scope of, 734–36

PHOTO CREDITS